1994

THE CANADIAN GLOBAL ALMANAC

1994

THE CANADIAN GLOBAL ALMANAC

John Robert Colombo
General Editor

Macmillan Canada
Toronto

Contents

CANADA

THE COUNTRY AT A GLANCE 1
SUPERLATIVE CANADIAN FACTS 2

THE LAND

LANDFORMS 3
VEGETATION 8
AGRICULTURE 10
CLIMATE 11
PROVINCES AND TERRITORIES 28
CANADIAN CITIES 35
NATIONAL PARKS 40

THE PEOPLE

POPULATION 42
VITAL STATISTICS 53
MIGRATION 63
POPULATION GROUPS 68
EDUCATION 72
FAMILIES AND INCOME 81

THE NATION

CANADIAN HISTORY 89
GOVERNMENT OF CANADA 114
POLITICS AND ELECTIONS 150
DEFENCE 161
SOCIAL SECURITY 164
CRIME AND JUSTICE 171
PUBLIC WORKS 174
FOREIGN AID 175

THE ECONOMY

GLOSSARY OF TERMS 178
ECONOMIC INDICATORS 179
TOURISM 192
BUSINESS AND LABOUR 193
SMALL BUSINESS 203
AGRICULTURE 204
NATURAL RESOURCES 208
ENERGY 212
FOREIGN TRADE 216
PERSONAL FINANCE 220

GLOBAL INFORMATION

GLOBAL SUPERLATIVES 235
GEOGRAPHY 236
POPULATION 240
ECONOMICS 244
INTERNATIONAL ORGANIZATIONS 250
HISTORY IN HEADLINES 259
WORLD MAPS 299
COUNTRIES OF THE WORLD 307

SCIENCE AND NATURE

ASTRONOMY AND SPACE 523
EARTH SCIENCES 536
PHYSICAL SCIENCES 546
INVENTION & SCIENTIFIC ACHIEVEMENT 553
ENVIRONMENT 557

ARTS AND ENTERTAINMENT

MOVIES	563
TELEVISION AND RADIO	569
POPULAR MUSIC	574
PERFORMING ARTS	584
GALLERIES AND MUSEUMS	590
BOOKS, MAGAZINES, NEWSPAPERS	592

SPORTS

OLYMPICS	601
HOCKEY	629
BASEBALL	643
FOOTBALL	658
BASKETBALL	673
OTHER SPORTS	675

QUICK REFERENCE

WEIGHTS AND MEASURES	692
DIET AND HEALTH	697
TRAVEL	707

OBITUARIES	711
NEWS EVENTS OF 1992–93	719
INDEX	744
1994 CALENDAR AND HOLIDAYS	760

Comments and Suggestions

Please feel free to send us your comments and any suggestions for subsequent editions. Many readers took the time to drop us notes and letters last year and the correspondence is most welcome, although it is not always possible to respond personally to each writer. Address all correspondence to the General Editor, *The Canadian Global Almanac*, c/o Macmillan Canada, 29 Birch Avenue, Toronto, Ontario M4V 1E2.

1994
THE CANADIAN GLOBAL ALMANAC

General Editor	JOHN ROBERT COLOMBO
Publisher and Editor-in-Chief	SUSAN GIRVAN
Founding Editor	JOHN FILION
Contributing Editors	BARBARA CZARNECKI *(Index)*
	MAGGIE DORNING *(Science)*
	MARGARET FILSHIE LEASK *(History)*
	MARTIN LEVIN *(Sports)*
	DAVID PHILLIPS *(Climate)*
Designer-Technician	JOE LOBO
Researchers	MATTHEW BEHRENS
	PAUL PELLIZZARI
	SONJA RUTHARD
	ELENA SIMONETTI
Cover Design	BRANT COWIE, ARTPLUS
Maps	JANE WHITNEY

A portion of the information in this publication is made available through the co-operation of Statistics Canada. Integral and/or adapted reproductions are published with permission of the Minister of Industry, Science and Technology. Readers wishing further information on any of the subjects credited "Statistics Canada" may obtain copies of related publications by contacting Publications Sales, Statistics Canada, Ottawa, Ontario, Canada K1A 0T6 or by calling (toll free in Canada) 1-800-267-6677; outside Canada, 1-613-951-7277. Readers may also facsimile orders by dialing 1-613-951-1584.

Canadian Cataloguing in Publication Data

The National Library of Canada has catalogued this publication as follows:

Main entry under title:

The Canadian global almanac

1992-
Annual
"A book of facts".
ISSN 1187-4570
ISBN 0-7715-9020-2 (1994)

1. Almanacs, Canadian (English).
2. Almanacs.

AY414.C36   031.02   C92-031173-3

Macmillan Canada wishes to thank the Canada Council and the Ontario Ministry of Culture and Communications for supporting its publishing program.

Macmillan Canada
A Division of Canada Publishing
Corporation
Toronto

Printed in Canada

Preface

CHANGE HAS ALWAYS BEEN the order of the day, but the last twelve months have seen Canadians mired almost in limbo. It has been a year of retrenchment, reassessment and the frustration that accompanies a time of waiting.

As the 1993 Almanac went to press, we were voting on the Charlottetown Accord. (*And* we were fresh from the first Canadian victory in the World Series.) As the 1994 Almanac goes to press, we are heading for the polls in an election that could refashion the political shape of the country. After months of more of the same—the continuation of the recession, more bad news for the East coast fishery, more crises in Eastern Europe—hang onto your hat: we'll have a new government, a peace accord in the Middle East and some new energy to move in new directions.

This year's Almanac has documented the news and activity of the past year to give you a snapshot, both of the fast-changing world and of the country that was and is. As you browse through this year's edition you'll notice that the past twelve months have also brought about many changes in the pages of the Almanac. Regular readers will notice that the book has a new look—a facelift courtesy of our growing capabilities in desktop production. The production changes have made the almanac easier on the eye: headings are bolder and typefaces are more varied to make the book easier to use and easier to read.

Regular and new readers of the Almanac may be assured that while we have given a lot of thought to the look of the book, we have also worked hard to enrich its contents. We continue our search for the most accurate and reliable sources of information. More and more tables are comparative to allow the reader to judge how things are now and how they have been changing. The Science section continues to grow. In fact, there are additions to most sections, including a glossary of weather terms, a look at national health care costs, more updates from recently released 1991 census data, a longer span for current events, and an ongoing commitment to reflect world history rather than just the history of the Western world.

As ever, the judge of the success of our efforts is the reader. We look forward to receiving your comments and suggestions. What's working well? What's not? What's especially valued? What's missing? Please address your responses and reactions to the General Editor, *The Canadian Global Almanac*, Macmillan Canada, 29 Birch Avenue, Toronto, Ontario M4V 1E2

In the meantime, welcome to 1994!

Colombo

John Robert Colombo
October 1993.

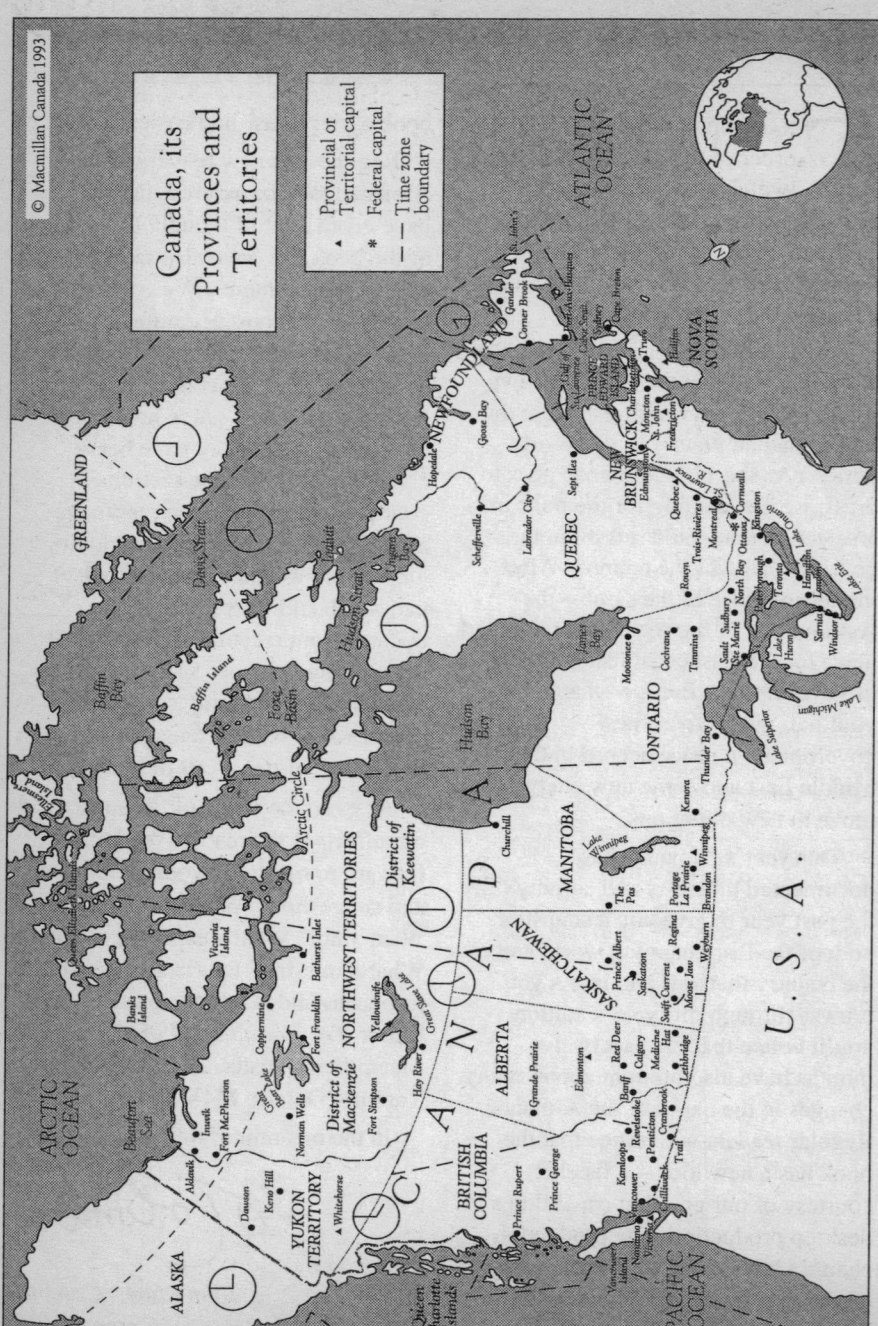

© Macmillan Canada 1993

Canada, its Provinces and Territories

▲ Provincial or Territorial capital
* Federal capital
--- Time zone boundary

The Country at a Glance

(as of October 1, 1993)

■ GENERAL

Motto:	A Mari Usque ad Mare (From Sea to Sea)
National Symbols:	the Maple Leaf and the Beaver (both official)
National Game:	lacrosse
Official Languages:	English and French
National Anthem:	O Canada
Royal Anthem:	God Save the Queen
Population:	27 296 000 (1991 census)
Capital City:	Ottawa, Ontario
Provinces:	10
Territories:	2

■ GEOGRAPHY

Area:	9 970 610 sq. km
Length of coastline:	243 792 km (longest in the world)
Length of border with U.S. inc. Alaska:	8 890 km
Longitudinal centre of Canada:	97°W (close to Winnipeg)
Latitudinal centre of Canada:	62°N (close to Yellowknife, NWT)
Geographic centre of Canada:	Arviat, NWT (60°06'30"N, 94°03'30"W)
Greatest distance east to west:	5 514 km (Cape Spear, Nfld. to the Yukon/Alaska border)
Greatest distance north to south:	4 634 km (Cape Columbia, Ellesmere Is. to Middle Is., Lake Erie)

■ POLITICS

Confederation:	July 1, 1867
Governor General:	His Excellency, the Right Honourable Ramon Hnatyshn
Prime Minister:	The Right Honourable Kim Campbell
Date of last general election:	Nov. 21, 1988
No. of Seats in the House of Commons:	295
No. of Seats in the Senate:	104
House of Commons General Information Inquiry:	613-992-4793
Senate General Inquiry:	1-800-267-7362 (toll free)

■ ECONOMY

Rate of inflation:	2.1% (1992)
Rate of unemployment:	11.3% (1992)
Goods and services tax:	7%, payable on most goods and services

■ SOCIETY

Life expectancy:	**males:** 73.0; **females:** 79.7
Average family income:	$53 131 (1991)
Average family size:	3.1 (1991)
Education:	compulsory to age 16
Health care:	universal publicly-sponsored system

What time is it?

If it's 12:00 noon in the Pacific Standard time zone, it is 1 p.m. Mountain Standard Time, 2 p.m. Central Standard Time, 3 p.m. Eastern Standard Time, 4:00 p.m. Atlantic Standard time, and 4:30 p.m. in Newfoundland.

Superlative Canadian Facts

Largest province		Quebec	1 540 680 sq. km
Smallest province		Prince Edward Island	5 660 sq. km
Largest city[1]:	by area	Gagnon, Que.	5 970 sq. km
	by population	Montreal, Que.	1 017 700 people
	by density	Montreal-Nord, Que.	8 187 people/sq. km
Smallest city[1]:	by area	L'Ile-Dorval, Que.	0.18 sq. km
	by population	Gagnon, Que.	5 people
	by density	Gagnon, Que.	0.0008 people/sq. km
Largest island		Baffin Island, NWT	507 451 sq. km
Northernmost point		Cape Columbia, Ellesmere Island, NWT	83° 06'N.–69°57'W.
Southernmost point		Middle Island, Lake Erie, Ont.	41° 41'N.–82°40'W.
Easternmost point		Cape Spear, Nfld.	47° 31'N.–52° 37'W.
Westernmost point		Yukon-Alaska boundary	141° 00'W.
Northernmost community		Grise Fiord, Ellesmere Island, NWT	76° 25'N.–82°54'W.
Southernmost community		Pelee Island South, Ont.	41° 45'N.–82°38'W.
Easternmost community		Blackhead, Nfld.	47°32'N.–52° 39'W.
Westernmost community		Beaver Creek, YT	62°23'N.–140° 52'W.
Highest city		Kimberley, BC	1 128 m
Highest community		Lake Louise, Alta.	1 540 m
Northernmost ice-free port		Stewart, BC	55°56'N.
Longest river		Mackenzie River, NWT	4 241 km
Largest lake (partly) in Canada		Superior, Ont. . . Total area 84 100 sq. km: 28 700 in Canada; 53 400 in U.S.	
Largest lake (entirely) in Canada		Great Bear Lake, NWT	31 328 sq. km
Deepest lake		Great Slave Lake, NWT	614 m
Highest mountain		Mt. Logan, YT	5 959 m
Highest waterfall		Della Falls, BC	440 m (more than one leap)
Greatest waterfall by volume		Horseshoe Falls, Niagara River, Ont.	5 365 cubic metres/second
Longest bridge		Pierre-Laporte Suspension Bridge, Que.	668 m
Longest covered bridge		at Hartland, NB	391 m
Longest tunnel		Mt. Macdonald Railway Tunnel, Rogers Pass, BC	14.6 km

Source: Energy, Mines and Resources Canada; Statistics Canada

(1) As of 1991 Census. The definition of city varies by province and, for Quebec, includes "ville".

Half an hour later in Newfoundland...

*D*uring the 19th century (and as long as there were clocks before that), every community around the world set its clocks based on local conditions—when the sun was directly overhead, it was noon. The coming of railways and telegraphs made this system unworkable and railway officials in North America tried to establish a uniform system of time to solve the problem. While US railways prepared to adopt uniform time zones in the US, a Scottish-born Canadian railway surveyor and inventor, Sir Sandford Fleming, proposed an international system that established 24 time zones around the world, with a one hour difference between zones.

In November of 1883, railway companies in North America adopted his system of standard time. At the International Prime Meridian Conference in Washington in 1884, 25 countries agreed to convert their timekeeping to "standard time". Greenwich Mean Time officially became the meridian of the system on January 1, 1885 and during the years following, more and more countries conformed to standard time.

When first adopted, each time zone was exactly 15° wide, but the boundaries have been altered to make more convenient divisions. Time zones west of Greenwich (Canada) are successively one hour earlier than the time in Greenwich—until the 180th meridian where they meet the time zones east of Greenwich. Therefore 15°W is Greenwich Mean Time -1 hour; 30°W is -2 hours; 45°W is -3 hours and 60°W (Sydney, NS) is -4 hours. St. John's, Newfoundland is 52 1/2°W of the meridian, in the middle of a zone and thus the time there is -3 1/2 hours GMT.

LANDFORMS OF CANADA

Canada is the largest country in the Western Hemisphere and the second largest in the world, with a total area of 9,970,610 sq. km. It stretches north to south from Cape Columbia on Ellesmere Island to Middle Island in Lake Erie, a distance of 4,634 km. The greatest east-west distance is 5,514 km from Cape Spear, Nfld., to the Yukon-Alaska border. Within this vast expanse, Canada contains an extremely wide variety of geographical features: the towering peaks of the Rockies, the flat Prairies, the rugged north and the gently rolling landscape of the east. But within this seemingly wide range of features, five areas with similar characteristics are found. These physiographic regions are commonly used to describe Canada and form the basis of Canada's geographical landforms and geological regions.

■ The Canadian Shield

Also known as the Precambrian Shield, this area is located in the central part of the continent. Viewed from the air it is a vast, inhospitable land of rocks, lakes and trees. It makes up roughly half of Canada's surface area, sweeping around Hudson Bay like a giant horseshoe, but also is the foundation for the rest of the continent.

The Canadian Shield has not always looked as it does today. Early in the Earth's history this area was the site of towering mountains, deep valleys and mighty rivers. The mountains were thrust up by volcanic activity as long as 3.8 billion years ago, during the Precambrian era. Over time, the forces of erosion—wind, water, freezing temperatures, ice—wore down the rocks that formed the mountain peaks and carried the materials away. Now all that remains are the roots of the once-mighty mountains.

The processes of volcanism present at the time of mountain-building caused minerals to form in the cooling rock of the Precambrian mountains. Deep inside the mountains, minerals such as gold, silver, copper and nickel came together into veins of ore. These ore bodies make the Shield a rich storehouse of mineral wealth.

■ The Appalachian Region

To the east of the Shield, this region was also once the site of massive mountain peaks. The rock that forms these peaks is not as old as the rock of the Shield, and is of a type that is more easily eroded. The Appalachian Region runs in a northeasterly direction from the southern United States to Newfoundland.

The mineral deposits found in the region reflect the complexity of the geology, and include gypsum, barite, salt, copper, zinc, lead, gold and silver. Since the end of the mountain-building period, erosion has worn off the tops of the mountains and filled the valleys with sediments, which gives the area its present-day less rugged appearance.

■ The Interior Plains

West of the Shield, rock which formed at the bottom of ancient lakes and seas gives the Prairies their distinctive flatness.

The Interior Plains occupy the central portion of the continent. Minerals found in the Interior Plains include potash, a substance produced when lakes and shallow seas evaporate, leaving deposits. Potash deposits in Saskatchewan are among the largest in the world. Coal, oil and natural gas were formed from organic materials trapped by the sedimentary layers during Palaeozoic times. An extension of the Interior Plains thrusts up between the Canadian Shield and the Appalachian Region, forming the Great Lakes-St. Lawrence Lowlands landform area. Soils throughout the Interior Plains are fertile, since the sedimentary materials that are found in the Plains break down easily.

Other lowland areas were formed during the Palaeozoic era as a result of the deposit of sediment which created the Interior Plains. The Hudson Bay Lowlands on the southwestern edge of Hudson Bay are relatively thin layers of sedimentary rock on top of the Precambrian Shield. The Arctic Lowlands, between the Shield and the Innuition Mountains of the high Arctic, are similar in age and characteristics to the material of the Interior Plains.

■ The Western Cordillera

As the Precambrian mountains eroded, the sedimentary layers were deposited over a great distance and formed the Appalachian Region to the east. These deposits also provided the material from which future landforms would be built to the west. These landforms are now known as the Western Cordillera.

When the continent started its westward movement about 200 million years ago, its leading edge was forced against the adjacent oceanic plate and the land moved overtop the ocean. Geologists speculate that the tremendous pressure exerted during this process caused the sedimentary layers of the plate's edge to buckle into a massive dome. Magma, the hot fluid substance below the Earth's crust, flowed into the dome and formed a core which eventually collapsed between 65 and 160 million years ago, breaking the rock layers. This core stretches along the edge of the continental plate and absorbs the pressure of the two plates as they press upon each other.

The Western Cordillera is an area of great complexity; rocks composed of different materials and through different processes are thoroughly mixed. The Coast Ranges which form the leading western edge of the continent are composed of both igneous and metamorphic rock. The interior of the Cordillera is a jumble of plateaus, folded and broken rock layers and recent volcanoes. The sedimentary materials of the Rockies on the eastern edge of the Cordillera were folded and broken during a period of mountain-building in Eocene times, some 40-65 million years ago.

The Cordillera contains minerals associated with all the processes involved in its creation. The igneous rocks of the western part of the Cordillera are a major source of minerals including lead, zinc, silver, copper and gold. The sedimentary deposits of the eastern Cordillera are responsible for the coal and petroleum found there.

■ Innuitian Region

Mountain-building shaped the landforms of the high Arctic during the Devonian period (about 405 million years ago). The most recent activities appear to have occurred about 30 million years ago, which was long after the mountain-building period that thrust up the Rocky Mountains in the Cordillera.

Little detail is known about this region because research is so difficult in the inhospitable climate, but some geologists have suggested mountain-building is the result of the North American plate advancing on the Eurasian plate.

The topography of this region is characterized by low plateau mountains, with ridges as high as 3,000 m. The area is composed mainly of sedimentary rocks but includes some metamorphic and volcanic rocks. For more information on geological time periods, see the chart in the Science and Nature Section.

Glaciation

*V*irtually all of Canada was subject to glaciation—during the Ice Age (1.5 million years ago), it's estimated that 97% of the country was covered by ice. The periodic advances of the glaciers stripped away the soil and helped to wear away the rocks at the surface. There were likely four major periods of glaciation, each lasting about 100,000 years, with long warm periods in between. As the ice melted and the glaciers retreated, the soils and rocks which had been suspended in the ice were deposited onto the surface below. These deposits, some of which are known as moraines, drumlins and outwash plains, contribute to the present-day topography of Canada.

Drainage patterns were shaped by glaciation, and the countless lakes and swamps of the Canadian Shield are a product of the poorly-developed drainage system resulting from the last glacial period about 10,000 years ago.

The Great Lakes

The Great Lakes form the largest body of fresh water in the world and with their connecting waterways are the largest inland water transportation unit. They enable shipping to reach the Atlantic via the St. Lawrence River; the Gulf of Mexico via the Illinois Waterway, from Lake Michigan to the Mississippi River; a third outlet connects with the Hudson River and thence the Atlantic via the New York State Barge Canal System.

	Superior	Michigan	Huron	Erie	Ontario
Length in km	563	494	332	388	311
Breadth in km	257	190	295	92	85
Deepest soundings in metres	405	281	229	64	244
Volume of water in cubic km	12 100	4 920	3 540	484	1 640
Area[1] (sq. km) in US	53 400	57 800	23 600	12 900	8 960
Area[1] (sq. km) in Canada	28 700	0	36 000	12 800	10 000
Total Area[1] (sq. km) US and Canada	82 100	57 800	59 600	25 700	18 960
National boundary line in km	430	0	446	404	281

Source: *Energy, Mines and Resources Canada*   (1) Does not include islands larger than 0.052 sq. km.

Largest Lakes in Canada

Lake	Area[1] (sq. km)	Lake	Area[1] (sq. km)
Superior, Ont.[2]	82 100	Winnipegosis, Man.	5 374
Huron, Ont.[3]	59 600	Nipigon, Ont.	4 848
Great Bear, NWT	31 328	Manitoba, Man.	4 624
Great Slave, NWT	28 568	Dubawnt, NWT	3 833
Erie, Ont.[4]	25 700	Lake of the Woods, Ont./Man.[6]	4 472
Winnipeg, Man.	24 387	Amadjuak, NWT	3 115
Ontario, Ont.[5]	18 960	Melville, Nfld	3 069
Athabasca, Sask.	7 935	Wollaston, Sask.	2 681
Reindeer, Sask./Man.	6 650	Lac Mistassini, Que.	2 335
Smallwood Reservoir, Nfld	6 527	Nueltin, NWT/Man.	2 279
Nettilling, NWT	5 542	Southern Indian, Man.	2 247

Source: *Energy, Mines and Resources Canada*

(1) Total area, including islands except for the Great Lakes, where area does not include islands larger than 0.052 sq. km. (2) Includes 53,400 sq. km in U.S. (3) Includes 23,600 sq. km in U.S. (4) Includes 12,900 sq. km in U.S. (5) Includes 8 960 sq. km in U.S. (6) Includes 1,322 sq. km in U.S.

Largest Islands in Canada

Island	Area (sq. km)	Island	Area (sq. km)
Baffin, NWT	507 451	Prince Patrick, NWT	15 848
Victoria, NWT	217 291	King William, NWT	13 111
Ellesmere, NWT	196 236	Ellef Ringnes, NWT	11 295
Newfoundland (main island)	108 860	Bylot, NWT	11 067
Banks, NWT	70 028	Cape Breton, N.S.	10 311
Devon, NWT	55 247	Prince Charles, NWT	9 521
Axel Heiberg, NWT	43 178	Anticosti Island, Que.	7 941
Melville, NWT	42 149	Cornwallis, NWT	6 995
Southampton, NWT	41 214	Graham, BC	6 361
Prince of Wales, NWT	33 339	Prince Edward Island (main island)	5 620
Vancouver, BC	31 285	Coats, NWT	5 498
Somerset, NWT	24 786	Amund Ringnes, NWT	5 255
Bathurst, NWT	16 042	Mackenzie King, NWT	5 048

Source: *Energy, Mines and Resources Canada*

Canada's Highest Waterfalls

Name	Vertical drop (metres)	Location	Latitude	Longitude
Della Falls[1]	440	Della Lake, BC	49° 27'	125° 32'
Takakkaw Falls[1]	254	From the Daly Glacier, BC	51° 30'	116° 28'
Hunlen Falls	253	Atnarko River, BC	52° 17'	125° 46'
Panther Falls	183	Nigel Creek, Alta	52° 10'	117° 03'
Helmcken Falls	137	Murtle River, BC	51° 57'	120° 11'
Bridal Veil Falls	122	Bridal Creek, BC	49° 11'	121° 44'
Virginia Falls	90	South Nahanni River, NWT	61° 36'	125° 44'
Montmorency, Chute	84	Rivière Montmorency, Que.	46° 53'	71° 09'
Ouiatchouan, Chute	79	Rivière Ouiatchouaniche, Que.	48° 26'	72° 10'
Churchill Falls	75	Churchill River, Nfld	53° 36'	64° 19'
Brandywine Falls	61	Brandywine Creek, BC	50° 02'	123° 07'
Niagara Falls				
American Falls	59	Niagara River, US	43° 05'	79° 05'
Horseshoe Falls	57	Niagara River, Ont.	43° 05'	79° 04'
Wilberforce Falls	49	Hood River, NWT	67° 06'	108° 47'

Source: *Energy, Mines and Resources Canada*   (1) Falls with more than one leap

Longest Rivers in Canada

River	Length (km)	Flows Into	River	Length (km)	Flows Into
Mackenzie	4 241	Arctic Ocean	Rivière Koksoak	874	Ungava Bay
Yukon	3 185	Bering Sea	Churchill (Nfld)	856	Atlantic Ocean
St. Lawrence	3 058	Gulf of St. Lawrence	Coppermine	845	Arctic Ocean
Nelson	2 575	Hudson Bay	Dubawnt	842	Hudson Bay
Columbia	2 000	Pacific Ocean	Winnipeg	813	Hudson Bay
Saskatchewan	1 939	Lake Winnipeg	Kootenay	780	Columbia R.
Peace	1 923	Lake Athabasca	Rivière Nottaway	776	James Bay
Churchill (Man.)	1 609	Hudson Bay	Rivière Rupert	763	James Bay
South Saskatchewan	1 392	Saskatchewan R.	Rivière Eastmain	756	James Bay
Fraser	1 370	Pacific Ocean	Attawapiskat	748	James Bay
North Saskatchewan	1 287	Saskatchewan R.	Kazan	732	Hudson Bay
Ottawa	1 271	St Lawrence R.	Grande rivière de la		
Athabasca	1 231	Lake Athabasca	Baleine	724	Hudson Bay
Liard	1 115	Mackenzie R.	Red Deer	724	Saskatchewan R.
Assiniboine	1 070	Red R.	Porcupine	721	Pacific Ocean
Severn	982	Hudson Bay	Hay	702	Great Slave Lake
Albany	982	James Bay	Rivière Saguenay	698	St. Lawrence R.
Back	974	Arctic Ocean	Anderson	692	Arctic Ocean
Thelon	904	Hudson Bay	Peel	684	Arctic Ocean
La Grande Rivière	893	James Bay	Fairford	684	Hudson Bay
Red	877	Lake Winnipeg	Saint John	673	Bay of Fundy

Source: *Energy, Mines and Resources Canada*

Water Use in Canada

*C**anadians are the world's second largest per capita users of water. It has been estimated that about 80 L of water per person per day is enough to maintain a reasonable quality of life. Water use in the average Canadian household is 360 L per person per day.*

Municipalities, agriculture, transportation, energy, recreation and industries are also major water-using sectors in Canada.

Highest Peaks in Canada

Mountain	Range	Prov./Terr.	Elev. (m)	Mountain	Range	Prov./Terr.	Elev. (m)
Mt. Logan	St. Elias Mtns	YT	5 959	Mt. Cook	St. Elias Mtns	YT/Alaska	4 194
Mt. St. Elias	St. Elias Mtns	YT/Alaska	5 489	Mt. Quincy Adams	St. Elias Mtns	BC/Alaska	4 133
Mt. Lucania	St. Elias Mtns	YT	5 226	Mt. Craig	St. Elias Mtns	YT	4 039
King Peak	St. Elias Mtns	YT	5 173	Mt. Waddington	Coast Mtns	BC	4 016
Mt. Steele	St. Elias Mtns	YT	5 067	Mt. Robson	Rocky Mtns	BC	3 954
Mt. Wood	St. Elias Mtns	YT	4 838	Mt. Root	St. Elias Mtns	BC/Alaska	3 901
Mt. Vancouver	St. Elias Mtns	YT/Alaska	4 785	Mt. Malaspina	St. Elias Mtns	YT	3 886
Mt. Macaulay	St. Elias Mtns	YT	4 663	Mt. Queen Mary	St. Elias Mtns	YT	3 886
Mt. Slaggard	St. Elias Mtns	YT	4 663	Mt. Badham	St. Elias Mtns	YT	3 848
Fairweather Mtn.	St. Elias Mtns	BC/Alaska	4 663	Mt. Tiedemann	Coast Mtns	BC	3 848
Mt. Hubbard	St. Elias Mtns	YT/Alaska	4 577	Combatant Mtn.	Coast Mtns	BC	3 756
Mt. Walsh	St. Elias Mtns	YT	4 505	Mt. Columbia	Rocky Mtns	Alta/BC	3 747
Mt. Alverstone	St. Elias Mtns	YT/Alaska	4 439	North Twin	Rocky Mtns	Alta	3 733
McArthur Peak	St. Elias Mtns	YT	4 344	Asperity Mtn.	Coast Mtns	BC	3 716
Mt. Augusta	St. Elias Mtns	YT/Alaska	4 289	Mt. Clemenceau	Rocky Mtns	BC	3 642
Mt. Kennedy	St. Elias Mtns	YT	4 235	Serra Peaks	Coast Mtns	BC	3 642
Avalanche Peak	St. Elias Mtns	YT	4 212	Mt. Alberta	Rocky Mtns	Alta	3 620
Mt. Strickland	St. Elias Mtns	YT	4 212	Mt. Assiniboine	Rocky Mtns	Alta/BC	3 618
Mt. Newton	St. Elias Mtns	YT	4 210				

Source: *Energy, Mines and Resources Canada*

Highest Point in Each Province and Territory

Province/Territory	Highest Point	Elev. (m)
Newfoundland	Mt. Caubvick[1]	1 652
Prince Edward Island	46° 20'—63° 25' (Queen's County)	142
Nova Scotia	46° 42'—60° 36' (Cape Breton Highlands)	532
New Brunswick	Mt. Carleton	817
Quebec	Mont D'Iberville[2]	1 652
Ontario	Ishpatina Ridge	693
Manitoba	Baldy Mtn.	832
Saskatchewan	Cypress Hills	1 468
Alberta	Mt. Columbia	3 747
British Columbia	Fairweather Mtn.	4 663
Yukon Territory	Mt. Logan	5 959
Northwest Territories	61° 52'—127° 42' (unnamed peak, Mackenzie Mtns.)	2 773

Source: *Energy, Mines and Resources Canada*

(1) On the Nfld./Que. border; also known as Mt. D'Iberville in Quebec; next highest point in Nfld is Cirque Mt. at 1,568 m. (2) On the Nfld/ Que. border; also known as Mt. Caubvick in Newfoundland; next highest point in Que. is Mont Jacques-Cartier at 1,268 m.

Mapping the Country

*T*he National Atlas of Canada has been providing geographical information about the country since the first edition in 1906. The Department of the Interior released the second edition in 1915, when Canada had just 7 million people and only 30% lived in the 15 towns and cities that had a population of 25,000 or more.

Later editions were published in 1958 and 1974 and reflected the need for more specialized geographical information. The fifth edition, published by Energy, Mines and Resources, is the first not published as a bound book. Instead, EMR will release a series of maps. The first installment came in January 1986 and the final collection will total some 200 maps. Users will also be able to access the material electronically, via a digital database.

VEGETATION

Coniferous forests dominated by spruce, fir and pine cover much of the Canadian landscape, sweeping across the continent in a broad band. Through the rest of the country there is a range of forest conditions. To the north, cold temperatures limit growth and the trees become small and fewer in number. At the tree line, trees grow only in sheltered river valleys. The tree line marks the northern extent of forests and the beginning of tundra conditions.

The massive spruce, fir and pine of the forests along the coast of British Columbia are encouraged by a friendly climate. The moisture-laden winds from the Pacific Ocean keep the land well-supplied with rain. Under these conditions tree growth is rapid: the soils are constantly being replenished with minerals by the rains, and plant decay is rapid in the damp conditions, thereby releasing more minerals for tree growth. With average monthly temperatures seldom going below freezing, the growing season is long. Coniferous trees thrive under such conditions.

The Interior Plains is one region of Canada that is not naturally covered by forests because there is not enough precipitation, or available moisture, to sustain tree growth. In Alberta, Saskatchewan and Manitoba, forests gradually give way from north to south through a transitional area called the park belt, which contains both trees and grassland, before yielding to grasslands. Within these provinces, there are areas where moisture levels are insufficient to support grasslands and even hardy grasses have difficulty growing. During the 1930s, the lack of rainfall in the Interior Plains led to "dust bowl" conditions because vegetation could not grow enough to anchor the soil.

The forests of south-eastern Canada are mixed, containing both coniferous and deciduous trees. Adequate rainfall and warm temperatures allow the less hardy species such as oak, maple, hickory and walnut to flourish in southern Ontario and Québec and the Maritime provinces.

The Arctic tundra is so very dry and cold that the growing season is very limited. The vegetation of the tundra consists of mosses, lichen, dwarf bushes and heather. These plants are able to grow because they have adapted to the difficult conditions through characteristics such as small size and slow growth. Some shrubs and lichen grow so slowly that their development must be measured in centimetres per century.

Spring and Fall Frost Dates in Canada

Frost occurs whenever temperatures fall to 0°C or lower. All dates and values are based on the available data during the period 1951-1980. Data reported from airport stations unless * designates city office station.

	1 in 10 Chance Last Spring Frost After Date	1 in 10 Chance First Fall Frost Before Date	Frost-free Period (days)	Growing Degree-Days Above 5°C[1]
Newfoundland				
Corner Brook*	June 10	Sept. 8	139	1 370
St. John's*	June 24	Sept. 19	131	1 196
Prince Edward Island				
Charlottetown	May 27	Oct. 6	151	1 626
Nova Scotia				
Halifax	May 28	Sept. 30	155	1 694
New Brunswick				
Fredericton	June 10	Sept. 13	126	1 770
Saint John	June 10	Sept. 18	139	1 499
Quebec				
Chicoutimi*	June 4	Sept. 18	135	1 655
Gaspé*	June 12	Sept. 11	123	1 428
Montreal	May 19	Sept. 26	157	2 113
Quebec	May 28	Sept. 14	137	1 690
Schefferville	June 27	Aug. 22	77	614 ▶

	1 in 10 Chance Last Spring Frost After Date	1 in 10 Chance First Fall Frost Before Date	Frost-free Period (days)	Growing Degree-Days Above 5°C[1]
▶ **Ontario**				
Kitchener*	May 25	Sept. 17	151	2 169
Moosonee*	July 6	July 30	70	1 107
Ottawa	May 25	Sept. 21	147	2 043
St. Catharines*	May 18	Oct. 5	173	2 429
Sudbury	June 11	Sept. 11	128	1 664
Thunder Bay	June 13	Aug. 29	104	1 425
Timmins	June 23	Aug. 19	91	1 408
Toronto	May 25	Sept. 18	149	2 127
Windsor	May 10	Oct. 3	177	2 533
Manitoba				
Churchill	July 7	Aug. 20	76	555
Flin Flon	June 10	Sept. 2	115	1 340
Winnipeg	June 10	Sept. 11	121	1 785
Saskatchewan				
Prince Albert	June 21	Aug. 17	95	1 412
Regina	June 14	Aug. 27	109	1 677
Saskatoon	June 10	Sept. 1	117	1 620
Alberta				
Banff*	June 30	Aug. 6	89	1 081
Calgary	June 10	Aug. 27	112	1 387
Edmonton	June 14	Aug. 13	105	1 328
Fort McMurray	June 30	Aug. 2	84	1 290
Peace River	June 23	Aug. 13	93	1 239
British Columbia				
Fort Nelson	June 7	Aug. 14	106	1 266
Penticton	May 23	Sept. 14	148	2 136
Prince George	July 1	Aug. 11	85	1 199
Prince Rupert	May 25	Sept. 28	156	1 148
Vancouver	Apr. 21	Oct. 13	216	1 994
Victoria	Apr. 30	Oct. 17	201	1 864
Yukon				
Dawson*	June 16	Aug. 6	91	1 015
Whitehorse	June 24	Aug. 13	82	897
Northwest Territories				
Alert*	July 15	July 16	4	35
Iqaluit	July 12	July 26	59	179
Resolute	July 15	July 16	9	33
Yellowknife	June 9	Sept. 3	111	1 027

Source: *Environment Canada*

(1) Growing degree days represent the average total number of heat units (daily mean temp. -5°C) during the growing season

Do You Know Your Zone?

*A*griculture Canada has designated ten plant hardiness zones for Canada, ranging from 0 (the coldest) to 9 (the mildest), and classified common Canadian shrubs and plants according to their ability to thrive (or not) in each zone's weather conditions.

Weather factors that affect a plant's survival include the lowest winter temperature, the length of frost-free growing time, the average amount of summer rainfall, the highest temperatures during the growing season and the average amount of snow cover and wind during the year. Other factors to consider are the age of the plants (young plants may need protection during their first winter), whether the growing area is much higher than the surrounding area, and how close the growing area is to the next zone boundary. These zones are not absolute, but they can tell you what should survive.

AGRICULTURE

There are four main types of farms in Canada: livestock farms, grain farms producing such crops as wheat and oats, mixed farms producing both grain and livestock, and special crop farms producing vegetables, fruits, tobacco and other products. Both the type and amount of farming within Canada is affected by climate and location.

■ The Atlantic Region

The Atlantic region is an area of diverse agricultural activity. Newfoundland, because of poorly developed soils and a difficult climate, has a limited agricultural industry supplying only local markets. Encouraged by a moist climate and silty, stone-free soils, farming is the leading industry on Prince Edward Island; potatoes are the main crop. The land also supports mixed grains and dairy farms.

Nova Scotia's main agricultural areas surround the Bay of Fundy and Northumberland Strait where they are protected from Atlantic gales; dairy farming and poultry production are common. Nova Scotia's Annapolis Valley is famous for fruit, mainly apples. In New Brunswick, potatoes and livestock are produced in the Saint John River valley, and there is mixed farming in the northwest of the province.

■ The Central Region

In Canada's central region, the fertile soils and moist climate of southern Ontario and Quebec support a thriving agricultural industry. Although these growing conditions allow a variety of crops, the population concentration in this area encourages specialization in products with high transportation costs. Dairy farms are concentrated around Montreal and in southwestern Ontario, supplying milk, butter and cheese to the major centres, such as London, Hamilton, Toronto, Kingston, Montreal and Quebec City. Vegetable crops are also grown near these centres. Farms specializing in poultry and egg production, sheep and hogs are also common.

The Niagara Peninsula, between Lakes Ontario and Erie, is a major fruit-growing centre. The moderating effects of the lakes delay the growth of the fruit trees in the spring until danger of frost is past. Tender fruit crops—peaches, pears, plums and cherries—as well as grapes thrive in these conditions. Tobacco grows well on the glacially-created sand plains of southwestern Ontario.

■ The Prairie Provinces

Manitoba, Saskatchewan and Alberta contain 80 percent of Canada's farmland. Here, a combination of flat, easily-worked land, fertile soils, long sunny summer days and sufficient precipitation encourages the healthy growth of high-quality grains. This area grows most of Canada's wheat, about 90 percent of its barley and rye, and more than 75 percent of its oats.

Manitoba grows canola/rapeseed and flax in addition to wheat and other grains. Mixed farming in the province emphasizes beef cattle. Dairy farms are common around Winnipeg. Saskatchewan grows about 60 percent of Canada's wheat and large quantities of other grains. Mixed farming, poultry, egg and livestock production contribute to the provincial economy. Alberta, also a major grain producer, has more beef cattle ranches than any other province. They are located mainly in the south of the province and in the foothills of the Rocky Mountains where the steep slopes and dry land is unsuited to growing crops. ▶

Measuring the Weather

An anemometer measures wind speed in km per hour. ▲ *A barometer measures atmospheric pressure in kilopascals.* ▲ *A Campbell Stokes recorder measures sunshine in hours.* ▲ *A rain gauge measures rainfall in millimetres.* ▲ *A ruler or a snow gauge measures snowfall in centimetres.* ▲ *A thermometer measures temperature in °C.* ▲ *A wet bulb thermometer measures humidity in °C/percent.* ▲ *A wind vane measures wind direction according to N E S W.*

► ■ **The Pacific Region**

In the Pacific region, only 2 percent of British Columbia is agricultural land. But the pockets of farmland are extremely productive. The lower mainland and the southern tip of Vancouver Island comprise the Georgia Strait agricultural region, an area concentrating on dairy farming and poultry raising to supply the province's population centres. Other crops include raspberries, strawberries, peas, tomatoes and flowers.

The Okanagan Valley contains 90 percent of British Columbia's orchards, producing grapes, apples and tender fruit such as peaches, plums, apricots and cherries. Here, local climatic and physiographic characteristics have resulted in conditions suitable for the orchard industry, although irrigation is often necessary and frost damage is a hazard. Beef cattle and sheep are raised in the interior of the province, where growing conditions are not suitable for crops requiring cultivation, but grazing can be carried out.

■ **The North**

Canada's North generally has soil and climatic conditions unsuited to agriculture. A small number of farms produce some dairy products, beef cattle and vegetables for the local market.

CLIMATE

Within Canada, climate is primarily affected by surrounding landforms, proximity to large bodies of water and the degree of latitude.

Landforms Air masses are forced to rise over mountains which lie in their path. As this happens, the air cools and its ability to retain moisture is reduced. Condensation then occurs and precipitation falls in the form of snow or rain. For instance, Prince Rupert on the western side of the Coastal Mountains receives over 2,500 mm of precipitation annually.

On the leeward side of the mountains, the air mass descends, warms and is able to once again retain moisture. Moreover, there may be little moisture left in the air mass. Thus precipitation is light and a rain-shadow effect is created. In a rain-shadow area, such as near Kamloops, BC, desert-like conditions exist.

Water Parts of Canada near large bodies of water have more moderate climates due to the differing abilities of land and water to gain or lose heat. Whereas water can act like a heat bank, releasing accumulated heat through the fall and early winter and warming the land nearby, the reverse is also true. In the spring and early summer, the water is cooler than the land and can keep the land temperature lower.

Wind direction also determines the degree to which this influence is felt. On the Pacific coast the prevailing westerlies blow off the water onto the land and the influence of the Pacific Ocean is keenly felt. On the Atlantic coast, the westerlies blow off the land onto the water so the effect of the Atlantic Ocean is not as pronounced. Victoria has a monthly low of 4.1°C and a range of only 11.5°C while Halifax has a monthly low of -3.6°C and a range of 22.4°C.

Latitude Latitude is the distance north or south of the equator and is expressed in degrees. Its effects on climate are twofold. Firstly, the curvature of the earth results in the sunlight spreading over a greater surface area which decreases the solar radiation per unit area of ground so that less warmth from the sun is felt. Secondly, solar radiation has to travel a greater distance through the atmosphere at higher latitudes which again reduces the amount of energy reaching the earth.

Other Factors Because the prevailing wind direction is from west to east, the air masses move eastward across the continent picking up moisture from lakes and rivers and releasing it further along. Therefore, generally, precipitation increases with greater distance eastward from the central continent: the average precipitation in Winnipeg is 526 mm, Toronto 762 mm, Montreal 946 mm and Halifax 1 282 mm.

Also, the Labrador Current affects climate on the Atlantic coast. This cold current within the Atlantic Ocean flows south along the coast of Newfoundland and Labrador and reduces the moderating effect of the ocean on the land. It also causes the thick Newfoundland fog when relatively warm air is cooled from below on contact with the cold waters.

A Glossary of Weather Terms

air mass: an extensive body of air with a fairly uniform distribution of moisture and temperature throughout

atmosphere: the envelope of air surrounding the earth. Most weather events are confined to the lower 10 km of the atmosphere.

atmospheric pressure: the force exerted on the earth by the weight of the atmosphere

blizzard: severe winter weather condition characterized by low temperatures, strong winds above 40 km/h, and visibility of less than 1 km due to blowing snow; condition lasts three hours or more

blowing snow: snow lifted from the earth's surface by the wind to a height of two metres or more. Blowing snow is higher than drifting snow.

bright sunshine: sunshine intense enough to burn a mark on recording paper mounted in the Campbell-Stokes sunshine recorder. The daily period of bright sunshine is less than that of visible sunshine because the sun's rays are not intense enough to burn the paper just after sunrise, near sunset and under cloudy conditions

Chinook (also snow-eater): a dry, warm, strong wind that blows down the eastern slopes of the Rocky Mountains in North America. The warmth and dryness are due principally to heating by compression as the air descends the mountain slope.

cold wave: an occurrence of dangerous cold conditions, when temperatures often dip below -18°C, that usually lasts longer than a few days

deep low: used to describe the central barometric pressure of a low [usually when it is about 975 millibars (97.50 kPa or less)]. Often has winds of gale to storm force around the low.

developing low: a low in which the central pressure is decreasing with time. Winds would normally increase as the low deepens.

dew point temperature: the temperature at which air becomes saturated, allowing condensation of water vapour as frost, fog, dew or mist

drizzle: precipitation consisting of numerous minute water droplets which appear to float; the droplets are much smaller than in rain.

filling low: a low in which the central pressure is increasing with time., i.e. the low is gradually weakening

flash floods: a very rapid rise of water with little or no advance warning, most often when an intense thunderstorm drops a huge rainfall on a fairly small area in a very short space of time.

fog: a cloud based at the earth's surface consisting of tiny water droplets or, under very cold conditions, ice crystals or ice fog; generally found in calm or low wind conditions. Under foggy conditions, visibility is reduced to less than one km.

freezing precipitation: supercooled water drops of drizzle, or rain which freeze on impact to form a coating of ice upon the ground or any objects they strike

front: the boundary between two different air masses which have originated from widely separated regions. A cold front is the leading edge of an advancing cold air mass, while a warm front is the trailing edge of a retreating cold air mass.

frost: the deposit of ice crystals that occurs when the air temperature is at or below the freezing point of water. The term frost is also used to describe the icy deposits of water vapor that may form on the ground or on other surfaces like car windshields, which are colder than the surrounding air and which have a temperature below freezing.

gale: a strong wind. A gale warning is issued for expected winds of 65 to 100 km/h (34 to 47 knots).

gust: a sudden, brief increase in wind speed, for generally less than 20 seconds

heat wave: a period with more than three consecutive days of maximum temperatures at or above 32°C

high pressure: a term for an area of high (maximum) pressure with a closed, clockwise (in the Northern Hemisphere) circulation of air

humidex: a measure of what hot weather "feels like." Air of a given temperature and moisture content is equated in comfort to air with a higher temperature and that of negligible moisture content. At a humidex of 30°C some people begin to experience discomfort.

hurricane: a tropical storm with wind speeds of 120 km/h (65 knots) or more that can be many thousands of square kilometres in size. The storms originate over the warm tropical ocean as a small low-pressure system. They have a life span of several days and occur most frequently between August and October.

ice pellets: precipitation consisting of fragments of ice, 5 mm or less in diameter, that bounce when hitting a hard surface, making a sound upon impact

inversion: the term refers to a temperature increase with height, where the usual pattern is a decrease in temperature within increasing height

isobar: a line on a weather map or chart connecting points of equal pressure. The large concentric lines on television or newspaper weather maps are isobars.

killing frost: a frost severe enough to end the growing season, usually when the air temperature falls below -2°C

land breeze: a small-scale wind set off when the air temperature over water is warmer than that over adjacent land. The land breeze develops at night and blows from the land out to the sea or onto the lake. Its counterpart is the sea or lake breeze.

low pressure: an area of low (minimum) atmospheric pressure that has a closed counter-clockwise circulation in the Northern Hemisphere

peak wind (gust): the highest instantaneous wind speed recorded for a specific time period

precipitation: any and all forms of water, whether liquid or solid, that fall from the atmosphere and reach the earth's surface. A day with measurable precipitation is a day when the water equivalent of the precipitation is equal to or greater than 0.2 mm.

probability of precipitation (POP): subjective numerical estimates of your chances of encountering measurable precipitation at some time during the forecast period. For example, a 40% probability of rain means there are four chances in 10 of getting wet. They cannot be used to predict when, where or how much precipitation will occur.

relative humidity: the ratio of water vapour in the air at a given temperature to the maximum which could exist at that temperature. It is usually expressed as a percentage.

ridge: an elongated area of high pressure extending from the centre of a high pressure region; the opposite of a trough.

sea breeze: a small-scale wind set off when the air temperature over land is greater than that over the adjacent sea. The sea breeze develops during the day and blows from the sea to the land. Its counterpart is the land breeze.

small craft warning: issued when winds over the coastal marine areas are expected to reach and maintain speeds of 20 to 33 knots

snow: precipitation consisting of white or translucent ice crystals and often agglomerated into snowflakes. A day with measurable snow is a day when the total snowfall is at least 0.2 cm.

squall: a strong, sudden wind which generally lasts a few minutes then quickly decreases in speed. Squalls are generally associated with severe thunderstorms.

storm track: the path taken by a low-pressure centre

storm warning: the wind warning that is issued to mariners when winds are expected to be 48 to 63 knots

thunderstorm: a local storm, usually produced by a cumulonimbus cloud, and always accompanied by thunder and lightning. A thunderstorm day is a day when thunder is heard or when lightning is seen (rain and snow need not have fallen).

tornado (also twister): a violently rotating column of air that is usually visible as a funnel cloud hanging from dark thunderstorm clouds. It is one of the least extensive of all storms, but in violence, it is the most destructive.

trough: an elongated area of low pressure extending from the centre of a low pressure region; the opposite of a ridge

typhoon: a severe tropical cyclone in the Pacific Ocean, counterpart of the Atlantic hurricane

waterspout: a small whirling storm over water which is spawned from the base of a thunderstorm. It is similar to but generally not as severe as a tornado.

weather advisory: issued when forecast conditions are expected to cause general inconvenience or concern, and do not pose a serious enough threat to require a weather warning. An advisory will often precede a warning.

Weatheradio: this is the name of Environment Canada's weather information broadcast network. The network has transmitters in every region and listeners need a receiver, which can be purchased from electronic equipment dealers, to pick up the broadcasts. Weatheradio signals warnings of severe weather automatically to receivers equipped with special alarm devices for that purpose.

westerlies (west-wind belt): the pronounced west-to-east motion of the atmosphere centred over middle latitudes from about 35 to 65° latitude.

wind chill: a simple measure of the chilling effect experienced by the human body when strong winds are combined with freezing temperatures. The larger the wind chill, the faster the rate of cooling. The wind chill factor is expressed in watts per square metre or in °C (an equivalent temperature).

wind direction: the direction from which the wind is blowing

Canadian Weather Highlights from July 1992 to June 1993

JULY 1992: In the middle of the year with very little summer, July had below normal temperatures across most of Canada. Only BC, the District of Mackenzie and the Yukon Territory could boast a warmer than normal July. Across the rest of Canada, July was more like early fall than mid-summer. At Medicine Hat and Winnipeg, July average temperatures were colder than any year since 1884, and Ontario experienced its coldest July this century. Overnight lows in Moosonee were below freezing at mid-month. For only the second time in the last 150 years, the maximum temperature in Toronto failed to reach 30°C. Frost was reported as far south as Sudbury, with patchy ground frost in south-central Ontario.

Early in July, temperatures in the Yukon soared to the mid-30s. The hot, unstable air resulted in severe thunderstorms near Whitehorse. A funnel cloud was sighted near the Alaska-Yukon border, while lightning touched off numerous forest fires. The heat wave rapidly melted the winter snowpack, contributing to record river and lake water levels and causing some flooding.

AUGUST 1992: Cool weather continued across the southern parts of Ontario and Manitoba. Alberta was seared by 30°C heat mid-month, and then a cold Arctic air mass gave snow and record-low temperatures to southern and central Alberta on Aug. 21. In Edmonton, the snowfall was the earliest since records began in 1884. Snow fell as far south and east as Swift Current, Sask. The snow and subsequent cold wave devastated grain crops just weeks before harvest.

Severe weather events were numerous in Aug., not surprising since this month is normally the peak of the summer severe weather season. On the 3rd, a hail storm near Lethbridge flattened crops, knocked birds out of trees and necessitated the use of snowplows to clear roads of 30 cm of hail. On the 4th, a hail storm destroyed a quarter of the Niagara Peninsula's fruit crop. Flash floods cost $10 million damage in SW Quebec. Near the end of Aug., the remnants of Hurricane Andrew moved into southern Ontario, drenching some areas with over 100 mm of rain in 24 hours.

SEPTEMBER 1992: Cool and wet weather continued into Sept. During the latter half of the month, however, some of the warmest weather of the year occurred in parts of eastern Canada. In early Sept., Alberta received its second major snowstorm of the summer. Adding to the woes, a widespread frost occurred on the morning of the 5th.

In the middle of Sept., warm, humid air surged northward bringing 30°C temperatures from the Great Lakes to New Brunswick. Severe thunderstorms hit south of Quebec City, damaging 20 homes and cutting power for 12 hours. Heavy rain caused local flooding in the Muskoka-Haliburton district of Ontario. In the Terrace/Kitimat region of BC, 155 mm of rain fell in 24 hours, a new September rainfall record for the area.

OCTOBER 1992: October was a another cool month across Canada. Overnight lows plunged below -10°C from eastern BC to northern Ontario. Temperatures in the Yukon dropped to -31°C, the territory's earliest minus thirty value on record.

Almost all of the country received snow during the week of October 12th: 32 cm in Prince George, BC; 33 cm in Pincher Creek, Alta.; 25 cm east of Lake Winnipeg; 35 cm in Kapuskasing, Ont.; flurries as far south as Toronto; 40 cm of snow in central Quebec; 20 cm in Labrador and 45 cm on Baffin Island. Heavy rains continued to fall along the northern coast of BC.

Between the 6th and 8th of October, Newfoundland was hit by a savage storm that dropped 80 mm of rain, 20 cm of snow and produced 140 km/hr winds that ripped down trees and destroyed the province's only drive-in threatre. A storm on the 20th dropped 100 mm of rain on Sydney and several centimetres of snow on Halifax.

NOVEMBER 1992: The West was mild and the East was cold. In the Mackenzie Valley, average temperatures were as much as six degrees above normal. In Newfoundland, record cold temperatures around 4°C below normal prevailed. In much of the West, the month started out extremely cold, but above normal temperatures prevailed during most of the month. Just a few days after hitting a low of -25°C, High Level, Alta. set a new record high of 4°C on the 27th.

November was a wet month for much of the country. In excess of 250 mm of rain fell in several BC coastal communities, while the interior received almost 75 mm, three times the normal rate. Frequent storms and cold air brought heavy snow to the Prairies and eastern Canada. Calgary and Winnipeg received from 15 to 25 cm of snow early in the month and more later on. In the middle of November, 10 to 20 cm of snow fell across Ontario and 25 to 30 cm fell in the Maritimes.

DECEMBER 1992: Major snowstorms dominated this month's weather. Vancouver surpassed its average annual snowfall of 55 cm by the end of the month. A record early-winter storm dumped 20 to 60 cm of snow between London and Peterborough. In Toronto, the heavy, wet snow downed many trees and powerlines.

The Maritimes experienced several 30 to 50 cm snowfalls during December; the worst storms occurred two days apart early in the month. Moncton and Charlottetown were particularly hard hit. Both storms disrupted highway travel and caused major power outages. Between Christmas and New Year's, daytime high temperatures failed to rise about -30°C across the Prairies and wind chill warnings were issued from Alberta to the Maritimes. Portions of Vancouver Island experienced their first white Christmas in more than 30 years. At the same time, cold air produced heavy snow squalls and closed many highways in southern Ontario.

On Christmas Day, parts of Newfoundland received 50 cm of snow, along with wind gusts in excess of 105 km/hr.

JANUARY 1993: Cold weather dominated BC for most of January. Logs iced up on the lower Fraser River and hampered efforts to supply sawmills. Snow remained on the ground for 23 consecutive days (Dec. 29 to Jan. 20) in Vancouver—the second longest period on record. Business boomed for body repair shops and stores carrying snow tires, salt and shovels. Victoria also endured cold and snow. There was a high incidence of burst water mains as nighttime temperatures hovered near -8°C. In coastal valleys, wind chill readings were in the -50°C range.

The new year started off with a major winter storm in Atlantic Canada. More than 25 cm of snow fell on parts of New Brunswick, PEI and Cape Breton Island on New Year's Eve. As a result of the icy roads and blowing snow, three people were killed and several were injured in accidents. Later in the month, between 20 and 40 cm of snow covered the ground across Nova Scotia. In Halifax, 25 cm of snow fell and following the storm, temperatures plunged to -28°C. On the 31st, three Lunenburg fishermen died and 11 had to be rescued when a scallop dragger sank after becoming top-heavy in the freezing spray. At the time of the sinking, the air temperature was about -20°C and wind speeds were 80 km/hr. Near the end of January, up to 60 cm of snow buried the western half of Newfoundland.

FEBRUARY 1993: Record low temperatures and heavy winter snows prevailed across eastern Canada. Monthly temperatures were two to five degrees below normal from Ontario eastward. New record low temperatures were set at Saint John, Fredericton, Moncton, Charlottetown and Halifax. February began with spring-like conditions over much of the West and continued mild for much of the month over the Yukon, where 10°C maximum occurred around mid-month. By the second week, below -30°C readings across the Prairies brought an abrupt end to the mildness.

Precipitation during February was notable for its abundance in the east and its scarcity in the west. Several Atlantic coast storms brought what seemed to be continuous moisture to residents of central and eastern Canada. In Kingston, the February snowfall total of 72 cm was the greatest since 1972. In northwestern Ontario, new record low snowfall totals occurred. Halifax experienced two rainfalls of over 50 mm, one setting a new record for a single day in February and resulting in flooded streets and basements.

In the western provinces, precipitation was below normal. In Vancouver, only 11 mm fell, helping to make the December to February amount of 232 mm the lowest winter precipitation total on record for the city. Light mountain snowpacks, down 60 to 80 percent from normal, forced spring water restrictions in the lower mainland area.

MARCH 1993: Overall, mean temperatures for March were above normal from the Pacific coast to northern Ontario, however the continuation of winter through most of the month resulted in below normal temperatures from the Great Lakes eastward to the Atlantic. For many areas this was the coldest March in the last 10 years. Although precipitation was below average in most areas, snowfalls were normal in the southern Prairies and parts of the Atlantic provinces.

The winter's biggest storm, tagged as the "storm of the century," struck eastern North America on the weekend of the 13th. Adding to already hefty snow on the ground totals, many areas now had more than 100 mm of snow to contend with on Monday. At the Ottawa weather station, 135 cm of snow lay on the ground on the 15th, more than at any time in its history. Adding to the severity of the storm was a major influx of cold air in its wake.

APRIL 1993: April began with above normal temperatures extending from the Pacific coast to Manitoba. Record high daytime temperatures occurred in Saskatchewan and the Yukon.

April precipitation was above normal across most of the southern half of the country. A late winter storm moved over the Great Lakes and then south of Nova Scotia, dropping 20 to 40 cm of snow and 10 to 20 mm of freezing rain from southern Ontario across southwestern Quebec and into the Maritimes. In the warm air that followed, widespread rainfalls of 10 to 30 mm added to rapidly melting snow to produce flooding in low-lying areas.

The year's first sign of summer severe weather occurred in southern Ontario. On the 20th, thunderstorms moved across Lake Huron, producing small hail, winds of 100 km/hr and a small tornado near the town of Bancroft.

MAY 1993: Mean temperatures for the month were as much as 4 degrees above normal in British Columbia and the Yukon, making this the warmest May on record in most locations. At some low mountain elevations, the excessive warmth melted the snowpack, creating flooding and mud slides. Shortly after one of the warmest Mother's Days on record, with daytime maximums surpassing 30°C in the eastern Prairies and northern Ontario, temperatures plunged across the central part of the country. In the Maritimes, temperatures were somewhat variable through May producing a near-normal monthly mean.

Precipitation during May was lower than normal from Alberta to Northern Ontario. The dry conditions allowed most of the spring seeding to be completed on time. Elsewhere, unsettled air masses and a few coastal storms produced precipitation totals somewhat above normal in BC, central Ontario and Newfoundland. Most significant of these events were the occurrence of 2 cm of hail in western Quebec on the 6th, a 98 mm rainfall in Stephenville during the second week and 20 cm of snow in the Sept. Iles and Gaspé areas around the middle of May.

JUNE 1993: June was not an especially pleasant start to summer across most of Canada. A pool of cool, moist air anchored off the Pacific Coast for much of the month, resulting in plenty of rain and limited sunshine throughout most of the West. Record rainfalls, more than double the normal amount, fell at Prince George and in the Okanagan in British Columbia. Across Alberta, several vigorous disturbances left record rainfall amounts on several days. At Edmonton, on the 23rd, the city recorded its lowest station pressure in 113 years, 91.13 kPa. Across Saskatchewan and Manitoba, June featured cool temperatures, late frosts and excessive rainfalls. One forest fire near the town of Lynn Lake, Manitoba spread rapidly though, and forced the evacuation of all residents.

Compared to 1992, the weather in June 1993 across Ontario and Quebec was gorgeous. Temperatures still lagged normal by one degree, however; sunshine totals were 10 to 40 hours below normal and heavy thunderstorms inflated rainfall totals to well above the norm.

June was wet and marginally cool across the Maritimes. Monthly rainfall at Moncton was 203 mm, a record for any June. The weather was generally cloudy, damp and cool across Newfoundland. St. John's received 186 mm of rain, about double its normal rainfall. A brief warm spell during mid-month pushed temperatures inland across the Island near 30°C.

Unlike the rest of Canada, the Yukon and the Western Arctic experienced warmer and drier than normal conditions throughout June. The last week was especially warm; at Alert on the northern tip of Ellesmere Island, the temperature rose to 11°C, while Eureka got to a high of 17°C.

Weather Records

	Canada	United States	World
Highest maximum air temperature	45.0˚ Midale and Yellowgrass, Sask. July 5, 1937	56.7˚ Death Valley, CA July 10, 1913	58.0˚ Al'azizyah, Libya Sept. 13, 1922
Lowest minimum air temperature	-63.0˚ Snag, YT Feb. 3, 1947	-62.1˚ Prospect Creek Camp, AK Jan. 23, 1971	-89.6˚ Vostok, Antarctica July 21, 1983
Coldest month	-47.9˚ Eureka, NWT Feb. 1979		
Highest sea-level pressure	107.96 kPa Dawson, YT Feb. 2, 1989	107.86 kPa Northway, AK Jan. 31, 1989	108.38 kPa Agata, Siberia USSR Dec. 31, 1968
Lowest sea-level pressure	94.02 kPa St. Anthony, Nfld Jan. 20, 1977	89.23 kPa Matecumbe Key, FL Sept. 2, 1935	87.64 kPa in eye of Typhoon June (Pacific Ocean, 17˚N, 138˚E) Nov. 19, 1975
Greatest precipitation in 24hrs	489.2 mm Ucluelet Brynnor Mines, BC Oct. 6, 1967	1090 mm Alvin, TX	1 869.9 mm Cilaos La Réunion Is. March 15, 1952
Greatest precipitation in one month	2 235.5 mm Swanson Bay, BC Nov. 1917	2 717.8 mm Kukui, HI March 1942	9 300 mm Cherrapunji, India July 1861
Greatest precipitation in one year	8 122.4 mm Henderson Lake, BC 1931	17 902.7 mm Kukui, HI 1982	26 461.2 mm Cherrarpunji, India Aug. 1860-July 1861
Greatest average annual precipitation	6 655 mm Henderson Lake, BC	11 684 mm Mt. Waialeaie, Kauai, HI	11 684 mm Mt. Waialeaie, Kauai, HI
Least annual precipitation	12.7 mm Arctic Bay, NWT 1949	0.0 Bagdad, CA Oct. 3, 1912 to Nov. 8, 1914	0.0 Arica, Chile—no rain for 14 years
Greatest average annual snowfall	1 433 cm Glacier Mt. Fidelity, BC	1 460.8 cm Rainer Paradise Ranger Station, WA	
Greatest snowfall in one season	2 446.5 cm Revelstoke/Mt. Copeland, BC 1971–72	2 850 cm Rainer Paradise Ranger Station, WA 1971–72	
Greatest snowfall in one month	535.9 cm Haines Apps. No 2, BC Dec. 1959	990.6 cm Tamarack, CA Jan. 1911	
Greatest snowfall in one day	118.1 cm Lakelse Lake, BC Jan. 17, 1974	193.0 cm Silver Lake, CO April 14–15, 1921	
Highest average annual number of thunderstorm days	34 days London, Ont.	96 days Fort Meyers, FL	322 days Bogor, Indonesia
Heaviest hailstone	290 g Cedoux, Sask.	758 g Coffeyville, KS Sept. 3, 1970	5 000 g Guangxi region of China May 1, 1986
Highest average annual wind speed	36 km/h Cape Warwick, Resolution Island, NWT	56.3 km/h Mt. Washington, NH	
Highest wind speed for 1 hr	201.1 km/h Cape Hopes Advance (Quaqtaq), Que. Nov. 18, 1931	362.0 km/h Mt. Washington, NH April 12, 1934	
Highest average hours of fog	1 890 hrs Argentia, Nfld	2 552 hrs Cape Disappointment, WA	

Source: *Environment Canada*

Weather Here and There

| Locations: | Temperature °C | | | | Annual Total | | | |
| | Winter | | Summer | | Snowfall cm | Precipitation mm | Wet days | Sunshine hours |
	High	Low	High	Low				
Vancouver	5.2	-0.2	21.9	12.6	60	1 113	163	1 920
Whitehorse	-16.4	-25.0	20.3	7.9	137	261	120	
Yellowknife	-24.7	-33.0	20.7	11.8	135	267	121	2 277
Calgary	-6.0	-17.6	23.3	9.4	153	424	113	
Saskatoon	-14.1	-24.3	25.4	11.5	113	349	108	2 450
Winnipeg	-14.3	-24.2	25.9	13.3	126	526	120	2 321
London	-2.7	-10.5	26.4	14.2	209	909	166	1 894
Ottawa	-6.4	-15.4	26.3	14.9	227	879	156	2 009
Toronto	-2.5	-10.9	26.8	14.2	131	762	137	
Montreal	-5.7	-14.6	26.1	15.6	235	946	162	2 054
Quebec	-7.3	-16.6	24.9	13.2	343	1 174	175	1 852
Fredericton	-3.8	-14.5	25.7	13.0	290	1 109	156	1 878
Halifax	-1.6	-10.3	23.3	13.0	271	1 491	166	1 885
Charlottetown	-3.0	-11.2	23.0	13.7	331	1 169	174	1 818
St. John's	-0.5	-7.2	20.2	10.7	359	1 514	217	1 497
Beijing	6.7	-16.1	36.3	15.9	30	623	66	2 706
Calcutta	33.4	7.0	34.8	23.4	—	1 592	102	2 528
London	6.0	2.0	22.0	14.0	—	594	107	1 514
Los Angeles	23.4	3.0	34.3	11.3	—	373	39	3 185
Mexico City	23.0	2.0	26.0	10.0	—	726	133	2 366
Miami	29.4	9.4	35.5	19.9	—	1 520	103	2 945
Moscow	-9.0	-16.0	23.0	13.0	161	575	181	1 597
New York	7.7	-6.3	34.4	15.4	77	1 076	121	2 564
Rome	12.3	3.4	30.9	17.7	—	749	76	2 491
Rio de Janeiro ...	26.7	13.7	30.9	19.3	—	1 093	131	2 351
Shanghai	11.6	-4.8	36.0	18.2	25	1 143	98	1 877
Sydney	19.7	3.9	29.3	14.7	—	1 205	152	2 440
Tokyo	13.8	-6.4	32.3	17.9	20	1 563	104	2 021

Source: *Environment Canada*

Weather Story of the Year: Hurricane Andrew

*T*he first hurricane of the 1992-93 season—Andrew—was a record breaker. It formed from a tropical wave crossing from the west coast of Africa to tropical North Atlantic on August 14. The wave moved west, going south of the Cape Verde Islands on August 15 and making the transition to tropical depression status when narrow, spiral-shaped bands of clouds developed around the rotating centre. Andrew reached storm intensity in the eastern Atlantic on August 17 and gained steadily in strength until it struck the Bahamas on August 23. High pressure to the north blocked the storm, forcing it west where it smashed into southern Florida early on August 24.

As the eye of the storm swept over southern Dade County, the winds were clocked at 145 mph, with gusts to 175 mph. Andrew cut a narrow but destructive swath through the area, doing $20 billion worth of damage and ensuring its place in the record books as the most expensive natural disaster in US history.

The storm weakened over Florida but regained strength in the Gulf of Mexico, returning to the mainland on August 26 to do another $1 billion in damage in south-central Louisiana.

In addition to property damage, the storm was blamed for 15 deaths in Florida and eight in Louisiana; however, experts noted that similar storms have claimed thousands of lives in other parts of the world. Good forecasting, the tight organization and high speed of the storm and the fact that it did not hit densely populated areas contributed to the low death toll.

Average Number of Days Per Year With the Most...

Frost | Smoke or Haze

Province	Average # Days	Station	Average # Days	Station
Newfoundland	259	Nain	25	St. John's A
Prince Edward Island ...	175	O'Leary	34	Summerside A
New Brunswick	215	Nine Mile Brk. (Camp 68)	42	Chatham A
Nova Scotia	194	Northeast Margaree	29	Greenwood A
Quebec	296	Cape Hopes Advance	118	St. Hubert A
Ontario	254	Winisk A	228	Windsor A
Manitoba	258	Churchill A	30	Winnipeg Int'l. A
Saskatchewan	238	Stony Rapids	8	Saskatoon
Alberta	269	Lake Louise	34	Edmonton Municipal A
British Columbia	280	Alexis Creek Tautri Creek	187	Vancouver Int'l. A
Yukon Territory	296	Komakuk Beach A	3	Dawson
Northwest Territories ...	340	Isachsen	7	Fort Smith A

Fog | Hail

Province	Average # Days	Station	Average # Days	Station
Newfoundland	206	Argentia A	0	—
Prince Edward Island ..	47	Charlottetown A	0	—
New Brunswick	106	Saint John A	0	—
Nova Scotia	127	Sable Island	0	—
Quebec	85	Cape Hopes Advance	2	Matagami A
Ontario	76	Mount Forest	1	Red Lake
Manitoba	48	Churchill A	3	Winnipeg Int'l. A
Saskatchewan	37	Collins Bay	2	Estevan A
Alberta	39	Whitecourt	7	Edson A
British Columbia	226	Old Glory Mountain	18	Cape Scott
Yukon Territory	61	Komakuk Beach A	2	Dawson A
Northwest Territories ...	196	Resolution Island	0	—

Thunderstorms | Blowing Snow

Province	Average # Days	Station	Average # Days	Station
Newfoundland	7	Daniels Harbour	45	Hopedale
Prince Edward Island ..	11	Summerside A	26	Summerside A
New Brunswick	13	Fredericton A	16	Chatham A
Nova Scotia	12	Debert A	21	Greenwood A
Quebec	27	St. Hubert	90	Border A
Ontario	34	Windsor A	38	Winisk A
Manitoba	26	Rivers A	64	Churchill A
Saskatchewan	25	Wynyard	32	Regina A
Alberta	26	Edmonton Int'l. A	15	Coronation A
British Columbia	24	Prince George	25	Old Glory Mountain
Yukon Territory	11	Snag	82	Komakuk Beach A
Northwest Territories ..	12	Fort Smith A	91	Resolute A

Source: *Environment Canada*

Provincial Weather Facts

Province	*C	Warmest Temperature Ever Recorded Date	Station	*C	Coldest Temperature Ever Recorded Date	Station
Newfoundland ...	41.7	Aug. 11, 1914	Northwest River	-51.1	Feb. 17, 1973	Esker 2
P.E.I.	36.7	Aug. 19, 1935	Charlottetown	-37.2	Jan. 26, 1884	Kilmahumaig
New Brunswick ..	39.4	Aug. 18, 1935	Nepisiguit Falls	-47.2	Feb. 2, 1955	Sisson Dam
Nova Scotia	38.3	Aug. 19, 1935	Collegeville	-41.1	Jan. 31, 1920	Upper Stewiacke
Quebec	40.0	July 6, 1921	Ville Marie	-54.4	Feb. 5, 1923	Doucet
Ontario	42.2	July 20, 1919	Biscotasing	-58.3	Jan. 23, 1935	Iroquois Falls
Manitoba	44.4	July 11, 1936	St. Albans	-52.8	Jan. 9, 1899	Norway House
Saskatchewan ...	45.0	July 5, 1937	Midale	-56.7	Feb. 1, 1893	Prince Albert
Alberta	43.3	July 21, 1931	Bassano Dam	-61.1	Jan. 11, 1911	Fort Vermilion
British Columbia .	44.4	July 16, 1941	Lillooet	-58.9	Jan. 31, 1947	Smith River
Yukon	36.1	June 14, 1969	Mayo	-63.0	Feb. 3, 1947	Snag
NWT	39.4	July 18, 1941	Fort Smith	-57.2	Dec. 26, 1917	Fort Smith

Source: *Environment Canada*

Province	Warmest Annual Temperature On Average *C	Station	Coldest Annual Temperature On Average *C	Station
Newfoundland	6.3	Holyrood Ultramar	-3.8	Wabush Lake A
Prince Edward Island	5.9	Charlottetown CDA	4.8	O'Leary
New Brunswick	6.2	St. Andrews	1.6	Upsalquitch Lake
Nova Scotia	7.6	Sable Island	4.9	Trafalgar
Quebec	7.6	Montreal Lafontaine	-7.2	Koartak
Ontario	9.7	Windsor University	-5.5	Winisk A
Manitoba	3.3	Morden CDA	-7.2	Churchill A
Saskatchewan	5.0	Maple Creek North	-4.6	Collins Bay
Alberta	5.9	Bow Island Rivers	-2.7	Fort Chipewyan A
British Columbia	10.7	Sumas Canal	-3.2	Cassiar Yukon
Territory	-1.0	Whitehorse Riverdale	-11.4	Komakuk Beach A
Northwest Territories	-2.2	Fort Liard	-19.7	Eureka

Source: *Environment Canada*

Average Annual Bright Sunshine

Province	Greatest hrs	Station	Least hrs	Station
Newfoundland	1 572	Churchill Falls A	1 303	St. Shotts
Prince Edward Island	1 967	Tignish	1 817	East Baltic
New Brunswick	2 010	Chatham A	1 373	Summit Depot
Nova Scotia	1 969	Shearwater A	1 449	Sable Island
Quebec	2 054	Montreal Int'l. A	1 158	Mont Logan
Ontario	2 203	Thunder Bay A	1 635	New Liskeard
Manitoba	2 460	Delta U	1 828	Churchill A
Saskatchewan	2 537	Estevan A	2 073	Cree Lake
Alberta	2 490	Coronation A	1 724	Banff
British Columbia	2 244	Cranbrook A	949	Stewart A
Yukon Territory	1 844	Whitehorse A	1 789	Watson Lake A
Northwest Territories	2 277	Yellowknife A	1 443	Mould Bay A

Source: *Environment Canada*

Average Annual Precipitation

Province	Greatest		Least	
	mm	Station	mm	Station
Newfoundland	1 699.7	Burgeo	739.8	Nain
Prince Edward Island	1 169.4	Charlottetown A	921.0	Montague
New Brunswick	1 444.4	Saint John A	909.6	Upsalquitch Lake
Nova Scotia	1 630.7	Ingonish Beach	973.7	Pugwash
Quebec	1 559.8	Mont Logan	295.9	Cape Hopes Advance
Ontario	1 191.1	West Guilford	569.0	Kenora TCPL
Manitoba	696.1	Peace Gardens	402.3	Churchill A
Saskatchewan	530.1	Brabant Lake	287.9	Nashlyn
Alberta	1 072.0	Waterton Park HQ	270.8	Empress
British Columbia	6 655.0	Henderson Lake	205.6	Ashcroft
Yukon Territory	590.6	Tuchitua	135.9	Komakuk Beach A
Northwest Territories	663.2	Cape Dyer A	61.0	Rea Point

Source: *Environment Canada*

Average Annual Snowfall

Province	Greatest		Least	
	mm	Station	mm	Station
Newfoundland	322.8	Woody Point	91.6	St. Shotts
Prince Edward Island	330.6	Charlottetown A	173.3	Montague
New Brunswick	448.8	Dawson Settlement	176.2	Southwest Head
Nova Scotia	406.7	Cheticamp	104.1	Baccaro
Quebec	648.4	Mont Logan	161.6	Havre aux Maisons
Ontario	430.0	Searchmount	74.0	Lakeview MOE
Manitoba	332.7	Island Lake	94.9	Lundar
Saskatchewan	348.6	Collins Bay	58.0	Aylesbury
Alberta	642.9	Columbia Icefield	59.9	Empress
British Columbia	1 433.0	Glacier NP Mt. Fidelity	20.4	Carnation Creek
Yukon Territory	365.7	Keno Hill	60.1	Komakuk Beach A
Northwest Territories	602.4	Cape Dyer A	28.6	Rea Point

Source: *Environment Canada*

Greatest Snow on the Ground Any Month

Province	Depth (cm)	Station	Province	Depth (cm)	Station
Newfoundland	313	Hopedale	Manitoba	175	Glenlea
Prince Edward Island	156	Charlottetown	Saskatchewan	224	Hudson Bay
New Brunswick	252	Harvey Station	Alberta	179	Parker Ridge
Nova Scotia	183	Nappan	British Columbia	450	Whistler Roundhouse
Quebec	259	Blanc-Sablon	Yukon Territory	149	Hour Lake
Ontario	219	Gravenhurst	Northwest Territories	241	Cape Dyer

Source: *Environment Canada*

Watches and Warnings

*E*nvironment Canada signals severe summer storms by issuing weather watches and warnings. If a watch is issued in your area, maintain your normal routine, but keep an eye out for threatening weather and listen for further information. When severe local storms are expected, or have actually been sighted or detected by radar, warnings are issued and updated. These may be either severe thunderstorm warnings or tornado warnings.

Wind

Province	Highest Wind Speed km/hr	Highest Wind Speed Station	Highest % of Calms km/hr	Highest % of Calms Station
Newfoundland	28.0 (W)	Bonavista	17.1	Wabush Lake A
Prince Edward Island	22.4 (SSW)	Summerside A	4.4	Summerside A
New Brunswick	22.4 (W)	Miscou Island (AUT)	11.8	Fredericton A
Nova Scotia	25.7 (W)	Sable Island	16.9	Greenwood A
Quebec	32.0 (NW)	Grindstone Island	20.4	Gaspé A
Ontario	21.0 (SW)	Bruce Ontario Hydro	30.2	White River
Manitoba	22.7 (WNW)	Churchill A	21.0	Norway House A
Saskatchewan	22.9 (W)	Swift Current A	12.8	La Ronge A
Alberta	21.5 (W)	Pincher Creek	39.7	High Level A
British Columbia	33.7 (NW)	Cape St. James	48.5	Quesnel A
Yukon Territory	14.1 (SSE)	Whitehorse A	57.5	Dawson A
Northwest Territories	35.3 (NW)	Resolution Island	35.1	Eureka

Source: *Environment Canada*

"Coldest Days" (Wind Chill)

Province	ET/WCF[1]	Location	Date	Temp (°C)	Wind (km/hr)
Newfoundland	-71/2814	Wabush Lake	Jan. 20, 1975	-41	40
Prince Edward Island	-57/2450	Charlottetown	Jan. 18, 1982	-32	37
Nova Scotia	-53/2309	Sydney	Jan. 18, 1982	-25	59
New Brunswick	-61/2547	Charlo	Jan. 18, 1982	-31	54
Quebec	-77/3001	Nitchequon	Jan. 20, 1975	-42	56
Ontario	-70/2753	Thunder Bay	Jan. 10, 1982	-36	54
Manitoba	-76/2938	Churchill	Jan. 18, 1975	-41	56
Saskatchewan	-70/2757	Swift Current	Dec. 15, 1964	-34	89
Alberta	-68/2740	Red Deer	Dec. 15, 1964	-35	61
British Columbia	-69/2749	Old Glory Mtn.	Dec. 15, 1964	-36	58
Yukon Territory	-83/3152	Komakuk Beach	Feb. 12, 1975	-50	40
Northwest Territories	-92/3357	Pelly Bay	Jan. 13, 1975	-51	56

Source: *Environment Canada*

(1) ET is equivalent wind chill temperature in °C. WCF is wind chill factor in watts/square metre

---

Calculating Wind Chill

You can calculate the wind chill equivalent temperature in degrees Celsius (°C) or the wind chill factor in watts per square metre for your own values of air temperature (°C) and wind speed in kilometres per hour, by using the following equations:

Wind Chill Equivalent Temperature (°C) [WET]:

$$WET = 33.0 - (10.45 + 10\sqrt{W} - W)((33.0 - T)/22.04)$$

Wind Chill Factor [WCF]:

$$WCF = 1.1626(5.2735 \times \sqrt{W} + 10.45 - 0.2778 W)(33.0 - T)$$

T = ambient air temperature in °C   W = wind speed in kilometres per hour

This calculation gives meaningful values of WET and WCF for any air temperature lower than 5°C, and for any wind speed between 7 and 80 kilometres per hour.

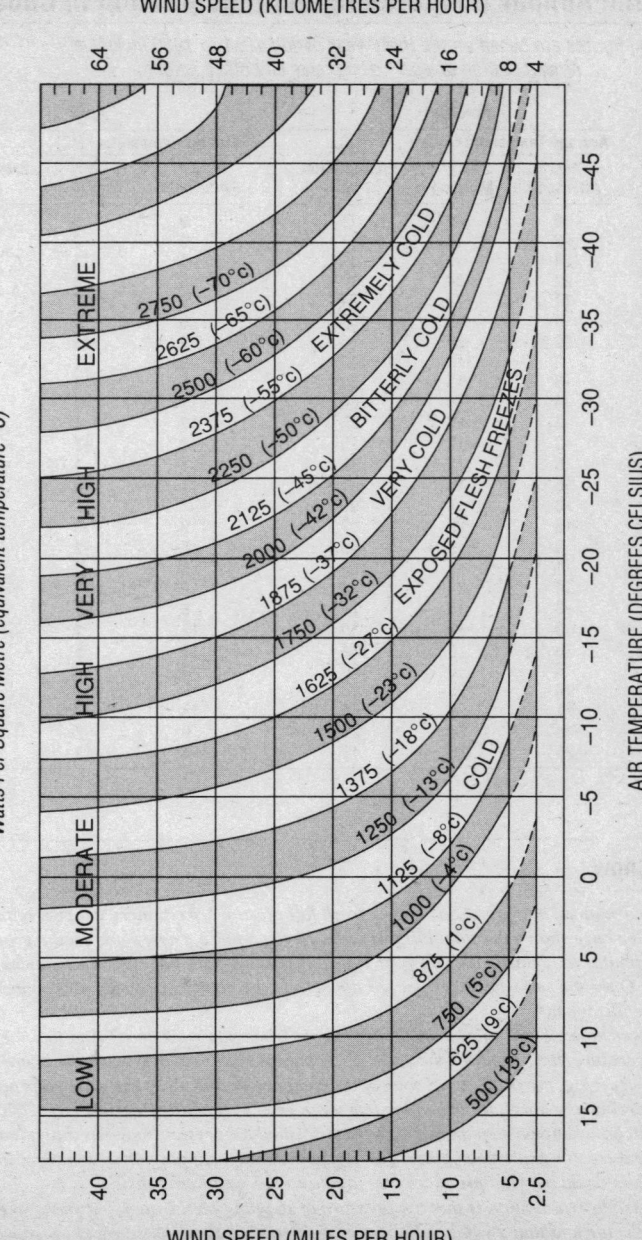

Wind Chill Factor

Watts Per Square Metre (equivalent temperature °C)

WIND SPEED (KILOMETRES PER HOUR)

64 56 48 40 32 24 16 8 4

EXTREME   HIGH   VERY HIGH   MODERATE   LOW

EXTREMELY COLD

BITTERLY COLD

VERY COLD

EXPOSED FLESH FREEZES

COLD

2750 (−70°c)
2625 (−65°c)
2500 (−60°c)
2375 (−55°c)
2250 (−50°c)
2125 (−45°c)
2000 (−42°c)
1875 (−37°c)
1750 (−32°c)
1625 (−27°c)
1500 (−23°c)
1375 (−18°c)
1250 (−13°c)
1125 (−8°c)
1000 (−4°c)
875 (1°c)
750 (5°c)
625 (9°c)
500 (13°c)

AIR TEMPERATURE (DEGREES CELSIUS)

−45 −40 −35 −30 −25 −20 −15 −10 −5 0 5 10 15

WIND SPEED (MILES PER HOUR)

40 35 30 25 20 15 10 5 2.5

■ To determine the wind chill factor, follow the temperature across and the wind speed up until the two lines intersect. The value of the wind chill factor can be interpolated using the labeled wind chill factor curves. ■ For example, at −10°C with a wind speed of 20 miles per hour, the point of intersection lies between 1500 (−23°C) and 1625 (−27°C), or approximately 1570 (−25°C).

■ It is not recommended that wind chill factors be calculated for wind speeds below 8 km an hour, since it is difficult to determine wind chill factors at these wind speeds and because other factors such as relative humidity become important.

Monthly and Annual Temperature and Precipitation in Canada

All figures are based on the thirty-year period 1951 to 1980 inclusive.
*Airport station unless * designates city office station.*

Station	January			April		
	Average Temperature (°C)		Total Precipitation (mm)	Average Temperature (°C)		Total Precipitation (mm)
	Mid Afternoon	Early Morning		Mid Afternoon	Early Morning	
Calgary, Alta.	-6	-18	16	9	-3	33
Charlottetown, PEI ..	-3	-11	117	6	-2	82
Churchill, Man.	-24	-31	15	-5	-15	23
Dawson, Yukon* ...	-27	-34	17	5	-9	10
Edmonton, Alta.	-11	-22	24	9	-3	20
Fredericton, NB	-4	-15	103	9	-1	80
Iqaluit, NWT	-22	-30	26	-9	-19	26
Halifax, NS	-2	-10	153	8	-1	115
Hamilton, Ont.	-3	-10	63	11	1	79
Kitchener, Ont.*	-4	-10	60	11	1	75
London, Ont.	-3	-11	75	12	1	81
Moncton, NB	-3	-13	125	8	-2	90
Montreal, Que.	-6	-15	72	11	1	74
Ottawa, Ont.	-6	-15	61	11	0	69
Quebec, Que.	-8	-17	90	8	-2	73
Regina, Sask.	-13	-23	17	9	-3	24
Saint John, NB	-3	-13	149	8	-2	107
St. John's, Nfld	-1	-7	156	5	-2	116
Saskatoon, Sask.	-14	-24	18	9	-3	21
Sault Ste. Marie, Ont.	-6	-15	74	8	-2	64
Toronto, Ont.	-3	-11	50	12	1	70
Vancouver, BC	5	0	154	13	5	60
Victoria, BC	6	0	154	13	4	39
Whitehorse, Yukon .	-16	-25	18	6	-5	10
Windsor, Ont.	-1	-9	55	13	3	83
Winnipeg, Man.	-14	-24	21	9	-2	39
Yellowknife, NWT ...	-25	-33	13	-1	-13	10

Sounds of Snow

*H*ave you ever noticed how quiet it is after a fresh fall of snow? Well, there's a real reason for that. Studies have shown that audibility is reduced when there's new snow on the ground. Fresh snow is similar to acoustic tiles on your walls or ceilings—it's full of tiny air spaces that soak up sound. Once the snow becomes packed down (and the air has escaped), this sound-deadening effect disappears.

Have you ever noticed that snow sometimes squeaks when you walk on it? And that the colder the temperature, the squeakier the snow is? One explanation is that when the temperature is a little below freezing, the pressure of your boots compresses and melts the snow, a process which doesn't create any noise. But when the temperature is well below freezing, say -20°C, the snow can't melt. So when you step on this snow, the crushed ice crystals move as individuals, slipping over and crashing into each other. The sudden rubbing, slipping or smashing of the dry, separated crystals could be what produces that familiar cold-weather creaking.

Another possible explanation is that the pressure of stepping on the air-filled snowflakes rapidly expels the air and that's what makes the characteristic squeak noise we know so well.

Station	July Average Temperature (°C) Mid Afternoon	July Average Temperature (°C) Early Morning	July Total Precipitation (mm)	October Average Temperature (°C) Mid Afternoon	October Average Temperature (°C) Early Morning	October Total Precipitation (mm)
Calgary, Alta.	23	9	65	12	-1	18
Charlottetown, PEI ..	23	14	84	12	4	106
Churchill, Man.	17	7	46	1	-4	43
Dawson, Yukon* ...	22	9	47	-1	-8	29
Edmonton, Alta.	22	9	92	11	-2	15
Fredericton, NB	26	13	89	13	2	97
Iqaluit, NWT	11	4	63	-2	-8	44
Halifax, NS	23	13	94	13	4	134
Hamilton, Ont.	26	15	71	14	5	61
Kitchener, Ont.*	26	15	84	14	5	69
London, Ont........	26	14	72	15	4	73
Moncton, NB	24	13	95	13	2	99
Montreal, Que.	26	16	90	13	4	76
Ottawa, Ont.	26	15	86	13	3	68
Quebec, Que.	25	13	117	11	2	91
Regina, Sask.	26	12	53	12	-2	19
Saint John, NB	22	12	103	12	3	128
St. John's, Nfld	20	11	75	10	3	146
Saskatoon, Sask. ...	25	12	54	11	-1	17
Sault Ste. Marie, Ont.	24	11	56	12	3	74
Toronto, Ont.	27	14	71	15	4	62
Vancouver, BC	22	13	32	14	6	114
Victoria, BC	22	11	18	14	6	78
Whitehorse, Yukon .	20	8	34	4	-3	22
Windsor, Ont.	28	17	83	16	6	57
Winnipeg, Man.	26	13	76	12	1	31
Yellowknife, NWT ..	21	12	34	1	-4	35

Source: *Environment Canada*

Network of Weather Watchers

*E*nvironment Canada has a national network of more than 2,500 unpaid weather observers who record the temperature and precipitation every day of the year. Volunteers are of all ages and walks of life—farmers, housewives, teachers, dentists, bankers... even prisoners. Many weather stations are operated by an individual; others are operated by schools, power companies, industrial firms and municipalities.

The routine of a volunteer observer rarely varies. Twice a day, every day, the volunteer reads two thermometers—a maximum and a minimum—recording the extremes since the last observation. A rain gauge sits on the ground nearby. The observer measures any rain collected since the last observation, then empties the gauge. In winter, the depth of freshly fallen snow is measured. Notes regarding the character of the weather during the day are recorded. Some observers also measure elements such as bright sunshine and wind speed.

At the end of each month a report is mailed to a regional office of Environment Canada. There, after verification, the data is sent to the Climate Centre in Downsview, Ontario where it is scrutinized again, processed and stored as a permanent record of Canada's climate.

Another corps of volunteers, severe weather watchers, maintain a sky watch for signs of hail, tornadoes, damaging winds or heavy rain, relaying sightings to the weather office. This simple task is vital for providing advance warning of dangerous conditions.

Environment Canada supplies and maintains the equipment for the observers and covers postage and other operating costs. In some parts of Canada, new observers and severe weather watchers are still needed. To join the volunteer program, contact the nearest Environment Canada weather office.

Annual Temperatures and Precipitation

(All figures are based on the thirty-year period 1951 to 1980 inclusive.)
Airport station unless * designates city office station.

Station	Average Temp (°C)	Total Precipitation (mm)	Total Snowfall (cm)	Station	Average Temp (°C)	Total Precipitation (mm)	Total Snowfall (cm)
Calgary, Alta.	3	424	153	Quebec, Que.	4	1 174	343
Charlottetown, PEI	5	1 169	331	Regina, Sask.	2	384	116
Churchill, Man.	-7	402	196	Saint John, NB	5	1 444	293
Dawson, Yukon*	-5	306	137	St. John's, Nfld	5	1 514	359
Edmonton, Alta.	2	467	138	Saskatoon, Sask.	2	349	113
Fredericton, NB	5	1 109	290	Sault Ste. Marie, Ont.	4	898	306
Iqaluit, NWT	-9	433	256	Toronto, Ont.	7	762	131
Halifax, NS	6	1 491	271	Vancouver, BC	10	1 113	60
Hamilton, Ont.	7	824	143	Victoria, BC	10	873	50
Kitchener, Ont.*	7	897	152	Whitehorse, Yukon	-1	261	137
London, Ont.	7	909	209	Windsor, Ont.	9	849	117
Moncton, NB	5	1 179	341	Winnipeg, Man.	2	526	126
Montreal, Que.	6	946	235	Yellowknife, NWT	-5	267	135
Ottawa, Ont.	6	879	227				

Source: *Environment Canada*

Greatest Number of Consecutive Days With Highest Temp Above 32°C

Province	# Days	Station	Starting Date
Newfoundland	3	Corner Brook	Aug. 10, 1936
Prince Edward Island	4	Charlottetown	Aug. 12, 1944
New Brunswick	8	Chipman	Aug. 11, 1944
Nova Scotia	7	Kentville	Aug. 11, 1944
Quebec	11	Nominingue	June 27, 1946
Ontario	22	Brantford	July 16, 1881
Manitoba	16	York Factory	June 27, 1878
Saskatchewan	22	Chaplin	July 4, 1894
Alberta	16	Peace River Crossing	July 17, 1925
British Columbia	31	Oliver/Hedley	July 14, 1971
Yukon Territory	4	Mayo	June 12, 1969
Northwest Territories	5	Hay River	July 31, 1984

Source: *Environment Canada*

What is Heat Lightning?

*O*n hot summer evenings, you've probably seen those broad areas of flashing light off in the distance. The sight is usually referred to as heat lightning or summer lightning. In fact, heat lightning is nothing more than ordinary streak lightning from a thunderstorm over the horizon. Instead of seeing individual strokes, a part of the sky will light up as cloud droplets scatter the light.

You can even see heat lightning under clear skies during hot summer evenings and, since you see the light flashes but don't hear any thunder, you might think that the lightning is somehow caused by the heat alone. That's not the case; thunder and lightning always happen at the same time. Although the light reaches your eyes almost instantaneously, the sound takes a much longer time to reach your ears. Lightning from distant thunderstorms can be seen as far away as 100 to 200 km, especially on the prairies, but the waves of sound generated by thunder farther than 20 km away become too widely dispersed to be heard by human ears.

Average Weather Data for Selected Major Airports in Canada

	Temperature °C				Precipitation	
	January		July		Annual Snowfall cm	Total Precipitation mm
Airport	High	Low	High	Low		
Victoria	6.0	0.1	21.7	10.8	50	873
Vancouver	5.2	-0.2	21.9	12.8	60	1 113
Calgary	-6.0	-17.6	23.3	9.4	153	424
Edmonton	-10.9	-22.0	22.4	9.2	138	467
Regina	-12.8	-23.2	26.1	11.7	116	384
Winnipeg	-14.3	-24.2	25.9	13.3	126	623
Toronto	-2.5	-10.9	26.8	14.2	131	762
Ottawa	-6.4	-15.4	26.3	14.9	227	879
Montreal	-5.7	-14.8	26.1	15.6	235	946
Quebec	-7.6	-16.8	24.9	13.2	343	1 174
Saint John	-2.6	-12.9	22.2	11.6	293	1 444
Halifax	-1.6	-10.3	23.3	13.0	271	1 491
Charlottetown	-3.0	-11.2	23.0	13.7	331	1 169
St. John's	-0.5	-7.2	20.2	10.7	359	1 514
Yellowknife	-24.7	-33.0	20.7	11.8	135	267
Whitehorse	-16.4	-25.0	20.3	7.9	137	261

	Wind			Sunshine		
Airport	Average Speed kn/hr	Prevailing Direction	Peak Wind km/hr	Bright Sunshine hours	sun	Possible Sunshine hours
Victoria	11.0	W	109	2 059		4 475
Vancouver	11.9	E	129	1 920		4 475
Calgary	16.2	W	127	2 314		4 483
Edmonton	13.3	S	148	2 316		4 488
Regina	20.7	SE	153	2 331		4 483
Winnipeg	18.6	S	129	2 321		4 482
Toronto	15.4	N	124	2 045		4 464
Ottawa	14.5	WNW	135	2 009		4 469
Montreal	15.6	WSW	161	2 054		4 465
Quebec	15.9	WSW	177	1 852		4 473
Saint John	18.6	S	146	1 866		4 452
Halifax	18.1	SSW	132	1 665		4 488
Charlottetown	19.3	W	177	1 618		4 467
St. John's	24.3	WSW	193	1 497		4 470
Yellowknife	15.6	E	106	2 277		4 644
Whitehorse	14.0	SSE	106	1 844		4 630

	Annual Number of Days						
Airport	Frost	Wet Weather	Thunder-storms	Freezing Precipitation	Smoke/ Haze	Blowing Snow	Fog
Victoria	60	155	2	—	33	—	28
Vancouver	55	163	6	1	187	—	45
Calgary	201	113	25	6	27	9	22
Edmonton	210	123	27	8	16	9	21
Regina	204	111	23	14	1	32	29
Winnipeg	195	120	27	12	30	25	20
Toronto	165	137	27	10	115	6	35
Ottawa	165	156	24	16	95	14	35
Montreal	156	162	25	13	108	16	20
Quebec	180	176	24	16	57	20	35
Saint John	173	163	11	12	26	14	108
Halifax	163	166	9	19	19	14	122
Charlottetown	169	174	9	17	17	26	47
St. John's	176	217	3	38	26	31	124
Yellowknife	226	121	5	13	5	10	21
Whitehorse	224	120	6	1	—	3	16

Source: *Environment Canada*

PROVINCES AND TERRITORIES

Latitude, Longitude, Elevation of Canadian Cities

City	Lat. N °	'	Long.W °	'	Elev. (m)	City	Lat. N °	'	Long.W °	'	Elev. (m)
Alert, NWT	82	30	62	22	31	Moose Jaw, Sask.	50	23	105	32	544
Brandon, Man.	49	51	99	57	409	Niagara Falls, Ont.	43	06	79	03	180
Brantford, Ont.	43	08	80	15	215	North Bay, Ont.	46	18	79	27	204
Burlington, Ont.	43	19	79	47	87	Ottawa, Ont.	45	26	75	41	56
Calgary, Alta.	51	02	114	03	1 045	Peterborough, Ont.	44	18	78	19	205
Charlottetown, PEI	46	14	63	07	9	Prince Rupert, BC	54	19	130	19	38
Churchill, Man.	58	45	94	10	29	Quebec, Que.	46	48	71	12	50
Dartmouth, NS	44	39	63	34	7	Regina, Sask.	50	27	104	36	577
Dawson, Yukon	64	03	139	26	369	Saint John, NB	45	16	66	03	8
Edmonton, Alta.	53	32	113	29	666	St. John's, Nfld	47	34	52	43	61
Fredericton, NB	45	57	66	38	9	Saskatoon, Sask.	52	07	106	39	484
Guelph, Ont.	43	32	80	14	325	Sault Ste. Marie, Ont.	46	30	84	20	180
Halifax, NS	44	38	63	34	18	Sherbrooke, Que.	45	24	71	53	191
Hamilton, Ont.	43	15	79	52	100	Sudbury, Ont.	46	29	80	59	347
Hull, Que.	45	25	75	42	56	Sydney, NS	46	08	60	11	62
Kingston, Ont.	44	13	76	28	80	Thunder Bay, Ont.	48	22	89	14	188
Kitchener, Ont.	43	26	80	29	335	Toronto, Ont.	43	39	79	23	91
LaSalle, Que.	45	25	73	39	34	Trois-Rivières, Que.	46	21	72	33	35
Laval, Que.	45	33	73	44	43	Vancouver, BC	49	18	123	04	43
Lethbridge, Alta.	49	41	112	49	910	Victoria, BC	48	25	123	21	17
London, Ont.	42	59	81	14	251	Whitehorse, Yukon	60	43	135	03	703
Moncton, NB	46	05	64	46	12	Winnipeg, Man.	49	53	97	08	232
Montreal, Que.	45	30	73	33	27	Yellowknife, NWT	62	28	114	22	205

Source: *Energy, Mines and Resources Canada (1981)*

Area[1] of Canadian Provinces and Territories

(sq. km)

	Land	Fresh Water	Total	% of total area	Forested land	Area North of treeline
Newfoundland	371 690	34 030	405 720	4.1	142 000	30 040
Island of Newfoundland	105 700	5 690	111 390	1.1	n.a.	—
Prince Edward Island	5 660	. . .	5 660	0.1	3 000	—
Nova Scotia	52 840	2 650	55 490	0.6	41 000	—
New Brunswick	72 090	1 350	73 440	0.7	65 000	—
Quebec	1 356 790	183 890	1 540 680	15.5	940 000	268 320
Ontario	891 190	177 390	1 068 580	10.7	807 000	17 610
Manitoba	548 360	101 590	649 950	6.5	349 000	19 680
Saskatchewan	570 700	81 630	652 330	6.5	178 000	—
Alberta	644 390	16 800	661 190	6.6	349 000	—
British Columbia	929 730	18 070	947 800	9.5	633 000	—
Yukon Territory	478 970	4 480	483 450	4.8	242 000	34 190
Northwest Territories	3 293 020	133 300	3 426 320	34.4	615 000	2 358 960
District of: Franklin	1 423 560	19 430	1 442 990	14.5	n.a.	1 463 860
District of: Keewatin	575 470	25 120	600 590	6.0	n.a.	454 800
District of: Mackenzie	1 293 990	88 750	1 382 740	13.9	n.a.	440 300
Canada	**9 215 430**	**755 180**	**9 970 610**	**100.0**	**4 364 000**	**2 728 800**

Source: *Energy, Mines and Resources Canada*

(1) Areas have been rounded to the nearest 10 sq. km; forested area has been rounded to nearest 1 000 sq. km; (—) = zero; . . . = too small to be included; (n.a.) not available

Newfoundland

☐ **CAPITAL:** St. John's, CMA pop. (1991) 171 859. **Date entered Confederation:** Mar. 31, 1949.

☐ **POPULATION (1991):** 568 474; **Pop. density:** 1.5 per sq. km. **Pop. urban** (1991): 53.6%. **Official Languages** (1991): 97% English; 3% bilingual. **Religious distrib.** (1981): 63% Protestant; 36% Catholic.

☐ **VITAL STATISTICS:** Rates (per 1,000 pop., 1990): **Birth:** 13.3; **Death:** male 7.7, female 5.8. **Life expectancy at birth** (1986): male 73; female 79.

☐ **MARITAL STATUS (1990):** 45% single; 49% married; 3% divorced and separated; 5% widowed. Rates (per 1,000 pop., 1991): **Marriage:** 6.6; **Divorce:** 1.8.

☐ **GEOGRAPHY:** **Total area** 405 720 sq. km; **Land area** 371 690 sq. km; **Forested land** 142 000 sq. km; **Length of coastline** 19 720 km. **Climate:** ranges from subarctic in Labrador and northern tip of island to humid continental with cool summers and heavy precipitation. **Topography:** Island of Newfoundland: highlands of the Long Range Mtns. (elev. 900 m) along w. coast; barren and rocky central plateau descends to lowlands towards the n. east; coast is deeply indented with bays and fjords. Labrador: mountainous in the n.; rugged coast and interior plateau.

☐ **ECONOMY:** **Gross Domestic Product** (1990): $8 787 million. **% change GDP** (1989–90): 27%. **Per capita GDP** (1990): $15 335. **Employment distrib.** (1992): services 35%; trade 19%; manu. 9%; primary ind. 7%; govt. 9%; transp., comm. and util. 8%; construc. 7%; finance 3%. **Unemployment rate** (1992): 20.2%. **Principal industries:** mining, manufacturing, fishing, logging and forestry, electricity production, tourism. **Metal production** (1991): $734 million: iron 97.4%. **Electricity production** (1991, mwh): 36 942 702: hydro 95.8%.

☐ **AGRICULTURE:** **Farm cash receipts** (1990): $68 million. Poultry 9%; dairy 14%; cattle 9%; vegetables 14%. **No. of farms** (1990): 725.

☐ **EDUCATION (1990–91):** No. of schools: 535 elem. and sec.; 13 post-sec. **Enrolment:** 127 400 elem. and sec.; 1 600 post-sec.

☐ **INTERNATIONAL AIRPORTS:** Gander.

☐ **PROVINCIAL DATA:** **Motto:** *Quaerite Prime Regnum Dei:* "Seek Ye First the Kingdom of God." **Flower:** Pitcher plant. **Bird:** Atlantic Puffin (unofficial). **Anthem:** Ode to Newfoundland. **Tartan:** Newfoundland Tartan.

☐ **POLITICS:** Premier: Clyde Wells (Lib.). **Leaders, opposition parties:** Jack Harris (NDP), L. Simms (Prog. Cons.). **Date of last general election:** May 3, 1993. **Lt. Governor:** Frederick W. Russell.

Prince Edward Island

☐ **CAPITAL:** Charlottetown, metro pop. (1991) 33 153. **Date entered Confederation:** July 1, 1873.

☐ **POPULATION (1991):** 129 765; **Pop. density:** 22.9 per sq. km. **Pop. urban** (1991): 39.9%. **Official Languages** (1991): 10% English; 9% bilingual. **Religious distrib.** (1981): 50% Protestant; 47% Catholic.

☐ **VITAL STATISTICS:** Rates (per 1,000 pop., 1990): **Birth:** 15.4; **Death:** male 9.5, female 8.0. **Life expectancy at birth** (1986): male 73; female 80.

☐ **MARITAL STATUS (1990):** 44% single; 49.1% married; 4% divorced and separated; 6% widowed. Rates (per 1,000 pop., 1988): **Marriage:** 7.6; **Divorce:** 2.1.

☐ **GEOGRAPHY:** **Total area** 5 660 sq. km; **Land area** 5 660 sq. km; **Forested land** 3 000 sq. km; **Length of coastline** 1 107 km. **Climate:** humid continental with temperatures moderated by maritime location. **Topography:** flat through gently rolling hills; sharply indented coastline; many streams but only small rivers and lakes.

☐ **ECONOMY:** **Gross Domestic Product** (1990): $1 991 million. **% change GDP** (1989–90): 4.7%. **Per capita GDP**(1990): $15 315. **Employment distrib.** (1992): services 37%; trade 16%; agr. 8%; govt. 10%; manu. 8%. **Unemployment rate** (1992): 17.7%. **Principal industries:** agriculture, tourism, fishing, manufacturing. **Electricity production** (1991, mwh): 71 384: steam 95.4%.

☐ **AGRICULTURE:** **Farm cash receipts** (1990): $270 million. **No. of farms** (1990): 2 361: field crops 25%; dairy 23%; cattle 23%; pigs 10%.

☐ **EDUCATION (1990–91):** No. of schools: 73 elem. and sec.; 3 post-sec. **Enrolment:** 24 850 elem. and sec.; 3 310 post-sec.

☐ **INTERNATIONAL AIRPORTS:** none.

☐ **PROVINCIAL DATA:** **Motto:** *Parva Sub Ingenti:* "The small under the protection of the great." **Flower:** Lady's slipper. **Bird:** Blue Jay. **Tree:** Red Oak.

☐ **POLITICS:** Premier: Catherine Callbeck (Lib.). **Leaders, opposition parties:** P. Mella (Prog. Cons.), L. Duchesne (NDP). **Date of last general election:** March 29, 1989. **Lt. Governor:** Marion Reid.

Nova Scotia

☐ **CAPITAL:** Halifax, metro pop. (1991) 320 501. **Date entered Confederation:** July 1, 1867.

☐ **POPULATION (1991): 899 942; Pop. density:** 16.2 per sq. km. **Pop. urban** (1991): 53.5%. **Official Languages** (1986): 92% English; 8% bilingual. **Religious distrib.** (1981): 58% Protestant; 37% Catholic.

☐ **VITAL STATISTICS:** Rates (per 1,000 pop., 1988): **Birth:** 13.8; **Death:** male 9.4, female 7.4. **Life expectancy at birth** (1986): male 72; female 79.

☐ **MARITAL STATUS (1986):** 44% single; 47% married; 4% divorced and separated; 6% widowed. **Rates** (per 1,000 pop., 1988): **Marriage:** 7.8; **Divorce:** 2.80.

☐ **GEOGRAPHY: Total area** 55 490 sq. km; **Land area** 52 840 sq. km; **Forested land** 41,000 sq. km; **Length of coastline** 5 934 km. **Climate:** humid continental with some moderating effects due to maritime location. **Topography:** Atlantic Uplands are segmented by river valleys; Cape Breton Is. rises from lowland in the s. to a high plateau; many rivers, lakes and jagged coastline.

☐ **ECONOMY: Gross Domestic Product** (1990): $17 017 million. **% change GDP** (1989–90): 5.6%. **Per capita GDP**(1990): $19 035. **Employ-ment distrib.** (1992): services 34%; trade 20%; manu. 13%; govt. 8%; transp., comm. and util. 8%; construc. 6%; finance 4%; primary ind. 4%; agr. 2%. **Unemployment rate** (1992): 13.1%. **Principal industries:** manufacturing, fishing and trapping, mining, agriculture, pulp and paper. **Metal production** (1991): $32.4 million: tin 77.8%. **Electricity production** (1991, mwh): 9 393 515.

☐ **AGRICULTURE: Farm cash receipts** (1988): $297 million: dairy 28%; poultry 12%; cattle 10%; pigs 9%; fruits 9%. **No. of farms** (1986): 3 170.

☐ **EDUCATION (1989–90): No. of schools:** 567 elem. and sec.; 25 post-sec. **Enrolment:** 168 920 elem. and sec.; 28 440 post-sec.

☐ **INTERNATIONAL AIRPORTS:** Halifax

☐ **PROVINCIAL DATA: Motto:** *Munit Haec et Altera Vincit:* "One defends and the other conquers." **Flower:** Mayflower. **Bird:** none. **Tree:** Red Spruce. **Gem:** Agate.

☐ **POLITICS: Premier:** John Savage (Lib.). **Leaders, opposition parties:** T.R.B. Donahoe (Prog. Cons.), Alexa McDonough (NDP). **Date of last general election:** May 25, 1993. **Lt. Governor:** Lloyd R. Crouse.

New Brunswick

☐ **CAPITAL:** Fredericton, metro pop. (1991) 71 869. **Date entered Confederation:** July 1, 1867.

☐ **POPULATION (1991): 723 900; Pop. density:** 9.9 per sq. km. **Pop. urban** (1991): 47.7%. **Official Languages** (1986): 59% English; 12% French; 30% bilingual. **Religious distrib.** (1981): 54% Catholic; 43% Protestant.

☐ **VITAL STATISTICS: Rates** (per 1,000 pop., 1991): **Birth:** 13.7; **Death:** male 8.7, female 6.6. **Life expectancy at birth** (1986): male 72; female 80.

Marital status (1991): 42% single; 49% married; 4% divorced and separated; 5% widowed. **Rates** (per 1,000 pop., 1990): **Marriage:** 7.0; **Divorce:** 2.34.

☐ **GEOGRAPHY: Total area** 73 440 sq. km; **Land area** 72 090 sq. km; **Forested land** 61,000 sq. km; **Length of coastline** 1 524 km. **Climate:** humid continental climate except along the shores where there is a marked maritime effect. **Topography:** northern upland; rolling central plateau; southern lowland plain with many rivers.

☐ **ECONOMY: Gross Domestic Product** (1990): $13 295 million. **% change GDP** (1989–90): 4.9%. **Per capita GDP**(1990): $18 389. **Employment distrib.** (1991): services 34%; trade 20%; manu. 13%; transp., comm. and util. 8%; govt. 8%; construc. 6%; primary ind. 4%; finance 4%; agr. 2%. **Unemployment rate** (1992): 12.8%. **Principal industries:** manufacturing, fishing, mining, forestry, pulp and paper, agriculture. **Metal production** (1991): $375 million: zinc 71.5%; silver 6.3%; lead 11.8%; cement 2%; copper 7.6%. **Electricity production** (1991, mwh): 15 807 472: steam 88.5%.

☐ **AGRICULTURE: Farm cash receipts** (1991): $254 million: dairy 22%; potatoes 21%; poultry 12%; cattle 10%; pigs 6%. **No. of farms** (1991): 3 252.

☐ **EDUCATION (1989–90): No. of schools:** 414 elem. and sec.; 13 post-sec. **Enrolment:** 140 971 elem. and sec.; 21 186 post-sec.

☐ **INTERNATIONAL AIRPORTS:** none.

☐ **PROVINCIAL DATA: Motto:** *Spem Reduxit:* "Hope was restored." **Flower:** Purple Violet. **Bird:** Black-capped Chickadee. **Tree:** Balsam Fir.

☐ **POLITICS: Premier:** Frank McKenna (Lib.). **Leaders, opposition parties:** Danny Cameron (interim) (CoR), Dennis Cochrane (Prog. Cons.), Elizabeth Weir (NDP). **Date of last general election:** Sept. 23, 1991. **Lt. Governor:** Gilbert Finn.

Quebec

☐ **CAPITAL:** Quebec, metro pop. (1991) 645 550. **Date entered Confederation:** July 1, 1867.

☐ **POPULATION (1991): 6 895 963; Pop. density:** 4.5 per sq. km. **Pop. urban** (1991): 77.6%. **Official Languages** (1986): 59% French; 6% English; 35% bilingual. **Religious distrib.** (1981): 88% Catholic; 6% Protestant; 2% Jewish; 1% Eastern Orthodox; 1% Eastern non-Christian.

☐ **VITAL STATISTICS: Rates** (per 1,000 pop., 1988): **Birth:** 13.0; **Death:** male 8.1, female 6.3. **Life expectancy at birth** (1986): male 72; female 79.

☐ **MARITAL STATUS (1986):** 43% single; 47% married; 5% divorced and separated; 5% widowed. **Rates** (per 1,000 pop., 1988): **Marriage:** 5.1; **Divorce:** 2.99.

☐ **GEOGRAPHY: Total area** 1 540 680 sq. km; **Land area** 1 356 790 sq. km; **Forested land** 940 000 sq. km; **Length of coastline** 10 839 km. **Climate:** varies from subarctic to continental. **Topography:** lowlands along the St. Lawrence R. valley separate the Laurentian Mtns. to the n. and the Appalachian Mtns. to the s.; Canadian Shield landscape dominates north.

☐ **ECONOMY: Gross Domestic Product** (1990): $154 066 million. **% change GDP** (1989–90): 2.9%. **Per capita GDP**(1990): $22 761. **Employment distrib.** (1992): services 36%; manu. 18%; trade 18%; transp., comm. and util. 7%; govt. 7%; finance 6%; construc. 5%; agr. 2%; primary ind. 1%; unclassified 1%. **Unemployment rate** (1992): 12.8%. **Principal industries:** manufacturing, electric power, mining, pulp and paper, transportation equipment. **Metal Production** (1991): $1.9 billion: gold 36.7%; copper 16.3%; zinc 8%. **Electricity production** (1991, mwh): 142 992 002: hydro 96.9%.

☐ **AGRICULTURE: Farm cash receipts** (1988): $3.4 billion: dairy 34%; pigs 16%; poultry 9%; cattle 6%; corn 4%. **No. of farms** (1986): 37 160.

☐ **EDUCATION (1989–90): No. of schools:** 2 855 elem. and sec.; 89 post-sec. **Enrolment:** 1 139 200 elem. and sec.; 273 900 post-sec.

☐ **INTERNATIONAL AIRPORTS:** Dorval; Mirabel.

☐ **PROVINCIAL DATA: Motto:** *Je me souviens:* "I remember." **Flower:** Lys blanc de jardin (White Garden (Madonna) Lily). **Bird:** Harfang des neiges (Snowy Owl).

☐ **POLITICS: Premier:** Robert Bourassa (Lib.). **Leaders, opposition parties:** Keith Henderson (Equality), Jacques Parizeau (Parti Quebecois). **Date of last general election:** Sept. 25, 1989. **Lt. Governor:** Martial Asselin.

Ontario

☐ **CAPITAL:** Toronto, metro pop. (1991) 3 893 046. **Date entered Confederation:** July 1, 1867.

☐ **POPULATION (1991): 10 084 885; Pop. density:** 9.4 per sq. km. **Pop. urban** (1991): 81.8%. **Official Languages** (1986): 86% English; 1% French; 12% bilingual. **Religious distrib.** (1981): 52% Protestant; 36% Catholic; 2% Eastern Orthodox; 2% Jewish.

☐ **VITAL STATISTICS: Rates** (per 1,000 pop., 1988): **Birth:** 14.6; **Death:** male 8.1, female 6.9. **Life expectancy at birth** (1986): male 73; female 80.

☐ **MARITAL STATUS (1986):** 42% single; 48% married; 5% divorced and separated; 5% widowed. **Rates** (per 1,000 pop., 1988): **Marriage:** 8.3; **Divorce:** 3.17.

☐ **GEOGRAPHY: Total area** 1 068 580 sq. km; **Land area** 891 190 sq. km; **Forested land** 807 000 sq. km; **Length of coastline** 1 210 km. **Climate:** ranges from humid continental in south to subarctic in far north; westerly winds bring winter storms; the Great Lakes moderate winter temperatures. **Topography:** Rugged, rocky Canadian Shield plateau is broken by lowlands around Great Lakes, St. Lawrence R. and Hudson Bay.

☐ **ECONOMY: Gross Domestic Product** (1990): $277 085 million. **% change GDP** (1989–90): 1.8%. **Per capita GDP** (1990): $28 439. **Employment distrib.** (1992): services 36%; manu. 18%; trade 16%; transp., comm. and util. 7%; govt. 6%; finance 7%; construc. 6%; agr. 2%; primary ind. .3%; unclassified .6%. **Unemployment rate** (1992): 10.8%. **Principal industries:** manufacturing, construction, agriculture, forestry, mining. **Metal production** (1991): $3.8 billion: nickel 32.2%; gold 27.2%; copper 18.7%; uranium 6.9%; zinc 7.2%. **Electricity production** (1991, mwh): 142 442 661: nuclear 49.7%; hydro 26.4%; steam 23%.

☐ **AGRICULTURE: Farm cash receipts** (1988): $5.6 billion: dairy 19%; cattle 18%; pigs 10%; poultry 7%; corn 6%. **No. of farms** (1986): 63 253.

☐ **EDUCATION (1989–90): No. of schools:** 5 281 elem. and sec.; 53 post-sec. **Enrolment:** 1 978 490 elem. and sec.; 303 700 post-sec.

☐ **INTERNATIONAL AIRPORTS:** Pearson (Toronto); Ottawa.

☐ **PROVINCIAL DATA:** Motto: *Ut Incepit Fidelis Sic Permanet:* "Loyal she began, loyal she remains." **Flower:** White trillium. **Bird:** Common Loon (unofficial). **Tree:** Eastern White Pine. **Gem:** Amethyst.

☐ **POLITICS: Premier:** Bob Rae (NDP). **Leaders, opposition parties:** Mike Harris (Prog. Cons.); Lyn McLeod (Lib.). **Date of last general election:** Sept. 6, 1990. **Lt. Governor:** Henry N. R. Jackman.

Manitoba

☐ **CAPITAL:** Winnipeg, metro pop. (1991) 652 354. **Date entered Confederation:** July 15, 1870.

☐ **POPULATION (1991): 1 091 942; Pop. density:** 1.7 per sq. km. **Pop. urban** (1991): 72.1%. **Official Languages** (1986): 90% English; 9% bilingual. **Religious distrib.** (1981): 57% Protestant; 31% Catholic; 2% Eastern Orthodox; 2% Jewish.

☐ **VITAL STATISTICS: Rates** (per 1,000 pop., 1988): **Birth:** 15.7; **Death:** male 9.4, female 7.4. **Life expectancy at birth** (1986): male 73; female 80.

☐ **MARITAL STATUS (1986):** 44% single; 47% married; 4% divorced and separated; 6% widowed. **Rates** (per 1,000 pop., 1988): **Marriage:** 7.3; **Divorce:** 2.76.

☐ **GEOGRAPHY: Total area** 649 950 sq. km; **Land area** 548 360 sq. km; **Forested land** 349 000 sq. km; **Length of coastline** 917 km. **Climate:** continental with seasonal extremes. **Topography:** the land rises gradually south and west from Hudson Bay; flat plateau through south central region; countless lakes, streams and bogs.

☐ **ECONOMY: Gross Domestic Product** (1990): $23 707 million. **% change GDP** (1989–90): 3.2%. **Per capita GDP** (1990): $21 710. **Employment distrib.** (1992): services 36%; trade 18%; manu. 10%; transp., comm. and util. 9%; agr. 8%; govt. 7%; finance 5%; construc. 5%; primary ind. 2%. **Unemployment rate** (1992): 9.6%. **Principal industries:** manufacturing, agriculture, food industry, mining, construction. **Metal production** (1991): $948 million: nickel 62.1%; copper 15.7%; zinc 11.9%; gold 4%. **Electricity production** (1991, mwh): 22 891 405: hydro 98.5%.

☐ **AGRICULTURE: Farm cash receipts** (1988): $1.8 billion: wheat 21%; cattle 15%; pigs 12%; canola-rapeseed 7%; flaxseed 4%. **No. of farms** (1986): 25 262.

☐ **EDUCATION (1989–90):** No. of schools: 844 elem. and sec.; 16 post-sec. **Enrolment:** 219 200 elem. and sec.; 23 580 post-sec.

☐ **INTERNATIONAL AIRPORTS:** Winnipeg.

☐ **PROVINCIAL DATA: Motto:** none. **Flower:** Prairie Crocus. **Bird:** Great Grey Owl. **Tartan:** Manitoba Tartan.

☐ **POLITICS: Premier:** Gary Filmon (Prog. Cons.). **Leaders, opposition parties:** Paul Edwards (Lib.), Gary Doer (NDP). **Date of last general election:** Sept. 11, 1990. **Lt. Governor:** George Johnson.

Saskatchewan

☐ **CAPITAL:** Regina, metro pop. (1991) 191 692. **Date entered Confederation:** Sept. 1, 1905.

☐ **POPULATION (1991): 988 928; Pop. density:** 1.5 per sq. km. **Pop. urban** (1991): 63%. **Official Languages** (1986): 95% English; 5% bilingual. **Religious distrib.** (1981): 57% Protestant; 31% Catholic; 2% Eastern Orthodox; 2% Jewish.

☐ **VITAL STATISTICS: Rates** (per 1,000 pop., 1988): **Birth:** 16.6; **Death:** male 9.3, female 6.7. **Life expectancy at birth** (1986): male 74; female 80.

☐ **MARITAL STATUS (1986):** 44% single; 47% married; 4% divorced and separated; 5% widowed. **Rates** (per 1,000 pop., 1988): **Marriage:** 6.7; **Divorce:** 2.44.

☐ **GEOGRAPHY: Total area** 652 330 sq. km; **Land area** 570 700 sq. km; **Forested land** 178 000 sq. km; **Climate:** continental, with cold winters and hot summers. **Topography:** gently rolling plains through south; higher, hilly plateaus in the s.w.; north is rugged Canadian Shield.

☐ **ECONOMY: Gross Domestic Product** (1990): $20 274 million. **% change GDP** (1989–90): 4.0%. **Per capita GDP** (1990): $20 274. **Employment distrib.** (1992): services 35%; trade 16%; govt. 7%; transp., comm. and util. 7%; manu. 5%; construc. 5%; finance 5%; primary ind. 3%; agri. 16%. **Unemployment rate** (1992): 8.2%. **Principal industries:** agriculture, mining, manufacturing, electric power, construction, chemical prod. **Metal production** (1991): $373 million: uranium 89.2%; gold 10.4%. **Electricity production** (1991, mwh): 13 598 251: steam 68.6%; hydro 31%.

☐ **AGRICULTURE: Farm cash receipts** (1988): $3.7 billion: wheat 38%; cattle 15%; canola-rapeseed 11%; barley 4%; pigs 3%. **No. of farms** (1986): 60 809.

☐ **EDUCATION (1989–90):** No. of schools: 1 012 elem. and sec.; 4 post-sec. **Enrolment:** 214 530 elem. and sec.; 23 450 post-sec.

☐ **INTERNATIONAL AIRPORTS:** none.

☐ **PROVINCIAL DATA:** Motto: *Multis E Gentibus Vires:* "from many peoples strength". **Flower:** Western Red Lily. **Bird:** Prairie sharp-tailed grouse. **Tree:** White Birch. **Tartan:** Saskatchewan Tartan.

☐ **POLITICS:** Premier: Roy Romanow (NDP). **Leaders, opposition parties:** Lynda Haverstock (Lib.), Rick Swenson (Prog. Cons.). **Date of last general election:** Oct. 21, 1991. **Lt. Governor:** Sylvia O. Fedoruk.

Alberta

☐ **CAPITAL:** Edmonton, metro pop. (1991) 839 924. **Date entered Confederation:** Sept. 1, 1905.

☐ **POPULATION (1991):** 2 545 553; **Pop. density:** 3.8 per sq. km. **Pop. urban** (1991): 79.8%. **Official Languages** (1986): 92% English; 6% bilingual. **Religious distrib.** (1981): 56% Protestant; 28% Catholic; 2% Eastern Orthodox; 2% Eastern non-Christian.

☐ **VITAL STATISTICS: Rates** (per 1,000 pop., 1988): **Birth:** 17.5; **Death:** male 6.6, female 5.0. **Life expectancy at birth** (1986): male 74; female 80.

☐ **MARITAL STATUS (1986):** 44% single; 47% married; 5% divorced and separated; 4% widowed. **Rates** (per 1,000 pop., 1988): **Marriage:** 8.1; **Divorce:** 3.60.

☐ **GEOGRAPHY: Total area** 661 190 sq. km; **Land area** 644 390 sq. km; **Forested land** 349 000 sq. km. **Climate:** great variance in temperatures between regions and seasons; summer highs between 16˚C and 32˚C; winters as low as -45˚C. **Topography:** Rocky Mtns. in s.w. to rolling prairie throughout southern region; far north is a forested plateau.

☐ **ECONOMY: Gross Domestic Product** (1990): $70 565 million. **% change GDP** (1989–90): 7.0%. **Per capita GDP** (1990): $28 546. **Employment distrib.** (1992): services 38%; trade 18%; transp., comm. and util. 7%; manu. 7%; agr. 7%; govt. 6%; primary ind. 6%; construc. 7%; finance 5%; 4 unclassified. **Unemployment rate** (1992): 9.5%. **Principal industries:** chemical products, mining, agriculture, food, manufacturing, construction, oil prod. and refinement. **Metal production** (1991): $3 billion: gold 15%. **Electricity production** (1991, mwh): 44 479 165: steam 90.6%.

☐ **AGRICULTURE: Farm cash receipts** (1988): $4.1 billion: cattle 34%; wheat 15%; canola-rapeseed 10%; pigs 6%; barley 6%. **No. of farms** (1986): 51 743.

☐ **EDUCATION (1989–90):** **No. of schools:** 1 710 elem. and sec.; 25 post-sec. **Enrolment:** 489 390 elem. and sec.; 71 950 post-sec.

☐ **INTERNATIONAL AIRPORTS:** Edmonton; Calgary.

☐ **PROVINCIAL DATA:** Motto: *Fortis et Liber:* "Strong and free." **Flower:** Wild Rose. **Bird:** Great horned owl. **Tree:** Lodge pole pine. **Tartan:** Alberta Tartan. **Stone:** Petrified wood.

☐ **POLITICS:** Premier: Ralph Klein (Prog. Cons.). **Leaders, opposition parties:** Laurence Decore (Lib.), Ray Martin (NDP). **Date of last general election:** Mar. 20, 1989. **Lt. Governor:** Gordon Towers.

British Columbia

☐ **CAPITAL:** Victoria, metro pop. (1991) 287 897. **Date entered Confederation:** July 20, 1871.

☐ **POPULATION (1991):** 3 282 061; **Pop. density:** 3.5 per sq. km. **Pop. urban** (1991): 80.4%. **Official Languages** (1986): 92% English; 6% bilingual. **Religious distrib.** (1981): 55% Protestant; 20% Catholic; 3% Eastern non-Christian; 1% Eastern Orthodox.

☐ **VITAL STATISTICS: Rates** (per 1,000 pop., 1988): **Birth:** 14.4; **Death:** male 8.3, female 6.8. **Life expectancy at birth** (1986): male 74; female 80.

☐ **MARITAL STATUS (1986):** 41% single; 48% married; 6% divorced and separated; 5% widowed. **Rates** (per 1,000 pop., 1988): **Marriage:** 8.2; **Divorce:** 3.55.

☐ **GEOGRAPHY: Total area** 947 800 sq. km; **Land area** 929 730 sq. km; **Forested land** 633 000 sq. km; **Length of coastline** 17 856 km. **Climate:** maritime with mild temperatures and abundant rainfall in the coastal areas; continental climate with temperature extremes in the interior and northeast. **Topography:** mostly mountainous; deep river valleys and gorges, except for the n.e. area which is an extension of the Great Plains; indented coast with numerous bays and islands.

☐ **ECONOMY: Gross Domestic Product** (1990): $80 706 million. **% change GDP** (1989–90): 4.7%. **Per capita GDP** (1990): $25 809. **Employment distrib.** (1992): services 38%; trade 19%; manu. 10%; transp., comm. and util. 8%; govt. 5%; finance 6%; construc. 8%; primary ind. 3%; agr. 2%; .5 unclassified. **Unemployment rate** (1992): 10.4%. **Principal industries:** forestry, wood and paper, mining, tourism, agriculture, fishing, manufacturing. **Metal production** (1991): $1.5 billion: copper 60.2%; zinc 10.6%; gold 16.1%. **Electricity production** (1991, mwh): 63 373 895: hydro 95%.

☐ **AGRICULTURE: Farm cash receipts** (1988): $1.1 billion: dairy products 22%; cattle 12%; poultry 11%; fruits 10%; vegetables 7%. **No. of farms** (1986): 13 699.

☐ **EDUCATION (1989–90):** No. of schools: 1 946 elem. and sec.; 25 post-sec. **Enrolment:** 551 770 elem. and sec.; 66 400 post-sec.

☐ **INTERNATIONAL AIRPORTS:** Vancouver; Victoria.

☐ **PROVINCIAL DATA: Motto:** _Splendor Sine Occasu:_ "Splendor without Diminishment." **Flower:** Dogwood. **Bird:** Stellar's Jay.

☐ **POLITICS: Premier:** Michael Harcourt (NDP). **Leader, opposition party:** Gordon Campbell (Lib.). **Date of last general election:** Oct. 17, 1991. **Lt. Governor:** David C. Lam.

Yukon Territory

☐ **CAPITAL:** Whitehorse, metro pop. (1991) 17 925. **Date entered Confederation:** June 13, 1898.

☐ **POPULATION (1991):** 27 797; **Pop. density:** .06 per sq. km. **Pop. urban** (1991): 58.8%. **Official Languages** (1986): 91% English; 9% bilingual.

☐ **VITAL STATISTICS:** Rates (per 1,000 pop., 1988): **Birth:** 20.1; **Death:** male 7.0, female 3.6.

☐ **MARITAL STATUS (1986):** 48% single; 44% married; 6% divorced and separated; 2% widowed. **Rates** (per 1,000 pop., 1988): **Marriage:** 8.2; **Divorce:** 3.20.

☐ **GEOGRAPHY: Total area** 483 450 sq. km; **Land area** 478 970 sq. km; **Forested land** 242 000 sq. km; **Length of coastline** 343 km. **Climate:** great variance in temperatures; warm summers, very cold winters; low precipitation. **Topography:** main feature is the Yukon plateau with 21 peaks exceeding 3 300 m; open tundra in the far north.

☐ **ECONOMY: Gross Domestic Product** (1990): $929 million. **% change GDP** (1989–90): 4.3%. **Per capita GDP** (1990): $35 731. **Principal industries:** mining, tourism. **Metal production** (1991): $335.5 million: gold 15.4%; zinc 57.1%; lead 23.8%. **Electricity production** (1991, mwh): 461 208: hydro 87.9%.

☐ **EDUCATION (1989–90):** No. of schools: 26 elem. and sec.; 1 post-sec. **Enrolment:** 5 110 elem. and sec.; 130 post-sec.

☐ **INTERNATIONAL AIRPORTS:** none.

☐ **PROVINCIAL DATA: Flower:** Fireweed. **Bird:** Common Raven.

☐ **POLITICS: Commissioner:** Ken McKinnon; **Govt. Leader:** John Ostashek (Yukon Party). **Leader, opposition party:** Willard Phelps (Prog. Cons.) **Date of last general election:** Oct. 19, 1992.

Northwest Territories

☐ **CAPITAL:** Yellowknife, metro pop. (1991) 15 179. **Date entered Confederation:** July 15, 1870.

☐ **POPULATION (1991):** 54 649; **Pop. density:** .02 per sq. km. **Pop. urban** (1991): 36.7%. **Official Languages** (1986): 81% English; 7% bilingual.

☐ **VITAL STATISTICS:** Rates (per 1,000 pop., 1988): **Birth:** 30.0; **Death:** male 5.2, female 3.2.

☐ **MARITAL STATUS (1986):** 57% single; 38% married; 3% divorced and separated; 2% widowed. **Rates** (per 1,000 pop., 1988): **Marriage:** 4.2; **Divorce:** 2.12.

☐ **GEOGRAPHY: Total area** 3 426 320 sq. km; **Land area** 3 293 020 sq. km; **Forested land** 615 000 sq. km; **Length of coastline** 111 249 km. **Climate:** extreme temperatures and low precipitation; arctic and sub-arctic. **Topography:** mostly tundra plains formed on the rocks of the Canadian Shield; the Mackenzie Lowland is a continuation of the Great Plains; the Mackenzie River Valley is forested.

☐ **ECONOMY: Gross Domestic Product** (1990): $2 120 million. **% change GDP** (1989–90): 2.3%. **Per capita GDP** (1990): $39 259. **Principal industries:** construction, utilities, services, tourism. **Metal production** (1991): $477.6 million: zinc 46.4%; gold 46.8%. **Electricity production** (1991, mwh): 571 977: hydro 42.4%; steam 41.5%.

☐ **EDUCATION (1989–90):** No. of schools: 72 elem. and sec.; 1 post-sec. **Enrolment:** 13 580 elem. and sec.; 180 post-sec.

☐ **INTERNATIONAL AIRPORTS:** none.

☐ **PROVINCIAL DATA: Flower:** Mountain Avens. **Bird:** none.

☐ **POLITICS: Commissioner:** Dan L. Norris; **Govt. Leader:** Nellie Cournoyea. **Date of last general election:** Oct. 15, 1991.

CANADIAN CITIES

Calgary, Alta

☐ **YEAR INCORPORATED:** 1893. **Population** (1991): 754 033; 49.9% male, 50.1% female. **Area:** 5 086 sq. km. **Pop. density:** 148.3 per sq. km. **Pop. growth** (1986–1991): 12.3%. **Pop. over 65:** 24 200 males; 34 475 females. **Pop. under 35:** 219 585 males; 214 785 females.

☐ **OFFICIAL LANGUAGES (1991):** 91.2% English; 0.2% French; 7% bilingual; 1.5% neither. **Immigrant pop.** (1991): 151 745, 20.1%. **Religious breakdown** (1991): 46% Protestant; 25% Catholic; 22% no affiliation; 4% Eastern non-Christian; 1% Jewish; 1% other.

☐ **AVG. INCOME (1985):** $27 893 males; $15 091 females; $45 624 families. **Avg. family size** (1991): 3.1 persons. **Single parent families** (1991): 12.8% of families.

☐ **CLIMATE:** Avg. temps. -12˚ (Jan.); 16˚ (July). **Avg. annual precip.** 300 mm. **Avg. annual snowfall:** 153 cm.

Chicoutimi–Jonquière, Que.

☐ **YEAR INCORPORATED:** 1976. **Population** (1991): 160 930; 49.5% male, 50.5% female. **Area:** 1 723.31 sq. km. **Pop. density:** 93 per sq. km. **Pop. growth** (1986–1991): 1.6%. **Pop. over 65:** 6 090 males; 8 525 females. **Pop. under 35:** 43 880 males; 42 445 females.

☐ **OFFICIAL LANGUAGES (1991):** .93% English; 98.0% French; .34% neither. **Immigrant pop.** (1991): 1 170, .72%. **Religious breakdown** (1991): 97% Catholic; 1.5% no affiliation; 1% Protestant; .1% Eastern non-Christian; .03% other.

☐ **AVG. INCOME:** n.a. **Avg. family size** (1991): 3.1 persons. **Single parent families** (1991): 13.4% of families.

☐ **CLIMATE:** Avg. temps. -15.8˚ (Jan.); 18˚ (July). **Avg. annual precip.** 641 mm. **Avg. annual snowfall:** 345 cm.

Edmonton, Alta

☐ **YEAR INCORPORATED:** 1904. **Population** (1991): 839 924; 49.8% male, 50.2% female. **Area:** 9 533 sq. km. **Pop. density:** 88.1 per sq. km. **Pop. growth** (1986–1991): 8.5%. **Pop. over 65:** 30 085 males; 41 125 females. **Pop. under 35:** 244 710 males; 238 700 females.

☐ **OFFICIAL LANGUAGES (1991):** 90.6% English; 0.1% French; 7.7% bilingual; 1.8% neither. **Immigrant pop.** (1991): 152 810, 18.2%. **Religious breakdown** (1991): 43% Protestant; 29% Catholic; 20% no affiliation; 4% Eastern non-Christian; 3% other; .5% Jewish.

☐ **AVG. INCOME (1985):** $24 304 males; $14 119 females; $40 465 families. **Avg. family size** (1991): 3.1 persons. **Single parent families** (1991): 14.2% of families.

☐ **CLIMATE:** Avg. temps. -15˚ (Jan.); 17˚ (July). **Avg. annual precip.** 353 mm. **Avg. annual snowfall:** 138 cm.

Halifax, NS

☐ **YEAR INCORPORATED:** 1841. **Population** (1991): 320 501; 48.7% male, 51.3% female. **Area:** 2 503 sq. km. **Pop. density:** 128 per sq. km. **Pop. growth** (1986–1991): 8.3%. **Pop. over 65:** 12 185 males; 18 185 females. **Pop. under 35:** 89 820 males; 89 910 females.

☐ **OFFICIAL LANGUAGES (1991):** 90.1% English; 0.1% French; 9.6% bilingual; 1.3% neither. **Immigrant pop.** (1991): 20 790, 6.5%. **Religious breakdown** (1991): 50% Protestant; 39% Catholic; 9% no affiliation; 1% Eastern non-Christian; .6% other; .5% Jewish.

☐ **AVG. INCOME (1985):** $23 797 males; $14 001 females; $41 005 families. **Avg. family size** (1991): 3.0 persons. **Single parent families** (1991): 14.0% of families.

☐ **CLIMATE:** Avg. temps. -6˚ (Jan.); 18˚ (July). **Avg. annual precip.** 1 224 mm. **Avg. annual snowfall:** 271 cm.

Hamilton, Ont.

☐ **YEAR INCORPORATED:** 1846. **Population** (1991): 599 760; 48.9% male, 51.1% female. **Area:** 1 359 sq. km. **Pop. density:** 441.5 per sq. km. **Pop. growth** (annual avg. 1986–1991): 7.7%. **Pop. over 65:** 32 085 males; 44 865 females. **Pop. under 35:** 154 415 males; 151 520 females.

☐ **OFFICIAL LANGUAGES (1991):** 91.9% English; 0.1% French; 6.6% bilingual; 3.4% neither. **Immigrant pop.** (1991): 139 560, 23.3%. **Religious breakdown** (1991): 47% Protestant; 35% Catholic; 13% no affiliation; 2% Eastern non-Christian; 2% other; .8% Jewish.

☐ **AVG. INCOME (1985):** $22 177 males; $11 669 females; $35 175 families. **Avg. family size (1991):** 3.1 persons. **Single parent families (1991):** 12.3% of families.

☐ **CLIMATE:** Avg. temps. -6° (Jan.); 21° (July).

Kitchener, Ont.

☐ **YEAR INCORPORATED:** 1912. **Population (1991):** 356 420; 49.3% male, 50.7% female. **Area:** 82 364 sq. km. **Pop. density:** 433 per sq. km. **Pop. growth (1986–1991):** 14.5%. **Pop. over 65:** 14 670 males; 21 790 females. **Pop. under 35:** 101 050 males; 98 255 females.

☐ **OFFICIAL LANGUAGES (1991):** 79.4% English; 1.3% French; 16.6% other. **Immigrant pop. (1991):** 75 980, 21.3%. **Religious breakdown (1991):** 50% Protestant; 33% Catholic; 11% no affiliation; 3% Eastern non-Christian; 1% other; .2% Jewish.

☐ **AVG. INCOME:** n.a. **Avg. family size (1991):** 3.1 persons. **Single parent families (1991):** 12.3% of families.

☐ **CLIMATE:** Avg. temps. -7.3° (Jan.); 19.9° (July). **Avg. annual precip.** 774 mm. **Avg. annual snowfall:** 158 cm.

London, Ont.

☐ **YEAR INCORPORATED:** 1855. **Population (1991):** 381 522; 48.3% male, 51.7% female. **Area:** 2 105 sq. km. **Pop. density:** 181.2 per sq. km. **Pop. growth (annual avg. 1986–1991):** 11.5%. **Pop. over 65:** 18 585 males; 27 565 females. **Pop. under 35:** 101 925 males; 102 195 females.

☐ **OFFICIAL LANGUAGES (1991):** 92.4% English; 0.2% French; 6.4% bilingual; 2.2% neither. **Immigrant pop. (1991):** 70 655, 19.3%. **Religious breakdown (1991):** 54% Protestant; 27% Catholic; 14% no affiliation; 2% Eastern non-Christian; 2% other; .6% Jewish.

☐ **AVG. INCOME (1985):** $24 133 males; $13 464 females; $39 975 families. **Avg. family size (1991):** 3.0 persons. **Single parent families (1991):** 13.4% of families.

☐ **CLIMATE:** Avg. temps. -7° (Jan.); 20° (July). **Avg. annual precip.** 726 mm. **Avg. annual snowfall:** 209 cm.

Montreal, Que.

☐ **YEAR INCORPORATED:** 1832. **Population (1991):** 3 127 242; 48.4% male, 51.6% female. **Area:** 3 509 sq. km. **Pop. density:** 891.2 per sq. km. **Pop. growth (1986–1991):** 7%. **Pop. over 65:** 136 735 males; 216 310 females. **Pop. under 35:** 805 070 males; 788 915 females.

☐ **OFFICIAL LANGUAGES (1991):** 9.6% English; 40.4% French; 48.3% bilingual; 1.7% neither. **Immigrant pop. (1991):** 520 530, 16.6%. **Religious breakdown (1991):** 78% Catholic; 8% Protestant; 5% no affiliation; 3% Eastern non-Christian; 3% Jewish; 3% other.

☐ **AVG. INCOME (1985):** $19 131 males; $12 481 females; $31 783 families. **Avg. family size (1991):** 3.0 persons. **Single parent families (1991):** 15.6% of families.

☐ **CLIMATE:** Avg. temps. -10° (Jan.); 21° (July). **Avg. annual precip.** 723 mm. **Avg. annual snowfall:** 235 cm.

Oshawa, Ont.

☐ **YEAR INCORPORATED:** 1924. **Population (1991):** 240 104; 49.7% male, 50.3% female. **Area:** 894.19 sq. km. **Pop. density:** 269 per sq. km. **Pop. growth (1986–1991):** 18.0%. **Pop. over 65:** 9 085 males; 12 555 females. **Pop. under 35:** 68 165 males; 66 695 females.

☐ **OFFICIAL LANGUAGES (1991):** 87.3% English; 2.1% French; 8.9% neither. **Immigrant pop. (1991):** 40 845, 17.0%. **Religious breakdown (1991):** 54% Protestant; 29% Catholic; 14% no affiliation; 1% Eastern non-Christian; 1% other; .2% Jewish.

☐ **AVG. INCOME:** n.a. **Avg. family size (1991):** 3.1 persons. **Single parent families (1991):** 11.8% of families.

☐ **CLIMATE:** Avg. temps. -5.7° (Jan.); 19.9° (July). **Avg. annual precip.** 755 mm. **Avg. annual snowfall:** 126 cm.

Ottawa-Hull

☐ **YEAR INCORPORATED:** 1854 (Ottawa). **Population (1991):** 920 857; 48.9% male, 51.0% female. **Area:** 5 138 sq. km. **Pop. density:** 179.2 per sq. km. **Pop. growth (1986–1991):** 12.4%. **Pop. over 65:** 35 200 males; 53 440 females. **Pop. under 35:** 250 405 males; 247 030 females.

☐ **OFFICIAL LANGUAGES (1991):** 46.8% English; 9.6% French; 42.6% bilingual; 1.0% neither. **Immigrant pop. (1991):** 134 755, 14.6%. **Religious breakdown (1991):** 57% Catholic; 27% Protestant; 10% no affiliation; 3% Eastern non-Christian; 1% Jewish; 1% other.

☐ **AVG. INCOME (1985):** $26 902 males; $16 448 females; $45 883 families. **Avg. family size (1991):** 3.0 persons. **Single parent families (1991):** 14.0% of families.

☐ **CLIMATE:** Avg. temps. -11˚ (Jan.); 21˚ (July). Avg. annual precip. 663 mm. Avg. annual snowfall: 227 cm.

Quebec, Que.

☐ **YEAR INCORPORATED:** 1832. Population (1991): 645 550; 48.2% male, 51.8% female. **Area:** 3 150 sq. km. **Pop. density:** 204.9 per sq. km. **Pop. growth** (1986–1991): 7.0%. **Pop. over 65:** 25 550 males; 43 315 females. **Pop. under 35:** 165 900 males; 162 445 females.

☐ **OFFICIAL LANGUAGES (1991):** 0.3% English; 72.0% French; 27.7% bilingual. **Immigrant pop.** (1991): 14 020, 2.2%. **Religious breakdown** (1991): 94% Catholic; 3.4% no affiliation; 2% Protestant; .4% Eastern non-Christian; .15% other; .02% Jewish.

☐ **AVG. INCOME (1985):** $19 748 males; $12 022 females; $32 276 families. **Avg. family size** (1991): 3.0 persons. **Single parent families** (1991): 14.9% of families.

☐ **CLIMATE:** Avg. temps. -12˚ (Jan.); 19˚ (July). Avg. annual precip. 836 mm. Avg. annual snowfall: 343 cm.

Regina, Sask.

☐ **YEAR INCORPORATED:** 1903. Population (1991): 191 692; 48.8% male, 51.2% female. **Area:** 3 422 sq. km. **Pop. density:** 56 per sq. km. **Pop. growth** (1986–1991): 2.8%. **Pop. over 65:** 8 400 males; 12 525 females. **Pop. under 35:** 54 165 males; 54 090 females.

☐ **OFFICIAL LANGUAGES (1991):** 93.9% English; 0.1% French; 5.6% bilingual; 0.4% neither. **Immigrant pop.** (1991): 15 895, 8.3%. **Religious breakdown** (1991): 49% Protestant; 33% Catholic; 14% no affiliation; 2% other; 1.25% Eastern non-Christian; .25% Jewish.

☐ **AVG. INCOME (1985):** $25 196 males; $14 202 females; $41 894 families. **Avg. family size** (1991): 3.1 persons. **Single parent families** (1991): 14.4% of families.

☐ **CLIMATE:** Avg. temps. -18˚ (Jan.); 19˚ (July). Avg. annual precip. 287 mm. Avg. annual snowfall: 116 cm.

St. Catharines–Niagara, Ont.

☐ **YEAR INCORPORATED:** 1876. Population (1991): 364 550; 48.7% male, 51.3% female. **Area:** 1 399.8 sq. km. **Pop. density:** 260 per sq. km. **Pop. growth** (1986–1991): 6.2%. **Pop. over 65:** 22 995 males; 31 595 females. **Pop. under 35:** 90 125 males; 88 205 females.

☐ **OFFICIAL LANGUAGES (1991):** 80.6% English; 3.7% French; 13.1% other. **Immigrant pop.** (1991): 67 875, 18.6%. **Religious breakdown** (1991): 51% Protestant; 37% Catholic; 10% no affiliation; 1.3% other; .7% Eastern non-Christian; .32% Jewish.

☐ **AVG. INCOME:** n.a. Avg. family size (1991): 3.0 persons. **Single parent families** (1991): 13.0% of families.

☐ **CLIMATE:** Avg. temps. -4.3˚ (Jan.); 21.7˚ (July). Avg. annual precip. 711 mm. Avg. annual snowfall: 114 cm.

Saint John, NB

☐ **YEAR INCORPORATED:** 1785. Population (1991): 124 981; 48.3% male, 51.7% female. **Area:** 2 905 sq. km. **Pop. density:** 43.0 per sq. km. **Pop. growth** (1986–1991): 3.1%. **Pop. over 65:** 6 095 males; 9 395 females. **Pop. under 35:** 33 290 males; 33 525 females.

☐ **OFFICIAL LANGUAGES (1991):** 89.1% English; 0.2% French; 10.6% bilingual; 0.1% neither. **Immigrant pop.** (1991): 5 295, 4.2%. **Religious breakdown** (1991): 54% Protestant; 40% Catholic; 6% no affiliation; .34% Eastern non-Christian; .31% other; .15% Jewish.

☐ **AVG. INCOME (1985):** $19 826 males; $11 008 females; $31 259 families. **Avg. family size** (1991): 3.1 persons. **Single parent families** (1991): 16.0% of families.

☐ **CLIMATE:** Avg. temps. -8˚ (Jan.); 17˚ (July). Avg. annual precip. 1 152 mm. **Avg. annual snowfall:** 293 cm.

St. John's, Nfld

☐ **YEAR INCORPORATED:** 1888. Population (1991): 171 859; 48.7% male, 51.3% female. **Area:** 1 130 sq. km. **Pop. density:** 152.1 per sq. km. **Pop. growth** (1986–1991): 6.2%. **Pop. over 65:** 6 375 males; 9 640 females. **Pop. under 35:** 49 250 males; 49 715 females.

☐ **OFFICIAL LANGUAGES (1991):** 95.2% English; 0% French; 4.3% bilingual; 0.2% neither. **Immigrant pop.** (1991): 4 770, 2.8%. **Religious breakdown** (1991): 49% Catholic; 47% Protestant; 2.9% no affiliation; .47% Eastern non-Christian; .19% other; .06% Jewish.

☐ **AVG. INCOME (1985):** $22 064 males; $12 562 females; $38 132 families. **Avg. family size** (1991): 3.3 persons. **Single parent families** (1991): 15.1% of families.

☐ **CLIMATE:** Avg. temps. -4° (Jan.); 16° (July). Avg. annual precip. 1 089 mm. Avg. annual snowfall: 359 cm.

Saskatoon, Sask.

☐ **YEAR INCORPORATED:** 1906. **Population** (1991): 210 023; 48.5% male, 51.5% female. **Area:** 4 749 sq. km. **Pop. density:** 44.2 per sq. km. **Pop. growth** (1986–1991): 4.7%. **Pop. over 65:** 8 920 males; 12 805 females. **Pop. under 35:** 60 425 males; 61 800 females.

☐ **OFFICIAL LANGUAGES (1991):** 93.1% English; 0.0% French; 6.3% bilingual; 0.6% neither. **Immigrant pop.** (1991): 17 120, 10.1%. **Religious breakdown** (1991): 51% Protestant; 31% Catholic; 14% no affiliation; 2% other; 1.25% Eastern non-Christian; .29% Jewish.

☐ **AVG. INCOME (1985):** $23 912 males; $12 982 females; $38 852 families. **Avg. family size** (1991): 3.1 persons. **Single parent families** (1991): 14.5% of families.

☐ **CLIMATE:** Avg. temps. -19° (Jan.); 19° (July). Avg. annual precip. 245 mm. Avg. annual snowfall: 113 cm.

Sherbrooke, Que.

☐ **YEAR INCORPORATED:** 1875. **Population** (1991): 139 194; 48.0% male, 52.0% female. **Area:** 916 sq. km. **Pop. density:** 152 per sq. km. **Pop. growth** (1986–1991): 7.1%. **Pop. over 65:** 5 990 males; 10 025 females. **Pop. under 35:** 36 705 males; 36 260 females.

☐ **OFFICIAL LANGUAGES (1991):** 2.3% English; 61.1% French; 21.1% bilingual; 0.1% neither. **Immigrant pop.** (1991): 5 165, 3.7%. **Religious breakdown** (1991): 89% Catholic; 5.6% Protestant; 4% no affiliation; .7% Eastern non-Christian; .23% other; .07% Jewish.

☐ **AVG. INCOME (1985):** $19 894 males; $11 484 females; $32 334 families. **Avg. family size** (1991): 3.0 persons. **Single parent families** (1991): 15.9% of families.

☐ **CLIMATE:** Avg. annual precip. 697 mm. Avg. annual snowfall: 323 cm.

Sudbury, Ont.

☐ **YEAR INCORPORATED:** 1930. **Population** (1991): 157 610; 49.2% male, 56.5% female. **Area:** 2 612.11 sq. km. **Pop. density:** 60 per sq. km. **Pop. growth** (1986–1991): 5.9%. **Pop. over 65:** 7 105 males; 9 330 females. **Pop. under 35:** 41 715 males; 41 875 females.

☐ **OFFICIAL LANGUAGES (1991):** 59.8% English; 27.5% French; 8.2% other. **Immigrant pop.** (1991): 12 840, 8.1%. **Religious breakdown** (1991): 65% Catholic; 27% Protestant; 7.2% no affiliation; .81% other; .51% Eastern non-Christian; .15% Jewish.

☐ **AVG. INCOME:** n.a. **Avg. family size** (1991): 3.1 persons. **Single parent families** (1991): 13.9% of families.

☐ **CLIMATE:** Avg. temps. -13.5° (Jan.); 19.1° (July). Avg. annual precip. 636 mm. Avg. annual snowfall: 267 cm.

Thunder Bay, Ont.

☐ **YEAR INCORPORATED:** 1970. **Population** (1991): 124 427; 49.4% male, 50.6% female. **Area:** 2 202.55 sq. km. **Pop. density:** 56.5 per sq. km. **Pop. growth** (1986–1991): 1.8%. **Pop. over 65:** 7 050 males; 9 505 females. **Pop. under 35:** 32 330 males; 31 765 females.

☐ **OFFICIAL LANGUAGES (1991):** 91.2% English; .2% French; .7% other. **Immigrant pop.** (1991): 16 235, 22.1%. **Religious breakdown** (1991): 46% Protestant; 41% Catholic; 11% no affiliation; 1.7% other; .52% Eastern non-Christian; .17% Jewish.

☐ **AVG. INCOME:** n.a. **Avg. family size** (1991): 3.0 persons. **Single parent families** (1991): 14.8% of families.

☐ **CLIMATE:** Avg. temps. -15.4° (Jan.); 17.6° (July). Avg. annual precip. 527.3 mm. Avg. annual snowfall: 213.0 cm.

Toronto, Ont.

☐ **YEAR INCORPORATED:** 1834. **Population** (1991): 3 893 046; 49.0% male, 51.0% female. **Area:** 5 584 sq. km. **Pop. density:** 697.2 per sq. km. **Pop. growth** (1986–1991): 13.4%. **Pop. over 65:** 165 335 males; 237 250 females. **Pop. under 35:** 1 044 835 males; 1 026 680 females.

☐ **OFFICIAL LANGUAGES (1991):** 88.2% English; 0.1% French; 8.0% bilingual; 3.7% neither. **Immigrant pop.** (1991): 1 468 620, 37.7%. **Religious breakdown** (1991): 36% Catholic; 35% Protestant; 15% no affiliation; 8% Eastern non-Christian; 4% Jewish; 3.3% other.

☐ **AVG. INCOME (1985):** $26 442 males; $16 750 females; $46 623 families. **Avg. family size** (1991): 3.1 persons. **Single parent families** (1991): 13.5% of families.

☐ **CLIMATE:** Avg. temps. -5° (Jan.); 22° (July). Avg. annual precip. 664 mm. Avg. annual snowfall: 139 cm.

Trois–Rivières, Que.

☐ **YEAR INCORPORATED:** 1857. **Population** (1991): 136 300; 48.1% male, 51.9% female. **Area:** 871.91 sq. km. **Pop. density:** 156.32 per sq. km. **Pop. growth** (1986–1991): 5.8%. **Pop. over 65:** 6 100 males; 9 935 females. **Pop. under 35:** 33 820 males; 33 655 females.

☐ **OFFICIAL LANGUAGES (1991):** 1.2% English; 97.3% French; .6% other. **Immigrant pop.** (1991): 1 725, 1.3%. **Religious breakdown** (1991): 96% Catholic; 2% no affiliation; 1.8% Protestant; .3% other; .22% Eastern non-Christian; .01% Jewish.

☐ **AVG. INCOME:** n.a. **Avg. family size** (1991): 2.9 persons. **Single parent families** (1991): 15.2% of families.

☐ **CLIMATE:** Avg. temps. -12.5˚ (Jan.); 19.8˚ (July). **Avg. annual precip.** 805 mm. **Avg. annual snowfall:** 242 cm.

Vancouver, BC

☐ **YEAR INCORPORATED:** 1886. **Population** (1991): 1 602 502; 49.2% male, 50.8% female. **Area:** 2 786 sq. km. **Pop. density:** 575.1 per sq. km. **Pop. growth** (1986–1991): 16.1%. **Pop. over 65:** 80 525 males; 114 905 females. **Pop. under 35:** 411 385 males; 404 190 females.

☐ **OFFICIAL LANGUAGES (1991):** 89.4% English; 0.0% French; 7.2% bilingual; 3.4% neither. **Immigrant pop.** (1991): 476 530, 29.7%. **Religious breakdown** (1991): 40% Protestant; 31% no affiliation; 19% Catholic; 8% Eastern non-Christian; 1.2% other; .9% Jewish.

☐ **AVG. INCOME (1985):** $22 491 males; $14 505 females; $39 905 families. **Avg. family size** (1991): 3.0 persons. **Single parent families** (1991): 12.6% of families.

☐ **CLIMATE:** Avg. temps. 3˚ (Jan.); 16˚ (July). **Avg. annual precip.** 1 055 mm. **Avg. annual snowfall:** 60 cm.

Victoria, BC

☐ **YEAR INCORPORATED:** 1862. **Population** (1991): 287 897; 47.9% male, 52.1% female. **Area:** 633 sq. km. **Pop. density:** 454.5 per sq. km. **Pop. growth** (1986–1991): 12.8%. **Pop. over 65:** 21 700 males; 31 785 females. **Pop. under 35:** 66 495 males; 65 660 females.

☐ **OFFICIAL LANGUAGES (1991):** 91.7% English; 0.0% French; 7.7% bilingual; .6% neither. **Immigrant pop.** (1991): 55 410, 19.2%. **Religious breakdown** (1991): 51% Protestant; 30% no affiliation; 16% Catholic; 2% Eastern non-Christian; .92% other; .3% Jewish.

☐ **AVG. INCOME (1985):** $19 131 males; $12 930 females; $30 498 families. **Avg. family size** (1991): 2.8 persons. **Single parent families** (1991): 12.5% of families.

☐ **CLIMATE:** Avg. temps. 3˚ (Jan.); 16˚ (July). **Avg. annual precip.** 823 mm. **Avg. annual snowfall:** 50 cm.

Windsor, Ont.

☐ **YEAR INCORPORATED:** 1892. **Population** (1991): 262 075; 48.7% male, 51.3% female. **Area:** 861.66 sq. km.² **Pop. density:** 304 per sq. km. **Pop. growth** (1986–1991): 3.2%. **Pop. over 65:** 13 350 males; 20 075 females. **Pop. under 35:** 68 850 males; 67 555 females.

☐ **OFFICIAL LANGUAGES (1991):** 76.0% English; 4.7% French; 15.3% other. **Immigrant pop.** (1991): 53 830, 20.5%. **Religious breakdown** (1991): 55% Catholic; 31% Protestant; 8% no affiliation; 3.3% other; 2.3% Eastern non-Christian; .6% Jewish.

☐ **AVG. INCOME:** n.a. **Avg. family size** (1991): 3.1 persons. **Single parent families** (1991): 15.3% of families.

☐ **CLIMATE:** Avg. temps. -5.0˚ (Jan.); 22.4˚ (July). **Avg. annual precip.** 788 mm. **Avg. annual snowfall:** 123 cm.

Winnipeg, Man.

☐ **YEAR INCORPORATED:** 1873. **Population** (1991): 652 354; 48.6% male, 51.4% female. **Area:** 3 295 sq. km. **Pop. density:** 198 per sq. km. **Pop. growth** (1986–1991): 4.3%. **Pop. over 65:** 33 235 males; 50 765 females. **Pop. under 35:** 174 920 males; 170 730 females.

☐ **OFFICIAL LANGUAGES (1991):** 88.0% English; 0.2% French; 10.5% bilingual; 1.3% neither. **Immigrant pop.** (1991): 113 165, 17.3%. **Religious breakdown** (1991): 43% Protestant; 34% Catholic; 16% no affiliation; 2.4% Eastern non-Christian; 2.3% other; 2.1% Jewish.

☐ **AVG. INCOME (1985):** $23 319 males; $12 826 females; $38 647 families. **Avg. family size** (1991): 3.0 persons. **Single parent families** (1991): 14.8% of families.

☐ **CLIMATE:** Avg. temps. -19˚ (Jan.); 20˚ (July). **Avg. annual precip.** 411 mm. **Avg. annual snowfall:** 126 cm.

NATIONAL PARKS

Park	Location	Size (sq. km)	Year est.	1991 Visitors	Description
Aulavik	northeast portion of Banks Is., NWT	12 200	(1992)[1]	n.a.	Thomsen River forms core of park marked by deep river canyons and desert-like badlands. Area supports high concentration of muskoxen.
Auyuittuq[2]	north shore of Baffin Is., NWT	21 469	1976	660	Located on the Arctic Circle; an isolated and very rugged wilderness area with mountains, fjords, tundra and permafrost.
Banff	Banff, Alta.	6 641	1885	4 160 000	The oldest national park; noted for ice-capped capped peaks, glaciers, hot springs, wildlife and skiing.
Bruce Peninsula	299 km northwest of Toronto, between Lake Huron and Georgian Bay	154	(1987)[1]	110 000	Niagara Escarpment, limestone cliffs on Georgian Bay. Includes Fathom Five National Marine Park: 19 islands, over 20 shipwrecks, clear water and distinctive under water geological features.
Cape Breton Highlands	across northern Cape Breton Is., NS	948	1936	540 000	The scenic Cabot Trail is characterized by a rugged shoreline with plunging cliffs.
Elk Island	45 km east of Edmonton, Alta.	194	1913	308 000	A large population of plains and wood bison, elk and moose inhabit the rolling woodlands and lakes.
Ellesmere Island[2]	northern tip of Canada	37 775	1988	470	Vast isolated high Arctic wilderness park. Mountains, glaciers, musk-oxen, Peary's caribou. Fragile permafrost environments.
Forillon	northeast tip of Gaspé Peninsula, Que.	240	1974	170 000	Rich variety of birds and animals; limestone cliffs, and the highest mountains in eastern Canada.
Fundy	southeastern shore on the Bay of Fundy, NB	206	1948	220 000	The giant tides of the Bay of Fundy, among the highest in the world, and a bold, irregular coastline.
Georgian Bay Islands	160 km northwest of Toronto, Ont.	25	1929	54 000	Endangered species, limestone cliffs, caves and archaeological sites are preserved on 77 islands.
Glacier	45 km east of Revelstoke, BC	1 349	1886	160 000	Glaciers, snowy peaks, avalanche slopes, turbulent rivers and grizzly bears are the main features.
Grasslands	100 km south of Swift Current, Sask.	906	(1975)[1]	2 400	Unique natural habitat of short-grass prairie; blacktailed prairie dogs, pronghorn antelope and the prairie falcon are found.
Gros Morne	west coast of Nfld	1 805	(1970)[1]	110 000	Gros Morne, spectacular fjords and the Long Range Mountains.
Ivvavik	northern tip of Yukon	10 168	1984	93	Migration route for Porcupine caribou herd; major North American waterfowl area; home to grizzly, black and polar bears
Jasper	340 km west of Edmonton, Alta.	10 878	1907	1 390 000	Contains the largest icefield in the Canadian Rockies—Columbia Icefield—and preserves the headwaters of major rivers, particularly the Athabasca.
Kejimkujik	central southwestern NS	404	1974	170 000	Gently rolling country with many lakes and rivers—provides good canoeing and camping
Kluane[2]	southwest corner of Yukon	22 013	1976	67 000	Features Mount Logan, Canada's highest peak, grizzly bears, dall sheep and whitewater rivers.
Kootenay	1 km east of Radium Hot Springs, BC	1 406	1920	1 180 000	Hot springs, alpine lakes, canyons, glaciers, 2 river valleys home to bighorn sheep, mountain goats.

Park	Location	Size (sq. km)	Year est.	1991 Visitors	Description
Kouchibouguac	eastern NB	239	1979	180 000	Swimming and sunbathing on the beaches and sand dunes; cycling, hiking trails; windsurfing.
La Mauricie	55 km north of Trois-Rivières, Que.	536	1977	230 000	Hilly terrain at the edge of the Canadian Shield; transitional forest vegetation from evergreens to deciduous.
Mingan Archipelago[2]	N of Anticosti Is. along the St. Lawrence shore, QC	151	1984	26 000	Interesting rock formations, plant species, nesting seabirds and whales, seals and porpoises.
Mount Revelstoke	Revelstoke, BC	260	1914	240 000	Dense rain forests, colorful alpine vegetation, lakes and deep snow.
Nahanni[2]	southwestern NWT	4 765	1976	1 400	Accessible only by air; site of Virginia Falls, whirlpools, hot springs, canyons and rapids.
North Baffin	eastern Arctic, northern Baffin Is. and Bylot Is.	22 252	(1992)[3]	n.a.	Spectacular fiords and glaciers, steep sea cliffs, huge colonies of seabirds and other wildlife.
Pacific Rim[2]	west coast of Vancouver Island	500	(1970)[1]	650 000	3 sections—Long Beach, Broken Group Islands and West Coast Trail; offers rain forest, beaches and scenic, rugged hiking.
Point Pelee	southernmost point of Ont.	15	1918	420 000	Extensive marshlands and beaches provide refuge for many migratory birds and butterfies.
Prince Albert	200 km north of Saskatoon, Sask.	3 874	1927	180 000	This mixture of forest land and lakes is home to woodland caribou, bison and a pelican nesting colony.
Prince Edward Island	north shore of PEI	22	1937	930 000	Saltwater beaches, sand dunes, high coastal cliffs, marshes, ponds and woodlands.
Pukaskwa	northeastern shore of Lake Superior	1 878	(1971)[1]	18 000	Impressive shoreline with 60 km of coastal hiking and white water canoe routes.
Riding Mountain	270 km northwest of Winnipeg, Man.	2 973	1929	330 000	Wildlife—wolf, elk, moose, black bear and beaver—abound.
St. Lawrence Islands	Thousand Island	2	1914	46 000	Thousand Islands landscape and the St. Lawrence River.
South Moresby (Gwaii Haanas)[2]	southern part of Queen Charlotte Islands, BC	1 495	(1987)[1]	n.a.	Canada's "Galapagos," home to 39 unique plants and animals; rugged coastline, rain forests.
Terra Nova	east coast of Nfld on Bonavista Bay	400	1957	210 000	Rolling forested hills; spongy bogs and inland ponds are bordered by a rugged coastline.
Vuntut	Old Crow Flats, northern Yukon	4 400	(1993)[1]	n.a.	Wetland area is Yukon's most important waterfowl habitat and home to porcupine caribou, grizzly bear, moose, muskrat and several species of fish. Vertebrate fossils found at over 56 sites within park.
Waterton Lakes	southwest corner of Alta.	505	1895	360 000	Transition from prairie grasslands to Rocky Mountains; a rich variety of wildlife.
Wood Buffalo	straddles the Alta.-NWT border	44 802	1922	8 600	Home to the largest free-roaming herd of bison; only naturally nesting whooping cranes, peregrine falcons and red-sided garter snakes.
Yoho	25 km east of Golden, BC	1 313	1886	690 000	Contains several of the highest peaks in the Rocky Mountains, icefields, waterfalls and a varied plant and animal life.

Source: *Environment Canada, Parks Services*

(1) Park created by federal/provincial agreement rather than federal enactment and administered by special legislation. (2) Park reserve, set aside for national park and under jurisdiction of Nation Parks Act, but lands, fish and wildlife are subject to future settlement of native land claims. (3) Agreement under negotiation; land has been designated for national park. (n.a.) not available.

THE PEOPLE

Population of Provinces and Territories

(thousands of persons)

	Canada	Nfld	PEI	NS	NB	Que	Ont	Man	Sask	Alta	BC	YT	NWT
1867	3 463	n.a.	88	364	271	1 123	1 525	15	*	*	32	*	45
1871	3 689	n.a.	94	388	286	1 191	1 621	25	*	*	36	*	48
1881	4 325	n.a.	109	441	321	1 360	1 927	62	*	*	49	*	56
1891	4 833	n.a.	109	450	321	1 489	2 114	153	*	*	98	*	99
1901	5 371	n.a.	103	460	331	1 649	2 183	255	91	73	179	27	20
1911	7 207	n.a.	94	492	352	2 006	2 527	461	492	374	393	9	7
1921	8 788	n.a.	89	524	388	2 361	2 934	610	756	589	525	4	8
1931	10 377	n.a.	88	513	408	2 875	3 432	700	922	732	694	4	9
1941	11 507	n.a.	95	578	457	3 332	3 788	730	896	796	818	5	12
1951	14 009	361	98	643	516	4 056	4 598	777	832	940	1 165	9	16
1961	18 238	458	105	737	598	5 259	6 236	922	925	1 332	1 629	15	23
1971	21 568	522	112	789	635	6 028	7 703	988	926	1 628	2 185	18	35
1976	22 993	558	118	829	677	6 235	8 265	1 022	921	1 838	2 467	22	43
1981	24 343	568	123	847	696	6 438	8 625	1 026	968	2 238	2 744	23	46
1986	25 354[1]	568	127	873[1]	710[1]	6 540[1]	9 114[1]	1 071[1]	1 010[1]	2 375[1]	2 889[1]	24	52
1991	27 297	568	130	900	924	6 896	10 085	1 092	989	2 546	3 282	28	58

Source: *Census of Canada*

(1) Includes estimates, rather than actual counts, for the population of some Indian reserves and settlements which were not completely enumerated. (*) Included with the Northwest Territories; n.a. not available.

Age Structure of the Population

	Total (000s)	% Under 5 Years	% 5–19 Years	% 20–44 Years	% 45–65 Years	% 65+ Years
1851	2 436	18.51	37.81	31.65	9.40	2.67
1861	3 230	16.82	37.22	32.73	10.16	3.03
1871	3 689	14.67	38.03	32.58	11.14	3.66
1881	4 325	13.85	36.02	33.94	12.14	4.12
1891	4 833	12.64	34.49	35.40	12.91	4.55
1901	5 372	12.03	32.74	36.17	14.02	5.06
1911	7 207	12.35	30.15	38.77	14.06	4.66
1921	8 788	12.05	31.51	36.62	15.04	4.79
1931	10 377	10.36	31.29	36.05	16.74	5.55
1941	11 507	9.1	28.39	37.19	18.63	6.67
1951	14 010	12.29	25.60	36.63	17.73	7.75
1956	16 081	12.34	27.39	35.35	17.20	7.74
1961	18 238	12.37	29.44	33.19	17.38	7.63
1966	20 015	10.98	31.14	32.41	17.77	7.69
1971	21 568	8.4	30.96	33.88	18.65	8.09
1976	22 993	7.5	28.31	36.24	19.12	8.71
1981	24 343	7.32	24.70	39.14	19.14	9.70
1986	25 310	7.15	21.76	41.17	19.26	10.66
1991	27 296	6.99	20.42	41.33	19.66	11.61

Source: *Census of Canada*

Male and Female Population by Age Group

(thousands of persons)

		Total Population	Under 5 Years	5–9 Years	10–14 Years	15–24 Years	25–34 Years	35–44 Years	45–54 Years	55–64 Years	65 Years and Over
1851	MALE	1 250	233	173	152	248	168	116	7 8	46	35
	FEMALE	1 186	218	173	146	252	161	103	67	38	30
1861	MALE	1 660	277	218	203	341	232	156	107	70	54
	FEMALE	1 570	266	211	196	337	224	141	92	59	44
1871	MALE	1 869	276	264	243	374	249	175	132	86	74
	FEMALE	1 820	265	255	233	385	256	171	120	73	61
1881	MALE	2 189	304	284	262	455	302	217	161	111	94
	FEMALE	2 136	295	278	251	464	301	212	153	100	84
1891	MALE	2 460	309	300	282	504	366	263	191	131	115
	FEMALE	2 373	302	292	272	499	354	246	180	122	105
1901	MALE	2 752	326	313	297	543	412	331	234	157	139
	FEMALE	2 620	320	306	285	530	386	299	214	148	133
1911	MALE	3 822	450	396	356	745	684	475	334	209	171
	FEMALE	3 385	440	389	346	653	535	388	286	184	165
1921	MALE	4 530	534	529	462	757	693	630	434	276	215
	FEMALE	4 258	525	521	452	761	650	532	366	246	206
1931	MALE	5 375	543	573	543	990	778	707	590	356	295
	FEMALE	5 002	531	560	531	962	717	627	485	306	281
1941	MALE	5 901	534	529	556	1 083	920	745	649	494.	391
	FEMALE	5 606	518	517	545	1 069	891	691	579	421	377
1951	MALE	7 089	879	714	575	1 070	1 066	950	728	557	551
	FEMALE	6 921	843	684	556	1 077	1 108	919	679	520	535
1956	MALE	8 152	1 012	920	732	1 154	1 209	1 079	838	588	623
	FEMALE	7 929	972	887	703	1 138	1 206	1 062	774	566	622
1961	MALE	9 219	1 154	1 064	948	1 316	1 258	1 191	959	655	674
	FEMALE	9 019	1 102	1 016	908	1 301	1 222	1 199	920	635	717
1966	MALE	10 054	1 129	1 173	1 071	1 656	1 249	1 275	1 041	743	717
	FEMALE	9 961	1 069	1 128	1 022	1 643	1 233	1 268	1 037	736	823
1971	MALE	10 795	930	1 152	1 181	2 016	1 462	1 286	1 132	854	782
	FEMALE	10 773	887	1 102	1 129	1 988	1 428	1 241	1 160	877	963
1976	MALE	11 450	889	967	1 165	2 262	1 823	1 315	1 226	928	876
	FEMALE	11 543	843	921	1 112	2 217	1 798	1 282	1 246	997	1 127
1981	MALE	12 068	914	912	985	2 356	2 105	1 497	1 257	1 030	1 011
	FEMALE	12 275	869	865	936	2 303	2 110	1 471	1 243	1 129	1 350
1986[1]	MALE	12 486	928	920	917	2 116	2 249	1 822	1 276	1 124	1 133
	FEMALE	12 824	882	875	870	2 062	2 278	1 819	1 269	1 204	1 564
1991	MALE	13 454	976	978	963	1 944	2 420	2 176	1 487	1 180	1 330
	FEMALE	13 842	931	930	915	1 887	2 446	2 196	1 479	1 220	1 840

Source: *Census of Canada*

(1) Excludes incompletely enumerated Indian reserves and settlements.

Canadian Population Projections by Age Group

(thousands of persons)

		Total Population	Under 5 Years	5–9 Years	10–14 Years	15–24 Years	25–34 Years	35–44 Years	45–54 Years	55–64 Years	65 Years and Over
2011	MALE	14 794	833	838	871	1 941	2 022	2 040	2 307	1 953	1 990
	FEMALE	15 531	789	794	823	1 858	1 963	2 002	2 377	2 113	2 810
2036	MALE	14 911	747	766	800	1 718	1 812	1 927	2 007	1 866	3 268
	FEMALE	16 087	708	726	758	1 639	1 754	1 883	1 999	1 943	4 677

Source: *Census of Canada*

Canadian Population by Country of Birth

	1911	1931	1951	1971	1986
Total Population	7 206 643	10 376 786	14 009 429	21 568 310	25 022 010
Total Foreign Born	752 732	1 220 379	2 059 911	3 295 535	3 900 910
Argentina[1]	—	—	—	—	8 365
Asia - Other	3 577	6 310	6 740	52 795	—
Australia..................	2 655	3 565	4 161	14 335	13 585
Austria[2]	67 502	37 391	37 598	40 450	30 635
Barbados[3]	—	—	—	—	13 795
Belgium	7 975	17 033	17 251	25 770	23 445
Brazil[1]	—	—	—	—	4 990
Cambodia[4]	—	—	—	—	12 430
Chile[1]	—	—	—	—	17 805
China.....................	27 083	42 037	24 166	57 150	119 190
Czechoslovakia	—	22 835	29 546	43 100	42 335
Denmark..................	4 937	17 217	15 679	28 045	23 980
Ecuador[1]	—	—	—	—	6 595
Egypt[1]	—	—	—	—	22 565
El Salvador[1]	—	—	—	—	11 245
Europe - Central[5]	129 421	317 350	—	—	—
Europe - Other[5]	6 951	4 926	7 619	85 550	—
Fiji[3]	—	—	—	—	12 305
Finland	10 987	30 354	22 035	24 930	19 415
France....................	17 619	16 756	15 650	51 655	53 345
Germany[6]	39 577	39 163	42 693	211 060	189 560
Greece	2 640	5 579	8 594	78 780	85 090
Guyana[3]	—	—	—	—	50 820
Haiti[1]	—	—	—	—	31 950
Hong Kong[3]	—	—	—	—	77 405
Hungary...................	—	28 523	32 929	68 495	61 280
India[3, 7]	4 491	—	3 934	43 645	130 060
Iran[1]	—	—	—	—	13 950
Ireland	92 874	107 544	24 110	38 490	25 900
Israel[1]	—	—	—	—	12 570
Italy......................	34 739	42 578	57 789	285 755	366 815
Jamaica[3]	—	—	—	—	87 605
Japan	8 425	12 261	6 239	9 485	12 030
Kenya[3]	—	—	—	—	10 570
Korea[4]	—	—	—	—	22 470
Laos[4]	—	—	—	—	11 770
Lebanon[1]	—	—	—	—	25 190
Malaysia[4]	—	—	—	—	9 210
Malta[3]	—	—	—	—	10 800
Mexico[1]	—	—	—	—	13 845
Morocco[1]	—	—	—	—	13 245
Netherlands	3 808	10 736	41 457	133 525	134 155
New Zealand[3]	903	—	—	—	7 490
Norway....................	20 968	32 679	22 969	16 350	9 270
Pakistan[1]	—	—	—	—	16 795
Philippines[4]	—	—	—	—	82 235
Poland[8]	—	171 169	164 474	160 040	156 805
Portugal[8]	—	—	—	—	138 635
Romania[9]	9 657	40 322	19 733	24 405	25 910
Russia[10]	100 971	—	—	—	—

▶

	1911	1931	1951	1971	1986
▶ South Africa[3]	1 166	2 235	2 057	—	18 780
Spain[8]	—	—	—	—	12 755
Sri Lanka[4]	—	—	—	—	9 370
Sweden	28 226	34 415	22 635	14 110	8 960
Switzerland[8]	—	6 076	6 414	13 895	15 995
Taiwan[4]	—	—	—	—	7 210
Tanzania[1]	—	—	—	—	14 030
Trinidad/Tobago[3]	—	—	—	—	40 000
Turkey[8]	1 861	—	—	—	10 360
Uganda[1]	—	—	—	—	9 375
USSR	—	114 406	188 292	160 120	109 445
United Kingdom	784 526	1 184 830	912 482	933 040	793 080
UK possessions / dependencies[5]	39 681	35 416	10 415	112 125	—
United States	303 680	344 574	282 010	209 640	282 025
Vietnam[4]	—	—	—	—	82 760
Yugoslavia[8]	—	17 110	20 912	78 285	87 755

Source: *Statistics Canada*

(1) Included in "Other countries" until 1986 census. (2) Includes Hungary (Austria-Hungary) in 1911 census. (3) British possessions/dependencies (see UK possessions) during various census years could incl. African, Asian, Caribbean, Mediterranean, and Pacific possessions as well as any territory in British North America prior to confederation with Canada (in the case of Newfoundland, this was not until 1949); many not reported separately until 1986 census. (4) Included in "Asia - Other" until 1986 census. (5) More detailed breakdown given in subsequent census data. (6) Total for Germany includes both East and West Germany. (7) Totals for India before 1986 include Pakistan. (8) Where not reported, included in "Europe - Other." (9) For 1911 census, also include Bulgaria. (10) For 1931, 1951, 1971 and 1986, see USSR. (—) = not reported.

Canadian Population Growth Components

(thousands)

Census Period	Births	− Deaths	= Natural Increase	Immigration	− Emigration	= Net Migration	Population Growth	Total population
1851–1861	1 281	670	611	352	170	182	793	3 230
1861–1871	1 370	760	610	260	410	-150	460	3 689
1871–1881	1 480	790	690	350	404	- 54	636	4 325
1881–1891	1 524	870	654	680	826	-146	508	4 833
1891–1901	1 548	880	668	250	380	-130	538	5 371
1901–1911	1 925	900	1 025	1 550	740	810	1 835	7 207
1911–1921	2 340	1 070	1 270	1 400	1 089	311	1 581	8 788
1921–1931	2 420	1 060	1 360	1 200	970	230	1 589	10 377
1931–1941	2 294	1 072	1 222	149	241	- 92	1 130	11 507
1941–1951	3 212	1 220	1 992	548	382	166	2 503	14 009
1951–1956	2 106	633	1 473	783	185	598	2 071	16 081
1956–1961	2 362	687	1 675	760	378	482	2 157	18 238
1961–1966	2 249	731	1 518	539	280	259	1 777	20 015
1966–1971	1 856	766	1 090	890	427	463	1 553	21 568
1971–1976	1 758	823	934	841	352	489	1 424	22 993
1976–1981	1 820	842	978	588	217	371	1 349	24 343
1981–1986	1 873	885	988	500	477	23	1 011	25 354
1986–1991	2 328	1 142	1 186	2 396	1 640	756	1 942[2]	27 297

Source: *Statistics Canada*

(1) At end of the census period. (2) Includes refugee claimants and non-permanent residents.

Canadian Urban and Rural Population

(thousands)

Year	Urban Total	Urban %	Rural Non-Farm	%	+ Farm	%	= Total	%
1871	722	19.6	n.a.	n.a.	n.a.	n.a.	2 967	80.4
1881	1 110	25.7	n.a.	n.a.	n.a.	n.a.	3 215	74.3
1891	1 537	31.8	n.a.	n.a.	n.a.	n.a.	3 296	68.2
1901	2 014	37.5	n.a.	n.a.	n.a.	n.a.	3 357	62.5
1911	3 273	45.4	n.a.	n.a.	n.a.	n.a.	3 934	54.6
1921	4 352	49.5	n.a.	n.a.	n.a.	n.a.	4 436	50.5
1931	5 469	52.7	1 670	16.1	3 238	31.2	4 908	47.3
1941	6 271	54.5	2 123	18.4	3 113	27.1	5 236	45.5
1951	8 817	62.9	2 423	17.3	2 769	19.8	5 192	37.1
1956	10 715	66.6	2 734	17.0	2 632	16.4	5 366	33.4
1961	12 700	69.6	3 465	19.0	2 073	11.4	5 538	30.4
1966	14 727	73.6	3 374	16.9	1 914	9.6	5 288	26.4
1971	16 410	76.1	3 738	17.3	1 420	6.6	5 158	23.9
1976	17 367	75.5	4 591	20.0	1 035	4.5	5 626	24.5
1981	18 436	75.7	4 867	20.0	1 040	4.3	5 907	24.3
1986	19 352	76.5	5 067	20.0	890	3.5	5 957	23.5
1991	20 907	76.6	n.a.	n.a.	n.a.	n.a.	6 390	23.4

Source: *Census of Canada*

Definitions: Urban: persons living in a built-up area having a population of 1 000 or more and a population density of 400 or more per sq. km; **Rural:** persons living outside "urban areas"; **Rural Farm:** persons living in rural areas who are members of households of farm operators; **Rural Non-Farm:** persons living in rural areas who are not members of households of farm operators.

(n.a.) not available.

Urban and Rural Population by Province

Province	1911 Rural	1911 Urban	1951 Rural	1951 Urban	1991 Rural	1991 Urban
Canada	3 924 394	3 280 444	5 174 555	8 473 458	6 389 724	20 907 135
Newfoundland[1]	n.a.	n.a.	n.a.	n.a.	264 023	304 451
PEI	78 758	14 970	73 744	24 685	77 952	51 813
NS	306 210	186 128	297 753	344 831	418 434	481 508
NB	252 342	99 547	300 686	215 011	378 686	345 214
Quebec	1 032 618	970 094	1 358 363	2 697 318	1 544 752	5 351 211
Ontario	1 194 785	1 328 489	1 346 443	3 251 099	1 831 043	8 253 842
Manitoba	255 249	200 365	336 961	439 580	304 767	787 175
Saskatchewan	361 067	131 365	579 258	252 470	365 531	623 397
Alberta	232 726	141 937	489 826	449 675	514 660	2 030 893
BC	188 796	203 684	371 739	793 471	641 922	2 640 139
Yukon	4 647	3 865	6 502	2 594	11 462	16 335
NWT	17 196	—	13 280	2 724	36 492	21 157

Source: *Statistics Canada, Census*

(1) Newfoundland joined confederation in 1949 and urban/rural split in population not included in 1951 census data.

Born at Sea

*C*ensus data for 1901 shows that 339 Canadians listed their birthplace as "At Sea;" by the 1911 census, that number had grown to 807. By the 1931 census, people born at sea were considered to be born somewhere within British possessions and therefore to be British born.

Population of Canadian Towns and Cities

(5,000 to 50,000 inhabitants)

Town or city classification is made according to the official designations adopted by provincial or federal authority. *Indicates a city; all others are towns.

	POPULATION		AREA
	1981	1991	(sq. km)
■ **NEWFOUNDLAND**			
Bay Roberts	• 4 512	5 474	24.36
Carbonear	5 335	5 259	11.81
Channel-Port aux Basques ..	5 988	5 644	37.43
Conception Bay South	10 856	17 590	59.70
Corner Brook*	24 339	22 410	147.37
Gander	10 404	10 339	101.16
Goulds	4 242	6162	18.79
Grand Falls-Windsor	14 666	14 693	56.66
Happy Valley-Goose Bay	7 103	8 610	306.42
Labrador City	11 538	9 061	6.47
Marystown	6 299	6 739	62.99
Mount Pearl	11 543	23 689	25.29
St. John's*	83 770	95 770	101.59
Stephenville	8 876	7 621	34.81
■ **PRINCE EDWARD ISLAND**			
Charlottetown*	15 282	15 396	6.99
Summerside	7 828	7 474	4.31
■ **NOVA SCOTIA**			
Amherst	9 864	9 742	15.29
Bedford	6 777	11 618	39.79
Bridgewater	6 669	7 248	13.35
Dartmouth*	62 277	67 798	58.58
Glace Bay	21 466	19 501	23.15
Halifax*	277 727	320 501	79.76
Kentville	4 974	5 506	17.12
New Glasgow	10 464	9 905	10.36
New Waterford	8 808	7 695	5.26
North Sydney	7 820	7 260	5.38
Stellarton	5 435	5 237	8.55
Sydney*	29 444	26 063	23.49
Sydney Mines	8 501	7 551	10.91
Truro	12 552	11 683	38.09
Yarmouth	7 475	7 781	11.14
■ **NEW BRUNSWICK**			
Bathurst*	15 705	14 409	90.94
Campbellton*	9 818	8 699	17.30
Chatham	6 779	6 544	10.36
Dieppe	8 511	10 463	52.90
Edmundston*	12 044	10 835	34.58
Fairvale	3 960	5 041	7.85
Fredericton*	43 723	46 466	129.58
Grand Falls (Grand-Sault) ...	6 203	6 083	17.73
Moncton*	55 743	57 010	141.09
Newcastle	6 284	5 711	14.09
Oromocto	9 064	9 325	22.26
Quispamsis	6 022	8 446	38.91
Riverview	14 907	16 270	34.26
Sackville	5 654	5 494	74.42
Saint John*	80 521	74 969	322.88

	POPULATION		AREA
	1981	1991	(sq. km)
■ **QUEBEC**			
Alma*	26 322	25 910	109.27
Amos*	9 421	13 783	108.05
Ancienne-Lorette*	12 935	15 242	7.87
Anjou*	37 346	37 210	13.65
Arthabaska*	6 827	7 584	8.94
Asbestos*	7 967	6 487	13.47
Aylmer*	26 695	32 244	91.21
Baie-Comeau*	12 866	26 012	352.27
Beaconsfield*	19 613	19 616	10.64
Beauharnois*	7 025	6 449	40.44
Beauport*	60 477	69 158	71.33
Bécancour*	10 247	10 911	434.29
Beloeil*	17 540	18 516	24.01
Blainville*	14 682	22 679	55.20
Boisbriand*	13 471	21 124	27.32
Bois-des-Filion*	4 943	6 337	3.92
Boucherville*	29 704	33 796	69.33
Brossard*	52 232	64 793	44.98
Buckingham*	7 992	10 548	14.46
Candiac*	8 502	11 064	16.47
Cap-de-la-Madeleine*	32 626	33 716	17.30
Cap-Rouge*	8 492	14 105	6.39
Carignan*	4 544	5 386	62.35
Chambly*	12 190	15 893	25.06
Charlemagne*	4 827	5 598	1.76
Charlesbourg*	68 326	70 788	67.36
Charny*	8 240	10 239	8.76
Châteauguay*	36 928	39 833	35.40
Chibougamau*	10 732	8 855	754.08
Chicoutimi*	60 064	62 670	156.66
Coaticook*	6 271	6 637	12.50
Côte-Saint-Luc*	27 531	28 700	7.21
Cowansville*	12 240	11 982	50.58
Delson*	4 935	6 063	7.15
Deux-Montagnes*	9 944	13 035	6.05
Dolbeau*	8 766	8 181	46.36
Dollard-des-Ormeaux*	39 940	39 940	15.05
Donnacona*	5 731	5 659	20.12
Dorion*	5 749	5 920	3.70
Dorval*	17 722	17 249	20.64
Drummondville*	27 347	35 462	31.01
Farnham*	6 498	6 146	24.70
Gaspé*	17 261	16 402	1 105.11
Gatineau*	74 988	92 284	272.11
Granby*	38 069	42 804	72.60
Grand-mère*	15 442	14 287	71.13
Greenfield Park*	18 527	17 652	4.58
Hampstead*	7 598	8 645	1.77
Hull*	56 225	60 707	37.07
Iberville*	8 587	9 352	4.90
Ile-Perrot*	5 945	8 064	4.87 ▶

	POPULATION 1981	1991	AREA (sq. km)		POPULATION 1981	1991	AREA (sq. km)
▶ Joliette*	16 987	17 396	22.14	Saint-Eustache*	29 716	37 278	70.03
Jonquière*	60 354	57 933	209.63	Saint-Félicien*	9 058	9 340	167.90
Kirkland*	10 476	17 495	10.34	Saint-Georges*	16 720	19 583	19.01
L'Assomption*	3 457	5 706	2.07	Saint-Hubert*	60 573	74 027	63.22
La Baie*	20 935	20 995	261.69	Saint-Hyacinthe*	38 246	39 292	36.63
La Prairie*	10 627	14 938	43.54	Saint-Jean-Chrysostome*	6 930	12 717	82.90
La Sarre*	8 861	8 513	148.30	Saint-Jean-sur-Richelieu*	35 640	37 607	47.40
La Tuque*	11 556	10 003	22.25	Saint-Jérôme*	25 123	23 384	15.79
Lac-Mégantic*	6 119	5 838	20.21	Saint-Lambert*	20 557	20 976	6.42
Lachenaie*	8 631	15 074	42.79	Saint-Laurent*	65 900	72 402	46.28
Lachine*	37 521	35 266	17.38	Saint-Léonard*	79 249	73 120	12.93
Lachute*	11 729	11 730	96.24	Saint-Luc*	8 815	15 008	51.22
LaSalle*	76 299	73 804	16.42	Saint-Nicolas*	5 074	7 600	36.93
Lauzon*	13 362	n.a.	16.40	Saint-Raphael de Ile Bizard	6 558	11 352	22.69
Laval*	268 335	314 398	245.40	Saint-Rédempteur*	4 463	5 862	3.46
Le Gardeur*	8 312	13 814	44.00	Saint-Rémi*	5 146	5 768	79.67
LeMoyne*	6 137	5 412	.96	Saint-Romuald*	9 849	9 830	18.34
Lévis*	17 895	39 452	16.70	Sainte-Agathe-des-Monts*	5 641	5 452	15.57
Longueuil*	124 320	129 874	42.68	Sainte-Anne-des-Monts*	6 062	5 652	106.27
Loretteville*	15 060	14 219	6.94	Sainte-Anne-des-Plaines*	7 651	10 787	92.23
Lorraine*	6 881	8 410	5.46	Sainte-Catherine*	6 372	9 805	9.06
Louiseville*	3 735	8 000	62.57	Sainte-Foy*	68 883	71 133	83.86
Magog*	13 604	14 034	15.26	Sainte-Julie*	14 243	20 632	47.91
Marieville	4 877	5 164	3.57	Sainte-Marie*	8 937	10 542	105.49
Mascouche*	20 345	25 828	107.95	Sainte-Marthe-sur-le-Lac*	5 586	7 410	9.01
Masson*	4 264	5 753	55.61	Sainte-Thérèse*	18 750	24 158	10.09
Matane*	13 612	12 756	24.35	Salaberry-de-Valleyfield*	29 574	27 598	35.74
Mercier*	6 352	8 227	45.89	Sept-Iles*	29 262	24 848	298.93
Mirabel*	14 080	17 971	492.26	Shawinigan*	23 011	19 931	26.27
Mistassini*	6 682	6 842	248.38	Shawinigan-Sud*	11 325	11 584	51.39
Mont-Joli*	6 359	6 265	9.11	Sherbrooke*	74 075	76 429	55.42
Mont-Laurier*	8 405	7 862	82.05	Sillery*	12 825	12 519	6.73
Mont-Royal*	19 247	18 212	7.43	Sorel*	20 347	18 786	9.65
Mont-Saint-Hilaire*	10 066	12 341	48.17	Terrebonne*	11 769	39 678	73.17
Montmagny*	12 405	11 861	125.77	Thetford Mines*	19 965	17 273	23.15
Montréal*	980 354	1 017 666	176.90	Tracy*	12 843	13 181	19.11
Montréal-Nord*	94 914	85 516	11.03	Trois-Rivières*	50 466	49 426	77.86
Montréal-Ouest*	5 514	5 180	1.63	Trois-Rivières-Ouest*	13 107	20 076	28.70
Otterburn Park*	4 268	6 046	5.21	Val-Belair*	12 695	17 181	68.54
Outremont*	24 338	22 935	3.68	Val d'Or	21 371	23 842	1 217.16
Pierrefonds*	38 390	48 735	24.40	Vanier*	10 725	10 833	4.66
Pincourt*	8 750	9 639	8.27	Varennes*	8 764	14 758	93.96
Plessisville*	7 249	6 952	4.34	Vaudreuil*	7 608	11 187	69.49
Pointe-Claire*	24 571	27 647	19.19	Verdun*	61 287	61 307	8.50
Port-Cartier*	8 191	7 383	74.47	Victoriaville*	21 838	21 495	16.13
Québec*	166 474	167 517	88.86	Westmount	20 480	20 239	3.96
Repentigny*	34 419	49 630	24.42	**■ ONTARIO**			
Rimouski*	29 120	30 873	75.68	Ajax	25 474	57 350	67.70
Rivière-du-Loup*	13 459	14 017	16.94	Alliston, Beeton, Tecumseth and Tottenham	16 191	20 239	269.55
Roberval*	11 429	11 628	147.05	Amherstburg	5 685	8 921	3.29
Rock Forest*	12 283	14 551	51.41	Ancaster	14 428	21 988	174.57
Rosemère*	7 778	11 198	10.20	Arnprior	5 828	6 679	8.52
Rouyn-Noranda	25 991	26 448	63.27	Aurora	16 267	29 454	49.16
Roxboro*	6 292	5 879	2.23	Aylmer	5 254	6 244	4.78
Saint-Antoine*	7 012	10 232	9.84	Barrie*	38 423	62 728	73.40
Saint-Basile-le-Grand*	7 658	10 127	34.83	Belleville*	34 881	37 243	29.13
Saint-Bruno-de-Montarville*	22 880	23 849	41.79	Bracebridge	9 063	12 308	632.09
Saint-Constant*	9 938	18 423	57.02	Bradford-West Gwillimbury	13 198	17 702	197.40 ▶
Saint-David-de-L'Auberivière*	5 380	n.a.	10.90				
Saint Emile	5 216	6 921	8.88				

	POPULATION 1981	1991	AREA (sq. km)		POPULATION 1981	1991	AREA (sq. km)
► Brampton*	149 030	234 445	265.04	New Liskeard	5 551	5 431	6.42
Brantford*	74 315	81 997	70.81	Newcastle	32 229	49 479	607.79
Brockville*	19 896	21 582	20.24	Newmarket	29 753	45 474	35.91
Burlington*	114 853	129 575	177.41	Niagara Falls*	70 960	75 399	212.02
Caledon	26 645	34 965	686.84	Niagara-on-the-Lake	12 186	12 945	131.11
Cambridge*	77 183	92 772	115.06	Nickel Centre	12 318	12 332	378.36
Carleton Place	5 626	7 432	5.64	North Bay*	51 268	55 405	312.88
Chatham*	40 952	43 557	27.52	North York*	559 521	562 564	176.87
Cobourg	11 385	15 079	15.89	Oakville	75 773	114 670	138.18
Colchester South	5 018	5 292	143.56	Onaping Falls	6 198	5 402	228.98
Collingwood	12 064	13 505	21.30	Orangeville	13 740	17 921	13.39
Cornwall*	46 144	47 137	63.49	Orillia*	23 955	25 925	22.90
Dryden	6 640	6 505	16.86	Oshawa*	117 519	129 344	143.41
Dundas	19 586	21 868	24.42	Ottawa*	295 163	313 987	110.15
Dunnville	11 353	12 131	302.92	Owen Sound*	19 883	21 674	20.29
East Gwillimbury	12 565	18 367	245.14	Paris	7 485	8 600	10.67
Elliot Lake	16 723	14 089	756.79	Parry Sound	6 124	6 125	14.98
Espanola	5 836	5 527	17.66	Pelham	11 104	13 328	124.52
Essex	6 295	6 759	6.48	Pembroke*	14 026	13 997	14.83
Etobicoke*	298 713	309 993	123.93	Penetanguishene	5 315	6 643	9.40
Fergus	6 064	7 940	6.87	Perth	5 655	5 574	8.92
Flamborough	24 470	29 616	489.90	Peterborough*	60 620	68 371	53.41
Fort Erie	24 096	26 006	168.30	Pickering	37 754	68 631	226.52
Fort Frances	8 906	8 891	26.05	Port Colborne*	19 225	18 766	122.82
Gananoque	4 863	5 209	9.01	Port Elgin	6 131	6 857	5.92
Georgina	20 111	29 746	286.27	Port Hope	9 992	11 505	10.00
Gloucester*	72 859	101 677	293.86	Rayside-Balfour	15 017	15 039	328.21
Goderich	7 322	7 452	6.74	Renfrew	8 283	8 134	12.25
Gravenhurst	8 532	9 988	524.01	Richmond Hill	37 778	80 142	99.42
Grimsby	15 797	18 520	68.12	Rockland	3 961	6 771	8.49
Guelph*	71 207	87 976	68.69	Sarnia*-Clearwater	50 892	74 376	32.76
Haldimand	16 866	20 573	638.15	Sault Ste. Marie*	82 697	81 476	221.52
Halton Hills	35 190	36 816	275.86	Scarborough*	443 353	524 598	187.70
Hamilton*	306 434	318 499	122.69	Simcoe	14 326	15 539	40.51
Hanover	6 316	6 711	6.49	Smiths Falls	8 831	9 396	8.26
Hawkesbury	9 877	9 706	8.16	St. Catharines*	124 018	129 300	94.43
Hearst	5 533	6 079	28.85	St. Marys	4 883	5 496	12.14
Huntsville	11 467	14 997	700.90	St. Thomas*	28 165	29 990	18.10
Ingersoll	8 494	9 378	10.20	Stoney Creek*	36 762	49 968	98.65
Iroquois Falls	6 339	5 999	689.94	Stratford*	26 262	27 666	20.33
Kanata*	19 728	37 344	132.19	Strathroy	8 748	10 566	13.89
Kapuskasing	12 014	10 344	83.92	Sturgeon Falls	6 045	5 837	5.79
Kenora	9 817	9 782	15.33	Sudbury*	91 829	92 884	262.73
Kincardine	5 778	6 585	7.65	Tecumseh	6 364	10 495	6.19
Kingston*	52 616	56 597	29.57	Thorold*	15 412	17 542	84.54
Kingsville	5 134	5 716	4.27	Thunder Bay*	112 486	113 946	322.86
Kirkland Lake	12 219	10 440	270.01	Tillsonburg	10 487	12 019	20.58
Kitchener*	139 734	168 282	135.13	Timmins*	46 114	47 461	3 004.39
Leamington	12 528	14 182	8.75	Toronto*	599 217	635 395	97.15
Lincoln	14 196	17 149	163.43	Trenton*	15 085	16 908	11.69
Lindsay	13 596	16 696	15.19	Valley East	20 433	21 939	518.03
Listowel	5 026	5 404	6.19	Vanier*	18 792	18 150	2.93
London*	254 280	303 165	162.21	Vaughan	29 674	111 359	275.34
Marathon	2 277	5 064	162.39	Walden	10 139	9 805	718 62
Markham	77 037	153 811	211.53	Wallaceburg	11 506	11 846	10.71
Midland	12 132	13 865	16.01	Wasaga Beach	4 705	6 224	52.10
Milton	28 067	32 075	367.20	Waterloo*	49 428	71 181	64.45
Mississauga*	315 056	463 388	273.86	Welland*	45 448	47 914	81.23
Nanticoke*	19 816	22 727	674.72	Westminster	5 952	6 826	224.69
Napanee	4 803	5 179	4.02	Whitby	36 698	61 281	142.99
Nepean*	84 361	107 627	217.02	Whitchurch-Stouffville	13 557	18 357	206.85 ►

	POPULATION 1981	1991	AREA (sq. km)
▶ Windsor*	192 083	191 435	119.87
Woodstock*	26 603	30 075	24.53
York*	134 617	140 525	23.18

■ MANITOBA

	POPULATION 1981	1991	AREA (sq. km)
Brandon*	36 242	38 567	74.50
Dauphin	8 971	8 453	11.94
Flin Flon* (part in Man. balance in Sask.)	7 894	7 119	11.55
Morden	4 579	5 273	10.53
Portage La Prairie*	13 086	13 186	24.03
Selkirk	10 037	9 815	24.71
Steinbach	6 676	8 213	25.24
The Pas	6 390	6 166	28.46
Thompson*	14 288	14 977	16.85
Winkler	5 046	6 397	16.17
Winnipeg*	564 473	616 790	571.60

■ SASKATCHEWAN

	POPULATION 1981	1991	AREA (sq. km)
Estevan*	9 174	10 240	17.67
Humboldt	4 705	5 089	11.65
Lloydminster*	15 031	7 241	39.38
Melfort*	6 010	5 628	14.66
Melville*	5 092	5 123	15.41
Moose Jaw*	33 941	33 593	45.30
North Battleford*	14 030	14 350	37.06
Prince Albert*	31 380	34 181	64.97
Regina*	162 613	179 178	110.06
Saskatoon*	154 210	186 058	132.23
Swift Current*	14 747	14 815	20.50
Weyburn*	9 523	9 673	13.70
Yorkton*	15 339	15 315	23.16

■ ALBERTA

	POPULATION 1981	1991	AREA (sq. km)
Airdrie*	8 414	12 456	13.37
Banff	5 768	5 688	4.86
Beaumont	2 638	5 042	5.59
Bonnyville	4 454	5 132	14.39
Brooks	9 421	9 433	15.81
Calgary*	592 743	710 677	534.82
Camrose*	12 570	13 420	24.43
Canmore	3 484	5 681	12.88
Coaldale	4 579	5 310	7.06
Cochrane	1 486	5 265	15.55
Crowsnest Pass	7 306	6 679	171.79
Drayton Valley	5 042	5 983	7.95
Drumheller*	6 508	6 277	28.48
Edmonton*	532 246	616 741	669.95
Edson	5 835	7 323	25.89
Fort McMurray*	31 000	34 706	56.61
Fort Saskatchewan*	12 169	12 078	32.94
Grande Prairie*	24 263	28 271	41.83
High River	4 792	6 269	10.42
Hinton	8 342	9 046	22.52
Innisfail	5 247	5 700	9.82
Lacombe	5 591	6 934	11.40
Leduc*	12 471	13 970	22.42
Lethbridge*	54 072	60 974	119.90
Lloydminster³*	15 031	10 042	39.38
Medicine Hat*	40 380	43 625	96.17

	POPULATION 1981	1991	AREA (sq. km)
Morinville	4 657	6 104	12.32
Okotoks*	3 847	6 720	11.67
Olds	4 813	5 542	9.79
Peace River	5 907	6 717	21.20
Ponoka	5 221	5 861	9.81
Red Deer*	46 393	58 134	51.74
Rocky Mountain House	4 698	5 461	10.82
Slave Lake	4 506	5 607	7.43
Spruce Grove	10 326	12 884	19.56
St. Albert*	31 996	42 146	33.63
Stony Plain	4 839	7 226	26.51
Taber	5 988	6 660	15.62
Vegreville	5 251	5 138	13.99
Wetaskiwin*	9 597	10 634	13.27
Whitecourt	5 585	6 938	25.40

■ BRITISH COLUMBIA

	POPULATION 1981	1991	AREA (sq. km)
Castlegar*	6 902	6 579	16.16
Colwood	10 540	13 463	17.91
Comox	6 607	8 253	7.88
Courtenay*	8 992	11 652	11.00
Cranbrook*	15 915	16 447	16.29
Dawson Creek*	11 373	10 981	20.30
Fernie*	5 444	5 012	13.64
Fort St. John*	13 891	14 156	19.53
Kamloops*	64 048	67 057	296.06
Kelowna*	59 196	75 950	212.56
Kimberley*	7 375	6 531	58.19
Langley*	15 124	19 765	10.18
Merritt*	6 110	6 253	8.34
Nanaimo*	47 069	60 129	88.20
Nelson*	9 143	8 760	6.51
New Westminster*	38 550	43 585	15.38
North Vancouver*	33 952	38 436	10.77
Parksville	5 216	7 306	10.66
Penticton*	23 181	27 258	40.79
Port Alberni*	19 892	18 403	17.51
Port Coquitlam*	27 535	36 773	26.91
Port Moody*	14 917	17 712	13.72
Prince George*	67 559	69 653	315.72
Prince Rupert*	16 197	16 620	53.56
Quesnel*	8 240	8 179	20.56
Revelstoke*	5 544	7 729	29.99
Richmond*	96 154	126 624	124.2
Sidney	7 946	10 082	5.02
Smithers	4 570	5 029	13.17
Terrace	10 914	11 433	19.21
Trail*	9 599	7 919	13.79
Vancouver*	414 281	471 844	112.94
Vernon*	19 987	23 514	22.67
Victoria*	64 379	71 228	18.78
White Rock*	13 550	16 314	5.05
Williams Lake	8 362	10 385	23.26

■ YUKON TERRITORIES

	POPULATION 1981	1991	AREA (sq. km)
Whitehorse*	14 814	17 925	413.48

■ NORTHWEST TERRITORIES

	POPULATION 1981	1991	AREA (sq. km)
Yellowknife*	9 483	15 179	102.38

Source: *Census of Canada*

n.a. not available

Population of Canadian Cities

(with 50,000+ population in 1991)

City	Year incorporated[1]	Population (000s) 1966	1976	1981	1986	1991
Ajax, Ont.	1955	9.4	20.8	38.4	48.3	62.7
Barrie, Ont.	1959	24.0	34.4	25.5	36.6	57.4
Beauport, Que.	1976	11.7	55.3	60.4	62.9	69.1
Brampton, Ont.	1974	36.3	103.5	149.0	188.5	234.4
Brantford, Ont.	1877	59.9	67.0	74.3	76.1	82.0
Brossard, Que.	1958	11.9	37.6	52.2	57.4	64.8
Burlington, Ont.	1974	65.9	104.3	114.9	116.7	129.6
Calgary, Alta.	1893	330.6	469.9	592.7	636.1	710.7
Cambridge, Ont.	1973	n.a.	72.4	77.2	79.9	92.8
Charlesbourg, Que.	1976	24.9	63.1	68.3	69.0	70.8
Chicoutimi, Que.	1976	32.5	57.7	60.1	61.0	62.7
Coquitlam, BC [2]	1891	40.9	55.5	61.1	69.3	n.a.
Dartmouth, NS	1961	58.7	65.3	62.3	65.2	n.a.
Delta, BC [2]	1879	20.7	64.5	74.7	79.6	n.a.
East York, Ont.[3]	1967	74.2	107.0	102.0	101.1	n.a.
Edmonton, Alta.	1904	376.9	461.4	532.2	574.0	616.7
Etobicoke, Ont.	1983	219.5	297.1	298.7	303.0	310.0
Gatineau, Que.	1975	17.7	73.5	75.0	81.2	92.3
Gloucester, Ont.	1981	23.2	56.5	72.9	89.8	101.7
Guelph, Ont.	1879	51.4	67.5	71.2	78.2	88.0
Halifax, NS	1841	86.8	117.9	114.6	113.6	67.8
Hamilton, Ont.	1846	298.1	312.0	306.4	306.7	318.5
Hull, Que.	1875	60.2	61.0	56.2	58.7	60.7
Jonquière, Que.	1976	29.7	60.7	60.4	58.5	57.9
Kamloops, BC	1973	10.8	58.3	64.0	61.8	67.1
Kelowna, BC	1973	17.0	52.0	59.2	61.2	76.0
Kingston, Ont.	1846	59.0	56.0	52.6	55.0	56.6
Kitchener, Ont.	1912	93.3	131.9	139.7	150.6	168.3
LaSalle, Que.	1958	48.3	76.7	76.3	75.6	73.8
Laval, Que.	1965	196.1	246.2	268.3	284.1	314.4
Lethbridge, Alta.	1906	37.2	46.8	54.1	58.8	61.0
London, Ont.	1855	194.4	240.4	254.3	269.1	303.2
Longueuil, Que.	1920	25.6	122.4	124.3	125.4	129.9
Markham, Ont.[4]	1971	7.8	56.2	77.0	114.6	153.8
Matsqui, BC [2]	1892	16.2	31.2	42.0	51.4	n.a.
Mississauga, Ont.	1974	93.5	250.0	315.1	374.0	463.4
Moncton, NB	1973	45.8	55.9	54.7	55.5	57.0
Montréal, Que.	1832	1 222.3	1 080.5	980.4	1 015.4	1 017.7
Montréal-Nord, Que.	1959	67.8	97.3	94.9	90.3	85.5
Nanaimo, BC	1874	15.2	40.3	47.1	49.0	60.1
Nepean, Ont.	1978	43.9	76.9	84.4	95.5	107.6
Niagara Falls, Ont.	1903	56.9	69.4	71.0	72.1	75.4
North Bay, Ont.	1925	23.6	51.6	51.3	50.6	55.4
North Vancouver, BC [2]	1891	48.1	63.5	65.4	68.2	n.a.
North York, Ont.	1979	399.5	558.4	559.5	556.3	562.6
Oakville, Ont.[4]	1857	52.8	69.0	75.8	87.1	114.7
Oshawa, Ont.	1924	78.1	107.0	117.5	123.7	129.3
Ottawa, Ont.	1854	290.7	304.5	295.2	300.8	314.0
Peterborough, Ont.	1905	56.2	59.7	60.6	61.0	68.4
Prince George, BC	1915	24.5	59.9	67.6	67.6	69.7
Québec, Que.	1832	167.0	177.1	166.5	164.6	167.5
Red Deer, Alta.	1913	26.2	32.2	46.4	54.4	58.1
Regina, Sask.	1903	131.1	149.6	162.6	175.0	179.2
Richmond, BC [2]	1879	50.5	80.0	96.1	108.5	n.a.
Richmond Hill, Ont.	1957	19.8	34.7	37.8	46.8	80.1 ▶

City	Year incorporated[1]	Population (000s)				
		1966	1976	1981	1986	1991
▶ Saanich, BC[2]	1906	58.8	73.4	78.7	82.9	n.a.
Saint-Hubert, Que.	1958	17.2	49.7	60.6	66.2	74.0
Saint John, NB	1785	51.6	86.0	80.5	76.4	75.0
Saint-Laurent, Que.	1955	59.5	64.4	65.9	67.0	72.4
Saint-Leonard, Que.	1963	25.3	78.5	79.4	75.9	73.1
Sainte-Foy, Que.	1955	48.3	71.2	68.9	69.6	71.1
St. Catharines, Ont.	1876	97.1	123.4	124.0	123.5	129.3
St. John's, Nfld.	1888	79.9	86.6	83.8	96.2	95.7
Sarnia-Clearwater, Ont.	1914	54.6	55.6	50.9	49.0	74.4[5]
Saskatoon, Sask.	1906	115.9	133.8	154.2	177.6	186.1
Sault Ste. Marie, Ont.	1912	74.6	81.0	82.7	80.9	81.5
Scarborough, Ont.	1983	278.4	387.1	443.4	484.7	524.6
Sherbrooke, Que.	1875	75.7	76.8	74.1	74.3	76.4
Sudbury, Ont.	1930	84.9	97.6	91.8	88.7	92.9
Surrey, BC[2]	1879	81.8	116.5	147.1	181.4	n.a.
Thunder Bay, Ont.	1970	104.5	111.5	112.5	112.3	114.0
Toronto, Ont.	1834	664.6	633.3	599.2	612.3	635.4
Vancouver, BC	1886	410.4	410.2	414.3	431.1	471.8
Vaughan, Ont.[4]	1971	n.a.	17.8	29.7	65.1	111.4
Verdun, Que.	1912	76.8	68.0	61.3	60.2	61.3
Victoria, BC	1862	57.5	62.6	64.4	66.3	71.2
Waterloo, Ont.	1948	29.9	46.6	49.4	58.7	71.2
Whitby, Ont.[4]	1855	17.3	28.1	36.7	45.8	61.3
Windsor, Ont.	1892	192.5	196.5	192.1	193.1	191.4
Winnipeg, Man.[6]	1873	257.0	560.9	564.5	594.6	616.8
York, Ont.	1983	134.7	141.4	134.6	135.4	140.5

Source: *Census of Canada*

(1) As a city, unless otherwise indicated by footnote. (2) District Municipality. (3) Borough. (4) Town. (5) 1991 includes Clearwater (6) Includes St. James-Assiniboia, Man.

Population of Census Metropolitan Areas in Canada

Statistics Canada defines a census metropolitan area (CMA) as a very large urban area, together with neighbouring urban and rural areas that have a high degree of economic and social integration with that large urban area. The urban area itself (or urbanized core) must have a population of at least 100,000 based on the previous census.

CMA	Population[1] (000s)					Land Area
	1951	1961	1971	1981	1991	1991
Calgary, Alta	142.3	279.1	403.3	592.6	754	5 085.8 sq. km
Chicoutimi-Jonquière, Que.	91.2	127.6	133.7	135.2	161	1 723.3 sq. km
Edmonton, Alta.	193.6	359.8	495.7	656.9	840	9 532.5 sq. km
Halifax, NS	138.4	193.4	222.6	277.7	321	2 503.1 sq. km
Hamilton, Ont.	281.9	401.1	498.5	542.1	600	1 358.5 sq. km
Kitchener, Ont.	107.5	154.9	226.8	287.8	356	823.6 sq. km
London, Ont.	167.7	226.7	286.0	283.7	382	2 105.1 sq. km
Montreal, Que.	1 539.3	2 215.6	2 743.2	2 828.3	3 127	3 508.9 sq. km
Oshawa, Ont.	n.a.	n.a.	120.3	154.2	240	894.2 sq. km
Ottawa-Hull, Ont.-Que.	311.6	457.0	602.5	718.0	921	5 138.3 sq. km
Quebec, Que.	289.3	379.1	480.5	576.0	646	3 150.3 sq. km
Regina, Sask.	72.7	113.7	140.7	164.3	192	3 421.6 sq. km
St. Catharines-Niagara, Ont.	189.0	257.8	303.4	304.4	365	1 399.8 sq. km
St. John's, Nfld.	80.9	106.7	131.8	154.8	172	1 130.0 sq. km
Saint John, NB	80.7	98.1	106.7	114.0	125	2 904.8 sq. km
Saskatoon, Sask.	55.7	95.6	126.4	154.2	210	4 749.4 sq. km
Sherbrooke, Que.	n.a.	n.a.	n.a.	125.2	139	915.8 sq. km
Sudbury, Ont.	80.5	127.4	155.4	149.9	158	2 612.1 sq. km ▶

CMA	Population[2] (000s)					Land Area
	1951	1961	1971	1981	1991	1991
▶ Thunder Bay, Ont.	73.7	102.1	112.1	121.4	124	2 202.6 sq. km
Toronto, Ont.	1 261.9	1 919.4	2 628.0	2 998.7	3 893	5 583.5 sq. km
Trois-Rivières, Que.	46.1	53.5	55.9	111.4	136	871.9 sq. km
Vancouver, B.C.	586.2	826.8	1 082.4	1 268.1	1 603	2 786.3 sq. km
Victoria, B.C.	114.9	155.8	195.8	233.5	288	633.4 sq. km
Windsor, Ont.	182.6	217.2	258.6	246.1	262	861.7 sq. km
Winnipeg, Man.	357.2	476.5	540.3	584.8	652	3 294.8 sq. km

Source: *Census of Canada*

(1) Population is based on a boundary CMA at time of that particular census. (n.a.) not available.

VITAL STATISTICS

Births in Canada, 1925–1992

	Live Births	Birth Rate[1]
1925	249 365	26.1
1930	250 335	23.9
1935	228 396	20.5
1940	252 577	21.6
1945	300 587	24.3
1950	372 009	27.1
1955	442 937	28.2
1960	478 551	26.8
1965	418 595	21.3
1970	371 988	17.5
1975	359 323	15.8
1980	370 709	15.5
1985	375 727	14.8
1986	372 913	14.7
1987	369 742	14.4
1988	376 795	14.5
1989	392 661	15.0
1990	405 474	15.2
1991	411 910	15.2
1992	404 290	14.7

Source: *Statistics Canada*   (1) Per 1,000 population.

Births by Province, 1992

	Live Births	Birth Rate[1]
Canada	404 290	14.7
Newfoundland	7 510	13.0
Prince Edward Island ..	1 890	14.5
Nova Scotia	11 990	13.2
New Brunswick	9 570	13.1
Quebec	97 520	14.1
Ontario	152 190	15.0
Manitoba	17 420	15.9
Saskatchewan	15 430	15.6
Alberta	42 580	16.6
British Columbia	46 040	13.9
Yukon Territory	570	20.2
Northwest Territories ..	1 580	20.2

Source: *Statistics Canada*   (1) Per 1,000 population.

Variable Birth Rates

*T*he birth rate in 1921, just after World War I, was 29 births per 1,000 population. By 1937, the rate had dropped 30%, down to 20 births per 1,000 population, but after World War II, the birth rate climbed back up to 28 births per 1,000 and what became known as the baby boom kept rates high for over a decade. By the 1970s, the birth rate began to drop again and has stayed at around 15 births per thousand since the mid-1980s.

This decline means that the fertility rate (the average number of children born to a woman during her lifetime) has dropped to 1.7 births per woman of child-bearing age. The fertility rate necessary to simply maintain the size of Canada's current population, without immigration, is 2.1.

Canadian[1] Births by Age of Mother, 1990

Age of Mother	Total Births	Order of birth[2]							
		1st	2nd	3rd	4th	5th	6th	7th	8+
under 15 years	239	233	6	—	—	—	—	—	—
15 years	836	810	26	—	—	—	—	—	—
16 years	2 310	2 178	129	2	—	—	1	—	—
17 years	4 328	3 897	405	22	2	—	—	—	—
18 years	6 554	5 490	950	107	5	2	—	—	—
19 years	9 148	7 000	1 863	253	25	5	1	—	—
20 years	11 384	7 871	2 852	568	78	8	4	1	—
21 years	13 287	8 483	3 747	862	166	26	1	—	1
22 years	15 628	9 210	4 735	1 333	293	51	5	—	1
23 years	18 892	10 727	5 941	1 696	412	93	19	4	—
24 years	22 536	12 264	7 403	2 187	522	126	25	3	5
25 years	27 641	14 423	9 275	2 993	721	167	41	15	5
26 years	30 930	15 045	11 076	3 616	870	233	55	24	9
27 years	32 471	14 377	12 259	4 366	1 076	287	70	24	11
28 years	32 113	13 299	12 291	4 752	1 263	336	128	27	17
29 years	31 103	11 503	12 431	5 190	1 402	400	104	47	25
30 years	28 594	9 546	11 624	5 301	1 485	426	122	55	33
31 years	24 524	7 535	9 894	4 964	1 454	442	148	48	39
32 years	20 422	5 784	8 122	4 462	1 436	363	140	58	57
33 years	16 564	4 435	6 438	3 813	1 258	353	146	71	50
34 years	13 248	3 329	5 059	3 117	1 142	330	139	68	63
35 years	10 609	2 546	3 835	2 626	991	348	131	49	83
36 years	7 970	1 941	2 772	1 908	822	288	98	68	73
37 years	5 729	1 311	1 905	1 394	658	234	96	58	73
38 years	4 026	913	1 354	955	436	181	73	47	67
39 years	2 730	627	862	633	317	132	65	40	54
40 years	1 701	390	547	362	189	81	46	28	58
41 years	1 054	238	300	219	145	60	38	15	39
42 years	643	114	162	155	86	45	28	19	34
43 years	321	55	87	67	45	25	17	11	14
44 years	137	31	24	20	25	12	6	8	11
45 years	59	10	10	11	10	5	5	2	6
46 years	24	1	6	2	6	2	1	1	5
47 years	8	2	1	1	1	—	1	—	2
48 years	8	1	2	2	—	—	1	1	1
49 years	—	—	—	—	—	—	—	—	—
50 years+	—	—	—	—	—	—	—	—	—
Age not stated	41	17	11	9	4	—	—	—	—
Total births	**397 812**[3]	**175 636**	**138 404**	**57 968**	**17 345**	**5 061**	**1 755**	**792**	**836**

Source: *Statistics Canada*

(1) Does not include Newfoundland; includes some data that could not be verified. (2) The order of birth takes into account all children born alive to the mother. (3) Includes 14 births where order of birth not stated.

Postponing Motherhood

*I**n 1971, 12% of the babies born had mothers under the age of 20, while mothers between the ages of 30 and 39 accounted for 20% of births. By 1989, only 6% of babies were born to mothers under 20 and in 1990, the number had dropped again, to 5.8%. In 1990, 33.8% of all births were to women in their 30s, but there was a dramatic drop-off to 1% for women in their 40s.*

Also in 1990, 21.6% of firstborns were to mothers in their 30s. In the early days of this trend to later parenthood, there was concern that older mothers would experience more birth complications. Experts now acknowledge that the age of the mother is a less important factor in a successful pregnancy than her general health, nutrition, medical history and the quality of her medical care.

Age of Mother at Birth of First Child[1]

Age of mother	1931	1950	1971	1990
Under 15	14	15	292	233
15–19	9 639	14 251	33 258	19 375
20–24	25 224	41 018	65 618	48 555
25–29	13 826	24 330	32 918	68 647
30–34	4 802	8 558	7 236	30 629
35–39	1 580	3 086	1 830	7 338
40–44	342	677	380	828
45 and over	27	37	15	14
Total first borns[2]	55 486	92 018	142 008	175 636

Source: *Statistics Canada*

(1) Excludes Newfoundland. (2) Includes births for which age of mother not stated.

Most Popular Baby Names in Canada, 1950–1990 [in order of popularity]

1950		1970		1990	
Boys	*Girls*	*Boys*	*Girls*	*Boys*	*Girls*
Robert	Linda	Michael	Lisa	Michael	Jessica
David	Patricia	David	Michelle	Matthew	Amanda
John	Barbara	Robert	Jennifer	Christopher	Sarah
James	Susan	Jason	Tracy	Andrew	Stephanie
William	Sharon	James	Tammy	Kyle	Samantha
Richard	Margaret	Christopher	Karen	Ryan	Ashley
Kenneth	Donna	John	Nicole	Joshua	Brittany
Donald	Judith	Richard	Christine	Daniel	Jennifer
Ronald	Carol	Kevin	Shannon	Jordan	Nicole
Douglas	Sandra	Mark	Susan	Justin	Kayla
Michael	Wendy	Steven	Angel	David	Melissa
Brian	Karen	William	Laura	Tyler	Megan
Gordon	Shirley	Paul	Sandra	James	Michelle
Thomas	Elizabeth	Brian	Tanya	Nicholas	Rebecca
Gary	Kathleen	Scott	Heather	Robert	Emily
Wayne	Heather	Darren	Kimberly	Adam	Laura
Peter	Brenda	Daniel	Patricia	Alexander	Danielle
Dennis	Janet	Kenneth	Brenda	Kevin	Alexandra
Bruce	Catherine	Andrew	Lori	Steven	Lauren
Daniel	Janice	Sean	Tracey	Joseph	Courtney
Larry	Marilyn	Gregory	Julie	Jonathan	Cassandra
Edward	Diane	Stephen	Kelly	Brandon	Rachel
George	Maureen	Deal	Cheryl	Eric	Lindsay
Gerald	Gail	Peter	Tara	John	Victoria
Patrick	Joan	Jeffrey	Andrea	Thomas	Marie

Expected Years of Life Remaining, 1921–86

| | At Birth | | At Age 20 | | At Age 40 | | At Age 60 | | At Age 80 | |
	Male	Female	Male	Female	Male	Female	Male	Female	Male	Female
1921[1]	n.a.	n.a.	49.1	49.2	32.2	33.0	16.6	17.1	6.0	6.1
1931	60.0	62.1	49.1	49.8	32.0	33.0	16.3	17.2	5.6	5.9
1941	63.0	66.3	49.6	51.8	31.9	34.0	16.1	17.6	5.5	6.0
1951	66.3	70.8	50.8	54.4	32.5	35.6	16.5	18.6	5.8	6.4
1956	67.6	72.9	51.2	55.8	32.7	36.7	16.5	19.3	5.9	6.8
1961	68.4	74.2	51.5	56.7	33.0	37.5	16.7	19.9	6.1	6.9
1966	68.8	75.2	51.5	57.4	33.0	38.2	16.8	20.6	6.4	7.3
1971	69.3	76.4	51.7	58.2	33.2	39.0	17.0	21.4	6.4	7.9
1976	70.2	77.5	52.1	59.0	33.6	39.7	17.2	22.0	6.4	8.2
1981	71.9	79.0	53.4	60.1	34.7	40.7	18.0	22.9	6.9	8.8
1986	73.0	79.7	54.3	60.7	35.5	41.2	18.4	23.2	6.9	8.9

Source: *Statistics Canada*

(1) Excludes Quebec. (n.a.) not available.

Canadian Life Expectancy

C *anadians of both sexes are living longer—in 1921 a male or female in their 20s could expect to live for another 49 years, while by 1986 the average 20-year-old male could expect another 54 years of life and his female counterpart could expect to live for another 60.7 years! This gap in life expectancy began in the1940s and grew until the 80s as the average woman's life expectancy grew at a faster rate than men's.*

By 1991, nearly 33% of Canada's population was over 45 years of age, with 19% of the population between 45-65 and 11% who were over 65. (In 1851, only 2.7% of the population was over 65.) The senior population is spread fairly evenly across the provinces, although Newfoundland and Alberta both have a smaller percentage of seniors that the national average.

Population Distribution by Age by Province[1]

(thousands of people)

	Total Population	Population 45-64	Population 65 or over	Percentage of Population 65 or over
Canada	26,309	4,984	2,764	11
Newfoundland	567	101	49	9
PEI	128	23	14	11
NS	875	163	98	11
NB	712	126	78	11
Quebec	6,712	1,328	661	10
Ontario	9,745	1,901	1,040	11
Manitoba	1,036	194	131	13
Saskatchewan	950	164	125	13
Alberta	2,455	398	193	8
BC	3,128	585	374	12

(1) Population projections based on 1986 Census.

Expected Years of Life Remaining, by Age, 1986

	Male		Female			Male		Female	
Age	% Dying[1]	Years of Life Remaining	% Dying[1]	Years of Life Remaining	Age	% Dying[1]	Years of Life Remaining	% Dying[1]	Years of Life Remaining
0	.86	73.04	.68	79.73	52 ..	.66	24.75	.38	30.08
1	.07	72.67	.06	79.27	53 ..	.74	23.92	.41	29.19
2	.05	71.72	.04	78.32	54 ..	.82	23.09	.45	28.31
3	.04	70.76	.03	77.35	55 ..	.91	22.28	.49	27.43
4	.04	69.79	.03	76.38	56 ..	1.01	21.48	.53	26.56
5	.03	68.81	.02	75.40	57 ..	1.11	20.69	.58	25.70
6	.02	67.83	.02	74.41	58 ..	1.22	19.92	.63	24.85
7	.02	66.85	.02	73.43	59 ..	1.34	19.16	.69	24.00
8	.02	65.86	.01	72.44	60 ..	1.47	18.41	.75	23.17
9	.02	64.87	.01	71.45	61 ..	1.61	17.68	.82	22.34
10	.02	63.88	.01	70.46	62 ..	1.77	16.96	.90	21.52
11	.02	62.89	.02	69.47	63 ..	1.95	16.25	.99	20.71
12	.03	61.91	.02	68.48	64 ..	2.14	15.57	1.08	19.91
13	.04	60.92	.02	67.49	65 ..	2.35	14.90	1.18	19.12
14	.06	59.95	.03	66.50	66 ..	2.57	14.24	1.29	18.34
15	.07	58.98	.03	65.52	67 ..	2.82	13.61	1.42	17.58
16	.09	58.02	.04	64.54	68 ..	3.09	12.99	1.56	16.82
17	.11	57.08	.04	63.57	69 ..	3.37	12.38	1.70	16.08
18	.12	56.13	.04	62.59	70 ..	3.67	11.80	1.87	15.35
19	.12	55.20	.04	61.62	71 ..	4.01	11.23	2.06	14.63
20	.13	54.27	.04	60.65	72 ..	4.38	10.68	2.28	13.93
21	.14	53.34	.04	59.67	73 ..	4.78	10.14	2.52	13.24
22	.14	52.41	.04	58.70	74 ..	5.21	9.63	2.79	12.57
23	.14	51.48	.04	57.72	75 ..	5.68	9.13	3.09	11.92
24	.14	50.55	.04	56.74	76 ..	6.19	8.65	3.42	11.28
25	.13	49.62	.04	55.77	77 ..	6.75	8.19	3.81	10.66
26	.13	48.68	.04	54.79	78 ..	7.34	7.74	4.23	10.07
27	.13	47.75	.04	53.81	79 ..	7.98	7.32	4.68	9.49
28	.13	46.81	.05	52.83	80 ..	8.67	6.91	5.17	8.93
29	.13	45.87	.05	51.86	81 ..	9.41	6.52	5.74	8.39
30	.13	44.92	.05	50.88	82 ..	10.22	6.14	6.38	7.87
31	.13	43.98	.05	49.91	83 ..	11.09	5.78	7.09	7.37
32	.14	43.04	.06	48.94	84 ..	12.02	5.44	7.86	6.90
33	.14	42.10	.06	47.96	85 ..	13.02	5.12	8.71	6.44
34	.14	41.16	.07	46.99	86 ..	14.09	4.81	9.65	6.01
35	.15	40.21	.07	46.02	87 ..	15.25	4.52	10.70	5.60
36	.15	39.27	.07	45.05	88 ..	16.49	4.24	11.84	5.21
37	.16	38.33	.08	44.09	89 ..	17.80	3.98	13.08	4.84
38	.17	37.39	.09	43.12	90 ..	19.20	3.73	14.42	4.49
39	.18	36.45	.10	42.16	91 ..	20.69	3.50	15.87	4.16
40	.20	35.52	.11	41.20	92 ..	22.28	3.28	17.47	3.85
41	.22	34.59	.13	40.25	93 ..	23.09	3.07	18.25	3.56
42	.24	33.66	.14	39.30	94 ..	23.08	2.85	18.21	3.25
43	.26	32.74	.16	38.33	95 ..	23.63	2.55	18.77	2.86
44	.28	31.82	.17	37.41	96 ..	26.08	2.19	21.36	2.41
45	.31	30.91	.19	36.48	97 ..	31.77	1.78	27.41	1.92
46	.35	30.01	.21	35.54	98 ..	42.75	1.38	39.08	1.46
47	.38	29.11	.23	34.62	99 ..	58.11	1.04	55.42	1.08
48	.43	28.22	.26	33.70	100 ..	74.80	0.78	73.18	0.80
49	.48	27.34	.28	32.78	101 ..	89.78	0.60	89.13	0.61
50	.53	26.47	.31	31.87	102 ..	100.00	0.50	100.00	0.50
51	.59	25.61	.34	30.97					

Source: *Statistics Canada*

(1) Represents the percentage of the population that will die before reaching the next age; in some cases totals do not equal 100% due to rounding of percentages to two decimal places.

Deaths in Canada, 1925–1992

	Deaths	Death Rates[1]				Deaths	Death Rates[1]		
		Both Sexes	Males	Females			Both Sexes	Males	Females
1925[2]	102 528	10.7	10.3	9.5	1975	167 404	7.3	8.5	6.2
1930[3]	113 283	10.8	11.2	10.2	1980	171 743	7.2	8.2	6.1
1935[3]	109 724	9.9	10.2	9.2	1985	181 323	7.2	8.0	6.3
1940[3]	114 717	9.8	10.5	9.0	1986	184 224	7.3	8.1	6.5
1945[3]	117 325	9.5	10.3	8.5	1987	184 953	7.2	8.0	6.4
1950	124 220	9.1	10.1	7.9	1988	190 011	7.3	8.1	6.5
1955	128 476	8.2	9.4	6.9	1989	190 965	7.3	8.1	6.5
1960	139 693	7.8	9.0	6.6	1990	196 050	7.2	n.a.	n.a.
1965	148 939	7.6	8.8	6.3	1991	191 700	7.2	n.a.	n.a.
1970	155 961	7.3	8.5	6.1	1992	198 980	7.3	n.a.	n.a.

Source: *Statistics Canada*

(1) Per 1,000 population. (2) Excludes Que., Nfld, Yukon and NWT. (3) Excludes Nfld, Yukon and NWT.

Deaths by Province, 1992

	Deaths	Death Rate[1]		Deaths	Death Rate[1]
Canada	**198 980**	**7.3**	Manitoba	9 190	8.4
Newfoundland	3 850	6.7	Saskatchewan	8 310	8.4
Prince Edward Island	1 220	9.3	Alberta	14 530	5.7
Nova Scotia	7 490	8.3	British Columbia	24 800	7.5
New Brunswick	5 580	7.7	Yukon Territory	120	4.3
Quebec	50 650	7.3	Northwest Territories	251	4.4
Ontario	72 990	7.2			

Source: *Statistics Canada*

(1) Rate per 1,000 population.

Social Trends for Seniors

*A*s Canadians live longer, new lifestyle patterns are emerging. Historically, aging parents lived with members of their extended family, however a 1990 survey indicated that more and more seniors are living on their own. Access to pensions, increased mobility and better general health has meant that the quality of life is very different for this age group than it was three (or even two) generations ago.

Some Canadians continue to work, perhaps part-time, either by choice or out of financial necessity, while many others retire before 65. The General Social Survey in 1989 found that 63% of Canadians who were retired had done so before reaching age 65, while 17% had retired at 65 and another 16% had continued to work after age 65.

Retired Canadians studied in the "Survey on Ageing and Independence" published in 1991 found that more than 70% of the seniors over age 60 reported good or excellent health and enjoyed such diverse activities as walking, reading, visiting friends and relatives, watching TV and travel. 69% of Canadians in the 65-69 age group had taken overnight trips during the 12 months prior to the survey (47% of the population aged 80 or over had done the same) and 16% of those in the 65-69 age group had had a holiday trip lasting four weeks or more during the same period.

Social networks of family and friends were important to the well-being of seniors, however the change in the structure of the family means that contact with family members and friends must be nurtured rather than taken for granted.

Leading Causes of Death Among Canadians

(death rate per 100,000 population)

1981

Age	Heart Disease Male	Heart Disease Female	Cancer Male	Cancer Female	Stroke Male	Stroke Female	Respiratory Disease Male	Respiratory Disease Female	Accidents Male	Accidents Female
less than 1	7.9	3.9	4.7	3.9	0.5	1.1	46.2	38.2	39.3	31.0
1-4	1.2	0.9	6.6	5.2	0.3	0	3.6	4.1	28.0	19.2
5-9	0.7	0.2	6.0	4.2	0.1	0.5	0.2	0.8	19.7	12.7
10-14	0.5	0.3	5.3	4.5	0.3	0.4	1.4	0.6	27.0	10.8
15-19	1.4	1.0	5.9	4.4	0.7	0.6	2.4	1.2	117.1	31.2
20-24	2.6	1.1	6.6	4.3	0.9	1.1	1.5	1.1	140.4	31.0
25-29	4.7	2.8	8.9	9.8	2.1	1.9	2.1	2.2	102.8	27.7
30-34	13.1	3.1	13.6	16.2	3.0	3.5	2.3	2.0	91.3	26.2
35-39	30.2	7.4	28.7	33.2	5.5	6.4	3.0	3.6	84.9	26.2
40-44	77.8	18.2	52.5	68.9	8.0	8.9	5.3	5.0	90.3	33.9
45-49	156.6	36.9	109.7	118.9	18.4	14.7	14.0	7.9	96.7	35.4
50-54	281.7	66.1	210.1	198.8	27.2	24.6	24.0	15.1	102.3	41.3
55-59	464.6	136.7	392.7	296.1	46.6	37.9	49.3	22.1	100.1	34.2
60-64	781.2	255.6	612.3	416.9	84.3	66.2	105.5	43.9	105.1	39.5
65-69	1 217.9	484.2	906.6	550.7	179.0	121.2	211.7	71.6	114.2	47.6
70-74	1 767.2	895.6	1 303.2	685.2	344.2	253.0	369.1	117.6	134.4	57.9
75-79	2 812.4	1 583.0	1 733.1	855.4	685.9	494.1	707.5	211.8	157.4	82.5
80-84	4 270.3	2 782.7	2 321.6	1 159.7	1 154.5	964.4	1 172.4	400.4	254.9	162.5
85+ years	7 431.4	6 008.2	2 671.5	1 435.2	2 325.8	2 288.8	2 283.3	1 006.5	491.9	406.4
TOTAL	**278.7**	**201.7**	**185.9**	**146.4**	**54.7**	**67.2**	**58.0**	**32.4**	**91.9**	**36.1**

1989

Age	Heart Disease Male	Heart Disease Female	Cancer Male	Cancer Female	Stroke Male	Stroke Female	Respiratory Disease Male	Respiratory Disease Female	Accidents Male	Accidents Female
less than 1	6.0	2.6	4.0	3.7	1.0	0.5	15.4	14.6	18.4	14.1
1-4	0.8	0.8	4.1	3.2	0.4	0.1	2.4	2.7	19.1	13.2
5-9	0.1	0.7	3.3	3.3	0.0	0.0	0.6	0.9	12.1	7.9
10-14	0.8	0.3	3.3	1.9	0.4	0.2	1.2	1.6	15.5	7.9
15-19	1.6	0.7	7.0	3.5	0.3	0.1	2.0	0.7	86.3	25.2
20-24	2.8	1.4	6.2	4.5	0.7	0.6	2.5	1.5	101.2	29.5
25-29	3.9	2.0	8.5	7.7	1.3	0.9	2.1	1.6	90.1	24.6
30-34	9.6	2.9	12.5	16.3	2.3	2.5	2.0	1.9	80.1	22.5
35-49	19.1	5.0	24.3	35.6	4.7	4.6	2.8	2.1	75.7	25.7
40-44	43.5	10.8	48.1	61.6	4.1	5.3	5.6	4.4	69.0	26.4
45-49	98.9	23.4	99.2	116.3	10.6	10.1	10.1	6.2	68.4	32.3
50-54	177.4	47.0	210.4	189.3	19.4	17.4	14.9	12.3	69.9	23.6
55-59	329.8	92.0	395.2	291.5	33.3	28.4	39.6	23.5	78.8	28.8
60-64	563.9	191.6	669.9	418.9	63.6	40.7	86.8	53.3	83.0	30.6
65-69	889.4	353.5	978.6	579.3	127.5	76.9	193.2	81.0	88.8	38.8
70-74	1 482.0	658.2	1 386.9	761.2	240.9	167.3	386.4	169.2	108.2	42.7
75-79	2 218.1	1 244.4	1 847.7	955.4	496.9	358.4	766.0	303.2	143.9	73.2
80-84	3 509.6	2 241.2	2 449.9	1 224.8	914.8	785.5	1 387.0	539.7	261.8	141.4
85+ years	6 232.5	5 197.6	3 105.3	1 567.6	1 920.5	1 918.0	3 042.0	1 536.8	545.9	402.4
TOTAL	**242.6**	**192.9**	**219.2**	**172.7**	**47.4**	**62.1**	**71.5**	**52.0**	**73.6**	**32.3**

Source: *Statistics Canada*   (1) Includes cases in which age was not specified. (—) = zero.

Causes of Accidental Death in Canada, 1991

Age Group	All Causes[1]	Motor Vehicle[2]	Falls	Poison	Fire	Drowning	Choking	Guns	Electro-cution
Less than 1	71	6	2	—	7	6	7	—	—
1-4	174	53	5	—	25	82	1	2	—
5-9	155	90	5	1	10	46	—	—	2
10-14	211	104	2	4	9	30	—	6	2
15-19	913	439	10	21	14	52	3	28	10
20-29	2 495	962	44	142	46	143	9	26	22
30-39	2 225	595	56	203	48	121	10	24	16
40-49	1 625	375	44	130	32	104	17	18	14
50-59	1 137	271	75	77	24	74	27	18	2
60-69	1 147	273	137	60	41	48	25	4	8
70-79	1 223	267	404	39	36	36	44	4	2
80-84	656	96	354	13	12	20	23	2	—
85+	1 200	61	915	9	14	18	32	—	—
Total[3]	13 232	3 592	2 053	699	318	780	198	132	78

Source: *Statistics Canada*

(1) Includes causes not specified in this table. (2) Includes both traffic and non-traffic accidents involving motor vehicles. (3) Includes cases for which the age was not stated. (—) = zero.

Suicides in Canada

The suicide rates below indicate the number of suicides per 100 000 population. The suicide rate among young Canadian men has risen dramatically over the past 20 years while that for women has remained approximately the same. Suicide rates for men are now more than three times higher than those for women in Canada. Experts attempting to explain the difference have speculated that men are less likely to seek help for their problems and are also likely to use more lethal means when attempting suicide.

	1951 Rate		1971 Rate		1991 Rate	
Age Groups	Male	Female	Male	Female	Male	Female
5–9 yrs.	—	—	0.1	—	0.1	—
10–14 yrs.	0.2	—	1.1	0.4	2.0	1.0
15–19 yrs.	2.6	1.0	12.7	3.1	22.7	6.5
20–24 yrs.	8.6	3.5	23.2	5.7	32.7	4.1
25–29 yrs.	8.1	3.1	22.2	5.7	29.7	7.1
30–34 yrs.	12.1	3.4	20.7	10.2	29.2	7.3
35–39 yrs.	12.3	4.2	24.5	9.9	27.2	7.0
40–44 yrs.	18.4	5.9	30.3	13.2	26.6	8.3
45–49 yrs.	19.9	7.6	29.2	14.9	25.7	7.7
50–54 yrs.	27.6	8.7	33.3	14.6	26.7	6.0
55–59 yrs.	26.0	8.3	33.5	13.3	23.7	7.2
60–64 yrs.	27.2	10.8	33.5	11.1	24.7	6.3
65–69 yrs.	25.9	8.8	23.6	9.6	n.a.	n.a.
70–74 yrs.	28.7	6.5	23.4	8.7	14.1[1]	3.9[1]
75–79 yrs.	30.8	9.6	28.6	4.9	n.a.	n.a.
80–84 yrs.	32.6	2.0	21.0	5.9	27.0[2]	0.8[2]
85 yrs. and over	30.8	3.4	31.1	1.2	38.4	2.0
Total Suicides[3]	**11.1**	**3.6**	**17.3**	**6.4**	**21.3**	**5.2**

Source: *Statistics Canada*

(1) 1991 data reported age 65-69 and 70-74 as one age group (2) 1991 data reported age 75-79 and 80-84 as one age group. (3) Includes cases for which the age was not specified. (—) = zero.

Abortions in Canadian Hospitals[1]

In 1969, an amendment to the Canadian Criminal Code legalized abortions in Canada, but only if performed by a doctor in an approved hospital, after a hospital committee had certified that continuation of a woman's pregnancy "would or would be likely to endanger her life or health." In Jan. 1988, the Supreme Court of Canada declared this law invalid because it violated a woman's constitutional right to life, liberty and security of the person as stated in the *Charter of Rights and Freedoms*. The Supreme Court decision left Canada without an abortion law.

In 1990 the federal government introduced new legislation which would have allowed abortions if a doctor had determined that a woman's physical or psychological health was threatened by the pregnancy. The legislation, which attracted opposition from both sides of the abortion debate, narrowly passed a vote in the House of Commons but was defeated on a tie vote in the Senate.

The table below shows the number of abortions performed in Canadian hospitals, with the approval of hospital abortion committees.

	1970	1975	1980	1985	1990
Canada	11 152	49 311	65 751	62 712	71 222
Newfoundland	25	176	539	415	429
Prince Edward Island	17	77	23	11	—
Nova Scotia	261	1 017	1 662	1 698	1 967
New Brunswick	72	379	467	310	518
Quebec	534	5 579	8 940	11 311	14 418
Ontario	5 568	24 921	30 900	27 335	31 350
Manitoba	238	1 298	1 587	2 285	2 672
Saskatchewan	215	1 282	1 572	1 173	1 261
Alberta	1 154	4 333	7 131	6 547	6 598
British Columbia	2 901	10 076	12 673	11 264	11 607
Yukon	6	77	125	95	148
Northwest Territories	n.a.	95	126	254	254
Not stated	161	1	6	14	—

Source: *Statistics Canada*

(1) Data shows province of residence of persons having abortions. (—) = zero; n.a. not available.

AIDS Deaths by Age

	1988		1991	
	male	female	male	female
0 - 4 yrs	1	2	2	3
5 - 9	—	—	–	1
10-14	1	1	1	—
15-19	—	1	4	—
20-24	19	5	10	2
25-29	77	4	115	13
30-34	128	8	228	8
35-39	121	8	243	7
40-44	112	2	227	10
45-49	73	3	132	7
50-54	35	1	69	3
55-59	18	3	32	4
60-64	17	6	25	1
65-69	7	2	7	4
70-74	3	1	9	2
75-79	2	—	1	—
80-84	—	—	—	—
85+	—	—	—	—
total	614	47	1 105	65

Source: *Statistics Canada*

AIDS-Related Deaths by Province

	1988		1989		1990		1991	
	male	female	male	female	male	female	male	female
Canada	**614**	**47**	**797**	**54**	**937**	**45**	**1 105**	**65**
Newfoundland	6	—	2	—	3	-	3	1
Prince Edward Island	—	—	1	—	1	—	2	—
Nova Scotia	12	1	9	2	13	—	17	1
New Brunswick	3	—	7	—	14	2	8	—
Quebec	202	33	280	28	319	24	346	37
Ontario	243	8	305	15	352	15	473	22
Manitoba	5	—	9	1	10	—	10	—
Saskatchewan	2	—	5	1	6	1	9	1
Alberta	31	1	45	2	43	—	70	1
British Columbia	110	4	134	5	176	3	167	2
Yukon Territory	—	—	—	—	—	—	—	—
Northwest Territories	—	—	—	—	—	—	—	—

Source: *Statistics Canada*

Cancer in Canada, 1992

	Number of New Cases[1]			Number of Deaths[1]		
	Total	Male	Female	Total	Male	Female
All cancers[2]	**115 000[3]**	**60 200**	**54 800**	**58 300**	**32 100**	**26 200**
Brain	2 030	1 150	880	1 430	810	620
Bladder	5 100	3 800	1 300	1 270	890	380
Breast	15 700	n.a.	15 700	5 200	n.a.	5 200
Cervix	1 450	n.a.	1 450	380	n.a.	380
Intestine & rectum	16 200	8 500	7 700	6 300	3 300	3 000
Kidney	3 600	2 100	1 500	1 300	790	510
Leukemia	3 200	1 800	1 400	2 040	1 150	890
Lung	19 300	12 800	6 500	15 700	10 700	5 000
Lymphatic system	6 400	3 500	2 900	3 050	1 600	1 450
Mouth & pharynx	3 210	2 300	910	1 090	790	300
Ovary	2 100	n.a.	2 100	1 300	n.a.	1 300
Pancreas	2 900	1 400	1 500	2 850	1 450	1 400
Prostate	12 000	12 000	n.a.	3 700	3 700	n.a.
Skin (Melanoma)	3 100	1 550	1 550	540	320	220
Stomach	3 000	1 900	1 100	2 190	1 400	790
Uterus	3 100	n.a.	3 100	600	n.a.	600
All other sites	12 610	7 400	5 210	9 360	5 200	4 160

Source: *Statistics Canada*

(1) Estimates. (2) Excludes an estimated 47,200 cases of non-melanoma skin cancer. (3) Breakdown by sex does not add to total due to rounding. (n.a.) not available or not applicable.

Deaths Due to Heart Disease and Strokes, 1991

	Total	Males	Females
Heart attack	23 623	13 779	9 844
Other heart disease	11 077	5 251	5 826
Stroke	14 194	6 035	8 159
Hypertension	1 230	467	763
Total	50 124	25 532	24 592

Source: *Statistics Canada*

MIGRATION

Canadian Immigration Totals, 1852–1992

Year	Total	Year	Total	Year	Total	Year	Total
1852	29 307	1888	88 766	1924	124 164	1960	104 111
1853	29 464	1889	91 600	1925	84 907	1961	71 689
1854	37 263	1890	75 067	1926	135 982	1962	74 586
1855	25 296	1891	82 165	1927	158 886	1963	93 151
1856	22 544	1892	30 996	1928	166 783	1964	112 606
1857	33 854	1893	29 633	1929	164 993	1965	146 758
1858	12 339	1894	20 829	1930	104 806	1966	194 743
1859	6 300	1895	18 790	1931	27 530	1967	222 876
1860	6 276	1896	16 835	1932	20 591	1968	183 974
1861	13 589	1897	21 716	1933	14 382	1969	161 531
1862	18 294	1898	31 900	1934	12 476	1970	147 713
1863	21 000	1899	44 543	1935	11 277	1971	121 900
1864	24 779	1900	41 681	1936	11 643	1972	122 006
1865	18 958	1901	55 747	1937	15 101	1973	184 200
1866	11 427	1902	89 102	1938	17 244	1974	218 465
1867	10 666	1903	138 660	1939	16 994	1975	187 881
1868	12 765	1904	131 252	1940	11 324	1976	149 429
1869	18 630	1905	141 465	1941	9 329	1977	114 914
1870	24 706	1906	211 653	1942	7 576	1978	86 313
1871	27 773	1907	272 409	1943	8 504	1979	112 096
1872	36 578	1908	143 326	1944	12 801	1980	143 117
1873	50 050	1909	173 694	1945	22 722	1981	128 618
1874	39 373	1910	286 839	1946	71 719	1982	121 147
1875	27 382	1911	331 288	1947	64 127	1983	89 157
1876	25 633	1912	375 756	1948	125 414	1984	88 239
1877	27 082	1913	400 870	1949	95 217	1985	84 302
1878	29 807	1914	150 484	1950	73 912	1986	99 219
1879	40 492	1915	36 665	1951	194 391	1987	152 098
1880	38 505	1916	55 914	1952	164 498	1988	161 929
1881	47 991	1917	72 910	1953	168 868	1989	192 001
1882	112 458	1918	41 845	1954	154 227	1990	214 230
1883	133 624	1919	107 698	1955	109 946	1991	230 781
1884	103 824	1920	138 824	1956	164 857	1992	248 200
1885	79 169	1921	91 728	1957	282 164		
1886	69 152	1922	64 224	1958	124 851		
1887	84 526	1923	133 729	1959	106 928		

Source: *Immigration Canada*

A Nation of Immigrants

*A*ccording to the 1991 census, Canada's population included 4.3 million immigrants. Nearly half (48%) of these residents arrived here before 1971, and another 24% arrived between 1971 and 1980. The number of immigrants enumerated in the 1986 census showed just a 2% growth in numbers since the count in 1981, reflecting a decrease in federal government target levels; however between 1986 and 1991, the immigrant population grew by 11%.

Although the actual number of immigrants has increased, the proportion of the Canadian population born elsewhere has remained between 15% and 16% for the last 40 years. This is a lower proportion than the period at the turn of the century when our government was encouraging settlement and growth, particularly in western Canada. In 1901, immigrants accounted for 13% of the population, but by 1911, after an intense recruiting campaign, 22% of the nation's people had been born in another country and made the trip to a new homeland.

Immigration[1] to Canada, 1956–91

	Total Immigrants	United States	Asia	Europe	Caribbean[3]	South America	Africa	Oceania
1956	164 857	9 777	3 537	145 554	1 351	1 551	1 079	1 924
1957	282 164	11 008	3 244	257 540	1 586	2 376	2 970	3 345
1958	124 851	10 846	4 223	102 279	1 519	2 168	1 355	2 344
1959	106 928	11 338	5 368	84 517	1 529	1 750	8 43	1 512
1960	104 111	11 247	4 002	82 922	1 542	1 823	8 33	1 657
1961	71 689	11 516	2 706	52 132	1 454	1 301	1 088	1 432
1962	74 586	11 643	2 593	53 790	1 842	1 103	2 171	1 384
1963	93 151	11 736	3 553	69 069	2 611	1 779	2 431	1 692
1964	112 606	12 565	6 121	82 798	2 467	2 257	3 874	2 303
1965	146 758	15 143	11 215	108 285	3 420	2 471	3 196	2 711
1966	194 743	17 514	13 835	148 410	4 357	2 604	3 661	4 057
1967	222 876	19 038	20 740	159 979	9 004	3 090	4 608	6 168
1968	183 974	20 422	21 686	120 702	8 129	2 693	5 204	4 815
1969	161 531	22 785	23 319	88 363	13 908	4 767	3 297	4 411
1970	147 713	24 424	21 170	75 609	13 371	4 943	2 863	4 385
1971	121 900	24 366	22 171	52 031	11 653	5 058	2 841	2 902
1972	122 006	22 618	23 325	51 293	9 218	4 309	8 308	2 143
1973	184 200	25 242	43 193	71 883	20 704	11 057	8 307	2 671
1974	218 465	26 541	50 566	88 694	25 276	12 528	10 450	2 594
1975	187 881	20 155	47 382	72 898	19 483	13 270	9 867	2 174
1976	149 429	17 315	44 328	49 903	16 198	10 628	7 752	1 886
1977	114 914	12 888	31 368	40 748	13 187	7 840	6 372	1 545
1978	86 313	9 945	24 007	30 075	9 240	6 782	4 261	1 233
1979	112 096	9 617	50 540	32 858	7 060	5 898	3 958	1 395
1980	143 117	9 926	71 602	41 168	8 141	5 433	4 330	2 497
1981	128 618	10 559	48 831	46 299	9 625	6 163	4 889	2 253
1982	121 147	9 360	41 686	46 156	10 317	6 871	4 513	2 119
1983	89 157	7 381	36 906	24 312	10 864	4 816	3 659	1 213
1984	88 239	6 922	41 920	20 901	9 706	4 085	3 552	1 151
1985	84 302	6 669	38 597	18 859	11 143	4 356	3 545	1 128
1986	99 219	7 275	41 600	22 709	14 947	6 686	4 770	1 227
1987	152 098	7 967	67 337	37 563	18 100	10 801	8 501	1 827
1988	161 929	6 537	81 136	40 689	15 108	7 255	9 380	1 822
1989	192 001	6 931	93 261	52 105	16 764	8 685	12 199	2 041
1990	213 334	6 057	111 195	51 667	19 459	8 888	13 426	2 642
1991	230 781	20 001[4]	119 955	48 055	12 922	10 582	16 087	3 135[5]

Source: *Immigration Canada*

(1) By country of last permanent residence. (2) Includes China and Hong Kong. (3) Includes Central America, Greenland and St. Pierre & Miquelon for 1956–76. (4) Includes Central America. (5) Includes Autralasia.

Popular Destinations

*A*ccording to the 1991 census, nearly one resident in four in Ontario and British Columbia has immigrated to Canada, and 33.8% of Canada's immigrants live in Toronto. Those figures translate into an immigrant population of 1,468,620 for the city and its surrounding area in 1991.

Toronto's share of immigrants has been rising steadily in the past decade—in the 1981 census, 29.4% of immigrants called the city home. Overall, Toronto's immigrants are predominantly from Italy, Jamaica, Portugal and the United Kingdom, however in the 10-year period since 1981, arrivals have more often been from China, Hong Kong, India and Poland.

In the 1991 census the five Canadian cities with the highest percentage of immigrants were Toronto, Vancouver, Hamilton, Kitchener and Windsor. The province of Ontario claimed 55% of immigrants to the country, by far the highest proportion; British Columbia came in second place with 17%.

Immigration by Province of Intended Destination

	Total immigrants[1]	Nfld	PEI	NS	NB	Que	Ont	Man	Sask	Alta	BC	YK	NWT
1956 ...	164 857	426	112	1 639	852	31 396	90 662	5 796	2 202	9 959	17 812	n.a.	n.a.
1960 ...	104 111	306	83	1 210	634	23 774	54 491	4 337	2 087	6 949	10 120	n.a.	n.a.
1965 ...	146 758	604	137	1 612	1 074	30 346	79 702	3 948	2 649	8 049	18 502	n.a.	n.a.
1970 ...	147 713	630	185	2 007	1 070	23 261	80 732	5 826	1 709	10 405	21 683	n.a.	n.a.
1975 ...	187 881	1106	235	2 124	2 093	28 042	98 471	7 134	2 837	16 277	29 272	n.a.	n.a.
1980 ...	143 117	541	190	1 616	1 207	22 538	62 257	7 683	3 603	18 839	24 437	n.a.	n.a.
1981 ...	128 618	483	128	1 405	990	21 182	55 032	5 370	2 402	19 330	22 095	n.a.	n.a.
1982 ...	121147	406	165	1 256	751	21 336	53 049	4 931	2 125	17 949	18 999	n.a.	n.a.
1983 ...	89 157	275	105	833	554	16 374	40 036	3 978	1 735	10 688	14 447	n.a.	n.a.
1984 ...	88 239	299	109	1 034	600	14 641	41 527	3 903	2 150	10 670	13 190	n.a.	n.a.
1985 ...	84 302	325	113	974	609	14 884	40 730	3 415	1 905	9 001	12 239	n.a.	n.a.
1986 ...	99 219	274	168	1 097	641	19 459	49 630	3 749	1 860	9 673	12 552	49	67
1987 ...	152 098	458	159	1 227	642	26 822	84 807	4 799	2 119	11 975	18 913	80	72
1988 ...	161 929	408	153	1 299	679	25 789	88 996	5 009	2 223	14 025	23 204	68	76
1989 ...	192 001	468	159	1 473	905	34 171	104 799	6 138	2 142	16 211	25 335	100	100
1990 ...	214 230	546	176	1 563	842	40 842	113 438	6 637	2 361	18 994	28 723	83	75
1991 ...	230 781	641	150	1 504	684	51 707	118 782	5 646	2 451	16 985	32 023	84	124
1992 ...	248 199	791	152	2 332	748	47 532	136 215	4 979	2 448	17 310	35 458	123	111

Source: *Immigration Canada*

Persons Granted Canadian Citizenship, 1920–1991[1]

1920	3 004	**1944**	12 827	**1968**	60 055
1921	10 507	**1945**	13 562	**1969**	59 900
1922	10 360	**1946**	9 047	**1970**	57 556
1923	7 589	**1947**	15 335	**1971**	63 669
1924	7 659	**1948**	11 410	**1972**	80 866
1925	13 288	**1949**	11 991[2]	**1973**	104 697
1926	15 403	**1950**	10 441	**1974**	130 278
1927	16 917	**1951**	10 301	**1975**	137 507
1928	13 466	**1952**	10 888	**1976**	117 276
1929	13 099	**1953**	13 562	**1977**	123 655
1930	21 221	**1954**	19 545	**1978**	223 214
1931	21 392	**1955**	58 711	**1979**	156 699
1932	32 517	**1956**	55 404	**1980**	118 590
1933	23 613	**1957**	95 462	**1981**	94 457
1934	21 908	**1958**	84 183	**1982**	87 468
1935	20 903	**1959**	71 280	**1983**	90 328
1936	30 679	**1960**	62 378	**1984**	109 504
1937	31 744	**1961**	56 476	**1985**	126 466
1938	27 455	**1962**	72 082	**1986**	103 800
1939	21 418	**1963**	69 468	**1987**	73 638
1940	18 207	**1964**	64 334	**1988**	58 810
1941	15 594	**1965**	63 844	**1989**	87 478
1942	14 213	**1966**	60 852	**1990**	104 267
1943	12 533	**1967**	59 968	**1991**	118 630

Source: *Multiculturalism and Citizenship Canada*

(1) For fiscal year ending Mar 31 for 1920 to 1951; calendar years 1952 onwards. (2) Does not include approx 359,000 Newfoundlanders who became Canadian citizens when Newfoundland became Canada's 10th province in 1949.

Refugees[1] to Canada, 1959–92

1959	3 047	1968	820	1977	1 061	1986	18 625
1960	2 329	1969	799	1978	775	1987	20 673
1961	1 813	1970	1 387	1979	27 740	1988	25 716
1962	1 733	1971	626	1980	40 361	1989	34 349
1963	2 024	1972	365	1981	14 996	1990	39 689
1964	2 279	1973	405	1982	16 908	1991	53 401
1965	2 131	1974	537	1983	13 643	1992	51 843
1966	2 058	1975	748	1984	15 400		
1967	1 499	1976	1 014	1985	16 550		

Source: *Immigration Canada*

(1) Represents total number of refugees admitted to Canada from abroad as Convention Refugees or members of Designated Classes and those admitted on the strength of Minister's Permits (who have been selected from abroad on an emergency basis and are not granted permanent residence on arrival but are allowed to remain in Canada for up to one year and may apply for permanent residence after arrival). Excludes Special Humanitarian Movements. (2) Up to March.

Refugees to Canada by Country[1]

	1980	1985	1986	1987	1988	1989	1992
Total Refugees	40 348	16 760	19 147	21 565	26 836	37 004	51 843
Eastern Europe	4 062	3 897	5 388	6 843	9 701	15 866	3 220
Czechoslovakia	1 015	764	697	762	725	830	146
Hungary	296	516	545	562	1 076	772	226
Poland	477	2 209	3 620	4 545	6 801	12 393	4 869
Romania	307	334	442	832	733	821	598
USSR	1 914	39	40	100	348	966	887
Indochina	34 637	6 163	6 065	5 874	6 952	9 018	9 017
Cambodia	3 261	1 593	1 665	1 546	1 492	1 992	—
Laos	6 264	360	617	438	823	648	50
Vietnam	25 112	4 210	3 783	3 890	4 637	6 378	2 266
Middle East	37	1 150	1 139	1 208	2 488	3 019	8 464
Iran	16	819	874	994	1 919	1 993	4 322
Iraq	5	294	183	130	443	797	1 518
Lebanon	10	16	26	30	32	81	1 829
Africa	191	1 061	1 249	1 436	2 269	3 197	9 607
Ethiopia	72	709	905	869	1 429	2 136	1 584
Ghana	—	51	38	29	61	76	1 262
Nigeria	2	1	5	13	10	10	204
Somalia	6	28	35	70	201	399	4 697
South Africa	16	17	53	34	40	30	79
Sudan	9	20	19	77	35	91	511
Uganda	3	113	54	73	117	93	147
Central America[3]	308	3 629	3 934	4 006	3 516	3 587	7 544
Cuba	293	55	41	20	5		97
El Salvador	1	2 491	2 459	2 368	2 091	2 263	4 004
Guatemala	2	546	710	549	391	462	1 193
Haiti	8	14	6	10	18	58	259
Honduras	—	50	39	25	32	132	462
Nicaragua	3	451	670	955	884	591	688
South America	396	289	407	492	335	430	1 823
Argentina	21	27	9	3	4	12	351
Chile	355	133	182	320	259	334	447
Guyana	1	83	154	104	35	35	123
Uruguay	14	26	22	8	5	15	124
Other	717	571	965	1 706	1 575	1 887	12 168
Afghanistan	7	346	539	801	960	1 003	895
Sri Lanka	1	123	265	599	206	230	7 965

Source: *Immigration Canada*

(1) By country of last permanent residence. Represents total number of refugees admitted to Canada from abroad as Convention Refugees or members of Designated Classes. Excludes Special Humanitarian Movements. (2) Preliminary figures. (3) Includes the Caribbean and Mexico. (—) = zero.

Special Refugee and Humanitarian Movements, 1947–92

1947–52	Post-War European Movement	186 150
1956–57	Hungarian Movement	37 149
1968–69	Czechoslovakian Movement	11 943
1970	Tibetans	228
1972–73	Ugandan Asians	7 069
1973–79	Special South American Program	7 016
1975	Cypriots	700
1975–78	Special Vietnamese/Cambodian Program	9 060
1976	Kurds from Iraq	98
1976–79	Lebanese Movement	11 321
1978–84	Argentine Political Detainee Program	9
1982–85	Polish Special Movement	9 365
1982—present	Iranian Special Movement	7 604[1]
1982—present	El Salvadoran Special Movement	6 370[1]
1983—present	Lebanese Special Movement	12 108[1]
1983—present	Sri Lankan Special Movement	10 843[1]
1984—present	Guatemalan Special Movement	2 405[1]
1992—present	Special Measures for Citizens of the Former Yugoslavia	1 334[2]

Source: *Immigration Canada*

(1) Figure represents preliminary total up to end of Dec. 1992. (2) Applications received affecting 9,800 people.

Where Canadians Move Within Canada

When Canadians move from one province to another, it tends to be directly related to economic conditions. This was most apparent from 1976–1981 when the resource boom in Alberta caused a large influx there from other provinces. But falling international oil prices in the early 1980s led to a reversal of this trend as Canadians moved east, especially to Ontario. In recent years, those moving to another province have tended to head to British Columbia.

The following table shows net interprovincial migration—the number of persons moving into a province minus the number of persons moving out of that province.

	Nfld	PEI	NS	NB	Que	Ont	Man	Sask	Alta	BC	YK	NWT
1956–61	-4 671	-1 099	-15 295	-5 270	-7 756	34 345	-15 957	-33 557	16 787	33 230	n.a.	n.a.
1961–66	-15 213	-2 969	-27 124	-25 680	-19 859	85 369	-23 471	-42 094	-1 983	77 747	n.a.	n.a.
1966–71	-19 344	-2 763	-16 396	-19 599	-122 736	150 712	-40 690	-81 399	32 005	114 964	n.a.	n.a.
1971–76	-1 857	3 754	11 307	16 801	-77 610	-38 560	-26 827	-40 752	58 571	92 285	988	1 900
1976–81	-18 983	- 829	-7 140	-10 351	-156 496	-57 826	-42 218	-9 716	186 364	122 625	-933	-4 497
1981–86	-15 051	751	6 895	-65	-81 254	121 767	-2 634	-2 974	-31 676	7 382	-2 775	-366
1986–91	-15 971	-771	-2 117	-5 246	-40 382	72 318	-36 454	-66 079	-41 438	138 860	1 219	-3 999
1992	-3 626	504	-2 132	-1 890	-15 497	-2 956	-6 513	-8 472	-1 278	41 240	1 232	-612

Source: *Statistics Canada*

Country of Origin in 1992

*P*reliminary statistics for immigration totals in 1992 show that the 248,199 newcomers to Canada came from:

Africa/Middle East	41,198
Asia/Pacific	118,354
Great Britain	6,931
Europe	37,166
South and Central America	37,395
United States	7,155

Canadian Emigration by Province

(number of persons moving from Canada)

	Canada[1]	Nfld	PEI	NS	NB	Que	Ont	Man	Sask	Alta	BC	YK	NWT
1961–66	432 100	10 971	2 436	17 172	13 972	124 877	147 896	21 595	21 378	31 972	38 934	n.a.	n.a.
1966–71	472 400	13 901	2 390	17 549	20 517	144 078	179 523	15 330	15 907	23 974	38 127	n.a.	n.a.
1971–76	357 200	3 501	393	4 857	3 358	82 085	163 312	12 501	9 073	26 254	51 866	n.a.	n.a.
1976–81	278 641	3 551	921	8 967	7 027	43 439	127 740	11 311	6 548	34 012	33 969	n.a.	n.a.
1981–82	45 338	261	48	432	874	6 963	21 184	1 570	780	6 769	6 374	n.a.	n.a.
1982–83	50 249	372	78	373	708	8 402	23 448	1 487	842	7 315	7 125	n.a.	n.a.
1983–84	48 826	253	87	398	665	8 146	22 319	1 745	954	7 200	6 981	n.a.	n.a.
1984–85	46 252	332	71	350	612	7 203	21 916	1 255	837	6 214	7 389	n.a.	n.a.
1985–86	44 816	245	66	371	710	6 141	22 385	1 299	936	5 677	6 893	n.a.	n.a.
1981–86	235 481	1 463	350	1 924	3 569	36 855	111 252	7 356	4 349	33 175	34 762	n.a.	n.a.
1986–87	51 040	496	62	541	867	6 408	24 849	1 833	805	7 434	7 640	n.a.	n.a.
1987–88	40 528	268	44	400	708	4 778	19 733	1 692	886	6 247	5 704	n.a.	n.a.
1988–89	37 437	178	32	404	749	4 542	18 224	2 027	810	5 324	5 006	n.a.	n.a.
1989–90	37 915	216	56	359	735	4 269	18 459	1 717	854	5 988	5 170	n.a.	n.a.
1990–91	39 236	174	57	440	748	4 760	19 101	2 107	844	5 619	5 296	n.a.	n.a.
1986–91	206 156	1 332	251	2 144	3 807	24 757	100 366	9 376	4 199	30 612	28 816	n.a.	n.a.
1991	43 125	280	94	873	768	5 902	18 451	1 945	775	7 682	6 231	69	51
1992	44 275	293	95	892	791	6 063	18 948	1 977	801	7890	6 408	67	50

Source: *Statistics Canada*
(n.a.) not available.

POPULATION GROUPS

Native Population of Canada

	1986				1991			
	Total Native Population[2]	Native Indian	Métis	Inuit	Total Population with Aboriginal Origins[1]	Native Indian	Métis	Inuit
Canada	711 725	548 945	151 605	36 460	1 002 675	783 980	212 650	49 255
Newfoundland	9 555	4 695	1 435	4 120	13 110	5 845	1 605	6 460
Prince Edward Island	1 290	1 115	160	30	1 880	1 665	185	75
Nova Scotia	14 225	13 060	1 110	315	21 885	19 950	1 590	770
New Brunswick	9 375	8 700	750	185	12 815	11 835	975	450
Quebec	80 945	68 585	11 435	7 360	137 615	112 590	19 480	8 480
Ontario	167 375	150 715	18 265	2 955	243 550	220 135	26 905	5 250
Manitoba	85 235	55 960	33 285	700	116 200	76 370	45 575	900
Saskatchewan	77 650	55 215	25 695	190	96 580	69 385	32 840	540
Alberta	103 925	68 965	40 125	1 125	148 220	99 650	56 310	2 825
British Columbia	126 625	112 790	15 295	1 035	169 035	149 570	22 295	1 990
Yukon	4 995	4775	220	65	6 390	5 870	565	170
Northwest Territories	30 530	9 380	3 825	18 360	35 390	11 100	4 310	21 355

Source: *Statistics Canada*

(1) The 1991 census question on ethnic or cultural origins gathered information on the number of people who reported North American Indian, Métis or Inuit origin as either a single response or in combination with other origins. (2) Census years previous to 1991 were marked by boycotts by aboriginal peoples; 1986 excluded approximately 45,000 individuals living on incompletely enumerated native reserves and settlements.

Status Indian Population[1], 1992

	Total Indian Population	On Reserve	Off Reserve	On Crown Land	Number of Bands
Canada	533 451	295 032	217 798	20 631	604
Atlantic Provinces	20 584	14 031	6 645	8	31
Quebec	52 582	36 138	15 347	1 077	39
Ontario	121 867	61 225	58 445	2 197	126
Manitoba	80 845	51 760	26 606	1 479	61
Saskatchewan	81 700	42 008	38 271	1 421	70
Alberta	66 065	41 094	22 811	2 160	43
British Columbia	90 769	48 106	42 360	303	196
Yukon	6 628	465	3 508	2 655	16
NWT	12 341	205	2 805	9 331	22

Source: *Dept. of Indian and Northern Affairs*

(1) Status Indians are those settled on reserves registered with the Department of Indian and Northern Affairs under the provisions of the Indian Act. (2) Total number of reserves is 2 284, but only 842 are inhabited.

Largest Native Bands in Canada

Band, Province	Population[1]	Band, Province	Population[1]
Six Nations of the Grand River, Ont.[2]	17 132	Fort Alexander, Man.	4 477
Kahnawake, Que.	7 659	Samson, Alta.	4 389
Mohawks of Akwesasne, Ont.	7 521	Cross Lake, Man.	4 232
Blood, Alta.	7 517	Norway House, Man.	4 212
Saddle Lake, Alta.	6 181	Siksika Nation, Alta.	4 197
Mohawks of the Bay of Quinte[3]	5 513	Bigstone Cree, Alta.	3 941
Lac La Ronge, Sask.	5 298	Onyota'a:ka, Ont.	3 864
Peguis, Man.	5 212	Montagnais du Lac St. Jean, Que.	3 815
Wikwemikong, Ont.	5 164	Sandy Bay, Man.	3 427
Peter Ballantyne, Sask.	4 842	Mistassini, Que.	2 919

Source: *Indian and Northern Affairs, Canada*

(1) As of Dec. 31, 1992. (2) This band consists of the following 13 groups: The Bay of Quinte Mohawks, Bearfoot Onondaga, Deleware, Konadaha Seneca, Lower Cayuga, Lower Mohawk, Niharondasa Seneca, Oneida, Onondaga Clear Sky, Tuscarora, Upper Cayuga, Upper Mohawk and Walker Mohawk. (3) This band is not part of the Six Nations of the Grand River.

Aboriginal Ancestry

The 1991 census marked the end of a series of census boycotts by Canada's native people and saw a 41% increase in the number of people acknowledging aboriginal ancestry as a result. Just over a million Canadians, or 3.7% of the total population claimed aboriginal ancestry, up from 2.8% in 1986.

The 1991 census marked the first time that people with aboriginal backgrounds were asked if they identified with their native ancestry and the data that has resulted has enabled demographers to better identify the characteristics of the aboriginal population. Those characteristics are in some cases very different from the non-aboriginal population, showing only 6 to 7% of the population over the age of 55, in marked contrast to 20% in that age group for Canada's total population. On the other hand, 38% of the aboriginal population is under the age of 15, compared with 21% of population in general.

Population by Official Languages

(percentage distribution)

	1961			1981			1991		
	English[1]	French[1]	Bilingual[2]	English[1]	French[1]	Bilingual[2]	English[1]	French[1]	Bilingual[2]
Canada	**67.4**	**19.1**	**12.2**	**67.0**	**16.6**	**15.3**	**67.1**	**15.2**	**16.3**
Newfoundland	98.5	0.1	1.2	97.6	...	2.3	96.5	.04	3.3
Prince Edward Island	91.1	1.2	7.6	91.7	0.2	8.1	89.6	.2	10.1
Nova Scotia	92.9	0.8	6.1	92.3	0.2	7.4	91.1	.02	8.6
New Brunswick	62.0	18.7	19.0	60.5	13.0	26.5	57.9	12.5	29.5
Quebec	11.6	61.9	25.5	6.7	60.1	32.4	5.5	58.0	35.4
Ontario	89.0	1.5	7.9	86.7	0.7	10.8	86.1	.5	11.4
Manitoba	89.6	0.9	7.4	90.3	0.3	7.9	89.4	.2	9.2
Saskatchewan	93.6	0.4	4.5	94.6	0.1	4.6	94.2	.05	5.2
Alberta	94.1	0.4	4.3	92.4	0.2	6.4	92.1	.1	6.6
British Columbia	95.3	0.2	3.5	92.8	0.1	5.7	91.6	.04	6.4
Yukon	93.5	0.3	5.6	91.9	...	7.9	90.5	.09	9.3
Northwest Territories	58.9	0.5	7.0	79.9	0.1	6.0	85.1	.1	6.1

Source: *Census of Canada*

(1) Refers to persons who speak either English or French, but not both. (2) Refers to persons who speak both English and French.
(...) = too small to be included.

Canadian Population by Mother Tongue[1]

(thousands of persons and percent of total population)

	1941	%	1951	%	1961	%	1971	%	1981	%	1991	%
English	6 448	56.0	8 281	59.1	10 661	58.5	12 974	60.2	14 918	61.3	16 170	60.0
French	3 355	29.2	4 069	29.0	5 123	28.1	5 794	26.9	6 249	25.7	6 503	24.1
Italian	80	0.7	92	0.7	340	1.9	538	2.5	529	2.2	511	1.9
German	322	2.8	329	2.3	564	3.1	561	2.6	523	2.2	466	1.7
Chinese	34	0.3	28	0.2	49	0.3	95	0.4	224	0.9	499	1.8
Ukrainian	313	2.7	352	2.5	361	2.0	310	1.4	292	1.2	187	.7
Portuguese	n.a.	n.a.	n.a.	n.a.	18	0.1	87	0.4	166	0.7	212	.8
Dutch	53	0.5	88	0.6	170	0.9	145	0.7	157	0.6	139	.5
Polish	129	1.1	129	0.9	162	0.9	135	0.6	128	0.5	190	.7
Greek	9	0.1	8	0.1	40	0.2	104	0.5	123	0.5	126	.5
Spanish	1		2		7	...	24	0.1	70	0.3	177	.7
Indo-Iranian	...	...	2	...	5	...	33	0.2	117	0.5	301	1.1
Aboriginal	131	1.1	166	1.2	167	0.9	180	0.9	146	0.6	173	.6
Hungarian	46	0.4	42	0.3	86	0.5	87	0.4	84	0.3	80	.3
Vietnamese	n.a.	n.a.	n.a.	n.a.	n.a.	n.a.	n.a.	n.a.	30	0.1	79	.3
Arabic	8	0.1	5	...	13	0.1	29	0.1	50	0.2	108	.4
Finnish	37	0.3	32	0.2	45	0.2	37	0.2	33	0.1	28	.1
Russian	52	0.5	39	0.3	43	0.2	32	0.1	31	0.1	35	.1
Yiddish	130	1.1	104	0.7	82	0.4	50	0.2	33	0.1	25	.09
Czech[2]	38	0.3	46	0.3	51	0.3	45	0.2	43	0.2	27	.09
Danish	19	0.2	16	0.1	35	0.2	27	0.1	26	0.1	22	.08
Japanese	22	0.2	18	0.1	18	0.1	17	0.1	20	0.1	30	.1
Armenian	n.a.	n.a.	n.a.	n.a.	n.a.	n.a.	n.a.	n.a.	17	0.1	26	.1
Norwegian	60	0.5	44	0.3	40	0.2	27	0.1	19	0.1	13	.05
Swedish	50	0.4	36	0.3	33	0.2	22	0.1	17	0.1	12	.04

Source: *Census of Canada*

(1) The language first spoken in childhood and still understood. (2) Includes Slovak.

(n.a.) not available. (...) = too small to be included.

Canadian Population by Religious Denominations

(thousands of persons)

	1941	%	1951	%	1961	%	1971	%	1981	%	1991	%
Total population	11 507	100.0	14 009	100.0	18 238	100.0	21 568	1 00 0	24 083	100.0	26 994	100.0
Adventist	18	0.2	21	0.1	26	0.1	29	0.1	42	0.2	52	.2
Anglican	1 754	15.2	2 061	14.7	2 409	13.2	2 543	11. 8	2 436	10.1	2 188	8.1
Bahai	n.a.	n.a.	n.a.	n.a.	n.a.	n.a.	n.a.	n.a.	8	...	15	.1
Baptist	484	4.2	520	3.7	594	3.3	667	3.1	697	2.9	663	2.5
Buddhist	16	0.1	8	0.1	12	0.1	16	0.1	52	0.2	163	.6
Christian and Missionary Alliance	4	...	6	...	18	0.1	24	0.1	34	0.1	59	.2
Christian Reformed[1]	n.a.	n.a.	n.a.	n.a.	62	0.3	83	0.4	77	0.3	85	.3
Churches of Christ, Disciples	21	0.2	15	0.1	20	0.1	16	0.1	15	0.1	18	.1
Confucian	22	0.2	6	...	5	...	2	...	n.a.	n.a.	.4	...
Doukhobor	17	0.1	13	0.1	13	0.1	9	...	7	...	5	...
Free Methodist	9	0.1	9	0.1	14	0.1	19	0.1	12	0.1	15	.1
Greek Orthodox	140	1.2	172	1.2	240	1.3	317	1.5	315	1.3	232	.9
Hindu	n.a.	n.a.	n.a.	n.a.	n.a.	n.a.	n.a.	n.a	.70	0.3	157	.6
Hutterite[2]	n.a.	n.a.	n.a.	n.a.	n.a.	n.a.	14	0.1	1 7	0.1	22	.1
Islam	n.a.	n.a.	n.a.	n.a.	n.a.	n.a.	n.a.	n.a.	98	0	253	.9
Jehovah's Witnesses	7	0.1	35	0.2	68	0.4	175	0.8	143	0. 6	168	.6
Jewish	169	1.5	205	1.5	254	1.4	276	1.3	296	1.2	318	1.2
Latter Day Saints	25	0.2	33	0.2	50	0.3	67	0.3	90	0.4	101	.4
Lutheran	402	3.5	445	3.2	663	3.6	716	3.3	703	2.9	636	2.4
Mennonite[3]	112	1.0	126	0.9	152	0.8	168	0.8	189	0.8	208	.8
Pentecostal	58	0.5	95	0.7	144	0.8	220	1.0	339	1.4	436	1.6
Presbyterian	831	7.2	782	5.6	819	4.5	872	4.0	812	3.4	636	2.4
Roman Catholic	4 806	41.8	6 069	43.3	8 343	45.7	9 975	46.2	11 210	46.5	12 204	45.2
Salvation Army	34	0.3	70	0.5	92	0.5	120	0.6	125	0.5	112	.4
Sikh	n.a.	n.a.	n.a.	n.a.	n.a.	n.a.	n.a.	n.a.	68	0.3	147	.5
Ukrainian Catholic[4]	186	1.6	191	1.4	190	1.0	228	1.1	191	0.8	128	.5
Unitarian	6	0.1	4	...	15	0.1	21	0.1	15	0.1	17	.1
United Church[5]	2 209	19.2	2 867	20.5	3 664	20.1	3 769	17. 5	3 758	15.6	3 093	11.5
No religion	19	0.2	60	0.4	95	0.5	930	4.3	1 752	7.3	3 386	12.5

Source: *Census of Canada.*

(1) Included with United Church 1931–1951. (2) Included with Mennonite 1931–61. (3) Includes Hutterite 1931–1961. (4) Includes Greek Catholic 1931–71. (5) Includes Christian Reformed 1931–1951. (...) = too small to be included; n.a. not available.

Reinventing the Family

*T**he structure of the Canadian family has undergone dramatic changes in the last 20 years. In the 1991 census, only 48% of families consisted of a married couple and their unmarried children—the first time the number has fallen below 50%. (In the 1981 census, the figure was 55%.) However, analysts were quick to point out that when 296,000 families with common-law spouses were added to the total, the number of two-parent families was back up to 52%.*

The change in the family's composition is a reflection of the variety of options open to Canadians, particularly women. More and more women are participating in the workforce and more effective birth control enables couples to either delay parenthood or remain childless. Fourteen percent of 1991 families were childless; families that did have children had fewer than families of previous generations. The number of women between 25 and 29 who either were or had been married but remained childless was 38%; in the 1971 census, that number stood at 21%. For married or formerly married women in the 35-39 age group, 13% had remained childless, while the 1971 census reported only 7% in the same category.

EDUCATION

Enrolment in Canadian Schools, 1992–93[1]

The number of students in Canadian schools increased for the 1992–93 school year, continuing a recent trend. The number of elementary and secondary students rose by approximately 51 500 Canada-wide, with the largest increases coming in Ontario, Alberta and British Columbia.

The gradual increase follows a sharp enrolment decline during the 1970s and early 1980s. Community college and university enrolment also increased in 1992-93.

	Elementary and Secondary[2]		Community Colleges		Universities	
	Enrolment[3]	Schools	Enrolment[3]	Schools	Enrolment[3]	Schools
Canada	5 287 730[4]	16 063	348 400	203	572 900	69
Newfoundland	123 170	508	4 250	12	13 200	1
Prince Edward Island ...	24 960	74	1 250	2	2 740	1
Nova Scotia	168 790	527	2 750	10	30 000	12
New Brunswick	141 650	450	3 450	8	19 000	5
Quebec	1 150 190	2 947	165 900	89	134 800	8
Ontario	2 085 320	5 804	105 700	32	233 700	22
Manitoba	220 040	852	4 240	10	21 160	6
Saskatchewan	207 500	957	3 500	1	23 100	3
Alberta	534 410	1 832	26 500	18	49 000	5
British Columbia	606 800	1 995	30 100	19	46 200	6
Yukon	5 700	29	260	1	—	—
Northwest Territories	15 900	80	500	1	—	—

Source: *Statistics Canada*

(1) Estimates. (2) Includes public, private and federal schools and schools for the blind and deaf. (3) Full-time. (4) Includes 3,300 overseas students (Dept. of National Defence). (—) = zero.

Educational Attainment[1] in Canada

(percentages)

	1971		1981		1991	
	Males	Females	Males	Females	Males	Females
Less than grade 9	33.2	31.4	20.8	20.6	13.6	14.2
High school	43.5	48.2	41.8	45.4	56.2	57.6
Some post-secondary	16.7	17.5	27.5	27.8	31.0	32.4
University degree	6.6	3.0	9.9	6.2	12.8	9.9
Bachelor	4.9	2.6	7.7	5.3	8.5	7.3
Master's or doctorate	1.7	0.4	2.2	0.8	4.3	1.5
Total Population[1] (000s)	7 474	7 579	9 152	9 458	10 422	10 883

Source: *Census of Canada*

(1) Population 15 years and over.

Where the Jobs Will Be

*I*t is expected that during the 1990s, 1.5 million new jobs will be created in Canada. The areas where the economy will grow are in computers and semi-conductors, pharmaceuticals and health-related fields, communications and telecommunications and the manufacture and use of environmental, weather and industrial measuring devices.

Education Spending[1] in Canada

(millions of dollars)

	1960	1965	1970	1975	1980	1985	1990	1993[2]
Canada[3]	1 706	3 400	6 624	11 061	19 975	32 116	44 170	54 170
Newfoundland	23	41	104	234	411	658	977	1 113
Prince Edward Island	6	11	26	53	85	127	178	216
Nova Scotia	57	103	230	363	629	1 027	1 389	1 538
New Brunswick	43	73	172	261	464	808	1 108	1 313
Quebec	448	981	1 700	3 222	6 114	8 863	10 757	13 444
Ontario	609	1 239	2 669	3 995	6 883	10 988	16 641	20 486
Manitoba	81	147	272	467	760	1 333	1 840	2 153
Saskatchewan	95	155	262	399	722	1 296	1 699	1 956
Alberta	157	285	,535	875	1 712	3 370	4 439	4 941
British Columbia	166	313	561	1 042	1 931	3 140	4 497	6 186
Yukon and NWT	n.a.	n.a.	n.a.	n.a.	n.a.	n.a.	655	735

Source: *Statistics Canada*

(1) From all sources of funding for academic years ending in the spring. (2) Estimates. (3) Provinces may not add up to Canadian total due to overseas and undistributed funds.

French Immersion Enrolment in Canada

French Immersion programs, through which non-francophone students take most or all of their subjects in French, have become increasingly popular in Canadian schools over the past decade. Most school boards offer early immersion (beginning in kindergarten) or middle immersion (usually starting in Grade 4). The goal of the program is to make students bilingual.

	1980–81		1986–86		1990–91	
	No. of Fr. Imm. Students	% of Total Enrolment[2]	No. of Fr. Imm. Students	% of Total Enrolment[2]	No. of Fr. Imm. Students	% of Total Enrolment[2]
Canada[1]	64 761	1.9	162 339	4.3	249 523	4.7
Newfoundland	392	0.3	2 015	1.4	4 269	3.5
Prince Edward Island	1 280	4.7	2 492	9.9	3 371	13.5
Nova Scotia	590	0.3	1 859	1.1	5 286	3.1
New Brunswick	5 532	3.6	14 530	10.1	16 693	11.8
Ontario	46 638	2.4	87 819	4.7	133 906	6.4
Manitoba	4 286	1.9	12 581	5.7	19 604	8.9
Saskatchewan	1 603	0.7	5 965	2.8	10 713	5.2
Alberta	n.a.	n.a.	19 017	4.1	26 924	5.0
British Columbia	4 368	0.8	15 590	3.0	27 984	4.6
Yukon	35	0.7	247	5.4	369	6.5
Northwest Territories	37	0.3	224	1.7	404	2.5

Source: *Statistics Canada*

(1) Includes elementary and secondary. (2) Excludes Quebec and Dept. of National Defence Schools overseas. For 1980–81 only, also excludes Alberta for which data was not available. (n.a.) not available.

Education Attainment and Employment

*E*mployment and Immigration Canada predicts that over 50% of the jobs that will be created in the 1990s will be in high-tech and specialized fields, requiring workers to have more than 16 years of training. This signals a dramatic change from the requirements as recent as 1986, when only 23% of the labour force held jobs that needed that much education.

Demand for those in highly-skilled and engineering fields will accelerate again at the end of the decade as large numbers of senior staff will be ready to retire.

Reading and Numeracy Skills of Canadians, 1989

(percentage of adult population)

A national survey of 9,500 Canadians aged 16 to 69 was conducted in October 1989 to assess literacy and numeracy skills. Both were defined as "the information processing skills necessary to use the printed material commonly encountered at work, at home and in the community." A series of tests designed to simulate real life tasks was used in the testing.

For literacy, tasks ranged from locating a word in a document (such as locating the expiry date on a driver's licence) to tasks such as reading a chart to determine eligibility for a benefit. Four levels of reading skills were classified. At Level 1, readers had difficulty dealing with printed materials. Level 2s could use materials for limited purposes such as finding a familiar word in a simple text. Level 3s could use materials in a variety of situations if the material and the required tasks were simple and clearly laid out; level 4 readers could meet everyday reading demands. The results showed that 62% of adult

Canadians had reading abilities sufficient to deal with everyday requirements and that their skills would enable them to use written material to find out more. But 16%, or 2.9 million adults, did not have sufficient reading skills to deal with the demands of everyday life.

Numeracy skills were also tested with common documents and forms—a swimming pool schedule, a bank deposit slip and a catalogue order form. Level 1 indicated very limited abilities; at most, numbers could be located and recognized in isolation or a short text. Level 2s could perform simple numerical operations such as addition and subtraction; level 3s could perform simple sequences of numerical operations and meet everyday demands. Again, 62% of adult Canadians had numeracy skills sufficient to handle everyday tasks; 14% were at level 1 and 24% functioned at level 2.

	Reading Skills				Numeracy Skills			
	Pop. (000s)	Level 1[1] (lowest)	Level 2	Level 3	Level 4 (highest)	Pop.[2] (000s)	Level 1 (lowest)	Level 2	Level 3 (highest)
Canada	18 024	7%	9%	22%	62%	17 206	14%	24%	62%
Atlantic Provinces	1 546	6	13	30	52	1 497	25	26	52
Newfoundland	384	7	17	36	39	369	29	26	45
Prince Edward Island	85	n.a.	n.a.	n.a.	n.a.	79	n.a.	n.a.	n.a.
Nova Scotia	594	5[3]	10	28	57	581	21	23	56
New Brunswick	483	6	12	26	56	468	22	24	54
Quebec	4 721	6	13	25	57	4 577	19	27	54
Ontario	6 689	9	8	21	62	6 228	11	25	64
Prairies	2 984	4	7	19	70	2 888	10	22	68
Manitoba	703	5[3]	73	23	65	678	13[3]	26	61
Saskatchewan	632	3[3]	53	19	72	620	9[3]	26	66
Alberta	1 649	4	73	17	71	1 589	8[3]	20	72
British Columbia	2 084	5	7	19	69	2 015	9	22	69

Sources: *Statistics Canada; National Literacy Secretariat*

(1) Includes persons who reported having no skills in either English or French. (2) Excludes persons who reported having no reading skills in either English or French and those whose reading skills were too limited to undertake the main test items. (3) Figure less reliable due to high sampling variability. (n.a.) not available.

Reading, Writing and Working

*I*n an industrial society such as Canada's (and in our "new economy" that is rapidly evolving), the ability to gather information and process it is particularly important.

Reading and numeracy skills—that is, the ability to work with both text and numbers—are more important than ever before as employment opportunities in the service sector and high-tech fields become the order of the day. Jobs in business, finance, education and health care services will require reading skills on more than just the basic level. While the table above indicates that in 1989, 62% of Canadians could function at the highest level and meet everyday requirements, the 16% (nearly 3 million people) at levels 1 and 2 will find it increasingly difficult to find a place in the global job market.

University Degrees[1] Awarded in Canada: Male and Female

(percentage distribution)

	1970 Males	1970 Females	1980 Males	1980 Females	1985 Males	1985 Females	1990 Males	1990 Females
Total Degrees	61.7	38.3	50.4	49.6	48.1	51.9	44.3	55.7
Education	46.6	53.4	31.9	68.8	28.7	71.3	29.2	70.8
Fine Arts	40.6	59.4	35.3	64.7	35.7	64.3	34.3	65.7
Humanities	n.a.	n.a.	39.9	60.1	38.9	61.1	37.2	62.8
English	n.a.	n.a.	29.0	71.0	26.8	73.2	27.7	72.3
History	n.a.	n.a.	54.3	45.7	55.7	44.3	54.6	45.4
Journalism	43.2	56.8	33.5	66.5	33.7	66.3	37.1	62.9
Theology	74.3	25.7	64.7	35.3	62.8	37.2	55.1	44.9
Social Sciences	n.a.	n.a.	57.2	42.8	50.1	49.9	45.6	54.4
Commerce	93.5	6.5	72.1	27.9	59.1	40.9	54.1	45.9
Economics	n.a.	n.a.	75.4	24.6	65.7	34.3	67.5	32.5
Geography	n.a.	n.a.	63.2	36.8	60.3	39.7	62.3	37.7
Law	92.9	7.1	65.0	35.0	55.4	44.6	52.8	47.2
Political Science	n.a.	n.a.	65.0	35.0	61.5	38.5	56.3	43.7
Psychology	n.a.	n.a.	31.0	69.0	26.6	73.4	24.2	75.8
Social Work	55.9	44.1	25.5	74.5	20.5	79.5	17.3	82.7
Sociology	n.a.	n.a.	32.7	67.3	27.7	72.3	23.7	76.3
Biological Sciences	n.a.	n.a.	49.5	50.5	44.0	56.0	43.0	57.0
Agriculture	93.6	6.4	65.7	34.3	58.0	42.0	58.7	41.3
Biology	n.a.	n.a.	55.0	45.0	49.6	50.4	48.2	51.8
Veterinary Medicine	94.0	6.0	60.5	39.5	48.2	51.8	36.9	63.1
Applied Sciences	n.a.	n.a.	92.4	7.6	88.4	11.6	86.7	13.3
Architecture	92.6	7.4	59.6	20.4	73.0	27.0	69.2	30.8
Engineering	98.9	1.1	94.3	5.7	90.4	9.6	88.3	11.7
Chemical	n.a.	n.a.	86.9	13.1	78.8	21.2	73.4	26.6
Civil	n.a.	n.a.	93.4	6.6	88.6	11.4	87.6	12.4
Electrical	n.a.	n.a.	96.5	3.5	94.3	5.7	91.8	8.2
Mechanical	n.a.	n.a.	97.5	2.5	94.5	5.5	92.8	7.2
Forestry	97.8	2.2	87.4	12.6	79.5	20.5	83.5	16.5
Health Sciences	n.a.	n.a.	40.7	59.3	34.4	65.6	29.8	70.2
Dentistry	94.9	5.1	83.3	16.7	77.2	22.8	64.2	35.8
Medicine	89.7	10.3	66.4	33.6	59.0	41.0	54.1	45.9
Nursing	2.7	97.3	4.9	95.1	3.3	96.7	4.4	95.6
Rehabilitation	2.2	97.8	8.8	91.2	10.4	89.6	15.1	84.9
Pure Sciences	n.a.	n.a.	71.6	28.4	70.7	29.3	71.2	28.8
Chemistry	n.a.	n.a.	69.4	30.6	64.2	35.8	63.3	36.7
Computer Sciences	n.a.	n.a.	75.2	24.8	72.9	27.1	80.2	19.8
Geology	n.a.	n.a.	78.5	21.5	78.8	21.2	74.1	25.9
Mathematics	n.a.	n.a.	63.4	36.6	62.2	37.8	60.3	39.7
Physics	n.a.	n.a.	89.0	11.0	84.5	15.5	84.9	15.1

Source: *Statistics Canada*   (1) Bachelor's and first professional degrees. (n.a.) not available.

Careers in the Future

*I*n 1993, the labour shortages were in the fields of engineering—specifically design and development, electrical and electronic engineers. Other shortages were cited in the fields of occupational therapy, physiotherapy, and the environment as well as computer-related jobs such as database, programmer and systems analysts.

The Conference Board of Canada predicts growth until the year 2000 in the health care field as well, citing speech therapists, nurses, social workers, occupational and physiotherapists as among those who will be needed.

Canadian Universities

Acadia University: Wolfville, N.S. B0P 1X0

Athabaska University: P.O. Box 10 000, Athabaska, Alta. T0G 2R0

Atlantic School of Theology: 640 Francklyn St., Halifax, N.S. B3H 3B5

Augustana University College: 4901-46 Ave., Camrose, Alta. T4V 2R3

Bishop's University: Lennoxville, Que. J1M 1Z7

Brandon University: Brandon, Man. R7A 6A9

Brock University: St. Catharines, Ont. L2S 3A1

Carleton University: Ottawa, Ont. K1S 5B6

Collège universitaire de Saint-Boniface: 200, avenue de la Cathédrale, Saint-Boniface, Man. R2H 0H7

Concordia University: 1455 de Maisonneuve Blvd. W., Montreal, Que. H3G 1M8

Dalhousie University: Halifax, N.S. B3H 3J5

The King's College: 10766-97 St., Edmonton, Alta. T5H 2M1

Lakehead University: Thunder Bay, Ont. P7B 5E1

Laurentian University of Sudbury: Sudbury, Ont. P3E 2C6

McGill University: 845 Sherbrooke St. W., Montreal, Que. H3A 2T5

McMaster University: Hamilton, Ont. L8S 4L8

Memorial University of Newfoundland: St. John's, Nfld. A1C 5S7

Mount Allison University: Sackville, N.B. E0A 3C0

Mount Saint Vincent University: Halifax, N.S. B3M 2J6

Queen's University: Kingston, Ont. K7L 3N6

Royal Military College of Canada: Kingston, Ont. K7K 5L0

Royal Roads Military College: Victoria, B.C. V0S 1B0

Ryerson Polytechnical Institute: 350 Victoria St., Toronto, Ont. M5B 2K3

St. Francis Xavier University: Antigonish, N.S. B2G 1C0

Saint Mary's University: Halifax, N.S. B3H 3C3

St. Thomas University: Box 4569, Fredericton, N.B. E3B 5G3

Simon Fraser University: Burnaby, B.C. V5A 1S6

Technical University of Nova Scotia: Box 1000, Halifax, N.S. B3J 2X4

Trent University: Peterborough, Ont. K9J 7B8

Trinity Western University: 7600 Glover Rd., Langley, B.C. V3A 6H4

University College of Cape Breton: Box 5300, Sydney, N.S. B1P 6L2

Université Laval: Quebec, Que. G1K 7P4

Université Sainte Anne: Point-de-l'êglise, N.S. B0W 1M0

Université de Moncton: Moncton, N.B. E1A 3E9

Université de Montréal: C.P. 6128, Succ. A., Montreal, Que. H3C 3J7

Université de Sherbrooke: Sherbrooke, Que. J1K 2R1

Université du Québec: 2875, boul. Laurier, Sainte-Foy, Que. G1V 2M3

University of Alberta: Edmonton, Alta. T6G 2E2

University of British Columbia: 2075 Wesbrook Mall, Vancouver, B.C. V6T 1W5

University of Calgary: 2500 University Dr. NW, Calgary, Alta. T2N 1N4

University of Guelph: Guelph, Ont. N1G 2W1

University of King's College: Halifax, N.S. B3H 2A1

University of Lethbridge: 4401 University Dr., Lethbridge, Alta. T1K 3M4

University of Manitoba: Winnipeg, Man. R3T 2N2

University of New Brunswick: Box 4400, Fredericton, N.B. E3B 5A3

University of Ottawa: Ottawa, Ont. K1N 6N5

University of Prince Edward Island: Charlottetown, P.E.I. C1A 4P3

University of Regina: Regina, Sask. S4S 0A2

University of Saskatchewan: Saskatoon, Sask. S7N 0W0

University of Toronto: Toronto, Ont. M5S 1A1

University of Victoria: Box 1700, Victoria, B.C. V8W 2Y2

University of Waterloo: Waterloo, Ont. N2L 3G1

University of Western Ontario: London, Ont. N6A 3K7

University of Windsor: Windsor, Ont. N9B 3P4

University of Winnipeg: 515 Portage Ave., Winnipeg, Man. R3B 2E9

Wilfrid Laurier University: Waterloo, Ont. N2L 3C5

York University: 4700 Keele St., North York, Ont. M3J 1P3

Canadian Colleges

■ Atlantic Provinces

Avalon Community College: P.O. Box 800, Carbonear, Nfld. A0A 1T0

Cabot Institute of Applied Arts & Technology: P.O. Box 1693, St. John's, Nfld. A1C 5P7

Central Newfoundland Community College: P.O. Box 745, Grand Falls, Nfld. A2A 2M4

Cobatec Community College: 60 Lorne St., Truro, N.S. B2N 3K3

Eastern Community College: P.O. Box 400, Burin, Nfld. A0E 1E0

Fisher Institute of Applied Arts & Technology: P.O. Box 822, Corner Brook, Nfld. A2H 6H6

Holland College: 140 Weymouth St., Charlottetown, P.E.I. C1A 4Z1

Institute of Fisheries and Marine Technology: Box 4920, St. John's, Nfld. A1C 5R3

Kingstec Community College: P.O. Box 487, Kentville, N.S. B4N 3X3

Labrador Community College: P.O. Box 3013, Stn. B, Happy Valley-Goose Bay, Nfld. A0P 1E0

New Brunswick Community College:

    Bathurst: Box 1, Bathurst, N.B. E2A 3Z2

    Campbellton: P.O. Box 309, Campbellton, N.B. E3N 3G7

    Dieppe: P.O. Box 4519, Dieppe, N.B. E1A 6G1

    Edmundston: P.O. Box 70, Edmundston, N.B. E3V 3K7

    Grand-Sault: P.O. Box 1270, Grand Falls, N.B. E0J 1M0

    Miramichi: P.O. Box 1053, Chatham, N.B. E1N 3W4

    Moncton: Box 2100, Stn. A, Moncton, N.B. E1C 8H9

    St. Andrews: P.O. Box 427, St. Andrews, N.B. E0G 2X0

    Saint John: Box 2270, Saint John, N.B. E2L 3V1

    Woodstock: P.O. Box 1175, Woodstock, N.B. E0J 2B0

Nova Scotia Agricultural College: P.O. Box 550, Truro, N.S. B2N 5E3

Nova Scotia Community College:

    I. W. Akerley Campus: 21 Woodlawn Rd., Dartmouth, N.S. B2W 2R7

    Annapolis Campus: P.O. Box 940, Middleton, N.S. B0S 1P0

    Burridge Campus: 372 Pleasant St., Yarmouth, N.S. B5A 2L2

    Cape Breton Adult Vocational Training Campus: P.O. Box 1042, Sydney, N.S. B1P 6J7

College of Geographic Sciences: P.O. Box 10, Lawrencetown, N.S. B0S 1M0

Cumberland Campus: P.O. Box 550, Springhill, N.S. B0M 1X0

Dartmouth Adult Vocational Training Campus: 10 Acadia St., Dartmouth, N.S. B2Y 2H3

Halifax Campus: 1825 Bell Rd., Halifax, N.S. B3H 2Z4

Hants Campus: P.O. Box 2079, Windsor, N.S. B0N 2T0

Institute of Technology: P.O. Box 2210, Halifax, N.S. B3J 3C4

Lunenburg Campus: 75 High St., Bridgewater, N.S. B4V 1V8

Nautical Institute: P.O. Box 1225, Port Hawkesbury, N.S. B0E 2V0

Pictou Campus: P.O. Box 820, Stellarton, N.S. B0K 1S0

Shelburne Campus: P.O. Box 760, Shelburne, N.S. B0T 1W0

Strait Campus: P.O. Box 2000, Port Hawkesbury, N.S. B0E 2V0

Sydney Campus: 365 Prince St., Sydney, N.S. B1P 5L2

Nova Scotia College of Art & Design: Halifax, N.S. B3J 3J6

Sir Wilfred Grenfell College: University Dr., Corner Brook, Nfld. A2H 6P9

Western Community College: P.O. Box 5400, Stephenville, Nfld. A2N 2Z6

■ Quebec

Cégep de l'Abitibi-Témiscamingue: C.P. 1500, Rouyn, Que. J9X 5E5

Cégep Ahuntsic: 9155 rue St-Hubert, Montréal, Que. H2M 1Y8

Cégep d'Alma: 675 boul. Auger ouest, Alma, Que. G8B 2B7

Cégep André-Laurendeau: 1111 rue Lapierre, LaSalle, Que. H8N 2J4

Cégep de Baie-Comeau: 537 boul. Blanche, Baie-Comeau, Que. G5C 2B2

Cégep Beauce-Appalaches: 116, rue est, Ville de Saint-Georges, Que. G5Y 3G1

Cégep de Bois-de-Boulogne: 10555, av. de Bois-de-Boulogne, Montréal, Que. H4N 1L4 ▶

▶ **College Régional Champlain:** C.P. 5000, Sherbrooke, Que. J1J 3R6

Cégep de Chicoutimi: 534 rue Jacques-Cartier est, Chicoutimi, Que. G7H 1Z6

Cégep de Drummondville: 960 rue St-Georges, Drummondville, Que. J2C 6A2

Cégep Edouard-Montpetit: 945 chemin de Chambly, Longueuil, Que. J4H 3M6

Cégep François-Xavier-Garneau: C.P. 6300, Québec, Que. G1T 2S5

Cégep de la Gaspésie et des Îles: C.P. 590, Gaspé, Que. G0C 1R0

Cégep de Granby: 235 St-Jacques, Granby, Que. J2G 3N1

Cégep Héritage: 205 rue Laurier, Hull, Que. J8X 3Y8

Cégep John Abbott: 21275 Lakeshore Road, Ste-Anne- de-Bellevue, Que. H9X 3L9

Cégep de Joliette-de-Lanaudière: 20, rue St-Charles sud, Joliette, Que. J6E 4T1

Cégep de Jonquière: 2505, rue St-Hubert, Jonquière, Que. G7X 7W2

Cégep de La Pocatière: 140, 4e av., La Pocatière, Comté de Kamouraska, Que. G0R 1Z0

Cégep de Lévis-Lauzon: 205, rue Mgr-Bourget, Lauzon, Que. G6V 6Z9

Cégep de Limoilou: 1300, 8e av., Québec, Que. G1K 7H3

Cégep Lionel-Groulx: 100, rue Duquet, Ste-Thérèse, Comté de Terrebonne, Que. J7E 3G6

Cégep de Maisonneuve: 3800, rue Sherbrooke est, Montréal, Que. H1X 2A2

Cégep de Matane: 616 av. St-Rédempteur, Matane, Que. G4W 3P7

Cégep Montmorency: 475, boul. de L'Avenir, Laval, Que. H7N 5H9

Cégep de l'Outaouais: C.P. 5220, Succ. A, Hull, Que. J8Y 6M5

Cégep de la Région de l'Amiante: 671, boul. Smith sud, Thetford Mines, Que. G6G 1N1

Cégep de Rimouski: 60 rue de l'Evàché ouest, Rimouski, Que. G5L 4H6

Cégep de Rivière-du-Loup: 80, rue Frontenac, Rivière- du-Loup, Que. G5R 1S8

Cégep de Rosemont: 6400, 16e av., Montréal, Que. H1X 2S9

Cégep de St-Félicien: 1105, boul. Hamel, St-Félicien, Que. G0W 2N0

Cégep de Ste-Foy: 2410, chemin Ste-Foy, Ste-Foy, Que. G1V 1T3

Cégep de St-Hyacinthe: 3000, rue Boullé, St-Hyacinthe, Que. J2S 1H9

Cégep St-Jean-sur-Richelieu: 30, boul. du Séminaire, St- Jean-sur-Richelieu, Que. J3B 7B1

Cégep de St-Jérôme: 455, rue Fournier, St-Jérôme, Que. J7Z 4V2

Cégep de St-Laurent: 625, boul. Ste-Croix, Ville St-Laurent, Que. H4L 3X7

Cégep de Sept-Îles: 175, rue de la Vérendrye, Sept-Îles, Que. G4R 5B7

Cégep de Shawinigan: 2263, boul. du Collège, Shawinigan, Que. G9N 6V8

Cégep de Sherbrooke: 475, rue Parc, Sherbrooke, Que. J1H 5M7

Cégep de Sorel-Tracy: 3000, boul. de la Mairie, Tracy, Que. J3R 5B9

Cégep de Trois-Rivières: 3500, rue de Courval, Trois-Rivières, Que. G9A 5E6

Cégep de Valleyfield: 169, rue Champlain, Valleyfield, Que. J6T 1X6

Vanier College: 821, boul. Ste-Croix, St-Laurent, Que. H4L 3X9

Cégep de Victoriaville: 475, rue Notre-Dame est, Victoriaville, Que. G6P 4B3

Cégep du Vieux-Montréal: C.P. 1444, Succ C, Montréal, Que. H2X 3M8

Dawson College: 3040 Sherbrooke St. W., Westmount, Que. H3Z 1A4

■ Ontario

Algonquin College of Applied Arts & Technology: 1385 Woodroffe Ave., Nepean, Ont. K2G 1V8

Cambrian College of Applied Arts & Technology: 1400 Barrydowne Rd., Stn. A, Sudbury, Ont. P3A 3V8

Canadore College of Applied Arts & Technology: Box 5001, North Bay, Ont. P1B 8K9

Centennial College of Applied Arts & Technology: Box 631, Stn. A, Scarborough, Ont. M1K 5E9

Centralia College of Agricultural Technology: Huron Park, Ont. N0M 1Y0

Conestoga College of Applied Arts & Technology: 299 Doon Valley Dr., Kitchener, Ont. N2G 4M4

Confederation College of Applied Arts & Technology: Box 398, Stn. F, Thunder Bay, Ont. P7C 4W1

Durham College of Applied Arts & Technology: Box 385, Oshawa, Ont. L1H 7L7

Fanshawe College of Applied Arts & Technology: 1460 Oxford St. E., London, Ont. N5W 5H1

George Brown College of Applied Arts & Technology: Box 1015, Stn. B, Toronto, Ont. M5T 2T9 ▶

▶ **Georgian College of Applied Arts & Technology:**
1 Georgian Dr., Barrie, Ont. L4M 3X9

Humber College of Applied Arts & Technology:
205 Humber College Blvd., Rexdale, Ont.
M9W 5L7

Kemptville College of Agricultural Technology:
Kemptville, Ont. K0G 1J0

Lambton College of Applied Arts & Technology:
1457 London Road, Sarnia, Ont. N7T 7K4

Loyalist College of Applied Arts & Technology:
Box 4200, Belleville, Ont. K8N 5B9

Mohawk College of Applied Arts & Technology:
Box 2034, Hamilton, Ont. L8N 3T2

New Liskeard College of Agricultural Technology:
New Liskeard, Ont. P0J 1P0

Niagara College of Applied Arts & Technology:
Woodlawn Road, Welland, Ont. L3B 5S2

Northern College of Applied Arts & Technology:
Box 2002, South Porcupine, Ont. P0N 1H0

Ontario Agricultural College: University of
Guelph, Guelph, Ont. N1G 2W1

Ontario College of Art: 100 McCaul St., Toronto,
Ont. M5T 1W1

Ridgetown College of Agricultural Technology:
Ridgetown, Ont. N0P 2C0

St. Clair College of Applied Arts & Technology:
2000 Talbot Rd. W., Windsor, Ont. N9A 6S4

**St. Lawrence College of Applied Arts &
Technology:** 2288 Parkedale Ave., Brockville,
Ont. K6V 5X3

Sault College of Applied Arts & Technology: 443
Northern Ave., Sault Ste. Marie, Ont. P6A 5L3

Seneca College of Applied Arts & Technology:
1750 Finch Ave. E., North York, Ont.
M2J 2X5

Sheridan College of Applied Arts & Technology:
1430 Trafalgar Rd., Oakville, Ont. L6H 2L1

**Sir Sandford Fleming College of Applied Arts &
Technology:** Brealey Drive, Peterborough, Ont.
K9J 7B1

■ Prairies

Alberta College of Art: 1407-14th Ave. N.W.,
Calgary, Alta. T2N 4R3

Assiniboine Community College: 1430 Victoria
Ave. E., Brandon, Man. R7A 5Z9

**The Banff Centre for the Arts & Centre for
Management:** P.O. Box 1020, Banff, Alta.
T0L 0C0

Carlton Trail Regional College: P.O. Box 720,
Humboldt, Sask. S0K 2A0

Cumberland Regional College: P.O. Box 2225,
Nipawin, Sask. S0E 1E0

Cypress Hills Regional College: 129-2nd Ave.
N.E., Swift Current, Sask. S9H 2C6

école technique et professionnelle: c/o Collège
universitaire de Saint-Boniface, 200, av. de la
Cathédrale, Saint-Boniface, Man. R2H 0H7

Fairview College: Box 3000, Fairview, Alta.
T0L 1L0

Grande Prairie Regional College: 10726-106th
Ave., Grande Prairie, Alta. T8V 4C4

Grant MacEwan Community College: 10030-
107th St., Edmonton, Alta. T5J 3E4

Keewatin Community College: 436 7th St. E.,
The Pas, Man. R9A 1M7

Keyano College: 8115 Franklin Ave., Fort
McMurray, Alta. T9H 2H7

Lakeland College: Vermillion Campus,
Vermillion, Alta. T0B 4M0

Lakeland College: P.O. Bag 6600, Lloydminster,
Sask. S9V 1Z3

Lethbridge Community College: 3000 College Dr.
S., Lethbridge, Alta. T1K 1L6

Medicine Hat College: 299 College Dr. S.E.,
Medicine Hat, Alta. T1A 3Y6

Mount Royal College: 4825 Richard Rd. S.W.,
Calgary, Alta. T3E 6K6

The Northern Alberta Institute of Technology:
11762- 106th St., Edmonton, Alta. T5G 2R1

Northlands College: P.O. Box 1000, Air Ronge,
Sask. S0J 3G0

North West Regional College: 1381-101st St.,
North Battleford, Sask. S9A 0Z9

Olds College: Olds, Alta. T0M 1P0

Parkland Regional College: P.O. Box 790,
Melville, Sask. S0A 2P0

Prairie West Regional College: P.O. Box 700,
Biggar, Sask. S0K 0M0

Red Deer College: Box 5005, Red Deer, Alta.
T4N 5H5

Red River Community College: 2055 Notre Dame
Ave., Winnipeg, Man. R3H 0J9

Saskatchewan Indian Community College: 401
Packham Place, Asimakaniseekan Askiy
Reserve, Sask. S7N 2T7

**Saskatchewan Institute of Applied Science and
Technology:**
   Kelsey Campus: P.O. Box 1520, Saskatoon,
   Sask. S7K 3R5
   Palliser Campus: P.O. Box 1420, Moose
   Jaw, Sask. S6H 4R4
   Wascana Campus: P.O. Box 556, Regina,
   Sask. S4P 3A3
   Woodland Campus: P.O. Box 3003, Prince
   Albert, Sask. S6V 6G1 ▶

▶ **Southeast Regional College:** 22-3rd St. N.E.,
Weyburn, Sask. S4H 0V9
The Southern Alberta Institute of Technology:
1301-16th Ave. N.W., Calgary, Alta. T2M 0L4

■ **British Columbia and Territories**

Arctic College: P.O. Box 1769, Yellowknife,
N.W.T. Y1A 2C6
B.C. Institute of Technology: 3700 Willingdon
Ave., Burnaby, B.C. V5G 3H2
Camosun College: 3100 Foul Bay Rd., Victoria,
B.C. V8P 5J2
Capilano College: 2055 Purcell Way, North
Vancouver, B.C. V7J 3H5
Cariboo College: Box 3010, Kamloops, B.C.
V2C 5N3
College of New Caledonia: 3330-22nd Ave.,
Prince George, B.C. V2N 1P8
Douglas College: P.O. Box 2503, New
Westminster, B.C. V3L 5B2
East Kootenay Community College: P.O. Box
8500, Cranbrook, B.C. V1C 5L7

Emily Carr College of Art & Design: 1399
Johnston St., Granville Island, Vancouver, B.C.
V6H 3R9
Fraser Valley College: 45600 Airport Rd.,
Chilliwack, B.C. V2P 6T4
Kwantlen College: Box 9030, Surrey, B.C.
V3T 5H8
Malaspina College: 900-5th St., Nanaimo, B.C.
V9R 5S5
North Island College: 156 Manor Dr., Comox,
B.C. V9N 6P7
Northern Lights College: 11401-8th St., Dawson
Creek, B.C. V1G 4G2
Northwest Community College: 5331 McConnell
Ave., Terrace, B.C. V8G 4C2
Okanagan College: 1000 KLO Rd., Kelowna,
B.C. V1Y 4X8
Selkirk College: P.O. Box 1200, Castlegar, B.C.
V1N 3J1
Vancouver Community College: Box 24700, Stn.
C, Vancouver, B.C. V5T 4N4
Yukon College: P.O. Box 2799, Whitehorse,
Yuk. Y1A 5K4

Continuing Education

*D*uring the past thirty years, enrolment in part-time post-secondary education has been
steadily on the increase. By late 1990, more than 705,000 Canadians classed as mature
students (between the ages of 25 and 64) were enrolled in an educational institution and over 70%
took their classes part time and held down a full-time job during the day. This group represents a
significant increase over the 378,000 attending classes on this basis at the same time in 1980.

Of the mature students, 65% were in the 25-34 age group, with 25% in the 30-34 age group.
Students in this category were most often back in class for job-related reasons: those wanting to
change jobs or increase promotion opportunities joined those needing to upgrade their skills to
keep up with new technology and innovations in an existing job. Other reasons for attendance
included education related to personal or family responsibilities.

Mature students in general tended to have a higher level of educational attainment than the
average Canadian—50% of the general population in the 25-64 age group had only a high school
education while 70% of mature students had some post-secondary education. The part-time
students were more likely to have a university degree than the full-time mature students.

Women accounted for 60% of the mature students, compared to 54% in 1980; part-time mature
students in general tended to be older than full-time mature students, with female part-time
students likely to be older than their male counterparts. These students came from all walks of life,
but were largely employed in teaching, clerical and service occupations.

Most older students were taking courses in post-secondary institutions. Enrolment in
universities has increased steadily with an emphasis on full-time studies, while part-timers are
more likely to attend community colleges and CEGEPS.

The increase in enrolment is largely a reflection of the fast pace of change in the workplace.
Jobs are changing or disappearing altogether at an unprecedented rate and many Canadians who
return to school part time are simply keeping up with the changing face of our economy.

FAMILIES AND INCOME

Marriages and Divorces in Canada

	Marriages				Divorces		
			Average Age at Marriage				Average Length of Marriage[2]
	Total	Rate[1]	Brides	Grooms	Total	Rate[1]	
1925	66 378	6.9	25.3	29.8	550	0.06	n.a.
1930	73 341	7.0	25.0	29.2	875	0.09	n.a.
1935	78 908	7.1	25.0	29.0	1 431	0.13	n.a.
1940	125 797	10.8	25.2	28.9	2 416	0.21	n.a.
1945	111 376	9.0	25.5	29.0	5 101	0.42	n.a.
1950	125 083	9.1	25.3	28.5	5 386	0.39	n.a.
1955	128 029	8.2	25.1	28.0	6 053	0.39	n.a.
1960	130 338	7.3	24.7	27.7	6 980	0.39	n.a.
1965	145 519	7.4	24.5	27.2	8 974	0.46	n.a.
1970	188 428	8.8	24.9	27.3	29 775	1.40	n.a.
1975	197 585	8.7	25.0	27.6	50 611	2.22	n.a.
1980	191 069	8.0	25.9	28.5	62 019	2.59	12.0
1981	190 082	7.8	26.2	28.8	67 671	2.78	12.1
1982	188 360	7.6	26.4	29.0	70 436	2.86	12.0
1983	184 675	7.4	26.0	29.4	68 567	2.76	12.0
1984	185 597	7.4	27.2	29.8	65 172	2.59	12.4
1985	184 096	7.3	27.4	30.0	61 980	2.44	12.5
1986	175 518	6.9	27.7	30.3	78 160	3.09	12.5
1987	182 151	7.1	28.4	31.1	90 985	3.55	12.4
1988	187 728	7.2	28.6	31.2	79 872	3.08	12.5
1989	190 640	7.3	28.8	31.4	80 716	3.08	12.4
1990	187 737	7.1	26.0	27.9	78 152	2.94	12.4
1991	172 251	6.2	26.2	28.2	77 031	2.82	n.a.

Source: *Statistics Canada*

(1) Rate per 1 000 population. (2) Refers to the average length (in years) of those marriages ending in divorce during the year stated. (n.a.) not available.

Marriages and Divorces by Province

	Marriages				Divorces	
	1981		1991		1990	
	Total	Rate[1]	Total	Rate[1]	Total	Rate[1]
Canada	190 082	7.8	172 251	6.4	78 152	2.94
Newfoundland	3 758	6.6	3 480	6.1	1 006	1.76
Prince Edward Island	849	6.9	876	6.7	276	2.12
Nova Scotia	6 632	7.8	5 845	6.5	2 414	2.71
New Brunswick	5 108	7.3	4 521	6.2	1 695	2.34
Quebec	41 005	6.4	28 922	4.2	20 398	3.02
Ontario	70 281	8.1	72 938	7.4	28 863	2.97
Manitoba	8 123	7.9	7 032	6.4	2 755	2.53
Saskatchewan	7 329	7.6	5 923	5.9	2 354	2.35
Alberta	21 781	9.7	18 612	7.4	8 483	3.44
British Columbia	24 699	9.0	23 691	7.4	9 735	3.11
Yukon Territory	235	10.2	196	7.3	81	3.12
Northwest Territories	282	6.2	215	3.9	92	1.70

Source: *Statistics Canada*

(1) Rate per 1,000 population.

Marital Status of the Canadian Population, 1992

Age Group	Total Population Male (000s)	Total Population Female (000s)	Single Male (%)	Single Female (%)	Married Male (%)	Married Female (%)	Widowed Male (%)	Widowed Female (%)	Divorced Male (%)	Divorced Female (%)
15 and over.......	10 576	11 099	31.3	24.4	61.5	59.3	2.3	10.3	4.9	6.1
15-19 years........	943.4	897.2	99.8	98.8	0.2	1.2	...	...	...	...
20-24 years........	1 011.9	967.3	90.1	77.0	9.6	22.2	...	0.1	0.3	0.7
25-29 years........	1 155.5	1 141.3	53.9	33.4	43.8	62.6	0.1	0.2	2.2	3.7
30-34 years........	1 224.9	1 235.1	24.9	15.7	69.6	77.3	0.1	0.4	5.3	6.7
35-39 years........	1 148.9	1 170.6	14.3	10.7	78.1	79.6	0.2	0.8	7.4	8.9
40-44 years........	1 031.4	1 042.2	9.6	7.9	81.6	79.9	0.4	1.4	8.4	10.7
45-49 years........	869.7	868.7	7.3	6.3	83.3	79.7	0.6	2.7	8.8	11.3
50-54 years........	676.2	680.8	6.4	5.6	84.3	79.0	1.2	5.4	8.1	10.0
55-59 years........	597.6	611.7	6.2	5.3	84.7	76.1	2.2	10.2	6.9	8.4
60-64 years........	570.1	604.3	6.5	5.5	84.1	70.0	3.8	17.7	5.7	6.9
65-69 years........	487.0	572.0	6.4	5.9	83.0	61.5	6.3	27.4	4.3	5.2
70-74 years........	372.1	483.4	6.0	6.5	80.5	50.1	10.1	39.5	3.4	3.9
75-79 years........	254.8	370.2	6.3	7.9	75.0	35.9	16.2	53.5	2.5	2.7
80-84 years........	145.1	247.7	6.7	9.2	65.9	22.7	25.6	66.4	1.8	1.7
85 years and over..	87.6	206.5	7.3	10.2	47.3	8.3	44.2	80.7	1.1	0.8

Source: *Statistics Canada*　　　　　　　　　　　　　　　　　　　(...) = too small to be included.

Lone-Parent Families by Province, 1991

Male Parent

Province	Total Lone-Parent Families	Total	Number of Children at Home 1	Number of Children at Home 2 +	Number of Children at Home 3 +
Canada	954 710	168 240	104 705	47 000	16 535
Newfoundland	17 920	3 390	1 970	950	470
Prince Edward Island	4 375	740	445	195	100
Nova Scotia	33 120	5 395	3 395	1 465	535
New Brunswick	26 545	4 580	2 855	1 285	440
Quebec	268 880	48 760	31 195	13 565	4 005
Ontario	342 805	59 000	36 215	16 800	5 985
Manitoba..............	37 365	6 485	3 930	1 795	760
Saskatchewan	30 230	5 335	3 230	1 420	685
Alberta................	83 005	14 675	8 880	4 080	1 710
British Columbia	107 375	19 135	12 190	5 235	1 710
Yukon Territory	1 040	230	145	65	20
Northwest Territories	2 045	520	255	140	120

Female Parent

Province	Total	Number of Children at Home 1	Number of Children at Home 2 +	Number of Children at Home 3 +
Canada	786 470	455 170	239 745	91 560
Newfoundland	14 530	7 875	4 460	2 195
Prince Edward Island	3 635	2 115	1 015	500
Nova Scotia	27 725	16 105	8 250	3 365
New Brunswick	21 965	12 775	6 685	2 500
Quebec	220 120	135 840	64 395	19 885
Ontario	283 805	161 465	87 915	34 420
Manitoba...........................	30 885	17 370	9 195	4 320
Saskatchewan	24 895	13 340	7 310	4 240
Alberta	68 335	36 765	21 910	9 660
British Columbia	88 245	50 295	27 935	10 010
Yukon Territory......................	810	470	250	90
Northwest Territories.................	1 530	745	415	375

Source: *1991 Census of Canada*

Composition of Canadian Families

(thousands)

	1961 No. of Families	%	1971 No. of Families	%	1981 No. of Families	%	1991 No. of Families	%
Total families[1]	4 147	100.0	5 071	100.0	6 325	100.0	7 356	100.0
Without children at home	1 217	29.3	1 545	30.5	2 013	31.8	2 580	35.1
With children at home	2 930	70.7	3 526	69.5	4 312	68.2	4 776	64.9
one child	839	20.2	1 045	20.6	1 580	25.0	1 945	26.4
two children	855	20.6	1 077	21.2	1 648	26.1	1 927	26.2
three children	557	13.4	677	13.4	730	11.5	691	9.4
four children	312	7.5	367	7.2	243	3.8	165	2.2
five children	162	3.9	186	3.7	70	1.1	33	0.4
six children[2]	206	5.0	84	1.7	25	0.4	10	0.1
seven children[2]	206	5.0	43	0.8	10	0.2	3	...
eight or more[2]	206	5.0	47	0.9	7	0.1	2	...
Lone parent families	385	9.3	471	9.3	653	10.3	955	13.0
lone female parent	305	7.4	371	7.3	541	8.6	786	10.7
lone male parent	80	1.9	100	2.0	112	1.8	168	2.3

Source: *Census of Canada*

(1) Based on the census family definition: a husband and wife (without children or with children who never married) or a parent with one or more children who never married, living together in the same home. (2) Includes six or more children.

Size of Families in Canada

(thousands of families)

	1951 No. of Families	Avg. Size	1961 No. of Families	Avg. Size	1971 No. of Families	Avg. Size	1981 No. of Families	Avg. Size	1991 No. of Families	Avg. Size
Canada	3 287	3.7	4 147	3.9	5 071	3.7	6 325	3.3	7 356	3.1
Newfoundland	75	4.4	89	4.7	108	4.4	135	3.8	151	3.3
Prince Edward Island	21	4.0	22	4.2	24	4.0	30	3.5	34	3.2
Nova Scotia	145	3.9	162	4.0	181	3.8	216	3.3	245	3.1
New Brunswick	112	4.1	125	4.3	140	4.0	177	3.4	198	3.1
Quebec	856	4.2	1 104	4.2	1 357	3.9	1 672	3.3	1 883	3.0
Ontario	1 163	3.4	1 511	3.6	1 882	3.6	2 279	3.2	2 727	3.1
Manitoba	191	3.6	216	3.7	236	3.6	262	3.2	286	3.1
Saskatchewan	196	3.7	212	3.8	216	3.7	246	3.3	258	3.2
Alberta	223	3.7	306	3.8	382	3.7	566	3.3	668	3.1
British Columbia	300	3.3	394	3.6	534	3.5	728	3.1	888	3.0
Yukon	5[1]	3.9[1]	7[1]	4.3[1]	11[1]	4.3[1]	6	3.3	7	3.1
Northwest Territories	5[1]	3.9[1]	7[1]	4.3[1]	11[1]	4.3[1]	9	4.0	13	3.7

Source: *Census of Canada*   (1) Includes both the Yukon and Northwest Territories.

Divorces in 1991

The number of divorces in Canada in 1991 decreased by 1.9% from the total in 1990, with 77,031 divorces granted during the year. This represents a divorce rate of 2.82 per 1,000, down from 2.94 the previous year. The Northwest Territories had the lowest divorce rate in 1991, with a rate of 1.51, with Newfoundland coming in at 1.6 for the second lowest.

Alberta once again had the highest divorce rate, although at 3.30 this was a drop from the previous year's rate of 3.44.

Average Family Income

The average Canadian family earned $53,131 in 1991, a real (after inflation) decrease of 2.6 percent from 1990. This continues a recent trend that is a departure from the previous decade—between 1984 and 1989, the standard of living of the average Canadian family improved, as real income rose 11 percent. This was partly due to a trend towards families with two or more wage earners. In 1989, less than a third of Canadian households relied on a single income.

Families in Ontario still tend to have the highest family income and those in the Maritimes the lowest. Families which include both a husband and wife tend to have higher than average incomes ($59 014) while those with single female parents earn, on average, far less ($22 186).

In the table below, family is defined as a husband and wife (with or without unmarried children), or a parent with one or more unmarried children, living in the same home.

	1971	1975	1980	1985	1991
Canada	**$10 113**	**$16 368**	**$27 246**	**$37 981**	**$53 131**
Newfoundland	6 855	12 359	20 374	29 022	41 654
Prince Edward Island	6 669	12 032	22 574	30 473	42 779
Nova Scotia	7 721	13 068	21 625	33 786	45 130
New Brunswick	7 882	13 283	21 021	31 196	44 323
Quebec	9 713	15 273	25 408	35 278	48 634
Ontario	11 154	17 772	28 313	41 291	58 634
Manitoba	9 083	14 869	25 029	35 576	46 621
Saskatchewan	7 762	15 784	26 315	35 453	45 930
Alberta	10 107	16 878	31 868	41 245	55 552
British Columbia	10 989	17 520	30 272	37 533	54 895

Source: *Statistics Canada*

Percentage Income Distribution in Canada by Gender[1]

(percent)

	1971		1981		1991	
	male	female	male	female	male	female
under $1 000	12.3	15.3	3.3	8.2	—	—
$1 000 - 2 499	24.1	33.4	—	—	4.5	7.9
2 500 - 4 999	20.4	24.4	11.4	26.3	3.8	7.5
5 000 - 6 999	16.1	14.0	7.5	14.1	—	—
7 000 - 9 999	15.9	8.5	8.9	13.2	10.2	18.2
10 000 - 14 999	8.3	3.4	13.8	17.3	12.0	19.0
15 000 - 17 499	2.9[2]	0.9[2]	—	—	5.1	7.0
17 500 - 19 999	—	—	14.6	10.6	4.5	5.4
20 000 - 22 499	—	—	—	—	4.9	4.9
22 500 - 24 999	—	—	14.0	5.2	4.4	4.3
25 000 - 29 999	—	—	10.2	2.7	9.1	8.4
30 000 - 34 999	—	—	16.4[3]	2.4[3]	8.6	5.7
35 000 - 39 999	—	—	—	—	7.2	3.7
40 000 - 44 999	—	—	—	—	6.0	2.5
45 000 - 49 999	—	—	—	—	4.6	1.8
50 000+	—	—	—	—	15.1	3.6

Source: *Statistics Canada*

(1) Data represents income of unattached individuals, i.e. not family income. (2) 1971 data reported as $15 000+ for final category. (3) 1981 data reported as $30 000+ for final category. (—) = not reported.

Personal Expenditure on Consumer Goods and Services

(per capita expenditure in dollars)

	1966	%	1975	%	1980	%	1990	%
Total	$1 896	100.0	$4 299	100.0	$7 171	100.0	$14 988	100.0
Rent and fuel	337	17.8	773	18.0	1 452	20.2	3 371	22.5
Food	331	17.5	641	14.9	970	13.5	2 344	15.6
Recreation equipment and services	70	3.7	245	5.7	401	5.6	995	6.6
Restaurants and hotels	110	5.8	294	6.8	500	7.0	951	6.4
Clothing	157	8.3	307	7.2	485	6.8	806	5.4
New and used cars	118	6.2	241	5.6	348	4.8	808	5.4
Financial, legal and other services	81	4.3	193	4.5	318	4.4	828	5.5
Household furnishings and supplies	82	4.3	213	5.0	358	5.0	694	4.6
Car repairs, parts and services	48	2.5	116	2.7	202	2.8	480	3.2
Gas and oil	51	2.7	130	3.0	244	3.4	466	3.1
Medical care	62	3.3	93	2.2	186	2.6	428	2.9
Education	44	2.3	124	2.9	209	2.9	417	2.8
Alcohol	68	3.6	155	3.6	230	3.2	397	2.7
Tobacco	53	2.8	90	2.1	134	1.9	327	2.2
Purchased transportation	31	1.6	78	1.8	150	2.1	309	2.1
Reading and entertainment supplies	31	1.6	74	1.7	127	1.8	243	1.6
Communications	27	1.4	62	1.4	115	1.6	235	1.5
Furniture	34	1.8	92	2.1	131	1.8	213	1.4
Household appliances	30	1.6	77	1.8	112	1.6	207	1.4
Domestic, childcare and other household services	23	1.2	41	1.0	73	1.0	229	1.5
Drugs	22	1.2	47	1.1	77	1.1	221	1.5
Toilet articles	18	0.9	36	0.8	62	0.9	137	0.9
Personal care	19	1.0	33	0.8	55	0.8	136	0.9
Jewellery, watches and repairs	11	0.6	36	0.8	63	0.9	88	0.6
Laundry and dry cleaning	13	0.7	15	0.3	22	0.3	44	0.3

Source: *Statistics Canada*

Whoever has the most toys...

*S*tatistics Canada's annual survey entitled "Household Facilities and Equipment" gives the top honours to Albertans in 1992 when it comes to possessions.

Canadians living in Alberta tend to have more rooms in their houses (6.26) than the national average (5.9), and as a result they own more things to put in them. More Albertans have VCRs than the national average (78.4% of Alberta households compared to 73.8%); they also have more camcorders (14% vs. 10.2%) and microwaves (81% vs. 76%) and are more likely to own two or more cars (28.4% compared to 25% nationally). Albertans also have more recreation equipment, leading the nation in ownership of downhill skis, bicycles and overnight camping equipment; although they dropped to second place when it came to CD players (BC came in first) and gas barbecues (behind Saskatchewan).

By contrast, citizens in Newfoundland have the most crowded living quarters with 3.2 people in each dwelling (compared to 2.63 across the nation) and these dwellings were the least likely to have microwave ovens, however Newfoundlanders may take comfort in the fact that they are by far more likely to have paid off their mortgage (68.3% of households in Newfoundland) than anyone else in Canada. (Only 50.6% of Canadian households can claim that status.)

Analysts note that residents of Alberta have the third highest level of disposable income in the country (just behind Ontario and BC). High disposable income plus lower than average housing and utility costs means there is more money available for the purchase of consumer goods.

Alberta's continued status as the only province without a provincial sales tax was also credited with increasing local buying power.

Home Electronics and Appliances Owned by Canadians

(percentage of households owning item)

Many consumer products which started out as luxury items during the early 1980s had become standard fixtures in the average household by the end of the decade.

In 1981, only 8 percent of households owned microwave ovens; by 1990, more than two-thirds (68.2%) of all households, and 84 percent of those with annual incomes above $70,000, owned them. In 1983, only 6.4 percent of households owned video cassette recorders; by 1990, 66.3 percent of all households, and 86.4 percent of those with incomes over $70,000, had VCRs.

During the 1990s, a similar trend is expected for camcorders, compact disc players and home computers.

Prairie families were most likely, and Atlantic province families least likely, to own technologically-new products. Alberta led the nation in ownership of CD players (18.2% of households), camcorders (6.7%), microwaves (76.9%) and home computers (20.1%). Residents of Prince Edward Island were least likely to own CD players (8.9% of households), camcorders (less than 1%) and home computers (8.9%). Microwaves were least popular in Newfoundland (56.6% of households).

	1960	1965	1970	1975	1980	1985	1990	1991
Air conditioners	n.a.	2.2	4.3	12.4	16.7	18.0	24.4	26.7
Automobiles	66.6	75.0	77.7	78.9	79.8	77.3	77.8	83.0
Camcorders	n.a.	n.a.	n.a.	n.a.	n.a.	n.a.	5.6	10.2
Clothes dryers	12.2	25.2	40.8	48.1	63.2	68.4	73.4	71.4
Compact disc players	n.a.	n.a.	n.a.	n.a.	n.a.	n.a.	15.4	26.9
Dishwashers	n.a.	2.7	7.5	15.2	28.6	37.1	42.0	44.2
Electric stoves	56.2	69.0	78.6	85.1	89.4	92.3	93.8	94.2
Electric washers	86.8	86.2	83.7	76.9	77.3	77.3	78.6	78.6
Freezers	11.5	22.6	33.2	41.8	51.0	57.0	57.6	57.9
Gas barbecues	n.a.	n.a.	n.a.	n.a.	n.a.	19.9[1]	45.9	50.5
Home computers	n.a.	n.a.	n.a.	n.a.	n.a.	n.a.	16.3	20.0
Microwave ovens	n.a.	n.a.	n.a.	0.8	8.0[2]	23.0	68.2	76.0
Radios	96.2	96.1	97.2	98.3	98.7	98.7	99.1	98.8
Refrigerators	90.3	95.8	98.4	99.3	99.6	99.2	99.5	99.4
Telephones	83.3	89.4	93.9	96.4	97.6	98.2	98.5	98.7
Television, cable	n.a.	n.a.	n.a.	40.4	54.8	62.5	71.4	71.4
Televisions	80.6	92.6	96.0	96.8	97.7	98.3	99.0	98.8
Televisions, color	n.a.	n.a.	12.1	53.4	81.1	91.4	96.9	97.5
Video recorders	n.a.	n.a.	n.a.	n.a.	n.a.	23.5	66.3	73.8
Number of households[3]	4 404	5 000	5 784	6 721	7 787	8 762	9 624	10 056

Source: *Statistics Canada*

(1) 1984 figure. (2) 1981 figure. (3) In thousands. (n.a.) not available.

When was the best time to get a raise?

The most rapid increases in wages (and purchasing power) took place after World War II when workers in the booming postwar economy won income increases of 34% during the 1940s, 42.5% during the 1950s and 36.8% in the 1960s. By contrast, in the 10 years between 1980 and 1990, real wages (adjusted for inflation) rose only 2%.

Wage growth ground nearly to a halt during the last 10 years due to a number of factors, including declining growth in productivity, increasing growth in the labour force and a ballooning debt. Inflation during the 1970s plus high unemployment in the 80s translated into almost no real wage increase for the average worker as the rise in prices (78%) meant it cost more to maintain the same standard of living. This meant that "real growth" or the increase in purchasing power was only 2%.

Low Income in Canada, 1991

In 1991, some 4,227,000 Canadians had low incomes. This includes some 1,210,000 children under 18 years of age.

The low-income cut-off level is set by Statistics Canada, using a standard that families or individuals who spend 56.2% or more of their pre-tax income on food, clothing and shelter are in financial difficulty.

The table below shows the minimum income level necessary to avoid financial hardship. It varies according to changes in the cost of living, family size and place of residence. For instance, in 1991 the poverty line for a family of 4 living in Vancouver was $29,661; for a family of 4 living in a rural area it was $20,192.

Family size[1]	Urban Areas Pop. Under 30 000	Pop. 30 000 to 99 999	Pop. 100 000 to 499 999	Pop. 500 000 or more	Rural Areas
1 person	11 695	12 829	13 132	14 951	10 179
2 persons	15 852	17 390	17 802	20 266	13 799
3 persons	20 149	22 103	22 626	25 761	17 539
4 persons	23 200	25 449	26 049	29 661	20 192
5 persons	25 347	27 805	28 462	32 406	22 062
6 persons	27 512	30 180	30 893	35 177	23 947
7 or more persons	29 593	32 463	33 230	37 833	25 757

Source: *Statistics Canada*

(1) Does not distinguish between adults and children as family members.

Canadian Residents Living Below the Poverty Line

(thousands of persons and families)

	1972	1975	1980	1985	1990
Single persons	642	832	1 041	1 026	992
Males	234	295	345	395	392
Females	408	537	696	631	600
Families	707	661	745	849	769
2 persons	275	266	291	299	79
3 persons	131	136	181	218	97
4 persons	118	117	145	181	62
5 or more persons	184	143	128	151	100
With children under 16 years	418	397	461	540	517
1 child	124	132	181	203	212
2 children	128	127	177	210	182
3 children	78	73	69	127[1]	123[1]
4 or more children	88	66	34	127[1]	—
Single parent families	n.a.	218[2]	252	271	286
Single male parent	n.a.	13[2]	15	17	19
Single female parent	n.a.	205[2]	237	254	267

Source: *Statistics Canada*

(1) 3 or more children. (2) 1976 data. (n.a.) not available.

THE NATION

The National Anthem: O Canada

The music of *O Canada* was composed by Calixa Lavallée and the lyrics were written in French by Adolphe-Basile Routhier in Quebec City. Originally called *Chant National* it was first performed at a banquet in Quebec City on June 24, 1880. The anthem grew in popularity in Quebec but was not heard in English until the early 1900s. There have been several English versions of the work, the most popular of which was written in 1908 by Robert Stanley Weir. In 1967 a Special Joint Committee of the Senate and the House of Commons was formed to recommend official versions of Canada's National and Royal Anthems. With a few minor changes, the official English version of *O Canada* is based on Weir's lyrics. On June 27, 1980 the House of Commons passed Bill C-36 designating both the music and lyrics of *O Canada* as Canada's national anthem. It was proclaimed July 1, 1980.

O Canada

O Canada! Terre de nos aïeux,

Ton front est ceint de fleurons glorieux!

Car ton bras sait porter l'épée,

Il sait porter la croix!

Ton histoire est une épopée

Des plus brillants exploits,

Et ta valeur, de foi trempée,

Protégera nos foyers et nos droits,

Protégera nos foyers et nos droits.

O Canada

O Canada! Our home and native land!

True patriot love in all thy sons command.

With glowing hearts we see thee rise,

The True North strong and free!

From far and wide, O Canada,

We stand on guard for thee.

God keep our land glorious and free!

O Canada, we stand on guard for thee.

O Canada, we stand on guard for thee!

The National Flag

The National Flag was adopted by Parliament Oct. 22, 1964 and proclaimed by Queen Elizabeth II. It was inaugurated on Feb. 15, 1965.

It is a red flag of the proportions two by length and one by width, containing in its centre a white square, the width of the flag, bearing a single, red, stylized maple leaf. The maple leaf has been looked upon as an emblem of Canada since the early 1700s. Red and white were declared Canada's official colours by King George V Nov. 21, 1921.

The National Flag is to be flown daily at all federal government buildings, airports and military bases and establishments within and outside Canada. When flown with other flags, it should be given a place of honour.

CANADIAN HISTORY

Circa 1000 Leif Ericsson and other Vikings visit Labrador and Newfoundland.

1497 John Cabot (Giovanni Caboto) claims Cape Breton Island (or possibly Newfoundland or Labrador) for Henry VII of England (June 24).

1498 Cabot makes his second voyage to North America.

1534 Jacques Cartier visits the Strait of Belle Isle (Newfoundland), and charts the Gulf of St Lawrence (landing in Gaspé July 14).

1535 Cartier sails up the St Lawrence River to Quebec and Montreal.

1541 Cartier and the Sieur de Roberval found Charlesbourg-Royal, the first French settlement in America.

1577 Martin Frobisher of England makes the first of his three attempts to find a north-west passage, sailing as far as Hudson Strait.

1600 King Henry IV of France grants a fur-trading monopoly in the Gulf of St Lawrence to a group of French merchants.

1605 Samuel de Champlain and the Sieur de Monts found Port Royal (Annapolis, NS).

1608 Champlain founds Quebec.

1609 Champlain supports the Algonquins against the Iroquois at Lake Champlain.

1610 Étienne Brûlé goes to live among the Huron and eventually becomes the first European to see Lakes Ontario, Huron and Superior. Henry Hudson explores Hudson Bay.

1617 Louis Hébert, the first habitant (farmer), arrives in Quebec.

1625 Jesuits arrive in Quebec to begin missionary work among the Indians.

1627 The Company of One Hundred Associates is founded (Apr. 29) to establish a French empire in North America.

1629 David Kirke captures Quebec for Britain (July 19).

1632 The Treaty of Saint-Germain-en-Laye returns Quebec to France.

1634–40 The Huron nation is reduced by half from European diseases (smallpox epidemic, 1639).

1637 Kirke is named first governor of Newfoundland.

1642 Montreal is founded (May 18) by the Sieur de Maisonneuve.

1649 The Jesuit Father Jean de Brébeuf is martyred by the Iroquois at St-Ignace (Mar. 16). The Iroquois disperse the Huron nation (1648–49).

1659 François de Laval, later to become Canada's first bishop, arrives in Quebec (June).

1660 Adam Dollard des Ormeaux makes his last stand against the Iroquois at Long Sault (May). The small party of French fights so well that the Iroquois decide not to attack Montreal.

1663 Quebec becomes a royal province.

1665 The Carignan-Salières regiment is sent from France to Quebec to deal with the Iroquois. Jean Talon becomes Quebec's intendant.

1667 Canada's first census counts 3,215 non-native inhabitants in 668 families.

1670 The Hudson's Bay Company is formed and granted trade rights over all territory draining into Hudson Bay (May 2).

1672 Count Frontenac becomes Governor of Quebec.

1673 Marquette and Jolliet explore the Mississippi to its junction with the Arkansas.

1674 Laval becomes first Bishop of Quebec.

1678–79 Dulhut explores the headwaters of the Mississippi.

1682 La Salle explores the Mississippi to its mouth.

1686 De Troyes and D'Iberville capture the English posts of Moose Fort (June 20). Rupert House (July 3) and Fort Albany (July 26) on James Bay.

1689 The Iroquois kill many French settlers at Lachine.

1690 Sir William Phips captures Port Royal (May 11). Frontenac repels Phips's attack on Quebec (Oct.).

1697 The Treaty of Ryswick restores the status quo in the struggle between England and France. All captured territory is returned.

1701 The **War of the Spanish Succession** begins in Europe; the conflict spreads to North America the following year.

1710 Francis Nicholson captures Port Royal for England.

1713 The **Treaty of Utrecht** confirms British possession of Hudson Bay, Newfoundland and Acadia (except Cape Breton Island). France starts building Fort **Louisbourg.**

1739 La Vérendrye expedition explores Lake Winnipeg.

1740 The **War of the Austrian Succession** pits Britain against France; the European conflict spreads to North America (**King George's War**) in 1744.

1745 Massachusetts Governor William Shirley takes the French fortress of **Louisbourg.**

1748 Louisbourg is returned to France by the **Treaty of Aix-la-Chapelle.**

1749 Britain founds **Halifax** to counter the French presence at Louisbourg.

1752 Canada's **first newspaper**, the Halifax *Gazette,* appears (Mar. 25).

1753 George **Washington**'s military expedition to the Monogahela is defeated by the French.

1754 Beginning of **French and Indian War** in America. Although war is not officially declared for another two years, this marks the final phase in the struggle between France and Britain in North America.

1755 Britain expels the **Acadians** from Nova Scotia, scattering them throughout her other North American colonies.

1756 Beginning of the **Seven Years' War** in Europe pits Britain against France. The Marquis **de Montcalm** assumes command of French troops in North America.

1758 The British under Generals Amherst and Wolfe take Louisbourg.

1759 **Wolfe takes Quebec**, defeating Montcalm on the Plains of Abraham (Sept. 13). Both generals are killed.

1760 General **James Murray** is appointed military governor of Quebec; he becomes civil governor in **1764.**

1763 France cedes its North American possessions to Britain by the **Treaty of Paris.** A Royal Proclamation imposes British institutions on Quebec (Oct.). This proclamation also serves as the cornerstone for relations between Canadian aboriginal peoples and the Canadian government, preserving land for their use and giving the government exclusive right to negotiate treaties.

1768 **Guy Carleton** succeeds Murray as governor of Quebec.

1769 Frances Brooke publishes *The History of Emily Montague*, a novel with descriptions of geography, climate and social culture in the New World.

1774 The **Quebec Act** provides for British criminal law but restores French civil law and guarantees religious freedom for Roman Catholic colonists.

1775 Americans under Montgomery capture Montreal (Nov.) and attack Quebec (Dec. 31).

1776 Under Carleton, Quebec withstands American siege until the appearance of a British fleet (May 6).

1778 Captain **James Cook** anchors in Nootka Sound, Vancouver Island (Mar. 29–Apr. 26).

1783 The American Revolutionary War ends; the border between Canada and the US is accepted between the Atlantic Ocean and Lake of the Woods.

1784 **United Empire Loyalists** arrive in Canada. The province of **New Brunswick** is created. The **North West Company** is formed.

1789 Alexander **Mackenzie** journeys to the Beaufort Sea, following what would later be named the Mackenzie River.

1791 **Constitutional Act** divides Quebec into Upper and Lower Canada.

1792 **George Vancouver** begins his explorations of the Pacific coast.

1793 Alexander **Mackenzie reaches** the **Pacific.**

1794 **Jay's Treaty** (Nov. 19) between the US and Britain promises British evacuation of the Ohio Valley forts. The treaty's appointment of officials to settle boundary disputes marks the beginning of international arbitration through its provisions for boundary settlements.

1797 **David Thompson** joins the North West Company as a surveyor and mapmaker.

1806 *Le Canadien*, Quebec nationalist newspaper, is founded.

1808 **Simon Fraser**, a North West Company employee, travels the river named after him to the Pacific.

1811 **David Thompson** charts the Columbia River to the Pacific coast.

1812 The US declares war on Britain (June 18), beginning the **War of 1812**. Americans under General William Hull invade Canada from Detroit (July 11). The Red River settlement is begun in Canada's northwest (Aug.–Oct.). Battle of Queenston Heights (Oct. 13): Canadian victory. British **General Isaac Brock** is killed in this battle.

1813 Americans burn York (Apr. 27). Battle of Stoney Creek (June 5): Canadian victory. Battle of Beaver Dams (June 23): Canadian victory; **Laura Secord**, driving a cow, passes American sentries and walks 32 km through dense bush to warn of American attack. Battle of Put-in-Bay, Lake Erie (Sept. 10): American victory. Battle of Moraviantown (Oct. 5): American victory; the Indian Chief **Tecumseh** is killed. Battle of Chateauguay (Oct. 25): Canadian victory. Battle of Crysler's Farm (Nov. 11): Canadian victory.

1814 Battle of Chippewa (July 5): American victory. Battle of Lundy's Lane (July 25): Canadian victory. A British naval force takes Washington (Aug. 24). Battle of Lake Champlain (Sept. 6–11): American victory. The **Treaty of Ghent** ends the War of 1812 (Dec. 24).

1816 Agents of the North West Company kill Robert Semple, governor of the Hudson's Bay Company's Red River colony, and 20 others at White Oaks (June 19).

1817 The **Rush-Bagot** agreement limits the number of battleships on the Great Lakes.

1818 The **49th parallel** is accepted as **Canada's border** with the US from Lake of the Woods to the Rocky Mountains.

1821 The Hudson's Bay Company and the North West Company are amalgamated as the HBC.

1829 The **Lachine** and **Welland Canals** are completed.

1835 **William Lyon Mackenzie** becomes the first mayor of Toronto.

1836 Opening of Canada's **first railway line,** from St. Johns, Que., to La Prairie, Que.

1837 Unsuccessful **rebellions** in Upper and Lower Canada are led by Mackenzie and Louis-Joseph Papineau.

1839 **Lord Durham's Report** recommends union of Upper and Lower Canada and the establishment of responsible government.

1841 The **Act of Union** unites Upper and Lower Canada.

1842 The Ashburton-Webster Treaty settles the Maine-New Brunswick border dispute.

1843 **Fort Victoria** is built to bolster Britain's claim to Vancouver Island.

1846 Great Britain ends a preferential trading policy with the British North American colonies and enters into a **limited free trade agreement** with the United States.

1848 **Responsible government** is achieved in the Canadas and in the Maritimes, thanks to the work of **Robert Baldwin** and **Joseph Howe**.

1849 The boundary of the 49th parallel is extended to the Pacific Ocean. Canada begins its policy of **official bilingualism**. All bills of the United Canada Parliament, now Quebec and Ontario, are given assent in both English and French.

1851 Britain transfers control of the colonial postal system to Canada.

1854 The **Reciprocity Treaty** between Canada and the U.S. is signed (June 6).

1857 Ottawa is named **Canada's capital** by Queen Victoria.

1860 Cornerstone of the **Parliament buildings** is laid (Sept. 1).

1861 The **Grand Trunk Railway** is completed.

1864 The **Charlottetown Conference** (Sept. 1–9) takes the first steps toward **Confederation**. The **Quebec Conference** (Oct. 10–27) sets out the basis for union.

1866 The **London Conference** (Dec. 4) passes resolutions which are redrafted to become the **British North America Act**. First raid into Canada by the **Fenians**, a radical Irish-American, anti-British group, takes place (June 2). The American government allows the **Reciprocity Treaty of 1854 to lapse**.

1867 Confederation. Britain's North American colonies are united by means of the **BNA Act** to become the **Dominion of Canada** (July 1). **Sir John A. Macdonald** is Canada's first prime minister. The BNA Act, now the **Constitution Act, 1867,** confirms the practice of **official bilingualism,** guaranteeing the use of French and English in the debates of the House of Commons and in the Senate, in federal courts and in publications of federal statutes. The provincial legislature, statutes and courts of Quebec are also made bilingual.

1868 Confederationist **Thomas D'Arcy McGee is assassinated** by a Fenian in Canada's first political assassination.

1869 Canada purchases Rupert's Land from the Hudson's Bay Company for £300,000.

1870 Louis Riel leads the Métis in resisting Canadian authority in Canada's northwest. The Métis negotiate with the Canadian government over the right to vote, land laws, the official use of both French and English and the provision of Roman Catholic and Protestant schools. The Manitoba Act creates the province of **Manitoba.**

1871 British Columbia joins Confederation upon the promise from Ottawa to build a **transcontinental railway.**

1872 Macdonald's Conservatives win federal re-election.

1873 Prince Edward Island joins Confederation. A period of economic depression begins. The North-West Mounted Police are formed. **Alexander Mackenzie** becomes Canada's second prime minister after **Macdonald resigns** over the **Pacific Scandal.**

1874 Liberals win federal election.

1875 The **Supreme Court of Canada** is established.

1876 The **Intercolonial Railway** linking central Canada and the Maritimes is completed (July 1). The **Indian Act of 1876** defines special status for aboriginal people living on land reserves and sets out land regulations. Status Indians have no vote in Canadian elections and are exempted from taxation.

1878 Conservatives under Macdonald win federal election.

1879 Macdonald introduces **protective tariffs** as part of his **National Policy.**

1880 Emily Stowe receives her medical licence after practising medicine in Toronto since her graduation from a New York medical school in 1867.

1881 The **Canadian Pacific Railway** is incorporated.

1884 Riel returns to Canada.

1885 Métis and the NWMP clash at Duck Lake (Mar. 26). The Métis are defeated at Batoche (May 9–12). The **last spike of the transcontinental railway** is driven at Craigellachie in Eagle Pass, BC, by Donald Smith (Nov. 7). Louis **Riel is hanged** in Regina (Nov. 16).

1887 Conservatives win federal election. Liberals choose **Wilfrid Laurier** as leader. The **first provincial premiers' conference** takes place in Quebec City.

1889 The **Dominion Women's Enfranchisement Association** is created to campaign for female voting rights in Canada.

1890 Manitoba Liberals under Thomas Greenway halt public funding of Catholic schools in Manitoba (Mar.).

1891 Conservatives win federal election. **Sir John A. Macdonald dies. Sir John Abbott** takes office as prime minister (June 16).

1892 Abbott resigns (Nov. 24). **Sir John Thompson** becomes prime minister (Dec. 5). He establishes the **Canadian Criminal Code.**

1894 Thompson dies (Dec. 12). **Sir Mackenzie Bowell** is asked by the governor general, the Earl of Aberdeen, to form the fourth Conservative government since 1891.

1896 The economic depression ends. Bowell resigns, calling his cabinet a "nest of traitors" (April 27). **Sir Charles Tupper** leads an interim government until the Liberals under Laurier win federal election on **Manitoba Schools Question** (June 23). Canada's minister of the interior, **Clifford Sifton,** develops an immigration plan that will bring farmers from central and eastern Europe to settle on the Prairies. Gold is discovered in the Klondike (Aug. 16).

1897 Gold Rush begins in the Klondike. **Clara Brett Martin** is the first woman admitted to the bar of Ontario.

1898 **Yukon** becomes a separate entity from the Northwest Territories. **Kit Coleman,** the first female Canadian war correspondent, covers the Spanish-American War for a Toronto newspaper.

1899 The first **Canadian troops** ever sent overseas are dispatched to the **Boer War** (Oct. 30).

1901 Marconi receives the **first transatlantic radio message** at St. John's, Newfoundland.

1903 Canada loses the **Alaska Boundary dispute** when British tribunal representative Lord Alverstone sides with the US (Oct. 20). In northern Ontario, Fred LaRose throws hammer at what he thinks are fox's eyes and hits world's richest silver vein.

1904 Liberals win federal election.

1905 The provinces of **Alberta** and **Saskatchewan** are formed.

1907 The **National Council of Women** calls for "equal pay for equal work."

1908 Liberals win federal election.

1909 The Department of External Affairs is formed. John McCurdy's Silver Dart is first heavier-than-air machine to achieve powered flight in Canada at Baddeck, NS. University of Toronto wins **first Grey Cup** football match.

1910 Laurier creates a Canadian navy via the Naval Service Bill.

1911 **Robert Borden** and the Conservatives win federal election, defeating Laurier on the Reciprocity issue.

1914 CP ship *Empress of Ireland* sinks in the St Lawrence in 14 minutes after being rammed in fog, with the loss of 1,014 lives (May 29). **Canada is automatically at war** with Germany when Britain declares war (Aug. 4). The first Canadian troops leave for England (Oct. 3). Parliament passes the **War Measures Act,** allowing suspension of civil rights during periods of emergency. European immigration to Canada increases. Over one million settlers come between 1911 and 1913, bringing total immigration to three million since 1891.

1915 Canadians face German gas attack at **Ypres,** Belgium (Apr. 22). John McCrae writes "In Flanders Fields."

1916 **Nellie McClung** succeeds in persuading the Manitoba government to grant women the right to vote and to hold office (Jan.). The Parliament buildings are destroyed by fire (Feb. 3). Canadian troops fight in the Battle of the **Somme** (July to Nov.); 24,713 Canadians and Newfoundlanders are killed. The unreliable, Canadian-made Ross rifle is withdrawn from war service (Aug.). **Emily Gowan Murphy** is the first woman magistrate appointed within the British Empire.

1917 **Income tax** is **introduced** as a "temporary wartime measure." Prime Minister Sir Robert Borden sits as a member of the Imperial War Cabinet (Feb. 23), giving Canada a voice in war policy. The Military Service Bill is introduced (June 11), leading to the **Conscription Crisis** between Quebec and English Canada. Unionist government under Borden wins federal election, in which **women vote** for the first time. **Louise McKinney** is elected to the Alberta legislature, the first woman in the British Commonwealth to hold such office. Canadians capture **Vimy Ridge,** France (Apr. 9–12). Canadians take **Passchendaele,** Belgium, (Nov. 7) in one of the war's worst battles; of the 20,000 Canadian troops sent into the two-week battle, 15,654 are killed or wounded. Explosion of a munitions ship in **Halifax harbour** wipes out two square miles (5.2 sq km) of Halifax, killing almost 2,000 and injuring 9,000 (Dec. 6).

1918 Canadians break through German trenches at Amiens (Aug. 8), "the black day of the German army." The period from this date until the end of the war becomes known as "Canada's Hundred Days." Armistice ends war (Nov. 11).

1919 Alcock and Brown take off from St. John's, Nfld, (June 14) on the first successful flight across the Atlantic to Cliften, Ireland. A **general strike paralyzes Winnipeg** (May–June), where an armed charge by the RCMP kills one person and injures 30 (June 21).

1920 **Canada joins** the **League of Nations** at its inception (Jan. 10). The flow of emigrants from the British Isles and Europe resumes, many going to urban centres. Federal legislation makes **women eligible** to sit in the **House of Commons.**

1921 Liberals under **Mackenzie King** defeat Conservatives under Arthur Meighen in federal election; the Progressive Party comes in second. **Agnes Macphail** becomes the first woman elected to Parliament. The world's fastest fishing schooner, the *Bluenose,* is launched at Lunenburg, NS. (Mar. 26). **Postwar economic depression** puts 300,000 men and women out of work—more than 15% of the work force.

1922 Canada declines to rally to Britain's side during the Chanak Crisis. Sir Frederick **Banting,** Dr Charles **Best,** Dr J.J.R. MacLeod and J.B. Collip share Nobel Prize for the **discovery of insulin.**

1923 The Canadian Northern and Canadian Transcontinental are merged to form the **Canadian National Railways.** Canada signs the Halibut Treaty with the US without a corroborating British signature. Mackenzie King leads opposition to a common imperial policy ("one voice for the empire") at an Imperial Conference in London.

1925 Although Conservatives win more seats in federal election, Mackenzie King's Liberals remain in power with the support of the Progressives.

1926 King's Liberals win federal election. An Imperial Conference defines British dominions as autonomous (Balfour Report).

1927 Britain's Privy Council awards Labrador to Newfoundland instead of to Quebec (Mar. 1). The Diamond Jubilee of Confederation (July 1) is marked by Canada's first coast-to-coast radio network broadcast. King's government, with the support of the Progressive Party, passes Canada's first **Old Age Pension Act.**

1928 The Supreme Court of Canada rules that, according to the British North America Act, women are not "persons" who could hold public office. This decision is reversed by British Privy Council in 1929.

1929 The **Great Depression** begins.

1930 **Cairine Wilson** is appointed Canada's first woman senator (Feb. 20). The Canadian Federation of Business and Professional Women's Clubs is organized. Conservatives under **R.B. Bennett** win federal election (Aug. 7).

1931 The **Statute of Westminster** (Dec. 11) grants Canada full legislative authority domestically and in external affairs. The Governor General becomes a representative of the crown.

1932 Ottawa Agreements provide for preferential trade between Canada and other Commonwealth nations. The **Co-operative Commonwealth Federation (CCF)** is founded at Calgary.

1933 One in five Canadians is unemployed.

1934 The Bank of Canada is formed. The **Dionne quintuplets** are born in Callander, Ont.

1935 Ten percent of Canadians rely on welfare or "relief." The **On to Ottawa Trek** by young men from government work camps ends in a riot at Regina (July 1). Liberals under Mackenzie King win federal election. The CCF win seven seats. Social Credit claims 17. **William Aberhart** leads Social Credit into office in Alberta.

1936 Union Nationale under **Maurice Duplessis** wins its first election in Quebec.

1937 The **Rowell-Sirois Commission** is appointed to investigate the financial relationship between the federal government and the provinces. First regular flight of **Trans Canada Air Lines** (Sept. 1).

1938 Franklin D. Roosevelt becomes first US President in office to visit Canada, meeting Mackenzie King at Kingston.

1939 **Canada declares war** on Germany (Sept. 10) after remaining neutral for a week following the British declaration. Quebec Premier Maurice Duplessis, who opposed Quebec participation in the war, is defeated by the Liberals on that issue (Oct. 26).

1940 **Unemployment insurance** is **introduced.** Liberals win federal election (Mar. 26). The Permanent Joint Board of Defence is formed between Canada and the US. **Thérèse Casgrain** wins women in Quebec the right to vote and to hold provincial office.

1941 Canadians are captured when Hong Kong falls to Japanese (Dec. 25); about 500 of the POWs subsequently die in Japanese camps. Immigration has changed Canadian demographic structure. Canadians of British ancestry now make up 49.7% of the population, of French descent 30.3% and of other ethnic backgrounds 20%.

1942 In Canada's first European war action, many Canadians are captured or killed in the disastrous **Dieppe** raid (Aug. 19). Canadians of Japanese descent are moved inland from the coast of British Columbia as "security risks"; their property is confiscated. A national plebiscite releases Mackenzie King from his pledge of no conscription but reveals deep divisions between Quebec and the rest of Canada.

1943 Canadians participate in the invasion of Sicily (July 10). Canadians win the Battle of Ortona (Dec. 20–28). **Ernest C. Manning** wins first of nine successive elections for the Social Credit in Alberta.

1944 Canadian troops push further inland than any other Allied unit on D-Day (June 6). Canadian forces fight as a separate army (July 23). Saskatchewan elects Tommy Douglas's CCF, the first socialist government in North America. Maurice Duplessis regains office for the Union Nationale in Quebec.

1945 War in Europe ends (May 5). One million Canadians fought in WW II; 42,042 were killed. Canadians killed while fighting for other Allied forces numbered 4,500. Liberals win federal election (June 11). First **family allowance payments** are **made** (June 20). Canada joins the **United Nations** (June 26). Igor Gouzenko defects from the Soviet Embassy in Ottawa (Sept. 5) and reveals the existence in Canada of a Soviet spy network. Canada's first nuclear reactor begins operations at Chalk River, Ont.

1947 Imperial Oil discovers the **Leduc oil field** (Feb. 13).

1948 **Louis St Laurent** succeeds Mackenzie King as prime minister (Nov. 15).

1949 Under Premier **Joey Smallwood**, **Newfoundland** becomes Canada's 10th province (Mar. 31). Canada joins NATO. Canadian appeals to Britain's Judicial Committee of the Privy Council are abolished: Canada's Supreme Court becomes final court of appeal. Liberals under St Laurent defeat Conservatives under George Drew in federal election (June 3).

1950 The Korean War begins (June 25); Canadian troops participate in the conflict as part of a United Nations force.

1951 The midcentury census reports Canada's population as 14,009,429. **Postwar immigration** to Canada exceeds 100,000 annually during the 1950s, primarily moving from central and eastern Europe to hold manufacturing jobs in urban centres. The Massey Royal Commission reports that Canadian cultural life is dominated by American influences. Revisions to the **Indian Act**, beginning in 1951, limit its coverage of aboriginal people. Indian women married to non-Indian men are excluded from the act. This provision was removed in 1985 after much protest of discrimination. **Charlotte Whitton** the first woman to be elected mayor of a major Canadian city, is elected in Ottawa.

1952 **Vincent Massey** becomes the first native-born Governor General of Canada. Canada's **first television** stations begin broadcasting in Montreal (Sept. 6) and Toronto (Sept. 8). **W.A.C. Bennett** begins **Social Credit's** administration in British Columbia.

1953 Canada's National Library is established in Ottawa (Jan. 1). The Stratford Festival opens (July 13). The **Korean War ends** (July 27); total Canadian casualties are 314 killed and 1,211 wounded. Liberals under St Laurent defeat Conservatives under Drew in federal election (Aug. 10).

1954 An economic slump interrupts the postwar boom. Canada's **first subway** opens in Toronto (Mar. 30). Roger Bannister and John Landy run the "miracle mile" at the British Empire Games in Vancouver (Aug.), the first time two men crack the four-minute barrier in the same race. Sixteen-year-old Marilyn Bell becomes the first person to swim Lake Ontario (Sept. 9). **Hurricane Hazel** hits Toronto, killing 83 people (Oct. 15). The Geneva Conference on the Far East invites Canada to join India and Poland in **supervising peace in Indochina**. This peacekeeping commitment continues for nearly 20 years to 1973.

1955 The Canadian Labour Congress is formed. The suspension of Montreal Canadiens' hockey star Maurice (Rocket) Richard leads to rioting in Montreal (Mar. 17).

1956 The Liberals use closure to limit the **Pipeline Debate** (May 8–June 6), a manoeuvre that contributes to their electoral defeat the following year.

1957 Conservatives under **John Diefenbaker** win federal election (June 10) and form minority government. Ellen Fairclough becomes the first woman federal cabinet minister. The Canada Council is created to help foster Canadian cultural life. **Lester B. Pearson wins Nobel Prize** (Oct.

12) for his role in resolving the Suez Crisis. Canadian supply and services troops are sent to work with a multinational UN force around the **Gulf of Aqaba**. They stay until 1967 and return there in 1973.

1958 Conservatives under Diefenbaker win 208 seats in federal election (Mar. 31). Coal mine disaster at Springhill, NS, results in death of 74 miners.

1959 The **Avro Arrow** project is terminated, with a loss of almost 14,000 jobs (Feb. 20). The **St. Lawrence Seaway** is **opened** (June 26).

1960 Liberals under **Jean Lesage** win provincial election in Quebec (June 22), inaugurating the **Quiet Revolution**. A **Canadian Bill of Rights** is approved by Parliament. Native people get the right to vote in federal elections. During the 1960s French is recognized as a language of instruction in elementary and secondary schools in New Brunswick, Ontario and Manitoba. It is recognized subsequently in other provincial jurisdictions.

1961 The **New Democratic Party** replaces the CCF.

1962 Conservatives are reduced to minority status in federal election (June 18). Social Credit wins 30 seats and NDP take 19 to control the balance of power in the House of Commons. The Saskatchewan NDP introduces the first Canadian **Medicare** plan (July 1), and is opposed by a doctors' strike. **Trans-Canada Highway** officially opens (Sept. 3). Canadian-made satellite *Alouette* is launched (Sept. 29), making Canada the third nation in space. Canada's last execution, the double hanging of Ronald Turpin and Arthur Lucas, takes place (Dec. 11), at the Don Jail in Toronto.

1963 Liberals under Pearson win federal election (Apr. 8), and form a minority government. The Quebec separatist group **Front de Libération du Québec (FLQ)** sets off a series of bombs in Montreal (Apr.–May). A TCA flight crashes in Quebec, killing all 118 people aboard (Nov. 29). The **Royal Commission on Bilingualism and Biculturalism** begins its work.

1964 Canadians get social insurance cards (Apr.). Northern Dancer becomes the first Canadian horse to win the Kentucky Derby (May 2). Canada ends difficult peacekeeping duties in the Congo (Zaïre) after four years of service with heavy casualties. Canadian troops join UN forces in Cyprus, a posting which continues until 1993.

1965 Canada gets a new flag (Feb. 15). The **Autopact** between Canada and the US is signed. Canadian Roman Catholic Churches begin to celebrate mass in English (Mar. 7). Liberals win federal election (Nov. 8) to continue as a minority government. Failure of an Ontario Hydro relay device at Queenston plunges eastern North America into a power blackout (Nov. 9).

1966 The **Munsinger Affair** becomes Canada's first major parliamentary sex scandal (Mar. 4). The **Canada Pension Plan** is established. The CBC begins colour television broadcasting (Oct. 1).

1967 The Canadian army, navy and air forces are **unified** to become the Canadian **Armed Forces** (Apr. 25). Montreal hosts a world's fair, **Expo 67** (opened Apr. 27). Canada celebrates its **Centennial** (July 1). French President Charles **de Gaulle** delivers his "Vive Québec Libre" speech in Montreal (July 24). The federal Department of Manpower and Immigration establishes the **"points system"** for immigrants. Patterns shift in the 1960s from European to Third World immigration as humanitarian objectives and family reunification policies increase multicultural immigration.

1968 Pierre Elliott Trudeau succeeds Pearson as Prime Minister (Apr. 6), and leads Liberals to majority in federal election (June 25). A Royal Commission on the Status of Women is appointed. Canadian divorce law is reformed.

1969 Saturday postal deliveries end (Feb. 1). Abortion law is liberalized (May). English and French become **official languages** of federal administration (July 9). New Brunswick declares official bilingualism. The breathalizer comes into use as a test for alcohol-impaired drivers (Dec. 1).

1970 The FLQ kidnaps British trade commissioner James Cross (Oct. 5), precipitating the **October Crisis**. Quebec labour and immigration minister Pierre Laporte is kidnapped (Oct. 10), and found murdered (Oct. 17). The federal government invokes the **War Measures Act** (Oct. 16), leading to the arrest of 465 people.

1971 A policy of **multiculturalism** is adopted by the federal government. Pierre Trudeau becomes the first prime minister to wed while in office when he marries 22-year-old Margaret Sinclair (Mar. 4). Canadian Gerhard Herzberg wins the Nobel Prize in chemistry for his studies of chemical reactions that help produce smog.

1972 Canada defeats the USSR in the first hockey series between the Soviets and Canadian professionals (Aug.–Sept.). Liberals win federal election with 109 seats to the Conservatives 107, with the NDP holding the balance of power at 31 (Oct. 30).

1973 The House of Commons passes a resolution (Jan. 5) criticizing US bombing of North Vietnam. Dr Henry Morgentaler is acquitted by a Montreal jury of having performed an illegal abortion (Nov. 13). The separatist Parti Québécois becomes the official Opposition in Quebec. Canadian troops are sent to the Middle East to serve with the United Nations Emergency Task Force there until 1979. Canada continues to send observers for the UN to the Golan Heights and to provide truce supervision personnel in Israel, Egypt, Lebanon, Jordan and Syria.

1974 Soviet ballet star Mikhail Baryshnikov defects in Montreal (June 29). Liberals under Trudeau win federal election and form majority government (July 8). **Pauline McGibbon** becomes the first female lieutenant-governor (Ont.) in the British Commonwealth.

1975 The **CN Tower**, the world's tallest free-standing structure at 553.339 metres, is completed in Toronto (Apr. 2). Federal government announces (July 18) its intention to screen foreign investment in Canada, via the Foreign Investment Review Agency (FIRA). Television cameras are allowed inside the House of Commons for the first time. Federal government imposes **wage and price controls** in an effort to fight inflation (Oct. 14). **Grace Hartman** is elected president of the Canadian Union of Public Employees.

1976 Canada announces 200-nautical-mile coastal fishing zone (June 4). **Death penalty** is **abolished** in a free vote (130–124) in Parliament (July 14). Montreal hosts **Olympic Games** (July 17–31). Team Canada wins the first **Canada Cup** hockey series (Sept. 15). The **Parti Québécois** under René Lévesque wins provincial election in Quebec (Nov. 15).

T. Eaton Company discontinues catalogue sales after 92 years.

1977 Prime Minister Trudeau and his wife Margaret separate (May 27). Quebec government pases Bill 101, restricting English-language schooling to children whose mother or father had attended English elementary school in Quebec (Aug. 26). Highway signs in most of Canada become metric (Sept. 6).

1978 **Soviet nuclear-powered satellite crashes** in Canadian north (Jan. 24). The federal government orders birth control pills sold in Canada to include a warning that women over 30 who smoke, and all women over 40, should not use them. Sun Life Assurance Co. announces a head office move from Montreal to Toronto because of language laws and political instability in Quebec.

1979 Conservatives under **Joe Clark** win federal election (May 22). Canada's first gold bullion coin, the Maple Leaf, goes on sale (Sept. 5). 220,000 people are evacuated from Mississauga, Ont., because of derailed tanker cars containing chlorine and other chemicals (Nov. 10). Supreme Court of Canada declares Manitoba and Quebec legislation creating unilingual courts and legislatures unconstitutional (Dec. 13). Federal Conservatives lose non-confidence vote on budget (Dec. 13), forcing the government's resignation. **Antonine Maillet** wins the prestigious French literary prize, the Prix Goncourt, for her novel *Pélagie-la-Charette*.

1980 Canada's ambassador to Iran, Ken Taylor, arranges the successful **escape of six American Embassy staff** from Tehran while their colleagues are held hostage (Jan. 28). Liberals win federal election (Feb. 18). Canada decides to boycott the Olympic Games in Moscow because of the Soviet invasion of Afghanistan. **Jeanne Sauvé** becomes the first female Speaker of the House of Commons (April 14). **Quebec votes "no"** to "sovereignty-association" (separatism) in a **referendum** (May 22). **O Canada** becomes Canada's national anthem (June 27). The Supreme Court awards Rosa Becker half the assets accumulated during a 19-year common-law relationship. **National Energy Program** is created to encourage oil self-sufficiency, increase Canadian ownership in the oil industry and obtain a larger share of Canadian energy revenues.

1981 Terry Fox dies of cancer at age 22 (June 29); his "Marathon of Hope," in which he tried to run across Canada on one leg after having lost the other to cancer, raised $25 million for cancer research. Quebec bans public signs in English (Sept. 23). The federal government and every province except Quebec reach agreement on a method for patriating Canada's constitution (Nov. 5). The 1981 census indicates significant increases in the percentage of new Canadians from Asia, the Caribbean and Latin America.

1982 The *Ocean Ranger,* an oil platform off the coast of Newfoundland, sinks with the loss of 84 lives (Feb. 15). Bertha Wilson becomes Canada's first woman to be appointed a justice of the Supreme Court (Mar. 4). The Quebec Court of Appeal rejects the Quebec government's claim of veto power over constitutional change (Apr. 7). Canada gains a new **Constitution** and **Charter of Rights and Freedoms** (Apr. 17). The charter entrenches bilingualism within federal jurisdictions and provides for minority language educational rights across Canada. Canada's GNP falls 4.8% in the worst recession since the Great Depression of the 1930s.

1983 Canadian pay-TV channels begin operation (Feb. 1). **Jeanne Sauvé** is Canada's first woman to be appointed Governor General (Dec. 23). Canada approves a US plan to test unarmed **cruise missiles** in western Canada beginning in 1984.

1984 Trudeau wins the 1984 Albert Einstein Peace Award for his globetrotting efforts to draw world leaders' attention to the disarmament talks. He is succeeded as prime minister by **John Turner** (June 30). Conservatives under **Brian Mulroney** win federal election with 211 seats, the largest majority in Canada's history (Sept. 4). The **Pope visits Canada** (Sept. 9–20). **Marc Garneau** becomes the first Canadian in space, aboard US space shuttle *Challenger* (Oct. 5). Council for the Northwest Territories recognizes the use of **aboriginal languages** as well as English and French. Yukon Territory passes similar language legislation in 1988.

1985 The voyage through the Northwest Passage of US icebreaker *Polar Sea* challenges Canada's **Arctic sovereignty**. Longtime premiers Bill Davis (Ont.), René Lévesque (Que.) and Peter Lougheed (Alta) retire. Prime Minister Mulroney and US

President Reagan declare mutual support for **Star Wars research** and **free trade** between the two nations at "Shamrock Summit" (Mar. 18) in Quebec City. The Liberals under Robert Bourassa defeat the Parti Québécois (Dec. 2). Ontario Liberals under David Peterson end four decades of Conservative rule.

1986 The Canadian dollar hits an all-time low of 70.20 cents US (Jan. 31). The **Expo 86** world's fair is held in Vancouver from May 2 to Oct. 13. The US imposes stiff tariffs (May 22) on imported Canadian shakes and shingles. Canada joins other Commonwealth nations (Aug. 5) in adopting **economic sanctions against South Africa** because of its apartheid policy. One hundred and fifteen **Tamil refugees** from Sri Lanka are found drifting in lifeboats off the coast of Newfoundland (Aug. 11). Canada receives a United Nations award (Oct. 6) for providing a haven for world refugees. Canadian John Polanyi shares the Nobel Prize for chemistry.

1987 The Bank of Canada rate drops to a 13-year low of 7.49% (Jan. 28); 6-month residential mortgages are as low as 7.5%. The **Meech Lake Accord**, proposing major constitutional amendments, is agreed to by Prime Minister Brian Mulroney and the 10 provincial premiers (Apr. 30). Ontario passes the first **pay equity legislation** for the private sector enacted in North America (June). A free vote in Parliament on restoration of **capital punishment** defeats the proposal 148–127 (June). A tornado kills 26 and injures 250 others in Edmonton (July 20). Team Canada wins the Canada Cup in a 6-5 victory over the Soviet Union (Sept. 15). A **free trade** agreement between Canada and the United States is reached (Oct. 3); the deal would still require ratification by both houses of Parliament and the US Congress. **Stock prices tumble** (Oct. 19) in Canada and throughout the world. The founding assembly of the **Reform Party** of Canada is held (Nov.)

1988 Canada is left without an **abortion law** (Jan. 28) when the Supreme Court rules that existing legislation is unconstitutional. The XV **Winter Olympics** open in Calgary (Feb. 13). Canadian sprinter **Ben Johnson** sets a world record and wins a gold medal at the Summer Olympics in Seoul (Sept. 24) but is stripped of both (Sept. 26) after testing positive for steroids. Brian Mulroney's Progressive Conservatives win a second consecutive majority in the **federal election** (Nov. 21), a bitter campaign fought over the impending free trade agreement with the US. Quebec's **French-only sign law** is struck down by the Supreme Court (Dec. 15) but is re-instated by Quebec (Dec. 21) using the "notwithstanding" clause in the Charter of Rights and Freedoms. Free trade legislation passes the House of Commons (Dec. 24) and the Senate (Dec. 30) two days before it is due to take effect. The "Kamloops Amendment" to the Indian Act grants band councils jurisdiction over all reserve land, including the power to impose taxes.

1989 The federal government announces a new **goods and services tax** (GST) to take effect Jan. 1991. Audrey McLaughlin becomes Canada's **first female national party leader** as the NDP chooses a successor to Ed Broadbent (Dec. 2). Fourteen **female university students are killed** by an anti-feminist gunman in Montreal (Dec. 6).

1990 Revisions to the Criminal Code provide choice of language in criminal hearings (Jan.). Several Quebec Conservative MPs, led by cabinet minister Lucien Bouchard (May 21), leave the government to form the pro-independence **Bloc Québécois**. The **Meech Lake Accord dies** when both Newfoundland and Manitoba fail to ratify the constitutional agreement by the deadline (June 23). Manitoba MLA **Elijah Harper** refuses the unanimous consent required for debate and a vote on the Meech Lake Accord because the accord does not provide special status for aboriginal peoples as it does for Quebec. Jean Chétien becomes leader of the federal Liberal party. A land dispute leads to a 78-day armed confrontation between Mohawk warriors and government forces at the Kanesatake reserve near **Oka**, Que. **Canada sends warships** to the Persian Gulf as part of the multinational force being assembled to force Iraq to withdraw from occupied Kuwait. Ontario elects its **first NDP government**, led by **Bob Rae** (Sept. 7). Brian Mulroney's Conservative government stacks the Senate (Sept. 27) with new appointees to ensure passage of the federal **goods and services tax** (GST), which becomes law Dec. 17 to take effect Jan. 1.

1991 Canadian military personnel participate with the Allied forces in the assault against Iraq beginning Jan. 16. (the **Gulf War**). After the war 300 Canadian military engineers join the UN mission patrolling the demilitarized zone between Iraq and Kuwait. Former Chicago Cubs pitcher **Ferguson Jenkins** becomes the first Canadian to be voted into baseball's hall of fame. Prime Minister Brian Mulroney and US President George Bush sign an **acid rain accord** with the goal of ending acid rain within ten years. **Rita Johnston** succeeds BC Premier **William Vander Zalm** as premier, the first woman to enter the provincial premier's office in Canada. Mulroney's government announces a **new constitutional reform package** promising aboriginal self-government within 10 years and guaranteed aboriginal representation in an elected Senate. Economists charge that Bank of Canada fight against inflation stalls economy; cross-border shopping reported up 57% in first six months of the year; Michael Harcourt and NDP defeat Socreds in BC; Roy Romanow and NDP oust Conservatives in Saskatchewan. **Gun control** bill passed, imposing tougher controls and banning imported military assault weapons; **Yukon First Nations** sign umbrella agreement on land claims and self-government; agreement reached on creation of Nunavut in Northwest Territories.

1992 Environment Canada officials warn of thinning **ozone** layers that will reduce atmospheric protection from the sun (Feb. 4); a year-long crisis in the Atlantic **fisheries** results in a two-year shutdown of the cod fishery (July 2), a five-year ban on commercial salmon fishing in Nfld. (Mar. 6) and international negotiations to protect the fish stocks; **Gwich'in Indians** sign a deal with Ottawa, giving them title to nearly 24 000 sq. km of land in the NWT and Yukon (Apr. 22); final talks on North American Free Trade Agreement (**NAFTA**) begin July 25 with final details announced Aug. 12, Prime Min. Mulroney signs the deal on Dec. 17; negotiations on **constitutional reform** take place throughout the year and an agreement (the Charlottetown Accord) that has Quebec's approval is announced Aug. 19 (proposals include Senate reform, an enlarged House of Commons and self-government for native people); a national referendum on the accord is held Oct. 26 and No side claims victory, killing the deal.

1993 See "News Events of the Year."

Quotes of the Year

Selected by John Robert Colombo

Here are some "quotable quotes"—the most memorable remarks made by Canadians between October 1992 and October 1993 (the Almanac year), arranged chronologically. The selection gives representation to both public figures and private commentators to the extent that their remarks made the headlines, lodged in the memory or illustrated subjects of importance.

1 "A bad day in Canada is better than a good day in any other country on the globe."

(Richard Berryman, columnist, paraphrasing a bumper sticker message, *The Hamilton Spectator*, Oct. 10, 1992.)

2 "The current mess shows the consequences of treating people as members of minorities with special rights rather than as people, all of whom should have the same rights."

(Unsigned article about the state of Canada with respect to challenges under the Charter of Rights and Freedoms and the movement to define Quebec's 'distinct culture,' *The Economist*, Oct. 17, 1992.)

3 "The role of the press used to be to provide a check on excessive political power, but now it's gone the other way. The genuine power to influence now rests with television, not the politicians. Governments rise and fall based on the impressions that are left with the public via this medium."

(Marjorie Nichols, columnist, *Mark My Words: the Memoirs of a Very Political Reporter* (1992) written with Jane O'Hara.)

4 "I want to ask you gentlemen, if I cannot give consent to my own death, then whose body is this? Who owns my life?"

(Sue Rodriguez, victim of a terminal illness, in her presentation to a House of Commons justice subcommittee urging amendments to the section of the Criminal Code that makes it a crime to assist in a suicide; quoted by Deborah Wilson in *The Globe and Mail*, Dec. 5,1992.)

5 "The best curriculum around to train Canadians how to cope with the future is to teach them how to be their own boss.... The most enlightened retraining policy a government can deliver is to give the unemployed, or anyone else, the generic skills to enable them to be self-employed."

(Diane Francis, columnist, *Maclean's*, Jan. 11, 1993.)

6 "When the history of the Mulroney government is written, the title can be 'Prime Minister of Canada, on loan from Washington.' I have never seen a head of state so contemptuous of preserving the sovereignty of a nation. It is just inconceivable, other than because of a personality failure, that a prime minister would consistently thumb his nose at history, evidence and public opinion."

(Ralph Nader, US consumer advocate, interviewed by Joe Chidly in *Maclean's*, Jan. 11, 1993.)

7 "Countries that have soldiers in charge seem, more often than not, to be the ones where democracy is but a flickering candle sitting in an open window with a forecast of rain."

(L.W. MacKenzie, Major-General in the Canadian Armed Forces, on his retirement, *The Globe and Mail*, Jan. 21, 1993.)

8 "Canada today is understood better as being composed of two quite different kinds of societies—an ethnic, European-style nation in Quebec, and a 'rest of Canada' that is well on the way to becoming a multi-ethnic World Nation."

(Richard Gwyn, columnist, "Home and Away," *The Toronto Star*, Jan. 31, 1993.)

9 "Non-white, non-Christian, non-French or non-English: let us stop in effect using those definitions to be synonymous with being non-Canadian."

(Dwight Wylie, Jamaican-born CBC Radio newscaster, address, Canadian Club of Toronto, Feb. 8, 1993, quoted by Peter Small in *The Toronto Star* the following day.)

10 "There's blood on the water."

(James Ross Fulton, MP, characterizing the James Bay II hydro-electric power development during an interview, Feb. 11, 1993. Hydro-Quebec was quick to denounce the suggestion; Fulton explained that he meant animal blood, not human blood.)

11 "Spanish will be the second language in Canada shortly after the start of the third millennium."

(Frank Ogden, futurologist, quoted by Ken MacQueen in *The Ottawa Citizen*, Feb. 13, 1993.)

12 "I often say, out on the lecture circuit, that if Greenpeace had started in any country other than Canada, the head office would still be in that country. Can you imagine the Germans or Brits or Americans or Spaniards giving up the title copyright? Not on your life."

(Bob Hunter, columnist, one of the founders of Greenpeace (now Greenpeace International, based abroad) in Vancouver, *Eye*, Feb. 18, 1993.)

13 "A millennium will date itself to the advent of computer technology. The impact of computers on human development will be as important as that of the Renaissance."

(Michael Greenberg, CEO of ISG Technologies, Inc., quoted by Daniel Stoffman in "Northern Bytes," *The Globe and Mail's Report on Business Magazine*, Mar. 1993.)

14 "Americans have great and noble principles and they go to hell trying to live up to them. Canadians also have great and noble principles, but they go to heaven figuring out ways to get around them."

(Noam Chomsky, US Linguist, quoted by Chris Dafoe in *The Globe and Mail*, Mar. 13, 1993.)

15 "In a planet of five to eight billion minds all hooked up together, there will be, finally, a place for everyone. The problem will not be how to eat. Rather it will be how to conduct the conversation."

(Dian Cohen and Guy Stanley, economic writers, *No Small Change: Succeeding in Canada's New Economy* (1993).)

16 "This has been the world's most competitive market. We had all of your television and all of ours.... Americans should cherish their Canadian experience, because they are going to see it proliferate all over the world."

(Moses Znaimer, executive, CITY-TV, quoted by Michael T. Malloy in "Global Entertainment," *The Wall Street Journal*, Mar. 26, 1993.)

17 "We don't *hafta* have NAFTA."

(Slogan of the Canadian Union of Public Employees in *The Canadian Forum*, Apr. 1993.)

18 "Most Canadian executives' idea of spirituality these days is to pray every night that they'll have a job the next morning."

(Peter C. Newman, columnist, "Business Watch," *Maclean's*, Apr. 12, 1993.)

19 "One can only be racist if one has power. Racism without power doesn't mean a damn thing. If you go into the ghetto you will find many blacks and whites who don't like each other. It's not a matter of power or racism. The fact is they just don't like each other. It's as simple as that. But don't call it racism."

(Arnold Auguste, publisher of the black weekly paper *Share*, distinguishing between bigotry and racism, quoted by Paul Palango, "City," *Eye*, May 6, 1993.)

20 "Don't mess with me. I've got tanks."

(Kim Campbell, Minister of National Defence and PC leadership candidate, quoted by Allan Fotheringham in *Maclean's*, May 10, 1993.)

21 "What I think this evening's debate reflects is a strong sense among the candidates that this race is a race within the family, and that at the end of the leadership campaign we will unite as a family to go forward and defeat not just the enemies of the Progressive Conservative party, but the enemies of Canada, and I use that term mildly I suppose."

(Kim Campbell, Minister of National Defence and Conservative leadership candidate, speaking at a leadership forum, Vancouver, May 13, 1993 and quoted by Rosemary Speirs in *The Toronto Star*, May 15, 1993. This is the origin of Campbell's so-called "enemies of Canada" remark which was directed against citizens who disagreed with policies of the Conservative party. It was disavowed by Jean Charest and other leadership contenders and then by Campbell herself, who explained to reporters, "It was not what I meant to say. As soon as it was out of my mouth, I realized I'd used a stronger word than I meant to use... I certainly wouldn't mean to offend anybody.")

22 "One of the absurdities of the Cold War is that 15 billion years of evolution could have ended in 15 minutes of nuclear war."

(Hubert Reeves, Quebec-born, Paris-based cosmologist and broadcaster, quoted by André Picard in *The Globe and Mail*, May 14, 1993.)

23 "The field of our dreams is flooded and frozen and has a net at either end."

(Joey Slinger, columnist, writing about hockey with an allusion to a baseball image associated with the novelist W.P. Kinsella, *The Toronto Star*, May 20, 1993.)

24 "You can be, these days, a popular prime minister or you can be an effective one. You can't be both."

(former Prime Min. Brian Mulroney, referring to himself and to British Prime Min. John Major, during a press conference at No. 10 Downing Street, London, England, May 11, 1993, quoted by Paul Koring in *The Globe and Mail* the following day.)

25 "Political leaders must understand they can stay too long and therefore run the risk of confusing their personal ambitions with the fundamental interests of the nation. I had seen it happen before and resolved it should not happen again. I, therefore, will be turning the government over to a new and younger generation of Canadians who can deal with these challenges, unburdened by the memory of past battles won or lost."

(former Prime Min. Brian Mulroney, in an address to Conservative party gathering, Ottawa, May 28, 1993, quoted by Susan Delacourt in *The Globe and Mail* the following day.)

26 "Our Lady of the Helicopters"

(sobriquet bestowed upon Conservative leadership contender Kim Campbell by Mordecai Richler, "Hail, Brian, and Farewell," *Saturday Night*, June 1993.)

27 "Ideas are harder to change than leaders. That may be because they matter more."

(Desmond Morton, historian, "A Time to Think About Leadership," *The Toronto Star*, June 6, 1993.)

28 "Canada is the only country in the world in which the majority is the moral guarantor of the minority."

(Laurier LaPierre, historian and broadcaster, CTV Network, July 2, 1993.)

29 "Life contains awful things. By the time you've reached a certain age, you notice."

(Margaret Atwood, author, "Why I Write," *Quill & Quire*, Aug. 1993.)

30 "The older I get, the better I used to be."

(Peter Gzowski, broadcaster and golfer for literacy, quoted by Alan Husak in *The Montreal Gazette*, Aug. 8, 1993.)

Fathers of Confederation

Union of the British North American colonies into the Dominion of Canada was discussed and its terms negotiated at three confederation conferences held at Charlottetown (C), Sept. 1, 1864; Quebec (Q), Oct. 10, 1864; and London (L), Dec. 4, 1866. The names of delegates are followed by the provinces they represented; Canada refers to what are now the provinces of Ontario and Quebec.

Adams G. Archibald, NS	C,Q,L
George Brown, Canada	C,Q
Alexander Campbell, Canada	C,Q
Frederick B.T. Carter, Nfld	Q
George-Étienne Cartier, Canada	C,Q,L
Edward B. Chandler, NB	C,Q
Jean-Charles Chapais, Canada	Q
James Cockburn, Canada	Q
George H. Coles, PEI	C,Q
Robert B. Dickey, NS	C,Q
Charles Fisher, NB	Q,L
Alexander T. Galt, Canada	C,Q,L
John Hamilton Gray, NB	C,Q
John Hamilton Gray, PEI	C,Q
Thomas Heath Haviland, PEI	Q
William A. Henry, NS	C,Q,L
William P. Howland, Canada	L
John M. Johnson, NB	C,Q,L
Hector L. Langevin, Canada	C,Q,L
Jonathan McCully, NS	C,Q,L
A.A. Macdonald, PEI	C,Q
John A. Macdonald, Canada	C,Q,L
William McDougall, Canada	C,Q,L
Thomas D'Arcy McGee, Canada	C,Q
Peter Mitchell, NB	Q,L
Oliver Mowat, Canada	Q
Edward Palmer, PEI	C,Q
William H. Pope, PEI	C,Q
John W. Ritchie, NS	L
J. Ambrose Shea, Nfld	Q
William H. Steeves, NB	C,Q
Sir Étienne-Paschal Taché, Canada	Q
Samuel Leonard Tilley, NB	C,Q,L
Charles Tupper, NS	C,Q,L
Edward Whelan, PEI	Q
R.D. Wilmot, NB	L

Canadian Disasters

Aug. 29, 1583: Canada's first recorded marine disaster took 85 lives when the *Delight* was wrecked on Sable Island.

Aug. 23, 1711: As many as 950 drowned when ships attached to the British fleet preparing to attack Quebec were grounded and sank on the rocks of Ile-aux-Oeufs.

Oct. 5, 1825: The Miramichi fire, north of New Brunswick's Miramichi River, destroyed the towns of Newcastle and Douglastown, and killed between 200–500 people.

May 17, 1841: On this date, several large boulders from Cap Diamant tumbled down the precipitous cliffs above the Lower Town of Quebec City and demolished eight houses, killing 32 people.

Oct. 27, 1854: In one of the earliest Canadian train disasters, a gravel train running near Baptiste Creek, 24 km west of Chatham, Ont., was hit by an express train on the same line. In the collision, 52 persons were killed and 48 seriously injured.

June 29, 1864: Near St-Hilaire, Que., a passenger train was unable to stop for an open drawbridge at the Beloeil bridge on the Richelieu River. The train plunged through the opening onto passing barges, killing 99 and injuring 100 people.

Apr. 1, 1873: Sailing from Liverpool to New York, the steamer *Atlantic* struck Meager's Rock off the coast of Nova Scotia and sank with the loss of 535 people.

May 13, 1873: Sixty men died when a fire and subsequent explosion in a coal mine at Westville, Pictou County, N.S., trapped firemen and workers. The mine was eventually sealed to starve the fire of oxygen and it was two years before all the bodies were recovered.

Aug. 25, 1873: The Great Nova Scotia Cyclone swept over Cape Breton Island. The hurricane destroyed 1,200 vessels and 900 buildings, demolished dykes, wharves and bridges and claimed 500 lives.

Feb. 21, 1891: In the first of several major disasters in the coal mines of Springhill, N.S., 125 men were killed in an explosion.

May 26, 1896: Fifty-five people were killed when a bridge at Point Ellice in Victoria, B.C., collapsed while a streetcar was passing over it. The bridge was too weak to support the weight of a recently built tramline.

Sept. 19, 1899: A massive rockslide from the cliffs above Quebec City's Lower Town demolished most of Champlain St, killing 45 people.

Apr. 29, 1903: Parts of the town of Frank, Alta., were obliterated by a sudden landslide when over 50 million tonnes of limestone came crashing down Turtle Mountain, crossed the four-km-wide valley floor and rolled up the other side of the valley. Approximately 50 people were killed. The landslide also sealed a mine entrance at the foot of the mountain and trapped 17 miners inside. The men were able to escape by digging a new tunnel to the surface.

Aug. 29, 1907: The Quebec Bridge, 11 km north of Quebec City, was the largest cantilevered bridge in the world at the time. As the bridge was nearing completion, the southern cantilever span collapsed, killing 75 workmen.

Mar. 5, 1910: A CPR work crew clearing the tracks from a previous snow slide in Rogers Pass, B.C., was hit by an avalanche. Sixty-two men were killed; one survived.

June 30, 1912: The worst tornado in Canadian history swept through Regina, Sask., killing 28 residents, injuring hundreds and causing $75 million damage (est. 1990 dollars).

May 29, 1914: The Canadian Pacific liner *Empress of Ireland* collided with a Norwegian coal ship in the St Lawrence River near Rimouski, Que., and sank in only 14 minutes with the loss of 1,014 lives. This was one of the worst naval disasters in history, with the eighth largest loss of life for a naval accident.

June 19, 1914: The worst coal mine disaster in Canadian history occurred at Hillcrest, Alta., when dust explosions killed 189 men.

July 29, 1916: A forest fire in northern Ontario, thought to have been started by lightning and locomotive sparks, engulfed the towns of Cochrane and Matheson, killing at least 233 persons.

Sept. 11, 1916: The Quebec Bridge was the scene of further tragedy when a new centre span being hoisted into position fell into the river below. Thirteen men were killed, bringing the loss of life during construction of the bridge to 88.

Dec. 6, 1917: Halifax was the scene of Canada's worst single disaster when a French munitions ship filled with explosives collided with a freighter in Halifax harbour. The French ship, the *Mont Blanc*, was split to the waterline; fuel oil spilled over its explosive cargo and started a fire in the hold. The crew abandoned ship without attempting to extinguish the fire.

In the explosion that followed, the *Mont Blanc* was tossed more than 1,000 m into the air. The explosion levelled homes and businesses in a large part of the city and set off explosives stockpiled on shore. The blast, heard as far away as Prince Edward Island, is thought to be the largest-ever accidental explosion, and the largest non-nuclear blast in history. More than 1,600 people were killed, 9,000 injured, and 6,000 left homeless. Property damage was estimated at $35 million.

Oct. 23, 1918: The Canadian Pacific steamship *Princess Sophia* ran onto Vanderbilt Reef while sailing from Alaska to Vancouver. The ship sank two days later on Oct. 25. All 343 aboard were drowned.

Jan. 9, 1927: A small fire that broke out in Montreal's Laurier Palace Theatre was quickly extinguished, but in the panic that ensued 12 people were crushed to death and 64 were asphyxiated, including many children.

Apr. 14, 1928: The 18-gun sloop *Acorn* sank near Halifax with 115 men on board.

Nov. 18, 1929: Newfoundland's Burin Peninsula was struck by a 4.5 m tidal wave. Property damage was extensive and 27 were killed.

Dec. 12, 1942: An arsonist set fire to the Knights of Columbus hostel in St. John's. Because the hostel had no emergency lighting, the doors opened inwards and exits were restricted, 99 people died and another 100 were seriously injured.

Sept. 9, 1949: A Quebec Airways DC-3 was sabotaged with a bomb and the plane exploded and crashed near St. Joachim, Que., killing 32 people. J.A. Guay and two accomplices were convicted of the crime and hanged.

Sept. 17, 1949: Seven hundred people were aboard the Great Lakes excursion ship *Noronic* when it caught fire and burned at its pier in Toronto harbour. The ship's fire hydrants were dry and no alarm was sent to the city fire department until 15 minutes after the blaze was discovered. In the meantime, the single exit became blocked by fire and 118 lives were lost.

Oct. 15, 1954: During the worst inland storm in Canadian history, Hurricane Hazel, over 10 cm of rain fell in Toronto in 12 hours. At that time, many houses in Toronto were built on low-lying flood plains. The storm and resulting floods caused 83 deaths and widespread property damage.

Nov. 1, 1956: A second major tragedy struck the coal mines at Springhill, N.S., when an accident killed 39 men.

June 17, 1958: Design errors in Vancouver's Second Narrows Bridge caused one section to collapse. The accident killed 18 men, including the two engineers that an investigation later determined were responsible for the errors.

Oct. 23, 1958: A third mining accident in Springhill, N.S,. killed 75 when a tunnel collapsed.

Nov. 19, 1963: A Trans Canada Airlines DC-8F crashed after takeoff from Dorval in Montreal, killing. 118.

July 5, 1970: At Toronto International Airport, an Air Canada DC-8 lost one starboard engine during a landing attempt. During the pilot's effort to take off and land again, the remaining starboard engine fell off. The aircraft crashed, killing all 109 persons aboard.

May 4, 1971: During a prolonged rainstorm in St-Jean-Vianney, Que., a giant sinkhole appeared in the ground. The hole swallowed 36 houses, several cars and a bus, and killed 31 people.

Sept. 1, 1972: The Blue Bird Bar in Montreal was set afire by three disgruntled patrons who had been ejected from the bar earlier in the evening. The blaze killed 37.

Nov. 10, 1975: The 218-m ore carrier *Edmund Fitzgerald*, based in Sault Ste Marie, broke apart during a storm on Lake Superior and sank in 156 m of water with all 29 members of the crew aboard. Two days later only two rubber rafts and some life preservers from the ship were found.

June 21, 1977: A fire that broke out in the cell block of the city police headquarters of St. John, N.B., was so hot that the locks on several cell doors were fused. Twenty prisoners were killed and 12 police officers who attempted to rescue the prisoners were injured.

Feb. 11, 1978: A Pacific Western Airlines aircraft crashed at Cranbrook, B.C., killing 43 people.

Aug. 4, 1978: The worst bus disaster in Canada occurred when the brakes on a chartered bus failed near Eastman, Que. The bus plunged into a lake, and 41 mentally and physically handicapped passengers were killed.

Dec. 31, 1979: Forty-four persons were killed during New Year's Eve celebrations at a social club in Chapais, Que., in a fire caused by a man playing with a lighter who set decorations ablaze.

Feb. 15, 1982: The ocean drilling rig *Ocean Ranger* overturned and sank during a storm while operating 265 km east of Newfoundland, killing 84 men. Inadequate safety procedures and equipment were later blamed for the accident.

May 31, 1985: A midafternoon tornado struck Barrie, Ont., killing 12, including four children. Property damage was in the hundreds of millions of dollars.

June 23, 1985: An Air India 747 flying from Toronto never reached its destination of London, England. Wreckage from the plane was found floating in the Atlantic, west of Ireland. The tragedy, thought to be caused by a bomb on board, killed 280 Canadians.

Dec. 12, 1985: In the worst air crash in Canada, an Arrow Airlines DC-8, after refueling in Gander en route to Hopkinsville, Ky., crashed seconds after takeoff, killing 256 passengers and crew.

Feb. 8, 1986: A 16-unit VIA Rail passenger train slammed head-on into a 118-unit CN freight train near Hinton, Alta. Twenty-six people were killed and dozens were seriously injured.

July 31, 1987: A tornado touched down in Edmonton, Alta., killing 26 people, injuring 250 others and causing an estimated $250 million damage.

Mar. 10, 1989: An Air Ontario jet crashed immediately after takeoff from Dryden, Ont., killing 24 people.

Dec. 6, 1989: Gunman Marc Lepine shot and killed 14 women and wounded 13 others at Montreal's l'École Polytechnique before killing himself. Lepine left a letter claiming he had attacked the female students because they were feminists.

Feb. 12, 1990: One of the worst tire fires in North America broke out near Hagersville, Ont., spewing oil and toxic smoke. The dump, which stored 14 million tires for recycling, burned for 16 days; the blaze was extinguished at a cost of $1.5 million.

May 9, 1992: Twenty-six miners died underground in the Westray coal mine near Plymouth, N.S., after a methane gas explosion. Fifteen bodies were recovered but the bodies of the remaining victims could not be reached in the debris.

July 16, 1993: Nineteen people died when a truck towing tanks of diesel fuel collided with a van carrying senior citizens near Lac-Bouchette, Que.

Prime Ministers of Canada

■ Sir John A. Macdonald

Canada's first prime minister, Sir John A. Macdonald, was born in Glasgow, Scotland, Jan. 11, 1815. At age 5 he came to Canada with his parents who settled at Kingston, Upper Canada.

Called to the bar in 1836, Macdonald practised law in Kingston, and then in Toronto. He established a reputation as a corporate lawyer, company director, and businessman.

He was elected to the Legislative Assembly of the Province of Canada in 1844, and was re-elected in 1848, 1851, 1854, 1857, 1861 and 1863. In 1864, he joined a coalition with George Brown, leader of the Upper Canadian reformers, dedicated to bringing about Confederation. That same year, Macdonald was a delegate to the Charlottetown and Quebec Conferences, and became the principal author of the Confederation resolutions agreed upon in Quebec. He was chairman of the London Conference (1866–67), and played a pivotal role in bringing about Confederation.

Macdonald became Canada's first prime minister when the Conservative party won a majority of seats in Parliament following the first post-Confederation general election in 1867. Though he was re-elected in 1872, Macdonald's second administration was marred by the "Pacific Scandal" in 1873, when the Liberal opposition charged that his government had awarded the C.P.R. contract to Sir Hugh Allan in return for political contributions. An investigation into these charges was held, and the government resigned on Nov. 5, 1873.

Macdonald's Liberal-Conservatives were re-elected Sept. 17, 1878, and Macdonald remained prime minister until his death in Ottawa on June 6, 1891.

During his first administration, the Dominion of Canada expanded to include the provinces of British Columbia, Prince Edward Island, and the newly-created Manitoba.

The building of the transcontinental railway is the most memorable feature of his second administration, but other accomplishments include the establishment of the "National Policy"—a system of tariff protection to aid the development of Canadian industries (1879)—and the increased settlement of the Western provinces that followed the construction of the railway.

■ Alexander Mackenzie

Alexander Mackenzie was born on Jan. 28, 1822 near Dunkeld, Perthshire, Scotland. He left school and became a stonemason at the age of 14.

He emigrated to Canada in 1842 and became a contractor at Lambton, Ontario and then editor of the *Lambton Shield*. From 1866–74, he was a major in the 27th Lambton Battalion Volunteer Infantry.

In 1861, Mackenzie was elected to the Legislative Assembly of the Province of Canada, where he gave his support to the Confederation plan. When George Brown was defeated in the 1867 election, Mackenzie became *de facto* leader of the Opposition, though it was not until after the 1872 elections that he formally accepted this title.

It was Mackenzie who led the attack on the Macdonald administration over the "Pacific Scandal"; when Macdonald resigned on Nov. 5, 1873, Mackenzie became prime minister.

During his 5-year term of office, Mackenzie introduced changes to election laws that included the secret ballot and universal male suffrage. The Supreme Court of Canada was established under Mackenzie's rule, and Wilfrid Laurier was brought into Mackenzie's cabinet.

Severe economic depression plagued Canada during the Mackenzie years, and in 1878, his Liberal party was routed at the polls.

Mackenzie retained his own seat, however, and was still a member of Parliament when he died Apr. 17, 1892, in Toronto.

■ Sir John Abbott

Sir John Joseph Caldwell Abbott was born Mar. 12, 1821 at St. Andrews, Lower Canada—the first prime minister to be born on Canadian soil.

After taking his law degree from University of McGill College, he was admitted to the bar in 1847 and practised law in Montreal. From 1855–80 he was dean of the Faculty of Law, McGill University.

Abbott was elected to the Legislative Assembly of the Province of Canada in 1857, re-elected in 1861 and 1863, and sat until Confederation. He was then elected to the

House of Commons in 1867, 1872, and 1874. He was last elected in 1882, and appointed to the Senate on May 12, 1887.

When Sir John A. Macdonald died in 1891, Abbott—though a senator—inherited the Conservative leadership. The three other leading Conservatives—Langevin, Tupper and Thompson— were unwilling or unable to assume the post. Abbott held the office of prime minister from June 16, 1891 until his resignation on Nov. 24, 1892. He died in Montreal on Oct. 30, 1893.

■ Sir John Thompson

Sir John Sparrow David Thompson was born in Halifax, N.S., on Nov. 10, 1845.

Thompson was called to the Nova Scotia bar in 1865, and was instrumental in founding Dalhousie Law School in 1883, where he eventually became a lecturer.

In May 1882, Thompson became premier of Nova Scotia, but when his government was defeated 2 months later, he retired from politics and became a judge of the Supreme Court of Nova Scotia.

Prime Minister Macdonald coaxed Thompson back into politics, making him Minister of Justice in 1885. When Macdonald died in 1891, Thompson declined the leadership, fearing that his conversion to Roman Catholicism in 1870 would hinder his party's fortunes. However, the following year, Thompson changed his mind, and on Dec. 5, 1892, he became prime minister.

Though prime minister for just over 2 years, Thompson was largely responsible for the establishment of the Criminal Code and penetentiary reforms. He very nearly succeeded in bringing Newfoundland into Confederation in 1894, and successfully negotiated fisheries clauses in the Treaty of Washington.

He died while still in office on Dec. 12, 1894.

■ Sir Mackenzie Bowell

Mackenzie Bowell was born at Rickinghall, Suffolk, England on Dec. 27, 1823, and came to Canada in 1832. In 1834, he became an apprentice printer at Belleville, Upper Canada, and was later editor and proprietor of the Belleville *Intelligencer*. He served in the Militia of the United Province of Canada during the American Civil War and the Fenian raids of 1866.

Bowell was elected to the House of Commons in 1867 for Hastings North, Ont., and was re- elected in 1872, 1874, 1878, 1887 and 1891.

As spokesman for the Orange Association of British America, Bowell was instrumental in having Louis Riel expelled from the Commons in 1874.

On Dec. 5, 1892, Bowell was appointed to the Senate and, after Thompson's death in 1894, was invited by the Governor General to form a government.

Perhaps the thorniest problem facing Prime Minister Bowell was the Manitoba Schools question. In 1890, Manitoba legislation had withdrawn school privileges from the Roman Catholic and primarily French minority in that province. By the time Bowell assumed office, attempts were being made to restore those lost school privileges by federal remedial legislation. Bowell was not equal to the political challenges facing him; he lost control of his cabinet ministers, several of whom eventually called for his resignation. Bowell denounced this cabinet rebellion as a "nest of traitors", but eventually he resigned on Apr. 27, 1896. He died in Belleville, Ont., on Dec. 10, 1917 at 93.

■ Sir Charles Tupper

Charles Tupper was born at Amherst, N.S., July 2, 1821. He took a degree in medicine at Edinburgh University. At the age of 22, he began practising medicine in Amherst, and became the first president of the Canadian Medical Association (1867–70).

The 1855 election that brought him to the Legislative Assembly of Nova Scotia was declared void on Feb. 24, 1857. He was subsequently re- elected in a by-election that same year and was elected again in 1859 and 1863.

Tupper was active in the Confederation movement, and was a delegate to the Charlottetown, Quebec and London Conferences. He was elected to the House of Commons in 1867, and re-elected 1870, 1872, 1874, 1878 and 1882. He resigned in 1884, and served as High Commissioner for Canada in the United Kingdom from May 28 of that year to Jan. 26, 1887. In 1887, he was re- elected to the House of Commons, but resigned the following year and again served as High Commissioner from May 23, 1888 to Jan. 14, 1896.

In 1896, following the rebellion of Bowell's

cabinet, Tupper became *de facto* leader of the administration until Bowell formally resigned on Apr. 27, 1896. At that time, the Governor General invited Tupper to form the government. Parliament was dissolved shortly thereafter and in the election that followed on June 23, Tupper's Conservatives were defeated. Tupper stayed on as leader of the Opposition until Feb. 5, 1901, then retired from public life. He died Oct. 30, 1915 at Bexley Heath, Kent, England.

■ Sir Wilfrid Laurier

Wilfrid Laurier was born at St-Lin, Canada East, Nov. 20, 1841. He first attended College de l'Assomption, and then took his degree from McGill University.

He was called to the bar of Lower Canada in 1865. He practised law at Montreal and at Arthabaskaville, Que.

First elected to the Legislative Assembly of Quebec in 1871, Laurier resigned in Jan. 1874 and later that year was elected to the House of Commons. He became leader of the Liberal Opposition in June 1887. Then, following the 1896 election that gave his party a 23-seat majority, Laurier became Canada's first French-speaking prime minister on July 11, 1896. The Liberals retained power in 1900, and won a landslide election victory in 1904.

Immigration increased during his time in office as Clifford Sifton, Laurier's minister of the interior from 1896–1905, mounted a powerful campaign to attract immigrants from Britain, the United States and Europe. In 1905, Laurier created the provinces of Alberta and Saskatchewan and established the boundaries of Manitoba. During Laurier's years in power the Canadian West became a major world wheat producer. In 1909, Laurier established the External Affairs Department.

His government's controversial support for the creation of a Canadian navy, and his unpopular attempt to enter into a reciprocal trade agreement with the United States (an agreement that would have reduced or eliminated duties on many imported goods) spelled trouble for Laurier in 1911. His party was defeated in the Sept. 21 election. He remained an Opposition M.P. until his death on Feb. 17, 1919 in Ottawa.

■ Sir Robert Borden

Robert Laird Borden was born at Grand Pré, N.S., June 26, 1854. At age 14 he gave up formal schooling to become an assistant master in classical studies. He taught classics and mathematics in New Jersey in 1873, before returning to Nova Scotia to study law. He was admitted to the Nova Scotia bar in 1878, and practised first in Halifax, then in Kentville, N.S.

Borden was elected to the House of Commons in 1896 and 1900 and became leader of the Conservative party on Feb. 6, 1901. He served as leader of the Opposition until 1911, when he led his party to victory in the Sept. 21 election.

Borden was prime minister throughout World War I and during the war years his government was accused of scandal over British munitions contracts and its staunch support of the Ross Rifle—a weapon known to jam in battle. Borden's government introduced the first federal income tax, nationalized Canadian railways and introduced conscription in 1917.

In the election of Dec. 17, 1917, Borden led a re-organized Union Government made up of Conservatives and pro-conscription Liberals to victory. Borden headed the Canadian delegation at the Paris Peace Conference in 1919, where the autonomy of Canada and other dominions within the British Commonwealth was successfully established. He resigned on July 10, 1920 and died in Ottawa June 10, 1937.

■ Arthur Meighen

Arthur Meighen was born at Anderson, Ont., June 16, 1874. Following his graduation from university in 1896, Meighen taught high school for a year, then moved to Winnipeg in 1898 to study law. He was called to the Manitoba bar in 1902, and practised at Portage La Prairie.

He was first elected to the House of Commons in 1908, re-elected in 1911, 1913 and 1917, defeated in 1921, and re-elected in 1922 and 1925.

Meighen first achieved national prominence in 1913 when he helped devise a closure rule which permitted the government to end debate on a bill which was to effect a $35-million contribution to the British navy. Prior to closure, the bill had been obstructed by a fierce and protracted Opposition party blockade.

Prime Minister Borden appointed Meighen his solicitor general on Oct. 2, 1915, and

Meighen held this post for 2 years. A strong supporter of conscription, Meighen essentially drafted Canada's 1917 Conscription bill, and put it into operation. He was also the chief draughtsman of the *Wartime Elections Act*.

When Borden resigned on July 10, 1920, Meighen succeeded him as prime minister. In the general election of Dec. 6, 1921, Meighen's party was defeated. Though his Conservatives won the most seats in the election of Oct. 29, 1925, the Liberals were able to stay in power with the support of Progressive and Labour members.

Following the resignation of William Lyon Mackenzie King's government on June 28, 1926, the Governor General invited Meighen to form a new ministry. This government was less than 3 months old, however, when it was defeated in the House of Commons (by only one vote) and Canadians again went to the polls.

Following a Liberal victory in the election of Sept. 14, 1926, Meighen resigned as Conservative leader in the House of Commons. He was appointed to the Senate on Feb. 3, 1932 during Richard Bennett's ministry and became government leader in the Senate. Then, following King's victory in 1935, he became Senate Opposition leader.

On Nov. 12, 1941, he once again became leader of the Conservative party, but failed in his bid to win a seat in the Commons in a federal by-election on Feb. 2, 1942. Following this defeat, he retired from politics and resumed his law practice in Toronto where he died Aug. 5, 1960.

■ Mackenzie King

William Lyon Mackenzie King, grandson of William Lyon Mackenzie, was born in Kitchener (then called Berlin) on Dec. 17, 1874.

He took his B.A. and law degrees from the University of Toronto, and also studied at the University of Chicago and Harvard University.

He served as deputy minister of labour from 1900–08.

He was first elected to the House of Commons in 1908, and succeeded Laurier as leader of the Liberal party in 1919. King became prime minister when the Liberals won the general election of Dec. 6, 1921.

Though Meighen's Conservatives won a majority of seats in the general election of Oct. 29, 1925, King stayed in office with the help of Progressive and Labour members who supported his proposed tariff reductions and old-age pension legislation. King had lost his York North seat in the 1925 election but returned to the House of Commons as the member for Prince Albert, Sask., following a by-election on Feb. 15, 1926. King's government was shaken in 1926 by the revelation that the Customs department was tainted with corruption and incompetence. In the furor that followed, King lost the support of many members of Parliament and, although never technically defeated in the House of Commons, decided that he could no longer hold his minority government. He appealed to the Governor General, Lord Byng, to dissolve Parliament, even though the government had not been defeated. Byng refused. King subsequently resigned on June 28, 1926, and the Governor General invited Arthur Meighen to form a government which was subsequently defeated in the House of Commons.

In the general election of Sept. 14, 1926, King's Liberals regained power and held it until 1930. But the disastrous fall in the price of wheat and other Canadian exports in 1929 soured Canadians on their government, and King was defeated by R.B. Bennett's Conservatives in the election of July 28, 1930.

Five years later, King was back in the prime minister's office, following the Liberal victory in the general election of Oct. 14, 1935. In the coming years, King, an ardent supporter of Canada's autonomy within the British Commonwealth was faced with the issue of Canada's participation in an impending European war. To soothe French-Canadian concerns over Canadian support of Great Britain, King promised there would be no conscription; Canada declared war in Sept. 1939. Later, however, heavy casualties in France and Italy in 1944 prompted King to break his promise and send conscripts overseas.

King's government began introducing postwar recovery legislation even before peace was declared. These measures included reconstruction plans and social security schemes such as mother's allowances.

King resigned as prime minister on Nov. 15, 1948, supporting Louis St. Laurent as his successor. In poor health in his final years, King died July 22, 1950 at Kingsmere, his estate in Wright County, Que.

■ Richard Bennett

Richard Bedford Bennett was born at Hopewell, N.B., July 3, 1870. Bennett studied law at Dalhousie University. He read and practised law in Chatham, N.B., from 1893–97, before moving to Calgary where he entered a legal partnership with Senator James A. Lougheed.

Bennett was first elected to the House of Commons in 1911. He served as minister of justice in Arthur Meighen's 1921 cabinet, and minister of finance and minister of mines in Meighen's 1926 government.

Bennett was chosen to replace Meighen as Conservative leader at the party convention in Winnipeg in 1927. He became prime minister following the Conservative victory in the election of July 28, 1930.

Bennett had the task of governing Canada during the worst years of the Depression. Virtually every measure his government attempted ended in failure. High unemployment levels continued despite Bennett's efforts to reduce them. Negotiations for a reciprocity treaty with the United States did not succeed. A plan of preferential tariffs agreed to in 1930 at the Imperial Conference did little to ease Canada's economic woes.

Then, in 1935, near the end of his term, Bennett took an unexpected step to the political left. He proclaimed that "the old order is gone" and that it was time for a new economic system. That new system was to include a state-planned economy, and new unemployment and health insurance legislation and old-age pension laws.

In the election of Oct. 14, 1935, Bennett's Conservatives suffered a devastating defeat, winning just 39 seats. Bennett remained in Opposition until 1937, when he retired to England. There he was given the title Viscount Bennett of Mickelham, Hopewell and Calgary.

Despite the overwhelming problems of the Great Depression, Bennett's term saw the creation of the Canadian Radio Broadcasting Corporation (the predecessor to the CBC) and the Bank of Canada. As well, it was during Bennett's tenure that the Statute of Westminster gave Canada increased autonomy in 1931.

Bennett died June 27, 1947.

■ Louis St. Laurent

Louis Stephen St. Laurent was born at Compton, Que., Feb. 1, 1882. Called to the Quebec bar in 1905, he practised law in Quebec City, and became Professor of Law at Université Laval. He was elected president of the Canadian Bar Association in 1930.

St. Laurent became justice minister in Mackenzie King's cabinet on Dec. 10, 1941. On Feb. 9, 1942, he was elected to the House of Commons in a by-election for Quebec East.

Originally planning to hold his cabinet post only during the war, St. Laurent was persuaded to stay on. On Dec. 10, 1946, he became secretary of state for external affairs. A firm believer in collective security, St. Laurent was one of the architects of the North Atlantic Treaty Organization (NATO). On Aug. 7, 1948, he accepted his party's nomination to be King's successor, and on Nov. 15 became prime minister.

While in power St. Laurent ended the practice of appealing court cases to the Judicial Committee of the Privy Council in England, and made the Supreme Court of Canada the final Canadian court of appeal. He won the acceptance of a new apportionment of taxes in 1956 and, in negotiation with President Truman, laid the foundation for a U.S.-Canada agreement to develop the St. Lawrence Seaway.

In 1958, he retired and returned to Quebec City to practise law. He died July 25, 1973.

■ John Diefenbaker

John George Diefenbaker was born at Neustadt, Ont., Sept. 18, 1895. He received his B.A. from the University of Saskatchewan in 1915, and his M.A. one year later.

After the outbreak of World War I, he joined the Canadian Officers' Training Corps, and served overseas as a lieutenant with the 105th 'Saskatoon Fusiliers' Regiment from 1916 to 1917.

Returning to Saskatchewan, he took his law degree from the University of Saskatchewan in 1919 and established a law practice at Wakaw. He later moved to Prince Albert.

After several unsuccessful attempts to gain a seat, first in the federal, then in Saskatchewan's provincial parliament, Diefenbaker was finally elected to the House of Commons in 1940. He was a candidate for leadership of the Progressive Conservative Party at the 1942 and 1948 conventions, but did not win the nomination until Dec. 14, 1956.

The PCs won the election of June 10, 1957

by a slim margin, and on June 21, John Diefenbaker officially became prime minister. A year later, he called an election, hoping to turn his Conservative minority government into a clear majority. He was overwhelmingly successful, winning 208 of the 265 seats in the Mar. 31, 1958 election. He fared less well in the 1962 election, when only 116 P.C.s were elected, and in the general election of 1963, a Liberal victory relegated Diefenbaker to the role of Opposition leader. Diefenbaker remained Conservative leader until Sept. 1967, when he was replaced by Robert Stanfield.

The Diefenbaker years (1957–63) saw the passage of the Canadian Bill of Rights, a "roads-to- resources" program to encourage the development of northern resources, legislation providing support for agriculture, encouragement of technical training and improved health and welfare programs. Regional development was emphasized by significant public works such as construction of the South Saskatchewan Dam, and simultaneous translation was introduced in the House of Commons.

Diefenbaker died Aug. 16, 1979 at his home in Rockliffe Park, Ottawa.

■ Lester Pearson

Lester Bowles Pearson was born at Newtonbrook, Ont., on Apr. 23, 1897. He took his B.A. at the University of Toronto, and his M.A. at Oxford University.

After serving overseas in World War I, he became a history professor at the University of Toronto, where he taught from 1924–1928. He joined Canada's foreign service in 1928, became Canada's ambassador to the U.N. in 1945, was appointed under-secretary of state for external affairs in 1946, and accepted the invitations of King and St. Laurent to become minister of external affairs in Sept. 1948.

In 1956, following the Anglo-French-Israeli invasion of Egypt, Pearson's work at the United Nations helped establish a U.N. Emergency Force which kept peace on the Israeli/Egyptian border for the next decade. His settlement of the Suez crisis brought him the Nobel Peace Prize in 1957—the only time a Canadian has been so honored.

Pearson was chosen leader of the Liberal Party Jan. 15, 1958. In the general election of Apr. 8, 1963, the Liberals won 129 seats in the House of Commons, and Pearson became the leader of a minority government.

In the 1965 election, the Liberals made slight gains, but were still short of a majority. Pearson announced his resignation in Dec. 1967 and, in Apr. 1968, was succeeded by Pierre Trudeau.

Under Pearson, the old age pension was extended and a national health plan created. He secured the adoption of a national flag and established the Royal Commission on Bilingualism and Biculturalism.

Though he retired in 1968, his international reputation prompted the World Bank to commission him to prepare a report on international aid programs.

He died in Ottawa, Dec. 27, 1972.

■ Pierre Trudeau

Pierre Elliott Trudeau was born in Montreal on Oct. 18, 1919. He attended the University of Montreal, Harvard University, Université de Paris and the London School of Economics. He was called to the Quebec bar in 1943. From 1949–51, he was a member of the Privy Council staff in Ottawa. In 1950, he co-founded the magazine *Cité Libre*. From 1952–1962, he practised law and was a journalist and broadcaster in Montreal. From 1962–1965 he was a law professor at the University of Montreal.

First elected to the House of Commons in 1965, Trudeau was named justice minister in Lester Pearson's cabinet in 1967. The following year, he won the Liberal leadership and became prime minister Apr. 19, 1968. In the general election of the same year, the Liberals won a solid majority.

During his first 4 years in power, Trudeau faced the "F.L.Q. Crisis"—the kidnapping of British diplomat James Cross and Quebec cabinet minister Pierre Laporte by the radical separatist organization Front de Libération du Québec. (Laporte was later murdered.) In response he invoked the War Measures Act, a statute giving the state broad powers of arrest and detention.

In the general election of 1972, Trudeau returned to power with a minority government. In 1974, he regained a majority.

In the general election of 1979, the Progressive Conservatives under Joe Clark won a narrow victory, and were able to form a minority government. Trudeau announced his intention to retire, but when the Clark government fell later that year, Trudeau led the

Liberals in the election and won a majority on Feb. 18, 1980.

Trudeau's final term in office was devoted to constitutional reform which, for the first time, allowed Canada's Parliament to amend the constitution without appeal to the U.K. government. A constitutionally-entrenched Charter of Rights and Freedoms was also introduced.

Trudeau's introduction of a National Energy Program led to bitter disputes between the federal government and the energy-producing provinces, particularly Alberta. The NEP was aimed at increasing Canadian control of the oil industry, promoting energy self-sufficiency and generating more federal revenues in the energy sector.

During his final year as prime minister Trudeau launched a world peace initiative, visiting more than 40 world leaders to appeal for peace and an end to the nuclear arms race.

In June of 1984, Trudeau resigned. He was succeeded by John Turner and left politics, eventually joining a Montreal law firm.

■ Joe Clark

Charles Joseph "Joe" Clark was born at High River, Alta., on June 5, 1939. He was educated at the University of Alberta.

Clark was first elected to the House of Commons in 1972. In 1976 he became leader of the Progressive Conservative Party and, in the general election of 1979, won enough seats to form a minority government. At 39, Clark was Canada's youngest prime minister. But his minority government fell in Dec. of that year on a vote of non-confidence on its proposed budget. In the Feb. 1980 election that followed, the Liberals returned to power.

At a national general meeting of the Conservative party in Jan. 1983, Clark received the support of only two-thirds of the delegates and called for a national party leadership convention. In June 1983, Clark lost the leadership to Brian Mulroney on the 4th ballot. He remained an MP and, when Mulroney became prime minister in 1984, Clark joined the cabinet as secretary of state for external affairs.

In 1991, he was appointed as minister responsible for constitutional affairs, and given the task of succeeding where the Meech Lake Accord had failed. Late 1991 and the first half of 1992 were marked by weeks of cross-country constitutional negotiations under Clark's guidance. In August, 1992 the Charlottetown

Accord—an agreement to amend the Constitution Act of 1982—was agreed upon by all first ministers. The text of the agreement was presented to Canadians and a national referendum was held on Oct. 26, 1992 on the issue of whether or not to approve the deal. The agreement was rejected by the majority of voters across the country.

In the spring of 1993, Clark announced his retirement from Canadian political life, effective as of the fall 1993 election.

■ John Turner

John Napier Turner was born at Richmond, Surrey, England on June 7, 1929. He attended the University of British Columbia, Oxford University and Université de Paris. He was called to the bar in England in 1953 and the bar in Quebec in 1954. He lectured for a time in the Faculty of Commerce at Sir George Williams University.

First elected to the House of Commons in 1962, Turner entered Lester Pearson's cabinet in 1965. He became minister of consumer and corporate affairs in 1967. In 1968 he was a candidate for the Liberal leadership, finishing 3rd on the final ballot.

In 1968, Turner was appointed minister of justice in Pierre Trudeau's cabinet. In 1972, he became minister of finance, a post he held until his resignation in Sept. 1975. In Feb. 1976 he left politics and joined a Toronto law firm.

Turner remained in private practice until Trudeau's retirement in 1984, when he successfully ran for leader of the Liberal Party and became prime minister on June 30, though he did not have a seat in the House of Commons. He dissolved Parliament July 9, and in the ensuing general election the Liberals were overwhelmingly defeated by the Progressive Conservatives.

As Leader of the Opposition, Turner used the Liberal majority in the Senate to block passage of the Conservatives' free trade legislation and force an election on the issue in 1988. The Conservatives won the election and were able to form another majority government.

Early in 1989, Turner announced plans to step down as leader; in June 1990, he was succeeded by Jean Chrétien.

■ Brian Mulroney

Martin Brian Mulroney was born at Baie Comeau, Que., Mar. 20, 1939. He attended St.

Francis Xavier University and Université Laval. Called to the bar of Quebec in 1965, Mulroney practised law in Montreal. In 1976, he joined the Iron Ore Company of Canada as executive vice-president, and was elected company president the following year.

Mulroney made an unsuccessful bid for the Progressive Conservative party leadership in 1976. In 1983 he ran again, defeating the incumbent leader, Joe Clark, on the 4th ballot.

A by-election for the Maritime riding of Central Nova brought Mulroney into Parliament as leader of the Opposition. In the general election of 1984, he led the Conservatives to victory, winning the largest number of seats (211) in Canadian history.

Mulroney's government took steps to attract more foreign investment and sought to strengthen ties with the United States. Mulroney's major initiatives between 1984 and 1988 were the Meech Lake Accord—a package of constitutional changes designed to end Quebec's boycott of the 1982 constitutional reform—and the negotiation of a free trade agreement with the United States.

In 1988, with free trade the central election issue, Mulroney won a second majority government. The free trade agreement subsequently received final approval and took effect in 1989.

Mulroney's plan for a new constitutional accord was halted in 1990 when Newfoundland and Manitoba did not ratify Meech Lake before the June 23 deadline. Negotiations to resolve the impasse recommenced shortly after.

In 1991, the Conservative government was sharply criticized for implementing a goods and services tax (GST) just as the country was facing an economic recession.

Much of 1992 was marked by intense negotiations to bring about a new constitutional agreement to replace the failed Meech Lake Accord. In August, agreement was reached amongst federal and provincial officials in what became known as the Charlottetown Accord. Proposals included new federal-provincial power sharing arrangements, provisions for native self-government and plans to redesign both the Senate and the House of Commons. A national referendum on the proposals was held on October 26, 1992 and the accord was rejected by voters.

The Conservatives under Mulroney continued their free trade initiative and finalized a North American free trade deal (NAFTA) with the US and Mexico.

On February 24, 1993 Mulroney announced his intention to retire and on June 25, 1993 he was replaced by Kim Campbell, newly-elected leader of the Conservative party.

■ Kim Campbell

Avril Phaedra (Kim) Campbell was born March 10, 1947 in Port Alberni, BC. She attended the University of British Columbia, earning an honours degree in political science.

Between 1970 and 1973, she studied Soviet government at the London School of Economics, returning to Canada in 1973. She began lecturing at UBC in political science in 1975 and went on to teach at Vancouver Community College before returning to UBC to study at the law faculty in 1980. Campbell served on the Vancouver school board beginning in 1980 and chaired the board in 1983. In 1983 she ran in the provincial election, contesting the riding of Vancouver Centre, but was defeated. In Sept. of 1985, she joined BC Premier William Bennett's office as a policy advisor. In May 1986, Campbell ran in the BC Socred leadership race and lost, however, in the October provincial election that year she won a seat in the legislature, representing the riding of Vancouver/Point Grey. She served in the provincial legislature until October of 1988 when she resigned her seat to contest the federal riding of Vancouver Centre. An ardent defender of free trade, Campbell narrowly defeated her NDP opponent and joined the junior ranks of Prime Min. Mulroney's cabinet with the Indian Affairs and Northern Development portfolio.

In a Feb. 1990 cabinet shuffle, Campbell was promoted to the Attorney General and Justice post and during her three-year tenure she brought 26 bills to the House of Commons, including a controversial gun control measure. In January of 1993 she became Minister of Defence and shortly thereafter, when Prime Min. Mulroney announced his intention to retire, Campbell became a candidate in the Conservative leadership contest. On June 13, 1993, she was elected to the Conservative leadership on the second ballot at the leadership convention and on June 25, she was sworn in as Canada's 19th Prime Minister.

GOVERNMENT OF CANADA

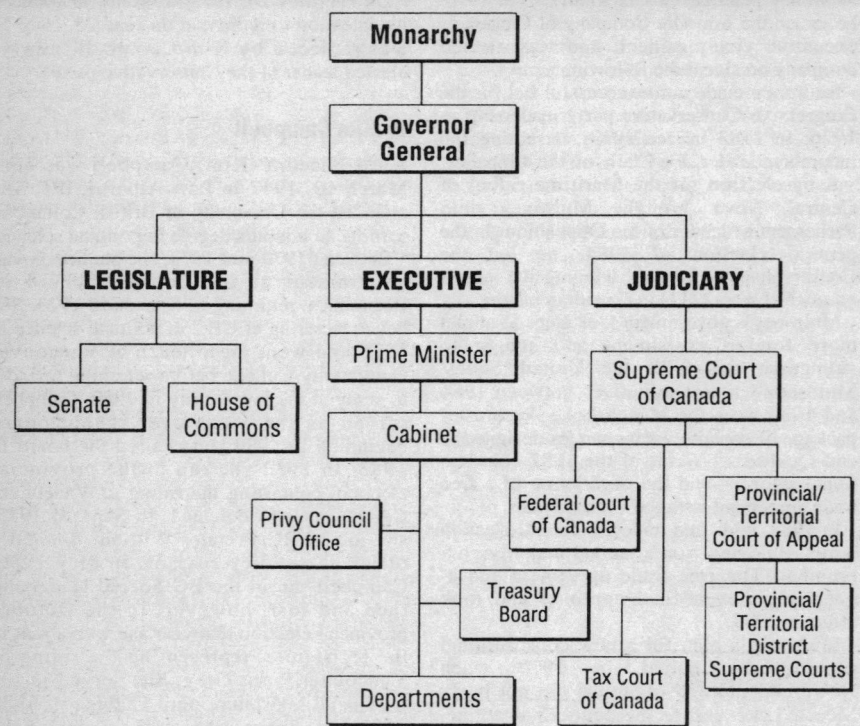

Canada is an independent, self-governing democracy whose form of government is a constitutional monarchy. There are three types of government power: legislative, executive and judicial. In Canada the legislative and executive powers are joined, while the judiciary remains separate. The executive proposes legislation, presents budgets and implements laws; the legislature adopts laws and votes on recommendations for taxes or other revenue; the judiciary interprets the laws.

■ The Monarchy

The British monarch (since June 2, 1953 Queen Elizabeth II) is Canada's official head of state through which the entire authority of the government is set in motion and in whose name laws are enacted. The Queen's role is set out in the *Constitution Act, 1867,* and that same act gives the monarch ultimate

authority over Canada's armed forces.

In practice, however, the Queen has little or no part to play in Canadian government. She appoints the Governor General, but does so only on the prime minister's recommendation. Once appointed, it is the Governor General who performs the monarch's duties, and these duties have been mainly ceremonial for many years. Only during royal visits does the Queen carry out those functions normally performed in her name by the Governor General, such as the opening of Parliament.

■ The Governor General

The Governor General is selected by the prime minister and formally appointed by the Queen to act as her representative in Canada. The appointment is usually for five years but has sometimes been extended to seven.

Bills passed in the House of Commons and

Senate do not become law until the Governor General has given them royal assent. The Governor General executes all orders-in-council and other state documents, appoints all superior court judges (on the advice of Cabinet) and summons, prorogues and dissolves Parliament (on the advice of the prime minister). Also, the Governor General invites the leader of the political party with the most support in the House of Commons to form a government. Thus, that leader becomes prime minister.

The Imperial Conferences of 1926 and 1930 established that the Governor General was not the representative or agent of the British government and should act only on the advice of the Canadian prime minister and Cabinet. Therefore, the Governor General is obliged to respect the principle of responsible government and to follow the wishes of Canada's elected representatives. Because of this, the role of the Governor General has become largely symbolic, with duties that are chiefly ceremonial.

Two members of the Royal Family have held the post: the Duke of Connaught (1911–16) and the Earl of Athlone (1940–46). The first Canadian Governor General was Vincent Massey (1952– 59).

The Legislature

Canada's legislature or Parliament consists of the Queen, an upper house, known as the Senate, and the House of Commons. Senators are appointed by the Governor General on the advice of the prime minister; the seats in the Senate are distributed on a regional basis; originally, there were 72 senators, but through the years the Senate has increased as the number of provinces and the population have grown. In 1975 the Senate was increased to 104 members; in 1990 Prime Minister Brian Mulroney employed a never-before- used section of the Constitution Act to increase the number to 112. The House of Commons is an elected assembly in which each member represents one of 295 electoral districts distributed according to population.

■ The Senate

The Senate is the Upper House of the Canadian Parliament through which all legislation must pass before it becomes law. Its members, appointed by the Governor General on the recommendation of the prime minister, hold office until age 75. (If appointed before June 1965 they hold office for life).

After 1975, there were 104 Senate seats apportioned on a regional basis: 24 from the Maritime provinces (Nova Scotia, 10; New Brunswick, 10; Prince Edward Island 4); 24 from Quebec; 24 from Ontario; 24 from the Western provinces (Manitoba, 6; Saskatchewan, 6; Alberta, 6; British Columbia, 6); 6 from Newfoundland; 1 each from the Northwest Territories and Yukon. In 1990, the number was temporarily increased to 112.

To be eligible for Senate appointment, a person must be a Canadian citizen, at least 30 years old, a resident of the province for which he or she is appointed, possess land in that province with an unencumbered value of $4 000 and have a net estate of $4 000. A Senator for Quebec must either be resident in the division for which he or she is appointed, or have property qualification there.

Technically, the Senate's legislative powers are equal to those of the House of Commons with two restrictions: first, on certain constitutional amendments, the Senate may delay resolutions of the House of Commons for up to 180 days, but cannot defeat them; second, the Senate cannot initiate money bills.

In practice, however, the Senate's chief role is to provide technical reviews of legislation proposed in the House of Commons rather than to initiate political action. These reviews are done by Senate committees, which inspect each bill clause-by-clause and hear evidence from groups or individuals who may be affected by the proposed legislation.

Historically, the Senate rarely used its powers to impede legislation originating from the elected House of Commons. From 1984 to 1990, however, the Liberal-dominated Senate attempted several times to stall or block legislation approved by the Conservative majority in the House of Commons. In 1990, when the Senate blocked his government's goods and services tax, Mulroney temporarily increased the size of the Senate and added eight new Conservatives, ensuring that the measure would be made law.

In recent years, there have been repeated calls, especially from the West, for constitutional reform which would include an elected Senate with more representation from the Western provinces and Newfoundland. Plans for discussions leading to a Senate overhaul are now part of other constitutional discussions.

■ The House of Commons

The House of Commons is Canada's 295-member elected federal assembly. Its members are chosen in general elections held at least once every five years. By-elections are held if a member dies or resigns between general elections.

All bills governing matters within federal jurisdiction must be passed by a majority of members of Parliament to become law.

Members of Parliament usually belong to a political party and will normally vote with that party on any proposed legislation. Occasionally, members will break with their party on a vote and will sometimes leave the party they were affiliated with when elected to sit as independents or to join another political party within the House. Members of Parliament can also be elected as independent candidates who do not belong to a political party.

The **prime minister** is the leader of the political party able to command the support of a majority of the members of the House of Commons. If no party holds a clear majority of seats, a "minority government" is formed, usually led by the party with the most seats in Parliament, provided it has enough support from the other parties to enable it to pass legislation.

When the House of Commons is in session it convenes at two o'clock daily and 11 o'clock on Fridays when the Speaker of the House takes the chair. After the mace is laid on the table in front of the Speaker and the daily prayer is read, business commences. Members of the government sit to the Speaker's right and the Opposition sits on the left. The leaders of other opposition parties sit on the left farther away from the Speaker's chair.

An important feature of Parliament is the daily question period at which time members question Cabinet ministers about their policies and actions. But most of Parliament's time is spent discussing proposed legislation introduced as "bills". Any member may introduce a bill, although this is usually done by a member of Cabinet. After readings in the House and detailed examination in committee, the bill will go for "third reading" in the House and if passed, will be forwarded to the Senate.

When a major piece of legislation introduced by the government is defeated in the House of Commons, the government is obliged to resign. The Governor General may then call on the leader of the Opposition to form a government but, in most cases, will call a general election so that the electorate can decide which party has the most public support for its policies.

The Executive

■ The Prime Minister

The Prime Minister is the pre-eminent figure in Canadian politics. The power and authority of the office come from the fact that the Prime Minister is the leader of the party (or group of parties) that has control of, if not a clear majority of seats in the House of Commons, at least more seats than any of the other parties. The Prime Minister is an elected Member of Parliament as well as national party leader and as such has a mandate to govern via programs and policies and to speak on behalf of Canada.

The Prime Minister has control over appointments, including appointing (and shifting) Cabinet members, senior staff in the public service and parliamentary secretaries; and appointing senators, judges, Lieutenant Governors, Privy Councillors, provincial administrators, and Speakers of the Senate. In addition, the Prime Minister recommends to the Monarchy the appointment of the Governor General. The Prime Minister has the authority to dissolve Parliament and can therefore control the timing of an election. The Prime Minister also controls the organization of government, including the power to: create or shut down Crown corporations; create, modify or merge Cabinet portfolios and bureaucratic agencies; and appoint Royal Commissions.

■ The Cabinet

The Cabinet is a group of government ministers who, chosen and led by the prime minister, determine executive policies and are responsible for them to the House of Commons. Cabinet members are usually given responsibility for heading specific areas of the government such as finance or foreign policy and will introduce legislation pertaining to them in the House of Commons. They will also explain or defend government actions when questioned in the House.

Cabinet ministers are generally chosen from members of the government's party in the House of Commons, although Senators are sometimes appointed to provide Cabinet representation from all parts of the country. When Senators join the Cabinet they do not usually head a government department because a Senator is constitutionally forbidden to introduce tax or "money bill" legislation.

There are five categories of cabinet ministers:

1. Department Ministers who assume responsibility for running one or more government departments.

2. Ministers with special parliamentary responsibilities.

3. Ministers without portfolios who do not have responsibility for running a department and are often appointed to balance regional representation in the Cabinet.

4. Ministers of state for designated purposes who formulate and develop new policies outside normal departmental responsibilities.

5. Other ministers of state who may assist departmental ministers, though the departmental minister remains legally responsible for the duties and functions performed by the minister of state.

■ The Privy Council Office

The Privy Council Office is directed by the senior member of the public service, the Clerk of the Privy Council, who also serves as the Secretary to the Cabinet. As part of the executive branch of government, the Office staffs the Cabinet secretariat and provides services to ensure the smooth functioning of the Cabinet and Cabinet meetings. In its advisory capacity, the Privy Council Office advises the Prime Minister on government appointments, relations with Parliament and the Monarchy, the roles and responsibilities of ministers and the organization of government. The Office assists in the co-ordination of policy, ensuring that new proposals are compatible both with existing policy and the government's objectives. During a transition period between gov-

ernments, the Privy Council Office assists in the winding down of outgoing administrations and the startup of the newly-elected government.

The Privy Council Office's primary responsibilities are to ensure the smooth functioning of the machinery of government and the decision-making process, provide support to the Cabinet, monitor developments throughout the government, and act as a broker to resolve governmental problems.

■ The Treasury Board

The Treasury Board is a committee of the Privy Council that reviews planned expenditures and programs proposed by the various government departments, and assigns priorities to each. The Board is responsible for preparing a long-range and comprehensive fiscal plan that projects government income and expenses for up to four years; it also prepares operational plans for departmental programs. The Board's estimates of the costs of existing programs, major statutory payments (such as transfer payments) and public debt charges form the basis of the Main Estimates, which are tabled by the first of March each year for review by various House committees.

The Treasury Board is also responsible for administrative policy; organization of the public service; and financial, expenditure and personnel management. In 1988, the Board was also given responsibility for the policies and programs of the Official Languages Act. The Board's Secretariat negotiates collective agreements with the federal public service, acting as employer on the government's behalf.

■ Departments

Legislation and government policies are administered through departments, departmental branches and corporations, corporations owned or controlled by the government, special boards and various commissions and advisory bodies. Departments and departmental corporations are accountable to a Cabinet minister and ultimately to Parliament; they perform research, administrative, advisory, supervisory or regulatory roles. Crown corporations usually operate in a competitive or commercial environment and some are accountable to Parliament through a minister as well.

The Canadian Judiciary

■ The Supreme Court of Canada

The Supreme Court of Canada is Canada's highest court of law. It was created by federal statute in 1875. Originally, Supreme Court decisions could be appealed to a special tribunal in England, but such appeals were abolished for criminal cases in 1933 and for civil cases in 1949. Since then, the Supreme Court of Canada has been the court of last resort for every case—criminal or civil— commenced in a Canadian court.

The Supreme Court has jurisdiction to hear appeals from the courts of appeal of each province, as well as from the Federal Court of Canada. The Court is also empowered to consider questions referred to it by the federal cabinet, and to rule on the legality of bills submitted by the government.

The *Constitution Act, 1982,* with its new Canadian Charter of Rights and Freedoms, has expanded the role of the courts in general, and of the Supreme Court in particular. Though it has always been within the power of Canadian courts to declare laws or other government actions invalid, this power had narrow limits prior to 1982. Legislation could only be struck down if the government introducing it had exceeded its legislative authority as defined in the *Constitution Act, 1867* (the BNA Act). In other words, the federal government was not permitted to legislate on matters within provincial legislative authority, and the provincial governments were not permitted to legislate on matters within federal legislative authority. As long as the legislation satisfied that test, it was valid.

But since the *Constitution Act* became law in 1982, the courts have had the power to strike down legislation or invalidate other government actions if they infringe or deny any of the fundamental rights and freedoms recognized by the Charter of Rights and Freedoms. This new power has made Supreme Court judges the watchdogs of Parliament and, ultimately, the guardians of our constitutionally-guaranteed rights. As the highest court in the land, it is the Supreme Court of Canada that has the final word on whether laws violate the Constitution.

The Supreme Court consists of 9 judges, including the Chief Justice. Three of the judges must be appointed from Quebec. By convention (although it is not legally required) 3 have usually been appointed from Ontario, 2 from the West and one from Atlantic Canada. All judges are appointed and paid by the federal government, and may hold office until age 75.

■ Federal Court of Canada

This Court consists of a trial division and a court of appeal and has jurisdiction over a small range of specialized areas such as admiralty law, income tax, patents and customs. Once called the Exchequer Court, the Federal Court is administered by the federal government.

■ Appellate Courts

When a decision of the provincial superior courts is to be appealed, these courts hear the appeal and decide upon it. An appeal is not a new trial; there are rarely any witnesses called and the judges do not rehear the whole case. Instead, they examine written transcripts of the trial and listen to legal arguments presented by the parties' lawyers. The appellate courts are provincial institutions and are called either the Court of Appeal, the Supreme Court Appeal Division or Appellate Division; the judges are appointed by the federal government.

■ Superior Court of Original Jurisdiction

This is the highest court at the provincial level, with jurisdiction to hear all civil and criminal cases, unless a statute specifically says otherwise. The name of the superior court differs among provinces. It can be called either the Court of Queen's Bench, the High Court of Justice or the Supreme Court Trial Division. The judges of these courts are appointed and paid by the federal government.

■ District or County Courts

These trial courts hear all but the most serious criminal matters and civil matters up to a certain dollar value. The judges of these courts are also appointed by the federal government.

■ Provincial Courts

This is the lowest rung of the judicial ladder. The jurisdiction of the provincial courts is limited by statute to the less serious criminal matters and civil cases involving relatively small sums of money. These judges are appointed and paid by the province in which they serve.

■ Federal and Provincial Legislative Authority

Because Canada is a federal state, legislative powers are divided between 2 levels of government: federal and provincial. (Municipal governments only exercise powers delegated to them by the provincial government).

Each level of government has a distinct sphere of authority. With a few exceptions, neither level is permitted to encroach on the legislative authority of the other.

The Constitution Act, 1867 (formerly called the British North America Act, 1867) lists the classes of subject over which the federal and provincial governments have exclusive authority. The federal government, in addition to a general power to make laws for the "peace, order and good government of Canada," has exclusive power in a number of areas including criminal law, unemployment insurance, postal service, regulation of trade, external relations, money and banking, transportation, citizenship, Indian affairs and defence. Matters exclusively within provincial legislative authority include property and civil rights, administration of justice, education, health and welfare, municipal institutions and matters of a merely local or private nature.

Many of the subject classes set out in the Constitution Act, 1867 are broadly worded, and considerable debate has arisen over which level of government has authority to pass certain laws. Confusion has also arisen over the proper distribution of powers to regulate matters that could not have been foreseen by the Fathers of Confederation, such as air travel, radio and television broadcasting, etc. These difficulties have led to long political debates and frequently to court challenges which arise when a person adversely affected by a particular law claims that the law is invalid because it is *ultra vires*—beyond the powers of the level of government that enacted it. Prior to the passing of the Constitution Act, 1982, only statutes found to be *ultra vires* could be declared inoperative by the Constitution. Now, there is an additional restraint on the federal parliament and the provincial legisla-

tures to comply with constitutional provisions, including the Canadian Charter of Rights and Freedoms.

■ The Provincial Governments

Canada's provinces have a system of government which parallels that of the federal government in several ways. A premier, like the prime minister, leads the government by virtue of being leader of the party with the most support in the provincial legislature and forms a Cabinet from the elected members of the governing party. Members of a provincial legislature, like members of the federal Parliament, represent constituencies and approve legislation within their constitutional jurisdiction. A lieutenant-governor, like the Governor General, gives royal assent to the laws passed by the legislature.

The major difference between the provincial and federal systems is that the provinces have no equivalent body to Canada's Senate.

■ Government in the Yukon and Northwest Territories

Both the Yukon and Northwest Territories are governed by elected representatives. Although the administration of each territory is technically in the hands of a commissioner appointed by the federal government, in practice, the commissioners' role has become much like that of the provincial lieutenant-governors' in that they follow the wishes of the territories' elected representatives when exercising their authority.

In the Northwest Territories, real executive power is in the hands of a 24-person elected assembly whose members run for office as independents rather than as members of political parties. This assembly then selects an 8-member executive council, one of whom is chosen to serve as Government Leader.

Yukon has a 16-member legislative assembly which operates on a political party system. As of Oct. 1989, the government leader (the leader of the political party supported by a majority of the assembly's elected representatives) is given the title premier. Executive power is in the hands of an executive council, which functions like a provincial Cabinet. Its members are appointed by Yukon's commissioner on the advice of the premier.

In both territories, the elected bodies have jurisdiction over such areas as education, housing, social services and renewable resources. A 1988 accord between the federal government and the Northwest Territories has opened the way for negotiation on the transfer of responsibility for oil and gas resource management and control of oil and gas revenues. Similar negotiations are underway between Yukon and the federal government.

In 1990, the Northwest Territories established six aboriginal languages (Dogrib, Chipewyan, Gwich'in, Cree, Slavey and Inuktitut) as Official Languages, in addition to English and French.

■ Mechanics of Government

Formation of Government General elections to choose House of Commons members occur at least every five years. But they may take place more often if the prime minister decides to call an election or if the governing party loses the support of the majority of members of the House.

Following an election, the Governor General calls upon the leader of the party with the greatest House of Commons support to become prime minister. This is almost always the leader of the party with the most seats in the House but, under unusual circumstances, it could be the leader of another party which is able to gain majority support in Parliament.

The prime minister selects the cabinet, usually from members of his party in the House of Commons. Formally, the prime minister and cabinet act as advisors to the Governor General. In practice, however, they wield executive power and the Governor General's role is mainly ceremonial.

Passage of Legislation To become law, proposed legislation (known as bills) must be passed by a majority of members in both the House of Commons and the Senate and must then be given royal assent by the Governor General. Most bills are introduced by members of the government in the House of Commons. Typically, a bill is given three "readings" in the House. The first reading is simply to introduce the bill. The second reading is accompanied by debate on the principle of the bill. The bill is then voted on and, if approved, is sent to a House committee composed of representatives of all parties to be considered clause-by-clause. The committee prepares a report and submits it to the House of Commons along with any proposed amendments. These amendments, plus any others

moved by any member of Parliament, are debated and usually voted on. A motion is then brought for the bill to be given third reading. If the vote is favorable, the bill is then introduced in the Senate where it undergoes a similar process. After a bill has been approved by both Houses, the Governor General gives it royal assent in a ceremony that takes place in the Senate chamber.

Defeat of a Government Between elections, a government can be forced to resign if it is defeated in a vote on a major government bill. When this happens the government is considered to have lost the support of the majority of Parliament's elected representatives. This typically occurs only when the party in power has formed a minority government—that is, if it holds more seats than any other single party but fewer seats than the combined Opposition parties. This last happened federally in 1979 when a minority Conservative government, elected earlier that year, introduced a budget which was defeated by the combined votes of the Liberal and New Democratic Party members in the House. Parliament was dissolved, an election was called and the Liberals regained power.

■ The Constitution of Canada

Canada's constitution consists of written documents and unwritten conventions. The written constitution is embodied in the Constitution Acts 1867–1982. The 1867 legislation (originally titled the British North America Act) was a British statute that established a federal state with a Parliament modelled on the British system. That Act assembled the colonies of Nova Scotia, New Brunswick and Canada (Ontario and Quebec) into the "Dominion of Canada," created a federal government in Ottawa, and divided the powers of government between Ottawa and the provinces.

The BNA Act gave Ottawa broad jurisdiction over internal matters, including unlimited powers of taxation, while allowing the provinces only a narrow field of local control. In general, the Canadian constitution of the late 19th century was a centralist document.

Under the BNA Act, Britain still had the power to veto Canadian laws or to enact statutes affecting Canada. But the British had no desire to raise revenue in Canada, for example, or to tax Canadians directly. This approach extended to trade and tariffs.

Gradually, the practice was established that where money was involved, even in trade treaties, Canada would determine its own policy.

The same was not true of political foreign policy. When Britain declared war on Germany in 1914, Canada, as part of the British Empire, was automatically at war, even though it had not been consulted on the matter. During this period, British courts also interpreted Canadian statutes, especially those involving the division of power between Ottawa and the provinces. As a result, the constitution's strong centralist thrust was altered to give more authority to the provinces.

The constitution was also adjusted more directly, through amendments. But because the BNA Act was a British statute, Canada could make formal changes to it only with the consent of the British Parliament. Ottawa tended to seek such amendments only when they did not affect provincial powers or when the provinces agreed with the changes. This process worked at least some of the time: 29 times, in fact, between 1870 and 1975. In 1940, for example, unemployment insurance became a federal responsibility through an amendment to the BNA Act.

In 1931, Britain attempted to tidy up relations with Canada and other self-governing dominions within the Commonwealth by passing the Statute of Westminster. The Statute conceded full powers over foreign affairs and trade to Canada. But because the federal and provincial governments could not agree on a method for amending the BNA Act at home, the British Parliament retained ultimate power over Canada's constitution. Until 1949, British courts continued to review Canadian constitutional cases.

From 1927 until 1982, a succession of federal governments attempted to resolve the problem by getting the provinces to agree to an amending formula. These negotiations failed as the provinces attempted to use them as a means of gaining concessions from Ottawa.

The catalyst in constitutional discussions during the late 20th century has been the province of Quebec, where successive provincial governments since 1960 have sought to expand the province's jurisdiction and limit that of the federal government. The rationale for the change has been Quebec's unique status as a French-speaking entity in North America—the only one with French speakers in the majority.

To protect French culture, the Quebec government requested more powers, over culture itself, but also over the economy and social institutions. Where a provincial power such as education had an international dimension, the Quebec government also asserted that it had the power to represent itself abroad without Ottawa's authority or intervention. Ottawa, alarmed that such representation could lead by stages to Quebec's complete independence, resisted the trend under prime ministers Lester Pearson and Pierre Trudeau.

Trudeau was determined to see the constitution patriated, but not at the cost of the federal government's basic jurisdiction. Without a strong central power, he argued, a country as sprawling and diverse as Canada would be fatally weakened and might disintegrate. In lengthy negotiations with the provinces, Trudeau was unable to gain agreement, even when he offered increased powers in return. In 1976, the election of the separatist Parti Québécois in Quebec made constitutional compromise even more unlikely. Instead, the government of Premier Réne Lévesque wanted "sovereignty-association" with Canada: political separation with economic union.

In 1980, the Quebec government risked a referendum on sovereignty-association and lost. Trudeau, who helped defeat sovereignty-association, promised constitutional renewal if Quebeckers chose to stay within Canada. Federal-provincial discussions became mired in disagreement through the summer of 1980. Then, in September, Trudeau announced that the federal government, with the support of only Ontario and New Brunswick, would ask the British parliament to amend the BNA Act so that the constitution could be patriated and a Charter of Rights and Freedoms established to protect individual liberties. Trudeau also sought to protect minority rights in education and the mobility rights of Canadian citizens. Finally, Trudeau changed the name of the constitution: the BNA Act became the Constitution Act, 1982.

It took 18 months to get the new amendments approved by the Canadian Parliament, work around the disagreement of eight provincial governments, and get the act through the British Parliament. But, in April 1982, the Constitution Act was proclaimed—although the consent of the Quebec government was never given. It was legal neverthe-less, although some observers felt its credibil-ity and acceptability were damaged by Quebec's abstention.

The Constitution Act, 1982, consolidated all the previous BNA Acts and added an amend-ing formula and a Charter of Rights and Freedoms. The Charter, which provided for basic democratic rights, also contained a "notwithstanding" clause that allowed Parliament or any provincial legislature to over-ride its provisions.

The amending formula provided for two types of constitutional change: the division of powers between the federal and provincial governments could be modified with the con-sent of the federal Parliament and seven provincial legislatures in provinces totalling more than 50 percent of the Canadian popula-tion; matters such as the composition of the Supreme Court or the status of English or French, however, required unanimous con-sent. No amendment could take longer than three years to be ratified by Ottawa and all 10 provinces.

This last point proved to be a major obstacle when the Conservative government of Brian Mulroney sought further constitutional reform to obtain Quebec's consent to the 1982 consti-tution. Under the new Liberal government of Premier Robert Bourassa, Quebec was pre-pared to accept the 1982 settlement, thus legitimizing it in the eyes of many critics, only if Ottawa and the other provinces agreed to modify the division of powers and to include a reference to Quebec as a "distinct society" in the constitution. In June 1987, in the "Meech Lake Accord," Mulroney and the 10 provincial premiers agreed to do just that. Ottawa conceded a provincial role in appoint-ments to the Supreme Court and Senate, con-ceded Quebec a role in setting immigration policy, and partly weakened the federal gov-ernment's ability to impose shared-cost pro-grams on the provinces.

Because parts of the Meech Lake agreement involved an amendment to the constitution of the Canadian Senate and the Supreme Court, unanimous provincial consent was required. The Meech Lake agreement lapsed when Newfoundland withdrew its ratification and Manitoba failed to ratify it within the three-year time limit. (June 23, 1990)

The failure of the Meech Lake accord plunged Canada into another constitutional crisis. Nationalism, sovereignty and total independence all acquired more support inside Quebec. The government of Quebec studied constitutional options during 1991, as did a number of federal commissions which travelled the country and consulted the population. Despite recommendations for sovereignty for Quebec, Quebec premier Robert Bourassa asked for further proposals from the federal government and scheduled a provincial referendum on those proposals to be held no later than October, 1992.

In September of 1991, Prime Min. Mulroney tabled a new constitutional plan with 28 proposals, and meetings and discussions concerning the plan lasted well into 1992. On Aug. 28, 1992 federal-provincial agreement was reached on revised proposals in Charlottetown, PEI and the resulting document became known as the Charlottetown Accord.

Proposals in the accord included provisions for: a smaller but elected Senate; an expanded House of Commons (337 seats instead of the present 295); annual First Ministers conferences; entrenchment of equalization payments to provinces to ensure each provincial government of sufficient revenues; recognition of the inherent right of Aboriginal peoples to self-government within Canada; recognition of Quebec as a distinct society; a transfer of responsibility for forestry, mining, telecommunications, regional development, municipal and urban affairs, culture within the province, tourism, housing and recreation to the provinces, with the federal government also committed to negotiating agreements with individual provinces concerning immigration.

The referendum in Quebec concerning the proposals was set for October 26, 1992 and the rest of the country followed suit with a national referendum on the same date on the question "Do you agree that the Constitution of Canada should be renewed on the basis of the agreement reached on August 28, 1992?"

Both the "yes" and the "no" sides waged a fierce campaign on the issue; the final, national verdict was 54.8% of votes cast for the "no" side and 44.9% for the "yes." Provincially, the Charlottetown Accord was approved by the Northwest Territories, Prince Edward Island, Newfoundland, New Brunswick and Ontario; the Yukon, Nova Scotia, Quebec, Manitoba, Saskatchewan, Alberta and British Columbia rejected it.

Text of the Canadian Charter of Rights and Freedoms

Whereas Canada is founded upon principles that recognize the supremacy of God and the rule of law:

■ Guarantee of Rights and Freedoms

1 The Canadian Charter of Rights and Freedoms guarantees the rights and freedoms set out in it subject only to such reasonable limits prescribed by law as can be demonstrably justified in a free and democratic society.

■ Fundamental Freedoms

2 Everyone has the following fundamental freedoms: (a) freedom of conscience and religion; (b) freedom of thought, belief, opinion and expression, including freedom of the press and other media of communication; (c) freedom of peaceful assembly; and (d) freedom of association.

■ Democratic Rights

3 Every citizen of Canada has the right to vote in an election of members of the House of Commons or of a legislative assembly and to be qualified for membership therein.

4 (1) No House of Commons and no legislative assembly shall continue for longer than five years from the date fixed for the return of the writs at a general election of its members. (2) In time of real or apprehended war, invasion or insurrection, a House of Commons may be continued by Parliament and a legislative assembly may be continued by the legislature beyond five years if such continuation is not opposed by the votes of more than one-third of the members of the House of Commons or the legislative assembly, as the case may be.

5 There shall be a sitting of Parliament and of each legislature at least once every twelve months.

■ Mobility Rights

6 (1) Every citizen of Canada has the right to enter, remain in and leave Canada. (2) Every citizen of Canada and every person who has the status of a permanent resident of Canada has the right (a) to move to and take up residence in any province; and (b) to pursue the gaining of a livelihood in any province. (3) The rights specified in subsection (2) are subject to (a) any laws or practices of general application in force in a province other than those that discriminate among persons primarily on the basis of province of present or previous residence; and (b) any laws providing for reasonable residency requirements as a qualification for the receipt of publicly provided social services. (4) Subsections (2) and (3) do not preclude any law, program or activity that has as its object the amelioration in a province of conditions of individuals in that province who are socially or economically disadvantaged if the rate of employment in that province is below the rate of employment in Canada.

■ Legal Rights

7 Everyone has the right to life, liberty and security of the person and the right not to be deprived thereof except in accordance with the principles of fundamental justice.

8 Everyone has the right to be secure against unreasonable search or seizure.

9 Everyone has the right not to be arbitrarily detained or imprisoned.

10 Everyone has the right on arrest or detention (a) to be informed promptly of the reasons therefor; (b) to retain and instruct counsel without delay and to be informed of that right; and (c) to have the validity of the detention determined by way of *habeas corpus* and to be released if the detention is not lawful.

11 Any person charged with an offence has the right (a) to be informed without unreasonable delay of the specific offence; (b) to be tried within a reasonable time; (c) not to be compelled to be a witness in proceedings against that person in respect of the offence; (d) to be presumed innocent until proven guilty according to law in a fair and public hearing by an independent

and impartial tribunal; (e) not to be denied reasonable bail without just cause; (f) except in the case of an offence under military law tried before a military tribunal, to the benefit of trial by jury where the maximum punishment for the offence is imprisonment for five years or a more severe punishment; (g) not to be found guilty on account of any act or omission unless, at the time of the act or omission, it constituted an offence under Canadian or international law or was criminal according to the general principles of law recognized by the community of nations; (h) if finally acquitted of the offence, not to be tried for it again and, if finally found guilty and punished for the offence, not to be tried or punished for it again; and (i) if found guilty of the offence and if the punishment for the offence has been varied between the time of commission and the time of sentencing, to the benefit of the lesser punishment.

12 Everyone has the right not to be subjected to any cruel and unusual treatment or punishment.

13 A witness who testifies in any proceedings has the right not to have any incriminating evidence so given used to incriminate that witness in any other proceedings, except in a prosecution for perjury or for the giving of contradictory evidence.

14 A party or witness in any proceedings who does not understand or speak the language in which the proceedings are conducted or who is deaf has the right to the assistance of an interpreter.

■ Equality Rights

15 (1) Every individual is equal before and under the law and has the right to the equal protection and equal benefit of the law without discrimination and, in particular, without discrimination based on race, national or ethnic origin, colour, religion, sex, age or mental or physical disability. (2) Subsection (1) does not preclude any law, program or activity that has as its object the amelioration of conditions of disadvantaged individuals or groups including those that are disadvantaged because of race, national or ethnic origin,

colour, religion, sex, age or mental or physical disability.

■ Official Languages of Canada

16 (1) English and French are the official languages of Canada and have equality of status and equal rights and privileges as to their use in all institutions of the Parliament and government of Canada. (2) English and French are the official languages of New Brunswick and have equality of status and equal rights and privileges as to their use in all institutions of the legislature and government of New Brunswick. (3) Nothing in this Charter limits the authority of Parliament or a legislature to advance the equality of status or use of English and French.

17 (1) Everyone has the right to use English or French in any debates and other proceedings of Parliament. (2) Everyone has the right to use English or French in any debates and other proceedings of the legislature of New Brunswick.

18 (1) The statutes, records and journals of Parliament shall be printed and published in English and French and both language versions are equally authoritative. (2) The statutes, records and journals of the legislature of New Brunswick shall be printed and published in English and French and both language versions are equally authoritative.

19 (1) Either English or French may be used by any person in, or in any pleading in or process issuing from, any court established by Parliament. (2) Either English or French may be used by any person in, or in any pleading in or process issuing from, any court of New Brunswick.

20 (1) Any member of the public in Canada has the right to communicate with, and to receive available services from, any head or central office of an institution of the Parliament or government of Canada in English or French, and has the same right with respect to any other office of any such institution where (a) there is a significant demand for communications with and services from that office in such language; or (b) due to the nature of the office, it is reasonable that communications with and services from that office be available in both English and French. (2) Any member of the public in New Brunswick has the right to communicate with, and to receive available services from, any office of an institution of the legislature or government of New Brunswick in English or French.

21 Nothing in sections 16 to 20 abrogates or derogates from any right, privilege or obligation with respect to the English and French languages, or either of them, that exists or is continued by virtue of any other provision of the Constitution of Canada.

22 Nothing in sections 16 to 20 abrogates or derogates from any legal or customary right or privilege acquired or enjoyed either before or after the coming into force of this Charter with respect to any language that is not English or French.

■ Minority Language Educational Rights

23 (1) Citizens of Canada (a) whose first language learned and still understood is that of the English or French linguistic minority population of the province in which they reside, or (b) who have received their primary school instruction in Canada in English or French and reside in a province where the language in which they received that instruction is the language of the English or French linguistic minority population of the province, have the right to have their children receive primary and secondary school instruction in that language in that province. (2) Citizens of Canada of whom any child has received or is receiving primary or secondary school instruction in English or French in Canada, have the right to have all their children receive primary and secondary school instruction in the same language. (3) The right of citizens of Canada under subsections (1) and (2) to have their children receive primary and secondary school instruction in the language of the English or French linguistic minority population of a province (a) applies wherever in the province the number of children of citizens who have such a right is sufficient to warrant the provision to them out of public funds of minority language instruction; and (b) includes, where the number of those children so warrants, the right to have them receive that instruction in minority language educational facilities provided out of public funds.

■ Enforcement

24. (1) Anyone whose rights or freedoms, as guaranteed by this Charter, have been infringed or denied may apply to a court of competent jurisdiction to obtain such remedy as the court considers appropriate and just in the circumstances. (2) Where, in proceedings under subsection (1), a court concludes that evidence was obtained in a manner that infringed or denied any rights or freedoms guaranteed by this Charter, the evidence shall be excluded if it is established that, having regard to all the circumstances, the admission of it in the proceedings would bring the administration of justice into disrepute.

■ General

25 The guarantee in this Charter of certain rights and freedoms shall not be construed so as to abrogate or derogate from any aboriginal, treaty or other rights or freedoms that pertain to the aboriginal peoples of Canada including (a) any rights or freedoms that have been recognized by the Royal Proclamation of October 7, 1763; and (b) any rights or freedoms that may be acquired by the aboriginal peoples of Canada by way of land claims settlement.

26 The guarantee in this Charter of certain rights and freedoms shall not be construed as denying the existence of any other rights or freedoms that exist in Canada.

27 This Charter shall be interpreted in a manner consistent with the preservation and enhancement of the multicultural heritage of Canadians.

28 Notwithstanding anything in this Charter, the rights and freedoms referred to in it are guaranteed equally to male and female persons.

29 Nothing in this Charter abrogates or derogates from any rights or privileges guaranteed by or under the Constitution of Canada in respect of denominational, separate or dissentient schools.

30 A reference in this Charter to a province or to the legislative assembly or legislature or a province shall be deemed to include a reference to the Yukon Territory and the Northwest Territories, or to the appropriate legislative authority thereof, as the case may be.

31 Nothing in this Charter extends the legislative powers of any body or authority.

■ Application of Charter

32. (1) This Charter applies (a) to the Parliament and government of Canada in respect of all matters within the authority of Parliament including all matters relating to the Yukon Territory and Northwest Territories; and (b) to the legislature and government of each province in respect of all matters within the authority of the legislature of each province. (2) Notwithstanding subsection (1), section 15 shall not have effect until three years after this section comes into force.

33 (1) Parliament or the legislature of a province may expressly declare in an Act of Parliament or of the legislature, as the case may be, that the Act or a provision thereof shall operate notwithstanding a provision included in section 2 or sections 7 to 15 of this Charter. (2) An Act or a provision of an Act in respect of which a declaration made under this section is in effect shall have such operation as it would have but for the provision of this Charter referred to in the declaration. (3) A declaration made under subsection (1) shall cease to have effect five years after it comes into force or on such earlier date as may be specified in the declaration. (4) Parliament or a legislature of a province may re-enact a declaration made under subsection (1). (5) Subsection (3) applies in respect of a re-enactment made under subsection (4).

■ Citation

34 This Part may be cited as the Canadian Charter of Rights and Freedoms.

Canadian Honours and Decorations

■ The Order of Canada

History Creation of the Order of Canada was announced by Prime Minister Lester B. Pearson in 1967. It was instituted on the centennial of Canadian Confederation, July 1, 1967.

Basis of Award To honour Canadians for outstanding achievement and service to their country or humanity at large. Appointments are announced twice annually, around July 1 and January 1. Investitures occur during the fall and spring when the awards are given by the Governor General.

Eligibility Every Canadian is eligible to become a member.

Membership There are three categories of membership: Companion of The Order of Canada (C.C.): no more than 15 may be appointed in any one year and the total number is not to exceed 150 living companions.

Officer of The Order of Canada (O.C.): not more than 46 appointments annually.

Member of The Order of Canada (C.M.): Designed to recognize service in a locality or a particular field of activity. Not more than 92 appointments annually.

Badge A six-armed cross in the form of a stylized snowflake with a ribbon in the same proportions of white and red which appear on the Canadian flag. Bears the words "Desiderantes Meliorem Patriam" (They Desire for a Better Country). Worn at the neck by Companions and Officers and on the left breast by Members.

■ The Order of Military Merit

History The Order was instituted in 1972.

Basis of Award To recognize exceptional service and conspicuous merit by regular and reserve members of Canada's Armed Forces.

Appointments are made by the Governor General on the recommendation of the minister of defence.

Eligibility Members of the Canadian Armed Forces, regular and reserve.

Membership Commander of the Order of Military Merit (C.M.M.): Commanders constitute 6% of the .1% of the Armed Forces who are annually eligible for an appointment.

Officer of the Order of Military Merit (O.M.M.): Of the .1%, 30% may be made Officers.

Member of the Order of Military Merit (M.M.M.): The balance of appointments are as Members.

Badge In the form of an enamelled blue cross having expanded arms, with a blue ribbon edged in gold. Bears the words "Merit Merite Canada". Worn at the neck by Commanders and on the left breast by Officers and Members.

■ Victoria Cross (V.C.)

History Approved by Queen Elizabeth II on February 2, 1993. The British Victoria Cross was created by Queen Victoria in 1856 and was awarded to Canadians in all wars until 1945. There have been 93 Canadian recipients of the British V.C.

Basis of Award In recognition of "the most conspicuous bravery, a daring or pre-eminent act of valour or self-sacrifice or extreme devotion to duty, in the presence of the enemy." The V.C. will be awarded by the Governor General on the advice of the Military Valour Advisory Committee. It is the highest order of precedence in Canadian honours.

Eligibility Members of the Canadian Forces or a member of an allied armed force that is serving with or in conjunction with the Canadian Forces on or after January 1, 1993. The V.C. may be awarded posthumously.

Badge The Cross is a bronze straight armed cross, suspended from a crimson ribbon. The face has, in the middle of the cross, a lion guardant standing on the Royal Crown, with the Latin inscription "Pro Valore." (For Valour) The date of the act for which the decoration is bestowed is engraved in a raised circle on the reverse.

■ The Star of Military Valour (S.M.V.)

History Approved by Queen Elizabeth II on February 2, 1993.

Basis of Award Awarded for distinguished and valiant service in the presence of the enemy.

Eligibility Members of the Canadian Forces or a member of an allied armed force that is serving with or in conjunction with the Canadian Forces on or after January 1, 1993. The S.M.V. may be awarded posthumously.

Badge A gold star with four points with a maple leaf in each of the angles, on the face of which a gold maple leaf is superimposed in the centre of a sanguine field surrounded by a silver wreath of laurel and on the reverse of which the Royal Cypher and Crown and the inscription "Pro Valore" shall appear. The Star shall be worn, suspended from a crimson ribbon with two white stripes, immediately after any order and before the Star of Courage.

■ The Medal of Military Valour (M.M.V.)

History Approved by Queen Elizabeth II on February 2, 1993.

Basis of Award Awarded for an act of valour or devotion to duty in the presence of the enemy.

Eligibility Members of the Canadian Forces or a member of an allied armed force that is serving with or in conjunction with the Canadian Forces on or after January 1, 1993. The M.M.V. may be awarded posthumously.

Badge A circular gold medal, on the face of which there shall be a maple leaf surrounded by a wreath of laurel and on the reverse of which the Royal Cypher and Crown and the inscription "Pro Valore" will appear. The medal shall be worn, from a crimson ribbon with three white stripes, immediately after the Meritorious Service Cross and before the Medal of Bravery.

■ The Cross of Valour (C.V.)

History Created in 1972, The Cross of Valour replaced all non-combattant commonwealth medals: the George Cross, the George Medal and the Queen's Gallantry Medal. The Cross of Valour takes precedence before all orders and other decorations except the Victoria Cross and the George Cross.

Basis of Award Awarded for instances of extraordinary heroism in circumstances of extreme peril.

Eligibility May be awarded to civilians or members of the Armed Forces. Only 15 have been awarded.

Badge A gold cross bearing the words "Valour Vaillance."

■ The Star of Courage (S.C.)

History Created in 1972.

Basis of Award Awarded for other outstandingly courageous actions and in cases where there is a greater degree of personal risk involved than to warrant a Medal of Bravery.

Eligibility May be awarded to civilians or members of the Armed Forces.

Badge A 4-pointed silver star with the word "Courage."

■ The Medal of Bravery (M.B.)

History   Created in 1972.

Basis of Award   Awarded for other outstandingly courageous actions.

Eligibility   May be awarded to civilians or members of the Armed Forces.

Badge   A circular silver medal with the words "Bravery Bravoure."

■ The Meritorious Service Cross (M.S.C.) (military and civilian)

History   Military division created in 1984; civilian division created in 1991.

Basis of Award   *Military division*: awarded in recognition of a military deed or activity that has been performed in an outstandingly professional manner, according to a rare high standard that brings considerable benefit or great honour to the Canadian Forces. *Civilian division*: awarded in recognition of the performance of a deed or activity performed in an outstandingly professional manner or according to an uncommonly high standard that brings considerable benefit or great honour to Canada.

Eligibility   A member of the Canadian and allied forces, persons serving in conjunction with the Canadian Forces or other persons, Canadian and foreigners.

Badge   A Greek cross of silver, ends splayed and convexed, ensigned with the Royal Crown. On the face appear a maple leaf within a circle and a laurel wreath between the arms. Recipients are entitled to use the letters "M.S.C." after their names.

■ The Meritorious Service Medal (M.S.M.) (military and civilian)

History   Created in 1991.

Basis of Award   *Military division*: awarded in recognition of a military deed or activity that has been performed in a highly professional manner or is of a very high standard that brings benefit or honour to the Canadian Forces. *Civilian division*: awarded in recognition of the performance of a deed or activity performed in a highly professional manner or of a very high standard that brings benefit or honour to Canada.

Eligibility   A member of the Canadian and allied forces, persons serving in conjunction with the Canadian Forces or other persons, Canadian and foreigners.

Badge   A circular medal of silver ensigned with the Royal Crown. On the face appears the design of the Cross. On the reverse appears the Royal Cypher and, within a double circle, the words "Meritorious Service Méritoire." Recipients are entitled to use the letters "M.S.M." after their names.

Decorations for Bravery, Rideau Hall, Ottawa

*O*n Friday, June 18, 1993, the Governor General presented 28 bravery decorations at an investiture ceremony.

The Star of Courage is awarded "for acts of conspicuous courage in circumstances of great peril" and six were awarded. Recipients were Suzanne-Marie Beaucher of Windsor, Quebec who was stabbed while rescuing a teenage girl from an attacker (June, 1992); Kelvin Brundrett (posthumous) of Baden, Ontario who died trying to save two skydivers whose parachutes had become entangled (July, 1991); Dana Frederick Dickieson (posthumous) of New Glasgow, PEI who rescued three people from a burning house but died trying to save his youngest son from the fire that claimed both their lives (February, 1990) ; Daniel Godin of Thunder Bay, Ontario who assisted fellow victims of a plane crash at Dryden, Ontario (March 1989); Stephen Anthony Lopez of Scarborough, Ontario who pulled a woman to safety from Toronto subway tracks (November, 1990) and Jocelyn McDonald of Minaki, Ontario who rescued her five-year-old playmate from an abductor (April, 1992).

Medals of Bravery were given "for acts of bravery in hazardous circumstances" and 22 were presented to Canadians from across the country for rescues both in war and peace. Acts of bravery in Bosnia-Hercegovina by Canadian Forces personnel were recognized as well as civilian rescues from burning buildings, capsized boats, bank robberies, mountaineering accidents, plane crashes, attacks by wild animals and the December 1989 shooting at L'École polytechnique in Montreal.

Governors General of Canada

Name	Date Appointed	Assumed Office	Term
Sir Charles Stanley, Viscount Monck	June 1, 1867	July 1, 1867	1867–69
Sir John Young, Baron Lisgar	Dec. 29, 1868	Feb. 2, 1869	1869–72
Frederick Temple Hamilton Blackwood, Earl of Dufferin	May 22, 1872	June 25, 1872	1872–78
John Douglas Sutherland Campbell, Marquess of Lorne	Oct. 5, 1878	Nov. 20, 1878	1878–83
Henry Charles Keith Petty-Fitzmaurice, Marquess of Lansdowne	Aug. 18, 1883	Oct. 23, 1883	1883–88
Frederick Arthur Stanley, Baron Stanley of Preston	May 1, 1888	June 11, 1888	1888–93
John Campbell Hamilton-Gordon, Earl of Aberdeen	May 22, 1893	Nov. 18, 1893	1893–98
Gilbert John Elliott Murray-Kynynmound, Earl of Minto	July 30, 1898	Nov. 12, 1898	1898–1904
Albert Henry George Grey, Earl Grey	Sept. 26, 1904	Dec. 10, 1904	1904–11
His Royal Highness The Prince Arthur, Field Marshall Duke of Connaught	Mar. 21, 1911	Oct. 13, 1911	1911–16
Victor Christian William Cavendish, Duke of Devonshire	Aug. 19, 19	Nov. 11, 1916	1916–21
Julian Byng, General Baron Byng of Vimy and of Thorpe	Aug. 2, 1921	Aug. 11, 1921	1921–26
Freeman Freeman-Thomas, Baron Willingdon of Ratton	Aug. 5, 1926	Nov. 2, 1926	1926–31
Vere Brabazon Ponsonby, Earl of Bessborough	Feb. 9, 1931	Apr. 4, 1931	1931–35
John Buchan, Baron Tweedsmuir	Aug. 10, 1935	Nov. 2, 935	1935–40
Alexander George Cambridge, Major General Earl of Athlone	Apr. 3, 1940	June 21, 1940	1940–46
Sir Harold George Alexander, Field Marshall Viscount Alexander of Tunis	Aug. 1, 1945	Apr. 18, 1946	1946–52
The Right Honourable Vincent Massey	Jan. 24, 1952	Feb. 22, 1952	1952–59
General the Right Honourable Georges P. Vanier	Aug. 1, 1959	Sept. 15, 1959	1959–67
The Right Honourable Daniel Roland Michener	Mar. 25, 1967	Apr. 15, 1967	1967–73
The Right Honourable Jules Léger	Oct. 5, 1973	Jan. 14, 1974	1973–79
The Right Honourable Edward Richard Schreyer	Dec. 7, 1978	Jan. 22, 1979	1979–83
The Right Honourable Jeanne Sauvé	Dec. 23, 1983	May 14, 1984	1984–90
The Right Honourable Ramon John Hnatyshyn	Oct. 6, 1989	Jan. 21, 1990	1990—

Prime Ministers of Canada

Prime Minister	Party	Term(s)	Born	P.M. at age	Died
Sir John A. Macdonald	Conservative	July 1, 1867–Nov. 5, 1873 Oct. 9, 1878–June 6, 1891	Jan. 11, 1815	52	June 6, 1891
Alexander Mackenzie	Liberal	Nov. 5, 1873–Oct. 9, 1878	Jan. 28, 1822	51	Apr. 17, 1892
Sir John Abbott	Conservative	June 15, 1891–Nov. 24, 1892	Mar. 12, 1821	70	Oct. 30, 1893
Sir John Thompson	Conservative	Nov. 25, 1892–Dec. 12, 1894	Nov. 10, 1845	48	Dec. 12, 1894
Sir Mackenzie Bowell	Conservative	Dec. 13, 1894–Apr. 27, 1896	Dec. 27, 1823	70	Dec. 10, 1917
Sir Charles Tupper	Conservative	Apr. 27, 1896–July 8, 1896	July 2, 1821	74	Oct. 30, 1915
Sir Wilfrid Laurier	Liberal	July 11, 1896–Oct. 6, 1911	Nov. 20, 1841	54	Feb. 17, 1919
Sir Robert Borden	Conservative/ Unionist	Oct. 1, 1917–July 10, 1920 Oct. 10, 1911–Oct. 12, 1917	June 26, 1854	57	June 10, 1937
Arthur Meighen	Unionist/ Conservative	June 29, 1926–Sept. 25, 1926 July 10, 1920–Dec. 29, 1921	June 16, 1874	46	Aug. 5, 1960
Mackenzie King	Liberal	Dec. 29, 1921–June 28, 1926 Sept. 25, 1926–Aug. 6, 1930 Oct. 23, 1935–Nov. 15, 1948	Dec. 17, 1874	47	July 22, 1950
Richard B. Bennett	Conservative	Aug. 7, 1930–Oct. 23, 1935	July 3, 1870	60	June 27, 1947
Louis St. Laurent	Liberal	Nov. 15, 1948–June 21, 1957	Feb. 1, 1882	66	July 25, 1973
John Diefenbaker	Prog. Cons.	June 21, 1957–Apr. 22, 1963	Sept. 18, 1895	61	Aug. 16, 1979
Lester Pearson	Liberal	Apr. 22, 1963–Apr. 20, 1968	Apr. 23, 1897	65	Dec. 27, 1972
Pierre Trudeau	Liberal	Apr. 20, 1968–June 4, 1979 Mar. 3, 1980–June 30, 1984	Oct. 18, 1919	48	
Joe Clark	Prog. Cons.	June 4, 1979–Mar. 3, 1980	June 5, 1939	39	
John Turner	Liberal	June 30, 1984–Sept. 17, 1984	June 7, 1929	55	
Brian Mulroney	Prog. Cons.	Sept. 17, 1984–June 25, 1993	Mar. 20, 1939	45	
Kim Campbell	Prog. Cons.	June 25, 1993—	Mar. 10, 1947	46	

The Canadian Cabinet

(as of September 1993)

Kim Campbell	Prime Minister
Perrin Beatty	Secretary of State for External Affairs
Pierre Blais	Minister of Justice and Attorney General of Canada; President of the Queen's Privy Council for Canada
Pauline A. Browes	Minister of Indian Affairs and Northern Development
Jean J. Charest	Deputy Prime Minister; Minister of Industry, Science and Technology; Minister of Consumer and Corporate Affairs
Mary Collins	Minister of National Health and Welfare; Minister responsible for the Status of Women
Jean Corbeil	Minister of Transport
Paul Dick	Minister of Supply and Services; Minister of Public Works
James Edwards	President of the Treasury Board
Tom Hockin	Minister of International Trade
Monique Landry	Secretary of State of Canada; Minister of Communications
Doug Lewis	Solicitor General of Canada; Leader of the Government in the House of Commons
Gilles Loiselle	Minister of Finance
Charles Mayer	Minister of Agriculture; Minister for Small Communities and Rural Areas
Peter L. McCreath	Minister of Veterans Affairs
Lowell Murray	Leader of the Government in the Senate
Robert D. Nicholson	Minister for Science; Minister responsible for Small Business
Ross Reid	Minister of Fisheries and Oceans; Minister for the Atlantic Canada Opportunities Agency
Larry Schneider	Minister of Western Economic Diversification
Thomas Siddon	Minister of National Defence
Barbara J. Sparrow	Minister of Energy, Mines and Resources; Minister of Forestry
Garth Turner	Minister of National Revenue
Bernard Valcourt	Minister of Employment and Immigration; Minister of Labour
Pierre H. Vincent	Minister of the Environment
Gerry Weiner	Minister of Multiculturalism and Citizenship

Supreme Court Justices of Canada

(as of September 1993)

Name	Date of Birth	Date Appointed	Appointed from
The Hon. Mr. Justice Antonio Lamer	July 8, 1933	Mar. 28, 1980[1]	Quebec Court of Appeal
The Hon. Mr. Justice Gérard V. La Forest	Apr. 1, 1926	Jan. 16, 1985	Court of Appeal of NB
The Hon. Madam Justice Claire L'Heureux-Dubé	Sept. 7, 1927	Apr. 15, 1987	Quebec Court of Appeal
The Hon. Mr. Justice John Sopinka	Mar. 19, 1933	May 24, 1988	private law practice
The Hon. Mr. Justice Charles Gonthier	Aug. 1, 1928	Feb. 1, 1989	Quebec Court of Appeal
The Hon. Mr. Justice Peter de Carteret Cory	Oct. 25, 1925	Feb. 1, 1989	Ontario Court of Appeal
The Hon. Madam Justice Beverley McLachlin	Sept. 7, 1943	Mar. 30, 1989	Supreme Court of BC
The Hon. Mr. Justice Frank Iacobucci	June 29, 1937	Jan. 7, 1991	Federal Court of Canada
The Hon. Mr. Justice John Charles Major	Feb. 20, 1931	Nov. 13, 1991	Alberta Court of Appeal

(1) Appointed Chief Justice July 1, 1990.

Members of Canada's Senate

(as of September 23, 1993; 104 Senators, 0 vacancies)

Senator	Birthdate	Date Appointed	Appointed by	Province
Willie Adams	June 22, 1934	Apr. 5, 1977	Trudeau	NWT
Raynell Andreychuk	Aug. 14, 1994	Mar. 11, 1993	Mulroney	Sask.
W. David Angus	July 21, 1937	June 10, 1993	Mulroney	Que.
Norm Atkins	June 27, 1934	July 2, 1986	Mulroney	Ont.
Jack Austin	Mar. 2, 1932	Aug. 19, 1975	Trudeau	BC
James Balfour	May 22, 1928	Sept. 13, 1979	Clark	Sask.
Gérald Beaudoin	Apr. 15, 1929	Sept. 26, 1988	Mulroney	Que.
Mario Beaulieu	Feb. 1, 1930	Aug. 30, 1990	Mulroney	Que.
Eric Arthur Berntson	May 16, 1941	Sept. 27, 1990	Mulroney	West[1]
Roch Bolduc	Oct. 9, 1928	Sept. 26, 1988	Mulroney	Que.
M. Lorne Bonnell	Jan. 4, 1923	Nov. 15, 1971	Trudeau	PEI
Peter Bosa	May 2, 1927	Apr. 5, 1977	Trudeau	Ont.
John Buchanan	Apr. 22, 1931	Sept. 12, 1990	Mulroney	NS
Pat Carney	May 26, 1935	Aug. 30, 1990	Mulroney	BC
Solange Chaput-Rolland	May 14, 1919	Sept. 26, 1988	Mulroney	Que.
Guy Charbonneau	June 21, 1922	Sept. 27, 1979	Clark	Que.
Ethel Cochrane	Sept. 23, 1937	Nov. 17, 1986	Mulroney	Nfld
Michel Cogger	Mar. 21, 1939	May 2, 1986	Mulroney	Que.
Erminie J. Cohen	July 23, 1926	June 4, 1993	Mulroney	NB
Gérald J. Comeau	Feb. 1, 1946	Aug. 30, 1990	Mulroney	NS
Anne C. Cools	Aug. 12, 1943	Jan. 13, 1984	Trudeau	Ont.
Eymard Corbin	Aug. 2, 1934	July 9, 1984	Turner	NB
Keith Douglas Davey	Apr. 21, 1926	Feb. 24, 1966	Pearson	Ont.
Paul David	Dec. 25, 1919	Apr. 16, 1985	Mulroney	Que.
Pierre De Bané	Aug. 2, 1938	June 29, 1984	Trudeau	Que.
Jean Noël Desmarais	Apr. 11, 1924	June 4, 1993	Mulroney	Ont.
Mabel Margaret DeWare	Sept. 9, 1926	Sept. 23, 1990	Mulroney	NB
Consiglio Di Nino	Jan. 24, 1938	Aug. 30, 1990	Mulroney	Ont.
C. William Doody	Feb. 26, 1931	Oct. 3, 1979	Clark	Nfld
Richard J. Doyle	Mar. 10, 1923	Mar. 19, 1985	Mulroney	Ont.
Douglas D. Everett	Aug. 12, 1927	Nov. 8, 1966	Pearson	Man.
John Trevor Eyton	July 12, 1934	Sept. 23, 1990	Mulroney	Ont.
Joyce Fairbairn	Nov. 6, 1939	June 29, 1984	Trudeau	Alta
John Michael Forrestall	Sept. 23, 1932	Sept. 27, 1990	Mulroney	Maritime[1]
Royce H. Frith	Nov. 12, 1923	Apr. 5, 1977	Trudeau	Ont.
Ronald D. Ghitter	Aug. 22, 1935	Mar. 25, 1993	Mulroney	Alta
Philippe D. Gigantès	Aug. 16, 1923	Jan. 13, 1984	Trudeau	Que.
Jerahmiel S. Grafstein	Jan. 2, 1935	Jan. 13, 1984	Trudeau	Ont.
B. Alasdair Graham	May 21, 1929	Apr. 27, 1972	Trudeau	NS
Normand Grimard	July 16, 1925	Sept. 27, 1990	Mulroney	Que.[1]
Leonard J. Gustafson	Nov. 10, 1993	May 26, 1993	Mulroney	Sask.
Stanley Haidasz	Mar. 4, 1923	Mar. 23, 1978	Trudeau	Ont.
Earl A. Hastings	Jan. 7, 1924	Feb. 24, 1966	Pearson	Alta
Daniel Hays	Apr. 24, 1939	June 29, 1984	Trudeau	Alta
Jacques Hébert	June 21, 1923	Apr. 20, 1983	Trudeau	Que.
Duncan J. Jessiman	June 5, 1923	May 26, 1993	Mulroney	Man.
Janis Johnson	Apr. 27, 1946	Sept. 27, 1990	Mulroney	West[1]
James Francis Kelleher	Oct. 2, 1930	Sept. 23, 1990	Mulroney	Ont.
William M. Kelly	July 21, 1925	Dec. 23, 1982	Trudeau	Ont.
Colin Kenny	Dec. 10, 1943	June 29, 1984	Trudeau	Ont.
Wilbert Joseph Keon	May 17, 1935	Sept. 27, 1990	Mulroney	Ont.[1]
Noel A. Kinsella	Nov. 28, 1939	Sept. 12, 1990	Mulroney	NB
Michael Kirby	Aug. 5, 1941	Jan. 13, 1984	Trudeau	NS
E. Leo Kolber	Jan. 18, 1929	Dec. 23, 1983	Trudeau	Que.
Daniel Lang	June 13, 1919	Feb. 14, 1964	Pearson	Ont.
Thérèse Lavoie-Roux	Mar. 12, 1928	Sept. 27, 1990	Mulroney	Que.[1]

Senator	Birthdate	Date Appointed	Appointed by	Province
▶ Edward M. Lawson	Sept. 24. 1929	Oct. 7, 1970	Trudeau	BC
Roméo LeBlanc	Dec. 18. 1927	June 29, 1984	Tudeau	NB
Marjory LeBreton	July 4, 1940	June 18, 1993	Mulroney	Ont.
P. Derek Lewis	Nov. 28, 1924	Mar. 23, 1978	Tudeau	Nfld
Paul Lucier	July 29, 1930	Oct. 23, 1975	Trudeau	Yukon
John Lynch-Staunton	June 19, 1930	Sept. 23, 1990	Mulroney	Que.
Finlay MacDonald	Jan. 4, 1923	Dec. 21, 1984	Mulroney	NS
John M. Macdonald	May 3, 1906	June 24, 1960	Diefenbaker	NS
Allan J. MacEachen	July 6, 1921	June 29, 1984	Trudeau	NS
Heath MacQuarrie	Sept. 18, 1919	Oct. 3, 1979	Clark	PEI
Len Marchand	Nov. 16, 1933	June 29, 1984	Trudeau	BC
Jack Marshall	Nov. 26, 1919	Mar. 23, 1978	Trudeau	Nfld
Michael Arthur Meighen	Mar. 25, 1939	Sept. 27, 1990	Mulroney	Ont.[1]
Gildas L. Molgat	Jan. 25, 1927	Oct. 7, 1970	Trudeau	Man.
Robert Muir	Nov. 10, 1919	Mar. 26, 1979	Trudeau	NS
Lowell Murray	Sept. 26, 1936	Sept. 13, 1979	Clark	Ont.
Pierre Claude Nolin	Oct. 30, 1950	June 18, 1993	Mulroney	Que.
Joan Neiman	Sept. 9, 1920	Sept. 1, 1972	Trudeau	Ont.
Donald H. Oliver	Nov. 16, 1938	Sept. 7, 1990	Mulroney	NS
H.A. (Bud) Olson	Oct. 6, 1925	Apr. 5. 1977	Trudeau	Alta
Gerald R. Ottenheimer	June 4, 1934	Dec. 30, 1987	Mulroney	Nfld
Raymond J. Perrault	Feb. 6, 1926	Oct. 5, 1973	Trudeau	BC
William J. Petten	Jan. 28, 1923	Apr. 8, 1968	Pearson	Nfld
Orville H. Philips	Apr. 5, 1924	Feb. 5, 1963	Diefenbaker	PEI
P. Michael Pitfield	June 18, 1937	Dec. 22, 1982	Trudeau	Ont.
Marcel Prud'homme	Nov. 30, 1934	May 26, 1993	Mulroney	Que.
Maurice Riel	Apr. 3, 1992	Oct. 5, 1973	Trudeau	Que.
Jean-Claude Rivest	Jan. 27, 1943	Mar. 11, 1993	Mulroney	Que.
Pietro Rizzuto	Mar. 18, 1934	Dec. 23, 1976	Trudeau	Que.
Fernand Roberge	July 19, 1940	May 26, 1993	Mulroney	Que.
Brenda Mary Robertson	May 23, 1929	Dec. 21, 1984	Mulroney	NB
Louis J. Robichaud	Oct. 21, 1925	Dec. 21, 1973	Trudeau	NB
Eileen Rossiter	July 14, 1929	Nov. 17, 1986	Mulroney	PEI
Gerry St. Germain	Nov. 6, 1937	June 23, 1993	Mulroney	BC
Jean-Maurice Simard	June 21, 1931	June 26, 1985	Mulroney	NB
Herbert O. Sparrow	Jan. 4, 1930	Feb. 9, 1968	Pearson	Sask.
Mira Spivak	July 12, 1934	Nov. 17, 1986	Mulroney	Man.
Richard J. Stanbury	May 2, 1923	Feb. 13, 1968	Pearson	Ont.
John B. Stewart	Nov. 19, 1924	Jan. 13, 1984	Trudeau	NS
Peter A. Stollery	Nov. 29, 1935	July 2, 1981	Trudeau	Ont.
Terrance R. Stratton	Mar. 16, 1938	Mar. 25, 1993	Mulroney	Man.
John Sylvain	June 7, 1924	Sept. 7, 1990	Mulroney	Que.
L. Norbert Thériault	Feb. 16, 1921	Mar. 26, 1979	Trudeau	NB
Andrew E. Thompson	Dec. 14. 1924	Apr. 6, 1967	Pearson	Ont.
David Tkachuk	Feb. 18, 1945	June 8, 1993	Mulroney	Sask.
Walter Patrick Twinn	Mar. 29, 1934	Sept. 27, 1990	Mulroney	Alta
Charlie Watt	June 29, 1944	Jan. 16, 1984	Trudeau	Que.
Dalia Wood	Aug. 21, 1924	Mar. 26, 1979	Trudeau	Que.

(1) Represents region rather than a province

Size of the Senate

*R*egional representation in the senate is as follows: Maritimes – 24 (PEI – 4; NS – 10; NB – 10); Que. – 24; Ont. – 24; West – 24 (Man. – 6; Sask. – 6; Alta – 6; BC – 6) Newfoundland and the territories are separate: Nfld - 6; YT - 1; NWT - 1, for a total of 104 members. In Sept. 1990, then Prime Min. Mulroney used a special provision to add 8 senators (two from each region) to bring the total to 112. To maintain regional representation (and reduce the senate to 104), provincial vacancies in the regions cannot be filled until representation is again 24.

Members of Parliament

(as of September 1993)

Correspondence to Members of Parliament should be addressed individually and may be sent postage free to the following address: (Name of M.P.), House of Commons, Ottawa, Ontario, K1A 0A6.

■ Newfoundland

Riding	Member	Party	Birthdate	First Elected[1]
Bonavista-Trinity-Conception	Fred Mifflin	Lib.	Feb. 6, 1939	1988
Burin-St. George's	Roger Simmons	Lib.	June 3, 1939	1988
Gander-Grand Falls	George S. Baker	Lib.	Sept. 4, 1942	1974
Humber-St. Barbe-Baie Verte	Brian Tobin	Lib.	Oct. 21, 1954	1980
Labrador	Bill Rompkey	Lib.	May 13, 1936	1972
St. John's East	Ross Reid	PC	July 31, 1952	1988
St. John's West	John C. Crosbie	PC	Jan. 30, 1931	1976*

■ Prince Edward Island

Riding	Member	Party	Birthdate	First Elected[1]
Cardigan	Lawrence MacAulay	Lib.	Sept. 9, 1946	1988
Egmont	Joe McGuire	Lib.	June 20, 1944	1988
Hillsborough	George Proud	Lib.	May 9, 1939	1988
Malpeque	vacant			

■ Nova Scotia

Riding	Member	Party	Birthdate	First Elected[1]
Annapolis Valley-Hants	Patrick Nowlan	Ind.	Nov. 10, 1931	1965
Cape Breton Highlands-Canso	Francis G. LeBlanc	Lib.	Dec. 22, 1953	1988
Cape Breton-East Richmond	Dave C. Dingwall	Lib.	June 29, 1952	1980
Cape Breton-The Sydneys	Russell MacLellan	Lib.	Jan. 16, 1940	1979
Central Nova	Elmer M. MacKay	PC	Aug. 5, 1936	1971*
Cumberland-Colchester	Bill Casey	PC	Feb. 19, 1945	1988
Dartmouth	Ron MacDonald	Lib.	June 23, 1953	1988
Halifax	Mary Clancy	Lib.	Jan. 13, 1948	1988
Halifax West	Howard E. Crosby	PC	Nov. 26, 1933	1978*
South Shore	Peter L. McCreath	PC	July 5, 1943	1988
South West Nova	Coline Campbell	Lib.	July 26, 1940	1988

■ New Brunswick

Riding	Member	Party	Birthdate	First Elected[1]
Acadie-Bathurst	Douglas Young	Lib.	Sept. 20, 1940	1988
Beauséjour	Jean Chrétien	Lib.	Jan. 11, 1934	1963
Carleton-Charlotte	Greg Thompson	PC	Mar. 28, 1947	1988
Fredericton-York-Sunbury	J. W. Bud Bird	PC	Mar. 22, 1932	1988
Fundy-Royal	Bob Corbett	PC	Dec. 14, 1938	1978
Madawaska-Victoria	Bernard Valcourt	PC	Feb. 18, 1952	1984
Miramichi	Maurice A. Dionne	Lib.	Aug. 16, 1936	1988
Moncton	George S. Rideout	Lib.	Jan. 2, 1945	1988
Restigouche–Chaleur	Guy H. Arseneault	Lib.	May 11, 1952	1988
Saint John	Gerry Merrithew	PC	Sept. 23, 1931	1984 ▶

▶ ■ **Quebec**

Riding	Member	Party	Birthdate	First Elected[1]
Abitibi	Guy St-Julien	PC	Feb. 19, 1940	1984
Ahuntsic	Nicole Roy-Arcelin	PC	Oct. 12, 1941	1988
Anjou-Rivière-des-Prairies	Jean Corbeil	PC	Jan. 7, 1934	1988
Argenteuil-Papineau	Lise Bourgault	PC	June 5, 1950	1984
Beauce	Gilles Bernier	PC	July 15, 1934	1984
Beauharnois-Salaberry	Jean-Guy Hudon	PC	Apr. 24, 1941	1984
Beauport-Montmorency-Orléans	Charles DeBlois	PC	May 27, 1939	1988
Bellechasse	Pierre Blais	PC	Dec. 30, 1948	1984
Berthier-Montcalm	vacant			
Blainville-Deux-Montagnes	Monique Landry	PC	Dec. 25, 1937	1984
Bonaventure-Îles-de-la-Madeleine	Darryl Gray	PC	Dec. 26, 1946	1984
Bourassa	Marie Gibeau	PC	July 11, 1950	1988
Brome-Missisquoi	Gabrielle Bertrand	PC	May 15, 1923	1984
Chambly	Phil Edmonston	NDP	n.a.	1990*
Champlain	Michel Champagne	PC	May 4, 1956	1984
Charlesbourg	Monique B. Tardif	PC	Jan. 8, 1936	1984
Charlevoix	Brian Mulroney	PC	Mar. 20, 1939	1983*
Châteauguay	Ricardo Lopez	PC	Feb. 13, 1937	1984
Chicoutimi	André Harvey	PC	Sept. 16, 1941	1984
Drummond	Jean-Guy Guilbault	PC	Mar. 14, 1931	1984
Frontenac	Marcel Masse	PC	May 27, 1936	1984
Gaspé	Charles-Eugène Marin	PC	Oct. 29, 1925	1984
Gatineau-La Lièvre	Mark Assad	Lib.	June 14, 1940	1988
Hochelaga-Maisonneuve	Allan Koury	PC	Nov. 22, 1930	1988
Hull-Aylmer	Gilles Rocheleau	Ind.[2]	Aug. 28, 1935	1988
Joliette	Gaby Larrivée	PC	Feb. 4, 1933	1988
Jonquière	Jean-Pierre Blackburn	PC	July 6, 1948	1984
Kamouraska-Rivière-du-Loup	André Plourde	PC	Jan. 12, 1937	1984
La Prairie	Fernand Jourdenais	PC	Mar. 25, 1933	1984
Lac-Saint-Jean	Lucien Bouchard	Ind.[2]	Dec. 22, 1938	1988*
Lachine-Lac-Saint-Louis	Bob Layton	PC	Dec. 25, 1925	1984
LaSalle-Émard	Paul Martin	Lib.	Aug. 28, 1938	1988
Laurentides	Jacques Vien	PC	Mar. 3, 1932	1988
Laurier-Sainte-Marie	Gilles Duceppe	Ind.[2]	n.a.	1990*
Laval Centre	Jacques Tétreault	PC	Apr. 8, 1929	1988
Laval-Est	Vincent Della Noce	PC	Nov. 18, 1943	1984
Laval-Ouest	Guy Ricard	PC	Aug. 2, 1942	1984
Lévis	Gabriel Fontaine	PC	Sept. 17, 1940	1984
Longueuil	Nic Leblanc	Ind.[2]	Nov. 15, 1941	1984
Lotbinière	Maurice Tremblay	PC	Apr. 23, 1944	1984
Louis-Hébert	Suzanne Duplessis	PC	June 30, 1940	1984
Manicouagan	Charles A. Langlois	PC	Mar. 22, 1938	1988
Matapédia-Matane	Jean-Luc Joncas	PC	Dec. 16, 1937	1984
Mégantic-Compton-Stanstead	François Gérin	Ind.	Aug. 3, 1944	1984
Mercier	Carole Jacques	PC	June 12, 1960	1984
Mont-Royal	Sheila Finestone	Lib.	Jan. 28, 1927	1984
Notre-Dame-de-Grâce	Warren Allmand	Lib.	Sept. 19, 1932	1965
Outremont	Jean-Pierre Hogue	PC	Nov. 24, 1927	1988
Papineau-Saint-Michel	André Ouellet	Lib.	Apr. 6, 1939	1967*
Pierrefonds-Dollard	Gerry Weiner	PC	June 26, 1933	1984
Pontiac-Gatineau-Labelle	Barry Moore	PC	Aug. 21, 1944	1984
Portneuf	Marc Ferland	PC	Apr. 15, 1942	1984
Québec	Gilles Loiselle	PC	May 20, 1929	1988
Québec-Est	Marcel R. Tremblay	PC	Mar. 30, 1943	1984
Richelieu	Louis Plamondon	Ind.[2]	July 31, 1943	1984
Richmond-Wolfe	Yvon Côté	PC	Mar. 16, 1939	1988
Rimouski-Témiscouata	Monique Vézina	PC	July 13, 1935	1984
Roberval	vacant			▶

▶ Rosemont .... Benoût Tremblay .... Ind.[2]   Mar. 16, 1948   1988
Saint-Denis .... vacant
Saint-Henri-Westmount. .... David Berger .... Lib.   Mar. 30, 1950   1979
Saint-Hubert .... Pierrette Venne .... Ind.[2]   Aug. 8, 1945   1988
Saint-Hyacinthe-Bagot. .... Andrée Champagne .... PC   July 17, 1939   1984
Saint-Jean .... Clément Couture .... PC   Aug. 2, 1939   1988
Saint-Laurent–Cartierville .... Shirley Maheu .... Lib.   Oct. 7, 1931   1988
Saint-Léonard .... Alfonso Gagliano .... Lib.   Jan. 25, 1942   1984
Saint-Maurice .... Denis Pronovost .... PC   May 3, 1953   1988
Shefford .... vacant
Sherbrooke .... Jean. J. Charest .... PC   June 24, 1958   1984
Témiscamingue. .... Gabriel Desjardins .... PC   Feb. 14, 1949   1984
Terrebonne .... Jean-Marc Robitaille .... PC   Sept. 11, 1955   1988
Trois-Rivières .... Pierre H. Vincent .... PC   Apr. 2, 1955   1984
Vaudreuil .... Pierre H. Cadieux .... PC   Apr. 6, 1948   1984
Verchères. .... Marcel Danis .... PC   Oct. 22, 1943   1984
Verdun-Saint-Paul .... Gilbert Chartrand .... PC   Nov. 3, 1954   1984

■ Ontario

Riding	Member	Party	Birthdate	First Elected[1]
Algoma.	Maurice Foster	Lib.	Sept. 8, 1933	1968
Beaches-Woodbine	Neil Young	NDP	Aug. 28, 1936	1980
Bramalea-Gore-Malton	Harry Chadwick	PC	Nov. 13, 1931	1988
Brampton.	John McDermid	PC	Mar. 17, 1940	1979
Brant.	vacant			
Broadview-Greenwood	Dennis Mills	Lib.	July 19, 1946	1988
Bruce-Grey.	Gus Mitges	PC	n.a.	1972
Burlington	William Kempling	PC	Feb. 5, 1921	1972
Cambridge.	Pat Sobeski	PC	July 25, 1951	1988
Carleton-Gloucester	Eugène Bellemare	Lib.	Apr. 6, 1932	1988
Cochrane-Superior.	Réginald Bélair	Lib.	Apr. 6, 1949	1988
Davenport	Charles Caccia	Lib.	Apr. 28, 1930	1968
Don Valley East.	Alan Redway	PC	Mar. 11, 1935	1984
Don Valley North.	Barbara Greene	PC	Sept. 1, 1945	1988
Don Valley West.	John Bosley	PC	May 4, 1947	1979
Durham	Ross Stevenson	PC	Oct. 1, 1942	1988
Eglinton-Lawrence	Joseph Volpe	Lib.	July 21, 1947	1988
Elgin-Norfolk.	Ken Monteith	PC	June 26, 1938	1988
Erie	Girve Fretz	PC	Mar. 4, 1927	1979
Essex-Kent.	Jerry Pickard	Lib.	Nov. 14, 1940	1988
Essex-Windsor.	Steven Langdon	NDP	July 15, 1946	1984
Etobicoke Centre.	Michael Wilson	PC	Nov. 4, 1937	1979
Etobicoke North	Roy MacLaren	Lib.	Nov. 26, 1934	1988
Etobicoke-Lakeshore	Patrick Boyer	PC	Mar. 4, 1945	1984
Glengarry-Prescott-Russell.	Don Boudria	Lib.	Aug. 30, 1949	1984
Guelph-Wellington	Bill Winegard	PC	Sept. 17, 1924	1984
Haldimand-Norfolk.	Bob Speller	Lib.	Feb. 29, 1956	1988
Halton-Peel	Garth Turner	PC	Mar. 14, 1949	1988
Hamilton East	Sheila Copps	Lib.	Nov. 27, 1952	1984
Hamilton Mountain.	Beth Phinney	Lib.	June 19, 1938	1988
Hamilton West	Stan Keyes	Lib.	May 5, 1953	1988
Hamilton-Wentworth	Geoff Scott	PC	Mar. 2, 1938	1978*
Hastings-Frontenac-Lennox & Addington .	Bill Vankoughnet	PC	Jan. 7, 1933	1979
Huron-Bruce.	Murray Cardiff	PC	June 10, 1934	1980
Kenora-Rainy River	Robert D. Nault	Lib.	Nov. 9, 1955	1988
Kent.	Rex Crawford	Lib.	Feb. 25, 1932	1988
Kingston & the Islands	Peter Milliken	Lib.	Nov. 12, 1946	1988
Kitchener	John Reimer	PC	July 16, 1936	1979
Lambton-Middlesex.	Ralph Ferguson	Lib.	Sept. 13, 1929	1988 ▶

▶ Lanark-Carleton	Paul Dick	PC	Oct. 27, 1940	1972
Leeds-Grenville	Jim Jordan	Lib.	Sept. 2, 1928	1988
Lincoln	Shirley Martin	PC	Nov. 20, 1932	1984
London East	Joe Fontana	Lib.	Jan. 13, 1950	1988
London-Middlesex	Terry Clifford	PC	Nov. 12, 1938	1984
London West	Tom Hockin	PC	Mar. 5, 1938	1984
Markham-Whitechurch-Stouffville	Bill Attewell	PC	Jan. 21, 1932	1984
Mississauga East	Albina Guarnieri	Lib.	June 23, 1953	1988
Mississauga South	Don Blenkarn	PC	June 17, 1930	1972
Mississauga-West	Bob Horner	PC	July 3, 1932	1984
Nepean	Beryl Gaffney	Lib.	Apr. 1, 1930	1988
Niagara Falls	Rob Nicholson	PC	Apr. 29, 1952	1984
Nickel Belt	John R. Rodriguez	NDP	Feb. 12, 1937	1972
Nipissing	Bob Wood	Lib.	May 11, 1940	1988
Northumberland	Christine Stewart	Lib.	Jan. 3, 1941	1988
Oakville-Milton	Otto Jelinek	PC	May 20, 1940	1972
Ontario	René Soetens	PC	Sept. 7, 1948	1988
Oshawa	Mike Breaugh	NDP	Sept. 13, 1942	1990*
Ottawa Centre	Mac Harb	Lib.	Nov. 11, 1953	1988
Ottawa South	John Manley	Lib.	Jan. 5, 1950	1988
Ottawa West	Marlene Catterall	Lib.	Mar. 1, 1940	1988
Ottawa-Vanier	Jean-Robert Gauthier	Lib.	Oct. 22, 1929	1972
Oxford	Bruce Halliday	PC	June 18, 1926	1974
Parkdale-High Park	Jesse Flis	Lib.	Nov. 15, 1933	1988
Parry Sound-Muskoka	Stan Darling	PC	July 16, 1911	1972
Perth-Wellington-Waterloo	Harry Brightwell	PC	Aug. 4, 1932	1984
Peterborough	Bill Domm	PC	July 24, 1930	1979
Prince Edward-Hastings	Lyle Vanclief	Lib.	Sept. 19, 1943	1988
Renfrew-Nipissing-Pembroke	Len Hopkins	Lib.	June 12, 1930	1965
Rosedale	David MacDonald	PC	Aug. 30, 1936	1965
Sarnia-Lambton	Ken James	PC	Aug. 5, 1934	1984
Sault Ste. Marie	Steve Butland	NDP	Mar. 26, 1941	1988
Scarborough Centre	Pauline A. Browes	PC	May 1, 1938	1984
Scarborough East	Bob Hicks	PC	June 4, 1933	1984
Scarborough West	Tom Wappel	Lib.	Feb. 9, 1950	1988
Scarborough-Agincourt	Jim Karygiannis	Lib.	May 2, 1955	1988
Scarborough-Rouge River	Derek Lee	Lib.	Oct. 2, 1948	1988
Simcoe Centre	Edna Anderson	PC	Nov. 9, 1922	1988
Simcoe North	Doug Lewis	PC	Apr. 17, 1938	1979
St. Catharines	Ken Atkinson	PC	Mar. 2, 1947	1988
St. Paul's	Barbara McDougall	PC	Nov. 12, 1937	1984
Stormont-Dundas	Bob Kilger	Lib.	June 29, 1944	1988
Sudbury	Diane Marleau	Lib.	June 21, 1943	1988
Thunder Bay-Atikokan	Iain Angus	NDP	June 1, 1947	1984
Thunder Bay-Nipigon	Joe Comuzzi	Lib.	May 5, 1933	1988
Timiskaming-French River	John A. MacDougall	PC	Apr. 21, 1947	1982*
Timmins-Chapleau	Cid Samson	NDP	Jan. 26, 1943	1988
Trinity-Spadina	Dan Heap	NDP	Sept. 24, 1925	1981*
Victoria-Haliburton	Bill Scott	PC	Oct. 6, 1921	1965
Waterloo	Walter McLean	PC	Apr. 26, 1936	1979
Welland-St. Catharines-Thorold	Gilbert Parent	Lib.	July 25, 1935	1988
Wellington-Grey-Dufferin-Simcoe	Perrin Beatty	PC	June 1, 1950	1972
Willowdale	Jim Peterson	Lib.	July 30, 1941	1988
Windsor West	Herb Gray	Lib.	May 25, 1931	1962
Windsor-St. Clair	Howard McCurdy	NDP	Dec. 10, 1932	1984
York Centre	Bob Kaplan	Lib.	Dec. 27, 1936	1968
York North	Maurizio Bevilacqua	Lib.	June 1, 1960	1988
York South-Weston	John Nunziata	Lib.	Jan. 4, 1955	1984
York-Simcoe	John E. Cole	PC	Aug. 4, 1942	1988
York West	Sergio Marchi	Lib.	May 12, 1956	1984 ▶

▶ ■ **Manitoba**

Riding	Member	Party	Birthdate	First Elected[1]
Brandon-Souris	Lee Clark	PC	Dec. 16, 1936	1983*
Churchill	Rod Murphy	NDP	Oct. 16, 1946	1979
Dauphin-Swan River	Brian White	PC	Jan. 17, 1951	1984
Lisgar-Marquette	Charlie Mayer	PC	Apr. 21, 1936	1979
Portage-Interlake	Felix Holtmann	PC	Dec. 5, 1944	1984
Provencher	Jake Epp	PC	Sept. 1, 1939	1972
Selkirk-Red River	David Bjornson	PC	July 7, 1947	1988
St. Boniface	Ronald J. Duhamel	Lib.	n.a.	1988
Winnipeg North Centre	David Walker	Lib.	Aug. 1, 1947	1988
Winnipeg North	Rey Pagtakhan	Lib.	Jan. 7, 1935	1988
Winnipeg South	Dorothy Dobbie	PC	Jan. 5, 1945	1988
Winnipeg St. James	John Harvard	Lib.	June 4, 1938	1988
Winnipeg-South Centre	Lloyd Axworthy	Lib.	Dec. 21, 1939	1979
Winnipeg-Transcona	Bill Blaikie	NDP	June 19, 1951	1979

■ **Saskatchewan**

Riding	Member	Party	Birthdate	First Elected[1]
Kindersley-Lloydminster	Bill McKnight	PC	July 20, 1940	1979
Mackenzie	Vic Althouse	NDP	Apr. 15, 1937	1980
Moose Jaw-Lake Centre	Rod Laporte	NDP	Oct. 24, 1953	1988
Prince Albert-Churchill River	Ray Funk	NDP	Feb. 13, 1948	1988
Regina-Lumsden	Les Benjamin	NDP	Apr. 29, 1925	1968
Regina-Qu'Appelle	Simon de Jong	NDP	Apr. 9, 1942	1979
Regina-Wascana	Larry Schneider	PC	Mar. 23, 1938	1988
Saskatoon-Clark's Crossing	Chris Axworthy	NDP	Mar. 10, 1947	1988
Saskatoon-Dundurn	Ron Fisher	NDP	July 22, 1934	1988
Saskatoon-Humboldt	Stan Hovdebo	NDP	Aug. 20, 1925	1979*
Souris-Moose Mountain	vacant			
Swift Current-Maple Creek-Assiniboia	Geoff Wilson	PC	Sept. 24, 1941	1979
The Battlefords-Meadow Lake	Len Taylor	NDP	Jan. 16, 1952	1988
Yorkton-Melville	Lorne Nystrom	NDP	Apr. 26, 1946	1968

■ **Alberta**

Riding	Member	Party	Birthdate	First Elected[1]
Athabasca	Jack Shields	PC	Dec. 25, 1929	1980
Beaver River	Deborah Grey	Ref.	July 1, 1952	1989*
Calgary Centre	Harvie Andre	PC	July 27, 1940	1972
Calgary North	Al Johnson	PC	Apr. 13, 1939	1988
Calgary Northeast	Alex Kindy	Ind.	Jan. 8, 1930	1984
Calgary Southeast	Lee Richardson	PC	Oct. 31, 1947	1988
Calgary Southwest	Barbara Sparrow	PC	July 11, 1935	1984
Calgary West	Jim Hawkes	PC	June 21, 1934	1979
Crowfoot	Arnold Malone	PC	Dec. 9, 1937	1974
Edmonton East	Ross Harvey	NDP	Apr. 25, 1952	1988
Edmonton North	Steve Paproski	PC	Sept. 23, 1928	1968
Edmonton Northwest	Murray W. Dorin	PC	May 21, 1954	1984
Edmonton Southwest	James Edwards	PC	Aug. 31, 1936	1984
Edmonton-Southeast	David Kilgour	Lib.	Feb. 18, 1941	1979
Edmonton-Strathcona	Scott Thorkelson	PC	Mar. 2, 1958	1988
Elk Island	Brian O'Kurley	PC	Mar. 7, 1953	1988
Lethbridge	Blaine Thacker	PC	Jan. 11, 1941	1979
Macleod	Ken G. Hughes	PC	Feb. 11, 1954	1988
Medicine Hat	Robert Porter	PC	Aug. 14, 1933	1984
Peace River	Albert Cooper	PC	June 19, 1952	1980 ▶

▶ Red Deer	Doug Fee	PC	July 21, 1944	1988
St. Albert	Walter Van De Walle	PC	July 20, 1922	1986*
Vegreville	Don Mazankowski	PC	July 27, 1935	1968
Wetaskiwin	Willie Littlechild	PC	Apr. 1, 1944	1988
Wild Rose	Louise Feltham	PC	Mar. 22, 1935	1988
Yellowhead	Joe Clark	PC	June 5, 1939	1972

■ British Columbia

Riding	Member	Party	Birthdate	First Elected[1]
Burnaby-Kingsway	Svend J. Robinson	NDP	Mar. 4, 1952	1979
Capilano-Howe Sound	Mary Collins	PC	Sept. 26, 1940	1984
Cariboo-Chilcotin	Dave Worthy	PC	Sept. 15, 1934	1988
Comox-Alberni	Robert E. Skelly	NDP	Apr. 14, 1943	1988
Delta	Stan Wilbee	PC	May 12, 1932	1988
Esquimalt-Juan de Fuca	David Barrett	NDP	Oct. 2, 1930	1988
Fraser Valley East	Ross Belsher	PC	Jan. 19, 1933	1984
Fraser Valley West	Robert L. Wenman	PC	June 19, 1940	1974
Kamloops	Nelson Riis	NDP	Jan. 10, 1942	1980
Kootenay East	Sid Parker	NDP	Sept. 15, 1930	1988
Kootenay West-Revelstoke	Lyle Kristiansen	NDP	May 9, 1939	1988
Mission-Coquitlam	Joy Langan	NDP	Jan. 23, 1943	1988
Nanaimo-Cowichan	David D. Stupich	NDP	Dec. 5, 1921	1988
New Westminster-Burnaby	Dawn Black	NDP	Apr. 1, 1943	1988
North Island-Powell River	Raymond Skelly	NDP	July 1, 1941	1979
North Vancouver	vacant			
Okanagan Centre	Al Horning	PC	June 11, 1939	1988
Okanagan-Shuswap	Lyle MacWilliam	NDP	July 31, 1949	1988
Okanagan-Similkameen-Merritt	Jack Whittaker	NDP	Nov. 13, 1944	1988
Port Moody-Coquitlam	Ian Waddell	NDP	Nov. 21, 1942	1979
Prince George-Bulkley Valley	Brian L. Gardiner	NDP	Aug. 18, 1955	1988
Prince George-Peace River	Frank Oberle	PC	Mar. 24, 1932	1972
Richmond	Tom Siddon	PC	Nov. 9, 1941	1978*
Saanich-Gulf Islands	Lynn Hunter	NDP	Jan. 20, 1947	1988
Skeena	Jim Fulton	NDP	Jan. 22, 1950	1979
Surrey North	Jim Karpoff	NDP	Oct. 14, 1937	1988
Surrey-White Rock-South Langley	Benno W. Friesen	PC	June 27, 1929	1974
Vancouver Centre	Kim Campbell	PC	Mar. 10, 1947	1988
Vancouver East	Margaret Anne Mitchell	NDP	July 17, 1925	1979
Vancouver Quadra	John N. Turner	Lib.	June 7, 1929	1962
Vancouver South	John A. Fraser	PC	Dec. 15, 1931	1972
Victoria	John F. Brewin	NDP	Sept. 14, 1936	1988

■ Yukon Territory

Riding	Member	Party	Birthdate	First Elected[1]
Yukon	Audrey McLaughlin	NDP	Nov. 7, 1936	1987*

■ Northwest Territories

Riding	Member	Party	Birthdate	First Elected[1]
Nunatsiaq	Jack I. Anawak	Lib.	Sept. 26, 1950	1988
Western Arctic	Ethel Blondin-Andrew	Lib.	Mar. 25, 1951	1988

(1) General election unless * indicating by-election. (2) Member of Bloc Québécois. (n.a.) not available. PC—Progressive Conservative; Lib.—Liberal; NDP—New Democratic Party; Ref.—Reform Party; Ind.—Independent; Ind. Cons.—Independent Conservative.

Salaries of Federal Political Figures

(as of June 30, 1993)

The **GOVERNOR GENERAL** receives $97 000 per year.

SENATORS.................... $64 800 plus $10 100 tax-free expense allowance and 64 travel points[2] per year.

The following senators receive as *extra* salary on top of their Senate salaries:

Leader of the Government .... $46 900 plus $2 000 car allowance.
Leader of the Opposition $23 900
Speaker of the Senate .... $31 100 plus $3 000 residence allowance and $1 000 car allowance.
Deputy Leader of the Government $14 900
Deputy Leader of the Opposition... $9 400
Government Whip $7 500
Opposition Whip.. $4 800

MEMBERS OF PARLIAMENT—$64 400 plus $21 300 tax-free expense allowance[1], and 64 travel points[2] per year.[3]

The following members of Parliament receive as *extra* salary on top of their MP salaries:

Prime Minister $69 920
Cabinet Ministers... $46 645
Speaker of the House $49 100
Deputy Speaker $25 700
Official Opposition Leader... $49 100
Other Party Leaders.. $29 500
Opposition House Leader.. $23 800
Other House Leaders.. $10 100
Government and Opposition Whips $13 200
Other Party Whips $7 500
Government and Opposition Deputy Whips $7 500
Deputy Chairman, Committees of the Whole House $10 500
Assistant Deputy Chairman, Committees of the Whole House $10 500
Parliamentary Secretaries... $10 500

(1) 24 MPs representing remote or distant ridings receive $26 200 tax-free expense allowance; 2 MPs representing NWT ridings receive $28 200 tax-free allowance. (2) One travel point represents a first-class return air trip anywhere in Canada and can be used by representatives or their spouses or a designated family member. (3) Members who travel in Canada on official business and are at least 100 km from their principal residences may claim $6 000 in food, accomodation, and incidental expenses.

■ **OFFICE BUDGET**

Each of the 295 elected Members has an office in both Ottawa and their riding, with staff to assist constituents with problems they may encounter when dealing with federal government departments and agencies. Each member's office budget covers staff salaries in Ottawa and constituency offices, as well as individuals or firms hired under contract. The budget is also intended to cover the costs of renting, equipping and maintaining constituency offices, as well as covering the costs of travel within the constituency and within the members' province.

A Member's office budget is set at $171,700; $174,700 or $177,600 according to the size of the constituency and its number of urban and/or rural polling divisions.

Geographic and Electoral Supplement: Members receive supplements to the main office budget if they represent large constituencies with over 70,000 voters (e.g. the riding of York North) and/or geographic boundaries over 8,000 sq. km (e.g. the riding of Nunatsiaq). These annual budgetary supplements cover the additional staff, operating and travel expenses required to serve the riding. Based on constituency characteristics, these supplements range from $5,380 to $21, 480 and may change after each general election as the riding demographics change. A Member may have more than one constituency office should he or she so desire, and many do.

Furniture and equipment allowance: Re-elected Members receive an allowance of up to $3,000 (per Parliament) to assist in purchasing office furniture and equipment for the constituency office. Newly-elected Members are entitled to up to $5,000 for their first Parliament for this purpose.

Other Services: To help meet the needs and requests of their constituents, Members are also given access to printing, translation, mail and other support services that help them respond to the thousands of letters and requests they receive. (Canadians may write to Members of Parliament free of charge from anywhere in Canada.) The services also allow Members to keep the public up-to-date on the events in Ottawa through a parliamentary report generally known as a "householder." Finally, Members are provided with desks, computers, typewriters, photocopiers and other office supplies and equipment required to run an efficient office in Ottawa.

■ PARLIAMENTARY PENSION PLAN

Members' pensions are provided for by law under the "Members of Parliament Retiring Allowances Act" and, like many pension plans, Members must make a financial contribution. Specifically, Members must contribute 11% of their annual Sessional Allowance (salary) of $64,400. For Members who are receiving additional salaries for extra duties such as Ministers, Whips or Parliamentary Secretaries, they have the option to contribute up to 11% of these salaries as well. The Act also provides that, upon ceasing to be a Member of the House of Commons, a former Member is immediately entitled to an annual pension after a minimum of six years of service. This pension is payable at the rate of 5% per year of service (i.e. a minimum of 30%: 6 x 5%) up to a maximum of 75% (15 years of service) of the average of the best consecutive six years of earnings. Members who serve less than six years must withdraw their contributions.

Indexing of a former Member of the House of Commons' pension begins only when he or she reaches the age of 60, except for extraordinary situations such as disability. Survivors' benefits are payable to spouses and dependent children. If a former Member in receipt of a pension is re-elected to the House of Commons or becomes a Senator, the pension allowance is suspended for the period in office.

Source: *Public Information Office, House of Commons*

Per Capita Legislative Costs

The following table apportions the costs of the various legislatures according to the population count in the 1991 census.

Jurisdiction	Legislative Budget 1991/92	Population (1991)	Cost of Each Legislature	Per Capita Total Per Capita Cost[1]
Canada: House of Commons........	$229 350 000	27 023 100	$ 8.49	$ 8.49
Canada: Senate......................	43 489 300	27 023 100	1.61	1.61
Newfoundland.........................	6 752 700	571 700	11.81	21.91
Prince Edward Island.................	2 542 100	129 900	19.57	29.67
Nova Scotia...........................	7 648 600	897 500	8.52	18.62
New Brunswick.......................	6 602 000	725 600	9.10	19.20
Quebec...............................	76 000 000	6 811 800	11.16	21.26
Ontario...............................	129 131 700	9 840 300	13.12	23.22
Manitoba.............................	9 749 800	1 092 600	8.92	19.02
Saskatchewan........................	14 435 700	995 300	14.50	24.60
Alberta...............................	23 346 717	2 501 400	9.33	19.43
British Columbia	24 711 000	3 185 900	7.76	17.86
Yukon Territory	2 196 000	26 500	81.33	91.43
Northwest Territories	9 209 000	54 000	170.54	180.64

Source: *Canadian Legislatures 1992, Robert J. Fleming*

(1) Includes the per capita costs of the Senate, House of Commons and the respective legislature.

Lieutenant-Governors of the Provinces

(as of June 1992)

Each of Canada's 10 provinces has a lieutenant-governor appointed by the Governor General on advice of the prime minister. The lieutenant-governor is the monarch's representative in the province and performs the same duties at the provincial level that the governor general performs at the federal level; the lieutenant-governor opens, prorogues and dissolves the provincial legislative assembly and gives royal assent to provincial legislation and provincial orders in council.

Lieutenant-governors are paid by the federal government and are usually appointed for a term of five years.

Province	Lieutenant-Governor	Birthdate	Date Sworn in
Newfoundland	Hon. Frederick W. Russell	Sept. 10, 1923	Nov. 5, 1991
Prince Edward Island	Hon. Marion Reid	Jan. 4, 1929	Aug. 16, 1990
Nova Scotia	Hon. Lloyd R. Crouse	Nov. 19, 1918	Feb. 20, 1989
New Brunswick	Hon. Gilbert Finn	Sept. 3, 1920	Aug. 13, 1987
Quebec	Hon. Martial Asselin	Feb. 3, 1924	Aug. 9, 1990
Ontario	Hon. Henry N.R. Jackman	June 10, 1932	Dec. 11, 1991
Manitoba	Hon. W. Yvon Dumont	Jan. 21, 1951	Mar. 5, 1993
Saskatchewan	Hon. Sylvia O. Fedoruk	May 5, 1927	Sept. 7, 1988
Alberta	Hon. Gordon Towers	July 5, 1919	Mar. 11, 1991
British Columbia	Hon. David C. Lam	Sept. 2, 1923	Sept. 9, 1988

n.a. not available

Provincial Premiers: An Historical Listing

(as of Sept. 1992)

■ Newfoundland

Premier	Term	Party	Elected or sworn in
Joseph R. Smallwood	1949–1972	Liberal	Apr. 1, 1949
Frank D. Moores	1972–1979	Conservative	Jan. 18, 1972
A. Brian Peckford	1979–1989	Conservative	Mar. 26, 1979
Tom Rideout	1989	Conservative	Mar. 22, 1989
Clyde Wells	1989—	Liberal	May 5, 1989

■ Prince Edward Island

Premier	Term	Party	Elected or sworn in
C. Pope	1873	Conservative	Apr., 1873
L. C. Owen	1873–76	Conservative	Sept., 1873
L. H. Davies	1876–79	Liberal (Coalition)	Aug.,1876
W. W. Sullivan	1879–89	Conservative	Apr. 25, 1879
N. McLeod	1889–91	Conservative	Nov., 1889
F. Peters	1891–97	Liberal	Apr. 27, 1891
A. B. Warburton	1897–98	Liberal	Oct., 1897
D. Farquharson	1898–1901	Liberal	Aug., 1898
A. Peters	1901–08	Liberal	Dec. 29, 1901
F. L. Haszard	1908–11	Liberal	Feb. 1, 1908
H. James Palmer	1911	Liberal	May 16, 1911
John A. Mathieson	1911–17	Conservative	Dec. 2, 1911
Aubin Arsenault	1917–19	Conservative	June, 21, 1917
J. H. Bell	1919–23	Liberal	Sept. 9, 1919
James D. Stewart	1923–27	Conservative	Sept. 5, 1923
Albert C. Saunders	1927–30	Liberal	Aug. 12, 1927
Walter M. Lea	1930–31	Liberal	May 20, 1930
James D. Stewart	1931–33	Conservative	Aug. 29, 1931
William J. P. MacMillan	1933–35	Conservative	Oct. 14, 1933

Walter M. Lea	1935–36	Liberal	Aug. 15, 1935
Thane A. Campbell	1936–43	Liberal	Jan. 14, 1936
J. Walter Jones	1943–53	Liberal	May 11, 1943
Alexander W. Matheson	1953–59	Liberal	May 25, 1953
Walter Shaw	1959–66	Prog. Conservative	Sept. 16, 1959
Alexander B. Campbell	1966–78	Liberal	July 28, 1966
William Bennett Campbell	1978–79	Liberal	Sept. 18, 1978
J. Angus MacLean	1979–81	Prog. Conservative	May 3, 1979
James M. Lee	1981–86	Prog. Conservative	Nov. 17, 1981
Joseph A. Ghiz	1986–93	Liberal	May 2, 1986
Catherine Callbeck	1993—	Liberal	Jan. 25, 1993

■ Nova Scotia

Premier	Term	Party	Elected or sworn in
H. Blanchard	1867	Conservative	July 4, 1867
William Annand	1867–75	Liberal	Nov. 7, 1867
P. C. Hill	1875–78	Liberal	May 11, 1875
S. H. Holmes	1878–82	Conservative	Oct. 22, 1878
John S. D. Thompson	1882	Conservative	May 25, 1882
W. T. Pipes	1882–84	Liberal	Aug. 3, 1882
W. S. Fielding	1884–96	Liberal	July 28, 1884
George H. Murray	1896–1923	Liberal	July 20, 1896
E. H. Armstrong	1923–25	Liberal	Jan. 24, 1923
E. N. Rhodes	1925–30	Conservative	July 16, 1925
Col. Gordon S. Harrington	1930–33	Conservative	Aug. 11, 1930
Angus L. Macdonald	1933–40	Liberal	Sept. 5, 1933
A. S. MacMillan	1940–45	Liberal	July 10, 1940
Angus L. Macdonald	1945–54	Liberal	Sept. 8, 1945
Harold Connolly	1954	Liberal	Apr. 13, 1954
Henry D. Hicks	1954–56	Liberal	Sept. 30, 1954
Robert L. Stanfield	1956–67	Prog. Conservative	Nov. 20, 1956
George Smith	1967–70	Prog. Conservative	Sept. 13, 1967
Gerald A. Regan	1970–78	Liberal	Oct. 28, 1970
John Buchanan	1978–90	Prog. Conservative	Oct. 5, 1978
Roger Bacon	1990–91	Prog. Conservative	Sept. 12, 1990
Donald Cameron	1991–93	Prog. Conservative	Feb. 9, 1991
John Savage	1993—	Liberal	June 11, 1993

■ New Brunswick

Premier	Term	Party	Elected or sworn in
Andrew Wetmore	1867–70	Confederation Party	1867
G.E. King	1870–71	Conservative	1870
George Hatheway	1871–72	Conservative	1871
G.E. King	1872–78	Conservative	1872
James Fraser	1878–82	Conservative	1878
D. L. Hanington	1882–83	Conservative	1882
Andrew Blair	1883–96	Liberal	1883
James Mitchell	1896–97	Liberal	July, 1896
Henry Emmerson	1897–1900	Liberal	Oct. 29, 1897
L. J. Tweedie	1900–07	Liberal	Aug. 31, 1900
William Pugsley	1907	Liberal	Mar. 6, 1907
Clifford Robinson	1907–08	Liberal	May 31, 1907
John Douglas Hazen	1908–11	Conservative	Mar. 24, 1908
James K. Flemming	1911–14	Conservative	Oct. 16, 1911
George J. Clark	1914–17	Conservative	Dec. 17, 1914
James Murray	1917	Conservative	Feb. 1, 1917
Walter E. Foster	1917–23	Liberal	Apr. 4, 1917
Peter Veniot	1923–25	Liberal	Feb. 28, 1923
John B. M. Baxter	1925–31	Conservative	Sept. 14, 1925
Charles D. Richards	1931–33	Conservative	May 19, 1931
Leonard Tilley	1933–35	Conservative	June 1, 1933
Allison Dysart	1935–40	Liberal	July 16, 1935

John McNair	1940–52	Liberal	Mar. 13, 1940
Hugh J. Flemming	1952–60	Prog. Conservative	Oct. 8, 1952
Louis J. Robichaud	1960–70	Liberal	July 12, 1960
Richard Hatfield	1970–87	Prog. Conservative	Nov. 12, 1970
Frank McKenna	1987—	Liberal	Oct. 27, 1987

■ Quebec

Premier	Term	Party	Sworn in
Pierre-Joseph-Olivier Chauveau	1867–73	Conservative	July 15, 1867
Gédéon Ouimet	1873–74	Conservative	Feb. 26, 1873
Charles E. Boucher deBoucherville	1874–78	Conservative	Sept. 22, 1874
Henri Joly	1878–79	Liberal	Mar. 8, 1878
J. Adolphe Chapleau	1879–82	Conservative	Oct. 31, 1879
J. Alfred Mousseau	1882–84	Conservative	July 31, 1882
John J. Ross	1884–87	Conservative	Jan. 23, 1884
L. Olivier Taillon	1887	Conservative	Jan. 25, 1887
Honoré Mercier	1887–91	Liberal	Jan. 27, 1887
Charles E. Boucher deBoucherville	1891–92	Conservative	Dec. 21, 1891
L. Olivier Taillon	1892–96	Conservative	Dec. 16, 1892
Edmund J. Flynn	1896–97	Conservative	May 11, 1896
F. Gabriel Marchand	1897–1900	Liberal	May 24, 1897
S. Napoléon Parent	1900–05	Liberal	Oct. 3, 1900
Lomer Gouin	1905–20	Liberal	Mar. 23, 1905
L. Alexandre Taschereau	1920–36	Liberal	July 9, 1920
Adélard Godbout	1936	Liberal	June 11, 1936
Maurice Duplessis	1936–39	Union Nationale	Aug. 26, 1936
Adélard Godbout	1939–44	Liberal	Nov. 8, 1939
Maurice Duplessis	1944–59	Union Nationale	Aug. 30, 1944
Paul Sauvé	1959–60	Union Nationale	Sept. 11, 1959
Antonio Barrette	1960	Union Nationale	Jan. 8, 1960
Jean Lesage	1960–66	Liberal	July 5, 1960
Daniel Johnson	1966–68	Union Nationale	June 16, 1966
Jean-Jacques Bertrand	1968–70	Union Nationale	Oct. 2, 1968
Robert Bourassa	1970–76	Liberal	May 12, 1970
René Lévesque	1976–85	Parti Québécois	Nov. 25, 1976
Pierre-Marc Johnson	1985	Parti Québécois	Oct. 3, 1985
Robert Bourassa	1985—	Liberal	Dec. 12, 1985

■ Ontario

Premier	Term	Party	Elected or sworn in
J.S. Macdonald	1867–71	Coalition	July 16, 1867
Edward Blake	1871–72	Liberal	Dec. 20, 1871
Oliver Mowat	1872–96	Liberal	Oct. 25, 1872
Arthur S. Hardy	1896–99	Liberal	July 25, 1896
George William Ross	1899–1905	Liberal	Oct. 21, 1899
Sir James P. Whitney	1905–14	Conservative	Feb. 8, 1905
Sir William Hearst	1914–19	Conservative	Oct. 2, 1914
Ernest C. Drury	1919–23	United Farmers of Ontario	Nov. 14, 1919
George Howard Ferguson	1923–30	Conservative	July 16, 1923
George Stewart Henry	1930–34	Conservative	Dec. 15, 1930
Mitchell F. Hepburn	1934–42	Liberal	July 10, 1934
George Daniel Conant	1942–43	Liberal	Oct. 21, 1942
Harry C. Nixon	1943	Liberal	May 18, 1943
George Drew	1943–48	Prog. Conservative	Aug. 17, 1943
Thomas L. Kennedy	1948–49	Prog. Conservative	Oct. 19, 1948
Leslie M. Frost	1949–61	Prog. Conservative	May 4, 1949
John P. Robarts	1961–71	Prog. Conservative	Nov. 8, 1961
William G. Davis	1971–85	Prog. Conservative	Mar. 1, 1971
Frank Miller	1985	Prog. Conservative	Feb. 8, 1985
David Peterson	1985–90	Liberal	June 26, 1985
Bob Rae	1990—	New Democratic	Oct. 1, 1990

■ Manitoba

Premier	Term	Party	Elected or sworn in
A. Boyd	1870–71	n.a.	Sept. 16, 1870
M. A. Girard	1871–72	Conservative	Dec. 14, 1871
H. H. Clarke	1872–74	n.a.	Mar. 14, 1872
M. A. Girard	1874	Conservative	July 8, 1874
R. A. Davis	1874–78	n.a.	Dec. 3, 1874
John Norquay	1878–87	Conservative	Oct. 16, 1878
D. H. Harrison	1887–88	Conservative	Dec. 26, 1887
T. Greenway	1888–1900	Liberal	Jan. 19, 1888
H. J. Macdonald	1900	Conservative	Jan. 8, 1900
Sir R. P. Roblin	1900–15	Conservative	Oct. 29, 1900
T. C. Norris	1915–22	Liberal	May 12, 1915
John Bracken	1922–43	Coalition[1]	Aug. 8, 1922
S. S. Garson	1943–48	Coalition	Jan. 8, 1943
D. L. Campbell	1948–58	Conservative	Nov. 11, 1948
Duff Roblin	1958–67	Prog. Conservative	June 16, 1958
Walter Weir	1967–69	Prog. Conservative	Nov. 25, 1967
Edward Schreyer	1969–77	New Democratic	July 15, 1969
Sterling Lyon	1977–81	Prog. Conservative	Nov. 24, 1977
Howard Pawley	1981–88	New Democratic	Nov. 30, 1981
Gary Filmon	1988—	Prog. Conservative	Apr. 26, 1988

■ Saskatchewan

Premier	Term	Party	Elected or sworn in
Walter Scott	1905–16	Liberal	Sept. 5, 1905
W. M. Martin	1916–22	Liberal	Oct. 20, 1916
C. A. Dunning	1922–26	Liberal	Apr. 5, 1922
J. G. Gardiner	1926–29	Liberal	Feb. 26, 1926
J. T. M. Anderson	1929–34	Conservative	Sept. 9, 1929
J. G. Gardiner	1934–35	Liberal	July 19, 1934
W. J. Patterson	1935–44	Liberal	Nov. 1, 1935
Tommy Douglas	1944–61	C.C.F.[2]	July 10, 1944
W. S. Lloyd	1961–64	C.C.F.—N.D.P.	Nov. 7, 1961
W. Ross Thatcher	1964–71	Liberal	May 22, 1964
Allan E. Blakeney	1971–82	New Democratic	June 30, 1971
Grant Devine	1982–91	Prog. Conservative	May 8, 1982
Roy Romanow	1991—	New Democratic	Nov. 1, 1991

■ Alberta

Premier	Term	Party	Elected or sworn in
Alex Rutherford	1905–10	Liberal	Sept. 2, 1905
A. L. Sifton	1910–17	Liberal	May 26, 1910
Charles Stewart	1917–21	Liberal	Oct. 30, 1917
Herbert Greenfield	1921–25	United Farmers of Alberta	Aug. 13, 1921
John E. Brownlee	1925–34	United Farmers of Alberta	Nov. 23, 1925
Richard G. Reid	1934–35	United Farmers of Alberta	July 10, 1934
William Aberhart	1935–43	Social Credit	Sept. 3, 1935
E. C. Manning	1943–68	Social Credit	May 31, 1943
Harry Strom	1968–71	Social Credit	Dec. 12, 1968
Peter Lougheed	1971–85	Prog. Conservative	Sept. 10, 1971
Don Getty	1985–92	Prog. Conservative	Nov. 1, 1985
Ralph P. Klein	1992—	Prog. Conservative	Dec. 14, 1992

■ British Columbia

Premier	Term	Party	Elected or sworn in
J. F. McCreight	1871–72	n.a.	Nov. 13, 1871
Amor De Cosmos	1872–74	n.a.	Dec. 23, 1872
G. A. Walkem	1874–76	n.a.	Feb. 11, 1874
A. C. Elliott	1876–78	n.a.	Feb. 1, 1876
G. A. Walkem	1878–82	n.a.	June 25, 1878
Robert Beaven	1882–83	n.a.	June 13, 1882
William Smithe	1883–87	n.a.	Jan. 29, 1883
A. E. B. Davie	1887–89	n.a.	May 1, 1887
John Robson	1889–92	n.a.	Aug. 2, 1889
Theodore Davie	1892–95	n.a.	July 2, 1892
J. H. Turner	1895–98	n.a.	Mar. 4, 1895
C. A. Semlin	1898–1900	n.a.	Aug. 15, 1898
Joseph Martin	1900	n.a.	Feb. 28, 1900
James Dunsmuir	1900–02	n.a.	June 15, 1900
E. G. Prior	1902–03	n.a.	Nov. 21, 1902
Richard McBride	1903–15	Conservative	June 1, 1903
William J. Bowser	1915–16	Conservative	Dec. 15, 1915
Harlan C. Brewster	1916–18	Liberal	Nov. 23, 1916
John Oliver	1918–27	Liberal	Mar. 6, 1918
John D. MacLean	1927–28	Liberal	Aug. 20, 1927
Simon F. Tolmie	1928–33	Conservative	Aug. 21, 1928
T. D. Pattullo	1933–41	Liberal	Nov. 15, 1933
John Hart	1941–47	Liberal[3]	Dec. 9, 1941
Byron Johnson	1947–52	Liberal[3]	Dec. 29, 1947
W. A. C. Bennett	1952–72	Social Credit	Aug. 1, 1952
David Barrett	1972–75	New Democratic Party	Sept. 15, 1972
William R. Bennett	1975–86	Social Credit	Dec. 22, 1975
Bill Vander Zalm	1986–91	Social Credit	Aug. 6, 1986
Rita Johnston	1991–91	Social Credit	Apr. 2, 1991
Michael Harcourt	1991–	New Democratic Party	Nov. 5, 1991

■ Yukon Territory

Government Leaders	Term	Party	Elected or sworn in
Chris Pearson	1978–85	Yukon Progressive Conservative	
Willard Phelps	1985	Yukon Progressive Conservative	
Tony Penikett	1985–92[4]	NDP	
John Ostashek	1992–	Yukon Party	

■ Northwest Territories

Government Leaders	Term	Party	Elected or sworn in
George Braden	1980–83	n.a.	July 25, 1980
Richard Nerysoo	1984–85	n.a.	Jan. 12, 1984
Nick Sibbeston	1985–87	n.a.	Nov. 5, 1985
Dennis Patterson	1987–91	n.a.	Nov. 12, 1987
Nellie Cournoyea	1991–	n.a.	Nov. 13, 1991

Source: *Historical Statistics of Canada; Provincial Archives*

(1) United Farmer/Progressive, 1922–27; Coalition, 1927–37; Liberal—Progressive, 1937–43. (2) Co-operative Commonwealth Federation. (3) Coalition. (4) From 1989–92, Government Leader was designated Premier. (n.a.) not available.

Cabinets of the Provinces and Territories

(as of September, 1993)

■ Newfoundland

Ministry or Portfolio	Minister
Premier	Clyde Wells
President of Council; President of Treasury Board; Finance	Winston Baker
Fisheries	Walter Carter
Employment and Labour Relations; Status of Women	Roger Grimes
Health	Dr. Hubert Kitchen
Justice	Edward Roberts

▶

▶ Social Services . . . . Tom Lush
Forestry and Agriculture . . . . Graham Flight
Industry, Trade and Technology . . . . Chuck Furey
Mines and Energy . . . . Dr. Rex Gibbons
Works, Services and Transportation . . . . John Efford
Municipal and Provincial Affairs; Housing . . . . Art Reid
Environment and Lands . . . . Patt Cowan
Education . . . . Chris Decker
Speaker of the House of Assembly . . . . Paul Dicks

■ New Brunswick

Ministry or Portfolio	Minister
Premier; President of Executive Council; Status of Women	Frank McKenna
Advanced Education and Labour	Vaughn Blaney
Agriculture	Gérald Clavette
Finance	Allan Maher
Economic Development and Tourism	Denis Losier
Education	Paul Duffie
Environment	Jane Barry
Fisheries and Aquaculture	Camille Thériault
Health and Community Services	Russell King, M.D.
Income Assistance, Minister of State for Literacy	Ann Breault
Intergovernmental Affairs, Justice, Attorney General	Edmond Blanchard
Municipal Affairs and Housing; Culture	Marcelle Mersereau
Natural Resources and Energy	Alan Graham
Minister of State for Mines and Energy	Doug Tyler
NB Power	Raymond Frenette
Solicitor General	Bruce Smith
Supply and Services	Laureen Jarrett
Transportation	Sheldon Lee

■ Nova Scotia

Ministry or Portfolio	Minister
Premier; President of Executive Council; Intergovernmental Affairs	John P. Savage, M.D.
Deputy Premier; Justice and Attorney General	J. William Gillis
Finance	J. Bernard Boudreau, Q.C.
Economic Development; Tourism and Culture	Ross Bragg
Education	John MacEachern
Health	Ronald D. Stewart, M.D.
Community Services	James A. Smith, M.D.
Transportation and Communications	Richard W. Mann
Municipal Affairs	Sandra L. Jolly
Natural Resources	Donald R. Downe
Supply and Services	F. Wayne Adams
Agriculture and Marketing	Wayne J. Gaudet
Environment	Robert S. Harrison
Civil Service Act; Status of Women	Eleanor E. Norrie
Housing and Consumer Affairs	Guy A.C. Brown
Fisheries	James A. Barkhouse
Labour; Youth Secretariat	Jay F. Abbass

■ Prince Edward Island

Ministry or Portfolio	Minister
Premier; President of Executive Council	Catherine S. Callbeck
Economic Development and Tourism	Robert J. Morrissey
Provincial Treasurer	Wayne D. Cheverie, Q.C.
Transportation and Public Works	Gordon E. MacInnis
Education and Human Resources	Keith Milligan
Environmental Resources	Barry W. Hicken
Agriculture, Fisheries and Forestry	Walter Bradley
Health and Social Services	Alan Buchanan

▶

▶ Provincial Affairs and Attorney-General .... Walter McEwen,Q.C.
Minister without Portfolio .... Jeannie Lea

■ Quebec

Ministry or Portfolio	Minister
Premier..	Robert Bourassa
Deputy Premier; Energy and Resources................................	Lise Bacon
Administration and the Public Service; Treasury Board.....................	Daniel Johnson
Agriculture, Fisheries and Food....................................	Yvon Vallières
Agriculture, Fisheries and Food; Regional Affairs......................	Yvon Picotte
Communications..	Lawrence Cannon
Cultural Communities and Immigration	Monique Gagnon-Tremblay
Culture	Liza Frulla
Education; Higher Education and Science.............................	Lucienne Robillard
Finance	Gérard D. Levesque
Finance	Louise Robic
Forests	Albert Côté
Government House Leader; Environment..............................	Pierre Paradis
Health and Social Services; Electoral Reform; Status of the Elderly..	Marc-Yvan Côté
Industry, Trade and Technology....................................	Gérald Tremblay
International Affairs	John Ciaccia
International Affairs; Francophone Affairs.............................	Guy Rivard
Justice; Canadian Intergovernmental Affairs..........................	Gil Rémillard
Labour; Cultural Communities	Normand Cherry
Manpower, Income Security and Skills Development......................	André Bourbeau
Municipal Affairs; Charter of French Language; Public Security..............	Claude Ryan
Native Affairs...	Christos Sirros
Recreation, Fish and Game	Gaston Blackburn
Revenue	Raymond Savoie
Status of Women; Family Policy....................................	Violette Trépanier
Supply and Services..	Robert Dutil
Tourism	André Vallerand
Transport	Robert Middlemiss
Transport	Sam Elkas

■ Ontario

Ministry or Portfolio	Minister
Premier; President of the Council; Intergovernmental Affairs....................	Bob Rae
Deputy Premier; Minister of Finance................................	Floyd Laughren
Labour	Bob Mackenzie
Municipal Affairs...	Ed Philip
Environment and Energy; Native Affairs	C.J. (Bud) Wildman
Education and Training	Dave Cooke
Health	Ruth Grier
Transportation; Francophone Affairs.................................	Gilles Pouliot
Natural Resources..	Howard Hampton
Northern Development and Mines	Shelley Martel
Housing..	Evelyn Gigantes
Attorney General; Women's Issues	Marion Boyd
Agriculture and Food	Elmer Buchanan
Economic Development and Trade...................................	Frances Lankin
Culture, Tourism and Recreation	Anne Swarbrick
Citizenship; Human Rights, Disabled, Seniors and Race Relations	Elaine Ziemba
Management Board of Cabinet; Government House Leader	Brian A. Charlton
Consumer and Commercial Relations	Marilyn M. Churley
Community and Social Services	Antonio V.G. Silipo
Solicitor General; Correctional Services	David Christopherson
Minister without Portfolio (Economic Development and Trade)	Richard Allen
Minister without Portfolio (Municipal Affairs)	Allan C. Pilkey
Minister without Portfolio (Health)	Shelley Wark-Martyn
Minister without Portfolio (Culture, Tourism and Recreation)	Shirley Coppen
Minister without Portfolio (Chief Government Whip)	Fred Wilson

▶

▶ Minister without Portfolio (Finance) .... Brad Ward
Minister without Portfolio (Education and Training) .... Mike Farnan

■ Manitoba

Ministry or Portfolio	Minister
Premier; President of Executive Council; Federal/Provincial Relations	Gary A. Filmon
Agriculture	Harry J. Enns
Deputy Premier; Industry, Trade and Tourism	James E. Downey
Energy and Mines	Donald W. Orchard
Natural Resources	Albert Driedger
Education and Training	Clayton S. Manness
Environment	James G. Cummings
Health	James C. McCrae
Consumer and Corporate Affairs	James A. Ernst
Highways and Transportation	Glen M. Findlay
Rural Development	Leonard Derkach
Government Services; Seniors	Gerald Ducharme
Family Services	Bonnie E. Mitchelson
Culture, Heritage and Citizenship	Harold Gilleshammer
Labour; Civil Service Act; French Language Services	Darren T. Praznik
Finance	Eric Stefanson
Urban Affairs	Linda McIntosh
Justice and Attorney-General	Rosemary Vodrey

■ Saskatchewan

Ministry or Portfolio	Minister
Premier; President of Executive Council	Roy Romanow, Q.C.
Deputy Premier; Provincial Secretary; Education, Training and Employment	Ed Tchorzewski
Economic Development	Dwain Lingenfelter
Energy and Mines	Doug Anguish
Health	Louise Simard
Environment and Resource Management	Bernhard Wiens
Municipal Government	Carol Carson
Justice and Attorney General	Robert Mitchell, Q.C.
Finance	Janice MacKinnon
Associate Minister of Finance; Crown Investments	John Penner
Agriculture and Food; Highways and Transportation	Darrel Cunningham
Labour	Ned Shillington
Social Services; Seniors	Pat Atkinson
Associate Minister of Health	Lorne Calvert
Saskatchewan Property Management Corporation	Eldon Lautermilch
Associate Minister of Education, Training and Employment	Keith Goulet

■ Alberta

Ministry or Portfolio	Minister
Premier; President of Executive Council; Intergovernmental Affairs	Ralph Klein
Advanced Education and Career Development	Jack Ady
Energy	Pat Black
Family and Social Services	Mike Cardinal
Labour	Stockwell Day
Provincial Treasurer	Jim Dinning
Environmental Protection	Brian Evans
Education	Halvar Jonson
Deputy Premier; Government House Leader; Economic Development and Tourism	Ken Kowalski
Community Development	Gary Mar
Health	Shirley McClellan

▶

▶ Minister without Portfolio	Dianne Mirosh
Agriculture, Food and Rural Development	Walter Paszkowski
Justice and Attorney General	Ken Rostad
Public Works, Supply and Services	Tom Thurber
Transportation and Utilities	Peter Trynchy
Municipal Affairs	Stephen West

■ British Columbia

Ministry or Portfolio	Minister
Premier; President of Executive Council	Michael Harcourt
Deputy Premier; Finance and Corporate Relations	Elizabeth Cull
Attorney General	Colin Gabelmann
Forests	Andrew Petter
Environment, Lands and Parks	Moe Sihota
Education	Art Charbonneau
Agriculture, Fisheries and Food	David Zirnhelt
Energy, Mines and Petroleum Resources	Anne Edwards
Skills, Training and Labour	Dan Miller
Small Business, Tourism and Culture	Bill Barlee
Municipal Affairs	Darlene Marzari
Health; responsible for Seniors	Paul Ramsey
Social Services	Joy MacPhail
Transportation and Highways	Jackie Pement
Employment and Investment	Glen Clark
Housing, Recreation and Consumer Services	Joan Smallwood
Government Services	Robin Blencoe
Aboriginal Affairs	John Cashore
Women's Equality	Penny Priddy

■ Yukon Territories

Ministry or Portfolio	Minister
Government Leader; Executive Council Office; Finance; Land Claims; Public Service Commission	John Ostashek
Renewable Resources; Workers' Compensation; Health and Safety Board; Yukon Liquor Corporation	Bill Brewster
Health and Social Services; Justice; Yukon Development Corporation; Yukon Energy Corporation	Willard Phelps
Education; Tourism; Women's Directorate	Doug Phillips
Economic Development; Government Services	John Devries
Community and Transportation Services; Yukon Housing Corporation	Mickey Fisher

■ Northwest Territories

Ministry or Portfolio	Minister
Government Leader; Executive Council; Energy, Mines and Petroleum Resources; Women's Directorate	Nellie J. Cournoyea
Government House Leader; Finance	John Pollard
Intergovernmental and Aboriginal Affairs; Justice	Stephen Kakfwi
Renewable Resources; Municipal and Community Affairs	Titus Allooloo
Government Services and Public Works	Don Morin
Education, Culture and Employment Programs	Richard Nerysoo
Health; Social Services	Rebecca Mike
Transportation, Safety and Public Services; Economic Development and Tourism	John Todd

POLITICS AND ELECTIONS

Winner of National Newspaper Award for Political Cartooning, 1992

SORRY I ASKED...

Source: Bruce MacKinnon, *The Halifax Chronicle Herald* and *The Mail Star, Oct. 28, 1992.*

Registered Federal Political Parties

(as of September 1993)

Bloc Québecois¹—Room 1475, 425 Maisonneuve Street West, Montréal, QC H3A 3G5; Tel: (514) 499-3000; Fax: (514) 499-3638; leader: Lucien Bouchard.

Canada Party¹—1216 12th Avenue East, Regina, SK S4N 0M5; Tel: (306) 757-0773; leader: Joseph A. Thauberger.

Canadian Party for Renewal¹—P.O. Box 382, Station "U," Etobicoke, ON M8Z 1P0; Tel: (416) 259-4649; Fax: (416) 234-8636; leader: Jeffrey Goodman.

Christian Heritage Party of Canada— 6369 Sundance Drive, Surrey, BC V3S 8A9; Tel: (604) 574-3456; Fax: (604) 574-9229; leader: Charles A. Cavilla.

Communist Party of Canada—1782 Keele Street, Toronto, ON M6M 3X1; Tel: (416) 651-8210; Fax: (416) 651-4078; leader: Miguel Figueron.

Confederation of Regions Western Party—Box 303, Bloomfield, ON K0K 1G0; Tel: (613) 476-5365; leader: Nora Galenzoski.

Liberal Party of Canada—Suite 200, 200 Laurier Avenue West, Ottawa, ON K1P 6M8; Tel: (613) 237-0740; Fax: (613) 235-7208; leader: The Hon. Jean Chrétien.

Libertarian Party of Canada—Suite 301, 1 St. John's Road, Toronto, ON M6P 1T7; Tel: (416) 763-3688; Fax: (416) 763-5306; leader: Hilliard Cox.

Marxist-Leninist Party of Canada¹—171 Dalhousie Street, Ottawa, ON K1N 7C7; Tel: (613) 235-7052; leader: Hardial Singh Bains.

National Party of Canada¹—200 - 250 Portage Avenue, P.O. Box 733, Winnipeg, MB R3C 2L4; Tel: (204) 949-2430; Fax: (204) 956-2784; leader: Mel Hurtig.

Natural Law Party of Canada¹— 500 Wilbrod Street, Ottawa, ON K1N 6N2; Tel: (613) 565-8517; leader: Neil Paterson.

New Democratic Party—310 Somerset Street West, Ottawa, ON K2P 0J9; Tel: (613) 236-3613; Fax: (613) 230-9950; leader: The Hon. Audrey McLaughlin.

Option Canada Party[1]—P.O. Box 8, 75 Harwood Road, Hudson Heights, QC J0P 1J0; Tel: (514) 458-2068; leader: John Robertson.

Parti Rhinocéros—6777 St-Dominique, Montréal, QC H2S 3B1; Tel: (514) 276-9403; leader: Dominique Langevin.

Parti Nationaliste du Québec[1]—19 St-Onge Street, Hull, QC J8Y 5T4; Tel: (819) 771-2092; leader: Louis Gravel.

Party for the Commonwealth of Canada—8259 St. Laurent Blvd., Montréal, QC H2P 2M1; Tel: (514) 385-5494; Fax: (514) 385-9130; leader: Gilles Gervais.

Populist Party for Canada[1]—231 - 2001 Highway 97 South, Kelowna, BC V1Z 3E3; Tel: (604) 768-4689; Fax: (604) 768-4689; leader: Benjamin S. Bissett.

Progressive Conservative Party of Canada—6th Floor, 275 Slater Street, Ottawa, ON K1P 5H9; Tel: (613) 238-6111; Fax: (613) 563-7892; leader: The Right Hon. Kim Campbell.

Reform of the Monetary Law[1]—3702 Mousseau Street, Montréal, QC H1K 2V5; Tel: (514) 354-5818; leader: Dollard Desjardins.

Reform Party of Canada—Suite 600, 833 4th Avenue SW, Calgary, AB T2P 0K5; Tel: (403) 269-1990; Fax: (403) 269-4077; leader: E. Preston Manning.

Social Credit Party of Canada—Box 100, Milton, ON L9T 2Y3; Tel: (416) 878-8461; leader: Kenneth L. Campbell.

The Green Party of Canada—831 Commercial Drive, Vancouver, BC V5L 3W6; Tel: (604) 254-8165; Fax: (604) 254-8166; leader: Chris Lea.

Source: *Elections Canada*

(1) Accepted for registration; such parties must field a minimum of 50 candidates in the next federal election in order to qualify.

Federal Election Results, 1867–1988

♣1867–1904	1867	1872	1874	1878	1882	1887	1891	1896	1900	1904
Canada										
Conservative	101	103	73	137	139	123	123	89	80	75
Liberal	80	97	133	69	71	92	92	117	133	139
Other	—	—	—	—	—	—	—	7	—	—
Prince Edward Island[1]										
Conservative	—	—	—	5	4	—	2	3	2	3
Liberal	—	—	6	1	2	6	4	2	3	1
Nova Scotia										
Conservative	3	11	4	14	15	14	16	10	5	—
Liberal	16	10	17	7	6	7	5	10	15	18
New Brunswick										
Conservative	7	7	5	5	10	10	13	9	5	6
Liberal	8	9	11	11	6	6	3	5	9	7
Quebec										
Conservative	45	38	32	45	48	33	30	16	7	11
Liberal	20	27	33	20	17	32	35	49	58	54
Other	—	—	—	—	—	—	—	5	—	—
Ontario										
Conservative	46	38	24	59	54	52	48	44	55	48
Liberal	36	50	64	29	37	40	44	43	37	38
Other	—	—	—	—	—	—	—	5	—	—
Manitoba[2]										
Conservative	—	3	2	3	2	4	4	4	4	3
Liberal	—	1	2	1	3	1	1	2	3	7
Other	—	—	—	—	—	—	—	1	—	—
British Columbia[3]										
Conservative	—	6	6	6	6	6	6	2	2	—
Liberal	—	—	—	—	—	—	—	4	4	7
Yukon[4]										
Conservative	—	—	—	—	—	—	—	—	—	1
Northwest Territories[2]										
Conservative	—	—	—	—	—	4	4	1	—	3
Liberal	—	—	—	—	—	—	—	2	4	7
Other	—	—	—	—	—	—	—	1	—	—

♦ 1908–1953

	1908	1911	1917[7]	1921	1925	1926	1930	1935	1940	1945	1949	1953
Canada												
Conservative	85	133	153	50	116	91	137	39	39	67	41	51
Liberal	133	86	82	117	101	116	88	171	178	125	190	170
Progressive	—	—	—	64	25	—	2	—	—	—	—	—
CCF	—	—	—	—	—	—	—	7	8	28	13	23
Social Credit	—	—	—	—	—	—	—	17	10	13	10	15
Other	3	2	—	4	3	38	18	11	10	12	8	6
Newfoundland[5]												
Conservative	—	—	—	—	—	—	—	—	—	—	2	—
Liberal	—	—	—	—	—	—	—	—	—	—	5	7
Prince Edward Island												
Conservative	1	2	2	—	2	1	3	—	—	1	1	1
Liberal	3	2	2	4	2	3	1	4	4	3	3	3
Nova Scotia												
Conservative	6	9	12	—	11	12	10	—	1	3	2	1
Liberal	12	9	4	16	3	2	4	12	10	8	10	10
CCF	—	—	—	—	—	—	—	—	1	1	1	1
New Brunswick												
Conservative	2	5	7	5	10	7	10	1	5	3	2	3
Liberal	11	8	4	5	1	4	1	9	5	7	7	7
Other	—	—	—	1	—	—	—	—	—	—	1	—
Quebec												
Conservative	11	27	3	—	4	4	24	5	—	1	2	4
Liberal	53	37	62	65	60	60	40	55	61	54	66	66
Other	1	1	—	—	1	1	1	5	4	10	5	5
Ontario												
Conservative	48	72	74	37	68	53	59	25	25	48	25	33
Liberal	36	36	8	21	12	23	22	56	55	34	56	50
Progressive	—	—	—	24	2	4	—	—	—	—	—	—
Other	2	1	—	—	—	2	1	1	2	—	2	2
Manitoba												
Conservative	8	8	14	—	7	—	11	1	1	2	1	3
Liberal	2	2	1	2	1	4	1	12	14	10	12	8
CCF	—	—	—	—	—	—	—	2	1	5	3	3
Progressive	—	—	—	12	7	4	—	—	—	—	—	—
Other	—	—	—	1	2	9	5	2	1	—	—	—
Saskatchewan[6]												
Conservative	1	1	16	—	—	—	8	1	2	1	1	1
Liberal	9	9	—	1	15	16	11	16	12	2	14	5
CCF	—	—	—	—	—	—	—	2	5	18	5	11
Progressive	—	—	—	15	6	5	2	—	—	—	—	—
Social Credit	—	—	—	—	—	—	—	—	2	—	—	—
Other	—	—	—	—	—	—	—	—	2	—	—	—
Alberta[6]												
Conservative	3	1	11	—	3	1	4	1	—	2	2	2
Liberal	4	6	1	—	4	3	3	1	7	2	5	4
Progressive	—	—	—	10	9	—	—	—	—	—	—	—
Social Credit	—	—	—	—	—	—	—	15	10	13	10	11
United Farmers of Alta.	—	—	—	—	—	11	9	—	—	—	—	—
Other	—	—	—	2	—	1	—	—	—	—	—	—
British Columbia												
Conservative	5	7	13	7	10	12	7	5	4	5	3	3
Liberal	2	—	—	3	3	1	5	6	10	5	11	8
CCF	—	—	—	—	—	—	—	3	1	4	3	7
Progressive	—	—	—	2	1	—	—	—	—	—	—	—
Social Credit	—	—	—	—	—	—	—	—	—	—	—	4
Other	—	—	—	1	—	1	2	2	1	2	1	—
Yukon and Northwest Territories												
Conservative	—	1	—	1	1	1	1	—	1	1	—	—
Liberal	1	—	—	—	—	—	—	—	—	—	1	2
Other	—	—	—	—	—	—	—	1	—	—	—	—

♣ 1957–1988

	1957	1958	1962	1963	1965	1968	1972	1974	1979	1980	1984	1988
Canada												
Conservative	112	208	116	95	97	72	107	95	136	103	211	169
Liberal	105	48	99	129	131	155	109	141	114	147	40	83
NDP (CCF)[8]	25	8	19	17	21	22	31	16	26	32	30	43
Social Credit	19	—	30	24	5	—	15	11	6	—	—	—
Other	4	1	1	—	11	15	2	1	—	—	1	—
Newfoundland												
Conservative	2	2	1	—	—	6	4	3	2	2	4	2
Liberal	5	5	6	7	7	1	3	4	4	5	3	5
NDP (CCF)	—	—	—	—	—	—	—	—	1	—	—	—
Prince Edward Island												
Conservative	4	4	4	2	4	4	3	3	4	2	3	—
Liberal	—	—	—	2	—	—	1	1	—	2	1	4
Nova Scotia												
Conservative	10	12	9	7	10	10	10	8	8	6	9	5
Liberal	2	—	2	5	2	1	1	2	2	5	2	6
NDP (CCF)	—	—	1	—	—	—	—	1	1	—	—	—
New Brunswick												
Conservative	5	7	4	4	4	5	5	3	4	3	9	5
Liberal	5	3	6	6	6	5	5	6	6	7	1	5
Other	—	—	—	—	—	—	—	1	—	—	—	—
Quebec												
Conservative	9	50	14	8	8	4	2	3	2	1	58	63
Liberal	63	25	35	47	56	56	56	60	67	74	17	12
NDP (CCF)	—	—	—	—	—	—	—	—	—	—	—	—
Social Credit	—	—	26	20	—	—	15	11	6	—	—	—
Other	3	—	—	—	11	14	1	—	—	—	—	—
Ontario												
Conservative	61	67	35	27	25	17	40	25	57	38	67	46
Liberal	20	14	43	52	51	64	36	55	32	52	14	43
NDP (CCF)	3	3	6	6	9	6	11	8	6	5	13	10
Other	1	1	1	—	—	1	1	—	—	—	1	—
Manitoba												
Conservative	8	14	11	10	10	5	8	9	7	5	9	7
Liberal	1	—	1	2	1	5	2	2	2	2	1	5
NDP (CCF)	5	—	2	2	3	3	3	2	5	7	4	2
Saskatchewan												
Conservative	3	16	16	17	17	5	7	8	10	7	9	4
Liberal	4	—	1	—	—	2	1	3	—	—	—	—
NDP (CCF)	10	1	—	—	—	6	5	2	4	7	5	10
Alberta												
Conservative	3	17	15	14	15	15	19	19	21	21	21	25
Liberal	1	—	—	1	—	4	—	—	—	—	—	—
NDP (CCF)	—	—	—	—	—	—	—	—	—	—	—	1
Social Credit	13	—	2	2	2	—	—	—	—	—	—	—
British Columbia												
Conservative	7	18	6	4	3	—	8	13	19	16	19	12
Liberal	2	—	4	7	7	16	4	8	1	—	1	1
NDP (CCF)	7	4	10	9	9	7	11	2	8	12	8	19
Social Credit	6	—	2	2	3	—	—	—	—	—	—	—
Yukon												
Conservative	—	1	1	1	1	1	1	1	1	1	1	—
Liberal	1	—	—	—	—	—	—	—	—	—	—	—
NDP (CCF)	—	—	—	—	—	—	—	—	—	—	—	1
Northwest Territories												
Conservative	—	—	1	—	—	—	—	—	1	1	2	—
Liberal	1	1	1	—	1	1	—	—	—	—	—	2
NDP (CCF)	—	—	—	—	—	—	1	1	1	1	—	—

(1) Entered Confederation July 1, 1873. (2) Entered Confederation July 15, 1870. (3) Entered Confederation July 20, 1871. (4) Entered Confederation June 13, 1898. (5) Entered Confederation Mar. 31, 1949. (6) Entered Confederation Sept. 1, 1905. (7) For the 1917 election, Conservative refers to "Unionists," a coalition of Conservatives and pro-conscription Liberals; Liberals, for the 1917 election, are sometimes called "Laurier Liberals" because of their support for Laurier's anti-conscription stand. (8) The New Democratic Party (NDP) replaced the Co-operative Commonwealth Federation (CCF) in Aug. 1961.

Federal Election 1988—Results by Province and Party

Province	Conservative	%	Liberal	%	New Democrat	%	Other[1]	%
Newfoundland	108 349	42.2	115 588	45.0	31 769	12.4	1 025	0.4
Prince Edward Island .	31 372	41.5	37 761	49.9	5 661	7.5	850	1.1
Nova Scotia	196 390	40.9	223 175	46.5	54 515	11.4	5 761	1.2
New Brunswick	155 056	40.4	173 967	45.4	35 790	9.3	18 758	4.9
Quebec...........	1 844 279	52.7	1 058 952	30.3	488 633	14.0	1 09 239	3.1
Ontario	1 787 291	38.2	1 819 095	38.9	939 928	20.1	1 33 716	2.8
Manitoba	200 100	36.9	198 408	36.5	115 638	21.3	28 795	5.3
Saskatchewan	190 597	36.4	95 295	18.2	231 358	44.2	6 503	1.2
Alberta	602 848	51.8	159 807	13.7	202 847	17.4	1 99 452	17.1
British Columbia	541 172	35.3	312 803	20.4	566 582	37.0	1 12 469	7.3
Yukon	4 524	35.3	1 450	11.3	6 594	51.4	255	2.0
NWT	5 585	26.4	8 771	41.4	5 993	28.3	833	3.9
Total votes	**5 667 563**	**43.0**	**4 205 072**	**31.9**	**2 685 308**	**20.4**	**617 656**	**4.7**
Seats	169	57.3	83	28.1	43	14.6	—	—

Source: *Elections Canada*

(1) Includes the Reform Party, Christian Heritage Party, Green Party, Confederation of Regions Western Party, Libertarian Party, Party for Commonwealth, Communist Party, Parti Rhinocéros, Social Credit Party, independents and those with no affiliation.

Voter Turnout at Canada's Federal Elections, 1867–1988

(percentage of eligible voters casting votes)

Year	Voter turnout[1]	Year	Voter turnout[1]	Year	Voter turnout[1]	Year	Voter turnout[1]
1867	73%	1904	84%	1940	71%	1968	76%
1872	70	1908	79	1945	76	1972	77
1874	75	1911	72	1949	75	1974	71
1878	71	1917	90	1953	68	1979	76
1882	72	1921	71	1957	75	1980	69
1887	70	1925	69	1958	81	1984	75
1891	65	1926	70	1962	80	1988	76
1896	61	1930	76	1963	80		
1900	79	1935	75	1965	76		

Source: *Elections Canada*

(1) Percentage of actual votes to eligible voters. In many early general elections, several electoral districts were won by acclamation; hence, no eligible voters nor actual votes were recorded. Furthermore, in some of the more remote districts, votes were cast but no voters' lists had been prepared.

Federal Election 1988 — Voter Turnout by Province

	Eligible voters	Actual votes cast[1]	Voter turnout[2]		Eligible voters	Actual votes cast[1]	Voter turnout[2]
Canada	17 639 001	13 386 783	76%	Manitoba	729 281	546 571	75%
Newfoundland	384 236	258 855	67	Saskatchewan	675 160	526 685	78
PEI	89 546	76 328	85	Alberta	1 557 669	1 170 586	75
Nova Scotia	644 353	483 523	75	British Columbia.	1 954 040	1 544 230	79
New Brunswick	508 741	388 831	76	Yukon	16 396	12 875	79
Quebec	4 740 091	3 624 451	76	NWT	30 113	21 450	71
Ontario	6 309 375	4 732 398	75				

Source: *Elections Canada*

(1) Valid and non-valid votes. (2) Percentage of actual votes to eligible voters.

Federal Political Party Leaders

■ Progressive Conservative[1] Party

Leader	Term
Sir John A. Macdonald	1854–July 6, 1891
Sir J.J.C. Abbott	June 16, 1891–Dec. 5, 1892
Sir John Thompson	Dec. 5, 1892–Dec. 12, 1894
Sir Mackenzie Bowell	Dec. 21, 1894–Apr. 27, 1896
Sir Charles Tupper	May 1, 1896–Feb. 5, 1901
Sir Robert Borden	Feb. 6, 1901–July 10, 1920
Arthur Meighen	July 10, 1920–Oct. 11, 1926
Hugh Guthrie[2]	Oct. 11, 1926–Oct. 12, 1927
R.B. Bennett	Oct. 12, 1927–July 7, 1938
R.J. Manion	July 7, 1938–May 13, 1940
R.B. Hanson[2]	May 13, 1940–Nov. 12, 1941
Arthur Meighen	Nov. 12, 1941–Dec. 11, 1942
John Bracken	Dec. 11, 1942–Oct. 2, 1948
George A. Drew	Oct. 2, 1948–Dec. 14, 1956
John G. Diefenbaker	Dec. 14, 1956–Sept. 9, 1967
Robert L. Stanfield	Sept. 9, 1967–Feb. 22, 1976
Joe Clark	Feb. 22, 1976–Feb. 8, 1983
Erik Nielsen[2]	Feb. 9, 1983–June 11, 1983
Brian Mulroney	June 11, 1983–June 13, 1993
Kim Campbell	June 13, 1993–

■ Liberal Party

Leader	Term
Robert Baldwin	1804–1858
Louis-H. Lafontaine	1807–1864
George Brown	1867–1872
Alexander Mackenzie	Mar. 6, 1873–Apr. 27, 1880
Edward Blake	May 4, 1880–June 2, 1887
Sir Wilfrid Laurier	June 1887–Feb. 17, 1919
Daniel D. McKenzie[2]	Feb. 1919–Aug. 1919
W.L. Mackenzie King	Aug. 7, 1919–Aug. 7, 1948
Louis St. Laurent	Aug. 7, 1948–Jan. 16, 1958
Lester B. Pearson	Jan. 16, 1958–Apr. 2, 1968
Pierre E. Trudeau	Apr. 6, 1968–June 16, 1984
John N. Turner	June 16, 1984–June 23, 1990
Jean Chrétien	June 23, 1990–

■ New Democratic Party[3]

Leader	Term
James S. Woodsworth	Aug. 1932–July 1942
M.J. Coldwell	July 1942–Aug. 1960
Hazen Argue	Aug. 1960–Aug. 1961
Tommy Douglas	Aug. 1961–Apr. 1971
David Lewis	Apr. 24, 1971–July 7, 1975
Ed Broadbent	July 7, 1975–Dec. 2, 1989
Audrey McLaughlin	Dec. 2, 1989–

(1) Name changed from Conservative to Progressive Conservative Dec. 1942. (2) Interim leader appointed to fill a vacancy until a party leadership convention could be held. (3) Prior to Aug. 1961 was called the Co-operative Commonwealth Federation.

Federal Political Party Leadership Conventions

■ Progressive Conservative Party, 1993

Candidates	First ballot	Second ballot
Kim Campbell	1 664	1 817
Jean Charest	1 369	1 630
Jim Edwards	307	—
Garth Turner	76	—
Patrick Boyer	53	—

■ Liberal Party, 1990

Candidates	First ballot
Jean Chrétien	2 662
Paul Martin	1 176
Sheila Copps	499
Tom Wappel	267
John Nunziata	64

■ New Democratic Party, 1989

Candidates	First ballot	Second ballot	Third ballot	Fourth ballot
Audrey McLaughlin	646	829	1 072	1 316
Dave Barrett	566	780	947	1 072
Steven Langdon	351	519	393	—
Simon de Jong	315	289	—	—
Howard McCurdy	256	—	—	—
Ian Waddell	213	—	—	—
Roger Lagassé	53	—	—	—

Ottawa, June 13, 1993

*T*he June Tory leadership convention was contested by five candidates: Patrick Boyer, member for Etobicoke-Lakeshore (Ontario); Kim Campbell, member for Vancouver Centre (BC); Jean Charest, member for Sherbrooke (Quebec); Jim Edwards, member for Edmonton Southwest (Alberta) and Garth Turner, member for Halton-Peel (Ontario). Of the five, only two had served in cabinet: Kim Campbell had been in various portfolios including Indian Affairs and Northern Development, Justice and Attorney General, and most recently she served as Minister of Defence. Jean Charest began as youth minister in 1986, moving to Fitness and Amateur Sport in 1988, and then took over the Environment ministry.

Once again the field was dominated by lawyers: Kim Campbell, Patrick Boyer and Jean Charest all hold law degrees, while Garth Turner and Jim Edwards came from the communications fields.

The dominant issues during the leadership campaign were the economy and attendant topics— unemployment, Canada's role in the global economy, NAFTA, government cutbacks and government spending and the deficit. Related topics included maintaining Canada's social security net while reigning in the deficit.

The subject of constitutional reform was on the back burner after many months of intense debate and attention. After the defeat of the Charlottetown Accord, all parties agreed that it was unlikely that a new deal could be reached until both politicians and the electorate had had a break from the discussions.

Provincial Election Results

■ Newfoundland

	1962	1966	1971	1972	1975	1979	1982	1985	1989	1993
Liberal	34	38	20	9	16	19	8	15	31	35
Progressive Conservative	7	4	21	33	30	33	44	36	21	16
New Democratic	—	—	—	—	—	—	—	1	—	1
Other	1	—	1	—	5	—	—	—	—	—
Size of legislature	42	42	42	42	51	52	52	52	52	52

■ Prince Edward Island

	1962	1966	1970	1974	1978	1979	1982	1985	1989	1993
Liberal	11	17	27	26	17	11	14	21	30	31
Progressive Conservative	19	15	5	6	15	21	18	11	2	1
Size of legislature	30	32	32	32	32	32	32	32	32	32

■ Nova Scotia

	1960	1963	1967	1970	1974	1978	1981	1984	1988	1993
Liberal	15	4	6	23	31	17	13	6	21	40
New Democratic[1]	1	—	—	2	3	4	1	3	2	3
Progressive Conservative[2]	27	39	40	21	12	31	37	42	28	9
Other	—	—	—	—	—	—	1	1	1	—
Size of legislature	43	43	46	46	46	52	52	52	52	52

■ New Brunswick

	1956	1960	1963	1967	1970	1974	1978	1982	1987	1991
Liberal	15	31	32	32	26	25	28	18	58	48
Progressive Conservative[3]	37	21	20	26	32	33	30	39	—	1
New Democratic	—	—	—	—	—	—	—	1	—	1
Confederation of Regions	—	—	—	—	—	—	—	—	—	8
Size of legislature	52	52	52	58	58	58	58	58	58	58

■ Quebec

	1956	1960	1962	1966	1970	1973	1976	1981	1985	1989
Crédit Social	—	—	—	—	12	2	1	—	—	—
Equality	—	—	—	—	—	—	—	—	—	4
Liberal	20	51	63	50	72	102	26	42	99	92
Parti Québécois[4]	—	—	—	—	7	6	71	80	23	29
Union Nationale	72	43	31	56	17	—	11	—	—	—
Other	1	1	1	2	—	—	1	—	—	—
Size of legislature	93	95	95	108	108	110	110	122	122	1 25

■ Ontario

	1959	1963	1967	1971	1975	1977	1981	1985	1987	1990
Liberal	22	24	28	20	36	34	34	48	95	36
New Democratic[5]	5	7	20	19	38	33	21	25	19	74
Progressive Conservative[3]	71	77	69	78	51	58	70	52	16	20
Size of legislature	98	108	117	117	125	125	125	125	130	130

■ Manitoba

	1959	1962	1966	1969	1973	1977	1981	1986	1988	1990
Liberal	—	13	14	4	5	1	—	1	20	7
Liberal and Liberal Progressive	11	—	—	—	—	—	—	—	—	—
New Democratic[5]	10	7	11	28	31	23	34	30	12	20
Progressive Conservative[6]	35	36	31	22	21	33	23	26	25	30
Other	1	1	1	3	—	—	—	—	—	—
Size of legislature	57	57	57	57	57	57	57	57	57	57

■ Saskatchewan

	1956	1960	1964	1967	1971	1975	1978	1982	1986	1991
Liberal	14	17	33	35	15	15	—	—	1	1
New Democratic[7]	36	38	25	24	45	39	44	8	25	55
Progressive Conservative[8]	—	—	1	—	—	7	17	56	38	10
Other	3	—	—	—	—	—	—	—	—	—
Size of legislature	53	55	59	59	60	61	61	64	64	66

■ Alberta

	1959	1963	1967	1971	1975	1979	1982	1986	1989	1993
Liberal	1	2	3	—	—	—	—	4	8	32
New Democratic[1]	—	—	—	1	1	1	2	16	16	—
Progressive Conservative[6]	1	—	6	49	69	74	75	61	59	51
Social Credit	62	60	55	24	4	4	—	—	—	—
Other	1	1	1	1	1	—	2	2	—	—
Size of legislature	65	63	65	75	75	79	79	83	83	83

■ British Columbia

	1960	1963	1966	1969	1972	1975	1979	1983	1986	1991
Liberal	4	5	6	5	5	1	—	—	—	17
New Democratic[5]	16	14	16	12	38	18	26	21	22	51
Progressive Conservative[6]	—	—	—	—	2	1	—	—	—	—
Social Credit	32	33	33	38	10	35	31	35	47	7
Other	—	—	—	—	—	—	—	1	—	—
Size of legislature	52	52	55	55	55	55	57	57	69	75

(1) Known as the Co-operative Commonwealth Federation until 1962. (2) Known as the Conservative Party until 1946. (3) Known as the Conservative Party until 1943. (4) Formed in 1968. (5) Known as the Co-operative Commonwealth Federation until 1961. (6) Known as the Conservative Party until 1944. (7) Known as the Co-operative Commonwealth Federation until 1967. (8) Known as the Conservative Party until 1945.

Provincial Party Leaders[1]

(as of September 1993)

■ Newfoundland

Progressive Conservative Party	Liberal Party	New Democratic Party
G. R. Ottenheimer 1966–69	Donald Jamieson 1979–82	Peter Fenwick 1981–89
Frank D. Moores 1970–79	Len Sterling 1982–84	Cle Newhook 1989–92
A. Brian Peckford 1979–89	Stephen Neary 1984–85	Jack Harris .... 1992—
Tom Rideout 1989–91	Leo Barry 1985–87	
Len Simms .... 1991—	Clyde Wells .... 1987—	

■ Prince Edward Island

Progressive Conservative Party	Liberal Party	New Democratic Party
Angus MacLean 1976–81	J. Walter Jones 1943–53	Aquinas Ryan 1974–77
James M. Lee 1981–87	Alexander W. Matheson 1953–65	Douglas Murray 1979–81
Leone Bagnall 1987–88	Alex Campbell 1965–78	David Burke 1982–83
Melbourne Gass 1988–90	Bennett Campbell 1978–81	Jim Mayne 1983–89
Pat Mella .... 1990—	Joseph Ghiz 1981–93	Larry Duchesne .... 1991—
	Catherine Callbeck .... 1993—	

■ Nova Scotia

Progressive Conservative Party[2]	Liberal Party	New Democratic Party[3]
Leonard Wm. Fraser 1940–46	Gerald A. Regan 1965–80	Michael J. McDonald 1952–63
Robert Stanfield 1948–67	A.M. (Sandy) Cameron 1980–85	No member elected 1963–66
George I. Smith 1967–71	Vincent J. MacLean 1985	James Aitchison 1966–68
John M. Buchanan 1971–90	J. William Gillis 1985–86	Jeremy Akerman 1968–80
Donald Cameron 1991–93	Vincent J. MacLean 1986–92	Alexa McDonough ...... 1980—
Terence R.B. Donahoe (acting) 1993—	John Savage .... 1992—	

■ New Brunswick

Progressive Conservative Party[4]	Liberal Party	Confederation of Regions
C. B. Sherwood 1960–66	Louis Robichaud 1958–71	Arch Pafford 1989–91
Charles Van Horne 1966–69	Robert Higgins 1971–78	Danny Cameron .... 1991—
Richard B. Hatfield 1969–87	Joe Daigle 1978–8	**New Democratic Party**
Malcolm MacLeod 1987–89	Doug Young 1982–83	Elizabeth Weir .... 1988—
Barbara Baird Filliter....... 1989–91	Frank McKenna .... 1985—	
Dennis Cochrane .... 1991—		

■ Quebec

Parti Québécois	Parti Libéral	Equality Party
René Lévesque 1968–85	Georges-Emile Lapalme . 1950–58	Robert M. Libman 1989–93
Pierre-Marc Johnson 1985–88	Jean Lesage 1958–70	Keith Henderson .... 1993—
Jacques Parizeau .... 1988—	Robert Bourassa 1970–77	
	Claude Ryan 1978–82	
	Robert Bourassa .... 1983—	

■ **Ontario**

Progressive Conservative Party	Liberal Party	New Democratic Party[5]
John Robarts 1961–71	Andrew E. J. Thompson 1964–66	Edward B. Joliffe 1942–53
William G. Davis 1971–85	Robert Nixon 1967–76	Donald C. MacDonald .. 1953–70
Frank Miller 1985	Stuart Smith 1977–81	Stephen H. Lewis 1970–78
Larry Grossman 1985–87	David Peterson 1982–90	Michael Cassidy 1978–82
Andrew Brandt 1987–90	Lyn McLeod 1992–	Bob Rae 1982–
Mike Harris 1990–		

■ **Manitoba**

Progressive Conservative Party[6]	Liberal Party	New Democratic Party[5]
Duff Roblin 1954–67	Robert Bend 1969–70	Lloyd Stinson 1952–60
Walter C. Weir 1967–70	Israel (Izzy) Asper 1970–75	A. Russell Paulley 1960–69
Sidney Spivak 1971–75	Charles Huband 1975–78	Edward R. Schreyer 1969–79
Sterling Lyon 1975–83	Doug Lauchlan 1980–82	Howard R. Pawley 1979–88
Gary Filmon 1983–	Sharon Carstairs 1984–93	Gary Doer 1988–
	Paul Edwards 1993–	

■ **Saskatchewan**

Progressive Conservative Party[7]	Liberal Party	New Democratic Party[5]
Alvin Hamilton 1949–57	Ross Thatcher 1961–71	John H. Brockelbank 1941–44
Martin Pederson 1958–68	Dave Steuart 1971–76	Tommy Douglas 1944–61
Ed Nasserden 1969–73	E.C. Ted Malone 1976–81	Woodrow Lloyd 1961–70
Dick Collver 1973–79	Ralph E. Goodale 1981–88	Allan Blakeney 1970–87
Grant Devine 1979–92	Lynda Haverstock 1989–	Roy Romanow 1987
Rick Swenson 1992–		

■ **Alberta**

Progressive Conservative Party[7]	Liberal Party	New Democratic Party[5]
W. J. C. Cam Kirby 1958–60	J. Walter Grant McEwan ... 1959–62	Chester A. Ronning 1939–42
Ernest Watkins 1960–62	David Hunter 1962–65	Elmer Roper 1942–55
Milt Harradance 1962–64	Mike Maccagno 1967–68	Neil Reimer 1955–67
Peter Lougheed 1965–85	Nick Taylor 1974–88	W. Grant Notley 1968–82
Donald R. Getty 1985–92	Laurence Decore 1988–	Ray Martin 1982–
Ralph P. Klein 1992–		

■ **British Columbia**

Social Credit		New Democratic Party	Liberal
W. A. C. Bennett	1952–73	Robert M. Strachan 1956–69	Jevington Blair Tothill .. 1979–81
Bill Bennett	1973–86	Thomas Berger 1969	Shirley McLoughlin 1981–83
Bill Vander Zalm	1986–91	Dave Barrett 1969–84	Arthur Lee 1984–87
Rita Johnston	1991–92	Bob Skelly 1984–87	Gordon Wilson 1987–93
Jack Weisgerber (interim)	1992–	Michael Harcourt 1987–	Gordon Campbell 1993–

(1) Includes up to 5 most recent leaders of the major parties; for years no leader is listed, the leadership was vacant or there was an interim leader. (2) Known as the Conservative Party until 1946. (3) Known as the Co-operative Commonwealth Federation until 1962. (4) Known as the Conservative Party until 1943. (5) Known as the Co-operative Commonwealth Federation until 1961. (6) Known as the Conservative Party until 1944. (7) Known as the Conservative Party until 1945.

DEFENCE

Canadian security policy is based on three elements: defence and collective security, arms control and disarmament, and the peaceful resolution of disputes. The Department of National Defence and the Canadian Forces support this policy by their contributions to strategic deterrence, conventional defence, sovereignty, peacekeeping and arms control.

In addition, the Department of National Defence provides special support to other government departments in areas such as search and rescue, fisheries patrols, enforcement of drug prohibitions, disaster relief, and aid to civil powers in law enforcement. These tasks are carried out both in emergencies and where it complements military surveillance and control responsibilities.

Canadian Regular Armed Forces Strength

Canada has an all-volunteer Armed Forces which, since 1968, has been a single body composed of what had been a separate army, navy and air force.

	Navy	Army	Air Force	Total Armed Forces		Navy	Army	Air Force	Total Armed Forces
1914	379	3 000	—	3 379	1945	92 529	494 258	174 254	761 041
1915	1 255	81 195	—	82 450	1950	9 259	20 652	17 274	47 185
1916	1 557	274 194	—	275 751	1951	11 082	34 986	22 359	68 427
1917	2 220	304 585	—	306 805	1952	13 505	49 278	32 611	95 394
1918	4 792	326 258	—	331 050	1953	15 546	48 458	40 423	104 427
1919	5 495	228 292	—	233 787	1955	19 207	49 409	49 461	118 077
1920	1 048	4 684	—	5 732	1960	20 675	47 185	51 737	119 597
1925	496	3 410	384	4 290	1965	19 756	46 264	48 144	114 164
1930	783	3 510	844	5 137	1970	—	—	—	93 353
1935	860	3 509	794	5 163	1975	—	—	—	79 817
1939	1 585	4 169	2 191	7 945	1980	—	—	—	80 166
1940	6 135	76 678	9 483	92 296	1985	—	—	—	83 740
1941	17 036	194 774	48 743	260 553	1990	—	—	—	87 976
1942	32 067	311 118	111 223	454 408	1991	—	—	—	87 319
1943	56 259	460 387	176 307	692 953	1992	—	—	—	84 792
1944	81 582	495 804	210 089	787 475	1993	—	—	—	78 376

Source: *Department of National Defence*

Senior Canadian Military Personnel

(as of September 1993)

Chief of the Defence Staff... Admiral John R. Anderson
Vice-Chief of the Defence Staff... Lt.–Gen. P.J. O'Donnell
Deputy Chief of the Defence Staff... Vice-Admiral L.E. Murray
Maritime Command.. Vice-Admiral P.W. Cairns
Maritime Command Pacific .... Rear-Admiral R.C. Waller
Mobile Command .... Lt.-Gen. Gordon Reay
Air Command .... Lt.-Gen. Scott Clements
Canadian Military Representative, North Atlantic Treaty Organization................. Vice-Admiral R.E. George
Deputy Commander-in-Chief, North American Aerospace Defence .... Lt.-Gen. B.L.M. Smith
Commander, Canadian Defence Liaison Staff (London) .... Brig.-Gen. D.M. Dean
Commander, Canadian Defence Liaison Staff (Washington) .... Rear-Admiral K.J. Summers
Chief of Staff to UN Secretary-General .... Maj.-Gen. J.M. Baril
Communication Command .... Brig.-Gen. R.K. Martineau
Canadian Forces Europe.. Brig.-Gen. J.C. Thibault
Training Systems Headquarters .... Brig.-Gen. H.C. Armstrong
Northern Region Headquarters .... Brig.-Gen. R. Dwayne Daly

Source: *Department of National Defence*

Canadian Defence Spending

(millions of dollars; fiscal years ending Mar. 31)

	Spending	%of Govt. spending		Spending	%of Govt. spending		Spending	%of Govt. spending
1910	6	7.4	1942	1 268	67.3	1981	5 049	8.7
1914	14	7.6	1943	2 563	58.4	1982	5 907	9.2
1915	72	29.3	1944	4 242	79.7	1983	7 041	9.7
1916	173	51.2	1945	4 000	76.2	1984	7 840	9.2
1917	312	62.3	1950	387	15.8	1985	8 767	9.3
1918	344	59.9	1951	787	27.1	1986	9 383	9.2
1919	439	63.1	1952	1 447	38.5	1987	9 955	9.3
1920	347	46.9	1953	1 959	42.2	1988	10 340	9.4
1925	13	3.7	1955	1 762	37.8	1989	11 200	9.4
1930	22	5.4	1960	1 537	24.5	1990	11 340	8.7
1935	14	2.9	1965	1 582	19.5	1991	12 005	8.8
1939	35	6.3	1970	1 791	11.9	1992	11 286	9.5
1940	126	18.5	1975	2 361	10.7			
1941	730	58.4	1980	4 375	8.6			

Source: *Department of National Defence*

Canadian Military Ranks

Army/Air Force

General Officers: General, Lieutenant-General, Major-General, Brigadier-General
Senior Officers: Colonel, Lieutenant-Colonel, Major
Junior Officers: Captain, Lieutenant, Second-Lieutenant
Non-commissioned Members: Chief Warrant Officer, Master Warrant Officer, Warrant Officer, Sergeant, Master Corporal, Corporal, Private

Navy

General Officers: Admiral, Vice-Admiral, Rear-Admiral, Commodore
Senior Officers: Captain (N), Commander, Lieutenant-Commander
Junior Officers: Lieutenant (N), Sub-Lieutenant, Acting Sub-Lieutenant
Non-commissioned Members: Chief Petty Officer 1st class, Chief Petty Officer 2nd class, Petty Officer 1st class, Petty Officer 2nd class, Master Seaman, Leading Seaman, Able Seaman

Canadian Forces Stations (CFS)

CFS Aldergrove: P.O. Box 4000, Aldergrove, British Columbia, V0X 1A0
CFS Alert: Belleville, Ontario, K0K 3S0
CFS Carp: P.O. Box 48, Carp, Ontario, K0A 1L0
CFS Debert: Debert, Nova Scotia, B0M 1G0
CFS Flin Flon: P.O. Box 338, Flin Flon, Manitoba, R8A 1N1
CFS Leitrim: P.O. Box 485, Station A, Ottawa, Ontario, K1N 8T3
CFS Masset: P.O. Box 2000, Masset, British Columbia, V0T 1M0
CFS Mill Cove: Hubbards, Nova Scotia, B0J 1T0
CFS St. John's: P.O. Box 2028, St. John's, Newfoundland, A1C 6B5
CFS Shelburne: Shelburne, Nova Scotia, B0T 1W0
Naval Radio Station: Newport Corner, Ellershouse Post Office, Hants County, Nova Scotia

Canadian Forces Bases (CFB) and Detachment Bases (BFC)

BFC Bagotville: .... Alouette, Quebec, G0C 1A0
CFB Borden: .... Borden, Ontario, L0M 1C0
CFB Calgary: .... Calgary, Alberta, T3E 1T8
.... Wainwright Detachment, Denwood, Alberta, T0B 1B0
CFB Chatham: .... Curtis Park, New Brunswick, E0C 2E0
CFB Chilliwack: .... Chilliwack, British Columbia, V0X 2E0
.... Vancouver Detachment, 4050 West 4th Avenue, Vancouver, British Columbia, V6R 1P6
CFB Cold Lake: .... Medley, Alberta, T0A 2M0
CFB Comox: .... Lazo, British Columbia, V0R 2K0
CFB Cornwallis: .... Cornwallis, Nova Scotia, B0S 1H0
CFB Edmonton: .... Lancaster Park, Alberta, T0A 2H0
CFB Esquimalt: .... FMO Victoria, British Columbia, V0S 1B0
.... Nanaimo Detachment, Nanaimo, British Columbia, V9R 5J9
CFB Gagetown: .... Oromocto, New Brunswick, E0G 2P0.
CFB Gander: .... P.O. Box 6000, Gander, Newfoundland, A1V 1X1
CFB Goose Bay: .... Goose Airport—Station A, Goose Bay, Newfoundland, A0P 1S0
CFB Greenwood: .... Greenwood, Nova Scotia, B0P 1N0
CFB Halifax: .... FMO Halifax, Nova Scotia, B3K 2X0
CFB Kingston: .... Kingston, Ontario, K0K 5L0
CFB Lahr[1]: .... CFPO 5000, Belleville, Ontario, K0K 3R0
CFB Moncton: .... Moncton, New Brunswick, E1C 8K4
BFC Montreal: .... St-Hubert, Quebec, J3Y 5T4
CFB Moose Jaw: .... Bushell Park, Saskatchewan, S0H 0N0
.... Dundurn Detachment, Dundurn, Saskatchewan, S0K 1K0
CFB North Bay: .... Hornell Heights, Ontario, P0H 1P0
CFB Ottawa: .... Ottawa, Ontario, K1A 0K5
CFB Petawawa: .... Petawawa, Ontario, K8H 2X3
BFC Saint-Jean: .... Richalain, Quebec, J0J 1R0
CFB Shearwater: .... Shearwater, Nova Scotia, B0J 3A0
CFB Shilo: .... Shilo, Manitoba, R0K 2A0
CFB Suffield: .... Ralston, Alberta, T0J 2N0
CFB Toronto : .... Downsview, Ontario, M3K 1Y6
.... London, Ontario, N5Y 4T7
CFB Trenton: .... Astra, Ontario, K0K 1B0
BFC Valcartier: .... Courcelette, Quebec, G0A 1R0
CFB Winnipeg: .... Westwin, Manitoba, R3J 0T0

(1) Closing Summer 1994

Defence Today

*C*anadian defence policy has changed to meet the realities of the post-Cold War world just as the environment in which Canada seeks its security has been changed by a new combination of factors. Recent events, including the conflicts in Somalia and Yugoslavia, suggest a trend toward instability, however, Canada, through its involvement in multilateral peacekeeping and related operations, is playing a major role in international efforts to address these problems.

The Canadian Forces is a unified tri-service under the Chief of the Defence Staff with navy, army and air force commanders located in Halifax, Montreal and Winnipeg respectively. The Department of National Defence is the military and civilian organization, under the direction of the Minister of National Defence in Ottawa.

At home, the Canadian Forces carry out a number of important roles. As a minimum requirement, the Government of Canada must have at its disposal armed forces that are capable of establishing a presence throughout Canada's territory, airspace and maritime approaches. This applies not only with respect to external intruders, but also to the ability of the Forces to contribute to other national priorities in such areas as search and rescue, fisheries protection, drug interdiction and environmental surveillance.

SOCIAL SECURITY

Canada Assistance Plan

The Canada Assistance Plan (CAP), introduced in 1966, is a cost-shared program in which the federal government pays 50 percent of shareable costs incurred by provinces, territories, and municipalities in providing social assistance and welfare services. The provinces are responsible for the design and administration of social assistance programs. While all these programs have key features in common, each is governed by its own set of regulations and these vary from province to province.

The primary objectives of the CAP are: 1) to support the provision by provinces of adequate assistance and institutional care for persons in need; 2) to support the provinces' ability to provide welfare services which aim to lessen, remove or prevent the causes and effects of poverty, child neglect, or dependence on public assistance.

The principal eligibility criterion for all welfare programs throughout the country is that applicants must be in need of social assistance. "Need" is determined on the basis of a test to ensure that individuals have insufficient means to support themselves and their dependents. The needs test takes into account budgetary requirements as well as the resources available to meet those needs.

Persons who benefit from assistance and welfare services include: one-parent families; mentally and physically disabled persons; the aged; children who are in care or who are in need of protection because of abuse or neglect; the unemployed; families/individuals in crisis; low-income workers; and battered women.

The Plan also provides for the federal government to pay half the shareable costs of work activity projects. Such agreements have been signed with all the provinces but not with the territories. Work activity projects are designed to improve the employability of persons who have difficulty finding or retaining jobs or in undertaking job training.

Source: *Health and Welfare Canada; National Council of Welfare*

Canada Assistance Plan[1] Payments

	Recipients[2]				Expenditures[3] ($000)			
	1970	1980	1990	1992	1970	1980	1990	1992
Canada	1 346 009	1 505 481	1 930 100	2 723 00	456 473	1 894 869	5 502 554	6 130 331
Newfoundland	85 698	53 003	47 900	59 800	20 289	43 187	101 049	132 858
Prince Edward Island	9 404	10 070	8 600	11 800	3 293	10 268	23 881	34 755
Nova Scotia	51 814	56 125	78 400	92 600	15 246	53 670	157 211	217 723
New Brunswick ...	54 343	71 952	67 200	78 200	11 795	66 403	158 936	206 936
Quebec	477 440	562 960	555 900	674 900	162 213	738 583	1 723 610	1 546 500
Ontario	354 913	404 516	675 700	1 184 700	132 257	472 570	1 761 482	2 158 841
Manitoba	58 667	53 439	66 900	80 900	19 260	60 181	194 497	253 126
Saskatchewan	55 578	46 990	54 100	60 400	17 233	60 060	152 857	177 035
Alberta	84 386	94 585	148 800	188 300	31 441	127 388	513 187	623 276
British Columbia ..	113 766	144 454	216 000	279 300	43 086	255 602	693 783	747 342
Yukon Territory	n.a.	7 387[4]	1 000	1 700	360	1 093	5 202	8 170
Northwest Territories	n.a.	7 387[4]	9 600	10 400	n.a.	5 865	16 859	23 774

Source: *Health and Welfare Canada*

(1) Expenditures shown are from the federal government only. (2) As of March. Because individuals may appear in more than one category, double counting may occur. (3) For fiscal years ending Mar. 31. Federal government payments are shown for the years in which they were made to the provinces. Some payments include reimbursements to the provinces for expenditures made during previous fiscal years. (4) Includes Yukon and Northwest Territories. (n.a.) not available or not applicable.

Unemployment Insurance

The Unemployment Insurance program, introduced by the federal government in 1940, has 2 objectives: to provide income protection for workers suffering temporary income interruptions and to facilitate the best possible match between unemployed workers and available jobs. The program covers most workers in Canada, major exclusions being the self-employed (except fishermen who are covered by special arrangement) and those who work less than 15 hours per week and earn less than 20 percent of the maximum insurable earnings ($149.00 per week in 1993).

To qualify for regular UI benefits, claimants must have suffered an interruption of earnings from employment and have accumulated 10 to 20 weeks of insurable employment. To receive benefits, a person must file a claim stating that they are willing to work and are looking for a job. Following a two-week waiting period, claimants are eligible to receive 57% of their average weekly insurable earnings up to a maximum of $425.00 per week in 1993. The longest period for which benefits can be claimed ranges from 17 to 50 weeks, depending on the length of previous employment as well as the regional unemployment rate in the area where they reside.

Maternity and sickness benefits are payable to persons who prove pregnancy or sickness with a medical certificate and who have 20 weeks of insurable employment. A maximum of 15 weeks of maternity benefits are payable as part of initial benefits. There are also 10 weeks of parental benefits which can be paid to the mother or the father of a natural or an adopted baby. To qualify, 20 weeks of insurable employment are also required.

The Unemployment Insurance program is financed through contributions from employer and employee. The basic employee premium rate for 1993 was $3.00 for each $100 of weekly insurable earnings. The employer premium is 1.4 times the employee rate. The maximum weekly insurable earnings in 1993 was $745.00. This amount is adjusted in accordance with the rate of increase in wages and salaries averaged over the most recent eight-year period.

Source: *Employment and Immigration Canada*

Unemployment Insurance Program Payments

Year	Claims[1] (000s)	Benefit payments ($000)	Weeks paid (000s)	Maximum weekly payment	Average weekly payment
1943	36.7	941	85	$14.40	$ 11.12
1945	296.4	14 576	1 224	14.40	11.91
1950	1 150.2	98 994	6 980	21.00	14.18
1955	1 929.8	228 860	12 375	30.00	18.49
1960	2 700.4	481 836	21 592	36.00	22.32
1965	1 628.2	312 110	12 718	36.00	24.54
1970	2 260.8	695 222	19 817	53.00	35.08
1975	2 857.2	3 146 497	37 327	123.00	84.64
1980	2 762.2	4 393 308	36 333	174.00	120.92
1985	3 312.4	10 266 888	59 788	276.00	171.05
1986	3 353.1	10 513 557	58 063	297.00	181.07
1987	3 220.8	10 440 709	54 875	318.00	190.26
1988	3 230.8	10 852 400	53 527	339.00	202.75
1989	3 215.2	11 528 036	53 399	363.00	215.88
1990	3 259.0	13 189 000	57 052	384.00	231.18
1991	3 876.5	17 685 617	71 460	408.00	243.91
1992	3 805.7	19 308 233	73 795	426.00	254.78

Source: *Statistics Canada*

(1) Initial and renewal.

Canada and Quebec Pension Plans

The Canada and Quebec Pension Plans were instituted in 1966 to provide benefits to Canadians who have contributed to the plan during their working lives. Both plans pay a monthly retirement benefit in addition to a one-time death benefit, survivor benefits for the spouse and dependent children of a deceased contributor and benefits to the severely disabled and their families.

Payments to the plan are made by all workers between the ages of 18 and the time they claim retirement (between the ages of 60 and 70). Payments are based on a contribution rate which in 1993 was 5.0 percent of "pensionable earnings." This payment is shared equally by employers and employees; self-employed persons must pay the entire amount themselves. The contribution rate is scheduled to increase steadily, reaching 9.1 percent in 2011. Contributions are not paid if income falls below an annual minimum ($3 300 in 1993) or on income above an annual maximum ($33 400 in 1993).

Retirement benefits from the plan are based on lifetime earnings and generally amount to 25 percent of average annual income, adjusted for inflation. The maximum monthly benefit at age 65 in 1993 was $667.36.

Source: *Health and Welfare Canada*

Spouses in a continuing marriage and partners in a common-law relationship may apply to receive an equal share of the retirement pension earned by both parties during their life together.

A provision that allows divorced couples to divide CPP credits earned during marriage was introduced in 1978. On Jan. 1, 1987, the provision was expanded to include legally-separated married spouses and those living in a common- law union. In March 1991 a further amendment allowed those previously denied a division due to a property waiver to have their situation remedied.

Since Jan. 1987, Canadians eligible for CPP benefits who retire before age 65 can receive partial pensions beginning as early as age 60. Those who begin collecting at 60 receive 70 percent of the amount they would be entitled to at age 65. For each month past age 60 that a person delays retirement, an additional half a percentage point is added—so that someone retiring at age 61 would receive 76 of their full (age 65) pension while someone postponing retirement to age 70 would receive 130 percent.

The Canada Pension Plan is administered by the federal government while the Quebec Pension Plan is administered by the Government of Quebec's Pension Board. Essentially the same rules and benefits apply to each.

Canada and Quebec Pension Plans Payments

	Canada Pension				Quebec Pension Plan			
	Benefi- ciaries[1]	Benefits paid[2] ($000)	Contrib- utors[4] (000s)	Avg. monthly retirement payments[1]	Benefi- ciaries[1] ($000)	Benefits paid[2] (000s)	Contrib- utors[4]	Avg. monthly retirement payments[1]
1971	251 853	$ 89 236	6 755	$ 23	79 649	$ 47 576	2 053	$ 25
1976	774 890	587 834	7 561	67	232 815	266 181	2 601	66
1981	1 274 306	2 010 924	8 626	144	406 069	704 798	2 793	148
1986	1 764 604	4 887 134	8 932	247	627 317	1 899 730	2 921	243
1987	1 974 417	5 721 315	9 269	270	666 847	2 132 658	3 031	258
1988	2 173 225	7 329 222	9 530	289	702 141	2 406 453	3 110	276
1989	2 335 711	8 445 044	9 600	306	736 176	2 663 521	3 152	292
1990	2 463 222	9 472 955	9 603	324	771 838	2 946 125	3 156	307
1991	2 584 986	10 541 912	9 630	342	809 409	3 182 379	3 110	323
1992	2 713 692	11 792 756	n.a.	363	845 846	3 605 378	3 064	341
1993	2 845 059	13 199 084	n.a.	370	883 610	3 860 717	n.a.	349

Source: *Health and Welfare Canada; Régie des Rentes du Québec; Statistics Canada*

(1) As of March. (2) For fiscal years ending Mar. 31. (3) From 1971 to 1978, data is for calendar years; Jan. 1979 to Mar. 1980, data is for 15 months; from 1981 to 1988, data is for fiscal years ending Mar. 31. (4) Calendar years. (n.a.) not available.

Old Age Security, Guaranteed Income Supplement and Spouse's Allowance

The Old Age Security (OAS) program, introduced in 1952, provides pensions to persons 65 years and older who meet Canadian residence requirements. Full monthly pensions ($374.44 per month as of April 1, 1992) are given to persons who have lived in Canada for 40 years since the age of 18; some persons who have lived in Canada for 10 consecutive years are also eligible for full pensions. Partial pensions, introduced in 1977, are based on the number of years a pensioner has lived in Canada.

The Guaranteed Income Supplement (GIS) was introduced in 1966 to assist those with little or no income other than their OAS pension. The amount of income supplement depends upon the pensioner's income, marital status and spouse's income. Generally, the maximum GIS payment is reduced by $1 for every $2 of income a pensioner has above his/her old age security pension. For example, in April 1993 a single pensioner with no personal income received OAS benefits of $381.60 per month and an income supplement of $453.49 per month. If this person had a private pension of $400 per month, the GIS would be reduced $200 to $253.49 per month.

Spouse's Allowance (SPA) benefits are payable to persons aged 60 to 64 whose spouses have died or those with low income whose spouse receives an Old Age Security pension. Like Guaranteed Income Supplement benefits, the amount of the SPA benefit is dependent on income and marital status. The maximum SPA benefit payable in April 1993 was $747.39 for widows and widowers and $676.99 for spouses of OAS pensioners.

Source: *Health and Welfare Canada*

Old Age Security Program Payments

	Number of Recipients[1] (000s)			Net Payments[2] ($000 000)			Average Yearly[3] payment per pensioner		
	OAS	GIS	SPA	OAS	GIS	SPA	OAS	GIS	SPA
1952	$643	$n.a.	$n.a.	$76	$n.a.	$n.a.	$n.a.	$n.a.	$n.a.
1961	905	n.a.	n.a.	592	n.a.	n.a.	n.a.	n.a.	n.a.
1966	1 106	n.a.	n.a.	927	n.a.	n.a.	n.a.	n.a.	n.a.
1971	1 720	860	n.a.	1 627	280	n.a.	956	340	n.a.
1976	1 957	1 087	54	2 976	923	35	1 537	863	1 788
1981	2 303	1 245	85	5 322	1 918	178	2 338	1 592	2 168
1986	2 652	1 330	142	8 858	3 319	348	3 385	2 555	3 105
1987	2 749	1 345	144	9 520	3 451	473	3 517	2 615	3 375
1988	2 835	1 357	140	10 248	3 618	483	3 659	2 702	3 474
1989	2 919	1 364	134	10 963	3 766	473	3 803	2 803	3 538
1990	3 006	1 359	127	11 804	3 888	461	3 974	2 907	3 652
1991	3 099	1 346	121	12 705	3 976	450	4 153	3 009	3 759
1992	3 180	1 329	116	13 808	4 139	446	4 386	3 171	3 927
1993	3 264	1 331	113	14 421	4 250	435	4 464	3 268	3 964

Source: *Health and Welfare Canada*

(1) As of March. (2) For fiscal years ending Mar. 31. (3) For fiscal years ending Mar. 31 using annual average number of recipients. (n.a.) not available or not applicable; OAS = Old Age Security; GIS = Guaranteed Income Supplement; SPA = Spouse's Allowance.

Veterans' Allowances and Disability Pensions

The War Veterans Allowances Act, approved in 1930, gives benefits to Canadian veterans who suffered disabilities or are unable to work as a result of injuries sustained in World War I, World War II or the Korean War. To qualify, the veteran must have lived in Canada for at least 10 years, be 60 years or older (younger if medical reasons warrant), and have little or no income. In June 1992, the maximum monthly allowance was $895.02 for a single veteran and $1 358.93 for a married veteran.

Source: *Health and Welfare Canada*

Allowances are also paid to civilians who served alongside the armed forces during a war; these include firefighters and the merchant marine. Counselling services, treatment services and emergency funds are also available to veterans and their spouses and children.

The Pension Act, 1919, gives compensation to armed forces personnel for disability or death related to military service. Since 1962, benefits have also been paid to civilians working with the armed forces during wartime. In some cases, benefits are paid to veterans of Commonwealth forces. The amount of the monthly pension varies according to the disability.

Number of Veterans Receiving Benefits

Year[1]	Disability Pensions[2] (by period of service)					Veterans Allowances		
	World War I	World War II	Korean War	Peacetime service	Surviving dependants	Veterans	Veterans' surviving dependants	Civilians[3]
1946	72 396	36 454	—	—	33 821	25 030	3 282	n.a.
1951	66 001	95 650	—	—	34 009	30 608	7 992	n.a.
1961	45 588	105 338	1 651	1 389	32 699	47 865	21 681	n.a.
1966	33 688	106 191	1 843	2 133	30 712	55 947	29 888	1 318
1971	22 298	102 666	2 010	3 344	28 808	48 384	32 749	2 822
1976	12 404	96 776	2 084	4 106	26 884	47 999	37 297	4 075
1981	6 581	90 840	2 139	5 793	25 141	51 175	38 897	4 446
1986	2 669	84 237	2 204	8 883	42 969	47 455	31 852	4 519
1987	2 123	83 153	2 125	9 842	43 691	47 101	30 891	4 408
1988	1 672	81 705	2 225	10 848	44 573	40 385	28 093	4 180
1989	1 319	80 295	2 251	11 870	45 467	34 226	26 153	3 903
1990	981	78 657	2 275	13 038	49 772	28 990	24 102	3 655
1991	732	77 203	2 271	14 314	52 515	23 852	22 039	3 293
1992	549	75 563	2 251	15 516	54 074	19 809	20 189	2 978
1993	387	73 573	2 245	16 754	54 805	16 591	18 544	2 808

Source: *Veterans Affairs Canada*

(1) As of March. (2) Includes recipients of Civilian War Disability pensions. (3) Includes surviving dependants. (—) = zero. (n.a.) not available.

Invasion of Sicily

*T*he fiftieth anniversary of the invasion of Sicily—the first major offensive of the Second World War—was on July 10, 1993. In 1943, 27,000 Canadian troops, mostly from the 1st Canadian Infantry Division and the 1st Army Tank Brigade, joined members of the British and American armies in a massive attack of the island.

The Canadians captured an airfield and a series of towns during the operation, which ended in victory on August 17.

Health Care

Total Estimated Provincial Health Care Expenditures[1], 1975–90

(millions of dollars)

Year	Nfld.	PEI	NS	NB	Quebec	Ontario
1975	207.5	43.5	281.5	215.1	2 661.5	3 271.0
1976	223.0	46.1	312.1	251.8	3 076.7	3 729.5
1977	237.0	51.8	344.7	278.7	3 333.9	3 999.2
1978	265.6	58.0	381.2	306.2	3 771.7	4 309.9
1979	308.1	64.2	426.7	347.2	4 194.2	4 655.4
1980	346.7	75.6	493.5	411.5	4 746.4	5 339.1
1981	409.3	87.1	610.8	501.0	5 442.9	6 319.1
1982	479.7	102.5	701.5	606.5	6 273.0	7 372.4
1983	528.1	112.1	763.9	634.9	6 823.3	8 240.9
1984	537.1	118.3	840.0	684.5	7 194.0	9 029.7
1985	570.7	124.7	908.3	720.1	7 625.7	9 993.4
1986	626.6	134.2	952.4	772.9	8 186.1	11 338.3
1987	673.2	145.4	1 033.3	860.4	8 950.7	12 502.2
1988	725.1	157.5	1 131.3	923.7	9 622.6	13 590.7
1989	774.7	170.6	1 240.3	1 012.7	10 378.3	15 282.1
1990	862.8	181.8	1 336.1	1 081.7	11 138.7	16 283.8

Year	Manitoba	Sask.	Alberta	BC	Yukon	NWT
1975	397.5	316.5	736.4	994.3	6.4	16.1
1976	467.1	380.5	836.7	1 118.8	9.6	19.9
1977	507.9	421.7	893.2	1 225.3	10.1	24.6
1978	531.2	454.7	1 063.5	1 418.7	11.8	29.2
1979	583.3	527.2	1 324.0	1 610.4	12.5	27.5
1980	676.8	631.2	1 573.3	2 049.5	14.0	29.9
1981	819.2	737.0	1 972.0	2 495.1	15.4	37.4
1982	948.0	900.9	2 579.5	2 807.7	24.7	55.6
1983	1 046.8	988.3	2 834.8	2 986.8	22.1	58.5
1984	1 121.7	1 035.5	2 848.5	3 120.9	24.0	63.1
1985	1 204.0	1 124.3	3 099.4	3 243.9	25.2	74.8
1986	1 292.6	1 262.0	3 391.5	3 516.3	28.4	96.6
1987	1 390.0	1 257.1	3 282.3	3 724.4	29.7	108.4
1988	1 487.4	1 313.5	3 585.2	4 051.1	34.7	163.6
1989	1 610.1	1 452.8	3 942.4	4 516.1	36.7	178.2
1990	1 741.9	1 658.1	4 127.9	5 119.8	n.a.	n.a.

Source: *Health and Welfare Canada*

(1) All health care expenditures made by the provinces including the respending of federal contributions. It does not include the spending of federal government departments (federal direct), WCB expenditures nor expenditures by local governments, private or company health insurance plans or out-of-pocket spending by individuals.

Total Estimated Provincial Health Expenditures by Function

(millions of dollars)

Year	Hospital Services	Medical Services	Extended Health Services	Other Health Services	Total[1]
1975	5 207.0	1 847.7	909.1	1 269.0	9 232.7
1976	5 967.5	2 061.3	1 114.6	1 407.6	10 550.9
1977	6 234.1	2 268.4	1 283.6	1 640.8	11 426.9
1978	6 804.0	2 569.6	1 506.0	1 857.4	12 737.0
1979	7 466.3	2 842.7	1 742.9	2 209.8	14 261.7
1980	8 751.3	3 323.3	2 027.1	2 566.5	16 668.3
1981	10 278.6	3 885.1	2 453.1	3 111.5	19 728.2
1982	12 142.4	4 473.3	2 746.9	3 638.2	23 000.8
1983	11 804.3	4 736.8	2 789.3	3 671.1	23 001.5
1984	13 703.3	5 507.5	3 137.1	4 413.5	26 761.4
1985	14 546.8	6 019.3	3 341.6	4 969.0	28 876.7
1986	15 884.6	6 708.0	3 628.5	5 603.1	31 824.2
1987	17 081.6	7 369.2	3 973.2	5 758.6	34 182.5
1988	18 365.4	7 931.7	4 461.6	6 288.6	37 047.2
1989	20 233.3	8 488.8	4 921.9	7 215.0	40 859.0

Source: *Health and Welfare Canada*

(1) Total may differ due to rounding.

Federal Contributions as a Percentage of Provincial Expenditures

Year	Nfld	PEI	NS	NB	Que	Ont
1974	39.1	43.8	42.4	46.1	38.8	37.0
1979	48.3	50.6	51.2	52.3	40.6	47.5
1984	46.5	46.0	44.1	44.2	39.0	41.1
1989	42.0	43.2	40.0	39.4	36.2	34.8

Year	Manitoba	Alberta	Sask	BC	Yukon	NWT	Total
1974	39.4	44.0	37.3	38.9	51.6	40.1	38.6
1979	45.8	46.6	42.7	42.5	48.9	42.1	44.0
1984	39.8	42.3	34.6	38.5	38.7	33.4	39.6
1989	37.2	38.5	34.3	37.8	38.1	16.4	35.8

Source: *Health and Welfare Canada*

CRIME AND JUSTICE

Canadian Law Enforcement

Policing in most Canadian provinces is carried out by municipal police forces and the Royal Canadian Mounted Police (R.C.M.P.). In addition, Ontario, Quebec and New-foundland have their own provincial forces. The two territories are policed solely by the R.C.M.P. In 1991 there were 56 774 police officers in Canada.

■ Municipal Police Forces

Each city and town is required by provincial law to have enough police to maintain law and order. Municipalities will either operate their own police forces, or contract with the R.C.M.P. or the provincial police force to provide the necessary police. In 1991 there were 31 790 independent municipal police officers.

■ Royal Canadian Mounted Police

The R.C.M.P. was founded as the North-West Mounted Police in 1873. The force is maintained by the federal government, and is the responsibility of the federal solicitor general. The R.C.M.P. has contracts with every province except Ontario and Quebec to provide police services to communities that do not maintain their own police forces. In those communities, the R.C.M.P. enforces all laws—federal, provincial and municipal. In 1991 there were 15 555 R.C.M.P. officers.

■ Ontario Provincial Police

The Ontario Provincial Police force is operated by the provincial government, and is the responsibility of Ontario's solicitor general. The O.P.P. enforces the Criminal Code and provincial statutes in those parts of Ontario where provincial law does not require municipal police forces. The force also maintains a traffic patrol on many of the province's highways, and enforces the Liquor Licence Act. As well, the O.P.P. provides municipal policing under contract. In 1991 there were 4 630 O.P.P. officers.

■ Quebec Police Force

The Quebec Police Force is similar to the O.P.P. in that it is a provincial force, with jurisdiction throughout the province. The force is responsible to Quebec's attorney general, and has a mandate to maintain peace, order and public safety throughout Quebec. It enforces criminal and provincial laws. In 1991 there were 4 431 Quebec Police Force officers.

■ Royal Newfoundland Constabulary

The Royal Newfoundland Constabulary (R.N.C.) was created in 1872. Although technically a provincial police force, R.N.C. policing is confined to the urban centres of St. John's, Labrador City and Corner Brook. The remainder of the province is policed by the R.C.M.P. In 1991 there were 368 R.N.C. officers.

Youth Crime

679,000 federal charges were laid in Canada in 1991 and 22% of them were against youth between the ages of 12 and 17. (Children under 12 are dealt with under provincial child welfare legislation.) 13% of the youth charges (18,800) were violence-related, an increase of 102% over the 9,300 violence-related charges laid in 1986, although the size of the population between 12 and 17 decreased 1.8% during the same period. By comparison, between 1986 and 1991, the rate of charges for violent offences laid against adults rose 45%.

Nearly half of the violent offence charges against youth were for minor assaults. By contrast, murder charges represented only a small proportion of the youth court cases (0.04%).

Over half of the youth accused in violent offence cases in 1991 were either 16 or 17 years old; 35% were 14-15 and and the remainder of the charges were against 12 and 13 year-olds. The majority of the accused were male (82%) although violent offence charges against females have increased from 15% in 1986 to 18% in 1991.

Number of Police[1], by Province

	1965		1975		1985		1991[5]	
	Police officers	Population per police officer	Police officers	Population per police officer	Police officers	Population per police officer	Police officers	Population per police officer
Canada[2]	32 010	620	50 663	452	53 464	477	56 774	476
Newfoundland	521	940	777	714	927	626	917	625
Prince Edward Is.	104	1 038	198	596	180	711	188	695
Nova Scotia	889	848	1 197	690	1 439	614	1 542	584
New Brunswick	582	1 058	1 105	610	1 175	613	1 298	560
Quebec	9 531	602	14 526	428	13 893	476	14 575	470
Ontario[3]	10 773	639	17 439	472	18 461	495	21 210	467
Manitoba	1 184	813	2 036	500	2 086	516	2 193	498
Saskatchewan[4]	1 114	855	1 846	497	1 964	519	1 996	498
Alberta	1 956	744	3 362	540	4 526	557	4 526	557
British Columbia	2 599	711	4 728	520	5 784	501	6 149	523
Yukon	56	268	83	263	116	196	117	230
Northwest Terr.	128	219	185	229	232	219	238	230

Source: *Statistics Canada*

(1) Full-time police officers as of Sept. 30, 1991. (2) Until 1987, this total included RCMP officers from HQ, N, and Depot Divisions, and police officers from CN Railways, CP Railways and Ports Canada. Beginning in 1987, officers from CN, CP, and Ports Canada were no longer included in this total. (3) Excludes police officers from RCMP HQ. (4) Excludes police officers from the RCMP Training Depot. (5) Preliminary figures.

Number of Inmates in Canadian Prisons[1]

Year	Federal prisons	Provincial prisons	Year	Federal prisons	Provincial prisons
1960	6 738	10 896	1986	11 106	15 787
1965	7 518	12 627	1987	10 557	16 077
1970	7 375	12 124	1988	11 030	16 436
1975	8 456	11 277	1989	11 415	18 116
1980	8 651	13 851	1990	11 289	17 944
1985	11 214	16 178	1991	11 783	18 944

Source: *Statistics Canada*   (1) Average number of offenders in custody daily during the fiscal year.

Homicides[1] in Canada, 1961–91

	Canada	Nfld	PEI	NS	NB	Que	Ont	Man	Sask	Alta	BC	Yukon	NWT
1961	233	1	1	6	2	52	89	15	14	18	34	1	—
1966	250	3	1	9	6	56	71	17	12	27	48	—	—
1971	473	2	—	16	10	124	151	33	29	45	61	—	2
1976	668	6	2	25	14	205	183	31	34	68	88	4	8
1981	648	4	1	11	17	186	170	41	29	73	110	1	5
1986	569	4	—	15	12	156	139	47	26	64	89	3	14
1987	642	5	—	14	20	174	204	44	30	73	76	—	2
1988	575	7	1	11	8	154	186	31	23	66	79	1	8
1989	649	4	1	15	18	214	170	43	22	65	89	2	6
1990	656	—	1	9	12	181	182	39	36	74	110	1	11
1991	753	11	2	21	17	180	244	43	21	84	127	—	3

Source: *Statistics Canada*

(1) Includes offences of murder, manslaughter and infanticide. One "offence" is counted for each victim. (—) = zero.

Canadian Criminal Offences and Crime Rate

There were more than 2.8 million Criminal Code non-traffic offences in 1991—an increase of eight percent over the previous year. The violent crime rate increased by eight percent over 1990, while the property crime rate increased nine percent.

Criminal Code offence rates increased in all provinces from 1990 to 1991. The rate for Narcotic Control Act offences decreased by five percent over the previous year.

	1991				
	No. of offences	Adults Charged male	female	Youth charged	Crime rate[1]
Total criminal code offences....................	2 898 814	397 457	83 773	208 702	10 736
Total crimes of violence........................	*296 838*	*109 762*	*12 915*	*26 827*	*1 099*
Homicides	753	508	47	54	3
Attempted murder	1 044	714	69	67	4
Assault[2]	256 790	99 576	12 126	23 349	950
Other sexual offences	3 933	1160	34	283	15
Abduction....................................	1 093	176	73	10	4
Robbery......................................	33 225	7 628	566	3 064	123
Total Property Crimes	*1 726 726*	*156 734*	*47 510*	*128 144*	*6 395*
Breaking and entering	434 600	37 479	1 732	34 495	1 610
Theft-motor vehicle	139 310	9 953	606	11 228	516
Theft-over $1,000............................	117 554	6 177	1 345	2 732	435
Theft-$1,000 or under	864 351	60 153	30 096	66 966	3 201
Possession of stolen goods	34 020	14 526	1 975	8 312	126
Fraud..	136 891	28 446	11 756	4 411	507
Total Other Crimes	*875 250*	*130 961*	*23 348*	*53 731*	*3 242*
Prostitution	10 568	5 075	5 596	500	39
Gaming and betting	1 386	1 061	156	11	5
Offensive weapons..........................	19 702	7 236	549	3 023	74
Other criminal code offences	843 594	117 589	17 047	50 197	3 124
Federal statutes[3]	**93 751**	**42 946**	**6 465**	**6 185**	**347**
Total Drug-related Offences	*57 123*	*35 549*	*5 321*	*3 249*	*212*
Heroin.......................................	1 363	735	258	12	5
Cocaine......................................	16 135	10 026	1 802	336	60
Other drugs..................................	4 148	2 088	303	239	15
Cannabis	33 275	21 724	2 819	2 466	123
Controlled drugs (trafficking).................	630	141	48	15	2
Restricted drugs.............................	1 572	835	91	181	6
Provincial statutes.............................	343 244	176 818	23 489	28 991	1 271
Municipal by-laws.............................	102 570	23 469	4 269	4 133	380
All offences	**3 438 199**	**640 690**	**117 996**	**248 011**	**12 734**

	1971				
	No. of offences	Adults Charged male	female	Youth charged	Crime rate[1]
Total criminal code offences....................	259 431	180 469	24 774	54 188	1 365.7
Total crimes of violence........................	*38 756*	*33 644*	*2 214*	*2 898*	*203.9*
Homicides	415	353	43	19	2.1
Attempted murder	278	235	33	10	1.5
Assault[2]	30 207	26 614	1 890	1 703	159
Other sexual offences	3 448	3 041	31	376	18.1
Robbery......................................	4 408	3 401	217	790	23.2
Total Property Crimes	*147 833*	*88 897*	*15 692*	*43 244*	*778.3*
Breaking and entering	36 512	20 884	639	14 989	192.2
Theft-motor vehicle	13 905	8 496	231	5 178	73.2
Theft-over $50	17 888	11 702	1 523	4 663	94.2 ▶

▶ Theft-$50 or under	52 127	25 910	10 166	16 051	274.4
Possession of stolen goods	9 965	7 584	658	1 723	52.5
Fraud	17 436	14 321	2 475	640	91.8
Total Other Crimes	*72 842*	*57 928*	*6 868*	*8 046*	*383.5*
Prostitution	2 011	401	1 595	15	10.6
Gaming and betting	3 137	2 885	231	21	16.5
Offensive weapons	4 738	4 220	178	340	24.9
Other criminal code offences	62 974	50 422	4 864	7 688	331.5
Federal statutes[3]	**21 897**	**19 669**	**1 184**	**1 044**	**115.3**
Total Drug-related Offences	16 397	13 499	1 630	1 268	86.2
LSD	2 134	1 751	162	221	11.2
Addicting drugs	1 168	903	237	28	6.1
Cannabis	12 453	10 314	1 143	996	65.5
Controlled drugs (trafficking)	642	531	88	23	3.4
Provincial statutes	236 024	211 955	15 209	8 860	1 242.3
Municipal by-laws	43 152	36 521	5 286	1 345	227.1
All offences	**560 504**	**448 614**	**46 453**	**65 437**	**2 950.4**

Source: *Statistics Canada*

(1) Per 100 000 population. (2) Includes sexual assault. (3) Also includes Bankruptcy Act, Canada Shipping Act, Customs Act, Excise Act, Immigration Act and other federal statutes

PUBLIC WORKS

Public Works Canada (PWC) was established to provide for the federal government's office and other properties and to offer expert advice and services concerning the provision, management, operation and disposal of federal property.

PWC acts as custodian of federal office buildings, specified land, bridges, highways, dry docks and dams, and the Parliamentary Precinct. The department is also a service agency that provides architectural and engineering services for planning, design, construction and project management of federal facilities; dredging and fleet services; real estate services such as appraisals and legal surveys of real property, market and investment analyses, acquisitions and disposals; and property management services.

PWC administers the following parliamentary statutes: Bridges Act, Dry Dock Subsidies Act, Expropriation Act, Government Property Traffic Act, Government Works Tolls Act, Municipal Grants Act, Ottawa River Act, Public Lands Grants Act, Public Works Act, Public Works Health Act, Surplus Crown Assets Act and Trans-Canada Highway Act.

Major Projects Completed or Ongoing in 1990-91

	Number of Projects	Estimated Cost ($M)
Atlantic Region		
New Brunswick, Prince Edward Island, Nova Scotia, Newfoundland	16	$ 154.3
Quebec Region	15	219.9
National Capital Region		
Ottawa-Hull to Rouyn-Noranda; from Cornwall to Gananoque	10	169.1
Ontario Region	10	201.9
Western Region		
Alberta, Saskatchewan, Manitoba, Northwest Territories	18	390.1
Pacific Region		
British Columbia, Yukon Territory	26	142.0

Source: *Public Works Canada*

Largest Projects by Region

Region	Client	Project	Estimated Cost ($M)
☐ Atlantic	RCMP	RCMP "B" Division HQ, St. John's, Newfoundland	$ 31.0
☐ Quebec	Canadian Space Agency	Space Agency HQ, St-Hubert, Quebec	72.2
☐ National Capital	Public Works Canada	National Archives Facility, Gatineau, Quebec	89.0
☐ Ontario	Department of National Defence	Land Militia Base, CFB Meaford	66.0
☐ Western	Health and Welfare and Agriculture Canada	Disease Control Centre, Winnipeg, Man. and Ottawa, Ont.	184.0
☐ Pacific	Public Works Canada	Alaska Highway Maintenance, British Columbia and Yukon	25.0

Source: *Public Works Canada*

FOREIGN AID

Canadian Official Development Assistance (ODA) totalled $3.1 billion in the 1990–91 fiscal year. About 78 percent of ODA is distributed through the Canadian International Development Agency (CIDA), whose primary goal is to help the poorest countries and people in the world to help themselves. CIDA places special priority on alleviating poverty, improving economic management, promoting the increased participation of women in development programs, encouraging environmentally sound development and ensuring secure food and energy supplies.

Canada's foreign aid projects started with contributions to the United Nations during the 1940s. In 1950, Canada supported the Colombo Plan, assistance aimed at the newly-independent Asian nations of India, Pakistan and Ceylon (now Sri Lanka). During the next 2 decades, Canadian aid expanded to include the Caribbean (1958), Commonwealth Africa (1959), Francophone Africa (1961) and Latin America (1964).

By the time CIDA was created in 1968, Canadian foreign aid had begun focussing on self-sufficiency rather than its earlier goal of encouraging rapid industrial development. During the 1970s, Canadian aid was aimed at improving social conditions in very poor countries by assisting in such areas as rural planning and public health.

Canadian Expenditure on Foreign Aid, 1950-1991

(millions of dollars)

	Foreign aid[1]	% of GNP		Foreign aid[1]	% of GNP		Foreign aid[1]	% of GNP
1950	13	.08	1964	65	.14	1978	1 050	.49
1951	13	.07	1965	101	.20	1979	1 166	.49
1952	27	.12	1966	123	.22	1980	1 291	.47
1953	8	.03	1967	214	.34	1981	1 307	.43
1954	14	.05	1968	193	.29	1982	1 489	.43
1955	16	.06	1969	212	.28	1983	1 670	.46
1956	29	.10	1970	279	.34	1984	1 812	.45
1957	30	.09	1971	346	.40	1985	2 097	.49
1958	62	.18	1972	398	.41	1986	2 174	.46
1959	72	.20	1973	525	.47	1987	2 522	.50
1960	70	.19	1974	591	.46	1988	2 624	.48
1961	76	.20	1975	750	.49	1989	2 947	.49
1962	61	.15	1976	910	.53	1990	2 850	.45
1963	58	.13	1977	972	.49	1991	3 021	.45
						1992	2 787	.41

Source: *Canadian International Development Agency*   (1) For fiscal year ending Mar. 31.

Canadian Foreign Aid, by Country

(millions of dollars; for fiscal year ending Mar. 31)

Country	1970[1]	1975[1]	1980[1]	1985[1]	1990[2]	1991[2]
Africa	**37.39**	**208.01**	**285.67**	**548.28**	**1 064.41**	**1 109.62**
Algeria	3.91	9.21	0.88	5.84	4.36	5.84
Angola	—	—	—	1.85	13.06	14.02
Botswana	—	7.20	3.56	7.56	16.29	10.99
Burkina Faso	—	4.02	18.09	11.21	22.52	24.22
Cameroon	2.29	4.58	15.29	33.36	44.92	43.18
Côte d'Ivoire	1.11	4.24	16.99	17.88	18.79	17.41
Egypt	—	—	27.78	10.73	37.72	46.49
Ethiopia	0.03	6.47	2.09	47.00	57.98	70.36
Gabon	n.a.	0.77	—	0.87	12.07	10.06
Ghana	4.44	13.17	17.97	45.97	63.53	56.68
Guinea	—	0.51	0.05	18.06	15.32	12.43
Kenya	1.99	5.20	12.78	38.71	35.74	49.34
Lesotho	—	0.62	7.02	4.67	12.49	10.63
Madagascar	0.25	0.48	3.86	1.03	16.40	14.34
Malawi	—	9.11	15.96	4.31	17.62	30.09
Mali	—	6.57	12.79	14.43	41.37	39.96
Morocco	0.50	4.86	2.58	8.58	39.73	50.75
Mozambique	—	—	0.06	13.14	41.86	46.22
Namibia	—	0.02	0.02	0.15	2.81	3.47
Niger	1.11	16.84	4.08	21.87	29.23	23.37
Nigeria	4.63	10.20	0.56	1.70	5.42	4.99
Rwanda	0.86	3.68	5.84	15.03	28.54	31.62
Senegal	1.98	5.69	8.76	20.35	79.66	44.11
Somalia	n.a.	n.a.	n.a.	n.a.	22.37	14.82
South Africa	n.a.	—	—	0.98	8.52	10.61
Sudan	—	—	2.40	22.19	30.95	43.58
Tanzania	2.24	38.34	27.64	44.93	46.53	54.48
Tunisia	7.24	11.72	10.87	6.53	10.97	12.83
Uganda	1.17	0.36	0.27	3.83	20.87	30.27
Zaire	0.96	6.33	8.18	24.33	48.73	36.30
Zambia	—	4.39	15.98	22.89	20.72	28.64
Zimbabwe	—	0.01	0.04	18.07	19.99	23.62
Asia	**140.93**	**244.25**	**234.62**	**410.85**	**812.04**	**822.85**
Afghanistan	0.02	1.78	7.02	n.a.	3.58	17.42
Bangladesh	—	69.13	65.18	105.76	201.03	190.47
China	—	—	—	13.51	94.87	124.53
India	88.61	96.40	42.60	90.08	93.15	83.96
Indonesia	2.33	19.52	11.75	37.05	73.77	59.60
Jordan	n.a.	—	—	0.66	22.95	24.80
Malaysia	1.57	1.61	1.75	3.17	8.28	9.77
Myanmar (Burma)	—	1.39	6.33	3.22	15.19	8.66
Nepal	—	0.07	6.74	10.08	28.13	30.37
Pakistan	32.76	32.23	67.17	66.30	99.07	73.10
Philippines	—	0.02	0.37	8.34	44.62	40.62
Sri Lanka	6.40	10.84	15.94	37.97	31.75	25.64
Thailand	2.26	0.41	6.79	22.02	36.19	38.29
Americas[3]	**n.a.**	**n.a.**	**66.18**	**197.93**	**343.3**	**348.55**
Argentina	n.a.	—	—	1.80	5.14	5.75
Bolivia	n.a.	0.99	1.01	3.28	19.17	25.72
Brazil	n.a.	1.44	2.39	8.38	14.31	11.87 ▶

Country	1970[1]	1975[1]	1980[1]	1985[1]	1990[2]	1991[2]
Chile	n.a.	0.30	—	4.67	6.00	5.84
Colombia	n.a.	1.74	7.11	7.97	20.10	15.76
Costa Rica	n.a.	0.15	0.17	8.07	16.17	10.64
Dominica	n.a.	0.56	1.95	9.57	7.17	3.51
Dominican Republic	n.a.	3.71	0.34	5.00	4.55	4.40
Ecuador	n.a.	3.33	0.30	1.58	6.95	9.84
El Salvador	n.a.	1.42	1.37	1.51	6.08	6.88
Guatemala	n.a.	0.02	2.94	2.39	7.65	7.38
Guyana	2.15	4.05	5.95	2.15	20.60	16.62
Haiti	n.a.	1.34	7.59	8.77	22.10	21.81
Honduras	n.a.	2.19	4.62	20.45	11.20	12.91
Jamaica	2.72	3.11	7.76	29.11	39.65	42.14
Mexico	n.a.	—	—	1.78	6.49	7.17
Nicaragua	n.a.	1.02	0.20	8.52	10.15	19.35
Peru	n.a.	1.61	4.02	16.90	30.59	30.51
Trinidad & Tobago	2.15	0.65	—	0.60	4.16	3.44
Oceania	**n.a.**	**n.a.**	**0.42**	**3.05**	**19.17**	**15.53**

Source: *Canadian International Development Agency*

(1) Includes only country-to-country aid—i.e., Canadian aid to specified countries. It does not include Canadian aid to international organizations such as the United Nations relief programs, international financial institutions dealing with foreign aid and the World Food Program. Country-to-country aid represents about ⅔ of all Canadian foreign aid. Includes only countries with $2.5 million or more in aid. (2) Includes country-to-country and multi-lateral aid to international organizations. (3) Includes Central America, the Caribbean and South America; — = zero; n.a. not available.

How We Compare – World Assistance to Developing Countries

(millions of U.S. dollars)

	1965		1975		1980		1985		1990	
Donor Country	Foreign aid	% of GNP[1]	Foreign aid	% of GNP[1]	Foreign aid	% of GNP[1]	Foreign aid	% of GNP[1]	Foreign aid	% of GNP[1]
Algeria	n.a.	n.a.	41	0.28	81	0.20	54	0.10	7	0.03
Australia	119	0.53	552	0.65	667	0.48	749	0.48	955	0.34
Austria	10	0.11	79	0.21	178	0.23	248	0.38	394	0.25
Belgium	102	0.60	378	0.59	595	0.50	440	0.55	889	0.45
Canada	**96**	**0.19**	**880**	**0.54**	**1 075**	**0.43**	**1 631**	**0.49**	**2 470**	**0.44**
Denmark	13	0.13	205	0.58	481	0.74	440	0.80	1 171	0.93
France	752	0.76	2 093	0.62	4 162	0.63	3 995	0.78	9 380	0.79
Italy	60	0.10	182	0.11	683	0.15	1 098	0.26	3 395	0.32
Japan	244	0.27	1 148	0.23	3 353	0.32	3 797	0.29	9 069	0.31
Kuwait	n.a.	n.a.	946	7.18	1 140	3.52	771	3.17	1 666	...
Libya	n.a.	n.a.	259	2.29	376	1.16	57	0.24	4	0.01
Netherlands	70	0.36	608	0.75	1 630	0.97	1 136	0.91	2 529	0.94
New Zealand	n.a.	n.a.	66	0.52	72	0.33	54	0.25	95	0.23
Nigeria	n.a.	n.a.	14	0.04	35	0.04	45	0.06	13	0.06
Norway	11	0.16	184	0.66	486	0.87	574	1.01	1 205	1.17
Qatar	n.a.	n.a.	338	15.58	277	4.16	8	0.15	1	0.02
Saudi Arabia	n.a.	n.a.	2 756	7.76	5 682	4.87	2 630	2.98	3 692	3.90
Sweden	38	0.19	566	0.82	962	0.78	840	0.86	2 012	0.90
Switzerland	12	0.09	104	0.19	253	0.24	302	0.31	750	0.31
United Arab Emirates	n.a.	n.a.	1 046	11.68	1 118	4.21	122	0.45	888	2.65
United Kingdom	472	0.47	904	0.39	1 854	0.35	1 530	0.33	2 638	0.27
United States	4 023	0.58	4 161	0.27	7 138	0.27	9 403	0.24	11 394	0.21
Venezuela	n.a.	n.a.	31	0.11	135	0.23	32	...	15	0.03
West Germany	456	0.40	1 689	0.40	3 567	0.44	2 942	0.47	6 320	0.42

Source: *World Development Report 1991, World Bank*

(1) Gross National Product. (n.a.) not available. (...) = too small to be included.

THE ECONOMY

Understanding the Economy: A Glossary of Terms

Appreciation: the increase in the value of a currency relative to other currencies under free market conditions.

Balanced budget: when a government's budget is balanced, all revenues equal expenditures in a budget year. Thus there is no surplus or deficit, but a national debt may still exist.

Balance of payments: a measure of all yearly business transactions between one country and the rest of the world. It is the difference between the value of exports and imports, as well as the difference between investment money coming into and leaving the country.

Bank of Canada: the sole money-issuing bank in Canada, acting as banker to all other financial institutions and the government. It is responsible for Canada's banking system, sets interest rates and regulates the money supply.

Bank rate: the interest rate at which the Bank of Canada is prepared to lend money to the chartered banks.

Cartel: a group of companies in a specific industry which band together to restrict output and increase prices in order to get higher profits. In Canada, cartels are illegal. The best known international cartel is the Organization of Petroleum Exporting Countries (OPEC).

Consumer price index: an indexed measure of the average prices of household goods to show inflationary trends; compiled monthly by Statistics Canada.

Cost of living: the cost of maintaining a particular standard of living measured in terms of purchased goods and services. The rise in the cost of living is the same as the rate of inflation.

Deficit spending: the practice whereby a government goes into debt to finance some of its expenditures.

Demand-side economics: a school of thinking which states that an economy can prosper through policies which tend to increase public and private spending on goods and services.

Depreciation: the decrease in the value of a currency relative to other currencies under free market conditions. This differs from a devaluation.

Depression: a long period of little business activity when prices are low, unemployment is high, and purchasing power decreases sharply.

Devaluation: the official lowering of the value of a nation's currency relative to foreign currencies.

Disposable income: income after taxes which is available to persons for spending and saving.

Equalization payments: transfers of tax revenues from the Canadian government to provinces with a higher proportion of lower income earners, to compensate them for their lower per capita tax revenues.

Exchange rate: the price of one currency relative to another country's currency.

Fiscal policy: the deliberate use of government budget measures (i.e., tax and spending policies) to alleviate economic problems such as low GNP, high unemployment and inflation.

Free trade: a system whereby the free movement of all goods and services, investment money and workers between countries is neither restricted nor encouraged by governments.

Gross domestic product (GDP): the value of all goods and services produced in a country.

Gross national product (GNP): the value of all goods and services produced by citizens of a country both inside and outside the country.

Inflation: a steady rise in the average level of prices in an economy.

Less developed countries (LDCs): also known as Third World countries, these are countries considered economically-underdeveloped relative to the western industrialized nations.

Minimum wage: a minimum hourly wage as set by federal or provincial legislation.

Monetary policy: the government's manipulation of interest rates and the money supply to achieve economic growth, employment and price stability.

Money supply: the amount of money in an economy, with money defined as all currency in circulation and chequing accounts.

National debt: the debt of the central government; in Canada's case, the federal government.

Per capita GNP: also known as per capita income, it is the nation's gross national product divided by its population.

Prime interest rate: the rate charged by chartered banks on short-term loans to large commercial customers with the highest credit rating.

Protectionism: government policies designed to restrict imports in order to protect domestic industries. These policies include customs duties (tariffs) and restrictions on the quantity of imports (quotas). ▶

178

▶ **Real GNP:** gross national product adjusted for inflation.

Recession: not as severe or as long-lasting as a depression but with the same general characteristics: a decline in real GNP for two consecutive quarters, with consequent unemployment and widespread softening in many sectors of the economy.

Stagflation: a high inflation rate combined with a high unemployment rate.

Supply-side economics: a school of thinking which states that an economy can prosper through policies affecting costs of production—that is, by giving production incentives to labor and greater financial rewards to investors.

Trade balance: the difference between the value of exports and imports.

Transfer payments: government payments to the provinces where no productive return is provided, such as old age pensions, unemployment insurance and welfare.

Wage-price controls: legislation whereby the government sets wage, salary and price increases in order to curb inflation.

Wage-price spiral: inflation brought about by increased wages which increase costs to the producers, who in turn increase prices. The increase in prices would cause labor to bargain for higher wages, resulting in a spiralling inflation.

ECONOMIC INDICATORS

Canadian Gross Domestic Product

(millions of dollars)

The gross domestic product (GDP) measures the value of all goods and services produced in Canada. The real (adjusted for inflation) change in the GDP shows year-to-year changes in economic activity and is considered a prime indicator of how well the nation's economy is performing.

	Current Dollars		Constant (1986) Dollars			Current Dollars		Constant (1986) Dollars	
	GDP	Annual % Change	Real GDP	Annual % Change		GDP	Annual % Change	Real GDP	Annual % Change
1926	5 354	n.a.	43 986	n.a.	1960	39 448	4.1	164 126	2.9
1927	5 777	7.9	48 108	9.4	1961	40 886	3.6	169 271	3.1
1928	6 279	8.7	52 527	9.2	1962	44 408	8.6	181 264	7.1
1929	6 400	1.9	52 997	0.9	1963	47 678	7.4	190 672	5.2
1930	6 009	-6.1	51 262	-3.3	1964	52 191	9.5	203 382	6.7
1931	4 975	-17.2	45 521	-11.2	1965	57 523	10.2	216 802	6.6
1932	4 079	-18.0	41 302	-9.3	1966	64 388	11.9	231 519	6.8
1933	3 723	-8.7	38 331	-7.2	1967	69 064	7.3	238 306	2.9
1934	4 186	12.4	42 318	10.4	1968	75 418	9.2	251 064	5.4
1935	4 514	7.8	45 357	7.2	1969	83 026	10.1	264 508	5.4
1936	4 879	8.1	47 437	4.6	1970	89 116	7.3	271 372	2.6
1937	5 477	12.3	51 635	8.9	1971	97 290	9.2	286 998	5.8
1938	5 523	0.8	52 354	1.4	1972	108 629	11.7	303 447	5.7
1939	5 880	6.5	56 265	7.5	1973	127 372	17.3	326 848	7.7
1940	6 987	18.8	63 722	13.3	1974	152 111	19.4	341 235	4.4
1941	8 532	22.1	72 214	13.3	1975	171 540	12.8	350 113	2.6
1942	10 497	23.0	84 925	17.6	1976	197 924	15.4	371 688	6.2
1943	11 282	7.5	88 164	3.8	1977	217 879	10.1	385 122	3.6
1944	12 068	7.0	91 385	3.7	1978	241 604	10.9	402 737	4.6
1945	12 063	0.0	89 170	-2.4	1979	276 096	14.3	418 328	3.9
1946	12 167	0.9	87 177	-2.2	1980	309 891	12.2	424 537	1.5
1947	13 940	14.6	91 665	5.1	1981	355 994	14.9	440 127	3.7
1948	15 969	14.6	93 056	1.5	1982	374 442	5.2	425 970	-3.2
1949	17 347	8.6	97 234	4.5	1983	405 717	8.4	439 448	3.2
1950	19 125	10.3	104 821	7.8	1984	444 735	9.6	467 167	6.3
1951	22 280	16.5	109 492	4.5	1985	477 988	7.5	489 437	4.8
1952	25 170	13.0	118 627	8.3	1986	505 666	5.8	505 666	3.3
1953	26 395	4.9	124 526	5.0	1987	551 597	9.1	526 730	4.2
1954	26 531	0.5	123 163	-1.1	1988	605 147	9.7	551 423	4.7
1955	29 250	10.2	134 889	9.5	1989	649 102	7.3	503 661	2.2
1956	32 902	12.5	146 523	-8.6	1990	671 577	3.5	502 691	-0.2
1957	34 467	4.8	150 179	2.5	1991	675 928	0.6	497 163	-1.1
1958	35 689	3.5	153 439	2.2	1992	688 541	1.9	502 097	1.0
1959	37 877	6.1	159 484	3.9					

Source: *Statistics Canada*

n.a. not available

Canadian Consumer Price Index by Year

1986 = 100

1915	9.4	1956	21.8	1969	30.0	1982	83.7
1920	17.3	1957	22.5	1970	31.0	1983	88.5
1925	13.9	1958	23.1	1971	31.9	1984	92.4
1930	13.9	1959	23.4	1972	33.4	1985	96.0
1935	11.1	1960	23.7	1973	36.0	1986	100.0
1940	12.2	1961	23.9	1974	39.9	1987	104.4
1945	13.9	1962	24.2	1975	44.2	1988	108.6
1950	19.0	1963	24.6	1976	47.5	1989	114.0
1951	21.1	1964	25.1	1977	51.3	1990	119.5
1952	21.6	1965	25.7	1978	55.9	1991	126.2
1953	21.4	1966	26.6	1979	61.0	1992	128.1
1954	21.5	1967	27.6	1980	67.2	1993	130.2
1955	21.5	1968	28.7	1981	75.5		

Source: *Statistics Canada* (1) As of June 1993.

Canadian Consumer Price Index by Item

1986 = 100

This table shows the relative costs, as far back as 1950, of categories of purchases made by Canadian consumers. To compare today's (1993) costs with those of another year, divide the 1993 index by the index for the year you wish to compare it with; then multiply that by your actual cost in the year for which you are making the comparison.

Example: you spent $40 per week on family food purchases in 1960. To calculate what that would be in today's dollars, divide the 1993 food index (123.4) by the 1960 food index (20.4). Now multiply the result by $40. The answer, $241.96, is what you now must spend to buy the same package of groceries that cost $40 in 1960.

	All Items	Food	Housing	Clothing	Trans- portation	Health and Personal Care	Recreation and Education	Tobacco and Alcohol
1950	19.0	17.1	19.0	30.3	18.0	15.7	20.7	19.0
1955	21.5	18.7	22.3	32.7	20.2	19.5	24.9	20.0
1960	23.7	20.4	24.2	33.7	24.0	23.8	29.3	21.5
1965	25.7	22.6	25.7	36.9	25.2	27.1	31.3	22.7
1970	31.0	26.9	31.8	43.4	30.0	33.4	38.9	27.3
1975	44.2	44.0	44.3	55.0	40.3	45.4	51.7	34.8
1976	47.5	45.2	49.2	58.1	44.7	49.3	54.8	37.2
1977	51.3	48.9	53.8	62.0	47.8	52.9	57.3	39.9
1978	55.9	56.5	57.9	64.4	50.6	56.7	59.6	43.1
1979	61.0	63.9	61.9	70.3	55.5	61.9	63.7	46.2
1980	67.2	70.8	66.9	78.6	62.6	68.0	69.7	51.4
1981	75.5	78.9	75.3	84.2	74.1	75.4	76.8	58.0
1982	83.7	84.6	84.7	88.9	84.5	83.4	83.4	67.0
1983	88.5	87.7	90.4	92.5	88.7	89.2	88.8	75.5
1984	92.4	92.6	93.8	94.7	92.5	92.7	91.8	81.6
1985	96.0	95.2	97.1	97.3	96.9	95.9	95.6	89.4
1986	100.0	100.0	100.0	100.0	100.0	100.0	100.0	100.0
1987	104.4	104.4	104.0	104.2	103.6	105.0	105.4	106.7
1988	108.6	107.2	108.6	109.6	105.6	109.6	111.3	114.6
1989	114.0	111.1	114.3	114.1	111.1	114.4	116.2	125.2
1990	119.5	115.7	119.5	117.3	117.3	120.0	121.3	136.1
1991	126.2	121.2	124.7	128.4	119.4	128.4	130.2	159.5
1992	128.1	120.8	126.4	129.5	121.8	131.3	131.9	169.0
1993	130.2	123.4	127.7	130.9	124.6	134.8	135.1	171.2

Source: *Statistics Canada* (1) As of June 1993.

Consumer Price Index by Category and Major City

City	1988	1991	1993[1]
St. John's	105.3	120.0	122.2
Charlottetown/Summerside	107.4	125.8	126.9
Halifax	107.4	125.2	126.2
Saint John	106.6	124.8	125.2
Quebec	107.5	125.4	127.5
Montreal	108.5	127.5	129.3
Ottawa	108.3	126.3	127.6
Toronto	110.9	128.7	129.7
Thunder Bay	107.6	125.0	127.0
Winnipeg	108.5	125.7	126.9
Regina	109.4	124.9	127.2
Saskatoon	109.7	124.4	126.3
Edmonton	107.1	124.6	126.6
Calgary	106.6	125.0	126.3
Vancouver	106.8	124.0	127.4
Victoria	106.4	123.9	126.4
Whitehorse	106.0	121.81	123.1
Yellowknife	106.9	123.81	124.5

Source: *Statistics Canada*   (1) As of June 1993.

Canadian Inflation Rate by Year

This table shows annual inflation rates, as measured by the percentage change in the Consumer Price Index (CPI) from one year to the next. The CPI, determined monthly by Statistics Canada, is a "weighted" average of the cost of a package of goods and services—such as food, clothing, housing and health care—normally purchased by Canadian households. Weighted average means that some items are given more importance according to the proportion of household income spent on them.

Prices increase for several reasons: rising production costs, limited availability of the commodity, unfavourable exchange rates pushing up import prices, excessive consumer demand and too much currency in the economy.

Year	Rate	Year	Rate
1915	2.2	1968	4.0
1920	16.1	1969	4.5
1925	1.5	1970	3.3
1930	-0.7	1971	2.9
1935	0.9	1972	4.7
1940	4.3	1973	7.8
1945	0.7	1974	10.8
1950	2.7	1975	10.8
1951	11.1	1976	7.5
1952	2.4	1977	8.0
1953	-0.9	1978	9.0
1954	0.5	1979	9.1
1955	0.0	1980	10.2
1956	1.4	1981	12.4
1957	3.2	1982	10.9
1958	2.7	1983	5.7
1959	1.3	1984	4.4
1960	1.3	1985	3.9
1961	0.8	1986	4.2
1962	1.3	1987	4.4
1963	1.7	1988	4.0
1964	2.0	1989	5.0
1965	2.4	1990	4.8
1966	3.5	1991	5.6
1967	3.8	1992	2.1

Source: *Statistics Canada*

Canadian Interest Rates, 1981–92

(average annual)

	Bank Rate	Prime Rate	Savings Rate[1]	Conventional 5 Year Mortgage	Govt. of Canada Average Bond Yield (10 yrs. and over)
1981	17.93	19.29	15.42	18.15	15.22
1982	13.96	15.81	11.50	17.89	14.26
1983	9.55	11.17	6.85	13.29	11.79
1984	11.31	12.06	7.69	13.59	12.75
1985	9.65	10.58	6.08	12.13	11.04
1986	9.21	10.52	6.02	11.21	9.52
1987	8.40	9.52	4.81	11.17	9.95
1988	9.69	10.83	5.69	11.65	10.22
1989	12.29	13.33	8.08	12.06	9.92
1990	13.05	14.06	8.77	13.35	10.85
1991	9.03	9.94	4.48	11.13	9.76
1992	6.78	7.48	2.27	9.51	8.77

Source: *Bank of Canada*   (1) Non-chequable savings account.

Federal Government Spending, 1971–92

(millions of dollars)

Department	1971–72	1981–82	1991–92
Agriculture	286.1	1 125.0	4 327.4
Atlantic Canada Opp. Agcy	—	—	293.5
Communications	21.7	1 134.0	1 997.1
Consumer and Corporate Affairs	23.9	95.0	180.3
Economic Development	—	13.0	—
Employment & Immigration	792.9	2 209.0	2 109.7
Energy, Mines & Resources	175.6	1 398.0	955.3
Environment	200.7	627.0	1 055.4
External Affairs	314.5	1 285.0	3 803.8
Finance	3 542.1	19 824.0	49 986.4
Fisheries and Oceans	—	441.0	756.9
Forestry	—	—	196.6
Governor General	1.2	4.0	10.6
Indian Aff. & Northern Dev.	426.6	1 507.0	4 020.1
Industry, Science & Technology	—	—	2 668.1
Industry, Trade and Commerce	362.7	990.0	—
Justice	28.7	200.0	723.9
Labour	17.3	71.0	277.4
National Defence	1 895.2	6 028.0	11 751.1
National Health and Welfare	2 706.1	17 818.0	36 034.3
National Revenue	185.3	816.0	2 166.1
Parliament	32.6	151.0	448.3
Post Office	413.3	1 156.0	—
Privy Council	15.5	64.0	207.5
Public Works	336.8	2 188.0	3 305.0
Regional Economic Expansion	346.4	745.0	—
Science and Technology	—	486.0	—
Secretary of State	867.8	2 264.0	3 546.2
Social Development	—	3.0	—
Solicitor General	260.1	1 184.0	2 389.6
Supply & Services	83.7	394.0	415.1
Transport	512.5	2 280.0	3 410.7
Treasury Board	438.4	318.0	483.6
Urban Affairs and Housing	129.9	—	—
Veterans Affairs	423.3	1 140.0	1 899.1
Western Economic Div	—	—	185.8
TOTAL	**14 840.9**	**67 958.0**	**139 604.7**

Source: *Public Accounts of Canada*

Per Capita National Debt, 1940–92

	(millions of dollars)		(dollars)	
Year[1]	Net Debt[2]	Interest on Debt	Net Debt Per Capita	Interest Per Capita
1940	3 271	139	288	12
1945	11 298	409	936	34
1950	11 645	440	849	32
1955	11 263	478	718	30
1960	12 089	736	677	41
1965	15 504	1 012	789	52
1970	16 943	1 676	796	79
1975	19 276	3 164	849	139
1980	72 159	8 494	2 853	353
1981	85 681	10 658	3 520	438
1982	100 553	15 114	4 090	615
1983	128 369	16 903	5 179	682
1984	160 768	18 077	6 436	724
1985	199 092	22 445	7 911	892
1986	233 496	25 441	9 210	1 003
1987	264 101	26 658	10 306	1 040
1988	292 184	29 028	11 276	1 120
1989	320 918	33 183	12 240	1 266
1990	357 811	38 820	13 484	1 472
1991	388 429	42 537	14 424	1 590
1992	423 072	41 020	15 469	1 499

Source: *Finance Canada*

(1) As of Mar. 31, on a public accounts basis. (2) Accumulated budgetary deficit (net recorded assets minus gross liabilities) since Confederation.

Federal Government Annual Surplus or Deficit[1]

(millions of dollars; fiscal year ending Mar. 31)

	Surplus or Deficit	% of GDP[2]		Surplus or Deficit	% of GDP[2]		Surplus or Deficit	% of GDP[2]
1957	-325	1.0[3]	1969	-400	0.5	1981	-13 522	4.4
1958	-196	0.6[3]	1970	332	0.4	1982	-14 872	4.2
1959	-877	2.5[3]	1971	-780	0.9	1983	-27 816	7.4
1960	-600	1.7[3]	1972	-1 542	1.6	1984	-32 399	8.0
1961	-529	1.4[3]	1973	-1 675	1.5	1985	-38 324	8.6
1962	-948	2.3	1974	-1 999	1.6	1986	-34 404	7.2
1963	-833	1.9	1975	-2 009	1.3	1987	-30 733	6.0
1964	-1 169	2.5	1976	-5 737	3.3	1988	-28 201	5.1
1965	-315	0.6	1977	-6 297	3.2	1989	-28 951	4.8
1966	-303	0.5	1978	-10 426	4.8	1990	-28 996	4.4
1967	-187	0.3	1979	-12 617	5.2	1991[4]	-30 618	4.6
1968	-711	1.0	1980	-11 501	4.2	1992	-34 643	5.0

Source: *Finance Canada*

(1) A minus (-) sign indicates a deficit. (2) GDP (Gross Domestic Product) represents the value of all goods and services produced in Canada. (3) Represents percentage of GNP.

Provincial Government Revenue and Spending

(millions of dollars)

	Newfoundland		Prince Edward Island		Nova Scotia		New Brunswick	
	1981	1991	1981	1991	1981	1991	1981	1991
■ Income								
Direct Taxes	832	1 865	177	474	1 524	3 764	1 169	2 800
Indirect Taxes	558	1 411	102	287	1 122	2 596	1 019	2 096
Other	182	614	59	159	472	1 293	267	874
Total Income	1 572	3 890	338	920	3 118	7 653	2 455	5 770
■ Annual Spending								
Goods and Services	1 125	2 277	370	718	3 013	5 813	1 822	3 676
Transfer payments	1 379	3 228	253	699	2 300	3 734	2 180	3 331
Interest on Public Debt	403	942	71	198	651	1 827	306	1 154
Total Spending	2 907	6 447	694	1 615	5 964	11 374	4 308	8 161
Surplus (Loss)	(1 335)	(2 557)	(356)	(695)	(2 846)	(3 721)	(1 853)	(2 391)

	Quebec		Ontario		Manitoba		Saskatchewan	
	1981	1991	1981	1991	1981	1991	1981	1991
■ Income								
Direct Taxes	17 652	37 644	23 413	63 892	2 018	4 429	2 138	3 826
Indirect Taxes	11 258	23 669	18 130	40 091	1 598	3 356	2 015	3 329
Other	3 440	8 571	7 450	12 197	749	1 888	1 305	1 781
Total Income	32 350	69 884	48 993	116 180	4 365	9 673	5 458	8 936
■ Annual Spending								
Goods and Services	18 124	33 807	23 497	53 453	2 886	5 780	2 516	4 688
Transfer payments	14 565	30 316	12 568	38 468	1 713	4 814	2 019	5 792
Interest on Public Debt	5 878	14 850	10 626	31 823	844	2 500	534	1 942
Total Spending	38 567	78 973	46 691	123 744	5 443	13 094	5 069	12 422
Surplus (Loss)	(6 217)	(9 089)	2 302	(7 564)	(1 078)	(3 421)	389	(3 486)

	Alberta		British Columbia		Yukon		NWT	
	1981	1991	1981	1991	1981	1991	1981	1991
■ Income								
Direct Taxes	9 551	14 212	7 961	17 601	88	171	139	383
Indirect Taxes	4 168	7 728	5 924	11 045	25	61	37	107
Other	7 335	7 513	2 247	6 044	42	85	72	177
Total Income	21 054	29 453	16 132	34 690	155	317	248	667
■ Annual Spending								
Goods and Services	6 372	12 984	7 733	14 136	192	376	451	1 159
Transfer payments	3 681	10 376	4 896	13 198	38	130	91	348
Interest on Public Debt	1 372	4 426	1 536	5 707	18	74	29	149
Total Spending	11 425	27 786	14 165	33 041	248	580	571	1 656
Surplus (Loss)	9 629	1 667	1 967	1 649	(93)	(263)	(323)	(989)

Source: *Statistics Canada*

Provincial Government Accumulated Surplus or Deficit

(millions of dollars; fiscal years ending Mar. 31)

Each year, most provincial governments spend more money than they receive in taxes and other income. This produces a debt (deficit) which continues to accumulate as this practice continues. In the table below, a minus sign represents an accumulated deficit; a plus sign represents an accumulated surplus.

	Nfld	PEI	NS	NB	Que	Ont	Man	Sask	Alta	BC
1978	-1 094	-105	-566	-760	-5 662	-8 116	-657	+713	+4 841	+1 443
1979	-1 365	-114	-731	-815	-6 711	-9 658	-707	+837	+7 656	+1 648
1980	-1 541	-119	-812	-813	-8 209	-10 696	-652	+913	+9 418	+1 962
1981	-1 533	-135	-966	-925	-10 904	-11 926	-730	+1 050	+11 045	+2 144
1982	-1 699	-135	-1 439	-1 079	-9 097	-13 524	-970	+1 176	+13 547	+1 948
1983	-1 866	-165	-1 820	-1 476	-12 467	-16 586	-1 375	+884	+13 354	+817
1984	-2 143	-161	-2 148	-1 751	-15 214	-19 625	-1 916	+599	+13 918	-125
1985	-2 415	-164	-2 594	-1 983	-19 158	-21 872	-2 373	+131	+15 591	-730
1986	-2 616	-169	-3 010	-2 232	-24 674	-26 591	-3 497	-631	+15 674	-1 404
1987	-2 751	-183	-3 239	-2 409	-27 973	-28 691	-4 499	-1 867	+11 814	-2 051
1988	-2 889	-202	-3 438	-2 827	-30 991	-30 478	-5 205	-2 486	+10 676	-1 970
1989	-2 817	-215	-3 502	-2 834	-32 213	-31 290	-4 517	-2 643	+8 740	-1 017
1990	—	-233	-4 500	-2 795	-33 446	-30 497	-4 508	-3 059	+6 625	-297

Source: *Statistics Canada 1991*

Canadian Direct Investment Abroad

(millions of dollars)

	1960	1970	1980	1990	1991
All Countries	2 468	6 188	26 967	87 886	94 435
Africa[1]	41	61	137	171	172
Australia	64	237	694	2 344	2 088
Austria	—	10	31	36	41
Bahamas	13	151	268	1 945	2 085
Belgium/ Luxembourg	2	40	74	625	852
Bermuda	5	136	1 003	1 973	2 612
Brazil	35	648	691	1 611	1 354
Denmark	—	3	80	46	34
France	24	82	289	1 671	1 715
Germany	10	77	276	837	868
Greece	—	1	30	89	89
Hong Kong	2	—	39	547	590
India	10	34	61	130	79
Indonesia	1	24	590	846	819
Ireland	4	43	233	939	1 102
Italy	8	53	125	368	853
Japan	15	48	109	770	1 721
Malaysia	—	2	19	63	113
Mexico	12	45	165	230	188
Middle East	3	7	233	166	118
Netherlands	2	52	300	1 528	1 602
Netherlands Antilles	—	6	153	60	45
Norway	23	68	64	56	24
Pacific Rim[2]	7	34	156	355	755
Panama	7	2	15	26	13
Portugal	—	1	10	110	162
Singapore	—	2	8	1 785	1 887
South Africa	28	73	159	19	14
South Korea	—	—	—	58	73
Spain	3	34	168	541	440
Sweden	3	2	10	25	13
Switzerland	12	21	291	1 134	1 057
Taiwan	—	—	16	162	143
United Kingdom	257	586	2 860	11 292	12 269
United States	1 618	3 273	16 781	52 800	54 639
Venezuela	40	12	59	55	90

Source: *Statistics Canada*

(1) Except South Africa. (2) Other than countries specified.

Foreign Investment in Canada

(millions of dollars)

	1960	1970	1980	1990	1991		1960	1970	1980	1990	1991
All Countries ...	13 582	27 374	64 708	126 588	131 630	Mexico	—	5	1	1	1
Africa[1]	23	180	139	11	9	Middle East[2] ...	—	—	40	81	72
Australia	7	12	74	782	711	Netherlands	102	452	1 219	3 111	3 174
Austria.........	—	3	18	221	389	Netherlands					
Bahamas.......	14	74	131	143	144	Antilles........	3	10	49	93	61
Belgium/						Norway.........	—	5	20	355	584
Luxembourg ..	194	260	681	537	596	Pacific Rim[3] ...	31	7	5	779	591
Bermuda.......	3	29	658	1 284	1 325	Panama........	9	17	99	117	123
Denmark.......	10	14	31	56	55	Saudi Arabia....	—	—	13	83	70
France.........	145	475	1 287	3 881	3 885	Singapore......	—	—	—	111	117
Germany.......	112	364	1 806	4 855	5 218	South Korea....	—	—	—	132	76
Greece.........	—	—	2	19	19	Spain..........	—	—	22	41	36
Hong Kong.....	—	20	51	1 309	2 306	Sweden........	33	126	322	1 010	1 045
India	—	5	1	8	8	Switzerland.....	129	353	960	3 021	3 212
Ireland.........	—	6	81	358	419	Taiwan	—	—	—	38	48
Israel..........	—	—	2	55	49	United Kingdom.	1 550	2 641	5 772	17 955	17 068
Italy...........	—	68	63	274	304	United States ...	11 210	22 054	50 368	80 931	83 775
Japan	—	103	605	4 138	5 345	Venezuela......	2	3	3	4	21
Malaysia	—	—	1	25	23						

Source:*Statistics Canada*

(1) Except South Africa. (2) Except for Saudi Arabia and Israel. (3) Other than countries specified.

Global Slowdowns

*T*he world's appetite for Canada's raw materials is slowing down as economies continue to shift and change. Major consumers of our exports—commodities such as coal, aluminum, lumber, wheat and fish—have traditionally been industrialized countries such as Japan and the US. In recent years, Japan in particular has been moving to more sophisticated types of businesses rather than concentrating on production.

More than 75% of Canada's exports still go to the US, but other international consumers are showing less demand for our natural resources as their economies move up the "value-added" chain. In the case of Japan, the rising value of their currency has hurt their exports and forced them to find cheaper ways to produce their goods. This often means that production is shifted to locales where the costs are lower, and therefore our markets in countries like Japan, Korea and other Asian nations need fewer raw materials.

One option to counter this trend could be for Canada itself to move up the value-added chain, doing more of the processing of raw materials before they leave the country instead of sending the work elsewhere. But as a highly-industrialized nation, Canada faces the same problems of high costs as its trading partners in the developed world.

Canada's Official Monetary Reserves

(millions of U.S. dollars)

	Total Reserves	US Dollars	Other Foreign Currencies	Gold	IMF Reserves[1]	Special Drawing Rights[2]
1965	3 036.9	1 519.9	12.8	1 150.8	353.4	—
1970	4 679.0	3 022.1	14.5	790.7	669.6	182.1
1975	5 325.6	3 207.1	15.7	899.4	648.0	555.4
1980	4 029.6	2 037.6	23.1	936.6	579.0	453.2
1981	4 371.1	2 865.3	95.8	833.7	402.4	174.0
1982	3 793.2	2 454.9	120.1	782.3	365.0	70.8
1983	4 205.4	2 373.8	368.2	739.1	703.3	21.0
1984	3 182.1	1 692.1	48.6	690.8	678.4	72.2
1985	3 275.6	1 523.9	50.1	773.0	710.8	217.9
1986	4 095.6	2 274.1	43.4	844.5	686.3	247.4
1987	8 203.2	6 163.3	54.5	919.5	660.6	405.2
1988	16 197.6	12 608.3	908.3	807.2	504.7	1 369.2
1989	16 795.8	11 489.3	2 660.9	740.6	527.7	1 377.4
1990	18 580.5	11 476.4	4 325.8	735.1	517.4	1 525.8
1991	16 901.4	9 439.7	4 639.9	649.0	592.3	1 581.6
1992	11 909.0	7 864.0	1 518.0	478.0	1 010.0	1 039.0

Source: *Bank of Canada*

(1) Canada, as a participating member, is required to hold reserves (primarily in Canadian dollars) with the International Monetary Fund (IMF). This pool of foreign currencies can be used by any member country to alleviate international trade balance problems. (2) Special Drawing Rights (SDRs) serve the same purpose as regular IMF reserves but are allocated differently and each country does not require IMF approval to use them. (—) = zero.

Foreign Currency Exchange Rates

	Canadian Dollars in US Dollars			Foreign Currency Units Per Canadian Dollar (annual averages)					
	High	Low	Average	British Pound	French Franc	German Mark	Swiss Franc	Japanese Yen	Italian Lira
1971	n.a.	n.a.	0.9903	0.4051	5.4555	3.4483	4.0717	343.4066	611.9951
1972	n.a.	n.a.	1.0096	0.4033	5.0891	3.2175	3.8551	305.8104	588.9282
1973	1.0127	0.9885	0.9999	0.4076	4.4307	2.6441	3.14 96	270.5628	581.3954
1974	1.0443	1.0044	1.0225	0.4370	4.9140	2.6420	3.03 49	298.1515	664.8936
1975	1.0095	0.9615	0.9830	0.4426	4.2070	2.4131	2.53 68	291.5452	641.0256
1976	1.0389	0.9588	1.0141	0.5615	4.8379	2.5510	2.53 36	300.5711	840.3361
1977	0.9985	0.8963	0.9403	0.5385	4.6189	2.1805	2.25 02	251.2563	829.8755
1978	0.9170	0.8363	0.8770	0.4568	3.9448	1.7572	1.55 47	182.4818	743.4944
1979	0.8778	0.8320	0.8536	0.4023	3.6311	1.5640	1.41 92	186.0465	709.2199
1980	0.8767	0.8249	0.8554	0.3677	3.6088	1.5518	1.43 14	192.9385	730.9942
1981	0.8506	0.8031	0.8340	0.4117	4.3346	1.8804	1.63 35	183.4862	942.5071
1982	0.8446	0.7680	0.8103	0.4634	5.3050	1.9662	1.64 18	201.3693	1 094.0919
1983	0.8208	0.7990	0.8114	0.5352	6.1576	2.0687	1.70 27	192.6782	1 228.5012
1984	0.8038	0.7486	0.7723	0.5780	6.7250	2.1911	1.80 93	183.2509	1 351.3514
1985	0.7587	0.7107	0.7325	0.5649	6.5232	2.1381	1.78 09	173.4004	1 392.7577
1986	0.7332	0.6913	0.7197	0.4905	4.9751	1.5564	1.28 72	120.5400	1 069.5187
1987	0.7721	0.7248	0.7541	0.4603	4.5290	1.3543	1.12 30	108.8376	997.5171
1988	0.8444	0.7688	0.8124	0.4560	4.8263	1.4229	1.18 44	104.0150	1 053.7407
1989	0.8652	0.8254	0.8445	0.5151	5.3821	1.5863	1.38 01	116.1980	1 157.4074
1990	0.8859	0.8275	0.8570	0.4806	4.6577	1.3824	1.18 62	123.6094	n.a.
1991	0.8934	0.8573	0.8728	0.4932	4.9044	1.4422	1.24 58	117.3709	1 078.7487
1992	0.8771	0.7729	0.8276	0.4694	4.3706	1.2892	1.1592	104.7120	1 016.2600

Source: *Bank of Canada*

n.a. not available.

Largest Canadian Financial Institutions[1], 1992

(millions of dollars)

Company (1991 rank)	Assets	Revenue	Employees	Major shareholders
Royal Bank of Canada (1)	138 293	12 199	50 893	Widely held
Canadian Imperial Bank of Commerce (2)	132 212	11 468	34 426	Widely held
Bank of Montreal (3)	109 035	8 847	32 126	Widely held
Bank of Nova Scotia (4)	97 661	8 420	29 888	Widely held
Toronto-Dominion Bank (5)	74 133	6 138	23 514	Widely held
Confédération caisses populaires Desjardins (6)	56 529	6 470	38 490	Members
CT Financial Services Inc. (7)	44 265	4 048	17 019	Imasco 98%
Caisse de dépôt et placement du Québec (9)	41 307	2 969	353	Quebec govt. 100%
National Bank of Canada (10)	40 045	3 713	11 962	Widely held
Power Financial Corp. (30)	26 094	5 867	7 600	Power 69%; Caisse de dépôt 12%

Source: *The Financial Post 500 Magazine*

(1) For the fiscal year ending Oct. 31, 1992.

Canada's Manufacturing Industries

	1985			1989		
	Value of Manufacturing[1]	No. of Businesses	No. of Employees	Value of Manufacturing[1]	No. of Businesses	No. of Employees
Total Manufacturing	248.5	36 854	1 305 159	308.8	39 150	1 495 937
Transportation	43.2	1 471	163 192	53.8	1 699	188 887
Food industries	32.8	3 228	135 226	38.0	3 385	145 804
Paper industries	18.1	688	86 477	25.8	746	90 781
Primary metal industries	17.0	435	80 989	22.9	523	82 110
Chemical Products	18.3	1 256	46 274	23.7	1 443	51 955
Electrical and Electronic Products	13.3	1 379	88 224	19.5	1 627	104 259
Metal Products	14.0	5 537	112 386	19.2	5 926	153 392
Wood Products	11.1	3 476	90 988	15.8	3 380	106 682
Petroleum and coal products	24.4	121	6 436	15.0	163	6 973
Printing and publishing	9.5	5 443	74 386	13.5	5 207	87 002
Machinery industries	7.5	1 815	53 286	11.0	2 173	72 519
Mineral products	5.9	1 532	38 763	8.0	1 688	46 019
Clothing industries	5.5	2 497	98 854	6.9	2 686	97 276
Other Manufacturing industries	5.1	1 235	51 865	6.3	3 427	60 492
Plastic Products	3.9	1 091	30 890	6.3	1 257	43 556
Beverage industries	4.9	304	17 445	5.8	274	15 828
Furniture and fixtures	3.4	1 727	42 576	4.9	1 845	55 784
Textile products	2.7	802	25 152	3.5	915	30 170
Primary textiles	2.7	215	19 589	3.1	221	18 428
Rubber industries	2.5	148	18 029	2.7	193	18 793
Tobacco industries	1.6	25	4 178	1.8	19	2 874
Leather industries	1.3	384	19 954	1.3	353	16 353

Source: *Statistics Canada*

(1) Millions of dollars.

Canadian Motor Vehicle Production

	Total	Passenger Cars	Trucks and Vans	% for Export
1961	386 923	323 638	63 285	3.3
1965	846 609	706 810	139 799	10.3
1970	1 159 504	923 437	236 067	75.1
1975	1 385 137	1 027 242	357 895	68.1
1980	1 323 999	820 114	503 885	70.0
1981	1 289 231	796 378	492 853	75.3
1982	1 293 417	851 431	441 986	86.8
1983[1]	1 524 413	968 867	555 546	83.3
1984[1]	1 829 384	1 180 085	649 299	83.9
1985[1]	1 932 738	1 077 935	854 803	81.5
1986[1]	1 854 125	1 061 365	792 760	83.2
1987[1]	1 635 681	810 086	825 595	81.4
1988[1]	1 954 198	1 024 807	929 391	83.4
1989[1]	1 829 590	894 539	935 051	85.2
1990[1]	1 635 055	833 660	801 395	87.7
1991[1]	1 679 764	864 096	815 668	85.7
1992[1]	1 802 375	1 078 819	723 556	88.3

Source: *Motor Vehicle Manufacturers' Association*

(1) Includes only member companies of the Motor Vehicle Manufacturers' Association, not comparable to previous years which include other non-member companies. Members include American Motors Canada Inc., Chrysler Canada Ltd., Ford Motor Co. of Canada, Ltd., General Motors of Canada Ltd., Mack Canada Inc., Navistar International Corp. Canada, Paccar of Canada Ltd., Volvo Canada Ltd., Western Star Trucks Inc.

Car Sales in Canada

(thousands of cars)

	Total cars sold	Domestic[1]		Foreign					
		Total	%	Total	%	Japanese	%	Other	%
1950	325	262	80.6	63	19.4	n.a.	n.a.	n.a.	n. a.
1955	387	365	94.3	22	5.7	n.a.	n.a.	n.a.	n.a.
1960	448	322	71.9	126	28.1	n.a.	n.a.	n.a.	n.a.
1965	709	634	89.4	75	10.6	n.a.	n.a.	n.a.	n.a.
1970	640	497	77.7	143	22.3	n.a.	n.a.	n.a.	n.a.
1975	989	836	84.5	154	15.5	96	9.7	58	5.8
1980	932	741	79.5	191	20.5	138	14.8	53	5.7
1985	1 137	795	69.9	342	30.1	199	17.5	143	12.6
1986	1 095	761	69.5	334	30.5	203	18.6	131	11.9
1987	1 065	701	65.8	364	34.2	243	22.9	121	11.3
1988	1 056	725	68.6	332	31.4	244	23.1	88	8.3
1989	988	671	67.9	317	32.1	246	24.7	73	7.4
1990	884	580	65.5	304	34.5	240	27.3	64	7.2
1991	873	573	65.6	300	34.5	238	27.3	62	7.1
1992	798	507	63.5	291	36.5	233	29.2	58	7.3

Source: *Statistics Canada*

(1) North American. (n.a.) not available.

Business Bankruptcies in Canada

	1991	1992	% change		1991	1992	% change
Newfoundland	149	170	+14%	Saskatchewan	583	527	-10%
Nova Scotia	662	829	+25%	Alberta	1 304	1 466	-12%
Prince Edward Island	23	39	+70%	British Columbia	1 288	1 051	-18%
New Brunswick	227	295	+30%	Yukon	3	0	—
Quebec	5 217	5 353	+3%	Northwest Territories	1	8	+800%
Ontario	3 629	4 240	+17%	Canada	13 496	14 317	+6%
Manitoba	410	339	-17%				

Source: *Consumer and Corporate Affairs Canada*

Retail Car Sales by Province – 1992

Manufacturer	Total	Nfld	PEI	NS	NB	Que
BMW	4 520	7	—	39	—	1 258
Chrysler	98 043	2 437	435	2 661	4 719	31 132
Ford	129 115	1 866	562	4 756	4 038	29 843
General Motors	266 232	5 565	973	8 709	6 987	65 871
Honda	84 644	738	150	2 105	1 324	32 503
Hyundai	18 920	460	144	1 123	275	9 449
Jaguar	581	—	—	8	—	104
Lada	1 077	19	41	3	—	662
Mazda	42 818	504	96	1 330	566	17 489
Mercedes-Benz	3 221	6	—	20	8	822
Nissan	30 825	163	109	758	338	12 116
Peugeot	15	—	—	—	—	3
Subaru	7 121	64	1	203	125	2 977
Suzuki	7 841	43	—	116	118	4 393
Toyota	71 772	799	189	1 735	1 556	27 946
Volkswagen	27 734	233	64	961	490	12 252
Volvo	3 450	13	—	73	38	758

Manufacturer	Ont.	Man	Sask	Alta	BC
BMW	2 001	51	34	190	940
Chrysler	36 250	2 407	1 707	9 666	6 629
Ford	56 063	4 091	3 199	12 263	12 434
General Motors	116 146	7 786	6 017	22 297	25 881
Honda	28 873	1 478	958	4 507	12 008
Hyundai	4 953	145	168	628	1 575
Jaguar	303	8	1	47	110
Lada	258	3	6	33	52
Mazda	14 315	572	367	1 837	5 742
Mercedes-Benz	1 415	29	30	202	689
Nissan	10 729	676	366	1 806	3 764
Peugeot	3	1	—	1	7
Subaru	1 729	93	57	484	1 388
Suzuki	2 112	269	43	212	535
Toyota	23 296	1 569	1 050	4 161	9 471
Volkswagen	9 329	414	201	1073	2 717
Volvo	1 382	49	3	150	984

Source: *Motor Vehicle Manufacturers' Association*

Building Construction in Canada

(millions of dollars)

	1960 Value	%	1970 Value	%	1980 Value	%	1990 Value	%	1992 Value	%
Total Construction ..	4 051	100.0	8 098	100.0	24 706	100.0	61 471	100.0	59 948	100.0
Residential	1 913	47.2	4 009	49.5	14 267	57.7	38 337	62.4	37 315	62.2
Single detached ...	n.a.	n.a.	1 367	16.9	5 533	22.4	15 405	25.1	11 130	18.6
Semi-detached	n.a.	n.a.	141	1.7	630	2.5	545	0.9	840	1.4
Apartments	n.a.	n.a.	1 250	15.4	2 395	9.7	5 869	9.5	4 874	8.1
Other	n.a.	n.a.	1 251	15.4	5 709	23.1	16 518	26.9	20 471	34.1
Industrial	452	11.2	1 000	12.3	2 096	8.5	3 437	5.6	2 777	4.6
Factories	366	9.0	848	10.5	1 774	7.2	3 131	5.1	2 573	4.3
Commercial	738	18.2	1 287	15.9	5 098	20.6	13 827	22.5	11 185	18.7
Hotels[1]	48	1.2	93	1.1	417	1.7	1 068	1.7	576	1.0
Office buildings ...	310	7.7	617	7.6	1 989	8.1	6 710	10.9	6 522	10.9
Stores	188	4.6	273	3.4	1 370	5.5	3 658	6.0	1 932	3.2
Theatres[2]	32	0.8	86	1.1	399	1.6	964	1.6	886	1.5
Institutional	615	15.2	1 330	16.4	1 831	7.4	3 837	6.2	5 964	9.9
Schools	347	8.6	890	11.0	908	3.7	1 653	2.7	3 569	5.9
Churches	70	1.7	29	0.4	78	0.3	145	0.2	104	0.2
Hospitals	154	3.8	263	3.2	544	2.2	1 085	1.8	1 352	2.3
Other	333	8.2	473	5.8	1 414	5.7	2 033	3.3	2 707	4.5
Farm buildings	168	4.1	208	2.6	749	3.0	752	1.2	924	1.5
Airports, bus and train stations	26	0.6	27	0.3	60	0.2	106	0.2	194	0.3

Source: *Statistics Canada*

(1) Includes clubs, restaurants, cafeterias and tourist cabins. (2) Includes arenas, amusement and recreation buildings. (n.a.) not available.

A Leader in Unemployment

*W*ith an unemployment rate of 11%, Canada is first in the Group of Seven leading industrialized nations in an unenviable category. And our governments, faced with soaring deficits and shrinking tax revenues, have few options available to help the 1.6 million Canadians who are officially out of work.

Canada's shrinking economy has perhaps been hardest on those trying to enter the workforce for the first time, often after years of preparation. Although statistically the problem of unemployment among younger workers is not as bad as it was in the 1982 recession, many analysts do not foresee the kind of growth in jobs that ended the downturn a decade earlier. As the economy begins a modest expansion corporations have been investing in equipment and technology, but there has been little growth when it comes to labour. New technology has tended to eliminate many entry level positions or stall the advancement of those already employed, halting the chain of promotion and revitalization. Furthermore, the number of jobs in the manufacturing sector continues to decline as production goes in search cheaper costs, leaving the service sector to spark growth in the workforce.

As a result of the high unemployment, the combined federal and provincial network of UIC, welfare and retraining programs for the jobless is bearing a burden it must strain to carry. In 1992, Ottawa paid $19.3 billion in unemployment insurance payments to approximately 3.8 million Canadians. Governments are searching for ways to amend existing programs and bring their spending under control without causing more hardship.

TOURISM

Tourism employs more people than any other industry and includes services provided to consumers for sightseeing, leisure and business travel (accommodation, transportation, food services, travel agents and tour operators, recreation and amusements).

In 1989 tourism accounted for 4% of Canada's GDP $25.0 billion. Canadians took approximately 80.3 million overnight trips in Canada that year and spent $17.8 billion; 12.2 million visitors from the United States spent $4.3 billion; and $2.9 billion came into the economy from 2.9 million overseas visitors.

International Visitors to Canada

	1972	1991		1972	1991
Total International Visitors	37 118	36 818	Market Share:		
Overnight	13 812	14 989	Total International Visitors	100%	100%
Sameday	23 306	21 906[1]	From the United States	98%	91%
			From Other Countries	2%	9%
Total Visitors from the United States	36 216	33 577			
Overnight	13 067	12 050	Overnight International Visitors	100%	100%
Sameday	23 149	21 603[1]	From the United States	95%	80%
			From Other Countries	5%	20%
Total Visitors from Other Countries	902	3 241			
Overnight	745	2 939			
Sameday	157	303[1]			

Source: *Statistics Canada*

(1) Estimated

Major Overseas Markets

	1972	1991[1]
Total Travellers from Overseas	477 000	3 241 000
Major Markets:		
United Kingdom	268 000	537 000
Japan	52 000	398 000
Germany[2]	89 000	277 000
France	68 000	307 000
Australia	n.a	100 000
Hong Kong	n.a	122 000
Italy	n.a	89 000

Source: *Statistics Canada*

(1) Estimated (2) 1991 shows visitors from united Germany

International Visitor Spending in Canada, 1990

	$ Million	Share	Average
Total Spending[1]	7 437 000	100%	—
Visitors from United States	368 000	59	$ 126
Visitors from other countries	069 000	41	943

Source: *Travel-log, Winter 1992*

(1) Includes international fares paid to Canadian carriers.

BUSINESS AND LABOUR

Canada's Largest Corporations, 1992[1]

Company (1991 Rank)	Revenue (millions)	Assets (millions)	Profit or Loss (−) (millions)	Employees	Major Shareholders
BCE Inc. (1)	$20 784	$48 312	$1 390	124 000	Widely held
General Motors of Canada Ltd. (2)	18 347	6 230	-72	41 318	General Motors, Detroit
Ford Motor Co. of Canada (3)	14 443	3 881	-363	21 800	Ford Motor, Dearborn 94%
George Weston Ltd. (4)	11 599	3 965	48	62 000	Wittington Investments 57%
Chrysler Canada Ltd. (8)	9.453	3 141	-48	13 800	Chrysler, Detroit
Alcan Aluminium Ltd. (6)	9 183	12 875	-135	46 000	Widely held
Canadian Pacific Ltd. (5)	8 963	20 223	-478	63 300	Widely held
Noranda Inc. (7)	8 538	14 370	79	48 000	Brascan 49%
Imasco Ltd. (26)	7 989	48 519	380	75 000	B.A.T. Industries, Britain 41%
Imperial Oil Ltd. (9)	7 968	13 192	195	10 152	Exxon, Irving TX 70%
Ontario Hydro (10)	7 768	46 671	312	29 000	Ontario govt. 100%
Seagram Co.2 (16)[2]	7 431	12 820	598	16 500	E. Bronfman 17%; C. Bronfman 16%
Thomson Corp. (13)	7 229	10 033	200	45 700	Woodbridge 71%
Hydro-Québec (14)	6 807	44 864	724	21 161	Quebec govt. 100%
IBM Canada Ltd. (15)	6 760	3 110	8	9 985	IBM, Armonk NY
Univa Inc. (11)[2]	6 701	1 465	32	18 700	Unigesco 26%; Empire 24%; Caisse dépôt 13%
Power Corp. of Canada (n.a.)	6 181	27 217	152	9 800	P. Desmarais & Assoc. 62%
Brascan Ltd. (12)	5 951	4 920	-113	n.a.	Brascan Holdings 49%
Hudson's Bay Co. (17)[2]	5 152	3 279	116	56 500	Woodbridge 25%
Oshawa Group Ltd.2 (20)[2]	5 011	1 158	41	17 335	Wolfe family 100%
Petro-Canada (18)	4 551	5 350	9	8 260	Federal govt. 70%
Shell Canada Ltd. (n.a.)	4 492	6 024	80	5 593	Shell Petroleum, The Netherlands
Bombardier Inc. (32)[2]	4 448	4 270	132	34 316	Bombardier family 63%
Canada Safeway Ltd. (n.a.)[2]	4 357	1 151	45	29 000	Safeway, Oakland CA
Canadian National Railway Co. (22)	4 051	7 051	-1 005	35 281	Federal govt. 100%

Source: *The Financial Post 500 Magazine, 1993*

(1) Figures represent fiscal year ending Dec. 1992 unless otherwise stated. (2) For fiscal year ending Jan. 1993.

Tops in Their Fields, 1992

(thousands of dollars)

■ **Agriculture**

Company (1991 rank)	Revenue
Canadian Wheat Board (1)	$3 503 910
Saskatchewan Wheat Pool (2)	1 872 344
Cargill Ltd. (3)	1 794 000
Coopérative Fédérée du Québec (4)	1 562 718
United Grain Growers (5)	1 034 268
Agropur Coopérative Agro-Alimentaire (7)	1 007 300
Alberta Wheat Pool (6)	995 489
XCAN Grain (9)	721 767
Manitoba Pool Elevators (8)	532 338
United Co-operatives of Ontario (10)	265 351

■ **Integrated Mines**

Company (1990 rank)	Revenue
Alcan Aluminium Ltd. (1)	$9 183 564
Inco Ltd. (2)	3 093 745
Noranda Minerals Inc. (n.a.)	2 245 900
Falconbridge Inc. (3)	1 650 780
Cominco Ltd. (4)	1 467 396
Rio Algom Ltd. (6)	1 028 145
Placer Dome Inc. (5)	1 020 000
American Barrick Resources Corp. (n.a.)	653 226
LAC Minerals Ltd. (8)	587 769
QIT-Fer et Titane Inc. (9)	431 000

▶ ■ **Forestry**

Company (1991 rank)	Revenue
Noranda Forest Inc. (n.a.)	$4 478 000
MacMillan Bloedel Ltd. (2)	3 039 300
Domtar Inc. (3)	1 884 000
Canadian Pacific Forest Products Ltd. (4) .	1 825 500
Abitibi-Price Inc. (1)	1 674 900
Repap Enterprises Inc. (4)	1 173 700
Weyerhaeuser Canada Ltd. (6)	1 000 000
Canfor Corp. (7)	976 331
Fletcher Challenge Canada Ltd. (5)	957 300
Cascades Inc. (8)	902 211

■ **Energy**

Company (1991 rank)	Revenue
Imperial Oil Ltd. (1)	$7 968 000
Ontario Hydro (2)	7 768 000
Hydro-Québec (3)	6 807 000
Petro-Canada (4)	4 551 000
Shell Canada (n.a.)	4 492 000
Amoco Canada Petroleum Co. (5)	3 826 000
TransCanada PipeLines Ltd. (6)	3 757 500
Total Petroleum (North America) Ltd. (8) .	3 476 916
NOVA Corp. of Alberta (7)	3 027 000
HorshamCorp. (n.a.)	2 709 788

■ **Transportation**

Company (1991 rank)	Revenue
Canadian National Railway Co. (1)	$4 051 459
Air Canada (2)	3 501 000
PWA Corp. (4)	2 877 000
Laidlaw Inc. (5)	2 253 935
Via Rail Canada Inc. (6)	487 087
Trimac Ltd. (7)	476 055
British Columbia Railway Co. (n.a.)	324 047
Federal Express Canada Ltd. (10)	253 000
Charterways Transportation Ltd. (n.a.)	223 597
Marine Atlantic Inc.	201 262

■ **Media**

Company (1991 rank)	Revenue
Thomson Corp. (1)	$7 229 800
Quebecor Inc. (2)	2 535 608
Maclean Hunter Ltd. (3)	1 634 600
Southam Inc .(4)	1 183 469
Rogers Communications Inc. (5)	1 148 678
Torstar Corp. (6)	921 127
Hollinger Inc. (7)	877 569
Groupe Vidéotron Ltée (8)	553 011
G.T.C. Transcontinental Group Ltd. (9) . . .	544 566
Canadian Broadcasting Corporation (10) .	376 732

■ **Heavy Manufacturing**

Company (1991 rank)	Revenue
Bombardier Inc. (1)	$4 448 000
Stelco Inc. (3)	2 202 860
United Dominion Industries Ltd. (n.a.)	2 064 512
Dofasco Inc. (2)	1 952 900
Dow Chemical of Canada Inc. (4)	1 463 487
General Electric Canada Inc. (6)	1 439 423
Pratt & Whitney Canada Inc. (5)	1 426 582
Du Pont Canada Inc. (7)	1 416 642
Ivaco Inc. (8)	1 094 340
Emco Ltd. (9)	1 037 763

■ **Auto & Parts**

Company (1991 rank)	Revenue
General Motors of Canada Ltd. (1)	$18 347 173
Ford Motor Co. of Canada (2)	14 443 100
Chrysler Canada Ltd. (3)	9 453 800
Honda Canada Inc. (4)	2 722 203
Magna International Inc. (5)	2 358 800
Toyota Canada Inc. (6)	1 618 309
Mazda Canada Inc. (7)	1 033 000
Goodyear Canada Inc. (8)	895 784
Nissan Canada Inc. (10)	794 855
Volkswagen Canada Inc. (9)	764 729

■ **Food & Beverage**

Company (1991 rank)	Revenue
George Weston Ltd. (1)	$11 599 000
Seagram Co. (2)	7 431 018
John Labatt Ltd. (3)	3 837 000
Maple Leaf Foods Inc. (4)	2 750 512
McCain Foods Ltd. (5)	2 741 671
Kraft General Foods Canada Inc. (7)	1 646 706
Nestlé Canada Inc. (10)	993 000
Coca-Cola Beverages Ltd.	894 967
Beatrice Foods Inc.	817 700
Burnsd Food (1985) Ltd.	670 000

■ **High-Tech**

Company (1991 rank)	Revenue
IBM Canada Ltd. (1)	$6 760 000
Digital Equipment of Canada Ltd. (3)	1 076 886
CAE Industries Ltd. (2)	1 045 812
SHL Systemhouse Inc. (4)	738 622
Hewlett-Packard (Canada) Ltd. (5)	632 641
Spar Aerospace	484 275
Honeywell Ltd. (8)	420 000
Mitel Corp. (7)	406 100
ISM Information Systems Management . . .	378 894
NCR Canada Ltd.	332 000 ▶

▶ ■ **Merchandising**

Company (1991 rank)	Revenue
Loblaw Cos.(n.a.)	$9 261 600
Univa Inc. (n.a.)	6 701 600
Hudson's Bay Co. (2)	5 152 216
Oshawa Group Ltd. (3)	5 011 400
Canada Safeway Ltd.	4 357 700
Sears Canada Inc. (4)	3 957 672
Canadian Tire Corp. (5)	3 221 864
Great Atlantic & Pacific Co. of Canada (6)	2 980 131
Westfair Foods Ltd.	2 414 701
Métro-Richelieu Inc. (7)	2 308 619

Source: *The Financial Post 500 Magazine, 1993*

■ **Conglomerates**

Company (1991 rank)	Revenue
BCE Inc. (1)	$20 784 000
Canadian Pacific Ltd. (2)	8 963 600
Noranda Inc. (3)	8 538 000
Imasco Ltd. (5)	7 989 800
Brascan Ltd. (4)	5 951 000
Jim Pattison Group (6)	2 914 000
Onex Corp. (8)	2 816 078
Molson Cos. (n.a.)	2 545 264
Empire Co. (7)	2 248 126
James Richardson & Sons Ltd.	1 831 850

Source: *The Financial Post 500 Magazine, 1993*

Largest Foreign-Owned Companies in Canada, 1992

(millions of dollars)

Company (1991 Rank)	Revenue	% Foreign-Owned	Parent
General Motors of Canada Ltd. (1)	$18 347	100	General Motors (U.S.)
Ford Motor Co. of Canada (2)	14 443	96	Ford Motor (U.S.)
Chrysler Canada Ltd. (3)	9 453	100	Chrysler (U.S.)
Imperial Oil Ltd. (4)	7 968	73	Exxon (U.S.)
IBM Canada Ltd. (5)	6 760	100	IBM (U.S.)
Shell Canada Ltd. (n.a.)	4 492	78	Shell Petroleum (Netherlands)
Canada Safeway (n.a.)	4 357	100	Safeway (U.S.)
Sears Canada Inc. (6)	3 957	61	Sears Roebuck (U.S.)
Amoco Canada Petroleum Co. (7)	3 826	100	Amoco (U.S.)
Total Petroleum (N.A.) Ltd. (10)	3 476	74	Total S.A. (France)

Source: *The Financial Post 500 Magazine, 1993*

Canadian Corporate Profits and Losses, 1992

(thousands of dollars)

Largest Profits

BCE Inc.	1 390 000
Hydro-Québec	724 000
Seagram Co.	598 038
Imasco Ltd.	380 400
TransCanada PipeLines Ltd.	328 700
Ontario Hydro	312 000
B.C. Hydro & Power Authority	220 000
American Barrack Resources	211 450
British Columbia Telephone Co.	205 700
Thomson Corp.	200 700

Largest Losses

Canadian National Railway Co.	1 005 242
Bramalea Ltd.	937 300
Amoco Canada Petroleum Co.	608 000
Trizec Corp. Ltd.	544 100
PWA Corp.	543 300
Canadian Pacific Ltd.	478 300
Ford Motor Co. of Canada	363 800
Gulf Canada Resources Ltd.	302 000
Southam Inc.	262 851
Mobil Oil Canada Ltd.	260 182

Source: *The Financial Post 500 Magazine, 1993*

Largest Canadian Subsidiaries,[1] 1992

(millions of dollars)

Company (1991 rank)	Sales	Assets	Major shareholder
Northern Telecom Ltd. (1)	10 166	11 902	BCE 52%
Loblaw Cos. (2)	9 261	2 474	George Weston 71%
Bell Canada (3)	7 862	18 414	BCE 100%
Noranda Forest Inc. (4)	4 478	6 076	Noranda 82%
Zellers Inc.[2] (5)	3 021	1 228	Hudson's Bay 100%
Westfair Foods Ltd. (6)	2 414	670	George Weston 71%
Noranda Minerals Inc. (n.a.)	2 245	4 725	Noranda 100%
Canadian Pacific Forest Products Ltd. (7)	1 825	3 000	Canadian Pacific 70%
Loeb Inc.[2] (9)	1 787	665	Univa 100%
Quebecor Printing Inc. (10)	1 745	1 549	Quebecor 95%

Source: *The Financial Post 500 Magazine, 1993*

(1) For fiscal year ending Dec. 1991, unless otherwise stated. (2) For fiscal year ending Jan. 1993. (n.a.) not available.

Canadian Business Directory

The following is a list of the addresses for the corporate headquarters of the 35 largest Canadian companies, based on the 1993 *Financial Post 500* ranking. (Corporate rank by revenues is shown in brackets).

☐ **Air Canada** (32)
Air Canada Centre, 7th floor
271 P.O. Box 14000
St-Laurent, Que. H4Y 1H4
President and CEO: Hollis Harris [transportation]

☐ **Alcan Aluminium Ltd** (6)
1188 Sherbrooke St W,
Montreal, Que. H3A 3G2
CEO: David Morton [resources]

☐ **Amoco Canada Petroleum Co.** (28)
PO Box 200, 240-4th Ave SW,
Calgary, Alta T2P 2H8
Chairman and President: T. Don Stacy [resources]

☐ **BCE Inc.** (1)
Suite 2100, 2000 McGill College Ave,
Montreal, Que. H3A 3H7
Chairman: J.V. Raymond Cyr [communications]

☐ **Bombardier Inc.** (23)
800 René-Lévesque Blvd W,
Montreal, Que. H3B 1Y8
Chairman and CEO: Laurent Beaudoin [mfg]

☐ **Brascan Ltd** (18)
Commerce Court West,
PO Box 48, Toronto, Ont. M5L 1B7
Chairman: J. Trevor Eyton [mgmt]

☐ **Canada Post Corp.** (29)
Sir Alexander Campbell Building,
Confederation Heights,
Ottawa, Ont. K1A 0B1
Chairman: Roger Beaulieu [services]

☐ **Canada Safeway Ltd** (24)
47th floor, 150-6 Ave SW,
Calgary, Alta T2P 2J6
CEO and President: R.H. Kinnie [food/bev.]

☐ **Canadian National Railway Co.** (25)
935 de La Gauchetière St W.,
PO Box 8100,
Montreal, Que. H3B 2M9
President and CEO: R.E. Lawless [transportation]

☐ **Canadian Pacific Ltd** (7)
PO Box 6042, Station "A,"
Montreal, Que. H3C 3E4
Chairman and CEO: W.W. Stinson [mgmt]

☐ **Canadian Tire Corp. Ltd.** (34)
P.O. Box 770, Station "K"
Toronto, Ont. M4P 2V8
Chairman: Hugh Macaulay [retail]

☐ **Canadian Wheat Board** (31)
423 Main Street, P.O. Box 816
Winnipeg, Man. R3C 2P5
Chief Commissioner: Lorne Hehn [food/bev]

☐ **Chrysler Canada Ltd** (5)
2450 Chrysler Centre,
PO Box 1621,
Windsor, Ont. N9A 4H6
President and CEO: G. Yves Landry [mfg]

☐ **Ford Motor Co. of Canada Ltd** (3)
The Canadian Road,
Oakville, Ont. L6J 5E4
Chairman and CEO: Kenneth W. Harrigan [mfg]

▶ ☐ **General Motors of Canada Ltd** (2)
1908 Colonel Sam Dr.,
Oshawa, Ont. L1H 8P7
President & General Manager: George A. Peapples [mfg]

☐ **George Weston Ltd** (4)
Suite 1901, 22 St Clair Ave E.,
Toronto, Ont. M4T 2S7
Chairman, President & CEO: W. Galen Weston [food/bev.]

☐ **Hudson's Bay Co.** (19)
Suite 500, 401 Bay St,
Toronto, Ont. M5H 2Y4
President: George J. Kosich [retail]

☐ **Hydro-Québec** (14)
75, René-Lévesque Blvd W.,
Montreal, Que. H2Z 1A4
Chairman and CEO: Richard Drouin [utility]

☐ **Imasco Ltd** (9)
Floor 20, 600 de Maisonneuve Blvd W.,
Montreal, Que. H3A 3K7
Chairman and CEO: Purdy Crawford [mgmt]

☐ **Inco Ltd.** (35)
P.O. Box 44, Royal Trust Tower
Toronto-Dominion Centre, 21st floor
Toronto, Ont. M5K 1N4
Chairman: Dr. Michael Sopko [resources]

☐ **IBM Canada Ltd** (15)
3500 Steeles Ave E,
Markham, Ont. L3R 2Z1
President and CEO: W.A. Etherington [tech.]

☐ **Imperial Oil Ltd** (10)
111 St Clair Ave W,
Toronto, Ont. M5W 1K3
Chairman and CEO: A.R. Haynes [resources]

☐ **John Labatt Ltd** (27)
451 Ridout St N,
London, Ont. N6A 5L3
Chairman: Samuel Pollock [food/bev.]

☐ **Noranda Inc.** (8)
PO Box 755, BCE Place,
Suite 4100, 181 Bay St,
Toronto, Ont., M5J 2T3
Chairman: Alfred Powis [resources]

☐ **Ontario Hydro** (11)
700 University Ave,
Toronto, Ont. M5G 1X6
Chairman: Maurice Strong [utility]

☐ **Oshawa Group Ltd** (20)
302 The East Mall,
Islington, Ont. M9B 6B8
Chairman and CEO: Allister P. Graham [food/bev.]

☐ **Petro-Canada** (21)
PO Box 2844,
Calgary, Alta. T2P 3E3
Chairman and CEO: Jim Stanford [resources]

☐ **Power Corp. of Canada** (17)
751 Square Victoria,
Montreal, Que. H2Y 2J3
Chairman and CEO: Paul Desmarais [mgmt]

☐ **Seagram Co. Ltd** (12)
1430 Peel St,
Montreal, Que. H3A 1S9
Chairman and CEO: Edgar M. Bronfman [food/bev.]

☐ **Sears Canada Inc.** (26)
222 Jarvis St,
Toronto, Ont. M5B 2B8
President and CEO: G. Joseph Reddington [retail]

☐ **Shell Canada Ltd** (22)
PO Box 100, Station "M,"
Calgary, Alta T2P 2H5
CEO: Charles Wilson [resources]

☐ **Thomson Corp.** (13)
65 Queen St W.,
Toronto, Ont. M5H 2M8
President and CEO: Michael W. Johnston [pub/prtg]

☐ **Total Petroleum (North America) Ltd.** (33)
Now part of Rigel Oil and Gas Ltd.
#1900, 255 5th Ave SW
Calgary, Alberta T2P 3G6
Chairman: Don West [resources]

☐ **TransCanada PipeLines** (30)
PO Box 1000, Station "M",
Calgary, Alta T2P 4K5
Chairman, President & CEO: G.J. Maier [resources]

☐ **Univa Inc.** (formerly Provigo) (16)
41st Floor, 1250 René-Lévesque Blvd W,
Montreal, Que. H3B 4X1
Chairman: Bertin F. Nadeau [food/bev.]

Source: *Financial Post 500 Magazine, 1993. The Blue Book of Canadian Business*

Labour Force of Canadian Metropolitan[1] Areas, 1991

(thousands)

	Population 15 Years and Over	Labour Force[2]	Participation Rate[3]	Employed	% Employed[4]	Un- employed	% Un- employed[5]
Toronto, Ont.	2 886	2 022	70.1	1 824	63.2	198	9.8
Montreal, Que.	2 438	1 590	65.2	1 396	57.2	195	12.2
Vancouver, B.C.	1 297	887	68.3	813	62.7	74	8.3
Ottawa-Hull, Ont.-Que.	682	485	71.1	450	65.9	35	7.3
Edmonton, Alta.	568	409	72.0	370	65.1	39	9.5
Calgary, Alta.	544	398	73.2	363	66.7	36	8.9
Winnipeg, Man.	498	339	67.9	305	61.1	34	10.0
Hamilton, Ont.	481	328	68.2	295	61.4	33	9.9
Quebec, Que.	480	321	66.7	292	60.8	29	9.0
Kitchener-Waterloo, Ont. . . .	263	193	73.5	175	66.6	18	9.4
St. Catharines-Niagara, Ont. .	255	164	64.2	145	56.8	19	11.5
London, Ont.	251	178	70.6	164	65.1	14	7.8
Halifax, N.S.	245	173	70.8	158	64.4	16	9.0
Victoria, B.C.	223	139	62.2	127	57.1	11	8.2
Windsor, Ont.	206	133	64.3	116	56.3	17	12.4
Oshawa, Ont.	154	109	70.8	99	63.9	11	9.6
Regina, Sask.	139	96	69.0	89	64.2	7	6.9
Saskatoon, Sask.	140	97	69.0	86	61.4	11	11.0
St. John's, Nfld.	127	84	66.1	73	57.4	11	13.1
Chicoutimi-Jonquière, Que. . .	110	66	59.9	58	52.8	8	11.9
Sudbury, Ont.	108	68	62.8	61	56.4	7	10.2
Sherbrooke, Que.	105	68	64.4	59	56.0	9	13.1
Thunder Bay, Ont.	102	67	65.8	61	59.6	6	9.4
Trois-Rivières, Que.	96	60	63.0	53	55.7	7	11.6
Saint John, N.B.	93	61	65.5	54	57.8	7	11.7

Source: *Statistics Canada*

(1) For census metro areas, which include neighboring municipalities from which the major urban centre draws its work force. (2) The labour force consists of employed workers and those who are unemployed but actively seeking work. (3) Participation rate is the percent of the total population aged 15 and over that makes up the labour force. (4) The percent of the total population aged 15 and over that is employed. (5) The percent of the labour force that is unemployed. (n.a.) not available.

Labour Force by Industry

(thousands)

Industry	Total Labour Force			% Unemployed		
	1971	1981	1991	1971	1981	1991
All Industries	5 845	11 645	13 513	8.7	8.5	10.2
Agriculture	372	462	441	9.6	6.4	8.1
Other primary industries	226	329	299	10.0	12.7	16.2
Manufacturing	1 339	2 236	2 051	8.5	10.6	12.5
Construction	514	726	833	10.6	16.0	22.5
Transportation, communication, utilities	564	940	993	5.8	5.6	7.6
Trade	838	2 035	2 419	9.1	6.6	9.4
Finance, insurance, real estate	183	622	816	7.8	4.3	4.8
Community, business and personal services	925	3 452	4 709	11.4	6.5	8.3
Public administration	483	783	886	4.8	6.2	6.5
Unclassified	402	61	66	—	—	—

Source: *Census, Statistics Canada*

Canadian Labour Force by Province, 1991

(thousands)

	Population 15 Years and Over	Labour Force[1]	Participation Rate[2]	Employed	% Employed[3]	Un- employed	% Un- employed[4]
Canada	**20 882**	**13 757**	**66.3**	**12 340**	**59.5**	**1 417**	**10.3**
Newfoundland	438	241	55.3	197	45.1	44	18.4
Prince Edward Island	97	64	65.1	53	54.2	11	16.8
Nova Scotia	692	422	61.3	371	53.9	51	12.0
New Brunswick	560	327	58.6	286	51.1	42	12.7
Quebec	5 382	3 392	63.4	2 987	55.8	405	11.9
Ontario	7 778	5 276	68.3	4 770	61.8	506	9.6
Manitoba	810	541	66.9	494	61.0	48	8.8
Saskatchewan	720	484	67.1	449	62.2	36	7.4
Alberta	1 889	1 357	72.5	1 246	66.5	111	8.2
British Columbia	2 516	1 652	66.4	1 489	59.9	163	9.9

Source: *Census, Statistics Canada*

(1) The labour force consists of employed workers and those who are unemployed but actively seeking work. (2) Participation rate is the percent of the total population aged 15 and over that makes up the labour force. (3) The percent of the total population aged 15 and over that is employed. (4) The percent of the labour force that is unemployed.

Labour Force by Age

(thousands)

	Population		Labour Force[1]		Employed		% Unemployed[2]	
	1971	1991	1971	1991	1971	1991	1971	1991
Both Sexes								
15 yrs. and over	14 870	20 740	8 639	13 757	8 104	12 340	6	10
15–24 yrs.	3 925	3 728	2 228	2 500	1 982	2 095	11	16
25 yrs. and over	10 950	17 020	6 410	11 257	6 121	10 246	5	9
Males								
15 yrs. and over	7 330	10 121	5 667	7 569	5 329	6 751	6	11
15–24 yrs.	1 966	1 896	1 232	1 308	1 083	1 062	12	19
25 yrs. and over	5 367	8 223	4 435	6 261	4 245	5 690	4	9
Females								
15 yrs. and over	7 541	10 626	2 972	6 188	2 775	5 589	7	10
15–24 yrs.	1 963	1 832	997	1 192	899	1 033	10	13
25 yrs. and over	5 583	8 795	1 975	4 996	1 876	4 556	5	9

Source: *Census, Statistics Canada*

(1) The labour force consists of employed workers and those who are unemployed but actively seeking work. (2) The percent of the labour force that is unemployed.

Changing Labour Force

The International Labour Organization, a UN agency, reports that part-time work has become the recent global employment trend. In September 1993 the ILO estimated that 60 million people in the industrialized countries, or one in seven workers, holds a part-time job.

The highest proportion of part-time workers is found in the Netherlands where 33% of the workforce falls into that category. It was also noted that many of the part-time jobs are held by women—25% of working women hold part-time jobs, compared to 4% of the men in the 24 industrialized countries (including Canada) in the survey.

Canadian Minimum Wages[1]

(hourly rate for experienced adult workers)

	1965	1970	1975	1980	1985	1990	1991	1993[2]
Federal[3]	$1.25	$1.65	$2.60	$3.25	$3.50	$4.00	$4.00	$4.00
Nfld	.70 (m)	1.25 (m)	2.20	3.15	4.00	4.25	4.75	4.75
	.50 (f)	1.00 (f)						
PEI	1.00	1.25 (m)	2.30	3.00	4.00	4.50	4.75	4.75
		.95 (f)						
NS	1.05 (m)	1.25 (m)	2.25	3.00	4.00	4.50	4.50	5.15
	.80 (f)	1.00 (f)						
NB	.80	1.15	2.30	3.35	3.80	4.50	5.00	5.00
Que	.85	1.40	2.80	3.65	4.00	5.30	5.30	5.70
Ont	1.00	1.50	2.40	3.00	4.00	5.40	6.00	6.35
Man	.85[4]	1.50	2.60	3.15	4.30	4.70	5.00	5.00
Sask	$38.00/wk	1.25	2.50	3.65	4.50	5.00	5.00	5.35
Alta	1.00	1.55	2.50	3.50	3.80	4.50	4.50	5.00
BC	1.00	1.50	2.75	3.65	3.65	5.00	5.00	6.00
Yukon	1.25	1.50	2.70	3.35	4.25	5.97	5.97	6.24
NWT	1.25	1.50	2.50	3.50	4.25	5.00	5.00	6.50

Minimum wage rates (1991)[2] for young workers and students: **PEI:** under 18, $4.35; **NS:** 14 to 18, $4.55; **Ont.:** students under 18, $5.90; **Alta.:** under 18, attending school, $4.50; **B.C.:** under 18, $5.00; **N.W.T.** under 16, $6.50 if distant from NWT highway system. The federal jurisdiction, Nfld., N.B., Que., Man., Sask., and Yukon do not have special rates for young workers and students.

Some provinces have different minimum wage rates for special categories of workers such as domestics and farm workers.

Source: *Labour Canada*

(1) Represents highest minimum rate in effect during the year. (2) As of July 1993. (3) Applies to work under federal government jurisdiction as defined by the Constitution Act, 1867, Sections 91 and 92. (4) .85 urban, .80 rural. (m) male. (f) female.

Unions with Largest Membership

	1980	1990	1993
Canadian Union of Public Employees (CUPE)	257 180	376 975	412 242
National Union of Provincial Government Employees (NUPGE)	195 754	301 217	307 592
United Food and Commercial Workers' International Union (UFCW)	120 000	170 000	170 000
National Automobile, Aerospace and Agricultural Implement Workers Union of Canada (CAW)	130 000	167 410	170 000
Public Service Alliance of Canada (PSAC)	155 731	162 772	171 091
United Steel Workers of America (USWA)	203 000	160 000	161 232
Communications, Energy and Paperworkers Union of Canada (CEP)	n.a.	n.a.	143 000
International Brotherhood of Teamsters, Chauffeurs, Warehousemen and Helpers of America (IB of TCW&H of A)	91 000	100 000	95 000
Fédération des affaires sociales inc. (FAS)	70 000	94 675	94 675
Fédération des enseignantes et enseignants des commissions scolaires (FCECS)	81 033	75 000	75 000
Service Employees International Union (SEIU)	65 000	75 000	75 000

Source: *Labour Canada*

Union Membership in Canada, 1961–93

(thousands)

	1961	1971	1981	1991	1992	1993
Total civilian labor force	6 055	8 395	11 573	13 681	13 757	13 797
Total union membership	1 447	2 231	3 487	4 068	4 089	4 071
% of civilian labor force	22.6	26.6	30.1	29.7	29.7	29.5
% in national unions	28.1	38.0	55.3	64.4[1]	65.1	65.8
%in international unions	71.9	62.0	44.7	31.0[1]	30.6	29.8

Source: *Labour Canada*   (1) Does not include directly chartered unions and independent local organizations.

Canadian Labour Unions Directory

(as of September 1, 1993)

☐ **Alberta Teachers' Association (ATA):** 11010-142 St., Edmonton, Alta. T5N 2R1

☐ **British Columbia Teachers' Federation (BCTF):** 2235 Burrard St., Vancouver, B.C. V6J 3H9

☐ **Canadian Brotherhood of Railway, Transport and General Workers (CBRT&GW):** 2300 Carling Ave., Ottawa, Ont. K2B 7G1

☐ **Canadian Union of Postal Workers (CUPW):** 377 Bank St., Ottawa, Ont. K2P 1Y3

☐ **Canadian Union of Public Employees (CUPE):** 21 Florence St., Ottawa, Ont. K2P 0W6

☐ **Communications, Energy and Paperworkers (CEP):** 350 Albert St., 19th Fl., Ottawa, Ont. K1R 1A4

☐ **Fédération CSN–Construction (CSN):** 1594, ave. de Lorimier, Montréal, Que. H2K 3W5

☐ **Fédération des affaires sociales inc. (FAS):** 1601 ave. de Lorimier, Montréal, Qué. H2K 4M5

☐ **Fédération des employées et employés de services publics inc. (FEESP):** 1601, ave. de Lorimier, Montréal, Que. H2K 4M5

☐ **Fédération des enseignantes et enseignants des commissions scolaires (FCECS):** 300–1170 boul. Lebourgneuf, Québec, Que. G2K 2G1

☐ **Fédération des infirmières et infirmiers du Québec (FIIQ):** 4e étage, 2050, rue De Bleury, Montréal, Qué. H3A 2J5

☐ **Fédération du commerce inc. (FC):** bureau 122, 1601 avenue de Lorimier, Montréal, Qué. H2K 4M5

☐ **Federation of Women Teachers' Associations of Ontario (FWTAO):** 3rd Fl., 1260 Bay St., Toronto, Ont. M5R 2B8

☐ **Hospital Employees Union (HEU):** 2006 West 10th Ave., Vancouver, BC V6K 2N5

☐ **Hotel Employees and Restaurant Employees International Union (HERE):** 1150–1140, boul. de Maisonneuve ouest, Montréal, Que. H3A 1MB

☐ **International Association of Machinists and Aerospace Workers (IAM):** Suite 300, 100 Metcalfe St., Ottawa, Ont. K1P 5M1

☐ **International Brotherhood of Electrical Workers (IBEW):** Suite 401, 45 Sheppard Ave. E., Willowdale, Ont. M2N 5Y1

☐ **International Brotherhood of Teamsters (IB of T):** 8000 boul. Langelier, suite 404, St. Léonard, Que.H1P 3K2

☐ **International Union of Operating Engineers (IUOE):** 401–4211 Kingsway, Burnaby, BC V5H 1Z6

☐ **IWA-Canada (IWA):** 500-1285 West Pender St., Vancouver, B.C. V6E 4B2

☐ **Labourers' International Union of North America (LIUNA):** Lower Level, 1145 Hunt Club Rd., Ottawa, Ont. K1V 0Y3

☐ **National Automobile, Aerospace and Agricultural Implement Workers Union of Canada (CAW):** 205 Placer Court, Willowdale, Ont. M2H 3H9

☐ **National Union of Public and General Employees (NUPGE):** Suite 204, 2841 Riverside Dr., Ottawa, Ont. K1V 8N4

☐ **Office and Professional Employees International Union (OPEIU):** 630–1265, rue Berri, Montréal, Qué. H2L 4C6

☐ **Ontario English Catholic Teachers' Association (OECTA):** 400–65 St. Clair Ave. E., Toronto, Ont. M4T 2Y8

▶

▶ ☐ **Ontario Nurses Association (ONA):** 600-85 Grenville St., Toronto, Ont. M5S 1B3

☐ **Ontario Secondary School Teachers' Federation (OSSTF):** 60 Mobile Dr., Toronto, Ont. M4A 2P3

☐ **Professional Institute of the Public Service of Canada (PIPS):** 53 Auriga Drive, Nepean, ont. K2E 8C3

☐ **Public Service Alliance of Canada (PSAC):** 233 Gilmour St., Ottawa, Ont. K2P 0P1

☐ **Service Employees International Union (SEIU):** 1 Credit Union Dr., Toronto, Ont. M4A 2S6

☐ **Syndicat des fonctionnaires provinciaux du Québec inc. (SFPQ):** 5100, boul. des Gradins, Québec, Que. G2J 1N4

☐ **United Association of Journeymen and Apprentices of the Plumbing and Pipe Fitting Industry of the United States and Canada (UA):** 702-310 Broadway Ave., Winnipeg, Man. R3C 0S6

☐ **United Brotherhood of Carpenters and Joiners of America (UBC):** Suite 807, 5799 Yonge St., Willowdale, Ont. M2M 3V3

☐ **United Food and Commercial Workers International Union (UFCW):** Suite 300, 61 International Blvd., Rexdale, Ont. M9W 6K4

☐ **United Steelworkers of America (USWA):** 7th Fl., 234 Eglinton Ave. E., Toronto, Ont. M4P 1K7

Source: *Labour Canada*

Employment in Canada's Industries by Province, 1992

(thousands)

	Canada	Nfld	PEI	NS	NB	Que	Ont	Man	Sask	Alta	BC
All Industries	12 241	187	45	361	289	2 954	4 716	484	441	1 240	1 516
Services[1]	4 408	69	19	127	100	1 066	1 687	174	152	451	564
Trade[2]	2 155	36	9	69	56	525	802	84	71	216	287
Manufacturing	1 788	16	4	41	36	516	841	51	26	92	165
Utilities[3]	922	17	4	29	25	222	330	43	31	94	127
Government[4]	834	17	5	33	24	208	314	36	30	80	88
Finance[5]	763	7	—	20	13	170	333	26	24	64	104
Construction	681	10	—	18	16	147	254	21	19	82	111
Agriculture	433	—	4	7	7	64	114	41	76	89	29
Primary[6]	257	15	—	17	12	36	41	8	12	72	42

Source: *Statistics Canada*

(1) Services refers to occupations in which a service is provided but no goods are produced—e.g. teaching, health care. (2) Trade is the sales and distribution network of merchandise. (3) Utilities comprise transportation, communications, electricity, gas and waterworks. (4) Government includes municipal, provincial and federal levels. (5) Finance includes insurance, real estate, banking and related activities. (6) Primary industries include fishing, trapping, forestry and mining.

Canadian Unemployment Rates

	1970	1975	1980	1985	1986	1987	1988	1989	1990	1991	1992
Canada	5.7	6.9	7.5	10.5	9.5	8.8	7.8	7.5	8.1	10 .3	11.3
Nfld	7.3	14.0	13.3	20.8	19.2	17.9	16.4	15.8	17.1	18.4	20.2
PEI	n.a.	8.0	10.6	13.3	14.3	13.2	13.0	14.1	14.9	16.8	17.7
NS	5.3	7.7	9.7	13.6	13.1	12.3	10.2	9.9	10 .5	12.0	13.1
NB	6.3	9.8	11.0	15.1	14.3	13.1	12.0	12.5	12.1	12.7	12.8
Que	7.0	8.1	9.8	11.8	11.0	10.3	9.4	9.3	10.1	11.9	12.8
Ont	4.4	6.3	6.8	8.0	7.0	6.1	5.0	5.1	6.3	9.6	10.8
Man	5.3	4.5	5.5	8.2	7.7	7.4	7.8	7.5	7.2	8.8	9.6
Sask	4.2	2.9	4.4	8.1	7.7	7.4	7.5	7.4	7.0	7.4	8.2
Alta	5.1	4.1	3.7	10.0	9.8	9.6	8.0	.7.2	7.0	8.2	9.5
BC	7.7	8.5	6.8	14.1	12.5	11.9	10.3	9.1	8.3	9.9	10.4

Source: *Statistics Canada*

SMALL BUSINESS

According to the federal government, the term small business describes firms with fewer than 100 employees in the manufacturing sector, and fewer than 50 employees in all other sectors. As the charts and tables below indicate, small business has been the major engine of growth of the Canadian economy during the past decade. Indeed, between 1979 and 1989, small businesses accounted for 2.1million new jobs—81 percent of all new job creation in Canada.

Small Business Share of Employment[1]

Year	Under 50 employees	Under 100 employees
1979	34.0.%	40.8%
1989	39.8	47.1

Source: *Industry, Science and Technology Canada*   (1) Includes self-employment, but not public administration

Small Business Share of Sales, Profits and Assets[1]

	1986	1987	1988
Sales	25.6%	27.9%	28.9%
Profits	25.1	27.1	28.1
Assets	19.3	22.8	19.4

Source: *Industry, Science and Technology Canada*   (1) Includes self-employment, but not public administration

Net New Jobs Created by Small Business, 1988–89

Sector	Net jobs created (thousands)	Firms with under 100 employees %	Firms with under 50 employees %
Business/Personal services	89.0	100	100
Community services	75.4	33	27
Unclassified	63.4	n.a.	n.a.
Retail trade	53.6	81	73
Construction	39.9	87	79
Transportation/Communications	39.5	38	35
Finance/Insurance/Real estate	31.7	91	86
Wholesale trade	30.6	90	82
Manufacturing	3.0	100	100
Primary	−1.8	n.a.	60
Mining	−5.9	21	3
Totals	418.5	83	75

Source: *Industry, Science and Technology Canada*   n.a. not available

Small Business Start-ups and Stops

Year	Start-ups	Stops	Net increase
1979–80	127 105	92 816	34 289
1980–81	134 769	95 996	38 773
1981–82	119 126	106 653	12 473
1982–93	145 154	102 251	42 903
1983–84	138 547	117 371	21 176
1984–85	152 213	110 520	41 693
1985–86	152 472	122 828	29 644
1986–87	161 285	127 085	34 200
1987–88	161 931	135 394	26 537
1988–89	165 980	140 054	25 926

Source: *Industry, Science and Technology Canada*

AGRICULTURE

Value[1] of Canadian Agricultural Products

(millions of dollars)

	Canada[2]	PEI	NS	NB	Que	Ont	Man	Sask	Alta	BC
1930	642	8	16	14	92	213	47	124	97	30
1935	533	5	15	11	71	161	36	110	99	23
1940	731	7	15	16	110	216	63	150	124	31
1945	1 656	16	27	33	217	443	151	406	291	72
1950	2 122	21	35	41	321	650	199	410	354	90
1955	2 239	24	41	37	360	724	173	416	357	107
1960	2 734	28	44	45	403	850	223	543	471	128
1965	3 818	41	51	60	507	1 102	342	887	664	164
1970	4 193	45	68	58	667	1 411	336	686	705	217
1975	10 177	86	114	99	1 383	2 688	946	2 531	1 900	429
1980	15 882	140	196	152	2 286	4 396	1 485	3 318	3 130	779
1985	19 507	171	257	216	3 066	4 987	1 995	4 011	3 776	1 027
1990	20 920	245	312	275	3 700	5 517	1 915	3 674	4 097	1 185
1991	21 285	239	307	255	3 651	5 402	1 980	4 003	4 172	1 216

Source: *Statistics Canada*

(1) Based on the gross cash returns to farmers from the sale of all agricultural products; excludes supplementary payments.
(2) Excludes Newfoundland, Yukon and Northwest Territories.

Farm Cash Receipts by Province, 1991[1]

(thousands of dollars)

	Canada	Nfld	PEI	NS	NB	Que
Cattle	3 834 578	2 402	29 373	35 544	25 439	305 971
Dairy products	3 141 002	—	39 254	85 998	56 234	1 168 920
Wheat	2 750 217	—	538	647	343	10 313
Pigs	1 837 346	80	77	2 620	14 939	565 057
Poultry	1 159 843	12 048	3 547	40 217	31 235	324 294
Canola	792 188	—	—	—	—	—
Nurseries	717 470	3 059	858	20 320	11 548	91 886
Vegetables	707 660	3 422	5 104	11 227	11 578	137 974
Eggs	483 219	8 760	2 945	23 356	15 125	90 929
Barley	465 534	—	3 074	174	1 173	21 803
Corn	452 283	—	—	—	—	158 129
Potatoes	372 153	850	96 839	5 777	54 016	46 254
Fruits	355 898	1 920	2 500	18 019	6 736	62 378
Tobacco	324 037	—	7 952	1 753	600	25 854
Soybeans	271 601	—	—	—	—	—
Other legumes	126 920	—	—	—	—	—
Forest products	84 155	136	501	6 309	7 009	35 729
Other seeds	77 687	—	—	—	—	125
Flaxseed	73 617	—	—	—	—	—
Maple products	55 402	—	—	676	1 366	45 527
Oats	53 394	—	270	114	864	9 243
Honey	49 782	—	112	605	454	4 703
Hay and clover	33 669	—	97	6	110	3 060
Sheep	33 371	223	181	1 292	344	6 025
Sugar beets	33 252	—	—	—	—	—
Furs	26 558	450	541	6 498	841	2 294
Rye	21 131	—	—	—	—	—
Wool	1 870	2	11	80	22	279	▶

	Ont	Man	Sask	Alta	BC
▶ Cattle	885 533	253 864	563 577	1 538 652	194 223
Dairy products	1 075 028	118 169	91 273	248 685	257 441
Wheat	44 082	522 976	1 537 958	618 710	6 738
Pigs	524 765	243 769	122 539	266 816	49 730
Poultry	412 413	54 907	35 132	99 976	146 074
Canola	9 824	123 370	346 151	308 990	3 853
Nurseries	398 265	15 000	8 535	40 000	127 999
Vegetables	360 598	16 696	—	41 237	119 824
Eggs	171 554	45 563	18 255	42 353	64 379
Barley	11 137	56 658	175 194	191 143	3 178
Corn	280 158	13 996	—	—	—
Potatoes	54 056	43 225	9 348	37 693	24 095
Fruits	150 578	—	—	—	103 888
Tobacco	287 878	—	—	—	—
Soybeans	271 601	—	—	—	—
Other legumes	31 800	35 519	43 605	16 396	—
Forest products	13 832	1 521	1 364	2 389	15 365
Other seeds	1 721	30 483	25 112	16 845	3 401
Flaxseed	—	35 760	33 195	4 662	—
Maple products	7 833	—	—	—	—
Oats	1 121	5 979	11 146	23 738	919
Honey	9 401	7 829	9 513	13 390	3 775
Hay and clover	2 251	872	3 771	18 795	4 707
Sheep	12 509	439	1 719	6 608	2 031
Sugar beets	—	12 375	—	20 877	—
Furs	9 814	1 105	65	836	4 114
Rye	295	3 825	12 511	4 574	26
Wool	373	60	169	772	102

Source: *Statistics Canada*

(1) For the crop year ending June 30. Does not include government subsidies and crop insurance payment. (—) = zero; n.a. not available

Canadian Grain Exports

(millions of metric tonnes; millions of dollars)

	1980	1987	1988	1989	1990	1991	1992
Wheat							
Gross production	19.2	31.4	26.0	16.0	24.6	32.7	32.0
Gross exports	15.6	20.8	23.5	12.4	17.2	21.9	25.1
Gross value of exports	n.a.	$3 224.0	$4 439.5	$2 578.9	$3 340.9	$3 796.9	$4 690.7
Canola/Rapeseed							
Gross production	2.5	3.8	3.8	4.3	3.1	3.3	4.2
Gross exports	1.4	2.1	1.8	1.9	2.0	1.9	1.9
Gross value of exports[1]	n.a.	$490.6	$607.4	$623.9	$612.8	$507.4	$504.7
Barley							
Gross production	11.3	14.6	14.0	10.2	11.7	13.9	11.6
Gross exports	3.2	6.7	4.6	2.9	4.5	4.8	3.3
Gross value of exports	n.a.	$448.2	$282.7	$573.1	$506.1	$450.4	$325.5
Flax/Linseed							
Gross production	0.4	1.0	0.7	0.4	0.5	0.9	0.6
Gross exports	0.6	0.7	0.6	0.5	0.5	0.5	0.5
Gross value of exports	n.a.	$147.3	$168.5	$201.8	$174.2	$98.2	$89.5
Oats							
Gross production	3.0	3.3	3.0	3.0	3.5	2.9	1.8
Gross exports	0.05	0.3	0.3	0.7	0.7	0.4	.3
Gross value of exports	n.a.	$44.9	$63.1	$159.7	$75.4	$38.7	$68.3

Source: *Statistics Canada*

(1) Rape or colza seeds, whether broken or not.

Canada's Share of the World Wheat Market[1]

(thousands of metric tonnes)

	1976 Wheat Imports	1976 Canadian Total	1976 Canadian Share (%)	1981 Wheat Imports	1981 Canadian Total	1981 Canadian Share (%)	1992 Wheat Imports	1992 Canadian Total	1992 Canadian Share (%)
All Countries[2]	63 105	12 810	20.3	94 116	17 067	18.1	118 140	25 383	21.5
United States	n.a.	n.a.	n.a.	n.a.	n.a.	n.a.	1 123	1 027	91.5
Venezuela	740	43	5.8	800	—	—	1 180	586	49.7
USSR	4 600	1 166	25.3	16 000	4 459	27.9	21 250	4 969	23.4
Iran	1 200	—	—	1 700	173	10.2	2 500	1 158	46.3
Cuba	922	814	88.3	1 030	1 014	98.4	1 074	192	17.9
United Kingdom	3 424	1 333	38.9	2 150	1 339	62.3	800	292	36.5
China	3 158	1 929	61.1	13 789	2 921	21.2	15 823	7 184	45.4
Japan	5 521	1 320	23.9	5 840	1 463	25.1	5 786	1 479	25.6
South Korea	1 993	55	2.8	1 998	17	0.9	4 396	745	16.9
India	3 804	148	3.9	50	40	80.0	100	—	—
Algeria	1 338	418	31.2	1 800	750	41.7	4 000	369	9.2
Belgium[3]	699	38	5.4	1 600	—	—	2 250	244	10.8
Brazil	2 911	975	33.5	3 893	1 426	33.2	4 165	1 824	43.8
Indonesia	1 155	151	13.1	1 500	—	—	2 300	632	27.5
Portugal	416	—	—	742	17	2.3	700	—	—
Italy	2 431	499	20.5	3 300	858	26.0	7 300	309	4.2
Syria	316	24	7.6	511	—	—	792	12	1.5
Greece	2	1	5.0	2	1	50.0	250	—	—
Egypt	4 028	219	5.4	5 600	12	0.2	5 781	105	1.8
East Germany	1 700	292	17.2	500	67	13.4	n.a.	n.a.	n.a.
France	187	30	16.0	700	12	1.7	200	—	—
Iraq	911	200	22.0	1 600	467	29.2	1 705	6	0.4
Mexico	1	—	—	1 240	38	3.1	739	511	69.1
Netherlands	1 373	167	12.2	1 400	28	2.0	1 700	11	0.6
Peru	718	94	13.1	813	—	—	1 125	90	8.0
Poland	2 225	804	36.1	3 962	1 165	29.4	123	—	—
Spain	107	—	—	303	25	8.3	1 548	—	—
Sri Lanka	750	77	10.3	650	—	—	665	—	—
West Germany	1 480	346	23.4	1 500	1	0.1	1 100	—	—

Source: *Statistics Canada*

(1) For the crop year ending June 30. (2) May include countries not listed here. (3) Includes Luxembourg.

(—) = zero; n.a. not available.

You say potato...

Canada is the second largest exporter of potatoes (Holland is far ahead) in the world and close to 70% of our exports are grown on Prince Edward Island.

Prince Edward Island was cultivating potatoes before 1771 (it was recorded that year that the harvest was a "phenomenal success"), and by 1800, PEI was exporting potatoes to Nova Scotia and New Brunswick.

By 1830, the potato was one of the Island's main exports and over the years the number of acres that are in potatoes has grown from 44,000 at the end of the 1800s to around 85,000 acres in the early 1990s. (The maximum acreage on the Island is estimated at 90,000.) The markets for potatoes range from central Canada to Brazil, Jamaica, Algeria and Italy.

The chief exports are seed potatoes and unprocessed product—researchers work year after year to perfect new varieties suited to particular conditions, while others ponder ways to process the potato (and create more jobs) before they leave the Island.

Vegetable Production, 1991

(thousands of dollars)

	Canada	Nfld	PEI	NS	NB	Que	Ont	Man	Alta	BC
Asparagus	5 963	—	—	—	—	1 434	3 980	193	—	356
Beans	16 987	—	28	n.a.	n.a.	6 964	6 361	—	—	1 186
Beets	5 715	116	0	231	48	1 797	2 714	191	184	434
Cabbage	35 991	960	313	1 517	770	13 289	13 336	1 484	1 336	2 986
Carrots	59 969	583	1 283	2 457	415	27 155	17 841	2 562	2 979	4 694
Cauliflower	19 894	—	120	841	901	5 711	7 132	1 518	722	2 949
Celery	12,563	—	—	—	—	6 468	4 878	320	—	897
Corn	64,955	—	172	918	1 007	18 050	38 435	1 050	2 389	2 934
Cucumbers[3]....	48 635	64	31	1 281	192	6 697	25 579	543	7 111	6 857
Lettuce	26 441	—	128	534	205	15 581	5 007	—	—	4 986
Mushrooms ...	149 753	([1])	([1])	([1])	([1])	([1])	74 410	([2])	([2])	44 581
Onions	43 971	—	—	—	—	12 858	26 125	2 215	901	1 872
Parsnips	1 689	—	173	119	—	—	595	625	—	177
Peas	24 782	n.a.	n.a.	n.a.	n.a.	6 927	8 458	n. a.	n.a.	3 153
Peppers	18 684	—	—	—	—	3 545	14 779	—	—	360
Potatoes.......	380 778	1 376	102 558	5 964	57 881	52 937	41 559	50 292	35 656	23 156
Radishes	4 639	—	—	—	—	2 298	1 641	—	—	700
Rutabagas	14 412	1 777	827	790	479	5 469	3 613	266	486	705
Spinach	2 272	—	—	—	—	960	658	—	—	654
Tomatoes[3]	136 152	325	32	1 469	1 623	15 825	104 812	160	608	11 216

Source: *Statistics Canada*

(1) Total production for the Maritimes and Quebec valued at $9.135 million. (2) Total production for the Prairies valued at $21.627 million. (3) Includes greenhouse products. (—) = zero. (n.a.) not available.

Fruit Production, 1991

(thousands of dollars)

	Canada	NS	NB	Que	Ont	BC
Apples	n.a.	10 650	2 778	n.a.	59 785	49 504
Blueberries[2]	46 674	15 718	4 675	12 538	1 090	9 968
Cranberries[3]	25 388	350	—	—	—	24 976
Grapes	30 611	119	—	—	26 613	3 879
Peaches	24 979	—	—	—	23 168	1 811
Pears	10 740	438	—	—	8 469	1 833
Plums & prunes	3 865	—	—	—	3 489	376
Raspberries	20 804	228	110	3 992	2 212	14 262
Sour cherries	5 840	—	—	—	4 968	872
Strawberries[1]	40 467	3 288	3 657	15 681	9 633	5 800
Sweet cherries	5 401	—	—	—	2 440	2 961

Source: *Statistics Canada*

(1) Includes Nfld.: $1.05 million; PEI: $1.3 million. (2) Includes Nfld.: $1.8 million (includes both cultivated and wild berries); PEI: $887,000. (3) Includes Nfld.: $62,000 (includes both cultivated and wild berries). (—) = zero.

NATURAL RESOURCES

Canadian Mining by Province, 1992[1]

(millions of dollars)

	Canada	Nfld	NS	NB	Que	Ont	Man	Sask	Alta	BC	YT	NWT
Metals												
Gold	2 086.8	...	—	...	590.0	979.2	34.8	24.3	.5	202.1	50.7	182.8
Copper	2 062.9	—	...	43.2	255.2	716.2	167.8	.3	—	880.1	—	—
Nickel	1 679.9	—	—	—	—	1 112.9	567.0	—	—	—	—	—
Zinc	1 727.2	—	...	426.8	147.4	276.1	123.4	...	—	188.2	302.9	261.5
Iron ore	1 129.4	680.2	—	—	...	...	—	—	—	1.3	—	—
Lead	230.9	—	...	56.1	—	...	...	—	—	53.6	91.3	28.4
Silver	173.2	...	—	36.1	20.8	32.1	6.6	...	—	56.3	17.8	3.5
Platinum metals	117.1	—	—	—	—	...	...	—	—	—	—	—
Cobalt	136.9	—	—	—	—	109.5	27.3	—	—	—	—	—
Tin	...	—	...	—	—	—	—	—	—	—	—	—
Tantalum	5.2	—	—	—	—	—	5.2	—	—	—	—	—
Cadmium	3.2	—	...	.3	.1	1.7	.3	...	—	.8	—	—
Columbium	...	—	—	—	...	—	—	—	—	—	—	—
Magnesium	...					...			...	—	—	—
Non-Metallics												
Cement	739.2	...	...	—	94.3	305.9	...	...	...	—	—	—
Sand and gravel[2]	637.0	11.6	20.4	14.6	93.2	206.5	28.2	21.0	101.4	128.0	5.2	3.4
Stone	507.6	5.0	19.8	13.4	205.8	218.6	8.7	—	4.3	28.8	—	3.4
Asbestos	235.8	4.6	—	—	224.8	—	—	—	—	6.3	—	—
Salt	253.8	—	...	...	...	140.5	—	25.2	15.3	—	—	—
Sulphur	131.4	—	—	—	—	—	—	—	115.2	—	—	—
Gypsum	79.2	...	55.1	—	—	14.0	...	—	—	...	—	—
Potash	963.3	—	—	...	—	—	—	...	—	—	—	—

Source: *Statistics Canada*

(1) Preliminary estimates. (2) Includes PEI production of $3.4 million. (—) = zero. (...) too small to count.

Value of Canada's Mineral Production

(millions of dollars)

	1950	1960	1970	1980	1990[1]	1991[1]	1992[1]
Gold	169.0	157.2	103.4	1 165.4	2 378.3	2 355.3	2 086.8
Copper	104.7	264.8	607.9	1 859.6	2 494.6	2 101.2	2 062.9
Coal	110.1	74.7	54.0	932.0	1 871.0	1 905.9	1 663.3
Nickel	112.1	295.6	528.2	1 497.4	2 024.0	1 828.2	1 807.6
Zinc	98.0	108.6	326.9	858.2	2 477.0	1 351.0	1 727.2
Iron ore	23.4	175.1	532.7	119.0	1 312.2	1 307.9	1 129.3
Potash	—	178.7	65.1	1 020.7	907.2	919.0	963.3
Cement	35.9	93.3	148.2	581.4	864.9	816.8	739.2
Sand and gravel[2]	36.4	111.2	129.5	508.4	794.1	631.4	637.0
Uranium	—	269.9	52.3	702.0	868.0	472.1	575.6

Source: *Statistics Canada*

(1) Preliminary estimates. (2) Includes production values for quartz. (—) = zero.

Mineral Production in Canada

(thousands of units)

	Unit of weight	1950	1960	1970	1980	1990	1992
Cement	t	15 188	5 250	7 208	10 270	11 745	8 484
Coal	t	17 363	9 989	15 063	36 677	68 332	64 550
Copper	kg	239 685	398 490	610 275	716 352	771 433	744 687
Gold	g	138 151	143 999	74 939	55 092	167 373	157 554
Iron ore	t	3 270	19 551	47 458	49 054	35 670	32 772
Nickel	kg	112 181	194 596	277 489	184 799	195 004	189 051
Potash	t	n.a.	n.a.	3 103	7 198	7 345	7 324
Sand and gravel	t	66 310	174 246	183 845	276 452	244 316	201 082
Uranium	kg	n.a.	11 564	3 724	6 739	9 720	9 057
Zinc	kg	284 154	369 107	1 135 708	883 683	1 179 372	1 193 607

Source: *Statistics Canada*   t = tonne; kg = kilogram; g = gram; n.a. not available.

Canadian Mineral Reserves, 1991[1]

(thousands of tonnes)

	Copper	Nickel	Lead	Zinc	Molybdenum	Silver	Gold
Canada	**11 203**	**5 792**	**6 317**	**20 091**	**193**	**23 227**	**1 548**
Newfoundland	—	—	—	—	—	4	39
Nova Scotia	11	—	29	76	—	—	—
New Brunswick	375	—	3 383	8 700	—	9 498	59
Quebec	775	—	28	1 224	—	1 311	343
Ontario	5 050	4 208	94	2 689	—	5 027	812
Manitoba	538	1 584	13	1 145	—	757	34
Saskatchewan	—	—	—	—	—	1	13
British Columbia	4 454	—	957	1 942	193	4 162	117
Yukon Territory	—	—	1 358	2 419	—	2 339	26
Northwest Territories	—	—	456	1 897	—	127	105

Source: *Energy, Mines and Resources Canada*   (1) As of Jan. 1. (—) = zero.

Canada's Logging Industry[1], 1990

	Value of Shipments		Value Added[2]	Businesses[3]		Employees[4]	
	($000)	%	($000)	No.	%	No.	%
Canada[5]	**8,113.8**	**100.0**	**3,177.2**	**8 447**	**100.0**	**39 242**	**100.0**
British Columbia	4 017.7	49.5	1 524.1	3 251	38.5	16 616	42.4
Quebec	1 649.3	20.3	699.0	2 070	24.5	10 341	26.3
Ontario	1 168.4	14.4	432.4	1 367	16.2	5 620	14.3
New Brunswick	557.9	6.9	230.8	787	9.3	2 829	7.2
Nova Scotia	196.2	2.4	78.3	305	3.6	990	2.5
Alberta	203.4	2.5	90.6	276	3.3	1 246	3.2
Newfoundland	135.9	1.7	58.9	100	1.1	899	2.3
Saskatchewan	102.6	1.3	32.7	131	1.6	284	0.7
Manitoba	78.9	1.0	28.0	137	1.6	373	1.0
Prince Edward Island	2.6	0.3	1.9	15	0.2	34	0.1

Source: *Statistics Canada*

(1) Includes primarily businesses involved in felling and bucking, bunching, yarding, forwarding, decking and loading of round wood, and in the recovery of lost logs, as well as businesses engaged in transporting primary wood products with specialized logging equipment. Also included are barking mills. (2) The value of shipments minus the cost of producing them. (3) Based on the number of business locations. (4) Production and related workers only. (5) Includes businesses located in the Yukon and N.W.T.

Canada's Wood Industries[1], 1990

	Value of Shipments		Value Added[2]	Businesses[3]		Employees	
	($000)	%	($000)	No.	%	No.	%
Canada	14 805.6	100.0	5 648.4	3 409	100.0	98 688	100.0
British Columbia	6 761 700	45.7	2 446 700	681	20.0	34 536	35.0
Quebec	3 404 000	23.0	1 339 800	1 237	36.3	25 454	25.8
Ontario	2 729 800	18.4	1 092 000	836	24.6	23 910	24.2
Alberta	933 400	6.3	399 700	208	6.1	6 179	6.3
New Brunswick	449 300	3.0	163 600	142	4.2	3 459	3.5
Manitoba	209 500	1.4	89 700	83	2.4	1 912	2.0
Saskatchewan	124 800	1.0	47 700	64	2.0	1 047	1.0
Nova Scotia	147 500	1.0	52 300	93	2.8	1 692	1.7
Prince Edward Island	13 500	0.1	4 800	18	0.5	137	0.1
Newfoundland	32 100	0.2	12 100	47	1.3	362	0.4

Source: *Statistics Canada*

(1) Includes sawmills, planing and shingle mills, veneer and plywood industries, and other millwork industries producing lumber for the manufacturing industry. (2) The value of shipments minus the cost of producing them. (3) Based on the number of business locations.

Canada's Fishing Industry, 1987

	Registered Fishermen	Catches		Fish Processing Industry	
		Tonnes	Landed Value ($000)	Businesses	Employees
Canada	94 128[1]	1 567 181	1 659 389	414	31 171[2]
Newfoundland	29 022	499 086	292 697	103	11 206
Prince Edward Island	4 771	42 812	68 312	22	985
Nova Scotia	15 921	475 998	524 194	106	7 226
New Brunswick	8 036	152 526	119 004	73	4 004
Quebec	6 944	97 161	126 195	40	2 529
Ontario	1 500	27 757	48 340	19	n.a.
Manitoba	n.a.	11 997	25 415	1	n.a.
Saskatchewan	n.a.	3 835	5 385	1	n.a.
Alberta	n.a.	1 887	2 330	1	n.a.
British Columbia	21 741	251 336	442 296	48	4 156
Northwest Territories	n.a.	1 513	2 258	—	n.a.

Source: *Dept. of Fisheries and Oceans*

(1) Includes 6 193 registered fishermen in the Prairie provinces and N.W.T. (2) Includes confidential provincial figures listed as not available. (—) = zero. (n.a.) not available.

More cutbacks for the Atlantic fishery

*I*n September 1993, the Fisheries Resource Conservation Council filed a report with the federal ministry that recommended more drastic cutbacks to the east coast fishery in the hope that they would allow the devastated fish stocks to recover for future generations.

Proposals included closing the cod fishery off the south coast of Newfoundland and the southern Gulf of St. Lawrence, and cutting the 1993 cod quotas for the rest of Newfoundland and southeast Nova Scotia by up to 50%. It was estimated that if all the recommendations were enacted, up to 12,000 people would be affected. While some would be able to find work in other fisheries, most would be dependent on compensation to replace lost income.

Canadian Commercial Fishing, 1989

	Atlantic Coast		Inland Waters		Pacific Coast	
	Tonnes	Landed Value ($000)	Tonnes	Landed Value ($000)	Tonnes	Landed Value ($000)
Grand Total	**497 515**	**1 284 036**	**51 198**	**82 690**	**272 305**	**416 294**
Alewife	11 186	4 185	1 958	776	—	—
Artic char	—	—	89	494	—	—
Bass	—	—	2 064	2 581	—	—
Burbot	—	—	37	3	—	—
Capelin	86 372	18 844	—	—	—	—
Carp	—	—	339	134	—	—
Catfish	1 994	515	71	73	—	—
Clam	13 281	10 415	—	—	7 668	19 996
Cod	422 471	217 697	—	—	9 143	4 519
Crab	24 494	47 284	—	—	1 522	6 089
Cusk	3 403	1 837	—	—	—	—
Eel	850	2 781	379	1 179	—	—
Flatfish	70 218	38 907	—	—	6 475	4 871
Haddock	26 022	25 339	—	—	—	—
Hake	14 228	6 507	—	—	66 100	10 000
Halibut	2 318	9 981	—	—	6 196	18 696
Herring[1]	222 233	30 928	—	—	41 008	76 320
Lobster	41 827	259 209	—	—	—	—
Mackerel	21 637	5 534	—	—	—	—
Oyster	551	3 628	—	—	3 473	3 409
Perch	—	—	8 572	27 194	—	—
Pickerel	—	—	8 491	19 634	—	—
Pike	—	—	3 853	3 170	—	—
Pollock	44 464	19 808	—	—	434	63
Redfish	76 126	21 985	—	—	24 453	14 983
Salmon	916	3 976	8	8	352	45
Sauger	—	—	2 730	4 844	—	—
Scallop	92 030	92 928	—	—	—	—
Shad	—	—	247	292	—	—
Shrimp	36 189	61 331	—	—	3 144	10 189
Skate	79	8	—	—	—	—
Smelt	1 472	1 208	7 384	2 770	—	1
Squid	2 280	568	—	—	—	—
Sturgeon	—	—	286	1 296	—	—
Sucker (mullet) ...	—	—	2 059	646	—	—
Sunfish	—	—	105	128	—	—
Tomcod	—	—	17	13	—	—
Trout, lake	—	—	1 093	1 402	—	—
Tullibee	—	—	1 118	1 463	—	—
Tuna	736	8 547	—	—	145	380
Turbot	16 675	11 951	—	—	609	116
Whitefish	—	—	9 385	13 217	—	—
Other fish	6 312	12 528	906	1 173	12 860	21 172
Miscellaneous.....	43 671	7 039	—	—	n.a.	5 391

Source: *Dept. of Fisheries and Oceans*   (1) Includes sardines. (—) = zero; n.a. not available.

ENERGY

Electricity Production in Canada

(percentage distribution of electricity production by type)

	1960	1970	1975	1980	1985	1990	1992
Hydro	92.6	76.5	74.0	68.4	67.4	62.9	62.2
Steam[1]	6.7	22.1	20.8	21.4	19.1	21.5	21.6
Nuclear	—	0.5	4.3	9.8	12.8	14.8	15.2
Internal combustion[2]	0.5	0.4	0.4	0.3	0.2	0.2	0.1
Gas turbine[3]	0.3	0.5	0.5	0.2	0.6	0.7	0.8
Total production, MWh[4] (000s)	114 378	204 723	273 392	367 306	447 182	465 744	501 523

Source: *Statistics Canada*

(1) Powered by natural gas and heavy fuel oil. (2) Produced from diesel fuel powering an internal-combustion engine. (3) Produced primarily from natural gas powering a turbine generator. (4) MWh = megawatt hours. (—) = zero.

Electricity Production by Province, 1992

(thousands of megawatt hours)

	Canada	Nfld	PEI	NS	NB	Que
Hydro	312 132.8	34 880.4	—	896.0	2 972.1	141 351.9
Steam[1]	108 409.0	1 730.5	33.5	8 821.8	8 134.8	867.5
Nuclear	76 021.0	—	—	—	4 834.6	4 600.0
Internal combustion[2]	716.1	69.3	—	—	-9	251.6
Gas turbine[3]	4 244.4	.5	.6	4.5	20.8	6.3
Total production	501 523.3	36 680.7	34.1	9 722.3	15 962.3	147 077.2
% by province	100.0	7.3	...	2.0	3.2	29.3

	Ont	Man	Sask	Alta	BC	YT/NWT
Hydro	39 718.6	26 433.6	3 054.6	1 584.8	60 555.0	685.8
Steam[1]	30 508.5	303.4	10 927.8	43 666.0	3 415.2	—
Nuclear	66 586.5	—	—	—	—	—
Internal combustion[2]	0.1	26.2	.2	19.6	69.7	279.4
Gas turbine[3]	1 703.8	—	144.3	2 250.0	17.7	95.9
Total production	138 517.5	26 763.1	14 126.8	47 520.3	64 057.6	1 062.3
% by province	27.6	5.3	2.8	9.5	12.8	2.1

Source: *Statistics Canada*

(1) Powered by natural gas and heavy fuel oil. (2) Produced from diesel fuel powering an internal-combustion engine. (3) Produced primarily from natural gas powering a turbine generator. (—) = zero. (...) = too small to be included.

Nuclear Generating Stations in Canada

Reactor	Province	Installed capacity (MW)	Approved	Operational	Energy Produced in 1992[1] (MWh)
Pickering A	Ontario	2 × 542	1964	1971	11 681 290
		2 × 542	1967	1972–73	
Pickering B	Ontario	4 × 540	1974	1983–86	14 067 420
Bruce A	Ontario	2 × 825	1969	1977–78	17 755 112
		2 × 815	1969	1977–79	
Bruce B	Ontario	2 × 885	1975	1984–85	25 175 900
		2 × 890	1975	1986–87	
Darlington	Ontario	4 × 935	1977	1990–92	5 354 376
Gentilly 2	Quebec	685	1973	1983	4 198 725[2]
Point Lepreau	New Brunswick	680	1974	1983	5 817 652[2]

Source: *Ontario Hydro*

(1) Gross figures, representing total energy produced by plants. (2) 1991 figure. (MW) = megawatt; (MWh) = megawatt hours.

Natural Gas Production[1] by Province

(millions of cubic metres and millions of dollars)

	1960		1970		1980		1990	
	Quantity	Value	Quantity	Value	Quantity	Value	Quantity	Value
Canada	14 814	53	52 432	292	69 820	5 737	98 771	5 692
New Brunswick	3	...	3	...	2	...	—	—
Ontario	481	7	483	6	363	27	449	47
Saskatchewan	1 036	4	1 522	7	1 203	20	5 648	306
Alberta	10 869	34	42 743	250	60 517	5 370	82 214	4 842
British Columbia	2 424	8	7 679	29	7 374	276	10 335	491
Northwest Territories....	1	...	2	...	361	44	124	7

Source: *Statistics Canada*

(1) Marketable natural gas. (...) = too small to be included. (—) = zero.

Oil Production[1] by Province

(thousands of cubic metres and millions of dollars)

	1960		1970		1980		1990	
	Quantity	Value	Quantity	Value	Quantity	Value	Quantity	Value
Canada...............	30 120	423	80 009	1 269	89 531	9 639	96 878	10 279
Ontario	160	3	167	3	93	10	247	44
Manitoba	757	11	939	15	564	55	740	115
Saskatchewan	8 249	104	14 256	200	9 368	866	12 460	1 558
Alberta	20 739	302	60 312	987	77 163	8 491	79 354	8 002
British Columbia	138	2	4 201	63	2 182	206	2 183	313
Northwest Territories ...	77	1	134	1	161	11	1 893	248

Source: *Statistics Canada*

(1) Marketable crude oil and equivalent.

Coal Production by Province

(thousands of tonnes and millions of dollars)

	1960 Quantity	1960 Value	1970 Quantity	1970 Value	1980 Quantity	1980 Value	1989 Quantity	1989 Value	1990 Quantity	1990 Value
Canada	9 989	75	15 063	86	36 688	932	70 527	1 743	68 331	1 823
Alberta.............	2 170	12	6 154	28	17 396	302	30 878	467	30 405	482
British Columbia	766	6	3 160	26	10 156	445	24 801	943	24 556	1 000
Saskatchewan	1 969	4	3 465	7	5 971	34	10 816	100	9 407	99
Nova Scotia	4 146	45	1 925	22	2 726	133	3 512	199	3 415	205
New Brunswick	933	9	359	3	439	17	520	34	548	37

Source: *Statistics Canada*

Canadian Energy Imports and Exports

		Crude Oil Quantity cu.m (000s)	Crude Oil Value ($million)	Natural Gas Quantity cu.m (millions)	Natural Gas Value ($million)	Coal Quantity tonnes (000s)	Coal Value ($million)	Electricity Quantity KWh (millions)	Electricity Value ($million)
1960	Imports	19 953	280	158	2	12 320	77	116	...
	Exports	6 712	94	2 579	18	774	7	5 639	16
1965	Imports	22 912	312	444	6	15 063	126	3 405	14
	Exports	17 164	280	11 442	104	1 119	13	3 379	15
1970	Imports	32 995	415	336	5	17 122	151	2 882	12
	Exports	38 280	649	21 759	206	4 004	30	5 147	34
1975	Imports	47 422	3 302	296	8	15 272	576	2 940	13
	Exports	41 707	3 052	26 896	1 092	11 697	478	7 216	104
1980	Imports	32 694	6 919	3	...	16 067	811	154	3
	Exports	12 426	2 899	22 972	3 984	14 311	794	28 323	773
1985	Imports	15 856	3 695	1	...	15 022	887	206	8
	Exports	27 886	5 972	26 155	4 011	27 572	1 996	41 531	1 425
1986	Imports	20 167	2 885	2	...	13 369	744	231	9
	Exports	33 617	3 775	21 389	2 524	25 900	1 851	35 271	1 086
1987	Imports	21 767	3 179	1	...	14 150	725	375	9
	Exports	35 776	4 855	27 672	2 527	25 466	1 670	45 318	1 200
1988	Imports	23 476	2 821	1	...	15 671	728	2 684	57
	Exports	40 973	4 038	36 254	2 954	29 450	1 944	30 442	894
1989	Imports	28 300	3 607	2	...	15 447	686	7 299	222
	Exports	37 458	4 462	37 870	3 023	31 801	2 082	18 459	662
1990	Imports	31 847	5 300	6	...	14 807	611	15 133	558
	Exports	33 055	5 532	47 373	3 267	31 995	2 110	16 231	538
1991	Imports	30 823	4 489	3	...	32 401	2 043	1 724	50
	Exports	39 167	5 503	44 844	3 339	29 307	1 849	19 784	557
1992	Imports	29 383	4 142	613	50	13 461	564	1 842	76
	Exports	46 582	6 682	56 551	4 361	25 910	1 667	26 217	714

Source: *Statistics Canada*

(—) = zero. (...) = too small to be included.

Household Heating by Province

(percentage of households)

	Oil		Gas		Electricity		Wood	
	1978	1990	1978	1990	1978	1990	1978	1990
Canada	**43.5**	**17.6**	**38.0**	**44.6**	**16.2**	**33.1**	**1.8**	**4.5**
Newfoundland	66.9	31.8	...	...	27.9	45.7	4.4	22.0
Prince Edward Island	91.2	77.8	n.a.	...	...	...	...	17.8
Nova Scotia	83.4	61.3	...	1.9	8.7	23.3	5.0	11.6
New Brunswick	72.5	28.3	n.a.	...	20.1	51.8	6.3	19.0
Quebec	62.4	22.8	6.8	6.9	27.8	65.3	2.4	5.0
Ontario	40.2	16.4	45.2	60.0	13.3	21.0	1.1	2.6
Manitoba	21.2	3.9	57.6	57.7	18.5	34.5	n.a.	2.6
Saskatchewan	22.9	8.7	74.3	83.2	1.7	5.3	...	2.8
Alberta	2.8	1.4	95.2	95.7	0.8	1.7	...	0.7
British Columbia	31.6	11.0	52.2	54.9	14.0	28.6	1.9	5.4

Source: *Statistics Canada*

n.a. not available; . . . = too small to be included.

Consumer Cost of Fuel

(annual averages)

	Regular Unleaded Gasoline [1]	Heating Oil [2]	Natural Gas [2]	Electricity [2]
	cents per litre	cents per litre	cents per cubic metre	cents per kilowatt hour
1971	11.2	4.7	3.6	n.a.
1975	15.9	8.2	4.8	n.a.
1976	17.7	9.5	6.3	n.a.
1977	19.2	11.0	7.4	n.a.
1978	20.0	12.5	8.5	2.8
1979	21.9	14.1	9.2	3.0
1980	25.9	17.1	10.6	3.3
1981	35.3	24.6	13.2	3.7
1982	42.9	30.1	15.4	4.1
1983	45.9	33.3	18.0	4.4
1984	48.4	35.5	18.5	4.8
1985	51.2	38.3	18.7	5.0
1986	44.8	30.4	18.9	5.2
1987	47.3	29.1	18.6	5.4
1988	47.4	30.5	18.4	5.6
1989	51.3	30.2	17.3	5.9
1990	58.0	35.9	17.8	6.3
1991	57.1	39.0	19.5	7.2

Source: *Energy, Mines and Resources Canada*

(1) Was leaded gasoline until 1990. (2) Residential sales. (n.a.) not available.

FOREIGN TRADE

Canadian Balance of International Payments

(millions of dollars)

The Canadian balance of payments is a measure of all yearly business transactions between Canada and the rest of the world. These transactions are listed in 2 accounts: current account and capital account. The current account keeps track of all Canadian payments for imported goods and services and of all money received for Canadian exports of goods and services. The capital account records all investment transactions (stocks, bonds, real estate, new companies, loans, foreign currency trading, interest payments) between Canada and other countries.

The balance of payments, the sum of the 2 accounts, shows whether Canada is experiencing a surplus (more money flowing into the country than out) or a deficit (more money leaving the country than coming in). In the short run, neither a deficit nor a surplus is necessarily bad or good. However, a persistent deficit might cause inflation by depreciating the Canadian dollar, or could lead to higher interest rates because Canada would be forced to borrow from foreign countries. A prolonged surplus might contribute to an increase in the value of the Canadian dollar, reducing foreign demand for Canadian exports and causing unemployment.

| Year | Balance of Payments[1] | Current Account | | | Capital Account | | |
		Receipts[2]	Payments	Balance[3]	Investment Inflow[4]	Investment Outflow[5]	Total Investment Balance[6]
1961	-167	7 892	8 830	-938	n.a.	n.a.	771
1965	271	11 693	12 792	-1 098	n.a.	n.a.	1 369
1970	316	21 907	20 874	1 033	1 860	2 577	-717
1975	1 326	42 076	46 707	-4 631	7 202	1 245	5 957
1980	1 176	93 893	95 024	-1 130	9 861	7 555	2 306
1981	8 457	103 931	110 061	-6 131	33 033	18 446	14 587
1982	2 111	105 556	102 732	2 824	5 929	6 642	-713
1983	5 692	112 244	109 177	3 066	11 237	8 611	2 626
1984	6 437	135 762	133 067	2 695	15 051	11 308	3 742
1985	6 218	146 019	148 011	-1 991	12 070	3 861	8 209
1986	2 574	150 244	160 399	-10 155	24 854	12 125	12 729
1987	3 087	158 239	167 407	-9 168	29 073	16 819	12 254
1988	4 039	177 985	188 146	-10 162	36 489	22 288	14 200
1989	5 382	180 083	196 772	-16 688	33 719	11 648	22 070
1990	-263	183 473	209 182	-25 709	34 712	9 266	25 446
1991	5 795	178 322	207 571	-29 249	43 062	8 018	35 044
1992	-1 254	194 125	222 689	-28 563	28 595	1 286	27 309

Source: *Statistics Canada*

(1) Sum of the current and capital account balances. (2) Money received for Canadian exports of goods and services. (3) Receipts minus payments. (4) Represents net foreign investment to Canada. (5) Represents net Canadian investment to other countries. (6) Investment inflow minus investment outflow.

Canadian Trade Balance[1]

(millions of dollars)

	1960	1970	1980	1985	1990	1991	1992
All Countries	-97	2 868	6 885	15 119	12 249	9 997	5 891
United States[2]	-651	983	728	21 039	23 399	23 238	22 024
USSR	5	93	1 468	1 577	940	1 245	994
Netherlands	32	202	1 211	365	794	1 120	827
Belgium[3]	29	140	764	204	688	650	644
Iran	-28	-26	17	-81	336	237	232
Algeria	...	19	352	9	229	179	53
Morocco	...	5	60	154	194	118	49
Egypt	1	38	101	162	64	99	40
Libya	...	3	-7	57	53	57	80
India	8	91	253	317	89	45	232
Spain	3	33	39	-292	-109	43	-1
Turkey	2	21	28	182	73	26	67
Romania	1	-1	-18	-9	-63	22	-5
Colombia	4	-2	135	73	79	17	98
Australia	64	56	157	310	136	14	-120
United Arab Emirates	-8	-7	-41	19	-28	13	51
Israel	4	1	53	45	20	11	-15
Lebanon	3	4	40	9	5	11	21
Peru	6	32	-40	-19	-67	6	-7
China	3	123	692	858	263	—	-315
Kenya	-2	-4	-4	2	43	-1	11
El Salvador	1	-1	-12	-26	-4	-3	-1
South Africa	42	59	-183	-79	20	-7	-9
Hungary	1	-2	-17	-20	-37	-20	-10
Philippines	15	27	-27	-80	5	-20	-71
Cuba	6	50	262	286	43	-22	-143
Poland	15	3	282	-27	-44	-25	-5
Yugoslavia	4	20	36	-3	-36	-26	-33
Chile	6	20	16	-48	17	-33	-57
Nicaragua	1	1	-16	-7	-52	-33	-22
Czechoslovakia	...	-20	64	-48	-53	-48	14
Venezuela	-159	-227	-1 533	-761	-292	-64	-9
Argentina	16	51	192	-29	-92	-66	-11
Switzerland	3	40	-101	-147	405	-68	475
Jamaica	-20	21	15	-98	-48	-82	-109
Brazil	-5	44	605	-125	-290	-89	-95
New Zealand	14	1	-36	30	-55	-101	-100
Malaysia	-133	-20	-71	5	-125	-140	-368
Singapore	-133	-9	97	-66	-147	-214	-325
South Korea	...	19	80	-866	-688	-222	-603
Hong Kong	6	-57	-358	-507	-379	-223	-377
Saudi Arabia	-34	-17	-2 330	213	-357	-260	-256
Nigeria	-2	-37	42	-172	-531	-516	-423
Sweden	1	-57	-138	-491	-572	-558	-587
Italy	26	42	363	-869	-780	-732	-660
United Kingdom	336	763	1 275	-515	-1 329	-1 155	-1 090
Taiwan	2	18	-325	-945	-1 313	-1 156	-1 517
France	24	-1	210	-686	-1 132	-1 256	-1 349
West Germany[4]	41	18	175	-1 559	-1 532	-1 302	-1 370
Mexico	18	49	152	-928	-1 124	-2 114	-1 981
Japan	69	231	1 469	-994	-1 302	-3 097	-3 345
East Germany[4]	...	-4	...	94	—	—	n.a.
Iraq	2	-10	-127	70	84	—	3.41

Source: *Statistics Canada*

(1) The trade balance is the value of merchandise exports minus the value of merchandise imports; it does not include services. Prior to 1980, imports were attributed to country of export/consignment. From 1980, imports are attributed to country of origin (the country in which the goods were grown, extracted or manufactured). (2) 1990 data not directly comparable to previous years due to improvements in data collection procedures which resulted in higher values for 1990. Also beginning in 1990, includes Puerto Rico and the U.S. Virgin Islands. (3) Includes Luxembourg. (4) From Oct. 1990 on, all data for reunified Germany is listed under West Germany. Figures for East Germany represent trade prior to Oct. 1990 only. (—) = zero; ... = too small to be included.

Canadian Imports by Country[1]

(millions of dollars)

	1970	%	1980	%	1990	%	1991	%	1992	%
Total Imports	13 952	100.0	69 273	100.0	135 922	100.0	135 284	100.0	147 865	100.0
United States[2]	9 917	71.1	47 445	68.5	87 803	64.6	86 235	63.7	96 397	65.1
Japan	582	4.2	2 904	4.2	9 517	7.0	10 249	7.0	10 757	7.3
United Kingdom	738	5.3	1 969	2.8	4 840	3.6	4 182	3.1	4 102	2.8
West Germany[3]	370	2.7	1 492	2.2	3 832	2.8	3 734	2.8	3 531	2.4
France	158	1.1	807	1.2	2 434	1.8	2 670	2.0	2 688	1.8
Mexico	47	0.3	342	0.5	1 730	1.3	2 574	1.9	2 751	1.9
Taiwan	52	0.4	578	0.8	2 109	1.6	2 212	1.6	2 469	1.7
South Korea	15	0.1	432	0.6	2 252	1.7	2 110	1.6	2 008	1.4
China	19	0.1	181	0.3	1 392	1.0	1 852	1.4	2 447	1.7
Italy	145	1.0	641	0.9	1 953	1.4	1 792	1.3	1 744	1.2
Hong Kong	78	0.6	557	0.8	1 059	0.8	1 021	0.8	1 134	0.8
Sweden	106	0.8	423	0.6	899	0.7	789	0.6	791	0.5
Brazil	49	0.4	357	0.5	790	0.6	706	0.5	715	0.5
Australia	146	1.0	521	0.8	767	0.6	664	0.5	750	0.5
Switzerland	81	0.6	488	0.7	648	0.5	661	0.5	651	0.4
Netherlands	79	0.6	230	0.3	721	0.5	599	0.4	598	0.4
Singapore	20	0.1	104	0.2	552	0.4	589	0.4	644	0.4
Saudi Arabia	24	0.2	2 643	3.8	635	0.5	540	0.4	542	0.4
Nigeria	45	0.3	63	0.1	561	0.4	518	0.4	473	0.3
Venezuela	339	2.4	2 212	3.2	562	0.4	482	0.4	334	0.2
Spain	34	0.2	197	0.3	496	0.4	461	0.3	436	0.3
Belgium[4]	52	0.4	237	0.3	550	0.4	447	0.3	428	0.3
Malaysia	34	0.2	166	0.2	380	0.3	436	0.3	598	0.4
India	40	0.3	106	0.2	227	0.2	240	0.2	278	0.2
USSR	9	0.1	72	0.1	185	0.1	233	0.2	269	0.2
Philippines	4	...	113	0.2	202	0.1	212	0.2	276	0.2
New Zealand	43	0.3	150	0.2	214	0.2	195	0.1	204	0.1
Chile	3	...	96	0.1	180	0.1	183	0.1	202	0.1
Jamaica	27	0.2	50	0.1	157	0.1	159	0.1	173	0.1
Cuba	9	0.1	163	0.2	130	0.1	153	0.1	256	0.2
Colombia	27	0.2	101	0.1	132	0.1	136	0.1	130	...
Argentina	9	0.1	40	0.1	140	0.1	130	0.1	112	...
Israel	14	0.1	62	0.1	125	0.1	127	0.1	131	...
South Africa	46	0.3	388	0.6	141	0.1	126	0.1	137	...
Morocco	...	...	10	...	40	...	71	0.1	76	...
Peru	4	...	96	0.1	126	0.1	71	0.1	95	...
Yugoslavia	7	0.1	34	...	94	0.1	71	0.1	56	...
Iran	34	0.2	24	...	21	...	68	0.1	126	...
Turkey	1	...	13	...	84	0.1	66	...	67	...
Czechoslovakia	27	0.2	64	0.1	70	0.1	65	...	60	...
Poland	12	0.1	75	0.1	79	0.1	63	...	57	...
Algeria	...	...	41	0.1	62	...	60	...	98	...
Nicaragua	1	...	31	...	63	...	46	...	31	...
Hungary	9	0.1	27	...	45	...	37	...	41	...
Romania	5	...	40	0.1	87	0.1	25	...	31	...
United Arab Emirates	7	0.1	86	0.1	58	...	24	...	3	...
El Salvador	4	...	27	...	19	...	16	...	12	...
Kenya	6	...	18	...	14	...	13	...	13	...
Egypt	...	...	29	...	9	...	12	...	58	...
Lebanon	1	...	...	...	3	...	4	...	4	...
Iraq	14	0.1	280	0.4	113	0.1	—	—	.59	...
East Germany[3]	4	0.1	11	...	22	...	—	—		
Libya	...	...	80	0.1	—	—				

Source: *Statistics Canada*

(1) Prior to 1980, imports were attributed to country of export/consignment. From 1980, imports are attributed to country of origin (the country in which the goods were grown, extracted or manufactured). (2) Beginning with 1990, includes Puerto Rico and the U.S. Virgin Islands. (3) From Oct. 1990 on, all data for reunified Germany is listed under West Germany. Figures for East Germany represent trade prior to Oct. 1990 only. (4) Includes Luxembourg.

(—) = zero; ... = too small to be included.

Canadian Exports by Country[1]

(millions of dollars)

	1970	%	1980	%	1990	%	1991	%	1992	%
Total Exports	**16 820**	**100.0**	**76 158**	**100.0**	**148 170**	**100.0**	**145 281**	**100.0**	**153 756**	**100.0**
United States[1]	10 900	64.8	48 173	63.3	111 202	75.0	109 473	75.4	118 421	77.0
Japan	813	4.8	4 373	5.7	8 215	5.5	7 152	4.9	7 412	4.8
United Kingdom	1 501	8.9	3 244	4.3	3 511	2.4	3 027	2.1	3 012	2.0
West Germany[2]	388	2.3	1 667	2.2	2 300	1.6	2 432	1.7	2 161	1.4
South Korea	19	0.1	512	0.7	1 563	1.1	1 888	1.3	1 405	1.0
China	142	0.8	873	1.1	1 654	1.1	1 852	1.3	2 132	1.3
Netherlands	281	1.7	1 441	1.9	1 515	1.0	1 719	1.2	1 425	1.0
USSR	102	0.6	1 540	2.0	1 125	0.8	1 478	1.0	1 263	0.8
France	157	0.9	1 017	1.3	1 302	0.9	1 414	1.0	1 339	0.9
Belgium[3]	192	1.1	1 001	1.3	1 237	0.8	1 097	0.8	1 072	0.7
Italy	187	1.1	1 004	1.3	1 173	0.8	1 060	0.7	1 084	0.7
Taiwan	18	0.1	253	0.3	796	0.5	1 056	0.7	952	0.6
Hong Kong	21	0.1	199	0.3	680	0.5	836	0.6	757	0.5
Australia	202	1.2	678	0.9	903	0.6	678	0.5	630	0.4
Brazil	93	0.6	962	1.3	499	0.3	617	0.4	620	0.4
Switzerland	41	0.2	387	0.5	1 053	0.7	593	0.4	1 126	0.7
Spain	67	0.4	236	0.3	387	0.3	504	0.3	435	0.3
Mexico	96	0.6	494	0.6	606	0.4	460	0.3	770	0.5
Venezuela	112	0.7	679	0.9	270	0.2	418	0.3	325	0.2
Singapore	11	0.1	201	0.3	405	0.3	375	0.3	319	0.2
Iran	8	...	41	0.1	357	0.2	305	0.2	358	0.2
Malaysia	14	0.1	95	0.1	256	0.2	296	0.2	230	0.1
India	131	0.8	359	0.5	316	0.2	285	0.2	510	0.3
Saudi Arabia	7	...	313	0.4	278	0.2	280	0.2	286	0.2
Algeria	19	0.1	393	0.5	291	0.2	239	0.2	151	0.1
Sweden	49	0.3	285	0.4	328	0.2	231	0.2	204	0.1
Philippines	31	0.2	86	0.1	206	0.1	192	0.2	205	0.1
Morocco	5	...	70	0.1	234	0.2	189	0.1	125	0.1
Colombia	25	0.1	236	0.3	211	0.1	153	0.1	228	0.1
Chile	23	0.1	112	0.1	197	0.1	150	0.1	145	0.1
Israel	15	0.1	115	0.2	145	0.1	138	0.1	116	0.1
Cuba	59	0.4	425	0.6	173	0.1	131	0.1	113	0.1
South Africa	105	0.6	205	0.3	161	0.1	119	0.1	128	0.1
Egypt	38	0.2	130	0.2	74	...	111	0.1	98	0.1
New Zealand	44	0.3	114	0.2	158	0.1	94	0.1	104	0.1
Turkey	22	0.1	41	0.1	157	0.1	92	0.1	134	0.1
Jamaica	48	0.3	65	0.1	109	0.1	77	0.1	64	...
Peru	36	0.2	56	0.1	58	...	77	0.1	88	0.1
Argentina	60	0.4	232	0.3	48	...	64	...	101	0.1
Libya	3	...	73	0.1	53	...	57	...	80	0.1
Romania	4	...	22	...	25	...	47	...	26	...
Yugoslavia	27	0.2	70	0.1	57	...	45	...	23	...
Poland	15	0.1	357	0.5	35	...	38	...	52	...
United Arab Emirates	...	...	45	0.1	30	...	37	...	54	...
Czechoslovakia	7	...	128	0.2	17	...	17	...	74	...
Hungary	7	...	10	...	8	...	17	...	31	...
Lebanon	5	...	40	0.1	8	...	15	...	25	...
El Salvador	3	...	15	...	15	...	13	...	11	...
Nicaragua	2	...	15	...	12	...	13	...	9	...
Kenya	2	...	14	...	56	...	12	...	24	...
Nigeria	8	...	105	0.1	30	...	2	...	50	...
East Germany[2]	...	...	11	...	23	...	—		—	
Iraq	4	...	153	0.2	197	0.1	—		4	...

Source: *Statistics Canada*

(1) 1990 data not directly comparable to previous years due to improvements in data collection procedures which resulted in higher values for 1990. Also beginning in 1990, includes Puerto Rico and the U.S. Virgin Islands. (2) From Oct. 1990 on, all data for reunified Germany is listed under West Germany. Figures for East Germany represent trade prior to Oct. 1990 only. (3) Includes Luxembourg. (—) = zero. (...) = too small to be included.

PERSONAL FINANCE

What's a Dollar Worth[1]?

This table shows how many current (1993) dollars it would take to equal the purchasing power of a single dollar in earlier years. For example, if you lived on $50 a week in 1950 and want to know what that would be by today's standards, multiply $50 times the relative value of a 1950 dollar ($6.85) and you have your answer: $342.50. The relative value of a dollar for the years listed was calculated according to changes in the cost of living in Canada as measured by the Consumer Price

Year	Value	Year	Value	Year	Value	Year	Value
1915	$13.85	1956	$5.97	1969	$4.34	1982	$1.56
1920	7.53	1957	5.79	1970	4.20	1983	1.47
1925	9.37	1958	5.64	1971	4.08	1984	1.41
1930	9.37	1959	5.56	1972	3.84	1985	1.36
1935	11.73	1960	5.49	1973	3.62	1986	1.30
1940	10.67	1961	5.45	1974	3.26	1987	1.25
1945	9.37	1962	5.38	1975	2.95	1988	1.20
1950	6.85	1963	5.29	1976	2.74	1989	1.14
1951	6.17	1964	5.19	1977	2.54	1990	1.09
1952	6.03	1965	5.07	1978	2.33	1991	1.03
1953	6.08	1966	4.89	1979	2.13	1992	1.02
1954	6.05	1967	4.72	1980	1.94	1993	1.00
1955	6.05	1968	4.54	1981	1.72		

(1) Based on June Consumer Price Index

Average Income in Selected Canadian Cities, 1990

City	Average Income[1]	Total Income ($000)	Number of Tax Returns
West Vancouver, B.C.	$57 302	1 300 589	22 700
Oakville, Ont.	44 382	2 807 811	63 260
Markham, Ont.	43 350	4 420 476	101 970
Richmond Hill, Ont.	41 241	1 843 885	44 710
Vaughan, Ont.	39 915	1 482 284	37 140
Burlington, Ont.	39 318	2 894 765	73 620
North York, Ont.	38 880	9 526 689	245 030
Whitby, Ont.	38 327	1 207 938	31 520
Nepean, Ont.	38 094	2 204 290	57 870
Toronto, Ont.	38 089	22 119 562	580 740
Pickering, Ont.	37 477	1 323 528	35 320
Newmarket, Ont.	37 235	979 697	26 310
Waterloo, Ont.	37 232	1 514 727	40 680
St. Albert, Alta.	37 024	873 386	23 590
Gloucester, Ont.	36 934	2 370 657	64 190
Ottawa, Ont.	36 488	7 011 394	192 160
Halton Hills, Ont.	36 050	795 129	22 060
North Vancouver, B.C.	36 045	2 361 351	65 510
Etobicoke, Ont.	35 813	4 502 202	125 710
Mississauga, Ont.	35 609	8 841 237	248 290
Dollard-des-Ormeaux, Que.	35 409	805 373	22 750
Ajax, Ont.	35 233	1 032 847	29 320
Calgary, Alta.	35 174	13 841 227	393 500
Newcastle, Ont.	$34 830	878 273	25 220
Vancouver, B.C.	34 858	9 612 513	275 760
Brampton, Ont.	33 127	4 145 518	125 140
London, Ont.	32 504	5 424 107	166 880
Halifax, N.S.	32 030	2 125 470	66 360
Edmonton, Alta.	31 452	10 160 700	323 050
Victoria, B.C.	31 406	4 526 794	144 140
Scarborough, Ont.	31 040	8 532 664	274 900
Regina, Sask.	30 898	2 940 701	95 180
Fredericton, N.B.	30 467	1 080 324	35 460
St. John's, Nfld.	30 095	1 484 370	49 320
Saskatoon, Sask.	30 035	2 830 557	94 240
Laval, Que.	29 681	4 964 672	167 270
Hamilton, Ont.	29 514	5 016 308	169 960
Winnipeg, Man.	29 268	9 967 308	340 550
Montreal, Que.	28 364	15 177 071	535 080
Saint John, N.B.	28 054	1 134 603	40 440
Quebec, Que.	27 930	2 439 568	87 350
Sydney, N.S.	27 768	511 296	18 410
Brandon, Man.	26 895	572 407	21 280
Drummondville, Que.	26 027	622 764	23 930
Montreal-Nord, Que.	24 409	928 759	38 050

Source: *Revenue Canada* (1) Average total income after business deductions, but before personal deductions.

Average Income in Canada

This table shows actual average income from 1971 to 1991 in addition to average income in constant dollars over the same period. Constant dollars are adjusted to remove the effects of inflation, thereby providing a realistic way of comparing incomes for different years. An increase in constant dollar income means that incomes have increased faster than the cost of living; a decrease in constant dollar income means that incomes have not kept pace with inflation.

| | Families[1] | | | | Individuals | | | |
| | Female Head | | Male Head | | Females | | Males | |
	Actual	Constant[2]	Actual	Constant[2]	Actual	Constant[2]	Actual	Constant[2]
1971	$5 486	$22 393	$10 486	$42 804	$3 597	$14 683	$5 136	$20 965
1973	6 687	26 066	12 910	50 323	4 267	16 633	6 206	24 191
1975	8 528	25 158	16 993	50 129	5 450	16 078	7 964	23 494
1977	10 691	27 134	20 544	52 141	6 923	17 571	9 919	25 174
1979	12 663	27 023	24 946	53 235	8 754	18 681	12 427	26 519
1980	13 982	27 083	28 533	55 268	8 364	16 201	16 917	32 768
1981	16 704	28 898	31 655	54 763	9 833	17 011	19 041	32 941
1982	17 439	27 205	34 357	53 596	10 551	16 460	19 905	31 052
1983	17 135	25 188	36 008	52 932	10 985	16 148	20 756	30 511
1984	19 578	27 605	37 487	52 857	11 764	16 587	21 125	29 786
1985	20 541	27 936	39 982	54 376	12 375	16 830	22 563	30 686
1986	21 396	27 858	42 390	55 192	13 247	17 248	23 846	31 047
1987	22 818	28 454	44 885	55 972	14 028	17 493	24 903	31 054
1988	23 656	28 364	47 763	57 268	14 886	17 848	26 403	31 657
1989	26 802	30 608	51 413	58 714	16 321	18 639	28 238	32 248
1990	26 721	29 099	53 264	58 004	17 269	19 198	29 108	31 699
1991	31 700	32 715	55 946	57 736	20 203	20 849	25 179	25 985

Source: *Statistics Canada*

(1) Based on the Census family definition: a husband and wife (without children or with children who never married) or a parent with one or more children who never married, living together in the same home. (2) Converted to 1993 dollars using the CPI with 1986 = 100.

Taxes of the Average Canadian Family, 1993[1]

Province	Total Taxes	Average Cash Income	Income Tax	Sales Tax	Property Tax	Liquor, Tobacco, Amusement and other Excise Taxes	Auto, Fuel and Motor Vehicle Licence Taxes	Social Security, Pension, Medical and Hospital Taxes	Other Taxes[2]
Canada	$22 946	$51 797	$8 381	$3 611	$2 040	$1 254	$743	$4 123	$2 795
Nfld.	16 652	46 475	5 692	3 809	630	1 301	747	2 483	1 989
P.E.I.	15 887	45 481	6 028	3 423	725	1 366	689	2 588	1 069
N.S.	17 627	42 164	6 928	3 305	1 069	1 224	696	2 810	1 594
N.B.	18 288	44 488	6 387	3 797	1 550	1 052	772	2 733	1 997
Que.	22 793	48 487	8 155	3 846	2 153	1 039	686	4 271	2 645
Ont.	27 233	59 580	10 112	4 136	2 758	1 304	843	4 929	3 151
Man.	19 943	45 410	7 015	3 150	1 673	1 427	680	3 777	2 221
Sask.	23 159	44 714	6 938	3 299	3 157	1 362	1 141	2 383	4 877
Alta.	24 047	51 594	8 168	1 711	2 757	1 503	671	3 870	5 399
B.C.	23 525	49 004	8 482	3 691	2 064	1 538	644	3 689	3 417

Source: *The Fraser Institute*

(1) Preliminary estimates. (2) Includes profits tax, natural resource taxes, import duties and other taxes.

Canadian Income Tax

Income tax was introduced in 1917 as a temporary measure to finance Canada's participation in World War I. The law introducing the tax (the Income War Tax Act) was shorter and much simpler than our current legislation. It imposed tax at graduated rates, ranging from 4% on the first $1 500 to 25% for income over $100 000.

This "temporary" tax was not repealed when the war ended. But on Jan. 1, 1949, the federal government removed "war" from the title and gave the statute the name it has today—the Income Tax Act. This act has been amended many times—most notably in 1972 when a major overhaul of the tax system broadened the tax base and introduced a tax on capital gains. This is still the basis of our federal income tax laws today.

In 1988, all personal exemptions and many deductions were changed to non-refundable tax credits. Unlike deductions, which reduce taxable income, credits are used to reduce the amount of tax payable. The term "non-refundable" refers to the fact that, although you can use these credits to reduce or eliminate your federal tax payable, any unused portion is not refundable to you. In some cases, however, you may be able to transfer the unused portion of the credits to someone else.

Because the credits are calculated by multiplying eligible amounts by 17%—the same as the lowest personal tax rate—the change makes no difference to those whose income falls within the lowest tax bracket. But it increases taxes for most of those with higher incomes.

For 1993, the federal income tax rates for individuals are: 17% on income up to $29 590; 26% on income between $29 590 and $59 180; and 29% on income in excess of $59 180.

Provincial Income Tax

Every province except Quebec collects income tax from its residents by "piggy-backing" on the federal tax. Each province imposes tax of a fixed percentage based on the amount of income tax an individual must pay to the federal government. The federal government collects the tax, then remits the appropriate amounts to the provincial governments.

Quebec, however, chooses to collect its own provincial income tax, so Quebec residents must file both the federal return filed by all Canadian taxpayers, and the Quebec provincial income tax return.

Filing Tax Returns

Though corporations must file tax returns each year, individuals need only file if they owe taxes or if they are eligible to claim tax credits such as the Child Tax Credit or the Goods and Services Tax Credit. Persons owing money must file a return by Apr. 30 of the year following the taxation year. Failure to do so makes you liable to a late-filing penalty of 5% of unpaid tax plus an additional penalty of 1% per month on the amount outstanding, to a maximum of 12 months, plus interest on amounts owing.

Source: *Revenue Canada*

Taxes Paid by Province, 1990

	Returns Filed	Total Income Assessed ($million)	New Federal Tax Payable ($million)	Net Provincial Tax Payable ($million)
Canada	13 795 990	433 602.6	59 562.2	23 928.7
Newfoundland	239 040	6 037.3	715.1	422.9
PEI	62 150	1 513.6	174.7	96.9
Nova Scotia	418 790	11 839.2	1 512.1	865.9
New Brunswick	332 890	8 851.1	1 093.9	626.2
Quebec	3 378 650	97 910.8	12 717.1	6.5
Ontario	5 361 460	181 980.8	26 251.5	13 308.8
Manitoba	529 260	14 831.8	1 846.7	1 140.3
Saskatchewan	446 890	12 506.2	1 530.8	948.0
Alberta	1 269 690	41 004.7	5 727.9	2 706.8
BC	1 690 060	54 849.1	7 605.0	3 723.7
Yukon	13 780	480.8	60.0	25.7
NWT	22 540	912.7	130.9	54.8
Outside Canada	30 800	884.3	196.5	2.1

Source: *Taxation Statistics, Revenue Canada*

Individual Income Tax Rates, 1993

Federal Tax

Taxable Income	Basic Federal Tax	Marginal Rate[1]
$ 1	$ 0	17%
29 590	5 030	26%
59 180	12 724	29%

(1) Excludes the federal surtax of 3 % of basic federal tax which generally constitutes the tax payable after deducting personal and dividend tax credits, but before deducting other credits. A further surtax of 5% applies to basic federal tax in excess of $12 500 (taxable income in excess of $62,193 assuming no other credits)

Quebec Tax[1]

Taxable Income	Basic Federal Tax	Marginal Rate[1]
$ 0	$ —	16%
7 000	1 120	19%
14 000	2 450	21%
23 000	4 340	23%
50 000	10 550	24%

(1) Residents of Quebec (as at Dec. 31) are entitled to a federal tax abatement of 16.5% of basic federal tax (after deducting personal and dividend tax credits), but must pay Quebec income tax at the indicated rates. Surtaxes at 5% of provincial tax over $5,000 plus 5% of provincial tax over $10,000 also apply.

Provincial Tax
(rates applied to basic federal tax)

Newfoundland	69.0%[1]	Saskatchewan	50.0%	[7]
Prince Edward Island	59.5%[2]	Alberta	45.5%	[8]
Nova Scotia	59.5%[3]	British Columbia	52.5%	[9]
New Brunswick	62.0%[4]	Northwest Territories	45.0%	
Ontario	58.5%[5]	Yukon Territories	50.0%[10]	
Manitoba	52.0%[6]	Non-residents	52.0%[11]	

(1) Increased from 64.5% to 69% effective Jan. 1, 1993. (2) To be increased by 10% of basic provincial tax in excess of $12,500. (3) To be increased by 10% of basic provincial tax in excess of $10 000. (4) To be increased by 8% of provinicial tax in excess of $13 500. (5) Increased from 55% to 58% effective Jan. 1, 1993. To be increased by 17% of provincial tax in excess of $5 500 plus 8% of provincial tax in excess of $8,000. (6) To be increased by a flat tax of 2% of net income plus, where net income exceeds $30 000, a surtax equal to the flat tax minus $600 and several other credits. (7) To be increased by a flat tax of 2% of net income plus a surtax of 15% of provincial tax (including the 2% flat tax) in excess of $4 000 and a surtax of 10% of provincial tax and flat tax. (8) To be increased by 8% of basic provincial tax in excess of $3 500, plus an additional tax equal to 0.5% of taxable income. (9) To be increased by 20% (30% for 1994) of provincial tax in excess of $5 300 plus 10% (20% for 1994) of provincial tax in excess of $9 000. (10) Basic rate increased from 45% to 50%, effective Jan. 1, 1993. To be increased by 5% of provincial tax in excess of $6,000.(11) Non-residents are subject to an additional federal tax of 52% in lieu of provincial tax.

Source: *Coopers & Lybrand*

Tax Freedom Day

Tax freedom day is the day of the year on which Canadians begin to work for themselves. Until that point, everything they earn is paid out in taxes levied by federal, provincial and municipal governments.

The concept of tax freedom day was developed by the Fraser Institute, a Vancouver-based, independent Canadian economic research organization. According to the Institute's calculations, the average Canadian family in 1992 had an income of $51,797, out of which it paid taxes totalling $22,946—a rate of 44 percent. This corresponds to the 162nd day of the year, June 11. In 1961, the earliest year covered by the Institute's calculations, the average Canadian family had earned enough to pay its taxes by May 3.

Tax freedom day falls on a different date in each province due to variations in provincial and municipal taxes. The earliest tax freedom day—May 8 — is in Prince Edward Island; the latest—July 8—is in Saskatchewan. Dates for all provinces are listed below.

Prince Edward Island	May 8	Ontario	June 16
Newfoundland	May 11	Alberta	June 19
New Brunswick	May 30	Quebec	June 21
Nova Scotia	June 2	British Columbia	June 24
Manitoba	June 10	Saskatchewan	July 8

Source: *The Fraser Institute*

1993 Personal Tax Credits

	Basic Amount	Federal Credit	Quebec Credit
Basic	$6 456	$1 098	$1 180
Age 65	3 482	592	450
Disability	4 233	720	450
Married[1]	5 380	915	1 180
Dependants[2] — 1st	—	—	520
— Other	—	—	450
Disabled dependant[3]	1 583	269	1 180
Single parent	—	—	260
Living alone	—	—	210
Charitable donations:			
First $250	—	17%	20%
Remainder	—	29%	20%
Medical expenses[5]	—	17%	20%
Education credit[6]	640	109	660
Health Services Fund	—	—	20%
CPP/QPP/UIC & tuition	—	17%	20%
Tuition	—	17%	(4)
Pension income	1 000	170	200
Dividends[7]	—	13.33%	8.87%

Source: *Coopers & Lybrand*

(1) The credit is reduced where the spouse or qualifying dependant has income in excess of $538. (2) Includes only those under 19 years of age at the end of the year. (3) Those over 18 years of age at the end of the year. Income in excess of $2 690 reduces the credit. (4) For Quebec, this amount is deductible from income. (5) Based upon the amount by which qualifying expenses exceed the lesser of $1 614 or 3% of net income. (6) The credit is actually $13.60 per month for federal purposes and $330 per term (not more than 2) for Quebec purposes. (7) The credit for taxable Canadian dividends is applied at the specified percentages to the grossed-up amount (125%) of dividends. Provincial taxes (other than Quebec) are then calculated on the net federal tax payable.

1993 Individual Tax Tables

This table shows the combined federal and provincial income taxes, including surtaxes and flat taxes, payable on the assumption that only the basic personal tax credit is available. The political contribution tax credit and provincial credits for homeowners, renters, sales tax, cost of living, children, and venture capital have not been taken into account.

Taxable Income

	$20 000	$30 000	$40 000	$50 000	$60 000	$70 000	$80 000	$90 000	$100 000
Nfld.	3 960	6 947	11 419	15 891	20 407	25 508	30 641	35 774	40 907
P.E.I.	3 742	6 564	10 789	15 014	19 279	24 105	28 963	33 820	38 824
N.S.	3 742	6 564	10 789	15 014	19 279	24 105	29 014	34 044	39 074
N.B.	3 799	6 664	10 954	15 244	19 576	24 474	29 404	34 334	39 348
Que.-Prov.[1]	2 530	4 770	7 174	9 589	12 197	14 837	17 477	20 117	22 757
Que.-Fed.[1]	1 992	3 494	5 743	7 992	10 263	12 884	15 538	18 191	20 845
Ont.	3 707	6 503	10 689	14 875	19 336	24 450	29 684	34 919	40 153
Man.[2]	3 939	6 861	11 291	15 721	20 190	25 198	30 238	35 278	40 318
Sask.[3]	4 078	7 042	11 388	15 941	20 535	25 698	30 893	36 087	41 282
Alta.[4]	3 519	6 148	10 059	14 026	18 070	22 646	27 253	31 860	36 467
B.C.	3 580	6 281	10 324	14 367	18 635	23 562	28 548	33 660	38 771
Yukon	3 523	6 180	10 158	14 136	18 152	22 772	27 426	32 081	36 735
N.W.T.	3 408	5 978	9 826	13 674	17 559	21 964	26 401	30 838	35 275

Source: *Coopers & Lybrand*

(1) Because taxable income differs for federal and Quebec purposes, Quebec taxpayers may have to determine the tax payable to each jurisdiction on separate lines of the table before totalling. (2) The tax payable for Manitoba includes the additional tax of 2% of net income on the assumption that net income is the same as taxable income. Where net income exceeds taxable income, the tax payable should be increased by 2% of the excess to more accurately approximate the liability. (3) The tax payable for Saskatchewan includes the flat tax of 2% on the assumption that net income is the same as taxable income. Where net income exceeds taxable income, the tax payable should be increased by 2% of the excess to more accurately approximate the liability. (4) The tax payable for Alberta includes the flat tax of 0.5% of taxable income.

Average Canadian Income and Taxes by Occupation, 1990

Occupation	Average Income[1]	Average Federal Tax	Number[2]	Occupation	Average Income[1]	Average Federal Tax	Number[2]
Self-employed doctors and surgeons	$123 159	$27 026	40 390	Provincial government employees	$33 413	$4 588	383 510
Self-employed dentists	104 684	21 308	9 410	Municipal government employees	31 421	4 281	738 870
Self-employed lawyers and notaries	97 075	20 349	24 050	Investors	30 707	3 747	1 271 070
Self-employed accountants	76 441	14 237	13 810	Business employees	27 430	3 460	1 046 300
Self-employed engineers and architects	52 574	9 310	5 900	Institutional employees	26 991	3 763	8 085 130
Teachers and professors	44 820	6 866	230 670	Self-employed salespeople	24 028	3 000	49 270
Provincial crown corp. employees	41 130	6 392	162 840	Property owners	21 854	2 891	152 220
Federal crown corp. employees	38 463	5 552	149 690	Fishermen	20 783	2 121	34 020
Federal government employees	38 239	5 768	314 650	Unclassified business employees	19 431	2 262	620 570
Armed forces employees	35 187	5 184	93 780	Farmers	18 012	1 543	239 230
Other self-employed professionals	34 685	5 358	89 960	Business proprietors	16 958	1 837	633 450
				Self-employed entertainers and artists	16 090	1 753	20 690
				Pensioners	15 672	1 189	2 358 040
				Unclassified	6 313	564	1 991 230

Source: *Revenue Canada*

(1) Average total income after business expense deductions but before personal deductions. (2) Based on number of tax returns.

Income Tax Collected from Individuals and Corporations

(millions of dollars)

Year[1]	Total Tax Collected[2]	Individual Income Tax	% of Total	Corporate Income Tax	% of Total	Cost of Collecting Tax
1950	1 300.8	622.0	47.8	603.2	46.4	28.1
1955	2 457.0	1 284.4	52.3	1 066.5	43.4	25.7
1960	3 148.2	1 752.2	55.7	1 234.2	39.2	31.8
1965	4 940.7	2 903.9	58.8	1 804.4	36.5	43.1
1970	10 988.4	7 661.9	69.7	3 080.0	28.0	82.5
1975	23 275.0	17 436.9	74.9	5 386.4	23.1	226.7
1980	37 328.7	27 935.1	74.8	8 511.6	22.8	388.8
1985	66 884.0	53 147.9	79.5	10 046.7	15.0	729.0
1986	72 857.7	59 658.8	81.9	9 983.0	13.7	774.7
1987	80 699.7	68 140.4	84.4	10 588.4	13.1	861.7
1988	93 914.8	80 589.3	85.8	12 035.2	12.8	922.6
1989	98 303.0	83 229.4	84.7	13 129.9	13.4	990.9
1990	109 003.3	92 726.1	85.1	14 635.5	13.4	1 138.3
1991	114 482.0	103 676.0	90.5	10 806.0	9.4	1 184.1
1992	122 041.0	112 814.0	92.4	9 227.0	7.6	1 237.0

Source: *Revenue Canada.*

(1) For fiscal year ending Mar. 31. (2) Includes non-resident tax, excess profits and special taxes, miscellaneous tax revenue, Canada Pension Plan contributions and Unemployment Insurance premiums.

Credit Card Costs

An estimated 46 million credit cards were in circulation in Canada in 1991, or 2.3 cards for every adult Canadian over the age of 18. Of those, more than 24 million were MasterCard or Visa, 14 million were cards issued by large department stores, and 3 million were gasoline cards. Other cards, such as American Express and enRoute, and cards issued by small financial institutions and retail stores constituted the remainder.

The total number of Visa and MasterCards more than doubled from 1981 to 1991—from 12 million to 24.3 million. MasterCard and Visa credit cards were used for more than 617 million transactions in 1991, 2.5 times the 1981 level. The volume of sales in 1991 was $40 billion, compared to $11 billion in 1981.

From 1986 to 1991, the number of merchant outlets in Canada accepting Visa or MasterCard increased by 50% to more than 857 000. The average sale per transaction charged to Visa and MasterCard increased from just under $42 in 1981 to almost $67 in 1991.

For the approximately 50 percent of credit card users who do not avoid interest charges by paying off their credit card balances each month, these cards are a relatively expensive form of credit. That's because the rate of interest is considerably higher than what's charged for other types of consumer loans. (In September 1992 the average interest rate for a two-year conventional consumer loan was 12% for amounts less than $5 000.)

Identifying the lowest credit card costs involves more than a comparison of interest rates and annual fees. Just as important is the way in which the interest charges are calculated. Some factors to consider:

The grace period: The number of days granted to pay your bill without being charged interest. The longer the grace period, the greater the financial benefit. There is no grace period for cash advances.

Calculation of interest: When you don't pay your balance in full, interest charges apply. But cards with the same annual interest rate can have very different interest charges, depending on whether the interest is charged from the date of purchase or from the date on which your monthly billing statement is issued. Obviously, the user pays more if the interest is charged from the earlier (purchase) date. You should also check whether interest is calculated on a daily or monthly basis.

Comparing Credit Cards

(as of April 1992)

Banks, Trust Companies and Credit Unions	Annual fees	Annual Interest rates	Grace period (days)	Interest calculated from date of[1]
MasterCard				
Bank of Montreal	none	18.0 %	21	purchase
Canada Trust	$ 8	17.75	22	purchase
CS CO-OP	none	17.75	21	purchase
National Bank	none	18.25	21	purchase
National Trust	none	17.50	21	statement
Niagara Credit Union	none	17.50	21	purchase
Shell/Royal Trust Vision	none	19.75	17[2]	purchase
VISA				
Bank of Nova Scotia	$ 6	17.25	21	purchase
Can. Imp. Bank of Commerce	$12	16.75	21	purchase
Central Guaranty	none	18.00	21	purchase
Centre Desjardins	$12	16.75	21	purchase
Laurentian Bank	$14	16.75	21	purchase
Montreal Trust	$12[3]	16.75	21	purchase
Royal Bank	$12[3]	16.75	21	purchase
Toronto Dominion Bank	$ 9	17.75	21	purchase
Vancouver City Savings	$12	16.75	21	purchase

▶

▶ Other Credit Cards	Annual fees	Annual Interest rates	Grace period (days)	Interest calculated from date of[4]
Canadian Tire	none	28.8%	30	statement
Eaton's	none	28.8	30	statement
enRoute	$38	22.0	30	statement
Home Hardware	none	28.8	30	statement
Hudson's Bay	none	28.8	25–30	statement
Petro-Canada	none	24.0	30	purchase
Sears	none	28.8	25–30	statement
Simpsons	none	28.8	25–30	statement
Ultramar	none	24.0	21	statement
Woodward's	none	26.4	25	statement
Zellers	none	28.8	25–30	statement

Charge Cards[5]	Annual fees	Annual Interest rates	Grace period (days)	Interest calculated from date of[1]
American Express	$55	n.a.	45	statement
Esso Petroleum Canada	none	24	30	statement
Husky Oil Ltd.	none	15	25	statement
Irving Oil	none	24	25	statement
Sunoco	none	24	25	statement

Source: *Consumer and Corporate Affairs Canada*

(1) Interest is calculated on a daily interest basis and payments immediately reduce the daily balance that is subject to interest. Interest is payable on the full daily balances up to the date of payment in full. (The exception is the Bank of Nova Scotia, which charges interest only up to the date of the most recent statement—when the statement is paid in full.) For the amounts of merchandise purchased that are included for the first time in the monthly statement balance, no interest is charged if the full balance is paid within the grace period. Interest is payable up to the date of payment in full. (2) 21 days in Quebec. (3) Under certain conditions, fee may be reduced or waived entirely. (4) Except for Canadian Tire, retail stores subtract payments equal to or exceeding 50 percent of the monthly balance before calculating interest charges. In Quebec, interest is calculated on a daily basis from the date of statement, which means that all payments reduce the balance that is subject to interest as of the date of payment. (5) These cards require payment in full each month by the payment due date.

Mortgage Rates by Year

	1-Year[1]	3-Year	5-Year
1981	18.1	18.19	18.38
1982	17.15	17.85	18.04
1983	11.17	12.67	13.23
1984	12.08	13.24	13.58
1985	10.44	11.65	12.13
1986	10.12	10.88	11.21
1987	9.86	10.71	11.17
1988	10.74	11.36	11.65
1989	12.77	12.17	12.06
1990	13.44	13.35	13.35
1991	10.22	11.00	11.13
1992	7.93	8.97	9.50

Sources: *Bank of Canada Review; Canada Mortgage and Housing Corp.; Canadian Bankers' Association*

(1) Does not include 1-year open.

The Effect of Interest Rate Changes on Mortgage Payments

The table below shows the monthly mortgage payment (principal and interest) for each $1 000 of mortgage debt. To calculate your payments at a given interest rate, choose the corresponding amount in the amortization column you select and multiply the amount by the number of thousands of dollars of debt. Example: if you want to know the cost per month to carry an $85 000 mortgage amortized over 25 years at 12.25%, multiply $10.49 by 85 and the result, $891.65, is your monthly payment. If the same mortgage was coming up for renewal at 12.75%, the new payment would be $922.25 ($10.85 × 85) or $30.60 more each month.

Monthly Payments for Each $1 000 of Mortgage

Interest Rate (%)	1 Year	2 Years	3 Years	5 Years	10 Years	15 Years	20 Years	25 Years
7.00	$86.48	$44.73	$30.83	$19.75	$11.56	$ 8.93	$ 7.69	$ 7.00
7.25	86.59	44.84	30.94	19.87	11.68	9.07	7.84	7.16
7.50	86.70	44.95	31.05	19.98	11.81	9.21	7.99	7.32
7.75	86.82	45.06	31.16	20.10	11.94	9.34	8.13	7.47
8.00	86.93	45.17	31.28	20.21	12.06	9.48	8.28	7.63
8.25	87.04	45.28	31.39	20.33	12.19	9.62	8.43	7.79
8.50	87.15	45.39	31.50	20.45	12.32	9.76	8.59	7.95
8.75	87.26	45.50	31.61	20.56	12.45	9.90	8.74	8.12
9.00	87.38	45.61	31.72	20.68	12.58	10.05	8.89	8.28
9.25	87.49	45.72	31.84	20.80	12.71	10.19	9.05	8.44
9.50	87.60	45.83	31.95	20.91	12.84	10.33	9.20	8.61
9.75	87.71	45.94	32.06	21.03	12.97	10.48	9.36	8.78
10.00	87.82	46.05	32.17	21.15	13.10	10.62	9.52	8.94
10.25	87.93	46.16	32.28	21.27	13.24	10.77	9.68	9.11
10.50	88.04	46.27	32.40	21.38	13.37	10.92	9.83	9.28
10.75	88.16	46.38	32.51	21.50	13.50	11.06	1 0.00	9.45
11.00	88.27	46.49	32.62	21.62	13.64	11.21	1 0.16	9.63
11.25	88.38	46.61	32.74	21.74	13.77	11.36	1 0.32	9.80
11.50	88.49	46.72	32.85	21.86	13.91	11.51	1 0.48	9.97
11.75	88.60	46.83	32.96	21.98	14.04	11.66	1 0.65	10.14
12.00	88.71	46.94	33.08	22.10	14.18	11.82	1 0.81	10.32
12.25	88.82	47.05	33.19	22.22	14.32	11.97	1 0.98	10.49
12.50	88.94	47.16	33.30	22.34	14.46	12.12	1 1.14	10.67
12.75	89.05	47.27	33.42	22.46	14.59	12.28	1 1.31	10.85
13.00	89.16	47.38	33.53	22.58	14.73	12.43	1 1.48	11.02
13.25	89.27	47.49	33.65	22.70	14.87	12.59	1 1.64	11.20
13.50	89.38	47.61	33.76	22.82	15.01	12.74	1 1.81	11.38
13.75	89.49	47.72	33.87	22.94	15.15	12.90	1 1.98	11.56
14.00	89.60	47.83	33.99	23.07	15.29	13.06	1 2.15	11.74
14.25	89.71	47.94	34.10	23.19	15.43	13.21	1 2.32	11.92
14.50	89.82	48.05	34.22	23.31	15.58	13.37	1 2.49	12.10
14.75	89.94	48.16	34.33	23.43	15.72	13.53	1 2.67	12.28
15.00	90.05	48.27	34.45	23.56	15.86	13.69	1 2.84	12.46
15.25	90.16	48.39	34.56	23.68	16.00	13.85	1 3.01	12.64
15.50	90.27	48.50	34.68	23.80	16.15	14.01	1 3.18	12.83
15.75	90.38	48.61	34.79	23.92	16.29	14.17	1 3.36	13.01
16.00	90.49	48.72	34.91	24.05	16.44	14.33	1 3.53	13.19

Source: *The Royal Bank of Canada*

Housing Affordability Table

The table below shows how expensive a home an individual or family could likely afford, using various income levels and mortgage interest rates — assuming a downpayment of 25% of the purchase price. As income rises, housing becomes more affordable; but it becomes less affordable as interest rates increase.

For example: most couples with a combined annual income of $60 000 would qualify for a mortgage on a home costing $186 916 at an 11% interest rate—provided they had a downpayment of $46 729 (25% of the purchase price). But at a 13% interest rate, the same couple earning the same income could only afford a $163 339 home.

The table assumes that mortgage payments, property taxes, heating costs and 50% of condominium fees should not exceed 32% of gross income (net income if self- employed). Most lending institutions use this percentage when calculating how large a mortgage you can afford. For this table, we have estimated annual costs of $1 800 for property taxes and $1 200 for heating. Most lenders will also require that your Total Debt Service Ratio (mortgage payments, property tax, heating costs, 50% of condo fees plus any other liabilities such as car loans or other debts) does not exceed 40% of gross income.

Mortgage Interest Rate (%)[1]	Annual Income							
	$30 000	$40 000	$50 000	$60 000	$70 000	$80 000	$90 000	$100 000
9.00	$88 567	$131 562	$174 396	$217 391	$260 386	$303 2 21	$346 216	$389 211
9.25	86 887	129 068	171 090	213 270	255 450	297 4 72	339 652	381 832
9.50	85 172	126 519	167 712	209 059	250 406	291 5 99	332 946	374 293
9.75	83 523	124 070	164 465	205 011	245 558	285 9 53	326 500	367 046
10.00	82 028	121 849	161 521	201 344	241 163	280 8 35	320 656	360 477
10.25	80 498	119 575	158 507	197 585	236 663	275 5 95	314 672	353 750
10.50	79 023	117 385	155 603	193 965	232 328	270 5 46	308 908	347 270
10.75	77 601	115 273	152 804	190 476	228 148	265 6 79	303 351	341 023
11.00	76 151	113 119	149 948	186 916	223 884	260 7 13	297 681	334 649
11.25	74 830	111 156	147 347	183 673	220 000	256 1 90	292 517	328 843
11.50	73 554	109 261	144 834	180 542	216 249	251 8 22	287 529	323 236
11.75	72 321	107 429	142 406	177 515	212 623	247 6 00	282 709	317 817
12.00	71 059	105 555	139 222	174 419	208 915	243 2 82	277 778	312 274
12.25	69 908	103 845	137 654	171 592	205 529	239 3 39	273 276	307 213
12.50	68 729	102 093	135 333	168 697	202 062	235 3 01	268 666	302 030
12.75	67 588	100 399	133 087	165 899	198 710	231 3 98	264 209	297 020
13.00	66 546	98 851	131 034	163 339	195 644	227 8 28	260 133	292 438
13.25	65 476	97 262	129 928	160 714	192 500	224 1 67	255 952	287 738
13.50	64 441	95 723	126 889	158 172	189 455	220 6 21	251 904	283 187
13.75	63 437	94 233	124 913	155 709	186 505	217 1 86	247 981	278 777

Source: *The Royal Bank of Canada*

(1) Compounded semi-annually. Mortgage payments based on a 25-year amortization.

Average Resale Value of Canadian Homes[1]

The average value of resale homes in Canada declined by almost $6 000 between 1990 and 1991, the second consecutive drop since the recession of the early 1980s. But the pattern varied widely from city to city.

In the Toronto area, average prices dropped more than 8 percent, while home values in such cities as Ottawa, Edmonton, Victoria and St. John's continued the decade's upward trend.

	1975	1980	1985	1988	1989	1990	1992
Canada	$47 201	$67 044	$80 775	$131 484	$148 737	$143 379	$150 732
Toronto, Ont.	57 583	75 620	109 093	229 635	273 698	254 890	214 971
Vancouver, B.C.	57 763	100 065	112 852	160 376	209 671	226 385	245 260
Mississauga, Ont.	61 977	80 340	99 674	200 297	239 981	224 449	195 762
Victoria, B.C.	n.a.	85 066	88 451	118 728	141 909	160 743	194 666
Hamilton, Ont.	45 103	54 834	72 972	135 221	163 249	165 742	151 038
Ottawa, Ont.	49 633	63 177	107 640	128 351	137 456	141 562	143 869
Calgary, Alta.	48 341	93 977	80 462	100 687	112 837	128 484	129 506
Montreal, Que.	35 266	49 419	70 563	104 071	110 015	111 956	113 688
Edmonton, Alta.	43 846	84 622	74 309	82 123	89 052	101 040	109 602
Halifax, N.S.	n.a.	53 160	79 350	92 204	93 444	97 238	102 021
St. John's, Nfld.	n.a.	53 246	66 642	77 099	83 273	88 939	91 959
Winnipeg, Man.	33 463	50 490	62 478	81 931	84 234	81 740	81 990
Saint John, N.B.	35 884	45 170	57 088	73 502	76 845	78 041	81 560
Regina, Sask.	33 880	48 628	61 403	69 389	72 078	71 054	72 372

Source: *The Canadian Real Estate Association*

(1) Average price of all homes sold on the Multiple Listing Service. (n.a.) not available.

Investment: A Glossary of Terms

Annual report: A report issued by a company to its shareholders at the end of the fiscal year. It contains a report on company operations and formal financial statements.

Bankers' acceptance: A commercial draft backed by the guarantee of a bank. The bankers' acceptance promises repayment on a certain date, usually not more than 90 days away, and bears a rate of return competitive with other chartered bank securities.

Bear market: A market in which prices are falling.

Bid and ask: The bid price is the highest price anyone is willing to pay to buy a stock; the ask is the lowest price anyone will accept to sell a stock. Together, the bid and ask prices are a "quote."

Blue chip stocks: Stocks with good investment qualities, usually common shares of well-established companies with good earnings records and long-time dividend payments.

Board Lot: A unit of trading. Board lots on The Toronto Stock Exchange are: under 10 cents each—1000 shares; between 10 cents and 99 cents each—500 shares; at and above $1 each—100 shares.

Bond: A written promise or IOU by the issuer to repay a fixed amount of borrowed money on a specified date, and to pay a set annual rate of interest in the meantime, generally at semi-annual intervals. Bonds are usually considered a safe investment because the borrower (whether a company or the government) must make interest payments before its money is spent on anything else.

Bull market: A market in which prices are rising.

Call: An option to buy a fixed amount of a certain stock at a specified price within a specified time.

Canada Savings Bonds: These are issued each fall, and are popular with small investors, because they come in denominations starting at $100. They are not traded. They have a term of several years, and a minimum guaranteed rate of interest. However, the government sets an effective rate during the issuing period each year, and adjusts it when necessary to conform with interest rate trends. Interest can be awarded yearly or compounded, depending upon which type of bond the purchaser buys.

Capital gain or loss: Profit or loss resulting from the sale of an asset, such as a security. The gain or loss is the difference between the buying and selling price of the security, with commissions figured in.

Commercial paper: Short-term negotiable securities issued by corporations which call for the payment of a specific amount of money at a given time.

▶

▶ **Common shares:** Securities issued by the company which represent part-ownership in the company. Common shares sometimes carry a voting privilege and entitle the holder to a share in the company's profits, usually issued in the form of dividends.

Convertible bond: A corporate bond (see below) which may be converted into a stated number of shares of the corporation's common stock. Its price tends to fluctuate with the price of the stock, as well as with changes in interest rates.

Corporate bonds: Evidence of debt by a corporation. The bond bears interest much like a government bond, and matures at a certain date in the future. Considered safer than the common or preferred stock of the same company.

Day Order: An order to buy or sell a security valid only for the day the order is given.

Dividend: A portion of a company's profit paid to the common and preferred shareholders. The amount is decided upon by the company's board of directors, and may be paid in cash or stock.

Equities: Common and preferred stocks, which represent a share in the ownership of a company.

Ex-dividend: Without dividend. The buyer of shares quoted ex-dividend is not entitled to receive an already declared dividend. When shares are un- dividend, the purchaser will receive the declared dividend.

Floor trader: A brokerage firm employee who works on the stock exchange trading floor, and is responsible for executing buy and sell orders on behalf of the firm and its clients.

Futures: Contracts to buy or sell specific quantities of a commodity or financial instrument with delivery delayed until some agreed-upon time in the future.

Government of Canada Bonds: These bear a fixed rate of interest and a maturation date in the future, and are traded on the market, with the price rising and falling in response to interest rate trends. Long-term government bonds are considered a safe investment. Provinces and municipalities may also issue long-term bonds.

Index: Statistical measure of the state of the stock market or economy, based on the performance of stocks or other components. Examples are the TSE 300 Composite Index and the Toronto 35 Index.

Limit order: An order to buy or sell securities in which the client has specified the price. The order can be executed only at the specified price or a better one.

Liquidity: The measure of how quickly an investor can turn securities into cash. A security is liquid if it can be bought and sold quickly with small price changes between transactions.

Long: A term signifying ownership of securities. "I am long 100 XYZ" means that the speaker owns 100 shares of XYZ.

Margin: The amount paid by clients when they use credit to buy a security, the balance being loaned by their brokers.

Market order: An order to buy a security immediately at the best possible price.

Money market: Part of the capital market established for short-term borrowing and lending of funds. Money market dealers conduct business over the telephone, and trade securities such as short-term (3years and less) government bonds, government treasury bills and commercial paper.

Mutual fund: A portfolio, or selection, of professionally bought and managed stocks in which you pool your money along with thousands of other people. A share price is based on net asset value, or the value of all the investments owned by the fund, less any debt, and divided by the total number of shares. The major advantage is less risk—your investment is spread out over many stocks, and if one or two do badly, the remainder may shield you from the losses. Bond funds are mutual funds that deal in the bond market exclusively. Money market mutual funds concentrate on debt instruments sold on the money market. Equity mutual funds place their investments in the common shares of companies.

Odd lot: A number of shares less than a board lot.

Open order: An order to buy or sell a security at a specified price, valid until executed or cancelled.

Over-The-Counter: The over-the-counter (OTC) or unlisted market is the market maintained by securities dealers for issues not listed on a stock exchange.

Penny stock: Low-priced, often speculative issues selling at less than $1 a share.

Preferred shares: Shares that carry dividends at fixed rates which must be paid before any dividends are paid to common shareholders.

Price/earnings ratio: A common stock's current market price divided by the company's annual per share earnings.

Prospectus: A legal document describing securities being offered for sale to the public. It must be prepared in accordance with provincial securities commission regulations.

Put: An option to sell a fixed amount of a certain stock at a specified price within a specified time.

Registered representative: A salesperson or broker employed by an investment firm. Salespersons must be registered with the provincial securities commission.

▶

▶ **Right:** A temporary privilege granted to existing common shareholders to purchase additional shares directly from the company at a stated price.

Settlement date: The date on which a securities buyer must pay for a purchase or a seller must deliver the securities sold. In general, settlement must be made on or before the fifth business day following the transaction date.

Short sale: The sale of shares which the seller does not own. The seller is speculating that the stock price will fall, in the hope of later purchasing the same number of securities at a lower price, thereby making a profit. Sellers must advise their brokers when they are selling short.

Stock yield: The percentage of the dividend paid in relation to the price of the stock. For example, a stock selling at $40 a share with an annual dividend of $2 a share yields five percent.

Transfer agent: A trust company appointed by a company to keep a record of the names, addresses and numbers of shares held by its shareholders. Transfer agents are often responsible for distributing dividend cheques.

Underwriting: The purchase for resale of a new issue of securities by an investment dealer or group of dealers.

Warrant: A certificate giving the holder the right to purchase securities at a stipulated price within a specified period of time. They are often detachable and may be traded separately.

Canadian Stock Exchange Trading

	Value traded	% of Canadian Total	% Value Change	Volume Traded	% of Canadian Total
Toronto					
1982	$17 670 332 337	80.0	-29.6	1 576 708 792	47.0
1987	100 224 304 252	77.3	+57.4	7 393 698 717	49.5
1992	76 161 051 067	74.8	+12.4	7 326 389 140	53.2
Montreal					
1982	2 773 415 534	12.5	-16.1	208 180 664	6.2
1987	21 875 596 915	16.9	+36.9	2 022 147 963	13.5
1992	21 063 915 203	20.7	+14.9	1 683 111 409	12.2
Vancouver					
1982	1 558 481 345	7.0	-59.6	1 442 747 544	43.0
1987	6 659 301 038	5.1	+48.3	4 795 142 825	32.1
1992	3 571 936 377	3.5	+3.1	3 899 206 755	28.3
Alberta					
1982	120 499 563	0.5	+71.8	126 130 894	3.7
1987	971 991 022	0.7	+104.2	740 753 453	4.9
1992	980 005 497	1.0	+72.9	867 960 979	6.3
Winnipeg					
1982	2 700 892	(1)	+195.4	2 017 108	0.1
1987	424 776	(1)	-23.2	150 032	(1)
1992	2 348 078	(1)	+100.5	15 112	(1)

Source: *Toronto Stock Exchange*   (1) Less than 1%.

Most Actively Traded Stocks, 1992

(based on Toronto Stock Exchange transactions)

Company	Shares Traded (millions)	Closing Price	High (for 52 weeks)	Low (for 52 weeks)
Nova Corp. Rv	118.8	$\$8\frac{3}{4}$	$\$9\frac{1}{8}$	$\$6\frac{3}{4}$
Transcan Pipelines	96.9	$17\frac{5}{8}$	$18\frac{1}{2}$	16
Laidlaw Cl B Nv	94.1	$11\frac{5}{8}$	$13\frac{1}{8}$	$\$8\frac{5}{8}$
Toronto Dominion Bank	94.0	$16\frac{5}{8}$	$19\frac{3}{4}$	$15\frac{3}{4}$
Placer Dome	93.5	$14\frac{3}{4}$	$15\frac{1}{2}$	$10\frac{3}{4}$
Bank of Nova Scotia	89.6	$23\frac{3}{4}$	$24\frac{3}{4}$	$19\frac{1}{8}$
Canadian Pacific Ltd.	87.0	$16\frac{1}{8}$	$19\frac{3}{8}$	$13\frac{1}{2}$
Royal Bank	82.5	$24\frac{5}{8}$	29	$21\frac{1}{2}$
BCE Inc.	78.7	$41\frac{1}{2}$	50	$40\frac{7}{8}$
Alcan Aluminium	78.5	$22\frac{5}{8}$	$26\frac{3}{8}$	$19\frac{1}{8}$

Source: *Toronto Stock Exchange*

Nv = Non-voting; Rv = Restricted voting.

Top 10 Stock Gainers and Losers, TSE 1992

52-Week Price Climb

Name of Stock	Open	Close	% Gain
United Reef Petroleums Ltd J	0.035	3.30	10 900
Southernera Resouces Ltd. J	0.08	5.0	6 150
Lytton Minerals Ltd J	0.07	2.08	3 367
Canhorn Mining Corp J	0.11	3.05	2 673
Osborn and Chappel Goldfields Ltd US, J	0.01	0.22	2 100
Pure Gold Resources Inc. J	0.03	0.44	2 100
Queenstake Resources Ltd	0.07	1.42	1 929
CanCapital Corp.	0.03	0.26	1 633
Tyler Resources Inc. J	0.06	0.76	1 167
Exall Resources Ltd J	0.15	1.38	1 050

52-Week Price Slide

Name of Stock	Open	Close	% Loss
Society Minhourem J	3.00	0.15	95
Claude Resources Inc. Pr J	3.40	0.25	93
Danio Industries	10.00	1.10	90
Peoples Jewellers Ltd	10.00	1.05	90
Timmins Nickel Inc. J	0.67	0.08	88
Claude Resources Inc. J	1.40	0.23	86
Petroleum Capital Energy Inc. J	0.10	0.03	85
Dynalta Energy Copr 10%RJ	3.00	0.50	82
Coscan Development	8.125	1.50	82
Pan Pacific Pete Inc. J	0.60	0.12	80

Source: *Toronto Stock Exchange*

Government of Canada Average Bond Yields, 1981–92

Year	1 to 3 Years	3 to 5 Years	5 to 10 Years	10 Years and Over
1981	15.97	15.68	15.29	15.22
1982	13.95	14.00	14.03	14.26
1983	10.18	10.61	11.11	11.79
1984	11.67	11.91	12.42	12.75
1985	10.12	10.39	10.78	11.04
1986	9.09	9.21	9.37	9.52
1987	9.19	9.42	9.55	9.95
1988	9.67	9.77	9.76	10.22
1989	10.71	10.20	9.83	9.92
1990	11.65	11.19	10.82	10.85
1991	8.99	9.16	9.36	9.76
1992	7.03	7.43	8.16	8.77

Source: *Bank of Canada*

Value of RRSP Holdings by Canadians

(millions of dollars)

1975	1 046	1984	5 672
1976	1 362	1985	6 499
1977	1 763	1986	7 307
1978	2 062	1987	8 361
1979	2 380	1988	9 414
1980	2 905	1989	11 812
1981	3 834	1990	14 362
1982	4 515	1991	13 424
1983	5 001		

Source: *Statistics Canada*

Toronto Stock Exchange (TSE) Price Index,[1] 1971–92

Year	High[2]	Date	Low[2]	Date	Year End	Net Change	Percent Change
1971	1 036.09	Apr. 16	879.80	Nov. 12	990.54	43.00	4.54
1972	1 226.58	Dec. 29	1 044.60	Jan. 7	1 226.58	236.04	23.83
1973	1 329.28	Oct. 31	1 122.34	May 18	1 193.56	-33.02	-2.69
1974	1 276.81	Mar. 15	821.10	Dec. 6	844.48	-349.08	-29.25
1975	1 081.96	July 18	862.74	Jan. 3	953.54	109.06	12.91
1976	1 106.17	May 13	920.15	Nov. 30	1 011.52	57.98	6.08
1977	1 068.53	July 20	957.58	Oct. 26	1 059.59	48.07	4.75
1978	1 336.34	Oct. 12	996.88	Jan. 30	1 309.99	250.40	23.63
1979	1 813.48	Dec. 31	1 310.31	Jan. 2	1 813.17	503.18	38.41
1980	2 405.65	Dec. 1	1 670.89	Mar. 27	2 268.70	455.53	25.12
1981	2 393.33	July 17	1 752.70	Sept. 28	1 954.24	-314.46	-13.86
1982	1 958.08	Dec. 31	1 332.22	July 8	1 958.08	3.84	0.20
1983	2 611.79	Sept. 12	1 926.44	Jan. 4	2 552.35	594.27	30.35
1984	2 594.59	Jan. 9	2 077.36	July 25	2 400.33	-152.02	-5.96
1985	2 902.17	Dec. 31	2 347.49	Jan. 7	2 900.60	500.27	20.84
1986	3 134.50	Apr. 29	2 744.00	Jan. 23	3 066.18	165.58	5.71
1987	4 118.94	Aug. 13	2 783.25	Nov. 10	3 160.05	93.87	3.06
1988	3 478.94	July 6	2 976.32	Feb. 8	3 389.99	229.94	7.28
1989	4 037.83	Oct. 6	3 353.13	Jan. 3	3 969.79	579.80	17.10
1990	4 020.86	Jan. 3	3 007.80	Oct. 16	3 256.75	-713.04	-17.96
1991	3 604.09	Nov. 12	3 150.88	Jan. 16	3 512.36	255.61	7.85
1992	3 672.58	Jan. 16	3 149.97	Oct. 5	3 350.44	-161.92	-4.61

Source: *Toronto Stock Exchange*

(1) A composite index of 300 leading stocks. The rise or fall of the index shows stock market trends. (2) High and low values are selected from the following time frames: 1958–70, month-end; 1971–75, month-end or weekly; 1976, daily close; 1977 on, intra-day values.

Global Superlatives

Largest continent	Asia	44 485 900 sq. km
Smallest continent	Australia	7 682 300 sq. km
Largest ocean	Pacific	166 241 000 sq. km
Smallest ocean	Arctic	9 485 000 sq. km
Deepest point of any ocean	Mariana Trench, Pacific Ocean	10 924 m
Largest sea	South China Sea	2 974 600 sq. km
Largest lake	Caspian Sea, CIS-Iran	371 000 sq. km
Deepest lake	Lake Baykal, Russia	1 620 m
Largest freshwater lake	Lake Superior, North America	82 100 sq. km
Highest major lake	Lake Titicaca, Bolivia-Peru, South America	3 809 m
Lowest major lake	Caspian Sea, CIS-Iran	-28 m
Largest island	Greenland, Denmark	2 175 600 sq. km
Longest reef	Great Barrier Reef, Australia-Papua New Guinea	2 027 km
Longest river	Nile, Africa	6 671 km
Largest nation	Russia	17 075 272 sq. km
Smallest nation	Vatican City	.44 ha. km
Most populous nation	People's Republic of China	pop. 1 133 682 501
Oldest city	Damascus, Syria	continuously inhabited since c. 2500 B.C.
Highest point	Mount Everest, Nepal-Tibet	8 848 m
Lowest point	Dead Sea, Israel-Jordan	-400 m
Highest city	Bogotá, Colombia	2 639 m
Coldest city	Norilsk, Russia	average temp. -10.9°C
Hottest city	Djibouti, Djibouti	average temp. 30°C
Coldest place	Plateau Station, Antarctica	-56.7°C
Hottest place	Dalol, Danakil Depression, Ethiopia	35°C avg.
Coldest recorded temperature	Vostok, Antarctica (Australian territory), July 21, 1983	-89.2°C
Hottest recorded temperature (shade)	Al-Aziziyah, Libya, Sept. 13, 1922	58°C
Wettest spot	Mount Waialeale, Kauai, Hawaii	avg. ann. rainfall of 16 800 mm
Driest spot	Atacama Desert, Chile	avg. ann. precipitation barely measurable
Greatest snowfall in 24 hrs	Silver Lake, Colorado, U.S., Apr. 14–15, 1921	193 cm
Greatest rainfall in 24 hrs	Cilaos, Reunion Island, Indian Ocean, Mar. 15–16, 1952	1 870 cm
Largest desert	Sahara, Africa	9 million sq. km
Largest waterfall (by volume)	Khone, Kampuchea-Laos	11 610 cu. m/sec.
Tallest waterfall	Angel Falls, Venezuela	807 m
Largest gorge	Grand Canyon, Colorado River, Arizona	349 km long; 6–20 km wide; 1.6 km deep
Deepest gorge	Colca River Canyon, Peru	3 223 m
Oldest tree	a bristlecone pine, Wheeler's Peak, Nevada	approx. age of 5 100 yrs.
Greatest tides	Bay of Fundy, Nova Scotia	14.5 m
Most devastating volcanic eruption	Tambora, Sumbawa, Indonesia, Apr. 5–7, 1815	92 000 deaths
Longest covered bridge	Hartland, New Brunswick	390.8 m
Longest bridge	Humber, crossing the River Humber, near Hull, England	(main span length) 1 410 m
Largest man-made lake	Owen Falls, Uganda	2 700 000 cu. m
Busiest airport	Chicago O'Hare	64 million passengers arriving and departing (1992)
Longest street	Yonge Street, from Toronto, Ont. to Rainy River (at. Man. border)	1 896.2 km
Largest car park	The West Edmonton Mall, Edmonton, Alberta	total vehicular capacity 20 000
Tallest building	Sears Tower, Chicago, Illinois	110 storeys, 443 m
Tallest free-standing structure	CN Tower, Toronto, Ont.	553.34 m
Most common language	Mandarin	approx. 750 million speakers
Most common religion	Christianity	(approx. 1/3 of world's pop.) 1 669 520 000

GEOGRAPHY

The Continents

Continent	Area (sq. km)	% of Earth's Land	Population	% of World Total
Asia	44 485 900	30.0	3 132 638 000	59.9
Africa	30 269 680	20.4	646 389 000	12.4
North America	24 235 280	16.3	416 664 500	8.0
South America	17 820 770	12.0	290 014 900	5.5
Antarctica	13 209 000	8.9	uninhabited	
Europe	10 530 750	7.1	715 233 800	13.7
Australia	7 682 300	5.2	16 820 000	.3
Islands of the Pacific	148 382	.1	9 636 000	.2

Source: *National Geographic Atlas of the World (1990)*

Highest and Lowest Points on Each Continent

Continent	Highest Point (metres)		Lowest Point (metres)	
Asia	Everest	8 848	Dead Sea	-400
South America	Aconcagua	6 960	Valdés Peninsula	-40
North America	McKinley (Denali)	6 194	Death Valley	-86
Africa	Kilimanjaro	5 895	Lake Assal	-156
Europe	El'brus	5 642	Caspian Sea	-28
Antarctica	Vinson Massif	4 897	—	-2 538
Australia	Kosciusko	2 228	Lake Eyre	-16

Source: *National Geographic Atlas of the World (1990)*

World's Highest Cities

City	Altitude	City	Altitude
Bogotá, Colombia	2 639 m	Calgary, Alta.	1 045 m
Addis Ababa, Ethiopia	2 450 m	Sao Paulo, Brazil	776 m
Mexico City, Mexico	2 309 m	Ankara, Turkey	686 m
Nairobi, Kenya	1 820 m	Edmonton, Alta.	666 m
Johannesburg, South Africa	1 734 m	Madrid, Spain	655 m

Source: *Global Atlas, Gage Educational Publishing Co.*

Oceans' Area and Depth

Ocean	Area (sq. km)	% of Earth's Water Area	Deepest Point	Depth (metres)
Pacific	166 241 000	46.0	Mariana Trench	10 924
Atlantic	86 557 000	23.9	Puerto Rico Trench	8 605
Indian	73 427 000	20.3	Java Trench	7 258
Arctic	9 485 000	2.6	Eurasia Basin	5 122

Source: *National Geographic Atlas of the World (1990)*

Major Seas of the World

Sea	Area (sq. km)	Average Depth (metres)	Sea	Area (sq. km)	Average Depth (metres)
South China	2 974 600	1 464	Sea of Japan	1 012 900	1 667
Caribbean	2 515 900	2 575	Hudson Bay	730 100	93
Mediterranean	2 510 000	1 501	East China	664 600	189
Bering	2 261 100	1 491	Andaman	564 900	1 118
Gulf of Mexico	1 507 600	1 615	Black	507 900	1 191
Sea of Okhotsk	1 392 100	973	Red	453 000	538

Source: *National Geographic Atlas of the World (1990)*

Largest Lakes of the World

Lake	Location	Area sq. mi.	Area sq. km
Caspian (Sea)	Iran/CIS	146 100	378 400
Superior	Canada/U.S.	31 760	82 260
Aral (Sea)	Kazakhstan-Uzbekistan	24 750	64 100
Victoria	Kenya/Tanzania/Uganda	24 300	62 940
Huron	Canada/U.S.	23 000	59 580
Michigan	U.S.	22 400	58 020
20 Tanganyika	Burundi/Tanzania/Zaire/Zambia	12 350	32 000
Baykal	Russia	12 160	31 500
Great Bear	NWT, Canada	12 030	31 150
Great Slave	NWT, Canada	11 030	28 570

Source: *World Facts and Figures, 1989; Victor Showers; John Wiley & Sons, Inc.*

Major Islands of the World

Island	Area (sq. km)	Island	Area (sq. km)
Greenland (Denmark)	2 175 600	Sumatra (Indonesia)	427 300
New Guinea (independent)	792 500	Honshu (Japan)	227 400
Borneo (Indonesia)	725 500	Great Britain (independent)	218 100
Madagascar (independent)	587 000	Victoria (Canada)	217 300
Baffin (Canada)	507 500	Ellesmere (Canada)	196 200

Source: *National Geographic Atlas of the World (1990)*

Highest Waterfalls in the World

Fall/Country	Height[1] (m)	Fall/Country	Height[1] (m)
Angel, Venezuela	807	Pilao, Brazil	524
Monge, Norway	774	Montoya, Venezuela	505
Itatinga, Brazil	628	Ribbon, United States	491
Ormeli, Norway	563	Great, Guyana	488
Tusse, Norway	533	Vestre Mardals, Norway	468

Source: *World Facts and Figures, 1989; Victor Showers; John Wiley & Sons Inc.*

(1) Height of the greatest individual leap.

Highest Mountains by Continent

Peak	Mountain Range or System	Location	Elevation[1] ft	Elevation[1] m	First Ascent
■ Africa					
Kibo	n.a.	Tanganyika, Tanzania	19 340	5 890	1889
Mawensi	n.a.	Tanganyika, Tanzania	17 100	5 210	1912
Batian	n.a.	Kenya	17 050	5 200	1899
Nelion	n.a.	Kenya	17 020	5 190	1929
Margherita	Ruwenzori	Uganda/Zaire	16 760	5 110	1906
Alexandra	Ruwenzori	Uganda/Zaire	16 700	5 090	1906
Albert	Ruwenzori	Zaire	16 690	5 090	1932
Savoia	Ruwenzori	Uganda	16 330	4 980	1906
Elena	Ruwenzori	Uganda	16 300	4 970	1906
Elizabeth	Ruwenzori	Uganda	16 170	4 930	1953
■ Antarctica					
—	Sentinel	Antarctica	16 860	5140	1966
Tyree	Sentinel	Antarctica	16 290	4970	1967
Shinn	Sentinel	Antarctica	15 750	4800	1966
Gardner	Sentinel	Antarctica	15 370	4690	1966
Epperly	Sentinel	Antarctica	15 100	4600	n.a.
Kirkpatrick	Queen Alexandra	Antarctica	14 850	4530	n.a.
Elizabeth	Queen Alexandra	Antarctica	14 700	4480	n.a.
Markham	Queen Elizabeth	Antarctica	14 290	4360	n.a.
Bell	Queen Alexandra	Antarctica	14 120	4300	n.a.
Mackellar	Queen Alexandra	Antarctica	14 100	4300	n.a.
■ Asia					
Everest (alt Qomolangma, Chumulangma)	Nepal Himalaya	China/Nepal	29 030	8 850	1953
K2 (alt Chogori, Dapsang, Godwin Austen)	Karakoram	Pakistan-held Kashmir	28 250	8 610	1954
Kangchenjunga (alt Kanchenjunga): highest peak	Nepal Himalaya	India/Nepal	28 170	8 590	1955
Lhotse (alt E1, Luozi, Lotzu)	Nepal Himalaya	China/Nepal	27 890	8 500	1956
Kangchenjunga: S peak	Nepal Himalaya	India/Nepal	27 800	8 470	n.a.
Makalu I	Nepal Himalaya	China/Nepal	27 790	8 470	1955
Kangchenjunga: W peak	Nepal Himalaya	India/Nepal	27 620	8 420	1973
Lhotse Shar (alt Lhotse: E peak)	Nepal Himalaya	China/Nepal	27 500	8 380	1970
Dhaulagiri I (alt Daulagiri I)	Nepal Himalaya	Nepal	26 810	8 170	1960
Cho Oyu (alt Zhuoaoyu, Choaoyu): highest peak	Nepal Himalaya	China/Nepal	26 750	8 150	1954
■ Europe					
Elbrus (for Elborus): W peak	Caucasus (off Kavkaz)	Russia	18 480	5630	1874
Elbrus: E peak	Caucasus	Russia	18 360	5 590	1829
Shkhara: E peak	Caucasus	Georgia/Russia	17 060	5 200	1888
Dykh(-Tau): W peak	Caucasus	Russia	17 050	5 200	1888
Dykh(-Tau): E peak	Caucasus	Russia	16 900	5 150	1938
Koshtan(-Tau)	Caucasus	Russia	16 880	5 140	1888
Shkhara: W peak	Caucasus	Georgia/Russia	16 880	5 140	n.a.
Pushkina	Caucasus	Russia	16 730	5 100	1938
Dzhangi(-Tau): NW peak	Caucasus	Georgia	16 570	5 050	1903
Kazbek: E peak	Caucasus	Georgia	16 560	5 050	1868 ▶

▶ ■ **North America**

McKinley: S peak	Alaska	Alaska, U.S.	20 320	6 190	1913
Logan: central peak	Saint Elias	Yukon, Canada	19 520	5 959	1925
Logan: W peak	Saint Elias	Yukon, Canada	19 470	5 930	1925
McKinley: N peak	Alaska	Alaska, U.S.	19 470	5 930	1910
Logan: E peak	Saint Elias	Yukon, Canada	19 420	5 920	1957
Citlaltepetl (alt Orizaba)	Neovolcanica	Puebla-Veracruz, Mexico	18 410	5 610	1848
Logan: N peak	Saint Elias	Yukon, Canada	18 270	5 570	1959
Saint Elias	Saint Elias	Canada/U.S.	18 010	5 490	1897
Popocatepetl	Neovolcanica	Puebla, Mexico	17 930	5 460	1520
Foraker	Alaska	Alaska, U.S.	17 400	5 300	1934

■ **Oceania**

Jaya (for Carstensz, Djaja, Sukarno)	Sudirman (for Nassau)	Irian Jaya, Indonesia	16 500	5 030	1936
Daam	Jayawijaya (for Djajawidjaja, Orange)	Irian Jaya, Indonesia	16 150	4 920	n.a.
Pilimsit (for Idenburg)	Sudirman	Irian Jaya, Indonesia	15 750	4 800	1962
Trikora (for Wilhelmina)	Jayawijaya	Irian Jaya, Indonesia	15 580	4 750	1913
Mandala (for Juliana)	Jayawijaya	Irian Jaya, Indonesia	15 420	4 700	1959
Wilhelm	Bismarck	Papua New Guinea	15 400	4 690	n.a.
Wisnumurti (for Jan Pieterszoon Coen)	Jayawijaya	Irian Jaya, Indonesia	15 080	4 590	n.a.
Yamin (for Prins Hendrik)	Jayawijaya	Irian Jaya, Indonesia	14 860	4 530	n.a.
Kubor	Kubor	Papua New Guinea	14 300	4 360	n.a.
Herbert	Bismarck	Papua New Guinea	14 000	4 270	n.a.

■ **South America**

Aconcagua	Andes	Mendoza, Argentina	22 840	6 960	1897
Ojos del Salado: SE peak	Andes	Argentina/Chile	22 560	6 870	1937
Bonete	Andes	La Rioja, Argentina	22 550	6 870	1913
Pissis	Andes	Catamarca, La Rioja, Argentina	22 240	6 780	1937
Huascaran: S peak	Blanca (Andes)	Peru	22 210	6 770	1932
Mercedario	Andes	San Juan, Argentina	22 210	6 770	1934
Llullaillaco	Andes	Argentina/Chile	22 100[1]	6 730	bef 1550
Libertador (for Cachi: N peak)	Andes	Salta, Argentina	22 050	6 720	1950
Ojos del Salado: NW peak	Andes	Argentina/Chile	22 050	6 720	1937
Tupungato	Andes	Argentina/Chile	21 900	6 670	1897

Source: *World Facts and Figures, 1989; Victor Showers; John Wiley & Sons, Inc.*

(1) Rounded figures except from some Canadian peaks from Energy, Mines and Resources Canada. n.a. not available or not applicable.

Longest Rivers in The World

River	Outflow and Location	Length mi.	Length km
Nile-Kagera-Ruvuvu-Luvironza	Mediterranean Sea, Egypt	4 140	6 670
Amazon-Ucayali-Tambo-Ene-Apurimac	Atlantic Ocean, Amapa-Para, Brazil	4 080	6 570
Yangtze	East China Sea, Jiangsu, China	3 720	5 980
Mississippi-Missouri-Jefferson-Beaverhead-Red Rock	Gulf of Mexico, Louisiana, U.S.	3 710	5 970
Yenisey-Angara-Selenga-Ider	Yenisey Gulf of Kara Sea, Russia	3 650	5 870
Amur-Argun-Kerulen	Tatar Strait, Russia	3 590	5 780
Ob-Irtysh	Gulf of Ob of Kara Sea, Russia	3 360	5 410
Plata-Parana-Grande	Atlantic Ocean, Argentina-Uruguay	3 030	4 880
Huang	Gulf of Chihli of Yellow Sea, Shandong, China	3 010	4 840
Congo-Lualaba	Atlantic Ocean, Angola-Zaire	2 880	4 630

Source: *World Facts and Figures, 1989; Victor Showers; John Wiley & Sons, Inc.*

POPULATION

The World's Most Populous Nations, 1992

China	1 188 000 000	Brazil	154 100 000
India	879 500 000	Pakistan	124 800 000
USSR (former)	284 500 000	Japan	124 500 000
United States	255 200 000	Bangladesh	119 300 000
Indonesia	191 200 000	Nigeria	115 700 000

Source: *The State of the World Population, 1993, U.N. Population Fund*

World's 20 Largest Cities, Ranked by Population Size, 1950–90

(millions of people)

	1950 City	Pop		1970 City	Pop		1990 City	Pop
1	New York, USA	12.3	1	New York, USA	16.2	1	Mexico City, Mexico	20.2
2	London, UK	8.7	2	Tokyo, Japan	14.9	2	Tokyo, Japan	18.1
3	Tokyo, Japan	6.7	3	Shanghai, China	11.2	3	Sao Paulo, Brazil	17.4
4	Paris, France	5.4	4	Mexico City, Mexico	9.4	4	New York, USA	16.2
5	Shanghai, China	5.3	5	London, UK	8.6	5	Shanghai, China	13.4
6	Buenos Aires, Argen.	5.0	6	Buenos Aires, Argen.	8.4	6	Los Angeles, USA	11.9
7	Chicago, USA	4.9	7	Los Angeles, USA	8.4	7	Calcutta, India	11.8
8	Moscow, USSR	4.8	8	Paris, France	8.3	8	Buenos Aires, Argen.	11.5
9	Calcutta, India	4.4	9	Beijing, China	8.1	9	Bombay, India	11.2
10	Los Angeles, USA	4.0	10	Sao Paulo, Brazil	8.1	10	Seoul, Korea	11.0
11	Beijing, China	3.9	11	Osaka, Japan	7.6	11	Beijing, China	10.8
12	Osaka, Japan	3.8	12	Moscow, USSR	7.1	12	Rio de Janeiro, Brazil	10.7
13	Milan, Italy	3.6	13	Rio de Janeiro, Brazil	7.0	13	Tianjin, China	9.4
14	Mexico City, Mexico	3.1	14	Calcutta, India	6.9	14	Jakarta, Indonesia	9.3
15	Philadelphia, USA	2.9	15	Chicago, USA	6.7	15	Cairo, Egypt	9.0
16	Bombay, India	2.9	16	Bombay, India	5.8	16	Moscow, USSR	8.8
17	Rio de Janeiro, Brazil	2.9	17	Milan, Italy	5.5	17	Delhi, India	8.8
18	Detroit, USA	2.8	18	Cairo, Egypt	5.3	18	Osaka, Japan	8.5
19	Naples, Italy	2.8	19	Seoul, Korea	5.3	19	Paris, France	8.5
20	Leningrad, USSR	2.6	20	Tianjin, China	5.2	20	Metro Manila, Philip.	8.5

Source: *The State of World Population, 1993, UN Population Fund*

20 Most Populous Cities (millions of people) in the Year 2000

T he UN Population Fund estimates that by the year 2000, the 20 most populous cities will be:

	City	Pop.		City	Pop.
1	Mexico City, Mexico	25.6	11	Delhi, India	13.2
2	Sao Paulo, Brazil	22.1	12	Buenos Aires, Argentina	12.9
3	Tokyo, Japan	19.0	13	Lagos, Nigeria	12.9
4	Shanghai, China	17.0	14	Tianjin, China	12.7
5	New York, USA	16.8	15	Seoul, Korea	12.7
6	Calcutta, India	15.7	16	Rio de Janeiro, Brazil	12.5
7	Bombay, India	15.4	17	Dhaka, Bangladesh	12.2
8	Beijing, China	14.0	18	Cairo, Egypt	11.8
9	Los Angeles, USA	13.9	19	Metro Manila, Philippines	11.8
10	Jakarta, Indonesia	13.7	20	Karachi, Pakistan	11.7

Populations in Danger

The organization Médecins sans Frontières (Doctors Without Borders) was founded in 1971 and is now the world's largest private organization for emergency medical aid. Its members provide emergency relief to all people in danger without discrimination.

In the 1992 edition of *Populations in Danger* the organization cited the ten population groups felt to face the most serious crises and the most desperate circumstances marked by war, population displacement, famine and epidemics.

Country	Dead/Missing	Refugees[1]	Context
Sudan	600 000 (since 1983)	760 000	Civil war between Moslem-supported government in north and black African population in the south.
Somalia	over 500 000 (since end of 1990)	over 4 million	Anti-government rebellion led to the collapse of the central government; clan warfare since the end of 1990 has uprooted much of the population; complete disruption of the economy has led to widespread famine.
Bosnia-Herzegovina (former Yugoslavia)	40 000 (June 1991 to July 1992)	2 million	Disintegration of Yugoslavia into Serbian, Croatian and Muslim ethnic groups attempting to secure national territory.
Mozambique	1 million (1977-1992)	5.5 million	18 years of civil war, complicated by recent drought and famine.
Myanmar (Burma)	no reliable statistics available	365 000 in Thailand and Bangladesh	Ethnic minorities have been targeted during 30-year period of economic mismanagement and political repression.
Sri Lanka	50 000 (1982-1992)	1 million	Tamil/Sinhalese conflict complicated by economic crisis. Sinhalese, Tamil and Muslim communities now locked in a conflict over territory.
Peru	25 000	600 000	Rural population victimized by Shining Path guerrillas allied with drug traffickers; widespread poverty, cholera epidemic.
Tuaregs of West Africa	3 000 (May 1990-April 1992)	100 000	Nomadic Tuaregs left without a state in 1960s when their territory divided amongst Algeria, Mali, Niger, Burkina Faso and Libya. In 1990, young Tuaregs began a series of rebellions in order to secure a political and national future.
Kurds in Iraq	180 000 (Oct. 1991- Dec. 1992)	2 million	25 million Kurds live in Iraq, Iran, Turkey, Syria and the former Soviet Union. Iraqi Kurds rose against Saddam Hussein at the end of the Gulf War. Hussein has retaliated with armed attacks, and embargoes on economic and humanitarian aid.
Caucasus: Nagomo-Karabakh	2 000	400 000	Long-standing conflict between Armenians and Azerbaijanis erupted in 1988 as Armenians in Azerbaijan attempted to establish political rights and annex the area of Nagorno-Karabakh to Armenia. Disruption of supplies complicated by severe winters.

Source: *Médecins sans Frontières*

(1) Includes displaced persons inside the borders of their country, as at Dec. 31, 1992.

Population Projections, by Region and for Selected Countries: 1990 to 2025

(in millions)

Region and Country	1990	2025	Region and Country	1990	2025
World total	**5 295.3**	**8 472.4**	Mauritania	2.0	5.0
More developed[1]	1 211.1	1 403.3	Niger	7.7	21.3
Less developed[1]	4 084.2	7 069.2	Nigeria	108.5	285.8
Africa	**642.6**	**1 582.5**	Senegal	7.3	17.1
Eastern Africa[2]	194.8	516.0	Sierra Leone	4.2	9.8
Burundi	5.5	13.4	Togo	3.5	9.4
Comoros	0.5	1.6	**Latin America**	**441.1**	**701.6**
Djibouti	0.4	1.2	Caribbean[2]	33.6	50.4
Ethiopia	49.8	130.7	Antigua and Barbuda	0.1	0.1
Kenya	23.6	63.8	Aruba	0.1	0.1
Madagascar	12.0	33.7	Bahamas	0.3	0.4
Malawi	9.6	24.9	Barbados	0.3	0.3
Mauritius	1.1	1.4	Cuba	10.6	13.0
Mozambique	14.2	36.3	Dominica	0.1	0.1
Reunion	0.6	0.9	Dominican Rep.	7.2	11.4
Rwanda	7.0	20.1	Grenada	0.1	0.1
Seychelles	0.1	0.1	Haiti	6.5	13.1
Somalia	8.7	23.4	Jamaica	2.4	3.5
Uganda	17.6	45.9	Puerto Rico	3.5	4.7
Tanzania	26.0	74.2	Saint Kitts and Nevis	...	...
Zambia	8.1	21.0	Saint Lucia	0.1	0.2
Zimbabwe	9.9	22.9	St. Vincent &		
Middle Africa	70.5	190.0	the Grenadines	0.1	0.2
Angola	9.2	26.6	Trinidad and Tobago	1.2	1.8
Cameroon	11.5	29.2	Central America	113.3	199.2
Cen. African Rep.	3.0	7.0	Belize	0.2	0.3
Chad	5.6	12.9	Costa Rica	3.0	5.6
Congo	2.2	5.8	El Salvador	5.2	9.7
Equatorial Guinea	0.4	0.8	Guatemala	9.2	21.7
Gabon	1.2	2.9	Honduras	5.1	11.5
Sao Tome and Principe	0.1	0.2	Mexico	84.5	137.5
Zaire	37.4	104.5	Nicaragua	3.7	9.1
Northern Africa[2]	140.5	280.4	Panama	2.4	3.9
Algeria	25.0	51.8	South America[2]	294.1	451.9
Egypt	52.4	93.5	Argentina	32.3	45.5
Libya	4.5	12.8	Bolivia	7.2	14.1
Morocco	25.1	47.5	Brazil	149.0	219.7
Sudan	25.2	60.6	Chile	13.2	19.8
Tunisia	8.1	13.4	Colombia	32.3	49.4
Southern Africa	43.1	85.3	Ecuador	10.5	18.6
Botswana	1.2	2.9	Guyana	0.8	1.1
Lesotho	1.7	3.8	Paraguay	4.3	9.2
Namibia	1.4	3.8	Peru	21.6	37.4
South Africa	37.9	73.2	Suriname	0.4	0.7
Swaziland	0.8	1.7	Uruguay	3.1	3.7
Western Africa[2]	193.7	510.8	Venezuela	19.3	32.7
Benin	4.6	12.4	**Northern America[2]**	**276.7**	**360.5**
Burkina Faso[3]	9.0	22.6	Canada	26.6	38.4
Cape Verde	0.4	0.8	United States	250.0	322.0
Côte d'Ivoire	12.0	37.9	**Asia**	**3 117.8**	**4 900.3**
Gambia	0.9	1.9	Eastern Asia[2]	1 350.5	1 762.2
Ghana	15.0	38.0	China[2]	1 153.5	1 539.8
Guinea	5.8	15.1	Hong Kong	5.7	6.4
Guinea-Bissau	1.0	2.0	Japan	123.5	127.0
Liberia	2.6	7.2	North Korea	21.8	33.3
Mali	9.2	24.6	South Korea	43.4	50.3 ▶

▶ Mongolia	2.2	4.6	Poland	38.2	43.8
South-Eastern Asia[2]	444.1	715.6	Romania	23.2	26.3
Brunei Darussalam	0.3	0.4	Northern Europe[2]	92.4	97.8
Cambodia	8.3	16.7	Denmark	5.1	5.1
Indonesia	184.3	283.3	Estonia	1.6	1.6
Laos	4.2	9.4	Finland	5.0	5.2
Malaysia	17.9	31.3	Iceland	0.3	0.3
Myanmar	41.8	75.6	Ireland	3.5	3.6
Philippines	62.4	105.1	Latvia	2.7	2.8
Singapore	2.7	3.3	Lithuania	3.7	4.1
Thailand	54.7	72.3	Norway United Kingdom	57.4	60.3
Vietnam	66.7	117.0	Southern Europe[2]	144.1	148.2
Southern Asia	1 191.1	2 135.8	Albania	3.3	4.5
Afghanistan	16.6	45.8	Andorra	. . .	0.1
Bangladesh	113.7	223.3	Greece	10.1	10.1
Bhutan	1.5	3.4	Italy	57.7	56.2
India	846.2	1 393.9	Malta	0.4	0.4
Iran	58.3	144.6	Portugal	9.9	10.1
Maldives	0.2	0.5	San Marino	. . .	. . .
Nepal	19.6	40.1	Spain	39.0	40.6
Pakistan	118.1	259.6	Yugoslavia	23.8	26.0
Sri Lanka	17.2	24.7	Western Europe	176.0	188.7
Western Asia[2]	131.9	286.6	Austria	7.7	8.3
Bahrain	0.5	1.0	Belgium	10.0	9.9
Cyprus	0.7	0.9	France	56.7	60.8
Iraq	18.1	46.3	Germany	79.5	83.9
Israel	4.7	8.1	Liechtenstein	. . .	. . .
Jordan	4.0	10.8	Luxembourg	0.4	0.4
Kuwait	2.1	2.8	Monaco	. . .	. . .
Lebanon	2.7	4.5	Netherlands	14.9	17.7
Oman	1.5	4.7	Switzerland	6.7	7.7
Qatar	0.4	0.7	**Soviet Union (former)**	**281.3**	**344.5**
Saudi Arabia	14.9	40.4	**Oceania**[2]	**26.7**	**41.3**
Syria	12.3	35.3	Australia	17.1	25.2
Turkey	56.0	92.9	Fiji	0.7	1.0
United Arab Emirates	1.6	2.8	Kiribati	0.1	0.1
Yemen	11.7	34.2	Nauru	. . .	. . .
Europe (excl. Soviet			New Zealand	3.4	4.3
Union)	**509.0**	**541.8**	Papua New Guinea	3.9	7.8
Eastern Europe	96.6	107.2	Solomon Islands	0.3	0.8
Bulgaria	9.0	8.8	Tonga	0.1	0.1
Czechoslovakia	15.7	17.9	Tuvalu	. . .	. . .
Hungary	10.6	10.4	Vanautu	0.2	0.3

Source: *World Population Prospects: The 1992 Revision, Population Division of the United Nations*

(1) Regions. (2) Includes areas not shown separately. (3) Formerly Upper Volta. (. . .) = too small to be included.

Growing Cities

*I*n *1950, 85% of the developing world's population lived in rural areas. By 1975, rural areas still accounted for nearly 75% of the population, but by the end of the 1990s, this number will likely be down to 60%. And by the early decades of the next century, more than half of the world's people will live in cities.*

During the 1990s, no less than 83% of the world's population growth is expected to take place in towns and cities. By the year 2000, in developing countries, the number of cities with more than 1 million people will increase to 300.

ECONOMY

The World's Largest Industrial Corporations, 1993

Company (1992 Rank)	Country	Sales (millions)	Profits (millions)	Employees
General Motors (1)	U.S.	$132 774.9	$-23 498.3[1]	750 000
Exxon (2)	U.S.	103 547.0	4 770.0	95 000
Ford Motor (3)	U.S.	100 785.6	-7 385.0[1]	325 333
Royal Dutch/Shell Group (4)	Brit./Netherlands	98 935.3	5 408.0	127 000
Toyota Motor (5)	Japan	79 114.2	1 812.6	108 167
IRI (6)	Italy	67 547.4	-3 811.2[2]	400 000
IBM (7)	U.S.	65 096.0	-4 965.0[1]	308 010
Daimler-Benz (8)	Germany	63 339.5	928.6	376 467
General Electric (9)	U.S.	62 202.0	4 725.0	268 000
Hitachi (10)	Japan	61 465.5	619.3	331 505
British Petroleum (11)	Britain	59 215.7	-808.4	97 650
Matsushita Electric Industrial (12)	Japan	57 480.8	307.7	252 075
Mobil (13)	U.S.	57 389.0	862.0[1]	63 700
Volkswagen (14)	Germany	56 734.1	49.9	274 103
Siemens (15)	Germany	51 401.9	1 136.1	413 000
Nissan Motor (16)	Japan	50 247.5	-448.7	143 754
Philip Morris (17)	U.S.	50 157.0	4 939.0	161 000
Samsung (18)	South Korea	49 559.6	374.2	188 558
Fiat (19)	Italy	47 928.7	446.8	285 482
Unilever (20)	Brit./Netherlands	43 962.6	2 278.6	283 000
ENI (21)	Italy	40 365.5	-767.1	124 032
Elf Aquitaine (22)	France	39 717.8	1 166.4	87 900
Nestlé (26)	Switzerland	39 057.9	1 916.9	218 005
Chevron (24)	U.S.	38 523.0	1 569.0[1]	49 245
Toshiba (17)	Japan	37 471.6	164.7	173 000

Source: *Fortune, ©1993 Time Inc. All rights reserved*
(1) Reflects a one-time accounting adjustment for cumulative liabilities. (2) *Fortune* est.

The Biggest Companies in the World by Industry

Industry	Company	Country	Sales (million)	Profits (million)
Aerospace	Boeing	U.S.	$ 30 414	$ 552.0[1]
Apparel	Levi Strauss Associates	U.S.	5 570	360.8
Beverages	Pepsico	U.S.	22 084	374.3[1]
Building materials	Saint-Gobain	France	14 297	448.8
Chemicals	E.I. Du Pont de Nemours	U.S.	37 386	-3 927.0[1]
Computers (incl. office equipment)	IBM	U.S.	65 096	-4 965.0[1]
Electronics	General Electric	U.S.	62 202	4 725.0
Food	Philip Morris	U.S.	50 157	4 939.0
Forest products	International Paper	U.S.	13 600	86.0[1]
Industrial and farm equipment	Mitsubishi Heavy Industries	Japan	23 011	649.7
Jewelry, watches	Citizen Watch	Japan	3 328	97.2
Metal Products	Pechiney	France	12 344	38.3
Metals	IRI	Italy	67 547	-3811.2[2]
Mining, crude oil production	Ruhrkohle	Germany	15 712	32.4
Motor vehicles and parts	General Motors	U.S.	132 775	-23 498.3[1]
Petroleum refining	Exxon	U.S.	103 547	4 770
Pharmaceuticals	Johnson & Johnson	U.S.	13 846	1 030.1
Publishing, printing	Matra-Hachette	France	10 416	66.8
Rubber and plastics products	Bridgestone	Japan	13 860	224.1
Scientific and photo. equipment	Eastman Kodak	U.S.	20 577	1 146.0[1]
Soaps, cosmetics	Procter & Gamble	U.S.	29 890	1 872.0
Textiles	Toray Industries	Japan	7 862	215.2
Tobacco	RJR Nabisco Holdings	U.S.	15 734	299.0
Toys, sporting goods	Nintendo	Japan	5 213	709.9
Transportation equipment	Hyundai Heavy Industries	S. Korea	6 518	387.9

Source: *Fortune, ©1993 Time Inc. All rights reserved*
(1) Reflects a one-time accounting adjustment for cumulative liabilities. (2) *Fortune* est.

The World's Largest Banks, 1992[1]

Bank (Head Office)	Total Assets (billions)	% Growth in Assets (since 1991)	Net Income (millions)	ShareHolders' Equity (millions)
Dai-Ichi Kangyo Bank[2] (Tokyo, Japan)	$493.4	3.7%	$ 372.6	$17 552.2
Fuji Bank[2] (Tokyo, Japan)	493.3	8.3	466.9	17 414.3
Sumitomo Bank[2] (Osaka, Japan)	490.9	5.8	168.9	19 641.4
Sanwa Bank[2] (Tokyo, Japan)	485.0	9.0	762.7	17 588.7
Sakura Bank[2,4] (Tokyo, Japan)	470.8	5.0	462.6	15 156.6
Mitsubishi Bank[2] (Tokyo, Japan)	460.8	6.6	503.1	15 789.7
Norinchukin Bank[2] (Tokyo, Japan)	379.1	21.9	344.5	2 814.1
Industrial Bank of Japan[2] (Tokyo, Japan)	370.0	11.0	328.0	12 244.3
Crédit Lyonnais[3] (Paris, France)	350.7	14.8	-349.0	15 383.9
Deutsche Bank (Frankfurt, Germany)	306.6	3.8	1 148.5	13 860.6
Crédit Agricole (Paris, France)	298.1	-2.7	995.0	14 534.8
Mitsubishi Trust & Banking[2] (Tokyo, Japan)	293.3	12.1	128.8	7 111.4
Tokai Bank[2] (Tokyo, Japan)	292.0	7.7	202.6	9 618.4
Long-term Credit Bank of Japan[2] (Tokyo, Japan)	290.4	13.6	186.2	9 662.9
Banque Nationale de Paris[3] (Paris, France)	283.7	3.1	450.7	10 249.1
Sumitomo Trust & Banking[2] (Osaka, Japan)	280.7	19.5	149.8	6 881.7
Bank of China[3] (Beijing, China)	279.4	21.8	2 249.0	11 785.0
Mitsui Trust & Banking[2] (Tokyo, Japan)	265.3	17.1	92.3	5 668.9
HSBC Holdings (Britain)	257.9	61.1	2 155.1	12 120.6
Société Générale (Paris, France)	256.9	9.7	617.1	7 257.8
Bank of Tokyo[2] (Tokyo, Japan)	254.8	3.1	303.2	8 833.4
ABN Amro Holding (Netherlands)	253.1	4.4	957.3	8 836.7
Asahi Bank[2] (Japan)	251.9	10.8	289.1	9 352.7
Daiwa Bank[2,5] (Japan)	224.2	14.6	135.1	5 070.7
Barclays Bank (London, U.K.)	222.7	-13.6	-605.4	7 987.1

Source: *Fortune, ©1993 Time Inc. All rights reserved*

(1) Data is for year ending Dec. 31, 1992; all figures are in U.S. dollars. (2) Figures are for fiscal year ending March 31, 1993. (3) Government owned. (4) Name changed from Mitsui Taiyo Kobe Bank April 1992. (5) Formed by a merger in April 1991 of Kyowa Bank and Saitama Bank.

World Exchange Trading Summary

(millions of US dollars)

	1990	1991	1992
New York[1]	$1 325 332.4	$1 520 164.0	$1 745 466.4
London[1]	543 392.5	553 922.0	662 990.9
Tokyo	1 287 694.2	882 973.5	476 976.1
Germany	508 706.7	404 648.8	454 205.5
Taiwan	711 737.0	386 031.2	250 330.8
Paris[1]	121 063.7	116 649.0	124 879.1
Osaka	243 822.9	138 548.7	120 936.2
Korea	75 625.1	85 091.8	116 072.5
Zurich	400 523.2	362 337.8	84 646.3
Midwest	71 304.4	74 504.1	84 355.7

Source: *Toronto Stock Exchange*   (1) Includes off-board trading

Leading Producers of Grains, 1991

(thousands of metric tons)

Country	Total	Percent of World Total	Country	Total	Percent of World Total
■ **Cereals**[1]			■ **Rice**		
World total	1 883 888	100.0%	World total	519 869	100.0%
China	392 919	20.9	China	187 450[2]	36.1
United States	279 923	14.9	India	110 945[2]	21.3
India	195 109	10.4	Indonesia	44 321	8.5
USSR	165 003	8.8	Bangladesh	28 575[2]	5.5
France	60 442	3.2	Thailand	20 040[2]	3.9
Canada	**55 969**	**3.0**	Vietnam	19 428[2]	3.7
Indonesia	50 732	2.7	Myanmar	13 201	2.5
Brazil	35 991	1.9	Japan	12 005[2]	2.3
Bangladesh	29 655	1.6	Philippines	9 670	1.9
Poland	27 861	1.5	Brazil	9 503	1.8
■ **Corn**			■ **Wheat**[3]		
World total	478 775	100.0%	World total	550 993	100.0%
United States	189 867[2]	39.7	China	95 003	17.2
China	93 350[2]	19.5	USSR	80 000	14.5
Brazil	22 604	4.7	India	54 522	9.9
Mexico	13 527	2.8	United States	53 915	9.8
France	12 787	2.7	France	34 483	6.3
Romania	10 493	2.2	**Canada**	**32 822**	**6.0**
Yugoslavia	8 800[2]	1.8	Turkey	20 400	3.7
USSR	8 500	1.8	Pakistan	14 505	2.6
India	8 200[2]	1.7	United Kingdom	14 300	2.6
South Africa	8 200	1.7	Australia	9 633	1.7

Source: Food and Agriculture Organization of the UN, *FAO Production Yearbook, 1991*

(1) Dry grain only, including mixed grains and buckwheat. Not including hay, feed, sileage, grazing grain. (2) Estimate. (3) Includes spelt, except for USSR figure.

Leading Producers of Meats, 1991

(thousands of metric tons)

Country	Total	Percent of World Total	Country	Total	Percent of World Total
■ **Beef and Veal**			■ **Lamb and Mutton**		
World total	51 452	100.0%	World total	7 006	100.0%
United States	10 531	20.5	USSR	875[1]	12.5
USSR	8 200	15.9	Australia	675	9.6
Brazil	2 800[1]	5.4	China	572[1]	8.2
Argentina	2 640[1]	5.1	New Zealand	550	7.9
West Germany	2 024	3.9	United Kingdom	382	5.5
France	1 934	3.8	Turkey	303[1]	4.3
Australia	1 760	3.4	Iran	240[1]	3.4
Mexico	1 550[1]	3.0	Spain	230	3.3
Italy	1 164[1]	2.3	Pakistan	229	3.3
Canada	**879[1]**	**1.7**	India	166	2.4 ▶

Country	Total	Percent of World Total	Country	Total	Percent of World Total
▶ ■ **Pork**			■ **Poultry**		
World total	70 852	100.0%	World total	40 891	100.0%
China	25 460	36.0	United States	11 503	28.1
United States	7 258	10.2	China	3 463	8.5
USSR	6 200	8.8	USSR	3 000	7.3
West Germany	3 320	4.7	Brazil	2 614	6.4
Poland	1 869[1]	2.6	Japan	1 417	3.7
Spain	1 850[1]	2.6	France	1 394	3.4
France	1 820[1]	2.6	United Kingdom	1 112	2.7
Netherlands	1 639[1]	2.3	Italy	1 105[1]	2.7
Japan	1 490[1]	2.1	Mexico	897	2.2
Denmark	1 255[1]	1.8	Spain	840[1]	2.1

Source: Food and Agriculture Organization of the UN, *FAO Production Yearbook*, 1991   (1) Estimate

Leading Producers of Livestock, 1991

(thousands of head[1])

Country	Total	Percent of World Total	Country	Total	Percent of World Total
■ **Cattle**			■ **Goats** (continued)		
World total	1 294 604	100.0%	Iran	23 500[2]	3.9
India	198 400[2]	15.2	Somalia	20 500[2]	3.4
Brazil	152 000[2]	10.8	Ethiopia	18 000	3.0
USSR	115 600	9.1	Sudan	15 277[2]	2.6
United States	98 896	7.6	Brazil	12 500	2.1
China	81 407	6.2	Turkey	10 977[2]	1.8
Argentina	50 080	3.9			
Ethiopia	30 000[2]	2.3	■ **Pigs**		
Mexico	29 847	2.2	World total	857 099	100.0%
Colombia	24 875	1.9	China	363 975	42.5
Bangladesh	23 500[2]	1.8	USSR	75 600	8.8
			United States	54 427	6.4
■ **Chickens (mil.)**			Brazil	35 000	4.1
World total	11 061	100.0%	West Germany	22 036	2.6
China	2 077[2]	18.8	Poland	21 868	2.6
United States	1 520[2]	13.7	Mexico	15 902	1.9
USSR	1 160[2]	10.5	Spain	16 100	1.9
Brazil	570[2]	5.2	Netherlands	13 788	1.6
Indonesia	590[2]	5.3	Romania	12 003	1.4
India	380[2]	3.4			
Japan	335[2]	3.0	■ **Sheep**		
Mexico	246[2]	2.2	World total	1 202 920	100.0%
France	213[2]	1.9	Australia	162 774	13.5
Nigeria	170[2]	1.5	USSR	134 000[2]	11.1
			China	112 820	9.4
■ **Goats**			New Zealand	57 000	4.7
World total	594 286	100.0%	India	55 700	4.6
India	112 000	18.8	Iran	45 000[2]	3.7
China	97 378	16.4	Turkey	40 553	3.4
Pakistan	36 673	6.2	South Africa	32 580	2.7
Nigeria	36 000[2]	6.1	Pakistan	30 160	2.5
			Argentina	27 552	2.3

Source: Food and Agriculture Organization of the UN, *FAO Production Yearbook*, 1991   (1) Except as indicated. (2) Estimate

Leading Producers of Fish, 1990

(metric tons)

Country	Live Weight	Percent of World Total	Country	Live Weight	Percent of World Total
World total	97 245 700	100.00%	Chile	5 195 418	5.3%
China	12 095 363	12.4	India	3 790 598	3.9
USSR	10 389 030	10.7	Indonesia	3 080 450[1]	3.2
Japan	10 353 555	10.6	South Korea	2 750 000	2.8
Peru	6 875 072	7.1	Thailand	2 650 000[1]	2.7
United States	5 856 003	6.0			

Source: Food and Agriculture Organization of the UN, *FAO Yearbook of Fishery Statistics, Catches and Landings, 1990* (1) Estimate.

Leading Producers of Dairy Products, 1991

(metric tons)

Country	Total	Percent of World Total	Country	Total	Percent of World Total
■ Butter and Ghee			**■ Cow Milk, Whole Fresh** (thousands)		
World total	7 450 408	100.0%	World total	464 468	100.0%
USSR	1 570 000	21.1	USSR	100 000	21.5
India	1 040 000[1]	14.0	United States	67 373	14.5
United States	634 000	8.5	India	27 000	5.8
France	500 000[1]	6.7	France	26 600	5.7
West Germany	420 000[1]	5.6	West Germany	23 500	5.1
Pakistan	298 134[1]	4.0	Brazil	15 300	3.3
New Zealand	292 000	3.9	Poland	15 050	3.2
East Germany	232 500[1]	3.1	United Kingdom	15 022	3.2
Poland	225 000[1]	3.0	Netherlands	11 220	2.4
Netherlands	165 000[1]	2.2	Italy	10 000	2.2
■ Cheese			**■ Hen Eggs**		
World total	14 163 370	100.0%	World total	35 374 528	100.0%
United States	3 090 100	21.8	China	6 845 000[1]	19.4
USSR	1 845 000[1]	13.0	USSR	4 400 000	12.4
France	1 425 000	10.1	United States	4 005 400	11.3
West Germany	1 135 297	8.0	Japan	2 466 000[1]	7.0
Italy	692 486	4.9	Brazil	1 400 000[1]	4.0
Netherlands	614 275	4.3	India	1 357 000[1]	3.8
Egypt	318 750[1]	2.3	Mexico	1 141 381	3.2
United Kingdom	310 000	2.2	France	942 000	2.7
Poland	292 780	2.1	Italy	707 000	2.0
Denmark	290 000	2.0	West Germany	660 000	1.9

Source: Food and Agriculture Organization of the UN, *FAO Production Yearbook, 1991* (1) Estimate.

Fishing Around the World

*T*he FAO reported that world fish production in 1990 declined by slightly more than 3%, 97.2 million tonnes. The decline is the first since 1977 and was attributed to declines in southeastern Pacific and North Atlantic fisheries.

Fish production in the developed countries was reported to have fallen for the third year in a row, by almost 3 million tonnes. Much of the decline was in East European countries experiencing economic restructuring. Fish production in the former USSR, for example, fell by almost 1 million tonnes, largely due to a reduction in their distant water fishing operations.

Leading Producers of Beverages and Beverage Crops, 1991

(thousands of metric tons)

Country	Total	Percent of World Total	Country	Total	Percent of World Total
■ Cocoa Beans			**■ Coffee, Green**		
World total	2 455	100.0%	World total	6 088	100.0%
Côte d'Ivoire	710	28.0	Brazil	1 497	24.6
Brazil	345	14.1	Colombia	870	14.3
Ghana	295	12.0	Indonesia	408	6.7
Malaysia	225	9.2	Mexico	299	4.9
Indonesia	214	8.7	Côte d'Ivoire	240	3.9
Ecuador	136	5.5	Guatemala	195	3.2
Nigeria	115	4.7	Uganda	180	2.9
Cameroon	95	3.9	India	173	2.8
Colombia	59	2.4	Ethiopia	168	2.8
Dominican Republic	50	2.0	Philippines	113	1.9
■ Tea			**■ Wine**		
World total	2 576	100.0%	World total	27 767	100.0%
India	730[1]	28.3	France	6 200	22.3
China	566	22.0	Italy	5 915	21.3
Sri Lanka	241	9.4	Spain	3 107	11.2
Kenya	204	7.9	USSR	1 800[1]	6.5
Indonesia	158	6.1	United States	1 490[1]	5.4
Turkey	136	5.3	Argentina	1 465[1]	5.3
USSR	118	4.6	West Germany	1 015[1]	3.7
Japan	90[1]	3.5	Portugal	991	3.6
Iran	45[1]	1.7	South Africa	963[1]	3.5
Bangladesh	38	1.5	Romania	600	2.2

Source: Food and Agriculture Organization of the UN, *FAO Production Yearbook, 1991*   (1) Estimate.

Food Aid Requirements in 1993

*T*he Food and Agriculture Organization of the United Nations (FAO) reported in its 1992 "State of Food and Agriculture" that the food situation in Africa continues, year after year, to be a concern.

In particular, widespread food shortages are affecting large expanses of southern and east Africa. Most of the problems have been attributed to recurring drought and the prevalence of civil disturbances. The FAO predicted that Ethiopia would continue to be at risk from famine and would require approximately 1 million tonnes of food aid. Somalia's problems, which stem largely from an ongoing civil war that has hampered the distribution of relief supplies and increased the numbers of deaths from starvation in the past, are no closer to political solution although UN forces have been able to establish supply lines. A shortage of rain has put thousands of citizens of Kenya at risk, while civil war in Sudan will negate the benefits of a record wheat harvest and the increases in sorghum and millet production. Displaced Sudanese in the western and southern parts of the country will need assistance in order to get adequate amounts of food.

Tanzania has had severe localized droughts while Sierra Leone's and Liberia's civil disturbances have cut back food cultivation and made international food assistance necessary.

Other trouble spots the FAO will be monitoring in 1993 include Angola, Botswana, Lesotho, Malawi, Mozambique, Namibia, Swaziland, Zambia and Zimbabwe in Southern Africa, as well as Afghanistan, Cambodia, Iraq, Albania, Armenia, Haiti, Jordan, Laos, Lebanon and Peru.

INTERNATIONAL ORGANIZATIONS

United Nations

The first United Nations declaration was signed by 22 Allied governments on January 1, 1942, and was an alliance against Germany, Italy and Japan. This anti-Axis coalition was converted into an international body in 1945 when 51 nations agreed to sign a United Nations Charter and form an organization that would "save succeeding generations from the scourge of war," as stated in the UN Charter. The Charter was drawn up at the Conference on International Organization held in San Francisco from Apr. 25 to June 26, 1945 and took effect Oct. 24, 1945. The UN succeeded the ineffectual League of Nations, taking over its physical assets. UN membership has grown to 184.

The UN has six principal parts, with the General Assembly—the central organ—acting as a world parliament. General Assembly meetings have been held in New York since 1946 when UN Headquarters were established there. The International Court of Justice in The Hague, Netherlands, is the only major UN organ not based in New York. Specialized agencies are located throughout the world.

General Information on the UN may be requested from the Public Inquiries Unit, Dept. of Public Information, Room GA-057A, United Nations, New York, NY 10017; or from the United Nations Association in Canada, 808-63 Sparks St., Ottawa, Ont., K1P 5A6.

■ Structure of the United Nations

General Assembly The General Assembly is the UN's forum for discussing issues, reviewing UN activities and setting the agenda for initiatives. All member states are represented, and each is entitled to one vote. Resolutions require a majority vote before adoption. A president, 21 vice-presidents and seven committee chairs head the Assembly, which sits from mid-September to mid- December. The seven committees study issues relating to: disarmament and security; economy and finance; social, humanitarian and cultural issues; UN administrative and budgetary matters; legal issues; and political and security issues such as peacekeeping, and report back to a plenary session of the Assembly.

The General Assembly sets UN policies, admits new members on recommendation of the Security Council, approves the budget and receives reports from all other UN bodies.

Security Council The Security Council has the power to act for the maintenance of peace and security. It can enforce military action or economic sanctions, and it can send peacekeeping units (the Blue Berets) to troubled areas. The Security Council may also try to negotiate a ceasefire in the case of conflicts.

The Council has 15 members, five permanent and 10 elected by the General Assembly for two- year terms. Decisions require nine affirmative votes, but all permanent members have the right to veto. The permanent members are: China, France, the United Kingdom, the United States and the Russian Federation. Canada served a fifth term as a member in 1989–1990. The Security Council is permanently in session and representatives are on call 24 hours a day, ready to confer in the event of an international crisis. The Secretary-General is an active participant in the Security Council.

Economic and Social Council The Economic and Social Council co-ordinates the economic and social work of the UN and its related agencies. It encourages economic growth in developing countries. The Council's 54 members hold two month- long sessions each year: one in New York, the other in Geneva. Each member is elected by the General Assembly for a three-year term.

Trusteeship Council The Trusteeship Council ensures that trust territories are preparing for self- government or independence. The Pacific Islands (administered by the US) is the only remaining trusteeship of the original 11.

International Court of Justice (World Court) The Inter-national Court of Justice is the UN's judicial body. The Security Council elects 15 judges to the Court for nine-year terms. No two members may be from the same nation. The Court, located in The Hague, Netherlands, only sits in judgement on disputes between states. Both member and non- member states may submit grievances (border disputes, resource access, breach of treaty, etc.). Countries can opt out of any proceeding, unless required to participate by treaty provisions. But after agreeing to become a party in a case, a nation must comply with the Court's decision, enforced by the Security Council.

Secretariat The Secretariat administers the programs and policies laid out by other UN bodies. The Secretary-General, heading the Secretariat, is responsible for the UN's administration and for alerting the Security Council to any threats to international peace and security, and acts as spokesperson for the UN. The Secretary-General is elected by the General Assembly and cannot be from one of the five permanent members of the Security Council.

Canadian Ambassadors to the United Nations

Ambassador	Date Appointed	Ambassador	Date Appointed
Andrew McNaughton	Jan. 1948	Yvon Beaulne	Jan. 1969
John Holmes	Jan. 1950	Saul Forbes Rae	June 1972
Gerald Riddell	June 1950	William Barton	May 1976
David Johnson	Oct. 1951	Michel Dupuy	Mar. 1980
Robert MacKay	June 1955	Gérard Pelletier	Aug. 1981
Charles Ritchie	Nov. 1957	Stephen H. Lewis	Oct. 1984
Paul Tremblay	May 1962	Yves Fortier	July 1988
George Ignatieff	Mar. 1966	Louise Fréchette	Jan. 1992

Source: *Dept. of External Affairs*

Canadian Representatives to International Organizations

(As of Oct. 1993)

European Communities Commission, Brussels	Gordon Smith, Amb., H.M.
FAO (Food and Agriculture Organization), Rome	Robert Andrigo, P.R.
Habitat (U.N. Centre for Human Settlements), Nairobi	Lucie Edward, P.R.
International Civil Aviation Organization, Montreal	Gilles H.J. Duguay, R.
Negotiations on Confidence and Security Building; Negotiations on Conventional Armed Forces in Europe, Vienna	H. David Peel, H.D., Amb.
North Atlantic Council, Brussels	James K. Bartleman, P.R., Amb.
Office of the U.N.; Conference on Disarmament, Geneva	Gerald E. Shannon, P.R., Amb.
Office of the U.N.; U.N. Industrial Development Organization, International Atomic Energy Agency, Vienna	Peter F. Walker, P.R., Amb.
Organization of American States, Washington	Jean-Paul Hubert, P.R., Amb.
Organization for Economic Co-Operation and Development, Paris	Anne-Marie Doyle, P.R., Amb.
UNEP (U.N. Environment Program), Nairobi	Lucie Edward, P.R.
UNESCO (U.N. Educational, Scientific and Cultural Organization), Paris	Marie Bernard-Meunier, P.R., Amb.
United Nations, New York	Louise Fréchette, P.R., Amb.

Source: *Dept. of External Affairs*

H.D. = Head of Delegation; H.M. = Head of Mission; Amb. = Ambassador; P.R. = Permanent Representative; P.O. = Permanent Observer; P.D. = Permanent Delegate; R.A. = Roving Ambassador; R. = Representative.

United Nations Secretaries-General

Secretary, Nation	Date Installed	Secretary, Nation	Date Installed
Trygve Lie, Norway	Feb. 1946	Kurt Waldheim, Austria	Dec. 1971
Dag Hammarskjold, Sweden	Apr. 1953	Javier Perez de Cuellar, Peru	Dec. 1981
U Thant, Burma	Nov. 1961	Boutros Boutros-Ghali, Egypt[1]	Jan. 1992

(1) Term ends Dec. 31, 1996

United Nations and Related Organizations

■ General Assembly

IAEA: International Atomic Energy Agency

INSTRAW: International Research and Training Institute for the Advancement of Women

UNCHS/HABITAT: UN Centre for Human Settlements

UNCTAD: UN Conference on Trade and Development

UNDP: UN Development Programme

UNEP: UN Environment Programme

UNFPA: United Nations Population Fund

UNHCR: Office of the UN High Commissioner for Refugees

UNICEF: UN Children's Fund

UNITAR: UN Institute for Training and Research

UNRWA: UN Relief and Works Agency for Palestine Refugees in the Near East

UNU: UN University

WFC: World Food Council

■ Security Council

MINURSO: UN Mission for the Referendum in Western Sahara

ONUMOZ: UN Operation in Mozambique

ONUSAL: UN Observer Mission in El Salvador

UNAVEM II: UN Angola Verification Mission II

UNDOF: UN Disengagement Observer Force

UNFICYP: UN Peace-keeping Force in Cyprus

UNIFIL: UN Interim Force in Lebanon

UNIKOM: UN Iraq-Kuwait Observation Mission

UNMOGIP: UN Military Observer Group in India and Pakistan

UNOMIG: UN Observer Mission in Georgia

UNOMUR: UN Observer Mission in Uganda-Rwanda

UNOSOM II: United Nations Operation in Somalia

UNPROFOR: UN Protection Force

UNTAC: UN Transitional Authority in Cambodia

UNTSO: UN Truce Supervision Organization

■ Secretariat

UNDRO: UN Disaster Relief Coordinator

■ Economic and Social Council

FAO: Food and Agriculture Organization

GATT: General Agreement on Tariffs and Trade

ICAO: International Civil Aviation Organization

IFAD: International Fund for Agricultural Development

ILO: International Labour Organization

IMF: International Monetary Fund

IMO: International Maritime Organization

ITU: International Telecommunications Union

UNESCO: UN Educational, Scientific and Cultural Organization

UNIDO: UN Industrial Development Organization

UPU: Universal Postal Union

WFP: World Food Programme

WHO: World Health Organization

WIPO: World Intellectual Property Organization

WMO: World Meteorological Organization

□ World Bank

IBRD: International Bank for Reconstruction and Development

IDA: International Development Association

IFC: International Finance Corporation

■ International Court of Justice

■ Trusteeship Council

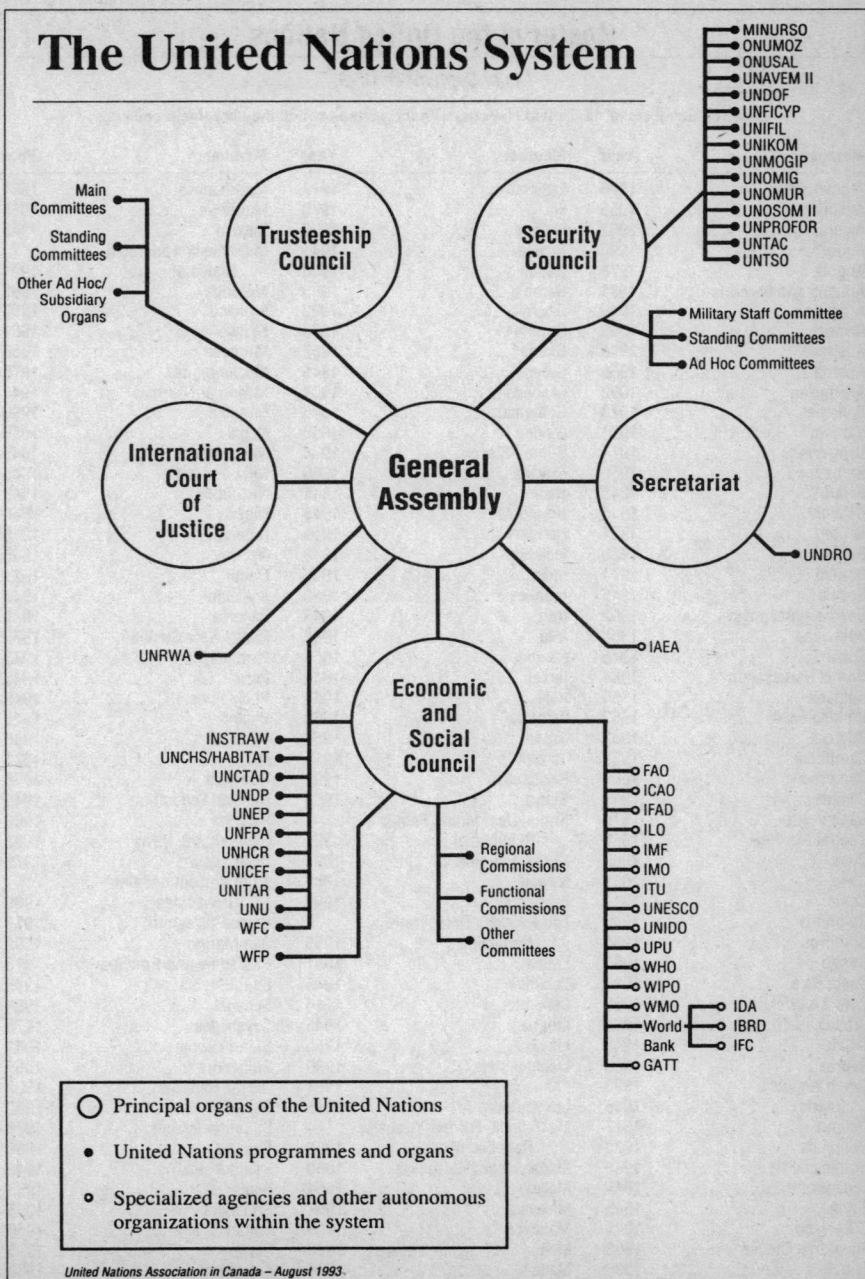

The United Nations System

- MINURSO
- ONUMOZ
- ONUSAL
- UNAVEM II
- UNDOF
- UNFICYP
- UNIFIL
- UNIKOM
- UNMOGIP
- UNOMIG
- UNOMUR
- UNOSOM II
- UNPROFOR
- UNTAC
- UNTSO

Trusteeship Council

Security Council

- Main Committees
- Standing Committees
- Other Ad Hoc/ Subsidiary Organs

- Military Staff Committee
- Standing Committees
- Ad Hoc Committees

International Court of Justice

General Assembly

Secretariat

- UNDRO

- UNRWA

- IAEA

Economic and Social Council

- INSTRAW
- UNCHS/HABITAT
- UNCTAD
- UNDP
- UNEP
- UNFPA
- UNHCR
- UNICEF
- UNITAR
- UNU
- WFC
- WFP

- Regional Commissions
- Functional Commissions
- Other Committees

- FAO
- ICAO
- IFAD
- ILO
- IMF
- IMO
- ITU
- UNESCO
- UNIDO
- UPU
- WHO
- WIPO
- WMO
- World Bank
  - IDA
  - IBRD
  - IFC
- GATT

○ Principal organs of the United Nations

● United Nations programmes and organs

○ Specialized agencies and other autonomous organizations within the system

United Nations Association in Canada – August 1993

Roster of the United Nations

(As of September 1993)

The 184 members of the United Nations, with the years in which they became members.

Member	Year	Member	Year	Member	Year
Afghanistan	1946	Ethiopia	1945	Mauritania	1961
Albania	1955	Fiji	1970	Mauritius	1968
Algeria	1962	Finland	1955	Mexico	1945
Andorra	1993	France	1945	Micronesia, Federated	
Angola	1976	Gabon	1960	States of	1991
Antigua and Barbuda	1981	Gambia	1965	Moldova	1992
Argentina	1945	Georgia	1992	Monaco	1993
Armenia	1992	Germany	1973	Mongolia	1961
Australia	1945	Ghana	1957	Morocco	1956
Austria	1955	Greece	1945	Mozambique	1975
Azerbaijan	1992	Grenada	1974	Myanmar (Burma)	1948
Bahamas	1973	Guatemala	1945	Namibia	1990
Bahrain	1971	Guinea	1958	Nepal	1955
Bangladesh	1974	Guinea-Bissau	1974	Netherlands	1945
Barbados	1966	Guyana	1966	New Zealand	1945
Belarus	1945	Haiti	1945	Nicaragua	1945
Belgium	1945	Honduras	1945	Niger	1960
Belize	1981	Hungary	1955	Nigeria	1960
Benin	1960	Iceland	1946	Norway	1945
Bhutan	1971	India	1945	Oman	1971
Bolivia	1945	Indonesia	1950	Pakistan	1947
Bosnia-Hercegovina	1992	Iran	1945	Panama	1945
Botswana	1966	Iraq	1945	Papua New Guinea	1975
Brazil	1945	Ireland	1955	Paraguay	1945
Brunei Darussalam	1984	Israel	1949	Peru	1945
Bulgaria	1955	Italy	1955	Philippines	1945
Burkina-Faso	1960	Jamaica	1962	Poland	1945
Burundi	1962	Japan	1956	Portugal	1955
Cambodia	1955	Jordan	1955	Qatar	1971
Cameroon	1960	Kazakhstan	1992	Romania	1955
Canada	1945	Kenya	1963	Russian Federation	1945
Cape Verde	1975	Korea, Democratic People's		Rwanda	1962
Central Afr. Rep.	1960	Republic of	1991	Saint Kitts & Nevis	1983
Chad	1960	Korea, Republic of	1991	Saint Lucia	1979
Chile	1945	Kuwait	1963	Saint Vincent and the	
China	1945	Kyrgyzstan	1992	Grenadines	1980
Colombia	1945	Lao People's Democratic		Samoa (Western)	1976
Comoros	1975	Republic	1955	San Marino	1992
Congo	1960	Latvia	1991	Sao Tome and Principe	1975
Costa Rica	1945	Lebanon	1945	Saudi Arabia	1945
Côte d'Ivoire	1960	Lesotho	1966	Senegal	1960
Croatia	1992	Liberia	1945	Seychelles	1976
Cuba	1945	Libya	1955	Sierra Leone	1961
Cyprus	1960	Liechtenstein	1990	Singapore	1965
Czech Republic	1993	Lithuania	1991	Slovak Republic	1993
Denmark	1945	Luxembourg	1945	Slovenia	1992
Djibouti	1977	Macedonia, Former Yugoslav		Solomon Islands	1978
Dominica	1978	Republic of	1993	Somalia	1960
Dominican Rep.	1945	Madagascar (Malagasy)	1960	South Africa[1]	1945
Ecuador	1945	Malawi	1964	Spain	1955
Egypt	1945	Malaysia	1957	Sri Lanka	1955
El Salvador	1945	Maldives	1965	Sudan	1956
Equatorial Guinea	1968	Mali	1960	Suriname	1975
Eritrea	1993	Malta	1964	Swaziland	1968
Estonia	1991	Marshall Islands	1991	Sweden	1946

Member	Year	Member	Year	Member	Year
Syria	1945	Turkmenistan	1992	Vanuatu	1981
Tajikistan	1992	Uganda	1962	Venezuela	1945
Tanzania	1961	Ukraine	1945	Vietnam	1977
Thailand	1946	United Arab Emirates	1971	Yemen	1947
Togo	1960	United Kingdom	1945	Yugoslavia[1]	1945
Trinidad & Tobago	1962	United States	1945	Zaire	1960
Tunisia	1956	Uruguay	1945	Zambia	1964
Turkey	1945	Uzbekistan	1992	Zimbabwe	1980

Source: *United Nations Association*

(1) Not permitted to participate in General Assembly deliberations.

Other International Organizations in the News

Association of Southeast Asian Nations (ASEAN) was created in 1967 to further the social, economic and agricultural progress of the region's non-communist countries. Original members are Indonesia, Malaysia, Philippines, Singapore and Thailand; Brunei joined in 1984. Based in Jakarta, ASEAN works for greater peace and security in the area. Summit meetings of heads of government, ministerial conferences and various committees organize for cooperation in research, trade and tourism of the member countries.

Caribbean Community (CARICOM) was created in 1973 as a common market for Barbados, Guyana, Jamaica and Trinidad and Tobago. It coordinates foreign policies of member states and organizes common services. Members now include Belize, Dominica, Grenada, St. Lucia, St. Vincent, Montserrat, Antigua and St. Kitts-Nevis.

La Francophonie is a term created in 1960 to define a community of 41 nations sharing the French language and culture. It is now commonly thought of as an informal grouping of mostly African francophone states, although Canada remains a participant. Heads of government, intergovernmental institutions and private organizations from francophone nations meet occasionally to promote economic and political cooperation. Conferences of francophone states have been held in 1969, 1986, and most recently in 1987 in Quebec, where Canada announced it would cancel $325 million in debt owed by seven French-speaking African nations. It also announced $1 million in aid to Chad and Lebanon.

League of Arab States (Arab League) was established in 1945 in Cairo to give Arab nations a united voice on political and economic issues and to mediate internal disputes. The original treaty was signed by Egypt, Iraq, Lebanon, Saudi Arabia, Syria, Jordan and Yemen. Membership now stands at 21 including: Algeria, Bahrain, Djibouti, Kuwait, Libya, Mauritania, Morocco, Oman, the Palestine Liberation Organization, Qatar, Somalia, Sudan, Tunisia and the United Arab Emirates. In 1948, the League opposed the formation of a Jewish state (Israel) in Palestine. In 1979, Egypt was suspended from the league for signing a peace treaty with Israel. As a result, the headquarters for the League moved from Cairo to Tunis. Egypt was re-admitted in 1989.

North Atlantic Treaty Organization (NATO) came into effect in 1949 as a military alliance of Western European and North American countries. The members agreed that agression against one country would be treated as an attack against all. They also united to solve political problems and settle internal disputes by peaceful means. The North Atlantic Council is the chief decision-making body of NATO, with a Defense Planning Committee, and a Military Committee making recommendations to it. Members are: Belgium, Canada, Denmark, France, Germany, Greece, Iceland, Italy, Luxembourg, Netherlands, Norway, Portugal, Spain, Turkey, the United Kingdom and the United States. Spain is the most recent member, joining in 1982, but its forces do not belong to the Integrated Military Structure of NATO. Similarly, France withdrew its forces from the Military Structure in 1966.

Organization for Economic Cooperation and Development (OECD) was established in 1961 to promote economic growth and to increase employment and standards of living in member nations. Its 24 members also work to expand world trade and provide aid for developing countries. Members are: Australia, Austria, Belgium, Canada, Denmark, Finland, France, West Germany, Greece, Iceland, Ireland, Italy, Japan, Luxembourg, Netherlands, New Zealand, Norway, Portugal, Spain, Sweden, Switzerland, Turkey, the United Kingdom and the United States.

Organization of American States (OAS) was established in 1948 to promote peace and development in the Western hemisphere. Based in Washington D.C., its 35 members include all the independent countries of the hemisphere except Cuba, which has been excluded from participation since 1962. Canada joined the OAS in 1990. The mandate of the OAS is based on a principle in the Monroe Doctrine, which defines an attack on one American state as an attack on all. The OAS tries to settle internal disputes independently, discouraging foreign intervention.

Organization of Petroleum Exporting Countries (OPEC) was founded in 1960 by major oil-producing nations to gain more control over the pricing and production of oil. Original members are Iran, Iraq, Kuwait, Saudi Arabia and Venezuela. Additional members include Algeria, Ecuador, Gabon, Indonesia, Libya, Nigeria, Qatar and the United Arab Emirates. Together they have up to 75 percent of the world's recoverable oil reserves. In the 1970s, OPEC raised oil prices, causing rapid inflation in the industrialized nations.

The European Community

The European Community (EC) is an organization of 12 democratic nations, striving for peace and prosperity through a united Europe. With more than 325 million people and 25 percent of the world's Gross National Product, it is the largest trading bloc in the world.

The EC was the brain-child of British Prime Minister Winston Churchill who proposed the establishment of a United States of Europe to speed economic recovery following the Second World War. The idea was revived in 1950 when French Foreign Minister Robert Schuman proposed joining the coal and steel industries of France and West Germany. He then opened the plan to any other democratic country in Europe. The result was the European Coal and Steel Community (ECSC) formed in 1951 by France, West Germany, Italy, Netherlands, Belgium and Luxembourg.

The ECSC boosted internal trade in steel by 129 percent in five years. Its success spurred the formation of a similar joint pool of resources for the entire economy. The same six nations formed the European Economic Community (EEC) in 1957, extending the common market to all sectors of the economy. The EEC favored dismantling trade barriers to allow the free movement of persons, services and capital between member countries. At the same time members formed the European Atomic Energy Agency (Euratom) to encourage the peaceful use of nuclear energy in Europe.

In 1967, the ECSC, Euratom and the EEC united to form a single commission that became the EC of today. In 1973, Denmark, Ireland and the U.K. became members, as did Greece in 1981 and Spain and Portugal in 1986.

From its inception, the European Community has been dedicated to "reducing the differences existing between the various regions and the backwardness of the less-favoured regions." To that end, the Community set up a number of structural funds such as the European Regional Development Fund and the Social Fund to make financial assistance available to those regions suffering from industrial decline, long-term unemployment or whose development is behind. Greece, Portugal, Ireland and parts of Spain and Italy have been targeted for aid that will bring their standards of living closer to that of other member states.

In 1986 EC members signed the Single European Act, designed to supplement the existing European treaties by proposing 282 measures covering all aspects needed for the creation of an internal market. The Act also reformed the way the EC institutions worked by making them more effective. The economic policies were to create a coherent economic unit, but also acknowledge the importance of environmental and social policy to the quality of life within the Community.

Since the signing and implementation of the Single Act, the European Council has gone on to negotiate a new treaty on economic and monetary union. What has become known as the Maastricht Treaty takes the integration process a step further, preparing the way for political union and the use of a common currency—the ecu (European currency unit). The treaty was ratified by all 12 member states and became effective Jan. 1, 1993, although the German provinces have challenged their federal government's right to pass such a

treaty on their behalf. Approval of the Maastricht Treaty paves the way for the Community to proceed with measures to :
- increase the powers of the European Parliament;
- create a common European currency by 1999 at the latest;
- extend the European Community's responsibilities to cover areas such as increased consumer protection; public health policy; the issuing of visas; the creation of major transport, telecommunications and energy infrastructures; education; culture; environmental protection; research and development; and
- develop a common foreign and security policy.

In early August 1993, progress toward a common currency was dealt a severe setback when the diverging economic goals of EC member countries (high interest rates in Germany to keep inflation in check vs. low interest rates needed to spur growth in France, Denmark, Spain and Belgium) made the restrictions on the variance in exchange rates (exchange-rate mechanism or ERM) unworkable. The pressure of buying and selling activity by currency speculators and investors forced the EC's monetary authorities to let the currencies float freely against each other in the market, thereby at least temporarily abandoning the ERM that was the cornerstone of the proposed European Monetary System.

Structure of the EC

The EC creates its own laws and policies through the following major organizations:

The Commission is the EC's executive and initiates proposed legislation. It consists of 17 members: two German, two Spanish, two French, two Italian, two British and one from each of the other EC countries. Members of the Commission are appointed for four years by mutual agreement of Community governments.

The European Parliament is the public forum for debating and questioning legislation in the EC. It has 518 deputies, elected every five years. There are 81 deputies from each of the four most populous countries (Germany, France, Italy, the U.K.); 60 from Spain; 25 from the Netherlands; 24 each from Belgium, Greece and Portugal; 16 from Denmark; 15 from Ireland; and six from Luxembourg. The Parliament is also responsible for passing or rejecting the EC's budget.

The Council of Ministers adopts and enacts EC legislation. Ministers from the governments of member states make the major Community policy decisions. The President of the Council changes every six months as each member state assumes the Presidency in rotation. Participants in meetings change according to the agenda: agriculture ministers, for instance, discuss farm prices; employment and economy ministers discuss employment problems. Each year, the Council holds two summits, at which the heads of member governments meet.

The Court of Justice interprets EC laws, acting as the Community's Supreme Court. Sitting in Luxembourg, the Court has 13 judges assisted by six advocates-general. Both groups are appointed for six years by mutual consent of the Member States.

The Economic and Social Committee advises the Commission and the Council on many issues and proposed policies. The consultative body has 189 members who represent employers, trade unions and other interested groups, such as farmers and consumers.

Roster of the European Community

(As of September 1993)

Member	Year Joined	Member	Year Joined
Belgium	1957	Italy	1957
Denmark	1973	Luxembourg	1957
France	1957	Netherlands	1957
Germany	1957	Portugal	1986
Greece	1981	Spain	1986
Ireland	1973	United Kingdom	1973

Source: *Commission of the European Communities*

The Commonwealth

The Commonwealth is a loosely-structured, voluntary association of 50 independent states which once formed part of the British Empire. Its roots can be traced to the early 1900s and the concept of autonomous nations within the Empire co-operating in such matters as foreign policy, out of a common allegiance to the Crown. The Commonwealth was more formally established in 1931 when the *Statute of Westminster* legally granted self-government to the Dominions within the Empire. Founding members were Britain, Canada, Newfoundland (which ceased to be an independent member upon entering Confederation in 1949), Australia, New Zealand and South Africa (which left in 1961 due to Commonwealth opposition to its racial policies).

The number of members grew quickly from the late 1940s into the 1960s as many Asian and African countries gained independence. In more recent years, many small Caribbean, Indian Ocean and Pacific Island countries have become member states. Current membership represents about a quarter of the world's population and about a third of the countries in the United Nations.

The Commonwealth has no written charter or constitution. It is a forum for pooling experience and expressing viewpoints. The highest level of Commonwealth consultation is the Heads of Government Meetings, held every 2 years. In 1971, the Commonwealth adopted 5 principles: the pursuit of international peace and order through the United Nations; the promotion of representative institutions and guarantees for personal freedom under the law; the recognition of racial equality and the need to combat racial discrimination; opposition to all forms of colonial domination and racial oppression; and dedication to lessening the disparities in wealth between different sections of mankind.

A central office, the Commonwealth Secretariat, was established in 1965 to facilitate coordination and consultation in all areas of Commonwealth joint endeavor. Funded by members under a system of assessed contributions, the Secretariat carries out economic, social and educational programs primarily for the benefit of developing Commonwealth countries.

Source: *Department of External Affairs*

Commonwealth Members[1]

Country	Year Joined	Country	Year Joined
Antigua and Barbuda	1981	Mauritius	1968
Australia	1931	Namibia	1990
Bahamas	1973	Nauru[2]	1968
Bangladesh	1972	New Zealand	1931
Barbados	1966	Nigeria	1960
Belize	1981	Pakistan[3]	1989
Botswana	1966	Papua New Guinea	1975
Britain	1931	St. Kitts and Nevis	1983
Brunei Darussalam	1984	St. Lucia	1979
Canada	1931	St.Vincent and The Grenadines	1979
Cyprus	1961	Seychelles	1976
Dominica	1978	Sierra Leone	1961
The Gambia	1965	Singapore	1965
Ghana	1957	Solomon Islands	1978
Grenada	1974	Sri Lanka	1948
Guyana	1966	Swaziland	1968
India	1947	Tanzania	1961
Jamaica	1962	Tonga	1970
Kenya	1963	Trinidad and Tobago	1962
Kiribati	1979	Tuvalu[2]	1978
Lesotho	1966	Uganda	1962
Malawi	1964	Vanuatu	1980
Malaysia	1957	Western Samoa	1970
Maldives	1982	Zambia	1964
Malta	1964	Zimbabwe	1980

(1) As of Oct. 1993. (2) Special Member of the Commonwealth. Has right to participate in all meetings and activities except meetings of Commonwealth Heads of Government. (3) Left the Commonwealth in 1972 in a dispute over the recognition of Bangladesh; became a member again Oct. 1, 1989.

HISTORY IN HEADLINES

■ Ancient History 5000 BC to AD 476

5000–3501: The earliest known cities are in Mesopotamia—in southwest Asia between the Tigris and Euphrates Rivers—a plain rendered fertile by canals; the Egyptian calendar is regulated by the sun and moon; Sumerian writing exists, in southern Mesopotamia on clay tablets, consisting of 2,000 pictograph signs; the Neolithic period in western Europe is characterized by polished stone weapons and tools and agriculturally-based settlements; Cretan ships appear in the Mediterranean Sea; copper alloys are used, and there is smelting of gold and silver in Sumer and Egypt; harps and flutes are played in Egypt; painted pottery appears along the Mediterranean; coloured ceramic ware from Russia reaches China.

3500–2001: The Middle Eastern Bronze Age begins (c. 3500 BC); the height of Sumerian civilization (in the region of the Euphrates River valley) is noted for having a numerical system, irrigated agriculture, poetry, potters' wheels, linen, wheeled vehicles, wedge-shaped (cuneiform) script, barley, bread, beer, use of metal coins as legal tender, oil-burning lamps, brick temples and medicine; the dynasty of Pharoahs as god-kings in Egypt begins (2200–525 BC); the Great Sphynx of Gizeh is built; wrestling is the first highly developed sport; glass beads are worn in Egypt; the bow and arrow is first used in warfare; the Yao dynasty is the first recorded in China (2500–2300); the Indus civilization begins in India; the earliest Egyptian mummies are made; equinoxes and solstices are calculated in China; the first library is in Egypt.

2000–1501: The Egyptian height of power and achievement (18th dynasty) features an irrigation system, contraceptives, bathrooms with a water supply, an alphabet of 24 signs, and the oldest form of a novel (*Story of Sinuhe*); the Persian empire begins (1750–1550); the first legal system and laws of a kingdom are set up by Hammurabi, king of Babylonia; the first of seven periods of Chinese literature begins; Stonehenge is built; Abraham, the patriarch of the Jewish religion, lives (c. 1800); Babylonia uses geometry as the basis for astronomical measurements, and

describes the signs of the Zodiac; religious dances are performed in Crete.

1500–1001: The Israelites, led by Moses, leave bondage in Egypt (eventually settling in Canaan in 1250), and receive the Ten Commandments and the world's first monotheistic belief at Mt Sinai; the decline of Egyptian power begins (1200–1090); Troy is destroyed during the Trojan War (1193–83) over Helen of Sparta (Greek legend); the Iron Age begins in the Mediterranean area (1000); obelisk structures are used as sundials in Egypt; the first Chinese dictionary is written; silk fabrics appear in China; leprosy spreads in India and Egypt; Phoenicia is the dominant trading power in the Mediterranean; the Mexican Sun Pyramid is built in Teotihuacan.

1000–901: Asiatic and Greek civilizations are linked by Phoenician trading; David is the king of the united kingdom of Judah and Israel (1000–960) with Jerusalem as its capital; David is succeeded by his son Solomon who presides over the height of Israel's ancient civilization (960–25); classical paganism reigns in Greece; pantheistic belief reigns in India (teaching reincarnation and the caste system); the Chou dynasty's rational philosophy reigns in China; Pinto Indians build huts in southwest North America; brush and ink painting appears in China; gold vessels and jewellery are made in northern Europe; the Hebrew alphabet and literature are developed; the Germanic peoples begin to migrate en masse.

900–601: Carthage is founded as a trading centre (813); *Iliad* and *Odyssey* are written and credited to the poet Homer (c. 800); according to legend, Rome is founded by the twins Romulus and Remus (753); the first recorded Olympic Games are held in Greece (776), and every four years thereafter during ancient times; the earliest record of music is a hymn on a Sumerian tablet; arts and crafts flourish in Asia Minor and Greece; a canal between the Nile River and the Red Sea is started under Pharoah Nechos; Etruscan art forms emerge in Tuscany; the Assyrians destroy Babylon and divert the Euphrates River to cover the site of the city; the Babylonians and their allies later destroy the Assyrian empire, which is then divided among the conquerors; the Acropolis, a fortified hill and religious centre, is built in Athens; limestone and marble are used in the construction of Greek temples; flutes and lyres accompany song; Greek choral and lyric poetry use strophe and antistrophe; Zoroaster, a religious teacher and prophet of ancient Persia, lives (c. 628–c. 551).

600–451: The Mayan civilization flourishes in Mexico; Nebuchadnezzer builds what may be the terraced Hanging Gardens of Babylon (600); Babylonian troops destroy the Jewish Temple at Jerusalem and take many Jews as slaves; Jews write the early books of the Bible during the Babylonian Captivity; Siddhartha Gautama, who becomes Buddha, the "enlightened" Indian philosopher and religious teacher, is born (563): at age 29 he renounces world luxuries and searches for enlightenment, which he attains at age 35 while meditating under a pipal tree at Bodh Gaya, and he teaches monks to continue his work; Confucius, the Chinese philosopher and teacher, is born (551); his moral and religious system governs China and is contained in the sayings of *Analects*; Cyrus II the Great of Persia conquers Babylon and surrounding areas and transforms Persia into a vast empire (c. 540): he frees the Jews from Babylon (536) and aids their return to Israel; Darius I divides the Persian empire into 20 provinces and introduces reforms including a common currency, regular taxes and a standing army; Solon's laws are adopted in Athens; Milo of Crotona, a legendary athlete, is crowned six times at the Olympic Games (536); Chinese feudal structure begins to weaken during Chou dynasty (c. 500–451); Greek cities are freed from Persian domination when the Greeks in Cyprus win the Persian Wars (490–49); the marble temple of Apollo is built at Delphi (478); the statue of Zeus, the centrepiece of the temple of Olympia, is built (460); Aeschylus writes *Prometheus Bound* (460); the *Fables of Aesop* is written by a former Phrygian slave.

450–301: The Greek Periclean Age unfolds with the philosophers Socrates and (his pupil) Plato, the dramatists Sophocles and Euripides and historians Thucydides and Herodotus; the beginning of the Indian empire is centred at Magadha (the "cradle of Buddhism"); the Torah becomes the moral code of the Jewish people; Celtic settlements begin in the British Isles; the Spartans use chemicals in warfare (charcoal, sulphur and pitch); the Parthenon, the masterpiece of Greek architecture, is built (447–32); the population of Greece reaches two million citizens and one million slaves; indigenous Indian civilization ends in Mexico; the Peloponnesian Wars between Athens and Sparta (431–04) end when the Spartan navy destroys the Athenian navy at Aegospotami: this leads to the decline of Athens as a great power; the first horoscopes are developed in Mesopotamia (c. 410); Socrates is put to death for state offences (399); Brennus leads the Gauls from northern Italy to sack Rome (390); Rome is rebuilt (387) and city walls are built around it (377); Plato, a Greek philosopher, founds the most influential school in the world, the Academy (c. 387); the use of catapults as weapons of war begins; Aristotle, the Greek philosopher, is born (384); Alexander the Great, son of Philip II of Macedon, is born (356); Shung-tse founds Chinese monist philosophy (the doctrine that the universe can be explained by one principle) (350); Corinth becomes a trading centre (338); Philip II is assassinated (336); Alexander succeeds his father and conquers Persia, Jerusalem and Tyre, extending his empire to the Indus River in India where his generals force him to turn back; Alexander dies in Babylon (323) and his empire is divided among his generals who fight civil wars for a time (beginning in 321); the Hellenistic period of Greek arts begins (330–20) and the leading Greek schools of thought are: Stoics, Epicureans and Cynics; Euclid writes *Elements*, a standard work on geometry (323); Alexandria is the centre of Greek learning.

300–151: The Mexican sun temple Atetello is built at Teotihuacan (300); accurate star maps are compiled by Chinese astronomers (c. 300); full equality between patricians and plebeians is mandated in Rome (287); Archimedes, the Greek mathematician, is born (287); the practical end of the history of Babylon coincides with Babylonian re-establishment in the new city of Seleucia (275); Manetho, the high priest of Egypt, writes a history of Egypt in Greek (275); the Colossus at Rhodes is completed (275); the Lighthouse of Pharos is completed at Alexandria (275); the First Punic War between the Carthaginians and the Romans (264–41) arises out of a dispute involving the Sicilian cities of Messana and Syracuse: the Romans win naval battles at Mylae (260) and Cape Ecnomus

(256) but lose in Africa (255); a Roman victory of the Aegadian Isles (241) brings a peace treaty that gives Sicily to Rome, but Rome reneges on the treaty and invades Sardinia and Corsica; the leap year is introduced into the Egyptian calendar (239); the Greeks and Romans play ball games, roll dice and play board games; the death of Sun-tsi marks the end of Chinese classical philosophy; the Great Wall of China (2,400 km long) is built to keep out invaders (215); the Second Punic War (218–01) opens when Hannibal and the Carthaginians conquer the Spanish city Saguntum, a Roman ally, and Rome declares war: Hannibal successfully invades Italy from the north (217) and makes an alliance with Philip V of Macedon (216), but is later defeated by the Romans at Zama (202) in Africa; Carthage surrenders its war fleet to Rome as well as its Spanish province; the Second Macedonian War (200–197) ends with the Romans under Flamius defeating Philip V of Macedon; the use of gears leads to the invention of the ox-driven water wheel for irrigation (200); an inscription is engraved on the Rosetta Stone (c. 200); Antiochus IV of Syria persecutes the Jews in Israel and desecrates their Temple of Jerusalem (168); the Jews revolt under Judas Maccabeus and repel the Syrians, then rededicate (Chanukah) the Temple (165); the inventor of trigonometry, Hipparchus of Nicaea, is born (160).

150–1 BC: During the Third Punic War (149–46) the Romans destroy Corinth and massacre the inhabitants of Carthage (due to alleged breach of treaty); the Roman Empire now consists of seven provinces; the Venus of Milo is sculpted (140); Cicero, the greatest Roman orator, is born (106); the first Chinese ships reach the east coast of India (100); the greatest of Roman poets, Virgil, is born (70): he pens the epic *Aeneid*; Horace, the lyric poet, is born (65); Julius Caesar, Roman military commander, organizes the First Triumvirate (60) with Pompey, commander-in-chief of the army, and Marcus Crassus; Caesar conquers the northern Gauls (55) and the Britons; Caesar and Pompey battle for control of Rome after Caesar crosses the Rubicon River and provokes a civil war; Caesar emerges victorious (48); the Julian calendar and leap year are adopted in Rome (46); Cleopatra, the last queen of Egypt, orders the death of Pompey; Caesar, now the dictator of Rome, is murdered by a group headed by Brutus and

Cassius Longinus (44); Mark Antony, Octavian and Lepidus form the Second Triumvirate and defeat Brutus and Cassius at Phillipi (42); Mark Antony returns to Egypt (38) where he and Cleopatra commit suicide after being defeated by Octavian at Actium (31); Octavian, retitled Augustus, is a virtual emperor of Rome (30–AD 14); Herod the Great is appointed king of Judea by the Romans (c. 40); the probable date of the birth of Jesus, the Jewish son of Mary, in Bethlehem (AD 4).

AD 1–150: Jesus, who is revered as the Son of God by his followers, the Christians, preaches for three years in Galilee (c. 30); in the third year of his preaching, Jesus is crucified in Jerusalem by Roman authorities at the request of local political and religious leaders; Caligula becomes emperor of Rome (37) and is known for his ruthlessness and insanity: he is assassinated by the Praetorian Guard (42) and is succeeded by Claudius I, who consolidates and reinvigorates the empire despite a paralysis (dies in 54); the apostle Paul sets out on his missionary travels (45) and spreads Christianity; Nero, emperor of Rome, is the first to persecute the Christians, for allegedly burning half of Rome (64); the Gospels according to Matthew, Mark and John are written; Jews revolt against Rome and the Romans destroy the second Temple at Jerusalem and enslave many inhabitants (70); 1,000 Jewish Zealots hold off the 15,000-member Roman legion for three years on the mountaintop fortress of Masada, and the Zealots commit suicide to escape capture (73); under Emperor Trajan, the Roman Empire reaches its greatest geographical extent when he conquers Dacia and much of Parthia (98–116); paper is made by the Chinese, though not for writing (by 100); Hadrian's Wall is built as the northern boundary and defence line of the Roman Empire (122–26); the medical authority until the 16th century, Greek physician and writer Galen, (c. 130–200) demonstrates that arteries carry blood (not air) and establishes the importance of the spinal cord by correlating earlier medical knowledge with his discoveries based on experiments and animal dissection; the earliest known Sanskrit inscriptions are made in India (150).

151–300: Ptolemy, a Greco-Egyptian thinker, compiles *Almagest*, the 13-volume work on ancient astronomy (earth-centred universe), mathematics, geography and science, which is influential to the 16th century; the oldest known Maya monuments are built (c. 164); the period of Neo-Platonism, the last of the Greek philosophies, begins (c. 200); silkworms are exported from Korea to China and then to Japan (c. 200); citizenship is granted to every freeborn subject in the Roman Empire (212); Afghanistan is invaded by the Huns (200); the Goths invade Asia Minor and the Balkan Peninsula (220); the end of the Han dynasty in China is followed by four centuries of division (220); the southern part of India breaks into several kingdoms; Rome celebrates its 1,000th anniversary (248); persecution of Christians increases and martyrs are revered as saints (c. 250); the first book of algebra is written by Diophantus of Alexandria (c. 250); the Goths attack the Black Sea area (257) as well as Athens, Sparta and Corinth (268); Pappus of Alexandria documents use of cogwheel, lever, pulley, screw and wedge (c. 285); Rome is partitioned into a western and an eastern empire; five distinct German dukedoms emerge (Saxons, Franks, Alemanni, Thuringians and Goths) (c. 300).

301–400: Constantine the Great reunites the western and eastern Roman Empires and becomes sole emperor (310–37); Constantine establishes toleration of Christianity with the Edict of Milan (313); the seat of the Roman Empire is moved to Constantinople (c. 331); the Basilican Church of St Peter is erected (330); Emperor Constantine is baptized on his deathbed (337) and is succeeded by his three sons, who again split Rome into two empires; the Huns invade Europe (360) and Russia (376); books begin to replace scrolls (360); Lo-Tsun, a Chinese monk, founds the Caves of the Thousand Buddhas in Kansu (360); Theodosius the Great becomes the last emperor of a united Roman Empire (392); Alaric, king of the Visigoths, invades Greece (396) and plunders Athens and the Balkans (398); the first definite records of Japanese history appear (400), although legend claims Japan was founded in 660 BC.

401–76: The Visigoths invade Italy (401); Alaric sacks Rome (410); Roman legions withdraw from Britain to defend Italy from the Visigoths (410); barbarians settle in Roman provinces (425); Attila becomes ruler of the Huns (433); St Augustine, Christian theologian, writes *The City of God* (411);

alchemy begins with the search for the Philosopher's Stone and the Elixir of Life as chief objects; pre-Inca culture develops in Peru; Venice is founded by refugees from Attila's Huns (452); the Vandals sack Rome (455) and destroy the Roman fleet at Cartegena (460); the Huns leave Europe (470); the Mayan civilization flourishes in southern Mexico (c. 470); the first Shinto religious shrines are built in Japan (478): they deal primarily with nature and ancestor worship; the German barbarian Odoacer takes Ravenna and deposes Emperor Romulus Augustulus, thereby ending the Western Roman Empire (476); Aryabhata, Hindu astronomer and mathematician, studies powers and roots of numbers (b. 476).

■ Middle or Dark Ages: 477–1450

477–529: Chi dynasty in southern China (479–502); Clovis, leader of the Franks (since 481), converts to Christianity (496); the first schism between the Western and Eastern Churches occurs when Pope Felix III excommunicates Patriarch Acacius of Constantinople (484–519); Armenian Church separates from Byzantium and Rome (491); the Moshica culture of the Chimic Indians flowers in Peru with agriculture, pottery and textiles; the Vatican Palace in Rome is first planned (500); Tamo carries tea from India to China (c. 500); Clovis kills Alaric II and annexes the Visigoth kingdom of Toulouse (507), and Clovis's realm is divided among his four sons upon his death (511); Emperor Wu-Ti converts to Buddhism and encourages the new religion in central China (517); Justinian I becomes the Byzantine Emperor (527): he is known for heavy taxes, public works and codifying Roman law; the Saxon kingdoms of Essex and Middlesex appear; Chosroes I is king of Persia (531–79) and encourages culture and art.

530–99: Arthur, the semi-legendary king of the Britons, is first mentioned at the Battle of Mt Badon (c. 540); the earliest Chinese roll paintings appear in Tun-huang (landscapes); war breaks out between Persia and the Byzantine Empire (539–62); St Gildas writes the first important source of early British history, *De excido et conquestu Brittaniae* (542); disastrous earthquakes occur around the world (543); the plague of Constantinople, imported by rats from Egypt and Syria, spreads throughout Europe and reaches Britain (547); the Golden Era of Byzantine art begins (550); Poles settle in western Galacia, Ukrainians in eastern Galacia (550); chess begins in India (c. 550); Buddhism is introduced into Japan by Emperor Shotoko Taishi (c.552–621), and the first Buddhist monastery in Japan is founded (587); Japanese prehistory ends and the Asuka period begins; Justinian sends missionaries to China and Ceylon to smuggle out silkworms and the European silk industry becomes a Byzantine state monopoly (553); Mohammed, the founder of Islam, is born (570); war is renewed between Persia and the Byzantine Empire (572–91), and again when Chosroes II ascends the throne of Persia (590–628); the plague ends after killing half the population of Europe (542–94); first verified account of decimal number system in India (595); probably the first English school is established at Canterbury (598); the authoritative Talmud Babli, a compilation of Jewish Oral Law with rabbinical interpretations, is compiled (c. 6th century).

600–749: Books printed in China (600); Czechs and Slovaks take up land in Bohemia and Moravia, Yugoslavs in Serbia (c. 600); smallpox spreads from India, via China and Asia Minor, to southern Europe; the oldest surviving wooden building in the world, the Horyuji temple and hospital, is completed in Japan (607); Mohammed experiences a religious vision on Mt Hira (610); "burning water" (petroleum) is used in Japan (615); orchestras are formed in China (619); porcelain is produced in China (620); the Hegira is named after Mohammed's flight from hostile Mecca to Yathrib (later renamed Medina), and is year one in the Muslim calendar (622); an encyclopedia of arts and sciences is written by Isidore of Seville (622); Shaka Trinity, the famous altarpiece of the Kondo in Japan, is built by Tori (623); Mohammed begins to dictate the Koran (the sacred book of Islam) in Arabic (625); the Byzantines decisively defeat the Persians at Nineveh (627); Mohammed captures Mecca and writes letters to world leaders explaining the Muslim faith (628); cotton is introduced in Arab countries (630); Buddhism becomes the state religion in Tibet (632); Medina is the seat of the first caliph (religious and political leader of Muslims) who is Abu Bekr, Mohammed's father-in-law; the Arabs attack Persia (633); Damascus is the new capital of the caliphs (635–70);

Jerusalem is conquered by the Arabs (637); the book-copying industry of the west is destroyed by the Arabs and the Alexandrian school ceases to be the centre of Western culture (641); the Arabs under Omar destroy the Persian Empire: the caliphs rule the area (until 1258), and Islam replaces the religion of Zoroaster; the Eastern Roman Empire is weakened by the Arab conquest of Egypt, Mesopotamia and Syria (642); the Dome of the Rock, a Muslim mosque, is begun in Jerusalem (643); the Muslim fleet destroys the Byzantine fleet at Lycia (655); Croats and Serbs settle in Bosnia (650); Chinese artists invent lamp-black ink and wood block printing (c. 650); Caliphs organize first news service (650); Japanese Buddhism and Shintoism are reconciled by the Korean-born priest Gyogi (c. 668–749); the Byzantines use "Greek Fire," a missile weapon of sulphur, rock, salt, resin and petroleum, against the Arabs at the siege of Constantinople (671–78); glass windows appear in English churches (674); the first Arab coinage is introduced (695); the Arabs destroy Carthage (697); Greek, instead of Latin, becomes the official language of the Eastern Roman Empire (700); the Arabs conquer Algiers (700) and virtually eliminate Christianity in northern Africa; mass migration of European peoples is followed by their subjection at the hands of property owners; China's population grows rapidly (700) and the first large urban developments appear there; the Great Mosque of Damascus is built (705); Buddhist monasteries in Japan become centres of civilization (710); the first written history of Japan, *Kojiki*, is compiled (712); the Lombard kingdom in northern Italy reaches its height (c. 600–c. 799); the Muslim empire now extends from the Pyrenees to China, with Damascus as its capital (715); the earliest Islamic paintings appear (715); Caliph Omar II grants tax exemption to all Muslim believers (717); the Chinese capital Ch'ang-an is the largest city in the world and Constantinople is the second largest (725); Casa Grande, a North American Indian fort and large irrigation works, is built in Arizona (725); Charles Martel (mayor of the Frankish court) wins victory over the Arabs in the battle of Tours and halts their westward advance (732); first printed newspaper published in Beijing (748).

750–849: Pueblos are built in southwest North America (750–900); Spain, under Arab influence, excels in mathematics, optics and chemistry (c. 750); Kiev, Russia, becomes known as a trading centre (750); the Turkish Empire is founded by a Tartar tribe in Armenia (760); Charlemagne becomes ruler of the Franks after the death of his father (Pepin the Short, son of Charles Martel) (768) and brother Carloman (771); Arabic learning flourishes under Harun-al-Rashid (790), peaks during reign of Caliph Mamun (813–33); the Byzantine Empress Irene overthrows her son Constantine (797), an act heralded by the Greek Church; Charlemagne is crowned Holy Roman Emperor (Western Empire) at Rome (800); the earliest records of Persian poetry and literature appear (800); the Vikings dominate Ireland (802); Arabic numerals are created under Indian influence (814); the Arabs conquer Crete, proceed as far as the Greek isles (826) and begin their conquest of Italy and Sardinia (827); Prince Mimir founds the Great Moravian Empire (830) from a confederation of Slavs in Bohemia, Moravia, Slovakia, Hungary and Transylvania; the Treaty of Verdun divides the Frankish Empire into France, Germany and Italy (843); paper currency in China creates inflation and state bankruptcy (845); Abu Tamman writes *Hamasa*, a collection of Arabian legends, proverbs and heroic stories (845); the Arabs sack Rome (846), damage the Vatican and destroy the Venetian fleet.

850–99: Salerno University is founded (850); the discovery of coffee is credited to Arabia (850); Jews settling in Germany develop the Yiddish language (c. 850); the first important Japanese painter, Kudara Kuwanari, dies (853); Norse pirates enter the Mediterranean and sack the coast up to Asia Minor (859); Iceland is discovered by the Northmen (861); Russian Northmen sack parts of France (861) and attack Constantinople (865); Basil I, the Byzantine Emperor, compiles the Basilican code (reforming finance and law and restoring the prestige of the military), and begins the Macedonian dynasty (867); Alfred the Great, king of England, recaptures London from the Danes (878); Emperor Charles III becomes king of France and once more unites the empire of Charlemagne (884), he is deposed (887) and there is a final separation of Germany and France; England's King Alfred establishes a regular militia and navy, extends the power of the king's courts and institutes fairs and markets (890).

900–99: The Vikings discover Greenland (900); the Mayans relinquish their settlements in the lowlands of Mexico and emigrate to the Yucatan peninsula (900); England is divided into shires with county courts in order to safeguard the civil rights of the inhabitants (900); the Arabian tales *A Thousand and One Nights* is begun (900); castles become the seats of the European nobility (900); Cordoba, Spain, is the seat of Arab learning, science, commerce and industry (930); Yenching becomes new capital city of China, later known as Beijing (938); revolts against imperial rule in Japan set off a period of civil war (939–1185); the Arab empire creates advanced postal and news services (942); the earliest record of the existence of a London bridge (963); a Chinese encyclopedia of 1,000 volumes is begun (978–84); the rule of nobles in Rome ends (980); Venice and Genoa carry on a flourishing trade between Asia and Western Europe (983); systematic musical notation develops (990); canonization of Christian saints begins.

1000–99: The heroic poem *Beowulf* is written in Old English by an unknown author (1000); Leif Ericsson, son of Eric the Red, sails to North America (1000); the Chinese invent gunpowder (1000); Mayan culture on the Yucatan peninsula achieves its zenith (1000); Sridhara, Indian mathematician, describes the importance of zero (1000); the Holy Sepulchre in Jerusalem is sacked by Muslims (1009); Danes under Canute control England (1016); Canute conquers Norway (1028); Jaroslav the Wise, Prince of Kiev (1020–54), codifies Russian law and builds cities, schools and churches; Byzantine power begins to decline (1025); Canute dies (1035) and his kingdom of England, Norway and Denmark is divided among his three sons; after murdering Duncan of Scotland, Macbeth becomes king (1040) and is later murdered by Malcolm (1057); time values are given to musical notes (1050); the separation of the Roman and Eastern Churches becomes permanent (1054); Westminster Abbey is consecrated (1065); William of Normandy is crowned William the Conqueror, of England (1066); the comet, later known as Halley's comet, appears (1066); She-tsung, Emperor of China, nationalizes agricultural production and distribution (1068); Constantine the African brings Greek medicine to the Western world (1071); the original Tower of London is built (1078); the Domesday Book, a survey of assessment for tax purposes, is compiled (1086); the start of the First Crusade (1096) is proclaimed by Pope Urban II to recapture the Holy Land from the Turks; Crusaders take Jerusalem (1099).

1100–99: Middle English supercedes Old English (1100); Islamic science begins to decline; secular music first appears; Robert of Normandy is appeased after invading England in the Treaty of Alton (1101); colonization of eastern Germany begins (1105); the earliest record of a miracle play is from Dunstable, England (1110): based on Scriptures and the lives of saints, they are widely performed until the 16th century; Bologna University founded (1119); the earliest account of a mariner's compass is by Alexander Neckham (1125); the Second Crusade begins (1146) and fails one year later; Paris University is founded (1150); Bologna Medical School is founded (1150); the first recorded fire and plague insurance is in Iceland (1151); the Japanese clans Taira and Minamoto fight each other (1156); Eric of Sweden conquers Finland (1157); Thomas à Becket is elected Archbishop of Canterbury (1162) in an effort to curb church power, but he later quarrels with King Henry II over growing royal power; Becket is murdered by Norman knights (1170) and buried at Canterbury; jails are ordered erected in all English counties and boroughs (1166); Oxford University is founded (1167); rules for the canonization of saints are established by Pope Alexander III (1170); first authenticated influenza epidemics occur (1173); the Campanile ("Leaning Tower") of Pisa is built (1174); Walter Map organizes the Arthurian legends in their present form (1176); all Jews are banished from France (1182); the Third Crusade (1189–93) fails to recapture Jerusalem from the Muslims; Moses Maimonides, Jewish philosopher, introduces Aristotle to modern western philosophy when he attempts to reconcile Aristotle's theories with those of Jewish philosophy in *Guide to the Perplexed* (1190), and he is also credited with organizing all Jewish law for the layman as well as religious educators.

1200–49: Cambridge University founded (1200); Islam takes root in India; the Fourth Crusade begins with crusaders from Venice fighting Constantinople and establishing a Latin Kingdom of Jerusalem (1204); St Francis of Assisi issues the first rules of his brotherhood of educators and missionaries, the Franciscans (1209); in the Children's Crusade (1212), thousands of children from Europe leave for the Holy Land, but most are either sold as slaves or die of hunger or disease; Genghis Khan becomes chief prince of the Mongols (1206) and conquers most of the Chinese empire of north China (1213–15) as well as Turkistan, Afghanistan and Transoxania (1218–24), and he raids Persia and Eastern Europe; Genghis Khan's empire is divided among his descendants upon his death (1227); the Council of St Albans is the precursor to the British Parliament (1213); King John puts his seal on England's Magna Carta at Runnymede under compulsion by the barons (1215): it defines the limitations of royal power and sets out basic civil rights; the Fifth Crusade fails in Egypt (1217–21); the oldest national flag in the world, Danneborg, is adopted by Denmark (1218); the form of the sonnet develops in Italian poetry (1221); Thomas Aquinas (1225–74) theorizes philosophical proofs for the existence of God and reconciles Greek ideas with Christian theology; the Sixth Crusade is led by Emperor Frederick II (1228); crusaders bring back leprosy to Europe (1230), and they secure a temporary truce with the Muslims; three later crusades against Muslims in the 13th century fail; coal is mined for the first time in Newcastle, England (1233); the Inquisition begins as the pope makes Dominicans responsible for putting an end to heresy (1233); Alexander Nevski made Grand Duke of Novgorod (1236).

1250–99: Kublai Khan becomes governor of China (1251) and ruler of the Mongol peoples (1259–94); he fails to conquer Japan (1274), southeast Asia and Indonesia, but he defeats the Sung dynasty of China (1279); instruments of torture are first used in the Inquisition (1252); the Sorbonne is founded by Robert de Sorbon as the Paris School of Theology (1254); the House of Commons is established in England (1258); Mongols control Baghdad, end caliphate (1258); Roger Bacon writes *"De computo naturali"* (1264); the glass mirror is invented (1278); Marco Polo, the Venetian explorer, journeys to China (1271–95) and is in the diplomatic service of Kublai Khan (1275–92); Florence, Italy, is the leading European city in commerce and finance (c. 1282); the Teutonic Order, a German military and religious order, conquers Prussia (1283) after killing the native "heathens" and replacing them with Germans; spectacles (eyeglasses) are invented (1290); the crusades end and the Knights of St John of Jerusalem settle in Cyprus (1291).

1300–99: Trade fairs at Bruges, Antwerp, Lyons and Geneva (c. 1300); Edward I of England standardizes the yard and the acre (1305); Dante composes his *Divina Commedia* (1307–21); mechanical clocks are driven by weights in Europe; Salic Law, excluding women from succession to the throne, is adopted in France (1317); No plays originate in Japan (1325); the Aztecs establish Mexico City (1327); the sawmill is invented (1328); weaving at York first documented (1331); the Hundred Years War between France and England begins (1337) as a dispute over lands held by the English crown in France: it later becomes a dispute over the French crown itself; the first scientific weather forecasts are attempted by William Merlee of Oxford (1337); the Black Death (bubonic plague) devastates Europe, killing about 75 million people, more than one-third of the population (1347–51); Boccaccio writes *Decameron* (1348–53), which is intended to be a diversion from the horrors of the plague; Timur the Lame (Tamerlaine) begins his conquest of Asia (1363); the Aztecs of Mexico build their capital, Tenochtitlan (1364); the Mongol Yüan dynasty in China is overthrown by the national Ming dynasty (1368–1644); the building of the Bastille begins in Paris (1369); "Robin Hood," the legendary hero who robbed the rich to help the poor, appears in English ballads and literature; The Great Schism in the Catholic Church begins (1378–1417) when, after the death of Pope Gregory XI, two popes are elected, one each at Rome and Avignon; Venice wins its Hundred Years War against Genoa (1256–1381); Briton John Wyclif calls for the reform of church practices (1379); he is condemned as a heretic (1380, 1382) and inspires the first English translation of the Latin Bible, the Wyclif Bible; Chaucer writes *The Canterbury Tales*; the rival southern and northern courts of Japan's divided imperial family reunite after 50 years of strife; Denmark, Sweden and Norway unite under Queen Margaret of Denmark (1397) in the Union of Kalmar.

1400–39: Russia's greatest icon painter, Andrei Rublex, creates *Trinity* (1411); England and France sign a perpetual peace treaty upon the marriage of Henry V and Catherine of Valois (1420); Joan of Arc and her French followers defeat the British at Orleans (1429) and march triumphantly to Paris: she is then taken prisoner by the Burgundians (1430) and condemned and executed (1431) in a political inquisition and trial; complete suits of metal armor plate replace chain mail in Europe (1430); China shuts out the western world and bans voyages there (1433) because Confucian doctrine sees little merit in trade; the Portugese find the way round Cape Bojador (on the west coast of Africa) under Henry the Navigator (1434); the Greek (Eastern or Byzantine) Church unites with the Roman church (1439) in order to save itself from the Turkish threat; Montezuma becomes ruler of the Aztecs in Mexico (1440) and begins to conquer surrounding tribes.

■ Renaissance: 1440–1650

1440–69: The rise of the Italian city-states heralds the Renaissance (1440–50), and the richest families (such as the Medici) vie with each other as patrons of art and learning (mainly in Florence); the first oil painter, Jan van Eyck, dies in Flanders (1441); France defeats England at Castillion, ending the Hundred Years War (1453), and the English give up everything except Calais, thus ending English rule in France; Zimbabwe, the great African kingdom, declines after 200 years of expansion (1450) because of food shortages; Constantinople, the old capital of the Byzantine empire, falls to the Ottomans (1453); a treaty unites rival Italian city-states (1454), requiring them to protect each other from outside aggression; Ming porcelain pottery appears in Europe (1460); the Bible is printed mechanically with metal type faces and oil-based ink by Johann Gutenberg (1455); the Wars of the Roses begin in England (1455) as a struggle for the throne between the houses of York and Lancaster, and end (1485) when Henry VII of the house of Lancaster prevails over Richard III; Plato's writings are translated into Latin at the Platonic Academy in Florence (1469).

1470–99: Music sheets, maps and posters are mechanically printed (1470s); Vlad the Impaler dies in Transylvania (1477) and the mass murderer becomes the source for

Dracula legends; Peruvian-centred Inca rule expands to include the entire Andean region (3,200 sq. km) under Pachacuti, and his son Topa Inca (1470), and it is characterized by terracing, irrigation, pantheistic religion with human sacrifice, advanced metalwork, tapestry making and construction; the Spanish Catholic Inquisition begins (1478); King Ferdinand V of Aragón and Queen Isabella I of Castile unite their crowns in Spain to ward off Alfonso V of Portugal (1479); Ivan the Great declares Russian independence (1480) from the Mongols when he refuses to continue paying them tribute; the first European manual of navigation and nautical almanac is prepared in Portugal by mathematical experts (1484) who calculate the latitude of the sun, based on the work of the Jewish astronomer Abraham Zacuto; the spread of witchcraft and heresy in Germany is attacked by Pope Innocent VIII (1484) and he authorizes Dominican inquisitors to torture and burn witches; the publication of an encyclopedia of witchcraft, *Malleus Maleficarum* (1486), adds to witch hunt hysteria; the Genoese seaman Christopher Columbus secures the sponsorship of Queen Isabella of Spain (1486) for his expedition to discover a western route to Asia (he sets sail with his three ships: Santa María, Pinta and Niña in 1492); the Aztecs of Mexico inaugurate the Great Temple of Tenochtitlan (1487) when they ritually sacrifice the hearts of 20,000 people; the Portugese explorer Bartholomew Dias rounds the Cape of Good Hope off South Africa (1488); Leonardo da Vinci is in his prime in Italy (1488) as an artist, scientist, inventor and philosopher, with inventions centuries ahead of their time (e.g., he conceives of flying machines and an apparatus to enable humans to breathe under water); the Great Wall of China is rebuilt by Ming emperors as a defence against attacks by northern Barbarians (1488); the first terrestrial globe is made by Martin Behaim, a German (1492); Jews are ordered by Spain's Catholic rulers to choose between expulsion or forced conversion (1492), and the rulers change the options to conversion or death (1498); Spain conquers Granada (1492), the last Muslim kingdom in Spain; Spain and Portugal sign a treaty dividing lands discovered in the new world, but Spain benefits the most from the treaty (1494); French armies in Italy bring a virus later identified as syphilis to Naples and the epidemic spreads through Europe (1495);

Columbus brings tobacco back from the new world (1496); the Chinese invent a toothbrush (1498); Vasco da Gama discovers a sea route round the Cape of Good Hope to India via the Indian Ocean (1498); the Italian navigator Amerigo Vespucci explores the northeast coast of South America (1499) and reports cannibals (1502); Portugal's Pedro Cabral discovers the east coast of Brazil and observes natives using stone to cut wood (1499).

1500–25: The discovery of plays and poems by Hroswitha of Gandersheim, a 10th-century saxoness, makes her the first European playwright since the Classical Age (1500); King Ferdinand of Spain sanctions a system of levying tribute payments from Indians in the new world and using Indians as forced labour (1501); Shi'ism becomes the state religion in Persia (1502) and Sunni Muslim dissenters are executed there; a hand-held timepiece, made possible by the invention of the coiled mainspring, is constructed by German locksmith Peter Henlein (1502); *David*, a 13-foot statue, is completed by Michelangelo Buonarrotti (1504) in Florence, Italy; Leonardo da Vinci paints the *Mona Lisa* (1505); Venice dominates Mediterranean trade (c. 1507); a map calls the new world "America" after Amerigo Vespucci (1507) and shows it as a distinct continent; the first great German artist, Albrecht Dürer (painter/engraver), creates his *Adam and Eve* oil painting (1507); Michelangelo paints the ceiling of the Sistine Chapel (1508–12); Sebastion Cabot sails around Cuba, proving it is an island (1508) and later reaches Hudson Bay in search of a northwest passage; the first African slaves are brought to the Americas (Cuba) (1510); Erasmus, the Dutch humanist, writes the satirical *In Praise of Folly* (1511); Juan Ponce de Léon claims Florida for Spain (1513) while searching for the Fountain of Youth; Niccolo Machiavelli writes *The Prince* (1513) which discusses the uses and abuses of power; Vasco Núñez de Balboa discovers the "South Sea," or Pacific Ocean, for Spain (1513); Spain orders new world natives to convert to Christianity under threat of enslavement or death (1514); Henry VIII of England puts forth measures to protect peasants from enclosure—the dividing and closing off of common land (1515); Sir Thomas More writes *Utopia*, which depicts an ideal state (1516); Martin Luther, a German Augustinian monk, writes his *95 Theses*, attacking the Catholic church's sale of indulgences granting the forgiveness of sins (1517) and nails it to the door of the Wittenberg church; English sailors complain to King Henry VIII about the growing number of French cod fishermen in Newfoundland (1517); the rule of Suleiman I the Magnificent sees the Ottoman Turks reach the zenith of their empire with the conquest of Egypt, Syria and Hungary (1520); Ferdinand Magellan begins a three-year voyage to circumnavigate the globe (1519); Hernando Cortes lands at Vera Cruz, Mexico, where Montezuma II and the Aztecs surrender (1519); chocolate is introduced to Europe from Mexico (1520); Nicholas Copernicus publishes his "Commentariolus" stating his theory that the earth revolves around the sun (1521); Martin Luther translates the Bible into German (1522).

1526–49: Lutheran German troops sack and burn Rome (1527); Hippocrates' ancient idea of the four humours governing bodily health is first disputed (1528); Henry VIII separates from the Church of Rome and becomes head of the English Church (1534) after he is refused an annulment of his first marriage; the Jesuit order of missionaries is founded by Ignatius Loyola (1534); Jacques Cartier searches for riches in North America along the St Lawrence River (1535); John Calvin, the French leader of the Protestant Reformation in Geneva, theorizes the concepts of predestination and God's omniscience (1536); the first mechanical artificial limbs appear for crippled war veterans (1539); the founder of the Sikh religion, Guru Nanak, dies in India (1539); Henry VIII becomes King of Ireland and Head of the Irish Church (1541); John Knox leads the Calvinist Reformation in Scotland (1541); oil is discovered in North America by the Spaniards (1543); Portugese traders are the first to sell guns to Japan (1543); Nostradamus, the French astrologer, begins making predictions (1547); Ivan IV (the Terrible) is crowned the first czar of Russia (1547): he calls the first national assembly (1549).

1550–99: Jesuit missionaries protect natives in the new world from slavery (1551); Ivan the Terrible defeats the Mongols (1552), and conquers as far as the Caspian Sea (1556); Lady Jane Grey is executed for treason in England by Queen Mary Tudor (1554), who becomes known as "Bloody Mary" after persecuting Protestants (1555); Mary restores papal authority in England and Wales (1554); Charles V relinquishes the Holy Roman Empire and Spain to his brother and son, and goes to a monastery (1556); an influenza epidemic hits Europe (1557); Elizabeth I becomes Queen of England (1558) and rejects papal power in England (1559); the Huguenot (Calvinist French Protestant) conspiracy occurs at Amboise: liberty of worship is promised in France (1560); the Edict of Orleans suspends persecution of Huguenots (1561); the Peace of Amboise ends the first War of Religion in France and the Huguenots are granted limited toleration (1563); Andreas Vesalius, the Flemish founder of modern anatomy, dies (1564); Nobunaga deposes the Japanese shogunate and centralizes the government (1567); the Iroquois Confederacy of five North American nations (Mohawk, Oneida, Onondaga, Cayuga, Seneca) is founded (c. 1570); Huguenots are massacred on St Bartholomew's Day in Paris (1572); the Dutch War of Independence begins (1572); the Union of Utrecht is the foundation of the Dutch Republic (1579); William of Orange accepts the sovereignty of northern Netherlands and is assassinated (1584); the first English colony in Newfoundland is founded (1582); Elizabeth of England orders Mary Queen of Scots beheaded for treason (1587); Christopher Marlowe completes *Dr. Faustus* (1588); the first Spanish Armada leaves for England and is defeated by the English under Charles Howard (1588); Sir Francis Drake, with 18,000 men, fails to take Lisbon for England (1589); William Shakespeare completes the play *Romeo and Juliet* (1594); the Second Spanish Armada leaves for England but is scattered by storms (1597); an English Act of Parliament calls for convicted criminals to serve their terms in the colonies (1597).

1600–49: France boasts the largest population in central Europe, with 16 million persons (1600); William Shakespeare completes *Hamlet* (1600); Dutch opticians invent the telescope (1600); the first modern public company is founded, the Dutch East India Company (1602); Guy Fawkes is arrested and accused of trying to blow up the House of Lords during James I's state opening of Parliament (The Gunpowder Plot, 1605); Fawkes is sentenced to death (1606); the first English settlement on the American mainland is founded at Jamestown, Virginia (1607);

Shakespeare writes his *Sonnets* (1609); the first cheques appear in Netherlands as "cash letters" (1608); the *King James Bible* is published (1611); Peter Paul Rubens paints *Descent from the Cross* (1611); the North American Indian princess Pocahantas marries English colonist John Rolfe (1614); Galileo Galilei, Italian astronomer, faces the Inquisition for the first time for renouncing the Ptolemaic system of the earth-centred universe and embracing the Copernican sun-centred system (1615); the Thirty Years War begins in Prague as Protestants rebel against Catholic oppression (1618); slavery in North America begins when the first Africans are brought to Virginia (1619) and the triangular slave trade starts (British goods are sent to west Africa and are traded for slaves, who are traded for agricultural staples in the new world, which are sent back to Britain); pilgrims arriving on the *Mayflower* found Plymouth Colony, Massachusetts (1620); patent law is created in England to protect inventors (1623); construction begins on the Taj Mahal mausoleum in Agra, North India (1628); Charles I dissolves the English Parliament for 11 years (1629); Cardinal Richelieu, chief minister of Louis XIII of France, rules France (1630–42); Galileo is forced by the Inquisition to cease promulgating the theories of Copernicus (1633); Japan forbids foreign books, Christianity and any European contacts (1637); René Descartes, called the father of modern philosophy, writes *Discourse on Method* (1637); the Ming dynasty in China ends and the Manchu dynasty takes power (1644–1912); Charles I of England, after a long struggle for power with Parliament (English Civil War 1642–48), is beheaded by Oliver Cromwell for treason (1649).

1650–99: Bishop James Ussher dates the creation of the world at Oct. 23, 4004 BC (1650); the wholesale massacre of North American Indians by European settlers begins (1650); Thomas Hobbes writes *Leviathan*, a defence of absolute monarchy in England (1651); Oliver Cromwell becomes Lord Protector in England, dissolves Parliament, divides England into 11 districts, prohibits Anglican services (1653) and readmits Jews to England after 365 years (1655); Blaise Pascal (French) develops the basic laws of probability (1654); the Portugese drive the Dutch out of Brazil (1654); the first London

opera house opens (1656); Dutch peasants (Boers) first settle in South Africa (1660); the Royal Society is founded in London to promote scientific discussion among great thinkers (1660); the earliest condemnation of industrial pollution, *The Inconvenience of the Air and Smoke of London Dissipated*, is written by John Evelyn (1661); Louis XIV (the Sun King) begins to build the palace at Versailles (1662); Jean Baptiste Colbert forms the North American colony of New France with Quebec as its capital (1663); the British annex New Netherlands from the Dutch and rename the main city New York (1664); Isaac Newton begins to experiment with gravity and develops calculus (1664–66); the cell is named and described by Briton Robert Hooke (1665); the French army uses the first hand grenades (1667); Portugal gains independence from Spain through the Treaty of Lisbon (1668); microorganisms are discovered by Anton van Leeuwenhoek (Dutch, 1669) who later observes bacteria (1683) for the first time; the Hudson's Bay Company is incorporated by a British royal charter to trade in the region of North America defined by those rivers which drain into Hudson Bay (1670); Dutch philosopher Baruch Spinoza writes *Ethics* (1675); the poems of Bashu (a pseudonym) popularize Japanese haiku poetry (1675); the *Declaration of the People of Virgina* by Nathaniel Bacon lends support to rebellion against authorities in the colonies (1676); Roman Catholics are excluded from both houses of Parliament in England (1678); the Habeas Corpus Amendment Act in England protects citizens from unjust imprisonment (1679); the French colonial empire of North America, reaching from Quebec to the mouth of the Mississippi River, is organized (1680); the large dodo bird with small, flightless wings becomes extinct (1680); Sir Isaac Newton writes *Principles of Natural Philosophy* (1687), which discusses universal gravitation; the Glorious Revolution establishes the constitutional monarchy in England (1688–89) and William of Orange III and Mary II ascend the throne; Peter the Great becomes Czar of Russia (1689); John Locke writes *Essay Concerning Human Understanding* and *Two Treatises on Civil Government* (1690).

1700–49: The War of the Spanish Succession to the childless Charles II, Hapsburg king of Spain, is fought (1701–14) between the

French Bourbons and Austrian Hapsburgs; rebellion occurs in Astrakhan against Czar Peter's westernization of Russia (1705); England and Scotland form Great Britain (1707); the Peace of Utrecht is signed between Spain and England: Spain cedes Gibraltar and Minorca to England (1713) and Philip of France retains the Spanish crown; D.G. Fahrenheit constructs a mercury thermometer with a temperature scale (1714); George F. Handel writes *Water Music* for King George I (1717); Daniel Defoe writes *The Life and Strange Surprising Adventures of Robinson Crusoe* (1719); the German composer and virtuoso organist J.S. Bach composes *The Brandenburg Concertos* (1721); Johnathan Swift writes *Gulliver's Travels* (1726); Benjamin Franklin, American statesman, scientist, printer and writer, writes *Poor Richard's Almanack* (1732); John Kay patents the fly shuttle loom, which revolutionizes weaving (1733); Alexander Pope, poet and English verse satirist, writes *Essay on Man* (1733); the modern classification system of plants and animals is introduced by Carolus Linnaeus (Swedish, 1735); Alaska is discovered by Victor Behring (1740); Frederick the Great introduces freedom of the press and freedom of worship in Prussia (1740); sign language for the deaf is created by Rodriguez Pereire (1749).

■ Industrial Revolution: 1750–1850

1750–99: Benjamin Franklin experimented with static electricity and invented the lightning conductor (1752); in the Seven Years War (1756–63) Britain declares war on France and, in the North American colonies, the French drive the British from the Great Lakes area (1756); the French lose Quebec to the British (1759) during the battle on the Plains of Abraham; Voltaire writes the philosophical novel *Candide* (1759); Catherine II (the Great) becomes czarina of Russia (1762); Swiss-French philosopher Jean Jacques Rousseau writes *Social Contract* (1762) which discusses his theory of "natural man"; the Peace of Paris (1763) ends the war between England and France and gives Canada to England; eight-year-old Mozart writes his first symphony (1764); the spinning jenny, which spins up to 120 threads at once is invented by Briton James Hargreaves (1764); the British Parliament passes the Stamp Act for taxing American colonies: Virginia and New York challenge the right of Britain to taxation without representation (1766); the Mason-Dixon Line is drawn by English surveyors between Pennsylvania and Maryland (1767) and is later the boundary between "slave" and "free" states; Daniel Rutherford and Joseph Priestley independently discover nitrogen (1772); the Bolshoi Ballet is founded in Russia (1773); during the Boston Tea Party American colonists protesting British taxes dress as Indians and dump the cargo of three tea ships in the Boston, Mass., harbor (1773); James Watt, Scottish inventor, perfects the steam engine (1775); the American Revolution begins (1775); the Second Continental Congress assembles at Philadelphia and appoints George Washington commander-in-chief of the American forces; the Americans proclaim the *Declaration of Independence* (July 4, 1776); Edward Gibbon writes *Decline and Fall of the Roman Empire* (1776); Adam Smith completes *Wealth of Nations* (1776); after the American victory in the Saratoga Campaign (1777) France entered into an alliance with the Americans (1778); Washington's army suffers at Valley Forge (1778); Hawaii is discovered by James Cook (1778); Franz Mesmer practices mesmerism (hypnotism) (1778); Spain joins the American War of Independence against Britain (1779); the Dutch support the American side (1780); Sir William Herschel discovers Uranus (1781); British General Cornwallis surrenders to the Americans (Oct. 1781) at the end of the Yorktown Campaign, and the Treaty of Paris recognizes American independence (1783); John Wesley writes the *Deed of Declaration,* the charter of Wesleyan Methodism (1784); the British colony of Australia is founded (1788); the French Revolution begins (1789); a Paris mob opposing the monarchy storms the Bastille jail; French royalists begin to emigrate; the French revolutionaries proclaim the Decrees of Aug. 4 and the *Declaration of the Rights of Man and of the Citizen;* the government limits the monarchy's power, abolishes the French feudal system, extends religious tolerance to Jews and protestants and reorganizes the Catholic Church; A.L. Lavoisier completes the *Table of Thirty-One Chemical Elements* (1790); the Constitutional Act divides Britain's Canadian colony into Upper Canada (English-speaking) and Lower Canada (French-speaking) (1791); Thomas Paine writes *The Rights of Man* in defence of the French Revolution (1791); the French King Louis XIV and Queen Marie Antoinette are beheaded for treason (Jan., 1793); the Reign of Terror (guillotine executions of prisoners) under the Jacobin government ends with the execution of Maximilien Robespierre; Robert Burns' *Auld Lang Syne* is published (1794); Edward Jenner discovers a smallpox vaccine (1796).

1800–09: Ottawa is founded (1800); Eli Whitney makes muskets with interchangeable parts (1800); the Library of Congress is established in Washington, DC by Thomas Jefferson (1800); the first battery is produced from zinc and copper plates by Alessandro Volto (1800); William Herschel discovers the existence of infrared solar rays (1800); the first submarine *Nautilus* is made by American civil engineer Robert Fulton (1801); the atomic theory of chemistry is put forth by John Dalton (1802); the US buys land from France in the Louisiana Purchase (1803); Henry Shrapnel invents the shell used in warfare (1803); Napoleon crowns himself emperor of the French empire (1804) and king of Italy (1805); modern Egypt is established when Mehemet Ali becomes Pasha (1805); morphine is isolated by F.W.A. Satürner (1805); Napoleon wins his greatest victory, at Austerlitz, over the Austrians and Russians allied against him (1805); the American frigate *Chesapeake* is stopped and boarded by British naval officers looking for deserters, almost causing a war (1807); Ludwig van Beethoven, the great German composer who brought together Classical and Romantic styles, performs his *Fifth Symphony* (written for Napoleon) and *Sixth Symphony* (1808); the first part of J.W. von Goethe's *Faust* is published (1808); Washington Irving writes *Rip van Winkle* (1809).

1810–19: Simón Bolívar becomes a leading figure in South American politics (1810) and liberates Greater Colombia (Panama, Venezuela, Ecuador and Colombia) (1819) and Peru (1824) from Spanish rule; a machine for spinning flax is invented by Philippe Girard (1812); German folklorist Jakob Grimm completes *Grimm's Fairy Tales* (1812–15); Napoleon Bonaparte's first military setback is in the Peninsular War (1808–14); and he later retreats from an unsuccessful invasion of Russia; the War of 1812 (1812–14) between Britain and the United States is foreshadowed by the battle at Tippecanoe (1811); Jane Austen writes *Pride and Prejudice* (1813), depicting English country life and mores; Austria, Russia and Prussia form an alliance against Napoleon and defeat him at Leipzig (1813) and recapture Paris (1814); Napoleon abdicates and is exiled to Elba Island; the War of 1812 continues in North America as the British capture Washington, DC (1814) but the Americans win battles at Fort McHenry, Thames (killing Tecumseh, an Indian ally of the British) and at Plattsburgh (1814); the British initiate peace in the Treaty of Ghent (1814) but this news travels too slowly to stop the Battle of New Orleans (1815), won by the Americans; Napoleon escapes from exile and returns to march on Paris; he is defeated at Waterloo (1815), abdicates again and is banished to St Helena Island; the German Confederation, dominated by Austria and Prussia, is created to replace the Holy Roman Empire (1815); Argentina declares its independence from Spain (1816); the classical economist David Ricardo (British) writes *The Principles of Political Economy and Taxation* (1817), discussing the determination of wage and value; Georg Hegel writes his all-embracing *Encyclopedia of the Philosophical Sciences* (1817); Mary Wollstonecraft Shelley writes *Frankenstein* (1818); Lord Byron begins *Don Juan* (1818–23); Chile proclaims its independence from Spain (1818); electromagnetism is discovered by Danish physicist Hans C. Oersted (1819); Greater Colombia (including Panama, Venezuela, Ecuador and Colombia) declares independence from Spain (1819).

1820–29: Andre Ampere (French) writes *Laws of Electrodynamic Action* (1820); Liberia is founded by the Washington Colonization Society, for the repatriation of black slaves (1820); Sir Walter Scott writes *Ivanhoe* (1820); John Keats writes *Ode to a Nightingale* (1820); an electric recording device for sound reproduction is invented by Sir Charles Wheatstone (1821); Peru and Guatemala declare their independence from Spain (1821); the Reign of Terror begins between the Greeks and the Turks (1821); Franz Liszt, the Hungarian pianist who revolutionizes Romantic music and invents the symphonic poem, makes his debut at age 11 in Vienna (1822); Brazil declares itself independent from Portugal (1822); the Monroe Doctrine closes the American continent to colonial settlement by European powers (1823); Spanish are defeated and Paris independence recognized (1824); Simón Bolívar creates his namesake, Bolivia (1825); the first steam-powered railroads carrying freight and passengers, operated by the the Stockton and Darlington Railway, run in England (1825); the Erie Canal opens, linking the Hudson River and the Great Lakes (1825); the first major American author, James Fenimore Cooper, writes *The Last of the Mohicans* (1826); Felix Mendelssohn composes the Overture to *A Midsummer Night's Dream* (1826); the great cholera epidemic begins in India (1826) and spreads from Russia into Central Europe; J. J. Audubon writes *Birds of North America* (1827); Noah Webster writes the *American Dictionary of the English Language* (1828); Uruguay declares independence from Brazil (1828); the Peace of Adrianople ends the Russo-Turkish war and Turkey acknowledges the independence of Greece (1829); Frederic Chopin, the Polish pianist, debuts in Vienna (1829); Venezuela withdraws from Greater Colombia and becomes independent (1829).

1830–39: Charles Lyell of Scotland divides the geological system into three groups: Eocene, Miocene and Pliocene (1830); Ecuador declares independence (1830); mass demonstrations in Swiss cities lead to liberal reforms (1831); Charles Darwin sails on the HMS *Beagle* as a naturalist, surveying South America, New Zealand and Australia (1831–36); the leading anti-slavery leader in the United States, W. L. Garrison, begins publishing *The Liberator* in Boston (1831); the wealthy middle classes emerging from the Industrial Revolution are enfranchised in Britain, doubling the number of voters (1832); the New England anti-slavery society is founded in Boston (1832); slavery is abolished in the British Empire (1833); the Spanish Inquisition, begun during the 13th century, is finally abolished (1834); France's leading writer, Victor Hugo, writes *The Hunchback of Notre Dame* (1834); the Poor Law Amendment Act decrees that no able-bodied person (displaced by the Industrial Revolution) in Great Britain shall receive assistance unless he or she enters a workhouse (1834); Hans Christian Anderson writes his first stories for children (1835); the American writer Ralph Waldo Emerson writes *Nature* (1836); the People's Charter initiates Britain's

first national working-class movement, calling for universal suffrage for men and voting by ballot (1836); the Dutch (Afrikaner) farmers begin "The Great Trek" of emigration across the Orange and Vaal Rivers, South Africa (1836); the first botanical textbook, *The Elements of Botany*, is written by American Asa Gray (1836); Victoria becomes Queen of Great Britain (1837); citizens stage unsuccessful rebellions in Lower and Upper Canada (1837); Louis Braille invents his reading system for the blind (1837); Charles Dickens's *Oliver Twist*, a critique of British industrial society, is a bestseller (1838); the first bicycle is invented by a Scot, Kirkpatrick Macmillan (1839); the cell-growth theory is put forth by Theodor Schwann (1839); ozone is discovered by Christian Schönbein, a German-Swiss chemist (1839); American Charles Goodyear develops the process of vulcanization, making the commercial use of rubber possible (1839); a photograph produced on a silver-coated copperplate treated with iodine vapor, the daguerreotype, is invented by Louis Daguerre and J. Niepce (French) (1839); the First Opium War between Britain and China begins (1839).

1840–49: New Zealand becomes a British colony (1840); philosopher Thomas Carlyle writes *On Heroes, Hero-Worship and the Heroic in History* in support of strong government (1841); the father of the guided tour, Thomas Cook (British), arranges his first trip (1841); showman P.T. Barnum gains fame after opening his American Museum of freak exhibitions (1841); the Webster-Ashburton Treaty between Britain and the US settles American border disputes with Canada (1842); the Treaty of Nanking ends the Opium War between Britain and China and confirms the cession of Hong Kong to Great Britain (1842); riots and strikes erupt in northern England's industrial areas (1842); Richard Wagner (German) finishes the opera *The Flying Dutchman* (1843); the amount of work required to produce a unit of heat, the joule, is determined by English physicist James P. Joule (1843); American social reformer Dorothea Dix reports on the shocking conditions in prisons and asylums, influencing the establishment of state hospitals for the insane in Europe and North America (1843); Samuel Morse's telegraph is used for the first time between Baltimore and Washington (1844); US troops are victorious over the Mexicans at

Palo Alto (1846), Congress formally declares war, US forces take Santa Fe and annex New Mexico; the Smithsonian Institution, a research and educational centre, is founded in Washington, DC (1846); ether is first used as an anaesthetic by dentist W.T. Morton (1846); sisters Charlotte and Emily Brontë publish *Jane Eyre* and *Wuthering Heights* respectively (1847); US forces capture Mexico City (1847) and the Treaty of Guadalupe Hidalgo ends the Mexican-US war (1848), the US acquires Texas and much of the surrounding territory in return for $15 million; gold discoveries in California lead to the first gold rush (1848); a revolt in Paris causes Louis Philippe to abdicate (1848); a revolution in Vienna brings Metternich's resignation (1848); revolutions in Venice, Berlin, Milan, Rome and Parma (1848); the first Public Health Act is introduced in Britain (1848); the first women's rights convention, organized by Elizabeth Stanton and Lucretia Mott, is held in Seneca Falls, New York (1848); the *Communist Manifesto* is issued by Germans Karl Marx and Friedrick Engels (1848), championing the working class and establishing socialist theory.

1850–59: Harriet Beecher Stowe writes her anti-slavery novel *Uncle Tom's Cabin* (1852); the Transvaal is granted self-government (1852); the Crimean War (1853–56) begins when Russia occupies Moldavia and Walachia and Turkey declares war, the Russians destroy the Turkish fleet off Sinope, and England, France and Sardinia join Turkey's fight; after a long siege the Russian base Sevastopol falls to the allied forces (1855), and after the allied victory at Balaklava, Russia recognizes the integrity of Turkey (1856); English nurse Florence Nightingale founds modern nursing while tending soldiers during the Crimean War (1853–56); the first hypodermic syringe is used by Alexander Wood (1853); Samuel Colt revolutionizes the manufacture of small arms (1853); Commander Matthew Perry negotiates the first American-Japanese treaty, permitting US ships to use two Japanese ports (1854); the Elgin Reciprocity Treaty between Great Britain and the US implements free trade between Canada and the US (1854); steel making becomes inexpensive when Henry Bessemer introduces a converter into his process for making steel (1855); pure cocaine is extracted from coca leaves (1856);

Gustave Flaubert, the French master of realistic novels, writes *Madame Bovary* (1856); Louis Pasteur discovers that fermentation is caused by micro-organisms (1857), and later invents pasteurization and discovers a vaccine for rabies; the first Neanderthal skeleton is found in a cave in Neander Valley (near Düsseldorf, Germany); the Indian Mutiny against British rule (1857) causes the British siege and capture of Delhi; the British Royal Navy destroys the Chinese fleet, and Britain and France take Canton (1857); Guiseppe Garibaldi forms the Italian National Association for the unification of Italy (1857); the Treaty of Tientsin ends the Anglo-Chinese war (1858); Charles Darwin writes *On the Origin of Species by Natural Selection*, explaining his theory of evolution (1859); the German National Association is formed to unite Germany under Prussia (1859); John Stuart Mill (British) writes his essay *On Liberty* (1859).

■ Modern Era

1860–64: Garibaldi and his redshirts sail from Genoa to take Palermo and Naples; Victor Emmanuel II (King of Sardinia) invades the Papal States and defeats the Papal troops, Garibaldi proclaims Emmanuel II king of Italy (1860); Anglo-French troops defeat the Chinese at Pa-li-Chau (1860) and sign the Treaty of Peking; the first Food and Drugs Act is enacted in Britain (1860); Lenoir constructs the first internal-combustion engine (1860); a primitive form of typewriter is created by American Christopher L. Sholes (1860); hundreds of thousands of Irish and British citizens flee their homelands following the potato famine (by 1860); Russian troops fire at anti-Russian demonstrators in Poland during the Warsaw Massacre (1861); the first machine-chilled cold storage unit is built by T. S. Mort (1861); Krupp begins arms production in Essen, Germany (1861); the Archaeopteryx, the skeleton linking reptiles and birds, is discovered at Solnhofen, Germany (1861); the American Civil War (1861–65) begins after Abraham Lincoln, who views slavery as evil, is elected president; South Carolina secedes in protest, followed by 10 other southern states, to form the Confederacy fighting for states' rights and opposing the abolition of slavery; Lincoln issues the Emancipation Proclamation (1862) calling for the freeing of black slaves in Confederate territory; the Red Cross voluntary relief organization is proposed by Jean Henri Dunant, a Swiss humanist (1862); the first form of a machine gun is invented by the American Richard Gatling (1862); Otto von Bismarck becomes the prime minister of Prussia (1862) and begins his system of alliances and alignments that result in German preeminence in Europe; Victor Hugo writes *Les Miserables* (1862); Leo Tolstoy writes *War and Peace* (1864); the Geneva Convention establishes the neutrality of battlefield medical facilities (1864); liberalism, socialism and rationalism are condemned in *Syllabus Errorum*, issued by Pope Pius IX (1864); Cheyenne and Arapahoe Indians are massacred at Sand Creek, Colorado (1864); the First International Workingmen's Association is founded by Karl Marx in London and New York (1864); Confederate forces surrender finally at Appomattox, Virginia (1865) marking the end of the war and victory for the Union; slavery in the US is abolished by the Thirteenth Amendment; US Pres. Lincoln is assassinated by the actor John Wilkes Booth (1865).

1865–69: Lewis Carroll (British) writes *Alice's Adventures in Wonderland* (1865); Joseph Lister initiates antiseptic surgery by using carbolic acid on a compound wound (1865); line geometry is invented by German mathematician Julius Plücker (1865); Gregor Mendel, an Austrian monk, describes his Law of Heredity (1865); Bismarck, the Prussian foreign minister, provoked the brief Austro-Prussian War by invading the duchies of Schleswig-Holstein and overrunning the German states allied with Austria; after seven weeks a peace settlement gave Schleswig-Holstein, Hanover, Hesse, Nasau and Frankfurt to Prussia and excluded Austria from influence in German affairs (1866); *Crime and Punishment* by Feodor Dostoevsky is published (1866); Alfred Nobel invents dynamite (1866); Johann Strauss popularizes the Viennese waltz with Blue Danube (1866); the underwater torpedo is invented by Robert Whitehead, an English engineer (1866); the fundamental law of biogenetics, *General Morphology,* is published by Ernst Haeckel (1866); Claude Monet, a French founder of Impressionism, paints *Camille* (1866); Russia sells Alaska to the US for $7.2 million (1867); Karl Marx writes *Das Kapital*, volume I (1867); the British North America Act establishes the Dominion of Canada and John A. Macdonald becomes prime minister (1867); Louisa May Alcott describes Victorian American life in *Little Women* (1868); a skeleton of Cro Magnon man from the Upper Paleolithic age (the first Homo sapiens in Europe, successor to the Neanderthal man) is found in France by Louis Lartet (1868); the first regular Trades Union Congress is held at Manchester, England (1868); Dmitri Mendeleyev formulates his periodic law for the classification of the elements (1869); John Stuart Mill writes *On the Subjection of Women* (1869); the major early treatise on eugenics, *Hereditary Genius*, is published by Francis Galton (1869); J.W. Hyatt invents celluloid (plastic) (1869); the First Nihilist Congress is held at Basel, Switzerland (1869); the strategically important Suez Canal opens (1869); the doctrine of papal infallibility is established by Pope Pius IX during Vatican Council I (1869–79).

1870–79: US industrialist John D. Rockefeller founds the Standard Oil Company (1870); T.H. Huxley, English biologist and educator, writes the *Theory of Biogenesis* (1870); the Franco-Prussian War begins (1870) and France under Napoleon III capitulates; William I, king of Prussia, is proclaimed the German Emperor at Versailles, and in the Peace of Frankfurt France cedes Alsace-Lorraine to Germany (1871); the Italian Law of Guarantees allows the Pope possession of the Vatican (1871); labour unions become legal in Britain (1871); Charles Darwin writes *The Descent of Man* (1871); the Great Fire ravages Chicago (1871); explorer Sir Henry M. Stanley is sent to find David Livingstone in Africa (1871); the first modern luxury liner, SS *Oceanic*, is launched (1871); Civil War in Spain ends with the Carlists' defeat (1872); the Three Emperors League is established in Berlin as an alliance between Germany, Russia and Austria-Hungary (1872); colour photographs are first developed (1873); James C. Maxwell writes *Electricity and Magnetism* (1873); Willhelm Wundt, known for the experimental method, writes *Physiological Psychology* (1873); under the direction of Benjamin Disraeli as prime minister, Britain expands its imperial power by annexing the Fiji islands (1874); Johannes Brahms composes the *Hungarian Dances* (1874); Johann Strauss II performs the operetta *Die Fleder-*

maus in Vienna (1874); Bosnia and Herzegovina rebel against Turkish rule (1875): Turkish sultan promises reforms (1875); Mary Baker Eddy writes *Science and Health* (1875) and she founds the Christian Science movement (1879); Georges Bizet performs *Carmen* in Paris (1875); British Queen Victoria is crowned empress of India (1876); Britain annexes the Transvaal (1877); US General George Custer is killed along with his cavalry by Cheyenne Indians in the Battle of the Little Bighorn (1876); Alexander Graham Bell constructs a telephone (1876); first national lawn tennis championship played at Wimbledon (1877); German historian Heinrich Treitschke begins a racial anti-semite movement (1878); Gilbert and Sullivan write *HMS Pinafore* (1878); British troops are massacred by Zulus in Isandhlwana, Africa (1879); the British occupy the Khyber Pass near Afghanistan and are massacred in Kabul (1879); Norwegian Henrik Ibsen completes the play *A Doll's House* (1879); Chile invades Bolivia and its ally Peru after Bolivia cancels a Chilean company's contract to exploit Bolivia's nitrate deposits (1879).

1880–84: Auguste Rodin sculpts *The Thinker* (1880); France annexes Tahiti (1880); Transvaal declares its independence from Britain and the Boers establish a republic after a brief war with Britain (1880–81); the first practical electrical lights are independently made by Thomas Edison and J.W. Swan (1880); the malaria parasite is discovered by Charles Laveran (1880); the first large steel furnace is developed by American steel baron Andrew Carnegie (1880); the Vatican opens its archives to scholars (1881); the first Japanese political parties are founded (1881); violent government-condoned attacks (pogroms) are carried out against Russian Jews (1881–1917) causing large-scale Jewish emigration to North America; the Federation of Organized Trades and Labor Unions of the US and Canada is formed (1881); Germany, Austria and Italy form an alliance (1882); the three-mile limit for territorial waters is agreed upon at the Hague Convention (1882); Peter I. Tchaikovsky composes the *1812 Overture* (1882); psychoanalysis begins when Joseph Breuer (Austrian) uses hypnosis to treat hysteria (1882); Thomas Edison designs the first hydroelectric plant in Wisconsin (1882); the Orient Express train between Paris and

Istanbul makes its first run (1883); *On the Size of Atoms* is published by British scientist William Thomson, later Lord Kelvin (1883); peace is restored between Peru and Chile (1883); Friedrich Nietzsche (German philosopher) begins *Thus Spake Zarathustra* (1884–91); gold is discovered in the Transvaal (1884) and this leads to the rise of Johannesburg; a truce is signed between Bolivia and Chile, with Bolivia forced to cede its only coastal territory to Chile (1884); the *Oxford English Dictionary* begins publication (1884–1928); the Berlin Conference of 14 nations on African affairs is held (1884).

1885–89: Karl Benz builds the single-cylinder engine for motor cars (1885); the individuality of fingerprints is proved by Sir Francis Galton (1885); the first Indian National Congress meets (1886); the Statue of Liberty is presented to the US by France (1886); steam is first used to sterilize surgical instruments by Ernst von Bergmann (1886); Irish politician Charles Parnell, the Fenians, and British Prime Min. William Gladstone try unsuccessfully to pass the first Irish Home Rule Bill to give Ireland control over domestic affairs (1886); Sir Arthur Conan Doyle writes the first Sherlock Holmes story, *A Study in Scarlet* (1887); William II (the Kaiser) becomes emperor of Germany (1888); Vincent Van Gogh paints the series of sunflowers (1888) and later, *Starry Night*; the electric motor is first constructed by Nikola A. Tesla and manufactured by George Westinghouse (1888); radio waves are discovered to be of the same family as light waves by the independently working Heinrich Hertz and Oliver Lodge (1888); Kodak box camera produced by George Eastman (1888); "Jack the Ripper" murders six women in London (1888); Alexander G. Eiffel designs the Eiffel Tower for the Paris World Exhibition (1889).

1890–94: The first Japanese general election is held (1890); German Chancellor Bismarck dismissed by Emperor William II (1890); the first moving picture shows appear in New York (1890); Oscar Wilde writes *The Picture of Dorian Gray* (1890); antitoxins are discovered by Emil von Behring (1890); the first entirely steel-framed building is erected in Chicago (1890); the Triple Alliance between Austria, Germany and Italy is renewed for 12 years (1891); Briton Thomas Hardy writes *Tess of the D'Ubervilles* (1891); Henri

Toulouse-Lautrec produces his first music hall posters (1891); *Experiments in Aerodynamics* is published by Samuel P. Langley (1891); the All-Deutschland Verband (Pan-Germany League) is founded (1891); Russia experiences widespread famine (1891); an earthquake in Japan kills ten thousand people (1891); the Java Man (*Pithecanthropus homo erectus*) is discovered by Dutch anthropologist Eugène Dubois, in Java (1891); Paul Gauguin (French) paints *By the Sea* in Tahiti (1892); Rudolph Diesel (German) patents his internal-combustion engine (1892); Tchaikovsky performs his *The Nutcracker* ballet score in St Petersburg (1892); Karl Benz constructs his four-wheel car (1893); Jewish French army captain Alfred Dreyfus is arrested under controversy and convicted of spying for Germany (1894); Rudyard Kipling writes *The Jungle Book* (1894); after Japan sends troops to Seoul, Korea, Japan declares war on China and defeats the Chinese at Port Arthur (1894); Emil Berliner develops a horizontal gramophone disc, replacing the record cylinder for sound reproduction (1894).

1895–99: The Chinese-Japanese war ends with Japan victorious: Formosa and Port Arthur are first ceded to Japan and later returned to China for payment (1895); H.G. Wells writes *The Time Machine* (1895); William B. Yeats writes *Poems* (1895); x-rays are discovered by William Röntgen (1895); Marchese Marconi invents radio telegraphy (1895); the principle of rocket reaction propulsion is developed by Konstantin Isiolkovski (1895); the first modern Olympics is held in Athens, Greece (1896); Anton Chekhov (Russian) writes *The Sea Gull* (1896); five annual Nobel prizes are established by Alfred Nobel for persons who have contributed the most in the fields of physics, physiology and medicine, chemistry, literature and peace (1896); Wilfrid Laurier becomes the first French Canadian prime minister of Canada (1896–1911); the Klondike gold rush in Bonanza Creek, Canada, begins (1896); Edmond Rostand writes *Cyrano de Bergerac* (1897); Queen Victoria celebrates her Diamond Jubilee (1897); French writer Emile Zola writes an open letter, *J'accuse*, condemning the Dreyfus espionage trial and he is imprisoned (1898), Col. Henry admits forging documents in the case (1898), and Captain Dreyfus is pardoned after a retrial (1899)—the case polarized French politics for

a decade; the US declares war on Spain over Cuba and destroys the Spanish fleet at Manila (1898); Spain cedes Cuba, Puerto Rico, Guam and the Philippines to the US for $20 million at the Treaty of Paris; Chinese Boxers, an anti-Western organization, is formed (1898); the Boer War begins as the South African Republic (Transvaal) and the Orange Free State unite against the British (1898); Marie and Pierre Curie discover radium and polonium (1898); German Count Ferdinand von Zeppelin builds his airship (1898); photographs using artificial light are first taken (1898); Marchese Marconi invents the radio (1899).

1900: The Boer War continues and Canadian troops set sail for South Africa to fight for England in their first foreign war; Boxer rebellion against Western influence, supported by the Dowager Empress Tzu-hsi, continues in China against Christian missionaries and foreigners; Sigmund Freud, the founder of psychoanalysis (Austrian), completes *The Interpretation of Dreams*; Wilhelm Wundt writes *Comparative Psychology*; Shintoism is reinstated in Japan to counter Buddhist influence; Commonwealth of Australia is created; Max Planck formulates the quantum theory; human speech is first transmitted via radio waves by the American scientist R.A. Fessenden; Holland's senate creates an international arbitration court at The Hague; millions are reported starving in India; botanist Hugo de Vries rediscovers Gregor Mendel's laws of heredity after 30 years; 10,000 Ashanti natives attack a British force of 400 at Cape Coast, Ghana, and are defeated.

1901: Queen Victoria dies and is succeeded by her son Edward VII; the Dutch Boers begin organized guerrilla warfare against the British; the Cuba Convention makes Cuba a US protectorate; US Pres. William McKinley is assassinated and is succeeded by Theodore Roosevelt; a treaty is signed to build the Panama Canal under US supervision; the hormone adrenaline is first isolated; Walter Nernst postulates the "third law of thermodynamics"; John Pierpont Morgan organizes the US Steel Corp., the first billion-dollar corporation; the Peace of Peking ends the Boxer uprising and China is forced to pay an indemnity of $333 million to the Allies to amend commercial treaties in favor of foreign nationals and to allow foreign troops to be posted in Peking; French physicist Henri Becquerel determines that atoms have internal structure; there are racial riots in New Orleans when American black leader Booker T. Washington is invited to the White House; the Trans-Siberian railroad reaches Port Arthur on the east coast of Russia; oil drilling begins in Persia (Iran).

1902: An Anglo-Japanese treaty recognizes the independence of China and Korea; the Treaty of Vereeniging ends the Boer War and the Orange Free State becomes a British colony; the Triple Alliance between Germany, Austria and Italy is renewed for another six years; the US acquires perpetual control over the Panama Canal; the Colonial Conference meets in London; the Committee of Imperial Defence meets in London for the first time; Jean Sibelius, Finnish composer and conductor, completes *Symphony No. 2*; Egypt's Aswan Dam is opened.

1903: The "Entente Cordiale" between England and France is established to counter German imperialism; the Russian Social Democratic Party splits into Mensheviks (led by Plechanoff) and Bolsheviks (led by Vladimir Lenin and Leon Trotsky); *The Conduction of Electricity through Gases* is published by Joseph John Thomson; Briton George Bernard Shaw writes *Man and Superman*; Orville and Wilbur Wright successfully fly a powered airplane near Kitty Hawk, North Carolina; the electrocardiograph, which records heart action, is invented by William Einthoven; Briton Emmeline Pankhurst founds the National Women's Social and Political Union and campaigns for women's right to vote; Albert I, Prince of Monaco, founds the International Peace Institute; Henry Ford founds the Ford Motor Company.

1904: The Russo-Japanese War breaks out over Korea and Manchuria; the Japanese besiege Port Arthur and occupy Seoul; the Russian fleet is partially destroyed off Port Arthur; the Russians are defeated at Mukden and Toushima Straits; Max Weber writes *The Protestant Ethic and the Birth of Capitalism*; the first performance of Giacomo Puccini's opera *Madame Butterfly* in Milan; the first radio transmission of music is at Graz, Austria; the general theory of radioactivity is postulated by Ernest Rutherford and Frederick Soddy; W.C. Gorgas eradicates yellow fever in the Panama Canal Zone; sili-

cones are discovered by F.S. Kipping.

1905: Albert Einstein publishes four papers detailing his special theory of relativity, the relationship between mass and energy, the Brownian theory of motion and another formulating the photon theory of light; the Russian city of Port Arthur surrenders to the Japanese; in Russia troops fire at peaceful protest marchers heading for the czar's Winter Palace in St Petersburg, and the event becomes known as "Bloody Sunday"; William II of Germany and Nicholas II of Russia sign the Treaty of Bjorko for mutual help in Europe; the Treaty of Portsmouth ends the Russo-Japanese War; a general strike in Russia in response to Bloody Sunday includes a sailors' mutiny on the battleship *Potemkin* and the creation of the first workers soviet in St Petersburg; Czar Nicholas establishes a constitutional government (the Imperial Duma); the Norwegian Parliament decides to separate from Sweden; the Anglo-Japanese alliance is renewed for 10 years; the Sinn Fein nationalist party is formed in Ireland; George Santayana writes his philosophical work *The Life of Reason*.

1906: Reform laws are proposed in Russia and the Imperial Duma is dissolved by the czar to end the radical change; the All India Muslim League is founded by Aga Khan; the term "allergy" is introduced by Clemens von Pirquet; the position of the magnetic North Pole is determined by Norwegian explorer Roald Amundsen; night-shift work for women is forbidden in many countries; the San Francisco earthquake kills 700 people and causes $400 million in property loss; Transvaal and Orange River colonies are granted self-government.

1907: The second Russian Duma meets in March; its radical proposals lead to its dissolution five months later; the US prohibits Japanese immigration; Lenin leaves Russia and founds the newspaper *The Proletarian*; Grigori Rasputin, a Russian mystic, gains influence with the royal family when he treats the hemophiliac son of Nicholas II; New Zealand becomes a dominion within the British Empire; Baden-Powell forms the Boy Scout movement; Korea becomes a Japanese protectorate; Russian artist Marc Chagall paints *Peasant Women*; Gustav Mahler (Austrian) composes *Symphony No. 8*; Ivan Pavlov (Russian) studies conditioned reflexes in dogs; the SS *Lusitania* beats the SS *Mauritania* in a race from Ireland to New York.

1908: Austria occupies Bosnia and Herzegovina; Bulgaria declares independence from Turkey; Isadora Duncan emerges as a popular modern dancer; the Zeppelin airship crashes near Echterdingen; General Motors Corporation is formed in the US; Henry Ford designs the inexpensive, standardized Model T automobile while pioneering assembly line techniques for autos; an earthquake in Sicily and Calabria kills 150,000; American Gertrude Stein writes *Three Lives*; French writer Anatole France completes the political satire *Penguin Island*; Canadian Lucy Maud Montgomery writes *Anne of Green Gables*.

1909: Turkey and Serbia acknowledge Austrian control of Bosnia and Herzegovina; sultan of Turkey is deposed and replaced by his brother; Ezra Pound writes *Exultations*; the first newsreels appear and director D.W. Griffith features Canadian-born Mary Pickford, who becomes the first film star; Sergei Diaghilev presents his *Ballets Russes*, revolutionizing dance, in Paris; Blériot flies from Calais to Dover in 37 minutes, Farman makes the first 100-mile flight; W.E. Du Bois cofounds the National Negro Committee which becomes the National Association for the Advancement of Colored People in 1910; Girl Guides organized in Britain; Thomas Hunt Morgan begins research in genetics; US explorer Robert E. Peary reaches the North Pole.

1910: The Union of South Africa becomes a dominion within the British Empire with Louis Botha as premier; China abolishes slavery; Japan takes over Korea; Montenegro becomes an independent kingdom; Portugal becomes a republic after a revolution ends the monarchy; Albania rebels against Turkish rule; Roger Fry arranges the Post-Impressionist Exhibition in London with works by Cezanne, van Gogh and Matisse; Igor Stravinsky performs his ballet score *The Firebird* in Paris; the South American tango is the dance craze in Europe and North America; the first deep-sea research expedition is undertaken by Murray and Hjort; the five-day work week is instituted in the US, making the "week-end" possible.

1911: US-Japanese and Anglo-Japanese commercial treaties are signed; Diaz surrenders power in Mexico but revolutions continue; the Kaiser's Hamburg speech promises Germany's "Place in the Sun"; war erupts between Turkey and Italy and aircraft are first used for offensive measures; a revolution in Central China is followed by the fall of the Manchu dynasty (in power since 1644) and the proclamation of a Chinese Republic; Sun Yat-sen is elected president and he appoints Chiang Kai-shek as his military adviser; Russian premier, Peter Stolypin, is assassinated; Roald Amundsen reaches the South Pole; Marie Curie is the first person to win a second Noble Prize, in chemistry; Rutherford formulates his theory of atomic structure.

1912: British dock workers, coal miners and transport workers strike; the German-Austro-Italian alliance is renewed again; Lenin becomes editor of *Pravda*; Sun Yat-sen founds Kuomintang (Chinese National Party); Montenegro declares war against Turkey and Bulgaria, Greece and Serbia mobilize; Carl Jung writes *The Theory of Psychoanalysis*; the term "vitamin" is coined by Polish chemist Kasimir Funk; Stefansson and Anderson explore Arctic Canada; Wilson's cloud chamber (particle detector) photographs lead to the detection of protons and electrons; the Royal Flying Corps (later RAF) is established in Britain; SS *Titanic* sinks on its first voyage after colliding with an iceberg: 1,513 people drown.

1913: The London Peace Treaty ending the First Balkan War is signed and Turkey loses all possessions in Europe except E. Thrace; the Second Balkan War breaks out as Bulgaria attacks Serbia and Greece; Russia declares war on Bulgaria, Bulgaria and Turkey settle a peace treaty and Turkey regains Thrace, Serbia invades Albania; Greece and Turkey make peace; police crack down on suffragette demonstrations led by Emmeline Pankhurst in London; Maxim Gorki, the father of Soviet literature, writes *My Childhood*; Charlie Chaplin first stars in movies; Niels Bohr formulates his theory of atomic structure; Albert Schweitzer, medical missionary, opens his famous hospital in Lambaréné, French Congo.

1914: Archduke Francis Ferdinand, heir to the Austrian throne, is assassinated in Sarajevo (capital of the Austro-Hungarian province of Bosnia) by a Serbian nationalist (June 28); Austria-Hungary challenges Serbia and declares war (July 28); Russia and France support Serbia and mobilize troops; Austria's ally Germany declares war on Russia and France in response; the members of the Triple Entente (Britain, France, Russia) declare war on Turkey after Turks attack Russia; Germany, Austria-Hungary and the Ottoman Empire (Turkey) form alliance of Central Powers, they are opposed by UK, members of British Empire, France, Russia, Belgium, Japan and Serbia (Allied Powers); Germany invades Belgium, attacks France, and establishes the Eastern Front against the Russians at Tannenberg and the Masurian Lakes; on the Western Front the Germans are held in check after battles at Marne River, France (Sept. 6); the First Battle of Ypres, Belgium, is waged to prevent the Germans from cutting British supply lines to France; Austria-Hungary fails in three attacks on Serbia and, after the Russians capture the province of Galicia, retreats to its own territory; by Nov. 14, 1914 there is a deadlock along the Western Front (stretching 720 km across Belgium and northeast France to the Swiss border) that remains throughout the war; Irish writer James Joyce writes *Dubliners* (1914); John B. Watson writes *Behavior: an Introduction to Comparative Psychology* (1914); the first successful heart surgery is performed on a dog by Dr. Alexis Carrel (1914); the Panama Canal opens (1914); millions of immigrants leave southern and eastern Europe between 1905 and 1914.

1915: The Allied Gallipoli Campaign to neutralize Turkey fails and Australian and New Zealand troops suffer heavy losses; the first German submarine (U-boat) attack is at Le Havre; the German blockade of England begins; at the Second Battle of Ypres, Canadian forces hold off the German advance while under heavy fire and attacks from chlorine gas and newly-introduced flame throwers; Italy joins the Allied Powers, declares war on Austria-Hungary (May 23) and an Italian Front soon opens; a German submarine sinks the *Lusitania* (May 7); the first Zeppelin air attack takes place on London; Ottoman-controlled Mesopotamia (now Iraq) surrenders to Britain; Italians fight Austria-Hungary in continuous battles at Isonzo (1915–17); Germans invade Warsaw and Brest-Litovsk; Allied troops land at Salonika; the first fighter airplane is constructed by Hugo Junkers; Henry Ford develops a farm tractor; the

dysentery bacillus is isolated by British chemist James Kendall; the first book advocating birth control, by American Margaret Sanger, is published, and the author is sent to jail.

1916: Germany stages a Zeppelin raid on Paris and declares war on Portugal; Portugal and Rumania later join the Allied Powers; in the Middle East, T.E. Lawrence leads an Arab revolt against Turkey; heavy casualties occur at Verdun (Feb. 21); British and German fleets clash at the Battle of Jutland (May 31–June 1); the 1st Newfoundland Regiment is annihilated along with 624,000 Allied troops during the offensive at the Somme (launched July 1); HMS *Hampshire* is sunk; Italy declares war on Germany; the Germans first use gas masks and steel helmets; peace notes are exchanged between Germany and the Allies; Lloyd George becomes British prime minister; blood for transfusion is first refrigerated; the theory of shell shock is put forth by F.W. Mott; an underwater ultrasonic source for submarine detection is built by Paul Langevin; Britain initiates daylight-saving time; US purchases the Virgin Islands for $25 million.

1917: The United States enters the war on the Allied side (Apr. 6); Germans withdraw on the Western Front; the Russian Black Sea fleet mutinies at Sebastopol; there is revolution in Russia in Feb. and the Czar abdicates (Mar. 16); Kerensky becomes Russian premier and continues the war effort; Canadian forces seize Vimy Ridge in northern France; Germany stages air attacks on England; Greece joins the Allies (July); China declares war on Germany and Austria; the British-led offensive at the Third Battle of Ypres (Passchendaele) fails (July 31); the Italian army is defeated at Caporetto by Austria-Hungary; Kerensky's government is overthrown in Petrograd in Oct. and Lenin is appointed Chief Commissar, Trotsky becomes Commissar for Foreign Affairs and Russia seeks peace with Germany; the first tank battle is at Cambrai; starvation sweeps Germany; Finland declares independence from Russia; the Allies execute dancer Mata Hari as a spy; Lord Arthur Balfour, the British Foreign Secretary, issues the Balfour Declaration stating British support for a Jewish national homeland in Palestine; women are arrested for suffrage activities in the US.

1918: Russia, the Ukraine and the Central Powers conclude the Treaties of Brest-Litovsk: the first one establishes the independence of the Ukraine, the second strips Russia of its Baltic and Polish possessions; Turks surrender to British at Jerusalem; US Pres. Wilson puts forth Fourteen Points for world peace (including a proposal for a League of Nations); Rumania signs a peace treaty with the Central Powers; Germany launches three final offensives on the Western Front (Mar. 21); Germans bomb Paris; the Second Battle of the Marne (July 15–Aug. 6) is won by the Allies; the Allies win victories on all fronts in the fall; the Japanese push into Siberia; Germany and Austria agree to retreat to their own territory before an armistice is signed; the Hungarian premier is assassinated; the Turkish and Austro-Hungarian empires and Bulgaria surrender to the Allies (Nov. 3); the German fleet mutinies at Kiel and the emperor flees; an armistice between the Allies and Germany is signed (Nov. 11); Germany agrees to the provisions of the Treaty of Versailles after the Allies threaten to invade; Emperor Charles of Austria loses the throne; the map of Europe is reshaped: Austria becomes a republic and the Serbo-Croatian-Slovene Kingdom of Yugoslavia is proclaimed; Poland and Czechoslovakia are created; Iceland becomes independent state; the Russian Revolution continues as Bolshevik workers take over government buildings, the Winter Palace and later Moscow and other cities; civil war between the Bolshevik (Red) and anti-Bolshevik (White) continues (until 1920); British, French and American troops intervene against the Reds; the British government abandons Home Rule for Ireland; ex-Czar Nicholas II and family are executed by Russian revolutionaries; Hsu-Shih-Chang becomes president of the Chinese Republic; women over 30 get the vote in Britain; controversy rages over the psychology of Freud and Jung; the true dimensions of the Milky Way are discovered by Harlow Shapley, an American astronomer.

1919: US Pres. Woodrow Wilson heads the first League of Nations meeting in Paris; the Peace Conference opens at Versailles; Benito Mussolini founds the Fasci del Combattimento in Italy; socialist governments are founded in Austria and Budapest, Hungary; the Treaty of Versailles is signed with Germany; the final treaty exacts heavy financial penalties on Germany, restricts the German army and navy, blames Germany for provoking the war and establishes the League of Nations; US refusal to ratify the treaty excludes it from League membership; the Allied peace treaty with Austria is signed at St Germain; the Treaty of Neuilly with Bulgaria is signed; the International Labor Congress in Washington endorses the eight-hour workday; the Red (Soviet) forces win successive battles in the Russian civil war; Soviets attack Finland; the first nonstop flight across the Atlantic is made from Newfoundland to Ireland by J.W. Alcock and A. Whitten Brown; Lady Astor is elected to Britain's Parliament, becoming the first female MP.

1920: The League of Nations is founded in Paris and establishes headquarters in Geneva; Russian civil war ends with Soviet victory; Great Britain gains control of Palestine from the Turks; The Hague becomes the International Court of Justice; the Little Entente between Czechoslovakia, Yugoslavia and Rumania is formed; the Treaty of Trianon is signed with Hungary; the Treaty of Sevres is signed with the Ottoman Empire; the 19th Amendment gives American women the vote; 200,000 Chinese die in an earthquake in Kansu province; the world population is 1.8 billion; Britain establishes separate parliaments for Northern and Southern Ireland; Adolph Hitler founds the Nazi party in Munich, Germany, and announces his 25-point program, blaming Germany's war defeat on Jews and Communists; Mohandas (Mahatma) Ghandi becomes India's leader in its struggle for independence from Britain; Prohibition goes into effect in the US, banning the sale and consumption of alcoholic beverages; a worldwide influenza epidemic, which began in 1918, leaves 22 million dead

1921: The first Indian Parliament meets; German reparations payments totalling $33.3 million are fixed by the Allies at a Paris conference; Hitler's storm troopers (SA) begin to terrorize ideological opponents; Mackenzie King is elected prime minister of Canada; British Broadcasting Company is founded (changed to the British Broadcasting Corporation in 1927); the Spanish prime minister and Japanese premier are assassinated; founder of Portuguese republic is murdered; ex-emperor Charles stages two failed coup attempts to regain Hungarian throne; Britain and Ireland sign a peace treaty; German mark falls and rapid inflation plagues the economy; coal is successfully hydrogenated into oil by Friedrich Bergius; the tuberculosis vaccine (B-C-G) is developed by Albert Calmette and Camille Guerin; the chromosome theory of heredity is put forth by American biologist Thomas Morgan; Albert Einstein wins Nobel Prize for Physics; Ku Klux Klan members terrorize blacks and black sympathizers in the southern US; one of the founders of modern aeronautics, Hermann J. Oberth, writes *The Rocket into Interplanetary Space.*

1922: Gandhi is sentenced to six years imprisonment for civil disobedience; German reconstruction minister Walter Rathenau is assassinated by German nationalists; the Arab Congress at Nablus rejects the British control of Palestine; Austria denounces "Anschluss" (union with Germany); Mussolini stages the March on Rome and forms a Fascist government; Irish Free State is proclaimed; the tomb of Tutankhamen is discovered by Lord Carnarvaron and Howard Carter; a self-winding wristwatch is invented by John Harwood (patented in 1924); a stock market "boom" begins in the US; Soviet states form the USSR; insulin, prepared by Canadian physicians Frederick Banting, Charles Best and John Macleod, is first given to diabetic patients.

1923: An earthquake kills 120,000 people in Tokyo and Yokohama; Adolph Hitler tries (and fails) to overthrow the German government ("Beer Hall Putsch"); Greek army overthrows monarch; Jewish philosopher Martin Buber writes the theological *I and Thou*; the theory of acids and bases is postulated by J.N. Brönsted; Lee de Forest demonstrates the process for motion pictures with sound; the first commercial airline, Aeroflot, is founded in the USSR.

1924: Ramsay MacDonald forms the first Labour government in Britain; Adolph Hitler writes *Mein Kampf* during an eight-month jail term; R.C. Andrews discovers skulls and skeletons of Mesozoic dinosaurs in the Gobi desert; Winston Churchill, having switched from the Liberals to the Conservatives, is named Chancellor of the Exchequer in Britain; in Russia, Lenin dies and Stalin, Zinoviev and Kamenev ally against Trotsky; the "Zinoviev letter," purported to be calling for a communist revolution in Britain, is published by the British Foreign Office; Greece becomes a republic; elections are held in Italy and Mussolini wins support of 65% of the electorate; leader of Italian socialists is murdered; Albanian Republic is founded; Sigmund Freud begins *Collected Writings* (12 vols. 1924–39); Ghandi fasts for 21 days, protesting feuding between Hindus and Muslims in India; British astronomer Arthur Eddington discovers that the luminosity of a star is approximately related to its mass; insecticides are used for the first time; a patent application for iconoscope (television) is filed by Russian-American inventor V.K. Zworkin; Danish polar explorer Knud Rasmussen completes the longest dog-sled journey ever made across the North American Arctic; British Imperial Airways begins commercial air flights.

1925: Locarno Conference creates a series of treaties between Germany, France, Belgium, Poland, UK, Italy and Czechoslovakia that set up a demilitarized zone in the Rhineland and confirmed borders between Belgium, France and Germany; Mrs Nellie Tayloe Ross of Wyoming becomes the first woman governor in the US; the United Church of Canada is founded; recognizable human features are transmitted by television by Scottish inventor John Logie Baird; Walter P. Chrysler founds the Chrysler Corporation; the (Franz) Fischer and (Hans) Tropsch synthesis leads to the industrial development of synthetic oil; Heisenberg, Bohr and Jordan develop quantum mechanics for atoms; the presence of cosmic rays in the upper atmosphere is discovered by US physicist Robert Andrews Millikan; the "flapper" era takes hold; an international convention condemns the illegal narcotics trade.

1926: Fascist youth organizations appear: "Balilla" in Italy and "Hitlerjugend" in Germany; Josef Pilsudski successfully stages a coup d'état in Poland and begins a military dictatorship; commerce in Britain is stopped by a general strike; Trotsky is expelled from Moscow; Hirohito succeeds his father Taisho as Emperor of Japan; Robert H. Goddard fires the first liquid fuel rocket; vitamin B is isolated by B. Jansen and W. Donath; Kodak produces the first 16mm movie film; British Imperial Chemical Industries (ICI) begins operations; H.L. Mencken writes *Notes on Democracy*; Turkish reforms include the abolition of polygamy, modernization of female attire and adoption of Latin alphabet (1926–28).

1927: The Allied military control of Germany ends; an economic conference in Geneva is attended by 52 nations; the economic system in Germany collapses ("Black Friday"); Trotsky expelled from the Communist Party in the USSR; Nazis on trial in Austria for political murder are acquitted and socialists riot in Venice to protest; the first film with sound, a "talkie," *The Jazz Singer*, stars Al Jolson; Lev Theremin invents the earliest electronic musical instrument; Charles Lindbergh flies the monoplane *Spirit of St Louis* in the first solo transatlantic flight, nonstop from New York to Paris in 33.5 hours; Canadian forests are the first sprayed with insecticides by airplanes; the first vehicular tunnel, the Holland Tunnel, links New York and New Jersey.

1928: The Supreme Court of Canada rules that women may not hold public office because they are not "persons" as defined by the British North America Act, but the British Privy Council overturns the decision in a landmark Commonwealth case in 1929; the Kellogg-Briand Pact outlawing war is signed by 65 states; Josef Stalin emerges as leader of Soviet Union; the first economic five-year plan begins in the USSR; Chiang Kai-Shek is elected president of China; over-production of coffee leads to the collapse of Brazil's economy; penicillin is discovered by Alexander Fleming (Scottish); American anthropologist Margaret Mead writes *Coming of Age in Samoa;* the first colour motion pictures are exhibited by George Eastman in Rochester, New York; J.L. Baird presents colour television; Mickey Mouse makes his Disney debut.

1929: The US Stock Exchange collapses on Oct. 28, Black Friday; the Great Depression, a world economic crisis, begins and is primarily caused by easy credit and stock market overspeculation, overproduction of goods and tariff and war-debt policies; six Chicago-area gangsters are machine-gunned to death in the St Valentine's Day Massacre; a dictatorship is established in Serbo-Croat-Slovene kingdom by the monarch and the country's name is changed to Yugoslavia; Trotsky is exiled from USSR; talks on Indian sovereignty begin betweeen Indian leaders and the Viceroy; the Lateran Treaty establishes the independence of Vatican City; precise timekeeping is made

possible with the quartz-crystal clocks by W.A. Morrison; the airship *Graf Zeppelin* flies around the world in 21 days.

1930: Austria and Italy sign a treaty of friendship; Britain, the US, Japan, France and Italy sign a treaty on naval disarmament; right-wing coalition comes to power in Germany, Nazis later capture 107 more seats in an election; right-wing government is formed in Poland; Catholic-Fascist units are established in Austria; revolution in Argentina brings new military dictatorship to power; the planet Pluto is discovered by C.W. Tombaugh at Lowell Observatory; a yellow fever vaccine is developed by South African microbiologist Max Theiler; photoflash bulb is introduced; the word "technocracy," meaning the domination of technology, comes into use.

1931: A financial crisis in central Europe is caused by the collapse of Austria's Credit-Anstalt; all German banks close following the bankruptcy of the German Danatbank; Britain abandons the gold standard; Fascist party is formed in Britain; the Statute of Westminster established the British Commonwealth of Nations as a free association of autonomous nations sharing a common allegiance to the British crown, and declared that British Parliament could no longer legislate for any member states unless requested to do so; US Pres. Hoover proposes a one-year moratorium for reparations and war debts; the first transAfrican railroad line is completed, Benguella-Katanga; the northern face of the Matterhorn is climbed for the first time by Franz and Toni Schmid.

1932: The Indian National Congress, a nationalist party dedicated to home rule, is declared illegal and its leader, Mahatma Gandhi, is arrested; the US criticizes Japanese aggression in Manchuria; the Nazis sweep the German Reichstag (Parliament) elections while WWI hero Hindenburg wins the Presidential election; Hitler refuses Hindenburg's offer to become Vice Chancellor, and the Austrian-born Hitler receives German citizenship; Franklin D. Roosevelt wins the US presidential election and proposes domestic reform programs to provide recovery and relief from the Great Depression ("New Deal"); the USSR suffers famine; Zuider Zee, a huge dam and drainage project in Holland, is completed; Amelia Earheart is the first woman to fly solo across the Atlantic; Japan conquers world markets by undercutting prices; about 30 million people are unemployed worldwide; the neutron is discovered by James Chadwick; vitamin D is discovered.

1933: Reichstag building is burned in Berlin and Hitler uses the event to justify banning opposition parties and labour unions; Hitler is appointed German Chancellor and granted dictatorial powers with the Enabling Law; Nazi Hermann Goering is named Prussian prime minister; Parliamentary government is suspended in Austria; starvation spreads in USSR; Paul Joseph Goebbels is named Hitler's Minister of Propaganda; Japan withdraws from the League of Nations; the first concentration camps are built by the Nazis in Germany to hold Jews and ideological opponents; books by non-Nazi and Jewish authors are burned in Germany; Germans begin to boycott and restrict Jewish services; an anti-Nazi treatise, *Judaism-Christendom-Germanism*, is published by Cardinal von Faulhaber in Munich; Assyrian Christians are massacred in Iraq; US goes off the gold standard and tries to stimulate its economy by creating The Tennessee Valley Authority to construct dams and generate electricity.

1934: A revolution in Austria overturns the Social Democrats and Austrian Chancellor is assassinated by the Nazis; a general strike takes place in France; the USSR is admitted to the League of Nations; Winston Churchill warns the British Parliament of the German air menace; Hitler oversees purge of his associates and many are executed; a national vote grants him the title Führer (leader); Stalin's purge of the Soviet Communist party begins and he reportedly oversees the murder of millions of people; German scientist Albert Einstein is persecuted by the Nazis for being Jewish and he flees, settling in the US; Japan renounces the Washington treaties of 1922 and 1930; Mao Tse-tung, leader of the Chinese Communists, heads the Long March.

1935: Nazis repudiate the Treaty of Versailles and reintroduce compulsory military service; the autonomous territory of Saarland votes for reunion with Germany; an Anglo-German Naval Agreement is concluded; Nazis implement the Nuremburg Laws against Jews, stripping them of civic rights and forbidding intermarriage with non-Jews; Mussolini invades Ethiopia, and the League of Nations retaliates by imposing sanctions; the Chaco

War, a bitter conflict between Paraguay and Bolivia begun in 1932 and fought over oil-rich but otherwise barren territory, ended after 100,000 lives were lost and both sides were exhausted (treaty not concluded until 1938); radar equipment to detect aircraft is built by Robert Watson Watt; oil pipelines between Iraq, Haifa and Tripoli open; Persia changes its name to Iran.

1936: King George V of England dies and is succeeded by Edward VIII; German troops occupy the Rhineland and Hitler wins the German elections with 99 percent of the vote; Italy, Austria and Hungary sign the Rome Pact; Britain, France and the US sign the London Naval Convention; an Austro-German convention acknowledges Austrian independence; the Spanish Civil War begins and Francisco Franco is appointed Chief of State by the Nationalist insurgents against the government's Loyalist republicans; Franco begins the siege of Madrid, rebels take Malaga and destroy Guernica and Gijon and Franco begins a naval blockade (1937); Heinrich Himmler is appointed head of the Gestapo, responsible for Nazi concentration camps (1936–45); King Edward VIII abdicates in order to marry American divorcee Wallis Simpson; Mussolini and Hitler proclaim the Rome-Berlin Axis; the Anti-Comintern Pact is signed by Germany and Japan; Chiang Kai-shek declares war on Japan; Dr Alexis Carrel develops an artificial heart; the airship *Hindenburg* burns at Lakehurst, New Jersey, after a transatlantic flight; black American athlete Jesse Owens upsets the Nazis when he wins four gold medals at the Olympic Games in Berlin.

1937: Poland refuses to return Danzig to Germany; the first worldwide radio broadcast is heard when George VI is crowned King of Great Britain; Roosevelt signs a US Neutrality Act, intended to keep the US out of a possible European war; Trotsky, exiled from Russia in 1929, is forced to leave Norway and settles in Mexico; aggressive Japanese war policy begins when Prince Konoye is named the Japanese premier, and the Japanese seize major Chinese cities (Beijing, Tianjin, Shanghai, Nanjing and Hangzhou), forcing Chiang Kai-shek and the Communists, under Mao Tse-tung and Chou En-lai, to unite; the Chinese government makes Chungking its capital; the Royal Commission on Palestine recommends the establishment of Arab and Jewish states; Stalin initiates a purge of Soviet generals and show trials of political leaders; Britain signs naval agreements with Germany and the USSR; Germany guarantees Belgian sovereignty; Italy joins the Anti-Comintern Pact and withdraws from the League of Nations; Japanese planes sink US gunboat in Chinese waters; Amelia Earheart disappears during a Pacific flight.

1938: Germany annexes Austria, "Anschluss" (Mar.); France calls up reservists; Great Britain, France and Italy agree to let Germany absorb the Sudetenland, Czechoslovakia, in a policy of appeasement (Munich Pact, Sept.) and Germany promises to cease its aggressive expansion; British foreign minister Anthony Eden resigns in protest against the appeasement policy and Winston Churchill also voices opposition; Franco begins an offensive against the Spanish Loyalists in Catalonia; anti-Jewish legislation is enacted in Italy; Kristallnacht, or "Night of Broken Glass," is a large-scale pogrom by the Nazis against German Jews; the US and Germany recall their respective ambassadors; Japan withdraws from the League of Nations and sets up a puppet Chinese government in Nanking; Howard Hughes flies around the world in less than four days.

1939: US Pres. Roosevelt demands assurances from Hitler and Mussolini that they have no plans to attack other states; Germany breaks the Munich Pact and occupies Bohemia and Moravia; Slovakia is placed under "protection"; Italy invades Albania; Germany renounces the nonaggression pact with Poland and naval agreement with England, and concludes a 10-year alliance with Italy and a nonaggression pact with the USSR, secretly dividing Poland; Germany stages a surprise (blitzkrieg) invasion of Poland, and annexes Danzig (Sept. 1); Britain and France declare war on Germany (Sept. 3); the Allied powers are Britain and France and the Axis powers are led by Germany; Canada declares war (Sept. 10); US Pres. Roosevelt announces US neutrality; Soviets invade Poland from the east (Sept. 17); Germans overrun western Poland and reach Brest-Litovsk and Warsaw and a puppet government is installed; France masses troops along the Maginot Line on the eastern frontier of France and Germany sends troops to its parallel Siegfried Line; the British Expeditionary

Force is sent to France; the USSR invades Finland and is expelled from the League of Nations; Japan occupies Hainan and blockades the British at Tientsin; the US renounces the Japanese trade agreement of 1911; the Spanish Civil War ends with Franco's Nationalists (supported by Hitler and Mussolini) victorious over the Loyalists (supported by the USSR); Spain joins the Anti-Comintern Pact and leaves the League of Nations; England and Poland sign a treaty of mutual assistance; women and children are first evacuated from London; the first helicopter is built by Russian-American Igor Sikorsky; the US economy booms from arms sales to Europe.

1940: Food rationing begins in Britain; Finland surrenders (Mar.) and signs a peace treaty with the USSR; Germany invades Norway and Denmark (Apr. 9); Winston Churchill becomes British prime minister (May 10); Norway falls (June); Germany invades Belgium, Luxembourg and the Netherlands (May 10); Holland and Belgium surrender to Germany and 340,000 Allied forces are trapped in Belgium, but most are evacuated from Dunkirk, a French seaport on the English channel (May 29 to June 3); Italy declares war on France and Britain; Germans attack France from the north and enter Paris (June 14); France concludes an armistice with Germany; southern France remains unoccupied until 1942 and is ruled by the Vichy government; USSR seizes Estonia, Latvia and Lithuania (summer); the Royal Navy sinks the French fleet in Oran; the Royal Air Force begins night bombing of Germany; the Battle of Britain in Aug. is the first battle fought completely in the air; Hitler begins bombing England (all-night blitzes) throughout fall and winter; Japan, Germany and Italy sign a military and economic pact; US destroyers are sold to Britain; Germany intensifies U-boat warfare; Italian forces attempt to take Egypt and Libya in order to cut off British access to Middle East oil and the Suez Canal; the British Eighth Army opens an offensive in North Africa and defeats the Italian forces; Trotsky is murdered in Mexico; Batista becomes president of Cuba; wall paintings dating to about 20,000 BC are discovered in France, the Lascaux caves; a giant cyclotron is built at the University of California for producing mesotrons from atomic nuclei.

1941: The British invade Ethiopia and defeat the Italians (by May); Germany opens a counter-offensive in North Africa to aid Italy; German General Rommel regains Libya and Egypt; Germans launch an airborne invasion against Crete, thereby securing an important base in the Mediterranean (by the end of May); England sinks the German battleship *Bismarck* in an effort to protect vital US shipments to Great Britain; Allies develop radar and sonar to track U-boats; German air raids over London continue; US freezes German and Italian assets in that country; Germans invade Russia (Operation Barbarossa, June 22); Churchill and Roosevelt sign the Atlantic charter (Aug. 14); German troops surround Leningrad and Moscow (Nov.), but an early, harsh winter saves the USSR; Marshal Timoshenko launches the Russian counter-offensive; the US ambassador to Japan warns Pres. Roosevelt of possible Japanese attack; Japanese bomb Pearl Harbor (Dec. 7) and the US and Britain declare war on Japan (Dec. 8); China declares war on the Axis (Dec. 9); Japan invades the Philippines; Germany and Italy declare war on the US; the US declares war on Germany and Italy; British Hong Kong surrenders to the Japanese; Henry Moore draws refugees in London air raid shelters while an official war artist; Dmitri Shostakovich writes *Symphony No. 7* during the German siege of Leningrad; German dramatist Bertolt Brecht writes *Mother Courage and Her Children* while in exile from the Nazis.

1942: Hitler's Final Solution, the systematic murder of Jews in the Nazi gas chambers (Holocaust) is in full force at death camps such as Auschwitz and Dachau; the 26 Allied nations agree not to make separate treaties with the Axis powers; Rommel breaks through British lines and reaches El Alamein (320 km from the Suez Canal); Montgomery (British Eighth Army) scores the first decisive defeat of Rommel at El Alamein; Germans reach Stalingrad, Russia; 400,000 American troops land in French North Africa; Rommel, in full retreat, loses Tobruk and Benghazi; Japan invades Burma, the Dutch East Indies, and captures Singapore; the British bomb Cologne and Lübeck; the US and Canada intern residents of Japanese heritage in camps; many American and Philippine prisoners die in the Japanese-forced Bataan Death March; Americans bomb Tokyo; Americans begin successful island-hopping strategy against Japan and win the battles of the Coral Sea and Midway; French navy loses in Toulon; British and Indian troops advance in Burma; Fermi achieves the first controlled nuclear chain reaction when he splits the atom; the Manhattan Project of intensive US atomic research begins; the first electronic brain or automatic computer is developed in the US; a recorder using plastic magnetic recording tape is invented by German engineers; Gandhi demands independence from Britain and is arrested.

1943: German troops surrender at Stalingrad (Feb. 2) and begin to withdraw from the Caucasus; Churchill and Roosevelt meet in Casablanca; the Japanese are driven from Guadalcanal by US troops; the British Eighth Army reaches Tripoli; Axis powers surrender in North Africa (Tunisia, May 13); Russians destroy the German army southwest of Stalingrad; Russians recapture Rostov and Kharkov; the Royal Air Force raids Berlin; US planes sink the 22-ship Japanese convoy in the Battle of the Bismarck Sea; British and US armies in Africa link up and Rommel retreats; an armed Jewish uprising begins in the overcrowded Warsaw ghetto, but it is crushed by German troops (1943–44) who massacre Jewish inhabitants; the RAF bombs Ruhr dams; US forces land in New Guinea; US recaptures Aleutians; Allies land in Sicily (July 10); Churchill, Roosevelt and Mackenzie King meet in Quebec; US troops bomb Ploesti oil fields in Rumania and enter Messina; Allies land in Salerno Bay and invade Italy, which surrenders unconditionally (Sept. 8); Russians take Kiev; Chinese Gen. and Mme Chiang Kai-shek meet with Roosevelt and Churchill in Cairo and pledge to liberate Korea after Japan is defeated; Churchill, Stalin and Roosevelt hold the Teheran Conference; Allied round-the-clock bombing of Germany begins; the first fully electronic computer is used by the British government to crack German military codes; penicillin is used to treat chronic diseases; Bengal is swept by famine; rationing of selected foods begins in the US; major US cities are troubled by race riots.

1944: Germany continues air raids on London; Russian offensives continue in the Ukraine and Crimea; Allies bomb Berlin; Monte Cassino and Rome are liberated by the Allies June 4; D-day landings in Normandy

(France, June 6): over 700 ships and 4,000 landing craft are involved and Canadian troops lead the trek from the Normandy beaches; Germans drop first flying bomb (V-1) on London; southern Japan is bombed by the US; US troops take Saigon; Russians capture 100,000 Germans at Minsk; German officers unsuccessfully attempt to assassinate Hitler; Russians reach Brest-Litovsk; Americans capture Guam from the Japanese; the British Eighth Army takes Florence; creation of a United Nations is discussed at the Dunbarton Oaks conference in Washington; Charles De Gaulle leads the Free French into Paris (Aug. 25); Allies liberate Belgium; the first V-2 rockets land in Britain; Churchill and Roosevelt meet in Quebec; Americans cross the German frontier near Trier; British airborne forces land at Eindhoven and Arnheim but have to withdraw; US troops land in the Philippines; Russians and Yugoslavs enter Belgrade; Russian Army occupies Hungary; Japanese suffer heavy losses in Battle of Leyte Gulf; Battle of the Bulge (Ardennes Forest) results in Allied victory; France regains Lorraine; Rommel commits suicide; Vietnam, under Ho Chi Minh, declares independence from France; American playwright Tennessee Williams completes *The Glass Menagerie*; quinine is synthesized; Richard Strauss completes the opera *Die Liebe der Danae* in Austria but its performance is cancelled when the Nazis shut down the theatres; French playwright Jean-Paul Sartre writes the existentialist work *Being and Nothingness*.

1945: Britain begins major offensive in Burma; Russians take Warsaw, Cracow and reach Oder River; Churchill, Roosevelt and Stalin meet at the Yalta Conference; Americans enter Manila; Russians take Budapest; British troops reach the Rhine; US air raids on Tokyo, Cologne and Danzig; Okinawa is captured; the British Second Army crosses the Rhine; the last German V-2 rocket falls on Britain; Franklin D. Roosevelt dies and is succeeded by Harry S. Truman; Russians reach Berlin; Bologna is captured; US and Soviet troops meet at Torgau and both liberate Nazi death camps, finding gas chambers and crematoriums; anti-Axis coalition agrees to set up new international body to replace ineffective League of Nations; new United Nations charter drawn up at conference in San Francisco (Apr.–June); Bremen, Genoa, Verona and Venice are captured by the Allies; the Allies cross the Elbe; Mussolini is killed by Italian partisans; Hitler commits suicide (Apr. 30); the German army on the Italian front surrenders; Berlin surrenders to the Russians (May 2) and Germany capitulates to the Allies (May 7); V-E Day (Victory in Europe) ends the war in Europe (May 8); Germany is divided into four zones by the Allies and the three-power occupation of Berlin begins; Churchill, Truman and Stalin meet at Potsdam; Clement Attlee replaces Churchill as prime minister of Great Britain in a Liberal landslide; the first atomic bomb is detonated near Alamogordo, New Mexico after being developed by J. Robert Oppenheimer, Enrico Fermi and others (July 16); the Soviet Union declares war on Japan and occupied Manchuria; the US drops atomic bombs on Hiroshima (Aug. 6) and Nagasaki (Aug. 9); Japan surrenders and World War II ends; war dead are estimated at 35 million plus victims of Nazi concentration camps; the Nuremburg trials of Nazi war criminals begin; the League of Nations holds its final meeting in Geneva and turns over its assets to the UN (Oct.); Charles De Gaulle is elected president of the French provisional government; Tito is chief of state of the newly created Federal People's Republic of Yugoslavia; Nationalists and Communists resume civil war in north China; the Arab League is founded to oppose the creation of a Jewish state; Shintoism is abolished in Japan; vitamin A is synthesized; black markets for food, clothing and cigarettes develop in Europe; the UN World Bank (International Bank for Reconstruction and Development) is founded with authorized share capital of $27 billion.

1946: Albania, Bulgaria, Hungary and Transjordan become sovereign states; the UN General Assembly holds its first session in London (Jan. 7), electing Trygve Lie of Norway as its first Secretary-General, and its permanent headquarters is made in New York; Juan Perón is elected president of Argentina; a Peace Conference of 21 nations is held in Paris; 12 leading Nazis are sentenced to death following the Nuremburg trials and others get life imprisonment; power in Japan is transferred from the Emperor to an elected assembly; the UN Atomic Energy Commission is formed to monitor member nations; after a referendum in Italy, the king abdicates, Italy becomes a republic and de

Gasperi becomes head of state; xerography (photocopying) is invented by Chester Carlson; Dr Benjamin Spock writes *Baby and Child Care*, the "baby boom" reference book.

1947: British coal industry is nationalized; *The Diary of Anne Frank* is published by Anne's father, the only member of the German-Jewish Frank family to survive the Holocaust; Burma proclaims its independence; Paris Peace treaties signed; the Dead Sea Scrolls, dating from about 22 BC to AD 100, are discovered in Wadi Qumran, Palestine; American Chuck Yeager flies the first airplane at supersonic speeds; the transistor is invented by Bell Telephone Laboratory scientists; the UN divides Palestine, which is under British mandate, into a Jewish and an Arab state (Nov. 1947) and the British withdraw six months later; India gains independence from Great Britain and is partitioned into India and East and West Pakistan.

1948: Gandhi is assassinated by a Hindu opposing his tolerance of Muslims; a Communist coup d'état takes place in Czechoslovakia (Feb. 25); the Marshall Plan providing $17 billion in aid for Europe is passed by the US Congress; Winston Churchill chairs the Hague Congress for European unity; the Jewish state of Israel is proclaimed with Chaim Weizmann as president and David Ben-Gurion as premier (May 14); neighbouring Arab states declare war (1948–49) on Israel but by the end of the conflict Israel succeeds in increasing its territory; the Berlin airlift by the west begins after the USSR imposes a land and water blockade (1948–Sept. 1949); bread rationing ends in Britain; the World Council of Churches is organized in Amsterdam; American biologist Alfred C. Kinsey writes *Sexual Behavior in the Human Male*; the first World Health Assembly meets in Geneva; the first port radar system is installed in Liverpool, England.

1949: Tianjin, China, falls to the Communists, Chiang Kai-shek resigns as president of China, and removes his Nationalist forces to Formosa; the Communist People's Republic is proclaimed under Mao Tse-tung, with Chou En-lai as premier; the North Atlantic Treaty establishing a defence alliance (NATO) is signed by all parties (Belgium, Canada, Denmark, France, Iceland, Italy, Luxembourg, the Netherlands, Norway,

Portugal, UK and US) in Washington; the Berlin blockade by the Soviet Union is lifted; the German Federal Republic (West Germany) comes into being with Bonn as its capital and Konrad Adenauer as Chancellor; republic of Eire is proclaimed with its capital in Dublin; Transjordan is renamed the Hashemite Kingdom of Jordan; the state of Vietnam, under Ho Chi Minh, is established at Saigon; civil war looms in Korea; the apartheid program of official racial discrimination is established in South Africa; the Democratic Republic is established in East Germany with Pieck as president; India becomes a federal republic with Pandit Nehru as prime minister; Indonesia gains sovereignty from Holland; the USSR tests its first atomic bomb; the US launches a guided missile to a height of 400 km, the highest altitude yet; George Orwell publishes *Nineteen Eighty-Four*.

1950: Communist China and Russia sign a treaty of friendship and mutual assistance, Britain also recognizes Communist China; 18 protesters are killed in anti-apartheid riots in South Africa; Vietnam, Laos and Cambodia gain independence from France; North Korea invades South Korea, capturing Seoul and forcing Pres. Syngman Rhee to flee; US Atomic Energy Commission begins work on hydrogen bomb; UN forces under Gen. Douglas MacArthur land in South Korea and push north of the 38th parallel, prompting Communist China to enter the war; US recognizes Vietnam, sends military supplies and instructors and signs pact for military assistance with Vietnam, Laos, Cambodia and France.

1951: North Korean forces reach the 38th parallel and capture Seoul: attempts to negotiate peace fail; Gen. MacArthur is replaced as commander in Korea for threatening massive retaliation against China; Winston Churchill forms the government in Britain; Remington Rand produces UNIVAC, the first large-scale, general-purpose computer; electricity is produced from atomic energy in the US; heart-lung machine devised by J. Andre-Thomas; penicillin and streptomycin available in US.

1952: Dwight D. Eisenhower is elected US president; Britain produces an atomic bomb; Elizabeth II becomes Queen of England; Egypt rocked by anti-British riots: premier resigns and the army seizes power; Mau-maus rebel in Kenya and government declares a state of emergency; first hydrogen bomb at Eniwetok Atoll in the Pacific; British Overseas Airways introduces the world's first jet passenger service from London to Rome; the first pocket-sized transistor radio is marketed by Sony in Japan.

1953: An armistice ending the Korean War is signed at Panmunjom; Soviet leader Joseph Stalin dies and is replaced by Malenkov; Sweden's Dag Hammarskjöld is elected UN secretary-general; the Soviet Union explodes a hydrogen bomb; Yugoslavia proclaims a new constitution and Marshall Tito becomes president; Egyptian generals establish a dictatorship and proclaim a republic; rebels from Vietnam attack Laos; Fidel Castro begins a campaign to overthrow Cuban dictator Fulgencio Batista; Ethel and Julius Rosenberg are executed after being convicted of passing American atomic secrets to the Soviet Union; Edmund Hillary and Tenzing Norgay become the first to scale Mt Everest; the first successful open heart surgery is performed in the US; researchers associate lung cancer with cigarette smoking.

1954: Vietnamese Communists defeat the French at Dien Bien Phu; racial segregation in public schools is banned by the US Supreme Court; Gammal Abdel Nasser becomes leader in Egypt; the US Senate censures Sen. Joseph McCarthy for launching a Communist witchhunt; Canada and the US plan a joint radar defence system in the north (Distant Early Warning, DEW Line); the US *Nautilus* becomes the first nuclear-powered submarine; Dr Jonas Salk begins inoculating children against polio; the oral contraceptive pill is introduced in the US; the first successful kidney transplant is performed in the US; Roger Bannister becomes the first to run a mile in less than four minutes.

1955: Churchill resigns in Britain and is succeeded by Anthony Eden; Bulganin succeeds Malenkov as Soviet premier; eight east-European Communist bloc countries adopt the Warsaw Pact mutual defence treaty; West Germany joins NATO; border clashes between Israel and Jordan increase; Juan Perón is ousted by a military coup in Argentina; the first optical fibres are produced in Britain.

1956: Nasser elected Egyptian president; Egypt seizes control of the Suez Canal; Israeli troops invade Egypt and push towards the canal; British and French forces invade Egypt; a United Nations force arrives in Egypt, prompting a cease-fire; UN truce proposals for dispute between Jordan and Israel accepted; Soviet Communist leader Nikita Khrushchev denounces Joseph Stalin's "cult of personality"; Soviet tanks and troops crush an anti-Communist rebellion in Hungary; Sudan becomes a democratic republic; Pakistan becomes an Islamic republic; Martin Luther King, Jr, leads the campaign against racial segregation in the US South; transatlantic telephone service begins; the first computer programming language (FORTRAN) is developed in the US.

1957: Israeli troops withdraw from Egypt and the Gaza Strip comes under UN jurisdiction; UN reopens the Suez Canal; the space race begins as the USSR launches the first earth-orbiting satellite *Sputnik 1*; Belgium, France, Italy, Luxembourg, the Netherlands and West Germany sign the Rome Treaty to extend the common market established for the steel industry to all sectors of the economy; Pres. Eisenhower warns that the US will oppose Communist takeovers in the Middle East; Harold Macmillan leads the new Conservative government in Britain; John Diefenbaker becomes Canada's prime minister.

1958: Nikita Khrushchev becomes Soviet premier; Charles De Gaulle is elected president of France; Pope Pius XII dies and is succeeded by John XXIII; the first US space satellite, *Explorer I*, is launched; scientists in the USSR send two dogs into space and return them safely; Egypt and Syria form the United Arab Republic; Iraq's King Faisal is assassinated in a military coup; Alaska becomes the 49th US state.

1959: Fidel Castro overthrows Fulgencio Batista and establishes a Communist government in Cuba, expropriating sugar mills owned by the US; Soviet Prem. Khrushchev visits the US; American Vice-Pres. Richard Nixon visits the Soviet Union and has the "kitchen debate" with Khrushchev; the USSR sends a space probe to the moon and photographs its hidden side; the St Lawrence Seaway opens; the first commercial photocopier is introduced; the Dalai Lama flees Tibet; Hawaii becomes the 50th state of the US.

1960: An American U-2 spy plane is shot

down over the USSR, prompting Soviet Prem. Nikita Khrushchev to cancel a Soviet-American summit meeting; 50 South African black protesters are massacred at Sharpeville; the Congo (Zaïre) gains independence from Belgium, sparking political instability and UN intervention; Cyprus becomes independent and Archbishop Makarios wins the first presidential election; Israeli agents capture former Gestapo chief Adolf Eichmann in Argentina and smuggle him to Israel for trial; Germany bans Neo-Nazi political groups; John F. Kennedy is elected US president; the first weather and communications satellites are launched in the US; the first heart pacemaker is developed.

1961: Soviet Major Yuri Gagarin becomes the first man in space; US breaks off diplomatic ties with Cuba; the US-backed Bay of Pigs invasion by Cuban exiles fails to topple Cuba's Fidel Castro; astronaut Alan Shepard becomes the first American in space with a sub-orbital flight; East Germany builds the Berlin Wall to stop its citizens from moving to the West; Kuwait becomes independent from Britain, which sends troops to counter Iraqi annexation threats; UN Sec.-Gen. Dag Hammarskjöld dies in a plane crash over Northern Rhodesia; UK applies for membership in the Common Market; the silicon chip is patented by Texas Instruments in the US.

1962: Fearing nuclear war, many North Americans build fallout shelters; John Glenn becomes the first American to orbit the earth; US establishes a military council in South Vietnam; the discovery of Soviet missile bases in Cuba leads to a US naval blockade; the Cuban Missile Crisis ends when Soviet leader Khrushchev agrees to dismantle the bases; UN troops quell rebellion in the Congo's Katanga province; Algeria, Uganda and Jamaica gain independence; the UN votes in favor of economic sanctions against South Africa; Pope John XXIII opens the Second Vatican Council which will modernize the Catholic church; the TV satellite *Telstar* is launched in the US.

1963: US Pres. John Kennedy is assassinated in Dallas and Lyndon Johnson succeeds him; the US, Soviet Union and Britain ban nuclear tests in the atmosphere; South Vietnamese leader Ngo Dinh Diem is assassinated following a military coup; US sends financial aid to South Vietnam; Zanzibar and Kenya gain independence; Dr. Martin Luther King leads the March on Washington seeking equality for US blacks; the "hot line" emergency communications link is established between the White House and the Kremlin; UK application to Common Market rejected after French opposition; British government rocked by the Profumo affair and the scandal forces the resignation of a senior minister; Pope John XXIII dies and is succeeded by Paul VI; archaeologists find the remains of a thousand-year-old Viking settlement in Newfoundland; the first liver and lung transplants are performed; Valentina Tereshkova becomes the first female astronaut.

1964: Harold Wilson becomes prime minister in Britain; Communist China announces it has developed an atomic bomb; the US escalates its military involvement in Vietnam following a reported North Vietnamese attack on US destroyers in the Gulf of Tonkin; the Palestine Liberation Organization (PLO) is formed; Zambia, Malta and Malawi become independent; the sultan of Zanzibar is banished and the country is declared a republic; Zanzibar unites with Tanganyika to form Tanzania; Northern Rhodesia declares independence and adopts the name Zambia; Leonid Brezhnev and Alexei Kosygin become Soviet leaders after Khrushchev is deposed; the first word processor is developed by IBM; the Beatles appear on the Ed Sullivan Show as "Beatlemania" sweeps North America.

1965: Ferdinand Marcos is elected president of the Philippines; Gambia and Rhodesia declare independence from Britain; Rhodesia's declaration is met with an oil embargo; a massive power failure blacks out most of the northeast US and eastern Canada; Pope Paul VI reaffirms the Catholic Church's opposition to birth control; a Soviet cosmonaut is the first to leave a spacecraft and "float" in space; two US Gemini capsules rendezvous in space.

1966: China's Red Guards demonstrate against western influences as Mao launches the Cultural Revolution; Indira Gandhi becomes India's prime minister; floods destroy art treasures in Florence, Italy; De Gaulle asks that NATO forces leave France; South African Pres. Hendrik Verwoerd is stabbed to death during a Parliamentary session; Lesotho and Guyana become independent; civilian protests against the Vietnam

War escalate in the US; government in Ghana overthrown by military coup; an artificial heart is successfully implanted for the first time by Dr Michael De Bakey in Houston; the Soviet Union lands an unmanned spacecraft on the moon.

1967: Israel defeats Egypt, Syria and Jordan in the Six Day War and occupies the Sinai Peninsula, Golan Heights, Gaza Strip and the east bank of the Suez Canal; Expo 67 world fair opens in Montreal; a Soviet cosmonaut becomes the first reported casualty of the space race; US manned space flights are suspended after astronauts Grissom, White and Chaffee die in Apollo capsule fire; race riots erupt in US cities during the "long hot summer"; Canada celebrates its centennial; Dr Christiaan Barnard of South Africa performs the world's first successful human heart transplant: the patient survives for 18 days.

1968: The US intelligence ship *Pueblo* is captured by North Korea; US civil rights leader Martin Luther King is assassinated in Memphis; presidential candidate Robert Kennedy is assassinated in Los Angeles; Soviet troops crush liberal reform in Czechoslovakia; a treaty limiting military use of outer space is signed by 62 nations; university student protest movement spreads worldwide; Richard Nixon is elected US president; Pierre Trudeau becomes prime minister in Canada; peace talks between the US and North Vietnam begin in Paris; British colony of Mauritius becomes independent; Pope Paul VI issues an encyclical banning artificial birth control; three US astronauts circle the moon and return to Earth; *Surveyor 7*, uncrewed, lands on moon.

1969: US astronaut Neil Armstrong becomes the first man to walk on the moon as *Apollo 12* lands on the lunar surface; Yasir Arafat becomes PLO chairman; North Vietnamese leader Ho Chi Minh dies at age 79; International Red Cross estimates that 1.5 million Biafrans have died, mostly by starvation, in the civil war with Nigeria; the US begins withdrawal of troops from Vietnam; Golda Meir becomes Israeli prime minister; the Concorde supersonic airliner makes its first flight; *Mariner* space probes transmit pictures of Mars back to earth.

1970: An earthquake kills about 30,000 people in Peru; US National Guardsmen kill four Kent State University students during anti-

war protests at the campus and two students are killed at Jackson State following similar demonstrations; the first complete synthesis of a gene is announced by University of Wisconsin scientists; Arab commandos hijack three jets bound for New York from Europe; the civil wars in Nigeria end when Biafra capitulates to the federal government; the Front de Libération du Québec (FLQ) kidnaps British trade commissioner James Cross, and kidnaps and murders Quebec cabinet minister Pierre Laporte; the Canadian federal government responds to this "October Crisis" by invoking the War Measures Act, temporarily suspending civil liberties in Canada; Israel and United Arab Republic declare a 99-day truce in latest conflict; Gambia becomes a republic; a cyclone and tidal wave hit the offshore islands in the Ganges Delta of East Pakistan, leaving at least 168,000 people dead and about 1 million homeless.

1971: US planes bomb Cambodia, attacking Vietcong supply routes; fighting in Indochina spreads to Laos and Cambodia; the US conducts large-scale bombing raids against North Vietnam; mainland China is admitted to the United Nations; women are granted the right to vote in Switzerland; violence in Northern Ireland escalates after Britain introduces policies of internment without trial; India fights with the Bengali rebels against Pakistan; the US and USSR sign a treaty banning nuclear weapons on the ocean floor; Algeria seizes majority control of all French oil and gas interests within its borders but promises restitution; Idi Amin takes control over Uganda; Mao Zedong's heir-apparent, Lin Piao, dies in a mysterious air crash; the USSR soft-lands a space capsule on Mars; a Los Angeles earthquake kills 60 people and causes $1 billion in damage; the hormone that controls human growth is synthesized by Dr. Choh Hao Li at the University of California.

1972: The world's largest diamond (969.8 carats) is unearthed in Sierra Leone; US Pres. Richard Nixon meets Mao Zedong in China; Britain imposes direct rule on Northern Ireland and 467 people are killed in violence between Catholics and Protestants; Ceylon becomes a republic and changes its name to Sri Lanka; Philippine Pres. Ferdinand Marcos assumes near-dictatorial powers; a Soviet spacecraft soft-lands on Venus; more than 70 nations sign a treaty prohibiting the stockpiling of biological weapons; the US conducts its heaviest B-52 bombing raids of the war against North Vietnam but continues to withdraw troops, despite lack of progress at Paris peace talks; Arab terrorists massacre 11 Israeli Olympic athletes in a stand-off with West German police at the summer Olympic games in Munich; Richard Leakey and Glynn Isaac discover a 2.5-million-year-old human skull in northern Kenya; a US federal grand jury indicts seven persons, including two former White House aids, on charges of conspiracy to break into the Democratic national headquarters (in the Watergate building) in Washington, DC; Richard Nixon is reelected as US president.

1973: A cease-fire agreement, intended to end the Vietnam war, is signed in Paris; fighting in the Middle East between Israeli and Arab forces (Yom Kippur War) is resolved by a shaky ceasefire; Arab oil-producing states cut petroleum exports to the US, western Europe and Japan because of their support of Israel; the US Senate begins televised hearings on the Watergate scandal and it is revealed that Pres. Nixon had secretly taped all conversations in his White House office; US vice-president resigns in an unrelated scandal; US combat involvement in Indochina officially ends as American planes halt their bombing of Cambodia; typhoon "Nora" leaves 800,000 Filipinos homeless on the island of Luzon; Great Britain, Ireland and Denmark formally join the Common Market; the Bahamas are granted independence from Britain after three centuries of colonial rule; Chilean Marxist Pres. Salvadore Allende is overthrown by a CIA-backed military junta which claims Allende commits suicide; Shah of Iran nationalizes foreign-owned oil companies.

1974: Oil-producing nations boost their prices and worldwide inflation accelerates as economic growth slows to near zero in most industrialized nations; the government of China launches a new "Cultural Revolution" program aimed at condemning both the Chinese philosopher Confucius and former Defence Minister Lin Piao; West German Chancellor Willy Brandt resigns after a scandal involving an East German spy; the Tower of London and the British Houses of Parliament are bombed by the Irish Republican Army; Soviet Nobel prize-winning author Aleksandr Solzhenitsyn is stripped of his citizenship and exiled; Portuguese dictatorship ended by military

coup and democratic reforms are initiated; rebels supported by Greece overthrow government in Cyprus: Turkish forces invade and take over much of the island; India explodes a nuclear device; Syria and Israel agree to the boundaries of a demilitarized zone in the Golan Heights and they begin troop withdrawals from the region; US Pres. Richard Nixon resigns to avoid impeachment by Congress for his coverup of the Watergate scandal; Gerald Ford is sworn in to replace Nixon; the US and Soviet Union reach a tentative agreement to limit the numbers of strategic offensive nuclear weapons and delivery vehicles; severe drought threatens millions in Africa; scientists warn of the effects of chloroflourocarbons (CFCs) on the ozone layer.

1975: Portugal's new constitution grants most power to the military; Angola, Cape Verde, Sâo Tomé and Principe and Mozambique gain independence from Portugal; Turkish Cypriots declare the establishment of a separate state in the northern half of the island; US evacuates as North Vietnam seizes Saigon; Egypt reopens the Suez Canal, which had been closed since the 1967 Arab-Israeli war; a UN Security Council resolution calling for the imposition of an arms embargo against South Africa is vetoed by the US, Great Britain and France; Generalissimo Franco, Spain's chief of state, dies and is replaced by King Juan Carlos I; Peru's president is ousted in a military coup and replaced by a general; a democratic republic is proclaimed in Laos; Papua New Guinea and Surinam become independent; civil war breaks out in Beirut between Christians and Muslims; rebels in Eritrea provoke battles with Ethiopian government.

1976: Chinese Prem. Chou En-lai and Communist Chinese leader Mao Zedong die within months of each other; riots against apartheid take place in the all-black township of Soweto outside of Johannesburg and spread to Cape Town in black townships and white areas; first reports surface that Libyan leader Col. Moammar Qaddafi is financing, training and arming a widespread terrorist network; the Parti Québécois wins power in Quebec's provincial election, raising the possibility of Quebec's secession from Canada; worldwide earthquakes kill an estimated 780,000 people; the Gang of Four (Mao Zedong's widow and three others) unsuccessfully attempt a coup in China; Venezuela nationalizes petroleum industry; president of Argentina overthrown by military junta; Spanish Sahara released from Spain's jurisdiction and divided between Morocco and Mauritania; North and South Vietnam reunited under Communist government; a military coup in Thailand topples the government; 9,000 refugees flee Angolan civil war.

1977: Cambodian refugees report economic and social disaster following the Communists' capture of Phnom Penh; Egypt severs diplomatic relations with Syria, Iraq, Libya, Algeria and South Yemen for attempting to disrupt its peace overtures to Israel; over 570 die in the world's worst aviation disaster when two Boeing 747s collide on the runway on the Canary Island of Tenerife; black South African leader Steven Biko dies in jail; French territories of Afars and Issa unite to form independent Republic of Djibouti; government of Pakistan is overthrown and martial law is imposed; Leonid Brezhnev becomes USSR president and Communist Party chief; Somalia-backed Eritrean guerrillas are stopped by Ethiopian army; Thailand government seized by military junta; Rhodesia's white government announces it will begin negotiations with black majority; cyclone in India leaves 20,000 dead and 2 million homeless; US unmanned spacecrafts *Voyager I* and *II* begin journeys to explore the outer solar system; the neutron bomb, which causes great loss of life but little property damage, is developed in the US.

1978: A Soviet-supported military junta takes power in Afghanistan and Soviet troops occupy the country; Lebanon is torn by Christian and Muslim militia activity as well as Palestinian guerrilla activity, and Arab League intervenes to restore peace; Israeli forces withdraw; Syria declares a unilateral cease-fire in and around Beirut, Lebanon; Egyptian Pres. Anwar Sadat and Israeli Prem. Menachem Begin sign peace accords, mediated by US Pres. Jimmy Carter; Shah Mohammed Riza Pahlevi of Iran imposes martial law to suppress anti-government demonstrations; leftist Sandinista guerrillas attempt to overthrow the government of Nicaraguan Pres. Anastasio Somoza; US establishes full diplomatic relations with Communist China; the first peaceful transfer of power takes place in Dominican Republic; Zaïre invaded by secessionist rebels: defence aid comes from other African nations, and France and Belgium after the massacre of Europeans; military junta seizes power in Honduras; army seizes government power in Bolivia; former Italian Prem. Aldo Moro is kidnapped and murdered by the Red Brigades, a revolutionary terrorist group; John Paul II (Karol Wojtyla) of Poland becomes the first non-Italian Pope in four centuries; the first "test-tube baby" (human baby conceived outside the womb) is born in England.

1979: Armed Islamic revolutionary followers of Ayatollah Khomeini overthrow the government of Iran and the Shah flees; students demanding the Shah's return to stand trial seize hostages at US embassy; a malfunction in the cooling system of a nuclear reactor at Three Mile Island in Pennsylvania, US, closes down the reactor and radiation escapes into the air; Conservative Margaret Thatcher becomes Britain's first female prime minister; a black government is formally installed in Rhodesia and its name is changed to Zimbabwe; China and the US establish formal commercial relations for the first time since 1949; Vietnamese army invades Cambodia and installs new government; St Lucia, St Vincent and the Grenadines become independent; coup in Grenada replaces government leader; president of Uganda, Idi Amin, overthrown; Egypt is expelled from Arab League after signing Camp David peace treaty; first elections for European Parliament held; the US-USSR SALT (Strategic Arms Limitation Treaty) Agreement is signed in Vienna; Iran nationalizes remaining privately-owned industries without compensation; sharp oil price increases contribute to high inflation worldwide; South Korean Pres. Park Chung Hee and his chief body guard are assassinated by a government official; emperor of Central African Empire overthrown; president of El Salvador is ousted by military coup.

1980: Soviet dissident Andrei Sakharov, a Nobel prize-winning physicist, is arrested in Moscow; human interferon, a promising natural disease-fighting substance, is made by gene splicing; Mt St Helens erupts in Washington, in a blast that sends debris 20 km up into the atmosphere and is heard over 300 km away; in a political comeback, Indira Gandhi wins a landslide victory in India's parliamentary elections; Soviet war in Afghanistan escalates as the US imposes an embargo on the sale of grain and high technology to the Soviet Union in response to the continued occupation of Afghanistan, and 50 nations boycott the Moscow Olympics in protest; Roman Catholic Archbishop Oscar Arnulfo Romero, an El Salvadoran reformer, is assassinated while saying mass; some 10,800 Cubans seek asylum in Peru's Cuban embassy and more than 125,000 Cubans escape by boat to the US; Liberian Pres. William Tolbert, Jr, is killed in a coup; military coup in Turkey unseats government; Zimbabwe gains independence from Britain; 350 Bengalis are massacred by native tribal people in India; black guerrillas successfully bomb two South African petroleum plants and a refinery; mass labour strikes in Poland force the government to allow independent trade unions, including Solidarity, led by Lech Walesa; 20 terrorist bomb attacks take place in France; the Iran-Iraq war begins when Iraqi fighter-bombers attack Iranian airfields and lay siege to its southwestern cities; 3,000 are killed in earthquakes centred in southern Italy; 20,000 die in two strong earthquakes in Algeria; *Voyager I* sends back the first pictures of Saturn; wreck of the *Titanic* found in North Atlantic.

1981: Aquired Immune Deficiency Syndrome (AIDS) is first recognized, in the US; in El Salvador, heavy fighting occurs between the government and leftist insurgents; the world's first reusable spacecraft, the Space Shuttle *Columbia*, is sent into space; clashes between Syrian troops and Christian militiamen in Lebanon are followed by Israeli bombing in support of Christian forces; artificial bone and skin are developed in the US; Pope John Paul II is shot and seriously wounded outside the Vatican by a Turkish terrorist; Israel is condemned worldwide after Israeli warplanes destroy an Iraqi atomic reactor near Baghdad; Irish prisoners in Belfast stage hunger strikes to force the British government to grant political prisoner status to Irish nationalist inmates, and some die; South African troops invade Angola in pursuit of guerrillas; Belize, formerly British Honduras, becomes independent from Britain; Pres. Anwar el-Sadat of Egypt is assassinated by Muslim extremists during a military parade; Israel formally annexes the Golan Heights; a five-day war between Ecuador and Peru erupts over a border dispute; Greece joins the European Community; Italian government rocked by revelation that nearly 1,000 key government, army and business leaders support a secret outlawed Masonic lodge; president of Bangladesh assassinated; Iranian president, prime minister and 29 others killed in bomb attack; 5,000 die when Indonesian ferry sinks in Java Sea; martial law is instituted in Poland in the face of continued labour unrest; the personal computer is introduced by IBM in the US.

1982: Argentina moves to reclaim Malvinas (the Falkland Islands) from UK by invading the territory; Britain defeats Argentina in the subsequent war; Canada gains the power to amend its own constitution from Britain; Israel withdraws from the Sinai and turns it over to Egypt, fulfilling their 1979 peace treaty; Israel invades Lebanon and the PLO leadership leaves Lebanon under UN protection; Lebanese Christian militiamen massacre Palestinians in refugee camps and Israel is accused of indirectly aiding the attack; Iran invades Iraq, but Iraq claims to have killed 27,000 Iranians in 18 days of battle; a series of IRA bombs explode in London, killing nine and wounding 51; western nations debate a proposed Soviet oil pipeline to western Europe; Lech Walesa, former leader of Solidarity, the outlawed Polish labour union, is freed after 11 months of imprisonment; military coups in Bangladesh and Guatemala force changes in government; Soviet leader Leonid Brezhnev dies and Yuri Andropov succeeds him; in Cambodia, support for Khmer Rouge grows as coalition against Vietnamese-backed government joined by Prince Sihanouk; up to 1,200 Afghan civilians and Soviet soldiers die in a tunnel explosion caused by the collision of two trucks; the first permanent artificial heart is transplanted into Dr Barney B. Clark, 61, in Utah; Mexican volcano, El Chichón, erupts, blasting debris into the stratosphere.

1983: Klaus Barbie, former chief of the German Gestapo in Lyons, France, during WW II is deported to France from Bolivia to face charges of "crimes against humanity"; Soviet citizens and diplomats accused of espionage are expelled from France, Spain, the US and Britain; the US government is accused of having illegally aided Nicaraguan rebels; anti-government protests increase in Chile, governed by Gen. Pinochet; Ethiopia appeals for aid to 4 million victims of drought and famine; Sri Lankan Sinhalese and Tamil forces clash, killing hundreds and destroying the homes of thousands of others; 1,200 die in an earthquake in Turkey; martial law is formally lifted in Poland; the Organization of Petroleum Exporting Countries (OPEC) agrees to cut crude oil prices for the first time in its 23-year-history; all 269 people aboard are killed when the Soviet Union shoots down a South Korean airliner, claiming that the plane had been on a spying mission and strayed into Soviet airspace; Benigno Aquino, opponent of Philippine Pres. Marcos, returns to Manila and is assassinated; 241 US Marines and sailors and 40 French paratroopers, members of a multinational peacekeeping force in Lebanon, are killed by suicide terrorists; the US and France support Chad's government against Libyan-supported guerrillas; Israeli withdrawal from Lebanon is followed by full-scale fighting between Lebanese ethnic and religious groups; US-led forces invade the small island of Grenada; US Cruise missiles in Europe are deployed in Britain despite Soviet and civilian opposition; white South Africans approve a new constitution granting limited political participation for persons of mixed race and Asians, but not for blacks, in a new tricameral legislature; Yasir Arafat and PLO guerrillas are evacuated from Lebanon to Tunis, under UN sponsorship; riots in Assam, India claim 5,000 lives and 300,000 refugees flee; the compact disc is introduced; after an 11-year journey, the *Pioneer 10* spacecraft leaves the solar system.

1984: Cholesterol is linked to heart disease following a 10-year study by US researchers; the Apple Macintosh with mouse enters the personal computer market; Konstantin Chernenko becomes Soviet leader following the death of Yuri Andropov; US astronauts fly free of the space shuttle *Challenger*, the first humans to do so without a tether; US and UN forces are withdrawn from Lebanon; French and American researchers, working separately, report that they have identified viruses which appear to be the cause of AIDS; Saudi, Greek and Swiss tankers are attacked by both Iran and Iraq in the Persian Gulf and Saudi Arabia shoots down two Iranian jets; hundreds die during a battle for the Golden Temple in Amritsar between Sikh militants and police in India; Indian Prime Min. Indira Gandhi is slain by two of her Sikh bodyguards in New Delhi and widespread violence follows; Daniel Ortega, Sandinista leader, wins in Nicaraguan elections; the international community sends aid to starving

Ethiopians; in a secret operation, Israel airlifts 25,000 Ethiopian Jews (Falashas) out of the Sudan; Britain and China finalize an agreement on Hong Kong's future, guaranteeing its capitalist system for 50 years after it is turned over to China in 1997; a Union Carbide chemical plant leak kills 2,500 in Bhopal, India; the European Space Agency launches the largest telecommunications satellite in the world.

1985: South African police kill 18 blacks commemorating the Sharpville massacre in 1960, 19 more are killed while participating in a funeral procession and later the government declares a state of emergency; Daniel Ortega becomes president of Nicaragua; US president urges military aid to Nicaraguan opposition forces but only humanitarian aid is approved; Mikhail Gorbachev succeeds Konstantin Chernenko as Soviet leader and he opens disarmament talks with the US; Iraq turns back an Iranian offensive, allegedly killing 30,000 to 50,000 Iranians; Shiite Muslim hijackers release hostages after 17 days of captivity in Beirut, having demanded the release of hundreds of Shiites detained by Israeli forces; Argentine president imposes drastic economic measures to cut 1,010 percent inflation rate; top French officials are linked to the bombing of a ship owned by Greenpeace; two leading Soviet KGB officials defect to Britain and the US, where both name Soviet spies in the two countries; a cyclone and tidal waves hit Bangladesh, killing 10,000; a Mexican earthquake kills more than 7,000 and causes widespread destruction, leaving thousands homeless; border dispute between Mali and Burkina Faso leads to war but is eventually referred to International Court of Justice; Nicaragua suspends civil rights; four Palestinians seize the Italian cruise ship *Achille Lauro* off the coast of Egypt, murdering a wheelchair-bound American; Reagan and Gorbachev meet at the first superpower summit in six years; 95 Colombians die when 60 rebels seize the Palace of Justice in Bogotá and take more than 300 persons hostage; 60 die when Arab gunmen hijack an Egyptian jetliner, in an act allegedly backed by Libya's leader Col. Muammar Qaddafi; a Colombian volcanic eruption kills 20,000 people; Guatemala elects its first civilian president following three decades of military rule; Uruguay's military government replaced by civilian government; Sudanese and Ugandan presidents ousted by military coups; terrorists kill 20 people at two airports (in Rome and Vienna), both at the ticket counters of El Al, Israel's national airline; Live Aid rock concert in London, UK and Philadelphia, US raises over $60 million for African famine relief.

1986: Portugal and Spain join the European Community; Jean-Claude Duvalier, Haiti's "president for life," flees to France in the face of nationwide protest; Portugal elects its first civilian president in 60 years; Gorbachev calls for "radical reform" of Soviet economy and reshapes the leadership of the Communist party; Philippine Pres. Ferdinand Marcos flees to the US after allegations of electoral fraud; his opponent, Corazon Aquino, succeeds Marcos as president; Swedish Prime Min. Olof Palme is assassinated; former UN secretary general Kurt Waldheim is elected president of Austria; US planes bomb Libya citing retaliatory measures after missile attacks; radiation is spread following the meltdown of the Chernobyl nuclear power plant in the USSR; South African forces attack alleged African National Congress (ANC) bases in neighbouring Botswana, Zambia and Zimbabwe; the *New York Times* first links Panama's General Manuel Noriega with drug and arms trafficking; US president acknowledges a secret and illegal arms deal with Iran: the "Iran-Contra Affair" involving the US sale of arms in exchange for hostages is first reported in a Lebanese newspaper; The US space shuttle *Challenger* explodes one minute after liftoff and all seven crew members die instantly; *Voyager 2* spacecraft passes Uranus.

1987: Soviet leader Mikhail Gorbachev begins a campaign for openness (glasnost) and reconstruction (perestroika); Tamil separatists kill hundreds of Sri Lankans, mostly Sinhalese, and clash with government forces; German pilot Mathias Rust, 19, embarrasses Soviets when he lands his single-engine Cessna in Red Square, Moscow; Moscow's Communist Party chief, Boris Yeltsin, is dismissed after criticizing Soviet leader Gorbachev; South Africa withdraws its troops from Angola; an Iraqi warplane's missile kills 37 US sailors in the Persian Gulf, and the US escorts Kuwaiti oil tankers despite danger posed by the Iran-Iraq war; 402 Iranian pilgrims to Mecca die in battles with Saudi police; 24 nations sign a treaty to protect the ozone layer; Portugal and China agree that the Portuguese colony of Macao will be returned to China in 1999; stock market prices plunge worldwide; the Palestinian intifadah (uprising) begins against Israeli authorities in the Gaza Strip and West Bank, and thousands of protesters are imprisoned; Syrian troops enter Beirut in an attempt to bring a cease-fire; Lebanese prime minister dies in a bomb attack; a military coup ousts coalition government in Chad; 2,000 die in the Philippines when a ferry sinks.

1988: Nicaraguan contras and the Sandinista government reach a cease-fire agreement; the US and Soviet Union sign a treaty on intermediate-range nuclear forces (INF); Soviet troops begin to pull out of Afghanistan after a nine-year occupation; nationalist groups in Soviet-controlled Azerbaijan and Armenia clash; Colombian drug cartels defy government attempts to bring them to justice, and fight among themselves; prime minister of Poland promises co-operation with non-communist groups; a US navy warship accidentally shoots down a commercial Iranian airliner over the Persian Gulf, killing all 290 persons aboard; the Soviet communist party backs Gorbachev's plan for perestroika; Canadian and US governments ratify a free trade agreement, to take effect Jan. 1, 1989; Iran and Iraq agree on a cease-fire to end their eight-year war; Iraq uses poison gas on its Kurdish minority and razes Kurdish villages; Libya and Chad formally end their war; Thailand and Laos do battle in a brief border dispute; Ethiopia and Somalia end 11 years of disputes over borders with a peace treaty; Solidarity supporters stage widespread strikes in Poland; Vietnamese troops leave Kampuchea; a military coup in Burma causes a change in leadership; Yugoslavia's inflation rate tops 250%, ethnic Albanians in Kosovo province demand freedom from Serbian rule; Benazir Bhutto, daughter of a former Pakistani president, becomes prime minister of Pakistan; 270 people die when a bomb blows up a Pan Am jetliner over Lockerbie, Scotland; 25,000 Armenians die during an earthquake.

1989: Iran's Ayatollah Khomeini calls for the execution of author Salman Rushdie for blaspheming the prophet Mohammed; the Soviet Union holds historic multicandidate parliamentary elections and Boris Yeltsin emerges as Russian leader; Japanese Prime Min.

Noboru Takeshita is toppled by financial scandal, Emperor Hirohita dies and is succeeded by his son; Chinese students lead more than one million in demonstrations for democratic reforms, but spreading unrest is checked by a government crackdown in Tiananmen Square that is suspected to have killed thousands; Hungary opens its border with Austria and moves toward political and economic reform; anti-Communist forces continue to battle the government in Afghanistan; fighting between Christians and Muslims in Beirut intensifies; 90 people die in ethnic violence in Soviet Uzbekistan; Poles participate in their first open election in 40 years and Solidarity wins a solid victory; the three Baltic states (Estonia, Latvia and Lithuania) protest Soviet domination; a Colombian presidential candidate is slain, prompting a renewed crackdown on illegal drug traffickers; thousands of East Germans flee to West Germany and the East German government proposes political reforms; Vietnamese forces withdraw from Cambodia; East German communist leader Erich Honecker is removed from power, he is later charged with corruption; thousands demonstrate in Czech-oslovakia and force the communist government to resign, Vaclav Havel is elected president; the spaceship *Atlantis* is launched on a journey to Jupiter; East Germany opens the Berlin wall after 28 years and lifts visa and emigration restrictions; Panama's General Noriega annuls presidential elections after an opposition party victory, the US invades Panama and Noriega goes into hiding; Romanian Pres. Nicolae Ceausescu is overthrown and executed with his wife for genocide, abuse of power and theft; 80 nations sign an agreement to limit production of chorofluorocarbons (CFCs) to protect the ozone layer; Paraguay's president is toppled by a military coup; the Exxon *Valdez* runs aground in Alaska and spills thousands of litres of oil; *Voyager 2* spacecraft reaches Neptune.

1990: Panama's Manuel Noriega surrenders to US authorities; violence erupts in Soviet Azerbaijan as Azerbaijanis attack Armenians; Bulgaria and Yugoslavia switch to multiparty systems; Violeta Chamorro defeats Sandinista leader Daniel Ortega to become the Nicaraguan president; South African government lifts restrictions on opposition organizations and declares amnesty for political pris-

oners, black leader Nelson Mandela is freed after 27 years in prison; the US, France, Great Britain and the Soviet Union reach agreement on a reunited Germany; Lithuania proclaims its sovereignty and Soviet troops move in; many Soviet communists are defeated by reformers in city council elections; Namibia gains independence from South Africa; newly-released Soviet documents prove Soviet secret police killed 15,000 Polish military officers in the Katyn forest massacre of 1940; the $1.5-billion Hubble Space Telescope is sent into space, but flawed light-gathering mirrors distort transmissions;   Iran's worst earthquake kills 40,000; more than 1,400 Muslim pilgrims to Mecca suffocate in a stampede in an overcrowded tunnel; the Ukraine declares its sovereignty within the Soviet Union; the two Germanys reunite, merging their economic, legal and political systems; Czechoslovakia and Romania hold their first free elections in the postwar era (Aug. 2); Iraq invades Kuwait over disagreements regarding oil production levels and appears ready to invade Saudi Arabia; the UN passes sweeping trade and financial sanctions against Iraq, and aid and troops pour into Saudi Arabia; Pakistani Prime Min. Benazir Bhutto is overthrown on charges of corruption and nepotism; civil war in black South African townships kills hundreds; the first human gene therapy for disease is done by blood transfusion; South Africa bans racial discrimination in public places; following a political challenge from within her own party, British Prime Min. Margaret Thatcher resigns and is succeeded by John Major; India's National Front coalition government is defeated and Chandra Shekhar becomes prime minister; Mozam-bique adopts a constitution allowing for a multiparty democracy; civil war in Chad ends with overthrow of president; a military coup in Bangladesh unseats the president; Soviet Pres. Mikhail Gorbachev proposes Union Treaty to restructure Soviet Union; Helmut Kohl elected Chancellor of Unified Germany; Lech Walesa elected president of Poland; African National Congress (ANC) holds first conference in South Africa in 31 years; Rev. Jean-Bertrand Aristide elected president of Haiti; Edward Shevardnadze resigns as Soviet foreign minister; Slovenia and Croatia initiate secession from Yugoslavian republic.

1991: Iraq ignores Jan. 15 deadline for withdrawal from Kuwait and Allied forces (including the US, Canada, Britain, France, Italy, Japan, Pakistan and members of the Arab League) launch a six-week air attack; Soviets suppress independence movements in Baltic republics; US and Italy begin rescue of foreigners trapped in Somalian civil war; limited integration of schools begins in South Africa and sweeping reforms of apartheid law are proposed; Allies launch ground assault on Iraqi forces and informal cease-fire follows; 1,200 killed in major earthquake in Pakistan and Afghanistan; Lithuanians vote to secede from Soviet Union; military seizes power in Thailand; Canada, the US and Mexico begin trade talks; Estonia and Latvia vote for independence from the Soviet Union; violent protests held in Belgrade to topple Yugoslavian government; Kuwaiti government forced to resign in wake of failure to establish post-war order; Mali government overthrown; UN cease-fire formally ends Gulf War (Apr.) and Kurds flee from Iraq; Soviet republic of Georgia votes for independence; thousands killed in cyclone in Bangladesh; cease-fire declared in Angola's 16-year civil war; Ethiopian Pres. Mengistu deposed; Rajiv Ghandi assassinated during Indian national election campaign; Albania's first non-Communist government confirmed; Boris Yeltsin elected president of Russia; Mt Pinatubo volcano erupts in Philippines; P.V. Narasimha Rao elected prime minister of India; Population Registration Act repealed in South Africa; fighting between Yugoslav military and Slovenian nationalists escalates; Israel agrees to take part in Middle East peace talks; Soviet hardliners attempt a coup against Mikhail Gorbachev: its failure results in the dissolution of the Communist party and a power struggle between Gorbachev and Russian leader Boris Yeltsin; rebels oust Haitian Pres. Jean-Bertrand Aristide; Serbia and Croatia reach political settlement but civil war continues; peace accord signed in El Salvador, paving the way to end of 11-year civil war; failed coup in Soviet Union speeds disintegration of the country as Lithuania, Estonia and Latvia act to enforce their independence; civil war in Croatia escalates; Philippine senate refuses to renew lease on US naval base; warring factions in Cambodia sign peace accord; members of EC and European Free Trade Area agree to create world's largest common market (European Economic Area) in 1993; Kiichi Miyazawa unseats Toshiki Kaifu as party leader and becomes prime minister of Japan; talks on new constitution begin in South Africa; rebels fighting in Somalia claim to have taken over Mogadishu and deposed the president; last oil well fire in Kuwait capped; Gorbachev resigns as USSR formally dissolved and CIS created; North and South Korea sign non-aggression pact; fighting escalates in Somalia; Slovenia and Croatia recognized as independent states by Germany; Islamic Salvation Front leads in Algerian elections; by year-end, cholera epidemic has killed 3,500 in Latin America and 12,500 in Africa.

1992: A Jan. military coup in Algeria gave power to a committee, which cancelled elections and outlawed its political rival, the Islamic Salvation Front (Mar.); in June the Algerian president was assassinated and power was assumed by the defense minister. In Afghanistan, the communist government backed by the former Soviet Union fell in Apr., after 14 years of fighting; interfactional fighting among the victorious mujaheddin continued throughout most of the year as rivals sought to secure power. Brazil was the site of the Earth Summit (June), which saw 100 world leaders and 30,000 participants gather in Rio de Janeiro to discuss worldwide environmental protection; the country was rocked by political unrest in Aug., which resulted in the end of the presidency of President Fernando Collor de Mello over an influence-peddling and bribery scandal. The European Community's Maastricht Treaty was first rejected by Denmark (June), then ratified by Irish (June) and French (Sept.) voters, and the Italian senate (Sept.). The leader of Colombia's drug cartel, Pablo Escobar, escaped from his custom-built prison during a bungled transfer (July) and stayed at large for the rest of the year. Czechoslovakia's president, Vaclav Havel, resigned on July 20 and the Parliament of Slovakia declared its sovereignty. An earthquake on Oct. 12 left 300 dead and thousands injured in Egypt. The Uruguay round of the GATT (General Agreement on Tariffs and Trade) negotiations remained stalled over the issue of farm subsidies. The president of Georgia was driven from office by fierce fighting around the capital (Jan.); by Mar., former Soviet foreign minister Eduard Shevardnadze had returned to assume legislative and executive power. Germany was plagued by riots and firebombings staged by right-wing extremists attacking foreign-born workers and refugees; German citizens rallied to protest. The OAS (Organization of American States) continued to try and reinstate Haiti's exiled president, Jean-Bertrand Aristide, without success. Israel's June national election resulted in a victory for the Labour Party and its leader, Yitzhak Rabin; in Aug., Rabin began to hint that compromise in the area of peace and territorial disputes might be possible. Italy continued an anti-Mafia crackdown despite the assassination of two prominent judges and a police investigator. In Iraq, the year was marked by a series of stand-offs with UN monitors attempting to enforce the terms of the Gulf War cease-fire. Jamaica's president Michael Manley resigned due to ill health and Percival Patterson was elected leader of the ruling party. Libya was the target of sanctions early in the year in an effort to force the surrender of suspects in the 1988 bombing of a Pan Am jet that crashed near Lockerbie, Scotland. A ruptured petrol pipeline in Mexico's working-class district of Guadalajara was blamed for an explosion that killed 200 and injured nearly 1,500 in Apr.. On Oct. 4, an El Al cargo plane crashed into two nine-storey apartment buildings close to the Netherland's Schipol airport. Nicaragua was hit by a powerful earthquake in Sept., which unleashed a series of tidal waves that killed 56 and left thousands homeless. Heavy rains and flash floods killed at least 650 people in northern and eastern Pakistan in Sept.. Peru's president, Alberto Fujimori, suspended sections of the country's constitution in Apr. and seized power, citing a need to root out corruption and combat the combined forces of the Shining Path guerrillas and various drug barons. Russia's first experiments with free markets triggered soaring inflation and shortages. Civil war in Somalia brought 4.5 million of its people to the brink of starvation; by Aug. the UN brought in forces to ensure that food was distributed to the hungry, but was unable to restore order; by Sept. the flights were targeted to remote villages in an effort to ensure that the hungry received the food. The government in South Africa continued to work towards a power-sharing agreement with the black majority after receiving nearly 70% support in a Mar. whites-only referendum; negotiations were broken off after hundreds of armed blacks attacked residents of the Boipatong settlement in June, killing 42 and tarnishing President de Klerk's government

with charges of collusion with the killers; in Sept. troops from the Ciskei homeland opened fire on ANC supporters massed at the border and talks on democratic reform were again delayed. Citizens in Thailand took to the streets in a series of demonstrations that forced Gen. Suchinda Kraprayoon to resign as the head of government by the end of May; at least 40 people were killed during the unrest but constitutional reforms were instituted and democratic elections were scheduled. In the United Kingdom, John Major's Conservative party won reelection to a fourth term with a reduced majority (Apr.); by Aug. the scandals of the royal family began to threaten the credibility of the monarchy; uncertainty over the fate of the Maastricht Treaty and pressure on UK currency forced a withdrawal from the European Monetary System in Sept. and a devaluation of the UK pound. In the United States, riots in Los Angeles in late Apr./early May left 42 dead, and damage was high; the US state of Florida was devastated by Hurricane Andrew (Aug.) which did an estimated $15 billion damage; on Oct. 12, the *Pioneer* spacecraft plunged into the scorching atmosphere surrounding the planet Venus and ended a 14-year space mission; in Nov., Republicans George Bush and Dan Quayle were defeated in their bid for reelection as the Democrats, under Bill Clinton and Al Gore, were elected to a four-year term. Yugoslavia continued to disintegrate: the UN Security Council deployed peacekeepers in Jan.; Croatia and Slovenia were given diplomatic recognition by the European community as well as 20 other countries (including Canada); by Feb., Serbia and Montenegro reached agreement on a common state retaining the Yugoslav flag, anthem and joint parliament; in Mar., citizens of the republic of Bosnia-Hercegovina voted for independence; however, ethnic fighting over Bosnian territory escalated throughout the year amid charges of "ethnic cleansing" and atrocities, and a series of cease-fires that rarely held for more than a few days; by the end of May, refugees began to arrive in neighbouring countries; in Sept., an attack on an Italian relief plane delivering supplies to Sarajevo forced the suspension of all flights for a month; on Sept. 22, Yugoslavia (Serbia and Montenegro) was expelled from the UN General Assembly.

1993: For 1993, see News Events of the Year.

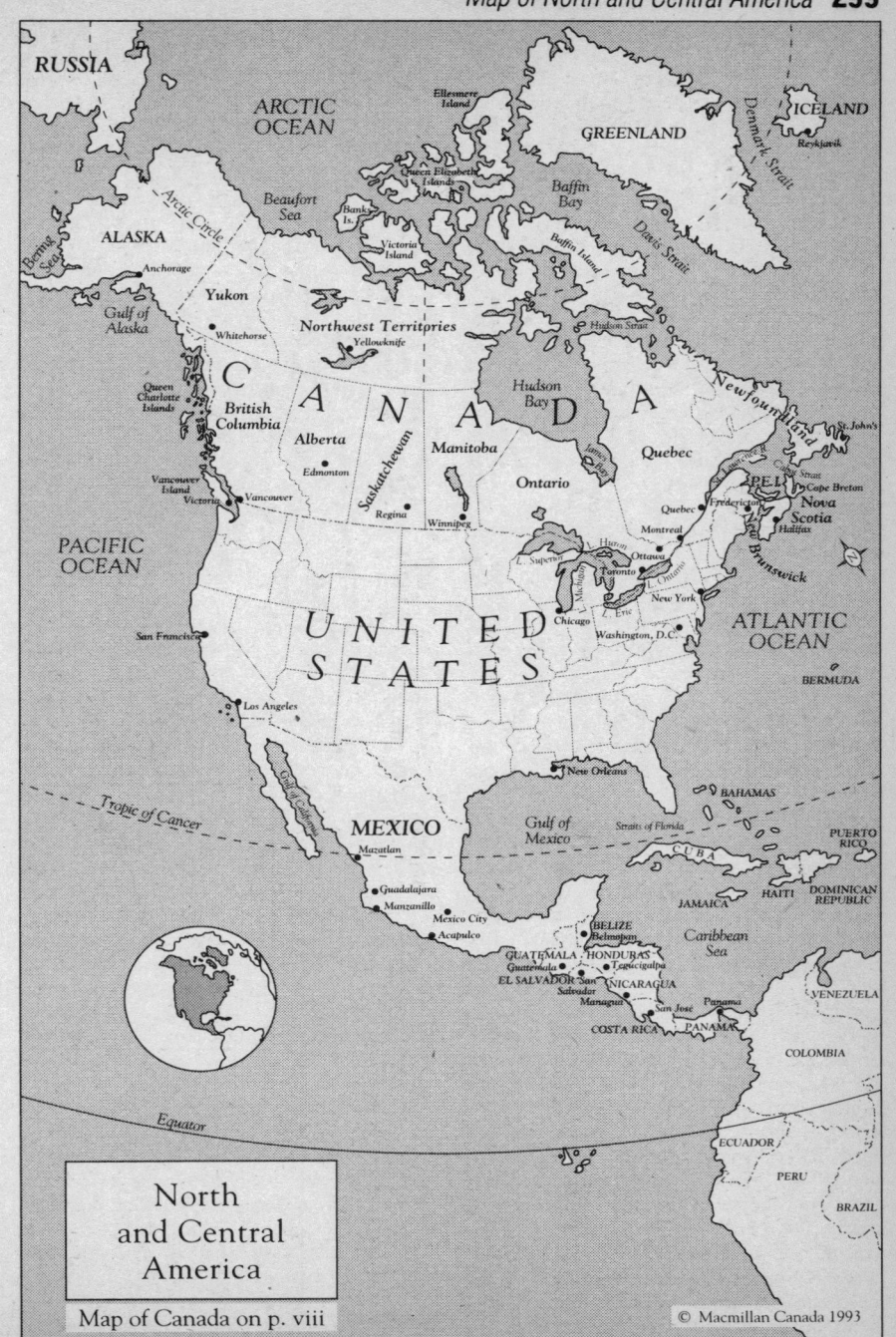

North
and Central
America

Map of Canada on p. viii

© Macmillan Canada 1993

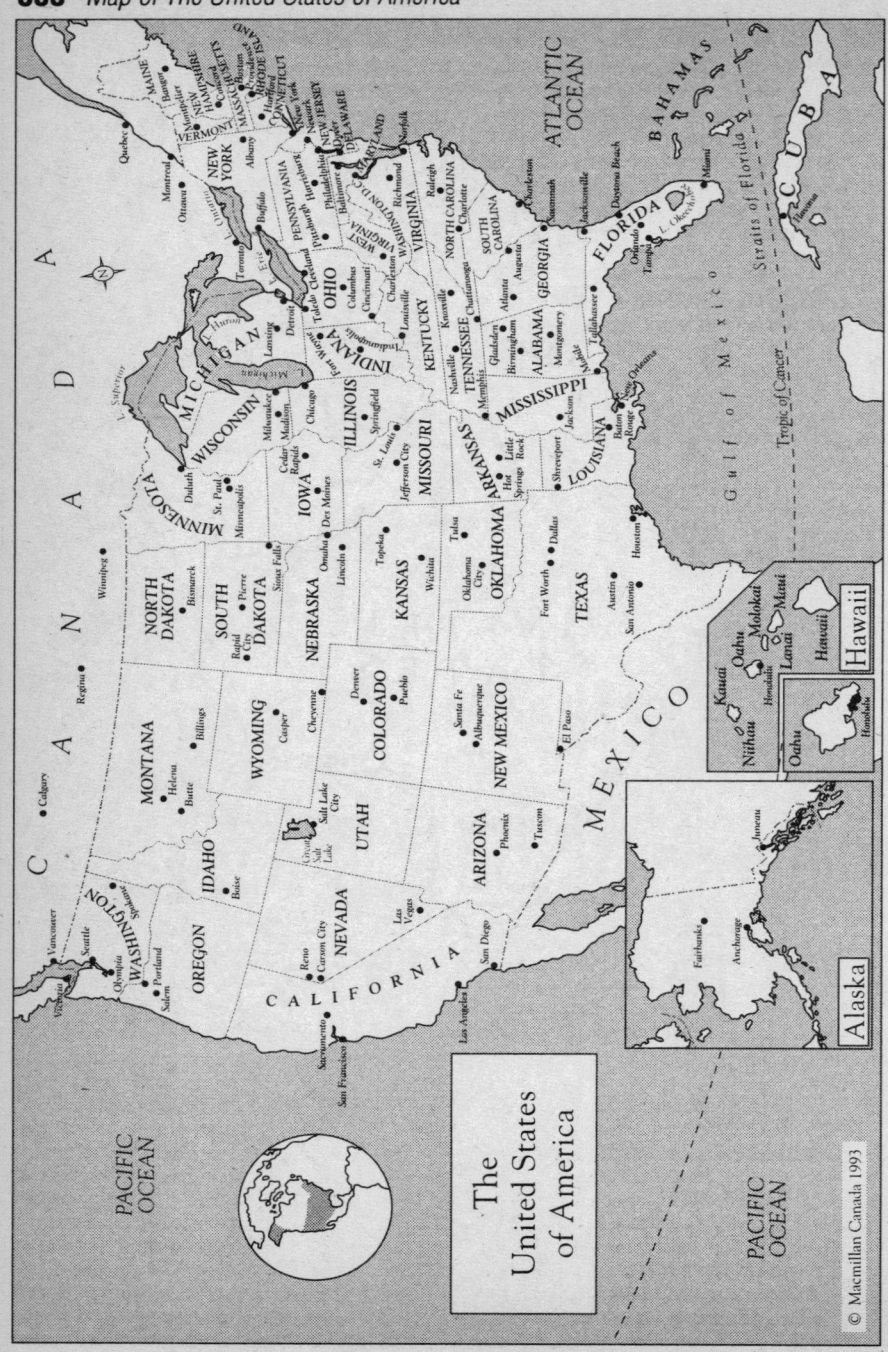

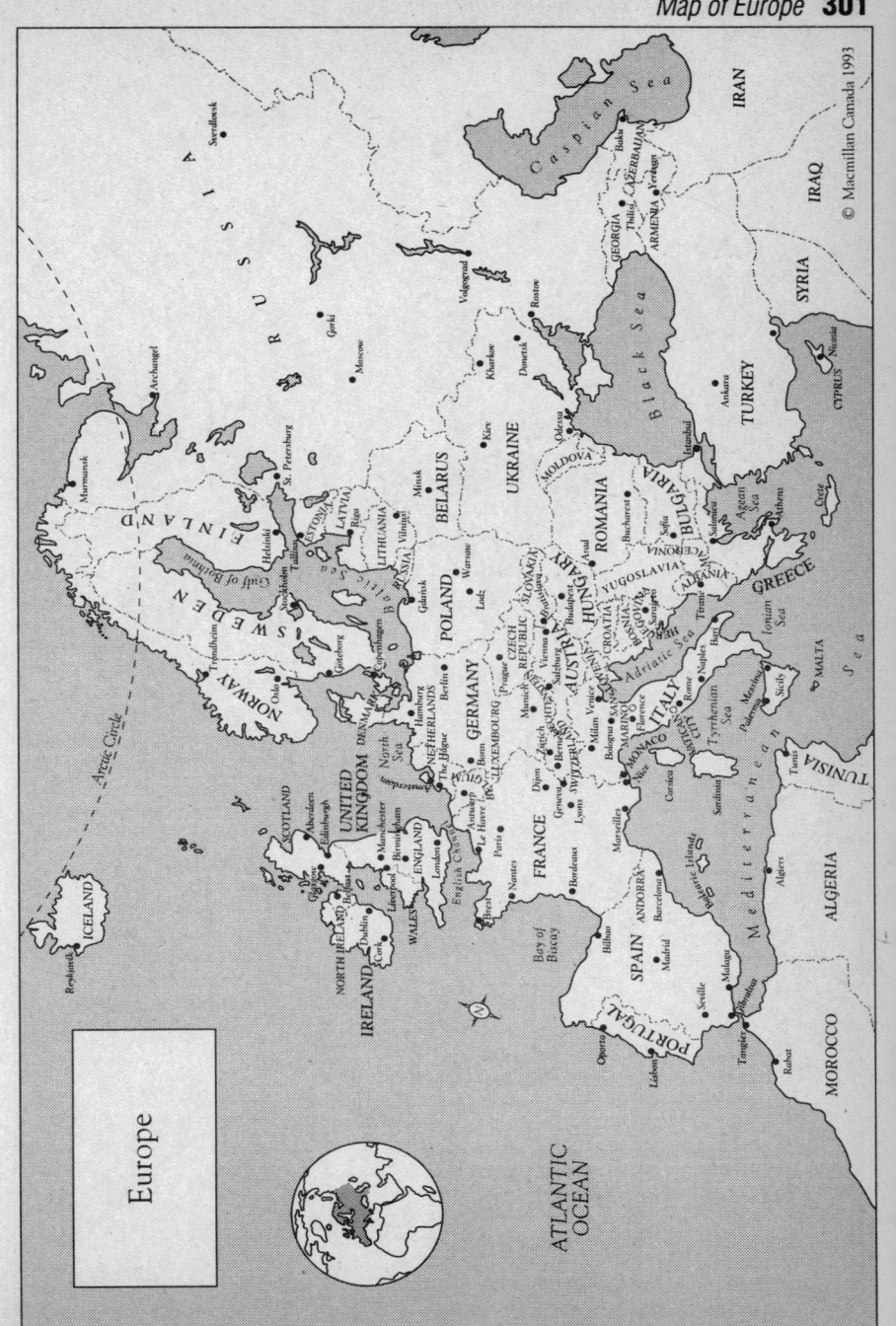

Europe

ATLANTIC OCEAN

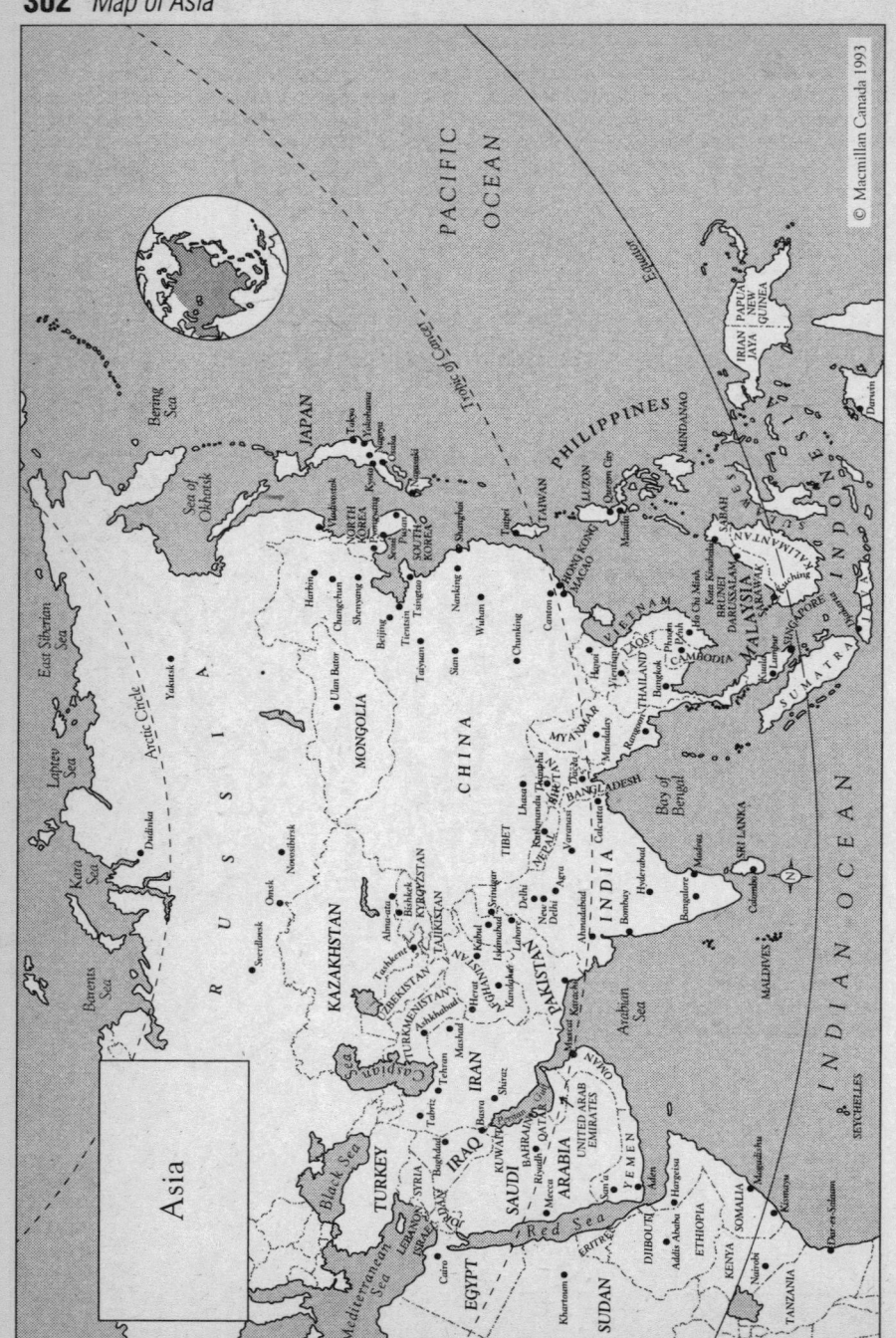

© Macmillan Canada 1993

Asia

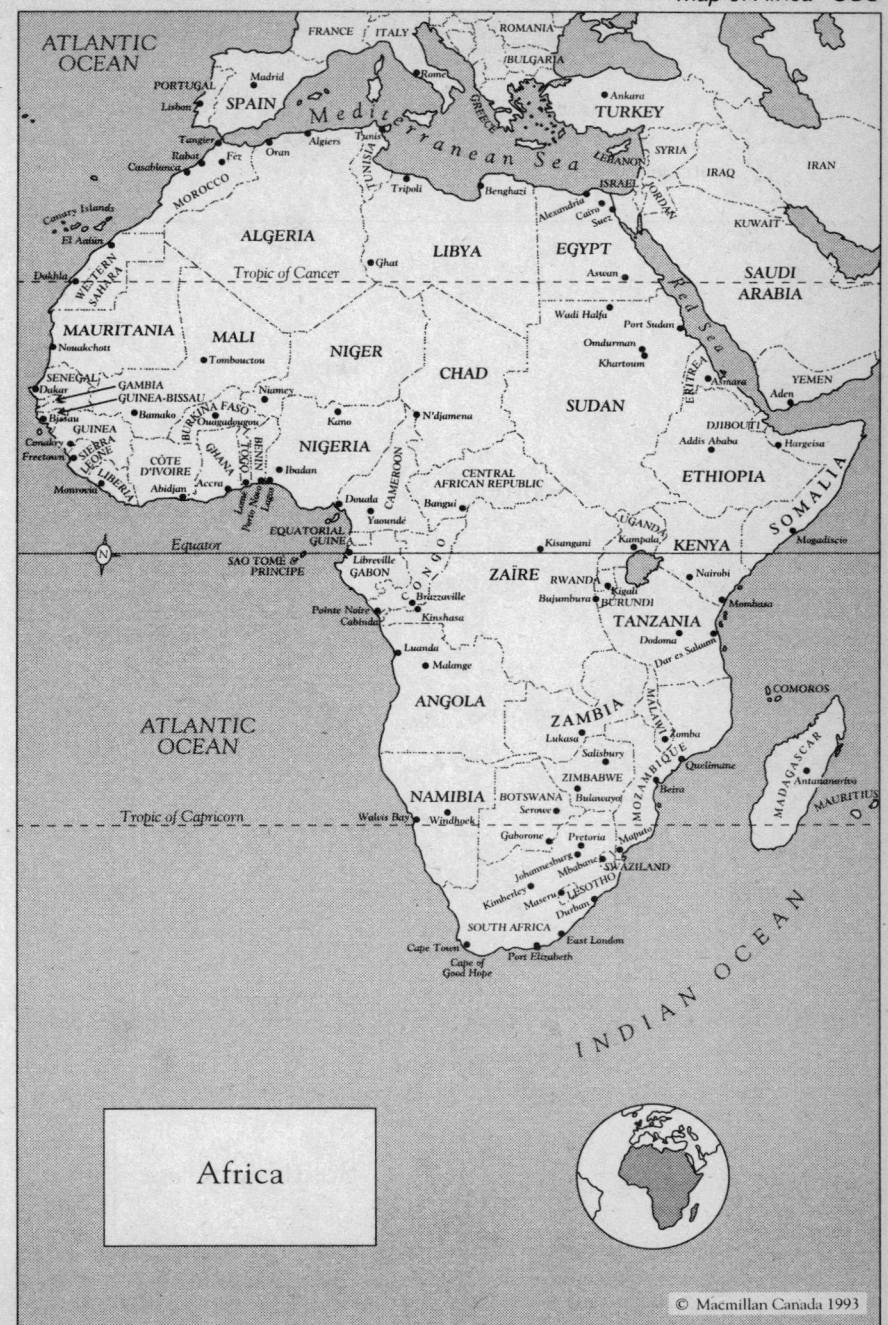

ATLANTIC
OCEAN

FRANCE
ITALY
ROMANIA
/BULGARIA
GREECE

PORTUGAL
Madrid
Rome
Ankara
TURKEY

Lisbon
SPAIN
M e d i t e r r a n e a n   S e a
Algiers
Tunis
LEBANON
SYRIA
IRAN

Tangier
Oran
ISRAEL
JORDAN
IRAQ

Rabat
Fez
Tripoli
Benghazi
KUWAIT

Casablanca
Alexandria
Cairo

MOROCCO
Suez

Canary Islands
El Aaiun
ALGERIA
LIBYA
EGYPT
SAUDI
ARABIA

Dakhla
Tropic of Cancer
Ghat
Aswan
Red Sea

WESTERN
SAHARA
Wadi Halfa
Port Sudan

MAURITANIA
MALI
NIGER
Omdurman
Khartoum
ERITREA
Asmara
YEMEN

Nouakchott
Tombouctou
Aden

SENEGAL
Niamey
Kano
CHAD
SUDAN
DJIBOUTI

Dakar
GAMBIA
BURKINA FASO
N'djamena
Addis Ababa
Hargeisa

GUINEA-BISSAU
Bamako
Ouagadougou

Bissau
NIGERIA
CENTRAL
AFRICAN REPUBLIC
ETHIOPIA
SOMALIA

Conakry
GUINEA
Ibadan

Freetown
SIERRA
LEONE
CÔTE
D'IVOIRE
GHANA
Accra
Lagos
Douala
CAMEROON
Bangui

Monrovia
LIBERIA
Abidjan
Porto Novo
Yaoundé
Kisangani
UGANDA
Kampala
KENYA

Equator
SAO TOMÉ &
PRINCIPE
EQUATORIAL
GUINEA
Libreville
GABON
CONGO
Brazzaville
ZAÏRE
RWANDA
Kigali
BURUNDI
Bujumbura
Nairobi
Mogadiscio

Pointe Noire
Cabinda
Kinshasa
TANZANIA
Dodoma
Mombasa

Luanda
Malange
Dar es Salaam
COMOROS

ATLANTIC
OCEAN
ANGOLA
ZAMBIA
Lusaka
MALAWI
Zomba
MOZAMBIQUE

Salisbury
Quelimane
MADAGASCAR
Antananarivo
MAURITIUS

ZIMBABWE
Bulawayo
Beira

Tropic of Capricorn
NAMIBIA
BOTSWANA
Serowe

Walvis Bay
Windhoek
Gaborone
Pretoria
Maputo

Johannesburg
Mbabane
SWAZILAND

Kimberley
Maseru
LESOTHO
Durban

SOUTH AFRICA
East London

Cape Town
Port Elizabeth
INDIAN OCEAN

Cape of
Good Hope

Africa

© Macmillan Canada 1993

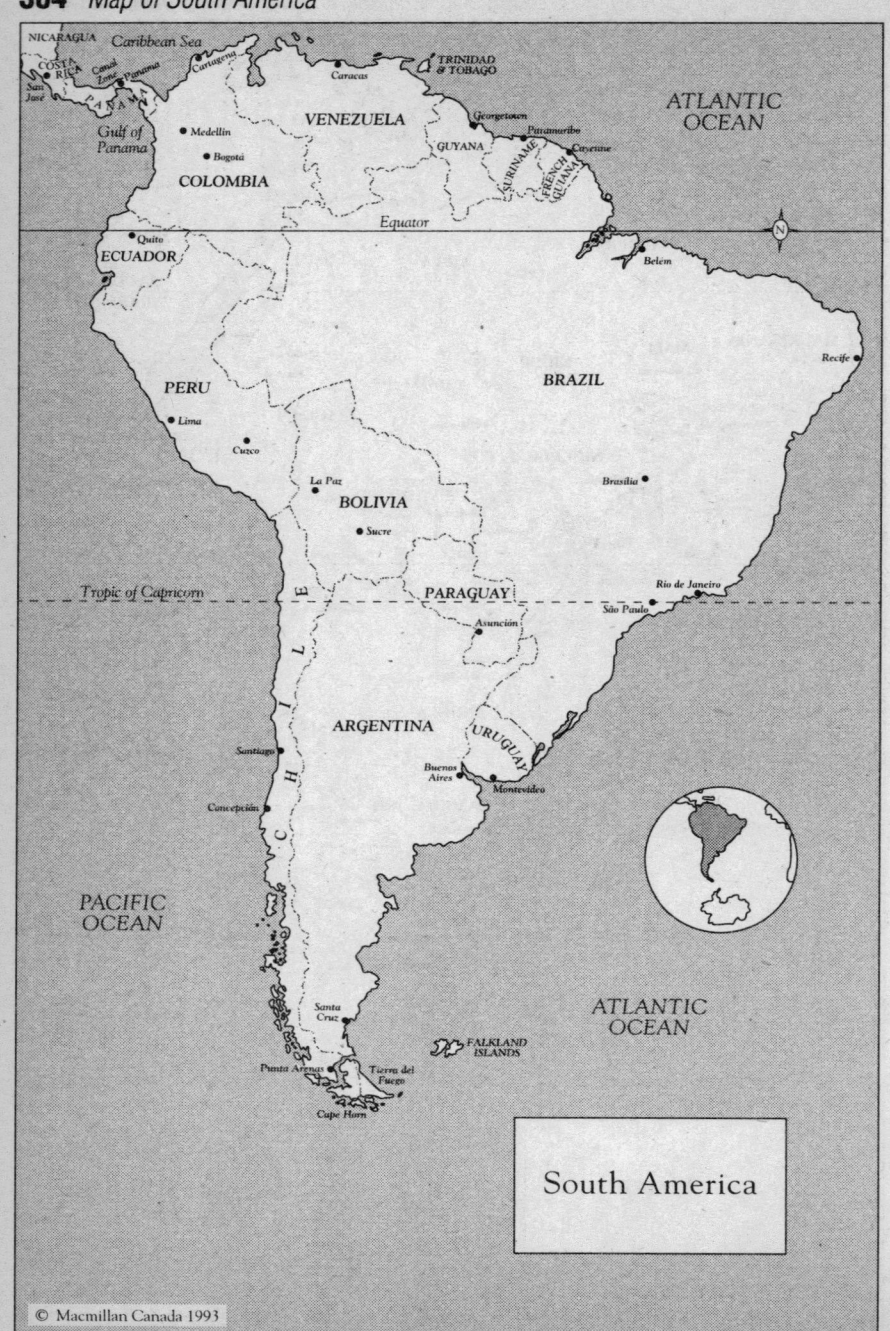

South America

© Macmillan Canada 1993

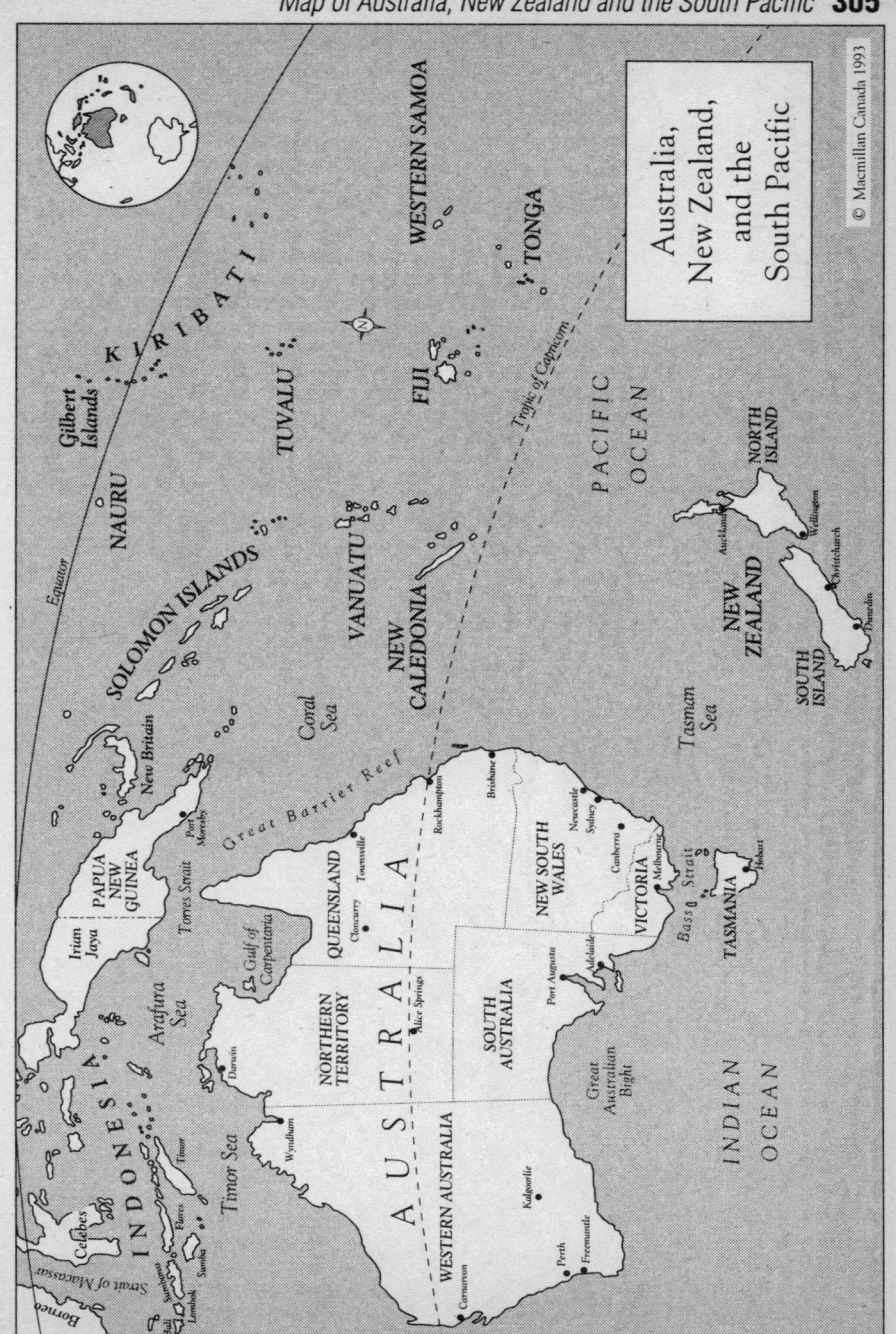

Australia,
New Zealand,
and the
South Pacific

© Macmillan Canada 1993

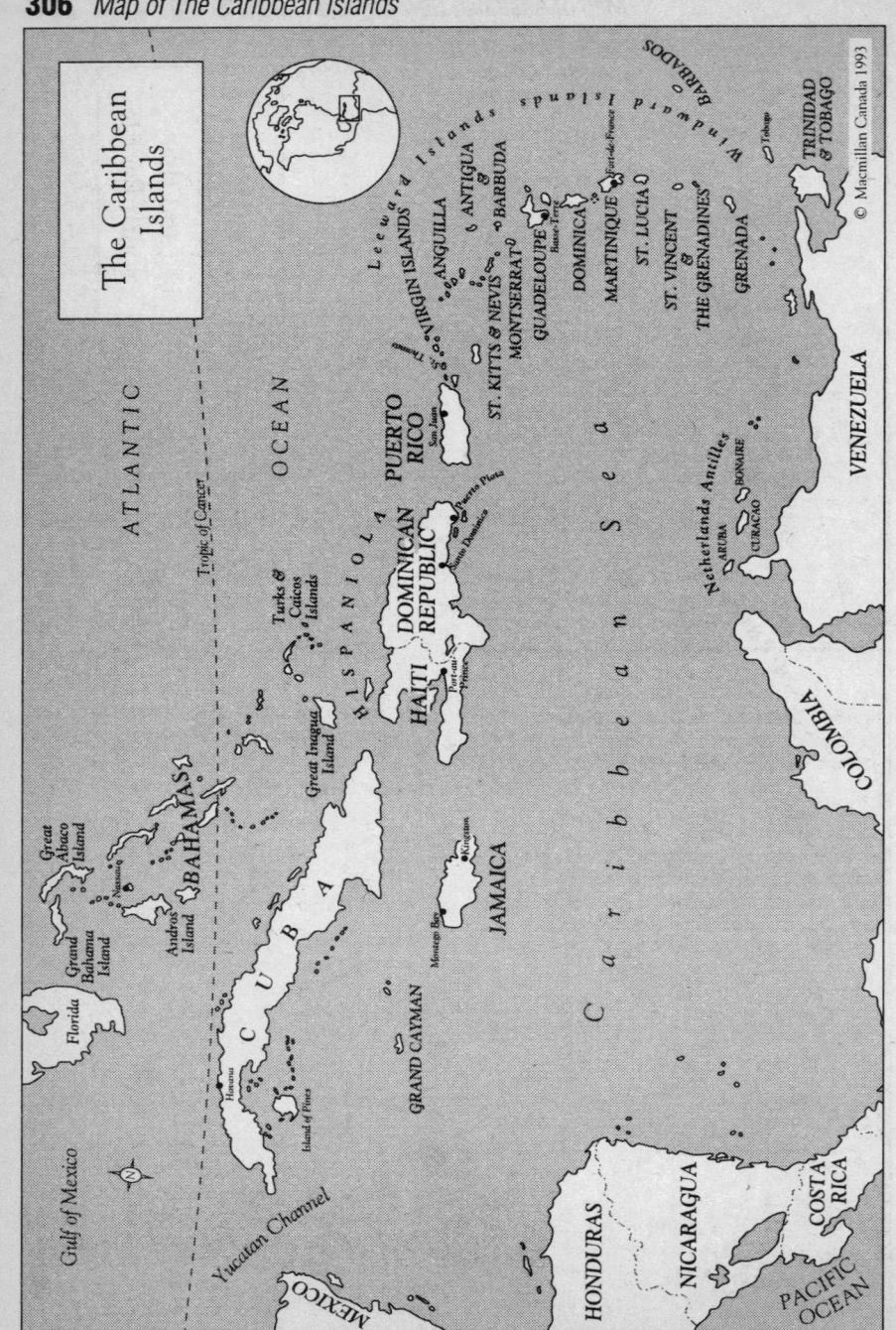

The Caribbean Islands

© Macmillan Canada 1993

THE STATISTICS SHOWN ARE INTENDED TO PRESENT an informative and comparative picture of the various nations of the world and their dependent territories. All data, including the geographic, population and government data, are taken from the latest available sources. The economic and finance/trade data indicate the size of the national economies and the amount of economic activity in the respective countries; health and education data, and communications and transportation data give some evidence of the quality of life and the state of the infrastructure in each nation. All dollar amounts are in US dollars.

The information contained in this section reflects data available up to and including October 1, 1993. Sources used for information include:

The Military Balance, 1991–92 (International Institute for Strategic Studies) • "Civil Aviation Statistics of the World"/ICAO Statistical Yearbook (ICAO) • Demographic Yearbook (UN) • Encyclopedia Britannica • External Affairs Canada • Government Finance Statistics Yearbook (International Monetary Fund) • "Human Development Report" (UN Development Programme) • International Financial Stats Yearbook (International Monetary Fund) • "Keesing's Record of World Events" • Monthly Bulletin of Statistics (UN Statistical Division) • "Population and Vital Statistics Report" (Dept. of International Economic and Social Affairs) • "Social Indicators of Development" (World Bank) • Statesman's Yearbook (Macmillan) • The World Media Handbook 1992-1994 (UN Programme Evaluation and Communication Research Unit) • World Bank Atlas (World Bank) • World Book Encyclopedia • "World Debt Tables 1992-1993" (World Bank) • "World Development Report" (World Bank) • "World Motor Vehicle Data" (Motor Vehicle Manufacturers Assoc. of the US Inc.) • "World Population" (UNESCO) • "World Population Data Sheet" (Population Reference Bureau Inc.) • World Resources 1992-1993 (World Resources Institute) • "World Tables 1992" (John Hopkins UP) • Worldwide Government Directory with International Organizations (Belmont Publications) • Year Book of Labour Statistics, (International Labour Office, Geneva).

Afghanistan

Long-Form Name: Republic of Afghanistan
Capital: Kabul
Population: 19,062,000 (1992)

■ GEOGRAPHY

Area: 652,090 sq. km
Coastline: none: landlocked
Climate: arid to semi-arid; cold winters and hot summers, considerable snowfall
Environment: damaging earthquakes occur in Hindu Kush mountains; soil degradation, desertification, overgrazing, deforestation, pollution
Terrain: mostly rugged mountains; plains in north and southwest
Land Use: 12% arable land; negligible permanent crops; 46% meadows and pastures; 3% forest and woodland; 39% other; includes negligible irrigated
Location: SW Asia (Middle East)

■ PEOPLE

Nationality: Afghan
Ethnic Groups: 50% Pathan, 25% Tajik, 9% Uzbek, 12–15% Hazara; minor ethnic groups include Charar Aimaks, Turkoman, Baloch and others

Languages: 50% Pushtu (official), 35% Afghan Persian (Dari), 11% Turkic languages (Primarily Uzbek and Turmen), 4% thirty minor languages (primarily Balochi and Pahai); much bilingualism
Religions: Islam (nearly 100% – majority Sunni Muslim)
Marriages: n.a.
Divorces: n.a.

■ GOVERNMENT

Leader(s): Pres. Burhanuddin Rabbani
Government Type: authoritarian
Administrative Divisions: 31 provinces
Independence: Aug. 19, 1919 (from UK)
National Holiday: Anniversary of the Suar Revolution, Apr. 27

■ ECONOMY

Overview: a poor country, largely dependent on farming (wheat) and livestock (sheep and goats). The economy is adversely affected by political and military disruptions
GNP: $3 billion, per capita $200; real growth rate 0% (1989 est.)
Inflation: 56.7% (1991)

Industries: small-scale production of textiles, soap, furniture, shoes, fertilizer and cement; handwoven carpets; natural gas, oil, coal, copper
Labour Force: 6,230,000 (1992); 61% agriculture and animal husbandry, 14% industry, 25% services and other
Unemployment: n.a.
Agriculture: largely subsistence farming and nomadic animal husbandry; cash products-wheat, fruits, nuts, karakul pelts, wool, mutton, barley, corn; production is limited due to the shortage of modern machinery, high-grade seed, and fertilizer
Natural Resources: natural gas, crude oil, copper, coal, salt, talc, barites, sulphur, lead, zinc, iron ore, slate, precious and semi-precious stones, especially lapis lazuli, amethysts, rubies

■ FINANCE/TRADE

Currency: afghani (Af)
International Reserves Excluding Gold: $227 million (1992)
Gold Reserves: 0.96 million fine troy ounces (1992)
Budget: revenues $962 million (1990); expenditures $3.2 billion, including capital expenditures of $296 million
Defence Expenditures: $286.56 million (1985)
External Debt: $1.8 billion (1989)
Exports: $235 million (1990); commodities: natural gas 55%, fruit and nuts 24%, handwoven carpets, wool, cotton, hides; partners: mostly USSR and Eastern Europe
Imports: $937 million (1990); commodities: food and petroleum products; partners: mostly USSR and Eastern Europe

■ HEALTH

Births: 44/1,000 population (1991)
Deaths: 20/1,000 population (1991)
Infant Mortality: 164 deaths/1,000 live births (1991)
Life Expectancy at Birth: 41 years male, 42 years female (1992)
No. of Physicians: 1.6/10,000 population (1992)

■ EDUCATION

Govt. Expenditure: 4.0% of govt. expenditure (1987)
Literacy: 29.4% (1992)

■ COMMUNICATIONS

Daily newspapers: 14 (1992)
Televisions: 8.1/1,000 inhabitants (1992)
Radios: 104/1,000 inhabitants (1992)
Telephones: 0.21/100 persons (1992)

■ TRANSPORTATION

Motor Vehicles: 70,000; 36,000 passenger cars.
Roads: 20,867 km; 2,608 km paved
Railway: No railways in the country, but the Oxus bridge, opened in 1982, brought Soviet Railways' track into the country. A 200 km line of 1,520 mm gauge has been authorized from Termez to Pul-i-Khumri.
Air Traffic: 212,000 passengers carried (1991)
Airports: 20

Canadian Embassy: C/o Canadian High Commission, Diplomatic Sector G-5, Islamabad; mailing address: GPO Box 1042, Islamabad, Pakistan. Tel: (011-92-51) 211-101-4

Albania

Long-Form Name: People's Socialist Republic of Albania
Capital: Tirana
Population: 3,360,000 (1992)

■ GEOGRAPHY

Area: 28,750 sq. km
Coastline: 362 km
Climate: mild temperate; cool, cloudy, wet winters; hot, clear, dry summers; interior is cooler and wetter, with severe winters
Environment: subject to destructive earthquakes; tsunami occur along southwestern coast; deforestation seems to be slowing
Terrain: mostly mountains and hills; small plains along coast
Land Use: 21 % arable land; 4% permanent crops; 15% meadows and pastures; 38% forest and woodland, including 30% scrub forest; 22% other; includes 1% irrigated
Location: SC Europe, bordering on Adriatic Sea

■ PEOPLE

Nationality: Albanian
Ethnic Groups: 90% Albanian, 8% Greek, 2% others (Vlachs, Gypsies, Serbs and Bulgarians) (1989 est.)
Languages: Albanian (Tosk is official dialect, also Gheg dialect), Greek
Religions: From April 1991, freedom of religion replaced official atheism. There is a large number of Muslims.
Marriages: 8.9 (per 1,000) (1987)
Divorces: 0.8 (per 1,000) (1987)

■ GOVERNMENT

Leader(s): Pres. Sali Berisha, Prime Min. Aleksander Meksi

Government Type: communist state (Stalinist)
Administrative Divisions: 26 districts
Independence: Nov. 28, 1912 (from Turkey); People's Socialist Republic of Albania declared Jan. 11, 1946
National holiday: Liberation Day, Nov. 29

■ ECONOMY

Overview: the poorest country in Europe, it is a Stalinist-type economy (central planning and state ownership of the means of production). It is largely self-sufficient in food and possesses considerable mineral resources
GNP: $3.8 billion, per capita $1,200; real growth rate n.a. (1989 est.)
Inflation: n.a.
Industries: food processing, textiles and clothing, lumber, oil, cement, chemicals, basic metals, hydroelectricity
Labour Force: 1,591,000 (1992); about 56% agriculture, 26% industry, 18% service (1989)
Unemployment: 9.1% (1991)
Agriculture: arable land per capita among lowest in Europe; one-half of work force engaged in farming; produces wide range of temperate-zone crops and livestock; claims self-sufficiency in grain output
Natural Resources: crude oil, natural gas, coal, chromium, copper, timber, nickel, petroleum

■ FINANCE/TRADE

Currency: lek (L)
International Reserves Excluding Gold: n.a.
Gold Reserves: n.a.
Budget: revenues $2.3 billion; expenditures $2.3 billion, capital expenditures n.a. (1989)
Defence Expenditures: $171.2 million (1990)
External Debt: n.a.
Exports: $378 million (1987); commodities: asphalt, bitumen, petroleum products, metals and metallic ores, electricity, oil, vegetables, fruits, tobacco; partners: Italy, Yugoslavia, Germany, Greece, Czechoslovakia, Poland, Romania, Bulgaria, Hungary
Imports: $255 million (1987); commodities: machinery, machine tools, iron and steel products, textiles, chemicals, pharmaceuticals; partners: Italy, Yugoslavia, Germany, Czechoslovakia, Romania, Poland, Hungary, Bulgaria

■ HEALTH

Births: 24/1,000 population (1991)
Deaths: 5/1,000 population (1991)
Infant Mortality: 50 deaths/1,000 live births (1991)

Life Expectancy at Birth: 70 years male, 76 years female (1992)
No. of Physicians: 10.5/10,000 population (1975)

■ EDUCATION

Govt. Expenditure: 11.1% of government expenditure (1988)
Literacy: 75%

■ COMMUNICATIONS

Daily newspapers: 2 (1992)
Televisions: 83.1/1,000 inhabitants (1992)
Radios: 172/1,000 inhabitants (1992)
Telephones: n.a.

■ TRANSPORTATION

Motor Vehicles: 3,500 passenger cars (1981)
Roads: 17,509 km ; paved n.a.
Railway: 569 km
Air Traffic: n.a.
Airports: 12

Canadian Embassy: C/o Kneza Milosa 75, 11000 Belgrade, Yugoslavia. Tel: (011-38-11) 644-666
Representative to Canada: C/o Permanent Mission of the Republic of Albania, 320 East 79th St, New York, NY 10021, USA. Tel. (212) 249-2059

Algeria

Long-Form Name: Democratic and Popular Republic of Algeria
Capital: Algiers
Population: 26,346,000 (1992)

■ GEOGRAPHY

Area: 2,381,740 sq. km
Coastline: 998 km
Climate: arid to semi-arid; mild, wet winters with hot, dry summers along coast; drier with cold winters and hot summers on high plateau; sirocco is a hot, dust/sand-laden wind especially common in summer
Environment: mountainous areas subject to severe earthquakes; desertification
Terrain: mostly high plateau and desert; some mountains; narrow, discontinuous coastal plain
Land Use: 3% arable land; negligible permanent crops; 13% meadows and pastures; 2% forest and woodland; cattle, sheep and goat grazing on grassland and shrub regions; includes negligible irrigated
Location: N Africa, bordering on Mediterranean Sea

■ PEOPLE

Nationality: Algerian
Ethnic Groups: 99% Arab-Berber, less than 1% European
Languages: Arabic (official), French, Berber dialects
Religions: 99% Sunni Moslem (state religion); 1% Christian and Jewish
Marriages: 5.7 (per 1,000) (1985)
Divorces: n.a.

■ GOVERNMENT

Leader(s): Pres. Ali Kafi, Prem. Redha Malek
Government Type: republic
Administrative Divisions: 48 "wilayat" (provinces) (1991)
Independence: July 5, 1962 (from France)
National Holiday: Anniversary of the Revolution, Nov. 1

■ ECONOMY

Overview: the economy is largely based on the exploitation of oil and natural gas products. Recently, reforms have been implemented to combat social and economic problems
GNP: $52.239 billion, per capita $2,020; real growth rate, 2.1% (1991)
Inflation: 16.7% (1990)
Industries: petroleum, light industries, natural gas, mining, electrical, petrochemical, food processing
Labour Force: 5,819,000 (1992); 11% industry, 14% agriculture, 75% services (1989)
Unemployment: 19% (1988)
Agriculture: accounts for 8% of GDP and employs 30% of labour force; must import more than 1/3 of its food
Natural Resources: crude oil, natural gas, iron ore, phosphates, uranium, lead, zinc, mercury

■ FINANCE/TRADE

Currency: dinar (DZD)
International Reserves Excluding Gold: $1,457 million (1992)
Gold Reserves: 5.58 million fine troy ounces (1992)
Budget: revenues $16.7 billion; expenditures $17.3 billion, including capital expenditures of $6.6 billion (1990)
Defence Expenditures: 5% of total expenditures (1988)
External Debt: $24.3 billion (1992)
Exports: $10.5 billion (1990); commodities: petroleum and natural gas 98%; partners: Netherlands, Czechoslovakia, Romania, Italy,

France, US
Imports: $13.2 billion (1990); commodities: capital goods 35%, consumer goods 36%, food 20%; partners: France 25%, Italy 8%, Germany 8%, US 6–7%

■ HEALTH

Births: 32/1,000 population (1991)
Deaths: 7/1,000 population (1991)
Infant Mortality: 57 deaths/1,000 live births (1991)
Life Expectancy at Birth: 65 years male, 67 years female (1992)
No. of Physicians: 4.3/10,000 population (1992)

■ EDUCATION

Govt. Expenditure: 27.0% of govt. expenditure (1989)
Literacy: 57.4% (1992)

■ COMMUNICATIONS

Daily newspapers: 12 (1992)
Televisions: 72.8/1,000 inhabitants (1992)
Radios: 232/1,000 inhabitants (1992)
Telephones: 3.8/100 inhabitants (1992)

■ TRANSPORTATION

Motor Vehicles: 1,250,000; 750,000 passenger cars (1990)
Roads: 71,452 km; 38,108 km paved
Railway: 3,810 km
Air Traffic: 3,385,000 passengers carried (1991)
Airports: 49

Canadian Embassy: 27 bis, rue Ali Massoudi, Hydra, Algiers 16000; mailing address: P.O. Box 225, Alger-Gare, Algiers, Algeria. Tel: (011-213-2) 60-66-11/60.61.90
Embassy in Canada: Embassy of the People's Democratic Republic of Algeria, 435 Daly Ave, Ottawa ON K1N 6H3. Tel: (613) 789-8505

American Samoa

Dependent Territory of the United States

Long-Form Name: Territory of American Samoa
Capital: Pago Pago (On Tutuila Island)
Population: 50,000 (1992); in 1990, some 85,000 Samoans lived in the US

■ GEOGRAPHY

Area: 197 sq. km
Coastline: 3,735 km

Climate: tropical maritime, plentiful rainfall, temperatures consistent throughout the year
Land Use: 23% tropical crop cultivation
Location: S Pacific Ocean, NW of Australia and New Zealand

■ PEOPLE

Nationality: American Samoan; nationals of the United States
Ethnic Groups: Polynesian and part-Polynesian
Languages: Samoan (a Polynesian dialect), English

■ GOVERNMENT

Leader(s): Gov. A.P. Lutali
Government Type: US dependency with democratically elected governor: unorganized unincorporated territory

■ ECONOMY

Overview: agriculture: taro, bread-fruit, yams, bananas, coconuts; livestock includes pigs, goats, poultry; industries: fish (tuna) canning
Exports: $308 million (1989): canned tuna, pet foods, crafts
Imports: $378 million (1989): building materials, fuel oil, machines and parts, alcoholic beverages, cigarettes
Currency: American dollar (US$)

Andorra

Long-Form Name: Principality of Andorra
Capital: Andorra-la-Vella
Population: 60,000 (1991)

■ GEOGRAPHY

Area: 470 sq. km
Coastline: none: landlocked
Climate: temperate; snowy, cold winters and warm, dry summers
Environment: deforestation, overgrazing
Terrain: rugged mountains dissected by narrow valleys
Land Use: 2% arable land; 0% permanent crops; 56% meadows and pastures; 22% forest and woodland; 20% other
Location: SW Europe

■ PEOPLE

Nationality: Andorran
Ethnic Groups: Catalan stock; 61% Spanish, 30% Andorran, 6% French, 3% other
Languages: Catalan (official); many also speak some French and Spanish
Religions: virtually all Roman Catholic

Marriages: 2.6 (per 1,000) (1987)
Divorces: n.a.

■ GOVERNMENT

Leader(s): co-Chiefs of State: François Mitterand (France) and Felipe González Márquez (Spain)
Government type: unique co-principality under formal sovereignty of president of France and Spanish bishop of Seo de Urgel, who are represented locally by officials called verguers
Administrative Divisions: 7 parishes
Independence: 1278 (from France and Spain)
National Holiday: Mare de Deu de Meritzell, Sept. 8

■ ECONOMY

Overview: tourism is the backbone of the economy, due to its duty-free status and year-round resorts. Most food is imported due to a scarcity of arable land
GNP: n.a.; per capita over $6,000 (1991)
Inflation: n.a.
Industries: tourism (particularly skiing), sheep, timber, tobacco, smuggling, banking
Labour Force: n.a.
Unemployment: n.a.
Agriculture: sheep raising, small quantities of tobacco, rye, wheat, barley, buckwheat, maize, oats and some vegetables, especially potatoes
Natural Resources: hydroelectricity, mineral water, timber, iron ore, lead

■ FINANCE/TRADE

Currency: French Franc, Spanish peseta (F Ptas)
International Reserves Excluding Gold: n.a.
Gold Reserves: n.a.
Budget: n.a.
Defence Expenditures: n.a.
External Debt: n.a.
Exports: $0.017 million (1986); commodities: electricity; partners: France and Spain
Imports: $531 million (1986); commodities: n.a.; partners: France and Spain

■ HEALTH

Births: 11/1,000 population (1991)
Deaths: 4/1,000 population (1991)
Infant Mortality: 7 deaths/1,000 live births (1991)
Life Expectancy at Birth: 74 years male, 81 years female (1991)
No. of Physicians: 112/10,000 population (1988)

■ EDUCATION

Govt. Expenditure: 15.8% of govt. expenditure (1986)

Literacy: 100%

■ COMMUNICATIONS

Daily newspapers: n.a.; 4 non-daily (1988)
Televisions: 148.9/1,000 inhabitants (1989)
Radios: 219/1,000 inhabitants (1989)
Telephones: n.a.

■ TRANSPORTATION

Motor Vehicles: 38,691; 34,168 passenger cars (1990)
Roads: n.a.
Railway: n.a.

Canadian Embassy: c/o 35, av Montaigne, 75008 Paris, France. Tel: (011-33-1) 44.43.32.00

Angola

Long-Form Name: People's Republic of Angola
Capital: Luanda
Population: 10,300,000 (1991)

■ GEOGRAPHY

Area: 1,246,700 sq. km
Coastline: 1,600 km
Climate: semi-arid in south and along coast to Luanda; north has cool, dry season (May to October) and hot, rainy season (Nov. to Apr.)
Environment: locally heavy rainfall causes periodic flooding on plateau; desertification, especially on coastal plain
Terrain: narrow coastal plain rises abruptly to vast interior plain
Land Use: 2% arable land; negligible permanent crops; 23% meadows and pastures; 43% forest and woodland; 32% other
Location: SW Africa

■ PEOPLE

Nationality: Angolan
Ethnic Groups: 37% Ovimbundu, 25% Kimbundu, 13% Bakongo, 2% Mestiço, 1% European
Languages: Portuguese (official); Bantu dialects spoken include Ovimbundu, Kimbundu, Bakongo and Chokwe
Religions: 68% Roman Catholic, 20% Protestant, 12% Animist
Marriages: n.a.
Divorces: n.a.

■ GOVERNMENT

Leader(s): Pres. José Eduardo dos Santos
Government type: Marxist people's republic
Administrative Divisions: 18 provinces

Independence: Nov. 11, 1975 (from Portugal)
National Holiday: Independence Day, Nov. 11

■ ECONOMY

Overview: subsistence agriculture is the main livelihood of the population, but oil production is the most lucrative activity. Recent internal war has weakened the economy
GNP: $5 billion, per capita $610; real growth rate 9.2% (1990)
Inflation: n.a.
Industries: petroleum, mining (phosphate rock, diamonds), fish processing, brewing, tobacco, sugar, textiles, cement, food processing, building construction
Labour Force: 4,081,000 economically active (1992); 74% agriculture, 10% industry, 16% services (1989)
Unemployment: 18.9% (1986)
Agriculture: cash crops—coffee, sisal, corn, cotton, sugar, manioc, tobacco; food crops-cassava, corn, vegetables, plantains, bananas and other local foodstuffs
Natural Resources: petroleum, diamonds, iron ore, phosphates, copper, feldspar, gold, bauxite, uranium

■ FINANCE/TRADE

Currency: kwanza (Kz)
International Reserves Excluding Gold: n.a.
Gold Reserves: n.a.
Budget: revenues $2.6 billion; expenditures $4.4 billion, including capital expenditures of $963 million (1990)
Defence Expenditures: $2.69 billion (1989)
External Debt: $7.1 billion (1990)
Exports: $2.9 billion (1989); commodities: oil, coffee, diamonds, sisal, fish and fish products, timber, cotton; partners: US, USSR, Cuba, Portugal, Brazil
Imports: $2.5 billion (1989); commodities: capital equipment (machinery and electrical equipment), food, vehicles and spare parts, textiles and clothing, medicines, substantial military deliveries; partners: US, USSR, Cuba, Portugal, Brazil

■ HEALTH

Births: 47/1,000 population (1991)
Deaths: 20/1,000 population (1991)
Infant Mortality: 151 deaths/1,000 live births (1991)
Life Expectancy at Birth: 42 years male, 46 years female (1992)
No. of Physicians: 0.6/10,000 population (1992)

■ EDUCATION

Govt. Expenditure: 10.7% of govt. expenditure (1989)
Literacy: 41.7% (1992)

■ COMMUNICATIONS

Daily newspapers: 1 (1992)
Televisions: 5.6/1,000 inhabitants (1992)
Radios: 53/1,000 inhabitants (1992)
Telephones: 0.76/100 inhabitants (1992)

■ TRANSPORTATION

Motor Vehicles: 175,000; 130,000 passenger cars (1990)
Roads: 72,309 km; 8,727 km paved
Railway: 2,992 km
Air Traffic: 456,000 passengers carried (1991)
Airports: 26

Canadian Embassy: c/o The Canadian High Commission, 45 Baines Ave, Harare; mailing address: P.O. Box 1430, Harare, Zimbabwe. Tel. (011-263-4) 733-881

Anguilla

Dependent Territory of the United Kingdom

Long-Form Name: Territory of Anguilla
Capital: The Valley
Population: 8,000 (1992)

■ GEOGRAPHY

Area: 155 sq. km
Climate: dry and sunny
Land Use: low rainfall limits agricultural potential
Location: West Indies

■ PEOPLE

Nationality: British
Ethnic Groups: of English ancestry, Black/mixed-Black
Languages: English (official)

■ GOVERNMENT

Leader(s): Gov. Alan W. Shave, Chief Min. Emile Gumbs
Government Type: separate dependency of Great Britain

■ ECONOMY

Overview: agriculture: pigeon peas, corn, sweet potatoes; fishing; livestock includes sheep, goats, cattle, poultry; tourism; main trading partner: United Kingdom

Currency: Eastern Caribbean dollar (EC$)

Antigua and Barbuda

Long-Form Name: Antigua and Barbuda
Capital: St. John's
Population: 80,000 (1991)

■ GEOGRAPHY

Area: 440 sq. km; includes Redonda (1.3 sq km)
Coastline: 153 km
Climate: tropical marine; little seasonal temperature variation
Environment: subject to hurricanes and tropical storms (July to Oct.); insufficient freshwater resources; occasional long periods of drought; deeply indented coastline provides many natural harbours
Terrain: mostly low-lying limestone and coral islands with some higher volcanic areas
Land Use: 18% arable land; 0% permanent crops; 7% meadows and pastures; 16% forest and woodland; 59% other
Location: Caribbean Islands

■ PEOPLE

Nationality: Antiguan
Ethnic Groups: almost entirely of black African origin; some British, Portuguese, Lebanese and Syrian origin
Languages: English (official), local dialects
Religions: Anglican (predominant), other Protestant sects, some Roman Catholic
Marriages: 4.1 (per 1,000) (1987)
Divorces: 0.5 (per 1,000) (1985)

■ GOVERNMENT

Leader(s): Prime Min. Vere C. Bird, Sr., Gov. Gen. Sir Wilfred Ebenezer Jacobs
Government type: parliamentary democracy
Administrative Divisions: 6 parishes, 2 dependencies
Independence: Nov. 1, 1981 (from UK)
National Holiday: Independence Day, Nov. 1

■ ECONOMY

Overview: tourism is the backbone of this service-oriented economy. A labour shortage is plaguing some sectors of the economy
GNP: $355 million, per capita $4,770; real growth rate 4.4% (1991)
Inflation: 7.1% (1988 est.)
Industries: tourism, construction, light manufacturing (clothing, alcohol, household appliances)

Labour Force: 30,000; 82% commerce and services, 11% agriculture, 7% industry (1983)
Unemployment: 5.0% (1988 est.)
Agriculture: expanding output of cotton, fruits, vegetables and livestock; other crops—bananas, coconuts, cucumbers, mangoes; not self-sufficient in food
Natural Resources: negligible; pleasant climate and beautiful beaches foster tourism

■ FINANCE/TRADE

Currency: East Caribbean dollar ($EC)
International Reserves Excluding Gold: $42 million (1992)
Gold Reserves: n.a.
Budget: revenues $92.8 million; expenditures $101 million, including capital expenditures (1990)
Defence Expenditures: n.a.
External Debt: $245.4 million (1987)
Exports: $22.0 million (1988); commodities: petroleum products 46%, manufactures 29%, food and live animals 14%, machinery and transport equipment 11%; partners: Trinidad and Tobago 40%, Barbados 8%, US 0.3%
Imports: $225.0 million (1988); commodities: food and live animals, machinery and transport equipment, manufactures, chemicals, oil; partners: US 27%, UK 14%, CARICOM 7%, Canada 4%, other 48%

■ HEALTH

Births: 18/1,000 population (1991)
Deaths: 6/1,000 population (1991)
Infant Mortality: 22 deaths/1,000 live births (1991)
Life Expectancy at Birth: 70 years male, 74 years female (1992)
No. of Physicians: n.a.

■ EDUCATION

Govt. Expenditure: 2.5% GNP (1984)
Literacy: 90%

■ COMMUNICATIONS

Daily newspapers: 1 (1992)
Televisions: 289.5/1,000 inhabitants (1992)
Radios: 276/1,000 inhabitants (1992)
Telephones: 14.4/100 inhabitants (1992)

■ TRANSPORTATION

Motor Vehicles: 17,000; 13,500 passenger cars (1990)
Railway: 64 km
Air Traffic: 755,000 passengers carried (1991)
Airports: 3

Canadian Embassy: C/o The Canadian High Commission, Bishop's Court Hill, St. Michael; mailing address: P.O. Box 404, Bridgetown, Barbados
Embassy in Canada: High Commission for Antigua and Barbuda, 112 Kent St, Ste 205, Place de Ville, Tower B, Ottawa ON K1P 5P2. Tel: (613) 234-9143, Fax: (613) 232-0539.

Argentina

Long-Form Name: Argentine Republic
Capital: Buenos Aires
Population: 33,100,000 (1992)

■ GEOGRAPHY

Area: 2,766,890 sq. km
Coastline: 4,989 km
Climate: mostly temperate; arid in southeast; sub-antarctic in southwest
Environment: Tucumán and Mendoza areas in Andes subject to earthquakes; pamperos are violent windstorms that can strike Pampas and northeast; irrigated soil degradation; desertification; air and water pollution in Buenos Aires
Terrain: rich plains of the Pampas in northern half, flat to rolling plateau of Patagonia in south, rugged Andes along western border
Land Use: 9% arable land; 4% permanent crops; 52% meadows and pastures; 22% forest and woodland; 13% other; includes 1% irrigated
Location: SE South America

■ PEOPLE

Nationality: Argentine or Argentinian
Ethnic Groups: 85% white, 15% mestizo, Indian, or other nonwhite groups
Languages: Spanish (official), English, Italian, German, French
Religions: 90% nominally Roman Catholic (less than 20% practising), 2% Protestant, 2% Jewish, 6% other
Marriages: 6.0 (per 1,000) (1983)
Divorces: n.a.

■ GOVERNMENT

Leader(s): Pres. Carlos Saùl Menem,

Government type: republic
Administrative Divisions: 22 provinces, 1 national territory and 1 district
Independence: July 9, 1816 (from Spain)
National Holiday: National Day, May 25

■ ECONOMY

Overview: though the country possesses abundant natural resources and a diversified industrial base, high inflation and burgeoning debt are weakening the economy
GNP: $91.211 billion, per capita $2,780; real growth rate -0.2% (1991)
Inflation: 171.7% (1991)
Industries: food processing (especially meat packing), motor vehicles, consumer durables, textiles, chemicals and petrochemicals, printing, metallurgy, steel
Labour Force: 11,548,000 (1992); 13% agriculture, 34% industry, 53% services (1989)
Unemployment: 7.3% (1989)
Agriculture: accounts for 15% of GNP (including fishing); produces abundant food for both domestic consumption and exports; among world's top five exporters of grain and beef; principal crops— wheat, corn, sorghum, soybeans, sugar beets
Natural Resources: fertile plains of the pampas, lead, zinc, tin, copper, iron ore, manganese, crude oil, uranium

■ FINANCE/TRADE

Currency: Austral ($a)
International Reserves Excluding Gold: $6,615 million (1991)
Gold Reserves: 4.12 million fine troy ounces (1991)
Budget: revenues $12.2 billion; expenditures $17.3 billion, including capital expenditures of $2.8 billion (1991)
Defence Expenditures: $770.98 million (1990)
External Debt: $46.1 billion (1990)
Exports: $11.972 billion (1992); commodities: meat, wheat, corn, oil seed, hides, wool; partners: US 14%, USSR, Italy, Brazil, Japan, Netherlands
Imports: $8.090 billion (1992); commodities: machinery and equipment, metals, chemicals, fuels and lubricants, agricultural products; partners: US 25%, Brazil, Germany, Bolivia, Japan, Italy, Netherlands

■ HEALTH

Births: 20/1,000 population (1991)
Deaths: 9/1,000 population (1991)
Infant Mortality: 31 deaths/1,000 live births (1991)
Life Expectancy at Birth: 66 years male, 73 years female (1992)
No. of Physicians: 26.7/10,000 population (1992)

■ EDUCATION

Govt. Expenditure: 10.0% of govt. expenditure (1989)
Literacy: 95.3% (1992)

■ COMMUNICATIONS

Daily newspapers: 194 (1992)
Televisions: 219.3/1,000 inhabitants (1992)
Radios: 673/1,000 inhabitants (1992)
Telephones: 12.13/100 inhabitants (1992)

■ TRANSPORTATION

Motor Vehicles: 5,784,500; 4,283,700 passenger cars (1990)
Roads: 213,050 km; 58,105 km paved
Railway: 34,586 km
Air Traffic: 4,532,000 passengers carried (1991)
Airports: 349

Canadian Embassy: Tagle 2828, 1425, Buenos Aires; mailing address: Casilla de Correo 3898, 1000 Buenos Aires, Argentina. Tel: (011-54-1) 805-3032
Embassy in Canada: Embassy of the Argentine Republic, Royal Bank Centre, 90 Sparks St, Ste 620, Ottawa ON K1P 5B4. Tel: (613) 236-2351, -4. Fax: (613) 235-2659.

Armenia

Long-Form Name: Republic of Armenia
Capital: Yerevan
Population: 3,489,000 (1992)

■ GEOGRAPHY

Area: 29,800 sq. km
Coastline: none: landlocked
Climate: severe winters; hot summers; dry year-round
Environment: prone to earthquakes; little land suitable for cultivation
Terrain: rugged highlands; 70% is mountains
Land Use: most farmland lies in the Aras Valley; animal herding predominant in the highlands
Location: SE Europe

■ PEOPLE

Nationality: Armenian
Ethnic Groups: 93.3% Armenians, 1.6% Russians, 2.6% Azerbaijanis, 1.7% Kurds
Languages: Armenian (official), Azerbaijan, Russian
Religions: predominantly Eastern Orthodox
Marriages: n.a.
Divorces: n.a.

■ GOVERNMENT

Leader(s): Pres. Levon Ter-Petrosyan, V. Pres. and Prime Min. Khosrov Harootunian
Government type: in transition to republic
Administrative Divisions: n.a.
Independence: declared Aug. 23, 1990
National Holiday: n.a.

■ ECONOMY

Overview: predominantly manufacturing and agriculture
GNP: $7.2 billion, per capita $2,150; real growth 2.9% (1991)
Inflation: n.a.
Industries: electrical equipment and machinery, chemicals, machine tools, vehicles
Labour Force: n.a.
Unemployment: n.a.
Agriculture: fruit, grapes, vegetables, tobacco, grains, beetroot, potatoes, geranium oil, cattle and sheep herding
Natural Resources: marble, precious metals, iron, tufa

■ FINANCE/TRADE

Currency: rouble (rbl.)
International Reserves Excluding Gold: n.a.
Gold Reserves: n.a.
Budget: 1989 revenues, 2,460 million roubles
Defence Expenditures: n.a.
External Debt: n.a.
Exports: cotton, fruit, olives, pomegranates, machine tools, instruments, shoes
Imports: n.a.

■ HEALTH

Births: 22.9/1,000 population (1989)
Deaths: 6.3/1,000 population (1989)
Infant Mortality: 20.4 deaths/1,000 live births (1989)
Life Expectancy at Birth: 69 years male, 75 years female (1992)
No. of Physicians: 14,200 (1989)

■ EDUCATION

Govt. Expenditure: n.a.
Literacy: n.a.

■ COMMUNICATIONS

Daily newspapers: 85 papers of all circulation types (1989)
Televisions: n.a.
Radios: n.a.
Telephones: n.a.

■ TRANSPORTATION

Motor Vehicles: n.a.
Railway: 820 km (1990)
Air Traffic: n.a.
Airports: n.a.

Canadian Embassy: C/o Starokonyushenny Per 23, Moscow 12100, Russian Federation . Tel: (011-7-95) 241-5070. Fax: (011-7-95) 241-9034.
C/o Embassy of the Russian Federation, 285 Charlotte St, Ottawa ON K1N 8L5. Tel: (613) 235-4341, 236-1413. Fax: (613) 236-6342.

Aruba

Dependent Territory of the Netherlands

Long-Form Name: Aruba
Capital: Oranjestad
Population: 62,000 (1992)

■ GEOGRAPHY

Area: 193 sq. km
Coastline: 68.5 km
Climate: tropical marine; little seasonal temperature variation
Environment: lies outside the Caribbean hurricane belt
Terrain: flat with a few hills; scant vegetation
Land Use: 0% arable land; 0% permanent crops; 0% meadows and pastures; 0% forest and woodland; 100% other
Location: off N coast of South America, bordering Atlantic Ocean

■ PEOPLE

Nationality: Aruban
Ethnic Groups: 80% mixed European/Caribbean Indian
Languages: Dutch (official), Papiamento (a Spanish, Portuguese, Dutch, English dialect), English (widely spoken), Spanish

■ GOVERNMENT

Leader(s): Prime Min. Nelson Oduber, Gov. Gen. Felipe B. Tromp
Government type: part of the Dutch realm; independence planned for 1996
Administrative Divisions: none (self-governing part of the Netherlands)
National Holiday: Flag Day, Mar. 18

■ ECONOMY

Overview: tourism is the mainstay
GNP: $620 million, per capita $10,000, real growth rate 16.7% (1988 est.)
Currency: Aruban florin (Af)

Australia

Long-Form Name: Commonwealth of Australia
Capital: Canberra
Population: 17,530,000 (1992)

■ GEOGRAPHY

Area: 7,686,850 sq. km; includes Macquarie Island
Coastline: 25,760 km
Climate: generally arid to semi-arid; temperate in south and east; tropical in north
Environment: subject to severe droughts and floods; cyclones along coast; limited freshwater availability; irrigated soil degradation; regular, tropical, invigorating, sea breeze known as the doctor occurs along west coast in summer; desertification
Terrain: mostly low plateau with deserts; fertile plain in southeast
Land Use: 6% arable land; negligible permanent crops; 58% meadows and pastures; 14% forest and woodland; 22% other; includes negligible irrigated
Location: divides Indian and Pacific Oceans

■ PEOPLE

Nationality: Australian
Ethnic Groups: 95% Caucasian, 4% Asian, 1% Aboriginal and other
Languages: English, native languages
Religions: 26% Anglican, 26% Roman Catholic, 24% other Christian; most of the rest do not profess a religion
Marriages: 7.1 (per 1,000) (1988)
Divorces: 2.5 (per 1,000) (1986)

■ GOVERNMENT

Leader(s): Prime Min. Paul Keating, Gov. Gen. Bill Hayden
Government type: federal parliamentary state
Administrative Divisions: 6 states, 2 territories; dependent areas inc.: Ashmore and Cartier Islands (uninhabited), Australian Antarctic Territory (uninhabited except for scientific staff), Cocos (Keeling) Islands, Coral Sea Islands Territory (uninhabited), Christmas Island (uninhabited), Heard and McDonald Islands (uninhabited), Norfolk Island

Independence: Jan. 1, 1901 (federation of UK colonies)
National Holiday: Australia Day, last Monday in Jan.

■ ECONOMY

Overview: successful Western-style capitalist economy and a major exporter of natural resources and agricultural products. Is looking to increase exports of manufactured goods
GNP: $287.765 billion, per capita $16,590; real growth rate 2.8% (1991)
Inflation: 3.2% (1991)
Industries: mining, industrial and transportation equipment, food processing, chemicals, steel, motor vehicles
Labour Force: 7,963,000 (1992); 78.3% services,16.4% industry, 5.3% agriculture (1989)
Unemployment: 9.6% (1991)
Agriculture: accounts for 5% of GNP and 37% of export revenues; world's largest exporter of beef and wool, second-largest for mutton, and among top wheat exporters; major crops—wheat, barley, sugar cane, fruit; livestock—cattle, sheep, poultry
Natural Resources: bauxite, coal, iron ore, copper, tin, silver, uranium, nickel, tungsten, mineral sands, lead, zinc, diamonds, natural gas, crude oil

■ FINANCE/TRADE

Currency: dollar ($A)
International Reserves Excluding Gold: $10,988 million (1992)
Gold Reserves: 7.93 million fine troy ounces (1991)
Budget: revenues $74.2 billion; expenditures $67.9 billion, including capital expenditures (1991)
Defence Expenditures: $7.01 billion (1990)
External Debt: $111.6 billion (1989)
Exports: $42.417 billion (1992); commodities: wheat, barley, beef, lamb, dairy products, wool, coal, iron ore; partners: Japan 26%, US 11%, New Zealand 6%, S Korea 4%, Singapore 4%, USSR 3%
Imports: $40.696 billion (1992); commodities: manufactured raw materials, capital equipment, consumer goods; partners: US 22%, Japan 22%, UK 7%, Germany 6%, New Zealand 4%

■ HEALTH

Births: 15/1,000 population (1991)
Deaths: 7/1,000 population (1991)
Infant Mortality: 8 deaths/1,000 live births (1991)

Life Expectancy at Birth: 73 years male, 80 years female (1992)
No. of Physicians: 22.9/10,000 population (1992)

■ EDUCATION

Govt. Expenditure: 7% of govt. expenditure (1988)
Literacy: 98.5%

■ COMMUNICATIONS

Daily newspapers: 68 (1992)
Televisions: 483.9/1,000 inhabitants (1992)
Radios: 1,262/1,000 inhabitants (1992)
Telephones: 51.72/100 inhabitants (1992)

■ TRANSPORTATION

Motor Vehicles: 9,776,600; 7,672,300 passenger cars (1990)
Roads: 860,927 km; 430,464 km paved
Railway: 39,971 km
Air Traffic: 21,244,000 passengers carried (1991)
Airports: 430

Canadian Embassy: The Canadian High Commission, Commonwealth Ave, Canberra A.C.T. 2600, Australia. Tel: (011-61-62) 273-3844
Embassy in Canada: Australian High Com-mission, 50 O'Connor St, Ste 710, Ottawa ON K1P 6L2. Tel: (613) 236-0841.

Austria

Long-Form Name: Republic of Austria
Capital: Vienna
Population: 7,880,000 (1992)

■ GEOGRAPHY

Area: 83,850 sq. km
Coastline: none: landlocked
Climate: temperate; continental, cloudy; cold winter with frequent rain in lowlands and snow in mountains; cool summers with occasional showers
Environment: because of steep slopes, poor soils and cold temperatures, population is concentrated on eastern lowlands
Terrain: mostly mountains with Alps in west and south; flat, with gentle slopes along eastern and northern margins
Land Use: 17% arable land; 1% permanent crops; 24% meadows and pastures; 39% forest and woodland; 19% other; includes negligible irrigated
Location: SC Europe

■ PEOPLE

Nationality: Austrian
Ethnic Groups: 99% German, 0.3 % Croatian, 0.2% Slovene, 0.1% others
Languages: German (official); Slovene, Hungarian, and a Croatian dialect also spoken
Religions: 89% Roman Catholic, 6% Protestant, 5% other
Marriages: 4.7 (per 1,000) (1988)
Divorces: 1.9 (per 1,000) (1987)

■ GOVERNMENT

Leader(s): Chanc. Franz Vranitzky, Pres. Thomas Klestil
Government type: federal republic
Administrative Divisions: 9 states
Independence: Nov. 12, 1918 (from Austro-Hungarian Empire)
National Holiday: National Day, Oct. 26

■ ECONOMY

Overview: prosperous, Western capitalist economy, as well as substantial welfare benefits and extensive nationalized industry
GNP: $157.528 billion, per capita $20,380; real growth rate 2.3% (1991)
Inflation: 3.3% (1991)
Industries: foods, iron and steel, machines, textiles, chemicals, electrical, paper and pulp, tourism, mining
Labour Force: 3,570,000 (1992); 64.7% services, 27.5% industry, 7.8% agriculture; an estimated 200,000 Austrians are employed in other European countries; foreign labourers in Austria number 177,840, about 6% of labour force (1989)
Unemployment: 5.8% (1992)
Agriculture: accounts for 4% of GDP (including forestry); principal crops and animals—grains, fruit, potatoes, sugar beets, sawn wood, cattle, pigs, poultry; 80–90% self-sufficient in food
Natural Resources: iron ore, crude oil, timber, magnesite, aluminum, lead, coal, lignite, copper, hydroelectricity

■ FINANCE/TRADE

Currency: schilling (S)
International Reserves Excluding Gold: $12,081 million (1992)
Gold Reserves: 19.81 million fine troy ounces (1992)
Budget: revenues $44.1 billion; expenditures $49.6 billion, including capital expenditures (1991)
Defence Expenditures: $1.54 billion (1990)

External Debt: $12.4 billion (1987)
Exports: $41.086 billion (1991); commodities: machinery and equipment, iron and steel, lumber, textiles, paper products, chemicals; partners: Germany 35%, Italy 10%, Eastern Europe 9%, Switzerland 7%, US 4%, OPEC 3%
Imports: $50.740 billion (1991); commodities: petroleum, foodstuffs, machinery and equipment, vehicles, chemicals, textiles and clothing, pharmaceuticals; partners: Germany 44%, Italy 9%, Eastern Europe 6%, Switzerland 5%, US 4%, USSR 2%

■ HEALTH

Births: 12/1,000 population (1991)
Deaths: 11/1,000 population (1991)
Infant Mortality: 5 deaths/1,000 live births (1991)
Life Expectancy at Birth: 73 years male, 79 years female (1992)
No. of Physicians: 25.8/10,000 population (1992)

■ EDUCATION

Govt. Expenditure: 9% of govt. expenditure (1989)
Literacy: 98%

■ COMMUNICATIONS

Daily newspapers: 34 (1992)
Televisions: 475.3/1,000 inhabitants (1992)
Radios: 622/1,000 inhabitants (1992)
Telephones: 50.0/100 inhabitants (1992)

■ TRANSPORTATION

Motor Vehicles: 3,691,749; 2,991,284 passenger cars (1990)
Roads: 108,586 km paved
Railway: 5,828 km
Air Traffic: 2,606,000 passengers carried (1991)
Airports: 11

Canadian Embassy: Dr. Karl Lueger Ring 10, A-1010 Vienna, Austria. Tel: (011-43-1) 533-3691
Embassy in Canada: Austrian Embassy, 445 Wilbrod St, Ottawa ON K1N 6M7. Tel: (613) 789-3429. -30. Fax: (613) 789-3431.

Azerbaijan

Long-Form Name: Republic of Azerbaijan
Capital: Baku
Population: 7,283,000 (1992)

■ GEOGRAPHY

Area: 86,600 sq. km
Coastline: n.a
Climate: Alpine to subtropical

Environment: n.a.
Terrain: fertile central lowlands
Land Use: grazing land in the Caucasus mountains; farming in lowlands
Location: SE Europe, bordering on Caspian Sea

■ PEOPLE

Nationality: Azerbaijani
Ethnic Groups: 82.7% Azerbaijani, 5.6% Russians, 5.6% Armenians, 2.4% Lezgins, 3.7% other
Languages: Azerbaijani (official), Armenian, Russian
Religions: predominantly Shia Moslem, with Armenian Apostolic minority
Marriages: n.a.
Divorces: n.a.

■ GOVERNMENT

Leader(s): Pres. Haydar Aliyev

Government type: in transition to republic
Administrative Divisions: n.a.; as part of the former Soviet Union, Azerbaijan consisted of 2 autonomous regions
Independence: declared Aug. 30, 1991
National Holiday: n.a.

■ ECONOMY

Overview: primarily industries and agriculture
GNP: $12.065 billion, per capita $1,670; real growth rate 1.9% (1991)
Inflation: n.a.
Industries: oil extraction and refining
Labour Force: n.a.
Unemployment: n.a.
Agriculture: cotton, grain, grapes, tea, citrus fruits, vegetables, sheep and horse breeding
Natural Resources: oil reserves, minerals, iron, aluminum

■ FINANCE/TRADE

Currency: rouble (rbl.), manat
International Reserves Excluding Gold: n.a.
Gold Reserves: n.a.
Budget: 1989 revenue, 3,808 million roubles
Defence Expenditures: n.a.
External Debt: n.a.
Exports: grain, cotton, rice, fruit, vegetables, oil extraction equipment
Imports: n.a.

■ HEALTH

Births: 25.6/1,000 population (1989)
Deaths: 6.2/1,000 population (1989)

Infant Mortality: 26.1 deaths/1,000 live births (1989)
Life Expectancy at Birth: 67 years male, 74 years female (1992)
No. of Physicians: 27,800 (1989)

■ EDUCATION

Govt. Expenditure: n.a.
Literacy: n.a.

■ COMMUNICATIONS

Daily newspapers: 158 daily newspapers of all circulation types (1989)
Televisions: n.a.
Radios: n.a.
Telephones: n.a.

■ TRANSPORTATION

Motor Vehicles: n.a.
Roads: n.a.
Railway: 2,040 km
Air Traffic: n.a.
Airports: 1

Canadian Embassy: C/o Starokonyushenny Per 23, Moscow 12100, Russian Federation . Tel: (011-7-95) 241-5070. Fax: (011-7-95) 241-9034. C/o Embassy of the Russian Federation, 285 Charlotte St, Ottawa ON K1N 8L5. Tel: (613) 235-4341, 236-1413. Fax: (613) 236-6342.

Bahamas

Long-Form Name: Commonwealth of the Bahamas
Capital: Nassau
Population: 260,000 (1992)

■ GEOGRAPHY

Area: 13,940 sq. km
Coastline: 3,542 km
Climate: tropical marine; moderated by warm waters of Gulf Stream
Environment: subject to hurricanes and other tropical storms that cause extensive flood damage
Terrain: long, flat coral formations with some low rounded hills
Land Use: 1% arable land; negligible permanent crops; negligible meadows and pastures; 32% forest and woodland; 67% other
Location: Caribbean Islands

■ PEOPLE

Nationality: Bahamian
Ethnic Groups: 85% black, 15% white

Languages: English; some Creole among Haitian immigrants
Religions: 29% Baptist, 23% Anglican, 22% Roman Catholic, smaller groups of other Protestants, Greek Orthodox and Jews
Marriages: 7.9 (per 1,000) (1987)
Divorces: 1.6 (per 1,000) (1986)

■ GOVERNMENT

Leader(s): Prime Min. Hubert Alexander Ingraham, Gov. Gen. Sir Henry Taylor
Government type: commonwealth
Administrative Divisions: 21 districts
Independence: July 10, 1973 (from UK)
National Holiday: Independence Day, July 10

■ ECONOMY

Overview: tourism and offshore banking are features of this stable, middle-income developing nation
GNP: $3.044 billion, per capita $11,720; real growth rate 3.3% (1991)
Inflation: 7.1% (1991)
Industries: banking, tourism, cement, oil refining and transshipment, salt production, rum, aragonite, pharmaceuticals, spiral weld, steel pipe
Labour Force: 132,600; 30% government, 25% hotels and restaurants, 10% business services, 5% agriculture (1986)
Unemployment: 11.7% (1989)
Agriculture: accounts for less than 5% of GDP; dominated by small-scale producers; principal products—citrus fruit, vegetables, poultry; large net importer of food
Natural Resources: salt, aragonite, timber

■ FINANCE/TRADE

Currency: Bahamian dollar ($B)
International Reserves Excluding Gold: $163 million (1992)
Gold Reserves: none
Budget: revenues $1.03 billion; expenditures $1.1 billion, including capital expenditures of $275 million (1991)
Defence Expenditures: n.a.
External Debt: $1.5 billion (1988)
Exports: $2.678 billion (1990); commodities: pharmaceuticals, cement, rum, crawfish; partners: US 90%, UK 10%
Imports: $2.920 billion (1990); commodities: foodstuffs, manufactured goods, mineral fuels; partners: Iran 30%, Nigeria 20%, US 10%, European Community 10%, Gabon 10%

■ HEALTH

Births: 19/1,000 population (1991)

Deaths: 5/1,000 population (1991)
Infant Mortality: 18 deaths/1,000 live births (1991)
Life Expectancy at Birth: 69 years male, 76 years female (1992)
No. of Physicians: 9.4/10,000 population (1992)

■ EDUCATION

Govt. Expenditure: 25.5% of govt. expenditure (1982)
Literacy: 95%

■ COMMUNICATIONS

Daily newspapers: 3 (1992)
Televisions: 224.9/1,000 inhabitants (1992)
Radios: 538/1,000 inhabitants (1992)
Telephones: 63.59/100 inhabitants (1992)

■ TRANSPORTATION

Motor Vehicles: 85,000; 70,000 passenger cars (1990)
Roads: n.a.
Railway: n.a.
Air Traffic: 1,090,000 passengers carried (1991)
Airports: 59

Canadian Embassy: c/o The Canadian High Commission, 30-36 Knutsford Blvd., Kingston 5; mailing address: P.O. Box 1500, Kingston 10, Jamaica. Tel: (809) 926-1500. Fax: (809) 926-1702
Embassy in Canada: High Commission for the Commonwealth of the Bahamas, 360 Albert St, Ste 1020, Ottawa ON K1R 7X7. Tel: (613) 232-1724. Fax: (613) 232-0097.

Bahrain

Long-Form Name: State of Bahrain
Capital: Manama
Population: 533,000 (1992)

■ GEOGRAPHY

Area: 690 sq. km
Coastline: 161 km
Climate: arid; mild, pleasant winters; very hot, humid summers
Environment: subsurface water sources being rapidly depleted (requires development of desalination facilities); dust storms; desertification
Terrain: mostly low desert plain rising gently to low central escarpment
Land Use: 2% arable land; 2% permanent crops; 6% meadows and pastures; 0% forest and woodland; 90% other; includes negligible irrigated

Location: Persian Gulf

■ PEOPLE

Nationality: Bahraini
Ethnic Groups: 63% Bahraini, 13% Asian, 10% other Arab, 8% Iranian, 6% other
Languages: Arabic (official); English also widely spoken; Farsi, Urdu
Religions: Moslem(60% Shi'a, 40% Sunni)
Marriages: 6.6 (per 1,000) ((1986)
Divorces: 1.1 (per 1,000) (1986)

■ GOVERNMENT

Leader(s): Prime Min. Khalifa bin Salman Al Khalifa, Amir 'Isa bin Sulman Al Khalifa
Government type: traditional monarchy
Administrative Divisions: 11 municipalities
Independence: Aug. 15, 1971 (from UK)
National Holiday: National Day, Dec. 16

■ ECONOMY

Overview: petroleum production and processing are the backbone of the economy and any change in the world oil market affects the economy
GNP: $3.679 billion, per capita $6,910; real growth rate 0.1% (1991)
Inflation: 0.9% (1991)
Industries: petroleum processing and refining, aluminum smelting, offshore banking, ship repairing
Labour Force: 220,000 (1992); 42% of labour force is Bahraini; 35% industry, 3% agriculture, 62% services (1989)
Unemployment: 3,286 (1991)
Agriculture: including fishing, accounts for less than 2% of GDP; not self-sufficient in food production; heavily subsidized sector produces fruit, vegetables, poultry, dairy products, shrimp and fish; fish catch 9,000 metric tons in 1987
Natural Resources: oil, associated and non-associated natural gas, fish

■ FINANCE/TRADE

Currency: Bahraini dinar (BD)
International Reserves Excluding Gold: $1,399 million (1992)
Gold Reserves: 0.15 million fine troy ounces (1990)
Budget: revenues $1.2 billion; expenditures $1.32 billion, including capital expenditures (1991)
Defence Expenditures: $201.92 million (1990)
External Debt: $1.1 billion (1989)

Exports: $3.404 billion (1991); commodities: petroleum 80%, aluminium 7%, other 13%; partners: US, United Arab Emirates, Japan, Singapore, Saudi Arabia
Imports: $4.066 billion (1991); commodities: non-oil 59%, crude oil 41%; partners: UK, Saudi Arabia, US, Japan

■ HEALTH

Births: 27/1,000 population (1991)
Deaths: 3/1,000 population (1991)
Infant Mortality: 17 deaths/1,000 live births (1991)
Life Expectancy at Birth: 70 years male, 74 years female (1992)
No. of Physicians: 12.2/10,000 population (1992)

■ EDUCATION

Govt. Expenditure: 15.51% of govt. expenditure (1991)
Literacy: 77.4% (1992)

■ COMMUNICATIONS

Daily newspapers: 3 (1992)
Televisions: 401.6/1,000 inhabitants (1992)
Radios: 527/1,000 inhabitants (1992)
Telephones: 28.91/100 inhabitants (1992)

■ TRANSPORTATION

Motor Vehicles: 128,086; 104,585 passenger cars (1990)
Roads: 203 km paved
Railway: n.a.
Air Traffic: 876,000 passengers carried (1991)
Airports: 1

Canadian Embassy: C/o The Canadian Embassy, Da'Aiah – Block 4, Al-Mutawakel St, Kuwait City; mailing address: P.O. Box 25281, 13113 (Safat), Kuwait City, Kuwait. Tel: (011-965) 256-3025
Representative to Canada: C/o The Embassy of the State of Bahrain, 3502 Int'l. Drive NW, Washington, DC 20008, USA

Bangladesh

Long-Form Name: People's Republic of Bangladesh
Capital: Dhaka
Population: 118,740,000 (1992)

■ GEOGRAPHY

Area: 144,000 sq. km
Coastline: 580 km
Climate: tropical; cool, dry winter (Oct. to Mar.); hot, humid summer (Mar. to June); warm, rainy monsoon (June to Oct.)
Environment: vulnerable to droughts; much of country routinely flooded during summer monsoon season; overpopulation; deforestation
Terrain: mostly flat alluvial plain; hilly in southeast
Land Use: 67% arable land; 2% permanent crops; 4% meadows and pastures; 16% forest and woodland; 11% other; includes 14% irrigated
Location: S Asia, bordering on Bay of Bengal

■ PEOPLE

Nationality: Bangladeshi
Ethnic Groups: 98% Bengali, 250,000 Biharis, less than 1 million tribals
Languages: Bangla (official), English widely used, 5% tribal dialects
Religions: 87% Moslem, about 12% Hindu, less than 1% Buddhist, Christian and other
Marriages: 9.0 (per 1,000) (1986)
Divorces: n.a.

■ GOVERNMENT

Leader(s): Pres. Abdur Rahman Biswas, Prime Min. Begum Khaleda Zia
Government type: unitary republic
Administrative Divisions: 64 districts
Independence: Dec. 16, 1971 (from Pakistan; Bangladesh formerly known as East Pakistan)
National Holiday: Independence Day, Mar. 26

■ ECONOMY

Overview: one of the poorest nations in the world; the economy is based on a small number of agricultural exports which are vulnerable to natural disasters. Few natural resources
GNP: $23.449 billion, per capita $220; real growth rate 4.2% (1991)
Inflation: 7.2% (1991)
Industries: jute manufacturing, food processing, cotton textiles, petroleum, urea fertilizer
Labour Force: 33,000,000 (1992); 56.5% agriculture, 33.7% services, 9.8% industry ; extensive export of labour to Saudi Arabia, UAE, Oman and Kuwait (1989)
Unemployment: 30% (1988 est.)
Agriculture: accounts for about 50% of GDP and 74% of both employment and exports; imports 10% of food grain requirements; world's largest exporter of jute; commercial products—jute, rice, wheat, tea, sugar cane, potatoes, beef, milk, poultry
Natural Resources: natural gas, uranium, arable land, timber

■ FINANCE/TRADE

Currency: taka (Tk)
International Reserves Excluding Gold: $1,825 million (1992)
Gold Reserves: 0.09 million fine troy ounces (1992)
Budget: revenues $2.2 billion; expenditures $3.9 billion, including capital expenditures of $1.6 billion (1989)
Defence Expenditures: $321.69 million (1990)
External Debt: $11.464 billion (1990)
Exports: $1.693 billion (1991); commodities: jute, tea, leather, shrimp, manufacturing; partners: US 25%, Western Europe 22%, Middle East 9%, Japan 8%, Eastern Europe 7%
Imports: $3.409 billion (1991); commodities: food, petroleum and other energy, nonfood consumer goods, semiprocessed goods and capital equipment; partners: Western Europe 18%, Japan 14%, Middle East 9%, US 8%

■ HEALTH

Births: 36/1,000 population (1991)
Deaths: 13/1,000 population (1991)
Infant Mortality: 118 deaths/1,000 live births (1991)
Life Expectancy at Birth: 54 years male, 53 years female (1992)
No. of Physicians: 1.6/10,000 population (1992)

■ EDUCATION

Govt. Expenditure: 10.5% of govt. expenditure (1989)
Literacy: 35.3% (1992)

■ COMMUNICATIONS

Daily newspapers: 72 (1992)
Televisions: 4.4/1,000 inhabitants (1992)
Radios: 41/1,000 inhabitants (1992)
Telephones: 0.1/100 inhabitants (1992)

■ TRANSPORTATION

Motor Vehicles: 128,000; 66,000 passenger cars (1990)
Roads: 8,064 km; 4,176 paved
Railway: 3,038 km (1988)
Air Traffic: 1,080,000 passengers carried (1991)
Airports: 15

Canadian Embassy: The Canadian High Commission, House CWN 16/A, Rd. 48, Gulshan, Dhaka 1212; mailing address: G.P.O. Box 569, Dhaka 1000, Bangladesh. Tel: (011-88-02) 607-071-7
Embassy in Canada: High Commission for the People's Republic of Bangladesh, 85 Range Rd, Ste 402, Ottawa ON K1N 8J6. Tel: (613) 236-0138, -9.

Barbados

Long-Form Name: Barbados
Capital: Bridgetown
Population: 260,000 (1992)

■ GEOGRAPHY

Area: 430 sq. km
Coastline: 97 km
Climate: tropical; rainy season (June to Nov.)
Environment: subject to hurricanes, especially June to Oct.
Terrain: relatively flat; rises gently to a central highland region
Land Use: 77% arable land; 0% permanent crops; 9% meadows and pastures; 0% forest and woodland; 14% other
Location: Caribbean islands

■ PEOPLE

Nationality: Barbadian
Ethnic Groups: 80% African, 16% mixed, 4% European
Languages: English
Religions: 70% Anglican, 9% Methodist, 4% Roman Catholic, 17% other, including Moravian
Marriages: 5.8 (per 1,000) (1986)
Divorces: 1.4 (per 1,000) (1986)

■ GOVERNMENT

Leader(s): Prime Min. Lloyd Erskine Sandiford, Gov. Gen. Dame Nita Barrow
Government type: parliamentary democracy
Administrative Divisions: 11 parishes
Independence: Nov. 30, 1966 (from UK)
National Holiday: Independence Day, Nov. 30

■ ECONOMY

Overview: has one of the highest standards of living of islands in the region; the tourist industry and traditional sugar cane cultivation are main parts of the economy
GNP: $1.711 billion, per capita $6,630; real growth rate 1.6% (1991)
Inflation: 6.3% (1991)
Industries: tourism, sugar, light manufacturing, component assembly for export
Labour Force: 137,000 (1992); 84.1% services, 10.2% industry, 5.7% agriculture (1989)
Unemployment: 17.1% (1991)

Agriculture: accounts for 10% of GDP; major cash crop is sugar cane; other crops—vegetables and cotton; not self-sufficient in food
Natural Resources: crude oil, fishing, natural gas

■ FINANCE/TRADE

Currency: Barbados dollar ($BDS)
International Reserves Excluding Gold: $149 million (1992)
Gold Reserves: none (1991)
Budget: revenues $501 million; expenditures $484 million, including capital expenditures of $113 million (1991)
Defence Expenditures: 0.7% GDP (1988)
External Debt: $635 million (1989)
Exports: $202 million (1991); commodities: sugar and molasses, electrical components, clothing, rum, machinery and transport equipment; partners: US 30%, CARICOM, UK, Puerto Rico, Canada
Imports: $695 million (1991); commodities: foodstuffs, consumer durables, raw materials, crude oil; partners: US 34%, CARICOM, Japan, UK, Canada

■ HEALTH

Births: 16/1,000 population (1991)
Deaths: 9/1,000 population (1991)
Infant Mortality: 23 deaths/1,000 live births (1991)
Life Expectancy at Birth: 70 years male, 76 years female (1992)
No. of Physicians: 8.9/10,000 population (1992)

■ EDUCATION

Govt. Expenditure: 18.64% of govt. expenditure (1989)
Literacy: 99.3% (1992)

■ COMMUNICATIONS

Daily newspapers: 2 (1992)
Televisions: 262.7/1,000 inhabitants (1992)
Radios: 878/1,000 inhabitants (1992)
Telephones: 57.46/100 inhabitants (1992)

■ TRANSPORTATION

Motor Vehicles: 45,000; 39,500 passenger cars (1990)
Roads: 1,570 km; 1,475 paved
Railway: none
Air Traffic: 1,320,000 passengers carried (1990)
Airports: 1

Canadian Embassy: The Canadian High Commission, Bishop's Court Hill, St. Michael, Barbados; mailing address: P.O. Box 404, Bridgetown, Barbados. Tel: (809) 429-3550. Fax: (809) 429-3780
Embassy in Canada: High Commission for Barbados, 124 O'Connor St, Suite 603, Ottawa ON K1P 5M9. Tel: (613) 236-9517, -8

Belarus

Long-Form Name: Republic of Belarus (or Byelorussia)
Capital: Minsk
Population: 10,295,000 (1992)

■ GEOGRAPHY

Area: 207,600 sq. km
Coastline: none; landlocked
Climate: n.a.
Environment: n.a.
Terrain: a hilly land of forests, lakes, rivers, and marshes; soil poor and sandy
Land Use: 25% forests and woodlands; 60% cultivated
Location: NC Europe

■ PEOPLE

Nationality: Belarus
Ethnic Groups: 79% Byelorussian, 12% Russian, 4% Polish, 2% Ukrainian, 1% Jews, 2% other
Languages: Byelorussian, Russian
Religions: predominantly Roman Catholic and Eastern Orthodox
Marriages: n.a.
Divorces: n.a.

■ GOVERNMENT

Leader(s): President Stanislav S. Shushkevich, Premier Vyacheslav M. Kebich
Government type: in transition to republic
Administrative Divisions: 6 regions
Independence: declared Aug. 24, 1991
National Holiday: n.a.

■ ECONOMY

Overview: strong emphasis on mining and agricultural, with growing manufacturing and services sector
GNP: n.a.
Inflation: n.a.
Industries: machinery, tools, refineries, fertilizer production
Labour Force: 5,327,000 (1989)
Unemployment: n.a.
Agriculture: potatoes, flax, rye, oats, barley, wheat, cattle breeding, pigs, potatoes, peat, forest resources
Natural Resources: oil, potassium

■ FINANCE/TRADE

Currency: rouble (rbl.)
International Reserves Excluding Gold: n.a.
Gold Reserves: n.a.
Budget: 1989 revenue, 11,022 million roubles
Defence Expenditures: n.a.
External Debt: n.a.
Exports: $390 million (Jan.–June 1992) agricultural and transport machinery, computers, refrigerators
Imports: $188 million (Jan.–June 1992)

■ HEALTH

Births: 15.0/1,000 population (1989)
Deaths: 10.1/1,000 population (1989)
Infant Mortality: 12.0 deaths/1,000 live births (1989)
Life Expectancy at Birth: 67 years male, 76 years female (1992)
No. of Physicians: 41,400 (1989)

■ EDUCATION

Govt. Expenditure: n.a.
Literacy: 97.9% (1992)

■ COMMUNICATIONS

Daily newspapers: 220 papers of all circulation types (1989), 28 dailies (1992)
Televisions: 255/1,000 inhabitants (1992)
Radios: 303/1,000 inhabitants (1992)
Telephones: n.a.

■ TRANSPORTATION

Motor Vehicles: n.a.
Railway: 5,590 km (1990).
Air Traffic: n.a.
Airports: n.a.

Canadian Embassy: C/o Starokonyushenny Per 23, Moscow 12100, Russian Federation. Tel: (011-7-95) 241-5070. Fax: (011-7-95) 241-9034.
Representative to Canada: C/o Embassy of the Russian Federation, 285 Charlotte St, Ottawa ON K1N 8L5. Tel: (613) 235-4341, 236-1413. Fax: (613) 236-6342.

Belau (Palau)

Dependent Territory of the United States

Long-Form Name: Republic of Belau (Palau)
Capital: Koror (on Koror Island)
Population: 16,000 (1992)

■ GEOGRAPHY

Area: 488 sq. km (26 islands and 300+ islets)
Climate: tropical, warm year-round; wet season, May to Dec., dry season, Jan. to April; typhoon-prone with violent winds and heavy rain, esp. in July
Land Use: northern islands of volcanic origin, fertile and extensively cultivated; southern islands too rugged for habitation
Location: W Pacific Ocean (Micronesia)

■ PEOPLE

Nationality: American
Ethnic Groups: Polynesian, Malayan, Melanesian, mixtures
Languages: Palauan, English (official)

■ GOVERNMENT

Leader(s): Pres. Kuniwo Nakamura, V. Pres. Tommy Remengesau
Government Type: outlying territory of the United States

■ ECONOMY

Overview: phosphate deposits on northern islands; some fishing; largely dependent on imports from US
Currency: American dollar (US$)

Belgium

Long-Form Name: Kingdom of Belgium
Capital: Brussels
Population: 9,998,000 (1992)

■ GEOGRAPHY

Area: 30,510 sq. km
Coastline: 64 km
Climate: temperate; mild winters, cool summers; rainy, humid, cloudy
Environment: air and water pollution
Terrain: flat coastal plains in northwest central rolling hills, rugged mountains of Ardennes Forest in southeast
Land Use: 24% arable land; 1% permanent crops; 20% meadows and pastures; 21% forest and woodland; 34% other; includes negligible irrigated
Location: NW Europe, bordering on North Sea

■ PEOPLE

Nationality: Belgian
Ethnic Groups: 55% Fleming, 33% Walloon, 12% mixed or other

Languages: Dutch or Flemish spoken in north (Flanders), French in south (Wallonia), both languages official; small English-speaking minority in the east
Religions: 75% Roman Catholic, remainder Protestant or other
Marriages: 5.7 (per 1,000) (1987)
Divorces: 1.9 (per 1,000) (1986)

■ GOVERNMENT

Leader(s): Prime Min. Jean-Luc Dehaene, King Albert II
Government Type: constitutional monarchy
Administrative Divisions: 9 provinces
Independence: Oct. 4, 1830 (from the Netherlands)
National Holiday: National Day, July 21

■ ECONOMY

Overview: a small, private-enterprise based economy possessing few natural resources, it is therefore highly vulnerable to the state of world markets
GNP: $192.370 billion, per capita $19,300; real growth rate 2.2% (1991)
Inflation: 3.2% (1991)
Industries: engineering and metal products, processed food and beverages, chemicals, basic metals, textiles, glass, petroleum, coal
Labour Force: 4,151,000 (1992); 78% services, 19.5% industry, 2.5% agriculture (1989)
Unemployment: 10.3% (1991)
Agriculture: accounts for 2% of GDP; emphasis on livestock production—beef, veal, pork, milk; major crops are sugar beets, fresh vegetables, fruits, grain and tobacco; net importer of farm products
Natural Resources: coal, natural gas

■ FINANCE/TRADE

Currency: Belgian franc (BF)
International Reserves Excluding Gold: $10,135 million (1992)
Gold Reserves: 25.04 million fine troy ounces (1992)
Budget: revenues $45 billion; expenditures $55.3 billion, including capital expenditures (1989)
Defence Expenditures: $3.07 billion (1991)
External Debt: $27.5 billion (1988)
Exports: $118.550 billion (1991) Belgium-Luxembourg Economic Union; commodities: iron and steel, transportation equipment, tractors, diamonds, petroleum products; partners: European Community 74%, US 5% Communist countries 2%
Imports: $121.271 billion (1991) Belgium-Luxembourg Economic Union; commodities: fuels, grains, chemicals, foodstuffs; partners: European Community 72%, US 5%, oil-exporting less developed countries 4%, Communist countries 3%

■ HEALTH

Births: 12/1,000 population (1991)
Deaths: 11/1,000 population (1991)
Infant Mortality: 6 deaths/1,000 live births (1991)
Life expectancy at birth: 72 years male, 79 years female (1992)
No. of physicians: 30.2/10,000 population (1992)

■ EDUCATION

Govt. Expenditure: 12% of govt. expenditure (1988)
Literacy: 98%

■ COMMUNICATIONS

Daily newspapers: 23 (1992)
Televisions: 447.1/1,000 inhabitants (1992)
Radios: 776/1,000 inhabitants (1992)
Telephones: 51.72/100 inhabitants (1992)

■ TRANSPORTATION

Motor Vehicles: 4,276,737; 3,833,294 passenger cars (1990)
Roads: 129,454 km; 124,267 km
Railway: 3,600 km
Air Traffic: 3,018,000 passengers carried (1991)
Airports: 12

Canadian Embassy: 2, Avenue de Tervuren, 1040 Brussels, Belgium. Tel: (011-32-2) 735-60-40. Fax: (011-32-2) 735-3383
Embassy in Canada: Embassy of Belgium, 80 Elgin St, 4th Floor, Ottawa ON K1P 1B7. Tel: (613) 236-7267.

Belize

Long-Form Name: Belize
Capital: Belmopan
Population: 198,000 (1992)

■ GEOGRAPHY

Area: 22,960 sq. km
Coastline: 386 km
Climate: tropical; very hot and humid; rainy season (May to Feb.)
Environment: frequent devastating hurricanes (Sept. to Dec.) and coastal flooding, especially in south; deforestation
Terrain: flat, swampy coastal plain; low mountains in south

Land Use: 2% arable land; negligible permanent crops; 2% meadows and pastures; 44% forest and woodland; 52% other; includes negligible irrigated

Location: Central (Latin) America, bordering on Caribbean Sea

■ PEOPLE

Nationality: Belizean

Ethnic Groups: 40% Creole, 33% Mestizo, 10% Maya, 8% Garifuna, 2% East Indian, 8% other

Languages: English (official), Spanish, Maya, Garifuna (Carib)

Religions: 60 % Roman Catholic, 30% Protestant sects, 10% Bahai and Muslim

Marriages: 6.0 (per 1,000) (1986)

Divorces: 0.4 (per 1,000) (1985)

■ GOVERNMENT

Leader(s): Prime Min. George Price, Gov. Gen. Dame Minita Elvira Gordon

Government Type: parliamentary

Administrative Divisions: 6 districts

Independence: Sept. 21, 1981 (from UK; Belize formerly known as British Honduras)

National Holiday: Independence Day, Sept. 21

■ ECONOMY

Overview: economy primarily based on agriculture and merchandising; sugar is the main crop

GNP: $389 million, per capita $2.050; real growth rate 5.3% (1991)

Inflation: 5.7% (1989)

Industries: sugar refining, clothing, timber and forest products, furniture, rum, soap, beverages, cigarettes, tourism

Labour Force: 51,500; 30% agriculture, 16% services, 15.4% government, 11.2% commerce, 10.3% manufacturing; shortage of skilled labour and all types of technical personnel (1985)

Unemployment: 14% (1988 est.)

Agriculture: accounts for 30% of GDP (including fish and forestry); commercial crops include sugar cane, bananas, cocoa, citrus fruits; expanding output of lumber and cultured shrimp; net importer of basic foods

Natural Resources: arable land potential, timber, fish

■ FINANCE/TRADE

Currency: Belize dollar ($BZ)

International Reserves Excluding Gold: $56 million (1992)

Gold Reserves: n.a.

Budget: revenues $87.4 million; expenditures $130.5 million, including capital expenditures of $53.5 million (1990)

Defence Expenditures: $9.94 million (1989)

External Debt: $140 million (1988)

Exports: $120 million (1991); commodities: sugar, clothing, seafood, molasses, citrus, wood and wood products; partners: US 47%, UK, Trinidad and Tobago, Canada

Imports: $251 million (1991); commodities: machinery and transportation equipment, food, manufactured goods, fuels, chemicals, pharmaceuticals; partners: US 55%, UK, Netherlands Antilles, Mexico

■ HEALTH

Births: 38/1,000 population (1991)

Deaths: 5/1,000 population (1991)

Infant Mortality: 35 deaths/1,000 live births (1991)

Life Expectancy at Birth: 67 years male, 72 years female (1992)

No. of Physicians: 4.5/10,000 population (1992)

■ EDUCATION

Govt. Expenditure: 16.1% of govt. expenditures (1992)

Literacy: 91.2% (1992)

■ COMMUNICATIONS

Daily newspapers: 5 (1992)

Televisions: 164.8/1,000 inhabitants (1992)

Radios: 580/1,000 inhabitants (1992)

Telephones: 15,917 (1990)

■ TRANSPORTATION

Motor Vehicles: 4,465; 1,692 passenger cars (1990)

Roads: 2,594 km; 344 km paved

Railway: none

Air Traffic: 765,430 passengers carried (1988)

Airports: 38

Canadian Embassy: The Canadian High Commission, 30-36 Knutsford Blvd., Kingston 5, Jamaica; mailing address: P.O. Box 1500, Kingston 10, Jamaica. Tel: (809) 926-1500. Fax: (809) 926-1702

Embassy in Canada: High Commission for Belize, 112 Kent St, Ste 2005, Place de Ville, Tower B, Ottawa ON K1P 5P2. Tel: (613) 232-7389. Fax: (613) 232-5804

Benin

Long-Form Name: Republic of Benin

Capital: Porto Novo (official); Cotonou (de facto)

Population: 4,918,000 (1992)

■ GEOGRAPHY

Area: 112,620 sq. km
Coastline: 121 km
Climate: tropical; hot, humid in south; semi-arid in north
Environment: hot, dry, dusty harmattan wind may affect north in winter; deforestation; desertification; recent droughts have severely affected marginal agriculture in north
Terrain: mostly flat to undulating plain; some hills and low mountains
Land Use: 12% arable land; 4% permanent crops; 4% meadows and pastures; 35% forest and woodland; 45% other; includes negligible irrigated
Location: WC Africa, bordering on South Atlantic Ocean

■ PEOPLE

Nationality: Beninese
Ethnic Groups: 99% African (42 ethnic groups, most important being Fon, Adja, Yoruba, Bariba); 5,500 Europeans
Languages: French (official); also Fon, Yoruba, Fulami, Bariba
Religions: majority Animist, 13% Islam, 15% Christian
Marriages: n.a.
Divorces: n.a.

■ GOVERNMENT

Leader(s): Pres. Nicéphore Soglo
Government Type: in transition to multi-party system
Administrative Divisions: 6 provinces
Independence: Aug. 1, 1960 (from France; Benin formerly Dahomey)
National Holiday: National Day, Nov. 30

■ ECONOMY

Overview: limited natural resources and a underdeveloped infrastructure characterize the economy; agriculture products are a major export
GNP: $1.848 billion, per capita $380; real growth rate 2.1% (1991)
Inflation: 4.3% (1988)
Industries: palm oil and palm kernel oil processing, textiles, beverages, petroleum
Labour Force: 2,200,000 (1992); 70.2% agriculture, 23.1% services, 6.6% industry (1989)
Unemployment: n.a.
Agriculture: small farms produce 90% of agricultural output; production is dominated by food crops—corn, sorghum, cassava, beans and rice; cash crops include cotton, palm oil and peanuts; poultry and livestock output has not kept up with consumption
Natural Resources: small offshore oil deposits, limestone, marble, timber

■ FINANCE/TRADE

Currency: Communauté financière africaine franc (CFAF)
International Reserves Excluding Gold: $230 million (1992)
Gold Reserves: 0.01 million fine troy ounces (1991)
Budget: revenues $168 million; expenditures $317 million, including capital expenditures of $97 million (1989)
Defence Expenditures: $38.36 million (1988)
External Debt: $1.262 billion (1990)
Exports: $226 million (1988); commodities: crude oil, fuels, cotton, palm products, cocoa; partners: Germany 36%, France 16%, Spain 14%, Italy 8%, UK 7%
Imports: $413 million (1988); commodities: foodstuffs, beverages, tobacco, petroleum products, cereals, chemicals, miscellaneous manufactured goods, intermediate goods, capital goods, light consumer goods; partners: France 34%, Netherlands 10%, Japan 7%, Italy 6%, US 5%

■ HEALTH

Births: 49/1,000 population (1991)
Deaths: 16/1,000 population (1991)
Infant Mortality: 119 deaths/1,000 live births (1991)
Life Expectancy at Birth: 45 years male, 49 years female (1992)
No. of Physicians: 0.6/10,000 population (1990)

■ EDUCATION

Govt. Expenditure: 36.8% of govt. expenditure (1980)
Literacy: 23.4% (1992)

■ COMMUNICATIONS

Daily newspapers: 1 (1992)
Televisions: 4.5/1,000 inhabitants (1992)
Radios: 89/1,000 inhabitants (1992)
Telephones: 0.37/100 inhabitants (1992)

■ TRANSPORTATION

Motor Vehicles: 38,000; 25,000 passenger cars (1990)
Roads: 7,546; 788 km paved
Railway: 586 km
Air Traffic: 64,000 passengers carried (1991)

Airports: 8
Canadian Embassy: The Canadian High
Commission, 4 Idowu-Taylor St, Victoria
Island; mailing address: P.O. Box 54506, Ikoyi
Station, Lagos, Nigeria
Embassy in Canada: Embassy of the Republic of
Benin, 58 Glebe Ave, Ottawa ON K1S 2C3.
Tel: (613) 233-4429, -4868, -5273.

Bermuda

Dependent Territory of the United States
Long-Form Name: Bermuda
Capital: Hamilton
Population: 62,000 (1992)

■ GEOGRAPHY

Area: 53 sq. km
Coastline: 103 km
Climate: subtropical; mild, humid; gales, strong
winds common in winter
Environment: ample rainfall, but no rivers or
freshwater lakes; consists of about 360 small
coral islands
Terrain: low hills separated by fertile depressions
Land Use: 0% arable land; 0% permanent crops;
0% meadows and pastures; 20% forest and
woodland; 80% other
Location: North Atlantic Ocean

■ PEOPLE

Nationality: Bermudan
Ethnic Groups: 61% black, 39% white and other
Languages: English

■ GOVERNMENT

Leader(s): Gov. Lord Waddington, Prem. John
WD. Swan
Government Type: dependent territory of the UK
Administrative Divisions: 9 parishes, 2 municipal-
ities
National Holiday: Bermuda Day, May 22

■ ECONOMY

Overview: a successful tourist industry accounts
for its high per capita income; most food is
imported
GNP: $1.3 billion, per capita $23,000; real
growth rate 2% (1989 est.)
Currency: Bermuda dollar ($Ber)

Canadian Embassy: c/o 501 Pennsylvania Ave
NW, Wahington, DC 20001 U.S.A.

Bhutan

Long-Form Name: Kingdom of Bhutan
Capital: Punakha (winter), Thimphu (summer)
Population: 1,612,000 (1992)

■ GEOGRAPHY

Area: 47,000 sq. km
Coastline: none: landlocked
Climate: varies; tropical in southern plains; cool
winters and hot summers in central valleys;
severe winters and cool summers in Himalayas
Environment: violent storms coming from the
Himalayas were the source of the country name
which translates as Land of the Thunder Dragon
Terrain: mostly mountainous with some fertile
valleys and savanna
Land Use: 2% arable land; negligible permanent
crops; 5% meadows and pastures; 70% forest
and woodland; 23% other
Location: S Asia

■ PEOPLE

Nationality: Bhutanese
Ethnic Groups: 60% Bhote, 25% ethnic Nepalese,
15% indigenous or migrant tribes
Languages: Bhotes speak various Tibetan
dialects-most widely spoken dialect is
Dzongkha (official); Nepalese speak various
Nepalese dialects
Religions: Mahayana Buddhism (state religion),
Hinduism (25%, mainly ethnic Nepalese)
Marriages: n.a.
Divorces: n.a.

■ GOVERNMENT

Leader(s): King Jigme Singye Wangchuk
Government Type: monarchy; special treaty rela-
tionship with India
Administrative Divisions: 3 regions, 1 division
Independence: Aug. 8, 1949 (from India)
National Holiday: National Day, Dec. 17

■ ECONOMY

Overview: agriculture and forestry are the
bedrock of the economy; it is poorly developed
due to omniscient rugged topography
GNP: $260 million, per capita $180; real growth
rate 9% (1991)
Inflation: 11.8% (1991)
Industries: cement, chemical products, mining,
distilling, food processing, handicrafts
Labour Force: 700,000 (1992); 92.5% agriculture, 2.8% industry; 4.7% services (1989)
Unemployment: n.a.

Agriculture: accounts for 50% of GDP; based on subsistence farming and animal husbandry; self-sufficient in food except for foodgrains; other production—rice, corn, root crops, citrus fruit, dairy and eggs
Natural Resources: timber, hydroelectricity, gypsum, calcium carbide

■ FINANCE/TRADE

Currency: ngultrum (Nu)
International Reserves Excluding Gold: $69 million (1991)
Gold Reserves: n.a.
Budget: revenues $99 million; expenditures $128 million, including capital expenditures of $65 million (1989)
Defence Expenditures: n.a.
External Debt: $80 million (1990)
Exports: $70.9 million (1989); commodities: cardamon, gypsum, timber, handicrafts, cement, fruit; partners: India 93%
Imports: $138.3 million (1989); commodities: fuel and lubricants, grain, machinery and parts, vehicles, fabrics; partners: India 67%

■ HEALTH

Births: 37/1,000 population (1991)
Deaths: 17/1,000 population (1991)
Infant Mortality: 135 deaths/1,000 live births (1991)
Life Expectancy at Birth: 46 years male, 49 years female (1992)
No. of Physicians: 1.0/10,000 population (1992)

■ EDUCATION

Govt. Expenditure: 10.66% of GNP (1991)
Literacy: 38.4% (1992)

■ COMMUNICATIONS

Daily newspapers: 1 (1992)
Televisions: n.a.
Radios: 15/1,000 inhabitants (1992)
Telephones: n.a.

■ TRANSPORTATION

Motor Vehicles: 7,002 registered vehicles (1989)
Roads: 1,316 km; 423 km paved
Railway: n.a.
Air Traffic: 8,000 passengers carried (1991)
Airports: 1

Canadian Embassy: The Canadian High Commission, 7/8 Shantipath, Chanakyapuri, New Delhi 110 021; mailing address: P.O. Box 5207, New Delhi, India. Tel: (011-91-11) 687-6500

Bolivia

Long-Form Name: Republic of Bolivia
Capital: La Paz (seat of government); Sucre (legal capital and seat of Judiciary)
Population: 7,830,000 (1992)

■ GEOGRAPHY

Area: 1,098,580 sq. km
Coastline: none: landlocked
Climate: varies with altitude; humid and tropical to cold and semi-arid
Environment: cold, thin air of high plateau is obstacle to efficient fuel combustion; overgrazing, soil erosion, desertification
Terrain: high plateau, hills, lowland plains
Land Use: 3% arable land; negligible permanent crops; 25% meadows and pastures; 52% forest and woodland; 20% other; includes negligible irrigated
Location: W South America

■ PEOPLE

Nationality: Bolivian
Ethnic Groups: 30% Quenchua, 25% Aymara, 25–30% mixed, 5–15% European
Languages: Spanish, Quechua and Aymara (all official)
Religions: 80% Roman Catholic; 20% Protestant, especially Methodist
Marriages: 4.8 (per 1,000) (1980)
Divorces: n.a.

■ GOVERNMENT

Leader(s): Pres. Jaime Paz Zamora
Government Type: republic
Administrative Divisions: 9 departments
Independence: Aug. 6, 1825 (from Spain)
National Holiday: Independence Day, Aug. 6

■ ECONOMY

Overview: a poor economy vulnerable to price fluctuations for its small number of exports, it relies heavily on coca, used for cocaine processing
GNP: $4.799 billion, per capita $650; real growth rate 0.5% (1991)
Inflation: 21.4% (1990)
Industries: mining, smelting, petroleum, food and beverage, tobacco, handicrafts, clothing; illicit drug industry reportedly produces the largest revenues
Labour Force: 2,283,000 (1992); 46.5% agriculture, 33.9% services, 19.2% industry (1989)
Unemployment: 19.0% (1990)

Agriculture: accounts for 20% of GDP (including forestry and fisheries); principal commodities— coffee, coca, cotton, corn, sugar cane, rice, potatoes, timber; self-sufficient in food
Natural Resources: tin, natural gas, crude oil, zinc, tungsten, antimony, silver, iron ore, lead, gold, timber

■ FINANCE/TRADE

Currency: peso Boliviano ($b)
International Reserves Excluding Gold: $208 million (1992)
Gold Reserves: 0.89 million fine troy ounces (1992)
Budget: revenues $2.5 billion; expenditures $2.8 billion, including capital expenditures of $850 million (1990)
Defence Expenditures: $179.53 (1989)
External Debt: $3.683 billion (1990)
Exports: $858 million (1991); commodities: metals 45%, natural gas 32%, coffee, soyabeans, sugar, cotton, timber and illicit drugs; partners: US 23%, Argentina
Imports: $942 million (1991); commodities: food, petroleum, consumer goods, capital goods; partners: US 15%

■ HEALTH

Births: 34/1,000 population (1991)
Deaths: 9/1,000 population (1991)
Infant Mortality: 83 deaths/1,000 live births (1991)
Life Expectancy at Birth: 58 years male, 64 years female (1992)
No. of Physicians: 6.5/10,000 population (1992)

■ EDUCATION

Govt. Expenditure: 18.65% government expenditure (1991)
Literacy: 77.5% (1992)

■ COMMUNICATIONS

Daily newspapers: 16 (1992)
Televisions: 98.4/1,000 inhabitants (1992)
Radios: 574/1,000 inhabitants (1992)
Telephones: 2.87/100 inhabitants (1992)

■ TRANSPORTATION

Motor Vehicles: 316,969; 261,082 passenger cars (1990)
Roads: 41,746 km; 1,099 km paved
Railway: 3,735 km
Air Traffic: 1,200,000 passengers carried (1991)
Airports: 590

Canadian Embassy: c/o The Canadian Embassy,

Federico Gerdes 130 (Antes Calle Libertad), Miraflores, Lima; mailing address: Casilla 18-1126, Lima 18, Peru. Tel: (011-51-14) 44-40-15. Fax (011-51-14) 44-43-47
Embassy in Canada: Embassy of Bolivia, 130 Albert St, Ste 504, Ottawa ON K1P 5G4. Tel: (613) 236-8237.

Bophuthatswana

Dependent Territory of South Africa

Long-Form Name: Republic of Bophuthatswana
Capital: Mmabatho
Population: 3,200,000 (1989); 47% live outside the Homeland

■ GEOGRAPHY

Area: 44,000 sq. km
Climate: semi-arid
Land Use: 6.6% dryland farming, remainder bushveld and grass veld, semi-arid and unsuitable for agriculture, good for grazing
Location: N South Africa, 6 discontinuous areas

■ PEOPLE

Nationality: South African
Ethnic Groups: Xhosa
Languages: Afrikaans, English, Setswana (official)

■ GOVERNMENT

Leader(s): Pres. Dr. Kgosi Lucas Manyane Mangope
Government Type: compromise between traditional chief-in-council and democratic electoral system; granted full independence from South Africa in 1977, but no other country recognizes the homeland as an independent state

■ ECONOMY

Overview: rich in minerals, especially platinum, asbestos, gold, calcite, granite, chrome, vanadium, limestone, diamonds; economically interdependent with South Africa
Currency: South African Rand (R)

Botswana

Long-Form Name: Republic of Botswana
Capital: Gaborone
Population: 1,390,000 (1992)

■ GEOGRAPHY

Area: 582,000 sq. km
Coastline: none: landlocked

Climate: sub-tropical to semi-arid; warm winters and hot summers
Environment: rains in early 1988 broke six years of drought that had severely affected the important cattle industry; overgrazing; desertification
Terrain: predominantly flat to gently rolling tableland; Kalahari Desert in southwest
Land Use: 2% arable land; 0% permanent crops; 75% meadows and pastures; 2% forest and woodland; 21% other; includes negligible irrigated
Location: SC Africa

■ PEOPLE

Nationality: Motswana (sing.), Batswana (pl.)
Ethnic Groups: 95% Batswana; about 4% Kalanga, Basarwa and Kgalagadi; about 1 % white
Languages: English (official), Setswana
Religions: majority indigenous beliefs, minority Christian
Marriages: 1.4 (per 1,000) (1986)
Divorces: n.a.

■ GOVERNMENT

Leader(s): Pres. Sir Quett Ketumile J. Masire, V. Pres. Festus Mogae
Government Type: parliamentary republic
Administrative Divisions: 10 districts
Independence: Sept. 30, 1966 (from UK; Botswana formerly known as Bechuanaland)
National Holiday: Botswana Day, Sept. 30

■ ECONOMY

Overview: economy based on mining (diamonds) and traditionally, cattle raising and crops, exhibits high unemployment
GNP: $3.335 billion, per capita $2,590; real growth rate 9.3% (1991)
Inflation: 11.8% (1991)
Industries: livestock processing; mining of diamonds, copper, nickel, coal, salt, soda ash, potash; tourism
Labour Force: 446,000 (1992); 52% services, 43.2% agriculture, 4.8 industry; 19,000 are employed in various mines in South Africa (1989)
Unemployment: 25% (1987)
Agriculture: accounts for only 5% of GDP; subsistence farming predominates; cattle raising supports 50% of the population; must import large share of food needs
Natural Resources: diamonds, copper, nickel, salt, soda ash, potash, coal, iron ore, silver, natural gas

■ FINANCE/TRADE

Currency: pula (P)
International Reserves Excluding Gold: $4,087 million (1992)
Gold Reserves: n.a.
Budget: revenues $1,719 million; expenditures $1,792 million, including capital expenditures n.a. (1992 estimate)
Defence Expenditures: $130.94 million (1990)
External Debt: $510 million (1990)
Exports: $1.285 billion (1990); commodities: diamonds 88%, copper and nickel 5%, meat 4%, cattle, animals products; partners: Switzerland, US, UK, other European Community—associated members of Southern African Customs Union
Imports: $1.873 billion (1990); commodities: foodstuffs, vehicles, textiles, petroleum products; partners: Switzerland

■ HEALTH

Births: 36/1,000 population (1991)
Deaths: 9/1,000 population (1991)
Infant Mortality: 43 deaths/1,000 live births (1991)
Life Expectancy at Birth: 55 years male, 62 years female (1992)
No. of Physicians: 1.5/10,000 population (1990)

■ EDUCATION

Govt. Expenditure: 20.52% of total govt. expenditures (1990)
Literacy: 73.6% (1992)

■ COMMUNICATIONS

Daily newspapers: 1 (1992)
Televisions: 11.9/1,000 inhabitants (1992)
Radios: 111/1,000 inhabitants (1992)
Telephones: 2.86/100 inhabitants (1992)

■ TRANSPORTATION

Motor Vehicles: 60,000; 25,000 passenger cars (1990)
Roads: 13,968 km; 2,328 km paved
Railway: 757 km
Air Traffic: 102,000 passengers carried (1991)
Airports: 28

Canadian Embassy: c/o The Canadian High Commission, 45 Baines Ave, Harare; mailing address: P.O. Box 1430, Harare, Zimbabwe. Tel: (011-263-4) 733-881. Fax: (011-263-4) 732-917

Representative to Canada: c/o Embassy of the Republic of Botswana, Intersat Bldg, 3400 International Dr. NW, Suite 7M, Washington, DC 20008 USA

Brazil

Long-Form Name: Federative Republic of Brazil
Capital: Brasilia
Population: 156,280,000 (1992)

■ GEOGRAPHY

Area: 8,511,965 sq. km; includes Arquipélago de Fernando de Noronha, Atol das Rocas, Ilha da Trindade, Ilhas Martin Vaz and Penedos de São Pedro e São Paulo
Coastline: 7,491 km
Climate: mostly tropical, but temperate in south
Environment: recurrent droughts in northeast; floods and frost in south; deforestation in Amazon basin; air and water pollution in Rio de Janeiro and São Paulo
Terrain: mostly flat to rolling lowlands in north; some plains, hills, mountains and narrow coastal belt
Land Use: 7% arable land; 1% permanent crops; 19% meadows and pastures; 67% forest and woodland; 6% other; includes negligible irrigated
Location: W South America

■ PEOPLE

Nationality: Brazilian
Ethnic Groups: Portuguese, Italian, German, Japanese, black, Amerindian; 55% white, 38% mixed, 6% black, 1% other
Languages: Portuguese (official), Spanish, English, French
Religions: 90% Roman Catholic (nominal)
Marriages: 6.6 (per 1,000) (1987)
Divorces: 0.2 (per 1,000) (1987)

■ GOVERNMENT

Leader(s): Pres. Itamar Franco, V. Pres. vacant
Government Type: federal republic
Administrative Divisions: 26 states and 1 federal district
Independence: Sept. 7, 1822 (from Portugal)
National Holiday: Independence Day, Sept. 7

■ ECONOMY

Overview: despite abundant natural resources, the economy has experienced runaway inflation and large foreign debt
GNP: $447.324 billion, per capita $2,920; real growth rate 2.5% (1991)

Inflation: 440.8% (1991)
Industries: textiles and other consumer goods, shoes, chemicals, cement, lumber, iron ore, steel, motor vehicles and auto parts, metalworking, capital goods, tin
Labour Force: 55,026,000 (1992); 54.7% services, 29.3% agriculture, 16% industry (1989)
Unemployment: 2.5% (Dec. 1989)
Agriculture: accounts for 12% of GDP; world's largest producer and exporter of coffee and orange juice concentrate and second-largest exporter of soybeans; self sufficient in food, except for wheat
Natural Resources: iron ore, manganese, bauxite, nickel, uranium, phosphates, tin, hydroelectricity, gold, platinum, crude oil, timber

■ FINANCE/TRADE

Currency: cruzeiro ($Cr)
International Reserves Excluding Gold: $20,805 million (1992)
Gold Reserves: 2.09 million fine troy ounces (1992)
Budget: revenues $36.5 billion; expenditures $48.2 billion, including capital expenditures of $4.6 billion (1988)
Defence Expenditures: $1.18 billion (1990)
External Debt: $82.098 billion (1990)
Exports: $31.622 billion (1991); commodities: coffee, metallurgical products, foodstuffs, iron ore, automobiles and parts; partners: US 28%, European Community 26%, Latin America 11%, Japan 6%
Imports: $21.010 billion (1991); commodities: crude oil, capital goods, chemical products, foodstuffs, coal; partners: Middle East and Africa 24%, European Community 22%, US 21%, Latin America 12%, Japan 6%

■ HEALTH

Births: 26/1,000 population (1991)
Deaths: 7/1,000 population (1991)
Infant Mortality: 68 deaths/1,000 live births (1991)
Life Expectancy at Birth: 62 years male, 68 years female (1992)
No. of Physicians: 9.3/10,000 population (1992)

■ EDUCATION

Govt. Expenditure: 3.14% of government expenditure (1990)
Literacy: 81.1% (1992)

■ COMMUNICATIONS

Daily newspapers: 366 (1992)
Televisions: 203.6/1,000 inhabitants (1992)

Radios: 373/1,000 inhabitants (1992)
Telephones: 9.54/100 inhabitants (1992)

■ TRANSPORTATION

Motor Vehicles: 13,063,345; 12,127,562 passenger cars (1990)
Roads: 1,676,857 km; 136,191 km paved
Railway: 30,643 km
Air Traffic: 19,015,000 passengers carried (1991)
Airports: 752

Canadian Embassy: Avendia das Nacoes, Lote 16, Brasilia–DF 70410-900; mailing address: Caixa Postal 00961, Brasilia DF 70359-970, Brazil. Tel: (011-55-61) 321-2171. Fax: (011-55-61) 321-4529
Embassy in Canada: Embassy of the Federative Republic of Brazil, 450 Wilbrod St, Ottawa ON K1N 6M8. Tel: (613) 237-1090. Fax: (613) 237-6144.

British Indian Ocean Territory

Dependent Territory of the United Kingdom

Long-Form Name: British Indian Ocean Territory
Capital: None; Victoria (Seychelles) is administrative headquarters
Population: 2,000 (1992); itinerant

■ GEOGRAPHY

Area: 60 sq. km
Climate: tropical maritime
Land Use: some coconut plantations
Location: Indian Ocean, the Chago Archipelago island group NE of Madagascar

■ PEOPLE

Nationality: n.a.
Ethnic Groups: n.a.
Languages: English

■ GOVERNMENT

Leader(s): Comm. T.G. Harris, Administrator R.G. Wells
Government Type: dependency of Great Britain

■ ECONOMY

Overview: agriculture: fishing, coconuts, guano fertilizer
Currency: n.a.

British Virgin Islands

Dependent Territory of the United Kingdom

Long-Form Name: British Virgin Islands
Capital: Road Town (on Tortola Island)
Population: 16,749 (1991)

■ GEOGRAPHY

Area: 130 sq. km; 40 islands and numerous small rocks and reefs
Climate: sub-tropical with modifying sea winds
Land Use: n.a.
Location: West Indies, NE of Puerto Rico

■ PEOPLE

Nationality: British
Ethnic Groups: various Hispanic strains, descendants of European settlers
Languages: English (official)

■ GOVERNMENT

Leader(s): Gov. Peter A. Penfold
Government Type: self-governing territory of United Kingdom

■ ECONOMY

Overview: very small export trade, mostly with American Virgin Islands and UK; very limited agriculture: fruits, vegetables, livestock, poultry; construction industry.
Budget: revenues $50,742,000; expenditures $46,040,700 (1991)
Currency: American dollar ($US)

Brunei Darussalam

Long-Form Name: Negara Brunei Darussalam
Capital: Bandar Seri Begawan
Population: 270,000 (1992)

■ GEOGRAPHY

Area: 5,770 sq. km
Coastline: 161 km
Climate: tropical; hot, humid, rainy
Environment: typhoons, earthquakes and severe floods occur
Terrain: flat coastal plain rises to mountainous east; hilly lowland in west
Land Use: 1% arable land; 1% permanent crops; 1% meadows and pastures; 79% forest and woodland; 18% other; includes negligible irrigated
Location: Indonesia (island of Borneo), bordering on South China Sea

■ PEOPLE

Nationality: Bruneian
Ethnic Groups: 64% Malay, 20% Chinese, 16% other
Languages: Malay (official), English and Chinese
Religions: Islam (official, mainly Sunni Muslims); majority of Chinese are Buddhist, Confucian or Daoist
Marriages: 7.4 (per 1,000) (1986)
Divorces: 0.9 (per 1,000) (1986)

■ GOVERNMENT

Leader(s): Sultan Sir Hassanal Bolkiah
Government Type: constitutional sultanate
Administrative Divisions: 4 districts
Independence: Jan. 1, 1984 (from UK)
National Holiday: National Day, Feb. 23

■ ECONOMY

Overview: economy is based on crude oil and natural gas exports and the per capita GDP is one of the highest for under-developed nations
GNP: $3.3 billion, per capita $9,600; real growth rate 2.5% (1989 est.)
Inflation: 2.5% (1989 est.)
Industries: petroleum, liquefied natural gas, construction
Labour Force: 89,000 (includes members of the army); 33% of labour force is foreign (1988); 50.4% production of oil, natural gas and construction; 47.6% trade, services and other; 2.0% agriculture, forestry and fishing (1984)
Unemployment: 2.5%, shortage of skilled labour (1989 est.)
Agriculture: imports about 80% of its food needs; principal crops and livestock include rice, cassava, bananas, buffaloes and pigs
Natural Resources: crude oil, natural gas, timber

■ FINANCE/TRADE

Currency: Brunei dollar ($B)
International Reserves Excluding Gold: n.a.
Gold Reserves: n.a.
Budget: revenues $1.2 billion; expenditures $1.4 billion, including capital expenditures of $230 million (1988)
Defence Expenditures: $229.025 million (1988)
External Debt: none
Exports: $1.894 billion (1989); commodities: crude oil, liquefied natural gas, petroleum products; partners: Japan 55%
Imports: $883 million (1991); commodities: machinery and transport equipment, manufactured goods, food, beverages, tobacco, con-

sumer goods; partners: Singapore 31%, US 20%, Japan 6%

■ HEALTH

Births: 22/1,000 population (1991)
Deaths: 4/1,000 population (1991)
Infant Mortality: 10 deaths/1,000 live births (1991)
Life Expectancy at Birth: 69 years male, 72 years female (1992)
No. of Physicians: 5.5/10,000 population (1992)

■ EDUCATION

Govt. Expenditure: 11.8% government expenditure (1980)
Literacy: 77.8% (1992)

■ COMMUNICATIONS

Daily newspapers: 1 (1992).
Televisions: 224.6/1,000 inhabitants (1992)
Radios: 234/1,000 inhabitants (1992)
Telephones: 19.38/100 inhabitants (1992)

■ TRANSPORTATION

Motor Vehicles: 112,087; 100,114 passenger cars (1990)
Railway: 13 km
Air Traffic: 307,000 passengers carried (1991)
Airports: 2

Canadian Embassy: c/o The Canadian High Commission, 80 Anson Rd, #1400; mailing address: Robinson Rd, P.O. Box 845, Singapore 9016. Tel: (011-65) 225-6363. Fax (011-65) 225-2450
Representative to Canada: c/o High Commission for Brunei Darussalam, 866 United Nations Plaza, Room 248, New York, NY 10017 USA. Tel: (212) 838-1600

Bulgaria

Long-Form Name: Republic of Bulgaria
Capital: Sofia
Population: 8,952,000 (1992)

■ GEOGRAPHY

Area: 110,910 sq. km
Coastline: 354 km
Climate: temperate; cold, damp winters; hot, dry summers
Environment: subject to earthquakes, landslides, deforestation, air pollution
Terrain: mostly mountains with lowlands in north and south

Land Use: 34% arable land; 3% permanent crops; 18% meadows and pastures; 35% forest and woodland; 10% other; includes 11% irrigated

Location: SC Europe, bordering on Black Sea

■ PEOPLE

Nationality: Bulgarian
Ethnic Groups: 85% Bulgarian, 9% Turk, 3% Gypsy, 3% Macedonian, 0.3% Armenian, 0.2% Russian, 0.6% other
Languages: Bulgarian (official), Turkish; secondary languages closely correspond to ethnic breakdown
Religions: 85% Bulgarian Orthodox, 13% Moslem (practised by Turkish and Pomak minorities), 0.8% Jewish, 0.7% Roman Catholic, 0.5% Protestant, Gregorian-Armenian and other
Marriages: 7.2 (per 1,000) (1987)
Divorces: 1.4 (per 1,000) (1987)

■ GOVERNMENT

Leader(s): Pres. Zhelyu Zhelev, Prime Min. Lyuben Beror, V. Pres. Blaga Dimitrova
Government Type: caretaker government
Administrative Divisions: 8 provinces, 1 city
Independence: Sept. 22, 1908 (from Turkey)
National Holiday: Anniversary of the Socialist Revolution in Bulgaria, Sept. 9

■ ECONOMY

Overview: heavily in debt with low growth, the economy is also hindered by antiquated industrial plants
GNP: $16.316 billion, per capita $1,840; real growth rate 1.7% (1991)
Inflation: 12% (1989)
Industries: food processing, machine and metal building, electronics, chemicals
Labour Force: 4,475,000 (1992); 37.9% industry, 16.5% agriculture, 45.6% services (1989)
Unemployment: 12% (1991)
Agriculture: accounts for 15% of GNP; climate and soil conditions support livestock raising and the growing of various grain crops, oilseeds, vegetables, fruits and tobacco; more than one-third of the arable land devoted to grain
Natural Resources: bauxite, copper, lead, zinc, coal, timber, arable land

■ FINANCE/TRADE

Currency: lev (pl. leva) (Lv)
International Reserves Excluding Gold: n.a.
Gold Reserves: n.a.
Budget: revenues $26 billion; expenditures $28 billion, including capital expenditures (1988)
Defence Expenditures: $2.01 billion (1990)
External Debt: $9.564 billion (1990)
Exports: $3.835 billion (1991); commodities: machinery and equipment 60.5%, agricultural products 14.7%, manufactured consumer goods 10.6%, fuels, minerals, raw materials and metals 8.5%, other 5.7%; partners: Socialist countries 82.5%, developed countries 6.8%, less developed countries 10.7%
Imports: $3.017 billion (1991); commodities: fuels, minerals, raw materials 45.2%, machinery and equipment 39.8%, manufactured consumer goods 4.6%, agricultural products 3.8%, other 6.6%; partners: Socialist countries 80.5%, developed countries 15.1%, less developed countries 4.4%

■ HEALTH

Births: 13/1,000 population (1991)
Deaths: 12/1,000 population (1991)
Infant Mortality: 13 deaths/1,000 live births (1991)
Life Expectancy at Birth: 66 years male, 75 years female (1992)
No. of Physicians: 36.2/10,000 population (1992)

■ EDUCATION

Govt. Expenditure: 6.21% government expenditure (1990)
Literacy: 95%

■ COMMUNICATIONS

Daily newspapers: 20 (1992)
Televisions: 249.1/1,000 inhabitants (1992)
Radios: 436/1,000 inhabitants (1992)
Telephones: 20/100 inhabitants (1992)

■ TRANSPORTATION

Motor Vehicles: 1,500,000; 1,300,000 passenger cars (1990)
Roads: 37,044 km; 33,828 km paved
Railway: 4,314 km
Air Traffic: 646,000 passengers carried (1991)
Airports: 3

Canadian Embassy: Kneza Milosa 75, 11000 Belgrade, Yugoslavia. Tel: (011-38-11) 644-666. Fax (011-38-11): 641-480
Embassy in Canada: Embassy of the People's Republic of Bulgaria, 325 Stewart St, Ottawa ON K1N 6K5. Tel: (613) 789-3215, -3523. Fax: (613) 789-3524.

Burkina Faso

Long-Form Name: Burkina Faso
Capital: Ouagadougou
Population: 9,490,000 (1992)

■ GEOGRAPHY

Area: 274,200 sq. km
Coastline: none: landlocked
Climate: tropical; warm,dry winters; hot, wet summers
Environment: recent droughts and desertification severely affecting marginal agricultural activities, population distribution, economy; overgrazing; desertification
Terrain: mostly flat to dissected, undulating plains; hills in west and southeast
Land Use: 10% arable land; negligible permanent crops; 37% meadows and pastures; 26% forest and woodland; 27% other; includes negligible irrigated
Location: WC Africa

■ PEOPLE

Nationality: Burkina-be
Ethnic Groups: more than 50 tribes; principal tribe is Mossi (about 2.5 million); other important groups are Gurunsi, Senufo, Lobi, Bobo, Mande and Fulani
Languages: French (official); tribal languages belong to Sudanic family, spoken by 90% of population
Religions: 45% indigenous beliefs, about 43% Moslem, 12% Christian (mainly Roman Catholic)
Marriages: n.a.
Divorces: n.a.

■ GOVERNMENT

Leader(s): Head of State, Head of Government & Chairman, Capt. Blaise Compaoré
Government Type: military council, established Oct. 31, 1987
Administrative Divisions: 30 provinces
Independence: Aug. 5, 1960 (from France; Burkina Faso formerly known as Upper Volta)
National Holiday: Anniversary of the Revolution, Aug. 4

■ ECONOMY

Overview: a poor economy with high population density and few natural resources, it relies heavily on subsistence agriculture
GNP: $3.213 billion, per capita $350; real growth rate 4% (1991)

Inflation: -0.5% (1990)
Industries: agricultural processing plants; brewery, cement and brick plants; a few other small consumer goods enterprises
Labour Force: 4,170,000 (1992); 86.6% agriculture, 4.3% industry, 9.1% services; 20% of male labour force migrates annually to neighbouring countries for seasonal employment (1989)
Unemployment: n.a.
Agriculture: cash crops—peanuts, shea nuts, sesame, cotton; food crops—sorghum, millet, corn, rice; livestock; not self-sufficient in food grains
Natural Resources: manganese, limestone, marble; small deposits of gold, antimony, copper, nickel, bauxite, lead, phosphates, zinc, silver

■ FINANCE/TRADE

Currency: Communauté financière africaine franc (CFAF)
International Reserves Excluding Gold: $386 million (1992)
Gold Reserves: 0.01 million fine troy ounces (1991)
Budget: revenues $275 million; expenditures $287 million, including capital expenditures (1989)
Defence Expenditures: $76.40 million (1990)
External Debt: $750 million (1990)
Exports: $95 million (1989); commodities: oilseeds, cotton, live animals, gold; partners: European Community 42%, Taiwan 17%, Ivory Coast 15%
Imports: $322 million (1989); commodities: grain, dairy products, petroleum, machinery; partners: European Community 37%, Africa 31%, US 15%

■ HEALTH

Births: 50/1,000 population (1991)
Deaths: 16/1,000 population (1991)
Infant Mortality: 119 deaths/1,000 live births (1991)
Life Expectancy at Birth: 51 years male, 52 years female (1992)
No. of Physicians: 0.2/10,000 population (1992)

■ EDUCATION

Govt. Expenditure: 17.5% of government expenditure (1989)
Literacy: 18.2% (1992)

■ COMMUNICATIONS

Daily newspapers: 4 (1992)
Televisions: 5.1/1,000 inhabitants (1992)
Radios: 26/1,000 inhabitants (1992)

Telephones: 0.2/100 inhabitants (1992)

■ TRANSPORTATION

Motor Vehicles: 25,000; 12,000 passenger cars (1990)
Roads: 11,242 km; 1,371 km paved
Railway: 494 km
Air Traffic: 124,000 passengers carried (1991)
Airports: 51

Canadian Embassy: c/o Immeuble Trade-Center, 23, rue Nogues, Le Plateau, Abidjan, Cote d'Ivoire. Tel: (011-225) 32-20-09. Fax (011-225) 22-05-30
Embassy in Canada: Embassy of Burkina Faso, 48 Range Rd, Ottawa ON K1N 8J4. Tel: (613) 238-4796, -7.

Burundi

Long-Form Name: Republic of Burundi
Capital: Bujumbura
Population: 5,780,000 (1992)

■ GEOGRAPHY

Area: 27,830 sq. km
Coastline: none: landlocked
Climate: temperate; warm; occasional frost in uplands
Environment: soil exhaustion; soil erosion; deforestation
Terrain: mostly rolling to hilly highland; some plains
Land Use: 43% arable land; 8% permanent crops; 35% meadows and pastures; 2% forest and woodland; 12% other; includes negligible irrigated
Location: EC Africa

■ PEOPLE

Nationality: Burundian
Ethnic Groups: Africans: 85% Hutu (Bantu), 14% Tutsi (Hamitic), 1% Twa (Pygmy)
Languages: Kirundi and French (official); Swahili used commercially
Religions: about 67% Christian (62% Roman Catholic, 5% Protestant), 32% indigenous beliefs, 1% Moslem
Marriages: n.a.
Divorces: n.a.

■ GOVERNMENT

Leader(s): Prime Min. Adrien Sibomana, Pres. Maj. Pierre Buyoya
Government Type: republic
Administrative Divisions: 15 provinces

Independence: July 1, 1962 (from UN trusteeship under Belgian administration)
National Holiday: Independence Day, July 1

■ ECONOMY

Overview: economy is heavily dependent on the coffee crop and therefore vulnerable to market conditions
GNP: $1.210 billion, per capita $210; real growth rate 4.3% (1991)
Inflation: 8.9% (1991)
Industries: light consumer goods such as blankets, shoes, soap; assembly of imports; public works construction; food processing
Labour Force: 2,820,000 (1992); 93% agriculture, 1.5% industry and commerce, 5.5% services (1989)
Unemployment: 14,471 (1990)
Agriculture: accounts for 60% of GDP; 90% of population dependent on subsistence farming; marginally self-sufficient in food production; cash crops—coffee, cotton, tea; food crops—corn, sorghum, sweet potatoes, bananas, manioc
Natural Resources: nickel, uranium, rare earth oxide, peat, cobalt, copper, platinum (not yet exploited), vanadium

■ FINANCE/TRADE

Currency: Burundi franc (FBu)
International Reserves Excluding Gold: $179 million (1992)
Gold Reserves: 0.02 million fine troy ounces (1992)
Budget: revenues $158 million; expenditures $204 million, including capital expenditures of $131 million (1989)
Defence Expenditures: $32.05 million (1988)
External Debt: $850 million (1990)
Exports: $91 million (1991); commodities: coffee 88%, tea, hides and skins; partners: European Community 83%, US 5%, Asia 2%
Imports: $248 million (1991); commodities: capital goods 31%, petroleum products 15%, foodstuffs, consumer goods; partners: European Community 57%, Asia 23%, US 3%

■ HEALTH

Births: 47/1,000 population (1991)
Deaths: 15/1,000 population (1991)
Infant Mortality: 109 deaths/1,000 live births (1991)
Life Expectancy at Birth: 50 years male, 54 years female (1992)
No. of Physicians: 0.5/10,000 population (1992)

■ EDUCATION

Govt. Expenditure: 16.7% of govt. expenditure (1988)
Literacy: 50.0% (1992)

■ COMMUNICATIONS

Daily newspapers: 1 (1992)
Televisions: 0.6/1,000 inhabitants (1992)
Radios: 57/1,000 inhabitants (1992)
Telephones: 0.2/100 inhabitants (1992)

■ TRANSPORTATION

Motor Vehicles: 19,500; 8,500 passenger cars (1990)
Roads: 5,594 km; 390 km paved
Railway: n.a.
Air Traffic: 8,000 passengers carried (1991)
Airports: 4

Canadian Embassy: C/o The Canadian Embassy, 17 Pumba Zone de Gombe Ave, Kinshasa; mailing address: P.O. Box 8341, Kinshasa, Zaïre. Tel: (011-243-12) 21-801, 907. Fax: (011-871) 156-0213
Embassy in Canada: Embassy of the Republic of Burundi, 151 Slater St, Ste 800, Ottawa ON K1P 5H3. Tel: (613) 236-8483, -9. Fax: (613) 563-1827.

Cambodia

Long-Form Name: State of Cambodia
Capital: Phnom Penh
Population: 9,050,000 (1992)

■ GEOGRAPHY

Area: 181,040 sq. km
Coastline: 443 km
Climate: tropical; rainy, monsoon season (May to Oct.); dry season (Dec. to Mar.); little seasonal temperature variation
Environment: a land of paddies and forests dominated by Mekong River and Tonle Sap
Terrain: mostly low, flat plains; mountains in southwest and north
Land Use: 16% arable land; 1% permanent crops; 3% meadows and pastures; 76% forest and woodland; 4% other; includes 1% irrigated
Location: SE Asia, bordering on the Gulf of Siam

■ PEOPLE

Nationality: Cambodian
Ethnic Groups: 90% Khmer (Cambodian), 5% Chinese, 5% other minorities
Languages: Khmer (official), French

Religions: 95% Theravada Buddhism, 5% Christianity
Marriages: n.a.
Divorces: n.a.

■ GOVERNMENT

Leader(s): Head of Government Prince Norodom Ranariddh, King Norodom Sihanouk
Government Type: Elections held May 1993under the supervision of the UN to establish a National Assembly
Administrative Divisions: 18 provinces, 1 autonomous municipality
Independence: Nov. 9, 1953 (from France)
National Holiday: CGDK-Independence Day, Apr. 17; PRK-Liberation Day, Jan. 7

■ ECONOMY

Overview: the economy has suffered badly due to internal war; the country has not been able to feed its people
GNP: $1.725 billion, per capita $200; real growth rate 0% (1991)
Inflation: n.a.
Industries: rice milling, fishing, wood and wood products, rubber, cement, gem mining
Labour Force: 3.76 million (1992); 74.4% agriculture, 6.7% industry, 18.9% services (1989)
Unemployment: n.a.
Agriculture: mainly subsistence farming except for rubber plantations; main crops—rice, rubber, corn; food shortages—rice, meat, vegetables, dairy products, sugar, flour
Natural Resources: timber, gemstones, some iron ore, manganese, phosphates, hydroelectricity potential

■ FINANCE/TRADE

Currency: riel (KR)
International Reserves Excluding Gold: n.a.
Gold Reserves: n.a.
Budget: n.a.
Defence Expenditures: n.a.
External Debt: $600 million (1989)
Exports: $32 million (1988); commodities: natural rubber, rice, pepper, wood; partners: Vietnam, USSR, Eastern Europe, Japan, India
Imports: $147 million (1988); commodities: international food aid, fuels, consumer goods; partners: Vietnam, USSR, Eastern Europe, Japan, India

■ HEALTH

Births: 38/1,000 population (1991)
Deaths: 16/1,000 population (1991)

Infant Mortality: 125 deaths/1,000 live births (1991)
Life Expectancy at Birth: 47 years male, 50 years female (1992)
No. of Physicians: n.a.

■ EDUCATION

Govt. Expenditure: n.a.
Literacy: 35.2% (1992)

■ COMMUNICATIONS

Daily newspapers: 1 (1992)
Televisions: 8.1/1,000 inhabitants (1992)
Radios: 107/1,000 inhabitants (1992)
Telephones: n.a.

■ TRANSPORTATION

Motor Vehicles: n.a.
Roads: 13,759 km; 2,716 km paved
Railway: 670 km, much inoperational since 1973
Air Traffic: n.a.
Airports: 5

Canadian Embassy: c/o Canadian Embassy, 12th Floor, Boonmitr Bldg., 138 Silom Rd, Bangkok 10500; mailing address: P.O. Box 2090, Bangkok 10500, Thailand. Tel: (011-66-2) 237-4126. Fax: (011-66-2) 236-6463

Cameroon

Long-Form Name: Republic of Cameroon
Capital: Yaoundé
Population: 12,240,000 (1992)

■ GEOGRAPHY

Area: 475,440 sq. km
Coastline: 402 km
Climate: varies with terrain from tropical along coast to semi-arid and hot in north
Environment: recent volcanic activity with release of poisonous gases; deforestation; overgrazing; desertification
Terrain: diverse with coastal plain in southwest, dissected plateau in centre, mountains in west, plains in north
Land Use: 13% arable land; 2% permanent crops; 18% meadows and pastures; 54% forest and woodland; 13% other; includes negligible irrigated
Location: WC Africa, bordering on South Atlantic Ocean

■ PEOPLE

Nationality: Cameroonian
Ethnic Groups: over 200 tribes of widely differing background; 31% Cameroon Highlanders, 19% Equatorial Bantu, 11% Kirdi, 10% Fulani, 8% Northwestern Bantu, 7% Eastern Nigritic, 13% other African, less than 1% non-African
Languages: English and French (official), 24 major African language groups, inc. Fang, Bamileke, Duala
Religions: 51% indigenous beliefs, 33% Christian, 16% Moslem
Marriages: n.a.
Divorces: n.a.

■ GOVERNMENT

Leader(s): Prime Min. Simon Achidi Achu, Pres. Paul Biya
Government Type : unitary republic; one-party presidential regime
Administrative Divisions: 10 provinces
Independence: Jan. 1, 1960 (from UN trusteeship under French administration; Cameroon formerly known as French Cameroon)
National Holiday: National Day, May 20

■ ECONOMY

Overview: an offshore oil industry has boosted the economy but the government is now emphasizing diversification, particularly in agriculture
GNP: $11.320 billion, per capita $940; real growth rate 2.1% (1991)
Inflation: 8.6% (1988)
Industries: crude oil products, small aluminum plant, food processing, light consumer goods industries, sawmills
Labour Force: 4.365 million (1992); 74% agriculture, 4.5% industry, 21.5% services (1989)
Unemployment: 7% (1985)
Agriculture: the agriculture and forestry sectors provide employment for the majority of the population, contributing nearly 25% to GDP and providing a high degree of self-sufficiency in staple foods
Natural Resources: crude oil, bauxite, iron ore, timber, hydroelectricity potential

■ FINANCE/TRADE

Currency: Communauté financière africaine franc (CFAF)
International Reserves Excluding Gold: $57 million (1992)
Gold Reserves: 0.30 million fine troy ounces (1992)
Budget: revenues $1.7 billion; expenditures $2.2 billion, capital expenditures n.a. (1989)
Defence Expenditures: $142.7 million (1989)
External Debt: $4.784 billion (1990)

Exports: $2,019 million (1990); commodities: petroleum products 56%, coffee, cocoa, timber, manufacturing; partners: European Community 50%, US 3%
Imports: $1.650 billion (1990); commodities: machines and electrical equipment, transport equipment, chemical products, consumer goods; partners: France 42%, Japan 7%, US 4%

■ HEALTH

Births: 41/1,000 population (1991)
Deaths: 15/1,000 population (1991)
Infant Mortality: 118 deaths/1,000 live births (1991)
Life Expectancy at Birth: 54 years male, 59 years female (1992)
No. of Physicians: 0.7/10,000 inhabitants (1980)

■ EDUCATION

Govt. Expenditure: 12% of govt. expenditure (1989)
Literacy: 54.1% (1992)

■ COMMUNICATIONS

Daily newspapers: 2 (1992)
Televisions: 2.1/1,000 inhabitants (1992)
Radios: 131/1,000 inhabitants (1992)
Telephones: 0.6/100 inhabitants (1992)

■ TRANSPORTATION

Motor Vehicles: 175,000; 93,000 passenger cars (1990)
Roads: 53,249 km; 3,328 km paved
Railway: 1,115 km
Air Traffic: 357,000 passengers carried (1991)
Airports: 43

Canadian Embassy: Canadian Embassy, Édifice Stamatiades, Place de l'Hôtel de Ville, Yaoundé; mailing address: CP 572, Yaoundé, Cameroon. Tel: (011-237) 23-02-03/22-18-22. Fax: (011-237) 22-10-90
Embassy in Canada: Embassy of the Republic of Cameroon, 170 Clemow Ave, Ottawa ON K1S 2B4. Tel: (613) 236-1522.

Canada

Long-Form Name: The Dominion of Canada
Capital: Ottawa
Population: 27,440,000 (1992 census)

■ GEOGRAPHY

Area: 9,970,610 sq. km
Coastline: 243,791 km
Climate: varies from temperate in south to sub-arctic and arctic in north
Environment: 80% of population concentrated within 160 km of US border; continuous permafrost in north a serious obstacle to development
Terrain: mostly plains with mountains in west and lowlands in southeast
Land Use: 5% arable land; negligible permanent crops; 3% meadows and pastures; 35% forest and woodland; 57% other; includes negligible irrigated
Location: N North America, bordering on North Atlantic Ocean, Arctic Ocean, North Pacific Ocean

■ PEOPLE

Nationality: Canadian
Ethnic Groups: 40% British, 27% French, 20% European, 11.5% other, 1.5% Indigenous
Languages: English and French (both official)
Religions: 48% Protestant, 47% Catholic, 5% other
Marriages: 7.1 (per 1,000) (1987)
Divorces: 3.1 (per 1,000) (1987)

■ GOVERNMENT

Leader(s): Prime Min. Kim Campbell, Gov. Gen. Ramon John Hnatyshyn
Government Type: confederation with parliamentary democracy
Administrative Divisions: 10 provinces, two territories
Independence: July 1, 1867 (from UK)
National Holiday: Canada Day, July 1

■ ECONOMY

Overview: abundant natural resources, skilled labour force, and high-tech industrialization characterize a market-oriented economy
GNP: $568.765 billion, per capita $21,260; real growth rate 3.1% (1991)
Inflation: 5.6% (1991)
Industries: processsed and unprocessed minerals, food products, wood and paper products, transportation equipment, chemicals, fish products, petroleum, natural gas
Labour Force: 13,360,000 (1992); 77.2% services, 19.4% industry, 3.4% agriculture (1989)
Unemployment: 10.3% (1991)
Agriculture: accounts for 3% of GDP; one of the world's major producers and exporters of grain (wheat and barley); key source of US agricultural imports; large forest resources cover 35% of total land area

Natural Resources: nickel, zinc, copper, gold, lead, molybdenum, potash, silver, fish, timber, wildlife, coal, crude oil, natural gas

■ FINANCE/TRADE

Currency: dollar ($ or $Can)
International Reserves Excluding Gold: $13,958 million (1992)
Gold Reserves: 10.21 million fine troy ounces (1992)
Budget: revenues $105.8 billion; expenditures $131.6 billion, capital expenditures n.a. (1990)
Defence Expenditures: $11.42 billion (1991)
External Debt: $247 billion (1987)
Exports: $134.223 billion (1992); commodities: newsprint, wood pulp, timber, grain, crude petroleum, natural gas, ferrous and nonferrous ores, motor vehicles; partners: US, Japan, UK, Germany, other European Community, USSR
Imports: $122.477 billion (1992); commodities: processed foods, beverages, crude petroleum, chemicals, industrial machinery, motor vehicles, durable consumer goods, electronic computers; partners: US, Japan, UK, Germany, other European Community, Taiwan, S Korea, Mexico

■ HEALTH

Births: 14/1,000 population (1991)
Deaths: 7/1,000 population (1991)
Infant Mortality: 7 deaths/1,000 live births (1991)
Life Expectancy at Birth: 73 years male, 80 years female (1992)
No. of Physicians: 19.6/10,000 population (1992)

■ EDUCATION

Govt. Expenditure: 2.92% government expenditure (1989)
Literacy: 99% (1992)

■ COMMUNICATIONS

Daily newspapers: 107 (1992)
Televisions: 626.3/1,000 inhabitants (1992)
Radios: 1,023/1,000 inhabitants (1992)
Telephones: 78.02/100 inhabitants (1992)

■ TRANSPORTATION

Motor Vehicles: 16,553,385; 12,622,038 passenger cars (1990)
Roads: 917,296 km; 269,206 km paved
Railway: 90,733 km
Air Traffic: 16,586,000 passengers carried (1991)
Airports: 512

Cape Verde

Long-Form Name: Republic of Cape Verde
Capital: Praia
Population: 384,000 (1992)

■ GEOGRAPHY

Area: 4,030 sq. km
Coastline: 965 km
Climate: temperate; warm, dry, very erratic summer precipitation
Environment: subject to prolonged droughts; harmattan wind can obscure visibility; volcanically and seismically active; deforestation; overgrazing
Terrain: steep, rugged, rocky, volcanic
Land Use: 9% arable land; negligible permanent crops; 6% meadows and pastures; negligible forest and woodland; 85% other; includes 1% irrigated
Location: Atlantic Ocean W of Africa

■ PEOPLE

Nationality: Cape Verdean
Ethnic Groups: approx. 71% Creole (mulatto), 28% African, 1% European
Languages: Portuguese and Crioulo, a blend of Portuguese and West African tongues
Religions: Roman Catholicism fused with indigenous beliefs
Marriages: 5.4 (per 1,000) (1975)
Divorces: n.a.

■ GOVERNMENT

Leader(s): Prime Min. Carlos Alberto Wahnon de Carvalho Veiga, Pres. Antonio Mascarenhas Monteiro
Government Type: republic
Administrative Divisions: 12 districts
Independence: July 5, 1975 (from Portugal)
National Holiday: Independence Day, July 5

■ ECONOMY

Overview: a service-oriented economy which suffers from a poor natural resource base, a high birth rate and a long drought
GNP: $285 million, per capita $750; real growth rate 4.8% (1991)
Inflation: 3.8% (1987)
Industries: fish processing, salt mining, clothing factories, ship repair
Labour Force: 141,000 (1992); 52% agriculture (mostly subsistence), 25% services, 23% industry (1989)
Unemployment: 25% (1988)

Agriculture: accounts for 16% of GDP; largely subsistence farming; bananas are the only export crop; annual food imports required; growth potential limited by poor soils and limited rainfall

Natural Resources: salt, basalt rock, pozzuolana, limestone, kaolin, fish

■ FINANCE/TRADE

Currency: Cape Verde escudo (C.V.Esc.)
International Reserves Excluding Gold: $63 million (1992)
Gold Reserves: n.a.
Budget: revenues $98.3 million; expenditures $138.4 million, including capital expenditures (1988)
Defence Expenditures: 11.8% GDP (1981)
External Debt: $140 million (1988)
Exports: $7 million (1989); commodities: fish, bananas, salt; partners: Portugal, Angola, Algeria, Belgium/Luxembourg, Italy
Imports: $112 million (1989); commodities: petroleum, foodstuffs, consumer goods, industrial products; partners: Portugal, Netherlands, Spain, France, US, Germany

■ HEALTH

Births: 48/1,000 population (1991)
Deaths: 10/1,000 population (1991)
Infant Mortality: 63 deaths/1,000 live births (1991)
Life Expectancy at Birth: 59 years male, 63 years female (1992)
No. of Physicians: 1.9/10,000 population (1990)

■ EDUCATION

Govt. Expenditure: 15.2% of govt. expenditure (1985)
Literacy: 66.5% (1992)

■ COMMUNICATIONS

Daily newspapers: 0; 3 non-daily
Televisions: n.a.
Radios: 158/1,000 inhabitants (1992)
Telephones: 0.81/100 inhabitants (1992)

■ TRANSPORTATION

Motor Vehicles: 14,500; 10,000 passenger cars (1990)
Roads: 2,249 km; 601 km paved
Railway: n.a.
Air Traffic: 177,000 passengers carried (1991)
Airports: 1

Canadian Embassy: C/o The Canadian Embassy, 4th Floor, Sorano Bldg, 45 boul. de la République, Dakar; mailing address: P.O. Box 3373, Dakar, Senegal. Tel: (011-221) 23-92-90. Fax (011-221) 23-87-49

Cayman Islands

United Kingdom Crown Colony

Long-Form Name: Cayman Islands
Capital: George Town (on Grand Cayman Island)
Population: 29,000 (1992)

■ GEOGRAPHY

Area: 260 sq. km (three islands: Grand Cayman, Little Cayman, Cayman Brac)
Climate: tropical maritime; cool season: Nov. to March, hurricane-prone July to Nov.
Land Use: subsistence agriculture, fishing
Location: Caribbean Sea, S of Cuba

■ PEOPLE

Nationality: British
Ethnic Groups: various Hispanic strains, descendants of European settlers
Languages: English (official)

■ GOVERNMENT

Leader(s): Gov. Michael Gore
Government Type: United Kingdom Crown Colony

■ ECONOMY

Overview: chiefly tourism, financial services; main export turtle products; imports: foodstuffs, manufactured items, textiles, building materials, cars, petroleum products
Exports: $3 million
Imports: $267 million
Currency: Cayman Island dollar (CI$)

Central African Republic

Long-Form Name: Central African Republic
Capital: Bangui
Population: 3,173,000 (1992)

■ GEOGRAPHY

Area: 622,440 sq. km
Coastline: none: landlocked
Climate: tropical; hot, dry winters; mild to hot, wet summers
Environment: hot, dry, dusty harmattan winds affect northern areas; poaching has diminished reputation as one of last great wildlife refuges; desertification

Terrain: vast, flat to rolling, monotonous plateau; scattered hills in northeast and southwest
Land Use: 3% arable land; negligible permanent crops; 5% meadows and pastures; 64% forest and woodland; 28% other
Location: C Africa

■ PEOPLE

Nationality: Central African
Ethnic Groups: about 80 ethnic groups, the majority of which have related ethnic and linguistic characteristics; 34% Baya, 27% Banda, 10% Sara, 21% Mandjia, 4% Mboum, 4% m'Baka; 6,500 Europeans, of whom 3,600 are French
Languages: French (official); Sangho (lingua franca and national language); Arabic, Hunsa, Swahili
Religions: 24% indigenous beliefs, 25% Protestant, 25% Roman Catholic, 15% Moslem, 11% other; animistic beliefs and practices strongly influence the Christian majority
Marriages: n.a.
Divorces: n.a.

■ GOVERNMENT

Leader(s): Prime Min. Thimothee Malendorna, Pres. Ange Felix Patassé
Government Type: republic, one-party presidential regime since 1986
Administrative Divisions: 16 prefectures, 1 capital commune
Independence: Aug. 13, 1960 (from France; formerly known as Central African Empire)
National Holiday: National Day (proclamation of the republic), Dec. 1

■ ECONOMY

Overview: subsistence agriculture is the backbone of the economy (mainly forestry). It suffers from a poor transportation infrastructure and a weak human resource base
GNP: $1.218 billion, per capita $390; real growth rate 1.2% (1991)
Inflation: 0.7% (1989)
Industries: sawmills, breweries, diamond mining, textiles, footwear, assembly of bicycles and motorcycles
Labour Force: 1.38 million (1992); 83.7% agriculture, 13.5% services, 2.8% industry (1989)
Unemployment: 8,221 (1988)
Agriculture: accounts for 40% of GDP; self-sufficient in food production except for grain; commercial crops—cotton, coffee, tobacco, timber; food crops—manioc, yams, millet, corn, bananas
Natural Resources: diamonds, uranium, timber, gold, oil

■ FINANCE/TRADE

Currency: Communauté financière africaine franc (CFAF)
International Reserves Excluding Gold: $119 million (1992)
Gold Reserves: 0.01 million fine troy ounces (1991)
Budget: revenues $132 million; expenditures $305 million, including capital expenditures (1989)
Defence Expenditures: $18.67 million (1988)
External Debt: $815 million (1990)
Exports: $74 million (1991); commodities: diamonds, cotton, coffee, timber, tobacco; partners: France, Belgium, Italy, Japan, US
Imports: $145 million (1991); commodities: food, textiles, petroleum products, machinery, electrical equipment, motor vehicles, chemicals, pharmaceuticals, consumer goods, industrial products; partners: France, other European Community, Japan, Algeria, Yugoslavia

■ HEALTH

Births: 44/1,000 population (1991)
Deaths: 18/1,000 population (1991)
Infant Mortality: 138 deaths/1,000 live births (1991)
Life Expectancy at Birth: 45 years male, 48 years female (1992)
No. of Physicians: 0.5/10,000 population (1990)

■ EDUCATION

Govt. Expenditure: 16.8% of govt. expenditure (1989)
Literacy: 37.7% (1992)

■ COMMUNICATIONS

Daily newspapers: 1 (1992)
Televisions: 3.4/1,000 inhabitants (1992)
Radios: 61/1,000 inhabitants (1992)
Telephones: 0.26/100 inhabitants (1992)

■ TRANSPORTATION

Motor Vehicles: 22,000; 12,000 passenger cars (1984)
Roads: 20,541 km; 622 km paved
Railway: none, but line of 800 km proposed for construction (1985)
Air Traffic: 118,000 passengers carried (1991)
Airports: 40

Canadian Embassy: c/o Canadian Embassy, Édifice Stamatiades, Place de l'Hôtel de Ville, Yaoundé; mailing address: CP 572, Yaoundé, Cameroon. Tel: (011-237) 23-02-03/22-18-22. Fax: (011-237) 22-10-90

Chad

Long-Form Name: Republic of Chad
Capital: N'Djamena
Population: 5,846,000 (1992)

■ GEOGRAPHY

Area: 1,284,000 sq. km
Coastline: none: landlocked
Climate: tropical in south, desert in north
Environment: hot, dry, dusty harmattan winds occur in north; drought and desertification adversely affecting south; subject to plagues of locusts
Terrain: broad, arid plains in centre, desert in north, mountains in northwest, lowlands in south
Land Use: 2% arable land; negligible permanent crops; 36% meadows and pastures; 11% forest and woodland; 51% others; includes negligible irrigated
Location: NC Africa

■ PEOPLE

Nationality: Chadian
Ethnic Groups: some 200 distinct ethnic groups, most of whom are Moslems in the north and centre, and non-Moslems in the south; some 150,000 non-indigenous, of whom 1,000 are French
Languages: French and Arabic (official); Sara and Sango in south; more than 100 different languages and dialects are spoken
Religions: 44% Moslem, 6% Christian, remainder indigenous beliefs, animism
Marriages: n.a.
Divorces: n.a.

■ GOVERNMENT

Leader(s): Prime Min. Joseph Yodemane, Pres. Col. Idriss Deby
Government Type: republic
Administrative Divisions: 14 prefectures
Independence: Aug. 11, 1960 (from France)
National Holiday: n.a.

■ ECONOMY

Overview: civil war, drought and food shortages have adversely affected the economy which is based on subsistence farming and fishing
GNP: $1.212 billion, per capita $220; real growth rate 6.3% (1991)
Inflation: 0.6% (1990)
Industries: cotton textile mills, slaughterhouses, brewery, natron (sodium carbonate)
Labour Force: 1.97 million (1992); 83% agriculture (engaged in unpaid subsistence farming, herding and fishing), 12% services, 5% industry (1989)
Unemployment: 10,715 (1989)
Agriculture: accounts for 45% of GDP; largely subsistence farming; cotton most important cash crop; food crops include sorghum, millet, peanuts, rice, potatoes, manioc; livestock—cattle, sheep, goats, camels; self-sufficient in food in years of adequate rainfall
Natural Resources: small quantities of crude oil (unexploited but exploration beginning), uranium, natron, kaolin, fish

■ FINANCE/TRADE

Currency: Communité financière africaine franc (CFAF)
International Reserves Excluding Gold: $84 million (1991)
Gold Reserves: 0.01 million fine troy ounces (1990)
Budget: revenues $78 million; expenditures $127 million, not including capital expenditures that are mostly financed by foreign aid donors (1989)
Defence Expenditures: $57.99 million (1989)
External Debt: $430 million (1990)
Exports: $141 million (1988); commodities: cotton 43%, cattle 35%, textiles 5%, fish; partners: France, Nigeria, Cameroon
Imports: $419 million (1988); commodities: machinery and transportation equipment 39%, industrial goods 20%, petroleum products 13%, foodstuffs 9%; partners: US, France

■ HEALTH

Births: 42/1,000 population (1991)
Deaths: 22/1,000 population (1991)
Infant Mortality: 134 deaths/1,000 live births (1991)
Life Expectancy at Birth: 45 years male, 47 years female (1992)
No. of Physicians: 0.3/10,000 population (1992)

■ EDUCATION

Govt. Expenditure: n.a.
Literacy: 29.8% (1992)

■ COMMUNICATIONS

Daily newspapers: 1 (1992)
Televisions: 1.0/1,000 inhabitants (1992)

Radios: 237/1,000 inhabitants (1992)
Telephones: 0.18/100 inhabitants (1992)

■ TRANSPORTATION

Motor Vehicles: 15,000; 8,500 passenger cars (1990)
Roads: 32,100 km; paved n.a.
Railway: n.a.
Air Traffic: 81,000 passengers carried (1991)
Airports: 51

Canadian Embassy: C/o The Canadian Embassy, Édifice Stamatiades, Place de l'Hôtel de Ville, Yaoundé; mailing address: CP 572, Yaoundé, Cameroon. Tel: (011-237) 23-02-03/22-18-22. Fax: (011-237) 22-10-90

Channel Islands

Dependent Territory of the United Kingdom

Long-Form Name: Channel Islands
Capital: St. Helier (Jersey), St. Peter Port (Guernsey)
Population: 143,000 (1992)

■ GEOGRAPHY

Area: 194 sq. km (2 islands: Jersey and Guernsey, with 7 island dependencies of Guernsey)
Climate: mild, with average precipitation
Land Use: fertile soil permits extensive cultivation
Location: English Channel, off the coast of France

■ PEOPLE

Nationality: British
Ethnic Groups: English, French
Languages: English (official), French (official only on Jersey), Norman-French dialect

■ GOVERNMENT

Leader(s): Jersey: Lt. Gov. & Commander-in-Chief Air Marshal Sir John Sutton; Guernsey: Lt. Gov. & Commander-in-Chief Capt. D.P.L. Hodgetts
Government type: largely self-governing dependency

■ ECONOMY

Overview: tourism, banking, financial services; agriculture inc. dairy cattle, cash crops, flowers, fern
Currency: Island parliament of Guernsey issues its own currency

Chile

Long-Form Name: Republic of Chile
Capital: Santiago
Population: 13,600,000 (1992)

■ GEOGRAPHY

Area: 742,000 sq. km
Coastline: 6,435 km
Climate: temperate; desert in north; cool and damp in south
Environment: subject to severe earthquakes, active volcanism, tsunami; Atacama Desert one of world's driest regions; desertification
Terrain: low coastal mountains; fertile central valley; rugged Andes in east
Land Use: 7% arable land; negligible permanent crops; 16% meadows and pastures; 21% forest and woodland; 56% other; includes 2% irrigated
Location: W South America

■ PEOPLE

Nationality: Chilean
Ethnic Groups: 95% European and European-Indian, 3% Indian, 2% other
Languages: Spanish
Religions: 89% Roman Catholic, 11% Protestant and small Jewish population
Marriages: 7.6 (per 1,000) (1987)
Divorces: 0.4 (per 1,000) (1985)

■ GOVERNMENT

Leader(s): Pres. Patricio Aylwin Azócar
Government Type: republic
Administrative Divisions: 13 regions
Independence: Sept. 18, 1810 (from Spain)
National Holiday: Independence Day, Sept. 18

■ ECONOMY

Overview: copper is the single largest export in this economy which has benefited from growth in industry, agriculture and construction
GNP: $28.897 billion, per capita $2,160; real growth rate 3.4% (1991)
Inflation: 21.8% (1991)
Industries: copper, other minerals, foodstuffs, fish processing, iron and steel, wood and wood products
Labour Force: 4,753,000 (1992); 63% services (including government), 18.3% industry; 18.7% agriculture (1989)
Unemployment: 5.3% (1991)

Agriculture: accounts for about 8% of GDP (including fishing and forestry); major exporter of fruit, fish and timber products; major crops— wheat, corn, grapes, beans, sugar beets, potatoes, fruit; self-sufficient in most foods
Natural Resources: copper, timber, iron ore, nitrates, precious metals, molybdenum

■ FINANCE/TRADE

Currency: peso ($CH)
International Reserves Excluding Gold: $8,865 million (1992)
Gold Reserves: 1.87 million fine troy ounces (1992)
Budget: revenues $6.6 billion; expenditures $7.1 billion, including capital expenditures of $575 million (1990)
Defence Expenditures: $541.41 million (1990)
External Debt: $10.339 billion (1990)
Exports: $8.924 billion (1991); commodities: copper 48%, industrial products 33%, molybdenum, iron ore, wood pulp, fishmeal, fruits; partners: European Community 34%, US 22%, Japan 10%, Brazil 7%
Imports: $7.424 billion (1991); commodities: petroleum, wheat, capital goods, spare parts, raw materials; partners: European Community 23%, US 20%, Japan 10%, Brazil 9%

■ HEALTH

Births: 21/1,000 population (1991)
Deaths: 6/1,000 population (1991)
Infant Mortality: 18 deaths/1,000 live births (1991)
Life Expectancy at Birth: 71 years male, 76 years female (1992)
No. of Physicians: 8.1/10,000 population (1992)

■ EDUCATION

Govt. Expenditure: 12% of govt. expenditure (1987)
Literacy: 93.4% (1992)

■ COMMUNICATIONS

Daily newspapers: 39 (1992)
Televisions: 200.6/1,000 inhabitants (1992)
Radios: 340/1,000 inhabitants (1992)
Telephones: 6.7/100 inhabitants (1992)

■ TRANSPORTATION

Motor Vehicles: 1,016,641; 706,641 passenger cars (1990)
Roads: 78,652 km; 10,388 km paved
Railway: 7,568 km
Air Traffic: 1,406,000 passengers carried (1991)
Airports: 129

Canadian Embassy: Ahumada 11, 10th Fl, Santiago, Chile; mailing address: Casilla 771, Santiago, Chile. Tel: (011-56-2) 696-2256. Fax: (011-56-2) 696-0738
Embassy in Canada: Embassy of Chile, 151 Slater St, Ste 605, Ottawa ON K1P 5H3. Tel: (613) 235-9940, -4402. Fax: (613) 235-1176.

China

Long-Form Name: People's Republic of China
Capital: Beijing (formerly Peking)
Population: 1,187,997,000 (1992)

■ GEOGRAPHY

Area: 9,536,020 sq. km
Coastline: 14,500 km
Climate: extremely diverse; tropical in south to subarctic in north
Environment: frequent typhoons (about five times per year along southern and eastern coasts), damaging floods, tsunamis, earthquakes; deforestation; soil erosion; industrial pollution; water pollution; desertification
Terrain: mostly mountains, high plateaus, deserts in west; plains, deltas and hills in east
Land Use: 10% arable land; negligible permanent crops; 31% meadows and pastures; 14% forest and woodland; 45% other; includes 5% irrigated
Location: SE Asia, bordering on South China Sea, Yellow Sea

■ PEOPLE

Nationality: Chinese
Ethnic Groups: 93% Han Chinese; 7% Zhuang, Uygur, Hui, Yi, Tibetan, Miao, Manchu, Omngo, Buyi, Korean and other nationalities
Languages: Mandarin and local dialects. The Tibetans, Uighurs, Mongols, and others have their own languages
Religions: Confucianism, Taoism and Buddhism; approx. 2–3% Moslem, 1% Christian
Marriages: n.a.
Divorces: n.a.

■ GOVERNMENT

Leader(s): Premier, State Council Li Peng, Pres. Yang Shangkun, V. Pres. Wang Zhen
Government Type: Communist Party-led state
Administrative Divisions: 22 provinces, 5 autonomous regions, 3 government-controlled municipalities
Independence: People's Republic established Oct. 1, 1949

National Holiday: National Day, Oct. 1

■ ECONOMY

Overview: the Soviet-style centrally planned economy has been recently altered to include increased local authority which has increased production; population control is vital

GNP: $424.012 billion, per capita $370; real growth rate 9.4% (1991)

Inflation: 1.3% (1990)

Industries: iron, steel, coal, machine building, armaments, textiles, petroleum

Labour Force: 680,000,000 (1992); 73.7% agriculture and forestry, 13.6% industry, 12.7% services,(1989)

Unemployment: 2.3% (1991)

Agriculture: accounts for 26% of GNP; among the world's largest producers of rice, potatoes, sorghum, peanuts, tea, millet, barley and pork; commercial crops include cotton, other fibers and oilseeds; produces variety of livestock products; self-sufficient in food

Natural Resources: coal, iron ore, crude oil, mercury, tin, tungsten, antimony, manganese, molybdenum, vanadium, magnetite, aluminum, lead, zinc, uranium, world's greatest hydroelectric potential

■ FINANCE/TRADE

Currency: renminbi yuan (¥RMB)

International Reserves Excluding Gold: $46,294 million (1992)

Gold Reserves: 12.7 million fine troy ounces (1992)

Budget: n.a.

Defence Expenditures: $6.06 billion (1990)

External Debt: $45.31 billion (1990)

Exports: $84.635 billion (1992); commodities: manufactured goods, agricultural products, oilseeds, grain (rice and corn), oil, minerals; partners: Hong Kong, US, Japan, USSR, Singapore, Germany

Imports: $80.315 billion (1992); commodities: grain (mostly wheat), chemical fertilizer, steel, industrial raw materials, machinery, equipment; partners: Hong Kong, Japan, US, Germany, USSR

■ HEALTH

Births: 22/1,000 population (1991)

Deaths: 7/1,000 population (1991)

Infant Mortality: 33 deaths/1,000 live births (1991)

Life Expectancy at Birth: 68 years male, 71 years female (1992)

No. of Physicians: 9.9/10,000 population (1992)

■ EDUCATION

Govt. Expenditure: 12.4% of government expenditure (1989)

Literacy: 73.3% (1992)

■ COMMUNICATIONS

Daily newspapers: 78 (1992)

Televisions: 26.7/1,000 inhabitants (1992)

Radios: 184/1,000 inhabitants (1992)

Telephones: 0.97/100 inhabitants (1992)

■ TRANSPORTATION

Motor Vehicles: 5,835,865; 1,664,010 passenger cars (1990)

Roads: 19,072 km; 9,536 km paved

Railway: 55,309 km

Air Traffic: 19,520,000 passengers carried (1991)

Airports: 92

Canadian Embassy: 19 Dong Zhi Men Wai St, Chaoyang District, Beijing 100600, China. Tel: (011-86-1) 532-3536. Fax (011-86-1) 532-4072

Embassy in Canada: Embassy of the People's Republic of China, 515 St Patrick St, Ottawa ON K1N 5H3. Tel: (613) 234-2706.

Christmas Island

Dependent Territory of Australia

Long-Form Name: Christmas Island
Capital: n.a.
Population: 1,770 (1991)

■ GEOGRAPHY

Area: 135 sq. km (land area); includes one of the largest coral islands in the Pacific

Climate: tropical, with little annual variation

Land Use: dry sandy soil does not permit much cultivation

Location: Indian Ocean (Line Islands)

■ PEOPLE

Nationality: Australian

Ethnic Groups: 60% Chinese, 15% Malay, 25% Austrian/European origin

Languages: English, Chinese, Oriental and European-speaking minorities

■ GOVERNMENT

Leader(s): administrator appointed by Australian Commonwealth Govt.

Government type: dependency

■ ECONOMY

Overview: extraction and export of rock phosphate dust
Currency: Australian dollar

Ciskei

Dependent Territory of South Africa

Long-Form Name: Republic of Ciskei
Capital: Bisho
Population: 2 million (1987); only 1 million live in Ciskei, the rest live and work in South Africa

■ GEOGRAPHY

Area: 9,000 sq. km
Climate: subtropical
Land Use: subsistence agriculture predominates
Location: SE South Africa, bordering on Indian Ocean

■ PEOPLE

Nationality: South African
Ethnic Groups: Xhosa
Languages: English, Xhosa

■ GOVERNMENT

Leader(s): Brig. Oupo Gqozo
Government type: dependency under constitutional, financial, and judicial control of South Africa; independence granted 1981, relinquished 1991

■ ECONOMY

Overview: agriculture: maize, wheat, cash crops, livestock, esp. sheep, goats, cattle, poultry; mineral resources largely underdeveloped; manufactured goods inc. textiles, timber and steel products, foodstuffs, leather; main trading partner: South Africa
Currency: South African Rand (R)

Cocos (Keeling) Islands

Dependent Territory of Australia

Long-Form Name: Cocos (Keeling) Islands
Capital: n.a.
Population: 603 (1990)

■ GEOGRAPHY

Area: 14.2 sq. km
Climate: tropical maritime
Land Use: primarily subsistence agriculture
Location: Indian Ocean, SW of Sumatra

■ PEOPLE

Nationality: Australian
Ethnic Groups: various Polynesian strains
Languages: English, local and tribal

■ GOVERNMENT

Leader(s): Administrator appointed by Gov.-Gen. of Australia
Government type: dependency placed under Australian govt. authority by Cocos (Keeling) Islands Act of 1955

■ ECONOMY

Overview: little industrial activity; agriculture limited to coconut cultivation
Currency: n.a.

Colombia

Long-Form Name: Republic of Colombia
Capital: Bogotá
Population: 33,424,000 (1992)

■ GEOGRAPHY

Area: 1,141,750 sq. km; includes Isla de Malpelo, Roncador Cay, Serrana Bank, and Serranilla Bank
Coastline: 3,208 km total (1,448 km North Pacific Ocean; 1,760 Caribbean Sea)
Climate: tropical along coast and eastern plains; cooler in highlands
Environment: highlands subject to volcanic eruptions; deforestation; soil damage from overuse of pesticides; periodic droughts
Terrain: mixture of flat coastal lowlands, plains in east, central highlands, some high mountains
Land Use: 4% arable land; 2% permanent crops; 29% meadows and pastures; 49% forest and woodlands; 16% other; includes negligible irrigated
Location: NW South America, bordering on Caribbean Sea, Pacific Ocean

■ PEOPLE

Nationality: Colombian
Ethnic Groups: 68% mestizo, 20% white, 5% black, 7% Indian
Languages: Spanish
Religions: 95% Roman Catholic
Marriages: 3.6 (per 1,000) (1981)
Divorces: n.a.

■ GOVERNMENT

Leader(s): Pres. César Gaviria Trujillo, Pres. Designate vacant

Government Type: republic; executive branch dominates government structure
Administrative Divisions: 23 departments, 5 commissariats and 4 intendancies
Independence: July 20, 1810 (from Spain)
National Holiday: Independence Day, July 20

■ ECONOMY

Overview: traditionally coffee has been the main export though other industries such as oil and coal are developing; drug-related violence is a threat to economic growth
GNP: $41.922 billion, per capita $1,280; real growth rate 3.2% (1990)
Inflation: 30.4% (1991)
Industries: textiles, food processing, oil, clothing and footwear, beverages, chemicals, metal products, cement; mining—gold, coal, emeralds, iron, nickel, silver, salt
Labour Force: 10,394,000 (1992); 76.9% services, 1.7% agriculture, 21.4% industry (1989)
Unemployment: 501,630 (1991)
Agriculture: accounts for 22% of GDP; crops make up two-thirds and livestock one-third of agricultural output; climate and soils permit a wide variety of crops, such as coffee, rice, tobacco, corn, sugar cane, cocoa beans, oilseeds, vegetables
Natural Resources: crude oil, natural gas, coal, iron ore, nickel, gold, copper, emeralds

■ FINANCE/TRADE

Currency: peso ($Col)
International Reserves Excluding Gold: $7,162 million (1992)
Gold Reserves: 0.21 million fine troy ounces (1992)
Budget: revenues $4.39 billion; expenditures $3.93 billion, including capital expenditures of $1.03 billion (1989)
Defence Expenditures: $904.06 million (1990)
External Debt: $14.68 billion (1990)
Exports: $7.269 billion (1991); commodities: coffee 30%, petroleum 24%, coal, bananas, fresh cut flowers; partners: US 36%, European Community 21%, Japan 5%, Netherlands 4%, Sweden 3%
Imports: $4.967 billion (1991); commodities: industrial equipment, transportation equipment, foodstuffs, chemicals, paper products; partners: US 34%, European Community 16%, Brazil 4%, Venezuela 3%, Japan 3%

■ HEALTH

Births: 26/1,000 population (1991)
Deaths: 5/1,000 population (1991)

Infant Mortality: 37 deaths/1,000 live births (1991)
Life Expectancy at Birth: 68 years male, 73 years female (1992)
No. of Physicians: 8.1/10,000 population (1992)

■ EDUCATION

Govt. Expenditure: 21.4% of govt. expenditure (1989)
Literacy: 86.7% (1992)

■ COMMUNICATIONS

Daily newspapers: 45 (1992)
Televisions: 108.1/1,000 inhabitants (1992)
Radios: 167/1,000 inhabitants (1992)
Telephones: 8.11/100 inhabitants (1992)

■ TRANSPORTATION

Motor Vehicles: 1,380,618; 715,315 passenger cars (1990)
Roads: 116,459 km; 11,418 km paved
Railway: 3,083 km
Air Traffic: 5,540,000 passengers carried (1991)
Airports: 197

Canadian Embassy: Calle 76, No. 11-52, Santafe de Bogotá, Colombia; mailing address: Apartado Aereo 53531, Santafe de Bogotá 2, Colombia. Tel: (011-57-1) 217-5555. Fax (011-57-1) 310-4509
Embassy in Canada: Embassy of Colombia, 360 Albert St, Ste 1130, Ottawa ON K1R 7X7. Tel: (613) 230-3760, -1. Fax: (613) 230-4416.

Comoros

Long-Form Name: Federal Islamic Republic of the Comoros
Capital: Moroni
Population: 585,000 (1992)

■ GEOGRAPHY

Area: 1,862 sq. km
Coastline: 340 km
Climate: tropical marine; rainy season (Nov. to May)
Environment: soil degradation and erosion; deforestation; cyclones possible during rainy season
Terrain: volcanic islands, interiors vary from steep mountains to low hills
Land Use: 35% arable; 8% permanent; 7% meadows; 16% forest; 34% other
Location: Indian Ocean E of Africa

■ PEOPLE

Nationality: Comorian
Ethnic Groups: Antalote, Cafre, Makoa, Oimatsaha, Sakalava
Languages: Shaafi Islam (a Swahili dialect), Malagasy, French, majority speaks Comoran
Religions: 99% Sunni Moslem, 1% Roman Catholic
Marriages: n.a.
Divorces: n.a.

■ GOVERNMENT

Leader(s): Pres. Said Mohamed Djohar
Government Type: independent republic
Administrative Divisions: 3 islands
Independence: July 6, 1975 (from France)
National Holiday: Independence Day, July 6

■ ECONOMY

Overview: agriculture is the main sector of the economy though it does not feed citizens adequately; one of the world's poorest countries
GNP: $245 million, per capita $500; real growth rate 2.6% (1991)
Inflation: 8.3% (1986)
Industries: perfume distillation
Labour Force: 230,000 (1992); 83% agriculture, 6% industry, 11% services (1989)
Unemployment: over 16% (1988 est.)
Agriculture: accounts for 40% of GDP; most of population works in subsistence agriculture and fishing; plantations produce cash crops for export— vanilla, cloves, perfume essences and copra; principal food crops—coconuts, bananas, cassava; large net food importer
Natural Resources: negligible

■ FINANCE/TRADE

Currency: Communauté financière africaine franc (CFAF)
International Reserves Excluding Gold: $22 million (1991)
Gold Reserves: n.a.
Budget: revenues $88 million; expenditures $92 million, including capital expenditures of $13 million (1990)
Defence Expenditures: 3% GDP (1981)
External Debt: $238 million (1988)
Exports: $18 million (1989); commodities: vanilla, cloves, perfume oil, copra; partners: US 53%, France 41%, Africa 4%, Germany 2%
Imports: $52 million (1987); commodities: rice and other foodstuffs, cement, petroleum products, consumer goods; partners: Europe 62% (France 22%, other 40%), Africa 5%,

Pakistan, China

■ HEALTH

Births: 47/1,000 population (1991)
Deaths: 12/1,000 population (1991)
Infant Mortality: 87 deaths/1,000 live births (1991)
Life Expectancy at Birth: 54 years male, 58 years female (1992)
No. of Physicians: 0.8/10,000 population (1992)

■ EDUCATION

Govt. Expenditure: 13.2% of govt. expenditure (1989)
Literacy: 47.9% (1992)

■ COMMUNICATIONS

Daily newspapers: 1 (1992)
Televisions: 0.3/1,000 inhabitants (1992)
Radios: 115/1,000 inhabitants (1992)
Telephones: 0.88/100 inhabitants (1992)

■ TRANSPORTATION

Motor Vehicles: 5,600 motor vehicles (1983)
Roads: 626 km; 175 km paved
Railway: n.a.
Air Traffic: 26,000 passengers carried (1991)
Airports: 4
Canadian Embassy: C/o The Canadian High Commission, Comcraft House, Hailé Sélassie Ave, Nairobi; mailing address: P.O. Box 30481, Nairobi, Kenya. Tel: (011-254-2) 214-804. Fax: (011-254-2) 226-987/216-485

Congo

Long-Form Name: People's Republic of the Congo
Capital: Brazzaville
Population: 2,368,000 (1992)

■ GEOGRAPHY

Area: 342,000 sq. km
Coastline: 169 km
Climate: tropical; rainy season (Mar. to June); dry season (June to Oct.); constant high temperatures and humidity; particularly enervating climate astride the Equator
Environment: deforestation; about 70% of the population lives in Brazzaville, Pointe Noire or along the railroad between them
Terrain: coastal plain, southern basin, central plateau, northern basin
Land Use: 2% arable land; negligible permanent; 29% meadows; 62% forest; 7% other

Location: WC Africa, bordering on South Atlantic Ocean

PEOPLE

Nationality: Congolese
Ethnic Groups: about 15 ethnic groups divided into some 75 tribes, almost all Bantu; most important ethnic groups are Kongo (48%) in south, Sangha (20%) and M'Bochi (12%) in the north, Teke (17%) in the centre; about 8,500 Europeans, mostly French
Languages: French (official); many African languages with Lingala and Kikongo most widely used
Religions: 50% Christian, 48% animist, 2% Moslem
Marriages: n.a.
Divorces: n.a.

GOVERNMENT

Leader(s): Prime Min. Claude Antoine Dacosta, Pres. Pascal Lissouba
Government Type: people's republic
Administrative Divisions: 9 regions, 1 capital district
Independence: Aug. 15, 1960 (from France; formerly known as Congo/Brazzaville)
National Holiday: National Day, Aug. 15

ECONOMY

Overview: oil revenues are responsible for one of the highest growth rates in Africa, though the country faces increasing foreign debts and is vulnerable to the oil market
GNP: $2.623 billion, per capita $1,120; real growth rate 3.1% (1991)
Inflation: 4.1% (1989)
Industries: crude oil, cement, sawmills, brewery, sugar mill, palm oil, soap, cigarettes
Labour Force: 781,000 (1992); 62.4% agriculture, 25.6% services, 11.9% industry (1989)
Unemployment: n.a.
Agriculture: accounts for 11% of GDP (including fishing and forestry); cassava accounts for 90% of food output; other crops—rice, corn, peanuts, vegetables; cash crops include coffee and cocoa; forest products important export earner; imports over 90% of food needs
Natural Resources: petroleum, timber, potash, lead, zinc, uranium, copper, phosphate, natural gas

FINANCE/TRADE

Currency: Communauté financière africaine franc (CFAF)
International Reserves Excluding Gold: $16 million (1992)
Gold Reserves: 0.01 million fine troy ounces (1991)
Budget: revenues $522 million; expenditures $767 million, including capital expenditures of $141 million (1989)
Defence Expenditures: $100.51 million (1987)
External Debt: $4.38 billion (1990)
Exports: $976 million (1990); commodities: crude petroleum 72%, lumber, plywood, coffee, cocoa, sugar, diamonds; partners: US, France, other European Community
Imports: $600 million (1990); commodities: foodstuffs, consumer goods, intermediate manufactures, capital equipment; partners: France, Italy, other European Community, US, Germany, Spain, Japan, Brazil

HEALTH

Births: 43/1,000 population (1991)
Deaths: 13/1,000 population (1991)
Infant Mortality: 108 deaths/1,000 live births (1991)
Life Expectancy at Birth: 52 years male, 55 years female (1992)
No. of Physicians: 1.3/10,000 population (1990)

EDUCATION

Govt. Expenditure: 9.8% of govt. expenditure (1989)
Literacy: 56.6% (1992)

COMMUNICATIONS

Daily newspapers: 1 (1992)
Televisions: 4.5/1,000 inhabitants (1992)
Radios: 109/1,000 inhabitants (1992)
Telephones: 1.29/100 inhabitants (1992)

TRANSPORTATION

Motor Vehicles: 48,000; 27,000 passenger cars (1990)
Roads: 11,970 km; 684 km paved
Railway: 513 km
Air Traffic: 227,000 passengers carried (1991)
Airports: 43

Canadian Embassy: C/o The Canadian Embassy, 17 Pumbe Zone de Gombe Ave, Kinshasa; mailing address: P.O. Box 8341, Kinshasa, Zaïre. Tel: (011-243-12) 21-801, 907. Fax: (011-871) 156-0213
Representative to Canada: C/o Ambassade de la République populaire du Congo, 4891 Colorado Ave, NW, Washington, DC 20011 USA

Cook Islands

Dependent Territory of New Zealand

Long-Form Name: Cook Islands
Capital: Avarua (on Rarotonga Island)
Population: 17,000 (1992)

■ GEOGRAPHY

Area: 293 sq. km
Climate: mild year-round
Land Use: fertile soil allows cultivation of cash crops
Location: S Pacific Ocean, NE of New Zealand

■ PEOPLE

Nationality: New Zealander
Ethnic Groups: Polynesian
Languages: English, Cook Islands Maori

■ GOVERNMENT

Leader(s): Queen's Rep. Apenera Short; New Zealand Rep. Tim Caughley; Prime Min. Hon. Geoffrey A. Henry
Government type: self-governing territory in free association with New Zealand, linked by common head of state (the Queen) and citizenship (New Zealand).

■ ECONOMY

Overview: agriculture: copra, fruits, tomatoes; livestock: pigs, goats; fishing
GNP: $620 million, per capita $10,000, real growth rate 16.7% (1988 est.)
Exports: $6.6 million, chiefly fresh fruits and vegetables, clothing, (1988)
Imports: $64.5 million, chiefly foodstuffs, manufactured goods, fuels (1988); chief trading partner: New Zealand
Currency: Cook Island dollar (at parity with New Zealand dollar)

Costa Rica

Long-Form Name: Republic of Costa Rica
Capital: San José
Population: 3,192,000 (1992)

■ GEOGRAPHY

Area: 51,100 sq. km; includes Isla del Coco
Coastline: 1,290 km
Climate: tropical; dry season (Dec. to Apr.); rainy season (May to Nov.)
Environment: subject to occasional earthquakes, hurricanes along Atlantic coast; frequent flooding of lowlands at onset of rainy season; active volcanoes; deforestation; soil erosion
Terrain: coastal plains separated by rugged mountains
Land Use: 6% arable; 7% permanent; 45% meadows; 34% forest; 8% other
Location: Central (Latin) America, bordering on Caribbean Sea, Pacific Ocean

■ PEOPLE

Nationality: Costa Rican
Ethnic Groups: 96% white (including mestizo), 2% black, 1% Indian, 1% Chinese
Languages: Spanish (official)
Religions: 95% Roman Catholic
Marriages: 7.8 (per 1,000) (1987)
Divorces: 1.0 (per 1,000) (1982)

■ GOVERNMENT

Leader(s): Pres. Rafael Angel Calderón Fournier
Government Type: democratic republic
Administrative Divisions: 7 provinces
Independence: Sept. 15, 1821 (from Spain)
National Holiday: Independence Day, Sept. 15

■ ECONOMY

Overview: external debt is high, many people are underemployed; coffee and banana crops are vital
GNP: $6.156 billion, per capita $1,930; real growth rate 3.4% (1991)
Inflation: 28.7% (1991)
Industries: food processing, textiles and clothing, construction materials, fertilizer, tourism
Labour Force: 1.023 million (1992); 18.2% industry and commerce, 56.4% services, 25.4% agriculture (1989)
Unemployment: 5.5% (1991)
Agriculture: accounts for 20–25% of GDP and 70% of exports; cash commodities—coffee, beef, bananas, sugar; normally self-sufficient in food except for grain; depletion of forest resources resulting in lower timber output
Natural Resources: hydroelectricity potential

■ FINANCE/TRADE

Currency: colón (pl. colones) (C/)
International Reserves Excluding Gold: $964 million (1992)
Gold Reserves: 0.39 million fine troy ounces (1992)
Budget: revenues $782 million; expenditures $917 million, including capital expenditures (1988)
Defence Expenditures: $62.67 million (1990)
External Debt: $3.077 billion (1990)

Exports: $1.543 billion (1991); commodities: coffee, bananas, textiles, sugar; partners: US 75%, Germany, Guatemala, Netherlands, UK, Japan
Imports: $1.853 billion (1991); commodities: petroleum, machinery, consumer durables, chemicals, fertilizer, foodstuffs; partners: US 35%, Japan, Guatemala, Germany

■ HEALTH

Births: 27/1,000 population (1991)
Deaths: 4/1,000 population (1991)
Infant Mortality: 15 deaths/1,000 live births (1991)
Life Expectancy at Birth: 75 years male, 79 years female (1992)
No. of Physicians: 10.5/10,000 population (1992)

■ EDUCATION

Govt. Expenditure: 19% of govt. expenditure (1990)
Literacy: 92.8% (1992)

■ COMMUNICATIONS

Daily newspapers: 4 (1992)
Televisions: 136.1/1,000 inhabitants (1992)
Radios: 259/1,000 inhabitants (1992)
Telephones: 16.7/100 inhabitants (1992)

■ TRANSPORTATION

Motor Vehicles: 250,000; 150,000 passenger cars (1990)
Roads: 35,566 km; 5,212 km paved
Railway: 700 km
Air Traffic: 504,000 passengers carried 1991
Airports: 63

Canadian Embassy: Flr 6, Cronos Building, Calle 3 y Avenida Central; mailing address: Apartado Postal 10303-1000, San José, Costa Rica. Tel: (011-506) 55-35-22. Fax: (011-506) 23-23-95
Embassy in Canada: Embassy of the Republic of Costa Rica, 135 York St, Ste 208, Ottawa ON K1N 5T4. Tel: (613) 234-5762.

Côte d'Ivoire (Ivory Coast)

Long-Form Name: Republic of Côte d'Ivoire
Capital: Yamoussoukro (previous capital was Abidjan; US does not recognize the change)
Population: 12,910,000 (1992)

■ GEOGRAPHY

Area: 322,460 sq. km
Coastline: 515 km
Climate: tropical along coast, semi-arid in far north; three seasons: warm and dry (Nov. to Mar.), hot and dry (Mar. to May), hot and wet (June to Oct.)
Environment: coast has heavy surf and natural harbors; severe deforestation
Terrain: mostly flat to undulating plains; mountains in northwest
Land Use: 9% arable; 4% permanent; 9% meadows; 26% forest; 52% other
Location: WC Africa, bordering on South Atlantic Ocean

■ PEOPLE

Nationality: Ivorian
Ethnic Groups: over 60 ethnic groups; most important are the Baoule 23%, Bete 18%, Senoufou 15%, Malinke 11% and Agni; about 2 million foreign Africans mostly Burkinabe; about 130,000 to 330,000 non-Africans (30,000 French and 100,000–300,000 Lebanese)
Languages: French (official), Akan, Kru, other indigenous languages
Religions: 17% indigenous, 38.7% Moslem, 27.5% Christian
Marriages: n.a.
Divorces: n.a.

■ GOVERNMENT

Leader(s): Prime Min. Alassane Ouattara, Pres. Félix Houphouët-Boigny
Government Type: republic; one-party presidential regime established 1960
Administrative Divisions: 34 departments
Independence: Aug. 7, 1960 (from France)
National Holiday: Independence Day, Dec. 7

■ ECONOMY

Overview: despite attempts to diversify, the economy is largely dependent on agriculture and related industries; highly sensitive to fluctuations in world prices for coffee and cocoa and to weather conditions
GNP: $8.523 billion, per capita $690; real growth rate 0.3% (1991)
Inflation: -0.7% (1990)
Industries: foodstuffs, wood processing, oil refinery, automobile assembly, textiles, fertilizer, beverage
Labour Force: 4,599,000 (1992), 65.2% agriculture, 8.3% industry, 26.5% services (1989)
Unemployment: 140,250 (1990)
Agriculture: most important sector, contributing one-third to GDP and 80% to exports; cash crops include coffee, cocoa beans, timber, bananas, palm kernels, rubber; food crops; not self-sufficient in bread grain and dairy products

Natural Resources: crude oil, diamonds, manganese, iron ore, cobalt, bauxite, copper

■ FINANCE/TRADE

Currency: Communauté financière africaine franc (CFAF)
International Reserves Excluding Gold: $11 million (1992)
Gold Reserves: 0.04 million fine troy ounces (1992)
Budget: revenues $2.8 billion; expenditures $4.1 billion, including capital expenditures (1989)
Defence Expenditures: $119.68 million (1987)
External Debt: $10.050 billion (1990)
Exports: $2.931 billion (1989); commodities: cocoa 30%, coffee 20%, tropical woods 11%, cotton, bananas, pineapples, palm oil; partners: France, Germany, Netherlands, US, Belgium, Spain
Imports: $2.185 billion (1989); commodities: manufactured goods and semifinished products 50%, consumer goods 40%, raw materials and fuels 10%; partners: France, other European Community, Nigeria, US, Japan

■ HEALTH

Births: 48/1,000 population (1991)
Deaths: 12/1,000 population (1991)
Infant Mortality: 97 deaths/1,000 live births (1991)
Life Expectancy at Birth: 52 years male, 55 years female (1992)
No. of Physicians: n.a.

■ EDUCATION

Govt. Expenditure: 21% of government expenditure (1984)
Literacy: 53.8% (1992)

■ COMMUNICATIONS

Daily newspapers: 2 (1992)
Televisions: 58.5/1,000 inhabitants (1992)
Radios: 139/1,000 inhabitants (1992)
Telephones: 1.06/100 inhabitants (1992)

■ TRANSPORTATION

Motor Vehicles: 262,000; 170,000 passenger cars (1990)
Roads: 54,496 km; 3,870 km paved
Railway: 677 km
Air Traffic: 175,000 passengers carried (1991)
Airports: 27

Canadian Embassy: Immeuble Trade-Center, 23 rue Nogues, Le Plateau; mailing address: 01 BP 4104, Abidjan 01, Côte d'Ivoire. Tel: (011-225) 32-20-09. Fax: (011-225) 22-05-30
Embassy in Canada: Embassy of the Republic of Côte d'Ivoire, 9 Marlborough Ave, Ottawa ON K1N 8C6. Tel: (613) 236-9919. Fax: (613) 230-7560.

Croatia

Long-Form Name: Republic of Croatia
Capital: Zagreb
Population: 4,760,300 (1991)

■ GEOGRAPHY

Area: 56,538 sq. km
Coastline: extensive Adriatic coastline
Climate: cold winters with much snow, cool, rainy summers
Environment: summer droughts
Terrain: mountainous region, extensively forested
Land Use: 8 million acres agricultural land, of which 63% is cultivated; 5 million acres forest land
Location: S Europe, bordering on Adriatic Sea

■ PEOPLE

Nationality: Croat
Ethnic Groups: Slavic (Croats, Serbs)
Languages: Serbo-Croat
Religions: majority Roman Catholic, Serbian Eastern Orthodoxy
Marriages: 29,399 (1989)
Divorces: n.a.

■ GOVERNMENT

Leader(s): Pres. Franjo Tudjman, Prime Min. Nikica Valentic
Government Type: parliamentary democracy
Administrative Divisions: n.a.
Independence: Dec. 21, 1990, secession from federal Yugoslovia
National Holiday: Independence Day, May 30, Anti-Fascism Struggle Commemoration Day, June 22

■ ECONOMY

Overview: tourism, manufacturing inc. chemicals, food products, petroleum, ships and textiles. War and internal strife have severely disrupted economy.
GNP: n.a.
Inflation: n.a.
Industries: mining, fertilizers, plastics, sugar, cotton fabrics, machinery

Labour Force: 3,049,000 (1989); 61% agriculture and animal husbandry, 14% industry, 25% services and other
Unemployment: 4.6% (1989)
Agriculture: wheat, maize, potatoes, plums, fish, livestock, esp. cattle, sheep, pigs, poultry
Natural Resources: coal, bauxite, brown coal and lignite, iron ore, china clay

■ FINANCE/TRADE

Currency: Kruna
International Reserves Excluding Gold: n.a.
Gold Reserves: n.a.
Budget: n.a.
Defence Expenditures: n.a.
External Debt: n.a.
Exports: machiney and transportation equipment and other manufactured goods; partners: mostly Italy, Germany, United States, Commonwealth of Independent States
Imports: machinery and transportation equipment, chemicals, raw materials

■ HEALTH

Births: 12.2/1,000 population (1989)
Deaths: 11.3/1,000 population (1989)
Infant Mortality: 11.3 deaths/1,000 live births (1989)
Life Expectancy at Birth: n.a.
No. of Physicians: n.a.

■ EDUCATION

Govt. Expenditure: n.a.
Literacy: n.a.

■ COMMUNICATIONS

Daily newspapers: n.a.
Televisions: n.a.
Radios: n.a.
Telephones: n.a.

■ TRANSPORTATION

Motor Vehicles: n.a.
Roads: n.a.
Railway: n.a.
Air Traffic: n.a.
Airports: n.a.

Canadian Embassy: C/o Kneza Milosa 75, 11000 Belgrade, Yugoslavia. Tel: (011-38-11) 644-666

Cuba

Long-Form Name: Republic of Cuba
Capital: Havana
Population: 10,811,000 (1992)

■ GEOGRAPHY

Area: 110,860 sq. km
Coastline: 3,735 km
Climate: tropical; moderated by trade winds; dry season (Nov. to Apr.); rainy season (May to Oct.)
Environment: averages one hurricane every two years
Terrain: mostly flat to rolling plains with rugged hills and mountains in the southeast
Land Use: 23% arable; 6% permanent; 23% meadows; 17% forest; 31% other
Location: West Indies, bordering on Caribbean Sea, Atlantic Ocean

■ PEOPLE

Nationality: Cuban
Ethnic Groups: 51% mulatto, 37% white, 11% black, 1% Chinese
Languages: Spanish
Religions: Christianity (majority Roman Catholic)
Marriages: 7.9 (per 1,000) (1988)
Divorces: 3.2 (per 1,000) (1987)

■ GOVERNMENT

Leader(s): Pres. of the Council of State Fidel Castro Ruz
Government Type: Communist state
Administrative Divisions: 14 provinces and 1 special municipality
Independence: May 20, 1902 (from Spain Dec. 10, 1898; administered by the US from 1898 to 1902)
National Holiday: Revolution Day, Jan. 1

■ ECONOMY

Overview: the Soviet-style, centrally planned and largely state-owned economy depends on agriculture, foreign trade (sugar) and Soviet aid, which may decline
GNP: $20.9 billion, per capita $2,000; real growth rate -1% (1989 est.)
Inflation: n.a.
Industries: sugar milling, petroleum refining, food and tobacco processing, textiles, chemicals, paper and wood products, metals (particularly nickel), cement, fertilizers, consumer goods, agricultural machinery
Labour Force: 4,461,000 (1992); 47.7% services, 28.5% industry, 23.8% agriculture (1989)
Unemployment: 6% overall, 10% for women (1989)

Agriculture: accounts for 11% of GNP (including fishing and forestry); key commercial crops— sugar cane, tobacco and citrus fruits; other products—coffee, rice, potatoes, meat, beans; world's largest sugar exporter; not self-sufficient in food
Natural Resources: cobalt, nickel, iron ore, copper, manganese, salt, timber, silica

■ **FINANCE/TRADE**

Currency: peso ($)
International Reserves Excluding Gold: n.a.
Gold Reserves: n.a.
Budget: revenues $12.46 billion; expenditures $14.45 billion, including capital expenditures (1990)
Defence Expenditures: $1.83 billion (1989)
External Debt: $6.8 billion (1989)
Exports: $3.585 billion (1991); commodities: sugar, nickel, shellfish, citrus, tobacco, coffee; partners: USSR 67%, Germany 6%, China 4%
Imports: $3.690 billion (1991); commodities: capital goods, industrial raw materials, food, petroleum; partners: USSR 71%, other Communist countries 15%

■ **HEALTH**

Births: 18/1,000 population (1991)
Deaths: 7/1,000 population (1991)
Infant Mortality: 12 deaths/1,000 live births (1991)
Life Expectancy at Birth: 74 years male, 78 years female (1992)
No. of Physicians: 18.9/10,000 population (1992)

■ **EDUCATION**

Govt. Expenditure: 12.8% government expenditure (1989)
Literacy: 94.0% (1992)

■ **COMMUNICATIONS**

Daily newspapers: 1 (1992)
Televisions: 203.4/1,000 inhabitants (1992)
Radios: 343/1,000 inhabitants (1992)
Telephones: 5.6/100 inhabitants (1992)

■ **TRANSPORTATION**

Motor Vehicles: 229,500 passenger cars (1987)
Roads: 21,174 km; 9,091 km paved
Railway: 12,915 km
Air Traffic: 831,000 passengers carried (1991)
Airports: 20

Canadian Embassy: Calle 30, No. 518 Esquina a7a, Avenida Miramar, Havana, Cuba; mailing address: Commercial Division, Box 500 (HVAN), Ottawa, Ontario K1N 8T7. Tel: (011-53-7) 33-2516. Fax: (011-53-7) 33-2044
Embassy in Canada: Embassy of the Republic of Cuba, 388 Main St, Ottawa ON K1S 1E3. Tel: (613) 563-0141. Fax: (613) 563-0068.

Cyprus

Long-Form Name: Republic of Cyprus
Capital: Nicosia
Population: 716,000 (1992)

■ **GEOGRAPHY**

Area: 9,250 sq. km
Coastline: 648 km
Climate: temperate, Mediterranean with hot, dry summers and cool, wet winters
Environment: moderate earthquake activity; water resource problems (no natural reservoir catchments, seasonal disparity in rainfall and most potable resources concentrated in the Turkish-Cypriot area)
Terrain: central plain with mountains to north and south
Land Use: 40% arable; 7% permanent; 10% meadows; 18% forest; 25% other
Location: Mediterranean Sea

■ **PEOPLE**

Nationality: Cypriot
Ethnic Groups: 80% Greek; 19% Turkish; 1% other
Languages: 80% Greek, Turkish, English
Religions: 78% Greek Orthodox; 18% Moslem; 4% Maronite, Armenian, Apostolic and other
Marriages: 7.3 (per 1,000) (1988)
Divorces: 0.5 (per 1,000) (1988)

■ **GOVERNMENT**

Leader(s): Pres. Georgios Vassiliou
Government Type: republic; Greek Cypriots control the only internationally-recognized government
Administrative Divisions: 6 districts; dependent areas inc.: Turkish Republic of Northern Cyprus
Independence: Aug. 16, 1960 (from UK)
National Holiday: Independence Day, Oct. 1

■ **ECONOMY**

Overview: a high growth rate, low inflation rate and manageable deficit characterize the economy
GNP: $6.135 billion, per capita $8,640; real growth rate 6% (1991)
Inflation: 5% (1991)

Industries: mining (iron pyrites, gypsum, asbestos); manufactured products—beverages, footwear, clothing and cement—are principally for local consumptions
Labour Force: 326,000 (1992); 67.4% services, 18.9% industry, 13.7% agriculture (1989)
Unemployment: 3.0% (1991)
Agriculture: accounts for 8% of GDP and employs 22% of labour force; major crops—potatoes, vegetables, barley, grapes, olives and citrus fruits; vegetables and fruit provide 25% of export revenues
Natural Resources: copper, pyrites, asbestos, gypsum, timber, salt, marble, clay earth pigment

■ **FINANCE/TRADE**

Currency: Cyprus pound (£ or £C)
International Reserves Excluding Gold: $1,154 million (1992)
Gold Reserves: 0.46 million fine troy ounces (1992)
Budget: revenues $1.2 billion; expenditures $1.4 billion, including capital expenditures of $178 million (1989)
Defence Expenditures: $155.29 million (1989)
External Debt: $2.8 billion (1988)
Exports: $952 million (1991); commodities: citrus, potatoes, grapes, wine, cement, clothing and shoes; partners: Middle East and North Africa 37%, UK 27%, other European Community 11%, US 2%
Imports: $2.621 billion (1991); commodities: consumer goods 23%, petroleum and lubricants 12%, food and feed grains, machinery; partners: European Community 60%, Middle East and North Africa 7%, US 4%

■ **HEALTH**

Births: 18/1,000 population (1991)
Deaths: 8/1,000 population (1991)
Infant Mortality: 10 deaths/1,000 live births (1991)
Life Expectancy at Birth: 74 years male, 78 years female (1992)
No. of Physicians: 13.4/10,000 population (1992)

■ **EDUCATION**

Govt. Expenditure: 11% of govt. expenditure (1991)
Literacy: 94% (1992)

■ **COMMUNICATIONS**

Daily newspapers: 14 (1992)
Televisions: 141.4/1,000 inhabitants (1992)
Radios: 289/1,000 inhabitants (1992)
Telephones: 33.3/100 inhabitants (1992)

■ **TRANSPORTATION**

Motor Vehicles: 192,700 passenger cars (1989)
Roads: 9,833 km; 4,255 km paved
Railway: n.a.
Air Traffic: 820,000 passengers carried (1991)
Airports: 3

Canadian Embassy: The Canadian High Commission to Cyprus, 220 Hayarkon St, Tel Aviv, 63405; mailing address: P.O. Box 6410, Tel Aviv 61063, Israel. Tel: (011-972-3) 527-2929. Fax: (011-972-3) 527-2333
Representative to Canada: c/o Embassy of Cyprus, 2211 R St, NW, Washington, DC 20008 USA

Czechoslovakia

As of Jan. 1, 1993 Czechoslovakia split into the Czech Republic and the Slovak Republic. Data on file is for the last year of Czechoslovakian state.

Long-Form Name: Czech Republic
Capital: Prague
Population: 15,731,000 (1990)

■ **GEOGRAPHY**

Area: 127,870 sq. km
Coastline: none: landlocked
Climate: temperate; cool summers; cold, cloudy, humid winters
Environment: infrequent earthquakes; acid rain; water pollution; air pollution
Terrain: mixture of hills and mountains separated by plains and basins
Land Use: 40% arable; 1% permanent; 13% meadows; 37% forest; 9% other
Location: C Europe

■ **PEOPLE**

Nationality: Czechoslovak
Ethnic Groups: 64% Czech, 31% Slovak, 4% Hungarian, 0.4% German, 0.4% Polish, 0.3% Ukrainian, 0.1% Russian, 0.2% other (Jewish, Gypsy)
Languages: Czech and Slovak (official), Hungarian
Religions: 70% Roman Catholic, 15% Protestant, 2% Orthodox, 13% other
Marriages: 7.9 (per 1,000) (1987)
Divorces: 2.5 (per 1,000) (1988)

■ **GOVERNMENT**

Leader(s): Czech Prime Min. Vaclav Klaus, Slovak Prime Min. Michel Kovac

Government Type: in transition from single republic to division into two separate republics

■ ECONOMY

Overview: economy is beginning the transition from a command to a market economy; deficient in energy and has an obsolete capital plant, though a skilled work force
GNP: $38.427 billion, per capita $2,450; real growth rate 0.7% (1991)
Inflation: 57.7% (1991)
Industries: iron and steel, machinery and equipment, cement, sheet glass, motor vehicles, armaments, chemicals, ceramics, wood, paper products, footwear
Labour Force: 8,386,000 (1992); 49.3% industry, 13.3% agriculture, 37.4% services (1989)
Unemployment: 6.6% (1991)
Agriculture: accounts for 15% of GNP (includes forestry); largely self-sufficient in food production; diversified crop and livestock production, including grains, potatoes, sugar beets, hops, fruit, hogs, cattle and poultry; exporter of forest products
Natural Resources: coal, timber, lignite, uranium, magnesite, iron ore, copper, zinc

■ FINANCE/TRADE

Currency: koruna (pl. koruny) (Kcs)
International Reserves Excluding Gold: $1,890 million (1992)
Gold Reserves: 3.29 million fine troy ounces (1992)
Budget: revenues $17.1 billion; expenditures $16.8 billion, including capital expenditures of $1.5 billion (1991)
Defence Expenditures: $4.32 billion (1990)
External Debt: $5.346 billion (1990)
Exports: $11.299 billion (1991); commodities: machinery and equipment 58.5%, industrial consumer goods 15.2%, fuels, minerals and metals 10.6%, agricultural and forestry products 6.1%, other products 15.2%; partners: USSR, Germany, Poland, Hungary, Yugoslavia, Austria, Bulgaria, Romania, US
Imports: $11.009 billion (1991); commodities: machinery and equipment 41.6%, fuels, minerals metals 32.2%, agricultural and forestry products 11.5%, industrial consumer goods 6.7%, other products 8%; partners: USSR, Germany, Poland, Hungary, Yugoslavia, Austria, Bulgaria, Romania, US

■ HEALTH

Births: 14/1,000 population (1991)
Deaths: 11/1,000 population (1991)

Infant Mortality: 11 deaths/1,000 live births (1991)
Life Expectancy at Birth: 68 years male, 75 years female (1992)
No. of Physicians: 36.1/10,000 population (1992)

■ EDUCATION

Govt. Expenditure: 1.88% of govt. expenditure (1990)
Literacy: 99%

■ COMMUNICATIONS

Daily newspapers: 30 (1992)
Televisions: 410/1,000 inhabitants (1992)
Radios: 583/1,000 inhabitants (1992)
Telephones: 25.0/100 inhabitants (1992)

■ TRANSPORTATION

Motor Vehicles: 3,508,120; 3,242,262 passenger cars (1990)
Roads: 74,548 km; 9,846 km paved
Railway: 13,362 km
Air Traffic: 837,000 passengers carried (1991)
Airports: 6

Canadian Embassy: Mickiewiczova 6, 125 33 Prague 6, Czechoslovakia. Tel: (011-42-2) 312-0251, -55. Fax: (011-42-2) 311-2791
Embassy in Canada: Embassy of the Czechoslovak Republic, 541 Sussex Dr, Ottawa ON K1N 6Z6. Tel: (613) 562-3877. Fax: (613) 562-3878.

Denmark

Long-Form Name: Kingdom of Denmark
Capital: Copenhagen
Population: 5,158,000 (1992)

■ GEOGRAPHY

Area: 43,070 sq. km; includes the island of Bornholm in the Baltic Sea and the rest of metropolitan Denmark, but excludes the Faroe Islands and Greenland
Coastline: 3,379 km
Climate: temperate; humid and overcast; mild, windy winters and cool summers
Environment: air and water pollution
Terrain: low and flat to gently rolling plains
Land Use: 61% arable land; negligible permanent; 6% meadows; 12% forest; 21% other
Location: N Europe, bordering on North Sea, Baltic Sea

■ PEOPLE

Nationality: Danish, Dane
Ethnic Groups: Scandinavian, Eskimo, Faroese, German
Languages: Danish, Faroese, Greenlandic (an Eskimo dialect); small German-speaking minority
Religions: 97% Evangelical Lutheran, 2% other Protestant and Roman Catholic, 1% other
Marriages: 6.3 (per 1,000) (1988)
Divorces: 2.9 (per 1,000) (1988)

■ GOVERNMENT

Leader(s): Prime Min. Poul Schlüter, Queen Margrethe II
Government Type: constitutional monarchy
Administrative Divisions: 15 counties and 1 city; dependent areas inc.: Faero Islands, Greenland (see Greenland entry for details)
Independence: became a constitutional monarchy in 1849
National Holiday: Birthday of the Queen, Apr. 16

■ ECONOMY

Overview: advanced agriculture and industry; extensive government welfare measures; highly dependent on foreign trade
GNP: $121.695 billion, per capita $23,660; real growth rate 2.2% (1991)
Inflation: 2.4% (1991)
Industries: food processing, machinery and equipment, textiles and clothing, chemical products, electronics, construction, furniture and other wood products
Labour Force: 2,852,000 (1992); 74.7% services, 20% industry, 5.3% agriculture (1989)
Unemployment: 10.6% (1991)
Agriculture: accounts for 7% of GNP and employs 1.8% of labour force (includes fishing); farm products account for nearly 16% of export revenues; principal products—meat, dairy, grain, potatoes, rape, sugar beets, fish; self-sufficient in food production
Natural Resources: crude oil, natural gas, fish, salt, limestone

■ FINANCE/TRADE

Currency: krone (pl. kroner) (DKr)
International Reserves Excluding Gold: $11,044 million (1992)
Gold Reserves: 1.66 million fine troy ounces (1992)
Budget: revenues $62.5 billion; expenditures $60 billion, including capital expenditures (1989)
Defence Expenditures: $2.6 billion (1990)

External Debt: $41.1 billion (1989)
Exports: $39.222 billion (1992); commodities: meat and meat products, dairy products, transport equipment, fish, chemicals, industrial machinery; partners: US 6%, Germany, Norway, Sweden, UK, other European Community, Japan
Imports: $33.398 billion (1992); commodities: petroleum, machinery and equipment, chemicals, grain and foodstuffs, textiles, paper; partners: US 7%, Germany, Netherlands, Sweden, UK, other European Community

■ HEALTH

Births: 12/1,000 population (1991)
Deaths: 11/1,000 population (1991)
Infant Mortality: 6 deaths/1,000 live births (1991)
Life Expectancy at Birth: 72 years male, 78 years female (1992)
No. of Physicians: 25.1/10,000 population (1992)

■ EDUCATION

Govt. Expenditure: 13.0% of govt. expenditure (1989)
Literacy: 99% (1992)

■ COMMUNICATIONS

Daily newspapers: 46 (1992)
Televisions: 528.3/1,000 inhabitants (1992)
Radios: 1,012/1,000 inhabitants (1992)
Telephones: 85.65/100 inhabitants (1992)

■ TRANSPORTATION

Motor Vehicles: 1,892,624; 1,590,570 passenger cars (1990)
Roads: 71,927 km paved
Railway: 88,670 km
Air Traffic: 4,582,000 passengers carried (1991)
Airports: 45

Canadian Embassy: Kr. Bernikowsgade 1, DK=1105 Copenhagen K, Denmark. Tel: (011-45-33) 12-22-99. Fax: (011-45-33) 14-05-85
Embassy in Canada: Embassy of the Kingdom of Denmark, 85 Range Rd, Ste 702, Ottawa ON K1N 8J6. Tel: (613) 234-0704, -0116, -0204.

Djibouti

Long-Form Name: Republic of Djibouti
Capital: Djibouti
Population: 467,000 (1992)

■ GEOGRAPHY

Area: 23,200 sq. km
Coastline: 314 km

Climate: desert; torrid, dry
Environment: vast wasteland
Terrain: coastal plain and plateau separated by central mountains
Land Use: 0% arable; 0% permanent; 9% meadows; negligible forest; 91% other
Location: E Africa, bordering on Gulf of Aden

■ PEOPLE

Nationality: Djiboutian
Ethnic Groups: 47% Somali (Issa); 37% Afar, 16% French, Arab, Ethiopian and Italian
Languages: French (official); Arabic, Somali and Afar widely used
Religions: 94% Moslem, 6% Christian
Marriages: n.a.
Divorces: n.a.

■ GOVERNMENT

Leader(s): Prime Min. Barkat Gourad Hamadou, Pres. Hassan Gouled Aptidon
Government Type: republic
Administrative Divisions: 5 districts
Independence: June 27, 1977 (from France; formerly known as French Territory of the Afars and Issas)
National Holiday: Independence Day, June 27

■ ECONOMY

Overview: based on service activities related to country's strategic location and status as a free trade zone; unemployment rate of over 50%
GNP: (GNP) $333 million, $1,070 per capita; real growth rate -0.7% (1986)
Inflation: 8% (1987)
Industries: limited to a few small-scale enterprises, such as dairy products and mineral-water bottling
Labour Force: n.a.
Unemployment: over 50% (1987)
Agriculture: accounts for 30% of GDP; scanty rainfall limits crop production to mostly fruit and vegetables; half of population pastoral nomads herding goats, sheep and camels; imports bulk of food needs
Natural Resources: geothermal areas

■ FINANCE/TRADE

Currency: Djibouti franc (DF)
International Reserves Excluding Gold: $83 million (1992)
Gold Reserves: n.a.
Budget: revenues $131 million; expenditures $154 billion, including capital expenditures of $25 million (1990)
Defence Expenditures: $36 million (1988)

External Debt: $250 million (1988)
Exports: $17 million (1991); commodities: hides and skins, coffee (in transit); partners: Middle East 50%, Africa 43%, Western Europe 7%
Imports: $214 million (1991); commodities: foods, beverages, transport equipment, chemicals, petroleum products; partners: European Community 36%, Africa 21%, Bahrain 14%, Asia 12%, US 2%

■ HEALTH

Births: 43/1,000 population (1991)
Deaths: 16/1,000 population (1991)
Infant Mortality: 117 deaths/1,000 live births (1991)
Life Expectancy at Birth: 46 years male, 49 years female (1992)
No. of Physicians: 2.4/10,000 population (1992)

■ EDUCATION

Govt. Expenditure: 10.7% of government expenditure (1989)
Literacy: 20%

■ COMMUNICATIONS

Daily newspapers: 1 (1992)
Televisions: 55.4/1,000 inhabitants (1992)
Radios: 88/1,000 inhabitants (1992)
Telephones: 2.4/100 inhabitants (1992)

■ TRANSPORTATION

Motor Vehicles: 15,000; 13,000 passenger cars (1990)
Roads: 2,900 km; 487 km paved
Railway: 100 km
Air Traffic: 131,000 passengers carried (1991)
Airports: 3

Canadian Embassy: C/o The Canadian Embassy, African Solidarity Insurance Building, 6th Floor, Churchill Ave, Addis Ababa; mailing address: P.O. Box 1130, Addis Ababa, Ethiopia. Tel: (011-251-1) 51-11-00. Fax: (011-251-1) 51-28-18
Representative to Canada: c/o Embassy of the Republic of Djibouti, 1156 15th St., NW, Ste 515, Washington, DC 20005 USA. Tel: (202) 331-0270

Dominica

Long-Form Name: Commonwealth of Dominica
Capital: Roseau
Population: 72,000 (1992)

■ GEOGRAPHY

Area: 750 sq. km
Coastline: 148 km
Climate: tropical; moderated by northeast trade winds; heavy rainfall
Environment: flash floods a constant hazard; occasional hurricanes
Terrain: rugged mountains of volcanic origin
Land Use: 9% arable; 13% permanent; 3% meadows; 41% forest; 34% other
Location: Caribbean Islands

■ PEOPLE

Nationality: Dominican
Ethnic Groups: mostly black; some Carib Indians
Languages: English (official); French patois widely spoken
Religions: 80% Roman Catholic; Anglican, Methodist
Marriages: n.a.
Divorces: n.a.

■ GOVERNMENT

Leader(s): Prime Min. (Mary) Eugenia Charles, Pres. Clarence Augustus Seignoret
Government Type: parliamentary democracy
Administrative Divisions: 10 parishes
Independence: Nov. 3, 1978 (from UK)
National Holiday: Independence Day, Nov. 3

■ ECONOMY

Overview: dependent on agriculture and vulnerable to climactic conditions;
GNP: $175 million, per capita $2,440; real growth rate 4.4% (1991)
Inflation: 1.4% (1990)
Industries: agricultural processing, tourism, soap and other coconut-based products, cigars, pumice mining
Labour Force: 25,000; 40% agriculture, 32% industry and commerce, 28% services (1984)
Unemployment: 10% (1989 est.)
Agriculture: accounts for 30% of GDP; principal crops—bananas, citrus fruit, coconuts, root crops; bananas provide the bulk of export earnings; forestry and fisheries potential not exploited
Natural Resources: timber

■ FINANCE/TRADE

Currency: East Caribbean dollar ($EC)
International Reserves Excluding Gold: $20 million (1992)
Gold Reserves: n.a.

Budget: revenues $48 million; expenditures $85 million, including capital expenditures of $41 million (1990)
Defence Expenditures: n.a.
External Debt: $63.6 million (1987)
Exports: $55 million (1991); commodities: bananas, coconuts, grapefruit, soap, galvanized sheets; partners: UK 72%, Jamaica 10%, OECS 6%, US 3%, other 9%
Imports: $118 million (1991); commodities: food, oils and fats, chemicals, fuels and lubricants, manufactured goods, machinery and equipment; partners: US 23%, UK 18%, CARICOM 15%, OECS 15%, Japan 5%, Canada 3%, other 21%

■ HEALTH

Births: 26/1,000 population (1991)
Deaths: 5/1,000 population (1991)
Infant Mortality: 13 deaths/1,000 live births (1991)
Life Expectancy at Birth: 73 years male, 79 years female (1992)
No. of Physicians: 3.4/10,000 population (1992)

■ EDUCATION

Govt. Expenditure: 10.6% of government expenditure (1989)
Literacy: 94.1% (1992)

■ COMMUNICATIONS

Daily newspapers: 2 (1992)
Televisions: 49.4/1,000 inhabitants (1992)
Radios: 507/1,000 inhabitants (1992)
Telephones: 9.1/100 inhabitants (1992)

■ TRANSPORTATION

Motor Vehicles: 4,250; 2,700 passenger cars (1990)
Railway: n.a.
Air Traffic: n.a.
Airports: 2

Canadian Embassy: C/o The Canadian High Commission, Bishop's Court Hill, St. Michael, Barbados; mailing address: P.O. Box 404, Bridgetown, Barbados. Tel: (809) 429-3550. Fax: (809) 429-3780

Dominican Republic

Long-Form Name: Dominican Republic
Capital: Santo Domingo
Population: 7,471,000 (1992)

■ GEOGRAPHY

Area: 48,440 sq. km
Coastline: 1,288 km
Climate: tropical maritime; little seasonal temperature variation
Environment: subject to occasional hurricanes (July to Oct.); deforestation
Terrain: rugged highlands and mountains with fertile valleys interspersed
Land Use: 23% arable; 7% permanent; 43% meadows; 13% forest; 14% other
Location: West Indies, bordering on Caribbean Sea, Atlantic Ocean

■ PEOPLE

Nationality: Dominican
Ethnic Groups: 73% mixed, 16% white, 11% black
Languages: Spanish
Religions: 95% Roman Catholic
Marriages: 3.3 (per 1,000) (1985)
Divorces: 1.2 (per 1,000) (1985)

■ GOVERNMENT

Leader(s): Pres. Joaquín Balaguer
Government Type: republic
Administrative Divisions: 29 provinces and 1 district
Independence: Feb. 27, 1844 (from Haiti)
National Holiday: Independence Day, Feb. 27

■ ECONOMY

Overview: agriculture is the backbone of the economy (sugar cane); tourism and a free trade zone help
GNP: $6.807 billion, per capita $950; real growth rate 1.9% (1991)
Inflation: 53.9% (1991)
Industries: tourism, sugar processing, feronickel and gold mining, textiles, cement, tobacco
Labour Force: 2,187,000 (1992); 45.7% agriculture, 38.8% services, 15.5% industry (1989)
Unemployment: 25% (1988)
Agriculture: accounts for 18% of GDP and employs 49% of labour force; sugar cane most important commercial crop, followed by coffee, cotton and cocoa; food crops; animal output; not self-sufficient in food
Natural Resources: nickel, bauxite, gold, silver

■ FINANCE/TRADE

Currency: Dominica peso ($RD)
International Reserves Excluding Gold: $390 million (1992)

Gold Reserves: 0.02 million fine troy ounces (1992)
Budget: revenues $413 million; expenditures $522 million, including capital expenditures of $218 million (1988)
Defence Expenditures: $60.62 million (1989)
External Debt: $3.440 billion (1990)
Exports: $651 million (1991); commodities: sugar, coffee, cocoa, gold, ferronickel; partners: US (including Puerto Rico) 74%
Imports: $1.721 billion (1991); commodities: foodstuffs, petroleum, cotton and fabrics, chemicals and pharmaceuticals; partners: US (including Puerto Rico) 36%

■ HEALTH

Births: 27/1,000 population (1991)
Deaths: 7/1,000 population (1991)
Infant Mortality: 60 deaths/1,000 live births (1991)
Life Expectancy at Birth: 66 years male, 69 years female (1992)
No. of Physicians: 5.7/10,000 population (1992)

■ EDUCATION

Govt. Expenditure: 10.17% of government expenditure (1990)
Literacy: 83.3% (1992)

■ COMMUNICATIONS

Daily newspapers: 10 (1992)
Televisions: 81.9/1,000 inhabitants (1992)
Radios: 168/1,000 inhabitants (1992)
Telephones: 2.1/100 inhabitants (1980).

■ TRANSPORTATION

Motor Vehicles: 270,000; 160,000 passenger cars (1990)
Roads: 17,390 km; 4,941 km paved
Railway: 518 km
Air Traffic: 648,000 passengers carried (1991)
Airports: 38

Canadian Embassy: C/o The Canadian Embassy, Maximo Gomez 30, Santo Domingo; mailing address: Apartado 2054, Santo Domingo, Dominican Republic. Tel: (809) 689-0002. Fax: (809) 862-2691

Ecuador

Long-Form Name: Republic of Ecuador
Capital: Quito
Population: 11,055,000 (1992)

■ GEOGRAPHY

Area: Area can only be estimated, as a portion of the frontier has not been delimited. One estimate is 270,670 sq. km, which excludes the litigation zone between Ecuador and Peru, but includes the Galapagos Islands.
Coastline: 2,237 km
Climate: tropical along coast becoming cooler inland
Environment: subject to frequent earthquakes, landslides, volcanic activity; deforestation; desertification; soil erosion; periodic droughts
Terrain: coastal plain, inter-Andean central highlands and flat to rolling eastern jungle
Land Use: 6% arable; 3% permanent; 17% meadows; 51% forest; 23% other
Location: NW South America, bordering on Pacific Ocean

■ PEOPLE

Nationality: Ecuadorian
Ethnic Groups: 55% mestizo (mixed Indian and Spanish), 25% Indian, 10% Spanish, 10% black
Languages: Spanish (official), Indian languages, especially Quechua
Religions: 80% Roman Catholic
Marriages: 6.2 (per 1,000) (1987)
Divorces: 0.4 (per 1,000) (1987)

■ GOVERNMENT

Leader(s): Pres. Rodrigo Borja Cevallos, V. Pres. José Francisco Merino López
Government Type: republic
Administrative Divisions: 21 provinces
Independence: May 24, 1822 (from Spain; Battle of Pichincha)
National Holiday: Independence Day, Aug. 10

■ ECONOMY

Overview: recovering from a major earthquake in 1987 which halted oil exports; vulnerable to international oil prices
GNP: $10.772 billion, per capita $1,020; real growth rate 2.0% (1991)
Inflation: 48.7% (1991)
Industries: food processing, textiles, chemicals, fishing, timber, petroleum
Labour Force: 3,287,000 (1992); 38.5% agriculture, 19.8% industry, 41.6% services and other activities (1989)
Unemployment: 8.0% (1989)
Agriculture: accounts for 18% of GDP and 35% of labour force (including fishing and forestry); leading producer and exporter of bananas and balsawood; crop and livestock sector; net importer of food-grain, dairy products and sugar
Natural Resources: petroleum, fish, timber

■ FINANCE/TRADE

Currency: sucre (S/.)
International Reserves Excluding Gold: $527 million (1992)
Gold Reserves: 0.44 million fine troy ounces (1992)
Budget: revenues $2.2 billion; expenditures $2.2 billion, including capital expenditures of $375 million (1991)
Defence Expenditures: $251.38 million (1990)
External Debt: $9.854 billion (1990)
Exports: $2.851 billion (1991); commodities: petroleum 47%, coffee, bananas, cocoa products, shrimp, fish products; partners: US 58%, Latin America, Caribbean, European Community countries
Imports: $2.399 billion (1991); commodities: transport equipment, vehicles, machinery, chemicals, petroleum; partners: US 28%, Latin America, Caribbean, European Community, Japan

■ HEALTH

Births: 30/1,000 population (1991)
Deaths: 7/1,000 population (1991)
Infant Mortality: 60 deaths/1,000 live births (1991)
Life Expectancy at Birth: 65 years male, 69 years female (1992)
No. of Physicians: 12.3/10,000 population (1992)

■ EDUCATION

Govt. Expenditure: 18.17% of government expenditure (1990)
Literacy: 85.8% (1992)

■ COMMUNICATIONS

Daily newspapers: 26 (1992)
Televisions: 82.3/1,000 inhabitants (1992)
Radios: 314/1,000 inhabitants (1992)
Telephones: 3.7/100 inhabitants (1992)

■ TRANSPORTATION

Motor Vehicles: 240,000; 77,000 passenger cars (1990)
Roads: 36,800 km; 6,200 km paved
Railway: 950 km
Air Traffic: 752,000 passengers carried (1991)
Airports: 49

Canadian Embassy: C/o The Canadian Embassy, Calle 76, No. 11-52, Santafe de Bogotá, Colombia; mailing address: Apartado Aereo

53531, Santafe de Bogotá 2, Colombia. Tel: (011-57-1) 217-5555. Fax (011-57-1) 310-4509
Embassy in Canada: Embassy of Ecuador, 50 O'Connor St, Ste 1311, Ottawa ON K1P 6L2. Tel: (613) 563-8206. Fax: (613) 235-5776.

Egypt

Long-Form Name: Arab Republic of Egypt
Capital: Cairo
Population: 54,842,000 (1992)

■ GEOGRAPHY

Area: 1,001,450 sq. km
Coastline: 2,450 km
Climate: desert; hot,dry summers with moderate winters
Environment: Nile is only perennial water source; increasing soil salinization below Aswan High Dam; hot, driving windstorm called khamisn occurs in spring; water pollution; desertification
Terrain: vast desert plateau interrupted by Nile valley and delta
Land Use: 3% arable; 2% permanent; 0% meadows; negligible forest; 95% other
Location: NE Africa, bordering on Mediterranean Sea, Red Sea

■ PEOPLE

Nationality: Egyptian
Ethnic Groups: 90% Eastern Hamitic stock; 10% Greek, Italian, Syro-Lebanese
Languages: Arabic (official); English and French
Religions: 80% Moslem (mostly Sunni), 20% Coptic Christian and other
Marriages: 9.1 (per 1,000) (1985)
Divorces: 1.6 (per 1,000) (1985)

■ GOVERNMENT

Leader(s): Prime Min. Atef Muhamed Sidki, Pres. Mohammad Hosni Mubarak
Government Type: republic
Administrative Divisions: 26 governorates
Independence: Feb. 28, 1922 (from UK; formerly known as United Arab Republic)
National Holiday: Anniversary of the Revolution, July 23

■ ECONOMY

Overview: urban population growth puts pressure on the agricultural sector; having difficulty with its debt servicing; vulnerable to oil prices
GNP: $33.068 billion, per capita $620; real growth rate 4.5% (1991)
Inflation: 19.8% (1991)

Industries: textiles, food processing, tourism, chemicals, petroleum, construction, cement, metals
Labour Force: 14,570,000; 54.1% services; 33.9% agriculture; 12% industry (1989); 2,500,000 Egyptians work abroad, mostly in Iraq and the Gulf Arab states (1988 est.)
Unemployment: 15% (1989 est.)
Agriculture: accounts for 20% of GNP and employs more than one-third of labour force; dependent on irrigation water from the Nile; world's fifth-largest cotton exporter; other crops include rice, corn, wheat, beans, fruit, vegetables; not self-sufficient in food
Natural Resources: crude oil, natural gas, iron ore, phosphates, manganese, limestone, gypsum, talc, asbestos, lead, zinc

■ FINANCE/TRADE

Currency: Egyptian pound (LE)
International Reserves Excluding Gold: $10,244 million (1992)
Gold Reserves: 2.43 million fine troy ounces (1992)
Budget: revenues $7 billion; expenditures $11.5 billion, including capital expenditures of $4 billion (1989)
Defence Expenditures: $1.57 billion (1990)
External Debt: $34.242 billion (1989)
Exports: $3.617 billion (1991); commodities: raw cotton, crude and refined petroleum, cotton yarn, textiles; partners: US, European Community, Japan, Eastern Europe
Imports: $7.754 billion (1991); commodities: foods, machinery and equipment, fertilizers, wood products, durable consumer goods, capital goods; partners: US, European Community, Japan, Eastern Europe

■ HEALTH

Births: 33/1,000 population (1991)
Deaths: 10/1,000 population (1991)
Infant Mortality: 82 deaths/1,000 live births (1991)
Life Expectancy at Birth: 58 years male, 61 years female (1992)
No. of Physicians: 13/10,000 population (1992)

■ EDUCATION

Govt. Expenditure: 13.39% of government expenditure (1989)
Literacy: 48.4% (1992)

■ COMMUNICATIONS

Daily newspapers: 8 (1992)
Televisions: 97.7/1,000 inhabitants (1992)

Radios: 322/1,000 inhabitants (1992)
Telephones: 2.9/100 inhabitants (1992)

■ **TRANSPORTATION**

Motor Vehicles: 725,000; 450,000 passenger cars (1990)
Roads: 46,067 km; 31,045 km paved
Railway: 4,607 km
Air Traffic: 2,602,000 passengers carried (1991)
Airports: 17

Canadian Embassy: 6 Mohamed Fahmy el Sayed St, Garden City, Cairo; mailing address: P.O. Box 2646, Cairo, Egypt. Tel: (011-20-2) 354-3110. Fax: (011-20-2) 356-3548
Embassy in Canada: Embassy of the Arab Republic of Egypt, 454 Laurier Ave E., Ottawa ON K1N 6R3. Tel: (613) 234-4931, -4935, -4958. Fax: (613) 234-9347.

El Salvador

Long-Form Name: Republic of El Salvador
Capital: San Salvador
Population: 5,396,000 (1992)

■ **GEOGRAPHY**

Area: 21,400 sq. km
Coastline: 307 km
Climate: tropical; rainy season (May to Oct.), dry season (Nov. to Apr.)
Environment: The Land of Volcanoes; subject to frequent and sometimes very destructive earthquakes; deforestation; soil erosion; water pollution
Terrain: mostly mountains with narrow coastal belt and central plateau
Land Use: 27% arable; 8% permanent; 29% meadows; 6% forest; 30% other
Location: Central (Latin) America, bordering on Pacific Ocean

■ **PEOPLE**

Nationality: Salvadorian
Ethnic Groups: 89% mestizo, 10% Indian, 1% white
Languages: Spanish
Religions: approx. 97% Roman Catholic, with activity by Protestant groups throughout the country
Marriages: 3.8 (per 1,000) (1985)
Divorces: 0.4 (per 1,000) (1985)

■ **GOVERNMENT**

Leader(s): Pres. (Felix) Alfredo Cristiani
Government Type: republic

Administrative Divisions: 14 departments
Independence: Sept. 15, 1821 (from Spain)
National Holiday: Independence Day, Sept. 15

■ **ECONOMY**

Overview: recently-ended (Feb. 1, 1992) guerrilla warfare hurt the economy, which is largely based on agriculture (coffee)
GNP: $5.697 billion, per capita $1,070; real growth rate 1.1% (1991)
Inflation: 14.4% (1991)
Industries: food processing, textiles, clothing, petroleum products, cement
Labour Force: 2,155,000 (1992); 8.2% agriculture, 21.8% industry, 70% services (1989)
Unemployment: 7.5% (1991)
Agriculture: accounts for 25% of GDP and 40% of labour force (including fishing and forestry); coffee most important commercial crop; other products—sugar cane, corn, rice, beans, oilseeds, beef, dairy products, shrimp; not self-sufficient in food
Natural Resources: hydroelectricity and geothermal power, crude oil

■ **FINANCE/TRADE**

Currency: colón (pl. colones) (C/)
International Reserves Excluding Gold: $422 million (1992)
Gold Reserves: 0.47 million fine troy ounces (1992)
Budget: revenues $751 million; expenditures $790 million, including capital expenditures (1990)
Defence Expenditures: $1.15 billion (1990)
External Debt: $1.898 billion (1990)
Exports: $496 million (1991); commodities: coffee 60%, sugar, cotton, shrimp; partners: US 49%, Germany 24%, Guatemala 7%, Costa Rica 4%, Japan 4%
Imports: $902 million (1991); commodities: petroleum products, consumer goods, foodstuffs, machinery, construction materials, fertilizer; partners: US 40%, Guatemala 12%, Venezuela 7%, Mexico 7%, Germany 5%, Japan 4%

■ **HEALTH**

Births: 34/1,000 population (1991)
Deaths: 7/1,000 population (1991)
Infant Mortality: 47 deaths/1,000 live births (1991)
Life Expectancy at Birth: 61 years male, 68 years female (1992)
No. of Physicians: 3.5/10,000 population (1992)

■ EDUCATION

Govt. Expenditure: 14.4% of government expenditure (1991)
Literacy: 73% (1992)

■ COMMUNICATIONS

Daily newspapers: 5 (1992)
Televisions: 87.1/1,000 inhabitants (1992)
Radios: 403/1,000 inhabitants (1992)
Telephones: 2.8/100 inhabitants (1992)

■ TRANSPORTATION

Motor Vehicles: 160,000; 80,000 passenger cars (1990)
Roads: 12,562 km; 1,798 km paved
Railway: 621 km
Air Traffic: 590,000 passengers carried (1991)
Airports: 35

Canadian Embassy: c/o The Canadian Embassy, Flr 6, Cronos Building, Calle 3 y Avenida Central; mailing address: Apartado Postal 10303-1000, San José, Costa Rica. Tel: (011-506) 55-35-22. Fax: (011-506) 23-23-95
Embassy in Canada: Embassy of El Salvador, 209 Kent St, Ste 504, Ottawa ON K2P 1Z8. Tel: (613) 238-2939.

Equatorial Guinea

Long-Form Name: Republic of Equatorial Guinea
Capital: Malabo
Population: 369,000 (1992)

■ GEOGRAPHY

Area: 28,050 sq. km
Coastline: 296 km
Climate: tropical; always hot, humid
Environment: subject to violent windstorms
Terrain: coastal plains rise to interior hills; islands are volcanic
Land Use: 8% arable; 4% permanent; 4% meadows; 51% forest; 33% other
Location: WC Africa, bordering on South Atlantic Ocean

■ PEOPLE

Nationality: Equatorial Guinean or Equatoguinean
Ethnic Groups: indigenous population of Bioko, primarily Bubi, some Fenandinos; Rio Muni, primarily Fang; less than 1,000 Europeans, mostly Spanish
Languages: Spanish (official), pidgin English, Fang, Bubi, Ndowe, Bujeba, Anobones and Corisqueño
Religions: natives all nominally Christian and predominantly Roman Catholic; some pagan practices retained (5%)
Marriages: n.a.
Divorces: n.a.

■ GOVERNMENT

Leader(s): Prime Min. Siale Bileka Silvestre
Government Type: republic
Administrative Divisions: 6 provinces
Independence: Oct. 12, 1968 (from Spain; formerly Spanish Guinea)
National Holiday: Independence Day, Oct. 12

■ ECONOMY

Overview: the economy is recovering from destruction by a past regime; subsistence agriculture, forestry and fishing predominate; little industry; undeveloped natural resources
GNP: $142 million, per capita $330; real growth rate 5.8% (1991)
Inflation: 1.1% (1990)
Industries: fishing, sawmilling
Labour Force: 180,000 (1992); 66% agriculture, 23% services, 11% industry (1989)
Unemployment: n.a.
Agriculture: cash crops—timber and coffee from Rio Muni, cocoa from Bioko; food crops—rice, yams, cassava, bananas, oil, palm nuts, manioc, livestock
Natural Resources: timber, crude oil, small unexploited deposits of gold, manganese, uranium

■ FINANCE/TRADE

Currency: Communité financière africaine franc (CFAF)
International Reserves Excluding Gold: $12 million (1992)
Gold Reserves: n.a.
Budget: revenues $23 million; expenditures $31 million, including capital expenditures (1988)
Defence Expenditures: n.a.
External Debt: $191 million (1988)
Exports: $41 million (1989); commodities: coffee, timber, cocoa beans; partners: Spain 44%, Germany 19%, Italy 12%, Netherlands 11%
Imports: $50 million (1988); commodities: petroleum, food, beverages, clothing, machinery; partners: Spain 34%, Italy 16%, France 14%, Netherlands 8%

■ HEALTH

Births: 42/1,000 population (1991)
Deaths: 16/1,000 population (1991)

Infant Mortality: 116 deaths/1,000 live births (1991)
Life Expectancy at Birth: 48 years male, 52 years female (1992)
No. of Physicians: n.a.

■ EDUCATION

Govt. Expenditure: 3.9% of government expenditure (1990)
Literacy: 50.2% (1992)

■ COMMUNICATIONS

Daily newspapers: 1 (1992)
Televisions: 8.7/1,000 inhabitants (1992)
Radios: 374/1,000 inhabitants (1992)
Telephones: n.a.

■ TRANSPORTATION

Motor Vehicles: 9,000; 5,500 passenger cars (1990)
Roads: n.a.
Railway: n.a.
Air Traffic: 14,000 passengers carried (1991)
Airports: 2

Canadian Embassy: The Canadian Embassy to Equatorial Guinea, P.O. Box 4037, Libreville, Gabon. Tel: (011-241) 74-34-64/65. Fax (011-241) 74-34-66

Estonia

Long-Form Name: Republic of Estonia
Capital: Tallinn
Population: 1,582,000 (1992)

■ GEOGRAPHY

Area: 45,100 sq. km
Coastline: 774 km
Climate: mild winters; long windy autumn; warm sunny summer; late and short spring
Environment: n.a.
Terrain: sloping coastal plain; islands account for 10% of the region
Land Use: 22% forests and woodland; 60 cultivated
Location: NE Europe, bordering on Baltic Sea

■ PEOPLE

Nationality: Estonian
Ethnic Groups: 65% Estonian, 28% Russian, 3% Ukrainian, 2% Byelorussian, 2% other
Languages: Estonian (official), Russian, English and German also spoken
Religions: Lutheran and Russian Orthodox
Marriages: n.a.

Divorces: n.a.

■ GOVERNMENT

Leader(s): Pres. Lennart Meri, Premier Mart Laar
Government Type: in transition to republic
Administrative Divisions: n.a.
Independence: declared Sept. 6, 1991
National Holiday: Independence Day, Feb. 24

■ ECONOMY

Overview: mining and manufacturing accounts for 75% of the country's economic output
GNP: $6.088 billion, $3,830 per capita; real growth rate 2.8% (1991)
Inflation: n.a.
Industries: electronics, electrical engineering, textiles, clothing, footwear
Labour Force: 795,500 (1990)
Unemployment: n.a.
Agriculture: dairy products, pork, poultry, eggs, fruit, vegetables
Natural Resources: fish, shale, phosphorites, limestone, peat, dolomite

■ FINANCE/TRADE

Currency: kroon (pl. kroons)
International Reserves Excluding Gold: n.a.
Gold Reserves: n.a.
Budget: n.a.
Defence Expenditures: n.a.
External Debt: n.a.
Exports: dairy products, fish, furniture, electrical power, meat
Imports: n.a.

■ HEALTH

Births: 14.2/1,000 population (1990)
Deaths: 12.4/1,000 population (1990)
Infant Mortality: 12.4/1,000 live births (1990)
Life Expectancy at Birth: 66 years male, 75 years female (1992)
No. of Physicians: n.a.

■ EDUCATION

Govt. Expenditure: n.a.
Literacy: n.a.

■ COMMUNICATIONS

Daily newspapers: 52 papers of all circulation types (1988)
Televisions: n.a.
Radios: n.a.
Telephones: n.a.

■ TRANSPORTATION

Motor Vehicles: n.a.
Railway: n.a.
Air Traffic: n.a.
Airports: n.a.

Canadian Embassy: c/o Pohjois Esplanadi, 25 B, 00100 Helsinki; mailing address: Box 779, 00101 Helsinki, Finland. Tel: (011-358-0) 171-141. Fax (011-358-0) 601-060

Ethiopia

Long-Form Name: People's Democratic Republic of Ethiopia
Capital: Addis Ababa
Population: 52,981,000 (1992)

■ GEOGRAPHY

Area: 1,221,900 sq. km
Coastline: 1,094 km
Climate: tropical with wide topographic-induced variation; prone to extended droughts
Environment: geologically active Great Rift Valley susceptible to earthquakes, volcanic eruptions; deforestation; overgrazing; soil erosion; desertification; frequent droughts; famine
Terrain: high plateau with central mountain range divided by Great Rift Valley
Land Use: 12% arable; 1% permanent; 40% meadows; 25% forest; 20% other
Location: E Africa, bordering on Red Sea

■ PEOPLE

Nationality: Ethiopian
Ethnic Groups: 40% Oromo, 32% Amhara and Tigrean, 9% Sidamo, 6% Somali, 4% Afar, 2% Gurage, 1% other
Languages: Amharic (official), Tigrinya, Orominga, Arabic, English (major foreign language taught in schools)
Religions: 45% Moslem, 40% Ehiopian Orthodox, 15% other
Marriages: n.a.
Divorces: n.a.

■ GOVERNMENT

Leader(s): Pres. Meles Zenawi, Premier Tamirat Laynie
Government Type: Communist state
Administrative Divisions: 24 administrative and 5 autonomous regions
Independence: oldest (at least 2,000 years) independent country in Africa and one of the oldest in the world

National Holiday: National Revolution Day, Sept. 12

■ ECONOMY

Overview: a centrally-planned state-run economy that is one of the poorest in Africa; economy is based on subsistence agriculture and is vulnerable to climactic conditions
GNP: $6.144 billion, per capita $120; real growth rate 1.5% (1991)
Inflation: 35.7% (1991)
Industries: cement, textiles, food processing, oil refinery
Labour Force: 21,000,000 (1992); 80% agriculture, 12% services, 8% industry, (1989)
Unemployment: 44,310 (1991); shortage of skilled labor
Agriculture: accounts for 45% of GDP even though frequent droughts, poor cultivation practices and state economic policies keep farm output low; famines not uncommon; estimated 50% of agricultural production at subsistence level
Natural Resources: small reserves gold, platinum, copper, potash

■ FINANCE/TRADE

Currency: birr (Br)
International Reserves Excluding Gold: $232 million (1992)
Gold Reserves: 0.11 million fine troy ounces (1992)
Budget: revenues $1.8 billion; expenditures $1.7 billion, including capital expenditures of $842 million (1988)
Defence Expenditures: $536.30 million (1989)
External Debt: $3.116 billion (1990)
Exports: $189 million (1991); commodities: coffee 60%, hides; partners: US, Germany, Djibouti, Japan, Yemen, France, Italy
Imports: $472 million (1991); commodities: food, fuels, capital goods; partners: USSR, Italy, Germany, Japan, UK, US, France

■ HEALTH

Births: 45/1,000 population (1991)
Deaths: 15/1,000 population (1991)
Infant Mortality: 114 deaths/1,000 live births (1991)
Life Expectancy at Birth: 46 years male, 48 years female (1992)
No. of Physicians: 0.1/10,000 population (1992)

■ EDUCATION

Govt. Expenditure: 10.58% of govt. expenditure (1988)
Literacy: 62.4% (1992)

■ COMMUNICATIONS

Daily newspapers: 2 (1992)
Televisions: 2.1/1,000 inhabitants (1992)
Radios: 188/1,000 inhabitants (1992)
Telephones: 0.3/100 inhabitants (1992)

■ TRANSPORTATION

Motor Vehicles: 64,000; 43,000 passenger cars (1990)
Roads: 23,216 km; 4,888 km paved (excluding urabn roads)
Railway: 733 km
Air Traffic: 636,000 passengers carried (1991)
Airports: 40

Canadian Embassy: African Solidarity Insurance Building, 6th Floor, Churchill Ave, Addis Ababa; mailing address: P.O. Box 1130, Addis Ababa, Ethiopia. Tel: (011-251-1) 51-11-00. Fax: (011-251-1) 51-28-18
Embassy in Canada: Embassy of the Transitional Government of Ethiopia, Place de Ville, 151 Slater St, Ste 210, Ottawa ON K1P 5P2. Tel: (613) 235-6637. Fax: (613) 235-4638.

Faeroe Islands

Dependent Territory of Denmark

Long-Form Name: Faeroe Islands
Capital: Tórshavn (island of Stremoy)
Population: 47,000 (1992)

■ GEOGRAPHY

Area: 1,399 sq. km (total of 18 islands and some reefs)
Climate: cold and windy
Land Use: 2% arable; potatoes are important crop; grazing, esp. for sheep and cattle
Location: Norwegian Sea (N Atlantic Ocean), N of Scotland

■ PEOPLE

Nationality: Danish
Ethnic Groups: Scandinavian
Languages: Faroese, Danish

■ GOVERNMENT

Leader(s): Chief Min. Jogvan Sundstein
Government Type: dependency with some degree of self-rule

■ ECONOMY

Overview: fishing main industry; steep coastline and treacherous currents make trading by sea difficult; exports: fish and fish products; chief trading partners: Denmark, Norway, Sweden, Germany, United States
Currency: Faroese krona (kr.)

Falkland Islands

Dependent Territory of the United Kingdom

Long-Form Name: Falkland Islands
Capital: Stanley (on East Falkland)
Population: 2,000 (1992)

■ GEOGRAPHY

Area: numerous islands covering 12,225 sq. km of ocean; total land area 6,682 sq km
Climate: damp, cool, temperate, strong winds esp. in spring
Land Use: mostly pastureland
Location: South Atlantic Ocean

■ PEOPLE

Nationality: British
Ethnic Groups: almost 100% British descent
Languages: English

■ GOVERNMENT

Leader(s): Gov. William H. Fullerton, Chief Exec. Ronald Sampson
Government Type: British dependency, although in 1990 Argentina declared Falklands and other British-held South Atlantic Islands part of new Argentine province Tierra del Fuego

■ ECONOMY

Overview: heavily agricultural, esp. sheep farming, with wool main product; fishing: illex squid; exports tend to outweigh imports in value; chief trading partner: United Kingdom
Currency: Falkland Islands pound (FKP), at parity with the British pound sterling

Fiji

Long-Form Name: Republic of Fiji
Capital: Suva
Population: 739,000 (1992)

■ GEOGRAPHY

Area: 18,270 sq. km
Coastline: 1,129 km
Climate: tropical marine; only slight seasonal temperature variation
Environment: subject to hurricanes from Nov. to Jan.; includes 332 islands of which approx. 110 are inhabited
Terrain: mostly mountains of volcanic origin

Land Use: 8% arable; 5% permanent; 3% meadows; 65% forest; 19% other
Location: Pacific Ocean, N of New Zealand

■ PEOPLE

Nationality: Fijian
Ethnic Groups: 46% Indian, 48% Fijian, 6% European, other Pacific Islanders, overseas Chinese and others
Languages: English (official); Fijian; Hindi
Religions: Christianity 50%, Hinduism 40%, Islam 10%
Marriages: 9.5 (per 1,000) (1985)
Divorces: 0.7 (per 1,000) (1979)

■ GOVERNMENT

Leader(s): Prime Min. Sitiveni Rabuka,Prime Min. Ratu Sir Penaia Ganilau
Government Type: declared a republic Oct. 6, 1987 following a military coup
Administrative Divisions: 14 provinces
Independence: Oct. 10, 1970 (from UK)
National Holiday: Independence Day, Oct. 10

■ ECONOMY

Overview: the economy, based on agriculture, has recovered from military coups, droughts and a drop in tourism
GNP: $1.377 billion, per capita $1,830; real growth rate 1.5% (1991)
Inflation: 6.5% (1991)
Industries: sugar, copra, tourism, gold, silver, fishing, clothing, lumber, small cottage industries
Labour Force: 250,000 (1992); 44.1% agriculture, 47.8% services, 8.1% industry (1989)
Unemployment: 5.9% (1991)
Agriculture: principal cash crop is sugar cane; coconuts, cassava, rice, sweet potatoes and bananas; small livestock sector includes cattle, pigs, horses and goats
Natural Resources: timber, fish, gold, copper, offshore oil potential

■ FINANCE/TRADE

Currency: Fiji dollar ($F)
International Reserves Excluding Gold: $307 million (1992)
Gold Reserves: none (1991)
Budget: revenues $314 million; expenditures $355 million, including capital expenditures of $81 million (1990)
Defence Expenditures: $25.15 million (1989)
External Debt: $398 million (1989)
Exports: $451 million (1991); commodities: sugar 49%, copra, processed fish, lumber; partners: UK 45%, Australia 21%, US 4.7%
Imports: $652 million (1991); commodities: food 15%, petroleum products, machinery, consumer goods; partners: US 48%, New Zealand, Australia, Japan

■ HEALTH

Births: 26/1,000 population (1991)
Deaths: 7/1,000 population (1991)
Infant Mortality: 19 deaths/1,000 live births (1991)
Life Expectancy at Birth: 62 years male, 67 years female (1992)
No. of Physicians: 4.9/10,000 population (1990)

■ EDUCATION

Govt. Expenditure: 22.31% of govt. expenditure (1992)
Literacy: 79% (1992)

■ COMMUNICATIONS

Daily newspapers: 2 (1992)
Televisions: 14.0/1,000 inhabitants (1992)
Radios: 573/1,000 inhabitants (1992)
Telephones: 8.3/100 inhabitants (1992)

■ TRANSPORTATION

Motor Vehicles: 56,000; 30,000 passenger cars (1990)
Roads: 4,293 km; 566 km paved
Railway: 643 km
Air Traffic: 414,000 passengers carried (1991)
Airports: 17

Canadian Embassy: C/o The Canadian High Commission, 61 Molesworth St, 3rd Floor, Wellington; mailing address: P.O. Box 12-49, Wellington, New Zealand. Tel: (011-64-4) 473-9577. Fax: (011-64-4) 471-2082
Representative to Canada: c/o Embassy of the Republic of Fiji, One United Nations Plaza, 26th Floor, New York, NY 10017 USA

Finland

Long-Form Name: Republic of Finland
Capital: Helsinki
Population: 5,008,000 (1992)

■ GEOGRAPHY

Area: 338,150 sq. km
Coastline: 1,126 km excluding islands and coastal indentations

Climate: cold temperate; potentially subarctic, but comparatively mild because of moderating influence of the North Atlantic Current, Baltic Sea and more than 60,000 lakes
Environment: permanently wet ground covers approx. 30% of land
Terrain: mostly low, flat to rolling plains interspersed with flats and low hills
Land Use: 8% arable; 0% permanent; negligible meadows; 76% forest; 16% other
Location: N Europe, bordering on Baltic Sea

■ PEOPLE

Nationality: Finnish, Finn
Ethnic Groups: Finn, Swede, Lapp, Gypsy, Tatar
Languages: 94% Finnish, 6% Swedish (both official); small Lapp-and Russian-speaking minorities; business language is English
Religions: 89% Evangelical Lutheran, 8% atheist, 1% Eastern Orthodox, 2% other
Marriages: 5.4 (per 1,000) (1987)
Divorces: 2.1 (per 1,000) (1987)

■ GOVERNMENT

Leader(s): Pres. Mauno Koivisto, Prime Min. Esko Aho
Government Type: republic
Administrative Divisions: 12 provinces
Independence: Dec. 6, 1917 (from Soviet Union)
National Holiday: Independence Day, Dec. 6

■ ECONOMY

Overview: the manufacturing sector and trade are vital to this highly industrialized, largely free market economy
GNP: $121.982 billion, per capita $24,400; real growth rate 2.9% (1991)
Inflation: 4.1% (1991)
Industries: metal manufacturing and shipbuilding, forestry and wood processing (pulp, paper), copper refining, foodstuffs, textiles, clothing
Labour Force: 2,552,000; 70.6% services, 21.1% industry, 8.3% agriculture (1989)
Unemployment: 7.5% (1992)
Agriculture: accounts for 8% of GNP (including forestry); livestock production, especially dairy cattle, predominates; forestry is an important export: earner main crops—cereals, sugar beets, potatoes; 85% self-sufficient, but short of food and fodder grains
Natural Resources: timber, copper, zinc, iron ore, silver

■ FINANCE/TRADE

Currency: markka (pl. markat) (Fmk)
International Reserves Excluding Gold: $5,213 million (1992)
Gold Reserves: 2.0 million fine troy ounces (1992)
Budget: revenues $35.1 billion; expenditures $33.1 billion, including capital expenditures of $1.4 million (1990)
Defence Expenditures: $1.94 billion (1990)
External Debt: $5.3 billion (1989)
Exports: $23.976 billion (1992); commodities: timber, paper and pulp, ships, machinery, clothing and footwear; partners: European Community 44.2% (UK 13%, Germany 10.8%), USSR 14.9%, Sweden 14.1%, US 5.8%
Imports: $21.169 billion (1992); commodities: foodstuffs, petroleum and petroleum products, chemicals, transport equipment, iron and steel, machinery, textile yarn and fabrics, fodder grains; partners: European Community 43.5% (Germany 16.9%, UK 6.8%), Sweden 13.3%, USSR 12.1%, US 6.3%

■ HEALTH

Births: 12/1,000 population (1991)
Deaths: 10/1,000 population (1991)
Infant Mortality: 6 deaths/1,000 live births (1991)
Life Expectancy at Birth: 71 years male, 79 years female (1991)
No. of Physicians: 22.6/10,000 population (1992)

■ EDUCATION

Govt. Expenditure: 14.86% of government expenditure (1990)
Literacy: 100%

■ COMMUNICATIONS

Daily newspapers: 66 (1992)
Televisions: 488.3/1,000 inhabitants (1992)
Radios: 998/1,000 inhabitants (1992)
Telephones: 61.66/100 inhabitants (1992)

■ TRANSPORTATION

Motor Vehicles: 2,217,729; 1,926,326 passenger cars (1990)
Roads: 85,214 km; 50,384 km paved
Railway: 6,492 km
Air Traffic: 3,999,000 passengers carried (1991)
Airports: 73

Canadian Embassy: Pohjois Esplanadi, 25 B, 00100 Helsinki; mailing address: Box 779, 00101Helsinki, Finland. Tel: (011-358-0) 171-141. Fax (011-358-0) 601-060
Embassy in Canada: Embassy of Finland, 55 Metcalfe St, Ste 850, Ottawa ON K1P 6L5. Tel: (613) 236-2380, -9. Fax: (613) 238-1474.

France

Long-Form Name: French Republic
Capital: Paris
Population: 57,182,000 (1992)

■ GEOGRAPHY

Area: 544,006 sq. km; includes Corsica and the rest of metropolitan France, but excludes the overseas administrative divisions
Coastline: 3,427 km (includes Corsica, 644 km)
Climate: generally cool winters and mild summers, but mild winters and hot summers along the Mediterranean
Environment: most of large urban areas and industrial centres in Rhône, Garonne, Seine or Loire River basins; occasional warm tropical wind known as mistral are in central south; air and water pollution
Terrain: mostly flat plains or gently rolling hills in north and west; remainder is mountainous, especially Pyrenees in south and Alps in east
Land Use: 32% arable; 2% permanent; 23% meadows; 27% forest; 16% other
Location: W Europe, bordering on Atlantic Ocean, Mediterranean Sea

■ PEOPLE

Nationality: French
Ethnic Groups: Celtic and Latin with Teutonic, Slavic, North African, Indochinese and Basque minorities
Languages: French (100% of population); rapidly declining regional dialects (Provençal, Breton, Alsatian, Corsican, Catalan, Basque, Flemish)
Religions: 90% Roman Catholic, 2% Protestant, 1% Jewish, 1% Moslem (North African workers), 6% unaffiliated
Marriages: 4.9 (per 1,000) (1988)
Divorces: 1.9 (per 1,000) (1987)

■ GOVERNMENT

Leader(s): Prime Min. Pierre Beregovoy, Pres. François Mitterand
Government Type: republic
Administrative Divisions: 22 regions; dependent areas inc.: French Polynesia, Guadeloupe, Guiana (French Guiana), Martinique (see Martinique enty for details), Mayotte, New Caledonia, Reunion, St. Pierre and Miquelon, Southern and Antarctic Territories, Wallis and Futuna Islands
Independence: unified by Clovis in 486, First Republic proclaimed in 1792

National Holiday: Taking of the Bastille, July 14

■ ECONOMY

Overview: the leading agricultural producer in Western Europe; highly diversified industrial sector; economic integration into the European Community has unknown consequences
GNP: $1,167.749 billion, per capita $20,600; real growth rate 2.3% (1991)
Inflation: 3.1% (1991)
Industries: steel, machinery, chemicals, automobiles, metallurgy, aircraft, electronics, mining, textiles, food processing, tourism
Labour Force: 25,404,000 (1992); 73.5% services, 19.8% industry; 6.7% agriculture (1989)
Unemployment: 9.3% (1991)
Agriculture: accounts for 4% of GNP (including fishing and forestry); one of the world's top five wheat producers; self-sufficient for most temperate-zone foods; shortages include fats and oils and tropical produce, but overall net exporter of farm products
Natural Resources: coal, iron ore, bauxite, fish, timber, zinc, potash

■ FINANCE/TRADE

Currency: franc (F or FF)
International Reserves Excluding Gold: $33,814 million (1992)
Gold Reserves: 81.85 million fine troy ounces (1992)
Budget: revenues $207.6 billion; expenditures $224.2 billion, including capital expenditures of $34 billion (1990)
Defence Expenditures: $37.34 billion (1991)
External Debt: $59.3 billion (1987)
Exports: $231.790 billion (1992); commodities: machinery and transportation equipment, chemicals, foodstuffs, agricultural products, iron and steel products, textiles and clothing; partners: Germany 15.8%, Italy 12.2%, UK 9.8%, Belgium/Luxembourg 8.9%, Netherlands 8.7%, US 6.7%, Spain 5.6%, Japan 1.8%, USSR 1.3%
Imports: $238.602 billion (1992); commodities: crude oil, machinery and equipment, agricultural products, chemicals, iron and steel products; partners: Germany 19.4%, Italy 11.5%, Belgium/ Luxembourg 9.2%, US 7.7%, UK 7.2%, Netherlands 5.2%, Spain 4.4%, Japan 4.1%, USSR 2.1%

■ HEALTH

Births: 14/1,000 population (1991)
Deaths: 9/1,000 population (1991)
Infant Mortality: 6 deaths/1,000 live births (1991)

Life Expectancy at Birth: 73 years male, 81 years female (1991)
No. of Physicians: 31.3/10,000 population (1992)

■ EDUCATION

Govt. Expenditure: 7% of govt. expenditure (1987)
Literacy: 99%

■ COMMUNICATIONS

Daily newspapers: 96 (1992)
Televisions: 35.6/1,000 inhabitants (1992)
Radios: 138/1,000 inhabitants (1992)
Phones: 60.87/100 inhabitants(1992)

■ TRANSPORTATION

Motor Vehicles: 28,460,000; 23,550,000 passenger cars (1990)
Roads: 796,425 km; 734,408 km paved
Railway:, 34,055 km
Air Traffic: 31,665,000 passengers carried (1991)
Airports: 417

Canadian Embassy: 35 av Montaigne, 75008 Paris France. Tel: (011-33-1) 44-43-32-00. Fax: (011-33-1) 44-43-34-98
Embassy in Canada: Embassy of France, 42 Sussex Dr, Ottawa ON K1M 2C9. Tel: (613) 789-1795. Fax: (613) 789-3484

French Guiana

Overseas Department of France

Long-Form Name: Guyane Française
Capital: Cayenne
Population: 104,000 (1992)

■ GEOGRAPHY

Area: 83,533 sq. km
Climate: tropical, warm and humid
Land Use: interior is uncultivated wilderness, with mineral and forest resources which have not been tapped; 31,000 acres under cultivation
Location: N South America, bordering on Atlantic Ocean

■ PEOPLE

Nationality: French
Ethnic Groups: 66% of Creole origin, remainder Black; small American Indian, Chinese, European, Indochinese, Lebanese, Syrian minorities
Languages: French (official), Creole patois

■ GOVERNMENT

Leader(s): Prefect of French Govt Jean-Pierre Lacroix, Pres. of General Council Elie Castor, Pres. of Regional Council Georges Othily
Government Type: overseas department

■ ECONOMY

Overview: agriculture: rice, manioc, sugar cane, livestock; forestry, fisheries, food processing industry; chief trading partners: France, EEC countries, Japan, United States
Exports: $70 million (1991)
Imports: $769 million (1991)
Currency: French franc

French Polynesia

Overseas Department of France

Long-Form Name: Territory of French Polynesia
Capital: Papeete (Windward Islands); Uturoa (Leeward Islands); Rikitea (Tuamotu Archipelago); Mataura (Austral or Tubuai Islands); Taiohae (Marquesas Island)
Population: 202,000 (1991)

■ GEOGRAPHY

Area: 3,265 sq. km, consisting of five island archipelagoes scattered widely over Eastern Pacific; uninhabited Clipperton Territory is a dependency of French Polynesia but does not form part of the territory
Climate: warm and humid
Land Use: high percentage of land area covered with coconut trees
Location: eastern Pacific Ocean

■ PEOPLE

Nationality: French
Ethnic Groups: Polynesian strains
Languages: French, Polynesian languages

■ GOVERNMENT

Leader(s): Pres. of Territorial Council Gaston Flosse
Government Type: French overseas territory

■ ECONOMY

Overview: agriculture: copra, tropical fruits grown for local consumption; chief trading partners: France, United Kingdom, United States
Exports: $127 million (1991)
Imports: $915 million (1991)
Currency: CFP franc

Gabon

Long-Form Name: Gabonese Republic
Capital: Libreville
Population: 1,237,000 (1992)

■ GEOGRAPHY

Area: 267,670 sq. km
Coastline: 885 km
Climate: tropical; always hot, humid
Environment: deforestation
Terrain: narrow coastal plain; hilly interior; savanna in east and south
Land Use: 1% arable; 1% permanent; 18% meadows; 78% forest; 2% other
Location: WC Africa, bordering on South Atlantic Ocean

■ PEOPLE

Nationality: Gabonese
Ethnic Groups: about 40 Bantu tribes, including four major tribal groupings (Fang, Eshira, Bapounou, Bateke); approx. 100,000 expatriate Africans and Europeans, including 27,000 French
Languages: French (official), Fang, Myene, Bateke, Bapounou/Eschira, Bandjabi
Religions: 60% Roman Catholic, 30% Protestant, 1% Muslim, remainder animist
Marriages: n.a.
Divorces: n.a.

■ GOVERNMENT

Leader(s): Prime Min. Casimir Oye-Mba, Pres. El Hadj Omar Bongo
Government Type: republic; one-party presidential regime since 1964
Administrative Divisions: 9 provinces
Independence: Aug. 17, 1960 (from France)
National Holiday: Renovation Day (Gabonese Democratic Party established), Mar. 12

■ ECONOMY

Overview: economy is dependent on oil, which has contributed to an increase in per capita income; agricultural and industrial sectors are relatively underdeveloped
GNP: $4.419 billion, per capita $3,780; real growth rate -0.9% (1990)
Inflation: 8.6% (1990)
Industries: sawmills, petroleum, food and beverages; mining of increasing importance (especially manganese and uranium)
Labour Force: 536,000 (1992); 75.5% agriculture, 10.8% industry, 13.7% services
Unemployment: n.a.
Agriculture: accounts for 8% of GDP (including fishing and forestry); cash crops—cocoa, coffee, palm oil; livestock not developed; importer of food; okoume (a tropical softwood) is the most important timber product
Natural Resources: crude oil, manganese, uranium, gold, timber, iron ore

■ FINANCE/TRADE

Currency: Communité financière africaine franc (CFAF)
International Reserves Excluding Gold: $188 million (1992)
Gold Reserves: 0.01 million fine troy ounces (1991)
Budget: revenues $1.1 billion; expenditures $1.5 billion, including capital expenditures of $277 million (1990)
Defence Expenditures: $145.79 million (1989)
External Debt: $2.945 billion (1990)
Exports: $2.474 billion (1990); commodities: crude oil 70%, manganese 11%, wood 12%, uranium 6%; partners: France 53%, US 22%, Germany, Japan
Imports: $0.767 billion (1989); commodities: foodstuffs, chemical products, petroleum products, construction materials, manufacturers, machinery; partners: France 48%, US 2.6%, Germany, Japan, UK

■ HEALTH

Births: 28/1,000 population (1991)
Deaths: 14/1,000 population (1991)
Infant Mortality: 104 deaths/1,000 live births (1991)
Life Expectancy at Birth: 51 years male, 54 years female (1992)
No. of Physicians: 3.6/10,000 population (1990)

■ EDUCATION

Govt. Expenditure: 21.7% of govt. expenditure (1985)
Literacy: 60.7% (1992)

■ COMMUNICATIONS

Daily newspapers: 1 (1992)
Televisions: 35.6/1,000 inhabitants (1992)
Radios: 138/1,000 inhabitants (1992)
Telephones: 1.12/100 inhabitants (1992)

■ TRANSPORTATION

Motor Vehicles: 38,000; 22,000 passenger cars (1990)
Roads: 7,762 km; 535 km paved
Railway: none

Air Traffic: 398,000 passengers carried (1991)
Airports: 39

Canadian Embassy: P.O. Box 4037 Libreville, Gabon. Tel: (011-241) 74-34-64, 65. Fax: (011-241) 74-34-66
Embassy in Canada: Embassy of the Gabonese Republic, 4 Range Rd, Ottawa ON K1N 8J5. Tel: (613) 232-5301, -2, -5570, -5649. Fax: (613) 232-6916.

Gambia

Long-Form Name: Republic of the Gambia
Capital: Banjul
Population: 908,000 (1992)

■ GEOGRAPHY

Area: 10,690 sq. km
Coastline: 80 km
Climate: tropical; hot, rainy season (June to Nov.); cooler, dry season (Nov. to May)
Environment: deforestation
Terrain: flood plain of the Gambia River flanked by some low hills
Land Use: 16% arable; 0% permanent; 9% meadows; 20% forest; 55% other
Location: W Africa, bordering on Atlantic Ocean

■ PEOPLE

Nationality: Gambian
Ethnic Groups: 99% African (42% Mandinka, 18% Fula, 16% Wolof, 10% Jola, 9% Serahuli, 4% other); 1% non-Gambian
Languages: English (official); Mandinka, Wolof, Fula, other indigenous vernaculars
Religions: 95% Moslem, 4% Christian, 1% indigenous beliefs
Marriages: n.a.
Divorces: n.a.

■ GOVERNMENT

Leader(s): Pres. Sir Dawda Kairaba Jawara, Prime Min. Saihou S. Sabally
Government Type: republic
Administrative Divisions: 5 divisions and 1 city (Banjul)
Independence: Feb. 18, 1965 (from UK)
National Holiday: Independence Day, Feb. 18

■ ECONOMY

Overview: a poor country, lacking in natural resources and possessing a limited agricultural base of peanut products; tourism is growing
GNP: $322 million, per capita $360; real growth rate 3.2% (1990)

Inflation: 8.6% (1991)
Industries: peanut processing, tourism, beverages, agricultural machinery assembly, woodworking, metalworking, clothing
Labour Force: 330,000 (1992) 84% agriculture, 7% industry, 9% services
Unemployment: n.a.
Agriculture: accounts for 30% of GDP and employs about 75% of the population; imports one-third of food requirements; major export crop is peanuts; forestry and fishing resources not fully exploited
Natural Resources: fish

■ FINANCE/TRADE

Currency: dalasi (D)
International Reserves Excluding Gold: $65 million (1992)
Gold Reserves: n.a.
Budget: revenues $69.3 million; expenditures $95.5 million, including capital expenditures of $21 million (1989)
Defence Expenditures: $3 million (1988)
External Debt: $330 million (1989)
Exports: $41 million (1991); commodities: peanuts and peanut products, fish, cotton lint, palm kernels; partners: Ghana 49%, Europe 27%, Japan 12%, US 1%
Imports: $221 million (1991); commodities: foodstuffs, manufacturers, raw materials, fuel, machinery and transport equipment; partners: Europe 55%, (European Community 39%, other 16%), Asia 20%, US 11%, Senegal 4%

■ HEALTH

Births: 48/1,000 population (1991)
Deaths: 17/1,000 population (1991)
Infant Mortality: 138 deaths/1,000 live births (1991)
Life Expectancy at Birth: 42 years male, 46 years female (1992)
No. of Physicians: 0.9/10,000 population (1990)

■ EDUCATION

Govt. Expenditure: 8.8% of government expenditure (1988)
Literacy: 27.2% (1992)

■ COMMUNICATIONS

Daily newspapers: 2 (1992)
Televisions: n.a.
Radios: 168/1,000 inhabitants (1992)
Telephones: 0.5/100 inhabitants (1992)

◼ TRANSPORTATION

Motor Vehicles: 8,000; 6,500 passenger cars (1990)
Roads: 2,523 km; 535 paved km
Railway: none
Air Traffic: n.a.
Airports: 1

Canadian Embassy: c/o Fourth Fl, Sorano Bldg, 45 boul. de la République, Dakar; mailing address: P.O. Box 3373, Dakar, Senegal. Tel: (011-221) 23-92-90. Fax: (011-221) 23-87-49
Representative to Canada: c/o High Commissioner for the Gambia, 1030 15th St NW, Ste 720, Washington DC 20005 USA. Tel: (202) 842-1356

Georgia

Long-Form Name: Republic of Georgia
Capital: Tbilisi
Population: 5,471,000 (1992)

◼ GEOGRAPHY

Area: 69,700 sq. km
Coastline: n.a.
Climate: Alpine to subtropical with warm, humid coastlands
Environment: n.a.
Terrain: Caucasus mountains; densely forested
Land Use: 35% forests and woodlands; 65% cultivated
Location: SE Europe, bordering on Black Sea

◼ PEOPLE

Nationality: Georgian
Ethnic Groups: 70.1% Georgian, 8.1% Armenian, 6.3% Russian, 5.7% Azerbaijani 3% Ossetian, 1.9% Greek, 1.8% Abkhazians, 1% Ukrainian
Languages: Georgian, Russian, Armenian
Religions: predominantly Eastern Orthodox
Marriages: n.a.
Divorces: n.a.

◼ GOVERNMENT

Leader(s): Chairman of Parliament Eduard A. Shevardnadze, Prime Minister Otar Patsatsia
Government Type: in transition to republic
Administrative Divisions: 2 autonomous regions
Independence: n.a.
National Holiday: n.a.

◼ ECONOMY

Overview: steel processing and light industry predominate; agriculture hindered by extensive wooded areas

GNP: $9 billion, $1,640 per capita; real growth rate 2.9% (1991)
Inflation: n.a.
Industries: coal and non-ferrous metals refining, machinery and instruments, electrical engineering, chemical production, food processing, vehicles, mining, esp. manganese, coal, baryta
Labour Force: n.a.
Unemployment: n.a.
Agriculture: grapes, tobacco, bay leaves, tea, citrus fruits, tung, silk, orchard fruits
Natural Resources: manganese deposits; sulphur and other medicinal springs, forest resources

◼ FINANCE/TRADE

Currency: Georgian rouble
International Reserves Excluding Gold: n.a.
Gold Reserves: n.a.
Budget: 4,067 million roubles (1989 revenues)
Defence Expenditures: n.a.
External Debt: n.a.
Exports: grain, fruit, vegetables, tea, electric mine cars, seamless pipes
Imports: n.a.

◼ HEALTH

Births: 16.7/1,000 population (1989)
Deaths: 8.6/1,000 population (1989)
Infant Mortality: 19.6 deaths/1,000 live births (1989)
Life Expectancy at Birth: 68 years male, 76 years female (1992)
No. of Physicians: 31,700 (1989)

◼ EDUCATION

Govt. Expenditure: n.a.
Literacy: n.a.

◼ COMMUNICATIONS

Daily newspapers: 149 papers of all circulation types (1989)
Televisions: n.a.
Radios: n.a.
Telephones: n.a.

◼ TRANSPORTATION

Motor Vehicles: n.a.
Railway: 1,570 km
Air Traffic: n.a.
Airports: n.a.

Canadian Embassy: c/o 23 Starokonyushenny Per, Moscow 12100, Russian Federation. Tel: (011-7-95) 241-5070. Fax: (011-7-95) 241-4400.

Germany

Long-Form Name: Federal Republic of Germany
Capital: Berlin; seat of government, Bonn
Population: 80,253,000 (1992)

■ GEOGRAPHY

Area: 356,950 sq. km
Coastline: 2,389 km
Climate: temperate; cool, wet summers; cool to cold cloudy winters with frequent rain and snow; occasional warm, tropical föhn wind
Environment: air and water pollution; significant deforestation in mountain regions due to environmental pollution
Terrain: flat plains; lowlands in north; central uplands; Bavarian Alps in southwest
Land Use: 35% arable land; 1% permanent crops; 17% meadows and pastures; 29% forest and woodland; 18% other
Location: NC Europe, bordering on North Sea, Baltic Sea

■ PEOPLE

Nationality: German
Ethnic Groups: primarily German; Slavic, Danish, and other minorities
Languages: German
Religions: 36% Protestant, 35% Roman Catholic in west, 7% in east; high percentage in east is unaffiliated
Marriages: 6.8/1,000 population (1988)
Divorces: 2.3/1,000 population (1988)

■ GOVERNMENT

Leader(s): Chanc. Helmut Kohl, Pres. Richard von Weizsäcker
Government Type: federal republic
Administrative Divisions: 16 states
Independence: former Federal Republic of Germany (west) had come into existence on Sept. 21, 1949; former German Democratic Republic (east), Oct. 1949; eastern and western halves were reunified on Oct. 3, 1990
National Holiday: German Unity Day, Oct. 3

■ ECONOMY

Overview: Former W Germany: highly urbanized with advanced market economy and strong exports; manufacturing and service industries dominate with imported raw materials and semi-manufactured products. Former E Germany: outmoded economy, slow pace of economic reform deters outside investors; FRG's legal, social welfare, and economic systems have been extended to the east. Unified Germany: slight nation-wide post reunification recession.
GNP: $1,516.785 billion, per capita $23,650; real growth rate 2.3% (1991)
Inflation: 3.5% (1991)
Industries: iron, steel, coal, chemicals, vehicles, ships, machinery, food and beverages, electronics
Labour Force: 48,651,000 (1992); 30.2% industry, 66.3% services, 3.5% agriculture (1989)
Unemployment: former W Germany 6.3% (1991); former E Germany 10.3% (1991)
Agriculture: agriculture, including fishing and forestry, accounts for about 3% of GDP; diversified crop and livestock farming, inc. wheat, potatoes, barley, sugar beets, fruit, livestock products; net importer of food
Natural Resources: iron ore, coal, potash, natural gas, salt, nickel, timber

■ FINANCE/TRADE

Currency: Deutsche Mark (DM)
International Reserves Excluding Gold: $90,996 million (1992)
Gold Reserves: 95.18 million fine troy ounces (1992)
Budget: former W Germany: revenues, $539 billion; expenditures, $563 billion, including capital expenditures of $11.5 billion; former E Germany: revenues, $147.0 billion; expenditures, $153.4 billion, capital expenditures n.a. (1988)
Defence Expenditures: $35.61 billion (1991)
External Debt: former W Germany $500 million (1988); former E Germany $20.6 billion (1989)
Exports: $429.953 billion (1992)
Imports: $408.529 billion (1992)

■ HEALTH

Births: 11/1,000 population (1991)
Deaths: 11/1,000 population (1991)
Infant Mortality: 7 deaths/1,000 live births (1991)
Life Expectancy at Birth: 72 years male, 78 years female (1992)
No. of Physicians: former W Germany: 26.5/10,000 population (1990); former E Germany: 22.8/10,000 population (1990)

■ EDUCATION

Govt. Expenditure: 8% of govt. expenditure (1989)
Literacy: 99%

■ COMMUNICATIONS

Daily newspapers: 358 (1992)
Televisions: 642.7/1,000 (1992)

Radios: 868/1,000 (1992)
Telephones: 46.04/100 (1992)

■ TRANSPORTATION

Motor Vehicles: 38,276,274; 35,512,083 passenger cars (1990)
Roads: 1,148,665 km; 884,850 km paved
Railway: 90,237 km
Air Traffic: 24,830,000 passengers carried (1991)
Airports: 655 (1991)

Canadian Embassy: Friedrich Wilhelm Strasse 18, D5300 Bonn 1, Germany. Tel. (011-49-228) 23 10 61. Fax: (011-49-228) 23 61 70
Embassy in Canada: Embassy of Germany, 1 Waverley St, Ottawa ON K2P 0T8. Tel: (613) 232-1101, -2, -3, -4, -5. Fax: (613) 594-9330.

Ghana

Long-Form Name: Republic of Ghana
Capital: Accra.
Population: 15,959,000 (1992)

■ GEOGRAPHY

Area: 239,460 sq. km
Coastline: 539 km
Climate: tropical; warm and comparatively dry along southeast coast; hot and humid in southwest; hot and dry in north
Environment: recent drought in north severely affecting marginal agricultural activities; deforestation; overgrazing; soil erosion; dry, northeasterly harmattan wind (Jan. to Mar.)
Terrain: mostly low plains with dissected plateau in south-central area
Land Use: 5% arable; 7% permanent; 15% meadows; 37% forest; 36% other
Location: WC Africa, bordering on South Atlantic Ocean

■ PEOPLE

Nationality: Ghanaian
Ethnic Groups: 99% black African (major tribes— 44% Akan, 16% Moshi-Dagomba, 13% Ewe, 8% Ga), 0.2% European and other
Languages: English (official); African languages include Akan, Moshi-Dagomba, Ewe and Ga
Religions: 30% indigenous beliefs, 30% Moslem, 40% Christian
Marriages: n.a.
Divorces: n.a.

■ GOVERNMENT

Leader(s): Chairman, Provisional National Defense Council Flt. Lt. (Ret.) Jerry John Rawlings
Government Type: military
Administrative Divisions: 10 regions
Independence: Mar. 6, 1957 (from UK, formerly known as Gold Coast)
National Holiday: Independence Day, Mar. 6

■ ECONOMY

Overview: international assistance boosts this economy, which depends on good harvests; population growth is a burden
GNP: $6.176 billion, per capita $400; real growth rate 3.1% (1991)
Inflation: 18% (1991)
Industries: mining, lumbering, light manufacturing, fishing, aluminum, food processing
Labour Force: 5,690,000 (1992); 59.3% agriculture, 11.1% industry, 29.6% services (1989)
Unemployment: 27,434 (Apr. 1989)
Agriculture: accounts for more than 50% of GDP; major cash crop is cocoa; other crops: rice, coffee, cassava, peanuts, corn; normally self-sufficient in food
Natural Resources: gold, timber, industrial diamonds, bauxite, manganese, fish, rubber

■ FINANCE/TRADE

Currency: cedi (C/)
International Reserves Excluding Gold: $351 million (1992)
Gold Reserves: 0.27 million fine troy ounces (1992)
Budget: revenues $821 million; expenditures $782 million, including capital expenditures of $151 million (1990)
Defence Expenditures: $45.39 million (1990)
External Debt: $2.670 billion (1990)
Exports: $880 million (1989); commodities: cocoa 60%, timber, gold, tuna, bauxite, and aluminium; partners: US 23%, UK, other European Community
Imports: $1,200 million (1989); commodities: petroleum 16%, consumer goods, foods, intermediate goods, capital equipment; partners: US 10%, UK, W Germany, France, Japan, S Korea, E Germany

■ HEALTH

Births: 46/1,000 population (1991)
Deaths: 13/1,000 population (1991)
Infant Mortality: 86 deaths/1,000 live births (1991)
Life Expectancy at Birth: 52 years male, 56 years female (1992)
No. of Physicians: 0.5/10,000 population (1992)

■ EDUCATION

Govt. Expenditure: 25.71% of govt. expenditure (1988)
Literacy: 60.3% (1992)

■ COMMUNICATIONS

Daily newspapers: 3 (1992)
Televisions: 14.5/1,000 inhabitants (1992)
Radios: 295/1,000 inhabitants (1992)
Telephones: 0.63/100 inhabitants (1992)

■ TRANSPORTATION

Motor Vehicles: 124,264; 82,152 passenger cars (1990)
Roads: 22,749 km; 5,747 km paved
Railway: 982 km
Air Traffic: 192,000 passengers carried (1991)
Airports: 3

Canadian Embassy: Canadian High Commission, 46 Independence Ave, Accra; P.O. Box 1639, Accra. Tel: (011-233-21) 228555. Fax: (011-233-21) 773-792
Embassy in Canada: High Commission for Ghana, 1 Clemow Ave, the Glebe, Ottawa ON K1S 2A9. Tel: (613) 236-0871, -2, -3. Fax: (613) 236-0874.

Gibraltar

Dependent Territory of United Kingdom

Long-Form Name: Gibraltar
Capital: Gibraltar
Population: 31,000 (1992)

■ GEOGRAPHY

Area: 6.5 sq. km, consisting of five island archipelagoes scattered widely over Eastern Pacific; uninhabited Clipperton Territory is a dependency of French Polynesia but does not form part of the territory
Climate: warm, temperate, low precipitation
Land Use: almost 100% bare limestone (Rock of Gibraltar) and/or built up; no farmland
Location: Iberian Peninsula of S Spain, bordering on Mediterranean Sea

■ PEOPLE

Nationality: British
Ethnic Groups: Genoese, Portuguese, Maltese, Spanish
Languages: English

■ GOVERNMENT

Leader(s): Gov. and Commander-in-Chief Adm. Sir Derek Reffell; Chief Min. José (Joe) Bossano
Government Type: dependency

■ ECONOMY

Overview: tourism most important; industries: construction materials, beverage bottling; re-exports: tobacco, petroleum, wine; exports of local products negligible; must import all food
Currency: Gibraltar pound

Greece

Long-Form Name: Hellenic Republic
Capital: Athens
Population: 10,182,000 (1992)

■ GEOGRAPHY

Area: 131,940 sq. km
Coastline: 13,676 km
Climate: temperate; mild, wet winter; hot, dry summers
Environment: subject to severe earthquakes; air pollution; archipelago of 2,000 islands
Terrain: mostly mountainous with ranges extending into sea as peninsulas or chains of islands
Land Use: 23% arable; 8% permanent; 40% meadows; 20% forest; 9% other
Location: S Europe, bordering on Adriatic Sea

■ PEOPLE

Nationality: Greek
Ethnic Groups: 98% Greek, 2% others
Languages: Greek (official); English, German and French widely understood
Religions: 98% Greek Orthodox, 1% Moslem, 1% other
Marriages: 6.3 (per 1,000) (1987)
Divorces: 0.9 (per 1,000) (1986)

■ GOVERNMENT

Leader(s): Prime Min. Constantinos Mitsotakis, Pres. Costantine Karamanlis
Government Type: presidential parliamentary government; monarchy rejected by referendum Dec. 8, 1974
Administrative Divisions: 51 departments (nomoi, singular-nomós)
Independence: 1827 (from the Ottoman Empire)
National Holiday: Independence Day (proclamation of the war of independence), Mar. 25

■ ECONOMY

Overview: a large commodity trade deficit is off-set by the successful tourism industry; a mixed capitalistic economy was administered by a socialist government in the 1980s
GNP: $65.504 billion, per capita $6,230; real growth rate 1.6% (1991)
Inflation: 19.5% (1991)
Industries: food and tobacco processing, textiles, chemicals, metal products, tourism, mining, petroleum
Labour Force: 3.825 million (1992); 56% services, 24.7% agriculture, 19.3% industry (1989)
Unemployment: 7.3% (1991)
Agriculture: accounts for 14% of GNP (including fishing and forestry); self sufficient in food; principal products—wheat, corn, barley, sugar beets, olives, tomatoes, wine, tobacco, potatoes, beef, mutton, pork, dairy products
Natural Resources: bauxite, lignite, magnesite, crude oil, marble

■ FINANCE/TRADE

Currency: drachma (Dr)
International Reserves Excluding Gold: $3,677 million (1992)
Gold Reserves: 3.43 million fine troy ounces (1992)
Budget: revenues $20.9 billion; expenditures $34.1 billion, including capital expenditures (1990)
Defence Expenditures: $4.52 billion (1991)
External Debt: $20 billion (1988)
Exports: $8.653 billion (1991); commodities: manufactured goods, food and live animals, fuels and lubricants, raw materials; partners: Germany 24%, Italy 14%, non-oil developing countries 11.8%, France 9.5%, US 7.1%, UK 6.8%
Imports: $21.582 billion (1991); commodities: machinery and transport equipment, light manufactures, fuels and lubricants, foodstuffs, chemicals; partners: Germany 22%, non-oil developing countries 14%, oil exporting countries 13%, Italy 12%, France 8%, US 3.2%

■ HEALTH

Births: 11/1,000 population (1991)
Deaths: 9/1,000 population (1991)
Infant Mortality: 10 deaths/1,000 live births (1991)
Life Expectancy at Birth: 73 years male, 78 years female (1992)
No. of Physicians: 28.5/10,000 population (1992)

■ EDUCATION

Govt. Expenditure: 6.1% of govt. expenditure (1987)
Literacy: 93.2% (1992)

■ COMMUNICATIONS

Daily newspapers: 117 (1992)
Televisions: 194.5/1,000 inhabitants (1992)
Radios: 419/1,000 inhabitants (1992)
Telephones: 50/100 inhabitants (1992)

■ TRANSPORTATION

Motor Vehicles: 2,522,628; 1,729,683 passenger cars (1990)
Roads: 34,832 km; 29,027 km paved
Railway: 2,494 km
Air Traffic: 4,937,000 passengers carried (1991)
Airports: 36

Canadian Embassy: 4 Ioannou Ghennadiou St, Athens 115 21. Tel: (011-30-1) 723-9515. Fax: (011-30-1) 724-7123
Embassy in Canada: Embassy of Greece, 76-80 MacLaren St, Ottawa ON K2P 0K6. Tel: (613) 238-6271, -2, -3. Fax: (613) 238-5676.

Greenland

Dependent Territory of Denmark

Long-Form Name: Grønland (Kalaallit Nunaat)
Capital: Nuuk (Godthab)
Population: 57,000 (1992)

■ GEOGRAPHY

Area: 2,186,000 sq. km
Coastline: 44,087 km
Climate: arctic to subarctic; cool summers, cold winters
Environment: sparse population confined to small settlements along coast; continuous permafrost over northern two-thirds of the island
Terrain: flat to gradually sloping icecap covers all but a narrow, mountainous, barren, rocky coast
Land Use: 0% arable land; 0% permanent crops; 1% meadow and pastures; negligible forest and woodland; 99% other
Location: N North America, bordering on Atlantic Ocean, Greenland Sea, Arctic Ocean, Baffin Bay

■ PEOPLE

Nationality: Greenlander
Ethnic Groups: 86% Greenlander (Inuit and Greenland-born Caucasians), 14% Danish

Languages: Inuit dialects, Danish

■ GOVERNMENT

Leader(s): Queen Margrethe II represented by High Commissioner Bent Klinte
Government Type: part of the Danish realm; self-governing overseas administrative division
Administrative Divisions: 3 municipalities
National Holiday: Birthday of the Queen, Apr. 16

■ ECONOMY

Overview: dependent on annual subsidy from the Danish government; fishing is the most important industry; mineral resource exploitation is limited to lead and zinc
GNP: $500 million, per capita $9,000; real growth rate 5% (1988)
Currency: danish krone (DKr)

Canadian Embassy: c/o Kr. Bernikowsgade 1, DK=1105 Copenhagen K, Denmark. Tel: (011-45-33) 12-22-99. Fax: (011-45-33) 14-05-85

Grenada

Long-Form Name: State of Grenada
Capital: St. George's
Population: 91,000 (1992)

■ GEOGRAPHY

Area: 380 sq. km
Coastline: 121 km
Climate: tropical; tempered by northeast trade winds
Environment: lies on edge of hurricane belt; hurricane season lasts from June to Nov.
Terrain: volcanic in origin with central mountains
Land Use: 15% arable; 26% permanent; 3% meadows; 9% forest; 47% other
Location: Caribbean Islands

■ PEOPLE

Nationality: Grenadian
Ethnic Groups: mainly of black African descent
Languages: English (official); some French patois
Religions: largely Roman Catholic; Anglican; other Protestant sects
Marriages: 3.3 (per 1,000) (1978)
Divorces: 0.4 (per 1,000) (1978)

■ GOVERNMENT

Leader(s): Prime Min. Nicholas Braithwaite, Gov. Gen. Paul Scoon
Government Type: parliamentary democracy

Administrative Divisions: 6 parishes and 1 dependency
Independence: Feb. 7, 1974 (from UK)
National Holiday: Independence Day, Feb. 7

■ ECONOMY

Overview: the economy is based on agriculture (spices, tropical plants) and tourism; unemployment is high
GNP: $198 million, per capita $2,180; real growth rate 4.9% (1991)
Inflation: 5.6% (1989)
Industries: food and beverage, textiles, light assembly operations, tourism, construction
Labour Force: 31% services, 24% agriculture, 8% construction, 5% manufacturing, 32% other (1985)
Unemployment: 26% (1988)
Agriculture: accounts for 20% of GDP and 90% of exports; bananas, cocoa, nutmeg and mace are major crops; small-scale farms predominate
Natural Resources: timber, tropical fruit, deep-water harbors

■ FINANCE/TRADE

Currency: East Caribbean dollar ($EC)
International Reserves Excluding Gold: $23 million (1992)
Gold Reserves: n.a.
Budget: revenues $54.9 million; expenditures $77.6 million, including capital expenditures of $16.6 million (1990)
Defence Expenditures: n.a.
External Debt: $108 million (1989)
Exports: $31.8 million (1988); commodities: nutmeg 35%, cocoa beans 15%, bananas 13%, mace 7%, textiles; partners: US 4%, UK, Germany, Netherlands, Trinidad and Tobago
Imports: $92.6 million (1988); commodities: machinery 24%, food 22%, manufactured goods 19%, petroleum 8%; partners: US 32%, UK, Trinidad and Tobago, Japan, Canada

■ HEALTH

Births: 35/1,000 population (1991)
Deaths: 7/1,000 population (1991)
Infant Mortality: 29 deaths/1,000 live births (1991)
Life Expectancy at Birth: 69 years male, 74 years female (1992)
No. of Physicians: 4.7/10,000 population (1992)

■ EDUCATION

Govt. Expenditure: 12.5% of govt. expenditure (1975)
Literacy: 85%

■ COMMUNICATIONS

Daily newspapers: 1 (1979)
Televisions: 148/1,000 inhabitants (1986)
Radios: 624/1,000 inhabitants (1989)
Telephones: 6.3/100 inhabitants (1992)

■ TRANSPORTATION

Motor Vehicles: 12,198 registered vehicles (1988)
Railway: n.a.
Air Traffic: n.a.
Airports: 3

Canadian Embassy: c/o The Canadian High Commission, Bishop's Court Hill, St. Michael, Barbados; mailing address: P.O. Box 404, Bridgetown, Barbados. Tel: (809) 429-3550. Fax: (809) 429-3780

Guadeloupe

Dependency of France

Long-Form Name: Guadeloupe
Capital: Basse-Terre (seat of govt.); each of the 7 inhabited islands has its own Chief Town
Population: 400,000 (1992)

■ GEOGRAPHY

Area: 1,779 sq. km, consisting of five island archipelagoes scattered widely over Eastern Pacific; uninhabited Clipperton Territory is a dependency of French Polynesia but does not form part of the territory
Climate: hot and humid May-Dec., cool and dry Dec.-April
Land Use: extensively cultivated
Location: Lesser Antilles (2 main islands, 5 small islands, one small island group called Iles des Saintes)

■ PEOPLE

Nationality: French
Ethnic Groups: 77% mulatto, 10% black, 10% mestizo
Languages: French, Creole dialect

■ GOVERNMENT

Leader(s): Commissioner of French Govt Yves Bonnet, Pres. of Regional Council Lucette Michaux-Chévry, President of Conseil Général Dominique Larifla
Government Type: dependency

■ ECONOMY

Overview: agriculture: inc. bananas, sugar cane, rum, flowers, livestock; vegetables and tobacco grown for local consumption; forestry, fisheries, tourism, food processing; chief trading partners: France, Martinique
Exports: $147 million (1991)
Imports: $1.644 billion (1991)
Currency: French franc

Guam

Unincorporated Outlying Territory of the United States

Long-Form Name: Territory of Guam
Capital: Agana
Population: 139,000 (1992)

■ GEOGRAPHY

Area: 541 sq. km
Climate: tropical maritime, with little seasonal variation, but typhoon-prone and suffers from earthquakes; wet all year
Land Use: interior is mountainous and volcanic hills dominate the south, but many forests in northern Guam have been cleared for farming and the construction of airfields; coconut trees grow throughout the island
Location: N Pacific Ocean, E of the Philippines

■ PEOPLE

Nationality: American
Ethnic Groups: mainly Chamorros (of Indonesian and Spanish descent) and Guamanian (Malay strain); also descendants from American, Italian, French, British, Japanese, Chinese, Filipino, Mexican settlers
Languages: English (official), Chamorro, Japanese

■ GOVERNMENT

Leader(s): Gov. Joseph F. Ada
Government Type: unincorporated outlying territory of the United States; executive powers of the legislature similar to those of an American state legislature

■ ECONOMY

Overview: agriculture: corn, coconuts, sweet potatoes, cucumbers, watermelons, beans, livestock, esp. cattle and pigs, fruits, vegetables, fish; industry: textile manufacture, cement, petroleum, printing, platics, ship repair; tourism of growing importance
Currency: American dollar

Guatemala

Long-Form Name: Republic of Guatemala
Capital: Guatamala City
Population: 9,745,000 (1992)

■ GEOGRAPHY

Area: 108,890 sq. km
Coastline: 400 km
Climate: tropical; hot, humid in lowlands; cooler in highlands
Environment: numerous volcanoes in mountains, with frequent violent earthquakes; Caribbean coast subject to hurricanes and other tropical storms; deforestation; soil erosion; water pollution
Terrain: mostly mountainous with narrow coastal plains and rolling limestone plateau (Petén)
Land Use: 12% arable; 4% permanent; 12% meadows; 40% forest; 32% other
Location: Central (Latin) America, bordering on Caribbean Sea, Pacific Ocean

■ PEOPLE

Nationality: Guatemalan
Ethnic Groups: 47% Ladino (mestizo-mixed Indian and European ancestry), 53% Indian
Languages: Spanish, but over 40% of the population speaks an Indian language as a primary tongue (20 Indian dialects, including Quiche, Cakchiquel, Kekchi)
Religions: predominantly Roman Catholic; also Protestant, traditional Mayan
Marriages: 5.3 (per 1,000) (1987)
Divorces: 0.2 (per 1,000) (1987)

■ GOVERNMENT

Leader(s): Pres. Ramiro de Leon Carpio
Government Type: republic
Administrative Divisions: 22 departments (departamento, pl. departamentos)
Independence: Sept. 15, 1821 (from Spain)
National Holiday: Independence Day, Sept. 15

■ ECONOMY

Overview: the inflation rate has dropped significantly as a result of government economic reforms, but political uncertainty casts a shadow over the agriculturally-based economy
GNP: $8.816 billion, per capita $930; real growth rate 1.0% (1991)
Inflation: 33.2% (1991)
Industries: sugar, textiles and clothing, furniture, chemicals, petroleum, metals, rubber, tourism
Labour Force: 2,628,000 (1992); 49.8% agriculture, 12.3% industry, 37.9% sevices (1989)
Unemployment: 13%, with 30–40% underemployment (1988 est.)
Agriculture: accounts for 25% of GDP; principal crops—sugar cane, corn, bananas, coffee, beans, cardamom; livestock—cattle, sheep, pigs, chickens; food importer
Natural Resources: crude oil, nickel, rare woods, fish, chicle

■ FINANCE/TRADE

Currency: quetzal (pl. quetzalas) (Q)
International Reserves Excluding Gold: $765 million (1992)
Gold Reserves: 0.12 million fine troy ounces (1992)
Budget: revenues $1.05 billion; expenditures $1.3 billion, including capital expenditures of $270 million (1989)
Defence Expenditures: $71.78 million (1990)
External Debt: 2.179 billion (1990)
Exports: $1.033 billion (1991); commodities: coffee 38%, bananas 7%, sugar 7%, cardamon 4%; partners: US 29%, El Salvador, Germany, Costa Rica, Italy
Imports: $1.674 billion (1991); commodities: fuel and petroleum products, machinery, grain, fertilizers, motor vehicles; partners: US 38%, Mexico, Germany, Japan, El Salvador

■ HEALTH

Births: 35/1,000 population (1991)
Deaths: 8/1,000 population (1991)
Infant Mortality: 58 deaths/1,000 live births (1991)
Life Expectancy at Birth: 60 years male, 65 years female (1992)
No. of Physicians: 4.6/10,000 population (1992)

■ EDUCATION

Govt. Expenditure: 20% of govt. expenditure (1989)
Literacy: 55.1% (1992)

■ COMMUNICATIONS

Daily newspapers: 5 (1992)
Televisions: 44.7/1,000 inhabitants (1992)
Radios: 64/1,000 inhabitants (1992)
Telephones: 1.61/100 inhabitants (1992)

■ TRANSPORTATION

Motor Vehicles: 230,000; 130,000 passenger cars (1990)
Roads: 13,176 km; 3,049 km paved

Railway: 893 km
Air Traffic: 165,000 passengers carried (1991)
Airports: 74

Canadian Embassy: Edificio Galerias Espana, 6th fl., 7A Avenida 11-59, Zona 9; mailing address: P.O. Box 400, Guatemala City, Guatemala; C.A. Tel: (011-502-2) 321411. Fax: (011-502-2) 321419
Embassy in Canada: Embassy of Guatemala, 130 Albert St, Ste 1010, Ottawa ON K1P 5G4. Tel: (613) 233-7237. Fax: (613) 233-0135.

Guinea

Long-Form Name: Republic of Guinea
Capital: Conakry
Population: 6,116,000 (1992)

■ GEOGRAPHY

Area: 245,860 sq. km
Coastline: 320 km
Climate: generally hot and humid; monsoonal-type rainy season (June to Nov.) with south-westerly winds; dry season (Dec. to May) with northeasterly harmattan winds
Environment: hot, dry, dusty harmattan haze may reduce visibility during dry season; deforestation
Terrain: generally flat coastal plain, hilly to mountainous interior
Land Use: 6% arable; negligible permanent, 12% meadows; 42% forest; 40% other
Location: W Africa, bordering on Atlantic Ocean

■ PEOPLE

Nationality: Guinean
Ethnic Groups: 40% Fuani, 26% Malike, 11% Sousou, 15 smaller tribes
Languages: French (official); each tribe has its own language; 8 official languages are taught in schools, including Fulani, Malinke, Soussou
Religions: 85% Moslem, 5% indigenous beliefs, 10% Christian
Marriages: n.a.
Divorces: n.a.

■ GOVERNMENT

Leader(s): Pres. Gen. Lansana Conté
Government Type: republic
Administrative Divisions: 33 provinces & 1 capital
Independence: Oct. 2, 1958 (from France; formerly known as French Guinea)
National Holiday: Anniversary of the Second Republic, Apr. 3

■ ECONOMY

Overview: although possessing numerous natural resources and potential for agricultural development, it is one of the poorest countries in the world
GNP: $2.669 billion, per capita $450; real growth rate n.a. (1991)
Inflation: 27% (1988)
Industries: bauxite mining, alumina, diamond mining, light manufacturing and agricultural processing industries
Labour Force: 3,100,000 (1992); 78.1% agriculture, 1.3% industry, 20.6% services (1989)
Unemployment: n.a.
Agriculture: accounts for 40% of GDP (includes fishing and forestry); mostly subsistence farming; principal products—rice, coffee, pineapples, palm kernels, cassava, sweet potatoes, timber; livestock— cattle, sheep and goats
Natural Resources: bauxite, iron ore, diamonds, gold, uranium, hydroelectricity, fish

■ FINANCE/TRADE

Currency: Guinea franc
International Reserves Excluding Gold: n.a.
Gold Reserves: n.a.
Budget: revenues $394 million; expenditures $548 million, including capital expenditures of $254 million (1989)
Defence Expenditures: n.a.
External Debt: 2.230 billion (1990)
Exports: $553 million (1988); commodities: alumina, bauxite, diamonds, coffee, pineapples, bananas, palm kernels; partners: US 33%, European Community 33%, USSR and Eastern Europe 20%, Canada
Imports: $509 million (1988); commodities: petroleum products, metals, machinery, transport equipment, foodstuffs, textiles and other grain; partners: US 16%, France, Brazil

■ HEALTH

Births: 47/1,000 population (1991)
Deaths: 21/1,000 population (1991)
Infant Mortality: 144 deaths/1,000 live births (1991)
Life Expectancy at Birth: 40 years male, 44 years female (1992)
No. of Physicians: 0.2/10,000 population (1990)

■ EDUCATION

Govt. Expenditure: 21.5% of govt. expenditure (1988)
Literacy: 24.0% (1992)

■ COMMUNICATIONS

Daily newspapers: 1 (1992)
Televisions: 5.4/1,000 inhabitants (1992)
Radios: 41/1,000 inhabitants (1992)
Telephones: n.a.

■ TRANSPORTATION

Motor Vehicles: 26,000; 13,500 passenger cars (1990)
Roads: 29,995 km; 1,229 km paved
Railway: 1,057 km
Air Traffic: 41,000 passengers carried (1991)
Airports: 11

Canadian Embassy: Coleah Quarter, Conakry; mailing address: P.O. Box 99, Conakry, Guinea. Tel: (011-224) 44-23-95. Fax: (011-224) 44-42-36
Embassy in Canada: Embassy of the Republic of Guinea, 483 Wilbrod St, Ottawa ON K1N 6N1. Tel: (613) 789-8444. Fax: (613) 789-7560.

Guinea-Bissau

Long-Form Name: Republic of Guinea-Bissau
Capital: Bissau
Population: 1,006,000 (1992)

■ GEOGRAPHY

Area: 36,120 sq. km
Coastline: 350 km
Climate: tropical; generally hot and humid; monsoon-type rainy season (June to Nov.) with southwesterly winds; dry season (Dec. to May) with northeasterly harmattan winds
Environment: hot, dry, dusty harmattan haze may reduce visibility during dry season
Terrain: mostly low coastal plain rising to savanna in east
Land Use: 11% arable; 1% permanent; 43% meadows; 38% forest; 7% other
Location: W Africa, bordering on Atlantic Ocean

■ PEOPLE

Nationality: Guinea-Bissauan
Ethnic Groups: approx. 99% African (30% Balanta, 20% Fula, 14% Manjaca, 13% Mandinga, 7% Papel); less than 1% European and mulatto
Languages: Portuguese (official); Crioulo (a Portuguese-based Creole), Balante and numerous African languages
Religions: 65% indigenous beliefs, 30% Moslem, 5% Christian
Marriages: n.a.
Divorces: n.a.

■ GOVERNMENT

Leader(s): Pres. Brig. Gen. João Bernardo Vieira, Prime Min. Carlos Correira
Government Type: republic; highly centralized one-party regime since Sept. 1974
Administrative Divisions: 9 regions (regiões, singular-região)
Independence: Sept. 24, 1973 (from Portugal; formerly known as Portuguese Guinea)
National Holiday: Independence Day, Sept. 24

■ ECONOMY

Overview: this poor country is focusing on agricultural development; exploitation of mineral deposits is hampered by a weak infrastructure and high costs
GNP: $194 million, per capita $190; real growth rate 3.3% (1991)
Inflation: n.a.
Industries: agricultural processing, beer, soft drinks
Labour Force: 460,000 (1992); 82% agriculture, 4% industry, 14% services (1989)
Unemployment: n.a.
Agriculture: accounts for over 50% of GDP, nearly 100% of exports and 80% of employment; rice is the staple; not self-sufficient in food; fishing and forestry not fully exploited; crops include corn, beans, cassava, cashew nuts, peanuts, palm kernels and cotton
Natural Resources: unexploited deposits of petroleum, bauxite, phosphates; fish, timber

■ FINANCE/TRADE

Currency: Guinea-Bissau peso (PG)
International Reserves Excluding Gold: n.a.
Gold Reserves: n.a.
Budget: revenues $22.7 million; expenditures $30.8 million, including capital expenditures of 18.0 million (1989)
Defence Expenditures: $4.43 billion (1989)
External Debt: $465 million (1989)
Exports: $15 million (1987); commodities: cashews, fish, peanuts, palm kernels; partners: Portugal, Spain, Switzerland, Cape Verde, China
Imports: $49 million (1987); commodities: capital equipment, consumer goods, semiprocessed goods, foods, petroleum; partners: Portugal, USSR, European Community, other Europe, Senegal, US

■ HEALTH

Births: 42/1,000 population (1991)
Deaths: 18/1,000 population (1991)

Infant Mortality: 125 deaths/1,000 live births (1991)
Life Expectancy at Birth: 40 years male, 43 years female (1992)
No. of Physicians: 1.4/10,000 population (1992)

■ EDUCATION

Govt. Expenditure: 2.7% of govt. expenditure (1989)
Literacy: 36.5% (1990)

■ COMMUNICATIONS

Daily newspapers: 1 (1992)
Televisions: n.a.
Radios: 39/1,000 inhabitants (1992)
Telephones: n.a.

■ TRANSPORTATION

Motor Vehicles: 5,700; 3,300 passenger cars (1990)
Roads: 4,118 km; 3,468 km paved
Railway: n.a.
Air Traffic: 21,000 passengers carried (1991)
Airports: 10

Canadian Embassy: c/o 4th Fl, Sorano Bldg, 45 boul. de la République; mailing address: P.O. Box 3373, Dakar, Senegal. Tel: (011-221) 23-92-90. Fax: (011-221) 23-87-49
Representative to Canada: c/o 918 16th St NW, Mezzinine Ste, Washington DC 20006 USA. Tel: (202) 872-4222

Guyana

Long-Form Name: Co-operative Republic of Guyana
Capital: Georgetown
Population: 808,000 (1992)

■ GEOGRAPHY

Area: 214,970 sq. km
Coastline: 459 km
Climate: tropical; hot, humid, moderated by northeast trade winds; two rainy seasons (May to mid-Aug., mid-Nov. to mid-Jan.)
Environment: flash floods a constant threat during rainy seasons; water pollution
Terrain: mostly rolling highlands; low coastal plain; savanna in south
Land Use: 3% arable; negligible permanent; 6% meadows; 83% forest; 8% other
Location: N South America, bordering on Atlantic Ocean

■ PEOPLE

Nationality: Guyanese
Ethnic Groups: 51% East Indian, 43% black and mixed, 4% Amerindian, 2% European and Chinese
Languages: English, Hindi, Urdu, Amerindian dialects
Religions: 50% Christian, 33% Hindu, 9% Moslem, 1% other
Marriages: n.a.
Divorces: n.a.

■ GOVERNMENT

Leader(s): Prime Min. and V. Pres. Sam Hinds, Pres. Cheddi Jagan
Government Type: republic
Administrative Divisions: 10 regions
Independence: May 26, 1966 (from UK; formerly known as British Guinea)
National Holiday: Republic Day, Feb. 23

■ ECONOMY

Overview: the government is focusing on an austere stabilization program after economic trouble in the 1980s
GNP: $233 million, per capita $290; real growth rate -3.8% (1991)
Inflation: 39.9% (1988)
Industries: bauxite mining, sugar, rice milling, timber, fishing (shrimp), textiles, gold mining
Labour Force: 380,000 (1992) 26% industry, 27% agriculture, 47% services (1989)
Unemployment: 9,209 (1987)
Agriculture: most important sector, accounting for 25% of GDP; sugar and rice are main crops; not self-sufficient in food; development potential exists for fishing and forestry
Natural Resources: bauxite, gold, diamonds, hardwood timber, shrimp, fish

■ FINANCE/TRADE

Currency: Guyana dollar ($G)
International Reserves Excluding Gold: $151 million (1992)
Gold Reserves: n.a.
Budget: revenues $65 million; expenditures $129 million, including capital expenditures of $6 million (1989)
Defence Expenditures: $14.4 million (1988)
External Debt: 1.8 billion (1988)
Exports: $255 million (1990); commodities: bauxite, sugar, rice, shrimp, gold, molasses, timber, rum; partners: UK 37%, US 12%, Canada 10.6%, CARICOM 4.8%

Imports: $512 million (1990); commodities: manufactures, machinery, food, petroleum; partners: CARICOM 41%, US 18%, UK 9%, Canada 3%

▨ HEALTH

Births: 23/1,000 population (1991)
Deaths: 7/1,000 population (1991)
Infant Mortality: 51 deaths/1,000 live births (1991)
Life Expectancy at Birth: 61 years male, 67 years female (1992)
No. of Physicians: 1.6/10,000 population (1992)

▨ EDUCATION

Govt. Expenditure: 8.1% of govt. expenditure (1987)
Literacy: 96.4% (1992)

▨ COMMUNICATIONS

Daily newspapers: 2 (1992)
Televisions: 31.4/1,000 inhabitants (1992)
Radios: 486/1,000 inhabitants (1992)
Telephones: 4.2/100 inhabitants (1992)

▨ TRANSPORTATION

Motor Vehicles: 33,000; 24,000 passenger cars (1990)
Roads: 8,383 km; 645 km paved
Railway: none
Air Traffic: 112,000 passenger carried (1991)
Airports: 43

Canadian Embassy: Canadian High Commission, High and Young Streets, Kingston, Georgetown; mailing address: P.O. Box 10880, Georgetown, Guyana. Tel: (011-592-2) 72081-5. Fax: (011-592-2): 58380
Embassy in Canada: High Commission for the Co-operative Republic of Guyana, Burnside Blvd, 151 Slater St, Ste 309, Ottawa ON K1P 5H3. Tel: (613) 235-7240, -9. Fax: (613) 235-1447.

Haiti

Long-Form Name: Republic of Haiti
Capital: Port-au-Prince
Population: 6,755,000 (1992)

▨ GEOGRAPHY

Area: 27,750 sq. km
Coastline: 1,771 km
Climate: tropical; semi-arid where mountains in east cut off trade winds

Environment: lies in the middle of the hurricane belt and subject to severe storms from June to Oct.; occasional flooding and earthquakes; deforestation
Terrain: mostly rough and mountainous
Land Use: 20% arable; 13% permanent; 18% meadows; 4% forest; 45% other
Location: West Indies, bordering on Caribbean Sea, Atlantic Ocean

▨ PEOPLE

Nationality: Haitian
Ethnic Groups: 95% black, 5% mulatto and European
Languages: French (official) spoken by only 10% of population; all speak Creole
Religions: 80% Roman Catholic (of which an overwhelming majority also practice Voodoo), 10% Protestant, 10% other
Marriages: n.a.
Divorces: n.a.

▨ GOVERNMENT

Leader(s): Pres.-in-exile Jean-Bertrand Aristide (to be re-instated Oct. 30/93) Robert Malvai
Government Type: republic
Administrative Divisions: 9 departments (départements)
Independence: Jan. 1, 1804 (from France)
National Holiday: Independence Day, Jan. 1

▨ ECONOMY

Overview: about 85% of the population live in absolute poverty, and do not have access to safe drinking water, medical care, or sufficient food; agriculture based on small-scale subsistence farming
GNP: $2.471 billion, per capita $370; real growth rate -0.6% (1991)
Inflation: 15.4% (1991)
Industries: sugar refining, textiles, flour milling, cement manufacturing, bauxite mining, tourism, light assembly industries based on imported parts
Labour Force: 3,130,000 (1992); 50.4% agriculture, 43.9% services, 5.7% industry (1989)
Unemployment: 339,680 (1990)
Agriculture: accounts for 32% of GDP and employs 65% of work force; mostly small-size subsistence farms; commercial crops include coffee and sugar cane; staple crops include rice, corn, sorghum and mangoes
Natural Resources: bauxite

■ FINANCE/TRADE

Currency: gourde (G)
International Reserves Excluding Gold: $18 million (1992)
Gold Reserves: 0.19 million fine troy ounces (1992)
Budget: revenues $300 million; expenditures $416 million, including capital expenditures of $145 million (1990)
Defence Expenditures: $16.9 million (1990)
External Debt: $745 million (1990)
Exports: $103 million (1991); commodities: light manufactures 65%, coffee 17%, other agriculture 8%, other products 10%; partners: US 77%, France 5%, Italy 4%, Germany 3%, other industrial 9%, less developed countries 2%
Imports: $347 million (1991); commodities: machines and manufactures 36%, food and beverages 21%, petroleum products 11%, fats and oils 12%, chemicals 12%; partners: US 65%, Netherlands Antilles 6%, Japan 5%, France 4%, Canada 2%, Asia 2%

■ HEALTH

Births: 43/1,000 population (1991)
Deaths: 15/1,000 population (1991)
Infant Mortality: 106 deaths/1,000 live births (1991)
Life Expectancy at Birth: 53 years male, 56 years female (1992)
No. of Physicians: 1.4/10,000 population (1992)

■ EDUCATION

Govt. Expenditure: 19.7% of govt. expenditure (1989)
Literacy: 53.0% (1992)

■ COMMUNICATIONS

Daily newspapers: 4 (1992)
Televisions: 4.5/1,000 inhabitants (1992)
Radios: 42/1,000 inhabitants (1992)
Telephones: 0.91/100 inhabitants (1992)

■ TRANSPORTATION

Motor Vehicles: 55,000; 33,000 passenger cars (1990)
Roads: 4,024 km; 944 km paved
Railway: 42 km
Air Traffic: n.a.
Airports: 6

Canadian Embassy: Édifice Banque de Nova Scotia, Delmas 18, Port-au-Prince, Haiti, WI; mailing address: C.P. 826, Port-au-Prince, Haiti. Tel: (011-509-1) 23-2358. Fax: (011-509-1) 23-8720

Embassy in Canada: Embassy of Haiti, 112 Kent St, Ste 212, Place de Ville, Tower B, Ottawa ON K1P 5P2. Tel: (613) 238-1628, -9. Fax (613) 238-2986.

Honduras

Long-Form Name: Republic of Honduras
Capital: Tegucigalpa
Population: 5,462,000 (1992)

■ GEOGRAPHY

Area: 112,090 sq. km
Coastline: 820 km
Climate: subtropical in lowlands, temperate in mountains
Environment: subject to frequent, but generally mild, earthquakes; damaging hurricanes along Caribbean coast; deforestation; soil erosion
Terrain: mostly mountainous in interior, narrow coastal plains
Land Use: 14% arable; 2% permanent; 30% meadows; 34% forest; 20% other
Location: Central (Latin) America, bordering on Caribbean Sea, Pacific Ocean

■ PEOPLE

Nationality: Honduran
Ethnic Groups: 90% mestizo (mixed Indian and European), 7% Indian, 2% black, 1% white
Languages: Spanish, Indian dialects
Religions: about 97% Roman Catholic; small Protestant minority
Marriages: 4.9 (per 1,000) (1983)
Divorces: 0.4 (per 1,000) (1983)

■ GOVERNMENT

Leader(s): Pres. Rafael Leonardo Callejas
Government Type: republic
Administrative Divisions: 18 departments (departamentos)
Independence: Sept. 15, 1821 (from Spain)
National Holiday: Independence Day, Sept. 15

■ ECONOMY

Overview: a high population growth rate, a high unemployment rate, a lack of basic services, and an export sector vulnerable to world prices (coffee, bananas)
GNP: $3.010 billion, per capita $570; real growth rate 2.6% (1991)
Inflation: 34% (1991)
Industries: agricultural processing (sugar and coffee), textiles, clothing, wood products
Labour Force: 1,580,000 (1992); 60.4% agriculture, 23.4% services, 16.1% industry (1989)

Unemployment: 72,135 unemployed, 30–40% underemployed (1991)
Agriculture: most important sector, accounting for nearly 30% of GDP, over 60% of the labor force and two-thirds of exports; main products include bananas, coffee, timber, beef, citrus fruit, shrimp; importer of wheat
Natural Resources: timber, gold, silver, copper, lad, zinc, iron ore, antimony, coal, fish

■ **FINANCE/TRADE**

Currency: lempira (L)
International Reserves Excluding Gold: $200 million (1992)
Gold Reserves: 0.02 million fine troy ounces (1992)
Budget: revenues $1,053 million; expenditures $949 million, including capital expenditures of $159 million (1989)
Defence Expenditures: $123.5 million (1990)
External Debt: 3.159 billion (1990)
Exports: $808 million (1991); commodities: bananas, coffee, shrimp, lobster, minerals, lumber; partners: US 52%, Germany 11%, Japan, Italy, Belgium
Imports: $880 million (1991); commodities: machinery and transport equipment, chemical products, manufactured goods, fuel and oil, foodstuffs; partners: US 39%, Japan 9%, CACM, Venezuela, Mexico

■ **HEALTH**

Births: 38/1,000 population (1991)
Deaths: 7/1,000 population (1991)
Infant Mortality: 56 deaths/1,000 live births (1991)
Life Expectancy at Birth: 62 years male, 66 years female (1992)
No. of Physicians: 6.6/10,000 population (1992)

■ **EDUCATION**

Govt. Expenditure: 19.5% of govt. expenditure (1987)
Literacy: 73.1% (1992)

■ **COMMUNICATIONS**

Daily newspapers: 4 (1992)
Televisions: 70.3/1,000 inhabitants (1992)
Radios: 384/1,000 inhabitants (1992)
Telephones: 1.42/100 inhabitants (1992)

■ **TRANSPORTATION**

Motor Vehicles: 133,000; 42,000 passenger cars (1990)
Roads: 12,106 km; 1,906 km paved
Railway: 785 km

Air Traffic: 447,000 passengers carried (1991)
Airports: 35

Canadian Embassy: Flr 6, Cronos Building, Calle 3 y Avenida Central; mailing address: Apartado Postal 10303-1000, San José, Costa Rica. Tel: (011-506) 55-35-22. Fax: (011-506) 23-23-95
Embassy in Canada: Embassy of the Republic of Honduras, 151 Slater St, Ste 900, Ottawa ON K1P 5H3. Tel: (613) 233-8900.

Hong Kong

Dependent Territory of United Kingdom

Long-Form Name: Hong Kong
Capital: Victoria
Population: 5,800,000 (1992)

■ **GEOGRAPHY**

Area: 1,040 sq. km
Coastline: 733 km
Climate: tropical monsoon; cool and humid in winter, hot and rainy from spring through summer, warm and sunny in fall
Environment: more than 200 islands; occasional typhoons; and water polution
Terrain: hilly to mountainous with steep slopes; lowlands in north
Land Use: 7% arable land; 1% permanent; 1% meadows; 12% forest; 79% other
Location: SE Asia, bordering on South China Sea

■ **PEOPLE**

Nationality: n.a. (no descriptive word)
Ethnic Groups: 98% Chinese, 2% other
Languages: Chinese (Cantonese), English

■ **GOVERNMENT**

Leader(s): Gov. Chris Patten; Chief Secretary Sir D.R. Ford
Government Type: colony of the UK; scheduled to revert to China July 1,1997
Administrative Divisions: none
National Holiday: Liberation Day, Aug. 29

■ **ECONOMY**

Overview: has a free-market economy and is autonomous in financial affairs; manufacturing is the base of the economy; natural resources are limited and food and raw materials must be imported; economic future unclear due to Chinese takeover in 1997
GNP: $77.302 billion, per capita $13,200; real growth rate 6.9% (1991)

Currency: Hong Kong dollar (HK$)

Canadian Embassy: Office of the Commission for Canada, 13th floor, Tower 1, Exchange Square, 8 Connaught Place, Hong Kong; mailing address: Office of the Commission for Canada, GPO Box 11142, Hong Kong

Hungary

Long-Form Name: Republic of Hungary
Capital: Budapest
Population: 10,512,000 (1992)

■ GEOGRAPHY

Area: 93,030 sq. km
Coastline: none: landlocked
Climate: temperate; cold, cloudy, humid winter; warm summer
Environment: levees are common along many streams, but flooding occurs almost every year
Terrain: mostly flat to rolling plains
Land Use: 54% arable; 3% permanent; 14% meadows; 18% forest; 11% other
Location: C Europe

■ PEOPLE

Nationality: Hungarian
Ethnic Groups: 97% Hungarian, 2% German, 1% Slovak, 0.3% Southern Slav, 0.2% Romanian
Languages: Hungarian (Magyar, official)
Religions: 68% Roman Catholic, 20% Calvinist, 5% Lutheran, 8% atheist and other
Marriages: 6.2 (per 1,000) (1987)
Divorces: 2.8 (per 1,000) (1987)

■ GOVERNMENT

Leader(s): Prime Min. Jozsef Antall, Pres. Arpad Goncz
Government Type: republic
Administrative Divisions: 19 counties and 1 capital city (Budapest)
Independence:
National Holiday: Anniversary of the Liberation, Apr. 4 (1945)

■ ECONOMY

Overview: Soviet-style economy which is attempting to decentralize and implement market-oriented enterprises; hampered by old capital plant and lack of funds
GNP: $28.244 billion, per capita $2,690; real growth rate 0.5% (1991)
Inflation: 28.3% (1990)
Industries: mining, metallurgy, engineering industries, processed foods, textiles, chemicals (especially pharmaceuticals)
Labour Force: 5,276,000 (1992); 47.8% services, 31.3% industry, 20.9% agriculture (1989)
Unemployment: 8.5% (1991)
Agriculture: accounts for about 15% of GNP (including forestry) and 19% of employment; highly diversified crop-livestock farming; main crops—wheat, corn, sunflowers, potatoes, sugar beets; livestock—hogs, cattle, poultry and dairy products; self-sufficient in food
Natural Resources: bauxite, coal, natural gas, fertile soils

■ FINANCE/TRADE

Currency: forint (Ft)
International Reserves Excluding Gold: $5,213 million (1992)
Gold Reserves: 0.11 million fine troy ounces (1992)
Budget: revenues $18.2 billion; expenditures $18.3 billion, including capital expenditures of $805 million (1989)
Defence Expenditures: $1.45 billion (1990)
External Debt: $18.046 billion (1990)
Exports: $10.301 billion (1991); commodities: capital goods 36%, foods 24%, consumer goods 18%, fuels and minerals 11%, other 11%; partners: USSR 48%, Eastern Europe 25%, developed countries 16%, less developed countries 8%
Imports: $11.532 billion (1991); commodities: machinery and transport 28%, fuels 20%, chemical products 14%, manufactured consumer goods 16%, agriculture 6%, other 16%; partners: USSR 43%, Eastern Europe 28%, less developed countries 23%, US 3%

■ HEALTH

Births: 12/1,000 population (1991)
Deaths: 13/1,000 population (1991)
Infant Mortality: 14 deaths/1,000 live births (1991)
Life Expectancy at Birth: 65 years male, 74 years female (1992)
No. of Physicians: 32.6/10,000 population (1992)

■ EDUCATION

Govt. Expenditure: 3.30% of govt. expenditure (1990)
Literacy: 98.9% (1992)

■ COMMUNICATIONS

Daily newspapers: 28 (1992)
Televisions: 403.9/1,000 inhabitants (1992)
Radios: 592/1,000 inhabitants (1992)
Telephones: 16.94/100 inhabitants (1992)

■ TRANSPORTATION

Motor Vehicles: 2,195,338; 1,944,553 passenger cars (1990)
Roads: 106,147 km; 52,934 km paved
Railway: 7,759 km
Air Traffic: 911,000 passengers carried (1991)
Airports: 2

Canadian Embassy: Budakeszi ut 32, H-1121 Budapest XII, Hungary. Tel.: (011-36-1) 176-7686. Fax: (011-36-1) 176-7689
Embassy in Canada: Embassy of the Republic of Hungary, 7 Delaware Ave, Ottawa ON K2P 0Z2. Tel: (613) 232-1711, -1549. Fax: (613) 232-5620.

Iceland

Long-Form Name: Republic of Iceland
Capital: Reykjavik
Population: 260,000 (1992)

■ GEOGRAPHY

Area: 103,000 sq. km
Coastline: 4,988 km
Climate: temperate; moderated by North Atlantic Current; mild, windy winters; damp, cool summers
Environment: subject to earthquakes and volcanic activity
Terrain: mostly plateau interspersed with mountain peaks, ice fields; coast deeply indented by bays and fjords
Land Use: negligible arable; 0% permanent; 23% meadows; 1% forest; 76% other
Location: NW Europe, bordering on Norwegian Sea, Atlantic Ocean

■ PEOPLE

Nationality: Icelander
Ethnic Groups: homogeneous mixture of descendants of Norwegians and Celts
Languages: Icelandic
Religions: Christianity (predominantly Protestant)
Marriages: 4.8 (per 1,000) (1987)
Divorces: 2.0 (per 1,000) (1987)

■ GOVERNMENT

Leader(s): Prime Min. David Oddsson, Pres. Vigdis Finnbogadóttir
Government Type: republic
Administrative Divisions: 27 lögsagnarumdoemi (divisions)
Independence: June 17, 1944 (from Denmark)
National Holiday: Anniversary of the Establishment of the Republic, June 17

■ ECONOMY

Overview: basically capitalistic but with extensive welfare measures and low unemployment; heavily dependent on fishing industry
GNP: $5.814 billion, per capita $22,580; real growth rate 2.4% (1991)
Inflation: 6.8% (1991)
Industries: fish processing, aluminum smelting, ferro-silicon production, hydroelectricity
Labour Force: 136,000 (1992); 55% commerce, finance and services, 14% other manufacturing, 6% agriculture, 8% fish processing, 5% fishing
Unemployment: 1.5% (1991)
Agriculture: accounts for about 25% of GDP (including fishing); fishing is the most important economic activity, contributing nearly 75% to export earnings; principal crops include potatoes and turnips; livestock—cattle, sheep; self-sufficient in crops
Natural Resources: fish, hydroelectric and geothermal power, diatomite

■ FINANCE/TRADE

Currency: króna (pl. krónur) (ISK)
International Reserves Excluding Gold: $498 million (1992)
Gold Reserves: 0.05 million fine troy ounces (1992)
Budget: revenues $1.6 billion; expenditures $1.66 billion, including capital expenditures (1990)
Defence Expenditures: n.a.
External Debt: $1.8 billion (1988)
Exports: $1.554 billion (1991); commodities: fish and fish products, animal products, aluminium, diatomite; partners: European Community 58.9% (UK 23.3%, Germany 10.3%), US 13.6%, USSR 3.6%
Imports: $1.720 billion (1991); commodities: machinery and transportation equipment, petroleum, foodstuffs, textiles; partners: European Community 58% (Germany 16%, Denmark 10.4%, UK 9.2%), US 8.5%, USSR 3.9%

■ HEALTH

Births: 17/1,000 population (1991)
Deaths: 7/1,000 population (1991)
Infant Mortality: 7 deaths/1,000 live births (1991)
Life Expectancy at Birth: 75 years male, 80 years female (1992)
No. of Physicians: 23/10,000 population (1990)

■ EDUCATION

Govt. Expenditure: 14.1% of govt. expenditure (1988)

Literacy: 100%

■ COMMUNICATIONS

Daily newspapers: 3 (1992)
Televisions: 318.7/1,000 inhabitants (1992)
Radios: 785/1,000 inhabitants (1992)
Telephones: 52.50/100 inhabitants (1992)

■ TRANSPORTATION

Motor Vehicles: 134,181; 119,731 passenger cars (1990)
Roads: 11,742 km; 2,163 km paved
Railway: n.a.
Air Traffic: 773,000 passengers carried (1991)
Airports: 97

Canadian Embassy: c/o The Canadian Embassy, Oscars Gate 20, Oslo 3, Norway; mailng address: 0244 Oslo, Norway. Tel: (011-47-2) 46-69-55. Fax: (011-47-2) 69-34-67
Representative to Canada: c/o Embassy of Iceland, 2022 Connecticut Ave NW, Washington DC 20008 USA

India

Long-Form Name: Republic of India
Capital: New Delhi
Population: 879,548,000 (1992), excluding the occupied areas of Jammu and Kashmir

■ GEOGRAPHY

Area: 3,166,830 sq. km
Coastline: 7,000 km
Climate: varies from tropical monsoon in south to temperate in north
Environment: droughts, flash floods, severe thunderstorms common; deforestation; soil erosion; overgrazing; air and water pollution; desertification
Terrain: upland plain (Deccan Plateau) in south, flat to rolling plain along the Ganges, deserts in west, Himalayas in north
Land Use: 55% arable; 1% permanent; 4% meadows; 23% forest; 17% other
Location: S Asia, bordering on Arabian Sea, Indian Ocean, Bay of Bengal

■ PEOPLE

Nationality: Indian
Ethnic Groups: 72% Indo-Aryan, 25% Dravidian, 3% Mongoloid and other
Languages: Hindi (official, spoken by 30%), English, 19 regional languages, including Bengali, Tlegu, Marathi, Tamil. Urdu, Gujarati, Malayalam, Kannada, Oriya, Punjabi, Assamese, Kashmiri, Sindhi and Sanskrit; 24 languages spoken by a million or more persons each; numerous other languages
Religions: 80% Hindu, 11% Moslem, 2% Christian, 2% Sikh, 0.7% Buddhist, 0.5% Jains, 0.4% other
Marriages: are not registered in India
Divorces: are not registered in India

■ GOVERNMENT

Leader(s): Pres. Shankar Dayal Sharma, Prime Min. P.V. Narasimha Rao
Government Type: federal republic
Administrative Divisions: 25 states and 7 union territories
Independence: Aug. 15, 1947 (from UK)
National Holiday: Anniversary of the Proclamation of the Republic, Jan. 26

■ ECONOMY

Overview: a mixture of traditional village farming and handicrafts, modern agriculture, old and new branches of industry and a multitude of support services; millions still live in poverty, hoping to benefit from modern farming techniques
GNP: $284.668 billion, per capita $330; real growth rate 5.5% (1991)
Inflation: 13.9% (1991)
Industries: textiles, food processing, steel, machinery, transportation equipment, cement, jute manufactures, mining, petroleum, power, chemicals, pharmaceuticals, electronics
Labour Force: 323,000,000 (1992); 62.6% agriculture, 10.8% industry, 26.6% services (1989)
Unemployment: 36,300,000 (1991)
Agriculture: accounts for 33% of GNP and employs 67% of labor force; self-sufficient in food grains; main crops—rice, wheat, oilseeds, cotton, jute, tea, sugar cane, potatoes; livestock— cattle, buffaloes, sheep, goats and poultry; in top 10 of fishing nations
Natural Resources: coal, iron ore, manganese, mica, bauxite, titanium ore, chromite, natural gas, diamonds, crude oil, limestone

■ FINANCE/TRADE

Currency: rupee (Rs)
International Reserves Excluding Gold: $4,854 million (1992)
Gold Reserves: 11.28 million fine troy ounces (1992)
Budget: revenues $34 billion; expenditures $54 billion, including capital expenditures of $13.3 billion (1991)
Defence Expenditures: $8.94 billion (1989)

External Debt: $61.097 billion (1990)
Exports: $17.366 billion (1991); commodities: tea, coffee, iron ore, fish products, manufactures; partners: European Community 25%, USSR and Eastern Euruope 17%, US 19%, Japan 10%
Imports: $20.252 billion (1991); commodities: petroleum, edible oils, textiles, clothing, capital goods; partners: European Community 33%, Middle East 19%, Japan 10%, US 9%, USSR and Eastern Europe 8%

■ HEALTH

Births: 29/1,000 population (1991)
Deaths: 10/1,000 population (1991)
Infant Mortality: 87 deaths/1,000 live births (1991)
Life Expectancy at Birth: 58 years male, 59 years female (1992)
No. of Physicians: 4.0/10,000 population (1992)

■ EDUCATION

Govt. Expenditure: 2.47% of govt. expenditure (1990)
Literacy: 48.2% (1992)

■ COMMUNICATIONS

Daily newspapers: 1,978 (1992)
Televisions: 27.0/1,000 inhabitants (1992)
Radios: 78/1,000 inhabitants (1992)
Telephones: 0.6/100 inhabitants (1992)

■ TRANSPORTATION

Motor Vehicles: 4,350,000; 2,300,000 passenger cars (1990)
Roads: 1,646,752 km; 779,040 km paved
Railway: 132,373 km
Air Traffic: 10,859,000 passengers carried (1991)
Airports: 179

Canadian Embassy: The Canadian High Commission, 7/8 Shantipath, Chanakyapuri, New Delhi 110 021; mailing address: The Canadian High Commission, P.O. Box 5208, New Delhi, India. Tel: (011-91-11) 687-6500
Embassy in Canada: High Commission for India, 10 Springfield Rd, Ottawa ON K1M 1C9. Tel: (613) 744-3751, -2, -3. Fax: (613) 744-0913.

Indonesia

Long-Form Name: Republic of Indonesia
Capital: Jakarta
Population: 191,170,000 (1992)

■ GEOGRAPHY

Area: (13,677 islands) 1,919,440 sq. km
Coastline: 54,716 km
Climate: tropical; hot, humid; more moderate in highlands
Environment: archipelago of 13,500 islands (6,000 inhabited); occasional floods, severe droughts and tsunamis; deforestation
Terrain: mostly coastal lowlands; larger islands have interior mountains
Land Use: 8% arable; 3% permanent crops; 7% meadows; 67% forest; 15% other
Location: SE Asia, bordering on Indian Ocean

■ PEOPLE

Nationality: Indonesian
Ethnic Groups: majority of Malay stock comprising 45% Javanese, 14% Sundanese, 8% Madurese, 8% coastal Malays, 26% other
Languages: Bahasa Indonesia (modified form of Malay; official); English and Dutch leading foreign languages; 25 local dialects, the most widely spoken of which is Javanese
Religions: 78% Islam, 11% Christianity, Hinduism, Buddhism
Marriages: 7.2 (per 1,000) (1984)
Divorces: 1.1 (per 1,000) (1984)

■ GOVERNMENT

Leader(s): Pres. Gen. (Ret.) Suharto, V. Pres. Gen. (ret'd) Sudharmono
Government Type: republic
Administrative Divisions: 24 provinces, 2 special regions and 1 special capital city district
Independence: Aug. 17, 1945 (from Netherlands; formerly known as Netherlands or Dutch East Indies)
National Holiday: Independence Day, Aug. 17

■ ECONOMY

Overview: a mixed economy with many socialist institutions and central planning but with a recent emphasis on deregulation and private enterprise; hampered by large population growth; possesses abundant natural wealth
GNP: $111.409 billion, per capita $610; real growth rate 5.8% (1991)
Inflation: 9.2% (1991)
Industries: petroleum, textiles, mining, cement, chemical fertilizer production, timber, food, rubber
Labour Force: 71 million (1992); 54.4% agriculture, 8% industry, 37.6 % services (1989)
Unemployment: 1,238,700 (1990)

Agriculture: subsistence food production; small-holder and plantation production for export; rice, cassava, peanuts, rubber, cocoa, coffee, copra, other tropical products
Natural Resources: crude oil, tin, natural gas, nickel, timber, bauxite, copper, fertile soils, coal, gold, silver

■ FINANCE/TRADE

Currency: rupiah (Rp)
International Reserves Excluding Gold: $10,413 million (1992)
Gold Reserves: 3.10 million fine troy ounces (1992)
Budget: revenues $17.2 billion; expenditures $23.4 billion, including capital expenditures of $8.9 billion (1991)
Defence Expenditures: $1.45 billion (1990)
External Debt: $44.974 billion (1990)
Exports: $29.142 billion (1991); commodities: petroleum and liquefied natural gas 40%, timber 15%, textiles 7%, rubber 5%, coffee 3%; partners: Japan 42%, US 16%, Singapore 9%, European Community 11%
Imports: $25.869 billion (1991); commodities: machinery 39%, chemical products 19%, manufactured goods 16%; partners: Japan 26%, European Community 19%, US 13%, Singapore 7%,

■ HEALTH

Births: 26/1,000 population (1991)
Deaths: 8/1,000 population (1991)
Infant Mortality: 73 deaths/1,000 live births (1991)
Life Expectancy at Birth: 58 years male, 63 years female (1992)
No. of Physicians: 1/10,000 population (1990)

■ EDUCATION

Govt. Expenditure: 9.07% of government expenditure (1990)
Literacy: 77.0% (1992)

■ COMMUNICATIONS

Daily newspapers: 60 (1992)
Televisions: 55.3/1,000 inhabitants (1992)
Radios: 144/1,000 inhabitants (1992)
Telephones: 0.58/100 inhabitants (1992)

■ TRANSPORTATION

Motor Vehicles: 2,591,087; 1,199,665 passenger cars (1990)
Roads: 232,252 km; 143,958 km paved
Railway: 6,910 km
Air Traffic: 10,386,000 passengers carried (1991)

Airports: 147

Canadian Embassy: Flr 5 Wisma Metropolitan-I, Jalan Jendral Sudirman Kav 29, Jakarta 12920; mailing address: P.O. Box 1052/JKT, Jakarta 10110, Indonesia. Tel: (011-62-21) 510-709. Fax: (011-62-21) 571-2251
Embassy in Canada: Embassy of the Republic of Indonesia, 287 MacLaren St, Ottawa ON K2P 0L9. Tel: (613) 236-7403. Fax: (613) 563-2858.

Iran

Long-Form Name: Islamic Republic of Iran
Capital: Tehran
Population: 61,565,000 (1992)

■ GEOGRAPHY

Area: 1,648,000 sq. km
Coastline: 3,180 km
Climate: mostly arid or semi-arid, subtropical along Caspian coast
Environment: deforestation; overgrazing; desertification
Terrain: rugged mountainous rim; high, central basin with deserts, mountains; small, discontinuous plains along both coasts
Land Use: 8% arable; negligible permanent; 27% meadows; 11% forest; 54% other
Location: SW Asia (Middle East), bordering on Persian Gulf

■ PEOPLE

Nationality: Iranian
Ethnic Groups: 51% Persian, 25% Azerbaijani, 9% Kurd, 8% Gilaki and Mazandarani, 2% Lur, 1% Baloch, 1% Arab, 3% other
Languages: Farsi (Persian, official, 45%), Turkish, Kurdish, Arabic
Religions: Islam (93% Shia, 5% Sunni), Christianity, Judaism, Zoroastrianism 2%
Marriages: 6.6 (per 1,000) (1988)
Divorces: 0.6 (per 1,000) (1988)

■ GOVERNMENT

Leader(s): Pres. Hojatolislam Ali Akbar Hashemi-Rafsanjani, Wali faqih, Commander-in-Chief of Armed Forces, Ayatollah Seyed Ali Khamenei
Government Type: theocratic republic
Administrative Divisions: 24 provinces
Independence: Apr. 1, 1979, Islamic Republic of Iran proclaimed
National Holiday: Islamic Republic Day, Apr. 1

■ ECONOMY

Overview: many aspects of economy were nationalized following the 1979 revolution but the new five-year plan (passed Jan. 1990) calls for many to be returned to the public sector; economy hurt by war with Iraq; country is looking to secure foreign loans
GNP: $127.366 billion, per capita $2,320; real growth rate 2.5% (1991)
Inflation: 17.1% (1991)
Industries: petroleum, petrochemicals, textiles, cement and other building materials, food processing (particularly sugar refining and vegetable oil production), metal fabricating (steel and copper)
Labour Force: 15,253,000 (1992); 36.4% agriculture, 32.8% industry, 30.8% services (1989)
Unemployment: 30% (1989)
Agriculture: principal products—rice, other grains, sugar beets, fruits, nuts, cotton, dairy products, wool, caviar; not self-sufficient in food
Natural Resources: petroleum, natural gas, coal, chromium, copper, iron ore, lead, manganese, zinc, sulphur

■ FINANCE/TRADE

Currency: rial (RIs)
International Reserves Excluding Gold: $5,168 million (1982)
Gold Reserves: 5.92 million fine troy ounces (1982)
Budget: revenues $63 billion, expenditures $80 billion, including capital expenditures of $23 billion (1990)
Defence Expenditures: $3.18 billion (1990)
External Debt: $1.797 billion (1990)
Exports: $12.3 billion (1988); commodities: petroleum 90%, carpets, fruits, nuts, hides; partners: Japan, Turkey, Italy, Netherlands, Spain, France, Germany
Imports: $9.454 billion (1988); commodities: machinery, military supplies, metal works, foodstuffs, pharmaceuticals, technical services, refined oil products; partners: Germany, Japan, Turkey, UK, Italy

■ HEALTH

Births: 44/1,000 population (1991)
Deaths: 9/1,000 population (1991)
Infant Mortality: 66 deaths/1,000 live births (1991)
Life Expectancy at Birth: 63 years male, 66 years female (1992)
No. of Physicians: 3.4/10,000 population (1992)

■ EDUCATION

Govt. Expenditure: 20.9% of govt. expenditure (1991)
Literacy: 54.0% (1992)

■ COMMUNICATIONS

Daily newspapers: 11 (1992)
Televisions: 65.8/1,000 inhabitants (1992)
Radios: 245/1,000 inhabitants (1992)
Telephones: 3.8/100 inhabitants (1992)

■ TRANSPORTATION

Motor Vehicles: 2,200,000; 1,600,000 passenger cars (1990)
Roads: 136,784 km; 56,032 km paved
Railway: 4,779 km
Air Traffic: 5,353,000 passengers carried (1991)
Airports: 34

Canadian Embassy: 57 Shahid Javad Sarafraz, Ostad-Motahari Ave, Tehran, 11365; mailing address: P.O. Box 11365-4647, Tehran, Iran. Tel: (011-98-21) 622623. Fax: (011-98-21) 623202
Embassy in Canada: Embassy of the Islamic Republic of Iran, 245 Metcalfe St, Ottawa ON K2P 2K2. Tel: (613) 235-4726. Fax: (613) 232-5712.

Iraq

Data does not reflect the dramatic change in economic and social conditions as a result of the 1991 Gulf War.
Long-Form Name: Republic of Iraq
Capital: Baghdad
Population: 19,290,000 (1992)

■ GEOGRAPHY

Area: 434,920 sq. km
Coastline: 58 km
Climate: desert; mild to cool winters with dry, hot, cloudless summers
Environment: development of Tigris-Euphrates river systems contingent upon agreements with upstream riparians (Syria and Turkey); air and water pollution; soil degradation (salinization) and erosion; desertification
Terrain: mostly broad plains; reedy marshes in southeast; mountains along borders with Iran and Turkey
Land Use: 12% arable; 1% permanent; 9% meadows; 3% forest; 75% other
Location: SW Asia (Near East), bordering on Persian Gulf

■ PEOPLE

Nationality: Iraqi
Ethnic Groups: 75–80% Arab, 15–20% Kurdish, 5% Turkoman (small minority)
Languages: Arabic (official), Kurdish (official in Kurdish region)
Religions: 97% Moslem (60–65% Shi'a, 32–37% Sunni), 3% Christian or other
Marriages: 8.5 (per 1,000) (1981)
Divorces: 0.1 (per 1,000) (1981)

■ GOVERNMENT

Leader(s): Prime Min. Muhammad Hamza al-Zubaidy, Pres. Saddam Hussein at-Takriti, V. Pres. Taha Mohieddin Maarouf and Taha Yassin Ramadan
Government Type: republic
Administrative Divisions: 18 governorates
Independence: Oct. 3, 1932 (from League of Nations mandate under British administration)
National Holiday: Anniversary of the Revolution, July 17

■ ECONOMY

Overview: industrial production and foreign trade is centrally planned and managed while some small-scale industry and services and most agriculture is left to private enterprise; war with Iran in the 1980s and the Gulf War has caused economic problems
GNP: $35 billion, per capita $1,940; real growth rate 5% (1989 est.)
Inflation: 30–40% (1989 est.)
Industries: petroleum, chemicals, textiles, construction materials, food processing
Labour Force: 5,119,000 (1992) 79.7% services, 12.5% agriculture, 7.8% industry (1989)
Unemployment: less than 5% (1989 est.)
Agriculture: accounts for less than 10% of GNP but 33% of labor force; principal products—wheat, barley, rice, vegetables, dates, other fruit, cotton, wool; livestock—cattle, sheep; not self-sufficient in food output
Natural Resources: crude oil, natural gas, phosphates, sulphur

■ FINANCE/TRADE

Currency: dinar
International Reserves Excluding Gold: n.a.
Gold Reserves: n.a.
Budget: revenues n.a., expenditures $35 billion, including capital expenditures (1989)
Defence Expenditures: $8.61 billion (1990)
External Debt: $40 billion (1988), excluding debt to Persian Gulf Arab States

Exports: $392 million (1990); commodities: crude oil and refined products, machinery, chemicals, dates; partners: US, Brazil, USSR, Italy, Turkey, France, Japan, Yugoslavia
Imports: $4.834 billion (1990); commodities: manufactures, food; partners: Turkey, US, Germany, UK, France, Japan, Romania, Yugoslavia, Brazil

■ HEALTH

Births: 46/1,000 population (1991)
Deaths: 7/1,000 population (1991)
Infant Mortality: 66 deaths/1,000 live births (1991)
Life Expectancy at Birth: 66 years male, 68 years female (1992)
No. of Physicians: 5.5/10,000 population (1992)

■ EDUCATION

Govt. Expenditure: 6.4% of government expenditure (1987)
Literacy: 59.7% (1992)

■ COMMUNICATIONS

Daily newspapers: 5 (1992)
Televisions: 68.4/1,000 inhabitants (1992)
Radios: 202/1,000 inhabitants (1992)
Telephones: 5.6/100 inhabitants (1992)

■ TRANSPORTATION

Motor Vehicles: 1,040,730; 672,205 passenger cars (1990)
Roads: 45,232 km; 38,273 km paved
Railway: 3,044 km
Air Traffic: 28,000 passengers carried (1991)
Airports: 2

Canadian Embassy: Hay Al-Mansour, Mahalla 609, Zuqaq 1, House 33, Baghdad; mailing address: P.O. Box 323, Central Post Office, Bagdad, Iraq. Tel: (011-964-1) 542-1459
Embassy in Canada: Embassy of the Republic of Iraq, 215 McLeod St, Ottawa ON K2P 0Z8. Tel: (613) 236-9177, -8.

Ireland

Long-Form Name: Republic of Ireland
Capital: Dublin
Population: 3,486,000 (1992)

■ GEOGRAPHY

Area: 68,890 sq. km
Coastline: 1,448 km
Climate: temperate maritime; modified by North Atlantic Current; mild winters, cool summers; consistently humid; overcast about half the time

Environment: deforestation
Terrain: mostly level to rolling interior plains surrounded by rugged hills and low mountains; sea cliffs on west coast
Land Use: 14% arable; negligible permanent; 71% meadows; 5% forest; 10% other
Location: NW Europe, bordering on Atlantic Ocean

■ PEOPLE

Nationality: Irish
Ethnic Groups: Celtic, with English minority
Languages: Irish (official first language, but use is limited) and English; English is the language generally used, with Gaelic spoken in a few areas, mostly along the western seaboard
Religions: 95% Roman Catholic, 5% Protestant
Marriages: 5.1 (per 1,000) (1987)
Divorces: illegal under Irish Law

■ GOVERNMENT

Leader(s): Prime Min. Albert Reynolds, Pres. Mary Robinson
Government Type: republic
Administrative Divisions: 26 counties
Independence: Dec. 6, 1921 (from UK)
National Holiday: St. Patrick's Day, Mar. 17

■ ECONOMY

Overview: a small, open economy that is trade dependent; unemployment is high but inflation has been considerably lowered and the deficit burden relieved
GNP: $37.738 billion, per capita $10,780; real growth rate 2.4% (1991)
Inflation: 3.2% (1991)
Industries: food products, brewing, textiles, clothing, chemicals, pharmaceuticals, machinery, transportation equipment, glass and crystal
Labour Force: 1,481,000 (1992) 68.6% services, 18.4% industry, 13% agriculture (1989)
Unemployment: 17.4% (1990)
Agriculture: accounts for 11% of GNP and 14.8% of the labor force; principal crops include turnips, barley, potatoes, sugar, beets, wheat; livestock— meat and dairy products; 85% self-sufficient in food; food shortages include bread grain, fruits, vegetables
Natural Resources: zinc, lead, natural gas, crude oil, barite, copper, gypsum, limestone, dolomite, peat, silver

■ FINANCE/TRADE

Currency: Irish pound (£ or £Ir)
International Reserves Excluding Gold: $3,440 million (1992)

Gold Reserves: 0.36 million fine troy ounces (1992)
Budget: revenues $11.3 billion; expenditures $11.7 billion, including capital expenditures of $1.6 billion (1990)
Defence Expenditures: $507.50 million (1990)
External Debt: $16.1 billion (1988)
Exports: $28.295 billion (1992); commodities: live animals, animal products, chemicals, data processing equipment, industrial machinery; partners: European Community 74% (U.K. 35%, Germany 11%, France 9%), US 8%
Imports: $22.486 billion (1990); commodities: food, animal feed, chemicals, petroleum and petroleum products, machinery, textiles, clothing; partners: European Community 66% (U.K. 42%, Germany 9%, France 4%), US 16%

■ HEALTH

Births: 15/1,000 population (1991)
Deaths: 9/1,000 population (1991)
Infant Mortality: 6 deaths/1,000 live births (1991)
Life Expectancy at Birth: 71 years male, 77 years female (1992)
No. of Physicians: 14.7/10,000 population (1992)

■ EDUCATION

Govt. Expenditure: 12.24% of govt. expenditure (1990)
Literacy: 99%

■ COMMUNICATIONS

Daily newspapers: 4 (1992)
Televisions: 271.0/1,000 inhabitants (1992)
Radios: 583/1,000 inhabitants (1992)
Telephones: 26.52/100 inhabitants (1992)

■ TRANSPORTATION

Motor Vehicles: 1.028,667; 796,408 passenger cars (1990)
Roads: 92,313 km; 86,733 km paved
Railway: 1,950 km
Air Traffic: 4,765,000 passengers carried (1990)
Airports: 19

Canadian Embassy: 65 St Stephen's Green, Dublin 2, Ireland. Tel: (011-353-1) 78-19-88
Embassy in Canada: Embassy of Ireland, 170 Metcalfe St, Ottawa ON K2P 1P3. Tel: (613) 233-6281. Fax: (613) 233-5835.

Isle of Man

Dependency of United Kingdom

Long-Form Name: Isle of Man

Capital: Douglas
Population: 69,000 (1992)

■ GEOGRAPHY

Area: 572 sq. km
Climate: temperate maritime
Land Use: most of island covered by farmland and moors; low mountain chain extends through island; 85% of cultivated land area used for farming, 68,000 acres farmland, 37,000 acres grazing
Location: Irish Sea, between England and Northern Ireland

■ PEOPLE

Nationality: British
Ethnic Groups: Celtic
Languages: English, Manx

■ GOVERNMENT

Leader(s): Pres. Sir Charles Kerruish
Government Type: Crown dependency administered in accordance with its own laws

■ ECONOMY

Overview: tourism, fishing; agriculture provides for local consumption only
Currency: has its own currency, on a par with British pound sterling

Israel

Long-Form Name: State of Israel
Capital: Jerusalem
Population: 5,131,000 (1992)

■ GEOGRAPHY

Area: 20,770 sq. km
Coastline: 273 km
Climate: temperate; hot and dry in desert areas
Environment: sandstorms may occur during spring and summer; limited arable land and natural water resources pose serious constraints; deforestation
Terrain: Negev desert in the south; low coastal plain; central mountains; Jordan Rift Valley
Land Use: 17% arable; 5% permanent; 40% meadows; 6% forest; 32% other
Location: SW Asia (Near East), bordering on Mediterranean Sea

■ PEOPLE

Nationality: Israeli
Ethnic Groups: 83% Jewish, 17% non-Jewish (mostly Arab)

Languages: Hebrew (official); Arabic used officially for Arab minority; European languages
Religions: 84% Judaism, 14% Islam (mostly Sunni Moslem), 2% Christian and Druze
Marriages: 6.9 (per 1,000) (1987)
Divorces: 1.2 (per 1,000) (1987)

■ GOVERNMENT

Leader(s): Prime Min. Yitzhak Rabin, Pres. Chaim Herzog
Government Type: republic
Administrative Divisions: 6 districts; annexed areas: Gaza Strip, West Bank
Independence: May 14, 1948 (from League of Nations mandate under British administration)
National Holiday: Independence Day; the Jewish calendar is lunar and the holiday may occur in Apr. or May

■ ECONOMY

Overview: a market economy with government participation; despite limited natural resources, country has strong agriculture and industry sectors; transfer payments and foreign loans offset the deficit; the Palestinian uprising and Russian immigration stifle growth
GNP: $59.128 billion, per capita $11,330; real growth rate 3.7% (1991)
Inflation: 19% (1991)
Industries: food processing, diamond cutting and polishing, textiles, clothing, chemicals, metal products, military equipment, transport equipment, electrical equipment, miscellaneous machinery, potash mining, high-technology electronics, tourism
Labour Force: 1,806,000 (1992); 75.3% services, 20.8% industry, 3.9% agriculture
Unemployment: 10.6% (1991)
Agriculture: accounts for 5% of GNP; largely self-sufficient in food production, except for bread grains; principal products—citrus and other fruits, vegetables, cotton; livestock products—beef, dairy and poultry
Natural Resources: copper, phosphates, bromide, potash, clay, sand, sulphur, asphalt, manganese, small amounts of natural gas and crude oil

■ FINANCE/TRADE

Currency: shekel (IS)
International Reserves Excluding Gold: $5,222 million (1992)
Gold Reserves: 0.01 million fine troy ounces (1992)
Budget: revenues $28.7 billion; expenditures $33.0 billion, including capital expenditures (1991)

Defence Expenditures: $6.16 billion (1990)
External Debt: $16.4 billion (1989)
Exports: $11.889 billion (1991); commodities: polished diamonds, citrus and other fruits, textiles and clothing, processed foods, fertilizer and chemical products, military hardware, electronics; partners: US, UK, Germany, France, Belgium, Luxembourg, Italy
Imports: $16.906 billion (1991); commodities: military equipment, rough diamonds, oil, chemicals, machinery, iron and steel, cereals, textiles, vehicles, ships, aircraft; partners: US, Germany, UK, Switzerland, Italy, Belgium, Luxembourg

■ HEALTH

Births: 21/1,000 population (1991)
Deaths: 6/1,000 population (1991)
Infant Mortality: 9 deaths/1,000 live births (1991)
Life Expectancy at Birth: 75 years male, 78 years female (1992)
No. of Physicians: 29/10,000 population (1990)

■ EDUCATION

Govt. Expenditure: 10.39% of govt. expenditure (1991)
Literacy: 96.4% (1992)

■ COMMUNICATIONS

Daily newspapers: 30 (1992)
Televisions: 265.5/1,000 inhabitants (1992)
Radios: 468/1,000 inhabitants (1992)
Telephones: 50.11/100 inhabitants (1992)

■ TRANSPORTATION

Motor Vehicles: 944,152; 786,266 passenger cars (1988)
Roads: 4,736 km paved
Railway: 532 km
Air Traffic: 2,047,000 passengers carried (1991)
Airports: 8

Canadian Embassy: 220 Hayarkon St, Tel Aviv, 63405; mailing address: P.O. Box 6410, Tel Aviv 61063, Israel. Tel: (011-972-3) 527-2929. Fax: (011-972-3) 527-2333
Embassy in Canada: Embassy of Israel, 50 O'Connor St, Ste 1005, Ottawa ON K1P 6L2. Tel: (613) 237-6450. Fax: (613) 237-8865.

Italy

Long-Form Name: Italian Republic
Capital: Rome
Population: 57,782,000 (1992)

■ GEOGRAPHY

Area: 301,270 sq. km; includes Sardinia and Sicily
Coastline: 4,996 km
Climate: predominantly Mediterranean; Alpine in far north; hot, dry in south
Environment: regional risks include landslides, mudflows, snowslides, earthquakes, volcanic eruptions, flooding, pollution; land sinkage in Venice; serious air and water pollution
Terrain: mostly rugged and mountainous; some plains, coastal lowlands
Land Use: 32% arable; 10% permanent; 17% meadows; 22% forest; 19% other
Location: S Europe, bordering on Adriatic Sea, Mediterranean Sea

■ PEOPLE

Nationality: Italian
Ethnic Groups: primarily Italian but population includes small clusters of German-, French- and Slovene-Italians in the north and Albanian-Italians in the south; Sicilians; Sardinians
Languages: Italian; parts of Trentino-Alto Adige region are predominantly German-speaking; significant French-speaking minority in Valle d'Aosta region; Slovene-speaking minority in the Trieste-Gorizia area
Religions: almost 100% nominally Roman Catholic
Marriages: 5.5 (per 1,000) (1988)
Divorces: 0.4 (per 1,000) (1988)

■ GOVERNMENT

Leader(s): Pres. Oscar Luigi Scalfaro, Prime Min. Carlo Azeglio Chiampi
Government Type: republic
Administrative Divisions: 20 regions
Independence: Mar. 17, 1861, Kingdom of Italy proclaimed
National Holiday: Anniversary of the Republic, June 2

■ ECONOMY

Overview: country is divided into a developed industrial north, and an undeveloped agricultural south; must curb pollution and improve communications system; must adjust to economic integration into the European community
GNP: $1,072.198 billion, per capita $18,580; real growth rate 2.4% (1991)
Inflation: 6.4% (1991)
Industries: machinery and transportation equipment, iron and steel, chemicals, food processing, textiles, motor vehicles

Labour Force: 23,339,000 (1992); 70.5% services, 20.4% industry, 9.1% agriculture (1989)
Unemployment: 11.0% (1990)
Agriculture: accounts for about 5% of GNP and 5% of the work force; self-sufficient in foods other than meat and dairy products; principal crops—fruits, vegetables, grapes, potatoes, sugar beets, soybeans, grain, olives
Natural Resources: mercury, potash, marble, sulphur, dwindling natural gas and crude oil reserves, fish, coal

■ FINANCE/TRADE

Currency: lira (Lit)
International Reserves Excluding Gold: $27,541 million (1992)
Gold Reserves: 66.67 million fine troy ounces (1992)
Budget: revenues $355 billion; expenditures $448 billion, including capital expenditures (1989)
Defence Expenditures: $21.31 billion (1991)
External Debt: n.a.
Exports: $169.399 billion (1991); commodities: textiles, wearing apparel, metals, transportation equipment, chemicals; partners: European Community 57%, US 9%, OPEC 4%
Imports: $183.850 billion (1991); commodities: petroleum, industrial machinery, chemicals, metals, foods, agricultural products; partners: European Community 57%, OPEC 6%, US 6%

■ HEALTH

Births: 11/1,000 population (1991)
Deaths: 10/1,000 population (1991)
Infant Mortality: 6 deaths/1,000 live births (1991)
Life Expectancy at Birth: 73 years male, 80 years female (1992)
No. of Physicians: 42.7/10,000 population (1992)

■ EDUCATION

Govt. Expenditure: 8% of government expenditure (1988)
Literacy: 97.1% (1992)

■ COMMUNICATIONS

Daily newspapers: 73 (1992)
Televisions: 422.9/1,000 inhabitants (1992)
Radios: 794/1,000 inhabitants (1992)
Telephones: 53.33/100 inhabitants (1992)

■ TRANSPORTATION

Motor Vehicles: 29,727,000; 27,300,000 passenger cars (1990)
Roads: 309,100 km paved
Railway: 19,251 km

Air Traffic: 18,910,000 passengers carried (1991)
Airports: 44

Canadian Embassy: Via G.B. de Rossi 27, 00161 Rome, Italy. Tel: (011-39-6) 841-5341. Fax: (011-39-6) 841-2479
Embassy in Canada: Embassy of Italy, 275 Slater St, 21st Flr, Ottawa ON K1P 5H9. Tel: (613) 232-2401, -2, -3.

Jamaica

Long-Form Name: Jamaica
Capital: Kingston
Population: 2,469,000 (1992)

■ GEOGRAPHY

Area: 11,425 sq. km
Coastline: 1,022 km
Climate: tropical; hot, humid; temperate interior
Environment: subject to hurricanes (especially July to Nov.); deforestation; water pollution
Terrain: mostly mountainous with narrow, discontinuous coastal plain
Land Use: 19% arable; 6% permanent; 18% meadows; 28% forest; 29% other
Location: West Indies, bordering on Caribbean Sea

■ PEOPLE

Nationality: Jamaican
Ethnic Groups: 76% African, 15% Afro-European, 3% East Indian and Afro-East Indian, 3% white, 1% Chinese and Afro-Chinese, 0.8% other
Languages: English (official), Creole
Religions: Christian (majority Anglican), Rastafarianism
Marriages: 4.3 (per 1,000) (1988)
Divorces: 0.4 (per 1,000) (1988)

■ GOVERNMENT

Leader(s): Prime Min. Percival J. Patterson, Gov. Gen. Howard Cooke
Government Type: parliamentary democracy
Administrative Divisions: 14 parishes
Independence: Aug. 6, 1962 (from UK)
National Holiday: Independence Day, first Monday in Aug.

■ ECONOMY

Overview: economy based on sugar, bauxite and tourism, and to a decreasing extent on illicit drugs
GNP: $3.365 billion, per capita $1,380; real growth rate 1.0% (1991)

Inflation: 51.1% (1991)
Industries: tourism, bauxite mining, textiles, food processing, light manufactures
Labour Force: 1,246,000 (1992); 25.3% agriculture, 11.5% industry, 63.2% services (1989)
Unemployment: 15.7% (1990)
Agriculture: accounts for about 9% of GDP, 30% of work force and 17% of exports; principal crops— sugar cane, bananas, coffee, citrus, potatoes and vegetables; not self-sufficient in grain, meat and dairy products
Natural Resources: bauxite, gypsum, limestone

■ FINANCE/TRADE

Currency: Jamaican dollar ($J)
International Reserves Excluding Gold: $151 million (1992)
Gold Reserves: none (1991)
Budget: revenues $1.0 billion; expenditures $1.1 billion, including capital expenditures $197 million (1990)
Defence Expenditures: $32.52 million (1990)
External Debt: $4.4 billion (1989)
Exports: $1.145 billion (1991); commodities: bauxite, alumina, sugar, bananas; partners: US 40%, UK, Canada, Trinidad and Tobago, Norway
Imports: $1.799 billion (1991); commodities: petroleum, machinery, food, consumer goods, construction goods; partners: US 46%, UK, Venezuela, Canada, Japan, Trinidad and Tobago

■ HEALTH

Births: 24/1,000 population (1991)
Deaths: 6/1,000 population (1991)
Infant Mortality: 18 deaths/1,000 live births (1991)
Life Expectancy at Birth: 71 years male, 75 years female (1992)
No. of Physicians: 4.9/10,000 population (1992)

■ EDUCATION

Govt. Expenditure: 12.9% of govt. expenditure (1989)
Literacy: 98.2% (1992)

■ COMMUNICATIONS

Daily newspapers: 4 (1992)
Televisions: 123.5/1,000 inhabitants (1992)
Radios: 409/1,000 inhabitants (1992)
Telephones: 7.13/100 inhabitants (1992)

■ TRANSPORTATION

Motor Vehicles: 112,000; 95,000 passenger cars (1990)
Roads: 17,550 km; 2,267 km paved

Railway: 310 km
Air Traffic: 894,000 passengers carried (1991)
Airports: 6

Canadian Embassy: The Canadian High Commission, Royal Bank Bldg, 30-36 Knutsford Blvd, Kingston 5; mailing address: The Canadian High Commission, P.O. Box 1500, Kingston 10, Jamaica, WI. Tel: (809) 926-1500. Fax: (809) 926-1702
Embassy in Canada: Jamaican High Commission, Standard Life Bldg., 275 Slater St, Ste 800, Ottawa ON K1P 5H9. Tel: (613) 233-9311, -4. Fax: (613) 233-0611.

Japan

Long-Form Name: Japan
Capital: Tokyo
Population: 124,491,000 (1992)

■ GEOGRAPHY

Area: 377,835 sq. km; includes Bonin Islands (Ogasawara-gunto), Daito-shoto, Minamijima, Okinotori-shima, Ryukyu Islands (Nansei-shoto) and Volcano Islands (Kazan-retto)
Coastline: 29,751 km
Climate: varies from tropical in south to cool temperate in north
Environment: many dormant and some active volcanoes; about 1,500 seismic occurrences (mostly tremors) every year; subject to tsunamis
Terrain: mostly rugged and mountainous
Land Use: 13% arable; 1% permanent; 1% meadows; 67% forest and woodland; 18% other
Location: E Asia, bordering on Sea of Japan, North Pacific Ocean

■ PEOPLE

Nationality: Japanese
Ethnic Groups: 99.4% Japanese, 0.6% other (mostly Korean)
Languages: Japanese
Religions: most Japanese observe both Shinto and Buddhist rites; about 16% belong to other faiths, including 0.8% Christian
Marriages: 5.7 (per 1,000) (1987)
Divorces: 1.3 (per 1,000) (1987)

■ GOVERNMENT

Leader(s): Prime Min. Morihiro Hosokawa, Emperor Tsegu no Miya Akihito
Government Type: constitutional monarchy
Administrative Divisions: 47 prefectures

Independence: 660 BC, traditional founding by Emperor Jimmu; May 3, 1947 constitutional monarchy established
National Holiday: Birthday of the Emperor, Dec. 23

■ ECONOMY

Overview: impressive economic growth and status as the third largest industrial economy in the world is due to government-industry cooperation and a strong work ethic; known for high-tech industry
GNP: $3,337.191 billion, per capita $26,920; real growth rate 4.3% (1991)
Inflation: 3.3% (1991)
Industries: metallurgy, engineering, electrical and electronic, textiles, chemicals, automobiles, fishing
Labour Force: 62,202,000 (1992); 69.2% services, 23.7% industry; 7.1% agriculture (1989)
Unemployment: 2.1% (1991)
Agriculture: accounts for 3% of GNP; highly subsidized and protected sector, with crop yields among highest in the world; main crops—rice, sugar beets, vegetables, fruit; animal products include pork, poultry, dairy and eggs; about 50% self-sufficient in food
Natural Resources: negligible mineral resources, fish

■ FINANCE/TRADE

Currency: yen (pl. yen) (¥)
International Reserves Excluding Gold: $71,263 million (1992)
Gold Reserves: 24.23 million fine troy ounces (1992)
Budget: revenues $449 billion; expenditures $532 billion, including capital expenditures $52 billion (1990)
Defence Expenditures: $28.73 billion (1990)
External Debt: n.a.
Exports: $340.483 billion (1992); commodities: manufactures 97% (including machinery 38%, motor vehicles 17%, consumer electronics 10%); partners: US 34%, Southeast Asia 22%, Western Europe 21%, Communist Countries 5%, Middle East 5%
Imports: $233.548 billion (1992); commodities: manufactures 42%, fossil fuels 30%, foodstuffs 15%, nonfuel raw materials 13%; partners: Southeast Asia 23%, US 23%, Middle East 15%, Western Europe 16%, Communist Countries 7%

■ HEALTH

Births: 10/1,000 population (1991)

Deaths: 7/1,000 population (1991)
Infant Mortality: 4 deaths/1,000 live births (1991)
Life Expectancy at Birth: 76 years male, 82 years female (1992)
No. of Physicians: 15.1/10,000 population (1992)

■ EDUCATION

Govt. Expenditure: 16.2% of government expenditure (1988)
Literacy: 99% (1992)

■ COMMUNICATIONS

Daily newspapers: 158 (1992)
Televisions: 610.4/1,000 inhabitants (1992)
Radios: 895/1,000 inhabitants (1992)
Telephones: 55.53/100 inhabitants (1992)

■ TRANSPORTATION

Motor Vehicles: 57,697,669; 34,924,172 passenger cars (1990)
Roads: 1,113,860 km; 757,560 km paved
Railway: 26,562 km
Air Traffic: 68,347,000 passengers carried (1991)
Airports: 81

Canadian Embassy: 7-3-38 Akasaka, Minato-ku, Tokyo 107, Japan. Tel: (011-81-3) 3408-2101. Fax: (011-81-3) 3470-7280
Embassy in Canada: Embassy of Japan, 255 Sussex Dr, Ottawa ON K1N 9E6. Tel: (613) 236-8541. Fax: (613) 563-9047.

Jordan

Long-Form Name: Hashemite Kingdom of Jordan
Capital: Amman
Population: 4,291,000 (1992)

■ GEOGRAPHY

Area: 89,200 sq. km
Coastline: 26 km
Climate: mostly arid desert; rainy season in west (Nov. to Apr.)
Environment: lack of natural water resources; deforestation; overgrazing; soil erosion; desertification
Terrain: mostly desert plateau in east, highland area in west; Great Rift Valley separates East and West Banks of the Jordan River
Land Use: 4% arable land; 0.5% permanent; 1% meadows; 0.5% forest; 94% other
Location: SW Asia (Near East)

■ PEOPLE

Nationality: Jordanian
Ethnic Groups: 98% Arab, 1% Circassian, 1% Armenian
Languages: Arabic (official); English widely understood among upper and middle classes
Religions: Islam (over 90% Sunni Moslem, Shia minority)
Marriages: 6.1 (per 1,000) (1987)
Divorces: 1.0 (per 1,000) (1987)

■ GOVERNMENT

Leader(s): Prime Min. Sharif Zaid Ibn Shaker, King Hussein ibn Talal I
Government Type: constitutional monarchy
Administrative Divisions: 8 governorates
Independence: May 25, 1946 (from League of Nations mandate under British administration; formerly known as Trans-Jordan)
National Holiday: Independence Day, May 25

■ ECONOMY

Overview: imports are outweighing exports and foreign aid makes up the difference; droughts are a potential threat
GNP: $3.881 billion, per capita $1,120; real growth rate 0.6% (1991)
Inflation: 8.2% (1991)
Industries: phosphate mining, petroleum refining, cement, potash, light manufacturing
Labour Force: 992,000 (1992); 10.2% agriculture, 64.2% services, 25.6% industry (1989)
Unemployment: 9–10% (Dec. 1989 est.)
Agriculture: accounts for 5% of GDP; principal products are wheat, barley, citrus fruit, tomatoes, melons, olives; livestock—sheep, goats, poultry; large net importer of food
Natural Resources: phosphates, potash, shale oil

■ FINANCE/TRADE

Currency: Jordanian dinar (JD)
International Reserves Excluding Gold: $767 million (1992)
Gold Reserves: 0.79 million fine troy ounces (1992)
Budget: revenues $1.05 billion; expenditures $1.6 billion, including capital expenditures (1991)
Defence Expenditures: $571.21 milion (1990)
External Debt: $6.486 billion (1990)
Exports: $902 million (1991); commodities: fruits and vegetables, phosphates, fertilizers; partners: Iraq, Saudi Arabia, India, Kuwait, Japan, China, Yugoslavia, Indonesia
Imports: $2.512 billion (1991); commodities: crude oil, textiles, capital goods, motor vehicles, foodstuffs; partners: European Community, US, Saudi Arabia, Japan, Turkey, Romania, China, Taiwan

■ HEALTH

Births: 46/1,000 population (1991)
Deaths: 5/1,000 population (1991)
Infant Mortality: 38 deaths/1,000 live births (1991)
Life Expectancy at Birth: 69 years male, 73 years female (1992)
No. of Physicians: 11.6/10,000 population (1992)

■ EDUCATION

Govt. Expenditure: 14.75% of govt. expenditure (1990)
Literacy: 80.1% (1992)

■ COMMUNICATIONS

Daily newspapers: 4 (1992)
Televisions: 77.2/1,000 inhabitants (1992)
Radios: 252/1,000 inhabitants (1992)
Telephones: 9.1/100 inhabitants (1992)

■ TRANSPORTATION

Motor Vehicles: 248,311; 161,884 passenger cars (1990)
Roads: 7,493 km; 5,530 km paved
Railway: 794 km
Air Traffic: 797,000 passengers carried (1991)
Airports: 3

Canadian Embassy: Pearl of Shmeisani Bldg., Shmeisani, Amman, Jordan; mailing address: P.O. Box 815403, Amman, Jordan. Tel: (011-962-6) 666-124. Fax: (011-962-6) 689-227
Embassy in Canada: Embassy of the Hashemite Kingdom of Jordan, 100 Bronson Ave, Ste 701, Ottawa ON K1R 6G8. Tel: (613) 238-8090.

Kazakhstan

Long-Form Name: Republic of Kazakhstan
Capital: Alma-Ata
Population: 17,048,000 (1992)

■ GEOGRAPHY

Area: 2,717,300 sq. km
Coastline:
Climate: dry desert climate; hot summers and cold winters
Environment: drought and desertification; lack of fresh water
Terrain: desert and steppe

Land Use: 30% cultivated; remainder predominantly grazing land
Location: C Asia, bordering on Caspian Sea

■ PEOPLE

Nationality: Kazakh
Ethnic Groups: 37.8% Russian, 39.7% Kazakh, 5.4% Ukrainian, 5.8% German, 2% Uzbeks, 2% Tatars; population includes over 100 nationalities
Languages: Kazakh (official), Russian, German, Ukrainian
Religions: primarily Sunni Muslim and Eastern Orthodox
Marriages: n.a.
Divorces: n.a.

■ GOVERNMENT

Leader(s): President Nursultan A. Nazarbayev, Premier Sergei Tereshchenko
Government Type: in transition to republic
Administrative Divisions: 19 regions
Independence: declared Dec. 16, 1991
National Holiday: n.a.

■ ECONOMY

Overview: predominantly mining and manufacturing; agriculture possible only with irrigation
GNP: $41.691 billion, $2,470 per capita; real growth rate 2.1% (1991)
Inflation: n.a.
Industries: coal refining, oil and natural gas extraction, mining
Labour Force: n.a.
Unemployment: n.a.
Agriculture: wheat, cotton, rice, vineyard and orchard crops, sheep, cattle
Natural Resources: fish, oil, natural gas, zinc, coal, lead, iron ore, rare metals, tungsten, copper, zinc, manganese

■ FINANCE/TRADE

Currency: rouble (rbl.)
International Reserves Excluding Gold: n.a.
Gold Reserves: n.a.
Budget: 1989 revenues: $14,254 million roubles
Defence Expenditures: n.a.
External Debt: n.a.
Exports: $969 million (Jan.-Sept. 1992): heat, karakul fleece, wool
Imports: $348 million (Jan.-Sept. 1992)

■ HEALTH

Births: 23.0/1,000 population (1989)
Deaths: 7.6/1,000 population (1989)

Infant Mortality: 26.0 deaths/1,000 live births (1989)
Life Expectancy at Birth: 64 years male, 73 years female (1992)
No. of Physicians: 68,000 (1989)

■ EDUCATION

Govt. Expenditure: n.a.
Literacy: n.a.

■ COMMUNICATIONS

Daily newspapers: 443 papers of all circulation types (1989)
Televisions: n.a.
Radios: n.a.
Telephones: n.a.

■ TRANSPORTATION

Motor Vehicles: n.a.
Railway: 14,460 km
Air Traffic: n.a.
Airports: n.a.

Canadian Embassy: C/o 23 Starokonyushenny Per, Moscow 12100, Russian Federation. Tel: (011-7-95) 241-5070. Fax: (011-7-95) 241-4400.

Kenya

Long-Form Name: Republic of Kenya
Capital: Nairobi
Population: 25,230,000 (1992)

■ GEOGRAPHY

Area: 582,650 sq. km
Coastline: 536 km
Climate: varies from tropical along coast to arid in interior
Environment: unique physiography supports abundant and varied wildlife of scientific and economic value; deforestation; soil erosion; desertification; glaciers on Mt. Kenya
Terrain: low plains rise to central highlands bisected by Great Rift Valley; fertile plateau in west
Land Use: 3% arable; 1% permanent; 7% meadows; 45% forest; 85% other
Location: E Africa, bordering on Indian Ocean

■ PEOPLE

Nationality: Kenyan
Ethnic Groups: 21% Kikuyu, 14% Luhya, 13% Luo, 11% Kakenjin, 11% Kamba, 6% Kisii, 6% Meru, 1% Asian, European and Arab

Languages: English and Swahili (official); Kikuyu and Luo are widely spoken, numerous indigenous languages
Religions: 25% Christianity, 6% Islam, remainder traditional
Marriages: n.a.
Divorces: n.a.

■ GOVERNMENT

Leader(s): Pres. Daniel Tarap Moi, V. Pres. George Saitoti
Government Type: republic
Administrative Divisions: 7 provinces and 1 area (Nairobi Area)
Independence: Dec. 12, 1963 (from UK; formerly known as British East Africa)
National Holiday: Independence Day, Dec. 12

■ ECONOMY

Overview: a large annual population growth and a shortage of arable land threaten economic growth; vulnerable to weather conditions
GNP: $8.505 billion, per capita $340; real growth rate 4.1% (1991)
Inflation: 14.8% (1991)
Industries: small-scale consumer goods (plastic, furniture, batteries, textiles, soap, cigarettes, flour), agricultural processing, oil refining, cement, tourism
Labour Force: 10,010,000 (1992); 81% agriculture, 6.8% industry, 12.1% services (1989)
Unemployment: n.a., but there is a high level of unemployment and underemployment
Agriculture: accounts for 30% of GDP, about 80% of the work force and over 50% of exports; cash crops include coffee, tea, sisal, pineapple; food products—corn, wheat, sugar cane, fruit, vegetables, dairy products; food output not keeping pace with population growth
Natural Resources: gold, limestone, diotomite, salt barytes, magnesite, feldspar, sapphires, fluorspar, garnets, wildlife

■ FINANCE/TRADE

Currency: Kenya shilling (KSh)
International Reserves Excluding Gold: $58 million (1992)
Gold Reserves: 0.08 million fine troy ounces (1992)
Budget: revenues $2.0 billion; expenditures $2.3 billion, including capital expenditures (1989)
Defence Expenditures: $275.42 million (1988)
External Debt: $4.810 billion (1990)
Exports: $1.125 billion (1991); commodities: coffee 20%, tea 18%, manufactures 15%, petroleum products 10%; partners: Western Europe 45%, Africa 22%, Far East 10%, US 4%, Middle East 3%
Imports: $1.802 billion (1991); commodities: machinery and transportation equipment 36%, raw materials 33%, fuels and lubricants 20%, food and consumer goods 11%; partners: Western Europe 49%, Far East 20%, Middle East 19%, US 7%

■ HEALTH

Births: 45/1,000 population (1991)
Deaths: 8/1,000 population (1991)
Infant Mortality: 69 deaths/1,000 live births (1991)
Life Expectancy at Birth: 59 years male, 63 years female (1992)
No. of Physicians: 1.0/10,000 population (1992)

■ EDUCATION

Govt. Expenditure: 19.89% of government expenditure (1990)
Literacy: 69.0% (1992)

■ COMMUNICATIONS

Daily newspapers: 5 (1992)
Televisions: 8.6/1,000 inhabitants (1992)
Radios: 95/1,000 inhabitants (1992)
Telephones: 1.54/100 inhabitants (1992)

■ TRANSPORTATION

Motor Vehicles: 300,000; 150,000 passenger cars (1990)
Roads: 65,840 km; 8,157 km paved
Railway: 3,088 km
Air Traffic: 760,000 passengers carried (1991)
Airports: 152

Canadian Embassy: The Canadian High Commission, Comcraft House, Hailé Sélassie Ave, Nairobi; mailing address: The Canadian High Commission, P.O. Box 30481, Nairobi, Kenya. Tel: (011-254-2). Fax: (011-254-2) 214-804/226-987
Embassy in Canada: High Commission for the Republic of Kenya, 415 Laurier Ave E, Ottawa ON K1N 6R4. Tel: (613) 563-1773, -4, -5, -6. Fax: (613) 233-6599.

Kiribati

Long-Form Name: Republic of Kiribati
Capital: Tarawa
Population: 74,000 (1992)

■ GEOGRAPHY

Area: 717 sq. km
Coastline: 1,143 km
Climate: tropical; marine, hot and humid, moderated by trade winds
Environment: typhoons can occur any time, but usually Nov. to Mar.; 10 of the 33 islands are inhabited
Terrain: mostly low-lying coral atolls surrounded by extensive reefs
Land Use: negligible arable; 51% permanent; 0% meadows; 3% forest; 46% other
Location: SW Pacific Ocean

■ PEOPLE

Nationality: Kiribatian
Ethnic Groups: Micronesian
Languages: English (official), I-Kiribati
Religions: 52% Roman Catholic, 41% Protestant (Congregational), some Seventh-Day Adventist and Baha'i
Marriages: n.a.
Divorces: n.a.

■ GOVERNMENT

Leader(s): Pres. Teatao Teannaki, V. Pres. Taomaki T. Iuta
Government Type: republic
Administrative Divisions: 3 units
Independence: July 12, 1979 (from UK; formerly known as Gilbert Islands)
National Holiday: Independence Day, July 12

■ ECONOMY

Overview: the economy has fluctuated widely in recent years and copra production and a good fish catch have provided a boost
GNP: $53 million, per capita $750; real growth rate 2.4% (1991)
Inflation: 3.1% (1988)
Industries: fishing, handicrafts
Labour Force: 40,000 (1992)
Unemployment: 2% (1985); considerable underemployment
Agriculture: accounts for 30% of GDP (including fishing); copra and fish contribute 95% to exports; subsistence farming predominates; food crops—taro, breadfruit, sweet potatoes, vegetables; not self-sufficient in food
Natural Resources: tuna fishing

■ FINANCE/TRADE

Currency: Australian dollar ($A)
International Reserves Excluding Gold: n.a.
Gold Reserves: n.a.

Budget: revenues $29.9 million; expenditures $16.3 million, including capital expenditures of $14.0 million (1990)
Defence Expenditures: n.a.
External Debt: $2 billion (1987)
Exports: $5.1 million (1988); commodities: fish 55%, copra 42%; partners: European Community 20%, Marshall Islands 12%, US 8%, American Samoa 4%
Imports: $21.5 million (1988); commodities: foodstuffs, fuel, transportation equipment; partners: Australia 39%, Japan 21%, New Zealand 6%, UK 6%, US 3%

■ HEALTH

Births: 33/1,000 population (1991)
Deaths: 12/1,000 population (1991)
Infant Mortality: 63 deaths/1,000 live births (1991)
Life Expectancy at Birth: 52 years male, 58 years female (1991)
No. of Physicians: 5.1/10,000 population (1992)

■ EDUCATION

Govt. Expenditure: 17.0% of government expenditure (1989)
Literacy: 90%

■ COMMUNICATIONS

Daily newspapers: 0 (1989)
Televisions: n.a.
Radios: 225/1,000 inhabitants (1989)
Telephones: n.a.

■ TRANSPORTATION

Motor Vehicles: n.a.
Railway: n.a.
Air Traffic: 25,000 passengers carried (1991)
Airports: 22

Canadian Embassy: The Canadian High Commission to Kiribati, C/o The Canadian High Commission, 61 Molesworth St, 3rd Fl, Wellington; mailing address: P.O. Box 12-049, Thorndon, Wellington, New Zealand

North Korea

Long-Form Name: Democratic People's Republic of Korea
Capital: Pyongyang (formerly Keijo)
Population: 22,618,000 (1992)

■ GEOGRAPHY

Area: 120,540 sq. km
Coastline: 2,495 km

Climate: temperate with rainfall concentrated in summer

Environment: isolated mountainous interior, nearly inaccessible and sparsely populated; late spring droughts often followed by severe flooding

Terrain: mostly hills and mountains separated by deep, narrow valleys; coastal plains wide in west, discontinuous in east

Land Use: 18% arable; 1% permanent; negligible meadows; 74% forest; 7% other

Location: E Asia, bordering on Yellow Sea, Sea of Japan

■ PEOPLE

Nationality: Korean
Ethnic Groups: Korean (racially homogeneous)
Languages: Korean
Religions: Buddhism and Confucianism; Daoism, Shamanism, Chonodogyu
Marriages: n.a.
Divorces: n.a.

■ GOVERNMENT

Leader(s): Premier Kang Song San, Pres. Kim Il Sung
Government Type: Communist state; one-man rule
Administrative Divisions: 9 provinces and 4 special cities
Independence: Sept. 9, 1948
National Holiday: Independence Day, Sept. 9

■ ECONOMY

Overview: a command economy which is almost completely socialized, with state-owned industry, and collectivization of agriculture.
GNP: $28 billion, per capita $1,240; real growth rate 3% (1989)
Inflation: n.a.
Industries: machine building, military products, electric power, chemicals, mining, metallurgy, textiles, food processing
Labour Force: 10,470,000 (1992); 42.8% agricultural, 26.9% services, 30.3% industry
Unemployment: officially none
Agriculture: accounts for about 25% of GNP and 36% of work force; principal crops—rice, corn, potatoes, soybeans, pulses; livestock and livestock products—cattle, hogs, pork, eggs; not self-sufficient in grain
Natural Resources: coal, lead, tungsten, zinc, graphite, magnesite, iron ore, copper, gold, pyrites, salt, fluorspar, hydroelectricity

■ FINANCE/TRADE

Currency: won (pl. won) (W)
International Reserves Excluding Gold: n.a.
Gold Reserves: n.a.
Budget: revenues $15.6 billion; expenditures $15.6 billion, including capital expenditures (1989)
Defence Expenditures: $5.23 billion (1990)
External Debt: $2.5 billion (1989)
Exports: $2.4 billion (1988); commodities: minerals, metallurgical products, agricultural products, manufactures; partners: USSR, China, Japan, Germany, Hong Kong, Singapore
Imports: $3.1 billion (1988); commodities: petroleum, machinery and equipment, coking coal, grain; partners: USSR, Japan, China, Germany, Hong Kong, Singapore

■ HEALTH

Births: 24/1,000 population (1991)
Deaths: 6/1,000 population (1991)
Infant Mortality: 30 deaths/1,000 live births (1991)
Life Expectancy at Birth: 66 years male, 72 years female (1992)
No. of Physicians: 23.9/10,000 population (1990)

■ EDUCATION

Govt. Expenditure: n.a.
Literacy: 95%

■ COMMUNICATIONS

Daily newspapers: 11 (1986)
Televisions: 14.0/1,000 inhabitants (1989)
Radios: 117/1,000 inhabitants (1989)
Telephones: n.a.

■ TRANSPORTATION

Motor Vehicles: 180,000 motor vehicles (1982)
Roads: 20,250 km; 360 km paved
Railway: 8,510 km
Air Traffic: 223,000 passengers carried (1991)
Airports: 7

Canadian Embassy: none

South Korea

Long-Form Name: Republic of Korea
Capital: Seoul
Population: 44,163,000 (1992)

■ GEOGRAPHY

Area: 98,480 sq. km
Coastline: 2,413 km

Climate: temperate, with rainfall heavier in summer than winter
Environment: occasional typhoons bring high winds and floods; earthquakes in southwest; air pollution in large cities
Terrain: mostly hilly and mountains; wide coastal plains in west and south
Land Use: 21% arable; 1% permanent; 1% meadows; 67% forest; 10% other
Location: E Asia, bordering on Yellow Sea, Sea of Japan

■ PEOPLE

Nationality: Korean
Ethnic Groups: homogeneous; small Chinese minority (about 20,000)
Languages: Korean; English widely taught in high school
Religions: Confucianism, Christianity, Buddhism, Daoism
Marriages: 8.6 (per 1,000) (1986)
Divorces: 0.8 (per 1,000) (1986)

■ GOVERNMENT

Leader(s): Prime Min. Hyun Soong Jong, Pres. Roh Tae Woo
Government Type: republic
Administrative Divisions: 9 provinces and 6 special cities
Independence: Aug. 15, 1948
National Holiday: Independence Day, Aug. 15

■ ECONOMY

Overview: dynamic growth is attributed to the planned development of an export-oriented economy in a strongly entrepreneurial society; labor unrest threatens to hurt its record of noninflationary growth
GNP: $274.464 billion, per capita $6,340; real growth rate 10.0% (1991)
Inflation: 9.7% (1991)
Industries: textiles, clothing, footwear, food processing, chemicals, steel, electronics, automobile production, ship building
Labour Force: 18,660,000 (1992); 55.5% services, 26.7% industry, 17.8% agriculture (1989)
Unemployment: 2.3% (1992)
Agriculture: accounts for 11% of GNP and 21% of work force (including fishing and forestry); main crops—rice, root crops, barley, vegetables, fruit; livestock and livestock products—cattle, hogs, chickens, milk, eggs; self-sufficient in food, except for wheat
Natural Resources: coal, tungsten, graphite, molybdenum, lead, hydroelectricity

■ FINANCE/TRADE

Currency: won (pl. won) (W)
International Reserves Excluding Gold: $17,121 million (1992)
Gold Reserves: 0.32 million fine troy ounces (1992)
Budget: revenues $38 billion; expenditures $38 billion, including capital expenditures (1991)
Defence Expenditures: $10.62 billion (1990)
External Debt: $17.814 billion (1990)
Exports: $71.898 billion (1991); commodities: textiles, clothing, electronic and electrical equipment, footwear, machinery, steel, automobiles, ships, fish; partners: US 33%, Japan 21%
Imports: $ 81.557 billion (1991); commodities: machinery, electronics and electronic equipment, oil, steel, transport equipment, textiles, organic chemicals, grains; partners: Japan 28%, US 25%

■ HEALTH

Births: 15/1,000 population (1991)
Deaths: 6/1,000 population (1991)
Infant Mortality: 23 deaths/1,000 live births (1991)
Life Expectancy at Birth: 67 years male, 75 years female (1992)
No. of Physicians: 8.7/10,000 population (1992)

■ EDUCATION

Govt. Expenditure: 16.2% of govt. expenditure (1992)
Literacy: over 96.3% (1992)

■ COMMUNICATIONS

Daily newspapers: 39 (1992)
Televisions: 207.3/1,000 inhabitants (1992)
Radios: 1,003/1,000 inhabitants (1992)
Telephones: 33.49/100 inhabitants (1992)

■ TRANSPORTATION

Motor Vehicles: 3,394,803; 2,074,922 passenger cars (1990)
Roads: 55,641 km; 34,173 km paved
Railway: 3,142 km
Air Traffic: 16,908,000 passengers carried (1991)
Airports: 12

Canadian Embassy: Flr 10, Kolon Building, 45 Mugyo-Dong, Jung-Ku, Seoul 100-170; mailing address: P.O. Box 6299, Seoul 100-662 Korea. Tel: (011-82-2) 753-2605. Fax: (011-82-2) 755-0686

Embassy in Canada: Embassy of the Republic of Korea, 151 Slater St, Flr 5, Ottawa ON K1P 5H3. Tel: (613) 232-1715, -6, -7. Fax: (613) 232-0928.

Kuwait

Data does not reflect the dramatic change in economic, political, and social conditions as a result of the 1991 Gulf War.

Long-Form Name: State of Kuwait
Capital: Kuwait City
Population: 1,970,000 (1992)

■ GEOGRAPHY

Area: 17,820 sq. km
Coastline: 499 km
Climate: dry desert; intensely hot summers; short, cool winters
Environment: some of world's largest and most sophisticated desalination facilities provide most of the water; air and water pollution; desertification
Terrain: flat to slightly undulating desert plain
Land Use: negligible arable; 0% permanent; 8% meadows; negligible forest; 92% other
Location: SW Asia (Middle East), bordering on Persian Gulf

■ PEOPLE

Nationality: Kuwaiti
Ethnic Groups: 28% Kuwaiti, 39% other Arab, 9% South Asian, 4% Iranian, 20% other
Languages: Arabic (official); Kurdish, Farsi, English (commercial) widely spoken
Religions: 95% Moslem(25% Shi'a, 70% Sunni), 15% Christian, Hindu, Parsi and other
Marriages: 5.3 (per 1,000) (1987)
Divorces: 1.4 (per 1,000) (1987)

■ GOVERNMENT

Leader(s): Prime Min. Sa'd al-'Abdallah al'Salim al-Sabah; Amir: Shaikh Jabir al-Ahmad al-Jabir al-Sabah
Government Type: nominal constitutional monarchy
Administrative Divisions: 4 governorates
Independence: June 19, 1961 (from UK)
National Holiday: National Day, Feb. 25

■ ECONOMY

Overview: the oil-dominated economy has been heavily dependent on foreign labor (about 80% of the work force); Iraq's invasion and the Gulf War have probably drastically affected the economy, as will calls for democratic reforms to this monarchic government
GNP: $20.5 billion, per capita $10,500; real growth rate 5% (1988)
Inflation: 3.3% (1989)
Industries: petroleum, petrochemicals, desalination, food processing, salt, construction
Labour Force: 835,000 (1992); 45% services, 20% construction, 12% trade, 9% manufacturing, 3% finance and real estate, 2% agriculture, 2% power and water, 1% mining and quarrying
Unemployment: 0% (1990)
Agriculture: virtually none; dependent on imports for food; about 75% of potable water must be distilled (adversely affected by the Gulf War) or imported
Natural Resources: petroleum, fish, shrimp, natural gas

■ FINANCE/TRADE

Currency: dinar (KD)
International Reserves Excluding Gold: $5,147 million (1992)
Gold Reserves: 2.54 million fine troy ounces (1992)
Budget: revenues $7.1 billion; expenditures $10.5 billion, including capital expenditures of $3.1 billion (1988)
Defence Expenditures: $1.504 billion (1990)
External Debt: $7.2 billion (1989)
Exports: $11.476 billion (1989); commodities: oil 90%; partners: Japan, Italy, Germany, US
Imports: $6.295 billion (1989); commodities: food, construction material, vehicles and parts, clothing; partners: Japan, US, Germany, UK

■ HEALTH

Births: 29/1,000 population (1991)
Deaths: 2/1,000 population (1991)
Infant Mortality: 15 deaths/1,000 live births (1991)
Life Expectancy at Birth: 72 years male, 76 years female (1992)
No. of Physicians: 15.6/10,000 population (1992)

■ EDUCATION

Govt. Expenditure: 12.1% of government expenditure (1987)
Literacy: 73.0% (1992)

■ COMMUNICATIONS

Daily newspapers: 8 (1992)
Televisions: 280.6/1,000 inhabitants (1992)
Radios: 337/1,000 inhabitants (1992)
Telephones: 18.92/100 inhabitants (1992)

■ TRANSPORTATION

Motor Vehicles: 630,000; 490,000 passenger cars (1990)
Roads: 4,277 km; paved km n.a.
Railway: n.a.
Air Traffic: 840,000 passengers carried (1991)
Airports: 1

Canadian Embassy: Da'Aiah - Block 4, Al-Mutawakel St, Kuwait City; mailing address: P.O. Box 25281, Safat, Kuwait City, 13113, Kuwait. Tel: (011-965) 256-3025. Fax: (011-965) 256-4167

Kyrgyzstan

Long-Form Name: Republic of Kyrgyzstan
Capital: Bishkek
Population: 4,518,000 (1992)

■ GEOGRAPHY

Area: 198,500 sq. km
Coastline: none; landlocked
Climate: glacial Alpine; moderate in valley regions
Environment: frequent severe earthquakes
Terrain: mountainous; 75% of land covered by snow and glaciers
Land Use: land is cultivated mainly in valleys, less than 25%
Location: C Asia

■ PEOPLE

Nationality: Kirghiz
Ethnic Groups: 52.4% Kirghiz, 21.5% Russian, 12.9% Uzbeks, 2.5% Ukrainian, 2.4% German, 1.6% Tatars
Languages: Kirghiz (official), Russian, Dungan
Religions: predominantly Sunni Muslim and Eastern Orthodox
Marriages: n.a.
Divorces: n.a.

■ GOVERNMENT

Leader(s): Pres. Askar Akayev; Chairman, Supreme Soviet: Medetkan Sherimkulov
Government Type: in transition to republic
Administrative Divisions: 6 regions
Independence: Sept. 1991
National Holiday: n.a.

■ ECONOMY

Overview: over 500 large, modern, industrial enterprises inc. sugar refineries, tanneries, cotton and wool-cleansing works, flour mills, tobacco factories; agricultural sector of the economy predominates
GNP: $6.9 billion, $1,550 per capita; real growth rate 4.1% (1991)
Inflation: n.a.
Industries: electronics, electrical engineering, silk making
Labour Force: n.a.
Unemployment: n.a.
Agriculture: wheat, barley, beets, cotton, fruit, vegetables, yaks, potatoes, livestock (mainly sheep); irrigation required
Natural Resources: mercury, antimony, zinc, tungsten deposits

■ FINANCE/TRADE

Currency: rouble (rbl.)
International Reserves Excluding Gold: n.a.
Gold Reserves: n.a.
Budget: 1989 revenues: 2,692 million roubles
Defence Expenditures: n.a.
External Debt: n.a.
Exports: agricultural products, antimony, silk, carpets, non-ferrous metals, electrical equipment
Imports: n.a.

■ HEALTH

Births: 30.4/1,000 population (1989)
Deaths: 7.2/1,000 population (1989)
Infant Mortality: 32.4 deaths/1,000 live births (1989)
Life Expectancy at Birth: 64 years male, 72 years female (1992)
No. of Physicians: 15,800 (1989)

■ EDUCATION

Govt. Expenditure: n.a.
Literacy: n.a.

■ COMMUNICATIONS

Daily newspapers: 122 papers of all circulation types (1989)
Televisions: n.a.
Radios: n.a.
Telephones: n.a.

■ TRANSPORTATION

Motor Vehicles: n.a.
Roads: n.a.
Railway: 370 km
Air Traffic: n.a.
Airports: 1

Canadian Embassy: C/o 23 Starokonyushenny Per, Moscow 12100, Russian Federation. Tel: (011-7-95) 241-5070. Fax: (011-7-95) 241-4400.

Representative to Canada: C/o Ambassador Designate of the Republic of Kyrgyzstan, 1511 K St NW, Ste 705, Washington DC 20005 USA. Tel: (202) 347-3732. Fax: (202) 347-3718

Laos

Long-Form Name: Lao People's Democratic Republic
Capital: Vientiane
Population: 4,469,000 (1992)

■ GEOGRAPHY

Area: 236,800 sq. km
Coastline: none: landlocked
Climate: tropical monsoon; rainy season (May to Nov.); dry season (Dec. to Apr.)
Environment: deforestation; soil erosion; subject to floods
Terrain: mostly rugged mountains; some plains and plateaus
Land Use: 4% arable land; negligible permanent crops; 3% meadows; 58% forest; 35% other
Location: SE Asia

■ PEOPLE

Nationality: Laotian
Ethnic Groups: 99% Laotian; Vietnamese, Chinese, European, Indian and Pakistani minorities
Languages: Lao (official), French, tribal languages
Religions: 85% Buddhist, 15% animist and other
Marriages: n.a.
Divorces: n.a.

■ GOVERNMENT

Leader(s): Pres. Nouhak Phoumsavan, Prime Min. Khamtai Siphandon
Government Type: Communist state
Administrative Divisions: 16 provinces and 1 municipality (Vientiane)
Independence: July 19, 1949 (from France)
National Holiday: National Day (proclamation of the Lao People's Democratic Republic), Dec. 2

■ ECONOMY

Overview: while traditionally a Communist centrally-planned economy with government ownership and control of productive enterprises, the government is now decentralizing control and encouraging some private enterprise; heavily dependent on foreign aid
GNP: $965 million, per capita $230; real growth rate 4.2% (1991)
Inflation: 35% (1989 est.)

Industries: tin mining, timber, electric power, agricultural processing
Labour Force: 2,240,000 (1992) 75.7% agriculture, 7.1% industry, 17.2% services (1989)
Unemployment: 15% (1989 est.)
Agriculture: accounts for 60% of GDP and employs most of the labor force; subsistence farming predominates; normally self-sufficient; principal crops—rice (80% of cultivated land), potatoes, vegetables, coffee, sugar cane, cotton
Natural Resources: timber, hydroelectricity, gypsum, tin, gold, gemstones

■ FINANCE/TRADE

Currency: new kip (NK)
International Reserves Excluding Gold: $43 million (1990)
Gold Reserves: n.a.
Budget: revenues $83 million; expenditures $188.5 million, including capital expenditures of $94 million (1990)
Defence Expenditures: $18.94 million (1989)
External Debt: $1.053 billion (1990)
Exports: $57.5 million (1989); commodities: electricity, wood products, coffee, tin; partners: Thailand, Malaysia, Vietnam, USSR, US
Imports: $219 million (1989); commodities: food, fuel oil, consumer goods, manufactures; partners: Thailand, USSR, Japan, France, Vietnam

■ HEALTH

Births: 37/1,000 population (1991)
Deaths: 15/1,000 population (1991)
Infant Mortality: 124 deaths/1,000 live births (1991)
Life Expectancy at Birth: 48 years male, 51 years female (1992)
No. of Physicians: 7.3/10,000 population (1992)

■ EDUCATION

Govt. Expenditure: 6.6% of government expenditure (1986)
Literacy: 83.9% (1992)

■ COMMUNICATIONS

Daily newspapers: 3 (1992)
Televisions: 5.0/1,000 inhabitants (1992)
Radios: 124/1,000 inhabitants (1992)
Telephones: 0.23/100 inhabitants (1992)

■ TRANSPORTATION

Motor Vehicles: 22,000; 18,000 passenger cars (1990)
Roads: 28,180 km; 1,895 km paved
Railway: n.a.

Air Traffic: 115,000 passengers carried (1991)
Airports: 13

Canadian Embassy: The Canadian Embassy to Laos, 12th Floor, Boonmitr Bldg., 138 Silom Rd, Bangkok 10500; mailing address: P.O. Box 2090, Bangkok 10500, Thailand. Tel: (011-66-2) 237-4126. Fax: (011-66-2) 236-6463
Representative to Canada: c/o Embassy of the People's Democratic Republic of Laos, 2222 S St NW, Washington DC 20008 USA. Fax: (202) 332-4923

Latvia

Long-Form Name: Republic of Latvia
Capital: Riga
Population: 2,679,000 (1992)

■ GEOGRAPHY

Area: 63,700 sq. km
Coastline: 472 km
Climate: mild with moderate rainfall
Environment: n.a.
Terrain: hilly, forested land with many lakes and shallow valleys
Land Use: 40% forest and woodland; 60% cultivated
Location: NE Europe, bordering on Baltic Sea

■ PEOPLE

Nationality: Latvian or Lett
Ethnic Groups: 54% Latvian, 33% Russian, 5% Belorussian, 3% Ukrainian, 3% Poles, 2% other
Languages: Latvian (official), Russian
Religions: Lutheran, Catholic, Russian Orthodox
Marriages: n.a.
Divorces: n.a.

■ GOVERNMENT

Leader(s): Pres. Anatolijs Gorbunovs, Premier Ivars Godmanis
Government Type: in transition to republic
Administrative Divisions: n.a.
Independence: declared Sept. 6, 1991
National Holiday: Independence Day, Nov. 18

■ ECONOMY

Overview: manufacturing accounts for 75% of economic production, agriculture less than 20%
GNP: $9.913 billion, per capita $3,410; real growth rate 3.4%
Inflation: n.a.
Industries: manufacturing of railroad cars, paper, woolen goods, electronics and engineering, food processing

Labour Force: 1,470,000 (1989)
Unemployment: n.a.
Agriculture: poor soil hinders agriculture products inc. grain, beets, potatoes, cattle and dairy farming, poultry, fishing
Natural Resources: forests, peat deposits

■ FINANCE/TRADE

Currency: rouble (rbl.)
International Reserves Excluding Gold: n.a.
Gold Reserves: n.a.
Budget: n.a.
Defence Expenditures: n.a.
External Debt: n.a.
Exports: vehicles, household appliances, electric power
Imports: n.a.

■ HEALTH

Births: 14.2/1,000 population (1990)
Deaths: 13.0/1,000 population (1990)
Infant Mortality: 13.7/1,000 live births (1990)
Life Expectancy at Birth: 65 years male, 75 years female (1992)
No. of Physicians: n.a.

■ EDUCATION

Govt. Expenditure: n.a.
Literacy: n.a.

■ COMMUNICATIONS

Daily newspapers: 121 papers of all circulation types (1988)
Televisions: n.a.
Radios: n.a.
Telephones: n.a.

■ TRANSPORTATION

Motor Vehicles: n.a.
Roads: n.a.
Railway: n.a.
Air Traffic: n.a.
Airports: n.a.

Canadian Embassy: C/o The Canadian Embassy, Tegelbacken 4 (Flr 7); mailing address: P.O. Box 16129; S-103 23 Stockholm 5, Sweden. Tel: (011-46-8) 613-9900. Fax: (011-46-8) 24 24 91.
Embassy in Canada: Consulate General, 700 Bay St, Ste 1900, Toronto, ON M5G 1Z6. Tel: (416) 408-2540.

Lebanon

Long-Form Name: Lebanese Republic
Capital: Beirut

Population: 2,838,000 (1992)

■ GEOGRAPHY

Area: 10,400 sq. km
Coastline: 225 km
Climate: Mediterranean; mild to cool, wet winters with hot, dry summers
Environment: rugged terrain historically helped isolate, protect and develop numerous factional groups based on religion, clan, and ethnicity; deforestation; soil erosion; air and water pollution; desertification
Terrain: narrow coastal plain; al Biqa' separates Lebanon and Anti-Lebanon Mountains
Land Use: 21% arable; 9% permanent; 1% meadow; 8% forest; 61% other
Location: SW Asia (Near East), bordering on Mediterranean Sea

■ PEOPLE

Nationality: Lebanese
Ethnic Groups: 93% Arab, 6% Armenian, 1% other
Languages: Arabic and French (both official); Armenian, English, Kurdish
Religions: Islam 57% (Sunni, Shia and Druse), Christian 43% (mainly Maronite; also, Armenian, Greek and Syrian sects and Protestants)
Marriages: n.a.
Divorces: n.a.

■ GOVERNMENT

Leader(s): Pres. Elias Hrawi, Prime. Min. Rafiq al-Hariri
Government Type: republic
Administrative Divisions: 5 governorates
Independence: Nov. 22, 1943 (from League of Nations mandate under French administration)
National Holiday: Independence Day, Nov. 22

■ ECONOMY

Overview: factional infighting has led to deterioration of the infrastructure and disrupted normal economic activity in what used to be the centre for Middle Eastern banking; high unemployment; growing shortages; international aid is vital
GNP: $2.3 billion, per capita $700; (1989 est.)
Inflation: 60% (1989 est.)
Industries: banking, food processing, textiles, cement, oil refining, chemicals, jewelry, some metal fabricating
Labour Force: 914,000 (1992); 27.4% industry, 58.4% services, 14.3% agriculture (1989)
Unemployment: 33% (1987 est.)

Agriculture: accounts for about one-third of GDP; principal products—citrus fruits, vegetables, potatoes, olives, tobacco, hemp (hashish), sheep and goats; not self-sufficient in grain
Natural Resources: limestone, iron ore, salt; water-surplus state in a water-deficit region

■ FINANCE/TRADE

Currency: Lebanese pound (LL)
International Reserves Excluding Gold: $1,496 million (1992)
Gold Reserves: 9.22 million fine troy ounces (1992)
Budget: revenues $120 million; expenditures $1.0 billion, including capital expenditures (1990)
Defence Expenditures: $140 million (1990)
External Debt: $545 million (1989)
Exports:
Imports: $2,457 billion (1989); commodities: n.a.; partners: Italy 14%, France 12%, US 6%, Turkey 5%, Saudi Arabia 3%

■ HEALTH

Births: 28/1,000 population (1991)
Deaths: 7/1,000 population (1991)
Infant Mortality: 48 deaths/1,000 live births (1991)
Life Expectancy at Birth: 66 years male, 70 years female (1992)
No. of Physicians: 14.9/10,000 population (1990)

■ EDUCATION

Govt. Expenditure: 16.8% of government expenditure (1985)
Literacy: 80.1% (1992)

■ COMMUNICATIONS

Daily newspapers: 10 (1992)
Televisions: 326.5/1,000 inhabitants (1992)
Radios: 834/1,000 inhabitants (1992)
Telephones: n.a.

■ TRANSPORTATION

Motor Vehicles: 300,000 passenger cars (1985)
Roads: 7,114 km; 5,690 km paved
Railway: 226 km
Air Traffic: 536,000 passengers carried (1991)
Airports: 1

Canadian Embassy: C/o Pearl of Shmeisani Bldg, Shmeisani, Amman, Jordan; mailing address: P.O. Box 815403, Amman, Jordan. Tel: (011-962-6) 666-124. Fax: (011-962-6) 689-227
Embassy in Canada: Embassy of Lebanon, 640 Lyon St S, Ottawa ON K1S 3Z5. Tel: (613) 236-5825, -55. Fax: (613) 232-1609.

Lesotho

Long-Form Name: Kingdom of Lesotho
Capital: Maseru
Population: 1,836,000 (1992)

GEOGRAPHY

Area: 30,350 sq. km
Coastline: none: landlocked
Climate: temperate; cool to cold, dry winters; hot, wet summers
Environment: population pressure forcing settlement in marginal agricultural areas results in overgrazing, severe soil erosion, soil exhaustion; desertification
Terrain: mostly highland with some plateaus, hills and mountains
Land Use: 10% arable; 0% permanent; 66% meadows; 0% forest; 24% other
Location: S Africa

PEOPLE

Nationality: Mosotho/Basotho (pl.)
Ethnic Groups: 99.7% Sotho; 1,600 Europeans, 800 Asians
Languages: Sesotho (southern Sotho) and English (official); also Zulu and Xhosa
Religions: 90% Christian, indigenous beliefs
Marriages: n.a.
Divorces: n.a.

GOVERNMENT

Leader(s): Prime Min. Ntsu Mokhele
Government Type: constitutional monarchy
Administrative Divisions: 10 districts
Independence: Oct. 4, 1966 (from UK: formerly known as Basutoland)
National Holiday: Independence Day, Oct. 4

ECONOMY

Overview: the economy is hampered by the geography of the country (small, landlocked and mountainous) and the lack of natural resources other than water; subsistence farming is the main occupation; labourers in South Africa make remittances
GNP: $1.053 billion, per capita $580; real growth rate 2.7% (1991)
Inflation: 15% (1989)
Industries: light manufacturing, milling, canning, leather, jute production, textiles, clothing, light engineering
Labour Force: 810,000 (1992); 23.3% agriculture, 33.1% industry, 43.6% services (1989)
Unemployment: 23% (1988)

Agriculture: very primitive, mostly subsistence farming and livestock; principal crops are corn, wheat, pulses, sorghum and barley
Natural Resources: some diamonds and other minerals, water, agricultural and grazing land

FINANCE/TRADE

Currency: maloti (M)
International Reserves Excluding Gold: $189 million (1992)
Gold Reserves: n.a.
Budget: revenues $280 million; expenditures $288 million, including capital expenditures (1992 estimate)
Defence Expenditures: $31.56 million (1986)
External Debt: $372 million (1989)
Exports: $55 million (1989); commodities: wool, mohair, wheat, cattle, peas, beans, corn, hides, skins, baskets; partners: South Africa 87%, European Community 10%
Imports: $526 million (1989); commodities: corn, building materials, clothing, vehicles, machinery, medicines, petroleum, oil and lubricants; partners: South Africa 87%, European Community 10%

HEALTH

Births: 36/1,000 population (1991)
Deaths: 10/1,000 population (1991)
Infant Mortality: 78 deaths/1,000 live births (1991)
Life Expectancy at Birth: 53 years male, 62 years female (1992)
No. of Physicians: 0.5/10,000 population (1992)

EDUCATION

Govt. Expenditure: 21.93% of government expenditure (1990)
Literacy: 58.6% (1992)

COMMUNICATIONS

Daily newspapers: 4 (1992)
Televisions: 2.9/1,000 inhabitants (1992)
Radios: 68/1,000 inhabitants (1992)
Telephones: 0.9/100 inhabitants (1992)

TRANSPORTATION

Motor Vehicles: 6,700 passenger cars (1986)
Roads: 4,250 km; 486 km paved
Railway: 3 km
Air Traffic: 56,000 passengers carried (1991)
Airports: 33

Canadian Embassy: c/o Canadian Embassy, 5th Flr, Nedbank Plaza, Church & Beatrix Streets, Arcadia, Pretoria 0007; mailing address: P.O. Box 26006, Arcadia, Pretoria 0007, South Africa. Tel: (011-27-12) 324-3970. Fax (011-27-12) 323-1564
Embassy in Canada: High Commission for the Kingdom of Lesotho, 202 Clemow Ave, Ottawa ON K1S 2B4. Tel: (613) 236-9449. Fax: (613) 238-3341.

Liberia

Long-Form Name: Republic of Liberia
Capital: Monrovia
Population: 2,751,000 (1992)

■ GEOGRAPHY

Area: 111,370 sq. km
Coastline: 579 km
Climate: tropical; hot, humid; dry winters with hot days and cool to cold nights; wet, cloudy summers with frequent heavy showers
Environment: West Africa's largest tropical rain forest, subject to deforestation
Terrain: mostly flat to rolling coastal plains rising to rolling plateau and low mountains in northeast
Land Use: 1% arable; 3% permanent; 2% meadows; 39% forest; 55% other
Location: WC Africa, bordering on South Atlantic Ocean

■ PEOPLE

Nationality: Liberian
Ethnic Groups: 95% indigenous African tribes, including Kpelle, Bassa, Gio, Kru, Grego, Mano, Krahn, Gola, Gbandi, Lom, Kissi, Vai and Bella; 5% descendants of repatriated slaves known as Americo-Liberians
Languages: English (official); 28 local languages of the Niger-Congo language group; English used by approx. 20%
Religions: 20% traditional, 15% Moslem, 65% Christian
Marriages: n.a.
Divorces: n.a.

■ GOVERNMENT

Leader(s): Pres. Amos Sawyer, Prime Min. Peter Naigoro (caretaker govt. appointed by the Economic Community of West African States (ECOWAS) until a freely elected govt. is formed)
Government Type: republic
Administrative Divisions: 13 counties
Independence: July 26, 1847

National Holiday: Independence Day, July 26

■ ECONOMY

Overview: the rubber industry and a growth in exports of forest products have boosted the economy; a producer and exporter of basic products; budget deficits, flight of capital and deterioration of some infrastructure hampers economic progress
GNP: $988 million, per capita $395; real growth rate 1.5% (1988)
Inflation: 9.1% (1989)
Industries: rubber processing, food processing, construction materials, furniture, palm oil processing, mining (iron ore, diamonds)
Labour Force: 910,000 (1992); 74.2% agriculture, 16.4% services, 9.4% industry (1989)
Unemployment: 43% urban (1988)
Agriculture: accounts for 40% of GDP (including fishing and forestry); principal products—rubber, timber, coffee, cocoa, rice, cassava, palm oil, sugar cane, bananas, sheep and goats; not self-sufficient in food, imports 25% of rice consumption
Natural Resources: iron ore, timber, diamonds, gold

■ FINANCE/TRADE

Currency: Liberian dollar ($L)
International Reserves Excluding Gold: $6 million (1989)
Gold Reserves: n.a.
Budget: revenues $242.1 million; expenditures $435.4 million, including capital expenditures of $29.5 million (1989)
Defence Expenditures: 28.07 million (1988)
External Debt: $1.127 billion (1990)
Exports: $550 million (1989); commodities: iron ore 61%, rubber 20%, timber 11%, coffee; partners: US, European Community, Netherlands
Imports: $335 million (1989); commodities: rice, mineral fuels, chemicals, machinery, transportation equipment, other foodstuffs; partners: US, European Community, Japan, China, Netherlands and ECOWAS

■ HEALTH

Births: 45/1,000 population (1991)
Deaths: 13/1,000 population (1991)
Infant Mortality: 124 deaths/1,000 live births (1991)
Life Expectancy at Birth: 53 years male, 56 years female (1992)
No. of Physicians: 1.1/10,000 population (1990)

■ EDUCATION

Govt. Expenditure: 11.04% of govt. expenditure (1988)
Literacy: 39.5% (1992)

■ COMMUNICATIONS

Daily newspapers: 7 (1992)
Televisions: 18/1,000 inhabitants (1992)
Radios: 225/1,000 inhabitants (1992)
Telephones: n.a.

■ TRANSPORTATION

Motor Vehicles: 12,000; 8,000 passenger cars (1990)
Roads: 9,355 km; 890 km paved
Railway: 568 km
Air Traffic: 32,000 passengers carried (1991)
Airports: 10

Canadian Embassy: C/o Canadian High Commission, 46 Independence Ave, Accra; P.O. Box 1639, Accra, Ghana. Tel: (011-233-21) 228555. Fax: (011-233-21) 773-792
Embassy in Canada: Embassy of the Republic of Liberia, Royal Trust Building, 160 Elgin St, Ste 2600, Ottawa ON K1N 8S3. Tel: (613) 232-1781

Libya

Long-Form Name: Great Socialist People's Libyan Arab Jamahiriya
Capital: Tripoli
Population: 4,875,000 (1992)

■ GEOGRAPHY

Area: 1,759,540 sq. km
Coastline: 1,770 km
Climate: Mediterranean along coast; dry, extreme desert interior
Environment: hot, dry, dust-laden ghibli is a southern wind lasting one to four days in spring and fall; desertification; sparse natural surface-water resources
Terrain: mostly barren, flat to undulating plains, plateaus, depressions
Land Use: 1% arable; 0% permanent; 8% meadows; 0% forest; 91% other
Location: N Africa, bordering on Mediterranean Sea

■ PEOPLE

Nationality: Libyan
Ethnic Groups: 97% Berber and Arab; some Greeks, Maltese, Italians, Egyptians, Pakistanis, Turks, Indians and Tunisians
Languages: Arabic (official); Italian and English widely understood in major cities, Berber
Religions: 97% Sunni Moslem, 2.5% Christian
Marriages: 4.3 (per 1,000) (1981)
Divorces: 1.1 (per 1,000) (1981)

■ GOVERNMENT

Leader(s): Col. Mu'ammar Abu Minyar al-Qadhafi (de facto chief of state); Senior Advisor: Major Abdel Salem Jalloud
Government Type: Jamahiriya (a state of the masses); in theory, governed by the populace through local councils; in fact, a military dictatorship
Administrative Divisions: 46 municipalities
Independence: Dec. 24, 1951 (from Italy)
National Holiday: Revolution Day, Sept. 1

■ ECONOMY

Overview: a socialist-oriented economy depends largely on revenues from the oil sector; cutbacks on imports due to declining oil revenues have led to shortages of foodstuffs and basic goods; must import 75% of its food needs
GNP: $20 billion, per capita $5,410; real growth rate 0% (1988 est.)
Inflation: 20% (1988 est.)
Industries: petroleum, food processing, textiles, handicrafts, cement
Labour Force: 1,076,000 (1992); 28.9% industry, 53% services, 18.1% agriculture (1989)
Unemployment: 2% (1988 est.)
Agriculture: accounts for 5% of GNP; cash crops— wheat, barley, olives, dates, citrus fruits, peanuts; 75% of food is imported
Natural Resources: crude oil, natural gas, gypsum

■ FINANCE/TRADE

Currency: Libyan dinar (LD)
International Reserves Excluding Gold: 5,330 million (1992)
Gold Reserves: 3.6 million fine troy ounces (1992)
Budget: revenues $8.1 billion; expenditures $9.8 billion, including capital expenditures of $3.1 billion (1989)
Defence Expenditures: $1.51 billion (1989)
External Debt: $2.1 billion (1988)
Exports: $6.1 billion (1988); commodities: petroleum, peanuts, hides; partners: Italy, USSR, Germany, Spain, France, Belgium/Luxembourg, Turkey
Imports: $5.911 billion (1988); commodities: machinery, transport equipment, food, manufactured goods; partners: Italy, USSR, Germany, UK, Japan

■ HEALTH

Births: 36/1,000 population (1991)
Deaths: 6/1,000 population (1991)
Infant Mortality: 62 deaths/1,000 live births (1991)
Life Expectancy at Birth: 65 years male, 70 years female (1992)
No. of Physicians: 14.4/10,000 population (1990)

■ EDUCATION

Govt. Expenditure: 20.8% of govt. expenditure (1986)
Literacy: 63.8% (1992)

■ COMMUNICATIONS

Daily newspapers: 1 (1992)
Televisions: 91.3/1,000 inhabitants (1992)
Radios: 224/1,000 inhabitants (1992)
Telephones: 13.19/100 inhabitants (1992)

■ TRANSPORTATION

Motor Vehicles: 775,000; 450,000 passenger cars (1990)
Roads: 31,672 km; 24,634 km paved
Railway: 3,167 km
Air Traffic: 1,884,000 passengers carried (1991)
Airports: 45

Canadian Embassy: Canadian Embassy, 3 rue du Sénégal, Place d'Afrique, 1002 Tunis Le Belvédère; mailing address: CP 31, Le Belvédère, 1002, Tunis, Tunisia. Tel: (011-216-1) 796-577. Fax: (011-216-1) 792-371
Representative to Canada: c/o Permanent Mission of Socialist People's Libyan Arab Jamahiriya to the UN, 309–315 St East 48th St, New York, New York 10017 USA

Liechtenstein

Long-Form Name: Principality of Liechtenstein
Capital: Vaduz
Population: 28,000 (1992)

■ GEOGRAPHY

Area: 160 sq. km
Coastline: none: landlocked
Climate: continental; cold, cloudy winters with frequent snow or rain; cool to moderately warm, cloudy, humid summers
Environment: variety of microclimatic variations based on elevation
Terrain: mostly mountainous (Alps) with Rhine Valley in western third
Land Use: 25% arable; 0% permanent; 38% meadows; 19% forest; 18% other

Location: C Europe

■ PEOPLE

Nationality: Liechtensteiner
Ethnic Groups: 95% Alemannic, 5% Italian and other
Languages: German (official), also Alemannic dialect
Religions: 87% Roman Catholic, 3% Protestant, 10% other
Marriages: 10.8 (per 1,000) (1986)
Divorces: 0.5 (per 1,000) (1976)

■ GOVERNMENT

Leader(s): Head of Govt. (Prime Min.) Hans Brunhart, Head of State Prince Hans Adam von und zu Liechtenstein II
Government Type: hereditary constitutional monarchy
Administrative Divisions: 11 communes
Independence: Jan. 23, 1719, Imperial Principality of Liechtenstein established
National Holiday: St. Joseph's Day, Mar. 19

■ ECONOMY

Overview: a prosperous economy based mainly on small-scale light industry and some farming; economy closely tied to that of Switzerland in a customs union; known for low business taxes and easy incorporation rules
GNP: n.a.
Inflation: 1.5% (1987 est.)
Industries: electronics, metal manufacturing, textiles, ceramics, pharmaceuticals, food products, precision instruments, tourism
Labour Force: 54% industry, trade and building, 42% services, 4% agriculture, fishing, forestry and horticulture
Unemployment: 0.1% (Dec. 1986)
Agriculture: livestock, vegetables, corn, wheat, potatoes, grapes
Natural Resources: hydroelectric potential

■ FINANCE/TRADE

Currency: Swiss franc (SwF)
International Reserves Excluding Gold: n.a.
Gold Reserves: n.a.
Budget: revenues $240 million; expenditures $197 million, including capital expenditures (1988)
Defence Expenditures: n.a.
External Debt: n.a.
Exports: $807 million (1986); commodities: small specialty machinery, dental products, stamps, hardware, pottery; partners: European Community 40%, EFTA 26% (Switzerland 19%)

Imports: n.a.; commodities: machinery, metal goods, textiles, foodstuffs, motor vehicles; partners: n.a.

■ HEALTH

Births: 13/1,000 population (1991)
Deaths: 7/1,000 population (1991)
Infant Mortality: 5 deaths/1,000 live births (1991)
Life Expectancy at Birth: 66 years male, 73 years female (1992)
No. of Physicians: n.a.

■ EDUCATION

Govt. Expenditure: n.a.
Literacy: 99.7% (1992)

■ COMMUNICATIONS

Daily newspapers: 2 (1992)
Televisions: 342.9/1,000 inhabitants (1992)
Radios: 718/1,000 inhabitants (1992)
Telephones: n.a.

■ TRANSPORTATION

Motor Vehicles: n.a.
Roads: n.a.
Railway: n.a.
Air Traffic: n.a.
Airports: none

Canadian Embassy: Canadian Embassy, 88 Kirchenfeldstrasse, CH-3005 Berne, Switzerland; mailing address: Box 3000, Berne 6, Switzerland. Tel: (011-41-31) 44-63-81. Fax: (011-41-31) 44-73-15

Lithuania

Long-Form Name: Republic of Lithuania
Capital: Vilnius
Population: 3,755,000 (1992)

■ GEOGRAPHY

Area: 65,200 sq. km
Coastline: n.a.
Climate: mild, with moderate precipitation
Environment: n.a.
Terrain: undulating glacial terrain; rivers, lakes, and swamps predominate
Land Use: 16% forests and woodland; 22% meadow and pasture; 49% arable; 13% unproductive
Location: NE Europe, bordering on Baltic Sea

■ PEOPLE

Nationality: Lithuanian
Ethnic Groups: 80% Lithuanian, 9% Russian, 7% Poles, 2% Byelorussian, 2% other
Languages: Lithuanian (official), Russian, Polish
Religions: predominantly Protestant, Roman Catholic, Russian Orthodox
Marriages: n.a.
Divorces: n.a.

■ GOVERNMENT

Leader(s): Pres. (acting): Algirdas Brazauskas, Prime Min Bronislovas Lubys
Government Type: in transition to republic
Administrative Divisions: n.a.
Independence: declared Mar. 1990
National Holiday: n.a.

■ ECONOMY

Overview: industrial activity accounts for 65% of economic output; agriculture makes up only 20%
GNP: $10.220 billion, $2,710 per capita; real growth rate 3.4%
Inflation: n.a.
Industries: heavy engineering, shipbuilding, production of building materials, nuclear and electric power production
Labour Force: 1,926,000 (1989)
Unemployment: n.a.
Agriculture: beef and dairy cattle and related products, pigs, poultry, grains, flax, potatoes, and other vegetables
Natural Resources: amber, oil reserves

■ FINANCE/TRADE

Currency: rouble (plan to re-introduce the Litas)
International Reserves Excluding Gold: n.a.
Gold Reserves: n.a.
Budget: n.a.
Defence Expenditures: n.a.
External Debt: n.a.
Exports: amber, electronics, furniture
Imports: n.a.

■ HEALTH

Births: 15/1,000 population (1991)
Deaths: 11/1,000 population (1991)
Infant Mortality: 14.3/1,000 live births (1991)
Life Expectancy at Birth: 67 years male, 76 years female (1992)
No. of Physicians: n.a.

■ EDUCATION

Govt. Expenditure: n.a.
Literacy: n.a.

■ COMMUNICATIONS

Daily newspapers: 147 papers of all circulation types (1988)

Televisions: n.a.
Radios: n.a.
Telephones: n.a.

■ TRANSPORTATION

Motor Vehicles: n.a.
Roads: n.a.
Railway: n.a.
Air Traffic: n.a.
Airports: none

Canadian Embassy: C/o The Canadian Embassy, Tegelbacken 4 (Flr 7); mailing address: P.O. Box 16129; S-103 23 Stockholm 5, Sweden. Tel: (011-46-8) 613-9900. Fax: (011-46-8) 24 24 91.
Representative to Canada: Consulate General, 235 Yorkland Blvd., Ste 502, Willowdale, ON M2J 4Y8. Tel: (416) 494-8313.

Luxembourg

Long-Form Name: Grand Duchy of Luxembourg
Capital: Luxembourg-Ville
Population: 378,000 (1992)

■ GEOGRAPHY

Area: 2,586 sq. km
Coastline: none: landlocked
Climate: modified continental with mild winters, cool summers
Environment: deforestation
Terrain: mostly gently rolling uplands with broad, shallow valleys; uplands to slightly mountainous in the north; steep slope down to Moselle floodplain in the southeast
Land Use: 24% arable; 1% permanent; 20% meadows; 21% forest; 34% other
Location: NW Europe

■ PEOPLE

Nationality: Luxembourger
Ethnic Groups: Celtic base, with French and German blend; also guest and worker residents
Languages: Letzeburgish (official), German (written language of commerce and press), French (administrative)
Religions: 95% Roman Catholic, 5% Protestant and Jewish
Marriages: 5.5 (per 1,000) (1988)
Divorces: 2.0 (per 1,000) (1987)

■ GOVERNMENT

Leader(s): Prime Min. Jacques Santer, Head of State, Jean, Grand Duke of Luxembourg
Government Type: constitutional monarchy
Administrative Divisions: 4 districts

Independence: 1839 (Grand Duchy)
National Holiday: National Day (public celebration of the Grand Duke's birthday), June 23

■ ECONOMY

Overview: a stable economy featuring moderate growth, low inflation and negligible unemployment; is in an economic union with Belgium for trade and most financial matters and is also closely connected economically with the Netherlands; financial sector is strong
GNP: $11.761 billion, per capita $31,080; real growth rate 4.2% (1991)
Inflation: 3.1% (1991)
Industries: banking, iron and steel, food processing, chemicals, metal products, engineering, tires, glass, aluminum
Labour Force: 155,000 (1992); 77.2% services, 19.1% industry, 3.7% agriculture (1989)
Unemployment: 1.3% (1990)
Agriculture: accounts for less than 3% of GDP (including forestry); principal products—barley, oats, potatoes, wheat, fruits, wine grapes; cattle-raising widespread
Natural Resources: iron ore (no longer exploited)

■ FINANCE/TRADE

Currency: Luxembourg franc (LuxF)
International Reserves Excluding Gold: n.a.
Gold Reserves: 0.43 million fine troy ounces (1992)
Budget: revenues $2.5 billion; expenditures $2.3 billion, including capital expenditures (1988)
Defence Expenditures: $100.23 million (1990)
External Debt: $131.6 million (1989)
Exports: $4.7 billion (1988); commodities: finished steel products, chemicals, rubber products, glass, aluminum, other industrial products; partners: European Community 75%, US 6%
Imports: $5.9 billion (1988); commodities: minerals, metals, foodstuffs, quality consumer goods; partners: Germany 40%, Belgium 35%, France 15%, US 3%

■ HEALTH

Births: 12/1,000 population (1991)
Deaths: 10/1,000 population (1991)
Infant Mortality: 7 deaths/1,000 live births (1991)
Life Expectancy at Birth: 71 years male, 78 years female (1992)
No. of Physicians: 18.1/10,000 population (1992)

■ EDUCATION

Govt. Expenditure: 9.96% of govt. expenditure (1990)
Literacy: 100%

■ COMMUNICATIONS

Daily newspapers: 5 (1992)
Televisions: 252.0/1,000 inhabitants (1992)
Radios: 623/1,000 inhabitants (1992)
Telephones: 50/100 inhabitants (1980)

■ TRANSPORTATION

Motor Vehicles: 211,123; 191,588 passenger cars (1990)
Roads: 5,100 km; 5,056 km paved
Railway: 273 km
Air Traffic: 406,000 passengers carried (1991)
Airports: 2

Canadian Embassy: C/o 2, Avenue de Tervuren, 1040 Brussels, Belgium. Tel: (011-32-2) 735-60-40. Fax: (011-32-2) 735-3383
Representative to Canada: c/o 2200 Massachusetts Ave NW, Washington DC 20008 USA

Macao

Dependent Territory of Portugal

Long-Form Name: Territory of Macao
Capital: n.a.
Population: 492,000 (1992)

■ GEOGRAPHY

Area: 16.92 sq. km (a peninsula and three small islands)
Climate: tropical maritime
Land Use: almost 100% built-up; almost no agricultural lands or fresh water resources
Location: SE coast of China, bordering on South China Sea

■ PEOPLE

Nationality: Portuguese
Ethnic Groups: Chinese 90%, Portuguese
Languages: Portuguese (official), Cantonese, English widely spoken

■ GOVERNMENT

Leader(s): Head of State Mario Soares (Pres. of Portugal), Gov. Gen. Vasco Rocha Vieira
Government Type: dependency: Chinese territory under Portuguese administration; Chinese govt. has power to veto any govt. policies and laws

■ ECONOMY

Overview: gambling and tourism; industry confined to textiles, fireworks, toy-making, plastics; imports almost all food and water from China
Exports: $1.655 million (1991)

Imports: $1.841 million (1991)
Currency: pataca (pl. patacas)

Madagascar

Long-Form Name: Democratic Republic of Madagascar
Capital: Antananarivo
Population: 12,827,000 (1992)

■ GEOGRAPHY

Area: 587,040 sq. km
Coastline: 4,828 km
Climate: tropical along coast, temperate inland, arid in south
Environment: subject to periodic cyclones; deforestation; overgrazing; soil erosion; desertification
Terrain: narrow coastal plain, high plateau and mountains in centre
Land Use: 4% arable; 1% permanent; 58% meadows; 26% forest; 11% other
Location: Indian Ocean, E of Africa

■ PEOPLE

Nationality: Malagasy
Ethnic Groups: basic split between highlanders of predominantly Malayo-Indonesian origin (Merina and Betsileo) and coastal tribes, collectively termed the Côtiers, with mixed African, Malayo-Indonesian and Arab ancestry (Betsimisaraka, Tsimihety, Antaiska, Sakalava)
Languages: French and Malagasy (official)
Religions: 52% indigenous beliefs; approx. 41% Christian, 7% Moslem
Marriages: n.a.
Divorces: n.a.

■ GOVERNMENT

Leader(s): Prime Min. Guy Razanamasy, Pres. Adm. Didier Ratsiraka
Government Type: republic
Administrative Divisions: 6 provinces
Independence: June 26, 1960 (from France; formerly known as Malagasy Republic)
National Holiday: Independence Day, June 26

■ ECONOMY

Overview: a poor country, hampered by high population growth and a GDP growth rate which is not keeping pace; agriculture is the basis of the economy; industrial development is hurt by government policies restricting imports of equipment and spare parts
GNP: $2,560 billion, per capita $210; real growth rate 0.5% (1991)

Inflation: 11.8% (1990)
Industries: agricultural processing (meat canneries, soap factories, breweries, tanneries, sugar refining), light consumer goods industries (textiles, glassware), cement, automobile assembly plant, paper, petroleum
Labour Force: 5,000,000 (1992); 80.9% agriculture, 6% industry, 13.2% services (1989)
Unemployment: n.a.
Agriculture: accounts for 40% of GDP; cash crops— coffee, vanilla, sugar cane, cloves, cocoa; food crops—rice, cassava, beans, bananas, peanuts; not self-sufficient in rice and wheat flour
Natural Resources: graphite, chromite, coal, bauxite, salt, quartz, tar sands, semi-precious stones, mica, fish

■ FINANCE/TRADE

Currency: Malagasy franc (FMG)
International Reserves Excluding Gold: $123 million (1992)
Gold Reserves: n.a.
Budget: revenues $390 million; expenditures $525 million, including capital expenditures of $240 million (1990)
Defence Expenditures: $35 million (1990)
External Debt: $3.677 billion (1990)
Exports: $306 million (1991); commodities: coffee 45%, vanilla 15%, cloves 11%, sugar, petroleum products; partners: France, Japan, Italy, Germany, US
Imports: $441 million (1991); commodities: intermediate manufactures 30%, capital goods 28%, petroleum 15%, consumer goods 14%, food 13%; partners: France, Germany, UK, other European Community, US

■ HEALTH

Births: 47/1,000 population (1991)
Deaths: 15/1,000 population (1991)
Infant Mortality: 95 deaths/1,000 live births (1991)
Life Expectancy at Birth: 53 years male, 56 years female (1992)
No. of Physicians: 1.0/10,000 population (1992)

■ EDUCATION

Govt. Expenditure: 17.23% of govt. expenditure (1991)
Literacy: 80.2% (1992)

■ COMMUNICATIONS

Daily newspapers: 8 (1992)
Televisions: 19.8/1,000 inhabitants (1992)
Radios: 198/1,000 inhabitants (1992)

Telephones: 0.44/100 inhabitants (1992)

■ TRANSPORTATION

Motor Vehicles: 79,792; 46,636 passenger cars (1990)
Roads: 14,676 km; 5,283 km paved
Railway: 1,057 km
Air Traffic: 315,000 passengers carried (1991)
Airports: 59

Canadian Embassy: The Canadian High Commission, 38 Mirambo St, Dar-es-Salaam; mailing address: P.O. Box 1022, Dar-es-Salaam, Tanzania. Tel: (011-255-51) 46000-9. Fax: (011-255-51) 46000 (ask for fax)
Embassy in Canada: Embassy of the Democratic Republic of Madagascar, 282 Somerset St W, Ottawa ON K2P 0J6. Tel: (613) 563-2506.

Malawi

Long-Form Name: Republic of Malawi
Capital: Lilongwe
Population: 10,356,000 (1992)

■ GEOGRAPHY

Area: 118,480 sq. km
Coastline: none: landlocked
Climate: tropical; rainy season (Nov. to May); dry season (May to Nov.)
Environment: deforestation
Terrain: narrow elongated plateau with rolling plains, rounded hills, some mountains
Land Use: 25% arable; negligible permanent; 20% meadows; 50% forest; 5% other
Location: SE Africa

■ PEOPLE

Nationality: Malawian
Ethnic Groups: Chewa, Nyanja, Tumbuko, Yao, Lomwe, Sena, Tonga, Ngoni, Ngonde, Asian, European
Languages: English and Chichewa (official); other languages important regionally
Religions: 50% Christian, remainder Islam, Hinduism, traditional beliefs
Marriages: n.a.
Divorces: n.a.

■ GOVERNMENT

Leader(s): Pres. Hastings Kamuzu Banda
Government Type: one-party republic
Administrative Divisions: 24 districts and 3 regions
Independence: July 6, 1964 (from UK; formerly known as Nyasaland)

National Holiday: Independence Day, July 6

■ ECONOMY

Overview: the underdeveloped economy is based on agriculture and operates in a relatively free enterprise environment; one of the world's least developed countries

GNP: $1.996 billion; per capita $230 real growth rate 3.5% (1991)

Inflation: 12.6% (1991)

Industries: agricultural processing (tea, tobacco, sugar), sawmilling, cement, consumer goods

Labour Force: 3,500,000 (1992); 81.8% agriculture, 3% industry, 15.2% services (1989)

Unemployment: n.a.

Agriculture: 40% of GDP; crops: tobacco, sugar cane, cotton, tea, corn; subsistence crops: cattle and goats

Natural Resources: limestone; unexploited deposits of uranium, coal and bauxite

■ FINANCE/TRADE

Currency: kwacha (K)

International Reserves Excluding Gold: $52 million (1992)

Gold Reserves: 0.01 million fine troy ounces (1991)

Budget: revenues $398 million; expenditures $510 million, including capital expenditures of $154 million (1991)

Defence Expenditures: $20.73 million (1988)

External Debt: $1.366 billion (1990)

Exports: $473 million (1991); commodities: tobacco, tea, sugar, coffee, peanuts; partners: US, UK, Zambia, South Africa, Germany

Imports: $705 million (1991); commodities: food, petroleum, semimanufactures, consumer goods, transportation equipment; partners: South Africa, Japan, US, UK, Zimbabwe

■ HEALTH

Births: 52/1,000 population (1991)

Deaths: 18/1,000 population (1991)

Infant Mortality: 136 deaths/1,000 live births (1991)

Life Expectancy at Birth: 48 years male, 50 years female (1992)

No. of Physicians: 0.9/10,000 population (1992)

■ EDUCATION

Govt. Expenditure: 8.83% of government expenditure (1989)

Literacy: 41.2% (1992)

■ COMMUNICATIONS

Daily newspapers: 1 (1992)

Televisions: n.a.

Radios: 237/1,000 inhabitants (1992)

Telephones: 0.3/100 inhabitants (1992)

■ TRANSPORTATION

Motor Vehicles: 32,000; 16,000 passenger cars (1990)

Roads: 15,400 km; 3,320 km paved

Railway: 1,007 km

Air Traffic: 118,000 passengers carried (1991)

Airports: 27

Canadian Embassy: c/o The Canadian High Commission, 1st Flr, Barclays Bank, North End Branch, Cairo Rd; mailing address: P.O. Box 313131, 10101 Lusaka, Zambia. Tel: (011-260-1) 228-811. Fax: (011-260-1) 22-51-60

Embassy in Canada: High Commission for Malawi, 7 Clemow Ave, Ottawa ON K1S 2A9. Tel: (613) 236-8931. Fax: (613) 236-1054.

Malaysia

Long-Form Name: Federation of Malaysia

Capital: Kuala Lumpur

Population: 18,792,000 (1992)

■ GEOGRAPHY

Area: 329,750 sq. km; inc. Sabah and Sarawak

Coastline: 4,675 km total (2,068 km Peninsular Malaysia, 2,607 km East Malaysia)

Climate: tropical; annual southwest (Apr. to Oct.) and northeast (Oct. to Feb.) monsoons

Environment: subject to flooding; air and water pollution

Terrain: coastal plains rising to hills and mountains

Land Use: 3% arable; 10% permanent; negligible meadows; 63% forest; 24% other

Location: SE Asia, bordering on South China Sea

■ PEOPLE

Nationality: Malaysian

Ethnic Groups: 59% Malay and other indigenous, 32% Chinese, 9% Indian

Languages: Bahasa Malaysia (official), English widely used, Chinese, Tamil and Iban spoken by minorities

Religions: Islam 53%, Buddhism 19%, Hinduism, Christianity, Animism

Marriages: n.a.

Divorces: n.a.

■ GOVERNMENT

Leader(s): Prime Min. Mahathir Sultan bin Mohamad, Paramount Ruler Azlan Muhibbuddin Shah
Government Type: Federation of Malaysia formed July 9, 1963; constitutional monarch nominally headed by the paramount ruler (king) and a bicameral Parliament
Administrative Divisions: 13 states and 2 federal territories
Independence: Aug. 31, 1957 (from UK)
National Holiday: National Day, Aug. 31

■ ECONOMY

Overview: the economy is vulnerable to recession or a fall in world commodity prices because of its high export dependence; the world's largest producer of semiconductor devices; the majority of the rural population subsists at the poverty level
GNP: $45.787 billion, per capita $2,490; real growth rate 5.6% (1991)
Inflation: 4.4% (1991)
Industries: rubber and oil palm processing and manufacturing, light manufacturing industries, electronics, tin mining and smelting, logging and processing timber, logging, petroleum production, agriculture processing, petroleum production and refining, logging
Labour Force: 7,070,000 (1992); 41.6% agriculture, 19.1% industry, 39.3% services (1989)
Unemployment: 7.9% (1989 est.)
Agriculture: Peninsular Malaysia—natural rubber, palm oil, rice; Sabah—mainly subsistence; main crops—rubber, timber, coconut, rice; Sarawak— main crops—rubber, timber, pepper; there is a deficit of rice in all areas
Natural Resources: tin, crude oil, timber, copper, iron ore, natural gas, bauxite

■ FINANCE/TRADE

Currency: ringgit ($M)
International Reserves Excluding Gold: $15,943 million (1992)
Gold Reserves: 2.35 million fine troy ounces (1992)
Budget: revenues $12.6 billion; expenditures $11.8 billion, including capital expenditures of $3.2 billion (1991)
Defence Expenditures: $1.56 billion (1990)
External Debt: $16.107 billion (1990)
Exports: $34.375 billion (1991); commodities: natural rubber, palm oil, tin, timber, petroleum, electronics, light manufactures; partners: Singapore, Japan, USSR, European Community, Australia, US
Imports: $36.699 billion (1991); commodities: food, crude oil, consumer goods, intermediate goods, capital equipment, chemicals; partners: Japan, Singapore, Germany, UK, Thailand, China, Australia, US

■ HEALTH

Births: 30/1,000 population (1991)
Deaths: 6/1,000 population (1991)
Infant Mortality: 29 deaths/1,000 live births (1991)
Life Expectancy at Birth: 69 years male, 73 years female (1992)
No. of Physicians: 5.2/10,000 population (1992)

■ EDUCATION

Govt. Expenditure: 19.30% of government expenditure (1991)
Literacy: 78.4% (1992)

■ COMMUNICATIONS

Daily newspapers: 47 (1992)
Televisions: 143.6/1,000 inhabitants (1992)
Radios: 428/1,000 inhabitants in (1992)
Telephones: 9.68/100 inhabitants (1992)

■ TRANSPORTATION

Motor Vehicles: 2,426,799; 1,811,141 passenger cars (1987)
Roads: 40,230 km; 27,700 km paved
Railway: 1,682 km
Air Traffic: 11,838,000 passengers carried (1991)
Airports: 49

Canadian Embassy: Flr 7, Plaza MBF, Jalan Ampang, 50450 Kuala Lumpur, Malaysia; mailing address: P.O. Box 10990, 50732 Kuala Lumpur, Malaysia. Tel: (011-60-3) 261-2000. Fax: (011-60-3) 261-3428
Embassy in Canada: High Commission for Malaysia, 60 Boteler St, Ottawa ON K1N 8Y7. Tel: (613) 237-5182, -3, -4. Fax: (613) 237-4852.

Maldives

Long-Form Name: Republic of Maldives
Capital: Malé
Population: 227,000 (1992)

■ GEOGRAPHY

Area: 300 sq. km
Coastline: 644 km

Climate: tropical; hot, humid; dry, northeast monsoon (Nov. to Mar.); rainy, southwest monsoon (June to Aug.)

Environment: 1,200 coral islands grouped in 19 atolls, future rise in ocean level could obliterate large parts of the country

Terrain: flat with elevations only as high as 2.5 metres

Land Use: 10% arable; 0% permanent; 3% meadows; 3% forest; 84% other

Location: Indian Ocean, S of India

■ PEOPLE

Nationality: Maldivian

Ethnic Groups: mixtures of Sinhalese, Dravidian, Arab and black

Languages: Dhivehi (Maldivian dialect of Sinhara; script derived from Arabic); English spoken by most government officials

Religions: Sunni Moslem

Marriages: 34.4 (per 1,000) (1981)

Divorces: 25.4 (per 1,000) (1981)

■ GOVERNMENT

Leader(s): Pres. Maumoun Abdul Gayoom

Government Type: republic

Administrative Divisions: 19 districts and 1 capital district

Independence: July 26, 1965 (from UK)'

National Holiday: Independence Day, July 26

■ ECONOMY

Overview: based on fishing, tourism and shipping; GDP growth has been increasing steadily

GNP: $101 million, per capita $460; real growth rate 10.2% (1991)

Inflation: 14% (1988 est.)

Industries: fishing and fish processing, tourism, shipping, boat building, some coconut processing, garments, woven mats, coir (rope), handicrafts

Labour Force: 25% agriculture, 15.8% industry, 59.2% services

Unemployment: n.a.

Agriculture: accounts for almost 30% of GDP (including fishing) fishing more important than farming; limited production of coconuts, corn, sweet potatoes; most staple foods must be imported

Natural Resources: fish

■ FINANCE/TRADE

Currency: rufiyaa (pl. rufiyaa) (Rf)

International Reserves Excluding Gold: $16 million (1991)

Gold Reserves: none (1991)

Budget: revenues $51 million; expenditures $50 million, including capital expenditures of $25 million (1988)

Defence Expenditures: $1.8 million (1984)

External Debt: $70 million (1988)

Exports: $54 million (1991); commodities: fish 57%, clothing 39%; partners: Thailand, Western Europe, Sri Lanka

Imports: $151 million (1991); commodities: intermediate and capital goods 47%, consumer goods 42%, petroleum products 11%; partners: Japan, Western Europe, Thailand

■ HEALTH

Births: 46/1,000 population (1991)

Deaths: 9/1,000 population (1991)

Infant Mortality: 72 deaths/1,000 live births (1991)

Life Expectancy at Birth: 62 years male, 59 years female (1992)

No. of Physicians: 0.7/10,000 population (1990)

■ EDUCATION

Govt. Expenditure: 11.27% of government expenditure (1990)

Literacy: 91.3% (1992)

■ COMMUNICATIONS

Daily newspapers: 2 (1992)

Televisions: 24.0/1,000 inhabitants (1992)

Radios: 115/1,000 inhabitants (1992)

Telephones: 1.4/100 inhabitants (1992)

■ TRANSPORTATION

Motor Vehicles: 509

Roads: n.a.

Railway: n.a.

Air Traffic: 9,000 passengers carried (1991)

Airports: 2

Canadian Embassy: c/o 6 Gregory's Rd, Colombo 7; mailing address: P.O. Box 1006, Colombo, Sri Lanka. Tel: (011-94-1) 69-58-41. Fax: (011-94-1) 68-70-49

Mali

Long-Form Name: Republic of Mali

Capital: Bamako

Population: 9,818,000 (1992)

■ GEOGRAPHY

Area: 1,240,000 sq. km

Coastline: none: landlocked

Climate: subtropical to arid; hot and dry Feb. to June; rainy, humid and mild June to Nov.; cool and dry Nov. to Feb.
Environment: hot, dust-laden harmattan haze common during dry seasons; desertification
Terrain: mostly flat to rolling northern plains covered by sand; savanna in south, rugged hills in northeast
Land Use: 2% arable; negligible permanent; 25% meadows; 7% forest; 66% other
Location: NW Africa

PEOPLE

Nationality: Malian
Ethnic Groups: 50% Mande (Bambara, Malinke, Sarakole), 17% Peul, 12% Voltaic, 6% Songhai, 5% Tuareg and Moor, 10% other
Languages: French (official); Bambara spoken by about 80% of the population; numerous African languages
Religions: 80% Moslem, 18% indigenous beliefs, 1% Christian
Marriages: n.a.
Divorces: n.a.

GOVERNMENT

Leader(s): Pres. Alpha Oumar Konare, Prime Min. Younoussi Toure
Government Type: republic; single-party constitutional government
Administrative Divisions: 7 regions & 1 capital district
Independence: Sept. 22, 1960 (from France; formerly French Sudan)
National Holiday: Anniversary of the Proclamation of the Republic, Sept. 22

ECONOMY

Overview: a poor country, 80% of its land area is desert or semidesert; 80% of the labor force is involved in agriculture and fishing; 10% of the population live as nomads
GNP: $2.412 billion, per capita $280; real growth rate 2.5% (1991)
Inflation: n.a.
Industries: small local consumer goods and processing, construction, phosphate, gold, fishing
Labour Force: 2,960,000 (1992); 85.5% agriculture, 12.5% services, 2% industry (1989)
Unemployment: n.a.
Agriculture: accounts for 50% of GDP; most production based on small subsistence farms; cotton and livestock products account for over 70% of exports; other crops—millet, rice, corn, vegetables, peanuts; livestock—cattle, sheep and goats
Natural Resources: gold, phosphates, kaolin, salt,

limestone, uranium; bauxite, iron ore, manganese, tin and copper deposits are known but not exploited

FINANCE/TRADE

Currency: Communauté Financière Africaine franc (MF)
International Reserves Excluding Gold: $290 million (1992)
Gold Reserves: 0.02 million fine troy ounces (1992)
Budget: revenues $329 million; expenditures $519 million, including capital expenditures of $178 million (1989)
Defence Expenditures: $63.82 million (1988)
External Debt: $2.306 billion (1990)
Exports: $271 million (1989); commodities: livestock, peanuts, dried fish, cotton, skins; partners: mostly franc zone and Western Europe
Imports: $500 million (1989); commodities: textiles, vehicles, petroleum products, machinery, sugar, cereals; partners: mostly franc zone and Western Europe

HEALTH

Births: 51/1,000 population (1991)
Deaths: 21/1,000 population (1991)
Infant Mortality: 114 deaths/1,000 live births (1991)
Life Expectancy at Birth: 43 years male, 46 years female (1992)
No. of Physicians: 0.4/10,000 population (1992)

EDUCATION

Govt. Expenditure: 9.04% of govt. expenditure (1988)
Literacy: 32.0% (1992)

COMMUNICATIONS

Daily newspapers: 2 (1992)
Televisions: 0.4/1,000 inhabitants (1992)
Radios: 39/1,000 inhabitants (1992)
Telephones: 0.17/100 inhabitants (1992)

TRANSPORTATION

Motor Vehicles: 31,000; 22,000 passenger cars (1990)
Roads: 16,120 km; 1,240 km paved
Railway: 620 km
Air Traffic: n.a.
Airports: 29

Canadian Embassy: c/o Immeuble Trade-Center, 23, rue Nogues, Le Plateau; mailing address: 01 BP 4104, Abidjan 01, Côte d'Ivoire. Tel: (011-225) 32-20-09. Fax: (011-225) 22-05-30

Embassy in Canada: Embassy of the Republic of Mali, 50 Goulburn Ave, Ottawa ON K1N 8C8. Tel: (613) 232-1501, -3264.

Malta

Long-Form Name: Republic of Malta
Capital: Valletta
Population: 359,000 (1992)

■ GEOGRAPHY

Area: 250 sq. km
Coastline: 140 km
Climate: Mediterranean with mild, rainy winters and hot, dry summers
Environment: numerous bays provide good harbors; fresh water very scarce, increasing reliance on desalination
Terrain: mostly low, rocky, flat to dissected plains; many coastal cliffs
Land Use: 38% arable; 3% permanent; 0% meadows; 0% forest; 59% other
Location: Mediterranean Sea, S of Sicily

■ PEOPLE

Nationality: Maltese
Ethnic Groups: mixture of Arab, Sicilian, Norman, Spanish, Italian, English
Languages: Maltese and English (official), Italian widely spoken
Religions: 98% Roman Catholic
Marriages: 7.1% (per 1,000) (1987)
Divorces: n.a.

■ GOVERNMENT

Leader(s): Prime Min. Eddie Fenech Adami, Pres. Vincent (Censu) Tabone
Government Type: parliamentary democracy
Administrative Divisions: none
Independence: Sept. 21, 1964 (from UK)
National Holiday: Freedom Day, Mar. 31

■ ECONOMY

Overview: manufacturing and tourism are important; economy is dependent on foreign trade and services (food, water and energy)
GNP: $2.598 billion, per capita $6,850; real growth rate 3.5% (1991)
Inflation: 2.5% (1991)
Industries: tourism, ship repair yard, clothing, construction, food manufacturing, textiles, footwear, clothing, beverages, tobacco
Labour Force: 146,000 (1992); 28.1% industry, 2.5% agriculture, 69.4% services (1989)
Unemployment: 3.7% (1989)
Agriculture: 20% self-sufficient overall; main products—potatoes, cauliflower, grapes, wheat, barley, tomatoes, citrus, cut flowers, green peppers, hogs, poultry, eggs; adequate supplies of vegetables, poultry, milk, pork products; seasonal or periodic shortages
Natural Resources: limestone, salt

■ FINANCE/TRADE

Currency: Maltese lira (LM)
International Reserves Excluding Gold: $1,213 million (1992)
Gold Reserves: 0.12 million fine troy ounces (1992)
Budget: revenues $1,020 million; expenditures $1,230 million, including capital expenditures of $380 million (1990)
Defence Expenditures: $25.57 million (1990)
External Debt: $90 million (1987)
Exports: $1.238 billion (1991); commodities: clothing, textiles, footwear, ships; partners: Germany 31%, UK 14%, Italy 14%
Imports: $2.114 billion (1991); commodities: food, petroleum, nonfood raw materials; partners: Germany 19%, UK 17%, Italy 17%, US 11%

■ HEALTH

Births: 15/1,000 population (1991)
Deaths: 8/1,000 population (1991)
Infant Mortality: 7 deaths/1,000 live births (1991)
Life Expectancy at Birth: 74 years male, 78 years female (1992)
No. of Physicians: 11.4/10,000 population (1990)

■ EDUCATION

Govt. Expenditure: 8.83% of govt. expenditure (1990)
Literacy: 85.7% (1992)

■ COMMUNICATIONS

Daily newspapers: 3 (1992)
Televisions: 740.7/1,000 inhabitants (1992)
Radios: 396/1,000 inhabitants (1992)
Telephones: 49.08/100 inhabitants (1992)

■ TRANSPORTATION

Motor Vehicles: 135,919; 114,682 passenger cars (1990)
Roads: 1,016 km; 956 km paved
Railway: n.a.
Air Traffic: 649,000 passengers carried (1991)
Airports: 1

Canadian Embassy: c/o Via G.B. de Rossi 27, 00161 Rome, Italy. Tel: (011-39-6) 841-5341. Fax: (011-39-6) 841-2479

Representative to Canada: c/o High Commission for the Republic of Malta, 2017 Connecticut Ave NW, Washington DC 20008 USA. Tel: (202) 462-3611, -12

Martinique

Overseas Department of France

Long-Form Name: Department of Martinique
Capital: Fort-de-France
Population: 359,572 (1990)

■ GEOGRAPHY

Area: 1,079 sq. km
Coastline: 290 km
Climate: warm and humid
Terrain: mountainous with indented coastline; dormant volcano
Land Use: 10% arable; 8% permanent; 30% meadows; 26% forest; 26% other
Location: Winward Islands, Caribbean

■ PEOPLE

Nationality: French
Ethnic Groups: majority Black, remainder a mix of Black African and Latin ancestry
Languages: French (official), majority speak Creole

■ GOVERNMENT

Leader(s): Pres. Regional Council Camille Darsieres, Pres. General Council Emile Maurice, French Govt. Commissioner Michel Morin
Government Type: overseas department of France

■ ECONOMY

Overview: industry: food processing, oil refining, chemical engineering; agriculture: pineapples, tobacco, cotton, bananas, sugar, rum, livestock; forest products; fishing; chief trading partners: France,. United Kingdom, Guadeloupe
GNP: $1.3 billion, per capita $3,650; real growth rate n.a. (1984)
Currency: French franc (F)

Canadian Embassy: c/o The Canadian High Commission, Huggins Bldg, 72 South Quay; Port-of-Spain; mailing address: P.O. Box 1246, Port of Spain, Trinidad and Tobago. Tel: (809) 623-7254. Fax: (809) 624-4016

Mauritania

Long-Form Name: Islamic Republic of Mauritania

Capital: Nouakchott
Population: 2,143,000 (1992)

■ GEOGRAPHY

Area: 1,030,700 sq. km
Coastline: 754 km
Climate: desert; constantly hot, dry, dusty
Environment: hot, dry, dust/sand-laden sirocco wind blows primarily in Mar. and Apr.; desertification; only perennial river is the Senegal
Terrain: mostly barren, flat plains of the Sahara; some central hills
Land Use: 38% meadows; 5% forest; 56% other, 1% arable
Location: NW Africa, bordering on Atlantic Ocean

■ PEOPLE

Nationality: Mauritanian
Ethnic Groups: 81% Moorish, 19% black
Languages: Hasaniya Arabic (national); French (official); Toucouleur, Fula, Sarakole, Wolof
Religions: nearly 100% Moslem
Marriages: n.a.
Divorces: n.a.

■ GOVERNMENT

Leader(s): Pres., Military Committee for National Salvation (CMSN); Chief of State Col. Maaouya Ould Sid'Ahmend Taya, Prime Min. Sidi Mohammed Ould Boubaker
Government Type: republic military seized power in bloodless coup July 10, 1978; a palace coup that took place on Dec. 24, 1984 brought President Taya to power
Administrative Divisions: 12 regions & 1 capital district
Independence: Nov. 28, 1960 (from France)
National Holiday: Independence Day, Nov. 28

■ ECONOMY

Overview: most of the population is engaged in agricultural and livestock production; substantial iron ores; threatened by foreign overexploitation of fishing areas
GNP: $1.026 billion, per capita $510; real growth rate 0.6% (1991)
Inflation: 1.4% (1988 est.)
Industries: fishing, fish processing, mining of iron ore and gypsum
Labour Force: 680,000 (1992) 69.4% agriculture, 21.7% services, 8.9% industry
Unemployment: 50% (1988 est.)
Agriculture: accounts for 29% of GDP (including fishing); largely subsistence farming, nomadic cattle and sheep herding except in Senegal river

valley; crops—dates, millet, sorghum, root crops; fish products number-one export; large food deficit in years of drought
Natural Resources: iron ore, gypsum, fish, copper, phosphate

■ FINANCE/TRADE

Currency: ouguiya (UM)
International Reserves Excluding Gold: $48 million (1992)
Gold Reserves: 0.01 million fine troy ounces (1991)
Budget: revenues $280 million; expenditures $364 million, including capital expenditures of $61 million (1989)
Defence Expenditures: 4.2% GDP (1987)
External Debt: $1.898 billion (1990)
Exports: $437 million (1989); commodities: iron ore, processed fish, small amounts of gum arabic and gypsum, unrecorded but numerically significant cattle exports to Senegal; partners: European Community 57%, Japan 39%, Ivory Coast 2%
Imports: $639 million (1990); commodities: foodstuffs, consumer goods, petroleum products, capital goods; partners: European Community 79%, Africa 5%, US 4%, Japan 2%

■ HEALTH

Births: 49/1,000 population (1991)
Deaths: 18/1,000 population (1991)
Infant Mortality: 94 deaths/1,000 live births (1991)
Life Expectancy at Birth: 46 years male, 49 years female (1992)
No. of Physicians: 0.8/10,000 population (1992)

■ EDUCATION

Govt. Expenditure: 33.2% of govt. expenditure (1985)
Literacy: 34% (1992)

■ COMMUNICATIONS

Daily newspapers: 1 (1992)
Televisions: 22.9/1,000 inhabitants (1992)
Radios: 143/1,000 inhabitants (1992)
Telephones: 0.3/100 inhabitants (1992)

■ TRANSPORTATION

Motor Vehicles: 15,000; 10,000 passenger cars (1990)
Roads: 7,215 km; 2,060 km paved
Railway: 722 km
Air Traffic: 210,000 passengers carried (1991)
Airports: 20

Canadian Embassy: C/o Immeuble Daniel Sorano, 4th Flr, 45 boul de la République; mailing address: P.O. Box 3373, Dakar, Senegal. Tel: (011-221) 23-92-90. Fax: (011-221) 23-87-49
Representative to Canada: c/o Permanent Mission of Mauritania to the UN, 9 East 77th St, New York NY 10021 USA

Mauritius

Long-Form Name: Mauritius
Capital: Port Louis
Population: 1,098,000 (1992)

■ GEOGRAPHY

Area: 2,040 sq. km; includes Agalega Islands, Cargados Carajos Shoals (St. Brandon), and Rodriques
Coastline: 177 km
Climate: tropical modified by southeast trade winds; warm, dry winter (May to Nov.); hot, wet, humid summer (Nov. to May)
Environment: subject to cyclones (Nov. to Apr.); almost completely surrounded by reefs
Terrain: small coastal plain rising to discontinuous mountains encircling central plateau
Land Use: 54% arable; 4% permanent; 4% meadows; 31% forest; 7% other
Location: Indian Ocean, E of Africa

■ PEOPLE

Nationality: Mauritian
Ethnic Groups: 68% Indo-Mauritian, 27% Creole, 3% Sino-Mauritian, 2% Franco-Mauritian
Languages: English (official), Creole
Religions: 55% Hindu, 28% Christian (mostly Roman Catholic with a few Anglicans), 17% Moslem
Marriages: 11.2 (per 1,000) (1987)
Divorces: 0.8 (per 1,000) (1987)

■ GOVERNMENT

Leader(s): Pres. Cassam Uteem, Prime Min. Sir Aneerood Jugnauth, Gov. Gen. Sir Veerasamy Ringadoo
Government Type: parliamentary democracy
Administrative Divisions: 9 administrative districts
Independence: Mar. 12, 1968 (from UK)
National Holiday: Independence Day, Mar. 12

■ ECONOMY

Overview: based on sugar, manufacturing (textiles) and tourism; features low unemployment and a high real growth rate
GNP: $2.623 billion, per capita $2,420; real growth rate 7.2% (1991)

Inflation: 7% (1991)
Industries: food processing (largely sugar milling), textiles, wearing apparel, chemical and chemical products, metal products, transport equipment, nonelectrical machinery, tourism
Labour Force: 440,000 (1992); 19% agriculture, 31.1% industry, 49.9% services (1989)
Unemployment: 10,589 (1991)
Agriculture: accounts for 14% of GDP; about 90% of cultivated land in sugar cane; other products— tea, corn, potatoes, bananas, pulses, cattle, goats, fish; net food importer, especially rice and fish
Natural Resources: arable land, fish

■ **FINANCE/TRADE**

Currency: rupee (Mau Rs)
International Reserves Excluding Gold: $820 million (1992)
Gold Reserves: 0.06 million fine troy ounces (1992)
Budget: revenues $477 million; expenditures $540 million, including capital expenditures of $112 million (1989)
Defence Expenditures: 0.2% GNP (1988)
External Debt: $739 million (1990)
Exports: $1.192 billion (1991); commodities: textiles 44%, sugar 40%, light manufactures 10%; partners: European Community 77%, US 15%
Imports: $1.575 billion (1991); commodities: manufactured goods 50%, capital equipment 17%, foodstuffs 13%, petroleum products 8%, chemicals 7%; partners: European Community, US, South Africa, Japan

■ **HEALTH**

Births: 19/1,000 population (1991)
Deaths: 6/1,000 population (1991)
Infant Mortality: 20 deaths/1,000 live births (1991)
Life Expectancy at Birth: 65 years male, 72 years female (1992)
No. of Physicians: 5.3/10,000 population (1992)

■ **EDUCATION**

Govt. Expenditure: 14.57% of govt. expenditure (1991)
Literacy: 82.8% (1992)

■ **COMMUNICATIONS**

Daily newspapers: 7 (1992)
Televisions: 214.6/1,000 inhabitants (1992)
Radios: 354/1,000 inhabitants (1992)
Telephones: 7.20/100 inhabitants (1992)

■ **TRANSPORTATION**

Motor Vehicles: 55,981; 46,793 passenger cars (1990)
Roads: 7,215 km; 2,060 km paved
Railway: n.a.
Air Traffic: 535,000 passengers carried (1991)
Airports: 1

Canadian Embassy: C/o The Canadian High Commission, 38 Mirambo St, Dar-es-Salaam; mailing address: P.O. Box 1022, Dar-es-Salaam, Tanzania. Tel: (011-255-51) 46000-9. Fax: (011-255-51) 46000 (ask for fax)
Representative to Canada: c/o Embassy of Mauritius, Suite 441, Van Ness Centre, 4301 Connecticut Avenue NW, Washington DC 20008 USA

Mayotte

Territorial Collectivity of France

Long-Form Name: Mayotte
Capital: n.a.; chief town is Mamoundzou
Population: 85,000 (1991)

■ **GEOGRAPHY**

Area: 373 sq. km
Climate: tropical maritime
Land Use: 20,000 acres under agricultural cultivation
Location: Mozambique Channel, off W coast of Africa

■ **PEOPLE**

Nationality: French
Ethnic Groups: Antalote, Cafre, Makoa, Oimatsaha, Sakalava
Languages: French (official), Mahorian

■ **GOVERNMENT**

Leader(s): Pres. General Council Younoussa Bamana, French Govt. Commissioner Akli Khider
Government Type: territorial collectivity

■ **ECONOMY**

Overview: industry: lobster, shrimp; agriculture: pineapples, bananas, mangoes, breadfruit, cassava, ylang-ylang, vanilla, coffee, spices; chief trading partners: United Kingdom, South Africa, Bahrain, Thailand, Réunion
Currency: French franc (F)

Mexico

Long-Form Name: United States of Mexico
Capital: Mexico City
Population: 88,153,000 (1992)

■ GEOGRAPHY

Area: 1,972,550 sq. km
Coastline: 9,330 km
Climate: varies from tropical to desert
Environment: subject to tsunamis along the Pacific coast and destructive earthquakes in the centre and south; natural water resources scarce and polluted in centre and extreme southeast; deforestation; erosion widespread; desertification; serious air pollution
Terrain: high, rugged mountains, low coastal plains, high plateaus and desert
Land Use: 12% arable, 1% permanent; 39% meadows; 24% forest; 24% other
Location: Central (Latin) America, bordering on Gulf of Mexico, Pacific Ocean

■ PEOPLE

Nationality: Mexican
Ethnic Groups: 60% mestizo (Indian-Spanish), 30% Amerindian or predominantly Amerindian, 9% white or predominantly white, 1% other
Languages: Spanish, also indigenous languages
Religions: 96% Roman Catholic, 3% Protestant
Marriages: 6.6 (per 1,000) (1985)
Divorces: 0.3 (per 1,000) (1985)

■ GOVERNMENT

Leader(s): Pres. Carlos Salinas de Gortari
Government Type: federal republic operating under a centralized government
Administrative Divisions: 31 states and 1 federal district
Independence: Sept. 16, 1810 (from Spain)
National Holiday: Independence Day, Sept. 16

■ ECONOMY

Overview: a mixture of state-owned industrial plants (mainly oil), private manufacturing and services and both large-scale and traditional agriculture; suffers from rapid population growth and large external debts due to falling petroleum prices
GNP: $252.381 billion, per capita $2,870; real growth rate 1.5% (1991)
Inflation: 22.7% (1991)
Industries: food and beverages, tobacco, chemicals, iron and steel, petroleum, mining, textiles, clothing, transportation equipment, tourism

Labour Force: 30,487,000 (1992); 57% services, 22.9% agriculture, 20.1% industry (1989)
Unemployment: 2.6% (1991)
Agriculture: accounts for 9% of GDP and over 25% of labor force; large number of small farms at subsistence level; major food crops—corn, wheat, rice, beans; cash crops—cotton, coffee, fruit, tomatoes
Natural Resources: crude oil, silver, copper, gold, lead, zinc, natural gas, timber

■ FINANCE/TRADE

Currency: peso ($Mex)
International Reserves Excluding Gold: $18,962 million (1992)
Gold Reserves: 0.75 million fine troy ounces (1992)
Budget: revenues $44.3 billion; expenditures $55.2 billion, including capital expenditures of $7.8 billion (1989)
Defence Expenditures: $678.41 million (1990)
External Debt: $97.2 billion (1990)
Exports: $27.180 billion (1991); commodities: crude oil, oil products, coffee, shrimp, engines, cotton; partners: US 66%, European Community 16%, Japan 11%
Imports: $38.062 billion (1991); commodities: grain, metal manufactures, agricultural machinery, electrical equipment; partners: US 62%, European Community 18%, Japan 10%

■ HEALTH

Births: 29/1,000 population (1991)
Deaths: 5/1,000 population (1991)
Infant Mortality: 29 deaths/1,000 live births (1991)
Life Expectancy at Birth: 68 years male, 76 years female (1991)
No. of Physicians: 6.7/10,000 population (1992)

■ EDUCATION

Govt. Expenditure: 12% of govt. expenditure (1989)
Literacy: 87.3% (1992)

■ COMMUNICATIONS

Daily newspapers: 286 (1992)
Televisions: 126.8/1,000 inhabitants (1992)
Radios: 242/1,000 inhabitants (1992)
Telephones: 11.08/100 inhabitants (1992)

■ TRANSPORTATION

Motor Vehicles: 9,882,490; 6,819,305 passenger cars (1990)
Roads: 232,760; 104,545 km paved
Railway: 20,910 km

Air Traffic: 14,901,000 passengers carried (1991)
Airports: 483

Canadian Embassy: Calle Schiller no. 529, Rincon del Bosque, 11580 Polanco Mexico, D.F.; mailing address: Apartado Postal 105-05, 11580 Mexico, Mexico. Tel: (011-525) 724-7900. Fax: (011-525) 724-7982
Embassy in Canada: Embassy of Mexico, 130 Albert St, Ste 1800, Ottawa ON K1P 5G4. Tel: (613) 233-8988, -9272, -9917. Fax: (613) 235-9123.

Moldova

Long-Form Name: Republic of Moldova
Capital: Kishinev
Population: 4,362,000 (1992)

■ GEOGRAPHY

Area: 33,700 sq. km
Coastline: none: landlocked
Climate: mild sunny winters; hot rainy summers; long dry autumns
Environment: n.a.
Terrain: hilly plains in north; southern steppe
Land Use: 85% cultivated, very fertile soil
Location: SE Europe, bordering on Black Sea

■ PEOPLE

Nationality: Moldavian
Ethnic Groups: 64.5% Moldavian, 13.9% Ukrainian, 13% Russian, 3.5% Gaguazi, 1.5% Jews, 2% other
Languages: Moldavian (official), Russian, Ukrainian
Religions: predominantly Eastern Orthodox, some Baptists and Roman Catholics
Marriages: n.a.
Divorces: n.a.

■ GOVERNMENT

Leader(s): Pres. Mircea Snegur, Prime Min. Andrei Sangheli
Government Type: in transition to republic
Administrative Divisions: 36 rural districts, 21 towns, 45 urban settlements
Independence: declared June 23, 1990
National Holiday: n.a.

■ ECONOMY

Overview: predominantly mining and manufacturing, with important agricultural sector
GNP: $9.529 billion, $2,170 per capita; real growth rate 2.7%
Inflation: n.a.

Industries: engineering, food processing, machinery, metalmaking
Labour Force: n.a.
Unemployment: n.a.
Agriculture: grapes and other fruits, vegetables, sugar, wheat and cereal grains, tobacco, oil, essential oil crops
Natural Resources: fish, lignite, phosphorites, gypsum

■ FINANCE/TRADE

Currency: rouble (rbl.), soon to be replaced by the leu (presently in preparation)
International Reserves Excluding Gold: n.a.
Gold Reserves: n.a.
Budget: 1989 revenues: 3,396 million roubles
Defence Expenditures: n.a.
External Debt: n.a.
Exports: $51 million (Jan.-Sept. 1992); wine, grapes, other agricultural products, machinery, pumps
Imports: $47 million (Jan.-Sept. 1992)

■ HEALTH

Births: 18.9/1,000 population (1989)
Deaths: 9.2/1,000 population (1989)
Infant Mortality: 20.7 deaths/1,000 live births (1989)
Life Expectancy at Birth: 66 years male, 72 years female (1992)
No. of Physicians: 17,500 doctors (1989)

■ EDUCATION

Govt. Expenditure: n.a.
Literacy: n.a.

■ COMMUNICATIONS

Daily newspapers: 200 papers of all circulation types (1989)
Televisions: n.a.
Radios: n.a.
Telephones: n.a.

■ TRANSPORTATION

Motor Vehicles: n.a.
Roads: n.a.
Railway: 1,150 km
Air Traffic: n.a.
Airports: n.a.

Canadian Embassy: c/o 36 Nicolae Iorga, Bucharest; mailing address: P.O. Box 2966 Post Office No. 22, 71118 Bucharest, Romania. tel: (011-40-1) 312.03.65. Fax: (011-40-1) 312.03.66.

Monaco

Long-Form Name: Principality of Monaco
Capital: Monaco
Population: 28,000 (1992)

■ GEOGRAPHY

Area: 1.9 sq. km
Coastline: 4.1 km
Climate: Mediterranean with mild, wet winters and hot, dry summers
Environment: almost entirely urban
Terrain: hilly, rugged, rocky
Land Use: 0% arable; 0% permanent; 0% meadows; 0% forest; 100% other
Location: S Europe, bordering on Mediterranean Sea

■ PEOPLE

Nationality: Monegasque
Ethnic Groups: 47% French, 16% Monegasque, 16% Italian, 21% other
Languages: French (official), English, Italian, Monegasque
Religions: 95% Roman Catholic
Marriages: 7.1 (per 1,000) (1979)
Divorces: 2.2 (per 1,000) (1979)

■ GOVERNMENT

Leader(s): Chief of State Prince Rainier III, Min. of State Jacques Dupont
Government Type: constitutional monarchy
Administrative Divisions: 4 districts
Independence: 1419, rule by the House of Grimaldi
National Holiday: National Day, Nov. 19

■ ECONOMY

Overview: a popular resort, attracting tourists to its casinos and pleasant climate; no income tax and low business taxes make it a tax haven; no data is published on the economy
GNP: n.a.
Inflation: n.a.
Industries: pharmaceuticals, food processing, precision instruments, glassmaking, printing, tourism
Labour Force: n.a.
Unemployment: full employment (1990)
Agriculture: n.a.
Natural Resources: none

■ FINANCE/TRADE

Currency: French franc (F)
International Reserves Excluding Gold: n.a.

Gold Reserves: n.a.
Budget: revenues $386 million; expenditures $426 million; including capital expenditures (1988)
Defence Expenditures: n.a.
External Debt: n.a.
Exports: n.a.
Imports: n.a.

■ HEALTH

Births: 7/1,000 population (1991)
Deaths: 7/1,000 population (1991)
Infant Mortality: 8 deaths/1,000 live births (1991)
Life Expectancy at Birth: 72 years male, 80 years female (1991)
No. of Physicians: 21.9/10,000 population (1982)

■ EDUCATION

Govt. Expenditure: 5.3% of govt. expenditure (1989)
Literacy: 99%

■ COMMUNICATIONS

Daily newspapers: 2 (1988)
Televisions: 785.7/1,000 inhabitants (1989)
Radios: 1,084/1,000 inhabitants (1989)
Telephones: 131.4/100 inhabitants (1985)

■ TRANSPORTATION

Motor Vehicles: 20,800; 17,000 passenger cars (1990)
Roads: n.a.
Railway: n.a.
Air Traffic: 43,000 passengers carried (1991)
Airports: 1

Canadian Embassy: c/o 35 av Montaigne, 75008 Paris France. Tel: (011-33-1) 44-43-32-00. Fax: (011-33-1) 44-43-34-98
Representative to Canada: c/o Consulate of Monaco, 1800 McGill College Ave, 14th Flr, Montreal, PQ H3A 3K9. Tel: (514) 849-0589.

Mongolia

Long-Form Name: Mongolian People's Republic
Capital: Ulan Bator
Population: 2,310,000 (1992)

■ GEOGRAPHY

Area: 1,565,000 sq. km
Coastline: none: landlocked
Climate: desert; continental (large daily and seasonal temperature ranges)
Environment: harsh and rugged

Terrain: vast semidesert and desert plains; mountains in west and southwest; Gobi desert in southeast
Land Use: 1% arable; 0% permanent; 79% meadows; 10% forest; 10% other
Location: C Asia

■ PEOPLE

Nationality: Mongolian
Ethnic Groups: 90% Mongol, 4% Kazakh, 2% Chinese, 2% Russian, 2% other
Languages: Kazakh and Khalkha Mongol is spoken by over 90% of population; minor languages include Turkic, Russian, Chinese and English
Religions: no state religion; 4% Buddhist Lamaism and Shamanism, Islam
Marriages: 7.8 (per 1,000) (1986)
Divorces: 0.5 (per 1,000) (1986)

■ GOVERNMENT

Leader(s): Prime Min. Puntsagiyn Jasray, Pres. Punsalmaagiyn Ochirbat, Vice Pres. Radnaasumbereliyn Gonchigdorj
Government Type: Communist state
Administrative Divisions: 18 provinces and 3 municipalities
Independence: Mar. 13, 1921 (from China; formerly known as Outer Mongolia)
National Holiday: People's Revolution Day, July 11

■ ECONOMY

Overview: traditionally based on agriculture and the breeding of livestock (has highest number of livestock per person in the world); recently extensive mineral resources have been developed
GNP: $1.7 billion, per capita $880 (1985 est.); average real growth rate 3.6% (1976–85 est.)
Inflation: n.a.
Industries: processing of animal products, building materials, food and beverage, mining (particularly coal)
Labour Force: 1,030,000 (1992); 39.9% agriculture, 21% industry, 39.2% services (1989)
Unemployment: n.a.
Agriculture: accounts for 90% of exports and provides livelihood for about 50% of the population; livestock raising predominates (sheep, goats, horses); crops—wheat, barley, potatoes, forage
Natural Resources: coal, copper, molybdenum, tungsten, phosphates, tin, nickel, zinc, wolfram, fluorspar, gold

■ FINANCE/TRADE

Currency: tugrik (Tug)
International Reserves Excluding Gold: n.a.
Gold Reserves: n.a.
Budget: deficit of $240 million (1991 est.)
Defence Expenditures: $249.44 million (1987)
External Debt: n.a.
Exports: $388 million (1985); commodities: livestock, animal products, wool, hides, fluorspar, nonferrous metals, minerals; partners: USSR 80%
Imports: $1 billion (1985); commodities: machinery and equipment, fuels, food products, industrial consumer goods, chemicals, building materials, sugar, tea; partners: USSR 80%

■ HEALTH

Births: 34/1,000 population (1991)
Deaths: 8/1,000 population (1991)
Infant Mortality: 48 deaths/1,000 live births (1991)
Life Expectancy at Birth: 62 years male, 67 years female (1992)
No. of Physicians: 22.7/10,000 population (1981)

■ EDUCATION

Govt. Expenditure: n.a.
Literacy: 80%

■ COMMUNICATIONS

Daily newspapers: 3 (1992)
Televisions: 37.5/1,000 inhabitants (1992)
Radios: 131/1,000 inhabitants (1992)
Telephones: n.a.

■ TRANSPORTATION

Motor Vehicles: n.a.
Roads: 46,950 km; 1,565 km paved
Railway: 1,878 km
Air Traffic: 554,000 passengers carried (1991)
Airports: 1

Canadian Embassy: c/o 19 Dong Zhi Men Wai St, Chaoyang District, Beijing 100600, China. Tel: (011-86-1) 532-3536. Fax (011-86-1) 532-4072
Representative to Canada: c/o Embassy of the Mongolian People's Republic, 10201 Iron Gate Road, Potomac, Maryland 20854 USA. Tel: (202) 485-3176

Montserrat

Crown Colony of the United Kingdom

Long-Form Name: Montserrat
Capital: Plymouth

Population: 11,000 (1992)

■ GEOGRAPHY

Area: 106 sq. km
Climate: tropical, no well-defined rainy season; June-Nov. hottest, prone to hurricanes
Land Use: mountainous islands not suited to much cultivation
Location: West Indies

■ PEOPLE

Nationality: British
Ethnic Groups: descendants of British, French, Irish settlers
Languages: English (official)

■ GOVERNMENT

Leader(s): Gov. David G.P. Taylor; Chief Min. Reuben Meade
Government Type: Crown colony

■ ECONOMY

Overview: manufacturing accounts for 85% of exports: leather goods, cotton clothing, electronics, plastic bags, tropical fruits, herbal teas, ornamental plants, tropical fruits; agriculture: self-sufficient in sea-island cotton, fruits, vegetables; livestock inc. sheep, goats, poultry; fishing
Currency: Eastern Caribbean dollar

Morocco

Long-Form Name: Kingdom of Morocco
Capital: Rabat
Population: 26,318,000 (1990)

■ GEOGRAPHY

Area: 459,000 sq. km
Coastline: 1,835 km
Climate: Mediterranean, becoming more extreme in the interior
Environment: northern mountains geologically unstable and subject to earthquakes; desertification
Terrain: mostly mountains with rich coastal plains
Land Use: 18% arable; 1% permanent; 28% meadows; 12% forest; 41% other
Location: N Africa, bordering on Atlantic Ocean

■ PEOPLE

Nationality: Moroccan
Ethnic Groups: 99.1% Arab-Berber, 0.7% non-Morrocan, 0.2% Jewish
Languages: Arabic (official); several Berber dialects; French is language of business, government, diplomacy and post primary education
Religions: 90% Sunni Moslem, 1.1% Christian, 0.2% Jewish, other
Marriages: n.a.
Divorces: n.a.

■ GOVERNMENT

Leader(s): Prime Min. Mohammed Karim Larmani, King Hassan II
Government Type: constitutional monarchy
Administrative Divisions: 36 provinces and 8 urban prefectures
Independence: Mar. 2, 1956 (from France)
National Holiday: National Day (anniversary of King Hassan II's accession to the throne), Mar. 3

■ ECONOMY

Overview: the economy is suffering due to high foreign debt, high unemployment and the country's vulnerability to external forces
GNP: $26.451 billion, per capita $1,030; real growth rate 4.3% (1991)
Inflation: 8.0% (1991)
Industries: phosphate rock mining and processing, food processing, leather goods, textiles, construction, tourism
Labour Force: 7,824,000 (1992); 45.6% agriculture, 29.4% services, 25% industry (1989)
Unemployment: 15% (1988)
Agriculture: 50% of employment and 30% of export value; not self-sufficient in food; cereal farming and livestock raising predominate; barley, wheat, citrus fruit, wine, vegetables, olives
Natural Resources: phosphates, iron ore, manganese, lead, zinc, fish, salt

■ FINANCE/TRADE

Currency: dirham (DH)
International Reserves Excluding Gold: $3,536 million (1992)
Gold Reserves: 0.7 million fine troy ounces (1992)
Budget: revenues $6.6 billion; expenditures $7.3 billion, including capital expenditures of $1.8 billion (1990)
Defence Expenditures: $1.34 billion (1990)
External Debt: $22.097 billion (1990)
Exports: $4.286 billion (1991); commodities: food and beverages 30%, semi-processed goods 23%, consumer goods 21%, phosphates 17%; partners: European Community 58%, India 7%, Japan 5%, USSR 3%, US 2%
Imports: $6.874 billion (1991); commodities: capital goods 24%, semiprocessed goods 22%, raw materials 16%, fuel and lubricants 16%, food and beverages 13%, consumer goods 10%;

partners: European Community 53%, US 11%, Canada 4%, Iraq 3%, USSR 3%, Japan 2%

■ HEALTH

Births: 30/1,000 population (1991)
Deaths: 8/1,000 population (1991)
Infant Mortality: 76 deaths/1,000 live births (1991)
Life Expectancy at Birth: 62 years male, 65 years female (1992)
No. of Physicians: 2.1/10,000 population (1992)

■ EDUCATION

Govt. Expenditure: 17.02% of govt. expenditure (1987)
Literacy: 49.5% (1992)

■ COMMUNICATIONS

Daily newspapers: 16 (1992)
Televisions: 69.6/1,000 inhabitants (1992)
Radios: 209/1,000 inhabitants (1992)
Telephones: 1.55/100 inhabitants (1992)

■ TRANSPORTATION

Motor Vehicles: 945,752; 663,802 passenger cars (1990)
Roads: 61,047 km; 29,835 km paved
Railway: 1,928 km
Air Traffic: 1,430,000 passengers carried (1991)
Airports: 29

Canadian Embassy: 13 bis, rue Jaafar As-Sadik; Rabat-Agdal; mailing address: CP 709, Rabat-Agdal, Morocco. Tel: (011-212-7) 77-28-80. Fax: (011-212-7) 77-28-87
Embassy in Canada: Embassy of the Kingdom of Morocco, 38 Range Rd, Ottawa ON K1N 8J4. Tel: (613) 236-7391, -2. Fax: (613) 236-6164.

Mozambique

Long-Form Name: Republic of Mozambique
Capital: Maputo
Population: 14,872,000 (1990)

■ GEOGRAPHY

Area: 801,590 sq. km
Coastline: 2,470 km
Climate: tropical to subtropical
Environment: severe drought and floods occur in south; desertification
Terrain: mostly coastal lowlands, uplands in centre, high plateaus in northwest, mountains in west
Land Use: 4% arable; negligible permanent; 56% meadows; 20% forest; 20% other

Location: E Africa, bordering on Mozambique Channel

■ PEOPLE

Nationality: Mozambican
Ethnic Groups: majority from indigenous tribal groups; about 10,000 Europeans, 35,000 Euro-Africans, 15,000 Indians
Languages: Portuguese (official); English; many indigenous dialects
Religions: 60% indigenous beliefs, 30% Christian, 10% Moslem
Marriages: n.a.
Divorces: n.a.

■ GOVERNMENT

Leader(s): Prime Min. Mário da Graça Machungo, Pres. Joaquím Alberto Chissano
Government Type: people's republic
Administrative Divisions: 10 provinces & 1 capital district
Independence: June 25, 1975 (from Portugal)
National Holiday: Independence Day, June 25

■ ECONOMY

Overview: internal disorders, lack of government administrative control and a growing foreign debt have contributed to the country's failure to exploit the economic potential of its agricultural, hydropower and transportation resources; depends on much foreign aid
GNP: $1.163 billion, per capita $70; real growth rate -1.1% (1990)
Inflation: 81.1% (1988)
Industries: food, beverages, chemicals (fertilizer, soap, paints), petroleum products, textiles, non-metallic mineral products (cement, glass, asbestos), tobacco
Labour Force: 8,440,000 (1992); 84.5% agriculture, 7.4% industry, 8.1% services (1989)
Unemployment: 40% (1988)
Agriculture: accounts for 50% of GDP, over 80% of labor force and about 90% of exports; cash crops—cotton, cashew nuts, sugar cane, tea, shrimp; other crops—cassava, corn, rice, tropical fruits; not self-sufficient in food
Natural Resources: coal, titanium

■ FINANCE/TRADE

Currency: metical (pl. meticais) (Mt)
International Reserves Excluding Gold: $253 million (1991)
Gold Reserves: n.a.
Budget: revenues $186 million; expenditures $239 million, including capital expenditures of $208 million (1988)

Defence Expenditures: $113.09 million (1990)
External Debt: $4.053 billion (1991)
Exports: $162 million (1991); commodities: shrimp 48%, cashews 21%, sugar 10%, copra 3%, citrus 3%; partners: US, Western Europe, Germany, Japan
Imports: $99 million (1991); commodities: food, clothing, farm equipment, petroleum; partners: US, Western Europe, USSR

■ **HEALTH**

Births: 46/1,000 population (1991)
Deaths: 17/1,000 population (1991)
Infant Mortality: 134 deaths/1,000 live births (1991)
Life Expectancy at Birth: 46 years male, 49 years female (1992)
No. of Physicians: 0.3/10,000 population (1990)

■ **EDUCATION**

Govt. Expenditure: n.a.
Literacy: 32.9% (1992)

■ **COMMUNICATIONS**

Daily newspapers: 2 (1992)
Televisions: 2.3/1,000 inhabitants (1992)
Radios: 41/1,000 inhabitants (1992)
Telephones: 0.41/100 inhabitants (1992)

■ **TRANSPORTATION**

Motor Vehicles: 111,500; 87,500 passenger cars (1990)
Roads: 26,453 km; 5,610 km paved
Railway: 3,367 km
Air Traffic: 283,000 passengers carried (1991)
Airports: 18

Canadian Embassy: c/o The Canadian High Commission, 45 Baines Ave, Harare; mailing address: P.O. Box 1430, Harare, Zimbabwe. Tel: (011-263-4) 733-881. Fax: (011-263-4) 732-917
Representative to Canada: c/o Embassy of the People's Republic of Mozambique, 1900 M St NW, Ste 570, Washington DC 20036 USA

Myanmar

Long-Form Name: Union of Myanmar (formerly Burma)
Capital: Rangoon
Population: 43,668,000 (1992)

■ **GEOGRAPHY**

Area: 678,500 sq. km
Coastline: 1,930 km
Climate: tropical monsoon; cloudy, rainy, hot, humid summers (southwest monsoon, June to Sept.); less cloudy, scant rainfall, mild temperatures, lower humidity during winter (northeast monsoon, Dec. to Apr.)
Environment: subject to destructive earthquakes and cyclones; flooding and landslides common during rainy season (June to Sept.); deforestation
Terrain: central lowlands ringed by steep, rugged highlands
Land Use: 15% arable land; 1% permanent crops; 1% meadows and pastures; 49% forest and woodland; 34% other; includes 2% irrigated
Location: SC Asia, bordering on Bay of Bengal

■ **PEOPLE**

Nationality: Burmese
Ethnic Groups: 68% Burmese, 9% Shan, 7% Karen, 4% Rakhine, 3% Chinese, 2% Mon, 2% Indian, 5% other
Languages: Myanmar (Burmese); minority ethnic groups have their own languages
Religions: 85% Buddhist, 15% animist beliefs, Moslem, Christian or other
Marriages: n.a.
Divorces: n.a.

■ **GOVERNMENT**

Leader(s): Prime Min. General Than Shwe
Government Type: military regime
Administrative Divisions: 7 divisions, 7 states
Independence: Jan. 4, 1948 (from UK)
National Holiday: Independence Day, Jan. 4

■ **ECONOMY**

Overview: economy is dependent on agriculture and is vulnerable to world market conditions (especially for rice)
GNP: $11 billion, per capita $280; real growth rate 0.2% (1988 est.)
Inflation: 32.3% (1991)
Industries: agricultural processing; textiles and footwear; wood and wood products; petroleum refining; mining of copper, tin, tungsten, iron; construction materials; pharmaceuticals; fertilizer
Labour Force: 18,000,000 (1992); 63.9% agriculture, 9.1% industry, 27% services (1989)
Unemployment: 555,250 (1990)
Agriculture: accounts for about 40% of GDP; self-sufficient in food; principal crops: rice, corn, oilseed, sugar cane, pulses; world's largest stand of hardwood trees; rice and teak account for 55% of exports; world's largest producer of opium poppies

Natural Resources: crude oil, timber, tin, antimony, zinc, copper, tungsten, lead, coal, some marble, limestone, precious stones, natural gas

■ FINANCE/TRADE

Currency: kyat (K)
International Reserves Excluding Gold: $289 million (1992)
Gold Reserves: 0.25 million fine troy ounces (1992)
Budget: revenues $4.9 billion; expenditures $5 billion, including capital expenditures of $0.7 billion (1989)
Defence Expenditures: $1.060 billion (1990)
External Debt: $4.447 billion (1990)
Exports: $412 million (1991); commodities: teak, rice, oilseed, metals, rubber, gems; partners: Southeast Asia, India, China, European Community, Africa
Imports: $616 million (1991); commodities: machinery, transport equipment, chemicals, food products; partners: Japan, European Community, CEMA, China, Southeast Asia

■ HEALTH

Births: 32/1,000 population (1991)
Deaths: 13/1,000 population (1991)
Infant Mortality: 95 deaths/1,000 live births (1991)
Life Expectancy at Birth: 56 years male, 60 years female (1992)
No. of Physicians: 2.7/10,000 population (1992)

■ EDUCATION

Govt. Expenditure: 15.91% of govt. expenditure (1990)
Literacy: 80.6% (1992)

■ COMMUNICATIONS

Daily newspapers: 2 (1992)
Televisions: 1.7/1,000 inhabitants (1992)
Radios: 81/1,000 inhabitants (1992)
Telephones: 0.21/100 inhabitants (1992)

■ TRANSPORTATION

Motor Vehicles: 73,000; 30,000 passenger cars (1990)
Roads: 27,820 km; 3,393 km paved
Railway: 3,257 km
Air Traffic: 319,000 passengers carried (1991)
Airports: 62

Canadian Embassy: c/o The Canadian Embassy, 12th Floor, Boonmitr Bldg., 138 Silom Rd, Bangkok 10500; mailing address: P.O. Box 2090, Bangkok 10500, Thailand. Tel: (011-66-2) 237-4126. Fax: (011-66-2) 236-6463
Embassy in Canada: Embassy of the Union of Myanmar, 85 Range Rd, Ste 902, Ottawa ON K1N 8J6. Tel: (613) 232-6434, -46. Fax: (613) 232-6435.

Namibia

Long-Form Name: Republic of Namibia
Capital: Windhoek
Population: 1,534,000 (1992)

■ GEOGRAPHY

Area: 824,290 sq. km
Coastline: 1,489 km
Climate: desert; hot, dry; rainfall sparse and erratic
Environment: inhospitable with very limited natural water resources; desertification
Terrain: mostly high plateau; Namib Desert along coast; Kalahari Desert in east
Land Use: 1% arable; negligible permanent crops; 64% meadows; 22% forest; 13% other
Location: SW Africa, bordering on South Atlantic Ocean

■ PEOPLE

Nationality: Namibian
Ethnic Groups: 86% black, 7% white, 8% mixed; about 50% of the population belong to the Ovambo tribe and 9% to the Kavangos tribe
Languages: white population: 60% Afrikaans, 33% German, 7% English (all official); several indigenous languages
Religions: 90% Christian, 10% traditional religions
Marriages: n.a.
Divorces: n.a.

■ GOVERNMENT

Leader(s): Prime Min. Hage Geingob, Pres. Sam Nujoma
Government Type: republic
Administrative Divisions: 26 districts
Independence: Mar. 21, 1990 (from South Africa)
National Holiday: Independence Day, Mar. 21

■ ECONOMY

Overview: economy is very dependent on the mining industry to extract and process minerals for export; world's fifth largest producer of uranium; rich diamond deposits
GNP: $2.051 billion, per capita $1,120; real growth rate 1.6% (1991)
Inflation: 15.1% (1989)

Industries: meat packing, fish processing, dairy products, mining (copper, lead, zinc, diamonds, uranium)
Labour Force: 537,000 (1992); 43.5% agriculture, 21.9% industry, 34.8% services (1989)
Unemployment: over 30% (1988)
Agriculture: accounts for 10% of GDP (including fishing); mostly subsistence farming; livestock raising major source of cash income; crops: millet, sorghum, peanuts; large unfulfilled fish catch potential
Natural Resources: diamonds, copper, uranium, gold, lead, tin, zinc, salt, vanadium, natural gas, fish; suspected deposits of coal and iron ore

■ FINANCE/TRADE

Currency: rand (R)
International Reserves Excluding Gold: n.a.
Gold Reserves: n.a.
Budget: revenues $794.1 million; expenditures $999.6 million, including capital expenditures (1991)
Defence Expenditures: $47.44 million (1990)
External Debt: $27 million (1990)
Exports: $935 million (1988); commodities: diamonds, uranium, zinc, copper, meat, processed fish, karakul skins; partners: South Africa
Imports: $856 million (1988); commodities: foodstuffs, manufactured consumer goods, machinery and equipment; partners: South Africa, Germany, UK, US

■ HEALTH

Births: 45/1,000 population (1991)
Deaths: 10/1,000 population (1991)
Infant Mortality: 69 deaths/1,000 live births (1991)
Life Expectancy at Birth: 59 years male, 61 years female (1992)
No. of Physicians: n.a.

■ EDUCATION

Govt. Expenditure: 22.20% of govt. expenditure (1991)
Literacy: 38.4% (1992)

■ COMMUNICATIONS

Daily newspapers: 5 (1989)
Televisions: 15.7/1,000 population (1989)
Radios: 133/1,000 population (1989)
Telephones: 4/100 inhabitants (1980)

■ TRANSPORTATION

Motor Vehicles: 103,715 registered motor vehicles (1986)
Roads: 54,400 km; 4,120 km paved

Railway: 2,390 km
Air Traffic: 455,000 passengers carried (1991)
Airports: 143

Canadian Embassy: 111-A Gloudina St, Ludwigsdorf, Windhoek 9000; mailing address: P.O. Box 2147, Windhoek 9000, Namibia. Tel: (011-264-61) 222-941. Fax: (011-264-61) 224-204
Representative to Canada: c/o Embassy of the Republic of Namibia, 1605 New Hampshire Ave NW, Washington DC 20009 USA

Nauru

Long-Form Name: Republic of Nauru
Capital: no capital city as such; government offices in Yaren District
Population: 10,000 (1992)

■ GEOGRAPHY

Area: 21 sq. km
Coastline: 30 km
Climate: tropical; monsoonal; rainy season (Nov. to Feb.)
Environment: only 53 km south of Equator
Terrain: sandy beach rises to fertile ring around raised coral reefs with phosphate plateau in centre
Land Use: 0% arable; 0% permanent; 0% meadows; 0% forest; 100% other
Location: Melanesia, Pacific Ocean

■ PEOPLE

Nationality: Nauruan
Ethnic Groups: 58% Nauruan, 26% other Pacific Islander, 8% Chinese, 8% European
Languages: Nauruan, a distinct Pacific Island language (official); English widely understood, spoken and used for most government and commercial purposes
Religions: Christian (two-thirds Nauruan Protestant, one-third Roman Catholic)
Marriages: 5.4 (per 1,000) (1976)
Divorces: n.a.

■ GOVERNMENT

Leader(s): Pres. Bernard Dowiyogo
Government Type: republic
Administrative Divisions: 14 districts
Independence: Jan. 31, 1968 (from UN trusteeship under Australia, New Zealand and UK; formerly known as Pleasant Island)
National Holiday: Independence Day, Jan. 31

■ ECONOMY

Overview: economy depends on revenues from the export of phosphates, the reserves of which are expected to be exhausted by the year 2000; most other resources are imported; has one of the highest per capita incomes in the Third World
GNP: over $90 million, per capita $10,000; real growth rate n.a. (1989)
Inflation: n.a.
Industries: phosphate mining, financial services, coconuts
Labour Force: n.a.
Unemployment: 0% (1990)
Agriculture: negligible; almost completely dependent on imports for food and water
Natural Resources: phosphates

■ FINANCE/TRADE

Currency: Australian dollar ($A)
International Reserves Excluding Gold: n.a.
Gold Reserves: n.a.
Budget: revenues $69.7 million; expenditures $51.5 million, including capital expenditures (1986)
Defence Expenditures: n.a.
External Debt: $33.3 million
Exports: $93 million (1984); commodities: phosphates; partners: Australia, New Zealand
Imports: $73 million (1984); commodities: food, fuel, manufactures, building materials, machinery; partners: Australia, UK, New Zealand, Japan

■ HEALTH

Births: 19/1,000 population (1991)
Deaths: 5/1,000 population (1991)
Infant Mortality: 41 deaths/1,000 live births (1991)
Life Expectancy at Birth: 64 years male, 69 years female (1991)
No. of Physicians: n.a.

■ EDUCATION

Govt. Expenditure: n.a.
Literacy: 99%

■ COMMUNICATIONS

Daily newspapers: n.a.
Televisions: n.a.
Radios: 633/1,000 inhabitants (1989)
Telephones: 18.9/100 inhabitants (1986)

■ TRANSPORTATION

Motor Vehicles: n.a.
Roads: n.a.
Railway: n.a.
Air Traffic: 59,000 passengers carried (1991)
Airports: 1

Canadian Embassy: c/o The Canadian High Commission, Commonwealth Ave, Canberra ACT 2600, Australia. Tel: (011-61-62) 273-3844

Nepal

Long-Form Name: Kingdom of Nepal
Capital: Kathmandu
Population: 20,577,000 (1992)

■ GEOGRAPHY

Area: 147,180 sq. km
Coastline: none: landlocked
Climate: varies from cool summers and severe winters in north to subtropical summers and mild winter in south
Environment: contains eight of the world's 10 highest peaks; deforestation; soil erosion; water pollution
Terrain: flat river plain of the Ganges in south, central hill region, rugged Himalayas in north
Land Use: 17% arable; negligible permanent; 13% meadows; 33% forest; 37% other
Location: SC Asia

■ PEOPLE

Nationality: Nepalese
Ethnic Groups: Newars, Indians, Tibetans, Gurungs, Magars, Tamangs, Bhotias, Rais, Limbus, Sherpas, as well as many smaller groups
Languages: Nepali (official); 20 languages divided into numerous dialects
Religions: only official Hindu state in world, although no sharp distinction between many Hindu and Buddhist groups; small groups of Moslems and Christians
Marriages: n.a.
Divorces: n.a.

■ GOVERNMENT

Leader(s): King Birendra Bir Bikram Shah Dev, Prime Min. Girija Prasad Koirala
Government Type: constitutional monarchy, but King Birendra exercises control over multitiered system of government
Administrative Divisions: 14 zones
Independence: 1768, unified by Prithyi Narayan Shah
National Holiday: Birthday of His Majesty the King, Dec. 28

■ ECONOMY

Overview: agriculture is the basis of this poor economy; suffers from an ongoing trade/transit dispute with India; agricultural production hasn't kept pace with high population growth

GNP: $3.453 billion, per capita $180; real growth rate 4.7% (1991)

Inflation: 15.6% (1991)

Industries: small rice, jute, sugar and oilseed mills, cigarette, textiles, cement, brick; tourism

Labour Force: 7,730,000 (1992); 93% agriculture, 6.5% services, 0.6% industry (1989)

Unemployment: 5%; underemployment estimated at 25–40% (1987)

Agriculture: accounts for 60% of GDP and 90% of work force; farm products—rice, corn, wheat, sugar cane, root crops, milk, buffalo meat; not self-sufficient in food, particularly in drought years

Natural Resources: quartz, water, timber, hydro-electric potential, scenic beauty; small deposits of lignite, copper, cobalt, iron ore

■ FINANCE/TRADE

Currency: rupee (NRs)

International Reserves Excluding Gold: $463 million (1992)

Gold Reserves: 0.15 million fine troy ounces (1992)

Budget: revenues $316.5 million; expenditures $618.5 million, including capital expenditures of $398 million (1991)

Defence Expenditures: $37.93 billion (1990)

External Debt: $1.557 billion (1990)

Exports: $273 million (1991); commodities: clothing, carpets, leather goods, grain; partners: India 38%, US 23%, UK 6%, other Europe 9%

Imports: $790 million (1991); commodities: petroleum products 20%, fertilizer 11%, machinery 10%; partners: India 36%, Japan 13%, Europe 4%, US 1%

■ HEALTH

Births: 39/1,000 population (1991)

Deaths: 15/1,000 population (1991)

Infant Mortality: 98 deaths/1,000 live births (1991)

Life Expectancy at Birth: 50 years male, 50 years female (1992)

No. of Physicians: 0.3/10,000 population (1992)

■ EDUCATION

Govt. Expenditure: 10.95% of govt. expenditure (1990)

Literacy: 25.6% (1992)

■ COMMUNICATIONS

Daily newspapers: 28 (1992)

Televisions: 1.6/1,000 inhabitants (1992)

Radios: 33/1,000 inhabitants (1992)

Telephones: 0.36/100 inhabitants (1992)

■ TRANSPORTATION

Motor Vehicles: n.a.

Roads: 6,475 km; 2,800 km paved

Railway: 103 km

Air Traffic: 672,000 passengers carried (1991)

Airports: 41

Canadian Embassy: C/o The Canadian High Commission, 7/8 Shantipath, Chanakyapuri, New Delhi 110 021; mailing address: The Canadian High Commission, P.O. Box 5208, New Delhi, India. Tel: (011-91-11) 687-6500

Representative to Canada: C/o Royal Nepalese Embassy, 2131 Leroy Place NW, Washington DC 20008 USA

Netherlands

Long-Form Name: Kingdom of the Netherlands

Capital: Amsterdam; seat of government: The Hague

Population: 15,158,000 (1992)

■ GEOGRAPHY

Area: 41,864 sq. km

Coastline: 451 km

Climate: temperate; marine; cool summers and mild winters

Environment: 27% of the land area is below sea level and protected from the North Sea by dikes

Terrain: mostly coastal lowland and reclaimed land (polders); some hills in southeast

Land Use: 25% arable;1% permanent; 34% meadows; 9% forest; 31% other

Location: NC Europe, bordering on North Sea

■ PEOPLE

Nationality: Dutch

Ethnic Groups: 96% Dutch, 4% Moroccans, Turks and others (1988)

Languages: Dutch, Frisian

Religions: 62% Christianity, of which Roman Catholic 36%, Protestant 26%; most of the rest do not profess a religion

Marriages: 6.1 (per 1,000) (1988)

Divorces: 1.8 (per 1,000) (1988)

■ GOVERNMENT

Leader(s): Prime Min. Ruud Lubbers, Queen Beatrix

Government Type: constitutional monarchy
Administrative Divisions: 12 provinces.
Dependent areas: Aruba, Netherland Antilles
Independence: 1579 (from Spain)
National Holiday: Queen's Day, Apr. 30

■ ECONOMY

Overview: a highly developed and affluent economy based on private enterprise; numerous government-backed welfare programs; trade and financial sectors are the strongest part of the economy; has a sizable budget deficit
GNP: $278.839 billion, per capita $18,560; real growth rate 2.1% (1991)
Inflation: 3.9% (1991)
Industries: agro-industries, metal and engineering products, electrical machinery and equipment, chemicals, petroleum, fishing, construction, microelectronics
Labour Force: 6,153,000 (1992); 78.4% services, 17.4% industry, 4.2% agriculture
Unemployment: 7.0% (1990)
Agriculture: accounts for 4% of GDP; animal production predominates; crops—grains, potatoes, sugar beets, fruits, vegetables; shortages of grain, fats and oils
Natural Resources: natural gas, crude oil, fertile soil

■ FINANCE/TRADE

Currency: guilder (f.)
International Reserves Excluding Gold: $21,937 million (1992)
Gold Reserves: 43.94 million fine troy ounces (1992)
Budget: revenues $68 billion; expenditures $76 billion, including capital expenditures of $7 billion (1990)
Defence Expenditures: $8.29 billion (1991)
External Debt: none
Exports: $139.944 billion (1992); commodities: agricultural products, processed foods and tobacco, natural gas, chemicals, metal products, textiles, clothing; partners: European Community 74.9% (Germany 28.3%, Belgium-Luxembourg 14.2%, France 10.7%, UK 10.2%), US 4.7%
Imports: $134.475 billion (1992); commodities: raw materials and semifinished products, consumer goods, transportation equipment, crude oil, food products; partners: European Community 63.8% (Germany 26.5%, Belgium-Luxembourg 23.1%, UK 8.1%), US 7.9%

■ HEALTH

Births: 13/1,000 population (1991)
Deaths: 8/1,000 population (1991)

Infant Mortality: 7 deaths/1,000 live births (1991)
Life Expectancy at Birth: 74 years male, 80 years female (1992)
No. of Physicians: 22.2/10,000 population (1992)

■ EDUCATION

Govt. Expenditure: 10.55% total govt. expenditures (1991)
Literacy: 99% (1992)

■ COMMUNICATIONS

Daily newspapers: 86 (1992)
Televisions: 484.8/1,000 inhabitants (1992)
Radios: 902/1,000 inhabitants (1992)
Telephones: 65.86/100 inhabitants (1992)

■ TRANSPORTATION

Motor Vehicles: 6,091,294; 5,509,174 passenger cars (1990)
Roads: 142,300 km; 125,215 km paved
Railway: 3,517 km
Air Traffic: 8,893,000 passengers carried (1991)
Airports: 15

Canadian Embassy: Parkstraat 25, 2514 JD The Hague, mailing address: P.O. Box 30820, 25 Parkstraat, 2500 GV The Hague, Netherlands. Tel: (011-31-70) 361-4111. Fax: (011-31-70) 356-1111
Embassy in Canada: Royal Netherlands Embassy, 350 Albert St, Ste 2020, Ottawa ON K1R 1A4. Tel: (613) 237-5030. Fax: (613) 237-6471

Netherlands Antilles

Dependent Territory of the Netherlands

Long-Form Name: Netherlands Antilles
Capital: Willemstad
Population: 175,000 (1992)

■ GEOGRAPHY

Area: 800 sq. km, 2 island groups
Climate: tropical maritime, short rainy season
Land Use: islands mostly too rocky for agriculture
Location: West Indies

■ PEOPLE

Nationality: Dutch
Ethnic Groups: West Indian, Hispanic
Languages: Dutch (official), Papiamento (derived from Dutch, Spanish, Portuguese), English

■ GOVERNMENT

Leader(s): Gov. Dr. Jaime M. Saleh; Prime Min. Maria-Liberia Peters
Government Type: dependency with internal self-government

■ ECONOMY

Overview: agriculture: livestock, esp. goats; fishing; most food must be imported; tourism; industries: limestone mining, crude oil, oil refining; Curaçao has one of the largest ship-repair dry docks in western hemisphere; chief trading partner: United Kingdom
Exports: $1.790 billion (1990)
Imports: $2.147 billion (1990)
Currency: Netherlands Antilles guilder

New Caledonia

Overseas Territory of France

Long-Form Name: New Caledonia and Dependencies
Capital: Nouméa
Population: 173,000 (1992)

■ GEOGRAPHY

Area: 18,576 sq. km (a peninsula and three small islands)
Climate: humid, subtropical maritime
Land Use: 677,000 acres pasture, 47,000 acres commercially cultivated, almost 1 million acres forest
Location: SW Pacific Ocean (Melanesia)

■ PEOPLE

Nationality: French
Ethnic Groups: Melanesians (40%); Europeans constitute the second-largest group; Indonesian, Polynesian, Vietnamese minorities
Languages: French (official), Melanesian, Polynesian languages

■ GOVERNMENT

Leader(s): Pres. of Territorial Congress Simon Loueckhote
Government Type: overseas territory

■ ECONOMY

Overview: agriculture inc. beef, poultry, coffee, fruits, vegetables; forest, fishery products; industry: nickel mining and smelting, chromite, cobalt, chemical plants, food processing, cement, hardware, clothing; one of the world's leading nickel producers; main trading partners: France, United Kingdom, Australia

Exports: $444 million (1991)
Imports: $863 million (1991)
Currency: CFP franc

New Zealand

Long-Form Name: New Zealand
Capital: Wellington
Population: 3,455,000 (1992)

■ GEOGRAPHY

Area: 268,680 sq. km
Coastline: 15,134 km
Climate: temperate with sharp regional contrasts
Environment: earthquakes are common though usually not severe
Terrain: predominately mountainous with some large coastal plains
Land Use: 2% arable, 0% permanent, 53% meadows and pastures, 38% forest and woodland, 7% other
Location: SE of Australia, bordering on Tasman Sea, Pacific Ocean

■ PEOPLE

Nationality: New Zealander
Ethnic Groups: 88% European, 8.9% Maori, 2.9% Pacific Islander, 0.2% other
Languages: English (official), Maori
Religions: 75% Christian, 18% unspecified, 7% Hindu, Confucian, other
Marriages: 7.5 (per 1,000) (1987)
Divorces: 2.7 (per 1,000) (1987)

■ GOVERNMENT

Leader(s): Gov. Gen. Catherine Tizard, Prime Min. Jim Bolger
Government Type: parliamentary democracy
Administrative Divisions: 93 counties, 9 districts, 3 town districts; dependent areas inc.: the Cook Islands, the Kermadec Islands, Nive, the Ross Dependency (uninhabited except for scientific personnel), Tokelau
Independence: Sept. 26, 1907 (from UK)
National Holiday: Waitangi Day, Feb. 6

■ ECONOMY

Overview: government has been reorienting an agrarian economy; inflation has been reduced; growth has been sluggish, unemployment has been at an all-time high
GNP: $41.626 billion, per capita $12,140; real growth rate 1.0% (1991)
Inflation: 6.1% (1990)

Industries: food processing, wool production, wood and paper products, textiles, machinery, transportation equipment, banking and insurance, tourism, mining
Labour Force: 1,570,900 (1992); 69.9% services, 20.1% industry, 10% agriculture (1989)
Unemployment: 10.3% (1991)
Agriculture: accounts for 9% of GNP and 10% of work force; livestock predominates: wool, meat, dairy products; crops: wheat, barley, potatoes, pulses, fruits and vegetables; surplus producer of farm products
Natural Resources: natural gas, iron ore, sand, coal, timber, hydroelectricity, gold, limestone

■ FINANCE/TRADE

Currency: New Zealand dollar (NZ$)
International Reserves Excluding Gold: $3,232 million (1992)
Gold Reserves: 0.00 million fine troy ounces (1992)
Budget: revenues $17.6 billion; expenditures $18.3 billion, including capital expenditures (1991)
Defence Expenditures: $826.27 million (1990)
External Debt: $17 billion (1989)
Exports: $9.873 billion (1992); commodities: wool, lamb, mutton, beef, fruit, fish, cheese, manufactures, chemicals, forestry products; partners: European Community 18.3%, Japan 17.9%, Australia 17.5%, US 13.5%
Imports: $9.219 billion (1992); commodities: petroleum, consumer goods, motor vehicles, industrial equipment; partners: Australia 19.7%, Japan 16.9%, European Community 16.9%, US 15.3%, Taiwan 3%

■ HEALTH

Births: 15/1,000 population (1991)
Deaths: 8/1,000 population (1991)
Infant Mortality: 10 deaths/1,000 live births (1991)
Life Expectancy at Birth: 72 years male, 78 years female (1992)
No. of Physicians: 17.4/10,000 population (1992)

■ EDUCATION

Govt. Expenditure: 13% of govt. expenditure (1988)
Literacy: 99% (1992)

■ COMMUNICATIONS

Daily newspapers: 35 (1992)
Televisions: 371.6/1,000 inhabitants (1992)
Radios: 922/1,000 inhabitants (1992)
Telephones: 71.74/100 inhabitants (1992)

■ TRANSPORTATION

Motor Vehicles: 1,867,745; 1,557,074 passenger cars (1990)
Roads: 93,232 km; 51,319 km paved
Railway: 4,245 km
Air Traffic: 5,371,000 passengers carried (1991)
Airports: 59

Canadian Embassy: The Canadian High Commission, 61 Molesworth St, 3rd Floor, Wellington; mailing address: P.O. Box 12049, Thorndon, Wellington, New Zealand. Tel: (011-64-4) 473-9577. Fax: (011-64-4) 471-2082
Embassy in Canada: New Zealand High Commission, Metropolitan House, 99 Bank St, Ste 727, Ottawa ON K1P 6G3. Tel: (613) 238-5991. Fax: (613) 238-5707.

Nicaragua

Long-Form Name: Republic of Nicaragua
Capital: Managua
Population: 3,955,000 (1992)

■ GEOGRAPHY

Area: 127,849 sq. km
Coastline: 910 km
Climate: tropical in lowlands, cooler in highlands
Environment: subject to destructive earthquakes, volcanoes, landslides and occasional severe hurricanes; deforestation; soil erosion; water pollution
Terrain: extensive Atlantic coastal plains rising to central interior mountains; narrow Pacific coastal plain interrupted by volcanoes
Land Use: 9% arable; 1% permanent; 43% meadows; 35% forest; 12% other
Location: Central (Latin) America, bordering on Caribbean Sea, Pacific Ocean

■ PEOPLE

Nationality: Nicaraguan
Ethnic Groups: 69% mestizo, 17% white, 9% black. 5% Indian
Languages: Spanish (official); English- and Indian-speaking minorities on Atlantic coast
Religions: 95% Roman Catholic, 5% Protestant
Marriages: 3.5 (per 1,000) (1986)
Divorces: 0.2 (per 1,000) (1986)

■ GOVERNMENT

Leader(s): Pres. Violeta Chamorro, V. Pres. Virgilio Reyes Godoy
Government Type: republic
Administrative Divisions: 16 departments
Independence: Sept. 15, 1821 (from Spain)

National Holiday: Independence Day, Sept. 15

■ **ECONOMY**

Overview: the economy is based on the export of coffee and cotton; government control is extensive, including the financial system, wholesale purchasing, production, sales, foreign trade and distribution of goods; many shortages; high inflation; large debt
GNP: $1.897 billion, per capita $340; real growth rate -1.4% (1991)
Inflation: 1,700% (1989)
Industries: food processing, chemicals, metal products, textiles, clothing, petroleum refining and distribution, beverages, footwear
Labour Force: 1,204,000 (1992); 37.7% services, 46.5% agriculture, 15.8% industry (1989)
Unemployment: 14.0% (1992)
Agriculture: accounts for 23% of GDP and 44% of work force; cash crops—coffee, bananas, sugar cane, cotton; food crops—rice, corn, cassava, citrus fruit, beans; variety of animal products—beef, veal, pork, poultry, dairy; war has lowered self sufficiency in food
Natural Resources: gold, silver, copper, tungsten, lead, zinc, timber, fish

■ **FINANCE/TRADE**

Currency: córdoba ($C)
International Reserves Excluding Gold: $167 million (1983)
Gold Reserves: 0.12 million fine troy ounces (1983)
Budget: revenues $244 million; expenditures $550 million, including capital expenditures of $73 million (1988)
Defence Expenditures: $318 million (1990)
External Debt: $8.067 billion (1990)
Exports: $250 million (1989); commodities: coffee, cotton, sugar, bananas, seafood, meat, chemicals; partners: CEMA 15%, OECD 75%, others 10%
Imports: $550 million (1989); commodities: petroleum, food, chemicals, machinery, clothing; partners: CEMA 55%, European Community 20%, Latin America 10%, others 10%

■ **HEALTH**

Births: 37/1,000 population (1991)
Deaths: 7/1,000 population (1991)
Infant Mortality: 60 deaths/1,000 live births (1991)
Life Expectancy at Birth: 59 years male, 65 years female (1992)
No. of Physicians: 6.4/10,000 population (1992)

■ **EDUCATION**

Govt. Expenditure: 12.0% of govt. expenditure (1987)
Literacy: 57.5% (1992)

■ **COMMUNICATIONS**

Daily newspapers: 3 (1992)
Televisions: 61.4/1,000 inhabitants (1992)
Radios: 247/1,000 inhabitants (1992)
Telephones: 1.65/100 inhabitants (1992)

■ **TRANSPORTATION**

Motor Vehicles: 74,085; 31,111 passenger cars (1990)
Roads: 16,110 km; 1,662 km paved
Railway: 320 km
Air Traffic: 130,000 passengers carried (1991)
Airports: 11

Canadian Embassy: C/o Flr 6, Cronos Building, Calle 3 y Avenida Central; mailing address: Apartado Postal 10303-1000, San José, Costa Rica. Tel: (011-506) 55-35-22. Fax: (011-506) 23-23-95
Embassy in Canada: Embassy of the Republic of Nicaragua, 170 Laurier Ave W, Ste 908, Ottawa ON K1P 5V5. Tel: (613) 234-9361. Fax: (613) 238-7666.

Niger

Long-Form Name: Republic of the Niger
Capital: Niamey
Population: 8,252,000 (1992)

■ **GEOGRAPHY**

Area: 1,267,000 sq. km
Coastline: none: landlocked
Climate: mostly hot, dry, dusty; tropical in extreme south
Environment: recurrent drought and desertification severely affecting marginal agricultural activities; overgrazing; soil erosion
Terrain: desert; hills in north
Land Use: 3% arable land; 0% permanent; 7% meadows; 2% forest; 88% other
Location: NC Africa

■ **PEOPLE**

Nationality: Nigerien
Ethnic Groups: 56% Hausa; 22% Djerma; 9% Fula; 8% Tuareg; 4% Beri Beri (Kanouri); 1% Arab, Toubou and Gourmantche; about 4,000 French expatriates
Languages: French (official); Hausa (50%), Djerma, also Tuareg, Fulani

Religions: 85% Moslem, remainder indigenous beliefs and Christians
Marriages: n.a.
Divorces: n.a.

■ GOVERNMENT

Leader(s): Prime Min. Amadou Cheiffou, Pres. Brig. Gen Ali Saibou
Government Type: republic; presidential system in which military officers hold key offices
Administrative Divisions: 7 departments
Independence: Aug. 3, 1960 (from France)
National Holiday: Republic Day, Dec. 18

■ ECONOMY

Overview: about 90% of the population is engaged in livestock rearing and farming; depends heavily on exploitation of uranium deposits, thus vulnerable to demand for uranium; increasing external debt is a problem
GNP: $2.361 billion, per capita $300; real growth rate -0.9% (1991)
Inflation: -7.8% (1991)
Industries: cement, brick, rice mills, small cotton gins, oilseed presses, slaughterhouses and a few other small light industries; uranium production began in 1971
Labour Force: 3,620,000 (1992); 85% agriculture, 2.7% industry, 12.3% services (1989)
Unemployment: 46.8% (1989)
Agriculture: accounts for roughly 40% of GDP and 90% of labor force; cash crops—cowpeas, cotton, peanuts; food crops—millet, sorghum, cassava, rice; livestock—cattle, sheep, goats; self-sufficient in food except in drought years
Natural Resources: uranium, coal, iron ore, tin, phosphates

■ FINANCE/TRADE

Currency: Communauté financière africaine franc (CFAF)
International Reserves Excluding Gold: $221 million (1992)
Gold Reserves: 0.01 million fine troy ounces (1991)
Budget: revenues $220 million; expenditures $446 million, including capital expenditures of $190 million (1989)
Defence Expenditures: $17.21 million (1989)
External Debt: $1.326 billion (1990)
Exports: $283 million (1990); commodities: uranium 76%, livestock, cowpeas, onions, hides, skins; partners: n.a.
Imports: $389 million (1990); commodities: petroleum products, primary materials, machinery, vehicles and parts, electronic equipment,

pharmaceuticals, chemical products, cereals, foodstuffs; partners: n.a.

■ HEALTH

Births: 50/1,000 population (1991)
Deaths: 16/1,000 population (1991)
Infant Mortality: 129 deaths/1,000 live births (1991)
Life Expectancy at Birth: 43 years male, 46 years female (1992)
No. of Physicians: 0.2/10,000 population (1992)

■ EDUCATION

Govt. Expenditure: 9.0% of government expenditure (1989)
Literacy: 28.4% (1992)

■ COMMUNICATIONS

Daily newspapers: 1 (1992)
Televisions: 4/1,000 inhabitants (1992)
Radios: 59/1,000 inhabitants (1992)
Telephones: 0.2/100 inhabitants (1992)

■ TRANSPORTATION

Motor Vehicles: 35,000; 17,000 passenger cars (1990)
Roads: 19,000 km; 3,800 km paved
Railway: n.a.
Air Traffic: 64,000 passengers carried (1991)
Airports: 20

Canadian Embassy: c/o Immeuble Trade-Center, 23, rue Nogues, Le Plateau; mailing address: 01 BP 4104, Abidjan 01, Côte d'Ivoire. Tel: (011-225) 32-20-09. Fax: (011-225) 22-05-30
Embassy in Canada: Embassy of the Republic of Niger, 38 Blackburn Ave, Ottawa ON K1N 8A2. Tel: (613) 232-4291, -2, -3. Fax: (613) 230-9808.

Nigeria

Long-Form Name: Federal Republic of Nigeria
Capital: Lagos
Population: 115,664,000 (1992)

■ GEOGRAPHY

Area: 923,770 sq. km
Coastline: 853 km
Climate: varies; equatorial in south, tropical in centre, arid in north
Environment: recent droughts in north severely affecting marginal agricultural activities; desertification; soil degradation, rapid deforestation
Terrain: southern lowlands merge into central hills and plateaus; mountains in southeast, plains in north

Land Use: 31% arable; 3% permanent; 23% meadows; 15% forest; 28% other
Location: WC Africa, bordering on South Atlantic Ocean

■ PEOPLE

Nationality: Nigerian
Ethnic Groups: more than 250 tribal groups; Hausa and Fulani of the north, Yoruba of the southwest and Ibos of the southeast make up 65% of the population; about 27,000 non-Africans
Languages: English (official); Hausa, Yoruba, Ibo, Fulani and several other languages also widely used
Religions: 50% Moslem, 40% Christian, 10% indigenous beliefs
Marriages: n.a.
Divorces: n.a.

■ GOVERNMENT

Leader(s): Ernest Shonekan (interim)
Government Type: military government from Dec. 1983 to Aug. 27, 1993 when interim government announced
Administrative Divisions: 21 states and 1 territory
Independence: Oct. 1, 1960 (from UK)
National Holiday: Independence Day, Oct. 1

■ ECONOMY

Overview: the economy is dependent on oil and vulnerable to oil prices; agricultural production has been poor recently; high inflationary pressures are a concern
GNP: $34.057 billion, per capita $290; real growth rate 1.4% (1991)
Inflation: 13% (1991)
Industries: crude oil, natural gas, coal, tin, columbite; palm oil, peanut, cotton, rubber, petroleum, wood, hides and skins; textiles, cement, building materials, food products, footwear, chemicals, printing, ceramics, steel
Labour Force: 42,000,000 (1992); 44.6% agriculture, 51.2% services, 4.2% industry (1989)
Unemployment: 57,094 (1990)
Agriculture: accounts for 28% of GNP and half of labor force; inefficient small-scale farming dominates; once a large net exporter of food and now an importer; cash crops—cocoa, peanuts, palm oil, rubber; food crops—corn, rice, sorghum, millet, cassava, yams
Natural Resources: crude oil, tin, columbite, iron ore, coal, limestone, lead, zinc, natural gas

■ FINANCE/TRADE

Currency: naira (N)

International Reserves Excluding Gold: $3,663 million (1992)
Gold Reserves: 0.69 million fine troy ounces (1992)
Budget: revenues $8.0 billion; expenditures $8.0 billion, including capital expenditures (1990)
Defence Expenditures: $272.46 million (1990)
External Debt: $33.709 billion (1990)
Exports: $13.67 billion (1990); commodities: oil 95%, cocoa, palm kernels, rubber; partners: European Community 51%, US 32%
Imports: $5.688 billion (1990); commodities: consumer goods, capital equipment, chemicals, raw materials; partners: European Community, US

■ HEALTH

Births: 46/1,000 population (1991)
Deaths: 16/1,000 population (1991)
Infant Mortality: 118 deaths/1,000 live births (1991)
Life Expectancy at Birth: 48 years male, 49 years female (1992)
No. of Physicians: 1.6/10,000 population (1992)

■ EDUCATION

Govt. Expenditure: 2.81% of govt. expenditure (1987)
Literacy: 50.7% (1992)

■ COMMUNICATIONS

Daily newspapers: 31 (1992)
Televisions: 28.6/1,000 inhabitants (1992)
Radios: 171/1,000 inhabitants (1992)
Telephones: 0.3/100 inhabitants (1992)

■ TRANSPORTATION

Motor Vehicles: 1,410,000; 785,000 passenger cars (1986)
Roads: 109,930 km; 30,484 km paved
Railway: 3,510 km
Air Traffic: 930,000 passengers carried (1991)
Airports: 46

Canadian Embassy: The Canadian High Commission, 4 Idowu Taylor St, Victoria Island, Lagos; mailing address: The Canadian High Commission, P.O. Box 54506, Ikoyi Station, Lagos, Nigeria. Tel: (011-234-1) 612-382. Fax: (011-234-1) 614-691
Embassy in Canada: High Commission for the Federal Republic of Nigeria, 295 Metcalfe St, Ottawa ON K2P 1R9. Tel: (613) 236-0521. Fax: (613) 236-0529.

Niue

Territory of New Zealand

Long-Form Name: Niue
Capital: Alofi
Population: 2,000 (1992)

■ GEOGRAPHY

Area: 258 sq. km, world's largest uplifted coral island
Climate: tropical maritime
Land Use: n.a.
Location: Pacific Ocean, NE of New Zealand

■ PEOPLE

Nationality: New Zealander
Ethnic Groups: Pacific Island tribes
Languages: English, Niuean

■ GOVERNMENT

Leader(s): Prem. Young Vivian
Government Type: self-governing territory

■ ECONOMY

Overview: agriculture inc. coconuts, honey, limes, root crops; chief trading partner: New Zealand
Currency: New Zealand dollar

Norfolk Island

Dependent Territory of Australia

Long-Form Name: Norfolk Island
Capital: Kingston
Population: 1,977 (1986)

■ GEOGRAPHY

Area: 35 sq. km
Climate: tropical maritime
Land Use: fertile soil, agricultural cultivation confined to citrus fruits, bananas, some vegetables
Location: S Pacific Ocean, NE of Australia

■ PEOPLE

Nationality: Australian
Ethnic Groups: majority descendants of Polynesians and British (the latter crew members of the British naval ship *Bounty*)
Languages: mixture of West Country English, Gaelic, Tahitian

■ GOVERNMENT

Leader(s): Admin. H. MacDonald; head of legislative assembly John Brown
Government Type: a largely self-governing dependency

■ ECONOMY

Overview: mainly export of indigenous fruits and vegetables
Currency: Australian dollar

Northern Marianas

Outlying Territory of the United States

Long-Form Name: The Commonwealth of the Northern Mariana Islands
Capital: Chalan Kanoa (largest town)
Population: 47,000 (1992)

■ GEOGRAPHY

Area: 477 sq. km (combined land area of 16 islands)
Climate: tropical maritime
Land Use: volcanic islands too mountainous for cultivation; chief agricultural use is grazing
Location: Pacific Ocean, E of the Philippines

■ PEOPLE

Nationality: American
Ethnic Groups: Pacific Island tribes, Oriental
Languages: English (official), Chamorro, Carolinian, Japanese

■ GOVERNMENT

Leader(s): Gov. Lorenzo (Larry) De Leon Guerrero; Lieut.-Gov. Benjamin Manglona
Government Type: outlying territory

■ ECONOMY

Overview: agriculture: livestock (cattle, tourism; imports greatly exceed export value
Currency: American dollar

Norway

Long-Form Name: Kingdom of Norway
Capital: Oslo
Population: 4,288,000 (1992)

■ GEOGRAPHY

Area: 324,220 sq. km
Coastline: 21,935 km (3,491 km mainland; 2,413 km large islands; 16,093 km long fjords, numerous small islands and minor indentations); one of the longest and most rugged coastlines in the world

Climate: temperate along coast, modified by North Atlantic Current; colder interior; rainy year-round on west coast

Environment: air and water pollution; acid rain

Terrain: glaciated; mostly high plateaus and rugged mountains broken by fertile valleys; small, scattered plains; coastline deeply indented by fjords; arctic tundra in north

Land Use: 3% arable; negligible meadows, 27% forest; 70% other

Location: N Europe, bordering on Norwegian Sea, North Sea

■ PEOPLE

Nationality: Norwegian

Ethnic Groups: Germanic (Nordic, Alpine, Baltic) and racial-cultural minority of 20,000 Lapps

Languages: Norwegian (official); small Lapp- and Finnish-speaking minorities

Religions: Christianity (predominantly Protestant)

Marriages: 5.0 (per 1,000) (1987)

Divorces: 2.0 (per 1,000) (1987)

■ GOVERNMENT

Leader(s): Prime Min. Gro Harlem Brundtland, King Harald V

Government Type: constitutional monarchy

Administrative Divisions: 19 counties; dependent areas inc.: Bouvet Island (uninhabited), Jan Mayen (uninhabited), Peter I Island (uninhabited), Queen Maud Land (uninhabited), Svalbard

Independence: Oct. 26, 1905 (from Sweden)

National Holiday: Constitution Day, May 17

■ ECONOMY

Overview: a prosperous capitalist nation which has extensive welfare measures; concerns are the aging population, increased economic integration with Europe and the balance between private and public influence in economic decisions

GNP: $102.885 billion, per capita $24,160; real growth rate 2.5% (1991)

Inflation: 3.4% (1991)

Industries: petroleum and gas, food processing, shipbuilding, pulp and paper products, metal, chemicals, timber, mining, textiles, fishing

Labour Force: 2,128,000 (1992); 77.8% services, 16.1% industry, 6.1% agriculture (1989)

Unemployment: 4.7% (1991)

Agriculture: accounts for 3.1% of GNP and 6.5% of labor force; among world's top 10 fishing nations; livestock output exceeds value of crops; over half of food needs imported

Natural Resources: crude oil, copper, natural gas, pyrites, nickel, iron ore, zinc, lead, fish, timber, hydropower

■ FINANCE/TRADE

Currency: krone (pl. kroner) (NKr)

International Reserves Excluding Gold: $16,619 million (1992)

Gold Reserves: 1.18 million fine troy ounces (1992)

Budget: revenues $47.9 billion; expenditures $48.7 billion, including capital expenditures (1990)

Defence Expenditures: $3.76 billion (1991)

External Debt: $18.3 billion (1989)

Exports: $34.801 billion (1992); commodities: petroleum and petroleum products 25%, natural gas 11%, fish 7%, aluminum 6%, ships 3.5%, pulp and paper; partners: UK 26%, EFTA 16.3%, less developed countries 14%, Sweden 12%, Germany 12%, US 6%, Denmark 5%

Imports: $25.797 billion (1992); commodities: machinery, fuels and lubricants, transportation equipment, chemicals, foodstuffs, clothing, ships; partners: Sweden 18%, less developed countries 18%, Germany 14%, Denmark 8%, UK 7%, Japan 5%

■ HEALTH

Births: 14/1,000 population (1991)

Deaths: 11/1,000 population (1991)

Infant Mortality: 7 deaths/1,000 live births (1991)

Life Expectancy at Birth: 73 years male, 80 years female (1992)

No. of Physicians: 22.2/10,000 population (1992)

■ EDUCATION

Govt. Expenditure: 9.4% of govt. expenditure (1990)

Literacy: 100% (1992)

■ COMMUNICATIONS

Daily newspapers: 83 (1992)

Televisions: 422.7/1,000 inhabitants (1992)

Radios: 796.7/1,000 inhabitants (1992)

Telephones: 62.20/100 inhabitants (1992)

■ TRANSPORTATION

Motor Vehicles: 1,942,558; 1,613,037 passenger cars (1990)

Roads: 93,051 km; 64,520 km paved

Railway: 4,280 km

Air Traffic: 8,857,000 passengers carried (1991)

Airports: 54

Canadian Embassy: The Canadian Embassy, Oscars Gate 20, Oslo 3, Norway; mailing address: 0244 Oslo, Norway. Tel: (011-47-2) 46-69-55. Fax: (011-47-2) 69-34-67

Embassy in Canada: Royal Norwegian Embassy, Royal Bank Centre, 90 Sparks St, Ste 532, Ottawa ON K1P 5B4. Tel: (613) 238-6571. Fax: (613) 238-2765.

Oman

Long-Form Name: Sultanate of Oman
Capital: Masqat or Muscat
Population: 1,637,000 (1992)

■ GEOGRAPHY

Area: estimated at 300,000 sq. km
Coastline: 2,092 km along the Arabian Sea and Gulf of Oman
Climate: dry desert; hot, humid along coast; hot, dry interior; strong southwest summer monsoon (May to Sept.) in far south
Environment: summer winds often raise large sandstorms and dust storms in interior; sparse natural freshwater resources
Terrain: vast central desert plain, rugged mountains in north and south
Land Use: negligible arable; negligible permanent; 5% meadows; 0% forest; 95% other
Location: SW Asia (Middle East), bordering on Arabian Sea

■ PEOPLE

Nationality: Omani
Ethnic Groups: almost entirely Arab, with small Balochi, Zanzibari and Indian groups
Languages: Arabic (official); English, Balochi, Urdu, Indian dialects
Religions: 75% Ibadhi Moslem; remainder Sunni Moslem, Shi'a Moslem, Hindu minority
Marriages: n.a.
Divorces: n.a.

■ GOVERNMENT

Leader(s): Sultan Qaboos bin Sa'id Al Said
Government Type: absolute monarchy; independent, with residual UK influence
Administrative Divisions: 7 planning regions
Independence: 1650, expulsion of the Portuguese
National Holiday: National Day, Nov. 18

■ ECONOMY

Overview: economy depends on the success of its oil industry which is fueled by 20 years' supply at the current rate of extraction; agriculture is the major employment

GNP: $8.787 billion, per capita $6,006; real growth rate 9.3% (1991)
Inflation: 2% (1988 est.)
Industries: crude oil production and refining, natural gas production, construction, cement, copper
Labour Force: 405,100 (1992); 50% agriculture, 21.8% industry, 28.6% services (1989); 58% of labor force are non-Omani
Unemployment: n.a.
Agriculture: accounts for 3.4% of GDP and 60% of the labor force (including fishing); less than 2% of land cultivated; largely subsistence farming (dates, limes, bananas, alfalfa, vegetables, camels, cattle); not self-sufficient in food
Natural Resources: crude oil, copper, asbestos, some marble, limestone, chromium, gypsum, natural gas

■ FINANCE/TRADE

Currency: Omani rial (RO)
International Reserves Excluding Gold: $1,609 million (1992)
Gold Reserves: 0.29 million fine troy ounces (1992)
Budget: revenues $3.5 billion; expenditures $4.3 billion, including capital expenditures of $675 million (1989)
Defence Expenditures: $1.39 billion (1990)
External Debt: $2.205 billion (1990)
Exports: $4.874 billion (1991); commodities: petroleum, re-exports, processed copper, dates, nuts, fish; partners: Japan, S Korea, Thailand
Imports: $3.194 billion (1991); commodities: machinery, transportation equipment, manufactured goods, food, livestock, lubricants; partners: Japan, United Arab Emirates, UK, Germany, US

■ HEALTH

Births: 41/1,000 population (1991)
Deaths: 6/1,000 population (1991)
Infant Mortality: 40 deaths/1,000 live births (1991)
Life Expectancy at Birth: 64 years male, 68 years female (1992)
No. of Physicians: 9.1/10,000 population (1990)

■ EDUCATION

Govt. Expenditure: 11.43% of government expenditure (1991)
Literacy: 20%

■ COMMUNICATIONS

Daily newspapers: 3 (1992)
Televisions: 761.8/1,000 inhabitants (1992)
Radios: 645/1,000 inhabitants (1992)

Telephones: 5.33/100 inhabitants (1992)

■ TRANSPORTATION

Motor Vehicles: 215,266; 140,000 passenger cars (1990)
Roads: 32,100 km; 5,400 km paved
Railway: n.a.
Air Traffic: 958,000 passengers carried (1991)
Airports: 7

Canadian Embassy: c/o Da'Aiah - Block 4, Al-Mutawakel St, Kuwait City; mailing address: P.O. Box 25281, Safat, Kuwait City, 13113, Kuwait. Tel: (011-965) 256-3025. Fax: (011-965) 256-4167

Pakistan

Long-Form Name: Islamic Republic of Pakistan
Capital: Islamabad
Population: 124,773,000 (1992)

■ GEOGRAPHY

Area: 796,095 sq. km
Coastline: 1,046 km along Gulf of Oman and Arabian Sea
Climate: mostly hot, dry desert; temperate in northwest; arctic in north
Environment: frequent earthquakes, occasionally severe especially in north and west; flooding along the Indus after heavy rains (July and Aug.); deforestation; soil erosion; desertification;
Terrain: flat Indus plain in east; mountains in north and northwest; Balochistan plateau in west
Land Use: 26% arable; negligible permanent; 6% meadows; 4% forest; 64% other
Location: SW Asia (Middle East), bordering on Arabian Sea

■ PEOPLE

Nationality: Pakistani
Ethnic Groups: Punjabi, Sindhi, Pashtun (Pathan), Balock, Nuhajir (immigrants from India and their descendents)
Languages: Urdu (national), Punjab, Sindhi, Pushto, English
Religions: 97% Moslem (77% Sunni, 20% Shi'a), 3% Christian, Hindu and other
Marriages: n.a.
Divorces: n.a.

■ GOVERNMENT

Leader(s): Prime Min. Moeen Qureshi (acting), Pres. Khan Ghulum Ishaq; national election Oct. 6, 1993.
Government Type: parliamentary with strong executive, federal republic
Administrative Divisions: 4 provinces, 1 tribal area and 1 territory
Independence: Aug. 15, 1947 (from UK; formerly West Pakistan)
National Holiday: Pakistan Day (proclamation of the republic), Mar. 23

■ ECONOMY

Overview: a poor economy faced with rapidly increasing population, sizable government deficits and heavy dependence on foreign aid; small-scale industry and agriculture is in private hands and most large-scale industry is now publicly-owned
GNP: $46.725 billion, per capita $400; real growth rate 6.5% (1991)
Inflation: 6.6% (1991)
Industries: textiles, food processing, beverages, petroleum products, construction materials, clothing, paper products, international finance, shrimp
Labour Force: 34,000,000 (1992); 49.6% agriculture, 12.4% industry, 38% services (1989)
Unemployment: 6.3% (1991)
Agriculture: 24% of GNP, over 50% of labor force; world's largest continuous irrigation system; cotton, wheat, rice, sugar cane, fruits, vegetables, livestock
Natural Resources: land, extensive natural gas reserves, limited crude oil, poor quality coal, iron ore, copper, salt, limestone

■ FINANCE/TRADE

Currency: Pakistani rupee (PRs)
International Reserves Excluding Gold: $850 million (1992)
Gold Reserves: 2.02 million fine troy ounces (1992)
Budget: revenues $5.6 billion; expenditures $8.3 billion, including capital expenditures of $2.7 billion (1991)
Defence Expenditures: $2.91 billion (1990)
External Debt: $16.532 billion (1990)
Exports: $6.471 billion (1991); commodities: rice, cotton, textiles, clothing; partners: European Community 31%, US 11%, Japan 11%
Imports: $8.427 billion (1991); commodities: petroleum, petroleum products, machinery, transportation, equipment, vegetable oils, animals fats, chemicals; partners: European Community 26%, Japan 15%, US 11%

■ HEALTH

Births: 43/1,000 population (1991)
Deaths: 13/1,000 population (1991)

Infant Mortality: 109 deaths/1,000 live births (1991)
Life Expectancy at Birth: 56 years male, 57 years female (1992)
No. of Physicians: 3.4/10,000 population (1992)

■ EDUCATION

Govt. Expenditure: 5.0% of government expenditure, or 2.0% of GNP in 1980; 2.6% of GNP in 1989
Literacy: 34.8% (1992)

■ COMMUNICATIONS

Daily newspapers: 183 (1992)
Televisions: 15.8/1,000 inhabitants (1992)
Radios: 86/1,000 inhabitants (1992)
Telephones: 0.7/100 inhabitants (1992)

■ TRANSPORTATION

Motor Vehicles: 909,576; 738,059 passenger cars (1990)
Roads: 114,640 km; 60,500 km paved
Railway: 9,075 km
Air Traffic: 5,198,000 million passengers carried (1991)
Airports: 34

Canadian Embassy: The Canadian High Commission, Diplomatic Enclave, Sector G-5, Islamabad; mailing address: The Canadian High Commission, G.P.O. Box 1042, Islamabad, Pakistan. Tel: (011-92-51) 211-101-4. Fax: (011-92-51) 211-540
Embassy in Canada: High Commission for the Islamic Republic of Pakistan, Burnside Bldg., 151 Slater St, Ste 608, Ottawa ON K1P 5H3. Tel: (613) 238-7881. Fax: (613) 238-7296.

Panama

Long-Form Name: Republic of Panama
Capital: Panama City
Population: 2,515,000 (1992)

■ GEOGRAPHY

Area: 77,082 sq. km
Coastline: 2,490 along Caribbean Sea and North Pacific Ocean (Gulf of Panama)
Climate: tropical; hot, humid, cloudy; prolonged rainy season (May to Jan.), short dry season (Jan. to May)
Environment: dense tropical forest in east and northwest
Terrain: interior mostly steep, rugged mountains and dissected, upland plains; coastal areas largely plains and rolling hills

Land Use: 6% arable; 2% permanent; 15% meadows; 54% forest; 23% other
Location: Central (Latin) America, bordering on Caribbean Sea, Pacific Ocean

■ PEOPLE

Nationality: Panamanian
Ethnic Groups: 70% mestizo (mixed Indian and European ancestry), 14% West Indian, 10% white, 6% Indian
Languages: Spanish (official)
Religions: over 93% Roman Catholic, 6% Protestant
Marriages: 5.2 (per 1,000) (1988)
Divorces: 0.7 (per 1,000) (1987)

■ GOVERNMENT

Leader(s): Pres. Guillermo Endara Galimany, V. Pres. Guillermo Ford Boyd
Government Type: centralized republic
Administrative Divisions: 9 provinces and 1 territory
Independence: Nov. 3, 1903 (from Colombia; became independent from Spain Nov. 28, 1821)
National Holiday: Independence Day, Nov. 3

■ ECONOMY

Overview: political instability, lack of credit and the erosion of business confidence have drastically hurt the economy; unemployment is high; exports are stagnant
GNP: $5.254 billion, per capita $2,180; real growth rate 0.3% (1991)
Inflation: 1.2% (1991)
Industries: manufacturing and construction activities, petroleum refining, brewing, cement and other construction materials, sugar mills, paper products
Labour Force: 873,000 (1992); 64.7% services, 25.4% agriculture, 9.9% industry (1989)
Unemployment: 15.7% (1991)
Agriculture: accounts for 10% of GDP; bananas, rice, corn, coffee, sugar cane, livestock, fishing, importer of food grain, vegetables, milk products
Natural Resources: copper, mahogany forests, shrimp

■ FINANCE/TRADE

Currency: balboa (B)
International Reserves Excluding Gold: $519 million (1992)
Gold Reserves: n.a.
Budget: revenues $1.7 billion; expenditures $1.8 billion, including capital expenditures of $70 million (1990)
Defence Expenditures: $75 million (1991)

External Debt: $3.987 billion (1990)
Exports: $342 million (1991); commodities: bananas 40%, shrimp 27%, coffee 4%, sugar, petroleum products; partners: US 90%, Central America and Caribbean, European Community
Imports: $1.695 billion (1991); commodities: foodstuffs 16%, capital goods 9%, crude oil 16%, consumer goods, chemicals; partners: US 35%, Central America and Caribbean, European Community, Mexico, Venezuela

■ HEALTH

Births: 26/1,000 population (1991)
Deaths: 5/1,000 population (1991)
Infant Mortality: 21 deaths/1,000 live births (1991)
Life Expectancy at Birth: 72 years male, 76 years female (1991)
No. of Physicians: 10.0/10,000 population (1992)

■ EDUCATION

Govt. Expenditure: 17.05% of govt. expenditure (1990)
Literacy: 88.1% (1992)

■ COMMUNICATIONS

Daily newspapers: 6 (1992)
Televisions: 164.6/1,000 inhabitants (1992)
Radios: 222/1,000 inhabitants (1992)
Telephones: 10.63/100 inhabitants (1992)

■ TRANSPORTATION

Motor Vehicles: 223,647; 150,903 passenger cars (1990)
Roads: 8,633 km; 2,775 km paved
Railway: 239 km
Air Traffic: 398,000 passengers carried (1991)
Airports: 51

Canadian Embassy: C/o Flr 6, Cronos Building, Calle 3 y Avenida Central; mailing address: Apartado Postal 10303-1000, San José, Costa Rica. Tel: (011-506) 55-35-22. Fax: (011-506) 23-23-95
Representative to Canada: c/o Embassy of Panama, 2862 McGill Terrace NW, Washington DC 20008 USA. Tel: (202) 483-1407. Fax: (202) 483-8413

Papua New Guinea

Long-Form Name: Independent State of Papua New Guinea
Capital: Port Moresby
Population: 4,056,000 (1992)

■ GEOGRAPHY

Area: 462,840 sq. km
Coastline: 5,152 km
Climate: tropical; northwest monsoon (Dec. to Mar.), southeast monsoon (May to Oct.); slight seasonal temperature variation
Environment: one of world's largest swamps along southwest coast; some active volcanos; frequent earthquakes
Terrain: mostly mountains with coastal lowlands and rolling foothills
Land Use: negligible arable; 1% permanent; negligible meadows; 71% forest; 28% other
Location: Pacific Ocean, Coral Sea N of Australia

■ PEOPLE

Nationality: Papua New Guinean
Ethnic Groups: predominantly Melanesian and Papuan; some Negrito, Micronesian and Polynesian
Languages: pidgin, English, Motu (all official); also some 700-800 local languages
Religions: Christianity, Pantheism
Marriages: n.a.
Divorces: n.a.

■ GOVERNMENT

Leader(s): Prime Min. Paias Wingti, Gov. Gen. Wiwa Korowi
Government Type: parliamentary democracy
Administrative Divisions: 20 provinces
Independence: Sept. 16, 1975 (from UN trusteeship under Australian administration)
National Holiday: Independence Day, Sept. 16

■ ECONOMY

Overview: country has abundant natural resources but exploitation has been hampered by the rugged terrain and the high cost of developing an infrastructure; subsistence agriculture and mining are important; receives world aid
GNP: $3.307 billion, per capita $820; real growth rate 1.7% (1991)
Inflation: 7.0% (1991)
Industries: copra crushing, oil palm processing, plywood processing, wood chip production, gold, silver, copper, construction, tourism
Labour Force: 1,570,000 (1992) 76.3% agriculture, 10.2% industry, 13.5% services (1989)
Unemployment: 5% (1988)

Agriculture: one-third of GDP; fertile soils and favourable climate permits cultivating a wide variety of crops; cash crops: coffee, cocoa, coconuts, palm kernels; other products: tea, rubber, sweet potatoes, fruit, vegetables, poultry, pork; net importer of food
Natural Resources: gold, copper, silver, natural gas, timber, oil potential

■ FINANCE/TRADE

Currency: kina (K)
International Reserves Excluding Gold: $277 million (1992)
Gold Reserves: 0.06 million fine troy ounces (1992)
Budget: revenues $867 million; expenditures $873 million, including capital expenditures of $119 million (1990)
Defence Expenditures: $49.82 million (1990)
External Debt: $1.509 billion (1990)
Exports: $1.283 billion (1991); commodities: gold, copper ore, coffee, copra, palm oil, timber, lobster; partners: Germany, Japan, Australia, UK, Spain, US
Imports: $1.403 billion (1991); commodities: machinery and transport equipment, fuels, food, chemicals, consumer goods; partners: Australia, Singapore, Japan, US, New Zealand, UK

■ HEALTH

Births: 34/1,000 population (1991)
Deaths: 11/1,000 population (1991)
Infant Mortality: 66 deaths/1,000 live births (1991)
Life Expectancy at Birth: 53 years male, 55 years female (1992)
No. of Physicians: 1.6/10,000 population (1992)

■ EDUCATION

Govt. Expenditure: 15.33% of govt. expenditure (1988)
Literacy: 52.0% (1992)

■ COMMUNICATIONS

Daily newspapers: 1 (1992)
Televisions: 2.1/1,000 inhabitants (1992)
Radios: 69/1,000 inhabitants (1992)
Telephones: 2.03/100 inhabitants (1992)

■ TRANSPORTATION

Motor Vehicles: 17,100 passenger cars (1987)
Roads: 19,440 km; 463 km paved
Railway: n.a.
Air Traffic: 907,000 passengers carried (1991)
Airports: 402

Canadian Embassy: c/o The Canadian High Commission, Commonwealth Ave, Canberra A.C.T. 2600, Australia. Tel: (011-61-62) 273-3844
Representative to Canada: c/o High Commission for Papua New Guinea, 1615 New Hampshire Ave NW, Ste 300, Washington DC 20009 USA. Tel: (202) 745-3680. Fax: (202) 745-3679

Paraguay

Long-Form Name: Republic of Paraguay
Capital: Asunción
Population: 4,519,000 (1992)

■ GEOGRAPHY

Area: 406,750 sq. km
Coastline: none: landlocked
Climate: varies from temperate in east to semi-arid in far west
Environment: local flooding in southeast (early Sept. to June); poorly drained plains may become boggy (early Oct. to June)
Terrain: grassy plains and wooded hills east of Río Paraguay; Gran Chaco region west of Río Paraguay mostly low, marshy plain near the river and dry forest and thorny scrub elsewhere
Land Use: 20% arable; 1% permanent; 39% meadows; 35% forest; 5% other
Location: C South America

■ PEOPLE

Nationality: Paraguayan
Ethnic Groups: 95% mestizo (Spanish and Indian), 5% white and Indian
Languages: Spanish (official), Guarani
Religions: 90% Roman Catholic; 10% Protestant
Marriages: 4.2 (per 1,000) (1986)
Divorces: n.a.

■ GOVERNMENT

Leader(s): Pres. Juan Carlos Wasmosy
Government Type: republic
Administrative Divisions: 19 departments
Independence: May 14, 1811 (from Spain)
National Holiday: Independence Days, May 14–15

■ ECONOMY

Overview: the economy is based on agriculture in the absence of significant mineral or petroleum resources; has a large hydropower potential; is vulnerable to climactic conditions and international commodity prices for agricultural exports
GNP: $5.374 billion, per capita $1,210; real growth rate 2.3% (1991)

Inflation: 24.3% (1991)
Industries: meat packing, oilseed crushing, milling, brewing, textiles, other light consumer goods, cement, construction
Labour Force: 1,410,000 (1992); 48.6% agriculture, 20.5% industry, 30.9% services
Unemployment: 5.1% (1991)
Agriculture: accounts for 25% GDP; cash crops: cotton, sugar cane; other crops: corn, wheat, tobacco, soybeans, cassava, fruits and vegetables; animal products: beef, pork, eggs, milk; surplus producer of timber; self-sufficient in most foods
Natural Resources: iron ore, manganese, limestone, hydropower, timber

■ FINANCE/TRADE

Currency: guaraní (pl. guaraníes) (G/)
International Reserves Excluding Gold: $643 million (1992)
Gold Reserves: 0.03 million fine troy ounces (1992)
Budget: revenues $1.2 billion; expenditures $1.2 billion, including capital expenditures of $487 million (1991)
Defence Expenditures: $60.59 million (1989)
External Debt: $1.736 billion (1990)
Exports: $959 million (1990); commodities: cotton, soybean, timber, vegetable oils, coffee, tung oil, meat products; partners: European Community 37%, Brazil 25%, Argentina 10%, Chile 6%, US 6%
Imports: $1.313 billion (1990); commodities: capital goods 35%, consumer goods 20%, fuels and lubricants 19%, raw materials 16%, foodstuffs, beverages and tobacco 10%; partners: Brazil 30%, European Community 20%, US 18%, Argentina 8%, Japan 7%

■ HEALTH

Births: 35/1,000 population (1991)
Deaths: 6/1,000 population (1991)
Infant Mortality: 47 deaths/1,000 live births (1991)
Life Expectancy at Birth: 65 years male, 69 years female (1992)
No. of Physicians: 6.9/10,000 population (1992)

■ EDUCATION

Govt. Expenditure: 11% of govt. expenditure (1987)
Literacy: 90.1% (1992)

■ COMMUNICATIONS

Daily newspapers: 5 (1992)
Televisions: 48.2/1,000 inhabitants (1992)

Radios: 169/1,000 inhabitants (1992)
Telephones: 2.6/100 inhabitants (1992)

■ TRANSPORTATION

Motor Vehicles: 110,000; 75,000 passenger cars (1990)
Roads: 11,390 km; 2,035 km paved
Railway: 447 km
Air Traffic: 309,000 passengers carried (1991)
Airports: 29

Canadian Embassy: c/o Ahumada 11, 10th Flr, Santiago, Chile; mailing address: Casilla 771, Santiago, Chile. Tel: (011-56-2) 696-2256. Fax: (011-56-2) 696-0738
Representative to Canada: 151 Slater St, Ste 401, Ottawa, ON K1P 5H3. Tel: (613) 567-1283. Fax: (613) 567-1679

Peru

Long-Form Name: Republic of Peru
Capital: Lima
Population: 22,451,000 (1992)

■ GEOGRAPHY

Area: 1,285,220 sq. km
Coastline: 2,414 km along South Pacific Ocean
Climate: varies from tropical in east to dry desert in west
Environment: subject to earthquakes, tsunamis, landslides, mild volcanic activity; deforestation; overgrazing; soil erosion; desertification; air pollution in Lima; shares control of Lago Titicaca, world's highest navigable lake, with Bolivia
Terrain: western coastal plain (costa), high and rugged Andes in centre (sierra), eastern lowland jungle of Amazon Basin (selva)
Land Use: 3% arable: negligible permanent; 21% meadows; 55% forest; 21% other
Location: W South America, bordering on Pacific Ocean

■ PEOPLE

Nationality: Peruvian
Ethnic Groups: 45% Indian; 37% mestizo (mixed Indian and European ancestry); 15% white; 3% black, Japanese, Chinese and other
Languages: Spanish and Quechua (official), Ayamara
Religions: predominantly Roman Catholic
Marriages: 6.0 (per 1,000) (1982)
Divorces: n.a.

■ GOVERNMENT

Leader(s): Pres. Alberto Kenyo Fujimori, Prime Min. Oscar de la Puente Raygada Albela
Government Type: republic; parts of constitution suspended in Apr. 1992; Congress dissolved; new elections set for Feb. 1993
Administrative Divisions: 24 departments and 1 constitutional province
Independence: July 28, 1821 (from Spain)
National Holiday: Independence Day, July 28

■ ECONOMY

Overview: economy is verging on hyperinflation and economic activity is contracting rapidly; deficit spending and poor relations with international lenders are problems; labor unrest has cut production; food shortages; world's largest producer of coca (for cocaine)
GNP: $38.295 billion, per capita $1,020; real growth rate -0.4% (1991)
Inflation: 409.5% (1991)
Industries: mining of metals, petroleum, fishing, textiles, clothing, food processing, cement, auto assembly, steel, shipbuilding, metal fabrication
Labour Force: 7.138 million (1992); 52.6% services, 35.1% agriculture, 12.3% industry (1989)
Unemployment: 5.8%; underemployment est. at 60% (1991)
Agriculture: accounts for 12% of GDP; commercial crops: coffee, cotton, sugar cane; other crops: rice, wheat, potatoes, plantains, coca; animal products: poultry, meats, dairy, wool; not self-sufficient in grain or vegetable oil; fish catch of 4.6 million metric tons
Natural Resources: copper, silver, gold, petroleum, timber, fish, iron ore, coal, phosphate, potash

■ FINANCE/TRADE

Currency: sol (pl. soles) (S/.)
International Reserves Excluding Gold: $2,664 million (1992)
Gold Reserves: 1.82 million fine troy ounces (1992)
Budget: revenues $1.3 billion; expenditures $2.1 billion, including capital expenditures (1990)
Defence Expenditures: 641.94 million (1990)
External Debt: $13.343 billion (1990)
Exports: $3.379 billion (1991); commodities: fishmeal, cotton, sugar, coffee, copper, iron ore, refined silver, lead, zinc, crude petroleum and byproducts; partners: European Community 22%, US 20%, Japan 11%, Latin America 8%, USSR 4%
Imports: $2.955 billion (1992); commodities:

foodstuffs, machinery, transport equipment, iron and steel semimanufactures, chemicals, pharmaceuticals; partners: US 23%, Latin America 16%, European Community 12%, Japan 7%, Switzerland 3%

■ HEALTH

Births: 28/1,000 population (1991)
Deaths: 8/1,000 population (1991)
Infant Mortality: 66 deaths/1,000 live births (1991)
Life Expectancy at Birth: 60 years male, 63 years female (1992)
No. of Physicians: 9.6/10,000 population (1992)

■ EDUCATION

Govt. Expenditure: 22.9% of govt. expenditure (1987)
Literacy: 85.1% (1992)

■ COMMUNICATIONS

Daily newspapers: 12 (1992)
Televisions: 94.6/1,000 inhabitants (1992)
Radios: 251/1,000 inhabitants (1992)
Telephones: 3.38/100 inhabitants (1992)

■ TRANSPORTATION

Motor Vehicles: 625,000; 395,000 passenger cars (1990)
Roads: 56,550 km; 6,426 km paved
Railway: 3,470 km
Air Traffic: 1,491,000 passengers carried (1991)
Airports: 162

Canadian Embassy: Federico Gerdes 130 (Antes Calle Libertad) Miraflores, Lima; mailing address: Casilla 18-1126, Correo Miraflores, Lima 18, Peru. Tel: (011-51-14) 44-40-15. Fax: (011-51-14) 44-43-47
Embassy in Canada: Embassy of Peru, 170 Laurier Ave W, Ste 1007, Ottawa ON K1P 5V5. Tel: (613) 238-1777, -9. Fax: (613) 232-3062.

Philippines

Long-Form Name: Republic of the Philippines
Capital: Manila
Population: 65,186,000 (1992)

■ GEOGRAPHY

Area: 300,000 sq. km
Coastline: 36,289 km
Climate: tropical marine; northeast monsoon (Nov. to Apr.); southwest monsoon (May to Oct.)

Environment: astride typhoon belt, usually affected by 15 and struck by five to six cyclonic storms per year; subject to landslides, active volcanoes, destructive earthquakes, tsunami; deforestation; soil erosion; water pollution
Terrain: mostly mountains with narrow to extensive coastal lowlands
Land Use: 26% arable; 11% permanent; 4% meadows; 40% forest; 19% other
Location: SE of China, bordering on South China Sea, Pacific Ocean

■ PEOPLE

Nationality: Filipino
Ethnic Groups: 92% Christian Malay, 4% Moslem Malay, 2% Chinese, 3% other
Languages: Pilipino (native national language based on Tagalog) and English (both official); Spanish also spoken, also 76 indigenous languages inc. Cebuano, Tagalog, Iloco, Ifugao
Religions: 83% Roman Catholic, 9% Protestant, 5% Moslem, 3% Buddhist and other
Marriages: 7.0 (per 1,000) (1987)
Divorces: n.a.

■ GOVERNMENT

Leader(s): Pres. Fidel Ramos, Pres. Joseph Estrada
Government Type: republic
Administrative Divisions: 14 regions, divided into 73 provinces and 61 chartered cities
Independence: July 4, 1946 (from US)
National Holiday: Independence Day (from Spain), June 12

■ ECONOMY

Overview: the agriculturally based economy is still recovering from the ouster of former President Marcos and several coup attempts; world's largest exporter of coconuts and coconut products
GNP: $46.138 billion, per capita $740; real growth rate 1.2% (1991)
Inflation: 18.7% (1991)
Industries: textiles, pharmaceuticals, chemicals, wood products, food processing, electronics assembly, petroleum refining, fishing
Labour Force: 22,000,000 (1992); 41.5% agriculture, 9.5% industry, 49% services (1989)
Unemployment: 8.1% (1990)
Agriculture: accounts for about one-third of GDP; major crops: rice, coconuts, corn, sugarcane, bananas, pineapple, mango; animal products: pork, eggs, beef: net exporter of farm products: fish catch of 2 million metric tons annually
Natural Resources: timber, crude oil, nickel, cobalt, silver, gold, salt, copper

■ FINANCE/TRADE

Currency: peso (P)
International Reserves Excluding Gold: $3,801 million (1992)
Gold Reserves: 2.79 million fine troy ounces (1992)
Budget: revenues $7.2 billion; expenditures $8.12 billion, including capital expenditures of $0.97 billion (1989)
Defence Expenditures: $978.98 million (1990)
External Debt: $24.108 billion (1989)
Exports: $8.840 billion (1991); commodities: electrical equipment 19%, textiles 16%, minerals and ores 11%, farm products 10%, coconut 10%, chemicals 5%, fish 5%, forest products 4%; partners: US 36%, European Community 19%, Japan 18%, ESCAP 9%, ASEAN 7%
Imports: $12.051 million (1991); commodities: raw materials 53%, capital goods 17%, petroleum products 17%; partners: US 25%, Japan 17%, ESCAP 13%, European Community 11%, ASEAN 10%, Middle East 10%

■ HEALTH

Births: 29/1,000 population (1991)
Deaths: 7/1,000 population (1991)
Infant Mortality: 54 deaths/1,000 live births (1991)
Life Expectancy at Birth: 63 years male, 66 years female (1992)
No. of Physicians: 1.5/10,000 population (1992)

■ EDUCATION

Govt. Expenditure: 16.14% of govt. expenditure (1991)
Literacy: 89.7% (1992)

■ COMMUNICATIONS

Daily newspapers: 38 (1992)
Televisions: 41.1/1,000 inhabitants (1992)
Radios: 136/1,000 inhabitants (1992)
Telephones: 1.64/100 inhabitants (1992)

■ TRANSPORTATION

Motor Vehicles: 1,219,471; 454,554 passenger cars (1990)
Roads: 158,400; 22,500 km paved
Railway: 1,080 km
Air Traffic: 5,438,000 passengers carried (1991)
Airports: 226

Canadian Embassy: Flr 11, Allied Bank Centre, 6754 Ayala Ave, Makati, Metro Manila, Philippines 1200; mailing address: P.O. Box 971, Makati CPO, Makati, Rizal, Metro Manila, Philippines 1299. Tel: (011-63-2) 815-9536. Fax: (011-63-2) 810-1699
Embassy in Canada: Embassy of the Philippines, 130 Albert St, Ste 606, Ottawa ON K1P 5G4. Tel: (613) 233-1121, -2, -3. Fax: (613) 233-4165.

Pitcairn Islands

Dependent Territory of the United Kingdom

Long-Form Name: Pitcairn Islands Group
Capital: n.a.; Adamstown is only settlement
Population: 61 (1991)

■ GEOGRAPHY

Area: 4.6 sq. km (Pitcairn and 3 small uninhabited islands)
Climate: mild, moist temperate
Land Use: rugged but fertile interior
Location: S Pacific Ocean, E of French Polynesia

■ PEOPLE

Nationality: British
Ethnic Groups: descendants of Polynesians and British (the latter crew members of the British naval ship *Bounty*)
Languages: Pitcairnese English

■ GOVERNMENT

Leader(s): Gov. David J. Moss; Island Magistrate Brian Young
Government Type: dependency

■ ECONOMY

Overview: imports: fuel oil, machinery, building materials; no exports other than small tourist trade with passing ships
Currency: Pitcairn dollar, at par with Zealand dollar

Poland

Long-Form Name: Republic of Poland
Capital: Warsaw
Population: 38,417,000 (1992)

■ GEOGRAPHY

Area: 312,680 sq. km
Coastline: 491 km along Baltic Sea
Climate: temperate with cold, cloudy, moderately severe winters with frequent precipitation; mild summers with frequent showers and thundershowers
Environment: plain crossed by a few north flowing, meandering streams; severe air and water pollution in south; historically, an area of conflict because of flat terrain and the lack of natural barrier on the North European Plain
Terrain: mostly flat plain, mountains along southern border
Land Use: 46% arable; 1% permanent; 13% meadows; 28% forest; 12% other
Location: NC Europe, bordering on Baltic Sea

■ PEOPLE

Nationality: Polish
Ethnic Groups: 98.7% Polish, 0.6% Ukrainian, 0.5% Byelorussian, less than 0.05% Jewish
Languages: Polish
Religions: 95% Roman Catholic (about 75% practising), 5% Russian Orthodox, Protestant and other
Marriages: 6.8 (per 1,000) (1989)
Divorces: 1.2 (per 1,000) (1989)

■ GOVERNMENT

Leader(s): Pres. Lech Walesa
Government Type: democratic state
Administrative Divisions: 49 provinces
Independence: Nov. 11, 1918, independent republic proclaimed
National Holiday: Constitution Day, May 3

■ ECONOMY

Overview: following sweeping political changes of 1989 which disrupted normal economic activity and increased shortages, the government adopted a "cold turkey" program for transforming the country to a market economy from a largely Soviet-style economy
GNP: $70.640 billion, per capita $1,830; real growth rate 1.2% (1991)
Inflation: 70.3% (1991)
Industries: machine building, iron and steel, extractive industries, chemicals, shipbuilding, food processing, glass, beverages, textiles
Labour Force: 19,704,000 (1992); 28.2% industry, 27.8% agriculture, 44% services (1989)
Unemployment: 11.5% (1991)
Agriculture: accounts for 15% GNP; 75% of output from private farms, 25% from state farms; low productivity; leading European producer of rye, rape seed and potatoes; wide variety of other crops and livestock; major exporter of pork products

Natural Resources: coal, sulphur, copper, natural gas, silver, lead, salt

■ FINANCE/TRADE

Currency: zloty (pl. zlotys) (Zl)
International Reserves Excluding Gold: $2,540 million (1991)
Gold Reserves: 0.47 million fine troy ounces (1991)
Budget: revenues $20.9 billion; expenditures $23.4 billion, including capital expenditures of $2.8 billion (1989)
Defence Expenditures: $2.54 billion (1990)
External Debt: $39.282 billion (1990)
Exports: $14.460 billion (1991); commodities: machinery and equipment 63%, fuels, minerals and metals 14%, manufactured consumer goods 14%, agricultural and forestry products 5%; partners: USSR 25%, Germany 12%, Czechoslovakia 6%
Imports: $14.261 billion (1991); commodities: machinery and equipment 36%, fuels, minerals and metals 35%, manufactured consumer goods 9%, agricultural and forestry products 12%; partners: USSR 23%, Germany 13%, Czechoslovakia 6%

■ HEALTH

Births: 14/1,000 population (1991)
Deaths: 9/1,000 population (1991)
Infant Mortality: 12 deaths/1,000 live births (1991)
Life Expectancy at Birth: 67 years male, 76 years female (1992)
No. of Physicians: 20.5/10,000 population (1992)

■ EDUCATION

Govt. Expenditure: 12.9% of govt. expenditure (1989)
Literacy: 98.8% (1992)

■ COMMUNICATIONS

Daily newspapers: 45 (1992)
Televisions: 291.5/1,000 inhabitants (1992)
Radios: 428/1,000 inhabitants (1992)
Telephones: 12.78/100 inhabitants (1992)

■ TRANSPORTATION

Motor Vehicles: 6,304,000; 5,260,000 passenger cars (1990)
Roads: 370,525 km; 227,630 km paved
Railway: 27,360 km (1990)
Air Traffic: 1,051,000 passengers carried (1991)
Airports: 11

Canadian Embassy: Ulica Jana Matejki 1/5, 00-481, Warsaw, Poland. Tel: (011-48-22) 29-80-51. Fax: (011-48-22)`29-64-57
Embassy in Canada: Embassy of the Republic of Poland, 443 Daly Ave, Ottawa ON K1N 6H3. Tel: (613) 789-0468. Fax: (613) 789-1218.

Portugal

Long-Form Name: Portuguese Republic
Capital: Lisbon
Population: 9,866,000 (1992)

■ GEOGRAPHY

Area: 92,080 sq. km; includes Azores and Madeira Islands
Coastline: 1,793 along North Atlantic Ocean
Climate: maritime temperate; cool and rainy in north, warmer and drier in south
Environment: Azores subject to severe earthquakes
Terrain: mountainous north, rolling plains in south
Land Use: 32% arable; 6% permanent; 6% meadows; 40% forest; 16% other
Location: SW Europe, bordering on North Atlantic Ocean

■ PEOPLE

Nationality: Portuguese (official); English, French
Ethnic Groups: homogeneous Mediterranean stock in mainland, Azores and Madiera Islands; citizens of black African descent who immigrated to mainland during decolonization number less than 100,000
Languages: Portuguese (official), English, French
Religions: 97% Roman Catholic, 1% Protestant, 2% other
Marriages: 7.0 (per 1,000) (1987)
Divorces: 0.9 (per 1,000) (1987)

■ GOVERNMENT

Leader(s): Prime Min. Aníbal Cavaco Silva, Pres. Mário Alberto Nobre Lopes Soares
Government Type: republic
Administrative Divisions: 18 districts and 2 autonomous regions; dependent areas: Macau (scheduled to become a Special Administrative Region of China in 1999)
Independence: 1140; independent republic proclaimed Oct. 5, 1910
National Holiday: Day of Portugal, June 10

■ ECONOMY

Overview: the economy has grown recently due to strong domestic consumption and investment spending; unemployment has declined but inflation remains high; government is promoting privatization measures

GNP: $58.451 billion, per capita $5,620; real growth rate 3.2% (1991)

Inflation: 11.4% (1991)

Industries: textiles and footwear; wood pulp, paper and cork; metalworking; oil refining; chemicals; fish canning; wine; tourism

Labour Force: 4,740,000 (1992); 57.3% services, 25.2% industry, 17.5% agriculture (1989)

Unemployment: 4.7% (1990)

Agriculture: accounts for 9% of GDP; small inefficient farms; imports more than half of food needs; major crops: grain, potatoes, olives, grapes; livestock sector: sheep, cattle, goats, poultry, meat, dairy products

Natural Resources: fish, forests (cork), tungsten, iron ore, uranium ore, marble

■ FINANCE/TRADE

Currency: escudo (Esc)

International Reserves Excluding Gold: $18,662 billion (1992)

Gold Reserves: 16.06 million fine troy ounces (1992)

Budget: revenues $21.6 billion; expenditures $23.8 billion, including capital expenditures of $6.9 billion (1990)

Defence Expenditures: $1.54 billion (1991)

External Debt: $14.432 billion (1990)

Exports: $17.905 billion (1992); commodities: cotton textiles, cork and cork products, canned fish, wine, timber and timber products, resin, machinery, applicances; partners: European Community 72%, other developed countries 13%, US 6%

Imports: $29.726 billion (1992); commodities: petroleum, cotton, foodgrains, industrial machinery, iron and steel, chemicals; partners: European Community 67%, other developed countries 13%, less developed countries 15%, US 4%

■ HEALTH

Births: 12/1,000 population (1991)

Deaths: 10/1,000 population (1991)

Infant Mortality: 13 deaths/1,000 live births (1991)

Life Expectancy at Birth: 71 years male, 78 years female (1992)

No. of Physicians: 24.3/10,000 population (1992)

■ EDUCATION

Govt. Expenditure: 10% of government expenditure (1987)

Literacy: 85.0% (1992)

■ COMMUNICATIONS

Daily newspapers: 28 (1992)

Televisions: 176.2/1,000 inhabitants (1992)

Radios: 216/1,000 inhabitants (1992)

Telephones: 21.91/100 inhabitants (1992)

■ TRANSPORTATION

Motor Vehicles: 2,198,000; 1,605,000 passenger cars (1988)

Roads: 52,000 km; 44,900 km paved

Railway: 3,600 km

Air Traffic: 3,572,000 passengers carried (1991)

Airports: 30

Canadian Embassy: Avendia da Liberdade 144/56, Flr 4, 1200 Lisbon, Portugal. Tel: (011-351-1) 347-4892. Fax: (011-351-1) 347-6466

Embassy in Canada: Embassy of Portugal, 645 Island Park Dr, Ottawa ON K1Y 0B8. Tel: (613) 729-0883, -2922. Fax: (613) 729-4236.

Puerto Rico

Dependent Territory of the United States

Long-Form Name: Commonwealth of Puerto Rico

Capital: San Juan

Population: 3,594,000 (1992)

■ GEOGRAPHY

Area: 8,959 sq. km

Coastline: 501 km

Climate: tropical marine, mild, little seasonal temperature variation

Environment: many small rivers and high central mountains ensure land is well watered; south coast relatively dry; fertile coastal plain belt in north; San Juan is one of the biggest and best natural harbors in the Caribbean

Terrain: mostly mountains with coastal plain belt in north; mountains precipitous to sea on west coast

Land Use: 8% arable; 9% permanent; 51% meadows; 25% forest; 7% other

Location: West Indies, bordering on Caribbean Sea, Atlantic Ocean

■ PEOPLE

Nationality: Puerto Rican

Ethnic Groups: almost entirely Hispanic

Languages: Spanish (official); English is widely understood

■ GOVERNMENT

Leader(s): Gov. Pedro J. Rossello
Government Type: commonwealth associated with US
Administrative Divisions: none
National Holiday: Constitution Day, July 25

■ ECONOMY

Overview: economy has benefited from heavy US investment; new industries include pharmaceuticals and electronics; tourism is important.
GNP: $22.498 billion, per capita $6,330; real growth rate 1.8% (1991)
Currency: US dollar ($)

Canadian Embassy: c/o Canadian Trade Commission, Plaza Scotia Bank, Flr 6, 273 Ponce de Leon, Hato Rey, Puerto Rico 00917. Tel: (809) 250-0367. Fax: (809) 250-0369

Qatar

Long-Form Name: State of Qatar
Capital: Doha
Population: 453,000 (1992)

■ GEOGRAPHY

Area: 11,437 sq. km
Coastline: 563 km
Climate: desert; hot, dry; humid and sultry in summer
Environment: haze, dust storms, sandstorms common; limited freshwater resources mean increasing dependence on large-scale desalination facilities
Terrain: mostly flat and barren desert covered with loose sand and gravel
Land Use: negligible arable; 0% permanent; 5% meadows; 0% forest; 95% other
Location: SW Asia (Middle East), bordering on Persian Gulf

■ PEOPLE

Nationality: Qatari
Ethnic Groups: 40% Arab, 18% Pakistani, 18% Indian, 10% Iranian, 14% other
Languages: Arabic (official); English is commonly used as second language
Religions: Islam (native Qataris – less than one-third of the population – principally adhere to orthodox Wahhabi sect of Sunni Moslems)
Marriages: 4.1 (per 1,000) (1987)
Divorces: 1.0 (per 1,000) (1987)

■ GOVERNMENT

Leader(s): Amir and Prime Min. Khalifa ibn Hamad Al Thani
Government Type: traditional monarchy
Administrative Divisions: 9 municipalities
Independence: Sept. 3, 1971 (from UK)
National Holiday: Independence Day, Sept. 3

■ ECONOMY

Overview: has one of the highest per capita GDP's in the world, due to oil revenues, reserves should not be completely depleted for about 25 years
GNP: $6.968 billion, per capita $15,860; real growth rate -6.6% (1991)
Inflation: 3.0% (1990)
Industries: crude oil production and refining, fertilizers, petrochemicals, steel, cement
Labour Force: 186,000 (1992); 3% agriculture, 28% industry, 69% services; 85% of labor force in private sector is non-Qatari (1989)
Unemployment: n.a.
Agriculture: farming and grazing on small scale, less than 2% of GDP; commercial fishing increasing in importance; most food imported
Natural Resources: crude oil, natural gas, fish

■ FINANCE/TRADE

Currency: Qatar riyal (QR)
International Reserves Excluding Gold: $694 million (1992)
Gold Reserves: 0.80 million fine troy ounces (1992)
Budget: revenues $1.8 billion; expenditures $3.4 billion, including capital expenditures of $400 million (1989)
Defence Expenditures: $934.07 million (1990)
External Debt: $1.1 billion (1989)
Exports: $2.2 billion (1988); commodities: petroleum products 90%, steel, fertilizers; partners: France, Germany, Italy, Japan, Spain
Imports: $1.326 billion (1989); commodities: foodstuffs, beverages, animal and vegetable oils, chemicals, machinery and equipment; partners: European Community, Japan, Arab countries, US, Australia

■ HEALTH

Births: 21/1,000 population (1991)
Deaths: 3/1,000 population (1991)
Infant Mortality: 24 deaths/1,000 live births (1991)
Life Expectancy at Birth: 69 years male, 74 years female (1992)

No. of Physicians: 17.4/10,000 population (1992)

■ EDUCATION

Govt. Expenditure: 7.2% of government expenditure (1980)
Literacy: 75.7% (1992)

■ COMMUNICATIONS

Daily newspapers: 4 (1992)
Televisions: 514.3/1,000 inhabitants (1992)
Radios: 510/1,000 inhabitants (1992)
Telephones: 36.26/100 inhabitants (1992)

■ TRANSPORTATION

Motor Vehicles: 162,377; 115,149 passenger cars (1990)
Roads: 1,555 km; 1,040 km paved
Railway: n.a.
Air Traffic: 876,000 passengers carried (1991)
Airports: 1

Canadian Embassy: c/o Da'Aiah - Block 4, Al-Mutawakel St, Kuwait City; mailing address: P.O. Box 25281, Safat, Kuwait City, 13113, Kuwait. Tel: (011-965) 256-3025. Fax: (011-965) 256-4167
Representative to Canada: c/o The Permanent Mission of Qatar to the UN, 747 Third Ave, 22nd Flr, New York, New York 10017 USA

Réunion

Overseas Department of France

Long-Form Name: Réunion
Capital: Saint-Denis
Population: 624,000 (1992)

■ GEOGRAPHY

Area: 2,512 sq. km; uninhabited islands of Juan de Nova, Europa, Bassas da India, Iles Glorieuses, Tromelin administered by Réunion but do not form part of the territory; Mauritius and the Seychelles claim Tromelin, Madagascar claims all 5 islands)
Climate: subtropical maritime, humid all year
Land Use: volcanic island; some cultivation of indigenous plants and cash crops such as corn
Location: Indian Ocean, E of Africa

■ PEOPLE

Nationality: French
Ethnic Groups: French Creoles, Indian and Chinese minorities
Languages: French (official), Creole vernacular

■ GOVERNMENT

Leader(s): Pres. General Council Eric Boyer, Pres. Regional Council Pierre Lagourgue, French Govt. Commissioner Jacques Dewatre
Government Type: overseas department

■ ECONOMY

Overview: agriculture: sugar, molasses, tea, tobacco, vanilla, corn, bananas, rum, livestock; forest products, fish; perfumes; industry: electricity, sugar refining, food processing, chemical engineering; chief trading partners: France, United Kingdom
Currency: French franc

Romania

Long-Form Name: Socialist Republic of Romania
Capital: Bucharest
Population: 23,372,000 (1992)

■ GEOGRAPHY

Area: 237,500 sq. km
Coastline: 225 km along Black Sea
Climate: temperate; cold, cloudy winters with frequent snow and fog; sunny summers with frequent showers and thunderstorms
Environment: frequent earthquakes most severe in south and southwest; geologic structure and climate promotes landslides, air pollution in south
Terrain: central Transylvanian Basin is separated from the plain of Moldavia on the east by the Carpathian Mountains and separated from the Walachian Plain on the south by the Transylvanian Alps
Land Use: 43% arable; 3% permanent; 19% meadows; 28% forest; 7% other
Location: SC Europe, bordering on Black Sea

■ PEOPLE

Nationality: Romanian
Ethnic Groups: 89% Romanian; 8% Hungarian; 2% German; 2% Ukrainian, Serb, Croat, Russian, Turk and Gypsy
Languages: Romanian (official), Hungarian, German; French and English also spoken
Religions: 85% Romanian Orthodox; 6% Roman Catholic; 4% Calvinist, Lutheran, Jewish, Baptist
Marriages: 7.1 (per 1,000) (1985)
Divorces: 1.4 (per 1,000) (1985)

■ GOVERNMENT

Leader(s): Prime Min. Nicolae Vacaroiu, Pres. Ion Iliescu

Government Type: in transition from communist state to republic
Administrative Divisions: 41 counties
Independence: 1881 (from Turkey); republic proclaimed Dec. 30, 1947
National Holiday: National Day of Romania, Dec. 1

■ ECONOMY

Overview: the new government is slowly loosening the tight central controls of Ceausescu's command economy; industry suffers from an aging capital plant and shortages of energy; agriculture sector has suffered from drought and mismanagement
GNP: $31.079 billion, per capita $1,340; real growth rate 0.3% (1991)
Inflation: 4.2 % (1990)
Industries: mining, timber, construction materials, metallurgy, chemicals, machine building, food processing, petroleum
Labour Force: 11,825,000 (1992); 43.5% industry, 30.5%% agriculture, 26% services (1989)
Unemployment: n.a.
Agriculture: 15% of GNP; major wheat and corn producer, sugar beets, sunflower seeds, potatoes, milk, eggs, meat
Natural Resources: crude oil (reserves being exhausted), timber, natural gas, coal, iron ore, salt

■ FINANCE/TRADE

Currency: leu (pl. lei) (n.a.)
International Reserves Excluding Gold: $246 million (1992)
Gold Reserves: 2.30 million fine troy ounces (1992)
Budget: revenues $28.4 billion; expenditures $28.4 billion, including capital expenditures of $12.3 billion (1989)
Defence Expenditures: $1.44 billion (1990)
External Debt: $19 million (1990)
Exports: $4.031 billion (1992); commodities: machinery and equipment 34.7%, fuels, minerals and metals 24.7%, manufactured consumer goods 16.9%, agricultural materials and forestry products 11.9%, other 11.6%; partners: USSR 27%, Eastern Europe 23%, European Community 15%, US 5%, China 4%
Imports: $5.394 billion (1992); commodities: fuels, minerals and metals 51%, machinery and equipment 26.7%, agricultural and forestry products 11%, manufactured consumer goods 4.2%; partners: Communist Countries 60%, non-Communist Countries 40%

■ HEALTH

Births: 16/1,000 population (1991)
Deaths: 10/1,000 population (1991)
Infant Mortality: 18 deaths/1,000 live births (1991)
Life Expectancy at Birth: 67 years male, 73 years female (1992)
No. of Physicians: 17.6/10,000 population (1992)

■ EDUCATION

Govt. Expenditure: 10.02% of governmemt expenditure (1991)
Literacy: 98% (1992)

■ COMMUNICATIONS

Daily newspapers: 34 (1992)
Televisions: 193.8/1,000 inhabitants (1992)
Radios: 195/1,000 inhabitants (1992)
Telephones: n.a.

■ TRANSPORTATION

Motor Vehicles: 1,100,000; 850,000 passenger cars (1990)
Roads: 75,050 km; 38,000 km paved
Railway: 11,425 km
Air Traffic: 1,149,000 passengers carried (1987)
Airports: 17

Canadian Embassy: 36, Nicolae Iorga, Bucharest; mailing address: P.O. Box 2966 Post Office No. 22, 71118 Bucharest, Romania. tel: (011-40-1) 312.03.65. Fax: (011-40-1) 312.03.66.
Embassy in Canada: Embassy of Romania, 655 Rideau St, Ottawa ON K1N 6A3. Tel: (613) 789-3709. Fax: (613) 789-4635

Russia

Long-Form Name: Russian Federation
Capital: Moscow
Population: 149,003,000 (1992)

■ GEOGRAPHY

Area: 44,224,250 sq. km
Coastline:
Climate: cold, windy, snowy winters; hot and dry summers; rainy, foggy autumn
Environment: cold desert in north; volcanic activity
Terrain: rolling western plains, north-south ridge of Ural Mountains, central plateau, rugged eastern uplands
Land Use: 30% forests and woodland; 25% cultivated; remainder steppe and cold desert
Location: E Europe, bordering on Barents Sea, Baltic Sea, Black Sea, Caspian Sea

■ PEOPLE

Nationality: Russian
Ethnic Groups: 81.5% Russians; 3.8% Tatars, 1.2% Chuvash, 0.9% Bashkir, 0.8% Belorussian, 0.7% Ukrainian, remainder inc. Chechens, Germans, Udmurts, Mari, Kazakhs, Avars, Jews and Armenians
Languages: Russian (official), Tartar, Ukrainian
Religions: Christianity (Russian Orthodox) with substantial Muslim populations and other religious minorities
Marriages: n.a.
Divorces: n.a.

■ GOVERNMENT

Leader(s): Pres. Boris N. Yeltsin, Prime Min. (interim) Viktor Chernomyrdin
Government Type: in transition to republic
Administrative Divisions: 6 territories, 49 regions, 16 autonomous republics, 5 autonomous regions, and 10 autonomous areas
Independence: declared July 12, 1991
National Holiday: Independence Day, June 12

■ ECONOMY

Overview: industry accounts for more than half of Russia's economic output; agriculture and service sector make up approximately 25% each
GNP: $479.546 billion, $3,220 per capita; real growth rate 2.0% (1991)
Inflation: n.a.
Industries: natural gas refining, steel and coal production and processing
Labour Force: 77,283,000 (1992)
Unemployment: n.a.
Agriculture: the former Russian Soviet Republic produced about 70% of the total industrial and agricultural output of the Soviet Union
Natural Resources: iron ore, coal, oil, gold, platinum, copper, zinc, lead, tin, rare metals

■ FINANCE/TRADE

Currency: ruble (rbl.)
International Reserves Excluding Gold: n.a.
Gold Reserves: n.a.
Budget: 1989 Budget balanced at 126,471 million roubles; in 1991–92 budgets were set every 3 months
Defence Expenditures: n.a.
External Debt: n.a.
Exports: $15.400 billion (Jan–June 1992)
Imports: $14.900 billion (Jan–June 1992)

■ HEALTH

Births: 14.6/1,000 population (1989)
Deaths: 10.7/1,000 population (1989)
Infant Mortality: 18.1 deaths/1,000 live births (1989)
Life Expectancy at Birth: 64 years male, 75 years female
No. of Physicians: 697,000 (1989)

■ EDUCATION

Govt. Expenditure: n.a.
Literacy: n.a.

■ COMMUNICATIONS

Daily newspapers: 4,772 papers of all circulation types (1989)
Televisions: n.a.
Radios: n.a.
Telephones: n.a.

■ TRANSPORTATION

Motor Vehicles: n.a.
Roads: n.a.
Railway: 87,090 km
Air Traffic: 128,275,000 passengers carried (1991)
Airports: n.a.

Canadian Embassy: Russian Federation Moscow, 23 Starokonyushenny Per, The Canadian Embassy. Tel: (011-7095) 241-4400. Fax: (011-7095) 241-9034.
Embassy in Canada: Embassy of the Russian Federation, 285 Charlotte St, Ottawa ON K1N 8L5. Tel: (613) 235-4341, 236-1413. Fax: (613) 236-6342.

Rwanda

Long-Form Name: Republic of Rwanda
Capital: Kigali
Population: 7,526,000 (1992)

■ GEOGRAPHY

Area: 26,340 sq. km
Coastline: none: landlocked
Climate: temperate; two rainy seasons (Feb. to Apr., Nov. to Jan.); mild in mountains with frost and snow possible
Environment: deforestation; overgrazing; soil exhaustion; soil erosion; periodic droughts
Terrain: mostly grassy uplands and hills; mountains in west
Land Use: 29% arable; 11% permanent; 18% meadows; 10% forest; 32% other
Location: EC Africa

■ PEOPLE

Nationality: Rwandese or Rwandan
Ethnic Groups: 90% Hutu, 9% Tutsi, 1% Twa (Pygmoid)
Languages: Kinyarwanda, French (official); Kiswahili used in commercial centres
Religions: 50% Christian (mostly Roman Catholic), 50% indigenous beliefs and other
Marriages: 2.6 (per 1,000) (1982)
Divorces: n.a.

■ GOVERNMENT

Leader(s): Pres. Maj. Gen. Juvénal Habyarimana, Prime Min. Dismas Nsengiyaremye
Government Type: republic; presidential system in which military leaders hold key offices
Administrative Divisions: 10 prefectures
Independence: July 1, 1962 (from UN trusteeship under Belgian administration)
National Holiday: Independence Day, July 1

■ ECONOMY

Overview: economy is dependent on coffee exports and foreign aid; deforestation and soil erosion are problems
GNP: $1.930 billion, per capita $260; real growth rate 0.5% (1991)
Inflation: 19.6% (1991)
Industries: mining of cassiterite (tin ore) and wolframite (tungsten ore), tin, cement, agricultural processing, small-scale beverage production, soap, furniture, shoes, plastic goods, textiles, cigarettes
Labour Force: 3,520,000 (1992); 92.8% agriculture, 4.3% services, 3% industry and commerce (1989)
Unemployment: n.a.
Agriculture: cash crops: coffee, tea, pyrethrum (insecticide made from chrysanthemums); main food crops: bananas, beans, sorghum, potatoes; stock raising; self-sufficiency declining; country imports foodstuffs as farm production fail to keep up with population growth
Natural Resources: gold, cassiterite (tin ore), wolframite (tungsten ore), natural gas, hydropower

■ FINANCE/TRADE

Currency: Rwandan franc (RF)
International Reserves Excluding Gold: $70 million (1992)
Gold Reserves: none (1991)
Budget: revenues $391 million; expenditures $491 million, including capital expenditures of $225 million (1989)
Defence Expenditures: $36.63 million (1990)

External Debt: $692 million (1990)
Exports: $110 million (1990); commodities: coffee 85%, tea, tin, cassiterite, wolframite, pyrethrum; partners: Germany, Belgium, Italy, Uganda, UK, France, US
Imports: $288 million (1990); commodities: textiles, foodstuffs, machines and equipment, capital goods, steel, petroleum products, cement and construction material; partners: US, Belgium, Germany, Kenya, Japan

■ HEALTH

Births: 57/1,000 population (1990)
Deaths: 18.2/1,000 population (1990)
Infant Mortality: 122 deaths/1,000 live births (1990)
Life Expectancy at Birth: 48 years male, 51 years female (1992)
No. of Physicians: 0.1/10,000 population (1992)

■ EDUCATION

Govt. Expenditure: 25.4% of govt. expenditure (1989)
Literacy: 50.2% (1992)

■ COMMUNICATIONS

Daily newspapers: 1 (1992)
Televisions: n.a.
Radios: 59/1,000 inhabitants (1992)
Telephones: 0.18/100 inhabitants (1992)

■ TRANSPORTATION

Motor Vehicles: 25,000; 15,000 passenger cars (1990)
Roads: 12,880 km; 900 km paved
Railway: n.a.
Air Traffic: 8,000 passengers carried (1991)
Airports: 7

Canadian Embassy: c/o 17 Pumbu Zone de Gombe Ave, Kinshasa, Zaïre; mailing address: P.O. Box 8341, Kinshasa, Zaïre. Tel: (011-243-12) 21-801. Fax: (011-871) 156-0213
Embassy in Canada: Embassy of the Rwandese Republic, 121 Sherwood Dr, Ottawa ON K1Y 3V1. Tel: (613) 722-5835, -7921. Fax: (613) 729-3291.

St. Helena

Dependent Territory of the United Kingdom

Long-Form Name: Territory of St. Helena
Capital: Jamestown
Population: 7,000 (1992)

■ GEOGRAPHY

Area: 121.2 sq. km
Climate: mild and fairly dry; little seasonal variation
Land Use: rough and mountainous volcanic wasteland; grasslands; less than one-third arable
Location: Atlantic Ocean, SW of Africa

■ PEOPLE

Nationality: British
Ethnic Groups: Europeans, East Indians, Africans
Languages: English (official)

■ GOVERNMENT

Leader(s): Gov. and Commander-in-Chief Alan Hoole
Government Type: dependency

■ ECONOMY

Overview: chief crops: New Zealand flax; fish curing; lacemaking; fibre mats only significant manufactured product; imports greatly exceed exports; chief trading partners: Ascension, United Kingdom,
Currency: British pound

Saint Kitts and Nevis

Long-Form Name: Federation of St. Kitts and Nevis
Capital: Basseterre
Population: 42,000 (1992)

■ GEOGRAPHY

Area: 360 sq. km
Coastline: 135 km
Climate: subtropical tempered by constant sea breezes; little seasonal temperature variation; rainy season (May to Nov.)
Environment: subject to hurricanes (July to Oct.)
Terrain: volcanic with mountainous interiors
Land Use: 22% arable; 17% permanent; 3% meadows; 17% forest; 41% other
Location: Caribbean Islands

■ PEOPLE

Nationality: Kittsian, Nevisian
Ethnic Groups: mainly of black African descent
Languages: English
Religions: Anglican, other Protestant sects, Roman Catholic
Marriages: 3.9 (per 1,000) (1977)
Divorces: 0.2 (per 1,000) (1977)

■ GOVERNMENT

Leader(s): Prime Min. Kennedy Alphonse Simmonds, Gov. Gen. Clement Athelston Arrindell
Government Type: constitutional monarchy
Administrative Divisions: 14 parishes
Independence: Sept. 19, 1983 (from UK)
National Holiday: Independence Day, Sept. 19

■ ECONOMY

Overview: traditionally dependent on the growing and processing of sugarcane and on remittances from overseas workers; tourism and export-oriented manufacturing are increasing
GNP: $156 million, per capita $3,960; real growth rate 4.5% (1991)
Inflation: 4.2% (1991)
Industries: sugar processing, tourism, cotton, salt, copra, clothing, footwear, beverages
Labour Force: n.a.
Unemployment: 20–25% (1987)
Agriculture: accounts for 10% of GDP; cash crop: sugarcane; subsistence crops: rice, yams, bananas; fishing potential but not fully exploited; most food imported
Natural Resources: negligible

■ FINANCE/TRADE

Currency: East Caribbean dollar ($EC)
International Reserves Excluding Gold: $30 million (1992)
Gold Reserves: n.a.
Budget: revenues $38.1 million; expenditures $68.1 million, including capital expenditures of $31.5 million (1991)
Defence Expenditures: n.a.
External Debt: $27.6 million (1988)
Exports: $30.3 million (1988); commodities: sugar, manufactures, postage stamps; partners: US 44%, UK 30%, Trinidad and Tobago 12%
Imports: $94.7 million (1988); commodities: foodstuffs, intermediate manufactures, machinery, fuels; partners: US 35%, UK 18%, Trinidad and Tobago 10%, Canada 6%, Japan 4%

■ HEALTH

Births: 24/1,000 population (1991)
Deaths: 10/1,000 population (1991)
Infant Mortality: 39 deaths/1,000 live births (1991)
Life Expectancy at Birth: 63 years male, 69 years female (1991)
No. of Physicians: 4.6/10,000 population (1992)

■ EDUCATION

Govt. Expenditure: 12.0% of govt. expenditure (1989)
Literacy: 97.6% (1992)

■ COMMUNICATIONS

Daily newspapers: n.a.
Televisions: 181.8/1,000 inhabitants (1992)
Radios: 580/1,000 inhabitants (1992)
Telephones: 7.61/100 inhabitants (1992)

■ TRANSPORTATION

Motor Vehicles: 4,903 passenger cars (1988)
Roads: n.a.
Railway: 58 km
Air Traffic: 98,263 passengers carried (1987)
Airports: 2

Canadian Embassy: C/o The Canadian High Commission, Bishop's Court Hill, St. Michael, Barbados; mailing address: P.O. Box 404, Bridgetown, Barbados. Tel: (809) 429-3550. Fax: (809) 429-3780

Saint Lucia

Long-Form Name: Saint Lucia
Capital: Castries
Population: 137,000 (1992)

■ GEOGRAPHY

Area: 620 sq. km
Coastline: 158 km
Climate: tropical, moderated by northeast trade winds; dry season from Jan. to Apr., rainy season from May to Aug.
Environment: subject to hurricanes and volcanic activity; deforestation; soil erosion
Terrain: volcanic and mountainous with some broad, fertile valleys
Land Use: 8% arable; 20% permanent; 5% meadow; 13% forest; 54% other
Location: Caribbean Islands

■ PEOPLE

Nationality: Saint Lucian
Ethnic Groups: 90% African descent, 6% mixed, 3% East Indian, 1% Caucasian
Languages: English (official), French patois
Religions: 90% Roman Catholic, 7% Protestant, 3% Anglican
Marriages: 3.1 (per 1,000) (1986)
Divorces: 0.4 (per 1,000) (1986)

■ GOVERNMENT

Leader(s): Prime Min. John Compton, Gov. Gen. Sir Stanislaus A. James
Government Type: parliamentary democracy
Administrative Divisions: 8 administrative regions
Independence: Feb. 22, 1979 (from UK)
National Holiday: Independence Day, Feb. 22

■ ECONOMY

Overview: depends on strong agricultural (bananas) and tourist industry sectors; expanding industrial base supported by foreign investment in manufacturing and activities such as data processing; vulnerable to droughts and tropical storms
GNP: $380 million, per capita $2,500; real growth rate 4.8% (1991)
Inflation: 6.1% (1991)
Industries: clothing, electronic component assembly, beverages, tourism, lime and coconut processing
Labour Force: 43% agriculture, 39% services, 18% industry and commerce (1983 est.)
Unemployment: 18.6% (1986)
Agriculture: accounts for 15% GDP; crops: bananas, coconuts, vegetables, citrus fruit, root crops, cocoa; imports food for the tourist industry
Natural Resources: forests, sandy beaches, minerals (pumice), mineral springs, geothermal potential

■ FINANCE/TRADE

Currency: EC dollar (EC$)
International Reserves Excluding Gold: $51 million (1992)
Gold Reserves: n.a.
Budget: revenues $131 million; expenditures $149 million, including capital expenditures of $71 million (1990)
Defence Expenditures: n.a.
External Debt: $39.5 million (1987)
Exports: $119 million (1989); commodities: bananas 67%, cocoa, vegetables, fruits, coconut oil, clothing; partners: UK 55%, CARICOM 21%, US 18%, other 6%
Imports: $221 million (1989); commodities: manufactured goods 22%, machinery and transportation equipment 21%, food and live animals 20%, mineral fuels, foodstuffs, machinery and equipment, fertilizers, petroleum products; partners: US 33%, UK 16%, CARICOM 14.8%, Japan 6.5%, other 29.7%

■ HEALTH

Births: 31/1,000 population (1991)
Deaths: 5/1,000 population (1991)
Infant Mortality: 18 deaths/1,000 live births (1991)
Life Expectancy at Birth: 69 years male, 74 years female (1992)
No. of Physicians: 2.6/10,000 population (1992)

■ EDUCATION

Govt. Expenditure: 7.2% of GNP (1986)
Literacy: 81.7% (1992)

■ COMMUNICATIONS

Daily newspapers: 1 (1992)
Televisions: 18.4/1,000 inhabitants (1992)
Radios: 667/1,000 inhabitants (1992)
Telephones: 12.14/100 inhabitants (1992)

■ TRANSPORTATION

Motor Vehicles: 11,000; 7,000 passenger cars (1990)
Roads: n.a.
Railway: n.a.
Air Traffic: n.a.
Airports: 2

Canadian Embassy: C/o The Canadian High Commission, Bishop's Court Hill, St. Michael, Barbados; mailing address: P.O. Box 404, Bridgetown, Barbados. Tel: (809) 429-3550. Fax: (809) 429-3780

Saint Pierre and Miquelon

Dependent Territory of the Netherlands

Long-Form Name: Iles Saint Pierre et Miquelon
Capital: Saint Pierre (chief town)
Population: 6,000 (1992)

■ GEOGRAPHY

Area: 242 sq. km, 8 small islands
Climate: moist, temperate summers, cold and snowy winters
Land Use: mostly barren rock unsuitable for cultivation; no agriculture
Location: N Atlantic Ocean, S of Newfoundland

■ PEOPLE

Nationality: French
Ethnic Groups: descendants of French settlers
Languages: French, English

■ GOVERNMENT

Leader(s): Prefect Karnel Khrissate; Pres. General Council Marc Plantegenest
Government Type: territorial collectivity with internal self-government

■ ECONOMY

Overview: agriculture: some vegetables and livestock for local consumption; industry: fishing; chief trading partners: United Kingdom, Canada, EEC

Currency: French franc

Saint Vincent and the Grenadines

Long-Form Name: Saint Vincent and the Grenadines
Capital: Kingstown
Population: 109,000 (1992)

■ GEOGRAPHY

Area: 388 sq. km
Coastline: 84 km
Climate: tropical; little seasonal temperature variation; rainy season (May to Nov.)
Environment: subject to hurricanes; Soufrière volcano is a constant threat
Terrain: volcanic, mountainous; Soufrière volcano on the island of St Vincent
Land Use: 38% arable; 12% permanent; 6% meadows; 41% forest; 3% other
Location: Caribbean Islands

■ PEOPLE

Nationality: Saint Vincentian
Ethnic Groups: mainly of black African descent; remainder mixed, with some white, East Indian, Carib Indian
Languages: English (official), some French patois
Religions: Anglican, Methodist, Roman Catholic, Seventh-Day Adventist
Marriages: 3.8 (per 1,000) (1986)
Divorces: 0.2 (per 1,000) (1980)

■ GOVERNMENT

Leader(s): Prime Min. James F. Mitchell, Gov. Gen. (Acting) David Jack
Government Type: constitutional monarchy
Administrative Divisions: 6 parishes
Independence: Oct. 27, 1979 (from UK)
National Holiday: Independence Day, Oct. 27

■ ECONOMY

Overview: overdependence on the weather-plagued banana crop as a major export earner has caused high unemployment (30% in 1990); has been unsuccessful in diversifying into new industries
GNP: $187 million, per capita $1,730; real growth rate 6.1% (1991)
Inflation: 2% (1988)
Industries: food processing (sugar, flour), cement, furniture, rum, starch, sheet metal, beverage
Labour Force: n.a.
Unemployment: 30% (1990)

Agriculture: accounts for 20% of GDP; provides bulk of exports; products: bananas, arrowroot (world's largest producer), coconuts, sweet potatoes, spices; small numbers of cattle, sheep, hogs, goats; small fish catch used locally
Natural Resources: negligible

■ FINANCE/TRADE

Currency: EC dollar ($EC)
International Reserves Excluding Gold: $31 million (1992)
Gold Reserves: n.a.
Budget: revenues $62 million; expenditures $67 million, including capital expenditures of $21 million (1990)
Defence Expenditures: n.a.
External Debt: $35 million (1987)
Exports: $63.8 million (1986); commodities: bananas, eddoes and dasheen (taro), arrowrrot starch, copra; partners: CARICOM 60%, UK 27%, US 10%
Imports: $87.3 million (1986); commodities: foodstuffs, machinery and equipment, chemicals and fertilizers, minerals and fuels; partners: US 37%, CARICOM 18%, UK 13%

■ HEALTH

Births: 27/1,000 population (1991)
Deaths: 6/1,000 population (1991)
Infant Mortality: 31 deaths/1,000 live births (1991)
Life Expectancy at Birth: 70 years male, 73 years female (1992)
No. of Physicians: 2.7/10,000 population (1992)

■ EDUCATION

Govt. Expenditure: 18.08% of govt. expenditure (1990)
Literacy: 95.6% (1992)

■ COMMUNICATIONS

Daily newspapers: 1 (1992)
Televisions: 78.9/1,000 inhabitants (1992)
Radios: 636/1,000 inhabitants (1992)
Telephones: 9.1/100 inhabitants (1992)

■ TRANSPORTATION

Motor Vehicles: 8,000; 5,000 passenger cars (1990)
Roads: n.a.
Railway: n.a.
Air Traffic: n.a.
Airports: 6

Canadian Embassy: C/o The Canadian High Commission, Bishop's Court Hill, St. Michael, Barbados; mailing address: P.O. Box 404, Bridgetown, Barbados. Tel: (809) 429-3550. Fax: (809) 429-3780

San Marino

Long-Form Name: Republic of San Marino
Capital: San Marino
Population: 23,000 (1992)

■ GEOGRAPHY

Area: 60 sq. km
Coastline: none: landlocked
Climate: Mediterranean; mild to cool winters; warm, sunny summers
Environment: dominated by the Appenines
Terrain: rugged mountains
Land Use: 17% arable; 0% permanent; 0% meadows; 0% forest; 83% other
Location: S Europe (E Italy)

■ PEOPLE

Nationality: Sanmarinese
Ethnic Groups: Sanmarinese, Italian
Languages: Slovene
Religions: Roman Catholic
Marriages: 8.7 (per 1,000) (1987)
Divorces: 1.0 (per 1,000) (1987)

■ GOVERNMENT

Leader(s): Capt. Regent Romeo Morri, Capt. Regent Marino Zanotti (until Apr. 1, 1993)
Government Type: republic
Administrative Divisions: 9 municipalities
Independence: 301 (by tradition)
National Holiday: Anniversary of the Foundation of the Republic, Sept. 3

■ ECONOMY

Overview: tourism and the sale of postage stamps are vital to the economy
GNP: $393 million, per capita $17,000; real growth rate 2% (1990 est.)
Inflation: 6.0% (1990)
Industries: wine, olive oil, cement, leather, textiles, tourism
Labour Force: 13,332 (1991)
Unemployment: 4.3% (1991)
Agriculture: products: wheat, grapes, corn, olives, meat, cheese, hides; small numbers of cattle, pigs, horses; depends on Italy for food imports
Natural Resources: building stones

■ FINANCE/TRADE

Currency: Italian lira (Lit)
International Reserves Excluding Gold: n.a.

Gold Reserves: n.a.
Budget: revenues $99.2 million (1983)
Defence Expenditures: n.a.
External Debt: n.a.
Exports: n.a.
Imports: n.a.

■ HEALTH

Births: 8/1,000 population (1991)
Deaths: 7/1,000 population (1991)
Infant Mortality: 8 deaths/1,000 live births (1991)
Life Expectancy at Birth: 73 years male, 79 years female (1992)
No. of Physicians: n.a.

■ EDUCATION

Govt. Expenditure: 10.7% of government expenditure (1984)
Literacy: 97%

■ COMMUNICATIONS

Daily newspapers: 16 (1988)
Televisions: 326.1/1,000 inhabitants (1989)
Radios: 583/1,000 inhabitants (1989)
Telephones: 62.5/100 inhabitants (1987)

■ TRANSPORTATION

Motor Vehicles: 22,519; 19,360 passenger cars (1990)
Roads: n.a.
Railway: n.a.
Air Traffic: n.a.
Airports: n.a.

Canadian Embassy: C/o The Canadian Embassy, Via G.B. de Rossi 27, 00161 Rome, Italy
Representative to Canada: C/o Consulate of San Marino, 27 McNider Ave, Montreal, PQ H2V 3X4. Tel: (514) 871-3833. Fax: (514) 876-4217.

Sao Tome and Principe

Long-Form Name: Democratic Republic of Sao Tome and Principe
Capital: Sao Tome
Population: 124,000 (1991)

■ GEOGRAPHY

Area: 1,000 sq. km
Coastline: 209 km
Climate: tropical; hot, humid; one rainy season (Oct. to May)
Environment: deforestation; soil erosion
Terrain: volcanic, mountainous
Land Use: 1% arable; 20% permanent; 1% meadows; 75% forest; 3% other

Location: South Atlantic Ocean, off WC African Coast

■ PEOPLE

Nationality: Sao Tomean
Ethnic Groups: mestiço, angolares (descendents of Angolan slaves), forros (descendents of freed slaves), servicais (contract laborers from Angola, Mozambique and Cape Verde), tongas (children of servicais born on the islands) and European (primarily Portuguese)
Languages: Portuguese (official), Crioulo
Religions: Roman Catholic, Evangelical Protestant, Seventh-Day Adventist
Marriages: 0.8 (per 1,000) (1985)
Divorces: n.a.

■ GOVERNMENT

Leader(s): Prime Min. Norberto José d'Alva Costa Alegre, Pres. Miguel Trovoada
Government Type: republic
Administrative Divisions: 7 districts
Independence: July 12, 1975 (from Portugal)
National Holiday: Independence Day, July 12

■ ECONOMY

Overview: the economy is hampered by overdependence on cocoa production; the value of imports generally exceeds the value of exports by a ratio of 4 to 1; imports 90% of food needs; government is attempting to restructure economy and reduce debt burden
GNP: $42 million, per capita $350; real growth rate -1.2% (1991)
Inflation: 4.2% (1986)
Industries: light construction, shirts, soap, beer, fisheries, shrimp processing
Labour Force: n.a.; most of population engaged in subsistence agriculture and fishing
Unemployment: n.a.
Agriculture: dominant sector of economy, primary source of exports; cash crops: cocoa (90%), coconuts, palm kernels, coffee; food products: bananas, papaya, beans, poultry, fish; not self-sufficient in food grain and meat
Natural Resources: fish

■ FINANCE/TRADE

Currency: dobra (Db)
International Reserves Excluding Gold: n.a.
Gold Reserves: n.a.
Budget: revenues $10.2 million; expenditures $36.8 million, including capital expenditures of $22.5 million (1989)
Defence Expenditures: 1.6% GDP (1980)
External Debt: $95 million (1988)

Exports: $5.0 million (1989); commodities: cocoa 90%, copra, coffee, palm oil; partners: Germany, Netherlands, China
Imports: $18.0 million (1989); commodities: machinery and electrical equipment 59%, food products 32%, fuels 9%; partners: Portugal, Germany, Angola, China

■ **HEALTH**

Births: 38/1,000 population (1991)
Deaths: 8/1,000 population (1991)
Infant Mortality: 60 deaths/1,000 live births (1991)
Life Expectancy at Birth: 64 years male, 67 years female (1992)
No. of Physicians: 5.0/10,000 population (1990)

■ **EDUCATION**

Govt. Expenditure: 18.8% of govt. expenditure (1986)
Literacy: 57.4% (1992)

■ **COMMUNICATIONS**

Daily newspapers: 1 (1992)
Televisions: n.a.
Radios: 256/1,000 inhabitants (1992)
Telephones: 2.44/100 inhabitants (1992)

■ **TRANSPORTATION**

Motor Vehicles: 2,600 passenger cars (1987)
Roads: n.a.
Railway: n.a.
Air Traffic: 22,000 passengers carried (1991)
Airports: 2

Canadian Embassy: C/o P.O. Box 4037 Libreville, Gabon. Tel: (011-241) 74.34.64, 65. Fax: (011-241) 74.34.66
Representative to Canada: C/o Permanent Mission of Sao Tomé and Principe to the UN, 801 Second Ave, Room 1504, New York, New York 10017 USA. Tel: (212) 697-4212

Saudi Arabia

Long-Form Name: Kingdom of Saudi Arabia
Capital: Riyadh (royal); Jeddah (administrative)
Population: 15,922,000 (1992)

■ **GEOGRAPHY**

Area: 2,149,690 sq. km
Coastline: 2,510 km along Red Sea and Persian Gulf
Climate: harsh, dry desert with great extremes of temperature
Environment: no perennial rivers or permanent water bodies; developing extensive coastal sea-water desalination facilities; desertification
Terrain: mostly uninhabited, sandy desert
Land Use: 1% arable; negligible permanent; 39% meadows; 1% forest; 59% other
Location: SW Asia (Middle East), bordering on Persian Gulf, Arabian Sea, Red Sea

■ **PEOPLE**

Nationality: Saudi
Ethnic Groups: 90% Arab, 10% Afro-Asian
Languages: Arabic (official); English (business language)
Religions: Islam (85% Sunni, 15% Shia)
Marriages: n.a.
Divorces: n.a.

■ **GOVERNMENT**

Leader(s): King and Prime Min. Fahd bin 'Abd al- 'Aziz Al Sa'ud
Government Type: monarchy
Administrative Divisions: 14 emirates
Independence: Sept. 23, 1932 (unification)
National Holiday: Unification of the Kingdom, Sept. 23

■ **ECONOMY**

Overview: has the largest reserves of petroleum in the world and is the largest exporter of petroleum; consumer prices have been dropping or showing little change in recent years
GNP: $105.133 billion, per capita $4,720; real growth rate 0.4% (1991)
Inflation: 4.9% (1991)
Industries: crude oil production, petroleum refining, basic petrochemicals, cement, small steel-rolling mill, construction, fertilizer, plastic
Labour Force: 4,081,000 (1992); 14.4% industry, 37.2% services, 48.5% agriculture (1989)
Unemployment: 0% (1989 est.)
Agriculture: accounts for about 10% of GDP; fastest growing economic sector; subsidized by government; products: wheat, barley, tomatoes, melons, dates, citrus fruits, mutton, chickens, eggs, milk; approaching self-sufficiency in food
Natural Resources: crude oil, natural gas, iron ore, gold, copper

■ **FINANCE/TRADE**

Currency: riyal (SRls)
International Reserves Excluding Gold: $5,935 million (1992)
Gold Reserves: 4.6 million fine troy ounces (1992)

Budget: revenues $31.5 billion; expenditures $38.1 billion, including capital expenditures of $6.9 billion (1990)
Defence Expenditures: $13.86 billion (1990)
External Debt: $18.9 billion (1989)
Exports: $44.417 billion (1990); commodities: petroleum and petroleum products 89%; partners: Japan 26%, US 26%, France 6%, Bahrain 6%
Imports: $24.069 billion (1990); commodities: manufactured goods, transportation equipment, construction materials, processed food products; partners: US 20%, Japan 18%, UK 16%, Italy 11%

■ HEALTH

Births: 37/1,000 population (1991)
Deaths: 6/1,000 population (1991)
Infant Mortality: 69 deaths/1,000 live births (1991)
Life Expectancy at Birth: 63 years male, 66 years female (1992)
No. of Physicians: 13.5/10,000 population (1992)

■ EDUCATION

Govt. Expenditure: 16.2% of government expenditure (1988)
Literacy: 62.4% (1992)

■ COMMUNICATIONS

Daily newspapers: 12 (1992)
Televisions: 276.5/1,000 inhabitants (1992)
Radios: 280/1,000 inhabitants (1992)
Telephones: 15.74/100 inhabitants (1992)

■ TRANSPORTATION

Motor Vehicles: 4,500,000; 2,350,000 passenger cars (1990)
Roads: 90,290 km; 34,400 km paved
Railway: 860 km
Air Traffic: 9,409,000 passengers carried (1991)
Airports: 23

Canadian Embassy: Diplomatic Quarter, Riyadh; mailing address: P.O. Box 94321, Riyadh 11693, Saudi Arabia. Tel: (011-966-1) 488-2288. Fax: (011-966-1) 488-0137
Embassy in Canada: Embassy of the Kingdom of Saudi Arabia, 99 Bank St, Suite 901, Ottawa ON K1P 6B9. Tel: (613) 234-4100, -1, -2, -3.

Senegal

Long-Form Name: Republic of Senegal
Capital: Dakar
Population: 7,736,000 (1992)

■ GEOGRAPHY

Area: 196,190 sq. km
Coastline: 531 km along the North Atlantic Ocean
Climate: tropical; hot, humid; rainy season (Dec. to Apr.) has strong southeast winds; dry season (May to Nov.) dominated by hot, dry harmattan wind
Environment: lowlands seasonally flooded; deforestation; overgrazing; soil erosion; desertification
Terrain: generally low, rolling, plains rising to foothills in southeast
Land Use: 27% arable; 0% permanent; 30% meadows; 31% forest; 12% other
Location: W Africa, bordering on Atlantic Ocean

■ PEOPLE

Nationality: Senegalese
Ethnic Groups: 36% Wolof, 13% Fulani, 19% Serer, 9% Toucouleur, 8% Diola, 9% Mandingo, 1% European and Lebanese, 2% other
Languages: French (official); Senegalo-Guinean, Mandé and Peulh language groups
Religions: 90% Moslem, 5% indigenous beliefs, 5% Christian (mostly Roman Catholic)
Marriages: n.a.
Divorces: n.a.

■ GOVERNMENT

Leader(s): Prime Min. Habib Thiam, Pres. Abdou Diouf
Government Type: republic under multi-party democratic rule
Administrative Divisions: 10 regions
Independence: Apr. 4, 1960 (from France)
National Holiday: Independence Day, Apr. 4

■ ECONOMY

Overview: tourism has emerged as a great boon to the economy; fishing is the main economic resource; mining (phosphate) has been hurt by reduced worldwide demand for fertilizers in recent years
GNP: $5.550 billion, per capita $720; real growth rate 2.9% (1991)
Inflation: -1.8% (1991)
Industries: fishing, agricultural processing, phosphate mining, petroleum refining, building materials
Labour Force: 3,192,000 (1992); 80.6% agriculture, 6.2% industry, 13.1% services (1989)
Unemployment: 7.5% (1988)

Agriculture: including fishing, accounts for 20% of GDP; major products: peanuts (cash crop), millet, corn, sorghum, rice, cotton, tomatoes, green vegetables; estimated two-thirds self-sufficient in food; fish catch of 299,000 metric tons (1987)

Natural Resources: fish, phosphates, iron ore

■ FINANCE/TRADE

Currency: Communauté financière africaine franc (CFAF)

International Reserves Excluding Gold: $12 million (1992)

Gold Reserves: 0.03 million fine troy ounces (1992)

Budget: revenues $921 million; expenditures $1 billion, including capital expenditures of $14 million (1989)

Defence Expenditures: $111.85 million (1990)

External Debt: $2.954 billion (1990)

Exports: $761 million (1988); commodities: manufactures 30%, fish products 27%, peanuts 11%, petroleum products 11%, phosphates 10%; partners: US, France, other European Community, Ivory Coast, India

Imports: $1.1 billion (1988); commodities: semimanufactures 30%, food 27%, durable consumer goods 17%, petroleum 12%, capital goods 14%; partners: US, France, other European Community, Nigeria, Algeria, China, Japan

■ HEALTH

Births: 44/1,000 population (1991)

Deaths: 13/1,000 population (1991)

Infant Mortality: 86 deaths/1,000 live births (1991)

Life Expectancy at Birth: 47 years male, 49 years female (1992)

No. of Physicians: 0.7/10,000 population (1990)

■ EDUCATION

Govt. Expenditure: 15% of govt. expenditure (1984)

Literacy: 38.3% (1992)

■ COMMUNICATIONS

Daily newspapers: 1 (1992)

Televisions: 35.1/1,000 inhabitants (1992)

Radios: 113/1,000 inhabitants (1992)

Telephones: n.a.

■ TRANSPORTATION

Motor Vehicles: 135,000; 92,000 passenger cars (1990)

Roads: 15,300 km; 4,510 km paved

Railway: 922 km

Air Traffic: 136,000 passengers carried (1991)

Airports: 16

Canadian Embassy: Immeuble Daniel Sorano, 4th Flr, 45, boul. de la République; mailing address: P.O. Box 3373, Dakar, Senegal. Tel: (011-221) 23 87 49. Fax: (011-221) 23-87-49

Embassy in Canada: Embassy of the Republic of Senegal, 57 Marlborough Ave, Ottawa ON K1N 8E8. Tel: (613) 238-6392.

Seychelles

Long-Form Name: Republic of Seychelles

Capital: Victoria

Population: 72,000 (1992)

■ GEOGRAPHY

Area: 455 sq. km

Coastline: 491 km

Climate: tropical marine; humid; cooler season during southeast monsoon (late May to Sept.); warmer season during northwest monsoon (Mar. to May)

Environment: lies outside the cyclone belt, so severe storms are rare; short droughts possible; no fresh water, catchments collect rain; 40 granitic and about 50 coralline islands

Terrain: Mahé Group is granitic, narrow coastal strip, rocky, hilly; others are coral, flat, elevated reefs

Land Use: 4% arable; 18% permanent; 0% meadows; 18% forest; 60% other

Location: Indian Ocean, NW of Madagascar

■ PEOPLE

Nationality: Seychellois

Ethnic Groups: Seychellois (mixture of Asians, Africans, Europeans)

Languages: Creole (official); English, French

Religions: 90% Roman Catholic, 8% Anglican, 2% other

Marriages: 8.7 (per 1,000) (1986)

Divorces: 0.6 (per 1,000) (1986)

■ GOVERNMENT

Leader(s): Pres. France Albert René

Government Type: republic

Administrative Divisions: none

Independence: June 29, 1976 (from UK)

National Holiday: Liberation Day (anniversary of coup), June 5

■ ECONOMY

Overview: the government is moving to reduce the high dependence on tourism by promoting the development of farming, fishing and small-scale manufacturing, yet it is also encouraging foreign investment in order to upgrade hotels and other services

GNP: $350 million, per capita $5,110; real growth rate 3.2% (1991)

Inflation: 1.9% (1991)

Industries: accounts for 7% GDP; mostly subsistence farming; cash crops: coconuts, cinnamon, vanilla; other products: sweet potatoes, cassava, bananas; broiler chickens; large share of food needs imported; expansion of tuna fishing under way

Labour Force: 31% industry and commerce, 21% services, 20% government, 12% agriculture, forestry and fishing, 16% other (1985)

Unemployment: 15% (1986)

Agriculture: accounts for 7% of GDP, mostly subsistence farming; cash crops: coconuts, cinnamon, vanilla; large share of food needs imported

Natural Resources: fish, copra, cinnamon trees

■ FINANCE/TRADE

Currency: Seychelles rupee (Sr)

International Reserves Excluding Gold: $26 million (1992)

Gold Reserves: n.a.

Budget: revenues $170 million; expenditures $173 million, including capital expenditures (1989)

Defence Expenditures: $12.4 million (1989)

External Debt: $178 million (1988)

Exports: $49 million (1991); commodities: fish, copra, cinnamon bark, petroleum products (re-exports); partners: France 63%, Pakistan 12%, Reunion 10%, UK 7%

Imports: $172 million (1991); commodities: manufactured goods, food, tobacco, beverages, machinery and transportation equipment, petroleum products; partners: UK 20%, France 14%, South Africa 13%, PDRY 13%, Singapore 8%, Japan 6%

■ HEALTH

Births: 23/1,000 population (1991)

Deaths: 7/1,000 population (1991)

Infant Mortality: 15 deaths/1,000 live births (1991)

Life Expectancy at Birth: 65 years male, 74 years female (1992)

No. of Physicians: 4.6/10,000 population (1992)

■ EDUCATION

Govt. Expenditure: 15.2% of govt. expenditure (1989)

Literacy: 57.7% (1992)

■ COMMUNICATIONS

Daily newspapers: 1 (1992)

Televisions: 73.5/1,000 inhabitants (1992)

Radios: 449/1,000 inhabitants (1992)

Telephones: 20.92/100 inhabitants (1992)

■ TRANSPORTATION

Motor Vehicles: 5,785; 4,301 passenger cars (1990)

Roads: n.a.

Railway: n.a.

Air Traffic: 243,000 passengers carried (1991)

Airports: 14

Canadian Embassy: C/o The Canadian High Commission, 38 Mirambo St, Dar-es-Salaam; mailing address: P.O. Box 1022, Dar-es-Salaam, Tanzania. Tel: (011-255-51) 46000-9. Fax: (011-255-51) 46000 (ask for fax)

Representative to Canada: C/o High Commissioner for the Seychelles, 820 Second Ave, Suite 900F, New York, New York 10017 USA. Tel: (212) 687-9766

Sierra Leone

Long-Form Name: Republic of Sierra Leone

Capital: Freetown

Population: 4,376,000 (1992)

■ GEOGRAPHY

Area: 73,326 sq. km

Coastline: 402 km

Climate: tropical; hot, humid; summer rainy season (May to Dec.); winter dry season (Dec. to Apr.)

Environment: extensive mangrove swamps hinder access to sea; deforestation; soil degradation

Terrain: coastal belt of mangrove swamps, wooded hill country, upland plateau, mountains in east

Land Use: 25% arable; 2% permanent; 31% meadows; 29% forest; 13% other

Location: WC Africa, bordering on South Atlantic Ocean

■ PEOPLE

Nationality: Sierra Leonean

Ethnic Groups: 99% native African (31% Temne, 34% Mende); 1% Creole, European, Lebanese and Asian; 13 tribes

Languages: English (official); regular use limited to literate minority; principal vernaculars are Mende in south and Temne in north; Krio is the language of the resettled ex-slave population of the Freetown area and is lingua franca
Religions: 30% Moslem, 25% Christian, 45% traditional beliefs
Marriages: n.a.
Divorces: n.a.

■ **GOVERNMENT**

Leader(s): Pres. Valentine E.M. Strasser
Government Type: republic under presidential regime
Administrative Divisions: 4 provinces
Independence: Apr. 27, 1961 (from UK)
National Holiday: Republic Day, Apr. 27

■ **ECONOMY**

Overview: the economic and social infrastructure is underdeveloped; subsistence agriculture is the backbone of the economy; problems include unemployment, rising inflation, large trade deficits
GNP: $904 million, per capita $210; real growth rate 1.1% (1991)
Inflation: 102.7% (1991)
Industries: mining (diamonds, bauxite, rutile), small-scale manufacturing (beverages, textiles, cigarettes, footwear), petroleum refinery
Labour Force: 1,440,000 (1992); 69.6% agriculture, 14.1% industry, 16.4% services (1989)
Unemployment: 2,432 (1986)
Agriculture: accounts for over 30% of GDP and two-thirds of the labor Force: largely subsistence farming; cash crops: coffee, cocoa, palm kernels; harvest of food staple rice meets 80% of domestic needs; annual fish catch averages 53,000 metric tons
Natural Resources: diamonds, titanium ore, bauxite, iron ore, gold, chromite

■ **FINANCE/TRADE**

Currency: leone (Le)
International Reserves Excluding Gold: $20 million (1992)
Gold Reserves: n.a.
Budget: revenues $134 million; expenditures $187 million, including capital expenditures of $32 million (1991)
Defence Expenditures: $5.13 million (1986)
External Debt: $606 million (1990)
Exports: $146 million (1991); commodities: rutile 50%, bauxite 17%, cocoa 11%, diamonds 3%, coffee 3%; partners: US, UK, Belgium, Germany, other Western Europe

Imports: $162 million (1991); commodities: capital goods 40%, food 32%, petroleum 12%, consumer goods 7%, light industrial goods; partners: US, European Community, Japan, China, Nigeria

■ **HEALTH**

Births: 46/1,000 population (1991)
Deaths: 20/1,000 population (1991)
Infant Mortality: 151 deaths/1,000 live births (1991)
Life Expectancy at Birth: 41 years male, 44 years female (1992)
No. of Physicians: 0.7/10,000 population (1992)

■ **EDUCATION**

Govt. Expenditure: 13.28% of govt. expenditure (1990)
Literacy: 20.7% (1992)

■ **COMMUNICATIONS**

Daily newspapers: 1 (1992)
Televisions: 9.9/1,000 inhabitants (1992)
Radios: 220/1,000 inhabitants (1992)
Telephones: n.a.

■ **TRANSPORTATION**

Motor Vehicles: 47,659; 35,870 passenger cars (1990)
Roads: 7,550 km; 1,175 km paved
Railway: 88 km
Air Traffic: n.a.
Airports: 13

Canadian Embassy: C/o Canadian High Commission, 46 Independence Ave, Accra; P.O. Box 1639, Accra, Ghana. Tel: (011-233-21) 228555. Fax: (011-233-21) 773-792
Representative to Canada: C/o High Commission for Sierra Leone, 1701 19th St NW, Washington DC 20009 USA

Singapore

Long-Form Name: Republic of Singapore
Capital: Singapore
Population: 2,769,000 (1992)

■ **GEOGRAPHY**

Area: 632.6 sq. km
Coastline: 193 km
Climate: tropical; hot, humid, rainy; no pronounced rainy or dry seasons; thunderstorms occur on 40% of all days (67% of days in Apr.)
Environment: mostly urban and industrialized

Terrain: lowland; gently undulating central plateau contains water catchment area and nature preserve
Land Use: 4% arable; 7% permanent; 0% meadows; 5% forest; 84% other
Location: SE Asia, bordering on South China Sea

■ PEOPLE

Nationality: Singaporean
Ethnic Groups: 76% Chinese, 15% Malay, 6% Indian, 2% other
Languages: Chinese (Mandarin), Malay, Tamil and English (official); Malay (national)
Religions: majority of Chinese are Buddhists or atheists; Malays nearly all Moslem(minorities are Christians, Hindus, Sikhs, Taoists, Confucianists)
Marriages: 9.4 (per 1,000) (1988)
Divorces: 1.1 (per 1,000) (1988)

■ GOVERNMENT

Leader(s): Prime Min. Goh Chok Tong, Pres. Wee Kim Wee
Government Type: republic within Commonwealth
Administrative Divisions: none
Independence: Aug. 9, 1965 (from Malaysia)
National Holiday: National Day, Aug. 9

■ ECONOMY

Overview: has an open entrepreneurial economy with strong service and manufacturing sectors and good international trading links; growth has traditionally run at high rates; per capita GDP is among the highest in Asia
GNP: $39.249 billion, per capita $12,890; real growth rate 7.1% (1991)
Inflation: 3.4% (1991)
Industries: petroleum refining, electronics, oil drilling equipment, rubber processing and rubber products, processed food and beverages, ship repair, entrepôt trade, financial services, biotechnology
Labour Force: 1,298,000 (1992); 29% industry, 0.5% agriculture, 70.5% services (1989)
Unemployment: 1.9% (1991)
Agriculture: minor importance in the economy; self-sufficient in poultry and eggs; must import most other food; major crops: rubber, copra, fruit, vegetables
Natural Resources: fish, deepwater ports

■ FINANCE/TRADE

Currency: Singapore dollar ($S)
International Reserves Excluding Gold: $39.534 billion (1992)

Gold Reserves: n.a.
Budget: revenues $8.0 billion; expenditures $7.2 billion, including capital expenditures of $2.4 billion (1990)
Defence Expenditures: $1.70 billion (1990)
External Debt: $5.2 billion (1988)
Exports: $63.471 billion (1992); commodities (includes transshipments to Malaysia): petroleum products, rubber electronics, manufactured goods; partners: US 24%, Malaysia 14%, Japan 9%, Thailand 6%, Hong Kong 5%, Australia 3%, Germany 3%
Imports: $72.181 billion (1992); commodities (includes transshipments from Malaysia): capital equipment, petroleum, chemicals, manufactured goods, foodstuffs; partners: Japan 22%, US 16%, Malaysia 15%, European Community 12%, Kuwait 1%

■ HEALTH

Births: 17.8/1,000 population (1991)
Deaths: 5/1,000 population (1991)
Infant Mortality: 8 deaths/1,000 live births (1991)
Life Expectancy at Birth: 72 years male, 77 years female (1992)
No. of Physicians: 7.1/10,000 population (1992)

■ EDUCATION

Govt. Expenditure: 19.88% of govt. expenditure (1990)
Literacy: 86.8% (1992)

■ COMMUNICATIONS

Daily newspapers: 8 (1992)
Televisions: 372.4/1,000 inhabitants (1992)
Radios: 306/1,000 inhabitants (1992)
Telephones: 45.59/100 inhabitants (1992)

■ TRANSPORTATION

Motor Vehicles: 411,740; 286,756 passenger cars (1989)
Roads: 2,742 km; 2,600 km paved
Railway: 37 km
Air Traffic: 7,745,000 passengers carried (1991)
Airports: 2

Canadian Embassy: Canadian High Commission, IBM Towers, 14th Flr, 80 Anson Rd, Singapore 0207; mailing address: Robinson Rd, P.O. Box 845, Singapore 9016. Tel: (011-65) 225-6363. Fax: (011-65) 225-2450
Representative to Canada: C/o High Commission for Singapore, Two United Nations Plaza, 25th Flr, New York, New York 10017 USA

Slovenia

Long-Form Name: Republic of Slovenia
Capital: Ljubljana
Population: 1,950,000 (1990)

■ GEOGRAPHY

Area: 20,251 sq. km
Coastline: n.a.
Climate: exceptionally cold winters with much snow, cool rainy summers
Environment: summer droughts
Terrain: mountainous, esp. in NW: Julian Alps; extensively forested; hilly plains in eastern and central region; numerous caves
Land Use: extensive forested regions; little fertile agricultural land
Location: southern Europe, bordering on Adriatic Sea

■ PEOPLE

Nationality: Slovene
Ethnic Groups: Slavic (Slovene)
Languages: Slovene, Serbo-Croatian
Religions: majority Roman Catholic
Marriages: n.a.
Divorces: n.a.

■ GOVERNMENT

Leader(s): Pres. Janez Drnovsek, Prime Min. Lojze Peterle
Government Type: parliamentary democracy
Administrative Divisions: n.a.
Independence: Oct. 8, 1991; recognized by EEC countries Jan. 15, 1992
National Holiday: Statehood Day, June 25; Day of Resistance, Apr. 27

■ ECONOMY

Overview: tourism has suffered due to internal strife; chief trading partners: Germany, Italy, former Soviet countries, France, Austria, United States
GNP: $7.150 billion (1991)
Inflation: n.a.
Industries: metallurgy, furniture, sports equipment, steel, cars, sugar, cement
Labour Force: 1,262,625 (1989)
Unemployment: 2.2% (1989)
Agriculture: 29% arable, 25% pasture, 2.5% vineyards; agriculture accounts for 4.5% of GNP (1991); products inc. wheat, maize, sugar beet, potatoes, cabbage, livestock (esp. cattle, sheep, pigs, poultry); fishing, forestry
Natural Resources: brown coal and lignite deposits

■ FINANCE/TRADE

Currency: Slovenian tolar (at parity with Yugoslav dinar)
International Reserves Excluding Gold: n.a.
Gold Reserves: n.a.
Budget: n.a.
Defence Expenditures: n.a.
External Debt: n.a.
Exports: $9.203 billion dinars (1989), inc. machinery, semi-finished goods, raw materials, electric motors, transportation equipment, clothing, foodstuffs
Imports: $8.565 billion dinars (1989), inc. raw materials, semi-finished goods, machinery, foodstuffs

■ HEALTH

Births: 12.5/1,000 population (1991)
Deaths: 9.9/1,000 population (1991)
Infant Mortality: 8.9 deaths/1,000 live births (1991)
Life Expectancy at Birth: n.a.
No. of Physicians: n.a.

■ EDUCATION

Govt. Expenditure: n.a.
Literacy: n.a.

■ COMMUNICATIONS

Daily newspapers: 3
Televisions: n.a.
Radios: n.a.
Telephones: n.a.

■ TRANSPORTATION

Motor Vehicles: 554,200 passenger cars (1989)
Roads: n.a.
Railway: n.a.
Air Traffic: n.a.
Airports: n.a.

Solomon Islands

Long-Form Name: Solomon Islands
Capital: Honiara(on island of Guadalcanal)
Population: 342,000 (1992)

■ GEOGRAPHY

Area: 27,540 sq. km
Coastline: 5,313 km
Climate: tropical monsoon; few extremes of temperature and weather
Environment: subject to typhoons, which are rarely destructive; geologically active region with frequent earth tremors

Terrain: mostly rugged mountains with some low coral atolls
Land Use: 1% arable; 1% permanent; 1% meadows; 93% pastures; 4% other
Location: Melanesia, Pacific Ocean

■ PEOPLE

Nationality: Solomon Islander
Ethnic Groups: 93% Melanesian, 4% Polynesian, 2% Micronesian, 0.8% European, 0.3% Chinese, 0.4% other
Languages: English (official), Pidgin, more than 80 local languages
Religions: 34% Anglican, 19% Roman Catholic, 17% South Seas Evangelical, 25% other Protestant
Marriages: n.a.
Divorces: n.a.

■ GOVERNMENT

Leader(s): Prime Min. Solomon Mamaloni, Gov. Gen. Sir George Lepping
Government Type: independent parliamentary state within Commonwealth
Administrative Divisions: 7 provinces and 1 town
Independence: July 7, 1978 (from UK; formerly known as British Solomon Islands)
National Holiday: Independence Day, July 7

■ ECONOMY

Overview: about 90% of the population depend on subsistence agriculture, fishing and forestry for at least part of their livelihood; a 1986 cyclone damaged the infrastructure; possesses an abundance of undeveloped mineral resources; little manufacturing activity
GNP: $184 million, per capita $560; real growth rate 6.7% (1991)
Inflation: 15.1% (1991)
Industries: copra, fish (tuna)
Labour Force: 32% agriculture, forestry and fishing; 25% services, 7% construction, manufacturing and mining; 5% commerce, transport and finance (1984)
Unemployment: n.a.
Agriculture: including fishing and forestry, accounts for approx. 75% of GDP; mostly subsistence farming; cash crops: cocoa, beans, coconuts, palm kernels, timber; other products: rice, potatoes, vegetables, fruit, cattle, pigs; not self-sufficient in food grains
Natural Resources: fish, forests, gold, bauxite, phosphates

■ FINANCE/TRADE

Currency: Solomon Islands dollar ($SI)

International Reserves Excluding Gold: $23 million (1992)
Gold Reserves: n.a.
Budget: revenues $44 million; expenditures $45 million, including capital expenditures of $22 million (1989)
Defence Expenditures: n.a.
External Debt: $128 million (1988)
Exports: $70 million (1990); commodities: fish 46%, timber 31%, copra 5%, palm oil 5%; partners: Japan 51%, UK 12%, Thailand 9%, Netherlands 8%, Australia 2%, US 2%
Imports: $92 million (1990); commodities: plant and machinery 30%, fuel 19%, food 16%; partners: Japan 36%, US 23%, Singapore 9%, UK 9%, New Zealand 9%, Australia 4%, Hong Kong 4%, China 3%

■ HEALTH

Births: 40/1,000 population (1991)
Deaths: 5/1,000 population (1991)
Infant Mortality: 39 deaths/1,000 live births (1991)
Life Expectancy at Birth: 60 years male, 61 years female (1992)
No. of Physicians: 1.3/10,000 population (1992)

■ EDUCATION

Govt. Expenditure: 12.4% of govt. expenditure (1984)
Literacy: 60%

■ COMMUNICATIONS

Daily newspapers: 1 (1992)
Televisions: n.a.
Radios: 117/1,000 inhabitants (1992)
Telephones: 2.19/100 inhabitants (1992)

■ TRANSPORTATION

Motor Vehicles: 3,629 registered motor vehicles (1986)
Roads: 2,066 km; 28 km paved
Railway: n.a.
Air Traffic: 69,000 passengers carried (1991)
Airports: 28

Canadian Embassy: c/o The Canadian High Commission, Commonwealth Ave, Canberra ACT 2600, Australia. Tel: (011-61-62) 273-3844
Representative to Canada: c/o High Commissioner for the Solomon Islands, 820-2nd Ave, Ste 800A, New York, New York 10017 USA . Tel: (212) 599-6193, -90

Somalia

Long-Form Name: Somali Democratic Republic
Capital:
Population: 9,204,000 (1992)

GEOGRAPHY

Area: 637,660 sq. km
Coastline: 3,025 km
Climate: desert; northeast monsoon (Dec. to Feb.), cooler southwest monsoon (May to Oct.); irregular rainfall; hot, humid periods (tangambili) between monsoons
Environment: recurring droughts; frequent dust storms over eastern plains in summer; deforestation; overgrazing; soil erosion; desertification
Terrain: mostly flat to undulating plateau rising to hills in north
Land Use: 2% arable; negligible permanent crops; 46% meadows; 14% forest; 38% other
Location: E Africa, bordering on Gulf Of Aden, Indian Ocean

PEOPLE

Nationality: Somali
Ethnic Groups: 85% Somali, rest mainly Bantu; 30,000 Arabs, 3,000 Europeans, 800 Asians
Languages: Somali (official); Arabic, Italian, English
Religions: almost entirely Sunni Moslem, small Christian community
Marriages: n.a.
Divorces: n.a.

GOVERNMENT

Leader(s): Prime Min. Omar Arteh Ghalib, Pres. Ali Mahdi Mohamed , V. Pres. Abdel-Qadir Adan Mohammed and Umar Ma'alim Mohammed (The United Somali Congress (USC) ousted the former regime on Jan. 27, 1991 and appointed Ali to lead a provisional govt. until a democratically elected govt. is established.)
Government Type: republic
Administrative Divisions: 18 regions
Independence: July 1, 1960 (from a merger of British Somaliland, which became independent from the UK on June 26, 1960, and Italian Somaliland, which became independent from the Italian-administered UN trusteeship on July 1, 1960, to form the Somali Republic)
National Holiday: Anniversary of the Revolution, Oct. 21

ECONOMY

Overview: nomads or semi-nomads who are dependent upon livestock for their livelihoods make up about 50% of the population; one of the world's least developed countries, possessing few resources; problems include high external debt, double-digit inflation and bitter civil war
GNP: $946 million, per capita $150; real growth rate -5.5% (1990)
Inflation: 81.9% (1988)
Industries: dominant sector, led by livestock raising (cattle, sheep, goats); crops: bananas, sorghum, corn, mangoes, sugarcane; not self-sufficient in food; fishing potential largely unexploited
Labour Force: 2,140,000 (1992); 75.6% agriculture, 8.4% industry, 16% services (1989)
Unemployment: n.a.
Agriculture: livestock raising dominant; crops: bananas, sorghum, corn, mangoes, sugar cane; not self-sufficient in food
Natural Resources: uranium and largely unexploited reserves of iron ore, tin, gypsum, bauxite, copper, salt

FINANCE/TRADE

Currency: Somali shilling (So.Sh.)
International Reserves Excluding Gold: $12 million (1989)
Gold Reserves: 0.02 million fine troy ounces (1989)
Budget: revenues $190 million; expenditures $195 million, including capital expenditures of $111 million (1989)
Defence Expenditures: $18.05 million (1989)
External Debt: $1.922 billion (1990)
Exports: $58 million (1988); commodities: livestock, hides, skins, bananas, fish; partners: US 0.5%, Saudi Arabia, Italy, Germany
Imports: $354 million (1988); commodities: textiles, petroleum products, foodstuffs, construction materials; partners: US 13%, Italy, Germany, Kenya, UK, Saudi Arabia

HEALTH

Births: 46/1,000 population (1991)
Deaths: 13/1,000 population (1991)
Infant Mortality: 116 deaths/1,000 live births (1991)
Life Expectancy at Birth: 44 years male, 48 years female (1992)
No. of Physicians: 0.5/10,000 population (1992)

■ EDUCATION

Govt. Expenditure: 2.8% of government expenditure (1986)
Literacy: 24.1% (1990)

■ COMMUNICATIONS

Daily newspapers: 1 (1988)
Televisions: 13.8/1,000 inhabitants (1989)
Radios: 41/1,000 inhabitants (1989)
Telephones: n.a.

■ TRANSPORTATION

Motor Vehicles: 32,000; 20,000 passenger cars (1990)
Roads: 21,680 km; 5,740 km paved
Railway: n.a.
Air Traffic: 46,000 passengers carried (1991)
Airports: 15

Canadian Embassy: C/o The Canadian High Commission, Comcraft House, Hailé Sélassie Ave, Nairobi; mailing address: The Canadian High Commission, P.O. Box 30481, Nairobi, Kenya. Tel: (011-254-2) 214-804. Fax: (011-254-2) 226-987

South Africa

Long-Form Name: Republic of South Africa
Capital: Pretoria (administrative), Cape Town (legislative), Bloemfontein (judicial)
Population: 39,818,000 (1992)

■ GEOGRAPHY

Area: 1,221,040 sq. km; includes Walvis Bay, Marion Island, and Prince Edward Island
Coastline: 2,881 km along Indian Ocean and South Atlantic Ocean
Climate: mostly semi-arid; subtropical along coast; sunny days, cool nights
Environment: lack of important arterial rivers or lakes requires extensive water conservation and control measures
Terrain: vast interior plateau rimmed by rugged hills and narrow coastal plain
Land Use: 10% arable; 1% permanent; 65% meadows; 3% forest; 21% other
Location: S Africa, bordering on Indian Ocean, South Atlantic Ocean

■ PEOPLE

Nationality: South African
Ethnic Groups: 74% black, 14% white, 9% coloured, 3% Indian
Languages: Afrikaans, English (official); many vernacular languages, including Zulu, Xhosa,

North and South Sotho, Tswana
Religions: most of whites, Coloureds and approx. 60% of blacks are Christian; approx. 60% of Indians are Hindu, 20% Moslem
Marriages: n.a.
Divorces: n.a.

■ GOVERNMENT

Leader(s): State Pres. Frederik Willem de Klerk
Government Type: republic
Administrative Divisions: 4 provinces, 10 homelands (4 independent and 6 other)
Independence: May 31, 1910 (from UK)
National Holiday: Republic Day, May 31

■ ECONOMY

Overview: there is great disparity in living standards between the white minority (favored) and the black majority, international embargoes against the country (because of its policy of apartheid) hurt the economy; has rich mineral resources (diamonds)
GNP: $90.953 billion, per capita $2,520; real growth rate 3.3% (1991)
Inflation: 15.3% (1991)
Industries: mining (world's largest producer of diamonds, gold, chrome), automobile assembly, metalworking, machinery, textile, iron and steel, chemical, fertilizer, foodstuffs
Labour Force: 12,434,000 (1992); 62% services, 13.6% agriculture, 24.4% industry (1989)
Unemployment: 8.6% (1991)
Agriculture: accounts for 6% of GDP; diversified agriculture, with emphasis on livestock; products: cattle, poultry, sheep, wool, milk, beef, corn, wheat; sugarcane, fruits, vegetables; self-sufficient in food
Natural Resources: gold, chromium, antimony, coal, iron ore, manganese, nickel, phosphates, tin, uranium, gem diamonds, platinum, copper, vanadium, salt, natural gas

■ FINANCE/TRADE

Currency: rand (R)
International Reserves Excluding Gold: $1,570 million (1992)
Gold Reserves: 6.65 million fine troy ounces (1992)
Budget: revenues $28.9 billion; expenditures $32.8 billion, including capital expenditures of 1.1 billion (1992 est.)
Defence Expenditures: $3.99 billion (1990)
External Debt: $21.2 billion (1988)

Exports: $17.150 billion (1991); commodities: gold 40%, minerals and metals 23%, food 6%, chemicals 3%; partners: Germany, Japan, UK, US, other European Community, Hong Kong
Imports: $17.608 billion (1991); commodities: machinery 27%, chemicals 11%, vehicles and aircraft 11%, textiles, scientific instruments, base metals; partners: US, Germany, Japan, UK, France, Italy, Switzerland

■ HEALTH

Births: 34/1,000 population (1991)
Deaths: 8/1,000 population (1991)
Infant Mortality: 51 deaths/1,000 live births (1991)
Life Expectancy at Birth: 61 years male, 67 years female (1992)
No. of Physicians: 5.3/10,000 population (1980)

■ EDUCATION

Govt. Expenditure: n.a.
Literacy: 71.1% (1980)

■ COMMUNICATIONS

Daily newspapers: 22 (1988)
Televisions: 101.4/1,000 inhabitants (1989)
Radios: 324/1,000 inhabitants (1989)
Telephones: 12.5/100 inhabitants (1992)

■ TRANSPORTATION

Motor Vehicles: 5,200,153; 3,375,277 passenger cars (1990)
Roads: 181,935 km; 52,505 km paved
Railway: 23,566 km (1989)
Air Traffic: 4,819,000 passengers carried (1991)
Airports: 156

Canadian Embassy: Canadian Embassy, 5th Flr, Nedbank Plaza, Church & Beatrix Streets, Arcadia, Pretoria 0007; mailing address: P.O. Box 26006, Arcadia, Pretoria 0007, South Africa. Tel: (011-27-12) 324-3970. Fax (011-27-12) 323-1564
Embassy in Canada: Embassy of the Republic of South Africa, 15 Sussex Dr., Ottawa ON K1M 1M8. Tel: (613) 744-0330.

Spain

Long-Form Name: Kingdom of Spain
Capital: Madrid
Population: 39,092,000 (1992)

■ GEOGRAPHY

Area: 504,750 sq. km; includes Balaeric Islands, Canary Islands, Ceuta, Melilla, Islas Chafarinas, Peñón de Vélez de la Gomera
Coastline: 4,964 km along Mediterranean Sea, Balearic Sea, Bay of Biscay, Strait of Gibraltar and North Atlantic Ocean
Climate: temperate; clear, hot summers in interior, more moderate and cloudy along coast; cloudy, cold winters in interior, partly cloudy and cool along coast
Environment: deforestation; air pollution
Terrain: large, flat to dissected rugged hills; Pyrenees in north
Land Use: 31% arable; 10% permanent; 21% meadows; 31% forest; 7% other
Location: SW Europe, bordering on Mediterranean Sea

■ PEOPLE

Nationality: Spanish
Ethnic Groups: composite of Mediterranean and Nordic types
Languages: Castilian Spanish; second languages include 17% Catalan (northeast),7% Galician (northwest), 2% Basque (north)
Religions: 99% Roman Catholic, 1% other sects
Marriages: 5.3 (per 1,000) (1986)
Divorces: 0.6 (per 1,000) (1982)

■ GOVERNMENT

Leader(s): Pres. Felipe González Márquez, King Juan Carlos I
Government Type: parliamentary monarchy
Administrative Divisions: 17 autonomous communities
Independence: 1492 (expulsion of the Moors and unification)
National Holiday: National Day, Oct. 12

■ ECONOMY

Overview: has been the fastest growing member of the European Economic Community (since joining in 1986) due largely to increased foreign and domestic investment; problems include the highest unemployment rate in Europe and inflation
GNP: $486.614 billion, per capita $12,460; real growth rate 3.2% (1991)
Inflation: 5.9% (1991)
Industries: textiles and apparel (including footwear), food and beverages, metals and metal manufacturing, chemicals, shipbuilding, automobiles, machine tools
Labour Force: 14,456,000 (1992); 67.7% services, 21.1% industry, 11.2% agriculture (1989)
Unemployment: 16.4% (1991)

Agriculture: accounts for 5% of GNP; major products: grain, vegetables, olives, wine grapes, sugar beets, citrus fruit, beef, pork, poultry, dairy; largely self-sufficient in food; fish catch of 1.4 million metric tons among top 20 nations
Natural Resources: coal, lignite, iron ore, uranium, mercury, pyrites, fluorspar, gypsum, zinc, lead, tungsten, copper, kaolin, potash, hydropower

■ FINANCE/TRADE

Currency: peseta (Ptas)
International Reserves Excluding Gold: $52.237 billion (1992)
Gold Reserves: 15.62 million fine troy ounces (1992)
Budget: revenues $100.1 billion; expenditures $111.6 billion, including capital expenditures (1990)
Defence Expenditures: $8.97 billion (1991)
External Debt: $32.7 billion (1988)
Exports: $60.182 billion (1991); commodities: foodstuffs, live animals, wood, footwear, machinery, chemicals; partners: European Community 66%, US 8%, other developed countries 9%
Imports: $93.314 billion (1991); commodities: petroleum, footwear, machinery, chemicals, grain, soybeans, coffee, tobacco, iron and steel, timber, cotton, transport equipment; partners: European Community 57%, US 9%, other developed countries 13%, Middle East 3%

■ HEALTH

Births: 11/1,000 population (1991)
Deaths: 8/1,000 population (1991)
Infant Mortality: 6 deaths/1,000 live births (1991)
Life Expectancy at Birth: 73 years male, 80 years female (1992)
No. of Physicians: 31.6/10,000 population (1992)

■ EDUCATION

Govt. Expenditure: 5.65% of govt. expenditure (1989)
Literacy: 95.8% (1992)

■ COMMUNICATIONS

Daily newspapers: 102 (1992)
Televisions: 388.7/1,000 inhabitants (1992)
Radios: 304/1,000 inhabitants (1992)
Telephones: 39.59/100 inhabitants (1992)

■ TRANSPORTATION

Motor Vehicles: 14,442,492; 11,995,640 passenger cars (1988)
Roads: 154,960 km; 151,930 km paved

Railway: 14,590 km
Air Traffic: 20,945,000 passengers carried (1991)
Airports: 39

Canadian Embassy: Calle Nunez de Balboa 35, 28001 Madrid; mailing address: Apartado 587, 28080 Madrid, Spain. Tel: (011-34-1) 431-4300. Fax: (011-34-1) 431-2367
Embassy in Canada: Embassy of Spain, 350 Sparks St, Ste 802, Ottawa ON K1R 7S8. Tel: (613) 237-2193, -4. Fax: (613) 236-1502.

Sri Lanka

Long-Form Name: Democratic Socialist Republic of Sri Lanka
Capital: Colombo
Population: 17,666,000 (1992)

■ GEOGRAPHY

Area: 65,610 sq. km
Coastline: 1,340 km along Indian Ocean, Bay of Bengal, Gulf of Mannar, Palk Bay
Climate: tropical; monsoonal; northeast monsoon (Dec. to Mar.); southwest monsoon (June to Oct.)
Environment: occasional cyclones, tornados; deforestation; soil erosion
Terrain: mostly low, flat to rolling plain; mountains in south-central interior
Land Use: 16% arable; 17% permanent; 7% meadows; 37% forest; 23% other
Location: Indian Ocean, S of India

■ PEOPLE

Nationality: Sri Lankan
Ethnic Groups: 74% Sinhalese; 18% Tamil; 7% Moor; 1% Burgher, Malay and Veddha
Languages: Sinhala (official); Sinhala and Tamil are the national languages; Sinhala spoken by about 74% of population, Tamil spoken by about 18%; English commonly used in government and spoken by about 10% of the population
Religions: 70% Buddhist, 15% Hindu (Tamil speakers), 7% Christian, 8% Moslem
Marriages: 7.9 (per 1,000) (1987)
Divorces: 0.3 (per 1,000) (1987)

■ GOVERNMENT

Leader(s): Pres. Dingiri Banda Wijetunge, Prime Min. Ranil Wickremasinghe
Government Type: republic
Administrative Divisions: 25 districts
Independence: Feb. 4, 1948 (from UK; formerly known as Ceylon)
National Holiday: Independence and National Day, Feb. 4

■ ECONOMY

Overview: economy based on agriculture, forestry and fishing; has had high rates of unemployment since the late 1970s
GNP: $8.665 billion, per capita $500; real growth rate 4% (1991)
Inflation: 12.2% (1991)
Industries: processing of rubber, tea, coconuts and other agricultural commodities; cement, petroleum refining, textiles, tobacco, clothing
Labour Force: 6,370,000 (1992); 42.6% agriculture, 11.7% industry, 45.7% services (1989)
Unemployment: 14.4% (1992)
Agriculture: accounts for 25% of GDP; most important staple crop is paddy rice; other field crops: sugarcane, grains, pulses, oilseeds, roots; spices; cash crops: tea, rubber, coconuts; animal products: milk, eggs, hides, meat; not self-sufficient in rice production
Natural Resources: limestone, graphite, mineral sands, gems, phosphates, clay

■ FINANCE/TRADE

Currency: rupee (SL Rs)
International Reserves Excluding Gold: $927 million (1992)
Gold Reserves: 0.16 million fine troy ounces (1992)
Budget: revenues $1.7 billion; expenditures $2.2 billion, including capital expenditures of $0.5 billion (1990)
Defence Expenditures: $439.31 million (1990)
External Debt: $4.911 billion (1990)
Exports: $1.965 billion (1991); commodities: tea, textiles and garments, petroleum products, coconut, rubber, agricultural products, gems and jewelery, marine products; partners: US 26%, Egypt, Iraq, UK, Germany, Singapore, Japan
Imports: $3.083 billion (1991); commodities: petroleum, machinery and equipment, textiles and textile materials, wheat, transportation equipment, electrical machinery, sugar, rice; partners: Japan, Saudi Arabia, US 5.6%, India, Singapore, Germany, UK, Iran

■ HEALTH

Births: 20/1,000 population (1991)
Deaths: 6/1,000 population (1991)
Infant Mortality: 21 deaths/1,000 live births (1991)
Life Expectancy at Birth: 68 years male, 73 years female (1992)
No. of Physicians: 1.8/10,000 population (1992)

■ EDUCATION

Govt. Expenditure: 8.32% of govt. expenditure (1991)
Literacy: 88.4% (1992)

■ COMMUNICATIONS

Daily newspapers: 21 (1992)
Televisions: 32.3/1,000 inhabitants (1992)
Radios: 194/1,000 inhabitants (1992)
Telephones: 1.01/100 inhabitants (1992)

■ TRANSPORTATION

Motor Vehicles: 320,235; 176,711 passenger cars (1990)
Roads: 25,850 km; 8,595 km paved
Railway: 1,476 km
Air Traffic: 893,000 passengers carried (1991)
Airports: 3

Canadian Embassy: 6 Gregory's Rd, Colombo 7; mailing address: P.O. Box 1006, Colombo 7, Sri Lanka. Tel: (011-94-1) 69-58-41. Fax: (011-94-1) 68-70-49
Embassy in Canada: High Commission for the Democratic Socialist Republic of Sri Lanka, 85 Range Rd, Ste 102-4, Ottawa ON K1N 8J6. Tel: (613) 233-8440, -9.

Sudan

Long-Form Name: Republic of the Sudan
Capital: Khartoum
Population: 26,656,000 (1992)

■ GEOGRAPHY

Area: 2,505,810 sq. km
Coastline: 853 km along Red Sea
Climate: tropical in south; arid desert in north; rainy season (Apr. to Oct.)
Environment: dominated by the Nile and its tributaries; dust storms; desertification
Terrain: generally flat, featureless plain; mountains in east and west
Land Use: 5% arable; negligible permanent; 24% meadows; 20% forest; 51% other
Location: NE Africa, bordering on Red Sea

■ PEOPLE

Nationality: Sudanese
Ethnic Groups: 52% black, 39% Arab, 6% Beja, 2% foreigners, 1% other
Languages: Arabic (official), Nubian, Ta Bedawie, diverse dialects of Nilotic, Nilo-Hamatic and Sudanic languages, English; program of Arabization in process

Religions: 70% Sunni Moslem (in north), 20% indigenous beliefs, 5% Christian (mostly in south and Khartoum)
Marriages: n.a.
Divorces: n.a.

■ GOVERNMENT

Leader(s): Prime Min. Lt. Gen. Omar Hassan Ahmad al-Bashir; Chairman, Revolutionary Command Council for National Salvation; Head of State and Prime Min. Lt. Gen. 'Umar Hasan Ahmad al-Bashir
Government Type: military; civilian government suspended and martial law imposed after June 30, 1989 coup
Administrative Divisions: 9 regions
Independence: Jan. 1, 1956 (from Egypt and UK; formerly known as Anglo-Egyptian Sudan)
National Holiday: Independence Day, Jan. 1

■ ECONOMY

Overview: a very poor country, hurt by civil war, chronic political instability, adverse weather and counterproductive governmental economic policies; international aid is helping the country manage a high foreign debt but creditors want economic reform
GNP: $10.107 billion (1991), per capita $340 (1987); real growth rate 0.3% (1991)
Inflation: 63.5% (1989)
Industries: cotton ginning, textiles, cement, edible oils, sugar, soap distilling, shoes, petroleum refining
Labour Force: 8,080,000 (1992); 63.4% agriculture, 4.3% industry, 32.3% services (1989)
Unemployment: 70,080 (1990)
Agriculture: accounts for 35% of GNP; untapped potential for higher farm production; two-thirds of land area suitable for crops and livestock; major products: cotton, oilseeds, sorghum, millet, wheat, gum arabic sheep; marginally self-sufficient in most foods
Natural Resources: modest reserves of crude oil, iron ore, copper, chromium ore, zinc, tungsten, mica, silver, crude oil

■ FINANCE/TRADE

Currency: Sudanese pound (LSd)
International Reserves Excluding Gold: $5 million (1992)
Gold Reserves: n.a.
Budget: revenues $514 million; expenditures $1.3 billion, including capital expenditures of $183 million (1989)
Defence Expenditures: $460 million (1990)
External Debt: $9.156 billion (1990)

Exports: $672 million (1989); commodities: cotton 43%, sesame, gum arabic, peanuts; partners: Western Europe 46%, Saudi Arabia 14%, Eastern Europe 9%, Japan 9%, US 3%
Imports: $1.2 billion (1989); commodities: petroleum products, manufactured goods, machinery and equipment, medicines and chemicals; partners: Western Europe 32%, Africa and Asia 15%, US 13%, Eastern Europe 3%

■ HEALTH

Births: 44/1,000 population (1991)
Deaths: 13/1,000 population (1991)
Infant Mortality: 85 deaths/1,000 live births (1991)
Life Expectancy at Birth: 52 years male, 53 years female (1992)
No. of Physicians: 1/10,000 population (1992)

■ EDUCATION

Govt. Expenditure: 15% of govt. expenditure (1985)
Literacy: 27.1% (1992)

■ COMMUNICATIONS

Daily newspapers: 3 (1992)
Televisions: 61.3/1,000 inhabitants (1992)
Radios: 235/1,000 inhabitants (1992)
Telephones: 0.4/100 inhabitants (1992)

■ TRANSPORTATION

Motor Vehicles: 173,422; 116,473 passenger cars (1990)
Roads: 7,520 km; 5,010 km paved
Railway: 5,262 km
Air Traffic: 363,000 passengers carried (1991)
Airports: 25

Canadian Embassy: C/o 6 Mohamed Fahmy El Sayed St, Garden City, Cairo; mailing address: P.O. Box 2646, Cairo, Egypt. Tel: (011-20-2) 354-3110. Fax: (011-20-2) 356-3548
Embassy in Canada: Embassy of the Republic of the Sudan, 85 Range Rd, Ste 407, Ottawa ON K1N 8J6. Tel: (613) 235-4000, -4999. Fax: (613) 235-6880.

Suriname

Long-Form Name: Republic of Suriname
Capital: Paramaribo
Population: 438,000 (1992)

■ GEOGRAPHY

Area: 163,820 sq. km
Coastline: 386 km along Atlantic Ocean

Climate: tropical; moderated by trade winds
Environment: mostly tropical rain forest
Terrain: mostly rolling hills; narrow coastal plain with swamps
Land Use: negligible arable: negligible permanent; negligible meadows; 87% forest; 3% other
Location: N South America, bordering on Atlantic Ocean

PEOPLE

Nationality: Surinamese
Ethnic Groups: 37% Hindustani (East Indian), 31% Creole (black and mixed), 15% Javanese, 10% Bush black, 3% Amerindian, 2% Chinese, 1% European, 1% other
Languages: Dutch (official), Hindustani 32%, Javanese 15%; the majority can speak the native language Sranang Tongo (taki-taki)
Religions: 27% Hindu, 20% Moslem, 23% Roman Catholic, 25% Protestant (predominantly Moravian), about 5% indigenous beliefs
Marriages: 6.7 (per 1,000) (1980)
Divorces: 1.1 (per 1,000) (1980)

GOVERNMENT

Leader(s): Pres. Runaldo R. Venetiaan, V. Pres. Jules Ajodhia (also head of govt.)
Government Type: republic
Administrative Divisions: 10 districts
Independence: Nov. 25, 1975 (from Netherlands; formerly known as Netherlands Guiana or Dutch Guiana)
National Holiday: Independence Day, Nov. 25

ECONOMY

Overview: the economy is vulnerable to world prices for its product bauxite as well as guerrilla activity which has targeted the economic infrastructure; it has been hurt by the cut off of Dutch development aid in 1982
GNP: $1.649 billion, per capita $3,610; real growth rate -2.2% (1991)
Inflation: 50% (1988 est.)
Industries: bauxite mining, alumina and aluminum production, lumbering, food processing, fishing
Labour Force: 135,000 (1992); 20% agriculture, 20% industry, 60% services (1989)
Unemployment: 24.15% (1988)
Agriculture: accounts for 11% of GDP; paddy rice planted on 85% of arable land and represents 60% of total farm output; other products: bananas, palm kernels, coconuts, plantains, peanuts, beef, chicken; shrimp and forestry products of increasing importance

Natural Resources: timber, hydropower potential, fish, shrimp, bauxite, iron ore and modest amounts of nickel, copper, platinum, gold

FINANCE/TRADE

Currency: Suriname guilder (Sf)
International Reserves Excluding Gold: $0 million (1992)
Gold Reserves: 0.05 million fine troy ounces (1992)
Budget: revenues $466 million; expenditures $716 million, including capital expenditures of $123 million (1989)
Defence Expenditures: $39 million (1989)
External Debt: $65 million (1989)
Exports: $232 million (1988); commodities: alumina, bauxite, aluminum, rice, wood and wood products, shrimp and fish, bananas; partners: Netherlands 28%, US 22%, Norway 18%, Japan 11%, Brazil 10%, UK 4%
Imports: $195 million (1988); commodities: capital equipment, petroleum, foodstuffs, cotton, consumer goods; partners: US 34%, Netherlands 20%, Trinidad and Tobago 8%, Brazil 5%, UK 3%

HEALTH

Births: 26/1,000 population (1991)
Deaths: 6/1,000 population (1991)
Infant Mortality: 39 deaths/1,000 live births (1991)
Life Expectancy at Birth: 67 years male, 72 years female (1992)
No. of Physicians: 7.9/10,000 population (1992)

EDUCATION

Govt. Expenditure: 18% of govt. expenditure (1986)
Literacy: 94.9% (1992)

COMMUNICATIONS

Daily newspapers: 2 (1992)
Televisions: 132.9/1,000 inhabitants (1992)
Radios: 633/1,000 inhabitants (1992)
Telephones: 10.45/100 inhabitants (1992)

TRANSPORTATION

Motor Vehicles: 48,000; 35,000 passenger cars (1990)
Roads: 9,500 km; 2,460 km paved
Railway: none
Air Traffic: 133,000 passengers carried (1991)
Airports: 38

Canadian Embassy: C/o The Canadian High Commission, Huggins Bldg, 72 South Quay; Port-of-Spain; mailing address: P.O. Box 1246, Port-of-Spain, Trinidad and Tobago. Tel: (809) 623-7254. Fax: (809) 624-4016

Representative to Canada: c/o Embassy of the Republic of Suriname, 4301 Connecticut Ave NW, Ste 108, Washington DC 20008 USA

Svalbard

Dependent Territory of Norway

Long-Form Name: Svalbard
Capital: n.a.; Longyearbyen is major transportation centre
Population: 3,544 (1989)

■ GEOGRAPHY

Area: 62,050 sq. km, 5 large islands, many smaller ones
Climate: arctic, tempered by mild Atlantic winds
Land Use: undeveloped except for mining establishments
Location: Arctic Ocean, midway between Norway and the North Pole

■ PEOPLE

Nationality: Norwegian
Ethnic Groups: Germanic (Nordic), Slavic minority
Languages: Norwegian

■ GOVERNMENT

Leader(s): under Norwegian govt. administration
Government Type: overseas dependency

■ ECONOMY

Overview: tourism most important; coal mining only industry
Currency: Norwegian krone

Swaziland

Long-Form Name: Kingdom of Swaziland
Capital: Mbabane
Population: 792,000 (1992)

■ GEOGRAPHY

Area: 17,360 sq. km
Coastline: none: landlocked
Climate: varies from tropical to near temperate
Environment: overgrazing; soil degradation; soil erosion
Terrain: mostly mountains and hills; some moderately sloping plains
Land Use: 8% arable; negligible permanent; 67%

meadows; 6% forest; 19% other
Location: S Africa

■ PEOPLE

Nationality: Swazi
Ethnic Groups: 97% African, 3% European
Languages: English and siSwati (official); government business conducted in English
Religions: 57% Christian, 43% indigenous beliefs
Marriages: n.a.
Divorces: n.a.

■ GOVERNMENT

Leader(s): Prime Min. Obed Mfanyana Dlamini, King Mswati III
Government Type: monarchy; independent member of Commonwealth
Administrative Divisions: 4 districts
Independence: Sept. 6, 1968 (from UK)
National Holiday: Somhlolo (Independence) Day, Sept. 6

■ ECONOMY

Overview: the economy is based on subsistence agriculture and is closely tied to that of its neighbor, South Africa, from which it receives 90% of its imports and to which it sends about one-third of its exports
GNP: $874 million, per capita $1,060; real growth rate 6.8% (1991)
Inflation: 11.0% (1990)
Industries: mining (coal and asbestos), wood pulp, sugar
Labour Force: 306,000 (1992); 74% agriculture, 17% services, 9% industry (1989); 24,000-29,000 employed in South Africa
Unemployment: n.a.
Agriculture: accounts for 25% of GDP; mostly subsistence agriculture; cash crops: sugarcane, citrus fruit, cotton, pineapple; other crops and livestock: corn, sorghum, peanuts, cattle, goats, sheep; not self-sufficient in grain
Natural Resources: asbestos, coal, clay, tin, hydroelectric power, forests and small gold and diamond deposits

■ FINANCE/TRADE

Currency: lilangeni (pl. emalangeni) (E)
International Reserves Excluding Gold: $309 million (1992)
Gold Reserves: n.a.
Budget: revenues $322.9 million; expenditures $325.5 million, including capital expenditures (1992 est.)
Defence Expenditures: 14% GNP (1988)

External Debt: $275 million (1987)
Exports: $443 million (1989); commodities: sugar, asbestos, wood pulp, citrus, canned fruit, soft drink concentrates; partners: South Africa, UK, US
Imports: $581 million (1989); commodities: motor vehicles, machinery, transport equipment, chemicals, petroleum products, foodstuffs; partners: South Africa, US, UK

■ HEALTH

Births: 44/1,000 population (1991)
Deaths: 12/1,000 population (1991)
Infant Mortality: 101 deaths/1,000 live births (1991)
Life Expectancy at Birth: 51 years male, 59 years female (1992)
No. of Physicians: 0.5/10,000 population (1990)

■ EDUCATION

Govt. Expenditure: 27.37% of govt. expenditure (1990)
Literacy: 55.2% (1992)

■ COMMUNICATIONS

Daily newspapers: 2 (1992)
Televisions: 16.4/1,000 inhabitants (1992)
Radios: 154/1,000 inhabitants (1992)
Telephones: 2.95/100 inhabitants (1992)

■ TRANSPORTATION

Motor Vehicles: 33,019; 24,899 passenger cars (1987)
Roads: 2,743 km; 521 km paved
Railway: 519 km
Air Traffic: 59,000 passengers carried (1991)
Airports: 4

Canadian Embassy: C/o Canadian Embassy, 5th Flr, Nedbank Plaza, Church & Beatrix Streets, Arcadia, Pretoria 0007; mailing address: P.O. Box 26006, Arcadia, Pretoria 0007, South Africa. Tel: (011-27-12) 324-3970. Fax (011-27-12) 323-1564
Embassy in Canada: High Commission for the Kingdom of Swaziland, 130 Albert St, Ste 1204, Ottawa ON K1P 5G4. Tel: (613) 567-1480.

Sweden

Long-Form Name: Kingdom of Sweden
Capital: Stockholm
Population: 8,652,000 (1992)

■ GEOGRAPHY

Area: 449,960 sq. km

Coastline: 3,218 km
Climate: temperate in south with cold, cloudy winters and cool, partly cloudy summers, subarctic in north
Environment: water pollution; acid rain
Terrain: mostly flat or gently rolling lowlands; mountains in west
Land Use: 7% arable; 0% permanent; 2% meadows; 64% forest; 27% other
Location: N Europe, bordering on Baltic Sea

■ PEOPLE

Nationality: Swedish
Ethnic Groups: homogeneous white population; small Lappish minority; about 12% foreign born of first-generation immigrants (Finns, Yugoslavs, Danes, Norwegians, Greeks, Turks)
Languages: Swedish (official), small Lapp- and Finnish-speaking minorities; immigrants speak native languages
Religions: 95% Evangelical Lutheran, 1% Roman Catholic, 4% other
Marriages: 5.2 (per 1,000) (1988)
Divorces: 2.3 (per 1,000) (1988)

■ GOVERNMENT

Leader(s): Prime Min. Carl Bildt, King Carl XVI Gustaf
Government Type: constitutional monarchy
Administrative Divisions: 24 provinces
Independence: June 6, 1809, constitutional monarchy established
National Holiday:

■ ECONOMY

Overview: a mixed system of high-tech capitalism and extensive welfare benefits; has benefited from neutrality in world wars; has essentially full employment and excellent communications systems; but faces loss of competitive edge
GNP: $218.934 billion, per capita $25,490; real growth rate 2.0% (1991)
Inflation: 9.3% (1991)
Industries: iron and steel, precision equipment (bearings, radio and telephone parts, armaments), wood pulp and paper products, processed foods, motor vehicles
Labour Force: 4,319,000 (1992); 3.3% agriculture, 21.8% industry, 74.9% services (1989)
Unemployment: 2.7% (1991)
Agriculture: animal husbandry predominates, with milk and dairy products accounting for 37% of farm income; main crops: grains, sugar beets, potatoes; 100% self-sufficient in grains and potatoes, 85% self-sufficient in sugar beets

Natural Resources: zinc, iron ore, lead, copper, silver, timber, uranium, hydropower potential

■ FINANCE/TRADE

Currency: krona (pl. kronor) (Skr)
International Reserves Excluding Gold: $20,722 million (1992)
Gold Reserves: 6.07 million fine troy ounces (1992)
Budget: revenues $60.1 billion; expenditures $56.7 billion, including capital expenditures (1989)
Defence Expenditures: $5.51 billion (1990)
External Debt: $17.9 billion (1988)
Exports: $56.020 billion (1992); commodities: machinery, motor vehicles, paper products, pulp and wood, iron and steel products, chemicals, petroleum and petroleum products; partners: European Community 52.1%, (Germany 12.1%, UK 11.2%, Denmark 6.8%), US 9.8%, Norway 9.3%
Imports: $49.515 billion (1992); commodities: machinery, petroleum and petroleum products, chemicals, motor vehicles, foodstuffs, iron and steel, clothing; partners: European Community 55.8%, (Germany 21.2%, UK 8.6%, Denmark 6.6%), US 7.5%, Norway 6%

■ HEALTH

Births: 13/1,000 population (1991)
Deaths: 11/1,000 population (1991)
Infant Mortality: 6 deaths/1,000 live births (1991)
Life Expectancy at Birth: 75 years male, 80 years female (1992)
No. of Physicians: 25.8/10,000 population (1992)

■ EDUCATION

Govt. Expenditure: 8.71% of govt. expenditure (1990)
Literacy: 99% (1992)

■ COMMUNICATIONS

Daily newspapers: 107 (1992)
Televisions: 470.5/1,000 inhabitants (1992)
Radios: 885/1,000 inhabitants (1992)
Telephones: 88.95/100 inhabitants (1992)

■ TRANSPORTATION

Motor Vehicles: 3,924,633; 3,600,518 passenger cars (1990)
Roads: 146,240 km; 103,940 km paved
Railway: 12,735 km
Air Traffic: 9,827,000 passengers carried (1991)
Airports: 189

Canadian Embassy: The Canadian Embassy, Tegelbacken 4 (Flr 7); mailing address: P.O. Box 16129; S-103 23 Stockholm 5, Sweden. Tel: (011-46-8) 613-9900. Fax: (011-46-8) 24 24 91
Embassy in Canada: Embassy of Sweden, Mercury Court, 377 Dalhousie St, Ottawa ON K1N 9N8. Tel: (613) 236-8553. Fax: (613) 236-5720.

Switzerland

Long-Form Name: Swiss Confederation
Capital: Berne
Population: 6,813,000 (1992)

■ GEOGRAPHY

Area: 41,290 sq. km
Coastline: none: landlocked
Climate: temperate, but varies with altitude; cold, cloudy, rainy/snowy winters; cool to warm, cloudy, humid summers with occasional showers
Environment: dominated by Alps
Terrain: mostly mountains (Alps in south, Jura in northwest) with a central plateau of rolling hills, plains and large lakes
Land Use: 10% arable; 1% permanent; 40% meadows; 26% forest; 23% other
Location: SC Europe

■ PEOPLE

Nationality: Swiss
Ethnic Groups: total population: 65% German, 18% French, 10% Italian, 1% Romansch, 6% other; Swiss nationals: 74% German, 20% French, 4% Italian, 1% Romansch, 1% other
Languages: 73.5% German, 20.1% French, 4.5% Italian (all official), 1% Raeto-Romansch
Religions: 49% Roman Catholic, 48% Protestant, 0.3% Jewish
Marriages: 6.6 (per 1,000) (1987)
Divorces: 1.8 (per 1,000) (1987)

■ GOVERNMENT

Leader(s): Pres. Rene Felber, V. Pres. Adolf Ogi
Government Type: federal republic
Administrative Divisions: 26 cantons
Independence: Aug. 1, 1291
National Holiday: Anniversary of the Founding of the Swiss Confederation, Aug. 1

■ ECONOMY

Overview: country has the highest per capita output, general living standards, education and science, healthcare and diet standards in Europe; important banking and tourist sectors; low inflation and negligible unemployment is due partly to government policies

GNP: $225.890 billion, per capita $33,510; real growth rate 2.2% (1991)
Inflation: 5.8% (1991)
Industries: machinery, chemicals, watches, textiles, precision instruments
Labour Force: 3,212,000 (1992); 63.8% services, 29.8% industry, 6.4% agriculture (1989)
Unemployment: 1.3% (1991)
Agriculture: dairy farming predominates; less than 50% self-sufficient; food shortages: fish, refined sugar, fats and oils (other than butter), grains, eggs, fruits, vegetables, meat
Natural Resources: hydropower potential, timber, salt

■ FINANCE/TRADE

Currency: Swiss franc (SwF)
International Reserves Excluding Gold: $33,255 million (1992)
Gold Reserves: 83.28 million fine troy ounces (1992)
Budget: revenues $24.0 billion; expenditures $23.8 billion, including capital expenditures (1990)
Defence Expenditures: $4.10 billion (1990)
External Debt: n.a.
Exports: $65.783 billion (1992); commodities: machinery and equipment, precision instruments, metal products, foodstuffs, textiles and clothing; partners: Europe 64% (European Community 56%, other 8%), US 9%, Japan 4%
Imports: $65.924 billion (1992); commodities: agricultural products, machinery and transportation equipment, chemicals, textiles, construction materials; partners: Europe 79% (European Community 72%, other 7%), US 5%

■ HEALTH

Births: 12/1,000 population (1991)
Deaths: 9/1,000 population (1991)
Infant Mortality: 5 deaths/1,000 live births (1991)
Life Expectancy at Birth: 74 years male, 81 years female (1992)
No. of Physicians: 14.4/10,000 population (1992)

■ EDUCATION

Govt. Expenditure: 18.8% of govt. expenditure (1988)
Literacy: 99% (1992)

■ COMMUNICATIONS

Daily newspapers: 98 (1992)
Televisions: 405.8/1,000 inhabitants (1992)
Radios: 851/1,000 inhabitants (1992)
Telephones: 90.0/100 inhabitants (1992)

■ TRANSPORTATION

Motor Vehicles: 3,297,237; 2,993,529 passenger cars (1990)
Roads: 73,830 km; paved km n.a.
Railway: 4,670 km
Air Traffic: 7,974,000 passengers carried (1991)
Airports: 10

Canadian Embassy: Canadian Embassy, 88 Kirchenfeldstrasse, CH-3005 Berne, Switzerland; mailing address: Box 3000, Berne 6, Switzerland. Tel: (011-41-31) 44-63-81. Fax: (011-41-31) 44-73-15
Embassy in Canada: Embassy of Switzerland, 5 Marlborough Ave, Ottawa ON K1N 8E6. Tel: (613) 235-1837, -8. Fax: (613) 563-1394.

Syria

Long-Form Name: Syrian Arab Republic
Capital: Damascus
Population: 13,276,000 (1992)

■ GEOGRAPHY

Area: 185,180 sq. km; including 1,295 sq. km of Israeli-occupied territory
Coastline: 193 km along Mediterranean Sea
Climate: mostly desert; hot, dry, sunny summers (June to Aug.) and mild, rainy winters (Dec. to Feb.) along coast
Environment: deforestation; overgrazing; soil erosion; desertification
Terrain: primarily semi-arid and desert plateau; narrow coastal plain; mountains in west
Land Use: 28% arable; 3% permanent; 46% meadows; 3% forest; 20% other
Location: SW Asia (Near East), bordering on Mediterranean Sea

■ PEOPLE

Nationality: Syrian
Ethnic Groups: 90% Arab; 10% Kurds, Armenians and other
Languages: Arabic (official), Kurdish, Armenian, Aramaic, Circassian; French widely understood
Religions: 90% Islam (of which 74% are Sunni, 16% Alawite, Druze and other Muslim sects); 10% Christian
Marriages: 9.4 (per 1,000) (1987)
Divorces: 0.7 (per 1,000) (1987)

■ GOVERNMENT

Leader(s): Pres. Lt.-Gen. Hafez al-Assad, V. Pres. Abdel Halim Khaddam, Zuheir Masharqa and Col. Rifaat Assad
Government Type: republic

Administrative Divisions: 14 districts
Independence: Apr. 17, 1946 (from League of Nations mandate under French administration; formerly known as United Arab Republic)
National Holiday: National Day, Apr. 17

■ ECONOMY

Overview: economic difficulties are due, in part, to severe drought in several recent years, costly but unsuccessful attempts to match Israel's military strength, a fall-off in Arab aid and insufficient foreign exchange earnings to buy needed imports
GNP: $14.234 billion, per capita $1,110; real growth rate 1.4% (1991)
Inflation: 7.7% (1991)
Industries: textiles, food processing, beverages, tobacco, phosphate rock mining, petroleum
Labour Force: 3,101,000 (1992); 62.9% services, 22% agriculture, 15.1% industry (1989)
Unemployment: n.a.
Agriculture: accounts for 27% of GDP; all major crops (wheat, barley, cotton, lentils, chickpeas) grown on rain-fed land causing wide swings in yields; animal products: beef, lamb, eggs, poultry, milk; not self-sufficient in grain or livestock products
Natural Resources: crude oil, phosphates, chrome and manganese ores, asphalt, iron ore, rock salt, marble, gypsum

■ FINANCE/TRADE

Currency: Syrian pound (LS)
International Reserves Excluding Gold: $143 million (1988)
Gold Reserves: 0.83 million fine troy ounces (1991)
Budget: revenues 4.8 billion; expenditures $5.5 billion, including capital expenditures of $2.1 billion (1990)
Defence Expenditures: $1.62 billion (1990)
External Debt: $14.959 billion (1990)
Exports: $3.143 billion (1991); commodities: petroleum, textiles, fruits and vegetables, phosphates; partners: Italy, Romania, USSR, US, Iran, France
Imports: $3.151 billion (1991); commodities: petroleum, machinery, base metals, foodstuffs and beverages; partners: Iran, Germany, USSR, France, Libya, US

■ HEALTH

Births: 43/1,000 population (1991)
Deaths: 5/1,000 population (1991)
Infant Mortality: 37 deaths/1,000 live births (1991)

Life Expectancy at Birth: 64 years male, 66 years female (1992)
No. of Physicians: 7.7/10,000 population (1992)

■ EDUCATION

Govt. Expenditure: 7.41% of govt. expenditure (1990)
Literacy: 64.5% (1992)

■ COMMUNICATIONS

Daily newspapers: 8 (1992)
Televisions: 58.7/1,000 inhabitants (1992)
Radios: 248/1,000 inhabitants (1992)
Telephones: 5.9/100 inhabitants (1992)

■ TRANSPORTATION

Motor Vehicles: 242,792; 112,259 passenger cars (1990)
Roads: 30,000 km; 23,330 km paved
Railway: 1,780 km
Air Traffic: 661,000 passengers carried (1991)
Airports: 7

Canadian Embassy: The Canadian Embassy, Lot 12, Mezzah Autostrade, Damascus; mailing address: P.O. Box 3394, Damascus, Syria. Tel: (011-963-11) 236-851. Fax: (011-963-11) 228-034

Representative to Canada: c/o Embassy of the Syrian Arab Republic, 2215 Wyoming Ave NW, Washington DC 20008 USA

Taiwan

Long-Form Name: Republic of China
Capital: Taipei
Population: 20,546,664 (1990)

■ GEOGRAPHY

Area: 35,980 sq. km; includes the Pescadores, Matsu and Quemoy
Coastline: 1,448 km
Climate: tropical; marine; rainy season during southwest monsoon (June to Aug.); cloudiness is persistent and extensive all year
Environment: subject to earthquakes and typhoons
Terrain: eastern two-thirds mostly rugged mountains; flat to gently rolling plains in west
Land Use: 24% arable; 1% permanent; 5% meadows; 55% forest; 15% other
Location: SE of China, bordering on South and East China Seas, Pacific Ocean

■ PEOPLE

Nationality: Chinese
Ethnic Groups: 84% Taiwanese, 14% mainland China, 2% aborigine
Languages: Mandarin Chinese (official); Taiwanese and Hakka dialects also used
Religions: 93% mixture of Buddhist, Islam, Confucian and Taoist, 5% Christian, 3% other
Marriages: n.a.
Divorces: n.a.

■ GOVERNMENT

Leader(s): Pres. Lee Teng-hui, Prem. Hao Po-ts'un
Government Type: one-party presidential regime; opposition political parties legalized in 1989
Administrative Divisions: 16 counties, 5 municipalities, 2 special municipalities
Independence: n.a.
National Holiday: National Day (Anniversary of the Revolution), Oct. 10

■ ECONOMY

Overview: capitalist economy with government guidance of investment and foreign trade; ranks as number 13 among major trading countries; steady industrialization
GNP: $150.8 billion, per capita $7,380; real growth rate 5.2% (1990)
Inflation: 5% (1989)
Industries: textiles, clothing, chemicals, electronics, food processing, plywood, sugar milling, cement, shipbuilding, petroleum
Labour Force: 41% industry and commerce, 32% services, 20% agriculture, 7% civil administration (1986)
Unemployment: 1.7% (1989)
Agriculture: accounts for 6% of GNP; heavily subsidized sector; major crops: rice sugarcane, sweet potatoes, fruits, vegetables; livestock: hogs, poultry, beef, milk, cattle; not self-sufficient in wheat, soybeans, corn; fish catch expanding, 1.1 million metric ton
Natural Resources: small deposits of coal, natural gas, limestone, marble and asbestos

■ FINANCE/TRADE

Currency: new taiwan dollar (NT$)
International Reserves Excluding Gold: $50,919 million (1990)
Gold Reserves: n.a.
Budget: revenues $30.3 billion; expenditures $30.1 billion, including capital expenditures (1991)
Defence Expenditures: $8.69 billion (1990)

External Debt: $1.0 billion (1989)
Exports: $66.2 billion (1989); commodities: textiles 16%, electrical machinery 19%, general machinery and equipment 14%, telecommunications equipment 9%, basic metals and metal products 5%, foodstuffs 0.9%, plywood and wood products 1.3%; partners: US 36.2%, Japan 13.7%
Imports: $52.2 billion (1989); commodities: machinery and equipment 15.9%, crude oil 5%, chemical and chemical products 11.1%, basic metals 7.4%, foodstuffs 2%; partners: Japan 31%, US 23%, Saudi Arabia 8.6%

■ HEALTH

Births: 16/1,000 population (1991)
Deaths: 5/1,000 population (1991)
Infant Mortality: 6 deaths/1,000 live births (1991)
Life Expectancy at Birth: 71 years male, 76 years female (1992)
No. of Physicians: 19,921 doctors (1990)

■ EDUCATION

Govt. Expenditure: n.a.
Literacy: 94%

■ COMMUNICATIONS

Daily newspapers: 139 (1990)
Televisions: 6.66 million (1991)
Radios: 13.6 million (1991)
Telephones: 14.7 million (1990)

■ TRANSPORTATION

Motor Vehicles: 2,800,000; 2,200,000 passenger cars (1990)
Roads: n.a.
Railway: 4,875 km
Air Traffic: 17.21 million passengers carried (1989)
Airports: 38

Canadian Embassy: Canadian Trade Office, Flr 13, 365 Fu Hsing North Rd, Taipei, Taiwan. Tel: (011-886-2) 713-7268. Fax: (011-886-2) 712-7244

Tajikistan

Long-Form Name: Republic of Tajikistan
Capital: Dushanbe
Population: 5,587,000 (1992)

■ GEOGRAPHY

Area: 143,100 sq. km
Coastline: none; landlocked

Climate: continental; severe winters in east; extremely hot summers; wet spring
Environment: lack of fresh water; little land suitable for cultivation
Terrain: mountains and glaciers constitute 93% of land area
Land Use: predominantly herding and nonagricultural
Location: C Asia

■ PEOPLE

Nationality: Tajik or Tadzhik
Ethnic Groups: 62.3% Tajik, 23.5% Uzbek, 7.6% Russian
Languages: Tajik (official), Uzbek, Russian
Religions: predominantly Sunni Muslim
Marriages: n.a.
Divorces: n.a.

■ GOVERNMENT

Leader(s): Pres. (acting) Imamoli Rakhmanov, Prime Min. Abdumalik Abdullojanov
Government Type: in transition to republic
Administrative Divisions: 3 regions, 43 rural districts, 18 towns, 49 urban settlements, 1 autonomous region
Independence: declared Aug. 25, 1990
National Holiday: n.a.

■ ECONOMY

Overview: mostly mining and manufacturing with strong agricultural sector
GNP: $5.669 billion, per capita $1,050; real growth rate 2.9% (1991)
Inflation: n.a.
Industries: aluminum and electrochemical plants, textile machinery, silk and carpet mills
Labour Force: n.a.
Unemployment: n.a.
Agriculture: cotton, grapes, fruit, grains, silkworm farming, cattle breeding, sheep, goats, pigs
Natural Resources: coal, oil, rare metals, rock crystal, mica, gold

■ FINANCE/TRADE

Currency: ruble (rbl.)
International Reserves Excluding Gold: n.a.
Gold Reserves: n.a.
Budget: 1989 revenues: 2.375 million roubles
Defence Expenditures: n.a.
External Debt: n.a.
Exports: textiles, carpets, machinery
Imports: n.a.

■ HEALTH

Births: 38.7/1,000 population (1989)

Deaths: 6.4/1,000 population (1989)
Infant Mortality: 43.3 deaths/1,000 live births (1989)
Life Expectancy at Birth: 67 years male, 72 years female (1992)
No. of Physicians: 14,900 doctors (1989)

■ EDUCATION

Govt. Expenditure: n.a.
Literacy: n.a.

■ COMMUNICATIONS

Daily newspapers: 74 daily newspapers of all circulation types (1989)
Televisions: n.a.
Radios: n.a.
Telephones: n.a.

■ TRANSPORTATION

Motor Vehicles: n.a.
Railway: 480 km (1990)
Air Traffic: n.a.
Airports: 1

Canadian Embassy: C/o Russian Federation Moscow, 23 Starokonyushenny Per, The Canadian Embassy. Tel: (011-7-95) 241-5070. Fax: (011-7-95) 241-4400.

Tanzania

Long-Form Name: United Republic of Tanzania
Capital: designated capital: Dodoma
Population: 27,829,000 (1992)

■ GEOGRAPHY

Area: 945,090 sq. km
Coastline: 1,424 km along Indian Ocean, lakes
Climate: varies from tropical along coast to temperate in highlands
Environment: lack of water and tsetse fly limit agriculture; recent droughts affected marginal agriculture; Kilimanjaro is highest point in Africa
Terrain: plains along coast; central plateau; highlands in north, south
Land Use: 5% arable; 1% permanent; 40% meadows; 47% forest; 7% other
Location: E Africa, bordering on Indian Ocean

■ PEOPLE

Nationality: Tanzanian
Ethnic Groups: mainland: 99% native African consisting of well over 100 tribes; 1% Asian, European and Arab
Languages: Swahili and English (official);

English primarily language of commerce, administration and higher education; Swahili widely understood and generally used for communication between ethnic groups
Religions: mainland: 33% Christian, 33% Moslem, 33% indigenous beliefs; Zanzibar: almost all Moslem
Marriages: n.a.
Divorces: n.a.

■ GOVERNMENT

Leader(s): Prime Min. John Malecela, Pres. Ali Hassan Mwinyi, V. Pres. John Malecela and Salmin Amour
Government Type: republic
Administrative Divisions: 25 regions
Independence: Tanganyika became independent on Dec. 9, 1961 (from UN trusteeship under British administration); Zanzibar became independent Dec. 19, 1963 (from UK); Tanganyika united with Zanzibar Apr. 26, 1964
National Holiday: Union Day, Apr. 26

■ ECONOMY

Overview: world aid is increasing the availability of imports and providing funds to rehabilitate this country's deteriorated economic infrastructure; this poor economy is heavily dependent on agriculture
GNP: $2.424 billion, per capita $100; real growth rate 2.0% (1991)
Inflation: 22.3% (1991)
Industries: primarily agricultural processing (sugar, beer, cigarettes, sisal twine), diamond mines, oil refineries, shoes, cement, textiles, wood products, fertilizer
Labour Force: 12,600,000 (1992); 85.6% agriculture, 4.5% industry, 9.9% services (1989)
Unemployment: n.a.
Agriculture: accounts for over 40% of GDP; topography and climatic conditions limit cultivated crops to only 5% of land area; cash crops: coffee, sisal, tea, cotton, pyrethrum (insecticide made from chrysanthemums), cashews, tobacco, cloves (Zanzibar)
Natural Resources: hydropower potential, tin, phosphates, iron ore, coal, diamonds, gemstones, gold, natural gas, nickel

■ FINANCE/TRADE

Currency: Tanzania shilling (TSh)
International Reserves Excluding Gold: $204 million (1991)
Gold Reserves: n.a.
Budget: revenues $495 million, expenditures $631 million, including capital expenditures of

$118 million (1990)
Defence Expenditures: $119.20 million (1989)
External Debt: $5.294 billion (1990)
Exports: $415 million (1990); commodities: coffee, cotton, sisal, cashew nuts, meat, tobacco, tea, diamonds, coconut products, pyrethrum, cloves; partners: Germany, UK, US, Netherlands, Japan
Imports: $1.021 billion (1990); commodities: manufactured goods, machinery and transportation equipment, cotton piece goods, crude oil, foodstuffs; partners: Germany, UK, US, Iran, Japan, Italy

■ HEALTH

Births: 50/1,000 population (1991)
Deaths: 15/1,000 population (1991)
Infant Mortality: 105 deaths/1,000 live births (1991)
Life Expectancy at Birth: 49 years male, 54 years female (1992)
No. of Physicians: 0.4/10,000 population (1992)

■ EDUCATION

Govt. Expenditure: 14.0% of government expenditure (1989)
Literacy: 90.4% (1992)

■ COMMUNICATIONS

Daily newspapers: 2 (1992)
Televisions: 1/1,000 inhabitants (1992)
Radios: 21/1,000 inhabitants (1992)
Telephones: 0.56/100 inhabitants (1992)

■ TRANSPORTATION

Motor Vehicles: 100,000; 45,000 passenger cars (1983)
Roads: 86,950 km; 3,780 km paved
Railway: 3,780 km
Air Traffic: 290,000 passengers carried (1991)
Airports: 62

Canadian Embassy: The Canadian High Commission, 38 Mirambo St, Dar-es-Salaam; mailing address: P.O. Box 1022, Dar-es-Salaam, Tanzania. Tel: (011-255-51) 46000-9. Fax: (011-255-51) 46000 (ask for fax)
Embassy in Canada: High Commission for the United Republic of Tanzania, 50 Range Rd, Ottawa ON K1N 8J4. Tel: (613) 232-1500, -9. Fax: (613) 232-5184.

Thailand

Long-Form Name: Kingdom of Thailand
Capital: Bangkok

Population: 56,129,000 (1992)

■ GEOGRAPHY

Area: 514,000 sq. km
Coastline: 3,219 km
Climate: tropical; rainy, warm, cloudy southwest monsoon (mid-May to Sept.); dry, cool, northeast monsoon (Nov. to mid-Mar.); southern isthmus always hot and humid
Environment: air and water pollution; land subsidence in Bangkok area
Terrain: central plain; eastern plateau (Khorat); mountains elsewhere
Land Use: 34% arable; 4% permanent; 1% meadows; 30% forest; 31% other
Location: SE Asia, bordering on Bay of Bengal, South China Sea

■ PEOPLE

Nationality: Thai
Ethnic Groups: 75% Thai, 14% Chinese, 11% other
Languages: Thai; English is the secondary language of the elite; small minorities speak Chinese, Malay, indigenous languages
Religions: 96% Buddhist (Theravada), 4% Moslem, 0.5% other
Marriages: 6.3 (per 1,000) (1986)
Divorces: 0.7 (per 1,000) (1986)

■ GOVERNMENT

Leader(s): Prime Min. Chuan Leekpai, King Phumiphon Adunlayadet (Rama IX)
Government Type: constitutional monarchy
Administrative Divisions: 73 provinces
Independence: 1238 (traditional founding date); never colonized
National Holiday: Birthday of His Majesty the King, Dec. 5

■ ECONOMY

Overview: improved weather, increased tourism, export-oriented investment and sound governmental fiscal and monetary policy have all contributed to impressive growth in this country; the government is refurbishing the infrastructure
GNP: $89.548 billion, per capita $1,580; real growth rate 7.8% (1991)
Inflation: 5.9% (1990)
Industries: tourism is the largest source of foreign exchange; textiles and garments, agricultural processing, beverages, tobacco, cement, other light manufacturing, such as jewelry; electric appliances and components, integrated circuits, furniture, plastics
Labour Force: 30 million (1992); 69.8% agricul-ture, 5.9%, 24.3% services (1989)
Unemployment: 6% (1989 est.)
Agriculture: accounts for 16% of GNP and 73% of labor force; leading producer and exporter of rice and cassava; other crops: rubber, corn, sugar cane, coconuts, soybeans; self-sufficient in food except for wheat
Natural Resources: tin, rubber, natural gas, tungsten, tantalum, timber, lead, fish, gypsum, lignite, fluorite

■ FINANCE/TRADE

Currency: baht (B)
International Reserves Excluding Gold: $20.127 billion (1992)
Gold Reserves: 2.47 million fine troy ounces (1992)
Budget: revenues $15.2 billion; expenditures $15.2 billion, including capital expenditures of $4.1 billion (1991)
Defence Expenditures: 2.9% GDP (1989)
External Debt: $12.572 billion (1990)
Exports: $28.395 billion (1991); commodities: textiles 12%, fishery products 12%, rice 8%, tapioca 8%, jewelery 6%, manufactured gas, corn, tin; partners: US 18%, Japan 14%, Singapore 9%, Netherlands, Malaysia, Hong Kong, China
Imports: $37.188 billion (1991); commodities: machinery and parts 23%, petroleum products 13%, chemicals 11%, iron and steel, electrical appliances; partners: Japan 26%, US 14%, Singapore 7%, Germany, Malaysia, UK

■ HEALTH

Births: 20/1,000 population (1991)
Deaths: 6/1,000 population (1991)
Infant Mortality: 37 deaths/1,000 live births (1991)
Life Expectancy at Birth: 64 years male, 69 years female (1992)
No. of Physicians: 1.6/10,000 population (1992)

■ EDUCATION

Govt. Expenditure: 20.19% of government expenditure (1991)
Literacy: 93.0% (1992)

■ COMMUNICATIONS

Daily newspapers: 40 (1992)
Televisions: 109.3/1,000 inhabitants (1992)
Radios: 182/1,000 inhabitants (1992)
Telephones: 1.9/100 inhabitants (1992)

■ TRANSPORTATION

Motor Vehicles: 2,813,865; 826,606 passenger cars (1990)
Roads: 73,500 km; 39,065 km paved
Railway: 3,960 km
Air Traffic: 7,709,000 million passengers carried (1991)
Airports: 31

Canadian Embassy: The Canadian Embassy, 12th Floor, Boonmitr Bldg, 138 Silom Rd, Bangkok 10500; mailing address: P.O. Box 2090, Bangkok 10500, Thailand. Tel: (011-66-2) 237-4126. Fax: (011-66-2) 236-6463
Embassy in Canada: Royal Thai Embassy, 180 Island Park Dr., Ottawa ON K1Y 0A2. Tel: (613) 722-4444. Fax: (613) 722-6624.

Togo

Long-Form Name: Republic of Togo
Capital: Lomé
Population: 3,763,000 (1992)

■ GEOGRAPHY

Area: 56,790 sq. km
Coastline: 56 km along Bight of Benin
Climate: tropical; hot, humid in south; semi-arid in north
Environment: hot, dry harmattan wind can reduce visibility in north during winter; recent droughts affecting agriculture; deforestation
Terrain: gently rolling savanna in north; central hills; southern plateau; low coastal plain with extensive lagoons and marshes
Land Use: 25% arable; 1% permanent; 4% meadows; 28% forest; 42% other
Location: WC Africa, bordering on South Atlantic Ocean

■ PEOPLE

Nationality: Togolese
Ethnic Groups: 37 tribes; largest and most important are Ewe, Mina and Kabyè; under 1% European and Syrian-Lebanese
Languages: French, both official and language of commerce; major African languages are Ewe and Mina in the south and Dagomba and Kabyè in the north
Religions: about 50% indigenous beliefs, 35% Christian, 15% Moslem
Marriages: 2.3 (per 1,000) (1979)
Divorces: n.a.

■ GOVERNMENT

Leader(s): Pres. Gen. Gnassingbé Eyadéma,
Prime Min. Joseph Kokov Koffigoh
Government Type: republic; one-party presidential regime
Administrative Divisions: 5 regions
Independence: Apr. 27, 1960 (from UN trusteeship under French administration; formerly known as French Togo)
National Holiday: Liberation Day (anniversary of coup), Jan. 13

■ ECONOMY

Overview: an underdeveloped country which is heavily dependent on subsistence agriculture and phosphate mining
GNP: $1.530 billion, per capita $410; real growth rate 1.8% (1991)
Inflation: 1.0% (1990)
Industries: phosphate mining, agricultural processing, cement, handicrafts, textiles, beverages
Labour Force: 1,400,000 (1992); 64.3% agriculture, 6.3% industry, 29.4% services (1989)
Unemployment: 2% (1987)
Agriculture: cash crops: coffee, cocoa, cotton; food crops: yams, cassava, corn, beans, rice, millet, sorghum, fish
Natural Resources: phosphates, limestone, marble

■ FINANCE/TRADE

Currency: Communauté financière africaine franc (CFAF)
International Reserves Excluding Gold: $362 million (1992)
Gold Reserves: 0.01 million fine troy ounces (1991)
Budget: revenues $330 million; expenditures $636 million, including capital expenditures of $101 million (1990)
Defence Expenditures: $43.41 million (1987)
External Debt: $1.096 billion (1990)
Exports: $245 million (1989); commodities: phosphates, cocoa, coffee, cotton, manufactures, palm kernels; partners: European Community 70%, Africa 9%, US 2%, other 19%
Imports: $472 million (1989); commodities: food, fuels, durable consumer goods, other intermediate goods, capital goods; partners: European Community 69%, Africa 10%, Japan 7%, US 4%, other 10%

■ HEALTH

Births: 49/1,000 population (1991)
Deaths: 13/1,000 population (1991)
Infant Mortality: 110 deaths/1,000 live births (1991)
Life Expectancy at Birth: 53 years male, 57 years female (1992)

No. of Physicians: 1.1/10,000 population (1992)

EDUCATION

Govt. Expenditure: 21.2% of govt. expenditure (1988)
Literacy: 43.3% (1992)

COMMUNICATIONS

Daily newspapers: 1 (1992)
Televisions: 5.8/1,000 inhabitants (1992)
Radios: 210/1,000 inhabitants (1992)
Telephones: 0.44/100 inhabitants (1992)

TRANSPORTATION

Motor Vehicles: 42,000; 26,000 passenger cars (1990)
Roads: 7,900 km; 1,930 km paved
Railway: 551 km
Air Traffic: 64,000 passengers carried (1991)
Airports: 8

Canadian Embassy: The Canadian High Commission, 4 Idowu Taylor St, Victoria Island, Lagos; mailing address: The Canadian High Commission, P.O. Box 54506, Ikoyi Station, Lagos, Nigeria. Tel: (011-234-1) 612-382. Fax (011-234-1) 614-691
Embassy in Canada: Embassy of the Republic of Togo, 12 Range Rd, Ottawa ON K1N 8J3. Tel: (613) 238-5916, -7.

Tokelau

Overseas Territory of New Zealand

Long-Form Name: Tokelau Islands
Capital: n.a.
Population: 2,000

GEOGRAPHY

Area: 10 sq. km, 3 atolls
Climate: tropical maritime
Land Use: little land is under cultivation
Location: S Pacific Ocean

PEOPLE

Nationality: New Zealander (British subjects)
Ethnic Groups: Polynesian
Languages: Polynesian dialect

GOVERNMENT

Leader(s): Administrator N.D. Walter
Government Type: overseas territory

ECONOMY

Overview: copra is only agricultural product of significance
Currency: New Zealand dollar

Tonga

Long-Form Name: Kingdom of Tonga
Capital: Nuku'alofa
Population: 97,000 (1992)

GEOGRAPHY

Area: 748 sq. km
Coastline: 419 km
Climate: tropical; modified by trade winds; warm season (Dec. to May), cool season (May to Dec.)
Environment: subject to cyclones (Oct. to Apr.); deforestation
Terrain: most islands have limestone base formed from uplifted coral formation; others have limestone overlying volcanic base
Land Use: 25% arable; 55% permanent; 6% meadows; 12% forest; 2% other
Location: Pacific Ocean, NE of New Zealand

PEOPLE

Nationality: Tongan
Ethnic Groups: Polynesian; about 300 Europeans
Languages: Tongan, English
Religions: Christian; Free Wesleyan Church claims over 30,000 adherents
Marriages: 6.6 (per 1,000) (1985)
Divorces: 0.6 (per 1,000) (1985)

GOVERNMENT

Leader(s): Prime Min. Baron Vaea, King Taufa'ahau Tupou IV
Government Type: hereditary constitutional monarchy
Administrative Divisions: three island groups, or 5 administrative divisions
Independence: June 4, 1970 (from UK; formerly known as Friendly Islands)
National Holiday: Emancipation Day, June 4

ECONOMY

Overview: the island remains dependent on external aid and remittances to sustain its trade deficit; the economy's base is agriculture though the country must import a high proportion of its food; tourism is the main source of hard currency
GNP: $110 million, per capita $1,100; real growth rate 2.2% (1991)
Inflation: 10.6% (1991)
Industries: tourism, fishing

Labour Force: 40,000 (1992)
Unemployment: n.a.
Agriculture: dominated by coconut, copra and banana production; vanilla beans, cocoa, coffee, ginger, black pepper
Natural Resources: fish, fertile soil

■ FINANCE/TRADE

Currency: pa'anga (P)
International Reserves Excluding Gold: $32 million (1992)
Gold Reserves: n.a.
Budget: revenues $30.6 million; expenditures $40.9 million, including capital expenditures of $22.5 million (1989)
Defence Expenditures: n.a.
External Debt: $31.8 million (1987)
Exports: $14 million (1991); commodities: coconut oil, desiccated coconut, copra, bananas, taro, vanilla beans, fruits, vegetables, fish; partners: New Zealand 54%, Australia 30%, US 8%, Fiji 5%
Imports: $59 million (1991); commodities: food products, beverages, tobacco, fuels, machinery, transport equipment, chemicals, building materials; partners: New Zealand 39%, Australia 25%, Japan 9%, US 6%, European Community 5%

■ HEALTH

Births: 26/1,000 population (1991)
Deaths: 7/1,000 population (1991)
Infant Mortality: 23 deaths/1,000 live births (1991)
Life Expectancy at Birth: 65 years male, 70 years female (1991)
No. of Physicians: 6.0/10,000 population (1990)

■ EDUCATION

Govt. Expenditure: 12.95% of government expenditure (1991)
Literacy: 90–95%

■ COMMUNICATIONS

Daily newspapers: 1 (1988)
Televisions: n.a.
Radios: 547/1,000 inhabitants (1989)
Telephones: 4.2/100 inhabitants (1992)

■ TRANSPORTATION

Motor Vehicles: 1,400 passenger cars (1987)
Roads: n.a.
Railway: n.a.
Air Traffic: 5,000 passengers carried (1991)
Airports: 6

Canadian Embassy: c/o The Canadian High Commission, 61 Molesworth St, 3rd Floor, Wellington; mailing address: P.O. Box 12-049, Wellington, New Zealand. Tel: (011-64-4) 473-9577. Fax: (011-64-4) 471-2082

Transkei

Dependent Territory of South Africa

Long-Form Name: Republic of Transkei
Capital: Umtata
Population: 2,876,122 (1985)

■ GEOGRAPHY

Area: 43,789 sq. km
Climate: mild, with rainy summers, dry winters
Land Use: grazing; 60% under cultivation, inc. 4,200 acres tea plantation; 173,000 acres indigenous forest; 151,000 acres exotic plantations; cash crops
Location: S Africa (SE South Africa)

■ PEOPLE

Nationality: South African
Ethnic Groups: Xhosa
Languages: English, Xhosa, Southern Sotho

■ GOVERNMENT

Leader(s): Pres. Paramount Chief Tutor N. Ndamase
Government Type: granted independence by South Africa Oct. 26, 1963, but no other country has recognized Transkei as an independent state

■ ECONOMY

Overview: agriculture inc. tea, forest products, livestock; industry: coal, titanium, black granite mining, some light industry
Currency: South African Rand

Trinidad and Tobago

Long-Form Name: Republic of Trinidad and Tobago
Capital: Port of Spain
Population: 1,265,000 (1992)

■ GEOGRAPHY

Area: 5,130 sq. km
Coastline: 362 km
Climate: tropical; rainy season (June to Dec.)
Environment: outside usual path of hurricanes and other tropical storms
Terrain: mostly plains with some hills and low mountains

Land Use: 14% arable; 17% permanent; 2% meadows; 44% forest; 23% other
Location: off N coast of South America, bordering on Atlantic Ocean

■ PEOPLE

Nationality: Trinidadian
Ethnic Groups: 41% black, 41% East Indian, 16% mixed, 2% white, Chinese, and other
Languages: English (official), Hindi, French, Spanish, Chinese
Religions: Christianity 60%, Hinduism 25%, Islam 6%
Marriages: 6.1 (per 1,000) (1987)
Divorces: 0.9 (per 1,000) (1987)

■ GOVERNMENT

Leader(s): Prime Min. Patrick Manning, Pres. Noor Mohammed Hassanali
Government Type: parliamentary democracy
Administrative Divisions: 8 counties, 3 municipalities and 1 ward
Independence: Aug. 31, 1962 (from UK)
National Holiday: Independence Day, Aug. 31

■ ECONOMY

Overview: the economy has suffered in recent years because of the sharp decline in the price of oil; the unemployment rate has risen due to the government's austerity programs; the government is seeking to diversify the country's export base
GNP: $4.525 billion, per capita $3,620; real growth rate 3.9% (1991)
Inflation: 3.9% (1991)
Industries: petroleum, chemicals, tourism, food processing, cement, beverage, cotton textiles
Labour Force: 501,000 (1992); 14.9% industry, 73.3% services, 11.8% agriculture (1989)
Unemployment: 22% (1989)
Agriculture: accounts for approx..3% of GDP; highly subsidized sector; major crops: cocoa and sugarcane; sugarcane acreage is being shifted into rice, citrus, coffee, vegetables; must import large share of food needs
Natural Resources: crude oil, natural gas, asphalt

■ FINANCE/TRADE

Currency: Trinidad and Tobago dollar ($TT)
International Reserves Excluding Gold: $150 million (1992)
Gold Reserves: 0.05 million fine troy ounces (1992)
Budget: revenues $1.5 billion; expenditures $1.7 billion, including capital expenditures (1991)
Defence Expenditures: $59 million (1989)

External Debt: $1.808 billion (1990)
Exports: $1.968 billion (1991); commodities (including re-exports): petroleum and petroleum products 70%, fertilizer, chemicals 15%, steel products, sugar, cocoa, coffee, citrus; partners: US 61%, European Community 15%, CARICOM 9%, Latin America 7%, Canada 3%
Imports: $1.659billion (1991); commodities: raw materials 41%, capital goods 30%, consumer goods 29%; partners: US 42%, European Community 21%, Japan 10%, Canada 6%, Latin America 6%, CARICOM 4%

■ HEALTH

Births: 21/1,000 population (1991)
Deaths: 6/1,000 population (1991)
Infant Mortality: 18 deaths/1,000 live births (1991)
Life Expectancy at Birth: 67 years male, 73 years female (1992)
No. of Physicians: 10.6/10,000 population (1992)

■ EDUCATION

Govt. Expenditure: 12.1% of government expenditure (1989)
Literacy: 94.9% (1992)

■ COMMUNICATIONS

Daily newspapers: 2 (1992)
Televisions: 301.3/1,000 inhabitants (1992)
Radios: 460/1,000 inhabitants (1992)
Telephones: 17.40/100 inhabitants (1992)

■ TRANSPORTATION

Motor Vehicles: 342,000; 272,000 passenger cars (1986)
Roads: 5,175 km; paved km n.a.
Railway: n.a.
Air Traffic: 1,345,000 passengers carried (1991)
Airports: 2

Canadian Embassy: The Canadian High Commission, Huggins Bldg, 72 South Quay; Port-of-Spain; mailing address: P.O. Box 1246, Port-of-Spain, Trinidad and Tobago. Tel: (809) 623-7254. Fax: (809) 624-4016
Embassy in Canada: High Commission for the Republic of Trinidad and Tobago, 75 Albert St, Ste 508, Ottawa ON K1P 5E7. Tel: (613) 232-2418, -9. Fax: (613) 232-4349.

Tunisia

Long-Form Name: Republic of Tunisia
Capital: Tunis
Population: 8,401,000 (1992)

■ GEOGRAPHY

Area: 163,610 sq. km
Coastline: 1,148 km along the Mediterranean Sea
Climate: temperate in north with mild, rainy winters and hot, dry summers; desert in south
Environment: deforestation; overgrazing; soil erosion; desertification
Terrain: mountains in north; hot, dry central plain; semi-arid south merges into the Sahara
Land Use: 20% arable; 10% permanent; 19% meadows; 4% forest; 4% other
Location: N Africa, bordering on Mediterranean Sea

■ PEOPLE

Nationality: Tunisian
Ethnic Groups: 98% Arab, 1% European, less than 1% Jewish
Languages: Arabic (official); Arabic and French (commerce)
Religions: 98% Moslem, 1% Christian, less than 1% Jewish
Marriages: 6.4 (per 1,000) (1986)
Divorces: 0.8 (per 1,000) (1985)

■ GOVERNMENT

Leader(s): Prime Min. Hamed Karoui, Pres. Gen. Zine El Abidine Ben Ali
Government Type: republic
Administrative Divisions: 23 governorates
Independence: Mar. 20, 1956 (from France)
National Holiday: National Day, Mar. 20

■ ECONOMY

Overview: two recent drought-induced crop failures have increased unemployment and strained the budget; increasing foreign debt is a problem but the country seems ready to implement structural reforms demanded by world creditors; labor unrest may occur
GNP: $12.417 billion, per capita $1,510; real growth rate 3.5% (1991)
Inflation: 8.2% (1991)
Industries: petroleum, mining (particularly phosphate and iron ore), textiles, footwear, food, beverages
Labour Force: 2,594,000 (1992); 21.6% agriculture, 16.3 % industry, 62.1% services (1989)
Unemployment: 25% (1989)
Agriculture: accounts for 16% of GDP; output subject to severe fluctuations because of frequent droughts; export crops: olives, dates, oranges, almonds; other products: grain, sugar beets, wine grapes, poultry, beef, dairy; not self-sufficient in food

Natural Resources: crude oil, phosphates, iron ore, lead, zinc, salt

■ FINANCE/TRADE

Currency: Tunisian dinar (D)
International Reserves Excluding Gold: $187 million (1992)
Gold Reserves: 0.22 million fine troy ounces (1992)
Budget: revenues $3.8 billion; expenditures $4.9 billion, including capital expenditures of $970 million (1991)
Defence Expenditures: $400.77 million (1990)
External Debt: $6.506 billion (1990)
Exports: $3.713 billion (1991); commodities: hydrocarbons, agricultural products, phosphates and chemicals; partners: European Community 73%, Middle East 9%, US 1%, Turkey, USSR
Imports: $5.189 billion (1991); commodities: industrial goods and equipment 57%, hyrocarbons 13%, food 12%, consumer goods; partners: European Community 68%, US 7%, Canada, Japan, USSR, China, Saudi Arabia, Algeria

■ HEALTH

Births: 26/1,000 population (1991)
Deaths: 5/1,000 population (1991)
Infant Mortality: 38 deaths/1,000 live births (1991)
Life Expectancy at Birth: 65 years male, 66 years female (1992)
No. of Physicians: 4.6/10,000 population (1992)

■ EDUCATION

Govt. Expenditure: 17.48% of government expenditure (1991)
Literacy: 65.3% (1992)

■ COMMUNICATIONS

Daily newspapers: 6 (1992)
Televisions: 75.1/1,000 inhabitants (1992)
Radios: 188/1,000 inhabitants (1992)
Telephones: 4.29/100 inhabitants (1992)

■ TRANSPORTATION

Motor Vehicles: 494,087; 320,101 passenger cars (1990)
Roads: 30,760 km; 18,450 km paved
Railway: 2,010 km
Air Traffic: 1,201,000 passengers carried (1991)
Airports: 12

Canadian Embassy: Canadian Embassy, 3, rue du Sénégal, Place d'Afrique, 1002 Tunis Le Belvédère; mailing address: CP 31, Le Belvédère, 1002, Tunis, Tunisia. Tel: (011-216-1) 796-577. Fax: (011-216-1) 792-371
Embassy in Canada: Embassy of the Republic of Tunisia, 515 O'Connor St, Ottawa ON K1S 3P8. Tel: (613) 237-0330, -2. Fax: (613) 237-7939.

Turkey

Long-Form Name: Republic of Turkey
Capital: Ankara
Population: 58,362,000 (1992)

■ GEOGRAPHY

Area: 780,580 sq. km
Coastline: 7,200 km along Black Sea and Mediterranean Sea
Climate: temperate; hot, dry summers with mild, wet winters; harsher in interior
Environment: subject to severe earthquakes, especially along major river valleys in west; air pollution; desertification
Terrain: mostly mountains; narrow coastal plain; high central plateau (Anatolia)
Land Use: 30% arable; 4% permanent; 12% meadows; 26% forest; 28% other
Location: SW Asia (Near East), bordering on Mediterranean Sea, Black Sea, Aegean Sea

■ PEOPLE

Nationality: Turkish
Ethnic Groups: 85% Turkish, 12% Kurd, 3% other
Languages: Turkish (official), Kurdish 7%, Arabic; English (business language)
Religions: 98% Moslem(mostly Sunni), 2% other (mostly Christian and Jewish)
Marriages: 8.5 (per 1,000) (1987)
Divorces: 0.4 (per 1,000) (1987)

■ GOVERNMENT

Leader(s): Prime Min. Suleyman Demirel, Pres. Turgut Özal
Government Type: republican parliamentary democracy
Administrative Divisions: 67 provinces
Independence: Oct. 29, 1923 (successor state to the Ottoman Empire)
National Holiday: Anniversary of the Declaration of the Republic, Oct. 29

■ ECONOMY

Overview: the economy has grown steadily since the early 1980s but inflation and interest rates remain high; a large budget deficit may hamper efforts to move from a centrally-controlled to a free market economy
GNP: $103.888 billion, per capita $1,820; real growth rate 5.4% (1991)
Inflation: 66% (1991)
Industries: textiles, food processing, mining (coal, chromite, copper, boron minerals), steel, petroleum, construction, lumber, paper
Labour Force: 23,696,000 (1992); 46.8% agriculture, 38.6% services, 14.6% industry; about 1,000,000 Turks work abroad (1989)
Unemployment: 7.4% (1991)
Agriculture: accounts for 20% GDP; products: tobacco, cotton, grain, olives, sugar beets, pulses, citrus fruit, variety of animal products; self-sufficient in food most years
Natural Resources: antimony, coal, chromium, mercury, copper, borate, sulphur, iron ore

■ FINANCE/TRADE

Currency: Turkish lira (LT)
International Reserves Excluding Gold: $5.676 billion (1992)
Gold Reserves: 4.05 million fine troy ounces (1992)
Budget: revenues $27.6 billion; expenditures $34.4 billion, including capital expenditures of $6.6 billion (1991)
Defence Expenditures: $4.40 billion (1991)
External Debt: $38.595 billion (1990)
Exports: $13.603 billion (1991); commodities: industrial products 70%, crops and livestock products 25%; partners: Germany 18.4%, Iraq 8.5%, Italy 8.2%, US 6.5%, UK 4.9%, Iran 4.7%
Imports: $20.019 billion (1991); commodities: crude oil, machinery, transport equipment, metals, pharmaceuticals, dyes, plastics, rubber, mineral fuels, fertilizers, chemicals; partners: Germany 14.3%, US 10.6%, Iraq 10.0%, Italy 7.0%, France 5.8%, UK 5.2%

■ HEALTH

Births: 28/1,000 population (1991)
Deaths: 6/1,000 population (1991)
Infant Mortality: 54 deaths/1,000 live births (1991)
Life Expectancy at Birth: 64 years male, 69 years female (1992)
No. of Physicians: 7.3/10,000 population (1992)

■ EDUCATION

Govt. Expenditure: 17.60% of govt. spending (1991)
Literacy: 80.7% (1992)

■ COMMUNICATIONS

Daily newspapers: 426 (1992)
Televisions: 173.6/1,000 inhabitants (1992)
Radios: 161/1,000 inhabitants (1992)
Telephones: 13.34/100 inhabitants (1992)

■ TRANSPORTATION

Motor Vehicles: 2,359,738; 1,649,879 passenger cars (1990)
Roads: 325,500 km; 46,050 km paved
Railway: 8,590 km
Air Traffic: 3,872,000 passengers carried (1991)
Airports: 39

Canadian Embassy: Nenehatun Caddesi 75, Gaziosmanpasa, 06700 Ankara, Turkey. Tel: (011-90-4) 436-1275. Fax: (011-90-4) 446-4437
Embassy in Canada: Embassy of the Republic of Turkey, 197 Wurtemburg St, Ottawa ON K1N 8L9. Tel: (613) 789-4044, -3440. Fax: (613) 789-3442.

Turkmenistan

Long-Form Name: Republic of Turkmenistan
Capital: Ashkhabad
Population: 3,861,000 (1992)

■ GEOGRAPHY

Area: 488,100 sq. km
Coastline: n.a.
Climate: long, extremely hot summers; short and cold winters; rainfall occurs only in the mountains
Environment: desertification; prone to earthquakes
Terrain: desert, southern mountains
Land Use: agriculture and mining occupy less than 20% of the land; remainder is uncultivated
Location: C Asia, bordering on Caspian Sea

■ PEOPLE

Nationality: Turkmen
Ethnic Groups: 72% Turkmen, 9.5% Russian, 9% Uzbek, 2.5% Kazakh
Languages: Turkmen (official), Russian, Uzbek, Kazakh
Religions: predominantly Sunni Muslim
Marriages: n.a.
Divorces: n.a.

■ GOVERNMENT

Leader(s): Prime Min. Khan Akhmedov
Government Type: in transition to republic
Administrative Divisions: 5 regions

Independence: declared Aug. 23, 1990
National Holiday: n.a.

■ ECONOMY

Overview: mining produces the greatest part of Turkmenistan's economic production value, but agriculture is the chief occupation
GNP: $6.387 billion, per capita $1,700; real growth rate 3.2%
Inflation: n.a.
Industries: oil production and refining, natural gas extraction, chemicals, electrical engineering, fertilizer, carpets, textiles and clothing
Labour Force: n.a.
Unemployment: n.a.
Agriculture: irrigation is mandatory for agriculture; products inc. cotton, grains, fruits, livestock, fishing
Natural Resources: extensive mineral deposits, inc. the world's largest sulfur deposits; oil, natural gas, potassium, salts

■ FINANCE/TRADE

Currency: rouble (rbl.); proposed introduction in late 1993 of new currency, the manat
International Reserves Excluding Gold: n.a.
Gold Reserves: n.a.
Budget: 1989 revenues: 1,934 million roubles
Defence Expenditures: n.a.
External Debt: n.a.
Exports: oil, electric power, clothing and textiles
Imports: n.a.

■ HEALTH

Births: 34.9/1,000 population (1989)
Deaths: 7.7/1,000 population (1989)
Infant Mortality: 54.8 deaths/1,000 live births (1989)
Life Expectancy at Birth: 62 years male, 68 years female (1992)
No. of Physicians: 12,800 doctors (1989)

■ EDUCATION

Govt. Expenditure: n.a.
Literacy: n.a.

■ COMMUNICATIONS

Daily newspapers: 66 papers of all circulation types (1989)
Televisions: n.a.
Radios: n.a.
Telephones: n.a.

■ TRANSPORTATION

Motor Vehicles: n.a.
Roads: n.a.

Railway: 2,120 km
Air Traffic: n.a.
Airports: n.a.

Canadian Embassy: C/o Russian Federation Moscow, Starokonyushenny Per 23, The Canadian Embassy, Moscow 12100, Russian Federation. Tel: (011-7095) 241-4400. Fax: (011-7095) 241-9034.

Turks and Caicos

Colony of the United Kingdom

Long-Form Name: The Turks and Caicos Islands
Capital: Grand Turk
Population: 13,000 (1992)

■ GEOGRAPHY

Area: 430 sq. km; 30+ small cays, of which only 6 are inhabited
Climate: equable climate with moderating winds; occasional hurricanes
Land Use: barren, sandy islands
Location: West Indies (S Atlantic Ocean), SE of Bahamas

■ PEOPLE

Nationality: British
Ethnic Groups: Black majority
Languages: English (official)

■ GOVERNMENT

Leader(s): Gov. M.J. Bradley, Chief Min. Washington Missick
Government Type: separate colony of the United Kingdom

■ ECONOMY

Overview: fishing is the most important activity; exports inc. lobster, conch, other fish products; imports inc. food and drink, tobacco, maufactured goods; chief trading partner: United States
Currency: n.a.

Tuvalu

Long-Form Name: Tuvalu
Capital: Funafuti
Population: 12,000 (1992)

■ GEOGRAPHY

Area: 26 sq. km
Coastline: 24 km

Climate: tropical; moderated by easterly trade winds (Mar. to Nov.); westerly gales and heavy rain (Nov. to Mar.)
Environment: severe tropical storms are rare
Terrain: very low-lying and narrow coral atolls
Land Use: 0% arable; 0% permanent; 0% meadows; 0% forest;100% other
Location: S Pacific Ocean, NE of Australia

■ PEOPLE

Nationality: Tuvaluan
Ethnic Groups: 96% Polynesian
Languages: Tuvaluan, English
Religions: 96% Christian, predominantly Protestant, 4% other
Marriages: n.a.
Divorces: n.a.

■ GOVERNMENT

Leader(s): Prime Min. Bikenibeu Paeniu, Gov. Gen. Toalipi Lati
Government Type: democracy
Administrative Divisions: none
Independence: Oct. 1, 1978 from UK (formerly known as Ellice Islands)
National Holiday: Independence Day, Oct. 1

■ ECONOMY

Overview: a small economy, no known mineral resources and few exports; receives money from the sale of stamps and coins and worker remittances as well as an international trust fund
GNP: $4.6 million, per capita $530; real growth rate n.a. (1989 est.)
Inflation: 3.9% (1990)
Industries: fishing, tourism, copra
Labour Force: n.a.
Unemployment: n.a.
Agriculture: coconuts, copra
Natural Resources: fish

■ FINANCE/TRADE

Currency: Australian dollar ($A)
International Reserves Excluding Gold: n.a.
Gold Reserves: n.a.
Budget: revenues $4.3 million; expenditures $4.3 million, including capital expenditures (1989)
Defence Expenditures: n.a.
External Debt: n.a.
Exports: $1.0 million (1983); commodities: copra; partners: Fiji, Australia, New Zealand
Imports: $2.8 million (1983); commodities: food, animals, mineral fuels, machinery, manufactured goods; partners: Fiji, Australia, New Zealand

■ HEALTH

Births: 29/1,000 population (1991)
Deaths: 10/1,000 population (1991)
Infant Mortality: 33 deaths/1,000 live births (1991)
Life Expectancy at Birth: 61 years male, 63 years female (1991)
No. of Physicians: 3.8/10,000 population (1986)

■ EDUCATION

Govt. Expenditure: n.a.
Literacy: less than 50%

■ COMMUNICATIONS

Daily newspapers: n.a.
Televisions: n.a.
Radios: 278/1,000 inhabitants (1989)
Telephones: 1.9/100 inhabitants (1987)

■ TRANSPORTATION

Motor Vehicles: n.a.
Roads: n.a.
Railway: n.a.
Air Traffic: n.a.
Airports: 1

Canadian Embassy: c/o The Canadian High Commission, 61 Molesworth St, 3rd Floor, Wellington; mailing address: P.O. Box 12-049, Wellington, New Zealand. Tel: (011-64-4) 473-9577. Fax: (011-64-4) 471-2082

Uganda

Long-Form Name: Republic of Uganda
Capital: Kampala
Population: 18,674,000 (1992)

■ GEOGRAPHY

Area: 236,860 sq. km
Coastline: none: landlocked
Climate: tropical; generally rainy with two dry seasons (Dec. to Feb., June to Aug.); semi-arid in northeast
Environment: straddles Equator; deforestation; overgrazing; soil erosion
Terrain: mostly plateau with rim of mountains
Land Use: 23% arable; 9% permanent; 25% meadows; 30% forest; 13% other
Location: EC Africa

■ PEOPLE

Nationality: Ugandan
Ethnic Groups: 99% African, 1% European, Asian, Arab
Languages: English (official); Luganda and Swahili widely used; other Bantu and Nilitic languages
Religions: 33% Roman Catholic, 33% Protestant, 16% Moslem, rest indigenous beliefs
Marriages: n.a.
Divorces: n.a.

■ GOVERNMENT

Leader(s): Prime Min. George Cosmas Adyebo, Pres. Yoweri Museveni
Government Type: republic
Administrative Divisions: 33 districts
Independence: Oct. 9, 1962 (from UK)
National Holiday: Independence Day, Oct. 9

■ ECONOMY

Overview: despite substantial natural resources, the economy has been ruined by years of political instability, mismanagement and civil war; the government has started a reform program which is partly aimed at lowering high inflation and increasing export earnings
GNP: $2.762 billion, per capita $160, real growth rate 5.9% (1991)
Inflation: 12% (1990)
Industries: sugar, brewing, tobacco, cotton textile, cement
Labour Force: 8,130,000 (1992); 85.9% agriculture, 4.4% industry, 9.7% services (1989)
Unemployment: n.a.
Agriculture: accounts for 57% of GDP; cash crops: coffee, tea, cotton, tobacco; food crops: cassava, potatoes, corn, millet, pulses; livestock products: beef, goat meat, milk, poultry; self-sufficient in food
Natural Resources: copper, cobalt, limestone, salt

■ FINANCE/TRADE

Currency: Uganda shilling (USh)
International Reserves Excluding Gold: $59 million (1992)
Gold Reserves: n.a.
Budget: revenues $365 million; expenditures $545 million, including capital expenditures of $165 million (1989)
Defence Expenditures: $74.13 million (1990)
External Debt: $2.301 billion (1990)
Exports: $201 million (1991); commodities: coffee 97%, cotton, tea; partners: US 25%, UK 18%, France 11%, Spain 10%
Imports: $197 million (1991); commodities: petroleum products, machinery, cotton piece goods, metals, transportation equipment, food; partners: Kenya 25%, UK 14%, Italy 13%

■ HEALTH

Births: 51/1,000 population (1991)
Deaths: 15/1,000 population (1991)
Infant Mortality: 94 deaths/1,000 live births (1991)
Life Expectancy at Birth: 50 years male, 52 years female (1992)
No. of Physicians: 0.01/10,000 population (1990)

■ EDUCATION

Govt. Expenditure: 22.5% government spending (1987)
Literacy: 48.3% (1992)

■ COMMUNICATIONS

Daily newspapers: 5 (1992)
Televisions: 8.3/1,000 inhabitants (1992)
Radios: 99/1,000 inhabitants (1992)
Telephones: 0.4/100 inhabitants (1992)

■ TRANSPORTATION

Motor Vehicles: 27,186; 12,284 passenger cars (1990)
Roads: 33,635 km; 7,340 km paved
Railway: 1,470 km
Air Traffic: 26,000 passengers carried (1991)
Airports: 10

Canadian Embassy: C/o The Canadian High Commission, Comcraft House, Hailé Sélassie Ave, Nairobi; mailing address: The Canadian High Commission, P.O. Box 30481, Nairobi, Kenya. Tel: (011-254-2) 214-804. Fax: (011-254-2) 226-987
Embassy in Canada: High Commission for the Republic of Uganda, 231 Cobourg St, Ottawa ON K1N 8J2. Tel: (613) 233-7797. Fax: (613) 789-0133.

Ukraine

Long-Form Name: Republic of the Ukraine
Capital: Kiev
Population: 52,158,000 (1992)

■ GEOGRAPHY

Area: 603,700 sq. km
Coastline: n.a.
Climate: cold winters; warm to hot summers; moderate rainfall in north; drier in southern regions
Environment: n.a.
Terrain: Carpathian mountains in west, marshy in north, remainder flat plains
Land Use: 80% cultivated
Location: SE Europe, bordering on Black Sea

■ PEOPLE

Nationality: Ukrainian
Ethnic Groups: 72.7% Ukrainian, 22.1% Russian, 1% Jews, 0.92 Belorussian
Languages: Ukrainian, Russian
Religions: predominantly Eastern Orthodox and Roman Catholic; Uniate Church re-legalized in 1991; also, Autocephalous Orthodox Church, Greek rite Catholic
Marriages: n.a.
Divorces: n.a.

■ GOVERNMENT

Leader(s): Pres. Leonid M. Kravchuk
Government Type: in transition to republic
Administrative Divisions: 25 regions
Independence: declared July 16, 1990
National Holiday: August 24 (independence day)

■ ECONOMY

Overview: mining and heavy industry, with very strong agricultural sector
GNP: $121.458 billion, per capita $2,340; real growth rate 2.7%
Inflation: n.a.
Industries: mining, manufacturing of machinery, food processing, chemicals, electric and electronic equipment
Labour Force: n.a.
Unemployment: n.a.
Agriculture: corn, wheat, sugar beets, sunflower seeds, barley, tobacco; livestock inc. cattle, pigs, goats, sheep
Natural Resources: coal, manganese, oil, gypsum, iron, lead, zinc, titanium

■ FINANCE/TRADE

Currency: rouble, to be replaced by a Ukrainian currency (grivna)
International Reserves Excluding Gold: n.a.
Gold Reserves: n.a.
Budget: 1989 revenues: 36,885 million roubles
Defence Expenditures: n.a.
External Debt: n.a.
Exports: $2.775 billion (Jan.-Sept. 1992): minerals, agricultural products, heavy machinery, vehicles, airplanes
Imports: $1.568 billion (Jan.-Sept. 1992)

■ HEALTH

Births: 12.1/1,000 population (1991)
Deaths: 12.9/1,000 population (1991)
Infant Mortality: 13.9 deaths/1,000 live births (1991)

Life Expectancy at Birth: 66 years male, 75 years female
No. of Physicians: n.a.

■ EDUCATION

Govt. Expenditure: n.a.
Literacy: 98.4% (1992)

■ COMMUNICATIONS

Daily newspapers: 1,763 papers of all circulation types (1989)
Televisions: 292/1,000 inhabitants (1992)
Radios: 781/1,000 inhabitants (1992)
Telephones: n.a.

■ TRANSPORTATION

Motor Vehicles: n.a.
Roads: n.a.
Railway: 22,730 km
Air Traffic: n.a.
Airports: n.a.

Canadian Embassy: C/o Zhowtneva Hotel, Office 808, Corpus 1, 5 Rosa Luxembourg St, Kiev, 22 252021 Ukraine. Tel: (011-7-044) 291-8978. Fax: (011-7-044) 291-8958.
Embassy in Canada: Embassy of Ukraine, 331 Metcalfe St, Ottawa ON K2P 2K3. Tel: (613) 230-2961. Fax: (613) 230-4765

United Arab Emirates

Long-Form Name: United Arab Emirates
Capital: Abu Dhabi
Population: 1,670,000 (1992)

■ GEOGRAPHY

Area: 83,600 sq. km
Coastline: 1,448 km along Persian Gulf and Gulf of Oman
Climate: desert; cooler in eastern mountains
Environment: frequent dust and sand storms; lack of natural freshwater resources being overcome by desalination plants; desertification
Terrain: flat, barren coastal plain merging into rolling sand dunes of vast desert wasteland; mountains in east
Land Use: negligible arable; negligible permanent crops; 2% meadows; negligible forest; 98% other
Location: SW Asia (Middle East), bordering on Persian Gulf

■ PEOPLE

Nationality: Emirian
Ethnic Groups: 19% Emirian, 23% other Arab, 50% South Asian (fluctuating), 8% other expatriates (includes Westerners and East Asians); less than 20% of the population are United Arab Emirates citizens (1982)
Languages: Arabic (official); Farsi and English widely spoken in major cities; Hindi, Urdu
Religions: 96% Moslem(16% Shi'a); 4% Christian, Hindu and other
Marriages: n.a.
Divorces: n.a.

■ GOVERNMENT

Leader(s): Pres. Zayid bin Sultan Al Nuhayyan, Prime Min. Maktum bin Rashid al- Maktum,
Government Type: federation with specified powers delegated to the United Arab Emirates central government and other powers reserved to member sheikhdoms
Administrative Divisions: 7 emirates
Independence: Dec. 2, 1971 (from UK; formerly known as Trucial States)
National Holiday: National Day, Dec. 2

■ ECONOMY

Overview: has an open economy tied to the world prices for oil and gas; currently has a high standard of living; crude oil reserves should last for over 100 years at present levels of production
GNP: $32.813 billion, per capita $19,860; real growth rate -1.8% (1991)
Inflation: 5–6% (1988 est.)
Industries: petroleum, fishing, petrochemicals, construction materials, some boat building, handicrafts, pearling
Labour Force: 784,000 (1992): 38% industry, 4.5% agriculture, 57.3% services (1989)
Unemployment: negligible (1988)
Agriculture: accounts for 1% of GNP; cash crop: dates; food products: vegetables, watermelons, poultry, eggs, dairy, fish; only 25% self-sufficient in food
Natural Resources: crude oil and natural gas

■ FINANCE/TRADE

Currency: UAE dirham (Dh)
International Reserves Excluding Gold: $5.885 billion (1992)
Gold Reserves: 0.80 million fine troy ounces (1992)
Budget: revenues $3.8 billion; expenditures $3.7 billion, including capital expenditures (1989)
Defence Expenditures: $1.59 billion (1990)
External Debt: $11 billion (1989)

Exports: $10.6 billion (1988); commodities: crude oil 75%, natural gas, re-exports, dried fish, dates; parnters: US, European Community, Japan
Imports: $13.746 billion (1991); commodities: food, consumer and capital goods; partners: European Community, Japan, US

■ HEALTH

Births: 30/1,000 population (1991)
Deaths: 3/1,000 population (1991)
Infant Mortality: 23 deaths/1,000 live births (1991)
Life Expectancy at Birth: 69 years male, 73 years female (1992)
No. of Physicians: 9.8/10,000 population (1992)

■ EDUCATION

Govt. Expenditure: 15% of govt. expenditure (1989)
Literacy: 53.5% (1992)

■ COMMUNICATIONS

Daily newspapers: 8 (1992)
Televisions: 108.5/1,000 inhabitants (1992)
Radios: 322/1,000 inhabitants (1992)
Telephones: 24.52/100 inhabitants (1992)

■ TRANSPORTATION

Motor Vehicles: 459,000; 302,000 passenger cars (1990)
Roads: 2,000 km; 1,840 km paved
Railway: n.a.
Air Traffic: 2,042,000 passengers carried (1991)
Airports: 5

Canadian Embassy: c/o Da'Aiah - Block 4, Al-Mutawakel St, Kuwait City; mailing address: P.O. Box 25281, Safat, Kuwait City, 13113, Kuwait. Tel: (011-965) 256-3025. Fax: (011-965) 256-4167

United Kingdom

Long-Form Name: United Kingdom of Great Britain and Northern Ireland
Capital: London
Population: 57,696,000 (1992)

■ GEOGRAPHY

Area: 244,820 sq. km
Coastline: 12,429 km along English Channel, North Sea, North Atlantic Ocean, Irish Sea
Climate: temperate; moderated by prevailing southwest winds over the North Atlantic Current; more than half of the days are overcast

Environment: pollution control measures improving air, water quality; because of heavily indented coastline, no location is more than 125 km from tidal waters
Terrain: mostly rugged hills and low mountains; level to rolling plains in east and southeast
Land Use: 29% arable; negligible permanent; 48% meadows; 9% forest; 14% other
Location: NW Europe, bordering on North Sea, Atlantic Ocean

■ PEOPLE

Nationality: British
Ethnic Groups: 82% English, 10% Scottish, 2% Irish, 2% Welsh, 2% Ulster, 3% West Indian, Indian, Pakistani and other
Languages: English, Welsh (about 20% of population of Wales), Scottish form of Gaelic (about 60,000 in Scotland)
Religions: 27.0 million Anglican, 5.3 million Roman Catholic, 2.0 million Presbyterian, 760,000 Methodist, 410,000 Jewish
Marriages: 6.7 (per 1,000) (1988)
Divorces: 2.8 (per 1,000) (1988)

■ GOVERNMENT

Leader(s): Prime Min. and First Lord of the Treasury John Major, Queen Elizabeth II
Government Type: constitutional monarchy
Administrative Divisions: 47 counties, 7 metropolitan counties, 26 districts, 9 regions and 3 island areas; dependent areas inc.: Anguilla, Bermuda, British Antarctic Territory (uninhabited except for variable population of research stations – about 300 persons), British Indian Ocean Territory, British Virgin Islands, Cayman Islands, Channel Islands, Falkland Islands, Gibraltar, Guernsey, Hong Kong, Isle of Man, Jersey, Montserrat, Pitcairn, Saint Helena, South Georgia (uninhabited except for scientific station and 500 persons in a whaling/sealing settlement), South Sandwich Islands (uninhabited), Turks and Caicos Islands
Independence: Jan. 1, 1801, United Kingdom established
National Holiday: Celebration of the Birthday of the Queen, second Saturday in June

■ ECONOMY

Overview: capitalistic with social welfare programs and some government ownership; the 1980s saw increased privatization and continuous growth; is a great trading power and financial centre which is energy-rich; may be affected by European economic integration

GNP: $963.696 billion, per capita $16,750; real growth rate 2.8% (1991)
Inflation: 5.9% (1991)
Industries: machinery and transportation equipment, metals, food processing, paper and paper products, textiles, chemicals, clothing, other consumer goods, motor vehicles, aircraft, shipbuilding, petroleum, coal
Labour Force: 27,766,000 (1992); 77.8% services, 2.1% agriculture, 20.1% industry (1989)
Unemployment: 8.1% (1991)
Agriculture: accounts for only 1.5% of GNP; highly mechanized and efficient farms; wide variety of crops and livestock products produced; about 60% self-sufficient in food and feed needs; fish catch of 665,000 metric tons (1987)
Natural Resources: coal, crude oil, natural gas, tin, limestone, iron ore, salt, clay, chalk, gypsum, lead, silica

■ **FINANCE/TRADE**

Currency: pound sterling (£ or £ stg)
International Reserves Excluding Gold: $38.485 billion (1992)
Gold Reserves: 18.67 million fine troy ounces (1992)
Budget: revenues $385.0 billion; expenditures $385.5 billion, including capital expenditures of $35 billion (1991)
Defence Expenditures: $35.95 billion (1990)
External Debt: $15.7 billion (1988)
Exports: $190.052 billion (1992); commodities: manufactured goods, machinery, fuels, chemicals, semifinished goods, transport equipment; partners: European Community 50.4% (Germany 11.7%, France 10.2%, Netherlands 6.8%), US 13%, Communist Countries 2.3%
Imports: $222.655 billion (1992); commodities: manufactured goods, machinery, semifinished goods, foodstuffs, consumer goods; partners: European Community 52.5% (Germany 16.6%, France 8.8%, Netherlands 7.8%), US 10.2%, Communist Countries 2.1%

■ **HEALTH**

Births: 14/1,000 population (1991)
Deaths: 11/1,000 population (1991)
Infant Mortality: 7 deaths/1,000 live births (1991)
Life Expectancy at Birth: 73 years male, 79 years female (1992)
No. of Physicians: 16.4/10,000 population (1990)

■ **EDUCATION**

Govt. Expenditure: 3.18% of govt. expenditure (1990)

Literacy: 99% (1992)

■ **COMMUNICATIONS**

Daily newspapers: 104 (1992)
Televisions: 434.3/1,000 inhabitants (1992)
Radios: 1,145/1,000 inhabitants (1992)
Telephones: 52.36/100 inhabitants (1992)

■ **TRANSPORTATION**

Motor Vehicles: 26,301,748; 22,527,963 passenger cars (1990)
Roads: 359,150 km paved
Railway: 17,115 km
Air Traffic: 42,861,000 passengers carried (1991)
Airports: 141

Canadian Embassy: Macdonald House, 1 Grosvenor Square, London, W1X OAB, England, UK. Tel: (011-44-71) 258-6600. Fax: (011-44-71) 258-6384
Embassy in Canada: British High Commission, 80 Elgin St, Ottawa ON K1P 5K7. Tel: (613) 237-1530. Fax: (613) 237-7980.

United States

Long-Form Name: United States of America
Capital: Washington, D.C.
Population: 255,159,000 (1992)

■ **GEOGRAPHY**

Area: 9,372,610 sq. km; includes only the 50 states and District of Colombia
Coastline: 19,924 km North Atlantic Ocean, Gulf of Mexico, North Pacific Ocean
Climate: mostly temperate, but varies from tropical (Hawaii) to arctic (Alaska); arid to semi-arid in west with occasional warm, dry chinook wind
Environment: pollution control measures improving air and water quality; acid rain; agricultural fertilizer and pesticide pollution; management of sparse natural water resources in west; desertification; tsunamis, volcanoes and earthquake activity around Pacific
Terrain: vast central plain, mountains in west, hills and low mountains in east; rugged mountains and broad river valleys in Alaska; rugged, volcanic topography in Hawaii
Land Use: 20% arable; negligible permanent; 26% meadows; 29% forest; 25% other
Location: North America, bordering on Pacific Ocean, Atlantic Ocean

■ **PEOPLE**

Nationality: American

Ethnic Groups: 84% white, 12% black, 3% other (1989)

Languages: predominantly English; sizable Spanish-speaking minority

Religions: 61% Protestant (21% Baptist, 12% Methodist, 8% Lutheran, 4% Presbyterian, 3% Episcopalian, 13% other Protestant), 25% Roman Catholic, 2% Jewish, 5% other, 7% none

Marriages: 9.7 (per 1,000) (1988)

Divorces: 4.8 (per 1,000) (1988)

■ GOVERNMENT

Leader(s): Pres. William Clinton

Government Type: federal republic

Administrative Divisions: 50 states and 1 district; dependent areas inc.: American Samoa, Baker Island, Federated States of Micronesia, Guam, Howland Island, Jarvis Island, Johnston Atoll, Kingman Reef, Marshall Islands, Midway Islands (inhabited by U.S. military personnel), Northern Marianas, Palau, Palymyra Atoll, Puerto Rico (for details see Puerto Rico entry), Virgin Islands (for details see Virgin Islands entry), Wake Island (military base)

Independence: July 4, 1776 (from England)

National Holiday: Independence Day, July 4

■ ECONOMY

Overview: a powerful and diversified economy, with high per capita GNP; the 1980s brought successive years of growth; problems may be the huge budget and trade deficits, large medical costs and inadequate investment in industry and infrastructure

GNP: $5,686.038 billion, per capita $22,560; real growth rate 3.1% (1991)

Inflation: 4.2% (1991)

Industries: highly diversified industry; petroleum, steel, motor vehicles, aerospace, telecommunications, chemicals, electronics, food processing, consumer goods, fishing, lumber, mining

Labour Force: 122,005,000 (1992); 2.8% agriculture, 18.4% industry, 78.8% services (1989)

Unemployment: 6.6% (1991)

Agriculture: accounts for 2% of GNP; favourable climate and soils support a wide variety of crops and livestock production; world's second-largest producer and top exporter of grain; surplus food producer; fish catch of 5.7 million metric tons (1987)

Natural Resources: coal, copper, lead, molybdenum, phosphates, uranium, bauxite, gold, iron, mercury, nickel, potash, silver, tungsten, zinc, crude oil, natural gas, timber

■ FINANCE/TRADE

Currency: US dollar ($ or $US)

International Reserves Excluding Gold: $61.173 billion (1992)

Gold Reserves: 261.81 million fine troy ounces (1992)

Budget: revenues $1,106 billion; expenditures $1,272 billion, including capital expenditures (1990)

Defence Expenditures: 5.8% GNP (1989)

External Debt: $532 billion (1988)

Exports: $447.829 billion (1992); commodities: capital goods, automobiles, industrial supplies and raw materials, consumer goods, agricultural products; partners: Canada 22.9%, Japan 11.8%

Imports: $548.295 billion (1992); commodities: crude and partly refined petroleum, machinery, automobiles, consumer goods, industrial raw materials, food and beverages; partners: Japan 19.6%, Canada 19.1%

■ HEALTH

Births: 15/1,000 population (1991)

Deaths: 9/1,000 population (1991)

Infant Mortality: 10 deaths/1,000 live births (1991)

Life Expectancy at Birth: 72 years male, 79 years female (1992)

No. of Physicians: 21.1/10,000 population (1992)

■ EDUCATION

Govt. Expenditure: 1.73% of govt. expenditure (1991)

Literacy: 99.5% (1992)

■ COMMUNICATIONS

Daily newspapers: 1,657 (1992)

Televisions: 813.6/1,000 inhabitants (1992)

Radios: 2,122/1,000 inhabitants (1992)

Telephones: 76.03/100 inhabitants (1992)

■ TRANSPORTATION

Motor Vehicles: 188,655,462; 143,549,627 passenger cars (1990)

Roads: 6,364,000 km; 3,627,000 km paved

Railway: 247,440 km

Air Traffic: 452,016,000 passengers carried (1991)

Airports: 5,268

Canadian Embassy: 501 Pennsylvania Ave, NW, Washington, DC 20001. Tel: (202) 682-1740. Fax: (202) 682-7726

Embassy in Canada: Embassy of the United States of America, 100 Wellington St, P.O. Box 866, Station "B," Ottawa ON K1P 5T1. Tel: (613) 238-5335.

Uruguay

Long-Form Name: Oriental Republic of Uruguay
Capital: Montevideo
Population: 3,130,000 (1992)

GEOGRAPHY

Area: 176,220 sq. km
Coastline: 660 km along South Atlantic Ocean
Climate: warm temperate; freezing temperatures almost unknown
Environment: subject to seasonally high winds, droughts, floods
Terrain: mostly rolling plains and low hills; fertile coastal lowland
Land Use: 8% arable; negligible permanent; 78% meadows; 4% forest; 10% other
Location: SE South America, bordering on Atlantic Ocean

PEOPLE

Nationality: Uruguayan
Ethnic Groups: 88% white, 8% mestizo, 4% black
Languages: Spanish
Religions: 66% nominally Roman Catholic, 2% Protestant, 2% Jewish, 30% other
Marriages: 7.2 (per 1,000) (1987)
Divorces: 1.4 (per 1,000) (1986)

GOVERNMENT

Leader(s): Pres. Luis Alberto Lacalle Herrera, VP Gonzala Aguirre Ramírez
Government Type: republic
Administrative Divisions: 19 departments
Independence: Aug. 25, 1828 (from Brazil)
National Holiday: Independence Day, Aug. 25

ECONOMY

Overview: economy is still recovering from a recession in the early 1980s; problems include high inflation rates, a large domestic debt and frequent strikes; growth in the agriculture and fishing sectors have spurred recovery
GNP: $8.895 billion, per capita $2,860; real growth rate 0.2% (1991)
Inflation: 102.0% (1991)
Industries: meat packing, oil refining, manufacturing, foodstuffs, engineering, transport equipment
Labour Force: 1,216,000 (1992); 15.3% agriculture, 18.2% industry, 66.5% services (1989)

Unemployment: 8.5% (1990)
Agriculture: meat processing, wool and hides, sugar, textiles, footwear, leather apparel, tires, cement, fishing, petroleum refining, wine
Natural Resources: soil, hydropower potential, minor minerals

FINANCE/TRADE

Currency: new peso (N$Ur)
International Reserves Excluding Gold: $354 million (1992)
Gold Reserves: 2.19 million fine troy ounces (1992)
Budget: revenues $1.2 billion; expenditures $1.4 billion, including capital expenditures of $165 million (1988)
Defence Expenditures: $150.19 million (1986)
External Debt: $3.044 billion (1990)
Exports: $1.590 billion (1991); commodities: hides and leather goods 17%, beef 10%, wool 9%, fish 7%, rice 4%; partners: Brazil 17%, US 15%, Germany 10%, Argentina 10%
Imports: $1.619 billion (1991); commodities: fuels and lubricants 15%, metals, machinery, transportation equipment, industrial chemicals; partners: Brazil 24%, Argentina 14%, US 8%, Germany 8%

HEALTH

Births: 17/1,000 population (1991)
Deaths: 10/1,000 population (1991)
Infant Mortality: 22 deaths/1,000 live births (1991)
Life Expectancy at Birth: 68 years male, 75 years female (1992)
No. of Physicians: 19.5/10,000 population (1992)

EDUCATION

Govt. Expenditure: 7.37% of govt. expenditure (1990)
Literacy: 96.2% (1992)

COMMUNICATIONS

Daily newspapers: 33 (1992)
Televisions: 227.2/1,000 inhabitants (1992)
Radios: 600/1,000 inhabitants (1992)
Telephones: 14.3/100 inhabitants (1992)

TRANSPORTATION

Motor Vehicles: 258,000; 175,000 passenger cars (1990)
Roads: 50,220 km; 1,060 km paved
Railway: 3,039 km
Air Traffic: 318,000 passengers carried (1991)
Airports: 27

Canadian Embassy: c/o Tagle 2828, Buenos Aires; mailing address: Casilla de Correo 3898, 1000 Buenos Aires, Argentina. Tel: (011-54-1) 805-3032
Embassy in Canada: Embassy of Uruguay, 130 Albert St, Ste 1905, Ottawa ON K1P 5G4. Tel: (613) 234-2727.

Uzbekistan

Long-Form Name: Republic of Uzbekistan
Capital: Tashkent
Population: 21,453,000 (1992)

■ GEOGRAPHY

Area: 447,400 sq. km
Coastline: none: landlocked
Climate: dry continental; warm to hot summers; cool to cold winters
Environment: n.a.
Terrain: deserts and semideserts, mountains
Land Use: 75% cultivated, including 206,000 hectares of orchards, 133,000 hectares of vineyards
Location: C Asia

■ PEOPLE

Nationality: Uzbek
Ethnic Groups: 70% Uzbek, 8.4% Russian, 2.4% Tartars, 4.7% Tajiks, 4.1% Kazakhs, 2.1% Kara-Kalpaks, 1% Crimean Tatars
Languages: Uzbek (official), Russian, Kazakh, Tajik, Tartar, Jagatai Turkish
Religions: predominantly Sunni Muslim and Eastern Orthodox
Marriages: n.a.
Divorces: n.a.

■ GOVERNMENT

Leader(s): Pres. Islam A. Karimov, Prem. Abdulkhashum Mutalov
Government Type: in transition to republic
Administrative Divisions: 12 regions, 1 autonomous republic
Independence: Dec. 1990
National Holiday: n.a.

■ ECONOMY

Overview: despite the need for irrigation, agriculture is the predominant economic sector
GNP: $28.255 billion, per capita $1,350; real growth rate 3.4% (1991)
Inflation: n.a.
Industries: chemicals and gas, machine building, metalmaking, textile manufacture, clothing, butter, preserves

Labour Force: n.a.
Unemployment: n.a.
Agriculture: cotton, almonds, fruit, livestock; 97% of all crops are grown on irrigated land
Natural Resources: gold, non-ferrous metals, coal, natural gas

■ FINANCE/TRADE

Currency: rouble (rbl.)
International Reserves Excluding Gold: n.a.
Gold Reserves: n.a.
Budget: 1989 revenues: 10,029 million roubles
Defence Expenditures: n.a.
External Debt: n.a.
Exports: $674 million (Jan.-Sept. 1992): cotton, agricultural products, machinery
Imports: $520 million (Jan.-Sept. 1992)

■ HEALTH

Births: 33.3/1,000 population (1989)
Deaths: 6.3/1,000 population (1989)
Infant Mortality: 38.1 deaths/1,000 live births (1989)
Life Expectancy at Birth: 66 years male, 72 years female (1992)
No. of Physicians: 72,400 (1989)

■ EDUCATION

Govt. Expenditure: n.a
Literacy: n.a.

■ COMMUNICATIONS

Daily newspapers: 276 papers of all circulation types (1988)
Televisions: n.a.
Radios: n.a.
Telephones: n.a.

■ TRANSPORTATION

Motor Vehicles: n.a.
Roads: n.a.
Railway: 3,460 km
Air Traffic: n.a.
Airports: n.a.

Canadian Embassy: C/o Russian Federation Moscow, Starokonyushenny Per 23, Moscow 12100, The Canadian Embassy. Tel: (011-7-95) 241-5070. Fax: (011-7-95) 241-4400.

Vanuatu

Long-Form Name: Republic of Vanuatu
Capital: Port Vila
Population: 157,000 (1992)

■ GEOGRAPHY

Area: 12,190 sq. km
Coastline: 2,528 km
Climate: tropical; moderated by southeast trade winds
Environment: subject to tropical cyclones or typhoons (Jan. to Apr.); volcanism causes minor earthquakes
Terrain: mostly mountains of volcanic origin; narrow coastal plains
Land Use: 1% arable; 5% permanent; 2% meadows; 1% forest; 91% other
Location: South Pacific Ocean, E of Australia

■ PEOPLE

Nationality: Vanuatuan
Ethnic Groups: 94% indigenous Melanesian, 4% French, remainder Vietnamese, Chinese and various Pacific Islanders
Languages: English and French (official); pidgin (known as Bislama or Bichelama)
Religions: most at least nominally Christian
Marriages: n.a.
Divorces: n.a.

■ GOVERNMENT

Leader(s): Prime Min. Maxim Carlot, Pres. Fred Timakata
Government Type: republic
Administrative Divisions: 11 regional councils
Independence: July 30, 1980 (from France and UK; formerly known as New Hebrides)
National Holiday: Independence Day, July 30

■ ECONOMY

Overview: economy is based on subsistence farming, fishing and tourism; few mineral deposits; tax revenues come largely from import duties
GNP: $175 million, per capita $1,120; real growth rate 2.6% (1991)
Inflation: 6.5% (1991)
Industries: food and fish freezing, meat canning
Labour Force: 61.1% agriculture, 1.3% industry, 37.6% services (1989)
Unemployment: n.a.
Agriculture: export crops: copra, cocoa, coffee and fish; subsistence crops: copra, taro, yams, coconuts, fruits and vegetables
Natural Resources: manganese, hardwood forests, fish

■ FINANCE/TRADE

Currency: vatu (VT)
International Reserves Excluding Gold: $42 million (1992)

Gold Reserves: n.a.
Budget: revenues $90.0 million; expenditures $103.0 million, including capital expenditures of $45.0 million (1989)
Defence Expenditures: n.a.
External Debt: $57 million (1988)
Exports: $20 million (1991); commodities: copra 37%, cocoa 11%, meat 9%, fish 8%, timber 4%; partners: Netherlands 34%, France 27%, Japan 17%, Belgium 4%, New Caledonia 3%, Singapore 2%
Imports: $83 million (1991); commodities: machines and vehicles 25%, food and beverages 23%, basic manufactures 18%, raw materials and fuels 11%, chemicals 6%; partners: Australia 36%, Japan 13%, New Zealand 10%, France 8%, Fiji 5%

■ HEALTH

Births: 36/1,000 population (1991)
Deaths: 5/1,000 population (1991)
Infant Mortality: 36 deaths/1,000 live births (1991)
Life Expectancy at Birth: 67 years male, 72 years female (1992)
No. of Physicians: 2.0/10,000 population (1992)

■ EDUCATION

Govt. Expenditure: 12.62% of govt. expenditure (1989)
Literacy: 52.9% (1992)

■ COMMUNICATIONS

Daily newspapers: 1 (1992)
Televisions: 8.5/1,000 inhabitants (1992)
Radios: 267/1,000 inhabitants (1992)
Telephones: 2.31/100 inhabitants (1992)

■ TRANSPORTATION

Motor Vehicles: 7,000; 4,200 passenger cars (1990)
Roads: n.a.
Railway: none
Air Traffic: 19,000 passengers carried (1991)
Airports: 33

Canadian Embassy: c/o The Canadian High Commission, Commonwealth Ave, Canberra ACT 2600, Australia. Tel: (011-61-62) 273-3844. Fax: (011-61-62) 273-3285
Embassy in Canada: Australian High Commission, 50 O'Connor St, Ste 710, Ottawa, ON K1P 6L2. Tel: (613) 746-4914.

Vatican City

Long-Form Name: State of the Vatican City
Capital: Vatican City
Population: 1,000 (1992)

■ GEOGRAPHY

Area: 0.438 sq. km
Coastline: none: landlocked
Climate: temperate; mild, rainy winters (Sept. to mid-May) with hot, dry summers (May to Sept.)
Environment: urban
Terrain: low hill
Land Use: 0% arable; 0% permanent; 0% meadows; 0% forest; 100% other
Location: S Europe (W Italy)

■ PEOPLE

Nationality: n.a. (no descriptive word)
Ethnic Groups: primarily Italians but also many other nationalities
Languages: Italian, Latin and various other languages
Religions: Roman Catholic
Marriages: n.a.
Divorces: n.a.

■ GOVERNMENT

Leader(s): Head, Roman Catholic Church, Pope John Paul II (Karol Wojtyla)
Government Type: monarchical-sacerdotal state
Administrative Divisions: none
Independence: Feb. 11, 1929 (from Italy)
National Holiday: Installation Day of the Pope (John Paul II), Oct. 22; also Christmas, Easter, Feast of Saints Peter and Paul (June 29), and other holy days of obligation

■ ECONOMY

Overview: economy is supported financially by contributions (known as Peter's pence) from Roman Catholics throughout the world, the sale of postage stamps, tourist mementos, fees for admission to museums and the sale of publications
GNP: n.a.
Inflation: n.a.
Industries: printing and production of a small amount of mosaics and staff uniforms; worldwide banking and financial activities
Labour Force: approx. 1,500 Vatican City employees divided into three categories: executives, office workers, salaried employees
Unemployment: n.a.
Agriculture: none

Natural Resources: none

■ FINANCE/TRADE

Currency: Vatican Lira (Lit) (at par with Italian lira)
International Reserves Excluding Gold: n.a.
Gold Reserves: n.a.
Budget: revenues $57 million; expenditures $113.7 million, including capital expenditures (1986)
Defence Expenditures: n.a.
External Debt: n.a.
Exports: n.a.
Imports: n.a.

■ HEALTH

Births: n.a.
Deaths: n.a.
Infant Mortality: n.a.
Life Expectancy at Birth: n.a.
No. of Physicians: n.a.

■ EDUCATION

Govt. Expenditure: n.a.
Literacy: 100%

■ COMMUNICATIONS

Daily newspapers: 1 (1988)
Televisions: n.a.
Radios: n.a.
Telephones: n.a.

■ TRANSPORTATION

Motor Vehicles: n.a.
Roads: n.a.
Railway: 850 m
Air Traffic: n.a.
Airports: none

Canadian Embassy: Via della Conciliazione 4/D, 00193 Rome, Italy. Tel. (011-6) 687-7503
Embassy in Canada: Apostolic Nunciature, 724 Manor Ave, Rockcliffe Park, Ottawa ON K1M 0E3. Tel: (613) 746-4914.

Venda

Dependent Territory of South Africa

Long-Form Name: Republic of Venda
Capital: Thohoyandou
Population: 459,986 (1985)

■ GEOGRAPHY

Area: 7,460 sq. km
Climate: dry subtropical to tropical

Land Use: too mountainous for extensive cultivation; 85% grazing, 10% dry-land agriculture
Location: S Africa (NE South Africa)

▪ PEOPLE

Nationality: South African
Ethnic Groups: Xhosa
Languages: Venda, English, Afrikaans

▪ GOVERNMENT

Leader(s): Pres. Brig. Gabriel Ramushwana
Government Type: parliamentary democracy; South Africa considers Venda an independent state, but no other country recognizes it as such

▪ ECONOMY

Overview: industry inc. chutney, furniture, sawmilling; relatively poor in mineral resources, with coal only significant mining industry; agriculture inc. maize, tea, sisal, groundnuts, coffee, fruits; chief trading partner: South Africa
Currency: South African Rand

Venezuela

Long-Form Name: Republic of Venezuela
Capital: Caracas
Population: 20,186,000 (1992)

▪ GEOGRAPHY

Area: 912,050 sq. km
Coastline: 2,800 km along Caribbean Sea
Climate: tropical; hot, humid; more moderate in highlands
Environment: subject to floods, rockslides, mud slides; periodic droughts; increasing industrial pollution in Caracas and Maracaibo
Terrain: Andes Mountains and Maracaibo lowlands in northwest; central plains (llanos); Guyana highlands in southwest
Land Use: 3% arable; 1% permanent; 20% meadows; 39% forest; 37% other
Location: N South America, bordering on Caribbean Sea

▪ PEOPLE

Nationality: Venezuelan
Ethnic Groups: 69% mestizo, 20% white, 9% black, 2% Indian
Languages: Spanish (official); Indian dialects spoken by approx. 200,000 Amerindians in the remote interior
Religions: 96% nominally Roman Catholic, 2% Protestant, 2% other
Marriages: 5.7 (per 1,000) (1987)
Divorces: 1.2 (per 1,000) (1987)

▪ GOVERNMENT

Leader(s): Pres. Carlos Andrés Pérez
Government Type: republic
Administrative Divisions: 20 states, 2 territories, 1 federal district and 1 federal dependency
Independence: July 5, 1811 (from Spain)
National Holiday: Independence Day, July 5

▪ ECONOMY

Overview: lower tariffs and price supports, a free market exchange rate and market-linked interest rates have thrown the economy into confusion, causing an 8% decline in GDP (1990); economy is based on petroleum
GNP: $52.775 billion, per capita $2,610; real growth rate 1.1% (1991)
Inflation: 34.2% (1991)
Industries: petroleum, iron-ore mining, construction materials, food processing, textiles, steel, aluminum, motor vehicle assembly
Labour Force: 6,860,000 (1992); 70.2% services, 17.3% industry, 12.5% agriculture (1989)
Unemployment: 10.4% (1992)
Agriculture: accounts for 6% GDP; products: corn, sorghum, sugarcane, rice, bananas, vegetables, coffee, beef, pork, milk, eggs, fish; not self-sufficient in food other than meat
Natural Resources: crude oil, natural gas, iron ore, gold, bauxite, other minerals, hydropower, diamonds

▪ FINANCE/TRADE

Currency: bolívar (Bs)
International Reserves Excluding Gold: $9.519 billion (1992)
Gold Reserves: 11.46 million fine troy ounces (1992)
Budget: revenues $8.4 billion; expenditures $8.6 billion, including capital expenditures of $5.9 billion (1989)
Defence Expenditures: $519.19 million (1990)
External Debt: $24.643 billion (1990)
Exports: $15.519 billion (1991); commodities: petroleum 81%, bauxite and aluminum, iron ore, agricultural products, basic manufactures; partners: US 50.3%, Germany 5.3%, Japan 4.1%
Imports: $9.963 billion (1991); commodities: foodstuffs, chemicals, manufactures, machinery and transport equipment; partners: US 44%, Germany 8.5%, Japan 6%, Italy 5%, Brazil 4.4%

▪ HEALTH

Births: 28/1,000 population (1991)
Deaths: 4/1,000 population (1991)

Infant Mortality: 26 deaths/1,000 live births (1991)
Life Expectancy at Birth: 67 years male, 73 years female (1992)
No. of Physicians: 14.3/10,000 population (1992)

■ EDUCATION

Govt. Expenditure: 8.8% of govt. expenditure (1989)
Literacy: 88.1% (1992)

■ COMMUNICATIONS

Daily newspapers: 56 (1992)
Televisions: 156.0/1,000 inhabitants (1992)
Radios: 432/1,000 inhabitants (1992)
Telephones: 9.33/100 inhabitants (1992)

■ TRANSPORTATION

Motor Vehicles: 2,184,000; 1,601,000 passenger cars (1990)
Roads: 104,000 km; 34,660 km paved
Railway: 365 km
Air Traffic: 6,626,000 passengers carried (1991)
Airports: 82

Canadian Embassy: Edificio Torre Europa, Septimo Piso, Avenida Francisco de Miranda, Campo Alegre, Caracas; mailing address: Apartado Postal 62.302, Caracas 1060-A, Venezuela. Tel: (011-58-2) 951-6166. Fax (011-58-2) 951-4950
Embassy in Canada: Embassy of Venezuela, 32 Range Rd, Ottawa ON K1N 8J4. Tel: (613) 235-5151. Fax: (613) 235-3205.

Vietnam

Long-Form Name: Socialist Republic of Vietnam
Capital: Hanoi
Population: 69,485,000 (1992)

■ GEOGRAPHY

Area: 329,560 sq. km
Coastline: 3,444 km (excluding islands) along the South China Sea (Gulf of Tonkin and Gulf of Thailand)
Climate: tropical in south; monsoonal in north with hot, rainy season (mid-May to mid-Sept.) and warm, dry season (mid-Oct. to mid-Mar.)
Environment: occasional typhoons (May to Jan.) with extensive flooding
Terrain: low, flat delta in south and north; central highlands; hilly, mountainous far north and northwest
Land Use: 22% arable; 2% permanent; 1% meadows; 40% forest; 35% other

Location: SE Asia, bordering on South China Sea

■ PEOPLE

Nationality: Vietnamese
Ethnic Groups: 85–90% predominantly Vietnamese; 3% Chinese; more than 60 ethnic minorities including Muong, Thai, Meo, Khmer, Man, Cham; other mountain tribes
Languages: Vietnamese (official), French, Chinese, English, Khmer, tribal languages (Mon-Khmer and Malayo-Polynesian)
Religions: Buddhist, Confucian, Taoist, Roman Catholic, indigenous beliefs, Islamic, Protestant
Marriages: n.a.
Divorces: n.a.

■ GOVERNMENT

Leader(s): Pres. Gen. Le Duc Anh, V. Pres. Nguyen Thi Binh, Prime Min. Gen. Vo Van Kiet
Government Type: Communist state
Administrative Divisions: 37 provinces, 3 municipalities
Independence: Sept. 2, 1945 (from France)
National Holiday: Independence Day, Sept. 2

■ ECONOMY

Overview: is a centrally planned, developing economy with extensive government ownership and control of production facilities; is dependent on foreign aid; problems are inflation and low per capita output
GNP: $14.2 billion, per capita $215; real growth rate 8% (1989 est.)
Inflation: 40% (1989 est.)
Industries: food processing, textiles, machine building, mining, cement, chemical fertilizer, glass, tires, oil, fishing
Labour Force: 33 million; 67.5% agriculture, 11.8% industry, 20.7% services (1989)
Unemployment: 25% (1989 est.)
Agriculture: accounts for half of GNP; rice, corn, potatoes make up 50% of farm output; commercial crops (rubber, soybeans, coffee, tea, bananas) and animal products other 50%; not self-sufficient in rice; fish catch of 900,000 metric tons (1988 est.)
Natural Resources: phosphates, coal, manganese, bauxite, chromite, offshore oil deposits, forests

■ FINANCE/TRADE

Currency: dong (pl. dong) (D)
International Reserves Excluding Gold: $10 million (1986)
Gold Reserves: 0.69 million fine troy ounces (1986)

Budget: revenues $892 million; expenditures $1.3 billion, including capital expenditures of $344 million (1990)

Defence Expenditures: $2.32 billion (1989)

External Debt: $16 billion (1989)

Exports: $1.1 billion (1988); commodities: agricultural and handicraft products, coal, minerals, ores; partners: USSR, Eastern Europe, Japan, Singapore

Imports: $2.5 billion (1988); commodities: petroleum, steel products, railroad equipment, chemicals, medicines, raw cotton, fertilizer, grain; partners: USSR, Eastern Europe, Japan, Singapore

■ HEALTH

Births: 29/1,000 population (1991)

Deaths: 8/1,000 population (1991)

Infant Mortality: 48 deaths/1,000 live births (1991)

Life Expectancy at Birth: 62 years male, 66 years female (1992)

No. of Physicians: 10.6/10,000 population (1992)

■ EDUCATION

Govt. Expenditure: n.a.

Literacy: 87.6% (1992)

■ COMMUNICATIONS

Daily newspapers: 4 (1992)

Televisions: 38.3/1,000 inhabitants (1992)

Radios: 107/1,000 inhabitants (1992)

Telephones: 0.2/100 inhabitants (1992)

■ TRANSPORTATION

Motor Vehicles: n.a.

Roads: 86,000 km; 9,560 km paved

Railway: 2.930 km

Air Traffic: 89,000 passengers carried (1991)

Airports: 4

Canadian Embassy: c/o The Canadian Embassy, 12th Floor, Boonmitr Bldg., 138 Silom Rd, Bangkok 10500; mailing address: P.O. Box 2090, Bangkok 10500, Thailand. Tel: (011-66-2) 237-4126. Fax: (011-66-2) 236-6463

Embassy in Canada: Embassy of the Socialist Republic of Vietnam, The Sandringham Apts., Ste 802, 85 Range Rd, Ottawa ON K1N 8J6. Tel: (613) 565-2292. Fax: (613) 565-2595.

Virgin Islands

Dependent Territory of the United States

Long-Form Name: Virgin Islands of the United States

Capital: Charlotte Amalie

Population: 107,000 (1992)

■ GEOGRAPHY

Area: 352 sq. km

Coastline: 188 km

Climate: subtropical, tempered by easterly trade winds, relatively low humidity, little seasonal temperature variation; rainy season May to Nov.

Environment: rarely affected by hurricanes; subject to frequent severe droughts, floods, earthquakes; lack of natural freshwater resources; St. Thomas has one of the best natural, deepwater harbors in the Caribbean

Terrain: mostly hilly to rugged and mountainous with little level land

Land Use: 15% arable; 6% permanent; 26% meadows; 6% forests; 47% other

Location: Caribbean Islands

■ PEOPLE

Nationality: Virgin Islander

Ethnic Groups: 74% West Indian (45% born in the Virgin Islands and 29% born elsewhere in the West Indies), 13% US mainland, 5% Puerto Rican, 8% other; 80% black, 15% white, 5% other; 14% of Hispanic origin

Languages: English (official), but Spanish and Creole are widely spoken

■ GOVERNMENT

Leader(s): Gov. Alexander Farrelly, Lt. Gov. Derek Hodge

Government Type: organized, unincorporated territory of the US administered by the Office of Territorial and International Affairs, US Department of the Interior

Administrative Divisions: 15 executive departments

National Holiday: Transfer Day (from Denmark to U.S.), Mar. 31

■ ECONOMY

Overview: tourism is the primary economic activity accounting for more than 70% of GDP and 70% of employment; some manufacturing; small agricultural sector

GNP: $1.03 billion, per capita $9,030 (1985)

Currency: US dollar ($)

Canadian Embassy: Canadian Consulate General, #400 South Tower, One CNN Center, Atlanta, GA 30303-2705, USA. Tel. (404) 577-6810. Fax: (404) 524-5046

Wallis and Futuna

Overseas Territory of France

Long-Form Name: Territory of the Wallis and Futuna Islands
Capital: Matu-Utu
Population: 15,400 (1988)

■ GEOGRAPHY

Area: 274 sq. km
Climate: tropical maritime
Land Use: agricultural cultivation is limited
Location: SW Pacific Ocean

■ PEOPLE

Nationality: French
Ethnic Groups: Polynesians, and descendants of French settlers
Languages: Wallisian, Futunian (Polynesian languages)

■ GOVERNMENT

Leader(s): Pres. of the Territorial Assembly Soane Mani Uhila
Government Type: overseas territory

■ ECONOMY

Overview: timbre; agriculture inc. copra, cassava, yams, taro roots, bananas; livestock inc. pigs and goats; considerable imports, few exports
Currency: CFP franc

Western Sahara

Long-Form Name: Western Sahara
Capital: El Aaiún (since Western Sahara has been under Moroccan occupation, El Aaiún has lost its significance as a capital city)
Population: 250,000 (1992); a further est. 165,000 Saharawis live in refugee camps in SW Algeria; large part of the population is nomadic

■ GEOGRAPHY

Area: 266,000 sq. km
Coastline: n.a.
Climate: Mediterranean to arid
Environment: desertification
Terrain: mostly barren rocky desert
Land Use: due to extensive desertification, less than 19% in agricultural use; vegetation scanty, except for patches of coarse grass and low bushes near the coast
Location: NW Africa, bordering on Atlantic Ocean

■ PEOPLE

Nationality: Saharawi
Ethnic Groups: Arabs, Berbers
Languages: Arabic, French, several Berber dialects
Religions: Islam (almost 100% Sunni Moslem)
Marriages: n.a.
Divorces: n.a.

■ GOVERNMENT

Leader(s): Pres. Mohammed Abdelaziz; Prime Min. Mahfoud Ali Beiba
Government Type: under Moroccan occupation
Administrative Divisions: 4 provinces
Independence: n.a.
National Holiday: n.a.

■ ECONOMY

Overview: economy severely disrupted by Moroccan occupation and ongoing guerrilla warfare
GNP: n.a.
Inflation: n.a.
Industries: phosphate mining
Labour Force: n.a.
Unemployment: n.a.
Agriculture: some grain production, livestock (esp. sheep, goats, camels)
Natural Resources: rich phosphate deposits

■ FINANCE/TRADE

Currency: dirham (DH)
International Reserves Excluding Gold: n.a.
Gold Reserves: n.a.
Budget: n.a.
Defence Expenditures: n.a.
External Debt: n.a.
Exports: phosphates main export product
Imports: most of the country's food supply must be imported

■ HEALTH

Births: n.a.
Deaths: n.a.
Infant Mortality: n.a.
Life Expectancy at Birth: n.a.
No. of Physicians: n.a.

■ EDUCATION

Govt. Expenditure: n.a.
Literacy: n.a.

COMMUNICATIONS

Daily newspapers: n.a.
Televisions: n.a.
Radios: n.a.
Telephones: n.a.

TRANSPORTATION

Airports: 2

Yemen

Long-Form Name: Republic of Yemen
Capital: Sana'a (political); commercial capital: Aden
Population: 12,535,000 (1992)

GEOGRAPHY

Area: 531,000 sq. km
Coastline: 1,906 km
Climate: hot, dry desert in the south to temperate in central region and north; harsh desert in the east
Environment: desertification, overgrazing, lack of natural fresh water, soil erosion
Terrain: narrow coastal plain; western mountains, northern desert interior
Land Use: 6% arable land; permanent crops negligible; 30% meadows & pastures; 7% forest & woodland; 57% other
Location: SW Asia (Middle East), bordering on Red Sea

PEOPLE

Nationality: Yemeni
Ethnic Groups: predominantly Arab; Afro-Arab, Indian, Somali and European minorities
Languages: Arabic
Religions: predominatly Moslem; Christian and Hindu minorities in the south
Marriages: n.a.
Divorces: n.a.

GOVERNMENT

Leader(s): Pres. Ali Abdallah Salih, V. Pres. Ali Salim al-Bid, Prime Min. Haider Abu Bakr al-Attas
Government Type: republic
Administrative Divisions: 11 provinces in north, 6 governorates in south
Independence: May 22, 1990
National Holiday: Proclamation of the Republic, May 22

ECONOMY

Overview: future economic level depends heavily on Western assistance. North: low level of domestic industry, dependent on imports; South: economic growth among the poorest of all Arab countries
GNP: $6.746 billion, per capita $540; real growth rate n.a. (1991)
Inflation: North, 16.9%; South, 0% (1989)
Industries: petroleum
Labour Force: 2,602,000; 62.5% agriculture, 11% industry, 26.4% services (1989)
Unemployment: North, 13% (1986); South, n.a.
Agriculture: in the north, agriculture accounts for 26% GDP and 7% of the labor force; main crops include fruit (grapes) and cotton; in the south, agriculture accounts for 17% GDP and 45% of the labor force; the main agricultural product is livestock (cattle, camels, sheep, goats, poultry)
Natural Resources: salt deposits

FINANCE/TRADE

Currency: during the transitional period following unification, the northern riyal and the southern dinar coexist
International Reserves Excluding Gold: North: $212 million, South: $58 million (1989)
Gold Reserves: North: n.a.; South: 0.04 million fine troy ounces (1988)
Budget: n.a.
Defence Expenditures: $1 billion (1990)
External Debt: $5.040 billion (1990)
Exports: North: $853 million, inc. crude oil, cotton, coffee, animal hides, vegetables. Partners: USA, Japan. South: $82.2 million, inc. cotton, animal hides, fish. Partners: Japan, Singapore. (1988)
Imports: North: $1.3 billion (1988), inc. textiles and other manufactured consumer goods, petroleum products, sugar, grain, flour, other foodstuffs, cement. Partners: Saudi Arabia, France, USA, Australia. South: $553.9 million (1989), inc. grain, consumer goods, crude oil, machinery, chemicals. Partners: nations of the former Soviet Union, UK, Ethiopia

HEALTH

Births: 51.2/1,000 population (1990)
Deaths: 21.2/1,000 population (1990)
Infant Mortality: 132/1,000 live births (1990)
Life Expectancy at Birth: 48 years male, 51 years female (1992)
No. of Physicians: North: 1.5/10,000 population (1990); South, n.a.

EDUCATION

Govt. Expenditure: 21.29% of govt. expenditure (1992)
Literacy: 38.8% (1992)

■ COMMUNICATIONS

Daily newspapers: 4 (1992)
Televisions: 79/1,000 population (1992)
Radios: 188/1,000 population (1992)
Telephones: n.a.

■ TRANSPORTATION

Motor Vehicles: 364,495; 145,390 passenger cars (1990)
Roads: 126,400 km; 10,090 km paved
Railway: n.a.
Air Traffic: 413,000 passengers carried (1991)
Airports: 19

Canadian Embassy: c/o Canadian Embassy, Diplomatic Quarter, Riyadh; mailing address: P.O. Box 94321, Riyadh 11693, Saudi Arabia. Tel: (011-966-1) 488-2288. Fax: (011-966-1) 488-0137
Embassy in Canada: Embassy of the Republic of Yemen, 350 Sparks St, Ste 1100, Ottawa ON K1R 7S8. Tel: (613) 232-8525. Fax: (613) 232-8276.

Yugoslavia

Long-Form Name: Socialist Federal Republic of Yugoslavia
Capital: Belgrade
Population: 10,500,000 (1992)

■ GEOGRAPHY

Area: 102,173 sq. km
Coastline: 3,955 km (including Croatia, Slovenia, offshore islands) along Adriatic Sea
Climate: temperate; hot, relatively dry summers with mild, rainy winters along coast; warm summer and cold winters inland
Environment: subject to frequent and destructive earthquakes
Terrain: mostly mountains with large areas of karst topography
Land Use: 28% arable, 25% meadows, 36% forest
Location: SC Europe, bordering on Adriatic Sea

■ PEOPLE

Nationality: Yugoslavian
Ethnic Groups: 36% Serb, 20% Croat, 9% Moslem, 8% Slovene, 8% Albanian, 6% Macedonian, 5% Yugoslav, 3% Montenegrin, 2% Hungarian, 4% other (1981 census)
Languages: Serbo-Croatian, Slovene, Macedonian (all official); Albanian, Hungarian
Religions: 41% eastern Orthodox, 32% Roman Catholic, 10% Moslem, 10% other

Marriages: 6.8 (per 1,000) (1988)
Divorces: 1.0 (per 1,000) (1988)

■ GOVERNMENT

Leader(s): Pres. Zoran Lilic (Federal Rep.), Prime Min. Radoje Kontic
Government Type: Federal republic in form
Administrative Divisions: 6 socialist republics
Independence: Dec. 1, 1918; independent monarchy established from the Kingdoms of Serbia and Montenegro; Socialist Federal Republic of Yugoslavia proclaimed Nov. 29, 1945. Republics of Croatia, Slovenia, Bosnia-Hercegovina and Macedonia declared independence. Republics of Montenegro, Serbia(which includes the autonomous provinces of Vojvodina and Kosovo-Metohija) continued as Republic of Yugoslavia. (Serbian Pres: Slobodan Milosevic) Ethnic groups in various states and republics have been involved in civil war since June 1991.
National Holiday: Proclamation of the Socialist Federal Republic of Yugoslavia, Nov. 29

■ ECONOMY

Overview: reformers are attempting to create an open market economy with still considerable state ownership of major industrial plants; the beleaguered economy may require massive economic investment and aid, and more privatization, presently disrupted by civil war
GNP: $70.038 billion, per capita $3,060; real growth rate -0.7% (1991)
Inflation: 117.4% (1991)
Industries: metallurgy, machinery and equipment, petroleum, chemicals, textiles, wood processing, food processing, pulp and paper, motor vehicles, building materials
Labour Force: 10,858,000 (1992); 28.7% agriculture, 23.6% industry, 47.7% services (1989)
Unemployment: 16.4% (1990)
Agriculture: diversified, with many small private holdings and large combines; main crops: corn, wheat, tobacco, sugar beets, sunflowers; occasionally a net exporter of corn, tobacco, foodstuffs, live animals
Natural Resources: coal, copper, bauxite, timber, iron ore, antimony, chromium, lead, zinc, asbestos, mercury, crude oil, natural gas, nickel, uranium

■ FINANCE/TRADE

Currency: new dinar (ND)
International Reserves Excluding Gold: $1.483 billion (1992)
Gold Reserves: 1.92 million fine troy ounces (1992)

Budget: revenues $6.4 billion; expenditures $6.4 billion, including capital expenditures (1990)
Defence Expenditures: $3.52 billion (1990)
External Debt: $13.492 billion (1992)
Exports: $9.548 billion (1991); commodities: raw materials and semimanufactures 50%, consumer goods 31%, capital goods and equipment 19%; partners: European Community 30%; CEMA 45%, less developed countries 14%, US 5%, other 6%
Imports: $11.804 billion (1991); commodities: raw materials and semimanufactures 79%, capital goods and equipment 15%, consumer goods 6%; partners: European Community 30%, CEMA 45%, less developed countries 14%, US 5%, other 6%

■ HEALTH

Births: 14/1,000 population (1991)
Deaths: 9/1,000 population (1991)
Infant Mortality: 21 deaths/1,000 live births (1991)
Life Expectancy at Birth: 69 years male, 74 years female (1992)
No. of Physicians: 18.2/10,000 population (1992)

■ EDUCATION

Govt. Expenditure: 32.5% of govt. expenditure (1980)
Literacy: 92.7% (1990)

■ COMMUNICATIONS

Daily newspapers: 28 (1989)
Televisions: 196.8/1,000 inhabitants (1989)
Radios: 245/1,000 inhabitants (1989)
Telephones: 16.7/100 inhabitants (1992)

■ TRANSPORTATION

Motor Vehicles: 4,439,360; 3,526,002 passenger cars (1990)
Roads: 122,270 km; 73,410 km paved
Railway: 9,360 km
Air Traffic: 1,888,000 passengers carried (1991)
Airports: 18

Canadian Embassy: Kneza Milosa 75, 11000 Belgrade, Yugoslavia. Tel: (011-38-11) 644-666. Fax: (011-38-11) 641-480.
Embassy in Canada: Embassy of the Socialist Republic of Yugoslavia, 17 Blackburn Ave, Ottawa ON K1N 8A2. Tel: (613) 233-6289. Fax: (613) 233-7850.

Zaïre

Long-Form Name: Republic of Zaïre
Capital: Kinshasa
Population: 39,882,000 (1992)

■ GEOGRAPHY

Area: 2,345,410 sq. km
Coastline: 37 km along South Atlantic Ocean
Climate: tropical; hot and humid in equatorial river basin; cooler and drier in southern highlands; cooler and wetter in eastern highlands
Environment: dense tropical rainforest in central river basin and eastern highlands; periodic droughts in south
Terrain: vast central basin is a low-lying plateau; mountains in east
Land Use: 3% arable; negligible permanent; 4% meadows; 78% forest; 15% other
Location: C Africa, just barely bordering on South Atlantic Ocean

■ PEOPLE

Nationality: Zairean
Ethnic Groups: over 200 African ethnic groups, the majority are Bantu; four largest tribes-Mongo, Luba, Kongo (all Bantu) and the Mangbetu-Azande (Hamitic)-make up 45% of the population
Languages: French (official), Lingala, Swahili, Kinggwana, Kikongo, Tshiluba
Religions: 50% Roman Catholic, 20% Protestant, 10% Kinbanguist, 10% Moslem, 10% other syncretic sects and traditional beliefs
Marriages: n.a.
Divorces: n.a.

■ GOVERNMENT

Leader(s): Prime Min. Etienne Tshisekedi, Pres. Marshal Mobutu Sese Seko
Government Type: republic with a strong presidential system
Administrative Divisions: 8 regions and 1 town
Independence: June 30, 1960 (from Belgium; formerly known as Belgian Congo, then Congo/Leopoldville, then Congo/Kinshasa)
National Holiday: Anniversary of the Regime (Second Republic), Nov. 24

■ ECONOMY

Overview: despite large mineral resources and one of the most developed and diversified economies in Sub-Saharan Africa, the country has a very low per capita GDP; increases in prices for copper and other minerals should help the economy

GNP: $8.123 billion, per capita $230; real growth rate 1.6% (1991)

Inflation: 2,154.5% (1991)

Industries: mining, mineral processing, consumer products (including textiles, footwear and cigarettes), processed foods and beverages, cement, diamonds

Labour Force: 13,080,000 (1992); 71.5% agriculture, 12.9% industry, 15.6% services (1989)

Unemployment: n.a.

Agriculture: cash crops: coffee, palm oil, rubber, quinine; food crops: cassava, bananas, root crops, corn

Natural Resources: cobalt, copper, cadmium, crude oil, industrial and gem diamonds, gold, silver, zinc, manganese, tin, germanium, uranium, radium, bauxite, iron ore, coal, hydroelectric potential

■ FINANCE/TRADE

Currency: zaire (Z)

International Reserves Excluding Gold: $160 million (1992)

Gold Reserves: 0.03 million fine troy ounces (1992)

Budget: revenues $685 million; expenditures $1.1 billion, excludes capital expenditures largely funded by foreign aid donors (1990)

Defence Expenditures: $66.82 million (1988)

External Debt: $8.851 billion (1990)

Exports: $832 million (1991); commodities: copper 37%, coffee 24%, diamonds 12%, cobalt, crude oil; partners: US, Belgium, France, Germany, Italy, UK, Japan

Imports: $713 million (1991); commodities: consumer goods, foodstuffs, mining and other machinery, transport equipment, fuels; partners: US, Belgium, France, Germany, Italy, Japan, UK

■ HEALTH

Births: 46/1,000 population (1991)

Deaths: 13/1,000 population (1991)

Infant Mortality: 99 deaths/1,000 live births (1991)

Life Expectancy at Birth: 50 years male, 54 years female (1992)

No. of Physicians: 0.7/10,000 population (1992)

■ EDUCATION

Govt. Expenditure: 6.4% of govt. expenditure (1988)

Literacy: 71.8% (1992)

■ COMMUNICATIONS

Daily newspapers: 7 (1992)

Televisions: 0.9/1,000 inhabitants (1992)

Radios: 101/1,000 inhabitants (1992)

Telephones: 0.09/100 inhabitants (1992)

■ TRANSPORTATION

Motor Vehicles: 190,000; 100,000 passenger cars (1990)

Roads: 150,100 km; 2,350 km paved

Railway: 5,400 km

Air Traffic: 150,000 passengers carried (1991)

Airports: 100

Canadian Embassy: 17 Pumbu Zone de Gombe Ave, Kinshasa, Zaïre; mailing address: P.O. Box 8341, Kinshasa 1, Zaïre. Tel: (011-243-12) 21-801. Fax: (011-871-12) 156-0213

Embassy in Canada: 18 Range Rd, Ottawa, ON K1N 8J3

Zambia

Long-Form Name: Republic of Zambia

Capital: Lusaka

Population: 8,638,000 (1992)

■ GEOGRAPHY

Area: 752,610 sq. km

Coastline: none: landlocked

Climate: tropical; modified by altitude; rainy season (Oct. to Apr.)

Environment: deforestation; soil erosion; desertification

Terrain: mostly high plateau with some hills and mountains

Land Use: 7% arable; negligible permanent crops; 47% meadows; 27% forest; 19% other

Location: SC Africa

■ PEOPLE

Nationality: Zambian

Ethnic Groups: 99% African, 1% European, 0.2% other

Languages: English (official); about 70 indigenous languages

Religions: 50–75% Christian, 1% Moslem and Hindu, remainder indigenous beliefs

Marriages: n.a.

Divorces: n.a.

■ GOVERNMENT

Leader(s): Pres. Frederick Chiluba, Vice-Pres. Levy Mwanawasa

Government Type: one-party state

Administrative Divisions: 9 provinces

Independence: Oct. 24, 1964 (from UK; formerly known as Northern Rhodesia)

National Holiday: Independence Day, Oct. 24

■ ECONOMY

Overview: basically the economy was in decline throughout the 1980s due to a sustained drop in copper production and ineffective economic policies; problems include a high inflation rate and high population growth

GNP: $3.394 billion, per capita $420; real growth rate 0.7% (1991)

Inflation: 92.6% (1991)

Industries: copper mining and processing, transport, construction, foodstuffs, beverages, chemicals, textiles and fertilizer

Labour Force: 2,640,000 (1992); 37.9% agriculture, 7.8% industry, 54.9% services (1989)

Unemployment: 15,896 (1989)

Agriculture: accounts for 15% GDP; crops: corn (food staple), sorghum, rice, peanuts, sunflower, tobacco, cotton, sugarcane, cassava; cattle, goats, beef, eggs produced; marginally self-sufficient in corn

Natural Resources: copper, cobalt, zinc, lead, coal, emeralds, gold, silver, uranium, hydropower potential

■ FINANCE/TRADE

Currency: kwacha (K)

International Reserves Excluding Gold: $185 million (1991)

Gold Reserves: 0.00 million fine troy ounces (1991)

Budget: revenues $1.5 billion; expenditures $1.5 billion, including capital expenditures of $300 million (1991)

Defence Expenditures: $186.01 million (1989)

External Debt: $4.784 billion (1990)

Exports: $1.292 billion (1990); commodities: copper, zinc, cobalt, lead, tobacco; partners: European Community, Japan, South Africa, US

Imports: $1.242 billion (1990); commodities: machinery, transportation equipment, foodstuffs, fuels, manufactures; partners: European Community, Japan, South Africa, US

■ HEALTH

Births: 49/1,000 population (1991)

Deaths: 12/1,000 population (1991)

Infant Mortality: 79 deaths/1,000 live births (1991)

Life Expectancy at Birth: 51 years male, 54 years female (1992)

No. of Physicians: 1.4/10,000 population (1992)

■ EDUCATION

Govt. Expenditure: 8.62% of govt. expenditure (1988)

Literacy: 72.8% (1992)

■ COMMUNICATIONS

Daily newspapers: 3 (1992)

Televisions: 24.6/1,000 inhabitants (1992)

Radios: 74/1,000 inhabitants (1992)

Telephones: 1.2/100 inhabitants (1992)

■ TRANSPORTATION

Motor Vehicles: 165,000; 98,000 passenger cars (1990)

Roads: 37,630 km; 6,775 km paved

Railway: 2,200 km

Air Traffic: 293,000 passengers carried (1991)

Airports: 70

Canadian Embassy: The Canadian High Commission, 1st Flr, Barclays Bank, North End Branch, Cairo Rd, Lusaka; mailing address: P.O. Box 313131, 10101 Lusaka, Zambia. Tel: (011-260-1) 228-811. Fax: (011-260-1) 22-51-60

Embassy in Canada: High Commission for the Republic of Zambia, 130 Albert St, Ste 1610, Ottawa ON K1P 5G4

Zimbabwe

Long-Form Name: Republic of Zimbabwe

Capital: Harare

Population: 10,583,000 (1992)

■ GEOGRAPHY

Area: 390,580 sq. km

Coastline: none: landlocked

Climate: tropical; moderated by altitude; rainy season (Nov. to Mar.)

Environment: recurring droughts; floods and severe storms are rare; deforestation; soil erosion; air and water pollution; desertification

Terrain: mostly high plateau with higher central plateau (high veld); mountains in east

Land Use: 7% arable; negligible permanent; 12% meadows; 62% forest; 19% other

Location: SC Africa

■ PEOPLE

Nationality: Zimbabwean
Ethnic Groups: 98% African (71% Shona, 16% Ndebele, 11% other), 1% white, 1% mixed and Asian
Languages: English (official); Shona and Ndebele
Religions: 50% syncretic (part Christian, part indigenous beliefs), 25% Christian, 24% indigenous beliefs, a few Moslem
Marriages: n.a.
Divorces: n.a.

■ GOVERNMENT

Leader(s): Exec. Pres. Robert Mugabe, V. Pres. Joshua Nkomo, Simon Vengesai Muzenda
Government Type: parliamentary democracy
Administrative Divisions: 8 provinces
Independence: Apr. 18, 1980 (from UK; formerly known as Southern Rhodesia)
National Holiday: Independence Day, Apr. 18

■ ECONOMY

Overview: the growth rate has been uneven in recent years due to year-to-year fluctuations in agricultural production; the annual population growth rate is running higher than economic growth
GNP: $6.220 billion, per capita $620; real growth rate 3.6% (1991)
Inflation: 24.3% (1991)
Industries: mining, steel, clothing and footwear, chemicals, foodstuffs, fertilizer, beverages, transportation equipment, wood products
Labour Force: 3,921,000 (1992); 64.7% agriculture, 5.6% industry, 29.7% services (1989)
Unemployment: at least 20% (1988 est.)
Agriculture: accounts for approx. 15% of GDP; 40% of land area divided into 6,000 large commercial farms and 42% in communal lands; crops: corn (food staple), cotton, tobacco, wheat, coffee, sugar cane, peanuts; livestock: cattle, sheep, goats, pigs
Natural Resources: coal, chromium ore, asbestos, gold, nickel, copper, iron ore, vanadium, lithium, tin

■ FINANCE/TRADE

Currency: Zimbabwe dollar ($Z)
International Reserves Excluding Gold: $222 million (1992)
Gold Reserves: 0.55 million fine troy ounces (1992)
Budget: revenues $2.7 billion; expenditures $3.3 billion, including capital expenditures of $330 million (1991)
Defence Expenditures: $361.45 million (1990)
External Debt: $2.449 billion (1990)
Exports: $1.723 billion (1990); commodities: agriculture 34% (tobacco 21%, other 13%), manufactures 19%, gold 11%, ferrochrome 11%, cotton 6%; partners: Europe 55% (European Community 41%, Netherlands 6%, other 8%), Africa 22% (South Africa 12%, other 10%), US 8%, Japan 4%
Imports: $1.85 billion (1990); commodities: machinery and transportation equipment 37%, other manufactures 22%, chemicals 16%, fuels 15%; partners: European Community 31%, Africa 29% (South Africa 21%, other 8%), US 8%, Japan 4%

■ HEALTH

Births: 41/1,000 population (1991)
Deaths: 8/1,000 population (1991)
Infant Mortality: 61 deaths/1,000 live births (1991)
Life Expectancy at Birth: 58 years male, 61 years female (1992)
No. of Physicians: 1.4/10,000 population (1992)

■ EDUCATION

Govt. Expenditure: 22% of govt. expenditure (1988)
Literacy: 66.9% (1992)

■ COMMUNICATIONS

Daily newspapers: 2 (1992)
Televisions: 26.6/1,000 inhabitants (1992)
Radios: 85/1,000 inhabitants (1992)
Telephones: 3.23/100 inhabitants (1992)

■ TRANSPORTATION

Motor Vehicles: 260,000; 178,000 passenger cars (1990)
Roads: 78,900 km; 13,280 km paved
Railway: 2,775 km
Air Traffic: 606,000 passengers carried (1991)
Airports: 33

Canadian Embassy: The Canadian High Commission, 45 Baines Ave, Harare; mailing address: P.O. Box 1430, Harare, Zimbabwe. Tel: (011-263-4) 733-881. Fax: (011-263-4) 732-917
Embassy in Canada: High Commission for the Republic of Zimbabwe, 332 Somerset St W, Ottawa ON K2P 0J9

ASTRONOMY AND SPACE

Astronomy has taught us that the universe is more complex than the ancients thought. Though less dependent on the "patterns" in the sky, we continue the exploration. The skies act not simply as a guide, but have become our latest frontier.

The Solar System

The solar system consists of the sun, at least nine planets and smaller bodies such as asteroids, comets and moons. The dominant member of this family is the sun, our nearest star. The sun is an enormous ball of hot, glowing gas, mostly hydrogen and helium. Its powerful pull of gravity holds the planets, asteroids and comets in orbit around it.

The planets have been known since people first turned their gaze skyward. The ancient Greeks called them "wanderers" because they moved through the sky relative to the fixed stars. Five planets can be seen without a telescope: Mercury, Venus, Mars, Jupiter and Saturn. They are visible because they reflect the light of the sun.

Until 1999, in order of distance from the sun, the planets are Mercury, Venus, Earth, Mars, Jupiter, Saturn, Uranus, Pluto and Neptune. Pluto is *usually* the most remote planet, over seven billion kilometres from the sun at its maximum distance, but from 1979 to 1999, its strange orbit brings it closer to the sun than Neptune.

All the planets revolve (orbit) around the sun in the same counter-clockwise direction. The closer to the sun, the greater their speed. Except for Pluto, all the orbits lie in nearly the same plane in space, like marbles rolling on a table top.

Our Place in the Universe Although the solar system seems enormous, it is quite small compared to the whole universe. Our sun is only one star among the hundreds of billions that make up our galaxy, the **Milky Way**. It takes our sun, with planets in tow, about 250 million years to orbit around the Milky Way just once. All the stars that we see at night are in a small, nearby portion of our galaxy. There may be billions of galaxies in the universe, each containing billions of stars of its own.

The Birth of the Solar System Approximately 4.6 billion years ago, (billions of years after the galaxies were formed), astronomers believe that a vast cloud of gas and dust collapsed and formed a spinning disk. Gravitation compacted so much material in the centre that extremely high pressures and temperatures lit a nuclear fire—our sun began to shine. Meanwhile, any remaining lumps of hot solids and gases slowly collected to become the planets, moons, asteroids and comets.

Our Solar System The planets of the solar system can be divided into two groups. The inner planets, Mercury, Venus, Earth and Mars, are the **terrestrial**, or Earth-like, planets. These are small rocky worlds with metal cores and thin atmospheres, except for airless Mercury. Jupiter, Saturn, Uranus and Neptune make up the realm of the **gas giants**. These planets do not have a solid surface, but are made up of layers of gases and clouds, possibly with rocky cores the size of Earth. The gas giants are huge: a thousand Earths could easily fit inside Jupiter. Saturn's rings may be the most famous feature of the solar system but rings are also found around Jupiter, Uranus and Neptune.

Pluto is unique and does not fit into either of these two groups. It is a tiny world of rock and ice, smaller than the Earth's moon, and with an extremely thin atmosphere.

Separating the terrestrial planets from the gas giants is the **asteroid belt**, a region of space between Mars and Jupiter where as many as 50 000 rocky objects may orbit the sun. Asteroids, often called minor planets, range from gravel-size, or smaller, to the 1000-km-wide Ceres. They may be the remains of a small, shattered planet.

Over 50 moons, or satellites, are found in the solar system. All the planets, except for Mercury and Venus, have at least one moon orbiting them. Some of these moons are fascinating worlds in their own right: **Phobos** and **Deimos**, the moons of Mars, may be captured asteroids; **Io**, one of Jupiter's moons, has many active volcanoes; **Europa**, another one of Jupiter's moons, may have a subterranean ocean; **Titan**, a moon of Saturn, has an atmosphere thicker than Earth's. Jupiter with its 16 known moons, Saturn with its 18 and

Uranus with its 15 are like miniature solar systems.

Exploring the Solar System Most of the planets have been visited by space probes from Earth: Mercury was visited in 1974 by *Mariner 10*, Soviet *Venera* spacecraft landed on Venus several times in the 1970's while *Viking 1* and 2 landed on Mars in 1976. The best spacecraft views of Jupiter and Saturn were obtained by *Voyager 1* and 2 in 1979 and 1980/81 respectively. *Voyager 2* went on to Uranus in 1986 and Neptune in August 1989. These spacecraft made discoveries unobtainable from the Earth: craters on Mercury, volca-noes and great valleys on Mars, Jupiter's ring and 10 new moons of Uranus were only a few.

Current missions include the American *Galileo* orbiter/atmospheric penetrator (Jupiter) and *Magellan* radar mapper (Venus), both of which were launched in 1989. *Magellan* is returning exquisitely-detailed images of the Venusian surface through the use of its imaging radar. *Galileo* will be arriving at Jupiter in 1995. The *Ulysses* mission, launched in 1990, will send a spacecraft over the poles of the sun in 1994 and 1995. Missions planned for the 1990s include visiting a comet, Titan and Mars.

Solar System at a Glance

	Distance from Sun (million km)	Equatorial diameter (km)	Gravity (Earth=1)	Mass (Earth=1)	Period of Orbit about the Sun	Period of Rotation on Axis (days)	Number of known Moons
Sun	—	1 392 000	27.9	332 830	—	25.38	—
Mercury	57.9	4 878	0.38	0.06	88.0 days	58.60	0
Venus	108.2	12 104	0.91	0.8	224.7 days	243.00	0
Earth	149.6	12 756	1.00	1.0	365.3 days	0.99	1
Mars	227.9	6 787	0.38	0.1	1.88 years	1.02	2
Jupiter	778.4	142 800	2.54	317.8	11.86 years	0.41	16
Saturn	1 423.8	120 000	1.08	95.2	29.63 years	0.42	17
Uranus	2 868.7	51 200	0.91	14.5	83.97 years	0.45	15
Neptune	4 492.1	48 680	1.19	17.2	164.80 years	0.67	8
Pluto	5 926.5	2 300	0.06	0.002	248.63 years	6.38	1

Source: *Global Atlas, Gage Educational Publishing Co.; Observer's Handbook, 1991, The Royal Astronomical Society of Canada*

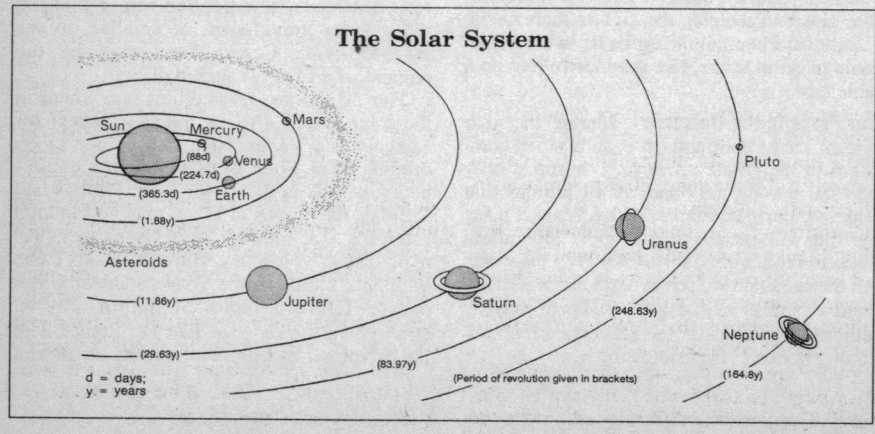

The Solar System

d = days;
y = years

(Period of revolution given in brackets)

Mars: Profile of a Planet

The Planet Mars, named for the Roman god of war, is the most Earth-like of all the planets in the solar system. Its surface may generally be considered a frozen desert, in some ways similar to the Antarctic. Midway in size between the Earth and Moon, and lacking oceans, Mars has a surface area approximately that of the land area of Earth. Its obvious red color is due to oxidation of material in the dusty soil, in fact, Mars has rusted.

The planet possesses an atmosphere of carbon dioxide at a pressure less than one percent of Earth's. Combined with Mars' greater distance from the sun, this thin atmosphere means that temperatures are generally quite low, ranging from a frigid -125°C at the pole to a balmy (for Mars) +23° at middle latitudes at noon during the summer. Martian seasons are similar to Earth's but last twice as long due to the planet's longer orbital period.

Surface Features As might be expected due to Mars' proximity to the asteroid belt, the surface is covered in craters of various sizes. There are, however, more fascinating features waiting to be explored:

Mountains—Barely perceptible from Earth as a bright spot, Olympus Mons is the highest mountain in the solar system. Standing 27 000 m tall, it is three times higher than Mount Everest! Placed on Earth, this volcano, up to 600 km across, would cover all of the Great Lakes. A volcano of even greater diameter is Alba Patera which measures some 1600 km across. While there are many other volcanic peaks on Mars, there is no evidence than any are currently active.

Valleys—Continuing the trend to large proportions is the Mariner Valley system, a huge network of cracks in the Martian crust that measures some 5000 km long. Individual canyons in the system may be 200 km wide and 7 km deep. In comparison, the Grand Canyon is 450 km long, 30 km across at its widest and 2 km deep.

Channels—Long sinuous channels, resembling dried-up river beds, are found on Mars and seem to indicate that water once flowed there (possibly no more recently than three billion years ago). This implies a more temperate climate once existed.

Polar Caps—At the pole experiencing winter, a large ice cap forms. This cap is composed of water ice and frozen carbon dioxide (dry ice). The cap is essentially the atmosphere itself, frozen solid due to the extreme cold.

Life on Mars? Mars is generally considered the most likely planet to harbor extraterrestrial life. Although the environment is harsh, simple terrestrial organisms have survived in artificially created Martian conditions. In the late 19th and early 20th centuries, observations of alleged canals inspired the idea that a civilization existed on Mars. The main proponent of this theory was the American astronomer Percival Lowell (1855–1915). His ideas were extremely controversial but inspired others to study the red planet. Intelligent life has been shown not to exist but the discovery of channels, indicating wetter, more hospitable conditions in the past, holds out some slim hope that microbial life may have existed and may yet survive. None was detected, however, when the *Viking* spacecraft landed in 1976 and carried out life-seeking tests.

Moons The moons are named for the mythical horses which drew the war god's chariot. They are oblong in shape: **Phobos** measures 27 by 21 by 19 km and **Deimos** 15 by 12 by 11 km. These objects probably represent asteroids captured by the gravity of Mars. Phobos is unusual in that it orbits Mars faster than it takes the planet to rotate; Phobos therefore rises in the west and sets in the east as seen from the Martian surface. The gravity of these moons is so weak that one could jump off them altogether by running at 11 km/hour!

Observing Mars American and Russian space probes have been observing the planet since the 1960s. American *Viking* (1975-6) and *Mariner* (1964-71) craft have confirmed surface craters and discovered evidence of surface water frost at the end of Mars's winters. On September 24, 1992 the United States launched the Mars *Observer* to help to understand why this planet, similar in many ways to earth, has evolved so differently. Among the questions American scientists and other experts hoped to answer were: whether Mars has a magnetic field, which minerals and chemicals form the planet's surface, and where the water responsible for the deep canyons and riverbeds on the planet has gone. Unfortunately, radio contact with *Observer* was lost on August 21, 1993, so the data *Observer* gathers may never be retrieved.

A Mars lander is due for launch in the fall of 1994. The lander will gather data on the climate and atmosphere, as well as the inner geological structure of the planet. Two small stations will be deployed from above the planet's surface and then parachuted separately down to the surface. After coming to rest, a protective casing separates from the lander and exposes the station. Then the station's petals open outward, permitting the instruments, including television, to carry out measurements.

Along with the instruments onboard each station will be a collection of science fiction stories, sounds and images on a compact disc that tells the story of humanity's fascination with Mars and its imagined Martians, from H.G. Wells to present day writers and artists. The disc is seen as a gift from our generation to future generations who may explore and perhaps settle, Mars.

Source: *The McLaughlin Planetarium, Toronto, Ont.*

Common Space Terms

Deploy To place something into position.

End Effector A robotic grasping device, for example, the "hand" of Canadarm.

Extravehicular Activity (EVA) Work done outside the pressurized part of the spacecraft.

Flyby The passage of a spacecraft past a moon or planet, without going into orbit.

Footprint The area on the Earth's surface within which a satellite's signal can be received.

Geosynchronous Orbit (geostationary) An orbit, about 35 900 km above the Earth's equator, in which a satellite revolves around the Earth at the same rate as the Earth rotates on its axis. Consequentially, the satellite appears to be stationary over a point on the Earth's surface.

Ionosphere Region of the Earth's atmosphere made up of several layers of ionized gases.

Magnetosphere The region above the ionosphere in which the Earth's magnetic field forms a magnetic shell around our planet. The outermost region of our atmosphere, it contains the Van Allen Belts.

Payload The cargo carried by a rocket or spacecraft.

Propellants The fuels and oxidizers burned in rocket engines to produce thrust.

Spacecraft Any vehicle designed to operate in space (placed in orbit or on a trajectory to another celestial body).

Space Shuttle The shuttle is a multipurpose vehicle which carries cargo to and from space.

Orbiter The reusable, main section of the shuttle that carries the crew and payload.

Thrust The propulsive force produced by a rocket engine during firing.

Transponder A radio repeater (receives a signal and transmits a response) carried on board communications satellites.

Weightlessness The condition in which no weight, caused by gravity or any other force, can be detected. A spacecraft in orbit falls endlessly around Earth or some other body, so that it and everything inside it is in freefall or weightless.

Van Allen Radiation Belt Two belts of high-energy charged particles trapped in the Earth's magnetic field. These doughnut-shaped zones are the source of the Aurora Borealis and the Aurora Australis.

Solar System Facts

1 *Due to a combination of Mercury's orbital and rotational motion, and its highly elliptical orbit, a suitably-located observer on the planet would see the sun moving westward, come to a complete stop, move backward, stop and then continue in the original direction.*

2 *Venus's rotation period is longer than its orbital period i.e. its day is longer than its year! In addition, Venus rotates backwards!*

3 *Jupiter's Great Red Spot is a whirlpool so immense that it could easily swallow the entire Earth!*

4 *Saturn's ring system, made largely of ice particles, is more than 270,000 km across but only a few metres thick. This is equivalent to having a piece of paper with the same area as North America.*

Some Astronomical Terms

Asteroid Any of the thousands of small, rocky objects that orbit the Sun. Some pass closer to the Sun than Earth does and others have orbits that take them well beyond Jupiter. The largest asteroid is one called Ceres.

Big Bang The primeval explosion that most astronomers think gave rise to the universe as we see it today, in which clusters of galaxies are moving apart from one another. Astronomers calculate the Big Bang happened about 15 to 20 billion years ago.

Black Hole An object whose gravitational pull is so strong that—within a certain distance of it— nothing can escape, not even light. Black holes are thought to result from the collapse of certain very massive stars, but other kinds have been postulated as well: **mini black holes**, for example, which might have been formed in the turbulence shortly after the Big Bang. **Supermassive black holes**—with masses millions of times the Sun's—may exist in the cores of large galaxies.

Comet A small chunk of ice, dust and rocky material (a few kilometres across) which, when it comes close enough to the Sun, can develop a tenuous "tail." The tail of a comet is made of gas and dust that have been driven off the comet's surface by the Sun's energy. The tail always points away from the Sun (no matter in what direction the comet is moving).

Eclipse The blocking of all or part of the light from one object by another.

Galaxy A large assemblage of stars (and sometimes interstellar gas and dust), typically containing millions to hundreds of billions of member stars. A galaxy is held together by the gravitational attraction of its member stars (and other material) to one another.

Light-Year The distance light travels in one year in a vacuum. Since light travels at a speed of about 300,000 km per second, a light-year is roughly 9.5 trillion km long.

Magnitude A way of expressing the brightness of astronomical objects, inherited from the Greeks. In the magnitude system, a lower number indicates a brighter object (for example, a 1st-magnitude star is brighter than a 3rd-magnitude star). Each step in magnitude corresponds to a brightness difference of about 2.5. Stars of the 6th magnitude are the faintest the unaided human eye can see.

Meteor A bit of solid debris from space, burning up in the Earth's atmosphere because of friction with the air. Before entering Earth's atmosphere, the body is called a meteoroid. If any of the object survives its fiery passage through the air, the parts that hit the ground are called **meteorites.**

Milky Way Galaxy A spiral galaxy, with a disk approximately 100,000 light-years across, containing roughly 400 billion stars. Our Sun is in the disk about two-thirds of the way from the centre. It takes about 200 million years to orbit the centre of the Milky Way once.

Neutron Star A crushed remnant left over when a very massive star explodes. Some neutron stars are known to spin very rapidly, at least at the beginning, and can be detected as **pulsars**: rapidly flashing sources of radio radiation or visible light. The pulses are produced by the spinning of a neutron star, much as a lighthouse beacon appears to flash off, on and off.

Nova A star that abruptly and temporarily increases its brightness by a factor of hundreds of thousands.

Orbit The path of one body around another (such as the Moon around the Earth) or around the centre of gravity of a number of objects (such as the Sun's 200-million-year path around the centre of our galaxy).

Planet A major object that orbits around a star.

Quasar One of a class of very distant (typically billions of light years away), extremely bright, and very small objects. Quasar means "quasi-star"— that is, something that looks like a star but can't actually be a star.

Red Giant A very large distended, and relatively cool star in the final stages of its life.

Solar System The Sun and all things orbiting it, including the nine major planets, their satellites, and all the asteroids and comets.

Supernova An explosion that marks the end of a very massive star's life. When it occurs, the star can outshine all the other stars in a galaxy in total for several days, and may leave behind a crushed core (perhaps a neutron star or a black hole).

White Dwarf The collapsed remnant of a relatively low-mass star (roughly one and a half times the Sun's mass and less), which has exhausted the fuel for its nuclear reactions and shines only by radiating its stored up heat.

Source: *The Astronomical Society of the Pacific, San Francisco, CA*

The Sky in 1994

Prepared by Ian G. McGregor
McLaughlin Planetarium, Toronto

▣ The Planets

Mercury is difficult to observe as it is never more than 28 degrees from the sun. In the northern hemisphere it is best observed for a few evenings after sunset in the spring and before sunrise for a few mornings in the autumn. Two favourable appearances of Mercury in the western sky after sunset will be from February 1 to 8, and an especially good one from May 15 to June 8. A favourable appearance in the eastern sky before sunrise will take place from October 31 to November 12.

Venus is not visible at the beginning of the year as it passes behind the sun in mid-January. It re-appears in the western sky after sunset in the early spring and will be near Mercury in late May, although it may not be easily observed until the early summer when it will be a brilliant "star" in the sky. Venus and Jupiter will be near each other in September. The planet is visible as the "evening star" until late October. On November 2, it passes between the earth and sun: Venus reappears in the east before sunrise in mid-November.

Mars will be a disappointing object for most of the year. Every two years the planet is favourably placed for observation from the earth at the time of opposition and 1994 is the in-between year. Mars moves rapidly around the sky during the year, beginning in Sagittarius and ending the year in Leo. It is lost in the sun's glare until the mid-spring when it appears as a rather ordinary-looking "star" in the east before sunrise. By year-end Mars is rising in the early evening with opposition in February 1995.

Jupiter begins the year as a bright object rising after midnight in the constellation of Libra. During the spring the planet retrogrades through the constellations of Libra and Virgo, reaching opposition on April 30 when it will rise at sunset and be visible all night. It will be very noticeable during the summer months. From July 21 to 23, the remains of Comet Shoemaker-Levy 9 are predicted to collide with the giant planet

causing tremendous explosions in the planet's atmosphere which will be observable from earth. By mid-autumn, Jupiter will be disappearing into the sunset glow. It is in conjunction with the sun on November 17 and is entering Scorpius at year-end.

Saturn is low in the southwest at sunset at the beginning of the year and disappears into the sun's glare in late January. It is in conjunction with the sun on February 21 and reappears in the east before sunrise by early May. This year the planet's rings are almost edge-on as seen from the Earth and the planet only appears as a brighter star. Opposition is on September 1 when the planet rises in the east at sunset and is visible all night. By the end of the year, Saturn is setting in the west before midnight. Saturn spends the year in eastern Aquarius.

Uranus, Neptune and Pluto are the three outermost planets in the solar system and require telescopic aid to be observed. They appear star-like in small instruments and move very slowly relative to the background stars. Uranus and Neptune appear near each other in eastern Sagittarius during the year. They are best observed from June to September.

Pluto is the faintest of the planets and very difficult to find. During 1994, it continues to move through Libra and is best observed between April and July. Pluto was at its minimum distance from the sun (4,290,240,000 km) in 1989. Currently closer to the sun than Neptune, it will again become the most distant of the known planets of the sun in 1999.

In 1992 and 1993 two large asteroids each about 150-200 km in size and in approximately circular orbits around the sun were discovered beyond the orbit of Pluto. Their existence suggests the presence of a second asteroid belt in the solar system and further reduces the possibility of other planetary size bodies orbiting the sun.

▣ Events

January

2	Earth at perihelion (147,099,700 km) at 1 am EST
3	Quadrantid meteor shower. Almost Last Quarter moon will interfere.

▶

▶
February

2	Mercury close to Saturn tonight

March

20	Spring equinox at 3:29 pm EST

April

3	Most provinces set clocks ahead one hour for daylight savings time. Saskatchewan uses standard time all year long.
22	Lyrid meteor shower. Full Moon interferes.
30	Jupiter at opposition. It rises at sunset and is visible all night.

May

5	Eta Aquarid meteor shower. Moon interferes.
10	Annular eclipse of the sun. See Eclipse table.
25	Partical eclipse of the moon. See Eclipse table.

June

21	Summer solstice at 10:49 am EDT

July

5	Earth at aphelion (152,099,700 km) at 3 pm. EDT
21-23	Comet Shoemaker-Levy 9 predicted to collide with Jupiter

August

12	Perseid meteor shower. An excellent display is expected this year as the 1993 shower was above average in activity and the moon will have set by the time peak activity occurs. Watch for many bright meteors. The much-anticipated big "shower" is not expected until 1995-1997.

September

1	Saturn at opposition. It rises at sunset and is visible all night.
23	Autumn equinox at 2:20 am EDT.

October

31	All provinces except Saskatchewan set clocks back one hour for a return to standard time.

November

3	Total eclipse of the sun. See Eclipse table.
18	Penumbral eclipse of the moon visible from all of North and South America.

December

14	Geminid meteor shower. An excellent shower although the almost Full Moon will interfere.
21	Winter solstice at 9:24 pm EST.

Phases of the Moon

(Eastern Standard Time)

New Moon		First Quarter		Full Moon		Last Quarter	
						Jan. 4	7:01 pm
Jan. 11	6:11 pm	Jan. 19	3:27 pm	Jan. 27	6:23 am	Feb. 3	3:07 am
Feb. 10	9:30 am	Feb. 18	12:48 pm	Feb. 25	8:16 pm	Mar. 4	11:54 am
Mar. 12	2:05 am	Mar. 20	7:15 am	Mar. 27	6:10 am	Apr. 2	9:55 pm
Apr. 10	8:18 pm	Apr. 18	10:35 pm	Apr. 25	3:45 pm	May 2	10:33 am
May 10	1:07 pm	May 18	8:50 am	May 24	11:40 pm	June 1	12:03 am
June 9	4:27 am	June 16	3:57 pm	June 23	7:34 am	June 30	3:31 pm
July 8	5:38 pm	July 15	9:12 pm	July 22	4:16 pm	July 30	8:41 am
Aug. 7	4:46 am	Aug. 14	1:58 am	Aug. 21	2:47 am	Aug. 29	2:41 am
Sept. 5	2:33 pm	Sept. 12	7:34 am	Sept. 19	4:01 pm	Sept. 27	8:24 pm
Oct. 4	11:56 pm	Oct. 11	3:18 pm	Oct. 19	8:18 am	Oct. 27	12:45 pm
Nov. 3	8:36 am	Nov. 10	1:14 am	Nov. 18	1:57 am	Nov. 26	2:04 am
Dec. 2	6:55 pm	Dec. 9	4:07 pm	Dec. 17	9:18 pm	Dec. 25	2:07 pm

Source: *McLaughlin Planetarium, Toronto*

Organizations

Canadian Astronomical Society (CAS): An organization of professional astronomers. Contact: Norman Broten, CAS Secretary, 48 Pineglen Crescent, Nepean, Ontario K2E 6X9.

Planetarium Association of Canada (PAC): Organization of planetariums across Canada. Contact: Phil Mozel, PAC Secretary, c/o McLaughlin Planetarium, 100 Queen's Park, Toronto, Ontario M5S 2C6.

Royal Astronomical Society of Canada (RASC): The Society is devoted to the advancement of astronomy and the allied sciences and has twenty-two centres across Canada. Address: 136 Dupont Street, Toronto, Ontario M5R 1V2 Tel: (416) 924-7973.

Space Junk

T *he consequence of thirty-five years of space exploration, more than 22,000 trackable pieces of space junk remain in orbit around the Earth. Of that number about 7,000 satellites have been catalogued; the rest are used rocket bodies, dead payloads, leftover junk (such as optics covers and discarded payload hardware), and debris resulting from years of rocket and payload fragmentation. Space junk poses an ever increasing hazard to spacecraft. Objects only 1mm in diameter travelling at 10 km/sec can penetrate most satellites and spacecraft.*

The behaviour of debris in orbit is closely monitored and "close approach" warnings are issued by the Space Defense Operations Centre in the US. An alert for collision avoidance is issued when two objects are within 5-8 km of each other. Shuttles are required to undertake avoidance procedures when debris is predicted within 2 km radially, 5 km downtrack, or 2 km out of orbital plane. Estimates are that space station "Freedom" would be required to make 20 such manoeuvres annually. The worst feature of the debris hazard is that there are now many thousands of pieces too small to be tracked, mostly resulting from the more than 100 explosions in space.

Eclipses in 1994

Four eclipses of the sun and moon take place during 1994. The event of most interest to Canadian observers is the May 10 eclipse of the sun.

May 10   **Annual Solar Eclipse**

Path of annularity crosses United States from the Pacific Ocean, passes through southern Ontario, parts of New Brunswick and most of Nova Scotia. All of North America experiences a partial eclipse of the sun. Maximum duration of annularity 6 minutes 13 seconds. The eclipse begins at 11:21 am EDT and ends 3:02 pm EDT. Toronto, Ontario is the largest Canadian city in the eclipse path, lying just inside the northern limit. Maximum eclipse here occurs at 1:24 pm EDT. Halifax lies near the centre-line of the path. At greatest eclipse, approximately 94% of the sun's diameter will be occulted by the moon.

Observers must take special precautions to observe the event as at no time during the eclipse will it be safe to observe with unprotected eyes. Contact major planetariums for observing information.

May 25   **Partial lunar eclipse**

Visible from all of North and South America.

November 3   **Total solar eclipse**

Mostly visible in the South Atlantic. The moon's shadow first touches the earth just off the coast of South America. Crosses Chile, Paraguay, Bolivia and Brazil, crosses the South Atlantic ocean and leaves the earth off the coast of South Africa. Maximum duration of totality 4 minutes 23 seconds.

November 18   **Penumbral lunar eclipse**

Visible from all of North and South America.

Source: *McLaughlin Planetarium, Toronto*

Major Satellite and Space Probe Launches

Space probes and satellites are instrument-carrying devices. Often overshadowed by crewed space-flight, the information they transmit has been the "engine" of space research.

Name	Launch	Accomplishment
Sputnik 1	Oct. 4, 1957	First artificial satellite to orbit Earth (USSR)
Explorer 1	Feb. 1, 1958	First US satellite; discovered Van Allen radiation belt
Score	Dec. 18, 1958	First satellite to send a recorded human voice into space (US)
Luna 3	Oct. 4, 1959	First photographic images of the dark side of the moon (USSR)
Tiros 1	Apr. 1, 1960	First weather satellite; crude cloud cover images (US)
Echo 1	Aug. 12, 1960	First communications satellite; voice and TV signals relayed by bouncing off satellite—a large balloon (US)
SO 1	Mar. 7, 1962	Orbiting Solar Observatory collected data on about 75 solar flares (US)
Telstar 1	July 10, 1962	Allowed first direct transmission of television images between the United Kingdom and the United States (US)
Mariner 2	Aug. 27, 1962	First successful interplanetary probe; passed Venus on Dec. 14 (109 days after launch) (US)
Alouette 1	Sept. 29, 1962	Launch of Canada's first satellite; first designed and built by a nation other than the US or the USSR; satellite gathered information on the ionosphere
Tiros 8	Dec. 21, 1963	Weather satellite carrying Automatic Picture Transmission (APT) equipment; allows local pictures to be received, using inexpensive portable ground stations (US)
Ariel 2	Mar. 27, 1964	First satellite to sample global distribution of ozone (UK/US)
Syncom 3	Aug. 19, 1964	First communications satellite in truly geostationary orbit (US)
Nimbus 1	Aug. 28, 1964	Earth orientation of weather satellite allows complete global cloud cover pictures every 24 hours; operated for 26 days (US)
Early Bird 1	Apr. 6, 1965	First commercial communications satellite; marked the beginning of global communications systems (US)
Molniya 1	Apr. 23, 1965	First Soviet communications satellite
Venera 3	Nov. 16, 1965	First space probe to make physical contact with another planet; probe crash landed on Venus (USSR)
Luna 9	Jan. 31, 1966	First photographic images transmitted from the surface of the Moon to Earth (USSR)
Surveyor 1	May 30, 1966	First successful soft lunar landing of a test vehicle (US)
Venera 7	Aug. 17, 1970	First probe to return signals from surface of Venus (USSR)
Mars 3	May 28, 1971	First soft landing of a probe on Mars (USSR)
Mariner 9	May 30, 1971	Enters Mars orbit on Nov. 13, and returns photographic images to Earth (US)
Pioneer 10	Mar. 3, 1972	First probe to explore Jupiter and its environment, and first to leave our solar system (US)

▶

Voyager Passes Over the Edge of Our Solar System

*T*he belief our solar system ended with the outermost planet has been overturned. Scientists now say the actual edge of our solar system is where solar wind, or electrically-charges particles spewed out by the sun collide with interstellar gas from distant stars.

Voyager 1 and 2 while cruising the outer reaches of the solar system began picking up intense radio signals in August 1992 that could only have come from such a collision. The radio source, although extremely powerful, has a very low frequency that can't be detected from Earth. The edge is estimated to be 13.5 billion to 18 billion kilometres from the sun—or three to four times farther out from the outermost planet.

During their fifteen years in outer space, the probes discovered at least 24 moons orbiting those planets, doubling the previously known number. Voyager 2 also discovered rings of debris around Uranus and Neptune.

Name	Launch	Accomplishment
▶ Landsat 1	July 23, 1972	First major Earth resources satellite; such satellites obtain (ERTS) information on Earth's land use, forestry, mineral, water and marine resources (US)
Anik A	Nov. 9, 1972	First domestic communications satellite in geostationary orbit (Canada)
Hermes (CTS)	Jan. 17, 1976	High-power communications satellite; first to demonstrate feasibility of direct-to-home television (Canada/US)
Voyager 2	Aug. 20, 1977	First scientific probe to study Jupiter and Saturn, including their satellites and the Rings of Saturn; first to flyby Uranus and Neptune; passed Neptune in late summer 1989 (US)
Seasat	June 26, 1978	Remote sensing satellite designed to study ocean currents and ice flow (US)
Solar Max	Feb. 14, 1980	Mission to study Sun activity during a period of maximum (SMM-A) activity for solar flares; failed satellite captured, repaired and successfully relaunched in April 1984 by astronauts on STS 41C shuttle mission (US)
SPOT	Feb. 21, 1986	*Système Probatoire d'observation de la Terre*—remote sensing satellite designed to record surface detail images of Earth; the area can be as small as 10 metres square (France)
Hubble Space Telescope	Apr. 24, 1990	First optical telescope to be placed in orbit around Earth; on deployment encountered difficulty in opening aperture door of telescope; in partial operation only (US)
GRO	Apr. 4, 1991	Gamma Ray Observatory is heaviest satellite deployed from an orbiter, released from Atlantis by the Canadarm; satellite investigating the sources of gamma rays in outer space (US)
UARS	Sept. 12, 1991	Upper Atmosphere Research Satellite deployed to collect substantial information on Earth's upper atmosphere, including the ozone layer (US)

Crewed Spaceflights—Selected Firsts

Mission	Launch	First
Vostok 1	Apr. 12, 1961	First person in space; Soviet cosmonaut, Yuri Gagarin
Freedom 7	May 5, 1961	First American in space; Alan Shepherd with a sub-orbital flight of 15 min.
Friendship 7	Feb. 20, 1962	First orbital flight by an American; John Glenn, 3 orbits
Vostok 6	June 16, 1963	First woman in space; Valentina Tereshkova, 48 orbits
Voskhod 2	Mar. 18, 1965	First space walk; Soviet cosmonaut Aleksei Leonov
Gemini 4	June 3, 1965	First US space walk; first use of personal propulsion unit
Gemini 6-A	Dec. 15, 1965	First space capsule rendezvous; comes within 2 m of Gemini 7
Gemini 10	July 18, 1966	First dual rendezvous; first docked vehicle maneuvers
Apollo 8	Dec. 21, 1968	First spacecraft in orbit about the Moon
Apollo 11	July 16, 1969	First lunar landing; Neil Armstrong places first footprints on the Moon on July 20
Soyuz 10	Apr. 23, 1971	First space station; cosmonauts dock with Salyut 1
Skylab 2	May 25, 1973	First Skylab launch with crew; established the Skylab orbital assembly in Earth orbit, and conducted a series of medical experiments
Soyuz 34	June 6, 1979	First spacecraft to be launched without a crew, and to return with a crew (from Salyut 6)
STS-1	Apr. 12, 1981	First space shuttle flight; Columbia proves reusable orbiter viable; first US landing on land
STS-5	Nov. 11, 1982	First deployment of satellites from a shuttle orbiter
STS-7	June 18, 1983	First use of Canadarm (Remote Manipulator System), deployed two communications satellites on second flight of Challenger; Sally Ride becomes first American woman in space
STS-41B	Feb. 3, 1984	First untethered space walks
Soyuz T-12	July 18, 1984	First woman to walk in space; Svetlana Savitskaya
STS-41G	Oct. 5, 1984	First Canadian in space; Marc Garneau, as a payload specialist, carried out a series of experiments onboard the sixth flight of Challenger
STS-31	Apr. 24, 1990	First optical telescope placed in Earth orbit; Hubble Space Telescope launched from Discovery.

Canadian Achievements Space Technology

Alouette Canada launched its first satellite on September 9, 1962. **Alouette 1** was the first satellite to return useful information on the ionosphere, the layer of the upper atmosphere that affects long-distance radio transmissions. Although designed to last one year, the satellite successfully transmitted data for over a decade.

STEM Antenna The STEM (storage tubular extendible member) antenna, designed at the National Research Council for Alouette, was the ingenious idea of George Klein. It consisted of a thin ribbon of steel rolled onto a spool for launch and then extended to form a long tube in orbit. Later produced by Spar Aerospace for NASA, STEMs were used on early spacecraft, including Alan Shepherd's sub-orbital flight in 1961.

Anik Canada was the first country to launch a satellite for domestic communications. Launched in 1972, **Anik A-1** made nationwide, real-time television possible. Reliable telephone service came to the North for the first time. Anik satellites continue to provide services to television networks, telephone systems to the Arctic, as well as private business networks, and allow a national newspaper to transmit copy to five printing plants across the country.

Hermes Canada worked with the United States on an experimental communications satellite system launched in 1976. Designed and built in Canada, **Hermes** operated at 10 times the power of previous communications satellites. Hermes proved that powerful satellites could bring low-cost television directly to remote areas anywhere on the globe. Teleconferencing was now feasible, and the world's first teleconferencing trials were carried out.

Canadarm Canadarm is the remote manipulator system designed and made in Canada for the US space shuttle program. About 15m long and 0.4m in diameter, it enables NASA astronauts to take satellites from their orbiter's cargo bay and position them accurately in space. Canadarm is also designed to grapple satellites already in orbit and place them in the cargo bay for return to Earth. Operated by two hand controls from the comfort of the orbiter's cabin, Canadarm is one of the most advanced robots in existence.

Canadarm was developed by the National Research Council in coordination with Spar Aerospace in Toronto, and made its first flight in 1981 on the second flight of the shuttle Columbia. It has since been tested and used extensively on subsequent flights. The initial $100 million system was donated by Canada to the US space program; new Canadarms are being sold to NASA for about $25 million each.

Canada's Astronauts

All Canadians were invited to enter a nation-wide competition to become astronauts and 4,300 applied. In December 1983, six were chosen. Two have since resigned and four more were appointed in June 1992, for a total of eight. The Canadian astronauts are research scientists who fly as payload specialists on shuttle missions. Trained by NASA in flight procedures, they operate NASA payloads, as well as their own.

Marc Garneau	launch on Oct. 5, 1984; carried out microgravity experiments
Steve MacLean	launch on Oct. 22, 1992; carried out microgravity and materials exposure experiments
Bob Thirsk	alternate, backup for Garneau
Bjarni Tryggvason	alternate, backup for MacLean
Roberta Bondar	launch on Jan. 22, 1992: carried out 43 life sciences experiments for 13 countries; resigned from the program Sept. 4, 1992
Ken Money	backup for Bondar, resigned July 1992
Dave Williams	appointed June 1992
Julie Payette	appointed June 1992
Major Chris Hadfield	appointed June 1992
Captain Michael McKay	appointed June 1992

Source: *Canadian Space Agency*

Constellations

Constellations are groups of stars that we on Earth see as patterns in the sky. Each pattern is named for a person, an animal or an object, usually from Greek mythology.

Astronomers use constellations to map directions in space. When citing a constellation to locate a star, astronomers use the possessive form instead of the common name; for example, Cancer (The Crab) is referred to as Cancri.

The largest constellation is Hydrus, followed by Virgo and Ursa Major. The smallest is Crux.

Constellation	Meaning
Andromeda	Daughter of Cassiopeia
Antlia	The Air Pump
Apus	Bird of Paradise
Aquarius	The Water-bearer
Aquila	The Eagle
Ara	The Altar
Aries	The Ram
Auriga	The Charioteer
Bootes	The Herdsman
Caelum	The Chisel
Camelopardalis	The Giraffe
Cancer	The Crab
Canes Venatici	The Hunting Dogs
Canis Major	The Big Dog
Canis Minor	The Little Dog
Capricornus	The Horned Goat
Carina	The Keel
Cassiopeia	The Queen
Centaurus	The Centaur
Cepheus	The King
Cetus	The Whale
Chamaeleon	The Chameleon
Circinus	The Compasses
Columba	The Dove
Coma Berenices	Berenice's Hair
Corona Australis	The Southern Crown
Corona Borealis	The Northern Crown
Corvus	The Crow
Crater	The Cup
Crux	The Cross
Cygnus	The Swan
Delphinus	The Dolphin
Dorado	The Goldfish
Draco	The Dragon
Equuleus	The Little Horse
Eridanus	A River
Fornax	The Furnace
Gemini	The Twins
Grus	The Crane (bird)
Hercules	The Son of Zeus
Horologium	The Clock
Hydra	The Water Snake (f)
Hydrus	The Water Snake (m)
Indus	The Indian
Lacerta	The Lizard
Leo	The Lion
Leo Minor	The Little Lion
Lepus	The Hare
Libra	The Balance
Lupus	The Wolf
Lynx	The Lynx
Lyra	The Lyre
Mensa	Table Mountain
Microscopium	The Microscope
Monoceros	The Unicorn
Musca	The Fly
Norma	The Square
Octans	The Octant
Ophiuchus	The Serpent-bearer
Orion	The Hunter
Pavo	The Peacock
Pegasus	The Winged Horse
Perseus	Rescuer of Andromeda
Phoenix	The Phoenix
Pictor	The Painter
Pisces	The Fishes
Piscis Austrinus	The Southern Fish
Puppis	The Stern
Pyxis	The Compass
Reticulum	The Reticle
Sagitta	The Arrow
Sagittarius	The Archer
Scorpius	The Scorpion
Sculptor	The Sculptor
Scutum	The Shield
Serpens	The Serpent
Sextans	The Sextant
Taurus	The Bull
Telescopium	The Telescope
Triangulum	The Triangle
Triangulum Australe	The Southern Triangle
Tucana	The Toucan
Ursa Major	The Great Bear[1]
Ursa Minor	The Little Bear[2]
Vela	The Sails
Virgo	The Maiden
Volans	The Flying Fish
Vulpecula	The Fox

(1) Commonly known as the Big Dipper. (2) Commonly known as The Little Dipper

Observatories in Canada

■ Maritime Region:

Burke-Gaffney Observatory: Saint Mary's University, Halifax, NS B3H 3C3. Open: Oct.-Mar., Sat. 7 pm; Apr.-Sept., Sat. 9 pm. Mon. eve. or day tours by arrangement. Tel: (902) 420-5633.

■ Central Canada:

David Dunlap Observatory: Richmond Hill, Ont. L4C 4Y6. open Tues. mornings 10 am throughout the year, Sat. evenings Apr.-Oct. by reservation. Tel: (416) 884-2112.

Helen B. Hogg Observatory: National Museum of Science and Technology. 1867 St. Laurent Blvd. Ottawa, Ont. K1A 0M8. Open: Oct.-June. Group tours Mon.-Thurs., Public visits Fri. (in French 2nd Fri.); Jul.-Aug.: Public visits: Tues. (French), Wed., Thurs. (English). Eve. tours by appt only. Tel: (613) 991-3073.

Hume Cronyn Observatory: University of Western Ontario, London, Ont. N6A 3K7. Tel: (519) 661-3183.

Observatoire astronomique du mont Mégantic: Notre-Dame-des-Bois, Que. J0B 2E0. Tel: (514) 343-6718 (information on summer programs).

Science North Solar Observatory: 100 Ramsey Lake Rd., Sudbury, Ont. P3A 2K3. Viewing of the solar spectrum and the Sun in hydrogen-alpha and white light in a darkened theatre. Open most days. Tel: (705) 522-3701.

■ Western Canada:

Climenhaga Observatory: Dept. of Physics and Astronomy, University of Victoria, Victoria, BC V8W 2H2. Tel: (604) 388-0001. Open daily.

Rothney Astrophysical Observatory: Physics and Astronomy Dept., University of Calgary, Calgary, Alta. T2N 1N4. Tel: (403) 220-5385.

Dominion Astrophysical Observatory: 5071 West Saanich Rd., Victoria, BC V8X 4M6. Open: May-Aug., daily 9:15 am-4:30 pm; Sept.-Apr., Mon.-Fri. 9:15 am-4:30 pm. Public observing: Sat. eve., Apr.-Oct. Tel: (604) 497-5321.

Dominion Radio Astrophysical Observatory: Penticton, BC V2A 6K3. Conducted tours: Sun., July-Aug. only, 2-5 pm. Visitors' centre open year-round during daytime. Tel: (604) 497-5321.

Gordon MacMillan Southam Observatory: 1100 Chestnut St., Vancouver, B.C. V6J 3J9. Open Fri.-Sun., and statutory holidays 12 pm- 5 pm and 7 pm-11 pm, weather and volunteer staff permitting. Tel: (604) 738-2855.

Devon Observatory: Dept. of Physics, University of Alberta, Edmonton, Alta. T6G 2J1.

University of Saskatchewan Observatory: Saskatoon, Sask. S7N 0W0. Tel.: (306) 966-6434.

University of British Columbia Observatory: 2219 Main Mall, Van., BC V6T 1W5. Free public observing on clear Sat. eve. Tel: (604) 224-6186 (observing) or (604) 228-2802 (tours).

Planetariums

■ Maritime Region:

Burke-Gaffney Planetarium: Saint Mary's University, Department of Astronomy, Halifax, NS B3H 3C3.

The Halifax Planetarium: The Education Section of the Nova Scotia Museum. Summer St., Halifax, NS B3H 3A6. Tel: (902) 429-1610. Located in the Sir James Dunn Building, Dalhousie Univeristy. Free public shows given on some evenings at 8 p.m. Group shows can be arranged.

■ Central Canada:

Doran Planetarium: Laurentian University, Ramsey Lake Rd., Sudbury, Ont. P3E 2C8. tel: (705) 675-1151, ext. 2222.

Dow Planetarium: 1000 St. Jacques St. W., Montreal, Que. H3C 1G7. Tel: (514) 872-4530. Live shows in French and English. Open daily.

London Regional Children's Museum: 21 Wharncliffe Rd. S., London, Ont. N6J 4G5. Tel. (519) 434-5726. Features a planetarium.

McLaughlin Planetarium: 100 Queen's Park, Toronto, Ont. M5S 2C6. Tel: (416) 586-5736 (for show times) or (416) 586-5751 (for sky information). Public shows Tues.-Fri. at 3:00 and 7:30. Additional shows on weekends and during summer. School shows. Astrocentre with solar telescope, and evening courses are available.

Seneca Planetarium: Seneca College, 1750 Finch Ave. E. Willowdale, Ont. M2J 2X5. Tel: (416) 491-5050. Entrance fee. Open winter, spring and fall.

■ Western Canada:

Calgary Centennial Planetarium: Alberta Science Centre, 701-11 St. S.W., P.O. Box 2100. Stn. M. Calgary, Alta. T2P 2M5. Tel: (403) 284-4060 or 221 3700.

Edmonton Space Sciences Centre: Coronation Park, 1121-142 St., Edmonton. Alta T5M 4A1. Tel: (403) 451-7722 or 452-9100. Features planetarium Star Theatre, IMAX film theatre, exhibit galleries, telescope shop and bookstore. Open daily.

H.R. MacMillan Planetarium: 1100 Chestnut St., Vancouver, B.C. V6J 3J9. Tel: (604) 736-3656. Open daily.

Manitoba Planetarium: Museum of Man and Nature. 190 Rupert Ave., Winnipeg, Man. R3B 0N2. Tel: (204) 956-2830 (switchboard). Shows daily except some Mondays. Museum gift shop has scientific books and equipment.

The Lockhart Planetarium: 394 University College, 500 Dysart Rd., Univesity of Manitoba, Winnipeg, Man. R3T 2M8. Tel: (204) 474-9785. By reservation only.

EARTH SCIENCES

The earth sciences include **geology** (the study of earth's origin and composition), **oceanography** (the study of ocean water, currents, life-forms and the ocean floor), **paleontology** (the study of fossils and ancient life-forms), and **meteorology** (the study of earth's atmosphere, including weather and climate). This section includes material on geology and paleontology. Meteorology can be found in the section on Climate (pp.11-27).

The Geological Survey of Canada

The Geological Survey of Canada (GSC) is Canada's first scientific agency, and one of the first of its kind in the world. The agency was created to survey and map mineral deposits in Canada's nearly 1 million square kilometres of land and freshwater lakes, and more than 6 million square kilometres of coastal boundaries.

The Survey began life in Montreal in 1842.

Under the first director William Edmond Logan, a Canadian businessman turned geologist, its initial task was a search for coal, the main industrial fuel at the time. The search, throughout Upper and Lower Canada, was unsuccessful, but Logan did find mineable deposits of copper and other metallic minerals.

Soon Survey geologists were undertaking expeditions westward. In the 1880s another director, George Mercer Dawson, became a noted ethnologist in Western Canada, as well as pioneer geologist. His reports included observations of the Haida people of British Columbia. During his expeditions he took many photographs of settlements and totem poles, capturing a glimpse of a vanishing landscape.

In 1992, the Geological Survey marked its 150th anniversary. It continues to provide Canadians with geoscientific knowledge about Canada and its offshore, its mineral and energy resources, and the natural conditions that affect land and seabed use.

Composition of the Earth

Core: The earth's core lies about 2,900 km below the surface, and consists of two layers: a solid inner core and an outer liquid layer. The inner core is a solid mass, 3,200 km in diameter, probably composed of compressed iron with small amounts of other metals such as nickel. The outer core (the only liquid layer) is about 3,470 km in radius and gives rise to earth's magnetic fields.

Mantle: Accounting for about 82% of earth's volume, the mantle is denser than the crust, and probably increases in density close to the core. The mantle extends from the core to about 90 km below the higher mountains, and to about 5 km beneath parts of the ocean crust.

Crust: The outside crust of planet earth ranges in thickness from 5 to 50 km. The relatively light, granite-like rock forming the continents overlies a thinner magnesium-iron layer that makes up the ocean floor. The continental blocks "float" on the denser layer forming the ocean bed.

Hydrosphere: A layer of water covering over 70% of the earth's crust, including all water on or near the surface of the planet.

Atmosphere: The lightest part of earth is the atmosphere, a gaseous envelope surrounding the planet. The atmosphere consists of nitrogen, oxygen, water vapour and argon. Less than 0.1% is composed of other gases. Gases have weight, so the atmosphere is densest near earth's surface, and thins towards the vacuum of space.

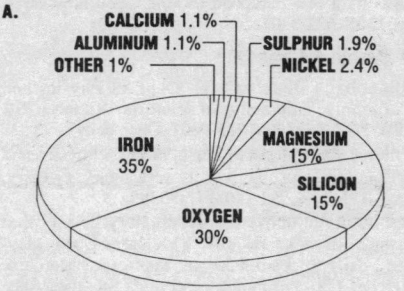

A.
CALCIUM 1.1%
ALUMINUM 1.1%
OTHER 1%
SULPHUR 1.9%
NICKEL 2.4%
IRON 35%
MAGNESIUM 15%
SILICON 15%
OXYGEN 30%

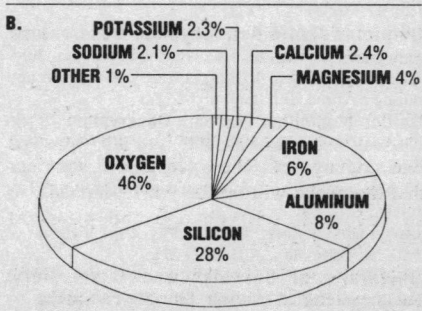

B.
POTASSIUM 2.3%
SODIUM 2.1%
OTHER 1%
CALCIUM 2.4%
MAGNESIUM 4%
OXYGEN 46%
IRON 6%
ALUMINUM 8%
SILICON 28%

▲
Relative abundance of elements by weight of elements in the whole earth (A) and in the earth's crust (B).

Common Geological Terms

Continental shelf: Submerged edge of continent, extending to depths of less than 200 metres, and largely made up of sedimentary rock.

Earthquake: A sudden motion or trembling in the earth caused by the release of slowly accumulated strain along a fault line or through volcanic activity.

Echo Sounding: A determination of water depth by measuring the time required for a sonic or ultrasonic signal to travel to the bottom of a body of water and back to the ship emitting the signal.

Epicentre: Point on the earth's surface directly above the focus of an earthquake, usually the location of the most severe damage.

Erosion: Breakdown and wearing away of rocks on the earth's surface by the action of water, waves, glaciers, wind and underground water.

Fault: a fracture in the earth's crust along which there has been displacement of the rock on either side, relative to one another.

Geothermal energy: energy that can be extracted from the earth's internal heat, usually in the form of emissions of hot water, steam, and gas.

Glacier: a large ice mass formed on land by recrystallisation of compacted snow.

Ice Field: An extensive area of interconnected glaciers. An ice field is known as pack ice when floating on the sea.

Igneous Rock: Rock formed when a mass of molten magma cools and solidifies on or below earth's surface. One of three main classes of rock.

Magma: Molten rocky material (mostly silica) beneath the earth's surface. Reaching the surface red hot through volcanic activity, it cools and becomes lava.

Metamorphic Rock: Rock formed when preexisting rocks are altered by marked changes in temperature, pressure, or shearing stress. One of three major rock groups.

Tectonic plates: Rigid outer layer of the earth's crust consists of about ten large plates, which "float" horizontally across the denser inner crust. The boundaries of these plates are zones of intense activity, and give rise to mountain building, volcanoes, changes in the ocean floor, and earthquakes.

Sedimentary rock: Rock formed from the accumulation of loose material deposited by water, wind and ice, and solidified by compaction.

Seismograph: a device that records the seismic vibrations of an earthquake. The wave disturbances caused by earthquakes have different speeds and require different lengths of time to reach the surface.

Tsunami: Particular form of ocean wave produced by an earthquake in the ocean floor, noted for its destructive force.

Volcano: A vent in the earth's crust through which magma, rock fragments, dust, gases, and ash are ejected from below earth's surface.

Earthquakes

Although the earth's surface seems completely stable, it is constantly moving and changing. Layers of rock in the earth's crust, called plates, push and pull each other until they bend or stretch.

Vibrations or "seismic waves" emanate from the source of the breakage out through the earth, causing the planet to quiver or ring like a tuning fork. The waves can be so minor that the quake will not be felt by humans, or so severe it will change the physical landscape of the area.

Earthquakes can happen all over the world, but they tend to reoccur along weaknesses in the crust, called faults. By studying the patterns of earthquakes, scientists determine the areas at greatest risk and compile the information in seismic zoning maps. In this way, building regulations can be applied to earthquake zones to minimize possible damage.

■ Measuring Earthquakes

The most common method of measuring an earthquake's magnitude is the Richter Scale. It estimates the force from recordings of seismic waves taken by an instrument called a seismometer. the scale is logarithmic, so that each numeric reading is ten times greater in recorded amplitude.

The intensity of an earthquake can also be measured through the Modified Mercalli Scale. In addition to mechanical recordings, it uses witness accounts to describe the effects of an earthquake.

Measuring Earthquakes

Richter		Modified Mercali	
2.5	Generally felt, but not recorded.	I	Not felt except by a very few
		II	Felt only by a few persons at rest, especially on upper floors of buildings
3.5	Felt by many people.	III	Felt noticeably indoors. Standing cars may rock slightly. Most people do not recognize.
		IV	During daytime felt by many indoors, outdoors by a few. Dishes, windows and doors disturbed; walls creak. At night, some awaken. Sensation like a heavy truck passing.
		V	Felt by nearly everyone; many awakened. Some dishes and windows broken; some objects over-turned. Trees, poles and other tall objects disturbed.
4.5	Some local damage may occur.	VI	Felt by all, many run outdoors. Heavy furniture moves; occasionally plaster falls and chimneys damaged. Overall damage slight.
		VII	Everyone runs outdoors. Well-built structures suffer negligible damage; slight to moderate damage in well-built homes; poorly constructed buildings suffer considerable damage. Noticed by people in moving cars.
6.0	A destructive earthquake	VIII	Damage slight in specially designed structures; considerable in ordinary substantial buildings, with partial collapse; great in poorly-built structures. Chimneys fall. Heavy furniture overturned. Disturbs people driving cars. Sand and mud ejected in small amounts.
		IX	Damage to specially designed structures considerable. Buildings shifted off foundations. Conspicuous ground cracks. Underground pipes broken.
7.0	A major earthquake, about 10 occur each year	X	Some well-built wooden structures destroyed; most masonry and frame structures destroyed. Ground badly cracked. Rails bent. Landslides considerable.
8.0	Great earthquake, occurs once every five to 10 years	XI	Few masonry structures remain standing. Bridges destroyed. Broad fissures in ground. Underground pipelines out of service. Earth slumps, and land slips in soft ground.
		XII	Damage total. Waves seen on ground surface. Lines of sight and levels distorted. Objects thrown upward into air.

How Hot is the Earth's Interior?

*S*cientists believe that temperatures increase fairly rapidly in the earth's mantle, from less than 1,000°C to perhaps 3,000°C at the core boundary; the rate of temperature rise slows down past the core boundry. Scientists estimate a maximum temperature of 4,300°C at the earth's centre—not quite as hot as the surface of the sun. The heat comes from the radioactivity of uranium, thorium and potassium. Also, some heat may remain from the early days of the planet.

World's Major Earthquakes

Date		Location	Deaths	Magnitude
1902	Dec. 16	Turkestan	4500	—
1905	Apr. 4	India, Kangra	19000	8.6
1905	Sep. 8	Italy, Calabria	2500	7.9
1906	Jan. 31	Colombia	1000	8.9
1906	Mar. 17	Formosa, Kaji	1300	7.1
1906	Apr. 18	U.S., San Francisco	700	8.5
1906	Aug. 17	Chile, Santiago	20000	8.6
1907	Jan. 14	Jamaica, Kingston	1600	6.5
1907	Oct. 21	Central Asia	12000	8.1
1908	Dec. 28	Italy, Messina	83000	7.5
1912	Aug. 9	Marmara Sea	1950	7.8
1915	Jan. 13	Italy, Avezzano	29980	7.5
1920	Dec. 16	China, Gansu	100000	8.6
1923	Sep. 1	Japan, Kwanto-Tokyo-Yokohama	143000	8.3
1925	Mar. 16	China, Yunnan	5000	7.1
1927	Mar. 7	Japan, Tango	3020	7.9
1927	May 22	China, near Xining	200000	8.3
1929	May 1	Iran	3300	7.4
1930	July 23	Italy	1430	6.5
1932	Dec. 25	China, Gansu	70000	7.6
1933	Mar. 2	Japan, Sanriku	2990	8.9
1933	Mar. 10	U.S., Long Beach	115	6.3
1934	Jan. 15	India, Behar-Nepal	10700	8.4
1935	Apr. 20	Formosa	3280	7.1
1935	May 30	Pakistan, Quetta	30000	7.6
1939	Jan. 25	Chile, Chillan	28000	8.3
1939	Dec. 26	Turkey, Erzincan	30000	7.6
1943	Sep. 10	Japan, Tottori	1190	7.4
1944	Dec. 7	Japan, Tonankai	1000	8.3
1945	Jan. 12	Japan, Mikawa	1900	7.1
1946	May 31	Turkey	1300	6.0
1946	Nov. 10	Peru, Ancash	1400	7.3
1946	Dec. 20	Japan, Tonankai	1330	8.4
1948	June 28	Japan, Fukui	5390	7.3
1949	Aug. 5	Ecuador, Ambato	6000	6.8
1950	Aug. 15	India, Assam, Tibet	1530	8.7
1954	Sep. 9	Algeria, Orleansville	1250	6.8
1956	June 9	Afghanistan	350–400	7.6
1957	July 2	Iran	1200	7.4
1957	Dec. 13	Iran	1130	7.3
1960	Feb. 29	Morocco, Agadir	15000	5.9
1960	May 22	Chile	5000	7.3
1962	Sep. 1	Iran, Qazvin		
1963	July 26	Yugoslavia, Skopje	1100	6.0
1964	Mar. 27	Southern Alaska	131	9.2
1966	Aug. 19	Turkey, Varto	2520	7.1
1968	Aug. 31	Iran	20000	7.3
1969	July 25	Eastern China	3000	5.9
1970	Mar. 28	Turkey, Gediz	1100	7.3
1970	May 31	Peru	66000	7.8
1972	Apr. 10	Southern Iran	5054	7.1
1972	Dec. 23	Nicaragua, Managua	5000	6.2
1975	Sep. 6	Turkey	2300	6.7
1976	Feb. 4	Guatemala	23000	7.5
1976	May 6	Northeastern Italy	1000	6.5
1976	June 25	Western Iran	422	7.1
1976	July 27	China, Tangshan	255000	8.0
1976	Aug. 16	Philippines, Mindanao	8000	7.9
1976	Nov. 24	Northwest Iran-USSR	5000	7.3

Date		Location	Deaths	Magnitude
▶ 1977	Mar. 4	Romania	1500	7.2
1977	Nov. 23	Argentina, San Juan Prov.	70	7.4
1978	Sep. 16	Iran	15000	7.8
1979	Dec. 12	near coast of Ecuador	600	7.9
1980	Oct. 10	Algeria	3500	7.7
1980	Nov. 23	Southern Italy	3000	7.2
1981	June 11	Southern Iran	3000	6.9
1981	July 28	Southern Iran	1500	7.3
1982	Dec. 13	Western Arabian Peninsula	2800	6.0
1983	Oct. 30	Turkey	1342	6.9
1985	Mar. 3	near coast of central Chile	177	7.8
1985	Sep. 19	Mexico, Michoacan	9500	8.1
1986	Oct. 10	El Salvador	1000	5.5
1987	Mar. 6	Colombia-Ecuador	1000	7.0
1988	Aug. 20	Nepal-India	1450	6.6
1988	Dec. 7	Turkey-USSR	25000	7.0
1989	Jan. 22	USSR, Tajik	274	5.3
1989	Aug. 1	Western Iran	120	5.8
1989	Oct. 18	U.S., Southern California	62	7.1
1989	Oct. 18	Northeastern China	29	5.3
1989	Oct. 29	Algeria	30	5.7
1989	Dec. 27	near S.E. coast of Australia	12	5.4
1990	Mar. 4	Pakistan	11	6.1
1990	Apr. 26	China, Qinghai Province	126	6.9
1990	May 30	Northern Peru	135	6.5
1990	May 30	Romania	9	6.7
1990	June 20	Western Iran	50000	7.7
1990	July 16	Luzon, Philippine Islands	1621	7.8
1990	Nov. 6	Southern Iran	22	6.8
1990	Dec. 13	Sicily	15	5.1

Source: *Energy, Mines and Resources Canada*

Major Earthquakes in Canada, 1970–92*

Date		Location	Magnitude	Damage
1970	June 24	West of Vancouver Island	7.0	
1971	March 13	West of Vancouver Island	6.4	
1971	March 26	Yukon—Alaska Border	5.8	
1972	July 5	West of Vancouver Island	5.7	
1972	July 23	West of Vancouver Island	5.8	
1972	July 30	Southeast Alaska. Felt in BC and the Yukon	7.6	
1972	Nov. 21	Melville Island NWT	5.7	
1973	July 1	Southeast Alaska. Felt in BC and the Yukon	6.1	
1974	Oct. 16	East of Newfoundland	5.8	
1975	Oct. 6	South of Newfoundland	5.7	
1976	Feb. 23	West of Vancouver Island	6.0	
1976	Dec. 20	West of Vancouver Island	6.7	
1978	June 2	West of Vancouver Island	5.7	
1979	Feb. 28	Yukon—Alaska Border	7.2	Minor
1980	Dec. 17	West of Vancouver Island	6.8	
1982	May 15	West of Vancouver Island	5.7	
1983	June 28	Yukon—Alaska Border	6.0	
1983	Oct. 28	Southern Utah. Felt in southern BC and Alberta	7.3	
1984	June 24	West of Vancouver Island	5.8	
1985	Oct. 5	Mackenzie Mountains, NWT	6.6	Major landslides
1985	Dec. 23	Mackenzie Mountains, NWT	6.9	

▶

Date		Location	Magnitude	Damage
1987	Nov. 17	Gulf of Alaska. Felt in BC and the Yukon	6.9	
1987	Nov. 23	Yukon—Alaska Border	5.7	
1987	Nov. 30	Gulf of Alaska. Felt in BC and the Yukon	7.6	
1987	Nov. 30	Gulf of Alaska	5.9	
1987	Dec. 1	Gulf of Alaska	5.7	
1988	March 6	Gulf of Alaska. Felt in BC and the Yukon	7.6	
1988	March 6	Gulf of Alaska	6.2	
1988	March 25	Mackenzie Mountains, NWT	6.0	
1988	Nov. 25	southern Quebec	6.5	Widespread minor damage
1989	March 13	northern Quebec	5.7	
1989	Dec. 25	northern Quebec	6.1	
1990	July 11	BC—Alaska Border	5.8	
1991	Dec. 19	west of Vancouver Island	5.7	
1992	Jan. 2	west of Vancouver Island	6.0	
1992	Jan. 4	Keewatin District, NWT	6.0	
1992	April 6	west of Vancouver Island	6.8	
1992	April 6	west of Vancouver Island	6.0	
1992	April 23	west of Vancouver Island	5.7	
1992	Aug. 7	Gulf of Alaska. Felt in the Yukon	6.5	

Source: *Geophysics Division, Geological Survey of Canada*   *Earthquakes in or near Canada with a magnitude of 5.7 or higher.

Worldwide Earthquakes, per year

Magnitude	Average number	Magnitude	Average number
8	2	5	3 000
7	20	4	15 000
6	100	3	more than 100 00

Source: *Energy, Mines and Resources Canada*

Geological Time Periods

The story of planet earth is one of continuous change. Fossils, rock records and radioactive dating show three marked changes in the patterns of plant and animal life. These times of change in the most recent 570 million years of the earth's history are divided by geologists into three eras: Paleozoic (ancient life); Mesozoic (age of reptiles); and Cenozoic (age of mammals). The more than 4 billion years before the start of the Paleozoic era are referred to as Precambrian time. Each geological unit is divided further: the eras into periods, the periods into epochs.

The names of the time periods are taken either from the geographic locality where the fossil information was best displayed or first studied, or from some characteristic of the geological formations. For example, the Jurassic period is named from the Jura Mountains of France and Switzerland, and the Carboniferous is named from the coal-bearing sedimentary rocks.

Era	Period	Epoch	Years Ago	Changes and Characteristics
Precambrian Time			4.5 bil.?	Cooling and melting of the earth's crust. Evidence of bacteria, the first known living things, about 3.5 billion years ago.
Paleozoic	Cambrian		575 mil.	Seas spread across North America. First fishes appear. Greatest development of invertebrates.
	Ordovician		480 mil.	Floods sometimes cover two-thirds of North America. Jawless fish appear. Algae become plentiful.
	Silurian		435 mil.	Coral reefs are formed. First amphibians and forests of fernlike trees appear.

▶

Era	Period	Epoch	Years Ago	Changes and Characteristics
▶	Devonian		405 mil.	Gas and oil are formed. Many kinds of fish in seas and fresh water. First insects appear.
	Carboniferous —Mississippian		350 mil.	Warm, moist climate produces great forests that later become coal beds. Fish and amphibians plentiful.
	—Pennsylvanian		310 mil.	Appalachian Mountains are formed. Large amounts of coal are formed. First reptiles appear.
	Permian		270 mil.	Ural Mountains are formed. Glaciers in southern hemisphere melt. Gas, oil and salt are formed. Reptiles developing.
Mezozoic	Triassic		225 mil.	Reptiles dominate the earth. First mammals appear.
	Jurassic		180 mil.	Shallow seas invade continents. Dinosaurs reach their largest size. First birds appear.
	Cretaceous		130 mil.	Seas spread over the land. Flowering plants appear. Dinosaurs die out. Most chalk deposits are made.
Cenozoic	Tertiary	Paleocene	65 mil.	Mountains become higher. Climates less uniform. Mammals, flowering plants become common.
		Eocene	50 mil.	Climate mild. Seas flood shores of continents. Primitive apes, early horses and elephants appear.
		Oligocene	38 mil.	Climate mild. Alps and Himalayas begin to rise. Many volcanoes. Oil and natural gas are formed.
		Miocene	27 mil.	Climate mild. Rocky Mountains and Sierra Nevadas forming. Flowering plants and trees resemble modern kinds.
		Pliocene	10 mil.	Climate cooling. Mountains rising in western Canada. Many volcanoes. Birds and mammals spread around the world. Humans appear near end of epoch.
	Quaternary	Pleistocene	1.5 mil.	Great ice sheets cover northern hemisphere. Climate cool. Mountains continue to rise in North America. Early humans reach Europe and North America.
		Recent, or Holocene	10 000	Glaciers melt and Great Lakes are formed. Climate warm. Humans live in most parts of the earth, develop agriculture, use metals, domesticate animals.

Source: *Gage Canadian Dictionary* by Walter S. Avis, et al. Copyright © 1983 Gage Publishing Limited. *Reproduced by permission.*

June Spelled Doom for Dinosaurs

Dinosaurs may have met their end one fateful day in June, according to a new study of the remains of water lilies. The study fleshes out, in chilling detail, some of the events that may have followed the catastrophic impact of a meteorite, now believed to have crashed into the earth near the Yucatan peninsula in Mexico.

The collision threw up huge clouds of dust and debris, blocking out the sun and sending temperatures falling from an average 19°C to -10°C. Water froze and many plants were killed, according to research by Dr. Jack Wolfe of the US Geological Survey in Denver.

The study, recently reported in *Nature*, suggests the effect of the "impact winter" may have been devastating for hundreds of species. The theory is based on a geological survey of an ancient lily pond at Teapot Dome, Wyoming, which contains remains of pond plant material that normally decays before being preserved as fossils. Analysis of hundreds of specimens enabled Wolfe to place the date of impact, thought to have occurred in early June.

The reconstructed time table of events in the Teapot Dome study suggests the impact winter ▶

▶ lasted only one to two weeks, given the survival of several aquatic species, and was followed immediately by greenhouse warming. Temperatures kept rising to more than 30°C, inaugurating a period of hot, wet conditions. This longer-lasting change may have had the greatest effect on plants and animals.

A later study of the Chicxulub crater in Mexico suggests that the impact winter may have lasted for months. Scientists studying the crater now feel that the meteor that collided with earth may have been 16 km in diameter and was travelling anywhere from 50,000 km/h (if it was an asteroid) to 160,000 km/h (if it was a comet) when it hit, blasting a crater nearly 320 km wide and throwing up a much larger cloud of dust and debris than was previously thought.

Source: *Royal Tyrrell Museum of Paleontology*

Dinosaur Skull First Found in Alberta

....

*I**n the spring of 1884, Joseph Tyrrell, a geologist with Geological Survey of Canada, arrived in Alberta looking for coal deposits. While studying exposed rocks at Kneehill Creek in the Drumheller area, he came face-to-face with a 70-million-year-old dinosaur skull. Later called Albertasaurus, it was the first dinosaur skull found anywhere in world.*

Tyrrell was not an expert on dinosaurs. Very few people in Canada were at the time. The existence of the huge reptiles had been established by British scientists only a few decades earlier. Tyrrell realized the skeleton should be preserved. He had the fossil bones loaded onto a buckboard and taken to Fort Calgary. The load was so heavy that the wagon axle broke, and several trips were necessary to cart the specimens out of the valley.

Minerals

Minerals are all around us—everything from ice on the sidewalk in winter to the salt you sprinkle on French fries. Each mineral species has a definite chemical composition and a crystal structure.Therefore, ice is mineral because it is solid, but water is not because it is liquid. Sea shells are not minerals because, although they are solid, they are organic—formed by living creatures.

The physical properties of minerals—their form and hardness—are easy to recognize. Specimens may be composed of large showy crystals or millions of tiny crystals fused together. The external shape (or habit) is determined by the internal arrangement of atoms. The atoms are joined together in a framework to form minute building blocks. Called the crystal structure, the arrangement of atoms is unique for each mineral. The habit is also partly the result of the environment in which a mineral grows. If there is enough space during growth, the mineral develops smooth external crystals. However, conditions are seldom ideal and more often than not, minerals grow together as masses of fibres, grains, plates or spheres. The hardness of a mineral—its resistance to scratching—is measured by the Mohs scale.

The optical properties of minerals—lustre, colour and transparency—are easily observed by the unaided eye; other optical properties are determined with microscopes. Lustre is the quality of light reflected from the surface of a mineral. For instance, the highly reflective surfaces of pyrite produce the metallic lustre characteristics of most sulphide minerals. Many silicates, carbonates and other minerals have a softer, but still bright, glassy or vitreous lustre. Minerals with surfaces that reflect light more diffusely, such as serpentine asbestos or cyanotrichite, are said to have silky or earthly lustres. Lustre is reliable means of distinguishing minerals.

Colour can also be very distinctive, but is ▶

Did You Know?

....

*M**ore than 380,000 Canadians worked in the minerals industries in 1990, a decrease of 2.9 per cent from 1989. Mineral manufacturing industries, such as Inco, Noranda, etc, employed 237,000 people; while 74,800 worked in mining and 75,500 in the smelting, refining and crude steel industries.*

▶ not always reliable in identifying most minerals because even minerals of the same species can occur in many colours. Quartz, which is quite common, can be as clear as water or the deepest purple because of flaws in the mineral's crystal structure. Colour can also be affected by the presence of major elements in the mineral: copper in azurite produces an intense azure blue; arsenic makes realgar appear red; and curite is coloured orange by uranium. Colour can also be produced by physical structure. When light strikes very thin layers within the structure of labradorite, the mineral glows with iridescent colours, an effect much like that of sunlight striking a film of gasoline on a puddle, causing a rainbow of colour.

Determining the chemical composition and crystal structure of minerals requires laboratory techniques and tools such as the electron microbe, a reliable tool for analysing chemical composition. Crystal structure is determined using an X-ray diffractometer. Other mineral properties such as magnetism, fluorescence and radioactivity are more easily detected: magnetite and pyrrhotite are noticeably magnetic; some minerals, such as scheelite, fluoresce strongly in ultra-violet light; and all uranium and thorium-bearing minerals are radioactive. The radiation can easily be detected with a Geiger counter or scintillometer.

Source: *Geological Survey of Canada*

Mohs Scale of Hardness

Mohs scale indicates the relative hardness of minerals. Each mineral listed is hard enough to scratch a smooth surface of those below it.

10	Diamond	5	Apatite
9	Corundum	4	Fluorite
8	Topaz	3	Calcite
7	Quartz	2	Gypsum
6	Orthoclase	1	Talc

Source: *Geological Survey of Canada*

Canada's Place as a World Producer

Mineral	World Rank	Mineral	World Rank
Zinc	1	Platinum	3
Asbestos	2	Sulphur	3
Magnesium	2	Cadmium	4
Nickel	2	Copper	4
Potash	2	Gold	5
Tantalum	2	Silver	5
Coal	3	Iron ore	7
Lead	3		

Source: *based on 1990 statistics, Statistics Canada*

What's in a Name?

*M*ore than 3,000 minerals have been recognized and each year the number increases by about 100. New mineral names are approved by the Commission of New Minerals and New Mineral Names, established in 1959 by the International Mineralogical Association. The mineralogist who conducted the study to determine a new mineral normally suggests its name.

Minerals can be named after a locality (Athabascaite), an institution (Mcgillite), the chemical composition (Cobaltite) or in honour of a person (Weloganite)—named for Sir William Logan, geologist and founder of the Geological Survey of Canada.

Source: *Wat on Earth, Spring 1992*

Earth Sciences Museums*

Maritime Region:

☐ **St. Lawrence Miner's Museum**
St. Lawrence, Nfld A0E 2V0. (709) 873-2222. No
charge. Open in summer.

☐ **Fundy Geological Museum**
4028 Eastern Avenue, Parrsboro, NS B0M 1S0. (902)
254-3814. No charge. Open May to June and Sept. to
Oct. - 5 days; summer - 7 days; winter by
appointment.

☐ **Inverness Miner's Museum**
Lower Railway Street, Inverness, NS B0E 1N0. (902)
258-2097. Entrance fee. Open all year.

☐ **Mineral and Gem Geological Museum**
1 Eastern Avenue, Parrsboro, NS B0M 1S0. (902)
254-2627. No charge. Open in summer and fall.

☐ **Springhill Miner's Museum**
Black River Road, Springhill, NS B0M 1X0. B0M 1X0
(902) 597-3449. Entrance fee. Open spring, summer
and fall.

Central Canada:

☐ **Alcan Museum**
1188 Sherbrooke Street West, Montreal, Quebec H3A
3G2. (514) 848-8187. No charge. Open all year.

☐ **Musée de Géologie**
Laval University, Pavillon Pouliot, 4th floor, Sainte
Foy, Quebec G1K 7P4. (418) 656-2193. No charge.
Open all year.

☐ **Musée minéralogique d'Asbestos**
104 Letendre Street, Asbestos, Quebec J1T 1E3.
(819) 879-6444. No charge. Open in summer.

☐ **Musée mineralogique et minier de la Région de
l'amiante**
671 Smith Blvd. South, Thetford Mines, Quebec G6G
5T3. Entrance fee. Open all year.

☐ **Musée régional mines de Malartic**
650 rue da la Paix, Abitibi East, Malartic, Quebec J0Y
1Z0. (819) 757-4677. Entrance fee. Open all year.

☐ **Biology and Earth Sciences Museum**
University of Waterloo, Waterloo, Ontario N2L 3G1.
(519) 885-1211, ext. 2469. No charge. Open all year.

☐ **Miller Museum of Geology and Minerology**
Queen's University, Dept. of Geological Sciences,
Miller Hall, Kingston, Ontario K7L 3N6. (613) 545-
2597. No charge. Open all year.

☐ **Oil Museum of Canada**
Oil Springs, 35 km southeast of Sarnia, Ontario N0N
1P0. (519) 834-2840. Entrance fee. Open in summer

and fall. Tours all year.

☐ **The Petrolia Discovery Foundation**
Blind Line, Petrolia, Ontario N0N 1R0. (519) 882-
0897. Entrance fee. Open in summer and fall.

☐ **Timmins Museum**
70 Legion Drive, South Porcupine, Ontario P4N 1B3.
(705) 235-5066. No charge. Open all year.

Western Canada:

☐ **Stonewall Quarry Park**
299 North Main Street, Stonewall, Manitoba R0C 2Z0.
(204) 467-5354. Entrance fee. Open all year.

☐ **Geological Museum**
University of Saskatchewan, Geological Sciences
Building, Saskatoon, Saskatchewan S7N 0W0. (306)
966-5683. No charge. Open all year.

☐ **Frank Slide Interpretive Centre**
1 km north of Frank, Alberta T0K 0E0. (403) 562-
7388. No charge. Open all year.

☐ **Museum of Geology**
University of Alberta, basement of Earth Sciences
Building, Edmonton Alberta T6G 2E3. (403) 492-
3265. No charge. Open all year.

☐ **Royal Tyrrell Museum of Palaeontology**
Midland Provincial Park, Drumheller, Alberta T0Y 0Y0.
(403) 823-7707. Entrance fee. Open all year.

☐ **Field Station of the Tyrrell Museum**
Dinosaur Provincial Park, Patricia, Alberta T0J 2K0.
(403) 378-4342. No charge. Open all year.

☐ **British Columbia Museum of Mining**
PO Box 188, Britannia Beach, BC V0N 1J0. Tel
(604) 688-8735. Entrance fee. Open in summer and
fall. All year for groups.

☐ **Manson Creek-Omenica Museum**
General Delivery, Manson Creek, BC V0J 2H0. Radio
telephone only. No charge. Open all year.

☐ **M.Y. Williams Geological Museum**
University of British Columbia, 6339 Stores Road,
Vancouver BC V6T 2B4. Tel
(604) 228-5586 No charge. Open all year.

☐ **Princeton and District Museums**
167 Vermilion Street, Princeton BC V0X 1W0. Tel
(604) 285-7588. No charge. Summer (30 June - 31
August)

☐ **Keno City Mining Museum**
Keno City, Yukon Y0B 1J0. (403) 995-2792. No
charge. Open in summer.

*Small museums, devoted entirely to one or more areas of the Earth Sciences

PHYSICAL SCIENCES

Physics and chemistry constitute the physical sciences. **Chemistry** concerns itself with the composition, properties, and reactions of substances. Organic chemistry, one of the two main branches of chemistry, specializes in the composition, properties, and reactions of hydrocarbon compounds. The other branch, inorganic chemistry, deals primarily with the elements and compounds that do not include hydrocarbons. **Physics** concerns itself with universal aspects of nature—forces, energy, structure of matter, and their interactions. Some of its particular fields are: plasma physics, optics and quantum optics, particle physics, geophysics, biophysics, and acoustics. As basic sciences, physics and chemistry permeate all sciences and technologies.

Common Chemistry Terms

Acid: a substance that in liquid form will turn blue litmus paper red, react with alkalis (bases) to form salts, and dissolve metals to form salts.

Alkali: Any compound that has chemical qualities of a base, such as reacting with acid to form salts.

Atomic Weight (Mass): The relative mass of an atom, based on a scale in which a specific carbon atom is assigned a mass value of 12.

Base: an alkaline substance, either molecular or ionic in form, that will accept or receive a proton from another chemical unit.

Catalyst: a substance that accelerates a chemical reaction without becoming a part of the end product of the reaction.

Compound: A substance formed by the combination of two or more chemical elements that cannot be separated from the combination by physical means. The constituent atoms, however, can usually be separated by means of chemical reactions.

Electron: A negatively-charged particle that moves in orbit about the nucleus of an atom.

Element: A substance composed of atoms with the same atomic number or the same number of protons in their nuclei.

Isotope: One of two or more atoms having the same atomic number, but a different mass number.

Mass Number: the atomic weight of an isotope, calculated from the number of protons and neutrons in the nucleus.

Matter: Anything that has weight or fills space, such as a solid, liquid, or gas.

Polymer: a huge molecule composed of repeating units of the same molecule.

Valence: a number that represents the combining power of an element, ion, or radical.

PROFILE—ABRAHAM GESNER, 1797–1864

*A*braham Gesner was a medical doctor who was more interested in rocks and chemistry, so he left medicine and his Nova Scotia home in 1837. Hired by New Brunswick as Provincial Geologist in 1838, Gesner was Canada's first official geologist and held the first such appointment in the British Empire. When he was laid off in 1842 due to government "downsizing," he opened Canada's first public museum in Saint John to display his mineral collection and to earn some badly needed cash.

Gesner is perhaps best known as the inventor of kerosene. In 1846 in Charlottetown, he demonstrated its use as a clean, bright lamp oil; it was an incredible improvement over whale oil, tallow or seal oil. Then he invented a process for distilling kerosene from the Albertite, and patented the process in 1854. Unfortunately Gesner was too late; a Scottish chemist had patented a similar process in England in 1850 and Gesner had to pay royalties to use his own process.

His misfortunes increased. In 1852, Gesner had become embroiled in a legal battle over the right to mine Albertite, the mineral used in his kerosene process. The case focused partly on what Albertite really was—whether it was a bitumen, and therefore not included in coal leases, as Gesner contended, or a coal, as the Albert Mining Company contended. The jury ruled it was a coal and Gesner not only lost the right to mine Albertite, he was ruined financially. (As we now know, the jury was wrong.) In 1854, Gesner left for New York and formed the North American Gaslight Company. Three years later, the first successful oil wells were drilled, and petroleum soon replaced kerosene. Gesner died in 1864.

Gairdner Awards

The Gairdner Foundation was established by James Arthur Gairdner, a Torontonian born in 1893. Gairdner was a scholar, an athlete and had a successful career in the investment business; he also had a lifelong interest in clinical medicine and medical research that lead him to believe that the achievements of medical scientists should be recognized. The Gairdner Foundation has given awards to medical scientists from many countries since 1959. The Foundation has honoured 230 scientists during its history and 40 of those have subsequently received a Nobel Prize for their work as well. The winners of the 1993 Gairdner International Awards were announced in March.

Dr. Mario R. Capecchi (University of Utah) and Dr. Oliver Smithies (University of North Caroline at Chapel Hill) for their independent work on a technique of gene targetting that is rapidly increasing our understanding of genetic diseases.

Dr. Alvan R. Feinstein (Yale University) for his contributions to clinical epidemiology. Modern clinical epidemiology is a scientific discipline for the study of the causes, diagnosis, prognosis and therapy of disease.

Dr. Stanley B. Prusiner (University of California) for his contributions to our understanding of brain degeneration.

Dr. Michel M. Ter-Pogossian (Washington University, St. Louis) is recognized for his contributions to the development of the PET scanner, which is useful in the study of brain function as well as the study of biochemical activity in other tissue.

Canada's Chemists Bring You— Recycled Roads

Asphalt road materials are complicated mixtures of oil-based compounds. In hot summer months, they tend to "flow," and ruts form in roads. In winter, the material becomes brittle and can snap like cold taffy. Ever increasing road traffic combines with unforgiving winters to produce annoying— and dangerous—bumps and potholes. When custom plastics are added to asphalt however, the long plastic molecules "knit" the asphalt together. The resulting road surface is stiffer and less prone to rutting in summer, but more flexible and less likely to crack in winter.

Imagine a pothole free world! A University of Toronto research team did. Led by chemical engineering professor Ray Woodhams and supported by the Ontario Centre for Materials Research (OCMR), one of Ontario's seven Centres of Excellence, they even added a new twist. Rather than using custom-made (and costly) plastics the way they do in Europe, they asked, "Why not use old plastic bottles, garbage bags or old tires?" By recycling these materials as asphalt modifiers, the life of roads could be doubled or tripled. The life of landfill sites and cars could also be extended. And best of all, the resulting asphalt itself would be recyclable.

After a decade of work, the research team was successful. For the first time ever, they were able to permanently stabilize poly-ethylene in asphalt, using a blend of polymers including recycled and plastic waste. Cold weather testing has proven successful, and the university-developed technology has been transferred to private industry. An exclusive license has been granted to small Ontario company, Polyphalt Ltd., for worldwide commercial development.

Green Ink

*N*orth America's first geochemist, Thomas Steery Hunt was one of the most versatile scientists of his time. A native of Norwich, Connecticut, he came to Canada in 1847 at the urging of Sir William Logan to join the Geological Survey as a chemist and mineralogist. The lab he established in Montreal introduced experimental chemistry in Canada. While a chemistry professor at McGill University in 1862, he invented the green ink used to print US and Canadian bank notes.

Common Physics Terms

Acceleration: the rate of change of velocity with respect to time.

Anode: The positive terminal of an electric current flow. In a vacuum tube, electrons flow from the cathode to the anode.

Cathode: The negative terminal of an electric current system. In vacuum tube, the filament serves as the source electrons.

Conduction: the transfer of heat by molecular motion from a source of high temperature to a region of lower temperature, tending towards a result of equalized temperatures.

Convection: The mechanical transfer of heated molecules of a gas or liquid from a source to another area, as when a room is warmed by the movement of air molecules heated by a radiator.

Electromotive Force: The force that causes the movement of electrons through an electrical circuit.

Energy: the ability to perform work. Energy may be changed from one form to another, as from heat to light, but normally it cannot be created or destroyed.

Force: the influence on a body that causes it to accelerate.

Heat: A form of energy that results from the disordered motion of molecules. As the motion becomes more rapid and disordered, the amount of heat is increased.

Mass: a measure of the amount of matter. Near the surface of earth, it is roughly equivalent to weight.

Momentum: the mathematical product of the mass of a moving object and its velocity.

Velocity: The speed with which an object travels over a specified distance during a measured amount of time.

Weight: The force on a body produced by the downward pull of gravity on it.

Did You Know?

*D*awson City was named for the noted Montreal geologist, George Mercer Dawson. Nicknamed "Klondike Dawson," he explored and mapped the Yukon nearly a decade before the Klondike gold discovery of 1896. Goldrush prospectors used his maps to blaze their trails.

Chemistry at 10^{-15} Seconds

*D*r. Geraldine Kenney-Wallace, chemist and president of McMaster University, is a pioneer in the field of ultrafast laser spectroscopy, at the pico (10^{-12}) and femto-second (10^{-15}) level. Her research enables the design of new systems for ultrafast switching and gating, so important to advances in microelectronic circuitry.

Food from Garbage

*C*ereal straws, sawdust and sugar cane waste are grist for one scientist's food mill. Dr. Moo-Young, a biotechnologist and biochemical engineer at the University of Waterloo, has devised a three-step process for converting these leftovers into nourishing food for farm animals. The resulting microbial biomass protein is roughly 50% protein, 25% carbohydrate, 10% fat, 10% lignin and 5% vitamins. It also has dietary fibre and no cholesterol.

Basic Laws of Physics

■ Newton's Laws of Motion

Newton's laws apply to objects in a vacuum, and are difficult to observe in the "real" world where forces such as friction affect all objects.

First Law: Any object at rest tends to stay at rest, and a body in motion will continue that motion with a constant velocity unless acted upon by some external unbalanced force.

Second Law: The acceleration of an object is directly proportional to the force acting upon it, and is inversely proportional to the mass of the object.

Third Law: Every action generates an equal and opposite reaction.

■ Gravity

When an object is dropped near the surface of the earth, it increases in speed as it falls. By rolling balls down inclined planes Galileo discovered that acceleration due to gravity is the same for all objects, independent of their weight (mass). For example, if you drop this book and a heavy dictionary simultaneously, they will reach to floor at the same time. You can try the same experiment with a heavy book and a single sheet of paper. The paper is affected by the resistance of the air. Then crumple the paper, and try again.

Gravity is the force that tends to attract objects to the centre of a cellestial body, such as the earth, the moon or Mars. The weight of an object at the earth's surface is mainly due to the force of gravity between the earth and the object. The force exerted by the earth varies with the object's distance from the centre of the earth. Therefore the weight of an object is not the same at the earth's surface as it is on the moon or in space.

■ Laws of Thermodynamics

Sadi Carnot (1796-1832) stated in his work *Reflections on the Motive Power of Fire* that mechanical energy could be produced by the simple transfer of heat.

First Law: In a closed system, energy appears to be conserved in all but nuclear reactions and other extreme conditions.

Second Law: In a closed system, heat never travels from a low to a higher temperature in a self sustaining process. In a closed system, entropy (disorder) always increases.

■ Two Basic Laws of Quantum Physics

Heisenberg's Uncertainty Principle: It is impossible to specify completely the position and momentum of a particle, such as an electron.

Pauli's Exclusion Principle: No two electrons of the same atom can have identical values for all four quantum numbers: at least one quantum number must be different.

■ Electricity

Ohm's Law: Electric current is directly proportional to the potential difference and inversely proportional to resistance. If current (I) is measured in amperes; potential difference (V) in volts, and resistance (R) in volts, the formula is as follows: $I = V/R$

From Fingerprints to Gemprint

*R**euniting stolen diamonds with their owners has long been a dilemma for police—thieves are understandably reluctant to reveal the source of their ill-gotten gains. Herman Wallner, a Canadian inventor, has come up with a solution—a "fingerprint" of the gem itself—the Gemprint. Like each person, each diamond is unique. When a low-density laser beam is passed through a gem, the diamond's distinctive light pattern can be projected onto a screen. A computer then scans, digitizes, and stores the pattern. Thanks to Wallner, the "jewelnappers" can be caught and the gems returned. Well, as long as their owners have had them "gemprinted."*

The Elements

(listed by name, symbol and atomic number)

An element is a substance composed of atoms that are chemically alike—each atom has an identical number of protons in its nucleus. Furthermore, there is no known process to break these elements down into more fundamental substances.

actinium	Ac	89	hafnium	Hf	72	praseodymium	Pr	59
aluminum	Al	13	hahnium	Ha	105	promethium	Pm	61
americium	Am	95	helium	He	2	protactinium	Pa	91
antimony	Sb	51	holmium	Ho	67	radium	Ra	88
argon	Ar	18	hydrogen	H	1	radon	Rn	86
arsenic	As	33	indium	In	49	rhenium	Re	75
astatine	At	85	iodine	I	53	rhodium	Rh	45
barium	Ba	56	iridium	Ir	77	rubidium	Rb	37
berkelium	Bk	97	iron	Fe	26	ruthenium	Ru	44
beryllium	Be	4	krypton	Kr	36	rutherfordium	Rf	104
bismuth	Bi	83	lanthanum	La	57	samarium	Sm	62
boron	B	5	lawrencium	Lr	103	scandium	Sc	21
bromine	Br	35	lead	Pb	82	selenium	Se	34
cadmium	Cd	48	lithium	Li	3	silicon	Si	14
calcium	Ca	20	lutetium	Lu	71	silver	Ag	47
californium	Cf	98	magnesium	Mg	12	sodium	Na	11
carbon	C	6	manganese	Mn	25	strontium	Sr	38
cerium	Ce	58	mendelevium	Md	101	sulfur	S	16
cesium	Cs	55	mercury	Hg	80	tantalum	Ta	73
chlorine	Cl	17	molybdenum	Mo	42	technetium	Tc	43
chromium	Cr	24	neodymium	Nd	60	tellurium	Te	52
cobalt	Co	27	neon	Ne	10	terbium	Tb	65
copper	Cu	29	neptunium	Np	93	thallium	Tl	81
curium	Cm	96	nickel	Ni	28	thorium	Th	90
dysprosium	Dy	66	niobium	Nb	41	thulium	Tm	69
einsteinium	Es	99	nitrogen	N	7	tin	Sn	50
erbium	Er	68	nobelium	No	102	titanium	Ti	22
europium	Eu	63	osmium	Os	76	tungsten	W	74
fermium	Fm	100	oxygen	O	8	uranium	U	92
fluorine	F	9	palladium	Pd	46	vanadium	V	23
francium	Fr	87	phosphorus	P	15	xenon	Xe	54
gadolinium	Gd	64	platinum	Pt	78	ytterbium	Yb	70
gallium	Ga	31	plutonium	Pu	94	yttrium	Y	39
germanium	Ge	32	polonium	Po	84	zinc	Zn	30
gold	Au	79	potassium	K	19	zirconium	Zr	40

Source: *Gage Canadian Dictionary*

It was all in the chemistry...

*O**n the evening of Friday, December 18, 1992 in Oakville, Manitoba, 29 of 41 CN freight cars jumped the track. The cars contained a potent cocktail of toxic and flammable chemicals—sulphuric acid, ethylene oxide, vinyl chloride, vinyl acetate, methanol, propane, sodium hydroxide and acetic anhydride.*

The freight cars holding the sulphuric acid and the sodium hydroxide substances ruptured and the Emergency Measures Organization ordered the immediate evacuation of the town. Fortunately, the railcars ruptured at the same time, and since they were positioned close together in the train (according to guidelines), when their contents spilled, the acid and the alkali neutralized each other. Given the cold weather, the substances reacted slowly; however, even if the spill had taken place in summer the result would not have differed. The mixing of suphuric acid with sodium hydroxide in July would still have resulted in heat, water and salt. The cleanup took a month, but due to happenstance, planning and chemistry, a greater disaster was averted.

Periodic Table of Elements

gases — *non-metals* — *other metals* — *transition metals* — *rare earth elements*

1	2	3	4	5	6	7	8	9	10	11	12	13	14	15	16	17	18
H 1, 1.00																	**He** 2, 4.00
Li 3, 6.94	**Be** 4, 9.01											**B** 5, 10.81	**C** 6, 12.01	**N** 7, 14.01	**O** 8, 15.99	**F** 9, 18.99	**Ne** 10, 20.17
Na 11, 22.98	**Mg** 12, 24.30											**Al** 13, 26.98	**Si** 14, 28.08	**P** 15, 30.97	**S** 16, 32.06	**Cl** 17, 35.45	**Ar** 18, 39.94
K 19, 39.00	**Ca** 20, 40.08	**Sc** 21, 44.95	**Ti** 22, 47.88	**V** 23, 50.94	**Cr** 24, 51.96	**Mn** 25, 54.93	**Fe** 26, 55.84	**Co** 27, 58.93	**Ni** 28, 58.69	**Cu** 29, 63.54	**Zn** 30, 65.39	**Ga** 31, 69.72	**Ge** 32, 72.59	**As** 33, 74.92	**Se** 34, 78.96	**Br** 35, 79.90	**Kr** 36, 83.80
Rb 37, 85.46	**Sr** 38, 87.62	**Y** 39, 88.90	**Zr** 40, 91.22	**Nb** 41, 92.90	**Mo** 42, 95.94	**Tc** 43, (98)	**Ru** 44, 101.07	**Rh** 45, 102.90	**Pd** 46, 106.42	**Ag** 47, 107.868	**Cd** 48, 112.41	**In** 49, 114.82	**Sn** 50, 118.71	**Sb** 51, 121.75	**Te** 52, 127.60	**I** 53, 126.90	**Xe** 54, 131.29
Cs 55, 132.90	**Ba** 56, 137.33	**La** 57, 138.90	**Hf** 72, 178.49	**Ta** 73, 180.94	**W** 74, 183.85	**Re** 75, 186.20	**Os** 76, 190.2	**Ir** 77, 192.22	**Pt** 78, 195.08	**Au** 79, 196.96	**Hg** 80, 200.59	**Tl** 81, 204.38	**Pb** 82, 207.2	**Bi** 83, 208.98	**Po** 84, (209)	**At** 85, (210)	**Rn** 86, (222)
Fr 87, (223)	**Ra** 88, 226.02	**Ac** 89, 227.02	**Unq** 104, (261)	**Unp** 105, (262)	**Unh** 106, (263)	**Uns** 107, (262)	**Uno** 108, (***)	**Une** 109, (***)	**Uun** 110, (***)								

Ce 58, 140.12	**Pr** 59, 140.90	**Nd** 60, 144.24	**Pm** 61, (145)	**Sm** 62, 150.36	**Eu** 63, 151.96	**Gd** 64, 157.25	**Tb** 65, 158.925	**Dy** 66, 162.50	**Ho** 67, 164.93	**Er** 68, 167.26	**Tm** 69, 168.93	**Yb** 70, 173.04	**Lu** 71, 174.96
Th 90, 232.03	**Pa** 91, 231.03	**U** 92, 238.02	**Np** 93, 237.04	**Pu** 94, (244)	**Am** 95, (243)	**Cm** 96, (247)	**Bk** 97, (247)	**Cf** 98, (251)	**Es** 99, (252)	**Fm** 100, (257)	**Md** 101, (258)	**No** 102, (259)	**Lr** 103, (260)

This is a table which shows the properties of the elements, in the order of their atomic mass or number, and arranged in horizontal rows (periods) and vertical columns (groups) to illustrate the occurance of similarities in the structure of their atoms. When the elements are arranged in this order, their chemical and physical properties show repeatable trends. This pattern in properties occurs periodically; that is the pattern is repeated in an orderly manner over time.

The order of the elements is that of their atomic numbers, the integers which are equal to the positive electrical charges of the atomic nuclei expressed in electronic units.

Loudness of Sounds

Intensity (decibels)	Loudness	Intensity (decibels)	Loudness
0	Threshold of hearing	70	Loud conversation
10 (1 bel)	Virtual silence	80	Door slamming
20	Quiet room	90	Busy typing room
30	Watch ticking at 1 m	100	Near loud motor horn
40	Quiet street	100	Pneumatic drill
50	Quiet conversation	120	Near airplane engine
60	Quiet motor at 1 m	130	Threshold of pain

A Pill for Diabetics.

*I**f insulin were taken by mouth, the digestive system would break it down and render it useless. Diabetics must therefore take insulin by injection. But a pill is on the horizon: Dr. Chris Orvig and his colleagues at the University of British Columbia in Vancouver have found a compound that mimics the action of insulin. In testing on diabetic rats, bis(maltolato)oxovanadium(IV) appears to pass through the digestive tract and find its way to body tissues intact.*

Science Centres and Museums

Maritime Region:

☐ **Electrical Engineering Museum**
University of New Brunswick, Dept. of Electrical Engineering, Head Hall, Fredericton, NB No charge. Open winter, spring and fall.

Central Canada:

☐ **Museum of Visual Science and Optometry**
University of Waterloo, Optometry Building, Columbia Street, Waterloo, Ontario N2L 3G1. Tel (519) 885-1211, ext. 3405. No charge. Open all year.

☐ **Hamilton Museum of Steam and Technology**
900 Woodward Avenue, Hamilton, Ontario L8H 7N2. Tel (416) 549-5225. Entrance fee. Open all year.

☐ **National Museum of Science and Technology**
1867 St. Laurent Blvd., Ottawa, Ontario K1G 5A3. Tel (613) 998-4566 Entrance fee. Open all year.

☐ **Ontario Science Centre**
770 Don Mills Road, Toronto, Ontario M3C 1T3. Tel (416) 429-4100. Open daily (except Christmas Day).

☐ **Science North**
100 Ramsay Lake Road, Sudbury, Ontario P3E 5S9. Tel (705) 522-3700 Entrance fee. Open all year.

Western Canada:

☐ **Alberta Science Centre**
701-11 Street SW, Calgary, Alberta T2P 2M5. Tel(403) 221-3700 No charge. Open all year.

☐ **Edmonton Space and Science Centre**
11211-142 Street, Edmonton, Alberta T5M 4A1. Tel(403) 452-9100 Entrance fee. Open all year.

☐ **Energeum**
640-5th Avenue S.W., Main Floor, Energy Resources Building, Calgary, Alberta T2P 3G4. Tel (403) 297-4293 No charge. Open all year.

☐ **Pacific Geoscience Centre**
9860 West Saanich Road, Sidney, BC V8L4B2. Tel(604) 363-6500 No charge. Open all year.

☐ **Science World**
1455 Quebec Street, Vancouver, BC V6A 3Z7. Tel (604) 687-8414   Entrance fee. Open daily, except Christmas Day.

Why does your newspaper turn yellow?

*N**ewsprint is made from a wood pulp, produced from groundwood that goes through very little chemical processing. The trouble is, this pulp contains lignin, a natural substance in trees that yellows when exposed to light and air.*

INVENTION AND SCIENTIFIC ACHIEVEMENT

Discoveries in technology, as well as achievements in science, are products of the human mind. Fascinated by ideas, inventors follow their curiosity. But they also possess the tenacity to overcome the many obstacles along the trail to discovery. Some remarkable Canadians and their contributions are noted in this section.

Canadian Nobel Laureates in Science and Medicine

1923	Dr. Frederick G. Banting	Medicine and Physiology	for the discovery of insulin
	Dr. J.J.R. Macleod		
1971	Dr. Gerhard Herzberg	Chemistry	for his contributions to the knowledge of electronic structure and geometry of molecules, particularly free radicals
1986	Dr. John Polyani	Chemistry	for contributions concerning the dynamics of elementary chemical reactions

Canadian Invention

The MacIntosh Apple In 1811, Scottish-born John McIntosh discovered wild apple trees on his farm near Dundela, Ontario. Of the several trees he transplanted, one produced a superior fruit. His son Alan went on to develop the variety, and McIntosh apples are now grown in many parts of North America. The original tree continued to bear fruit for 90 years.

Undersea Cable Frederick Gisbourne developed a method of insulating wire to make it saltwater resistant. Then in 1852, he successfully laid the first undersea telegraph cable in North America, linking New Brunswick and Prince Edward Island. Gisbourne also proposed a cable linking North America and Europe. With the financial backing of American industrialist Cyrus Field, the Atlantic Cable, connecting Ireland and Newfoundland, was completed in 1866.

The Railway Sleeping Car In 1857, Samuel Sharp designed and built the world's first railway sleeping car. The car had berths with spring mattresses and curtains for privacy. Sharp's invention was improved on by the American, George Pullman.

Standard Time In 1878, Sir Sandford Fleming, Canada's foremost railway surveyor and construction engineer, realized the new national railroad made local time keeping obsolete. He devised a method whereby the world is divided into 24 time zones. His system of Standard Time was adopted by the International Prime Meridian Conference in Washington, DC, in 1884, and is still used today.

First Radio Voice Message Reginald Fessenden, from East Bolton, Quebec, discovered a way to send actual sounds via radio waves. In 1906, he transmitted the world's first radio broadcast from his transmitter at Brant Rock, Massachusetts. Sailors aboard ships of the United Fruit Company in the Caribbean found themselves listening to a Christmas Eve broadcast of music and voice. Fessenden produced the program himself, and even sang and played carols on his violin.

Gas Mask In 1915, Dr. Cluny Macpherson designed the first gas mask, to protect troops from gas attacks during World War I.

The Snowmobile Fifteen-year-old Armand Bombardier built a prototype snowmobile in 1922 at his home in Valcourt, Quebec. Over the years, he refined the design and was granted a patent in 1937. At first he produced commercial vehicles, but in 1959 Bombardier perfected a sports model, the Ski-doo.

The First AC Radio Tube In 1925, Ted Rogers, a Torontonian, introduced the world's first batteryless radio. Gone were the days when programs faded away as batteries "died." The modern "plug in" radio was born. Rogers also built the world's first all-electric, batteryless broadcast station, CFRB.

The Variable Pitch Propeller Wallace Turnbull, an aeronautical engineer, worked on the variable pitch propeller in his home workshop in Rothesay, New Brunswick. This propeller was the first that could be adjusted in the air and adapted to the differing aerodynamic conditions of takeoff, climbing ▶

▶ and diving. Pilots could adjust the propeller's blades for takeoff and again during flight. It was successfully tested by the RCAF at Camp Borden in 1927.

Pablum Toronto doctors Alan Brown, F. Tisdall and T. Drake, working at the Hospital for Sick Children, became concerned about infant nutrition during the Depression. After much research and testing, they produced a precooked cereal—the now famous Pablum.

Table Hockey Dan Munroe created and built the first table hockey game to amuse his three children. In 1932 he patented the game, and first sold it through the T. Eaton Company. The Munroe family manufactured the first games by hand.

The Bush Plane The world's first bush aircraft was designed and built in Montreal by Robert Noorduyn in 1935. Norseman aircraft are noted for their performance in rugged terrain, and were known as "workhorses" of the North. Some are still in use.

The Paint Roller In 1940, Norman Breakey invented the paint roller in Toronto. Breakey revolutionized home decorating, but was unable to reap the financial benefits of his invention.

Electronic Synthesizer In 1945, the world's first electronic synthesizer, the Sackbut, was designed and built by Hugh Le Caine in his home studio. A research physicist with the National Research Council, Le Caine was also a composer. His piece "Dripsody," using only the sound of single drop of water, is recognized as an electronic music classic.

Cobalt Bomb In 1951, Dr. Harold Johns, working with others, created the "Cobalt-60 bomb" for the treatment of cancer. Cobalt radiation therapy units have revolutionized cancer treatment worldwide.

Laser Sailboat The Laser sailboat was designed and built in 1970 by three Canadian Olympic sailors: Bruce Kirby, Hans Fogh and Ian Bruce. An extremely stable, small pleasure craft, the Laser has given thousands of people their first introduction to sailing. The craft is now used throughout the world.

Steak Monitor The challenge of cooking T-bone steaks for hungry workers at the Great Lakes Power Company provided the impetus for Cathy Denomme of Wawa, Ontario to come up with a better way. Denomme is the inventor of No-Misteak, a handy device that, when pressed against cooking meat, registers its doneness.

Flat Electric Wall Plug In 1989, Bob Dickie of King City, Ontario invented a revolutionary wall plug—it's flat. The first major change to wall plugs in 75 years, the FlatPlug extends only one-quarter inch from the wall. The power cord exits and travels parallel to the wall. Dickie was motivated to create a safer plug while watching his two-year-old daughter at play.

Patents

If you have an idea for a new gizmo, what is required to have it patented? The Patent Office judges the idea based the following criteria:

1) the gizmo must be the first of its kind in the world;
2) the gizmo must be useful, and most importantly, it must work;
3) the gizmo must be obviously ingenious to others familiar with the field.

A patent gives you the right to exclude others from making, using or selling an invention from the day the patent is granted until 20 years after filing. Patents also provide useful technical information to the public.

Although individual inventors still apply for patents, the majority of applications now come from large corporations. Patents are granted by individual countries; so the protection of a Canadian patent extends throughout Canada alone. Patent rights in the United States or elsewhere must be applied for separately in the individual countries.

A list of the patents applied for and granted in Canada is issued once a week in The Patent Office Record. Among the 394 patents applied for during the week of 13 to 19 September 1992 are:

- ☐ an illuminated collar for pets
- ☐ a system for detecting the edge of an image
- ☐ a self-locking syringe
- ☐ a process for producing magnetic paint
- ☐ a remotely resettable time lock
- ☐ a process for painting snow

- [ ] a raising structure for lifting manhole covers
- [ ] and, a spiral football.

Patent applications to the Canadian Patent Office from 13 to 19 September 1992, inventions by country of origin

Country	Percent of applications*
United States	41
Japan	18
Canada	11
Germany	11
France	5
United Kingdom	4

Switzerland	3
Italy	2
Netherlands	2

* Ireland, Israel, Finland, Venezuela, Belgium, Austria, Denmark, Poland, South Africa, and Sweden share the remaining 3 percent.

Canadian Patent Firsts

1824 No. 1, first patent filed - Noah Cushing of Québec City, for a two compartment "washing and fulling machine."

1855 No. 429, first patent filed by a woman—Ruth Adams of Toronto, for a "reverse cooking stove."

Manning Awards

The Manning Awards were established to recognize and encourage innovation in Canada by honouring individuals who have created and promoted a new concept, process or product, which is beneficial to Canada and society. Administered by the Calgary-based, Ernest C. Manning Foundation, the awards are presented annually on the birthday of the former Alberta premier. Winners were announced September 22, 1993.

- [ ] **Ms. Dusanka Filipovic** (Toronto, Ontario) won the 1993 Principal Award for developing and patenting what has become known as "blue bottle" technology, which eliminates emissions of chlorofluorocarbons (CFCs) from equipment being repaired or abandoned. It is the only existing system that can capture all CFCs, preventing any escape to the atmosphere. Both the captured CFCs and the blue bottles themselves can be re-used.

- [ ] **Dr. David Schindler** (University of Alberta) won the 1993 Award of Distinction for his work at the Experimental Lakes Association program near Kenora, Ontario. His studies have led to recognition of the need to ban phosphates in detergents and he has also been influential in shaping legislation controlling sulphur dioxide emissions into the atmosphere.

Innovation Awards:

- [ ] **Fred Dimmick** (Parry Sound, Ontario) for patented illuminated signs that are reliable and energy efficient.

- [ ] **Yves Potvin** (Vancouver, BC) for his creation of meatless hot dogs and burgers that contain no cholesterol, low saturated fat and no preservatives.

Young Canadian Innovation Awards for 1993

- [ ] **Nathan Litke** (St. Catharines, Ontario): painting by computer
- [ ] **Samir Gupta** and **Denis Tsui** (Montreal, Quebec): fibre-optic biosensor for cell monitoring
- [ ] **Holly Pekau** (Calgary, Alberta): bioinorganic tracers
- [ ] **Francois Bouffard** and **Dany Theriault** (Levis, Quebec): plastic film electrostatic parabolic mirror

Science and Engineering Hall of Fame

Sixteen Canadians have been inducted into the Canadian Science and Engineering Hall of Fame. The inductees are outstanding researchers, inventors, and innovators who have won worldwide recognition for their accomplishments. The Hall of Fame portrait gallery is located at the National Research Council laboratories on Sussex Drive in Ottawa. Inductees are announced each October.

The Inductees

Maude Abbott (1869-1940)	- pathologist and specialist in congenital heart disease
Sir Frederick Banting (1891-1941)	- co-discoverer of insulin and Nobel laureate
Alexander Graham Bell (1847-1922)	- inventor of the telephone
J. Armand Bombardier (1907-1964)	- inventor of the snowmobile
Reginald Fessenden (1866-1932)	- pioneer in the development of the radio
Sir Sandford Fleming (1827-1915)	- architect of the transcontinental railway and inventor of standard time
Gerhard Herzberg (1904-)	- astrophysicist and Nobel laureate
Sir William Logan (1798-1875)	- first director of the Geological Survey of Canada
Elsie MacGill	- aeronautical engineer, oversaw WWII production of Hawker Hurricane fighter aircraft
Frere Marie-Victorinr (1885-1944)	- botanist, author and teache
Andrew GL MacNaughton (1887-1966)	- inventor of cathode-ray detection finder and military leader
Margaret Newton (1887-1971)	- plant pathologist, who developed techniques to combat wheat rust
Joseph-Alphonse Ouimet	- inventor, engineer and CBC president
Wilder Penfield (1891-1976)	- neurosurgeon who developed surgical treatments for epilepsy
John Polanyi (1929-)	- Nobel laureate whose work contributed to the development of laser chemistry
Wallace Turnbull (1870-1954)	- inventor of the variable pitch propellor

Organizations

Canadian Patent Office: A government agency that provides information to people wishing to file patents. Address: Commissioner of Patents, Consumer and Corporate Affairs Canada, 50 Victoria Street, Place du Portage, Phase 1, Hull, Québec. K1A 0C9

Canadian Industrial Innovation Centre: An organization helping Canadian innovators to develop their ideas. Address: 156 Columbia Street West, Waterloo, Ontario. N2I 3L3

Networks of Centres of Excellence in Canada: A federal program supporting the successful transfer of innovative research and development to private industry. Address: 200 Kent Street, Ottawa, Ontario. K1A 1H5

Women Inventors Project: A non-profit organization providing information to women inventors and to teachers. Address: 1 Greensboro Drive, Suite 302, Etobicoke, Ontario. M9W 1C8

Infant Evacuation Stretcher

Watching television coverage of the 1985 Mexico City earthquake, Wendy Murphy was touched by a pitiful sight—two rescuers carrying a large stretcher, with a tiny infant covered by a small rag rolling around on it. The image shook her. The Toronto research technician felt there must be a better way to rescue babies so she picked up a pencil and started drawing. A relative urged her to take out a patent on the resulting design, which she did. But it took another potential tragedy to prompt her to turn the drawing into a prototype. In 1987 there was a fire at the Hospital for Sick Children, where Murphy worked. Afterwards she told hospital officials about her idea; they ordered ten. The world's first infant evacuation stretcher was delivered to the hospital in spring 1990. Named "WEEVAC 6," the stretcher can transport six babies at a time.

THE ENVIRONMENT

The Earth Summit

The United Nations Conference on Environment and Development (the "Earth Summit") was held in Rio de Janeiro June 3 to 14, 1992. The Summit marked the 20th anniversary of the first environmental symposium sponsored by the UN, the United Nations Conference on the Human Environment, held in Stockholm in 1972.

The Stockholm Conference signalled the beginning of worldwide concern about the environment and resulted in the founding of the United Nations Environment Program. Since 1972, international co-operation has increased as nations deal with environmental issues that do not respect national boundaries, and Canada has joined in ratifying the following international agreements: the Geneva Convention on Long-range Transboundary Air Pollution (1979); the Helsinki Agreement, a 21- nation commitment to reduce sulphur dioxide emissions (1985); the Montreal Protocol on Substances that Deplete the Ozone Layer (1987); and the Basel Convention on Transboundary Movements of Hazardous Wastes (1989).

The focus of the Earth Summitt was on the relationship between the environment and economic development. During negotiations prior to the Summit, leaders were intent on devising a plan for sustainable development worldwide. The five main documents presented and signed at the Summit were:

Rio Declaration: A non-binding statement of principles to help define environmental policy.

Statement of Forest Priniciples: A non-binding statement of principles concerning the protection of forests.

Agenda 21: An non-binding 800-page document detailing proposals for protecting the environment without hampering economic development.

Convention on Climate Change ("Global Warming Convention"): A legally-binding treaty concerning climate change, including specific details about targets and timetables for reducing emissions of carbon dioxide and other greenhouse gases. The Convention also deals with the terms governing the way environmentally-sound technologies will be transferred to developing countries. This treaty was signed by 153 countries (including Canada).

It was not signed by: Albania, Cambodia, Czechoslovakia, Equatorial Guinea, Fiji, Iran, Iraq, Kuwait, Libya, Laos, Malaysia, Mali, Panama, Qatar, Saudi Arabia, Sierre Leone, South Africa, Syria, Turkey, United Arab Emirates and some states from the former USSR.

Biodiversity Convention: A legally-binding treaty concerning the protection of endangered species of plants and wildlife, and the financial aid available to developing countries to enable them to comply with the terms of the Convention. The treaty also deals with the terms under which developed countries will have access to biological resources found in areas such as the tropical forests in developing countries; the terms under which developing countries will have access to environmentally-sound technology and other new technologies based on materials and resources found in their territories; and the question of ownership and use of patent rights of the biotechnology produced from such materials. This treaty was signed by 156 countries (including Canada).

It was not signed by: Albania, Cambodia, Czechoslovakia, Equatorial Guinea, Fiji, Iraq, Kiribati, Libya, Laos, Mali, Saudi Arabia, Sierre Leone, Singapore, South Africa, Syria, Vietnam, United States and some states from the former USSR.

Did You Know?

The world's most accurate instrument for measuring ozone in the upper atmosphere—the Brewer Ozone Spectro-photometer—was designed by researchers at the Atmospheric Environment Service of Environment Canada. The device is now used by ozone monitoring stations worldwide.

Endangered Species in Canada[1]

An endangered species is any native species of plant or animal whose existence in Canada is threatened with imminent exitinction.

Species	Critical habitat

■ Birds

Species	Critical habitat
Eskimo Curlew	for breeding: tundra and lichen woodland
Harlequin Duck, Eastern population	coastal waters of Maritimes and New England
Henslow's Sparrow	Ontario
Kirtland's Warbler	dense jack pine stands
Loggerhead Shrike	old fields in eastern Man., Ont. and Que.
Mountain Plover	flat, heavily grazed grasslands of southern Alta and Sask.
Piping Plover	along beaches, close to the water
Sage Thrasher	breeds in southern interior BC, southeast Alta., southwest Sask.
Spotted Owl	old growth timber in southwest BC
Whooping Crane	breeding: generally Wood Buffalo National Park

■ Fish

Species	Critical habitat
Acadian Whitefish	Tusket and Petit rivers in southern NS
Aurora Trout	small lakes; however, no species left in wild
Salish Sucker	Campbell and Salmon rivers headwaters, BC

■ Mammals

Species	Critical habitat
Beluga (White Whale) St. Lawrence River stock	St. Lawrence estuary
Southeast Baffin stock	shallow coastal waters and river mouths; complete range unknown
Ungava Bay stock	Ungava Bay, northern Quebec
Bowhead Whale	winter: southern edge of pack ice
Eastern Cougar (mountain lion)	mixed and coniferous forest
Peary Caribou	Arctic tundra; with grasses and lichens
Right Whale	coasts of N. America, both Atlantic and Pacific, from tropics to sub-arctic
Sea Otter	Pacific Coast
Vancouver Island Marmot	alpine and subalpine areas, steep slopes, talus debris and open meadows
Wolverine, Eastern population	East of Hudson Bay and James Bay

■ Reptile

Species	Critical habitat
Blanchard's Cricket Frog	wet areas on Pelee Island and Point Pelee, Lake Erie
Blue Racer	Pelee Island, Ont.
Lake Erie Water Snake	western Lake Erie islands, Ont.
Leatherback Turtle	nesting: beaches

■ Plants

Species	Critical habitat
Cucumber Tree	9 sites in southwestern Ont.
Eastern Mountain Avens	generally in the Maritime provinces
Eastern Prickly Pear Cactus	southwestern Ont.
Engelmann's Quillwort	southern edge of Canadian Shield in Ont.
Furbish's Lousewort (herb)	banks of the upper Saint John R., NB
Gattinger's Agalinis	delta islands of St. Clair river in southwestern Ont.
Heart-Leaved Plantain	one site remains on the eastern shore of L. Huron; moist depressions in undisturbed deciduous woodland

▶

Species	Critical habitat
▶ Hoary Mountain Mint	one site in Ont.
Large Whorled Pogonia	only 2 known locations in Ont.
Pink Coreopsis (herb)	only in the Tusket R. valley, NS
Pink Milkwort (herb)	2 sites only in Lambton County, Ont.
Slender Bush Clover	one site in Windsor, Ont.
Slender Mouse-ear-cress	mixed grassland, southeast Alta to southwest Sask.
Small White Lady Slipper (orchid)	tall grass prairie, bogs, swampy meadows, remnant prairies, edge of thickets
Small Whorled Pogonia (orchid)	one site Elgin County, Ont.
Skinner's Agalinis	delta islands of St. Clair river in southwestern Ont.
Southern Maidenhair Fern	Fairmont Hot Springs, BC
Spotted Wintergreen	St. Williams and Wasaga areas in S. Ont.
Thread-leaved Sundew	only 3 small colonies in peat bogs in NS
Water-pennywort	only found at Wilson's Lake and Kejimkujik Lake in southeastern NS
White Prairie Gentian	only 20 plants in one southern Ont. site
Western Fringed Prairie Orchid	Manitoba
Wood Poppy	Ontario

Source: *Commitee on the Status of Endangered Wildlife in Canada*
(1) Status as of April 1993.

Pollution of the World's Oceans

POLLUTANTS	North Sea	Mediterranean Sea	Indian Ocean	Southeast Pacific Ocean	North Atlantic Ocean	North Pacific Ocean	Caribbean Sea	South Atlantic Ocean	South Pacific Ocean
Agricultural pesticides and fertilizers, runoff		■	■	■	■	■	■		
Food and beverage processing	■	■	■			■	■	■	■
Industries, chemical	■	■	■			■	■		
Industries, metal	■	■	■			■	■	■	
Industries, petrochemical	■	■	■			■	■	■	
Mining			■		■	■	■		■
Petroleum, drilling	■				■	■	■	■	■
Petroleum, transportation	■			■	■	■	■	■	
Pulp and paper manufacturing						■	■		
Radioactive wastes	■	■	■			■	■	■	
Sea-salt extraction			■				■		
Sewage	■	■	■		■	■	■	■	■
Sewage sludge, dumping	■					■	■		
Silt from coastal development				■	■			■	
Thermal sources				■		■	■	■	

Source: *Global Atlas*, Gage Educational Publishing Company

Names of Animal Babies

Adult name	A baby is known as:	Adult name	A baby is known as:
Ape or monkey	an infant	Harp or hooded seal	a whitecoat
Bat	a batling	Horse	a foal
Bear	a cub	Kangaroo	a joey
Beaver	a kit or pup	Koala	a cub or gum baby
Chicken	a chick	Moose	a calf
Crane	a craneling	Owl	an owlet
Dolphin	a cub	Parrot	a chick
Cat (domestic)	a cub, kit, kitling, kitten or pussy	Pheasant	a chick
Deer	a fawn	Pigeon	a squab
Dog (domestic)	a pup, puppy or whelp	Porcupine	a porcupette
Donkey	a colt or foal	Porpoise	a cub
Duck	a duckling	Rabbit	a fawn or kit
Eagle	an eaglet	Sheep	a lamb, hog, shearling, tag or teg
Elephant	a calf	Swan	a cygnet
Goat	a fawn or kid	Swine (domestic)	a garrow, grice, piglet or shoat
Goose	a gosling	Turkey	a poult
Hawk	an eyas	Zebra	a colt or fawn

Source: *Metro Toronto Zoo*

Animal Facts

Mammal group (species)	Length (avg. m)	Height (avg. m)	Weight (avg. kg)	Gestation (avg.)	Lifespan (avg.)	Status (in wild)
Ape (Barbary)	0.6	n.a.	7	7mo	20	OK
Baboon (Hamadryas)	0.7	n.a.	18	6mo	17	OK
Bear (Grizzly)	2.6	2.8	336	8mo	25	OK
Bear (Polar)	2.6	1.4	410	8mo	25	Vulnerable
Beaver (Canadian)	0.6	n.a.	23	128 d	20	OK
Bobcat	0.8	n.a.	8	80 d	11	OK
Caribou (Woodland)	1.7	1.3	214	140 d	15	OK
Cheetah (African)	1.7	.8	52	90 d	n.a.	Vulnerable
Cougar	2.1	n.a.	70	94 d	20	Endangered
Deer (White Tailed)	1.8	1.0	98	200 d	15	OK
Devil (Tasmanian)	0.7	n.a.	7	31 d	8	OK
Elephant (African)	n.a.	2.9	4615	20mo	60	Vulnerable
Gibbon (White-Handed)	0.5	n.a.	7	206 d	30	OK
Giraffe (Masai)	4.0	3.1	1175	450 d	18	OK
Gorilla (Lowland)	n.a.	1.5	208	9mo	43	Vulnerable
Hippo (River)	4.2	1.5	3750	234 d	n.a.	OK
Jaguar	1.7	n.a.	102	99 d	20	Endangered
Lion (African)	2.1	1.0	205	108 d	23	OK
Lynx (Canadian)	0.9	0.6	16	60 d	15	OK
Monkey (Spider)	0.5	n.a.	7	139 d	n.a.	Vulnerable
Moose	2.8	1.7	700	246 d	20	OK
Orangutan (Sumatran)	1.4	1.5	58	8–9mo	35	Endangered
Otter (River)	0.7	n.a.	10	11mo	19	OK
Panda (Red)	0.6	n.a.	5	120 d	n.a.	Unknown
Rhino (Indian)	3.2	1.6	3000	19mo	50+	Endangered
Sheep (Dall's)	1.5	1.0	83	165 d	18	Vulnerable
Tiger (Siberian)	2.3	n.a.	250	105 d	16	Endangered
Wolf (Arctic)	1.5	1.0	40	4mo	14	OK

Source: *Metro Toronto Zoo*

n.a. = not available or not applicable

Groups of Animals

Animal name	When you'd rather not say a "bunch of", try the group name:	Animal name	When you'd rather not say a "bunch of", try the group name:
Ants	colony	Martens	richness
Apes or monkeys	troop	Mice	nest
Bears	sloth or sleuth	Owls	parliament
Beavers	colony		
Boars	sounder		
Butterflies	flight	Pheasants	covey (on ground), bouquet (rising), nide (nye) (large covey), nest or brood (family)
Cats	clouder or clowder, clutter, cluster (tame), kindle (young)		
Chickens	brood	Pigs	drove or litter
Colts	rag	Ponies	string
Crows	murder or murmuration	Porpoises	school
Deer	bevy	Poultry	run
Dogs	kennel	Prairie dogs	coterie
Donkeys	pace		
Ducks	brace, flock, paddling (swimming), raft or team (in flight)	Ravens	unkindness
		Rhinoceroses	crash
		Roaches	shoal
Eagles	convocation		
Eels	swarm		
Elephants	herd	Salmon	run
Elk	gang	Sandpipers	murmuration
		Snakes	bed
Ferrets	business	Sparrows	host
Finches	charm	Squirrels	drag (dray)
Flies	business	Storks	mustering
Frogs	army	Swallows	flight
Goats	tribe	Swine	den, drift, sounder or doylt (tame)
Gorillas	band		
Grasshoppers	cluster		
Hens	brood	Toads	knot
Hogs	drift	Trout	hover
		Turkeys	rafter
Jackrabbits	husk	Turtles	bale
Jays	band		
Jellyfish	smack		
Kittens	kindle or litter	Wasps	nest
		Whales	gam, pod, or herd (sperm)
Larks	exaltation, ascension or bevy		
Leopards	leap	Woodpeckers	descent
Lions	pride	Wrens	herd

Source: *Metro Toronto Zoo*

Zoos and Aquariums*

Maritime Region:

☐ **Aquarium and Marine Centre**
2nd Avenue, Shippigan, NB E0B 2P0. Tel: (506) 336-4771. Entrance fee. Open May to September.

☐ **Cherry Brook Zoo**
Saint John, NB E2L 3W2. Tel: (506) 634-1440. Entrance fee. Open all year.

Central Canada:

☐ **Aquarium du Québec**
1675, avenue du Parc, Sainte-Foy, Quebec G1W 4S3 Tel: (418) 659-5266. Entrance fee. Open all year.

☐ **The Biodøme de Montréal**
An environmental museum. 4777, avenue Pierre-de-Coubertin, Montréal, Quebec H1V 1B3. Entrance fee. Open all year.

☐ **Jardin Zoologique de Québec**
8191, avenue du Zoo, Charlesbourg, Quebec G1G 4G4. Tel: (418) 622-0313. Entrance fee. Open all year.

☐ **Parc safari Africain**
823 Rt. 202, Hemmingford, Quebec J0L 1H0 Tel: (514) 247-2727. Entrance fee. Open mid-May to Labour Day.

☐ **Société Zoologique de Granby**
347, rue Bourget, Granby, Quebec J2G 1E8. Tel: (514) 372-5531. Entrance fee. Open May to September.

☐ **African Lion Safari**
R.R#1, Cambridge, Ontario N1R 5S2. Tel: (519) 623-2620. Entrance fee. Open summer.

☐ **Jungle Cat World**
R.R.#1, Orono, Ontario L0B 1M0. Tel: (416) 983-5016. Entrance fee. Open March to November.

☐ **Metro Toronto Zoo**
Meadowvale Road, Scarborough, Ontario M1E 4R5. Tel; (416) 392-5900. Entrance fee. Open all year.

☐ **Riverview Park and Zoo**
Peterborough, Ontario K9J 6Z5. Tel: (705) 748-9300 No charge. Open all year.

Western Canada:

☐ **Assiniboine Park Zoo**
2355 Corydon Avenue, Winnipeg, Manitoba R3P 0R5. Tel: (204) 888-3634. No charge. Open all year.

☐ **Forestry Farm Zoo**
Saskatoon, Saskatchewan S7N 2H0. Tel: (306) 975-3382. Entrance fee. Open all year.

☐ **Calgary Zoo, Botanical Garden and Prehistoric Park**
1300 ZOO Road, Calgary, Alberta T2E 7V6. Tel: (403) 232-9300. Entrance fee. Open all year.

☐ **Valley Zoo**
Edmonton, Alberta T5J 2R7. Tel: (403) 496-6911. Entrance fee. Open all year.

☐ **Crystal Garden**
713 Douglas Street, Victoria, BC V8W 1N8. Tel: (604) 386-1356. Entrance fee. Open all year.

☐ **Kamloops Wildlife Park**
East Trans Canada Highway, Kamloops, BC V2C 5L7. Tel: (604) 573-3242. Entrance fee. Open all year.

☐ **Okanagan Game Farm**
Kaleden, BC V2A 6J9. Tel: (604) 497-5405. Entrance fee. Open all year.

☐ **Vancouver Game Farm**
5048, 264 Street, Aldergrove, BC V0X 1A0. Tel: (604) 856-6825. Entrance fee. Open all year.

☐ **Vancouver Public Aquarium**
Stanley Park, Vancouver, BC V6B 3X8. Tel: (604) 658-3364. Entrance fee. Open all year.

*Accredited by the Canadian Association of Zoological Parks and Aquariums

MOVIES

Genie Awards, 1982–92

The Genie Awards have been presented since 1980 by the Academy of Canadian Cinema and Television to honor achievement in the Canadian film industry. Awards apply to films released in the previous year. Voting is conducted in a two-step process whereby the winners are chosen by all academy members from among the five nominees selected in each category by their respective craft branches. These awards were presented Nov. 22, 1992.

1982

Picture .... *Ticket to Heaven*
Actor .... Nick Mancuso, *Ticket to Heaven*
Actress .... Margot Kidder, *Heartaches*
Sup. Actor .... Saul Rubinek, *Ticket to Heaven*
Sup. Actress .... Denise Filiatrault, *Les Plouffe*
Director .... Gilles Carle, *Les Plouffe*

1983

Picture .... *The Grey Fox*
Actor .... Donald Sutherland, *Threshold*
Actress .... Rae Dawn Chong, *Quest for Fire*
Sup. Actor ... R. H. Thomson, *If You Could See What I Hear*
Sup. Actress .... Jackie Burroughs, *The Grey Fox*
Director .... Phillip Borsos, *The Grey Fox*

1984

Picture .... *The Terry Fox Story*
Actor .... Eric Fryer, *The Terry Fox Story*
Actress .... Martha Henry, *The Wars*
Sup. Actor .... Michael Zelniker, *The Terry Fox Story*
Sup. Actress .... Jackie Burroughs, *The Wars*
Director .... Bob Clark, *A Christmas Story;* David
.... Cronenberg, *Videodrome*

1985

Picture .... *The Bay Boy*
Actor .... Gabriel Arcand, *Le Crime d'Ovide Plouffe*
Actress .... Louise Marleau, *La Femme de l'hôtel*
Sup. Actor .... Alan Scarfe, *The Bay Boy*
Sup. Actress .... Linda Sorensen, *Draw!*
Director .... Micheline Lanctôt, *Sonatine*

1986

Picture .... *My American Cousin*
Actor .... John Wildman, *My American Cousin*
Actress .... Margaret Langrick, *My American Cousin*
Sup. Actor .... Alan Arkin, *Joshua Then and Now*
Sup. Actress ...... Linda Sorensen, *Joshua Then and Now*
Director .... Sandy Wilson, *My American Cousin*

1987

Picture .... *The Decline of the American Empire*
Actor .... Gordon Pinsent, *John and the Missus*
Actress .... Martha Henry, *Dancing in the Dark*
Sup. Actor ....: Gabriel Arcand, *The Decline of the American Empire*
Sup. Actress .... Louise Portal, *The Decline of the American Empire*
Director .... Denys Arcand, *The Decline of the American Empire*

1988

Picture .... *Un Zoo la nuit*
Actor .... Roger Le Bel, *Un Zoo la nuit*
Actress .... Sheila McCarthy, *I've Heard the Mermaids Singing*
Sup. Actor .... Germaine Houde, *Un Zoo la nuit*
Sup. Actress .... Paule Baillargeon, *I've Heard the Mermaids Singing*
Director .... Jean-Claude Lauzon, *Un Zoo la nuit*

1989

Picture .... *Dead Ringers*
Actor .... Jeremy Irons, *Dead Ringers*
Actress .... Jackie Burroughs, *A Winter Tan*
Sup. Actor .... Remy Girard, *Les Portes tournantes*
Sup. Actress .... Colleen Dewhurst, *Obsessed*
Director .... David Cronenberg, *Dead Ringers*

1990

Picture .... *Jesus de Montréal*
Actor .... Lothaire Bluteau, *Jesus de Montréal*
Actress .... Rebecca Jenkins, *Bye Bye Blues*
Sup. Actor .... Remy Girard, *Jesus de Montréal*
Sup. Actress .... Robyn Stevan, *Bye Bye Blues*
Director .... Denys Arcand, *Jesus de Montréal*

1991

Picture .... *Black Robe*
Actor .... Remy Girard, *Amoureux fou*
Actress .... Pascale Montpetit, *H*
Sup. Actor .... August Schellenberg, *Black Robe*
Sup. Actress .... Danielle Proulx, *Amoureux fou*
Director .... Bruce Beresford, *Black Robe*

1992

Picture .... *Naked Lunch*
Actor .... Tony Nardi, *La Sarrasine*
Actress .... Janet Wright, *Bordertown Café*
Sup. Actor .... Michael Hogan, *Solitaire*
Sup. Actress .... Monique Mercure, *Naked Lunch*
Director ....: David Cronenberg, *Naked Lunch*
Original Screenplay .... Jean-Claude Lauzon, *Léolo*
Adapted Screenplay ...... David Cronenberg, *Naked Lunch*
Cinematography .... Peter Suschitzky, *Naked Lunch*
Film Editing .... Michel Arcand, *Léolo*
Art Direction .... Carol Spier, *Naked Lunch*
Costume Design .... François Barbeau, *Léolo*
Overall Sound .... Bryan Day, Peter Maxwell, David Appleby, Don White, *Naked Lunch*
Sound Editing . David Evans, Wayne Griffin, Jane Tattersall, Tony Currie, Andy Malcolm, Rick Cadger, *Naked Lunch* ▶

▶ Music Score..Richard Grégoire, *Being at Home with Claude*
Original Song.... Ron Hynes, "Final Breath," *Secret Nation*
Feature Documentary.................. *Deadly Currents*

Short Documentary .... *A Song for Tibet*
Live Action Short Drama .... *Battle of the Bulge*
Animated Short................................ *Strings*

Festival of Festivals, 1993

(Toronto International Film Festival)

The 18th annual festival was held from Sept. 9 to 18 in 1993, showing more than 290 films from around the world. This is widely regarded as North America's major film festival.

People's Choice Award .... *The Snapper* (UK)
International Critics' Award .... *Strapped* (USA)
Best Canadian Feature Film .... *Kanehsatake: 270 Years of Resistance*
Metro Media Award.. *Naked* (UK)
Best Canadian Short Film .... *Save My Lost Nigga Soul*

Source: *Festival of Festivals*

Montreal World Film Festival, 1993

The sixteenth annual Festival des Films du Monde was held from Aug. 26th to Sept. 6th in 1993.

Grand Prix of the Americas .... *Trahir* (Romania-France)
Special Grand Prix of the Jury .... *And the Band Played On* (U.S.)
Best Director .... Claude Lelouch, *Tout ça...pour ça*, Juanma Ulloa, *La Madre Muerta* (tie)
Best Actress .... Carla Gravina, *Il Lungo Silenzio*
Best Actor .... Johan Leysen, *Trahir*, Denis Mercier, *The Sex of the Stars* (tie)
Best Scenario .... Michael Jenkins & Richard Barrett, *The Heartbreak Kid*
Best Short Film .... *Quien Mal Anda, Mal Acaba* (Spain)
International Critics Prize.. *Consuming Sun* (China)

Source: *Montreal World Film Festival*

The Cannes Film Festival Awards, 1983–93

1983

Best Film............... *The Ballad of Narayama* (Japan)
Special Grand Jury Prize... *Monty Python, The Meaning of Life* (Great Britain)
Best Director .... (not awarded)[1]
Best Actor.... Gian Maria Volonte, *The Death of Mario Ricci*
Best Actress........ Hanna Schygulla, *The Story of Piera*

1984

Best Film........ *Paris, Texas* (international collaboration)
Special Grand Jury Prize.......... *Diary For My Children* (Hungary)
Best Director . Bertrand Tavernier, *A Sunday in the Country*
Best Actor.... Francisco Rabal, Alfredo Landa, *Los Santos Innocentes*
Best Actress .... Helen Mirren, *Cal*

1985

Best Film .... *Father's Gone on a Business Trip* (Yugoslavia)
Special Grand Jury Prize................... *Birdy* (USA)
Best Director .... André Techine, *Rendez-vous*
Best Actor .... William Hurt, *Kiss of the Spider Woman*
Best Actress. Cher, *Mask;* Norma Aleandro, *Official Version*

1986

Best Film.................... *The Mission* (Great Britain)

Special Grand Jury Prize......... *The Sacrifice* (Sweden)
Best Director.............. Martin Scorsese, *After Hours*
Best Actor ... Michel Blanc, *Tenue de Soirée;* Bob Hoskins, *Mona Lisa*
Best Actress .... Barbara Sukowa, *Rosa Luxemburg;* Fernanda Torres, *Speak to Me of Love*

1987

Best Film .... *Under Satan's Sun* (France)
Special Grand Jury Prize................ *Repent* (USSR)
Best Director........ Wim Wenders, *The Wings of Desire*
Best Actor .... Marcello Mastroianni, *Black Eyes*
Best Actress................. Barbara Hershey, *The Bayou*

1988

Best Film................. *Pelle The Conqueror* (Denmark)
Special Grand Jury Prize..... *A World Apart* (Great Britain)
Best Director........... Fernando E. Solanas, *The South*
Best Actor .... Forest Whitaker, *Bird*
Best Actress.Barbara Hershey, Jodhi May and Linda Mvusi, *A World Apart*

1989

Best Film................ *sex, lies and videotape* (USA)
Special Grand Jury Prize ..... *Trop Belle Pour Toi* (France); *Cinema Paradiso* (Italy)
Best Director........ Emir Kusturica, *Time of the Gypsies* ▶

▶ Best Actor . . . . James Spader, *sex, lies and videotape*
Best Actress . . . . Meryl Streep, *A Cry In The Dark*

1990

Best Film . . . . Wild at Heart (USA)
Special Grand Jury Prize . . . Tilaï (Burkina Faso); *The Sting of Death* (Japan)
Best Director . . . . Pavel Loungine, *Taxi Blues*
Best Actor . . . . Gerard Depardieu, *Cyrano de Bergerac*
Best Actress . . . . Krystyna Janda, *Interrogation*

1991

Best Film . . . . Barton Fink (USA)
Special Grand Jury Prize . . . . La belle noiseuse (France)
Best Director . . . . Joel Coen & Ethan Coen, *Barton Fink*
Best Actor . . . . John Turturro, *Barton Fink*

Best Actress . . . . . Irène Jacob, *The Double Life of Veronica*

1992

Best Film . . . . The Best Intentions (Switzerland)
Special Grand Jury Prize . . . . Il Ladro di Bambini (Italy)
Best Director . . . . Robert Altman, *The Player*
Best Actor . . . . Tim Robbins, *The Player*
Best Actress . . . . Pernilla August, *The Best Intentions*

1993

Best Film . . (tie) *The Piano*, (New Zealand), *Farewell To My Concubine* (China)
Special Grand Jury Prize . . . Faraway, So Close! (Germany)
Best Director . . . . Mike Leigh, *Naked*
Best Actor . . . . David Thewlis, *Naked*
Best Actress . . . . Holly Hunter, *The Piano*

Source: *Embassy of France*

(1) The Cannes Festival Jury is not obliged to select a winner in any category except that of Best Film.

Motion Picture Academy Awards (Oscars), 1927–92

1927–28
Picture . . . . Wings, Paramount
Actor . . . . Emil Jannings, *The Way of All Flesh*
Actress . . . . Janet Gaynor, *7th Heaven*
Director . . . . . Frank Borzage, *7th Heaven*; Lewis Milestone, *Two Arabian Knights*

1928–29
Picture . . . . The Broadway Melody, MGM
Actor . . . . Warner Baxter, *In Old Arizona*
Actress . . . . Mary Pickford, *Coquette*
Director . . . . Frank Lloyd, *The Divine Lady*

1929–30
Picture . . . . All Quiet on the Western Front, Universal
Actor . . . . George Arliss, *Disraeli*
Actress . . . . Norma Shearer, *The Divorcee*
Director . . . Lewis Milestone, *All Quiet on the Western Front*

1930–31
Picture . . . . Cimarron, RKO
Actor . . . . Lionel Barrymore, *A Free Soul*
Actress . . . . Marie Dressler, *Min and Bill*
Director . . . . Norman Taurog, *Skippy*

1931–32
Picture . . . . Grand Hotel, MGM
Actor . . . . . Fredric March, *Dr. Jekyll and Mr. Hyde*; Wallace Beery, *The Champ* (tie)
Actress . . . . Helen Hayes, *Sin of Madelon Claudet*
Director . . . . Frank Borzage, *Bad Girl*
Special . . . . Walt Disney, *Mickey Mouse*

1932–33
Picture . . . . Cavalcade, Fox
Actor . . . . Charles Laughton, *The Private Life of Henry VIII*
Actress . . . . Katharine Hepburn, *Morning Glory*
Director . . . . Frank Lloyd, *Cavalcade*

1934
Picture . . . . It Happened One Night, Columbia
Actor . . . . Clark Gable, *It Happened One Night*
Actress . . . . Claudette Colbert, *It Happened One Night*
Director . . . . Frank Capra, *It Happened One Night*

1935
Picture . . . . Mutiny on the Bounty, MGM
Actor . . . . Victor McLaglen, *The Informer*
Actress . . . . Bette Davis, *Dangerous*
Director . . . . John Ford, *The Informer*

1936
Picture . . . . The Great Ziegfeld, MGM
Actor . . . . Paul Muni, *The Story of Louis Pasteur*
Actress . . . . Luise Rainer, *The Great Ziegfeld*
Sup. Actor . . . . Walter Brennan, *Come and Get It*
Sup. Actress . . . . Gale Sondergaard, *Anthony Adverse*
Director . . . . Frank Capra, *Mr. Deeds Goes to Town*

1937
Picture . . . . Life of Emile Zola, Warner Bros.
Actor . . . . Spencer Tracy, *Captains Courageous*
Actress . . . . Luise Rainer, *The Good Earth*
Sup. Actor . . . . Joseph Schildkraut, *Life of Emile Zola*
Sup. Actress . . . . Alice Brady, *In Old Chicago*
Director . . . . Leo McCarey, *The Awful Truth*

1938
Picture . . . . You Can't Take It With You, Columbia
Actor . . . . Spencer Tracy, *Boys Town*
Actress . . . . Bette Davis, *Jezebel*
Sup. Actor . . . . Walter Brennan, *Kentucky*
Sup. Actress . . . . Fay Bainter, *Jezebel*
Director . . . . Frank Capra, *You Can't Take It With You*

1939
Picture . . . . Gone With the Wind, Selznick International
Actor . . . . Robert Donat, *Goodbye, Mr. Chips*
Actress . . . . Vivien Leigh, *Gone With the Wind*
Sup. Actor . . . . Thomas Mitchell, *StageCoach*
Sup. Actress . . . . Hattie McDaniel, *Gone With the Wind*
Director . . . . Victor Fleming, *Gone With the Wind*

1940
Picture . . . . Rebecca, Selznick International
Actor . . . . James Stewart, *The Philadelphia Story*
Actress . . . . Ginger Rogers, *Kitty Foyle*
Sup. Actor . . . . Walter Brennan, *The Westerner*
Sup. Actress . . . . Jane Darwell, *The Grapes of Wrath* ▶

▶ Director . . . . John Ford, *The Grapes of Wrath*

1941
Picture . . . . *How Green Was My Valley*, 20th Cent.-Fox
Actor . . . . Gary Cooper, *Sergeant York*
Actress . . . . Joan Fontaine, *Suspicion*
Sup. Actor. . . . . . Donald Crisp, *How Green Was My Valley*
Sup. Actress . . . . Mary Astor, *The Great Lie*
Director . . . . John Ford, *How Green Was My Valley*

1942
Picture . . . . *Mrs. Miniver*, MGM
Actor . . . . James Cagney, *Yankee Doodle Dandy*
Actress . . . . Greer Garson, *Mrs. Miniver*
Sup. Actor. . . . . Van Heflin, *Johnny Eager*
Sup. Actress . . . . Teresa Wright, *Mrs. Miniver*
Director . . . . William Wyler, *Mrs. Miniver*

1943
Picture . . . . *Casablanca*, Warner Bros.
Actor. . . . . Paul Lukas, *Watch on the Rhine*
Actress . . . . Jennifer Jones, *The Song of Bernadette*
Sup. Actor. . . . . Charles Coburn, *The More the Merrier*
Sup. Actress. . . . . Katina Paxinou, *For Whom the Bell Tolls*
Director. . . . . Michael Curtiz, *Casablanca*

1944
Picture . . . . *Going My Way*, Paramount
Actor. . . . . Bing Crosby, *Going My Way*
Actress . . . . Ingrid Bergman, *Gaslight*
Sup. Actor. . . . . Barry Fitzgerald, *Going My Way*
Sup. Actress. . . Ethel Barrymore, *None But the Lonely Heart*
Director . . . . Leo McCarey, *Going My Way*

1945
Picture . . . . *The Lost Weekend*, Paramount
Actor. . . . . Ray Milland, *The Lost Weekend*
Actress . . . . Joan Crawford, *Mildred Pierce*
Sup. Actor. . . . . . . James Dunn, *A Tree Grows in Brooklyn*
Sup. Actress . . . . Anne Revere, *National Velvet*
Director . . . . Billy Wilder, *The Lost Weekend*

1946
Picture . . . . . . *The Best Years of Our Lives*, Goldwyn, RKO
Actor . . . . Fredric March, *The Best Years of Our Lives*
Actress . . . . Olivia de Havilland, *To Each His Own*
Sup. Actor . . . Harold Russell, *The Best Years of Our Lives*
Sup. Actress . . . . Anne Baxter, *The Razor's Edge*
Director . . . . . . William Wyler, *The Best Years of Our Lives*

1947
Picture . . . . *Gentleman's Agreement*, 20th Century-Fox
Actor . . . . Ronald Colman, *A Double Life*
Actress . . . . Loretta Young, *The Farmer's Daughter*
Sup. Actor. . . . . . . Edmund Gwenn, *Miracle on 34th Street*
Sup. Actress . . . . . . Celeste Holm, *Gentleman's Agreement*
Director . . . . Elia Kazan, *Gentleman's Agreement*

1948
Picture . . . *Hamlet*, Two Cities Film, Universal International
Actor. . . . . Laurence Olivier, *Hamlet*
Actress. . . . . Jane Wyman, *Johnny Belinda*
Sup. Actor . . . . . . Walter Huston, *Treasure of Sierra Madre*
Sup. Actress . . . . Claire Trevor, *Key Largo*
Director . . . . John Huston, *Treasure of Sierra Madre*

1949
Picture . . . . *All the King's Men*, Columbia.

Actor . . . . Broderick Crawford, *All the King's Men*
Actress . . . . Olivia de Havilland, *The Heiress*
Sup. Actor . . . . Dean Jagger, *Twelve O'Clock High*
Sup. Actress. . . Mercedes McCambridge, *All the King's Men*
Director . . . Joseph L. Mankiewicz, *A Letter to Three Wives*

1950
Picture . . . . *All About Eve*, 20th Century-Fox
Actor. . . . . Jose Ferrer, *Cyrano de Bergerac*
Actress. . . . . Judy Holliday, *Born Yesterday*
Sup. Actor. . . . . George Sanders, *All About Eve*
Sup. Actress . . . . Josephine Hull, *Harvey*
Director . . . . Joseph L. Mankiewicz, *All About Eve*

1951
Picture . . . . *An American in Paris*, MGM
Actor . . . . Humphrey Bogart, *The African Queen*
Actress . . . . Vivien Leigh, *A Streetcar Named Desire*
Sup. Actor . . . . Karl Malden, *A Streetcar Named Desire*
Sup. Actress . . . . . . Kim Hunter, *A Streetcar Named Desire*
Director . . . . George Stevens, *A Place in the Sun*

1952
Picture . . . . *The Greatest Show on Earth*, C.B. DeMille, Paramount
Actor. . . . . Gary Cooper, *High Noon*
Actress . . . . Shirley Booth, *Come Back, Little Sheba*
Sup. Actor . . . . Anthony Quinn, *Viva Zapata!*
Sup. Actress . . Gloria Grahame, *The Bad and the Beautiful*
Director . . . . John Ford, *The Quiet Man*

1953
Picture . . . . *From Here to Eternity*, Columbia
Actor . . . . William Holden, *Stalag 17*
Actress . . . . Audrey Hepburn, *Roman Holiday*
Sup. Actor . . . . Frank Sinatra, *From Here to Eternity*
Sup. Actress . . . . Donna Reed, *From Here to Eternity*
Director . . . . Fred Zinnemann, *From Here to Eternity*

1954
Picture . . . *On the Waterfront*, Horizon-American, Columbia
Actor . . . . Marlon Brando, *On the Waterfront*
Actress . . . . Grace Kelly, *The Country Girl*
Sup. Actor . . . . . . Edmond O'Brien, *The Barefoot Contessa*
Sup. Actress. . . . . Eva Marie Saint, *On the Waterfront*
Director . . . . Elia Kazan, *On the Waterfront*

1955
Picture . . . *Marty*, Hecht and Lancaster's Steven Prods., U.A.
Actor . . . . Ernest Borgnine, *Marty*
Actress . . . . Anna Magnani, *The Rose Tattoo*
Sup. Actor . . . . Jack Lemmon, *Mister Roberts*
Sup. Actress. . . . . Jo Van Fleet, *East of Eden*
Director . . . . Delbert Mann, *Marty*

1956
Picture . . . *Around the World in 80 Days*, Michael Todd, U.A.
Actor . . . . Yul Brynner, *The King and I*
Actress . . . . Ingrid Bergman, *Anastasia*
Sup. Actor . . . . Anthony Quinn, *Lust for Life*
Sup. Actress . . . . . . Dorothy Malone, *Written on the Wind*
Director . . . . George Stevens, *Giant*

1957
Picture . . . . *The Bridge on the River Kwai*, Columbia
Actor. . . . . . . Alec Guinness, *The Bridge on the River Kwai*
Actress . . . . . . Joanne Woodward, *The Three Faces of Eve*
Sup. Actor. . . . . Red Buttons, *Sayonara* ▶

▶ Sup. Actress . . . . Miyoshi Umeki, *Sayonara*
Director . . . . David Lean, *The Bridge on the River Kwai*

1958
Picture . . . . *Gigi*, Arthur Freed Production, MGM
Actor . . . . David Niven, *Separate Tables*
Actress . . . . Susan Hayward, *I Want to Live*
Sup. Actor . . . . Burl Ives, *The Big Country*
Sup. Actress . . . . Wendy Hiller, *Separate Tables*
Director . . . . Vincente Minnelli, *Gigi*

1959
Picture . . . . *Ben-Hur*, MGM
Actor . . . . Charlton Heston, *Ben-Hur*
Actress . . . . Simone Signoret, *Room at the Top*
Sup. Actor . . . . Hugh Griffith, *Ben-Hur*
Sup. Actress . . . . Shelley Winters, *The Diary of Anne Frank*
Director . . . . William Wyler, *Ben-Hur*

1960
Picture . . . . *The Apartment*, Mirisch Co., U.A.
Actor . . . . Burt Lancaster, *Elmer Gantry*
Actress . . . . Elizabeth Taylor, *Butterfield 8*
Sup. Actor . . . . Peter Ustinov, *Spartacus*
Sup. Actress . . . . Shirley Jones, *Elmer Gantry*
Director . . . . Billy Wilder, *The Apartment*

1961
Picture . . . . *West Side Story*, Mirisch Pictures, U.A.
Actor . . . . Maximilian Schell, *Judgment at Nuremberg*
Actress . . . . Sophia Loren, *Two Women*
Sup. Actor . . . . George Chakiris, *West Side Story*
Sup. Actress . . . . Rita Moreno, *West Side Story*
Director . . . Jerome Robbins, Robert Wise, *West Side Story*

1962
Picture . . . . *Lawrence of Arabia*, Columbia
Actor . . . . Gregory Peck, *To Kill a Mockingbird*
Actress . . . . Anne Bancroft, *The Miracle Worker*
Sup. Actor . . . . Ed Begley, *Sweet Bird of Youth*
Sup. Actress . . . . Patty Duke, *The Miracle Worker*
Director . . . . David Lean, *Lawrence of Arabia*

1963
Picture . . . *Tom Jones*, Woodfall Prod., U.A.-Lopert Pictures
Actor . . . . Sidney Poitier, *Lilies of the Field*
Actress . . . . Patricia Neal, *Hud*
Sup. Actor . . . . Melvyn Douglas, *Hud*
Sup. Actress . . . . Margaret Rutherford, *The V.I.P.s*
Director . . . . Tony Richardson, *Tom Jones*

1964
Picture . . . . *My Fair Lady*, Warner Bros.
Actor . . . . Rex Harrison, *My Fair Lady*
Actress . . . . Julie Andrews, *Mary Poppins*
Sup. Actor . . . . Peter Ustinov, *Topkapi*
Sup. Actress . . . . Lila Kedrova, *Zorba the Greek*
Director . . . . George Cukor, *My Fair Lady*

1965
Picture . . . . *The Sound of Music*, 20th Century-Fox
Actor . . . . Lee Marvin, *Cat Ballou*
Actress . . . . Julie Christie, *Darling*
Sup. Actor . . . . Martin Balsam, *A Thousand Clowns*
Sup. Actress . . . . Shelley Winters, *A Patch of Blue*
Director . . . . Robert Wise, *The Sound of Music*

1966
Picture . . . . *A Man for All Seasons*, Columbia
Actor . . . . Paul Scofield, *A Man for All Seasons*
Actress . . . Elizabeth Taylor, *Who's Afraid of Virginia Woolf?*
Sup. Actor . . . . Walter Matthau, *The Fortune Cookie*
Sup. Actress . . . . . Sandy Dennis, *Who's Afraid of Virginia
Woolf?*
Director . . . . Fred Zinnemann, *A Man for All Seasons*

1967
Picture . . . . . . *In the Heat of the Night*, Mirisch Corp., U.A.
Actor . . . . Rod Steiger, *In the Heat of the Night*
Actress . . . . . Katharine Hepburn, *Guess Who's Coming to
Dinner*
Sup. Actor . . . . George Kennedy, *Cool Hand Luke*
Sup. Actress . . . . Estelle Parsons, *Bonnie and Clyde*
Director . . . . Mike Nichols, *The Graduate*

1968
Picture . . . . *Oliver!*, Columbia
Actor . . . . Cliff Robertson, *Charly*
Actress . . . . Katharine Hepburn, *The Lion in Winter*, Barbra
. . . . Streisand, *Funny Girl* (tie)
Sup. Actor . . . . Jack Albertson, *The Subject Was Roses*
Sup. Actress . . . . Ruth Gordon, *Rosemary's Baby*
Director . . . . Sir Carol Reed, *Oliver!*

1969
Picture . . . . *Midnight Cowboy*, United Artists
Actor . . . . John Wayne, *True Grit*
Actress . . . . Maggie Smith, *The Prime of Miss Jean Brodie*
Sup. Actor . . . Gig Young, *They Shoot Horses, Don't They?*
Sup. Actress . . . . Goldie Hawn, *Cactus Flower*
Director . . . . John Schlesinger, *Midnight Cowboy*

1970
Picture . . . . *Patton*, 20th Century-Fox
Actor . . . . George C. Scott, *Patton* (refused)
Actress . . . . Glenda Jackson, *Women in Love*
Sup. Actor . . . . John Mills, *Ryan's Daughter*
Sup. Actress . . . . Helen Hayes, *Airport*
Director . . . . Franklin J. Schaffner, *Patton*

1971
Picture . . . . *The French Connection*, 20th Century-Fox
Actor . . . . Gene Hackman, *The French Connection*
Actress . . . . ,Jane Fonda, *Klute*
Sup. Actor . . . . Ben Johnson, *The Last Picture Show*.
Sup. Actress . . . . Cloris Leachman, *The Last Picture Show*
Director . . . . William Friedkin, *The French Connection*

1972
Picture . . . . *The Godfather*, Paramount
Actor . . . . Marlon Brando, *The Godfather* (refused)
Actress . . . . Liza Minnelli, *Cabaret*
Sup. Actor . . . . Joel Grey, *Cabaret*
Sup. Actress . . . . Eileen Heckart, *Butterflies Are Free*
Director . . . . Bob Fosse, *Cabaret*

1973
Picture . . . . *The Sting*, Universal
Actor . . . . Jack Lemmon, *Save the Tiger*
Actress . . . . Glenda Jackson, *A Touch of Class*
Sup. Actor . . . . John Houseman, *The Paper Chase*
Sup. Actress . . . . Tatum O'Neal, *Paper Moon*
Director . . . . George Roy Hill, *The Sting* ▶

1974
Picture .... *The Godfather Part II*, Paramount
Actor .... Art Carney, *Harry and Tonto*
Actress . . . Ellen Burstyn, *Alice Doesn't Live Here Anymore*
Sup. Actor .... Robert De Niro, *The Godfather Part II*
Sup. Actress ...... Ingrid Bergman, *Murder on the Orient Express*
Director ..... Francis Ford Coppola, *The Godfather Part II*

1975
Picture ... *One Flew Over the Cuckoo's Nest*, United Artists
Actor ... Jack Nicholson, *One Flew Over the Cuckoo's Nest*
Actress ..... Louise Fletcher, *One Flew Over the Cuckoo's Nest*
Sup. Actor .... George Burns, *The Sunshine Boys*
Sup. Actress .... Lee Grant, *Shampoo*
Director ... Milos Forman, *One Flew Over the Cuckoo's Nest*

1976
Picture .... *Rocky*, United Artists
Actor .... Peter Finch, *Network*
Actress .... Faye Dunaway, *Network*
Sup. Actor .... Jason Robards, *All the President's Men*
Sup. Actress .... Beatrice Straight, *Network*
Director .... John G. Avildsen, *Rocky*

1977
Picture .... *Annie Hall*, United Artists
Actor ...... Richard Dreyfuss, *The Goodbye Girl*
Actress...................... Diane Keaton, *Annie Hall*
Sup. Actor .... Jason Robards, *Julia*
Sup. Actress .... Vanessa Redgrave, *Julia*
Director...................... Woody Allen, *Annie Hall*

1978
Picture .... *The Deer Hunter*, Universal
Actor .... Jon Voight, *Coming Home*
Actress.................... Jane Fonda, *Coming Home*
Sup. Actor .... Christopher Walken, *The Deer Hunter*
Sup. Actress .... Maggie Smith, *California Suite*
Director .... Michael Cimino, *The Deer Hunter*

1979
Picture .... *Kramer vs. Kramer*, Columbia
Actor .... Dustin Hoffman, *Kramer vs. Kramer*
Actress .... Sally Field, *Norma Rae*
Sup. Actor .... Melvyn Douglas, *Being There*
Sup. Actress ...... Meryl Streep, *Kramer vs. Kramer*
Director .... Robert Benton, *Kramer vs. Kramer*

1980
Picture .... *Ordinary People*, Paramount
Actor..................... Robert De Niro, *Raging Bull*
Actress .... Sissy Spacek, *Coal Miner's Daughter*
Sup. Actor .... Timothy Hutton, *Ordinary People*
Sup. Actress ..... Mary Steenburgen, *Melvin and Howard*
Director .... Robert Redford, *Ordinary People*

1981
Picture .... *Chariots of Fire*, Warner Bros.
Actor..................... Henry Fonda, *On Golden Pond*
Actress ...... Katharine Hepburn, *On Golden Pond*
Sup. Actor .... John Gielgud, *Arthur*
Sup. Actress .... Maureen Stapleton, *Reds*
Director........................... Warren Beatty, *Reds*

1982
Picture........................... *Gandhi*, Columbia

Actor .... Ben Kingsley, *Gandhi*
Actress .... Meryl Streep, *Sophie's Choice*
Sup. Actor .... Louis Gossett, Jr., *An Officer and a Gentleman*
Sup. Actress .... Jessica Lange, *Tootsie*
Director .... Richard Attenborough, *Gandhi*

1983
Picture .... *Terms of Endearment*, Paramount
Actor .... Robert Duvall, *Tender Mercies*
Actress .... Shirley MacLaine, *Terms of Endearment*
Sup. Actor .... Jack Nicholson, *Terms of Endearment*
Sup. Actor .... Linda Hunt, *The Year of Living Dangerously*
Director........ James L. Brooks, *Terms of Endearment*

1984
Picture .... *Amadeus*, Orion
Actor.................... F. Murray Abraham, *Amadeus*
Actress .... Sally Field, *Places in the Heart*
Sup. Actor .... Haing S. Ngor, *The Killing Fields*
Sup. Actress ...... Peggy Ashcroft, *A Passage to India*
Director..................... Milos Forman, *Amadeus*

1985
Picture .... *Out of Africa*, Universal
Actor .... William Hurt, *Kiss of the Spider Woman*
Actress .... Geraldine Page, *The Trip to Bountiful*
Sup. Actor................... Don Ameche, *Cocoon*
Sup. Actress ...... Anjelica Huston, *Prizzi's Honor*
Director.............. Sydney Pollack, *Out of Africa*

1986
Picture .... *Platoon*, Orion
Actor .... Paul Newman, *The Color of Money*
Actress........ Marlee Matlin, *Children of a Lesser God*
Sup. Actor ...... Michael Caine, *Hannah and Her Sisters*
Sup. Actress ..... Dianne Wiest, *Hannah and Her Sisters*
Director .... Oliver Stone, *Platoon*

1987
Picture .... *The Last Emperor*, Columbia
Actor .... Michael Douglas, *Wall Street*
Actress .... Cher, *Moonstruck*
Sup. Actor........... Sean Connery, *The Untouchables*
Sup. Actress .... Olympia Dukakis, *Moonstruck*
Director .... Bernardo Bertolucci, *The Last Emperor*

1988
Picture .... *Rain Man*, United Artists
Actor...................... Dustin Hoffman, *Rain Man*
Actress .... Jodie Foster, *The Accused*
Sup. Actor............ Kevin Kline, *A Fish Called Wanda*
Sup. Actress ..... Geena Davis, *The Accidental Tourist*
Director .... Barry Levinson, *Rain Man*

1989
Picture.............. *Driving Miss Daisy*, Warner Bros.
Actor .... Daniel Day Lewis, *My Left Foot*
Actress .... Jessica Tandy, *Driving Miss Daisy*
Sup. Actor .... Denzel Washington, *Glory*
Sup. Actress.............. Brenda Fricker, *My Left Foot*
Director .... Oliver Stone, *Born on the Fourth of July*

1990
Picture .... *Dances With Wolves*, Orion
Actor .... Jeremy Irons, *Reversal of Fortune*
Actress .... Kathy Bates, *Misery* ▶

▶ Sup. Actor . . . . Joe Pesci, *Good Fellas*
Sup. Actress . . . . Whoopi Goldberg, *Ghost*
Director . . . . Kevin Costner, *Dances With Wolves*

1991

Picture . . . . *The Silence of the Lambs*, Orion
Actor . . . . Anthony Hopkins, *The Silence of the Lambs*
Actress . . . . Jodie Foster, *The Silence of the Lambs*
Sup. Actor . . . . Jack Palance, *City Slickers*
Sup. Actress . . . . Mercedes Ruehl, *The Fisher King*
Director . . . . . Jonathan Demme, *The Silence of the Lambs*

1992

Picture . . . . *Unforgiven*, Clint Eastwood, producer
Actor . . . . Al Pacino, *Scent of A Woman*
Actress . . . . Emma Thompson, *Howards End*
Sup. Actor . . . . Gene Hackman, *Unforgiven*
Sup. Actress . . . . Marisa Tomei, *My Cousin Vinny*
Director . . . . Clint Eastwood, *Unforgiven*
Foreign-Language Film . . . . *Indochine*, France
Original Screenplay . . . . Neil Jordan, *The Crying Game*
Screenplay Adaptation . . . . Ruth Prawer Jhabvala,
Howards End
Cinematography . . . . Philippe Rousselot, *A River Runs*

Through It
Editing . . . . Joel Cox, *Unforgiven*
Original Score . . . . Alan Menken, *Aladdin*
Original Song . . . . Alan Menken, Tim Rice,
"Whole New World," *Aladdin*
Art Direction . . . . Luciana Arrighi, *Howards End*
Set Decoration . . . . Ian Whittaker, *Howards End*
Costume Design . . . . . Eiko Ishioka, *Bram Stoker's Dracula*
Sound . . . . Chris Jenkins, Doug Hemphill, Mark Smith,
Simon Kaye, *The Last of the Mohicans*
Sound Effects Editing . . . Tom C. McCarthy, David E. Stone,
Bram Stoker's Dracula
Makeup . . . . Greg Cannom, Michele Burke, Matthew W.
Mungle, *Bram Stoker's Dracula*
Visual Effects . . . Ken Ralston, Doug Chiang, Doug Smythe,
Tom Woodruff, *Death Becomes Her*
Documentary Feature . . . . Barbara Trent and David Kasper,
producers, *The Panama Deception*
Documentary Short Subject . . . *Educating Peter*, Thomas C.
Goodwin and Gerardine Wurzburg, producers
Short Film, Animated . . . . Joan C. Gratz, *Mona Lisa*
Descending A Staircase
Short Film, Live . . . . Sam Karmann, *Omnibus*

Source: *Academy of Motion Picture Arts and Sciences*

1992 Oscar Nominations

Picture: *The Crying Game; A Few Good Men; Howards End; Scent of A Woman; Unforgiven.*

Actor: Robert Downey, Jr., *Chaplin;* Clint Eastwood, *Unforgiven;* Al Pacino, *Scent of A Woman;* Stephen Rea, *The Crying Game;* Denzel Washington, *Malcolm X.*

Actress: Catherine Deneuve, *Indochine;* Mary McDonnell, *Passion Fish;* Michelle Pfeiffer, *Love Field;* Susan Sarandon, *Lorenzo's Oil;* Emma Thompson, *Howards End.*

Supporting Actor: Jaye Davidson, *The Crying Game;* Gene Hackman, *Unforgiven;* Jack Nicholson, *A Few Good Men;* Al Pacino, *Glengarry Glen Ross;* David Paymer, *Mr. Saturday Night.*

Supporting Actress: Judy Davis, *Husbands and Wives;* Joan Plowright, *Enchanted April;* Vanessa Redgrave, *Howards End;* Miranda Richardson, *Damage;* Marisa Tomei, *My Cousin Vinny.*

Director: Neil Jordan, *The Crying Game;* James Ivory, *Howards End;* Robert Altman, *The Player;* Martin Brest, *Scent of A Woman;* Clint Eastwood, *Unforgiven.*

Foreign-Language Film: *Close to Eden*, Russia; *Daens*, Belgium; *Indochine*, France; *A Place in the World*, Uruguay; *Schtonk*, Germany.

Original Screenplay: Neil Jordan, *The Crying Game;* Woody Allen, *Husbands and Wives;* George Miller and Nick Enright, *Lorenzo's Oil;* John Sayles, *Passion Fish;* David Webb Peoples, *Unforgiven.*

Screenplay Adaptation: Peter Barnes, *Enchanted April;* Ruth Prawer Jhabvala, *Howards End;* Michael Tolkin, *The Player;* Richard Friedenberg, *A River Runs Through It;* Bo Goldman, *Scent of A Woman.*

Cinematography: Stephen H. Burum, *Hoffa;* Tony Pierce-Roberts, *Howards End;* Robert Fraisse, *The Lover;* Philippe Rousselot, *A River Runs Through It;* Jack N. Green, *Unforgiven.*

Original Song: Robert Kraft and Arne Glimcher, "Beautiful Maria of My Soul," *The Mambo Kings;* Alan Menken and Howard Ashman, "Friend Like Me," *Aladdin;* David Foster and Linda Thompson, "I Have Nothing," *The Bodyguard;* Jud Friedman and Allan Rich, "Run to You," *The Bodyguard;* Alan Menken and Tim Rice, "Whole New World," *Aladdin.*

Source: *Academy of Motion Picture Arts and Sciences*

TELEVISION AND RADIO

The Early Days of Canadian Television

Canadian television got off to a belated and somewhat shaky start in 1952 as stations signed on in Montreal Sept. 6 and two days later in Toronto, where the first image was the CBC logo upside down and backwards. As viewers huddled in front of flickering TV sets,

the picture quickly faded to black while the logo was reversed and the countdown to sign-on was restarted.

Both the Toronto and Montreal stations—which were joined by a third in Vancouver by the end of 1952—began with 18 hours of weekly programming, almost all of it Canadian. Performers in early productions included Don Harron, Barbara Hamilton and Lorne Greene. A young Norman Jewison was stage director of "The Big Revue," a variety show. Hockey Night in Canada, with Foster Hewitt handling the play-by-play, was one of the first shows to compete in popularity with American-based programs such as the Jackie Gleason Show.

Before the start of CBC television broadcasts, there were fewer than 150 000 television sets in the country—all with antennas pointed towards the United States, where the first stations had been launched five years earlier. Sales doubled each year during the mid 1950s so that, by 1956, more than half of Canadian households owned a TV.

An early boost to sales was the coronation of Queen Elizabeth in 1953. The CBC rewarded its early viewers by winning the transatlantic race to be the first North American station to broadcast the royal event. The network recorded the seven-hour BBC broadcast on kinescope film and developed it in minutes using a special process called "hot kine." The film was flown across the Atlantic in three shipments by a combination of RAF bomber, RCAF jet and helicopter. It aired in Canada at 4:14 p.m. EDT, less than four hours after the ceremony had ended.

Other notable CBC broadcasts during the early years included exclusive coverage of Roger Bannister's "miracle mile" at the 1954 British Empire and Commonwealth Games in Vancouver and the first live coverage of a federal election in 1957.

The early years were also not without controversy. The Nov. 1952 airing of Lister Sinclair's "Hilda Morgan," a play dealing openly with the experiences of an unwed mother, caused waves of moral indignation. In Parliament, opposition leader George Drew called for government intervention "to prevent filth of that kind" on Canada's airwaves.

The nation's first private station—Sudbury's CKSO—went on the air in Oct. 1953 and was quickly followed by others as the number of Canadian stations grew to 26 by 1955. By 1958, an electronic highway costing $50 million had linked stations on the east and west coasts.

Longest–Running Canadian TV Shows

(up to the end of the 1992–93 season)

Program (Network)	Seasons	Program (Network)	Seasons
Hockey Night in Canada (CBC)	41 (1952–)	This Land	19 (1967–86)
CFL Football	41 (1952–)	Canada AM (CTV)	21 (1972–)
Country Canada/Country Calendar	39 (1954–)	The Beachcombers	19 (1972–91)
Front Page Challenge	36 (1957–)	Market Place	21 (1972–)
The Nature of Things	33 (1960–)	Meeting Place	21 (1972–)
Wide World of Sports	33 (1960–)	What's New	18 (1972–90)
The Friendly Giant	27 (1958–85)	the 5th estate	18 (1975–)
Hymn Sing	28 (1965–)	Definition	16 (1974–90)
The Tommy Hunter Show	27 (1965–92)	Live It Up	13 (1977–90)
Romper Room	26 (1966–92)	Sportsweekend	14 (1979–)
W-5	27 (1966–)	What's Cooking	12 (1977–89)
Mr. Dressup	26 (1967–)	Headline Hunters	11 (1972–83)
Man Alive	26 (1967–)	Don Messer's Jubilee	10 (1959–69)
Question Period	25 (1968–)	Juliette	10 (1956–66)
Expos Baseball (CBC)	19 (1971–90)		

The Gemini Awards, 1993

The Gemini Awards were established in 1986 to honor outstanding contributions to the Canadian television industry. Given out annually by the Academy of Canadian Cinema and Television, the Geminis grew out of the former ACTRA Awards, last presented in 1985. These awards were presented Mar. 7, 1993.

Drama series	**ENG**
Dramatic mini-series	**Conspiracy of Silence**
Comedy series	**The Kids in the Hall**
Variety series	**The Best of Just for Laughs: Montreal International Comedy Festival**
TV movie	**Scales of Justice, "Regina vs Nelles"**

Actor (dramatic series) .... **Cedric Smith,** Road to Avonlea, "Friends and Relations"
Actor (dramatic program or mini-series) .... **Michael Mahonen,** Conspiracy of Silence
Supporting actor .... **Jonathan Welsh,** ENG, "Secrets"
Actress (drama series) .... **Sara Botsford,** ENG, "The Best Defense"
Actress (dramatic program or mini-series) .... **Kate Nelligan,** Diamond Fleece
Supporting actress .... **Brooke Johnson,** Conspiracy of Silence
Guest performance in a series .... **Kate Nelligan,** Road to Avonlea, "After the Honeymoon"
Performance (performing arts program or series) .... **Barenaked Ladies,** Ear to the Ground, "Barenaked Ladies"
Performance (comedy program or series) ...... **Dave Foley, Bruce McCullogh, Kevin McDonald, Mark McKinney, Scott Thompson,** The Kids in the Hall, "Asleep on the Job"
Performance (variety program or series) .... **Anne Murray, k.d. lang,** Country Gold
Animated program or series .... **The adventures of Tintin**
Children's program or series .... **Shining Time Station**
Documentary series .... **The Valour and the Horror**
Information series .... **The 5th Estate**
Light information series .... **Life: The Program**
Sports program .... **Sports Weekend**
Youth program or series .... **The Jellybean Odyssey**
Documentary program .... **Timothy Findley: Anatomy of a Writer**
Performing arts program .... **Cirque du soleil: Nouvelle expérience**
Short dramatic program .... **Scales of Justice, "Regina vs Stewart"**
Variety program .... **Brian Orser: Night Moves**

Source: *Academy of Canadian Cinema and Television*

The Most–Watched Television Programs in Canada[1]

(by adults 18+; Aug. 1992–May 1993)

Canadian

1. World Series 91/92 (CTV)
2. American League Playoffs (CTV)
3. CTV Sunday Movie (CTV)
4. Au Nom de Pere et du Fils (TVA)
5. Roseanne (CTV)
6. SC7 Shehaweh (RC)
7. CTV Monday Movie (CTV)
8. Home Improvement (CTV)
9. Scoop (RC)
10. Unsolved Mysteries (CTV)

American

1. 60 Minutes (CBS)
2. Roseanne (ABC)
3. Home Improvement (ABC)
4. Murphy Brown (CBS)
5. Murder She Wrote (CBS)
6. Coach (ABC)
7. NFL Monday Night Football (ABC)
8. CBS Sunday Movie (CBS)[2]
8. Cheers (NBC)
9. Full House (ABC)

Source: *A.C. Nielsen Co. of Canada.*

(1) Based on five or more telecasts. (2) Both Cheers and the CBS Sunday Movie had the same audience size.

The Emmy Awards, 1992–93

Drama Series .... **Picket Fences,** CBS
Actor (drama series) .... **Tom Skerritt,** Picket Fences, CBS
Actress (drama series) .... **Kathy Baker,** Picket Fences, CBS
Supporting actor (drama series) .... **Chad Lowe,** Life Goes On, ABC
Supporting actress (drama series) .... **Mary Alice,** I'll Fly Away, NBC
Directing (drama series) .... **Barry Levinson,** Homicide – Life on the Street NBC
Writing (drama series) .... **Tom Fontana,** Homicide – Life on the Street NBC
Comedy Series .... **Seinfeld,** NBC
Actor (comedy series) .... **Ted Danson,** Cheers, NBC
Actress (comedy series) .... **Roseanne Arnold,** Roseanne, ABC
Supporting actor (comedy series) .... **Michael Richards,** Seinfeld, NBC
Supporting actress (comedy series) .... **Laurie Metcalf,** Roseanne , ABC
Directing (comedy series) .... **Betty Thomas,** Dream On, "For Peter's Sake," HBO
Writing (comedy series) .... **Larry David,** Seinfeld, "A Contest," NBC
Miniseries .... **Prime Suspect 2,** PBS
Actor (miniseries or special) .... **Robert Morse,** Tru, PBS

Actress (miniseries or special) .... **Holly Hunter,** The Positively True Adventures of the Alleged Texas-Cheerleader Murdering Mom, HBO
Supporting actor (miniseries or special) .... **Beau Bridges,** The Positively True Adventures of the Alleged Texas-Cheerleader Murdering Mom, HBO
Supporting actress (miniseries or special) .... **Mary Tyler Moore,** Stolen Babies, Lifetime
Directing (miniseries or special) .... **James Sadwith,** Sinatra, CBS
Variety (music or comedy) special .... **Saturday Night Live,** NBC
Individual performance (variety or music) .... **Dana Carvey,** Saturday Night Live, NBC
Directing (variety or music) .... **Walter C. Miller,** The 1992 Tony Awards, CBS
Informational series .... **Healing and the Mind With Bill Moyers,** PBS
Animated program .... **Batman: The Series,** FBC
Children's program (series) .... **Avonlea,** The Disney Channel
Children's program (special) .... **Beethoven Lives Upstairs,** HBO
Outstanding TV Movie .... (tie) **Stalin, Barbarians at the Gate,** HBO

Average Hours Per Week of Television Viewing,[1] 1990

	Total Population	Men Age 18+	Women Age 18+	Teens Age 12–17	Children Age 2–11
Canada	23.3	22.4	26.5	17.7	19.4
Nfld	25.5	24.2	29.3	20.9	22.7
PEI	23.6	21.3	28.1	18.2	20.0
NS	23.9	22.2	27.5	18.8	20.9
NB	24.6	22.7	28.3	19.7	21.8
Que.	25.7	24.3	29.8	19.1	21.4
Ont.	22.1	21.3	25.1	17.0	18.7
Man.	23.1	23.1	25.7	16.5	20.3
Sask.	22.8	22.1	26.3	16.9	19.6
Alta	22.1	22.2	25.0	16.6	18.2
BC	21.8	21.9	24.4	16.5	16.6

Source: *Statistics Canada*

(1) Only at-home viewing is included.

TV Viewing Time By Type of Program, 1991

PROVINCE	News and Public Affairs	Documentary	Academic	Social/Recreational	Religion	Sports	Variety and Game	Music and Dance	Comedy	Drama	Other
NFLD	24.1	1.0	1.1	2.4	0.4	5.9	7.0	1.1	18.6	32.5	5.9
PEI	27.2	1.1	1.0	2.8	0.3	6.7	5.2	1.3	18.6	26.9	9.0
NS	24.1	1.5	1.1	1.8	0.3	5.6	5.9	1.7	18.7	29.7	9.6
NB	22.3	1.4	1.1	2.2	0.3	5.2	7.6	1.5	18.8	31.4	8.1
QUE	24.0	1.9	2.1	1.7	0.3	5.3	17.5	1.5	10.7	28.6	6.4
ONT	21.5	1.6	0.8	2.3	0.2	7.6	6.9	0.9	19.6	30.3	8.3
MAN.	21.7	1.6	1.0	2.3	0.4	9.2	6.6	0.9	20.2	27.3	8.8
SASK	24.0	1.0	0.9	1.8	0.5	8.1	6.3	1.1	19.2	27.7	9.2
ALTA	21.1	1.4	0.8	1.4	0.4	10.0	4.8	0.7	20.2	28.1	11.0
BC	23.8	1.6	0.8	1.1	0.3	9.9	6.0	0.7	18.3	27.9	9.6

Television Networks and Cable Services

Alberta Educational Communications Authority: 3720-76 Ave, Edmonton, Alta. T6B 2N9

American Broadcasting Company (ABC): 77 W 66th St, New York, NY 10023

Arts & Entertainment Network (A&E): 235 E 45th St, New York, NY 10017

Atlantic Television System & Atlantic Satellite Network: Box 1653, Halifax, N.S. B3J 2Z4

C-SPAN: 400 N. Capitol St. NW, Washington, DC 20001

Cable News Network (CNN): 1 CNN Centre, Box 105366, Atlanta, GA 30348-5366

Canadian Broadcasting Corporation (CBC): Box 8478, Ottawa, Ont. K1G 3J5

Canal Famille: 2100 Sainte-Catherine ouest, Bureau 800, Montreal, Que. H3H 2T3

Cathay International Television Inc.: 494 W 49th Ave, Vancouver, B.C. V5Y 2P7

Chinavision Canada Corporation: 160 Duncan Mill Rd., Don Mills, Ont. M3B 1Z5

Columbia Broadcasting System (CBS): 51 W 52nd St, New York, NY 10019

CTV Television Network Ltd.: 42 Charles St E, Toronto, Ont. M4Y 1T5

The Family Channel Inc.: BCE Place, 181 Bay St., Box 787, Toronto, Ont. M5J 2T3

First Choice Canadian Communications Corporation: 98 Queen St E, Toronto, Ont. M5C 1S6

Fox Broadcasting Co.: Box 900, Beverly Hills, CA 90213

Global Television Network: 81 Barber Greene Rd, Don Mills, Ont. M3C 2A2

Home Team Sports: 7700 Wisconsin Ave., Bethesda, MD 20814

Home Theatre: (A division of Allarcom Pay TV Ltd.), #200-5324 Calgary Trail, Edmonton, Alta. T6H 4J8

Inuit Broadcasting Corporation: 251 Laurier Ave W, Ste 703, Ottawa, Ont. K1P 5J6

Knowledge Network: 4355 Mathissi Place, Burnaby, B.C. V5G 4S8

The Learning Channel: 1525 Wilson Blvd, Ste 550, Rosslyn, VA 22209

MuchMusic Network: 299 Queen St W, Toronto, Ont. M5V 2Z5

MusiquePlus: 209 Sainte-Catherine est, Montreal, Que. H2X 1L2

The Nashville Network: 250 Harbor Dr, Stamford, CT 06904-2210

National Broadcasting Company (NBC): 30 Rockefeller Plaza, New York, NY 10020

Okalakatiget Society: Box 160, Nain, Nfld. A0P 1L0

Premier Choix TVEC Inc.: 2100 Sainte-Catherine ouest, #800 Montreal, Que. H3H 2T3

Public Broadcasting Service (PBS): 1320 Braddock Place, Alexandria, VA 22314

Radio-Canada International: Box 6000, Montreal, Que. H3C 3A8

Le Reseau des Sports: 1755 Boul. René-Lévesque est, Bur. 300, Montreal, Que. H2K 4P6

Société de radio-télévision du Quebec (Radio-Quebec): 800, rue Fullum, Montreal, Que. H2K 3L7

The Sports Network (TSN): 1155 Leslie St, Don Mills, Ont. M3C 2J6

Superchannel: 200-5324 Calgary Trail, Edmonton, Alta. T6H 4J8

Telelatino Network Inc.: 5125 Steeles Ave W, Weston, Ont. M5B 1M2

TVOntario (TVO): Box 200, Stn Q, Toronto, Ont. M4T 2T1

Vision TV: 315 Queen St E, Toronto, Ont. M5A 1S7

The Weather Channel: 2600 Cumberland Pkwy., Atlanta, GA 30339

YTV Canada Inc.: 64 Jefferson Ave, Unit 18, Toronto, Ont. M6K 3H3

Ten Early Highlights of Canadian Radio

1919 .... First broadcast by XWA Montreal, the first licensed radio station in North America.
1920 .... XWA broadcast its first regularly scheduled programs.
1923 .... First hockey play-by-play on CKCK Regina.
1924 .... First Dominion Observatory time signals.
1924 .... First livestock market reports.
1924 .... First Stanley Cup broadcast.
1932 .... First Christmas Day broadcast from Buckingham Palace.
1933 .... Canadian Press began providing daily news bulletins.
1936 ..... Live telephone reports on trapped miners in Nova Scotia heard on 58 Canadian stations and 650 in the US.
1941 .... CBC National News Service began regular scheduled broadcasts.

POPULAR MUSIC

The Juno Awards, 1983–93

The Juno Awards were established in 1975 to honor achievement in the Canadian recording industry. The name was chosen to honor Pierre Juneau, former head of the Canadian Radio-television and Telecommunications Commission (CRTC) which instituted "Canadian content" requirements in the nation's broadcast industry.

Nominations for most major Juno categories are determined by record sales, although the actual winners are selected by a vote of members of the Canadian Academy of Recording Arts & Sciences.

There were no awards presented in 1988. Following the Nov. 1987 awards, the presentation of the Junos was moved from the fall to the spring so that the next awards were presented in the spring of 1989. The 1989 awards cover 1988 releases.

The 1993 awards were announced Mar. 21, 1993.

Canadian Entertainer of the Year
1987 .... Bryan Adams
1989 .... Glass Tiger
1990 .... The Jeff Healey Band
1991 .... The Tragically Hip
1992 .... Bryan Adams
1993 .... The Tragically Hip

Album of the Year
1983/84 .... *Cuts Like a Knife*, Bryan Adams
1985 .... *Reckless*, Bryan Adams
1986 .... *The Thin Red Line*, Glass Tiger
1987 .... *Shakin' Like A Human Being*, Kim Mitchell
1989 .... *Robbie Robertson*, Robbie Robertson
1990 .... *Alannah Myles*, Alannah Myles
1991 .... *Unison*, Celine Dion
1992 .... *Mad Mad World*, Tom Cochrane
1993 .... *Ingenue*, k.d. lang

Single of the Year
1983/84 .... "Rise Up," The Parachute Club
1985 .... "Never Surrender," Corey Hart
1986 ..... "Don't Forget Me (When I'm Gone)," Glass Tiger
1987 .... "Someday," Glass Tiger
1989 .... "Try," Blue Rodeo
1990 .... "Black Velvet," Alannah Myles
1991 .... "Just Came Back," Colin James
1992 .... "Life Is a Highway," Tom Cochrane
1993 ... "Beauty and the Beast," Celine Dion/Peabo Bryson

Female Vocalist of the Year
1983/84 .... Carole Pope
1985 .... Luba

1986 .... Luba
1987 .... Luba
1989 .... k.d. lang
1990 .... Rita MacNeil
1991 .... Celine Dion
1992 .... Celine Dion
1993 .... Celine Dion

Male Vocalist of the Year
1983/84 .... Bryan Adams
1985 .... Bryan Adams
1986 .... Bryan Adams
1987 .... Bryan Adams
1989 .... Robbie Robertson
1990 .... Kim Mitchell
1991 .... Colin James
1992 .... Tom Cochrane
1993 .... Leonard Cohen

Group of the Year
1983/84 .... Loverboy
1985 .... The Parachute Club
1986 .... Honeymoon Suite
1987 .... Tom Cochrane & Red Rider
1989 .... Blue Rodeo
1990 .... Blue Rodeo
1991 .... Blue Rodeo
1992 .... Crash Test Dummies
1993 .... Barenaked Ladies

Most Promising Female Vocalist of the Year
1983/84 .... Sherry Kean
1985 .... k.d. lang ▶

▶ 1986 .... Kim Richardson
1987 .... Rita MacNeil
1989 .... Sass Jordan
1990.............................. Alannah Myles
1991 .... Sue Medley
1992.............................. Alanis
1993.............................. Julie Masse

Most Promising Male Vocalist of the Year
1983/84.............................. Zappacosta
1985 .... Paul Janz
1986 .... Billy Newton-Davis
1987 .... Tim Feehan
1989 .... Colin James
1990.............................. Daniel Lanois
1991 .... Andy Curran
1992 .... Keven Jordan
1993.............................. John Bottomley

Most Promising Group of the Year
1983/84 .... The Parachute Club
1985 .... Idle Eyes
1986 .... Glass Tiger
1987.............................. Frozen Ghost
1989 .... Barney Bentall & The Legendary Hearts
1990.............................. The Tragically Hip
1991.............................. The Leslie Spit Treeo
1992.............................. Infidels
1993.............................. Skydiggers

Country Female Vocalist of the Year
1983/84 .... Anne Murray
1985.............................. Anne Murray
1986.............................. Anne Murray
1987.............................. k.d. lang
1989.............................. k.d. lang
1990.............................. k.d. lang
1991.............................. Rita MacNeil
1992.............................. Cassandra Vasik
1993.............................. Michelle Wright

Country Male Vocalist of the Year
1983/84.............................. Murray McLauchlan
1985.............................. Murray McLauchlan
1986.............................. Murray McLauchlan
1987.............................. Ian Tyson
1989.............................. Murray McLauchlan
1990.............................. George Fox
1991.............................. George Fox
1992.............................. George Fox
1993.............................. Gary Fjellgaard

Country Group or Duo of the Year
1983/84.............................. The Good Brothers
1985.............................. The Family Brown
1986.............................. Prairie Oyster
1987.............................. Prairie Oyster
1989.............................. The Family Brown
1990.............................. The Family Brown
1991.............................. Prairie Oyster
1992.............................. Prairie Oyster
1993.............................. Tracey Prescott & Lonesome Daddy

Best Hard Rock Album
1991.............................. *Presto*, Rush
1992.............................. *Roll the Bones*, Rush

1993...................... *Doin' the Nasty*, Slik Toxik

Rap Recording of the Year
1991 .... "Symphony in Effect," Maestro Fresh-Wes

1992 .... "My Definition of a Boombastic Jazz Style,"
Dream Warriors
1993.......................... *Keep It Slammin'*, Devon

Best Dance Recording
1990 .... "I Beg Your Pardon (I Never Promised You a
Rose Garden)," Kon Kan
1991 .... "Don't Wanna Fall in Love," Jane Child
1992........ "Everyone's a Winner (Chocolate Movement
Mix)," Bootsauce
1993 . "Love Can Move Mountains (Club Mix)," Celine Dion

Best Jazz Album
1983/84 .. *All In Good Time*, Rob McConnell and The Boss
The Boss Brass
1985............ *A Beautiful Friendship*, Don Thompson
1986 .... *Lights of Burgundy*, Oliver Jones
1987.. *If You Could See Me Now*, The Oscar Peterson Four
1989 .... *Looking Up*, The Hugh Fraser Quintet
1990........ *Skydance*, Jon Ballantyne Trio featuring Joe
Henderson
1991 .... *Two Sides*, Mike Murley
1992..... *For the Moment*, Renee Rosnes; *In Transition*,
Brian Dickinson; *The Brass Is Back*, Rob
McConnell and The Boss Brass
1993.............................. *My Ideal*, P.J. Perry

Best R&B/Soul Recording
1985 .. "Lost Somewhere Inside Your Love," Liberty Silver
1986 ... "Love Is a Contact Sport," Billy Newton-Davis
1987.................... "Peek-A-Boo," Kim Richardson
1989.......................... "Angel," Erroll Star
1990........... "Spellbound," Billy Newton-Davis
1991 .... "Dance to the Music (Work Your Body),"
Simply Majestic Featuring B. Kool
1992.................... "Call My Name," Love & Sas
1993 .... "Once in a Lifetime," Love & Sas

Best Reggae/Calypso Recording
1985....... *Heaven Must Have Sent You*, Liberty Silver &
Otis Gayle
1986........... *Revolutionary Tea Party*, Lillian Allen
1987 .... *Mean While*, Leroy Sibbles
1989........... *Conditions Critical*, Lillian Allen
1990........... *Too Late To Turn Back Now*, Sattalites
1991 .... *Soldiers We Are All*, Jayson & Friends

Best World Beat Recording
1992 .... *The Gathering*, Various Artists
1993 .... *Spirits of Havana*, Jane Bunnett

Best Roots and Traditional Album
1989...... *The Return of the Formily Brothers*, The Amos
Garrett, Doug Sahm, Gene Taylor Band
1990........ *Je Voudrais Changer D'Chapeau*, La Bottine
Souriante
1991 .... *Dance & Celebrate*, Bourne & MacLeod
1992..... *Saturday Night Blues*, Various Artists; *The Visit*,
Loreena McKennitt
1993..... *Jusqu'aux P'tites Heures*, La Bouttine Souriante

Instrumental Artist(s) of the Year
1983/84.............................. Liona Boyd ▶

▶ 1985 . . . . The Canadian Brass
1986 . . . . David Foster
1987 . . . . David Foster
1989 . . . . David Foster
1990 . . . . Manteca
1991 . . . . Ofra Harnoy
1992 . . . . Shadowy Men on a Shadowy Planet
1993 . . . . Ofra Harnoy

Best Classical Recording
1983/84 . . . . . . *Ballades op. 10, Rhapsodies op. 79*, Glenn
Gould, A. Brahms

Best Classical Album (solo or chamber ensemble)
1985 . . . . *W.A. Mozart—String Quartets*, The Orford
String Quartet
1986 . . . *Stolen Gems*, James Campbell and Eric Robertson
1987 . . . . *Schubert, Quintet in C*, The Orford String
Quartet, Ofra Harnoy
1989 . . . . *Schubert: Arpeggione Sonata*, Ofra Harnoy
1990 . . . . *20th Century Original Piano Transcriptions*,
Louis Lortie
1991 . . *Schafer: Five String Quartets*, Orford String Quartet
1992 . . . . . *Franz Liszt: Années de Pelerinage*, Louis Lortie
1993 . . . . *Beethoven: Piano Sonatas*, Louis Lortie

Best Classical Album (large ensemble)
1985 . . . . . *Ravel: Ma Mère L'oye/Pavane Pour Une Infante
Defunte/Valses Nobles et Sentimentales*,
l'Orchestre Symphonique de Montréal, Charle Dutoit
1986 . . . . *Holst: The Planets*, Toronto Symphony,
Andrew Davis
1987 . . . . . *Holst: The Planets*, l'Orchestre Symphonique de
Montréal, Charles Dutoit
1989 . . . . *Bartok: Concerto for Orchestra; Music for
Strings, Percussion and Celesta*, Montreal
Symphony and Orchestra, Charles Dutoit
1990 . . . . . . *Boccherini: Cello Concertos and Symphonies*,
Tafelmusik Baroque Orchestra
1991 . . . . *Debussy: Images, Nocturnes*, Orchestre
Symphonique de Montréal, Charles Dutoit
1992 . . . . *Debussy: Pelleas et Melisande*, Orchestre
Symphonique de Montréal, Charles Dutoit
1993 . . . . *Handel: Excerpts from Floridante*, Tafelmusik

Best Classical Composition
1987 . . . . . . *Pages of Solitary Delights*, Maureen Forrester
with the McGill Symphony Orchestra, Donal
Steven, Composer
1989 . . . . *Songs of Paradise*, Alexina Louie
1990 . . . . *Concerto For Harp and Chamber Orchestra/
Morawetz Harp Concertos*, Oskar Morawetz
1991 . . . . *String Quartet No. 5 'Rosalind'*, R. Murray
Schafer
1992 . . . . *Concerto For Piano & Chamber Orchestra*,
Michael Conway Baker
1993 . . . . *Concerto for Flute and Orchestra*, R. Murray
Schafer

Best Children's Album
1983/84 . . . . *Rugrat Rock*, Rugrats
1985 . . . . *Murmel Murmel Munsch*, Robert Munsch
1986 . . . . *10 Carrot Diamond*, Charlotte Diamond
1987 . . . . *Drums*, Bill Usher
1989 . . . . *Fred Penner's Place*, Fred Penner; *Lullaby
Berceuse*, Connie Kaldor & Carmen Campagne
1990 . . . . . . *Beethoven Lives Upstairs*, Susan Hammond &
Barbara Nichol
1991 . . . . *Mozart's Magic Fantasy*, Susan Hammond/
Classical Kids
1992 . . . . *Vivaldi's Ring of Mystery*, Susan Hammond/
Classical Kids
1993 . . . . *Waves of Wonder*, Jack Grunsky

Composer of the Year
1985 . . . . Bryan Adams/Jim Vallance
1986 . . . . Jim Vallance
1987 . . . . Jim Vallance
1989 . . . . Tom Cochrane
1990 . . . . David Tyson, Christopher Ward
1991 . . . . David Tyson
1992 . . . . Tom Cochrane
1993 . . . . k.d. lang/Ben Mink

Producer of the Year
1983/84 . . . . Bryan Adams
1985 . . . . David Foster
1986 . . . . David Foster
1987 . . . . Daniel Lanois
1989 . . . . Daniel Lanois and Robbie Robertson
1990 . . . . Bruce Fairbairn
1991 . . . . David Tyson
1992 . . . . Bryan Adams
1993 . . . . . . k.d. lang/Ben Mink (Greg Penny, co-producer)

Best Video of the Year
1983/84 . . . *Sunglasses At Night* (Corey Hart), Rob Quartly
1985 . . . . *A Criminal Mind* (Gowan), Rob Quartly
1986 . . . . *How Many (Rivers to Cross)* (Luba), Greg
Masvak
1987 . . . . *Love Is Fire* (The Parachute Club), Ron Berti
1989 . . . . *Try* (Blue Rodeo), Michael Buckley
1990 . . . . . . *Boomtown* (Andrew Cash), Cosimo Cavallaro
1991 . . . . *Drop the Needle* (Maestro Fresh-Wes), Joel
Goldberg
1992 . . . . . *Into the Fire* (Sarah McLachlan), Phil Kates
1993 . . . . . *Closing Time* (Leonard Cohen), Curtis Wehrfritz

Hall of Fame Award
1978 . . . . Guy Lombardo, Oscar Peterson
1979 . . . . Hank Snow
1980 . . . . Paul Anka
1981 . . . . Joni Mitchell
1982 . . . . Neil Young
1983 . . . . Glenn Gould
1984 . . . . Crewcuts, Diamonds, Four Lads
1985 . . . . Wilf Carter
1986 . . . . Gordon Lightfoot
1987 . . . . The Guess Who
1989 . . . . The Band
1990 . . . . Maureen Forrester
1991 . . . . Leonard Cohen
1992 . . . . Ian & Sylvia
1993 . . . . Anne Murray

Source: *Canadian Academy of Recording Arts & Sciences*

CASBY Awards, 1992

The CASBY (Canadian Artists Selected By You) Awards were established in 1981 by Toronto radio station CFNYto pay tribute to Canadian musicians with awards chosen by the audience, rather than by the industry. These awards were presented Nov. 15, 1992.

Favourite Group	**Barenaked Ladies**
Favourite Live Act	**Barenaked Ladies**
Favourite Album	***These Days,*** The Grapes of Wrath
Favourite Male Vocalist	**Gord Downie,** The Tragically Hip
Favourite Female Vocalist	**Sarah McLachlan**
Favourite Song	**"I Am Here,"** The Grapes of Wrath
Favourite Reggae/Ska Group	**King Apparatus**
Favourite New Group, Western Canada	**Pure**
Favourite New Group, Central Canada	**Moxy Fruvous**
Favourite New Group, Eastern Canada	**Sloan**
Favourite Debut Album	***Gordon,*** Barenaked Ladies
Favourite Writers/Lyricists	**Jim Cuddy** and **Greg Keelor,** Blue Rodeo
Favourite Music Producer	**Michael Phillip-Wojewoda,** *Gordon,* Barenaked Ladies
Favourite Album Art	**Rebecca Baird** and **Kenny Baird,** *Lost Together,* Blue Rodeo
Special Achievement Award	**Teenage Head**

Source: *CFNY*

Canadian Country Music Association Awards, 1993

Awards and citations from the CCMA are presented during Country Music Week, which was held in Hamilton from Sept. 13th to 18th, 1993. These were the eleventh annual awards, the first to be broadcast in the US and Europe.

Entertainer of the Year	**Michelle Wright**
Single of the Year	**"He Would Be Sixteen,"** Michelle Wright
Album of the Year	***Bad Day For Trains,*** Patricia Conroy
Song of the Year	**"Backroads,"** Charlie Major
Female Vocalist of the Year	**Michelle Wright**
Male Vocalist of the Year	**George Fox**
Vocal Duo or Group	**Rankin Family**
Vocal Collaboration	**Cassandra Vasik and Russell deCarle**
Vista (Rising Star) Award	**Rankin Family**
Video of the Year	**"He Would Be Sixteen,"** Michelle Wright
Top Selling Album (Foreign or Domestic)	***Some Gave All,*** Billy Ray Cyrus

Source: *Canadian Country Music Association*

The Grammy Awards, 1982–92

Grammy winners are selected annually by the 6,000 voting members of The Recording Academy, based on artistic and/or technical excellence. Best male and female vocals from 1980 to 1989 are for best contemporary or pop vocal. The titles for song of the year are followed by the names of the songwriters. The 1993 Grammy winners will be announced Mar. 1, 1994.

Best Record

1982 "Rosanna," Toto
1983 "Beat It," Michael Jackson
1984 "What's Love Got to Do with It," Tina Turner
1985 "We Are the World," USA For Africa
1986 "Higher Love," Steve Winwood
1987 "Graceland," Paul Simon
1988 "Don't Worry, Be Happy," Bobby McFerrin
1989 "Wind Beneath My Wings," Bette Midler
1990 "Another Day In Paradise," Phil Collins
1991 "Unforgettable," Natalie Cole (with Nat King Cole)
1992 "Tears in Heaven," Eric Clapton

Best Album

1982 *Toto IV*, Toto
1983 *Thriller*, Michael Jackson
1984 *Can't Slow Down*, Lionel Richie
1985 *No Jacket Required*, Phil Collins
1986 *Graceland*, Paul Simon
1987 *The Joshua Tree*, U2
1988 *Faith*, George Michael
1989 *Nick of Time*, Bonnie Raitt
1990 *Back On The Block*, Quincy Jones
1991 *Unforgettable*, Natalie Cole
1992 *Unplugged*, Eric Clapton

Best Song

1982 "Always on My Mind," Johnny Christopher, Mark James, Wayne Carson
1983 "Every Breath You Take," Sting
1984 "What's Love Got to Do with It," Graham Lyle, Terry Britten
1985 "We Are the World," Michael Jackson, Lionel Richie
1986 "That's What Friends Are For," Burt Bacharach, Carole Bayer Sager
1987 "Somewhere Out There," Barry Mann, Cynthia Weil, James Horner
1988 "Don't Worry, Be Happy," Bobby McFerrin
1989 "Wind Beneath My Wings," Larry Henley, Jeff Silbar
1990 "From A Distance," Julie Gold
1991 "Unforgettable," Irving Gordon
1992 "Tears in Heaven," Eric Clapton, Will Jennings

Best Male Vocal

1982 "Truly," Lionel Richie
1983 *Thriller*, Michael Jackson
1984 "Against All Odds," Phil Collins
1985 *No Jacket Required*, Phil Collins
1986 "Higher Love," Steve Winwood
1987 *Bring On the Night*, Sting
1988 "Don't Worry, Be Happy," Bobby McFerrin
1989 "How Am I Supposed to Live Without You," Michael Bolton
1990 "Oh, Pretty Woman," Roy Orbison
1991 "When a Man Loves a Woman," Michael Bolton
1992 "Tears in Heaven," Eric Clapton

Best Female Vocal

1982 "You Should Hear How She Talks About You," Melissa Manchester
1983 "Flashdance…What a Feeling," Irene Cara
1984 "What's Love Got to Do with It," Tina Turner
1985 "Saving All My Love for You," Whitney Houston
1986 *The Broadway Album*, Barbra Streisand
1987 "I Wanna Dance with Somebody (Who Loves Me)," Whitney Houston
1988 "Fast Car," Tracy Chapman
1989 "Nick of Time," Bonnie Raitt
1990 "Vision Of Love," Mariah Carey
1991 "Something to Talk About," Bonnie Raitt
1992 "Constant Craving," k.d. lang

Best New Artist

1982 Men At Work
1983 Culture Club
1984 Cyndi Lauper
1985 Sade
1986 Bruce Hornsby and the Range
1987 Jody Watley
1988 Tracy Chapman
1989[1] Withdrawn
1990 Mariah Carey
1991 Mark Cohn
1992 Arrested Development

Source: *National Academy of Recording Arts & Sciences*

(1) Initially awarded to Milli Vanilli who later admitted they had not performed on any of their recordings.

Top Records in Canada, 1992

Hit Singles

1. "Sometimes Love Just Ain't Enough," Patty Smyth & Don Henley
2. "To Be With You," Mr. Big
3. "Song Instead of A Kiss," Alannah Myles
4. "If You Asked Me To," Celine Dion
5. "Layla," Eric Clapton
6. "One," U2
7. "I'll Be There," Mariah Carey
8. "This Used to Be My Playground," Madonna
9. "The One," Elton John
10. "Tears in Heaven," Eric Clapton

Adult Contemporary Tracks

1. "Beauty and the Beast," Celine Dion & Peabo Bryson
2. "Nothing Broken But My Heart," Celine Dion
3. "If You Asked Me To," Celine Dion
4. "Restless Heart," Peter Cetera
5. "The One," Elton John
6. "Just Another Day," Jon Secada
7. "Hold On My Heart," Genesis
8. "This Used to Be My Playground," Madonna
9. "Missing You Now," Michael Bolton
10. "Sometimes Love Just Ain't Enough," Patty Smyth & Don Henley

Country Tracks

1. "Achy Breaky Heart," Billy Ray Cyrus
2. "What's She Doing Now," Garth Brooks
3. "She Is His Only Need," Wynonna Judd
4. "Love's Got a Hold on You," Alan Jackson
5. "Cafe on the Corner," Sawyer Brown
6. "Take It Like a Man," Michelle Wright
7. "Is There Life Out There," Reba McEntire
8. "I Saw The Light," Wynonna Judd
9. "If I Didn't Have You," Randy Travis
10. "Seminole Wind," John Anderson

Albums

1. *Classic Queen*, Queen
2. *Waking Up The Neighbours*, Bryan Adams
3. *Gordon*, Barenaked Ladies
4. *Mad Mad World*, Tom Cochrane
5. *Achtung Baby*, U2
6. *Some Gave All*, Billy Ray Cyrus
7. *Unplugged*, Eric Clapton
8. *Nevermind*, Nirvana
9. *Blood Sugar Sex Magik*, Red Hot Chili Peppers
10. *Adrenalize*, Def Leppard

Dance Tracks

1. "Rhythm is A Dancer," Snap
2. "Jump," Kriss Kross
3. "Set Me Free," Clubland
4. "Justified & Ancient," The KLF w/ Tammy Wynette
5. "Twilight Zone," 2 Unlimited
6. "We Got a Love Thang," Ce Ce Peniston
7. "Too Funky," George Michael
8. "I'm Too Sexy," RSF
9. "Everybody's Free," Rozalla
10. "Please Don't Go," Double You

Canadian Content Albums

1. *Gordon*, Barenaked Ladies
2. *Mad Mad World*, Tom Cochrane
3. *Fully Completely*, The Tragically Hip
4. *Lost Together*, Blue Rodeo
5. *Rockinghorse*, Alannah Myles
6. *Black Eyed Man*, Cowboy Junkies
7. *Barenaked Ladies*, Barenaked Ladies
8. *Harvest Moon*, Neil Young
9. *Ingénue*, k.d. lang
10. *The Future*, Leonard Cohen

Source: *RPM Weekly*

Number of New Recordings

With Canadian Content

Type of music	1987–88	1989–90	1991–92
Adult-oriented Pop Music	74	198	244
Top 40/Rock, Disco	155	149	228
Classical and related	36	76	80
Jazz	19	24	18
Country and Folk	57	107	192
Children's	12	6	180
Other (includes unspecified)	68	55	159
Total	421	615	1,101

▶

Without Canadian Content

Type of music	1987–88	1989–90	1991–92
Type of music	1987–88	1989–90	1991–92
Adult-oriented Pop Music	417	725	623
Top 40/Rock, Disco	801	1 741	2 818
Classical and related	267	607	1 362
Jazz	543	220	488
Country and Folk	177	150	233
Children's	35	24	135
Other (includes unspecified)	222	357	746
Total	2 462	3 824	6 405

Source: *Statistics Canada*

Top–Selling[1] Canadian Record Albums, 1975–93

1 Million + Sales
Bryan Adams, *Reckless*
Corey Hart, *Boy In The Box*

900 000 + Sales
Tom Cochrane, *Mad Mad World*

600 000 + Sales
Anne Murray, *Greatest Hits*
Alannah Myles, *Alannah Myles*
Barenaked Ladies, *Gordon*

500 000 + Sales
Loverboy, *Loverboy*
Platinum Blonde, *Alien Shores*
Trooper, *Hot Shots*
Zamfir, *The Lonely Shepherd*

400 000 + Sales
Glass Tiger, *The Thin Red Line*
Rush, *Moving Pictures*
The Tragically Hip, *Fully Completely*

300 000 + Sales
Bryan Adams, *Cuts Like a Knife*
Bryan Adams, *Into The Fire*
Blue Rodeo, *Diamond Mine*
Corey Hart, *First Offense*
Harmonium, *L'Heptade*
Honeymoon Suite, *The Big Prize*
Honeymoon Suite, *Honeymoon Suite*
Loverboy, *Get Lucky*
Bob & Doug McKenzie, *The Great White North*
Rita MacNeil, *Now the Bells Ring*
Kim Mitchell, *Shakin' Like a Human Being*
Anne Murray, *Christmas Wishes*
Raffi, *Singable Songs For The Very Young*

Ginette Reno, *Je Ne Suis Qu'une Chanson*

200 000 + Sales
Aldo Nova, *Aldo Nova*
April Wine, *Greatest Hits*
April Wine, *The Nature of The Beast*
Angele Arsenault, *Libre*
Blue Rodeo, *Outskirts*
Gerry Boulet, *Rendez-vous doux*
Marie Carmen, *Miel Et Venin*
Chilliwack, *Hit Express*
Tom Cochrane and Red Rider, *Victory Day*
Burton Cummings, *Best of Burton Cummings*
Burton Cummings, *Dream of a Child*
The Emeralds, *Bird Dance*
Glass Tiger, *Diamond Sun*
Gowan, *Strange Animal*
Harmonium, *Harmonium*
Corey Hart, *Fields of Fire*
Headpins, *Turn it Loud*
The Jeff Healey Band, *See The Light*
Heart, *Dreamboat Annie*
Dan Hill, *Longer Fuse*
Honeymoon Suite, *Racing After Midnight*
Gordon Lightfoot, *Gord's Gold*
Loverboy, *Keep it Up*
The Rankin Family, *Fare Thee Well Love*
Rita MacNeil, *Flying On Your Own*
Rita MacNeil, *Home I'll Be*
Rita MacNeil, *Reason to Believe*
Rita MacNeil, *Rita*
Loreena McKennitt, *The Visit*
Marjo, *Celle Qui Va*
Alannah Myles, *Rockinghorse*
Platinum Blonde, *Standing in the Dark*

Powder Blues, *Uncut*
Prism, *Armageddon*
Raffi, *More Singable Songs*
Raffi, *Baby Beluga*
Robbie Robertson, *Robbie Robertson*
Roch Voisine, *Helene*

The Rovers, *The Rovers' 20th Anniversary*
Rush, *2112*
Sharon, Lois and Bram, *One Elephant, Deux Elephants*
Jennifer Warnes, *Famous Blue Raincoat*
Neil Young, *Harvest Moon*

Source: *Canadian Recording Industry Association*

(1) Includes only Canadian sales of over 200,000, based on certification by the Canadian Recording Industry Association, as of August 1993, of recordings that meet Canadian content standards by satisfying three of the following four criteria: music by a Canadian; performed by a Canadian artist; Canadian production; lyrics by a Canadian. Includes records, tapes and compact discs.

Record Sales in Canada by Format

(millions of units shipped)

	1972	1977	1982	1987	1992
7" singles	16.8	19.8	12.3	5.6	—
12" singles	—	—	—	0.6	0.3
Cassette singles	—	—	—	—	1.5
LPs	29.4	46.0	36.5	14.2	—
8-track tapes	5.9	15.0	1.4	—	—
Cassettes	1.0	4.5	18.2	31.5	23.6
CDs	—	—	—	6.2	26.3

Source: *Canadian Recording Industry Association*   (—) = zero

Top–Selling[1] Canadian Record Singles, 1975–93

Artist	Record Title	Canadian Sales
Northern Lights	"Tears Are Not Enough"	300 000+
The Rovers	"Wasn't That a Party"	200 000+
Bryan Adams	"Diana"[2]	100 000+
Alain Barrière	"Tue T'en Vas"	100 000+
Claudja Barry	"Boogie Woogie Dancin' Shoes"	100 000+
Corey Hart	"Never Surrender"	100 000+
Irish Rovers	"The Unicorn"	100 000+
Anne Murray	"You Needed Me"	100 000+
Platinum Blonde	"Crying Over You"	100 000+
J & R Williams	"La Danse des Canards"	100 000+

Source: *Canadian Recording Industry Association*

(1) Includes only Canadian sales of over 50,000, based on certification by the Canadian Recording Industry Association, as of August 1993, of recordings that meet Canadian content standards by satisfying three of the following four criteria: music by a Canadian; performed by a Canadian artist; Canadian production; lyrics by a Canadian. (2) An extended play single.

Canadian Music Video Awards, 1993

Best Director .... **Jeth Weinrich**, "I Would Die for You," Jann Arden
Best Director of Photography .... **Miroslaw Baszak**,"Livin' in the 90s," Barney Bentall and The Lengendary Hearts
Best Editor .... **Michelle Czukar**, "Courage," Tragically Hip
Best Video .... **"Locked in the Trunk of a Car,"** Tragically Hip
Best Rap Video .... **"Jungleman,"** The Maximum Definitive
Best R&B/Soul Video .... **"Supernatual,"** John James
Best Dance Video .... **"Won't Give Up My Music,"** Lisa Lougheed
Best Alternative Video .... **"Blast,"** Pure
Best Metal Video .... **"Under the Influence,"** Sven Gali
Best Adult Contemporary Video .... **"Because of Love,"** Mae Moore
Best Country Video .... **"I'm Gonna Drive You Out of My Mind,"** Charlie Major
VideoFACT Award .... **"Just Don't Say,"** Funkasaurus

Source: *MuchMusic Network*

MTV Video Music Awards, 1993

Best Video of the Year	**"Jeremy,"** Pearl Jam
Best Male Video	**"Are You Gonna Go My Way,"** Lenny Kravitz
Best Female Video	**"Constant Craving,"** k.d. lang
Best Group Video	**"Jeremy,"** Pearl Jam
Best Metal/Hard Rock Video	**"Jeremy,"** Pearl Jam
Best New Artist in a Video	**"Plush,"** Stone Temple Pilots
Best Video from a Film	**"Would?,"** Alice in Chains
Best Rap Video	**"People Everyday,"** Arrested Development
Best Dance Video	**"Free Your Mind,"** En Vogue
Best R&B Video	**"Free Your Mind,"** En Vogue
Best Direction in a Video	**"Jeremy,"** Pearl Jam
Best Choreography in a Video	**"Free Your Mind,"** En Vogue
Best Special Effects in a Video	**"Steam,"** Peter Gabriel
Best Alternative Video	**"In Bloom,"** Nirvana
Breakthrough Video	**"Kiko & The Lavender Moon,"** Los Lobos
Best Art Direction in a Video	**"Rain,"** Madonna
Best Editing in a Video	**"Steam,"** Peter Gabriel
Best Cinematography in a Video	**"Rain,"** Madonna
Viewer's Choice Award, US	**"Livin' on the Edge,"** Aerosmith
Viewer's Choice Award, Asia	**"Pretty Child,"** Indus Creed
Viewer's Choice Award, Brasil	**"Sera Que E Isso Que Eu Necessito,"** Titas
Viewer's Choice Award, Europe	**"Killer/Papa Was A Rolling Stone,"** George Michael
Viewer's Choice Award, MTV Internacional	**"America,"** Luis Miguel

Source: *MTV: Music Television*

The Rock and Roll Hall of Fame

The Rock and Roll Hall of Fame was established in 1984 to preserve and enhance the status of rock and roll as an art form. The Rock and Roll Hall of Fame and Museum, featuring exhibits on each of the member performers, is scheduled to open in 1995 in Cleveland, Ohio.

The members, chosen by a group of pop music experts, are listed below, followed by the years in which they were elected. Members in the early influences category are not listed.

■ **ARTISTS**

LaVern Baker (1991)
Hank Ballard (1990)
The Beach Boys (1988)
The Beatles (1988)
Chuck Berry (1986)
Bobby "Blue" Bland (1992)
Booker T. & The MG's (1992)
James Brown (1986)
Ruth Brown (1993)
The Byrds (1991)
Johnny Cash (1992)
Ray Charles (1986)
The Coasters (1987)
Eddie Cochran (1987)
Sam Cooke (1986)
Cream (1993)
Creedence Clearwater Revival (1993)
Bobby Darin (1990)
Bo Diddley (1987)
Dion (1989)
Fats Domino (1986)
The Doors (1993)
The Drifters (1988)
Bob Dylan (1988)

The Everly Brothers (1986)
The Four Seasons (1990)
The Four Tops (1990)
Aretha Franklin (1987)
Marvin Gaye (1987)
Bill Haley (1987)
Buddy Holly (1986)
The Jimi Hendrix Experience (1992)
John Lee Hooker (1991)
The Impressions (1991)
The Isley Brothers (1992)
Etta James (1993)
B.B. King (1987)
The Kinks (1990)
Jerry Lee Lewis (1986)
Little Richard (1986)
Frankie Lyman and the Teenagers (1993)
Clyde McPhatter (1987)
Van Morrison (1993)
Ricky Nelson (1987)
Roy Orbison (1987)
Carl Perkins (1987)
Wilson Pickett (1991)
The Platters (1990)
Elvis Presley (1986)

Otis Redding (1989)
Jimmy Reed (1991)
Smokey Robinson (1987)
The Rolling Stones (1989)
Sam & Dave (1992)
Simon and Garfunkel (1990)
Sly and the Family Stone (1993)
The Supremes (1988)
The Temptations (1989)
Ike and Tina Turner (1991)
Big Joe Turner (1987)
Muddy Waters (1987)
The Who (1990)
Jackie Wilson (1987)
Stevie Wonder (1989)
The Yardbirds (1992)

Leonard Chess (1987)
Dick Clark (1993)
Lamont Dozier, Brian Holland & Eddie Holland (1990)
Ahmet Ertegun (1987)
Leo Fender (1992)
Alan Freed (1986)
Milt Gabler (1993)
Gerry Goffin & Carole King (1990)
Berry Gordy, Jr. (1988)
Bill Graham (1992)
Jerry Leiber & Mike Stoller (1987)
Doc Pomus (1992)
Phil Spector (1989)
Sam Phillips (1986)
Jerry Wexler (1987)

■ **NON-PERFORMERS**
Dave Bartholomew (1991)
Ralph Bass (1991)

■ **LIFETIME ACHIEVEMENT AWARDS**
Nesuhi Ertegun (1991)
John Hammond (1986)

Source: *Rock and Roll Hall of Fame Foundation*

Major Canadian Jazz Festivals

■ **du Maurier Ltd. Downtown Jazz**,

June 24–July 3, 1994, Toronto,

Jim Galloway, Artistic Director.

366 Adelaide St. E, #334,

Toronto, Ont. M5A 3X9

■ **du Maurier Ltd. International Jazz Festival**,

June 24–July 3, 1994, Vancouver,

Ken Pickering, Artistic Director.

435 West Hastings St.,

Vancouver, BC Y6B 1L4

■ **du Maurier Ltd. Saskatchewan Jazz Festival**,

Saskatoon, Jim Hill, Artistic Director,

Bessborough Hotel, Ste. 701,

601 Spadina Cres. E,

Saskatoon, Sask. S7K 3G8

■ **du Maurier Ltd. Jazz City Festival**,

Edmonton, Marc Vasey, Festival Director.

10516 Seventy Seven Ave.,

Edmonton Alta. T6E 1M1

■ **du Maurier Ltd. Atlantic Jazz Halifax**,

Paul Simons, Artistic Director.

PO Box 33043, Halifax, NS B3L 4T6

■ **Montreal International Jazz Festival**,

Andre Menard, Artistic Director.

822 Sherbrooke E,

Montreal, Que. H2L 1K4

■ **Les Nuits Black Internationales De Jazz**,

Quebec City. CP 3114, Succ. Saint-Roch,

Quebec, Que. G1K 6X9

■ **Festival International de Jazz D'Ottawa.**

BP 3104, Succ. D, Ottawa Ont. K1P 6H7

■ **Festi-Jazz de Rimouski.**

CP 1294, Rimouski, Que. G5L 8M2

PERFORMING ARTS

Canadian Orchestras

Brampton Symphony Orchestra: 24 Alexander St., Brampton, Ont. L6V 1H6. Steve Riches, conductor.

Brantford Symphony Orchestra: P.O. Box 101, Brantford, Ont. N3T 5M3. Stanley Saunders, conductor.

Calgary Philharmonic Orchestra: 205-8th Ave. S.E., Calgary, Alta. T2G 0K9. Mario Bernardi, conductor.

Cathedral Bluffs Symphony: 37 Earl Road, Scarborough, Ont. M1M 1E9. Clifford Foole, conductor.

Chamber Players of Toronto: 24 Ryerson Ave., #209, Toronto, Ont. M5T 2P3. Paavo Jarvi, musical director.

Chatham Symphony Orchestra: P.O. Box 396, Chatham, Ont. N7M 5K5. Allen Kosmala, conductor.

Chebucto Symphony Orchestra: P.O. Box 332, Dartmouth, N.S. B2Y 3Y5. Edmond Agopian, conductor.

Civic Orchestra of Victoria: P.O. Box 6478, Depot 1, Victoria, B.C. V8P 5M4. Robert Cooper, conductor.

CJRT Radio Orchestra: 297 Victoria St., Toronto, Ont. M5B 1W1. Paul Robinson, conductor.

Crowsnest Pass Symphony: P.O. Box 268, Blairmore, Alta. T0K 0E0. Dick Burgman, conductor.

Deep River Symphony Orchestra: P.O. Box 1496, Deep River, Ont. K0J 1P0. James Wegg, conductor.

East York Symphony Orchestra: 110 Rumsey Rd., Toronto, Ont. M4G 1P2. Douglas M. Sanford, conductor.

Eastern Ontario Concert Orchestra: P.O. Box 102, Belleville, Ont. K8N 4Z9. Gordon Craig, conductor.

Edmonton Philharmonic Society: 18244-80A Ave., Edmonton, Alta. T5T 0T7. George Maylor, conductor.

Edmonton Symphony Orchestra: 10010-109 St., Edmonton, Alta. T5J 1M4. Uri Mayer, conductor.

Esprit Orchestra: Chalmers Bldg., 35 McCaul St., #410, Toronto, Ont. M5T 1V7. Alex Pauk, conductor.

Etobicoke Philharmonic Orchestra: 19 Hilldowntree Rd., Islington, Ont. M9A 2Z4. Tak-Ng Lai, conductor.

Fanshawe Community Orchestra: 1551 Ryersie Rd., London, Ont. N6G 2S2. Douglas M. Sanford, conductor.

Fraser Valley Symphony: Box 122, Abbotsford, B.C. V2S 4N3. David R. Rushton, conductor.

Georgian Bay Symphony: P.O. Box 133, Owen Sound, Ont. N4K 5P1. Clyde Mitchell, conductor.

Hamilton Philharmonic Orchestra: P.O. Box 2080, Station A, Hamilton, Ont. L8N 3Y7. Victor Feldbrill, conductor.

Hart House Orchestra: Hart House, University of Toronto, 7 Hart House Circle, Toronto, Ont. M5S 1A1. Errol Gay, conductor.

Huronia Symphony: P.O. Box 904, Barrie, Ont. L4M 4X6. Clyde Mitchell, conductor.

International Symphony Orchestra of Sarnia and Port Huron: 774 London Rd., Sarnia, Ont. N7T 4Y1. Zdzislaw Kopac, conductor.

Kamloops Symphony Orchestra: Box 57, Kamloops, B.C. V2C 5K3. Bruce Rodney Dunn, conductor.

Kingston Symphony Orchestra: 120Montreal St., #210, Kingston, Ont. K7L 5C8. Glen Fast, conductor.

Kitchener-Waterloo Chamber Orchestra: P.O. Box 937, Waterloo, Ont. N2J 4C3. Graham Coles, conductor.

Kitchener-Waterloo Community Orchestra: P.O. Box 938, Waterloo, Ont. N2J 4C3. Edit Haboczki, conductor.

Kitchener-Waterloo Symphony: 101 Queen St. N., Kitchener, Ont. N2H 6P7. Raffi Armenian, conductor.

Kootenay Chamber Orchestra: P.O. Box 512, Cranbrook, B.C. V1C 4J1. Ronald Edinger, conductor.

Lethbridge Symphony: P.O. Box 1101, Lethbridge, Alta. T1J 4A2. Stewart Grant, conductor.

Manitoba Chamber Orchestra: 202-1317A Portage Ave., Winnipeg, Man. R3G 0V3. Simon Streatfield, conductor.

McGill Chamber Orchestra: 1745 Cedar Ave., Montreal, Que. H3G 1A7. Alexander Brott, conductor.

Medicine Hat Youth & Community Orchestra: P.O. Box 1295, Medicine Hat, Alta. T1A 7N1. Carl Duguid, conductor.

Mississauga Symphony Orchestra and Sinfonia Mississauga: 161 Lakeshore Rd. W., Mississauga, Ont. L5H 1G3. John Barnum, conductor.

Montreal Chamber Orchestra: 5825 Esplanade Ave., Montreal, Que. H2T 3A2. Wanda Kuluzny, conductor.

Nanaimo Symphony Orchestra: P.O. Box 661, Nanaimo, B.C. V9R 5L9. Lloyd Blackman, conductor.

National Arts Centre Orchestra: P.O. Box 1534, Station B, Ottawa, Ont. K1P 5W1. Trevor Pinnock, conductor.

National Youth Orchestra of Canada: 1032 Bathurst St., Toronto, Ont. M5R 3G7.

Newfoundland Symphony Orchestra: Arts & Culture Centre, Prince Philip Dr., St. John's, Nfld. A1C 5P9. Mario Duschenes, conductor.

Niagara Symphony Orchestra: P.O. Box 401, St. Catharines, Ont. L2R 6V9. Ermanno Florio, conductor.

North Bay Symphony Orchestra: 269 Main St. W., #106, North Bay, Ont. P1B 2T8. Nurhan Arman, conductor.

North York Concert Orchestra: 10 Prestwick Cres., Willowdale, Ont. M2H 1M9. Steve Riches, conductor.

North York Symphony Orchestra: 1210 Sheppard Ave. E., Ste. 109, North York, Ont. M2K 1E3. Kerry Stratton, conductor.

Northumberland Orchestra Society: P.O. Box 1012, Cobourg, Ont., K9A 4W4. Matthew Jaskiewicz, conductor.

Oakville Symphony Orchestra: 297 Lakeshore Rd. E., #1, Oakville, Ont. L6J 1J3. David Miller, conductor.

Okanagan Symphony Orchestra: P.O. Box 1120, Kelowna, B.C. V1Y 7P8. Leonard Camplin, conductor.

Orchestra London Canada Inc.: 520 Wellington St., London, Ont. N6A 3P9. Uri Mayer, conductor.

Orchestre symphonique de Laval: 1395, boul. de la Concorde ouest, Ville de Laval, Que. H7N 5W1. Paul Andre Boivin, conductor.

Orchestre symphonique de Montréal: 85, rue St-Catherine ouest, #900, Montréal, Que. H2X 3P4. Charles S. Dutoit, conductor.

Orchestre symphonique de Québec: 130, Grande-Allée ouest, Québec, Que. G1R 2G7. Pascal Verrot, conductor.

Orchestra symphonique du Saguenay-Lac-St-Jean Inc.: 202, rue Jacques-Cartier est, Chicoutimi, Que. G7H 6R8. Jacques Clement, conductor.

Orchestre des Jeunes du Québec: 1501 Jeanne-Mance, Montreal, Que. H2X 1G9

Orchestre symphonique de Sherbrooke: 14, rue Alexandre, Sherbrooke, Que. J1H 4S6. Marc David, conductor.

Orchestre symphonique de Trois-Rivières: C.P. 1281, Trois-Rivières, Que. G9A 5K8. Gilles Bellemare, conductor.

Orchestre symphonique Régional d'Abitibi-Témiscamingue: C.P. 2305, Rouyn-Noranda, Que. J9X 5A9. Jacques Marchand, conductor.

Oshawa Symphony Orchestra: P.O. Box 444, Oshawa, Ont. L1H 7L5. Winston Webber, conductor.

Ottawa Symphony Orchestra: P.O. Box 3644, Station C, Ottawa, Ont. K1Y 4J7. David Currie, conductor.

Peterborough Symphony Orchestra: P.O. Box 1135, Peterborough, Ont. K9J 7H4. Zdzislaw Kopac, conductor.

Prince Edward Island Symphony Orchestra: P.O. Box 185, Charlottetown, PEI C1A 7K4. Brian Ellard, conductor.

Prince George Symphony Orchestra: 2880-15th Ave., Prince George, B.C. V2M 1T1. John Unsworth, conductor.

Pro Arte Orchestra: 1692 Danforth Ave., Toronto, Ont. M4C 1H8. Victor Di Bello, conductor.

Red Deer Orchestra: P.O. Box 754, Red Deer, Alta. T4N 5H2. Claude Lapalme, conductor.

Regina Symphony Orchestra: 200 Lakeshore Dr., Regina, Sask. S4P 3V7. Vladimir Conta, conductor.

Richmond Community Orchestra: P.O. Box 94284, Richmond, B.C. V6Y 2A2. Charles Willett, conductor.

Royal Conservatory Orchestra: (Orchestral Training Program), 273 Bloor St. W., Toronto, Ont. M5S 1W2

Saskatoon Symphony: P.O. Box 1361, 703 Hotel Bessborough, Saskatoon, Sask. S7K 3N9. Daniel Swift, conductor.

Sault Symphony Orchestra: P.O. Box 695, Sault Ste. Marie, Ont. P6A 5N2. John Wilkinson, conductor.

Scarborough Philharmonic Orchestra: 3663 Danforth Ave., Scarborough, Ont. M1N 2G2. Christopher Kitts, conductor.

Scotia Chamber Players: 1541 Barrington St., #317, Halifax, N.S. B3J 1Z5

Sir Ernest MacMillan String Ensemble: 9 Suter Cres., Dundas, Ont., Marta Hidy, conductor.

Sudbury Symphony Orchestra: 111 Larch Street, 9th Fl., Sudbury, Ont. P3E 4T5. Metro Kozak, conductor.

Symphony Hamilton: P.O. Box 7439, Ancaster, Ont. L9G 4G4. Clyde H. Mitchell, conductor.

Symphony New Brunswick: P.O. Box 6249, 2A-32 King St., Saint John, N.B. E2L 4R7. Nurhan Arman, conductor.

Symphony Nova Scotia: 1646 Barrington St., Halifax, N.S. B3J 2A3. Georg Tintner, conductor.

Tafelmusik Baroque Orchestra: 427 Bloor St. W., Toronto, Ont. M5S 1X7. Jeanne Lamon, conductor.

Te Deum Orchestra: 105 Victoria St., Dundas, Ont. L9H 2C1. Richard Birney-Smith, conductor.

Thunder Bay Symphony Orchestra: P.O. Box 2004, 953 Oliver Road, Thunder Bay, Ont. P7B 5E7. Glenn Mossop, conductor.

Timmins Symphony Orchestra: Box 1365, Timmins, Ont. P4N 7N2. Geoff Lee, conductor.

Toronto Chinese Philharmonic Orchestra: 39 Laurentide Dr., Don Mills, Ont. M3A 3C8. Tak Ng-Lai, conductor.

Toronto Philharmonic Orchestra: 35McCaul St., #411, Toronto, Ont. M5T 1V7. Jacob Harnoy, artistic director.

Toronto Sinfonietta: 2655 Bloor St. W., #210, Toronto, Ont. M8X 1A3. Mathew Jaskiewicz, conductor.

The Toronto Symphony: 60 Simcoe St., Ste. C116, Toronto, Ont. M5J 2H5. Gunther Hurbig, conductor.

University of Toronto Symphony Orchestra: Faculty of Music, U of T, 80 Queen's Park Cres., Toronto, Ont. M5S 1A1. Pierre Hétu, conductor.

University of Western Ontario Orchestra: Faculty of Music, UWO, London, Ont. N6A 3K7. Prof. Jerome Summers, conductor.

Vancouver Philharmonic Orchestra: P.O. Box 35406, Station E, Vancouver, B.C. V6M 4G5.

Vancouver Symphony Orchestra: 601 Smithe St., Vancouver, B.C. V6B 5G1. Sergiu Comissiona, conductor.

Victoria Symphony Orchestra: 846 Broughton St., Victoria, B.C. V8W 1E4. Peter McCoppin, conductor.

Wilfrid Laurier University Symphony: Faculty of Music, 75 University Ave. W., Waterloo, Ont. N2L 3C5. Paul Pulford, conductor.

Windsor Symphony Orchestra: 174-198 Pitt St. W., 3rd Floor, Windsor, Ont. N9A 5L4. Susan Haig, conductor.

Winnipeg Symphony Orchestra: 555Main St., Rm. 101, Winnipeg, Man. R3B 1C3. Bramwell Tovey, conductor.

York Symphony Orchestra: Box 355, Richmond Hill, Ont. L4C 4Y6. Roberto Declara, conductor.

Source: *Association of Canadian Orchestras*

Canadian Opera Companies

Atelier Lyrique: 1157 Ste. Catherine St. E., Montreal, Que. H2L 2G2. Bernard Uzan, music dir.

Calgary Opera Association: #800, 125-9 Ave. S.E., Calgary, Alta. T2G 0P8. David A. Speers, gen. dir.

Canadian Opera Co.: 227 Front St. E., Toronto, Ont., M5A 1E8. Brian Dickie, gen. dir.

Edmonton Opera Association: #320, 10232-112 St., Edmonton, Alta. T5K 1M4. Irving Guttman, gen. dir.

Manitoba Opera Association: Box 31027, 393 Portage Ave., Winnipeg, Man. R3B 3K9. Bruce H. Lang, exec. dir.

Opera Atelier–Canada's Baroque Theatre Co.: 2 Bloor St. W., Cumberland Terrace, Upper Level, Toronto, Ont. M4W 3E2. Jeannette Zingg and Marshall Pynkoski, dirs.

Opera Hamilton: 2 King St. W., Plaza Level, Hamilton,

Ont. L8P 1A1. Daniel Lipton, art. dir.

Opera Lyra: Arts Court, 2 Daly Avenue, Ottawa, Ont. K1N 6E2. Jeanette Aster, art. dir.

L'Opéra de Montréal: 260, Boulevard de Maisonneuve ouest, Montreal, Que. H2X 1Y9. Bernard Uzan, gen. dir.

Opéra de Québec: 580 Grand-Allée est, #575, Québec, Que. G1R 3B4. Guy Bélanger, art. dir.

Pacific Opera Victoria: 1316B Government St., Victoria, B.C. V8W 1Y8. Timothy Vernon, art. dir.

Saskatoon Opera: 509 Copelang Cr., Saskatoon, Sask. S7N 2Z4.

Vancouver Opera Association: 500-845 Cambie St., Vancouver, B.C. V6B 4Z9. Carole Anne Currie, assoc. art. dir.

Major Contemporary and Jazz Dance Companies

(artistic director in brackets)

Les Ballets Jazz de Montréal: 3450 rue St-Urbain, Montreal, Que. H2X 2N5 (William Whitener)

Contemporary Dancers Incorporated: 109 Pulford St., Winnipeg, Man. R3L 1X8 (Tom Stroud)

Dancemakers: 927 Dupont St., Toronto, Ont. M6H 1Z1 (Serge Bennathan)

Danse Partout: 880 Père-Marquette, Quebec, Que. G1S 2A4 (Luc Tremblay)

Decidedly Jazz Danceworks: P.O. Box 4626, Stn. "C," Calgary, Alta. T2T 5P1 (Vicki Willis)

Desrosiers Dance Theatre: 629 Eastern Ave., Toronto, Ont. M4M 1E4 (Robert Desrosiers)

Fortier Danse Création: 2600, rue Bennett, #302, Montreal, Que. H1V 3S4 (Paul-André Fortier)

La Fondation de danse Margie Gillis: 3575 boul. St. Laurent, #502, Montreal, Que. H2X 2T7 (Margie Gillis)

Danny Grossman Dance Company: 511 Bloor St. W., Toronto, Ont. M5S 1Y4 (Danny Grossman)

Le Groupe de la Place Royale: 2 Daly Ave., Ste. 2,

Ottawa, Ont. K1N 6E2 (Peter Boneham)

Karen Jamieson Dance Company: 242 E. 10th Ave., Vancouver, B.C. V5T 1Z5 (Karen Jamieson)

Kompany!: #810, 10136-100th St., Edmonton, Alta. T5J 0P1 (Ron Schuster)

Judith Marcuse Dance Company: 106-206 E. 6th Ave., Vancouver, B.C. V5T 1J8 (Judith Marcuse)

Mascall Dance: 1130 Jarvis St., Vancouver, B.C. V6E 2C7 (Jennifer Mascall)

Montanaro Danse: 24, ave. du Mont-Royal ouest, #601, Montreal, Que. H2T 2S2 (Michael Montanaro)

0 Vertigo: 4455 rue de Rouen, Montreal, Que. H1V 1H1 (Ginette Laurin)

La Fondation Jean-Pierre Perreault: 981 rue Cherrier, Montreal, Que. H2L 1J2 (Jean-Pierre Perreault)

Gina Lori Riley Dance Enterprises: 210-384 Pitt St. E., Windsor, Ont. N9A 2V7 (Gina Lori Riley)

Toronto Dance Theatre: 80 Winchester St., Toronto, Ont. M4X 1B2 (David Earle) Source: Dance in Canada

Major Ballet Companies

(artistic director in brackets)

Alberta Ballet: 1-10645 63 Ave., Edmonton Alta. T2S 0B8 (Ali Pourfarrokh)

Ballet British Columbia: 502-68 Water St., Vancouver, B.C. V6B 1A4 (John Alleyne)

Les Grands Ballets Canadiens: 4816 rue Rivard, Montreal, Que. H2J 2N6 (Lawrence Rhodes)

The National Ballet of Canada: 157 King St. E., Toronto, Ont. M5C 1G9 (Reid Anderson)

Ottawa Ballet: P.O. Box 366, Stn. "A," Ottawa, Ont. K1N 8V3 (Frank Augustyn)

Royal Winnipeg Ballet: 380 Graham Ave., Winnipeg, Man. R3C 4K2 (John Meehan) Source: Dance in Canada

National Dance Service Organizations

■ **Association Acadiennne des Artistes Professionnels de Nouveau Brunswick**
c/o DansEncorps,
140 Botsford St., Moncton, NB
E1C 4X4
Tel: (506) 855-0998

■ **Association for Dance in Universities and Colleges in Canada**
c/o Centre for the Arts,
Simon Fraser University,
Burnaby, BC V5A 1S6
Tel: (604) 291-3363

■ **Canadian Arts Presenters Association**
189 Laurier Ave. E,
Ottawa, Ont.
K1N 6P1

■ **Canadian Association of Professional Dance Organizations**
c/o 751 Ch. DuLac St. Louis,
Ville de Lery, Que.
J6N 1A4
Tel: (514) 699-8322

■ **Canadian Dance Teachers Association**
6033 Shawson Dr., Unit 38,
Mississauga, Ont.
L5T 1H8
Tel: (416) 564-2139

■ **Candance Network**
179 Richmond St. W,
Toronto, Ont.
M5V 1V3
Tel: (416) 204-1082

■ **Dancer Transition Centre**
66 Charles St. E, 2nd Flr.,
Toronto, Ont.
M4Y 2R3
Tel: (416) 928-9177

■ **Royal Academy of Dancing/Canada**
3284 Yonge St., Ste. 404,
Toronto, Ont.
M4N 2L6
Tel: (416) 489-2813

■ **US/Canada Performance Initiative**
179 Richmond St. W,
Toronto, Ont.
M5V 1V3
Tel: (416) 204-1082

Major Theatre Companies in Canada

(artistic directors in brackets)

Alberta Theatre Projects: 220-9th Ave SE, Calgary, Alta. T2G 5C4 (Michael Dobbin)

Arbour Theatre Company: Box 100, 220 Simcoe St., Peterborough, Ont. K9J 6Y5 (Brian Richmond)

Arts Club Theatre: 1585 Johnston St, Vancouver, B.C. V6H 3R9 (Bill Millerd)

Belfry Theatre: 1292 Gladstone Ave, Victoria, B.C. V8T 1G5 (Glynis Leyshon)

Canadian Stage Company: 26 Berkeley St, Toronto, Ont. M5A 2W3 (Bob Baker)

Centaur Theatre Company: 453, rue Saint-François-Xavier, Montreal, Que. H2Y 2T1

Citadel Theatre: 9828-101A Ave, Edmonton, Alta. T5J 3C6 (Robin Phillips)

La Compagnie Jean Duceppe: 1400 rue Saint-Urbain, Montreal, Que. H2X 2M5 (Michel Dumont)

Factory Theatre: 125 Bathurst St, Toronto, Ont. M5V 2R2 (Katherine Kaszas)

Globe Theatre: 1801 Scarth St, Regina, Sask. S4P 2G9 (Susan Ferley)

Grand Theatre: 471 Richmond St, London, Ont. N6A 3E4 (Martha Henry)

Great Canadian Theatre Company: 910 Gladstone Ave, Ottawa, Ont. K1R 6Y4 (Arthur Milner)

Gryphon Theatre: Box 454, Barrie, Ont. L4M 4T7 (Uwe Meyer)

Magnus Theatre Company Northwest Incorporated: 101 N. Syndicate Ave., Ste. 303, Thunder Bay, Ont. P7C 3V4 (Mario Crudo)

Manitoba Theatre Centre: 174 Market Ave, Winnipeg, Man. R3B 0P8 (Steven Schipper)

Mermaid Theatre of Nova Scotia: Box 2697, 132 Garrish St, Windsor, N.S. B0N 2T0 (Sara Lee Lewis)

National Arts Centre: Box 1534, Stn. B, Ottawa, Ont. K1P 5W1

Neptune Theatre Foundation: 1593 Argyle St, Halifax, N.S. B3J 2B2 (Linda Moore)

Persephone Theatre: 2802 Rusholme Rd, Saskatoon, Sask. S7L 0H2 (Tibor Fehergyhazi)

Prairie Theatre Exchange: 389 Portage Ave, Flr 3, Unit Y30, Winnipeg, Man. R3B 3H6

Royal Alexandra Theatre: 260 King St W, Toronto, Ont. M5V 1H9

Sudbury Theatre Centre: P.O. Box 641, Stn. B, Sudbury, Ont. P3E 4P8 (Gord McCall)

Sunshine Theatre Company: Box 443, Kelowna, B.C. V1Y 7P1 (Gregory Tuck)

Tamahnous Theatre: 222-275 Woodland Ave., Vancouver, B.C. V5L 3S7 (Teri Snelgrove)

Tarragon Theatre: 30 Bridgman Ave, Toronto, Ont. M5R 1X3 (Urjo Kareda)

Theatre Aquarius: 190 King William St., Hamilton, Ont. L8R 1A8 (Peter Mandia)

Theatre Calgary: 220-9th Ave. SE, Calgary, Alta. T2G 5C4 (Brian Rintoul)

Théâtre de la Bordée: 1105, rue Saint-Jean, #201, Quebec, Que. G1R 1S3 (Jean-Jacqui Boutet)

Théâtre du Nouveau Monde: 137, Saint-Ferdinand, #201, Montreal, Que. H4C 2S7 (Lorraine Pintal)

Théâtre du Rideau Vert: 355 Gilford, Montreal, Que. H2T 1M6 (Guillermo de Andrea)

Le Théâtre du Trident: 580, ave Grande-Allée est, #20, Quebec, Que. G1R 2K2 (Roland Lepage)

Theatre Network: 10708-124th St, Edmonton, Alta. T5M 0H1 (Ben Henderson)

Theatre New Brunswick: Box 566, Fredericton, N.B. E3B 5A6 (Michael Shamata)

Theatre Newfoundland and Labrador: Box 655, 90 West St., Corner Brook, Nfld. A2H 6G1

Theatre Passe Muraille: 16 Ryerson Ave, Toronto, Ont. M5T 2P3 (Susan Serran)

Theatre Plus: 70 The Esplanade, 2nd Flr, Toronto, Ont. M5E 1B3 (Duncan McIntosh)

25th Street Theatre: 7-420 Duchess St, Saskatoon, Sask. S7K 0R1 (Tom Bentley-Fisher)

Vancouver Playhouse: 543 West 7th Ave, Vancouver, B.C. V5Z 1B4 (Larry Lillo)

Young People's Theatre: 165 Front St E, Toronto, Ont. M5A 3Z4 (Maja Ardal)

Summer Theatre in Canada

Arbour Theatre: 220 Simcoe St., Peterborough, Ont. K9J 6Y5 (Brian Richmond)

Blyth Festival: P.O. Box 10, Blyth, Ont. N0M 1H0 (Peter Smith)

Charlottetown Festival: P.O. Box 848, Charlottetown, P.E.I. C1A 7L9 (Jacques Lemay)

Huron Country Playhouse: R.R. #1, Grand Bend, Ont. N0M 1T0 (Max Reimer)

Kawartha Summer Theatre: P.O. Box 161, Lindsay, Ont. K9V 4S1 (Diane Nyland Proctor)

Lighthouse Festival Theatre: P.O. Box 1208, Port Dover, Ont. N0A 1N0 (Simon Johnston)

Muskoka Festival: P.O. Box 1055, Gravenhurst, Ont. P1P 1X2 (Ron Ulrich)

Nanaimo Festival: P.O. Box 626, Nanaimo, B.C. V9R 5L9 (Michael McLaughlin)

Rainbow Theatre: P.O. Box 282, Parry Sound, Ont. P2A 2X4

Red Barn Theatre: P.O. Box 291, Jackson's Point, Ont. L0E 1L0 (D'Arcy M. Gordon)

Shaw Festival Theatre: P.O. Box 774, Niagara-on-the-Lake, Ont. L0S 1J0 (Christopher Newton)

Showboat Festival Theatre: P.O. Box 454, Port Colborne, Ont. L3K 5X7

Stephenville Festival: 149 Montana Dr., 2nd Flr., Stephenville, Nfld. A2N 2T4

Stratford Shakespearean Festival: P.O. Box 520, Stratford, Ont. L3V 6K8 (David William)

Sunshine Festival Theatre Company: 20 Mississauga St. W., Orillia, Ont. L3V 6K8

Thousand Islands Playhouse: P.O. Box 241, Gananoque, Ont. K7G 2T8 (Greg Wanlerss)

Upper Canada Playhouse: P.O. Box 852, Morrisburg, Ont. K0C 1X0 (Marshall Button)

Government Expenditures on Culture, 1990–91

(thousands of dollars)

	Federal	Provincial	Municipal
Libraries	39 733	688 426	899 301
Museums	160 658	201 886	28 705
Public archives.......................	66 221	26 354	9 365
Historic parks and sites	77 167	76 960	10 267
Nature/provincial parks	178 624	62 984	n.a.
Other heritage resources	165 145	28 940	n.a.
Arts education	4 037	70 937	n.a.
Literary arts	235 246	19 812	n.a.
Performing arts	109 520	122 203	16 819
Visual arts and crafts	15 530	33 009	n.a.
Film and video	255 446	69 811	n.a.
Broadcasting	1 456 002	211 483	n.a.
Sound recording	5 195	1 872	n.a.
Multiculturism	9 376	35 819	n.a.
Multidisciplinary activities	97 662	92 013	n.a.
Other	13 665	45 940	272 823
Total expenditures	**2 889 228**	**1 788 447**	**1 237 280**

Source:*Statistics Canada*   (n.a.) – not available.

Provincial Government Expenditures on Culture, by Province or Territory

(in thousands of dollars)

Province or Territory	1986–87	1988–89	1990–91
Newfoundland	20 061	22 004	23 529
Prince Edward Island	9 908	10 839	10 760
Nova Scotia	37 261	57 180	60 444
New Brunswick	22 660	27 276	27 631
Quebec	405 349	468 311	536 387
Ontario.............................	465 524	516 715	597 833
Manitoba...........................	67 055	67 439	79 198
Saskatchewan	59 615	59 764	62 385
Alberta.............................	171 411	156 075	160 373
British Columbia	153 175	160 807	209 463
Yukon	6 284	6 918	7 744
Northwest Territories	4 643	6 302	12 700
Total..............................	**1 422 946**	**1 559 630**	**1 788 447**

Source:*Statistics Canada*

Federal Government Expenditures on Culture, by Province or Territory

(in thousands of dollars)

Province or Territory	1986–87	1988–89	1990–91
Newfoundland	47 768	48 772	54 899
Prince Edward Island	10 764	11 512	14 339
Nova Scotia	71 191	79 304	97 846
New Brunswick	43 069	43 524	50 732
Quebec	710 587	844 238	877 511
Ontario	889 907	953 504	1 056 530
Manitoba	67 090	75 432	86 098
Saskatchewan	47 903	47 322	55 974
Alberta	123 741	134 393	151 325
British Columbia	116 608	161 063	144 195
Yukon	8 724	13 537	12 800
Northwest Territories	28 760	30 505	32 757
Other (1)	285 757	303 199	254 222
Total	**2 450 869**	**2 746 305**	**2 889 228**

Source: *Statistics Canada*   (1) includes national organizations, foreign countries, and unallocated expenditures.

GALLERIES AND MUSEUMS

The Group of Seven

The Group of Seven held its first exhibition at the Art Gallery of Toronto in May 1920. The original members included J.E.H. MacDonald, Lawren Harris, A.Y. Jackson, Arthur Lismer, F.H. Varley, Frank Johnston and Franklin Carmichael.

In 1924, Johnston resigned from the Group and, in 1926, A.J. Casson was invited to join. In the later years of the Group, two new members, Edwin Holgate and Lionel Lemoine FitzGerald, were added. The Group held its final exhibition in Dec. 1931 and disbanded in 1932.

Tom Thomson, who drowned in 1917, was never a member of the Group of Seven, though his boldly-colored works depicting the rugged landscape of northern Ontario became associated with its style of painting.

By breaking with the traditional, European, painting style popular in Canada in the 1920s, The Group of Seven made a huge impact on Canadian art. Although originally reviled by critics, the Group had gained wide acceptance and popularity by the 1930s. Today, the Group's paintings are exhibited in every major gallery in Canada.

J.E.H. **MacDonald** (1873–1932)

Lawren **Harris** (1885–1970)

Alexander Young (A.Y.) **Jackson** (1882–1974)

Arthur **Lismer** (1885–1969)

Frederick Horsman **Varley** (1881–1969)

Frank Hans **Johnston** (1888–1949)

Frank **Carmichael** (1890–1945)

Alfred Joseph (A.J.) **Casson** (1898–1992)

Edwin **Holgate** (1892–1977)

Lionel Lemoine **FitzGerald** (1890–1956)

Tom **Thomson** (1877–1917)

Source: *Looking at Landscape*, Dwight Siegner, The McMichael Canadian Art Collection

Major Public Art Galleries in Canada

Art Gallery of Greater Victoria: 1040 Moss St., Victoria, B.C. V8V 4P1

Art Gallery of Nova Scotia: P.O. Box 2262, Halifax, N.S. B3J 3C8

Art Gallery of Ontario: 317 Dundas St. W., Toronto, Ont. M5T 1G4

Art Gallery of Windsor: 445 Riverside Dr. W., Windsor, Ont. N9A 6T8

Beaverbrook Art Gallery: P.O. Box 605, Fredericton, N.B. E3B 5A6

Confederation Centre Art Gallery and Museum: P.O. Box 848, Charlottetown, P.E.I. C1A 7L9

Dunlop Art Gallery: P.O. Box 2311, Regina, Sask. S4P 3Z5

Edmonton Art Gallery: 2 Sir Winston Churchill Sq., Edmonton, Alta. T5J 2C1

London Regional Art Gallery: 421 Ridout St. N., London, Ont. N6A 5H4

McMichael Canadian Collection: Islington Ave., Kleinburg, Ont. L0J 1C0

Montreal Museum of Fine Arts: 3400, avenue du Musée, Montreal, Que. H3G 1K3

Musée du Québec: Parc des Champs de Bataille, 1, rue Wolfe/Montcalm, Quebec, Que. G1R 5H3

National Gallery of Canada: 380 Sussex Dr., Ottawa, Ont. K1N 9N4

Thunder Bay Art Gallery: P.O. Box 1193, Station F, Thunder Bay, Ont. P7C 4X9

Vancouver Art Gallery: 750 Hornby St., Vancouver, B.C. V6Z 2H7

Winnipeg Art Gallery: 300 Memorial Blvd., Winnipeg, Man. R3C 1V1

Major Public Museums in Canada

British Columbia Provincial Museum: 675 Belleville St., Victoria, B.C. V8V 1X4

Canadian Museum of Civilization: 100 Laurier St., Hull, Que. J8X 4H2

Canadian Museum of Contemporary Photography: P.O. Box 465, Station A, Ottawa, Ont. K1N 9N6

Canadian Museum of Nature: P.O. Box 3443, Station D, Ottawa, Ont. K1P 6P4

Canadian War Museum: 330 Sussex Dr., Ottawa, Ont. K1A 0M8

Glenbow-Alberta Institute: 130-9th Ave. SE, Calgary, Alta. T2G 0P3

Manitoba Museum of Man and Nature: 190 Rupert Ave., Winnipeg, Man. R3B 0N2

McCord Museum: 690, rue Sherbrooke ouest, Montreal, Que. H3A 1E9

Musée de la Civilisation: 86, côte de la Montagne, Quebec, Que. G1K 4E3

New Brunswick Museum: 277 Douglas Ave., Saint John, N.B. E2K 1E5

Newfoundland Museum: 285 Duckworth St., St. John's, Nfld. A1C 1G9

Nova Scotia Museum: 1747 Summer St., Halifax, N.S. B3H 3A6

Prince of Wales Northern Heritage Centre: Dept. of Culture and Communications, Govt. of the Northwest Territories, Yellowknife, N.W.T. X1A 2L9

Provincial Museum of Alberta: 12845-102nd Ave., Edmonton, Alta. T5N 0M6

Royal Ontario Museum: 100 Queen's Park, Toronto, Ont. M5S 2C6

Saskatchewan Museum of Natural History: Wascana Park, Regina, Sask. S4P 3V7

Vancouver Museum: 1100 Chestnut St., Vancouver, B.C. V6J 3J9

BOOKS, MAGAZINES, NEWSPAPERS

The Governor General's Literary Awards, 1981–92

The Governor General's Literary Awards, Canada's foremost literary prizes, are presented annually to recognize and reward Canadian writers. The awards were initiated in 1937 by the Canadian Authors' Association with the agreement of Governor General Baron Tweedsmuir (novelist John Buchan), and were administered by the Association until 1958.

The Awards are now administered by the Canada Council which appoints juries composed of literary specialists who select the best English and French-language works in each of 6 best categories: drama, fiction, poetry, non-fiction, and beginning in 1987, children's literature (text and illustration) and translation. The juries review all books by Canadian authors, illustrators and translators published in Canada or abroad during the previous year (Oct. 1—Sept. 30). In the case of translation, the original work must also be a Canadian-authored title. Winners receive a medal from the Governor General, $10,000 and a specially-bound copy of their award-winning book. The 1991 winners were announced Dec. 3.

English

—1981—

Fiction . . . . *Home Truths: Selected Canadian Stories*, Mavis Gallant
Non-fiction . . . . *Caribou and the Barren-lands*, George Calef
Poetry . . . . *The Collected Poems of F.R. Scott*, F.R. Scott
Drama . . . . *Blood Relations*, Sharon Pollack

—1982—

Fiction . . . . Man Descending, Guy Vanderhaeghe
Non-fiction . . . . *Louisbourg Portraits: Life in an Eighteenth-Century Garrison Town*, Christopher Moore
Poetry . . . . *The Vision Tree: Selected Poems*, Phyllis Webb
Drama . . . . *Billy Bishop Goes To War*, a play by John Gray with Eric Peterson, John Gray

—1983—

Fiction . . . . *Shakespeare's Dog*, Leon Rooke
Non-fiction . . . . *Byng of Vimy: General and Governor General*, Jeffrey Williams
Poetry . . . . *Settlements*, David Donnell
Drama . . . . *Quiet in the Land*, Anne Chislett

—1984—

Fiction. . . . . *The Engineer of Human Souls*, Josef Skvorecky
Non-fiction . . . . *The Private Capital: Ambition and Love in the Age of Macdonald and Laurier*, Sandra Gwyn
Poetry. . . . . *Celestial Navigation*, Paulette Jiles
Drama. . . . . *White Biting Dog*, Judith Thompson

—1985—

Fiction . . . . *The Handmaid's Tale*, Margaret Atwood
Non-fiction . . . . *The Regenerators: Social Criticism in Late Victorian English Canada*, Ramsay Cook
Poetry. . . . . *Waiting for Saskatchewan*, Fred Wah
Drama . . . . *Criminals in Love*, George F. Walker

—1986—

Fiction. . . . . *The Progress of Love*, Alice Munro
Non-fiction . . . . *Northrop Frye on Shakespeare*, Northrop Frye
Poetry. . . . . *The Collected Poems of Al Purdy*, Al Purdy
Drama . . . . *Doc*, Sharon Pollack

—1987—

Fiction. . . . . *A Dream Like Mine*, M.T. Kelly
Non-fiction. . . . . *The Russian Album*, Michael Ignatieff
Poetry . . . . *Afterworlds*, Gwendolyn MacEwen
Drama . . . . *Prague*, John Krizanc
Translation . . . . *Enchantment and Sorrow: The Autobiography of Gabrielle Roy*, Patricia Claxton
Children's Literature (Illustration) . . . *Rainy Day Magic*, Marie-Louise Gay
Children's Literature (Text) . . . . *Galahad Schwartz and the Cockroach Army*, Morgan Nyberg

—1988—

Fiction . . . . *Nights Below Station Street*, David Adams Richards
Non-fiction . . . . *In the Sleep Room*, Anne Collins
Poetry . . . . *Furious*, Erin Mouré
Drama . . . . *Nothing Sacred*, George F. Walker
Translation. . . . . *Second Chance*, Philip Stratford
Children's Literature (Illustration) . . . . *Amos's Sweater*, Kim LaFave ▶
Children's Literature (Text) . . . . *The Third Magic*, Welwyn Wilton Katz ▶

—1989—

Fiction . . . . *Whale Music*, Paul Quarrington
Non-fiction. . . . . . *Willie: The Life of W. Somerset Maugham*, Robert Calder
Poetry . . . . *The Word for Sand*, Heather Spears
Drama . . . . *The Other Side of the Dark*, Judith Thompson
Translation . . . . *On the Eighth Day*, Wayne Grady
Children's Literature (Illustration) . . . *The Magic Paintbrush*, Robin Muller
Children's Literature (Text) . . . . *Bad Boy*, Diana Wieler

—1990—

Fiction . . . . *Lives of the Saints*, Nino Ricci
Non-fiction . . . . *Trudeau and Our Times*, Stephen Clarkson
Poetry . . . . *No Time*, Margaret Avison
Drama . . . . *Goodnight Desdemona (Good Morning Juliet)*,
Ann-Marie MacDonald
Translation . . . . *Yellow-Wolf and Other Tales*
of the Saint Lawrence, Jane Brierley
Children's Literature (Illustration) . . . . *The Orphan Boy*, Paul Morin
Children's Literature (Text) . . . . *Redwork*, Michael Bedard

—1991—

Fiction. . . . . *Such a Long Journey*, Rohinton Mistry
Non-fiction . . . . *Occupied Canada*, Robert Hunter and Robert Calihoo
Poetry . . . . *Night Field*, Don McKay
Drama . . . . *Amigo's Blue Guitar*, Joan MacLeod
Translation . . . . *A Dictionary of Literary Devices*, Albert W. Halsall
Children's Literature (Illustration). . . . . *Doctor Kiss Says Yes*,
Joanne Fitzgerald
Children's Literature (Text) . . . . *Pick-Up Sticks*, Sarah Ellis

—1992—

Fiction. . . . . *The English Patient*, Michael Ondaatje
Non-fiction. . . . . *Revenge of the Land: A century of greed, tragedy*
and murder on a Saskatchewan Farm, Maggie Siggins
Poetry. . . . . *Inventing the Hawk*, Lorna Crozier
Drama . . . . *Possible Worlds, A Short History of Night*, John Mighton
Translation. . . . . *Imagining the Middle East*, Fred A. Reed
Children's Literature (Illustration) . . . . *Waiting for the Whales*,
Ron Lightburn
Children's Literature (Text) . . . . *Hero of Lesser Causes*, Julie Johnston

French

—1981—

Fiction . . . . *La province lunaire*, Denys Chabot

Non-fiction . . . . *L'échappée des discours de l'oeil*, Madeleine Ouellette-Michalska

Poetry . . . . *Visages*, Michel Beaulieu

Drama . . . . *C'était avant la guerre à l'Anse à Gilles*, Marie Laberge

—1982—

Fiction . . . . *Le cercle des arènes*, Roger Fournier

Non-fiction . . . . *Le marxisme des années soixante: une saison dans l'histoire de la pensée critique*, Maurice Lagueux

Poetry . . . . *Forages*, Michel Savard

Drama . . . . *HA ha!...*, Réjean Ducharme

—1983—

Fiction . . . . *Laura Laur*, Suzanne Jacob

Non-fiction . . . . *Le contrôle social du crime*, Maurice Cusson

Poetry . . . . *Un goût de sel*, Suzanne Paradis

Drama . . . . *Syncope*, René Gingras

—1984—

Fiction . . . . *Agonie*, Jacques Brault

Non-fiction . . . . *Le XXe siècle: Histoire du catholicisme québécois*, Jean Hamelin et Nicole Gagnon

Poetry . . . . *Double Impression*, Nicole Brossard

Drama . . . . *Ne blâmez jamais les Bédouins*, René-Daniel Dubois

—1985—

Fiction . . . . *Lucie ou un midi en novembre*, Fernand Ouellette
Non-fiction. . . . . *La littérature contre elle-même*, François Ricard
Poetry. . . . . *Action Writing*, André Roy
Drama . . . . *Duo pour voix obstinées*, Maryse Pelletier

—1986—

Fiction . . . . *Les silences du corbeau*, Yvon Rivard
Non-fiction . . . . *Le réalism socialiste: une esthétique impossible*,
Régine Robin
Poetry . . . . *L'écouté*, Cecile Cloutier
Drama. . . . . *La visite des sauvages*, Anne Legault

—1987—

Fiction . . . . *L'Obsédante Obèse et autres agressions*,
Gilles Archambault
Non-fiction . . . . *La Petite Noirceur*, Jean Larose
Poetry. . . . . *Les Heures*, Fernand Ouellette
Drama . . . . *Un oiseau vivant dans la gueule*, Jeanne-Mance Delisle
Translation . . . . *L'homme qui se croyait aimé, ou La vie secrete d'un
premier ministre*, Ivan Steenhout and Christiane Teasdale
Children's Literature (Illustration) . . . . . . *Venir au monde*, Darcia Labrosse
Children's Literature (Text) . . . . *Le Don*, David Schinkel and
Yves Beauchesne

—1988—

Fiction. . . . . *Le Silence ou le Parfait Bonheur*, Jacques Folch-Ribas
Non-fiction . . . . *Écrire dans la maison du père*, Patricia Smart
Poetry . . . . *Papiers d'épidémie*, Marcel Labine
Drama. . . . . *Le Chien*, Jean Marc Dalpé
Translation . . . . *Nucléus*, Didier Holtzwarth
Children's Literature (Illustration) . . . *Les Jeux de Pic-mots*, Philippe Béha
Children's Literature (Text). . . . . *Cassiopée ou L'été polonais*,
Michèle Marineau

—1989—

Fiction . . . . *La Rage*, Louis Hamelin
Non-fiction. . . . . *L'Intolérance : une problématique générale*, Lise Noël
Poetry . . . . *Monème*, Pierre Desruisseaux
Drama. . . . . *Mademoiselle Rouge*, Michel Garneau
Translation. . . . . *Les Âges de l'amour*, Jean Antonin Billard

Children's Literature (illustration) ...... *Benjamin et la saga des oreillers*,
Stéphane Poulin
Children's Literature (Text) .... *Temps mort*, Charles Montpetit

—1990—

Fiction .... *La Mauvaise Foi*, Gérald Tougas
Non-fiction .... *Dans l'oeil de l'aigle*, Jean François Lisée
Poetry .... *Les Cendres bleues*, Jean-Paul Daoust
Drama .... *Le Voyage magnifique d'Emily Carr*, Jovette Marchessault
Translation .... *Le Second Rouleau*, Charlotte and Robert Melançon
Children's Literature (Illustration) .... *Les fantaisies de l'oncle Henri*,
Pierre Pratt
Children's Literature (Text) ...... *La Vraie Histoire du chien de Clara Vic*,
Christiane Duchesne

—1991—

Fiction .... *La Croix du Nord*, André Brochu
Non-fiction .... *Le Jaguar et le Tamanoir*, Bernard Arcand
Poetry .... *Chant pour un Québec Iointain*, Madeleine Gagnon
Drama .... *Mon oncle Marcel qui vague vague près du métro Berri*,
Gilbert Dupuis
Translation .... *Les Enfants d'Aataentsic: l'histoire du peuple huron*,
Jean-Paul Sainte-Marie and Brigitte Chabert Hacikyan
Children's Literature (Illustration) .... *Un champion*, Sheldon Cohen
Children's Literature (Text) .... *Deux heures et demie avant Jasmine*,
François Gravel

—1992—

Fiction .... *L'enfant chargé de songes*, Anne Hébert
Non-fiction ...... *La Radissonie. Le pays de la baie James*, Pierre Turgeon
Poetry .... *Andromède attendra*, Gilles Cyr
Translation .... *La mémoire postmoderne. Essai sur l'art
canadien contemporain*, Jean Papineau
Children's Literature (Illustration) .... *Simon et la ville de carton*,
Gille Tibo
Children's Literature (Text) .... *Victor*, Christiane Duchesne

Source: The Canada Council

Bestselling Books in Canada, 1992

(Canadian books in bold type)

Fiction

1. **Generation X, Douglas Coupland**
2. **The English Patient , Michael Ondaatje**
3. **Such a Long Journey, Rohinton Mistry**
4. *Gerald's Game*, Stephen King
5. *The Wastelands: Dark Tower 3*, Stephen King
6. **Lives of the Saints, Nino Ricci**
7. *No Greater Love*, Danielle Steel
8. *The Elf Queen of Shannara*, Terry Brooks
9. *Road to Omaha*, Robert Ludlum
10. *Scarlett: The Sequel to Margaret Mitchell's Gone With the Wind*, Alexandra Ripley

Non-fiction

1. **Oh Canada! Oh Quebec!, Mordecai Richler**
2. *Revolution From Within*, Gloria Steinem
3. *Silent Passage*, Gale Sheehy
4. *The Popcorn Report*, Faith Popcorn
5. *Stolen Continents*, Ronald Wright
6. *The Great Reckoning*, James Dale Davidson and Lord William Rees-Mogg
7. *Diana: Her True Story*, Andrew Morton
8. *Backlash*, Susan Faludi
9. *The Culture of Contentment*, John Kenneth Galbraith
10. **The Betrayal of Canada, Mel Hurtig**

Source: *The Globe and Mail*

The Booker Prize, 1981–92

The Booker Prize recognizes the best work of English fiction published in the Commonwealth, South Africa and Ireland. It is sponsored by Booker McConnell Ltd., an international food and agriculture business, and administered by the Booker Prize Book Trust, a British educational charity. Since 1984, the value of the Booker Prize has been £15,000.

Year	Author	Title
1981	Salman Rushdie	*Midnight's Children*
1982	Thomas Keneally	*Schindler's Ark*
1983	J.M. Coetzee	*Life & Times of Michael K*
1984	Anita Brookner	*Hotel du Lac*
1985	Keri Hulme	*The Bone People*
1986	Kingsley Amis	*The Old Devils*
1987	Penelope Lively	*Moon Tiger*
1988	Peter Carey	*Oscar and Lucinda*
1989	Kazuo Ishiguro	*The Remains of the Day*
1990	A.S. Byatt	*Possession*
1991	Ben Okri	*The Famished Road*
1992 (joint winners)	Michael Ondaatje	*The English Patient*
	Barry Unsworth	*Sacred Hunger*

Pulitzer Prizes, 1992

The winners of these annual American literary awards were announced on April 13, 1993.

Fiction	Robert Olen Butler, *A Good Scent from a Strange Mountain*
Nonfiction	Gary Wills, *Lincoln at Gettysburg: The Words That Remade America*
Poetry	Louise Gluck, *The Wild Iris*
Drama	Tony Kushner, *Angels in America: Millenium Approaches*
Biography	David McCullough, *Truman*
History	Gordon S. Wood, *The Radicalism of the American Revolution*
Music	Christopher Rouse, *Trombone Concerto*

Top Canadian Daily Newspapers

Newspaper	Circulation[1]		
	Daily[2]	Weekend	
Toronto Star (all day)	499 683	737 513 (Sat.)	507 282 (Sun.)
The Globe and Mail (m)	311 171[5]		
Le Journal de Montréal (m)	293 687	342 553 (Sat.)	311 713 (Sun.)
Toronto Sun (m)	256 422	186 600 (Sat.)	453 355 (Sun.)
Montreal: La Presse (m)	195 940	329 335 (Sat.)	193 501 (Sun.)
Vancouver Sun (m)	202 987[3]	266 399 (Sat.)	
Vancouver Province (m)	179 261		221 195 (Sun.)
Ottawa Citizen (all day)	170 489	225 227 (Sat.)	156 456 (Sun.)
Edmonton Journal (m)	162 862[4]	195 860 (Fri.)	154 077 (Sun.)
Winnipeg Free Press (e)	147 391	225 310 (Sat.)	138 948 (Sun.)
Montreal Gazette (m)	156 968	229 954 (Sat.)	146 786 (Sun.)
Hamilton Spectator (e)	133 931		
Calgary Herald (m)	119 591[3]	160 113 (Fri.)	116 738 (Sun.)
London Free Press (m)	111 373	137 829 (Sat.)	
Quebec: Le Journal (m)	105 237	115 469 (Sat.)	100 949 (Sun.)
Quebec: Le Soleil (m)	96 280	139 501 (Sat.)	83 224 (Sun.)
Halifax Chronicle-Herald (m)	99 805		
Windsor Star (e)	84 784		
Edmonton Sun (m)	84 723		125 125 (Sun.)
Victoria Times-Colonist (m)	78 367		76 030 (Sun.)

Sources: *Audit Bureau of Circulations; The Globe and Mail*

(1) Average paid daily circulation for 6 months ending Mar. 31, 1993, unless otherwise indicated. (2) Monday to Saturday unless otherwise indicated. (3) Monday to Thursday. (4) Monday to Thursday plus Saturday. (5) Based on audited circulation six days a week for 1992. (m) morning; (e) evening.

National Newspaper Awards, 1992

These annual awards were announced in Toronto on April 21, 1993.

Editorial Writing	**Andrew Coyne,** *The Globe and Mail*
Spot News Photography	**Pat McGrath,** *The Ottawa Citizen*
Feature Photography	**Andrew Stawicki,** *The Toronto Star*
Spot News Reporting	**David Staples** and **Greg Owens,** *Edmonton Journal*
International Reporting	**Jan Wong,** *The Globe and Mail*
Sports Writing	**Michael Clarkson,** *Calgary Herald*
Feature Writing	**Pierre Foglia,** *La Presse*
Columns	**Dave Brown,** *The Ottawa Citizen*
Sports Photography	**Mike Cassese,** *The Toronto Star*
Enterprise Reporting	**Paulette Peirol** and **Michael Den Tandt,** *Kingston Whig-Standard*
Critical Writing	**Val Ross,** *The Globe and Mail*
Layout and Design	**Eric Nelson,** *The Globe and Mail*
Editorial Cartooning	**Bruce MacKinnon,** *Halifax Chronicle-Herald and Mail-Star*
Business Reporting	**Jacquie McNish,** *The Globe and Mail*
Special Projects	*Calgary Herald*

Source: *Canadian Daily Newspaper Association*

Top Canadian Paid–Circulation Magazines[1]

Magazine	Circulation[2]
Reader's Digest (Canadian English edition)	1 311 955
Chatelaine (English language edition)	904 454
TV Guide	837 800
Maclean's	592 827
Canadian Living	578 755
Time (Canadian edition)	363 587
Sélection du Reader's Digest (Canadian French edition)	325 774
TV Hebdo	237 681
Canadian Geographic	237 462
Chatelaine (French language edition)	218 450
Flare	191 205
L'Actualité	191 084
Select Homes Magazine	170 248
Equinox	164 065
Harrowsmith	153 116

Source: *Audit Bureau of Circulations*

(1) Paid circulation magazines are sold by subscription and delivered through the mail and/or sold at newsstands. (2) Average paid circulation per issue for 6months ending June 30, 1993, unless otherwise indicated.

National Magazine Awards, 1993

These annual awards were presented on April 23 by the National Magazine Awards Foundation. In 1993 there were gold and silver awards in 28 categories, including writing, design and photography.

Profiles: Carole Corbeil, "The Indiscreet Charm of Jean-Claude Lauzon," *Saturday Night*

Humour: Paul Quarrington, "Poaching With My Old Guy," *Harrowsmith*

Fashion Features: Manuel Rodenkirchen, Dimitri Mavrikis, Susie Sheffman, "Under Statements," *Flare*

Business Writing: Jennifer Wells, "The Fault Line," *Report on Business Magazine*

Science, Health and Medicine: Kate Fillion, "Fertility Rights, Fertility Wrongs," *Toronto Life*

Service Journalism: Max Burns, "Johnny be good," *Cottage Life*

Illustration: Douglas Fraser, "Climate of Fear," *Western Living*

Public Issues: Jennifer Wells, "The Fault Line," *Report on Business Magazine*

Poetry: Mia Anderson, "from The Shambles," *The Malahat Review*

Still-Life Photography: David Street, "Sitting Pretty," *City & Country Home*

Fiction: Yann Martel, "The Time I Heard the Private Donald J. Rankin String Concerto...," *The Malahat Review*

Column Writing: John Fraser, "The Last Laugh/The Last Refuge/On a Wing and a Prayer," *Saturday Night*

Arts and Leisure: Ian Brown, "The Beach Boys," *Destinations*

Portrait Photography: José Crespo, "Characters: Ihor Holubizky," *Hamilton This Month*

Magazine Covers: Jocelyne Fournel & Suzanne Langevin, "Mordecai Richler," *MTL*

Conceptual Photography: Mika Lada, "Scouts & Guides," *Today's Parent*

Spot Illustration: Rodney Frost, "Discovering Canadian Literature," *Imperial Oil Review*

Editorial Package: Ann Johnston and Maclean's staff, "Measuring Excellence," *Maclean's*

Travel Features: Hélène de Billy, "La ville de l'espoir," *Enroute*

Essays and Personal Journalism: Carole Corbeil, "The Indiscreet Charm of Jean-Claude Lauzon," *Saturday Night*

Environmental Journalism: John Lorinc, "The Reckoning," *Canadian Business*

Photojournalism: Robert Semeniuk, "Under Fire," *Equinox*

University of Western Ontario President's Medal for Excellence in Magazine Articles: Carole Beaulieu, "Dans le ventre de la métropole," *L'Actualité*

Foundation Award for Overall Editorial Excellence: *Cottage Life*

Foundation Award for Outstanding Achievement: Barbara Moon, *Saturday Night*

A Canadian Sports Chronology, 1993

January 1—September 30, 1993

■ January

Jan 1: Canada wins hockey's Spengler Cup in Davos, Switzerland with a 6-5 overtime win over Farjestads of Sweden.

Jan 5: Canadian trotter Billyjojimbob finishes third in voting for 1992 Trotter of the Year. Winner is Alf Palema, winner of the $1.38 million Hambletonian.

—Reggie Jackson, the charismatic slugger who earned the nickname "Mr. October" for his World Series exploits, is the only player elected to baseball's Hall of Fame, with 93.6% of the votes cast.

—Nikki Dryden of Victoria wins the gold medal in the 1000-metre freestyle in the first meet of the 1993 World Cup swimming circuit at Shanghai. Four days later, she repeats in Beijing. At the same meet, Marcel Gery of Toronto, a member of the bronze medal relay team at Barcelona, wins the 100-metre butterfly.

Jan 10: Sprinter Bruny Surin of Montreal, who barely missed a bronze medal in the 100 metres at the Barcelona Olympics in 1992, breaks the 55-metre record at the Dartmouth Relays in Hanover, NH with a time of 6.17 seconds. (On Feb. 5, he will tie the Canadian 60-metre record (6.52) in a meet at Berlin.)

—Andy Capicik of Toronto, in his first season with the men's freestyle ski team, wins the aerials competition at a World Cup meet in Whistler, BC.

Jan 14: Basketball's Michael Jordan and tennis star Monica Seles are named Associated Press male and female athlete of the year for the second straight year. Manon Rheaume of Quebec City, the first female to play professional hockey, is eighth.

Jan 18: Indy Car drivers Scott Goodyear of Newmarket, Ont. and John Jones of Thunder Bay join the lifetime millionaire's list. Goodyear's winnings reach $2,146,947; Jones is at $1,040,860.

Jan 19: A combined Ontario Hockey League/Western Hockey League team defeats Quebec 7-5 in the Canadian Hockey League junior all-star game at Montreal.

Jan 20: Canada is ousted from the World League of Volleyball for failure to obtain a signed television contract. It is replaced by Finland.

Jan 23: Bruny Surin's 21.08 second clocking sets a Canadian indoor record at the University of Sherbrooke track meet.

Jan 27: Wally Buono, who guided the Calgary Stampeders to the Grey Cup, is only the second Canadian coach to win the Annis Stukus Award as the CFL coach of the year. Cal Murphy of Winnipeg won in 1983 and '84.

—Larry Walker of the Montreal Expos, a 26-year-old outfielder from Maple Ridge, BC, is named Canada's "Baseball Man of the Year" in voting by the Montreal and Toronto chapters of the Baseball Writers' Association of America. Walker batted .301 with 23 home runs and 93 runs batted in, won a Gold Glove for fielding, and was an All-star.

Jan 30: Nathalie Lambert of Montreal sets a world record of 46.44 seconds in winning the women's 500 metres at a short track speed skating meet in Hamar, Norway.

■ February

Feb 1: Gary Bettman, a 42-year-old lawyer from New York, becomes the first commissioner of the National Hockey League.

—Canada-one, the four-man bobsled team captained by Chris Lori, is third in a World Cup race in Cortina D'Ampezzo, Italy. Lori eventually finishes second in the overall standings.

Feb 3: Marge Schott, the foot-in-mouth owner of baseball's Cincinnati Reds, is fined $25,000 and suspended as owner for one year for "using language that is racially and ethnically offensive." Schott, 64, had made remarks offensive to blacks and Jews.

Feb 4: Mark Tewksbury, who became Canada's darling when he won the 100-metre backstroke at the Barcelona Olympics, retires from competition. Tewksbury remains busy with youth swimming and endorsements.

Feb 5: Lloyd Eisler and Isabelle Brasseur win their fourth national pairs title at the Canadian figure skating championships in Hamilton.

Feb 6: Kurt Browning reclaims his title as king of Canadian figure skating, edging Elvis Stoyko of Richmond Hill, Ont. in the finals. The ice dancing title is won by newcomers Shae-Lynn Bourne, 17, of Chatham, Ont. and Victor Kraatz, 21, of Qualicum Beach, BC.

—The Wales Conference defeats the Campbell Conference in a 16-6 shoot-out in the NHL all-star game in Montreal. Mike Gartner of the New York Rangers scores four goals and is named Most Valuable Player.

—Arthur Ashe, who opened the doors for black professional tennis players, dies of pneumonia related to the AIDS virus in New York City.

Feb 7: Sprinters Bruny Surin and Ben Johnson both win races in Europe. Surin takes the 60 metres in 5.74 seconds at an invitational race in Stuttgart, while Johnson wins a 50-metre race in Grenoble in 5.65. Three days later, Johnson wins a 60-metre race in Ghent, Belgium in 6.6 seconds while Surin embarks on a string of victories at the same distance: in Madrid, 6.5 seconds and Lievin, France, 6.45 seconds.

—Josee Chouinard of Laval, Que wins the women's singles at the Canadian figure skating championships.

Feb 10: Kate Pace of North Bay, Ont. overcomes a broken wrist to win the women's downhill in the world alpine ski championships at Shizukuishi, Japan.

Feb. 13: Myriam Bedard of Loretteville, Que., a surprise bronze medallist in the biathlon at the 1992 Winter Olympics, is the first Canadian to win an international biathlon event with a victory in the 7.5 kilometre sprint in Borovets, Bulgaria.

Feb 17: Silken Laumann, the rowing star who won a bronze medal in single sculls at the 1992 Summer Olympics despite a broken leg, wins the 1992 Harry Jerome Comeback Award, for an athlete who returns to competition after overcoming an injury or illness.

Feb 16-20: The Canadian alpine ski championships are held in St-Jovite, Que. Michelle McKendry-Ruthven wins her third straight super-giant slalom, while Eric Villard captures the men's event. Other women's winners: Melanie Turgeon, giant slalom; Nancy Gee, slalom; Kerrin Lee-Gartner, downhill.

Men's winners: John Mealey, downhill; Rob Crossan, slalom; Thomas Grandi, giant slalom.

Feb 18: Canadians sweep the downhill races at the US alpine ski championships at Winter Park, Colo. Cary Mullen of Banff takes the men's and Lindsey Roberts of Rossland, BC the women's.

Feb 20: Lisa Walters of Prince Rupert, BC, defends her title in the Hawaiian Ladies Open Golf tournament with a 6-under-par 210.

Feb 22: Mike Spracklen, the coach who was instrumental in making Canada an international rowing power, leaves for a position with the US national team. He is replaced by Australian coach Brian Richardson.

Feb 24: Three notable pass catchers are named to the Canadian Football Hall of Fame: Peter Dalla Riva of the Montreal Alouettes, Whit Tucker of Ottawa Rough Riders and Calgary Stampeder's Herman Harrison.

Feb 25: Toronto's Woodbine race track is awarded the prestigious Breeder's Cup for 1996. The Cup, a series of seven races, has $10 million in purses.

—Julie Howard of Brantford, Ont. breaks the Canadian record for the 100-metre backstroke (1minute, 1.1 second) at a meet in Saint John.

Feb 26: Danny Gallivan, the long-time voice of the Montreal Canadiens, dies at 75 in Montreal.

■ March

Mar 5: Sprinter Ben Johnson, once again caught using steroids, is banned from track competition for life.

Mar 6: Sandra Peterson snaps a 13-year drought for Saskatchewan curlers by winning the Scott Tournament of Hearts in Brandon, beating Maureen Bonar of Manitoba 7-6 in an extra end.

Mar 5-6: Canada wins two diving medals at a competition in Rostock, Germany. Jason Napper of Thunder Bay takes silver in the men's one-metre. Paige Gordon of West Vancouver does the same in the women's 10-metre tower event.

Mar 7: Calgary defeats Montreal 3-0 (15-12, 15-4, 15-13) to win the CIAU men's volleyball title. Winnipeg is the women's champion, 3-0 (15-12, 15-8, 15-4) over Alberta.

—Swimmer Nancy Sweetnam of Lindsay,

Ont. sets her third Canadian record in two days at the national university championships in Toronto. Her 2 minutes 10.9 seconds in the 200-metre individual medley is just .30 off the world record. Her earlier marks came in the 200-metre breaststroke (2:25.69) and the 400-metre medley (4:38.61).

Mar 11-13: Kurt Browning and Elvis Stoyko become the first Canadians to finish one-two in the world figure skating championships, held in Prague. It is Browning's fourth world title. In pairs, Isabelle Brasseur of St-Jean-sur-Richelieu, Que and Lloyd Eisler of Seaforth, Ont. finally capture their elusive first gold medal. In women's skating, Karen Preston of Mississauga, Ont. and Josee Chouinard of Laval, Que, finish eighth and ninth, behind winner Oksana Baiul of Ukraine.

Mar 12: Just a week after Ben Johnson's lifetime ban, sprinter Bruny Surin wins the 60 metres in the world's indoor track championships at Toronto's Skydome. His 6.5 seconds ties the meet record, and edges Namibia's Frank Fredericks.

Mar 13: Olympic hurdles champion Mark McKoy wins the 60-metre hurdles at the world indoor track and field championships with a Canadian and event record time of 7.41 seconds.

—Kate Pace wins the women's downhill at a World Cup race in Lillehammer, Norway in 1 minute, 50.6 seconds.

Mar 14: Winnipeg wins the women's CIAU basketball championship, 70-63 over Victoria.

—Phillipe LaRoche of Lac Beauport, Que, defends his world freestyle ski title, winning the aerials competition in Altenmarkt, Austria.

—Ontario's Russ Howard wins curling's Labatt Brier, skipping his rink to a 5-3 win over BC's Rick Folk.

Mar 18: Serge Lajoie, a defenceman for the Alberta Golden Bears, wins the Senator Joseph A. Sullivan Trophy as the outstanding player in Canadian university hockey.

Mar 20: Mario Lemieux, despite missing a substantial part of the hockey season after being diagnosed with Hodgkin's disease, has his second consecutive four-goal game in the Pittsburgh Penguin's 9-3 win over the Philadelphia Flyers.

Mar 21: The Acadia Axemen capture the Canadian university hockey title with a 12-1 demolition of the University of Toronto before a crowd of 7,842 at Maple Leaf Gardens.

—The St. Francis Xavier X-Men win their first national university basketball title, defeating McMaster Marauders 72-64 in Halifax.

Mar 23: Winnipeg Jets rookie Teemu Selanne scores twice and adds an assist to break Peter Stastny's 1980-81 NHL rookie scoring record of 109 points. The Finnish sensation earlier broke Mike Bossy's rookie record for goals (53) and finishes with 76, tying for the NHL lead with Buffalo's Alexander Mogilny.

Mar 25: Kerrin Lee-Gartner of Calgary, winner of the downhill at the 1992 Winter Olympics, finishes third on the World Cup downhill circuit. Katia Seizinger of Germany is first.

Mar 27: Canada loses twice to Scotland in the finals of the world junior curling championships at Grindelwald, Switzerland. The men's rink is beaten 9-5 and the women 7-3.

Mar 28: The Toronto Aeros women's hockey team wins its second national hockey title in three years, defeating defending champion Edmonton Chimos 4-3 in Ottawa.

■ **April**

Apr 3: Canadian centre Jim Montgomery scores three times to lead Maine to a 5-4 victory over defending champion Lake Superior State in the US college hockey final.

—Claude Bourbonnais of Ile-Perrot, Que wins the Valvoline 200 Grand Prix auto race in Phoenix.

Apr 4: The rinks of Russ Howard of Penetanguishene, Ont. and Sandra Peterson of Regina give Canada a sweep in the world curling championships in Geneva. Howard beats Scotland's David Smith, the 1991 world champion, 8-4, while Peterson bests Germany, skipped by Regina native Janet Strayer, 5-3.

Apr 5: The North Carolina Tar Heels defeat the Michigan Wolverines 77-71 to win the US collegiate basketball championship.

Apr 7: The Pittsburgh Penguins tie the NHL record of 15 consecutive victories with a 4-3 overtime win over the Montreal Canadiens.

Apr 10: The fledgling Ottawa Senators win their first, and only, road game of the season, defeating the New York Islanders 5-3. The Senators' 38 straight road losses break the record of 37, set by the 1974-75 Washington Capitals.

—Making her first start of the season in goal for the Atlanta Knights of the International Hockey league, Manon Rheaume, pro hockey's only woman goalie, allows six goals on 31 shots.

Apr 11: Bernhard Langer of Germany wins his second Masters golf championship with a score of 277.

Apr 14: In only his fourth professional fight, Olympic silver medallist Mark Leduc of Toronto wins Canada's super-lightweight boxing title with an easy 12-round decision over Andy Wong of Windsor.

Apr. 18: Paul Tracy of Toronto wins his first Indy car race, with a victory at Long Beach, Cal. over Bobby Rahal. Also in Long Beach, Claude Bourbonnais, Jacques Villeneuve from Bertierville, Que. and David Empringham of Toronto take the top three positions in a Formula Atlantic race. Three weeks later, Villeneuve wins the Super Prix of Atlanta while Bourbonnais takes the June 5 Miller Genuine Draft 200 in Milwaukee.

—Canada's 3-1 victory over Honduras in a World Cup qualifying match is tainted when Honduras president Rafael Callejas threatens to cut his team's funding if it loses.

Apr 23: Former basketball superstar Magic Johnson, forced to retire when he contracted the HIV virus, becomes part of a group bidding for a National Basketball Association franchise in Toronto.

Apr 30: Team Canada, undefeated in the round-robin of the world hockey championships in Germany, loses 7-4 to Russia in the semi-finals. The team also loses the consolation final, 5-1 to the Czech Republic.

■ May

May 1: Sea Hero, a 13 to 1 underdog ridden by Jerry Reynolds, wins the Kentucky Derby at Churchill Downs over favourite Prairie Bayou.

May 2: Lizanne Bussieres-Chafe of London, Ont. wins the women's section of the Pittsburgh Marathon in a time of 2 hours, 35 minutes, 39 seconds.

May 8: Heavyweight boxer Lennox Lewis, who won an Olympic Gold Medal for Canada but now fights as a British citizen, defends his World Boxing Council crown with a unanimous 12-round decision in Las Vegas over Tony Tucker.

May 15: Prairie Bayou, ridden by Mike Smith, recovers from a disappointing Kentucky Derby performance to win the Preakness at Pimlico.

May 20: Arsenal defeats Sheffield Wednesday 2-1 in extra time at Wembley Stadium to win the 112th FA Cup. A 1-1 draw five days earlier had forced a replay.

May 22: Winners at the Canadian synchronized swimming championships in Montreal: senior duet, Karen Fonteyne and Cari Read, Calgary; senior solo, Lisa Alexander, Mississauga, Ont; team, Calgary Aquabelles.

May 23: The Sault Ste. Marie Greyhounds of the Ontario Hockey League win the Memorial Cup, emblematic of junior hockey supremacy, with a 4-2 win over the Peterborough Petes, also of the OHL.

May 29: Canada scores its first-ever rugby win over England with the national team's 15-12 victory in Burnaby, BC.

May 30: Cape Breton Islanders win the American Hockey League's Calder Cup with a 7-2 win over the Rochester Americans to take the series 4-1.

■ June

June 1: Canada's women's diving team is third behind China and Germany in a World Cup competition in Beijing.

June 5: Julie Krone is the first female jockey to win a triple crown race, guiding Colonial Affair to victory in the Belmont Stakes at Aqueduct. The race is marred by the death of Preakness winner Prairie Bayou, destroyed after fracturing a leg.

June 9: The Montreal Canadiens win their record 24th Stanley Cup, defeating the Los Angeles Kings 4-1 to win the finals in five games. Goaltender Patrick Roy wins the Conn Smythe Trophy as the playoff's most valuable player. After dropping the first game of their opening round with Quebec in overtime, the Canadiens reel off an astounding 10 straight overtime wins among their 16 victories.

June 13: Alain Prost of France wins the Canadian Grand Prix Formula One auto race at Montreal's Circuit Gilles-Villeneuve.

June 13: Patty Sheehan wins the LPGA tournament at Bethesda, Md, shooting 275.

June 17: NHL award winners for the 1992-93 season: Hart Trophy (MVP), Mario

Lemieux, Pittsburgh Penguins; Norris trophy (top defenceman), Chris Chelios, Chicago Black Hawks; Vezina Trophy (top goalie), Ed Belfour, Chicago; Lady Byng Trophy (gentlemanly conduct), Pierre Turgeon, NY Islanders; Selke Trophy (top defensive forward), Doug Gilmour, Toronto Maple Leafs; Calder Trophy (top rookie), Teemu Selanne, Winnipeg Jets; Jack Adams Award (top coach), Pat Burns, Toronto.

June 20: Canadian paddlers earn 21 medals, including seven gold, at the Paris International Regatta. World champion Renn Crichlow of Nepean, Ont. wins gold in the men's 200, 500, and 1000-metre kayak singles.

—The Chicago Bulls defeat the Phoenix Suns 99-98 to capture the NBA championship in six games. It is the Bulls' third straight championship as megastar Michael Jordan wins his third straight playoff MVP.

—Lee Janzen shoots a record-tying 272 to win the US Open golf tournament at Springfield, NJ.

June 26: Presidential Ball wins the $1 million North America Cup at Toronto's Greenwood race track. The pacer, driven by Ron Waples, posts the fastest mile ever (1:51) for a three-year-old in Canada.

June 27: Alexander Daigle, a centre from Victoriaville, Que. is taken by the Ottawa Senators as the first choice in the National Hockey League draft.

■ July

July 3: Grant Connell of Vancouver just misses becoming the first Canadian tennis player (other than a junior) to win a Wimbledon title when he and American partner Pat Galbraith lose to the number one pair of Australians Mark Woodforde and Todd Woodbridge, 7-5, 6-3, 7-6 (7-4) in the finals at the All England Club. Stefi Graf and Pete Sampras, the top seeds, win the women's and men's titles.

July 7: The Sacramento Gold Miners become the first non-Canadian team to play in the CFL, losing their opener to the Rough Riders 32-23 in Ottawa.

July 10: Patricia Hy wins the Canadian women's tennis championship over Rene Simpson-Alter 64, 6-3 at the Ontario Racquet Club in Mississauga.

July 11: Andrew Sznajder wins his sixth Canadian tennis championship, defeating Daniel Nestor, 6-2, 4-6, 6-3.

—Peteski wins the 134th Queen's Plate in Toronto by six lengths. The three-year-old is ridden by Craig Perret.

—Paul Tracy wins his second Indy car race, the Cleveland Grand Prix.

July 18: Paul Tracy is the first Canadian winner of the Molson Indy in Toronto. Before a record crowd of 66,225, he defeats Emerson Fittipaldi of Brazil.

—Greg Norman wins the British Open at Sandwich, England. His 267 is two strokes better than Nick Faldo.

July 25: Miguel Indurain of Spain coasts to his third straight victory in the Tour de France, cycling's most prestigious race.

—Lauri Merlen wins the US Women's Open at Carmel, Indiana with a score of 280.

July 26: The CFL awards a franchise to Las Vegas, which will begin play in 1994.

July 27: Seattle Mariners' Ken Griffey Jr. ties a major league record by homering in his eighth consecutive game, providing the only run in a 5-1 loss to the Minnesota Twins.

July 28: The New York Mets Anthony Young ends a record 27-game losing streak as the Mets beat the Florida Marlins 5-4.

■ August

Aug 1: Peteski wins his second race in Canada's Triple Crown, the Prince of Wales Stakes at Fort Erie. He is ridden by Dave Penna while regular jockey Craig Perret sits out a 15-day suspension for conduct detrimental to racing.

Aug. 7-8: Derek Porter, who stroked Canada's men's eights to Olympic gold at Barcelona, wins the single sculls at the Royal Canadian Henley Regatta in St. Catharines, Ont. The Ned Hanlan trophy for the men's eights goes to a University of Victoria crew, while the University of Western Ontario wins the women's eights.

Aug 8: Ten thousand fans and 2,000 athletes combine to open the Canada Summer Games in Kamloops, BC.

Aug 12: Quarterback Danny Barrett of the BC Lions sets a CFL record for yards passing in a single game. His 601 yards breaks the 39-year-old record of 586 set by Montreal's Sam Etcheverry in 1954 and leads the Lions to a 55-38 trouncing of the Toronto Argonauts.

—In an effort to head off a possible late-season strike by players, major league baseball owners pledge not to lock players out nor to attempt to change the existing system of arbitration and free agency before the start of the 1994 season.

Aug 15: Despite setting a Canadian record of 10.02 seconds in the 100-metres, Bruny Surin finishes fifth (in the same time as fourth place Carl Lewis) at the world track and field championships in Stuttgart, Germany. Linford Christie of Britain, a venerable 33, wins in 9.87 seconds, just one-hundredth of a second off Lewis's record time. Robert Esmie of Sudbury makes his major track debut, reaching the semi-finals and clocking a personal best 10.23 seconds. Freddie Williams of Brampton, Ont. advances to the 800-metres finals in a Canadian record 1 minute, 45.13 seconds.

—Canada's dream of a spot in soccer's 1994 World Cup ends in Sydney, as Australia wins a 4-1 shoot-out as Mark Schwarzer, a third-string goaltender, stops four of five Canadian kicks. The teams were tied 3-3 after trading 2-1 home victories.

—A young Canadian swim team wins six medals at the Pan Pacific swim championships in Kobe, Japan. Five of the medals are bronze, while veteran Jon Cleveland of Calgary wins a silver in the men's 200-metre breaststroke.

—Paul Azinger wins his first major golf championship by defeating Greg Norman on the second playoff hole in the PGA Championship at Toledo, Ohio. The two had tied at 272.

Aug. 16: Cambest sets a record for a mile by a harness horse, winning in 1 minute, 46.2 seconds at the Springfield, Ill. Fairgrounds.

Aug. 17: Rosey Edeh of LaSalle, Que. sets a Canadian record in the 400-metre hurdles. Her 54.53 seconds qualifies her for the finals in the world championships at Stuttgart.

Aug 19: In the women's 400-metre hurdles finals, Britain's Sally Gunnell sets a world record of 52.74 seconds, bettering the 52.94 of Russia's Maria Stepanova. Rosey Eedh finishes seventh at 55.19. Michael Smith of Toronto fouls on all attempts in the long jump and is eliminated from the decathlon, in which he was a favourite.

—Just days after resigning as chairman of the Ottawa Senators of the NHL, Bruce Firestone denies conspiring with four of his players to throw the last game of the season in order to ensure Ottawa the first pick in the amateur draft.

—The Canadian Motorsport Hall of Fame opens in Montreal. The 10 inductees include drivers Bill Brack, John Cannon, Billy Foster, Bob McLean, Peter Ryan, Gilles Villeneuve and Eppie Wietzes; builders Chuck Rathgeb and Players Ltd. (a long-time sponsor of car racing); and Bill Sadler, a designer.

Aug 20: Tanya Dubnicoff of Winnipeg becomes the first Canadian woman to win a world cycling championship with a victory in the sprint at Hamar, Norway.

—Britain's Colin Jackson sets a world record of 12.91 seconds in winning the 110-metre hurdles at the world track championships in Stuttgart.

Aug 21: Ontario leads the medal standings as the Canada Summer Games end in Kamloops, BC. Ontario's 45 golds edges Quebec's 43 and BC's 36.

—Anne Montminy of Point-Claire, Que. wins the gold medal in the women's 10-metre tower event at the 16- to 18-year-old diving championships in London, England. Montminy earlier won gold in the same event at the World University Games in Buffalo.

Aug 22: Peteski, the three-year-old son of Affirmed, captures Canadian racing's Triple Crown with a six-length victory in the Breeders' Stakes at Toronto's Woodbine. With Peteski the prohibitive favourite, only four horses run. Jockey is Craig Parret; trainer is Roger Attfield; owner is Earle Mack, the first American owner to win the Triple Crown.

—Paul Tracy wins his fourth Indy car race of the season, edging Nigel Mansell in the Texaco-Vavoline 200 at Elkhart Lake, Wis.

—Canada wins its first and only medal at the world track & field championships as the men's 4x100-metre relay team captures bronze in a Canadian record time of 37.83 seconds. Team members are Robert Esmie of Sudbury, Glenroy Gilbert of Ottawa, Bruny Surin and Atlee Mahorn of Montreal.

—Steffi Graf of Germany, world's top-ranked women's tennis player, defeats Jennifer Capriati of the US 6-1,6-0 6-3 to win the Canadian Open title in Toronto. Leila Neiland of Latvia and Jana Novotna of the Czech Republic take the doubles title, 6-1, 6-2 over Arantxa Sanchez Vicario of Spain and Helena Sukova of the Czech Republic.

Aug 23: Joe Carter of the Toronto Blue Jays ties the American League record with the fifth three-home run game of his career in a 9-8 loss to the Cleveland Indians.

Aug 25: Canada's representative at the Little League world series at Williamsport, Pa., is eliminated. North Vancouver's Lynn Valley loses 4-3 to the Far East representative. Eventual winner for the second straight year is Long Beach, Ca.

Aug 26: Chris Wilson, the Winnipeg wrestler eliminated from medal contention at the Barcelona Olympics by a controversial judging decision, is victimized again at the world wrestling championships in Toronto. A high-ranking Armenian official convinces judges to reverse a decision that had given Wilson a victory over a Russian opponent. Wilson ultimately wins the bronze medal in the light-weight (68-kg) division.

Aug 28: Canada wins gold in the team event at the world junior synchro swimming championships in Leeds, England. Kasia Kulesza of Montreal finishes second in solo.

—Canadians win three medals in the world canoeing championships in Copenhagen. Former world champion Renn Crichlow wins silver in the 500-metre kayak. Steve Giles of Echo Lake, NS earns bronze in the 500-metre canoe. Caroline Brunet of Lac Beauport, Que. becomes the first Canadian woman to win a world championship medal with a bronze in the K1 500-metre.

Aug 29: Brandie Burton wins the du Maurier Classic in London, Ont with a first playoff hole victory over Betsy King. The two tied at 277 for 72 holes.

Aug 31: Jean Beliveau, one of hockey's greatest players and goodwill ambassadors, retires on his 62nd birthday after 43 years with the Montreal Canadiens.

■ September

June 1: Canada's women's diving team is third behind China and Germany in a World Cup competition in Beijing.

Aug 29: Al Unser Jr., wins the Molson Indy Vancouver, finishing 11.2 seconds ahead of the runner-up, Bobby Rahal.

Sept 2: An NHL inquiry rules that stories of a conspiracy by Ottawa Senators players and management to ensure they finished last and could claim first pick in the entry draft are

untrue, and fine the club's former chairman for statements concerning the matter.

—Marlene Streit clinches the Canadian senior women's golf championship, winning her 15th Canadian title.

Sept 4-5: Canadian rowers star at the world rowing championships in Roudnice, in the Czech Republic as Michelle Darvill of Mississauga, Ont., the men's lightweight eights and Derek Porter of Victoria, BC all win gold medals, and Marnie McBean of London, Ont. wins a silver. Wendy Wiebe of St. Catharines and Colleen Miller of Winnipeg win a gold in lightweight double sculls; the lightweight women's coxless fours wins a silver and the Canadians also win a bronze in the women's coxless four.

Sept 5: Algerian runner Noureddine Morceli runs the mile in 3:44.39 at an international track meet in Rieti, Italy. Morceli breaks the old world record of 3:46.32 set by Steve Cram of the UK in a 1985 race in Oslo. Morceli also holds the world record for 1500 metres.

Sept 12: David Frost of South Africa wins the Canadian Open Golf Championship at Glen Abbey with a one-shot win over Fred Couples.

Sept 19: The winner of Canada's Triple Crown, Peteski, beats a strong field in the Molson Export Million by 4 1/2 lengths.

Sept 23: The International Olympic Committee casts their ballots for the site of the Olympic Games in the year 2000. From a field of five possible locations—Berlin, Istanbul, Sydney, Manchester and Beijing—IOC members choose Sydney, Australia.

Sept 27: Toronto Blue Jays clinch their fifth American League East title with a 2-0 victory over the Milwaukee Brewers. The Jays advance to the American League Championship for a series against the Chicago White Sox.

Sept 30: The NBA expansion committee recommends that a basketball franchise be awarded to Professional Basketball Franchise (Canada) Inc., whose principals include former Ontario premier David Peterson and food services magnate John Bitove Jr. The team will begin play in the 1995-96 season. A decision on a similar team bid from a Vancouver-based group is tabled until November.

OLYMPICS

Year	Location	Date of competition	Competitors Men	Women	Nations Represented	Unofficial Winners
1896	Athens, Greece	Apr. 6–15	311	0	13	United States
1900	Paris, France	May 20–Oct. 28	1 319	11	22	United States
1904	St. Louis, United States	July 1–Nov. 23	681	6	12	United States
1906[1]	Athens, Greece	Apr. 22–May 2	877	7	20	United States
1908	London, England	Apr. 27–Oct. 31	1 999	36	23	United States
1912	Stockholm, Sweden	May 5–July 22	2 490	57	28	United States
1916	Cancelled because of World War I					
1920	Antwerp, Belgium	Apr. 20–Sept. 12	2 543	64	29	United States
1924	Paris, France	May 4–July 27	2 956	136	44	United States
1928	Amsterdam, Netherlands	May 17–Aug. 12	2 724	290	46	United States
1932	Los Angeles, United States	July 30–Aug. 14	1 281	127	37	United States
1936	Berlin, Germany	Aug. 1–16	3 738	328	49	Germany
1940	Cancelled because of World War II					
1944	Cancelled because of World War II					
1948	London, England	July 29–Aug. 14	3 714	385	59	United States
1952	Helsinki, Finland	July 19–Aug.3	4 407	518	69	United States
1956	Melbourne, Australia[2]	Nov. 22–Dec. 8	2 958	384	67	USSR
1960	Rome, Italy	Aug. 25–Sept. 11	4 738	610	83	USSR
1964	Tokyo, Japan	Oct. 10–24	4 457	683	93	United States
1968	Mexico City, Mexico	Oct. 12–27	4 750	781	112	United States
1972	Munich, West Germany	Aug. 26–Sept. 10	5 848	1 299	122	USSR
1976	Montreal, Canada	July 17–Aug. 1	4 834	1 251	92[3]	USSR
1980	Moscow, USSR	July 19–Aug. 3	4 265	1 088	81	USSR
1984	Los Angeles, United States	July 28–Aug. 12	5 458	1 620	141	United States
1988	Seoul, South Korea	Sept. 17–Oct. 2	7 105	2 476	160	USSR
1992	Barcelona, Spain	July 25–Aug. 9	n.a.	n.a.	n.a.	Unified Team
1996	Atlanta, United States					
2000	Sydney, Australia					

(1) 1906 Games were not recognized by the International Olympic Committee. (2) The equestrian events were held in Stockholm, Sweden, June 10–17, 1956. (3) Most sources list this figure as 88. Cameroon, Egypt, Morocco and Tunisia all boycotted the 1976 Olympics; however, their athletes had already competed before the boycott was officially announced. (n.a.) not available.

Final Medal Standings of the Summer Olympics, 1992

(Barcelona, Spain, July 25–Aug. 9, 1992)

Country	Gold	Silver	Bronze	Total	Country	Gold	Silver	Bronze	Total
Unified Team	45	38	29	112	Bulgaria	3	7	6	16
United States	37	37	37	108	Netherlands	2	6	7	15
Germany	33	21	28	82	Sweden	1	7	4	12
China	16	22	16	54	New Zealand	1	4	5	10
Cuba	14	6	11	31	North Korea	4	0	5	9
Hungary	11	12	7	30	Kenya	2	4	2	8
South Korea	12	5	12	29	Czechoslovakia	4	2	1	7
France	8	5	16	29	Norway	2	4	1	7
Australia	7	9	11	27	Turkey	2	2	2	6
Spain	13	7	2	22	Denmark	1	1	4	6
Japan	3	8	11	22	Indonesia	2	2	1	5
Britain	5	3	12	20	Finland	1	2	2	5
Italy	6	5	8	19	Jamaica	0	3	1	4
Poland	3	6	10	19	Nigeria	0	3	1	4
Canada	6	5	7	18	Brazil	2	1	0	3
Romania	4	6	8	18	Morocco	1	1	1	3 ▶

Country	Gold	Silver	Bronze	Total	Country	Gold	Silver	Bronze	Total
Ethiopia	1	0	2	3	Slovenia	0	0	2	2
Latvia	0	2	1	3	Switzerland	1	0	0	1
Belgium	0	1	2	3	Mexico	0	1	0	1
Croatia	0	1	2	3	Peru	0	1	0	1
Iran	0	1	2	3	Taiwan	0	1	0	1
Independent1	0	1	2	3	Argentina	0	0	1	1
Greece	2	0	0	2	Bahamas	0	0	1	1
Ireland	1	1	0	2	Colombia	0	0	1	1
Algeria	1	0	1	2	Ghana	0	0	1	1
Estonia	1	0	1	2	Malaysia	0	0	1	1
Lithuania	1	0	1	2	Pakistan	0	0	1	1
Austria	0	2	0	2	Philippines	0	0	1	1
Namibia	0	2	0	2	Puerto Rico	0	0	1	1
South Africa	0	2	0	2	Qatar	0	0	1	1
Israel	0	1	1	2	Suriname	0	0	1	1
Mongolia	0	0	2	2	Thailand	0	0	1	1

(1) Yugoslavians competed as individual athletes.

Canada's Olympic Gold Medalists, 1900–92

■ Winter Olympic Games

1920 Winnipeg Falcons, Ice Hockey (Although the Olympic Winter Games did not begin until 1924, ice hockey was an official event at the 1920 Olympic Games.)

1924 Toronto Granites, Ice Hockey

1928 University of Toronto Graduates, Ice Hockey

1932 Winnipeg Hockey Team, Ice Hockey

1948 Barbara Ann **Scott,** Women's Figure Skating; **RCAF Flyers,** Ice Hockey

1952 Edmonton Mercurys, Ice Hockey

1960 Anne **Heggtveit,** Alpine Skiing, Women's Slalom; Barbara **Wagner** & Robert **Paul,** Pairs Figure Skating

1964 Vic **Emery,** John **Emery,** Douglas **Anakin** & Peter **Kirby,** Four-Man Bobsled

1968 Nancy **Greene,** Alpine Skiing, Women's Giant Slalom

1976 Kathy **Kreiner,** Alpine Skiing, Women's Giant Slalom

1984 Gaetan **Boucher,** Speed Skating, Men's 1 000 m; Gaetan **Boucher,** Speed Skating, Men's 1 500 m

1992 Kerrin **Lee-Gartner,** Alpine Skiing, Women's Downhill; Sylvie **Daigle,** Nathalie **Lambert,** Annie **Perreault,** Angela **Cutrone,** Speed Skating, Women's Short Track Relay; Philippe **Laroche,** Freestyle Skiing, Men's Aerials (demonstration)

■ Summer Olympic Games

1900 George **Orton,** 2 500 Steeplechase (Although a Canadian citizen, he represented the University of Pennsylvania; Canada did not officially appear at the Olympics until 1904.)

1904 Étienne **Desmarteau,** 56-pound Weight Throw; George **Lyon,** Golf; **The Galt Association Football Club,** Football (Soccer); **The Winnipeg Shamrocks Lacrosse Club,** Lacrosse 190; William **Sherring,** Marathon (The 1906 Games are not officially recognized by the I.O.C.)

1908 Walter **Ewing,** Trapshooting; Robert **Kerr,** Men's 200 m Run; **The All Canadas,** Lacrosse

1912 George **Goulding,** 10 000 m Walk; George **Hodgson,** Swimming, Men's 400 m Freestyle; George **Hodgson,** Swimming, Men's 1 500 m Freestyle

1920 Albert **Schneider,** Boxing, Welterweight; Earl **Thomson,** Men's 110 m Hurdles

1928 Ethel **Catherwood,** Women's High Jump; Percy **Williams,** Men's 100 m Run; Percy **Williams,** Men's 200 m Run; Women's Relay Team (Fanny **Rosenfeld,** Ethel **Smith,** Florence **Bell** & Myrtle **Cook**), Women's 4 x 100 m Relay

1932 Horace **Gwynne,** Boxing, Bantamweight; Duncan **McNaughton,** Men's High Jump

1936 Francis **Amyot,** Canoeing, Canadian Singles 1 000 m

1952 George **Genereux,** Trapshooting

1956 Gerald **Ouellette,** Small-Bore Rifle (Prone); University of British Columbia Team (Archibald **McKinnon,** Lorne **Loomer,** Walter **D'Hondt** & Donald **Arnold,** Rowing, Four-Oared Shell without Coxswain

1964 George **Hungerford** & Roger **Jackson,** Rowing, Pair-Oared Shell without Coxswain

▶ **1968** Equestrian Team (James **Elder,** James **Day** & Thomas **Gayford**), Grand Prix (Jumping)

1984 Alex **Baumann,** Swimming, Men's 200 m Individual Medley; Alex **Baumann,** Swimming, Men's 400 m Individual Med-ley; Sylvie **Bernier,** Women's Spring-board Diving; Larry **Cain,** Canoeing, Canadian Singles 500 m; Victor **Davis,** Swimming, 200 m Breaststroke; Hugh **Fisher** & Alwyn **Morris,** Canoeing, Kayak Pairs 1 000 m; Lori **Fung,** Rhythmic Gymnastics, All-Around; Anne **Otten-brite,** Swimming, Women's 200m Breast-stroke; Linda **Thom,** Women's Sport Pistol; National Team (Patrick **Turner,** Kevin **Neufeld,** Mark **Evans,** Grant **Main,** Paul **Steele,** J. Michael **Evans,** Dean **Crawford,** Blair **Horn** & Brian **Mc-Mahon**), Eight-Oared Shell with Coxswain

1988 Lennox **Lewis,** Boxing, Super heavyweight; Carolyn **Waldo,** Synchronized Swimming, Solo; Carolyn **Waldo** & Michelle **Cameron,** Synchronized Swimming, Duet

1992 Marnie **McBean** and Kathleen **Heddle,** Rowing, Women's Pairs; Mark **McKoy,** Track, Men's 110 m Hurdles; Mark **Tewksbury,** Swimming, Men's 100 m Backstroke; Women's Fours, Rowing (Kirsten **Barnes,** Brenda **Taylor,** Jessica **Monroe,** Kay **Worthington**); Men's Eights, Rowing (John **Wallace,** Bruce **Robertson,** Michael **Forgeron,** Darren **Barber,** Robert **Marland,** Michael **Rascher,** Andy **Crosby,** Derek **Porter,** Terry **Paul**); Women's Eights, Rowing (Kirsten **Barnes,** Brenda **Taylor,** Megan **Delehanty,** Shannon **Crawford,** Marnie **McBean,** Kay **Worthington,** Jessica **Monroe,** Kathleen **Heddle,** Lesley **Thompson**)

Canada's 1992 Summer Olympic Medal Winners

■ Gold

Rowing, Women's Pairs Marnie McBean, Toronto, Ont., and Kathleen Heddle, Vancouver, B.C.

Rowing, Women's Fours Kirsten Barnes, Victoria, B.C.; Brenda Taylor, Sidney, B.C.; Jessica Monroe, North Vancouver, B.C.; Kay Worthington, Toronto, Ont.

Rowing, Women's Eights with Coxswain Kirsten Barnes, Victoria, B.C.; Brenda Taylor, Sidney, B.C.; Megan Delehanty, Vancouver, B.C.; Shannon Crawford, Toronto, Ont.; Marnie McBean, Toronto, Ont.; Kay Worthington, Toronto, Ont.; Jessica Monroe, North Vancouver, B.C.; Kathleen Heddle, Vancouver, B.C.; Lesley Thompson, London, Ont.

Rowing, Men's Eights with Coxswain John Wallace, Burlington, Ont.; Bruce Robertson, Victoria, B.C.; Michael Forgeron, West Vancouver, B.C.; Darren Barber, Victoria, B.C.; Robert Marland, Mississauga, Ont.; Michael Rascher, Fernie, B.C.; Andy Crosby, Hamilton, Ont.; Derek Porter, Victoria, B.C.; Terry Paul, Victoria, B.C.

Swimming, Men's 100 m Backstroke Mark Tewksbury, Calgary, Alta.

Track and Field, Men's 110 m Hurdles Mark McKoy, Toronto, Ont.

■ Silver

Boxing, Light Welterweight Mark Leduc, Toronto, Ont.

Synchronized Swimming, Solo Sylvie Frechette, Montreal, Que.

Synchronized Swimming, Duet Penny and Vicky Vilagos, Montreal, Que.

Taekwondo (demonstration sport) Marcia King, London, Ont.

Track and Field, 20 km Racewalk Guillaume Leblanc, Rimouski, Que.

Wrestling, Super Heavyweight Jeff Thue, Port Moody, B.C.

■ Bronze

Boxing, Middleweight Chris Johnson, Kitchener, Ont.

Cycling, Indivdual Sprint Curt Harnett, Thunder Bay, Ont.

Judo, Middleweight Nicolas Gill, Montreal, Que.

Rowing, Women's Single Sculls Silken Laumann, Mississauga, Ont.

Swimming, Men's 4 x 100-Metre Medley Relay Mark Tewksbury, Calgary, Alta.; Jon Cleveland, Calgary, Alta.; Marcel Gery, Toronto, Ont.; Stephen Clarke, Brampton, Ont.

Track and Field, 3 000 m Angela Chambers, Victoria, B.C.

Yachting, Star Ross MacDonald, Vancouver, B.C. and Eric Jesperson, Sidney, B.C.

Summer Olympic Games Champions, 1896–1992

(*indicates Olympic record; **indicates Olympic and world record)

■ Men's Track and Field Events

100-Metre Run

1896	Thomas Burke, U.S.	12.0
1900	Francis jarvis, U.S.	11.0
1904	Archie Hanh, U.S.	11.0
1908	Reginald Walker, South Africa	10.8
1912	Raph Craig, U.S.	10.8
1920	Charles Paddock, U.S.	10.8
1924	Harold Abrahams, Great Britain	10.6
1928	**Percy Williams, Canada**	10.8
1932	Eddie Tolan, U.S.	10.3
1936	Jessie Owens, U.S.	10.3
1948	Harrison Dillard, U.S.	10.3
1952	Lindy Remigino, U.S.	10.4
1956	Bobby Morrow, U.S.	10.5
1960	Armin Hary, Germany	10.2
1964	Bob Hayes, U.S.	10.0
1968	Jim Hines, U.S.	9.95
1972	Valery Borzov, USSR	10.14
1976	Hasely Crawford, Trinidad	10.06
1980	Allan Wells, Great Britain	10.25
1984	Carl Lewis, U.S.	9.99
1988	Carl Lewis, U.S.	9.92*
1992	Linford Christie, Great Britain	9.96

200-Metre Run

1900	John Tewksbury, U.S.	22.2
1904	Archie Hahn, U.S.	21.6
1908	**Robert Kerr, Canada**	22.6
1912	Ralph Craig, U.S.	21.7
1920	Allen Woodring, U.S.	22.0
1924	Jackson Scholz, U.S.	21.6
1928	**Percy Williams, Canada**	21.8
1932	Eddie Tolan, U.S.	21.2
1936	Jesse Owens, U.S.	20.7
1948	Melvin Patton, U.S.	21.1
1952	Andrew Stanfield, U.S.	20.7
1956	Bobby Morrow, U.S.	20.6
1960	Livio Berruti, Italy	20.5
1964	Henry Carr, U.S.	20.3
1968	Tommie Smith, U.S.	19.83
1972	Valery Borzov, USSR	20.00
1976	Donald Quarrie, Jamaica	20.23
1980	Pietro Mennea, Italy	20.19
1984	Carl Lewis, U.S.	19.80
1988	Joe Deloach, U.S.	19.75
1992	Mike Marsh, U.S.	20.01*

(set Olympic record of 19.73 in semi-finals)

400-Metre Run

1896	Thomas Burke, U.S.	54.2
1900	Maxey Long, U.S.	49.4
1904	Harry Hillman, U.S.	49.2
1908	Wyndham Halswelle, Great Britain	50.0
1912	Charles Reidpath, U.S.	48.2
1920	Bevil Rudd, South Africa	49.6
1924	Eric Liddell, Great Britain	47.6
1928	Ray Barbuti, U.S.	47.8
1932	William Carr, U.S.	46.2
1936	Archie Williams, U.S.	46.5
1948	Arthur Wint, Jamaica	46.2
1952	George Rhoden, Jamaica	45.9
1956	Charles Jenkins, U.S.	46.7
1960	Otis Davis, U.S.	44.9
1964	Michael Larrabee, U.S.	45.1
1968	Lee Evans, U.S.	43.86*
1972	Vincent Matthews, U.S.	44.66
1976	Alberto Juantorena, Cuba	44.26
1980	Viktor Markin, USSR	44.60
1984	Alonzo Babers, U.S.	44.27
1988	Steven Lewis, U.S.	43.87
1992	Quincy Watts, U.S.	43.50*

800-Metre Run

1896	Edwin Flack, Australia.	2:11.0
1900	Alfred Tysoe, Great Britain	2:01.2
1904	James Lightbody, U.S.	1:56.0
1908	Mel Sheppard, U.S.	1:52.8
1912	Ted Meredith, U.S.	1:51.9
1920	Albert Hill, Great Britain	1:53.4
1924	Douglas Lowe, Great Britain	1:52.4
1928	Douglas Lowe, Great Britain	1:51.8
1932	Thomas Hampson, Great Britain	1:49.7
1936	John Woodruff, U.S.	1:52.9
1948	Mal Whitfield, U.S.	1:49.2
1952	Mal Whitfield, U.S.	1:49.2
1956	Thomas Courtney, U.S.	1:47.7
1960	Peter Snell, New Zealand	1:46.3
1964	Peter Snell, New Zealand	1:45.1
1968	Ralph Doubell, Australia	1:44.3
1972	Dave Wottle, U.S.	1:45.9
1976	Alberto Juantorena, Cuba	1:43.5
1980	Steve Ovett, Great Britain	1:45.4
1984	Joaquim Cruz, Brazil	1:43.0*
1988	Paul Ereng, Kenya	1:43.45
1992	William Tanui, Kenya	1:43.66

1 500-Metre Run

1896	Edwin Flack, Australia	4:33.2
1900	Charles Bennett, Great Britain	4:06.2
1904	James Lightbody, U.S.	4:05.4
1908	Mel Sheppard, U.S.	4:03.4
1912	Arnold Jackson, Great Britain	3:56.8
1920	Albert Hill, Great Britain	4:01.8
1924	Paavo Nurmi, Finland	3:53.6
1928	Harry Larva, Finland	3:53.2
1932	Luigi Beccali, Italy	3:51.2
1936	Jack Lovelock, New Zealand	3:47.8
1948	Henry Eriksson, Sweden	3:49.8
1952	Josef (Josy) Barthel, Luxembourg	3:45.1
1956	Ron Delany, Ireland	3:41.2
1960	Herb Elliott, Australia	3:35.6
1964	Peter Snell, New Zealand	3:38.1
1968	Kipchoge Keino, Kenya	3:34.9

1972	Pekka Vasala, Finland	3:36.3
1976	John Walker, New Zealand	3:39.17
1980	Sebastian Coe, Great Britain	3:38.4
1984	Sebastián Coe, Great Britain	3:32.53*
1988	Peter Rono, Kenya	3:35.96
1992	Fermin Cacho Ruiz, Spain	3:40.12

3 000-Metre Steeplechase

1920	Percy Hodge, Great Britain	10:00.4
1924	Ville Ritola, Finland	9:33.6
1928	Toivo Loukola, Finland	9:21.8
1932	Volmari Iso-Hollo, Finland	10:33.4
	(About 3 460 m extra lap by error)	
1936	Volmari Iso-Hollo, Finland	9:03.8
1948	Thore Sjöstrand, Sweden	9:04.6
1952	Horace Ashenfelter, U.S.	8:45.4
1956	Chris Brasher, Great Britain	8:41.2
1960	Zdzislaw Krzyszkowiak, Poland	8:34.2
1964	Gaston Roelants, Belgium	8:30.8
1968	Amos Biwott, Kenya	8:51.0
1972	Kipchoge Keino, Kenya	8:23.6
1976	Anders Gärderud, Sweden	8:08.2
1980	Bronislaw Malinowski, Poland	8:09.7
1984	Julius Korir, Kenya	8:11.80
1988	Julius Kariuki, Kenya	8:05.51*
1992	Matthew Birir, Kenya	8:08:84

5 000-Metre Run

1912	Johannes Kolehmainen, Finland	14:36.6
1920	Joseph Guillemot, France	14:55.6
1924	Paavo Nurmi, Finland	14:31.2
1928	Ville Ritola, Finland	14:38.0
1932	Lauri Lehtinen, Finland	14:30.0
1936	Gunnar Höckert, Finland	14:22.2
1948	Gaston Reiff, Belgium	14:17.6
1952	Emil Zátopek, Czechoslovakia	14:06.6
1956	Vladimir Kuts, USSR	13:39.6
1960	Murray Halberg, New Zealand	13:43.4
1964	Bob Schul, U.S.	13:48.8
1968	Mohamed Gammoudi, Tunisia	14:05.0
1972	Lasse Viren, Finland	13:26.4
1976	Lasse Viren, Finland	13:24.76
1980	Miruts Yifter, Ethiopia	13:21.0
1984	Said Aouita, Morocco	13:05.59*
1988	John Ngugi, Kenya	13:11.70
1992	Dieter Baumann, Germany	13:12.52

10 000-Metre Run

1912	Johannes Kolehmainen, Finland	31:20.8
1920	Paavo Nurmi, Finland	31:45.8
1924	Ville Ritola, Finland	30:23.2
1928	Paavo Nurmi, Finland	30:18.8
1932	Janusz Kusoci;aanski, Poland	30:11.4
1936	Ilmari Salminen, Finland	30:15.4
1948	Emil Zátopek, Czechoslovakia	29:59.6
1952	Emil Zátopek, Czechoslovakia	29:17.0
1956	Vladimir Kuts, USSR	28:45.6
1960	Ptyor Bolotnikov, USSR	28:32.2
1964	Billy Mills, U.S.	28:24.4
1968	Naftali Temu, Kenya	29:27.4
1972	Lasse Viren, Finland	27:38.4
1976	Lasse Viren, Finland	27:40.38

1980	Miruts Yifter, Ethiopia	27:42.7
1984	Alberto Cova, Italy	27:47.54
1988	M. Brahim Boutaib, Morocco	27:21.46*
1992	Khalid Skah, Morocco	27:46.7

Marathon

1896	Spiridon Louis, Greece	2:58:50
1900	Michel Théato, France	2:59:45
1904	Thomas Hicks, U.S.	3:28:63
1908	John Hayes, U.S.	2:55:18.4
1912	Kenneth McArthur, South Africa	2:36:54.8
1920	Johannes Kolehmainen, Finland	2:32:35.8
1924	Albin Stenroos, Finland	2:41:22.6
1928	Boughèra El Ouafi, France	2:32:57.0
1932	Juan Zabala, Argentina	2:31:36.0
1936	Kee-Chung Sohn (Kitei Son), Japan/Korea	
		2:29:19.2
1948	Delfo Cabrera, Argentina	2:34:51.6
1952	Emil Zátopek, Czechoslovakia	2:23:03.2
1956	Alain Mimoun, France	2:25:00.0
1960	Abebe Bikila, Ethiopia	2:15:16.2
1964	Abebe Bikila, Ethiopia	2:12:11.2
1968	Mamo Wolde, Ethiopia	2:20:26.4
1972	Frank Shorter, U.S.	2:12:19.8
1976	Waldemar Cierpinski, E. Germany	2:09:55.0
1980	Waldemar Cierpinski, E. Germany	2:11:03.0
1984	Carlos Lopes, Portugal	2:09:21.0*
1988	Gelindo Bordin, Italy	2:10.32
1992	Hwang Young-cho, S. Korea	2:13:23.0

20-Kilometre Walk

1956	Leonid Spirin, USSR	1:31:27.4
1960	Vladimir Golubnichiy, USSR	1:34:07.2
1964	Kenneth Mathews, Great Britain	1:29:34.0
1968	Vladimir Golubnichiy, USSR	1:33:58.4
1972	Peter Frenkel, E. Germany	1:26:42.4
1976	Daniel Bautista, Mexico	1:24:40.6
1980	Maurizio Damilano, Italy	1:23:35.5
1984	Ernesto Canto, Mexico	1:23:13.0
1988	Jozef Pribilinec, Czechoslovakia	1:19:57.0*
1992	Daniel Plaza, Spain	1:21:45.0

50-Kilometre Walk

1932	Thomas Green, Great Britain	4:50:10
1936	Harold Whitlock, Great Britain	4:30:41.4
1948	John Ljunggren, Sweden	4:41.52
1952	Giuseppe Dordoni, Italy	4:28:07.8
1956	Norman Read, New Zealand	4:30:42.8
1960	Donald Thompson, Great Britain	4:25:30.0
1964	Abdon Pamich, Italy	4:11:12.4
1968	Christoph Höhne, E. Germany	4:20:13.6
1972	Bernd Kannenberg, W. Germany	3:56:11.6
1980	Hartwig Gauder, E. Germany	3:49:24.0
1984	Raúl González, Mexico	3:47:26.0
1988	Viacheslav Ivanenko, USSR	3:38:29.0*
1992	Andrei Perlov, Unified Team	3:50:13.0

110-Metre Hurdles

1896	Thomas Curtis, U.S.	17.6
1900	Alvin Kraenzlein, U.S.	15.4
1904	Frederick Schule, U.S.	16.0
1908	Forrest Smithson, U.S.	15.0

1912	Frederick Kelly, U.S.	15.1
1920	**Earl Thomson, Canada**	14.8
1924	Daniel Kinsey, U.S.	15.0
1928	Sydney Atkinson, South Africa	14.8
1932	George Saling, U.S.	14.6
1936	Forrest Towns, U.S.	14.2
1948	William Porter, U.S.	13.9
1952	Harrison Dillard, U.S.	13.7
1956	Lee Calhoun, U.S.	13.5
1960	Lee Calhoun, U.S.	13.8
1964	Hayes Jones, U.S.	13.6
1968	Willie Davenport, U.S.	13.3
1972	Rod Milburn, U.S.	13.24
1976	Guy Drut, France	13.30
1980	Thomas Munkelt, E. Germany	13.39
1984	Roger Kingdom, U.S.	13.20
1988	Roger Kingdom, U.S.	12.98*
1992	**Mark McKoy, Canada**	13.12

400-Metre Hurdles

1900	John Tewksbury, U.S.	57.6
1904	Harry Hillman, U.S.	53.0
1908	Charles Bacon, U.S.	55.0
1920	Frank Loomis, U.S.	54.0
1924	F. Morgan Taylor, U.S.	52.6
1928	Lord David Burghley, Great Britain	53.4
1932	Robert Tisdall, Ireland	51.7
1936	Glenn Hardin, U.S.	52.4
1948	Roy Cochran, U.S.	51.1
1952	Charles Moore, U.S.	50.8
1956	Glenn Davis, U.S.	50.1
1960	Glenn Davis, U.S.	49.3
1964	Rex Cawley, U.S.	49.6
1968	David Hemery, Great Britain	48.12
1972	John Akii-Bua, Uganda	47.82
1976	Edwin Moses, U.S.	47.64
1980	Volker Beck, E. Germany	48.70
1984	Edwin Moses, U.S.	47.75
1988	Andre Phillips, U.S.	47.19
1992	Kevin Young, U.S.	46.78**

High Jump

1896	Ellery Clark, U.S.	1.81 m
1900	Irving Butler, U.S.	1.90 m
1904	Samuel Jones, U.S.	1.80 m
1908	Harry Porter, U.S.	1.90 m
1912	Alma Richards, U.S.	1.93 m
1920	Richmond Landon, U.S.	1.93 m
1924	Harold Osborn, U.S.	1.98 m
1928	Robert King, U.S.	1.94 m
1932	**Duncan McNaughton, Canada**	1.97 m
1936	Cornelius Johnson, U.S.	2.03 m
1948	John Winter, Australia	1.98 m
1952	Walter Davis, U.S.	2.04 m
1956	Charles Dumas, U.S.	2.12 m
1960	Robert Shavlakadze, USSR	2.16 m
1964	Valery Brumel, USSR	2.18 m
1968	Dick Fosbury, U.S.	2.24 m
1972	Yuri Tarmak, USSR	2.23 m
1976	Jacek Wszola, Poland	2.25 m
1980	Gerd Wessig, E. Germany	2.36 m
1984	Dietmar Mögenburg, W. Germany	2.35 m

1988	Guennadi Avdeenko, USSR	2.38 m*
1992	Javier Soto-Mayor, Cuba	2.34 m

Long Jump

1896	Ellery Clark, U.S.	6.35 m
1900	Alvin Kraenzlein, U.S.	7.18m
1904	Meyer Prinstein, U.S.	7.34 m
1908	Frank Irons, U.S.	7.48 m
1912	Albert Gutterson, U.S.	7.60 m
1920	William Petersson, Sweden	7.15 m
1924	William De Hart Hubbard, U.S.	7.44 m
1928	Edward Hamm, U.S.	7.73 m
1932	Edward Gordon, U.S.	7.64 m
1936	Jesse Owens, U.S.	8.06 m
1948	Willie Steele, U.S.	7.82 m
1952	Jerome Biffle, U.S.	7.57 m
1956	Gregory Bell, U.S.	7.83 m
1960	Ralph Boston, U.S.	8.12 m
1964	Lynn Davies, Great Britain	8.07 m
1968	Bob Beamon, U.S.	8.90 m*
1972	Randy Williams, U.S.	8.24 m
1976	Arnie Robinson, U.S.	8.35 m
1980	Lutz Dombrowski, E. Germany	8.54 m
1984	Carl Lewis, U.S.	8.54 m
1988	Carl Lewis, U.S.	8.72 m
1992	Carl Lewis, U.S.	8.67 m

100-Metre Relay

1912	Great Britain	42.4
1920	United States	42.2
1924	United States	41.0
1928	United States	41.0
1932	United States	40.0
1936	United States	39.8
1948	United States	40.6
1952	United States	40.1
1956	United States	39.5
1960	Germany	39.5
1964	United States	39.0
1968	United States	38.2
1972	United States	38.19
1976	United States	38.33
1980	USSR	38.26
1984	United States	37.83
1988	USSR	38.19
1992	United States	37.40**

400-Metre Relay

1908	United States (medley relay)	3:29.4
1912	United States	3:16.6
1920	Great Britain	3:22.2
1924	United States	3:16.0
1928	United States	3:14.2
1932	United States	3:08.2
1936	Great Britain	3:09.0
1948	United States	3:10.4
1952	Jamaica	3:03.9
1956	United States	3:04.8
1960	United States	3:02.2
1964	United States	3:00.7
1968	United States	2:56.16*
1972	Kenya	2:59.8

1976	United States	2:58.65
1980	USSR	3:01.1
1984	United States	2:57.91
1988	United States	2:56.16
1992	United States	2:55.74**

Pole Vault

1896	William Hoyt, U.S.	3.30 m
1900	Irving Baxter, U.S.	3.30 m
1904	Charles Dvorak, U.S.	3.50 m
1908	Alfred Gilbert, U.S.	
	Edward Cooke, U.S.	3.71 m
1912	Harry Babcock, U.S.	3.95 m
1920	Frank Foss, U.S.	4.09 m
1924	Lee Barnes, U.S.	3.95 m
1928	Sabin Carr, U.S.	4.20 m
1932	William Miller, U.S.	4.31 m
1936	Earle Meadows, U.S.	4.35 m
1948	Guinn Smith, U.S.	4.30 m
1952	Robert Richards, U.S.	4.55 m
1956	Robert Richards, U.S.	4.56 m
1960	Don Bragg, U.S.	4.70 m
1964	Fred Hansen, U.S.	5.10 m
1968	Bob Seagren, U.S.	5.40 m
1972	Wolfgang Nordwig, E. Germany	5.50 m
1976	Tadeusz Slusarski, Poland	5.50 m
1980	Wladyslaw Kozakiewicz, Poland	5.78 m
1984	Pierre Quinon, France	5.75 m
1988	Sergey Bubka, USSR	5.90 m*
1992	Maxim Tarassov, Unified Team	5.80 m

Hammer Throw

1900	John Flanagan, U.S.	49.73 m
1904	John Flanagan, U.S.	51.23 m
1908	John Flanagan, U.S.	51.92 m
1912	Matt McGrath, U.S.	54.74 m
1920	Pat Ryan, U.S.	52.87 m
1924	Fred Tootell, U. S.	53.295 m
1928	Patrick O'Callaghan, Ireland	51.39 m
1932	Patrick O'Callaghan, Ireland	53.92 m
1936	Karl Hein, Germany	56.49 m
1948	Imre Németh, Hungary	56.07 m
1952	József Csérmák, Hungary	60.34 m
1956	Harold Connolly, U.S.	63.19 m
1960	Vasily Rudenkov, USSR	67.10 m
1964	Romuald Klim, USSR	69.74 m
1968	Gyula Zsivótsky, Hungary	73.36 m
1972	Anatoly Bondarchuk, USSR	75.50 m
1976	Yuri Sedykh, USSR	77.52 m
1980	Yuri Sedykh, USSR	81.80 m
1984	Juha Tiainen, Finland	78.08 m
1988	Serguei Litvinov, USSR	84.80 m*
1992	Andrey Abduvaliyev, Unified Team	82.54 m

Discus Throw

1896	Robert Garrett, U.S.	29.15 m
1900	Rudolf (Rezsö) Bauer, Hungary	36.04 m
1904	Martin Sheridan, U.S.	39.28 m
1908	Martin Sheridan, U.S.	40.89 m
1912	Armas Taipale, Finland	45.21 m
1920	Elmer Niklander, Finland	44.685 m
1924	Clarence "Bud" Houser, U.S.	46.15 m

1928	Clarence "Bud" Houser, U.S.	47.32 m
1932	John Anderson, U.S.	49.49 m
1936	Ken Carpenter, U.S.	50.48 m
1948	Adolfo Consolini, Italy	52.78 m
1952	Sim Iness, U.S.	55.03 m
1956	Al Oerter, U.S.	56.36 m
1960	Al Oerter, U.S.	59.18 m
1964	Al Oerter, U.S.	61.00 m
1968	Al Oerter, U.S.	64.78 m
1972	Ludvik Dan;abek, Czechoslovakia	64.40 m
1976	Mac Wilkins, U.S.	67.50 m
1980	Viktor Rashchupkin, USSR	66.64 m
1984	Rolf Dannenberg, W. Germany	66.60 m
1988	Jurgen Schult, E. Germany	68.82 m*
1992	Romas Ubartas, Lithuania	65.12 m

Triple Jump

1896	James Connolly, U.S.	13.71 m
1900	Meyer Prinstein, U.S.	14.47 m
1904	Meyer Prinstein, U.S.	14.35 m
1908	Timothy Ahearne, Great Britain/Ireland	14.92 m
1912	Gustaf Lindblom, Sweden	14.76 m
1920	Vilho Tuulos, Finland	14.50 m
1924	Anthony Winter, Australia	15.52 m
1928	Mikio Oda, Japan	15.21 m
1932	Chuhei Nambu, Japan	15.72 m
1936	Naoto Tajima, Japan	16.00 m
1948	Arne A°hman, Sweden	15.40 m
1952	Adhemar Ferriera da Silva, Brazil	16.22 m
1956	Adhemar Ferriera da Silva, Brazil	16.35 m
1960	Józef Schmidt, Poland	16.81 m
1964	Józef Schmidt, Poland	16.85 m
1968	Viktor Saneyev, USSR	17.39 m
1972	Viktor Saneyev, USSR	17.35 m
1976	Viktor Saneyev, USSR	17.29 m
1980	Jaak Uudmaë, USSR	17.35 m
1984	Al Joyner, U.S.	17.26 m
1988	Hristo Markov, Bulgaria	17.61 m
1992	Mike Conley, U.S.	18.17 m

(wind-aided; earlier set Olympic record 17.63 m)

16 lb Shot Put

1896	Robert Garrett, U.S.	11.22 m
1900	Richard Sheldon, U.S.	14.10 m
1904	Ralph Rose, U.S.	14.81 m
1908	Ralph Rose, U.S.	14.21 m
1912	Pat McDonald, U.S.	15.34 m
1920	Ville Pörhölä, Finland	14.81 m
1924	Clarence "Bud" Houser, U.S.	14.99 m
1928	John Kuck, U.S.	15.87 m
1932	Leo Sexton, U.S.	16.00 m
1936	Hans Woellke, Germany	16.20 m
1948	Wilbur Thompson, U.S.	17.12 m
1952	Parry O'Brien, U.S.	17.41 m
1956	Parry O'Brien, U.S.	18.57 m
1960	William Nieder, U.S.	19.68 m
1964	Dallas Long, U.S.	20.33 m
1968	Randy Matson, U.S.	20.54 m
1972	Wladyslaw Komar, Poland	21.18 m
1976	Udo Beyer, E. Germany	21.05 m
1980	Vladimir Kiselyov, USSR	21.35 m
1984	Alessandro Andrei, Italy	21.26 m

1988	Ulf Timmermann, E. Germany	22.47 m*
1992	Mike Stulce, U.S.	21.70 m

Javelin

1908	Erik Lemming, Sweden	54.82 m
1912	Erik Lemming, Sweden	60.64 m
1920	Jonni Myyrä, Finland	65.78 m
1924	Jonni Myyrä, Finland	62.96 m
1928	Eric Lundkvist, Sweden	66.60 m
1932	Matti Järvinen, Finland	72.71 m
1936	Gerhard Stöck, Germany	71.84 m
1948	Kai Rautavaara, Finland	69.77 m
1952	Cy Young, U.S.	73.78 m
1956	Egil Danielson, Norway	85.71 m
1960	Viktor Tsibulenko, USSR	84.64 m
1964	Pauli Nevala, Finland	82.66 m
1968	Jümanis Lümusis, USSR	90.10 m
1972	Klaus Wolfermann, W. Germany	90.48 m
1976	Miklos Németh, Hungary	94.58 m*
1980	Dainis Kula, USSR	91.20 m
1984	Arto Härkönen, Finland	86.76 m
1988	Tapio Korjus, Finland	84.28 m
1992	Jan Zelezny, Czechoslovakia	89.66 m

Decathlon

		Points
1904	Thomas Kiely, Ireland	6 036[1]
1908	not held	
1912	Hugo Wieslander, Sweden	7 724[2]
1920	Helge Lövland, Norway	6 803
1924	Harold Osborn, U.S.	7 711
1928	Paavo Yrjölä, Finland	8 053
1932	James Bausch, U.S.	8 462
1936	Glenn Morris, U.S.	7 900
1948	Robert Mathias, U.S.	7 139
1952	Robert Mathias, U.S.	7 887
1956	Milton Campbell, U.S.	7 937
1960	Rafer Johnson, U.S.	8 392
1964	Willi Holdorf, Germany	7 887
1968	Bill Toomey, U.S.	8 193
1972	Nikolai Avilov, USSR	8 454
1976	Bruce Jenner, U.S.	8 617
1980	Daley Thompson, Great Britain	8 495
1984	Daley Thompson, Great Britain	8 798*[3]
1988	Christian Schenk, E. Germany	8 488
1992	Robert Zmelik, Czechoslovakia	8 611

Former point systems used prior to 1964.

(1) All 10 events held on same day. (2) Jim Thorpe of the U.S. won the 1912 Decathlon with 8 412 pts. but was disqualified and had to return his medals because he had played professional baseball prior to the Olympic games. The medals were restored posthumously in 1982. (3) Scoring change effective Apr., 1985.

■ Women's Track and Field Events

100-Metre Run

1928	Elizabeth Robinson, U.S.	12.2
1932	Stella Walsh (Stanislawa Walasiewicz), Poland.	11.9
1936	Helen Stephens, U.S.	11.5
1948	Francina "Fanny" Blankers-Koen, Netherlands	11.9
1952	Marjorie Jackson, Australia	11.5
1956	Betty Cuthbert, Australia.	11.5

1960	Wilma Rudolph, U.S.	11.0
1964	Wyomia Tyus, U.S.	11.4
1968	Wyomia Tyus, U.S.	11.0
1972	Renate Stecher, E. Germany	11.07
1976	Annegret Richter, W. Germany	11.08
1980	Lyudmila Kondratyeva, USSR	11.06
1984	Evelyn Ashford, U.S.	10.97
1988	Florence Griffith-Joyner, U.S.	10.54
1992	Gail Devers, U.S.	10.82

200-Metre Run

1948	Francina "Fanny" Blankers-Koen, Netherlands	24.4
1952	Marjorie Jackson, Australia	23.7
1956	Betty Cuthbert, Australia	23.4
1960	Wilma Rudolph, U.S.	24.0
1964	Edith McGuire, U.S.	23.0
1968	Irena Szewi;aanska, Poland	22.5
1972	Renate Stecher, E. Germany	22.40
1976	Bärbel Eckert, E. Germany	22.37
1980	Bärbel Wockel (Eckert), E. Germany	22.03
1984	Valerie Brisco-Hooks, U.S.	21.81
1988	Florence Griffith-Joyner, U.S.	21.34*
1992	Gwen Torrence, U.S.	21.81

400-Metre Run

1964	Betty Cuthbert, Australia	52.0
1968	Colette Besson, France	52.0
1972	Monika Zehrt, E. Germany	51.08
1976	Irena Szewi;aanska, Poland	49.29
1980	Marita Koch, E. Germany	48.88
1984	Valerie Brisco-Hooks, U.S.	48.83
1988	Olga Bryzguina, USSR	48.65*
1992	Marie-Jose Perec, France	48.83

800-Metre Run

1928	Lina Radke, Germany	2:16.8
1960	Lyudmila Shevtsova, USSR	2:04.3
1964	Ann Packer, Great Britain	2:01.1
1968	Madeline Manning, U.S.	2:00.9
1972	Hildegard Falck, W. Germany	1:58.55
1976	Tatyana Kazankina, USSR	1:54.94
1980	Nadezhda Olizarenko, USSR	1:53.42*
1984	Doina Melinte, Romania	1:57.6
1988	Sigrun Wodars, E. Germany	1:56.10
1992	Ellen Van Langen, Netherlands	1:55.54

1 500-Metre Run

1972	Lyudmila Bragina, USSR	4:01.4
1976	Tatyana Kazankina, USSR	4:05.48
1980	Tatyana Kazankina, USSR	3:56.6
1984	Gabriella Dorio, Italy	4:03.25
1988	Paula Ivan, Romania	3:53.96*
1992	Hassiba Boulmerka, Algeria	3:55.30

3 000-Metre Run

1984	Maricica Puic;aba, Romania	8:35.96
1988	Tatiana Samolenko, USSR	8:26.53*
1992	Elena Romanova, Unified Team	8:46.04

10 000-Metre Run

1988	Olga Bondarenko, USSR	31:05.21*
1992	Derartu Tulu, Ethiopia	31:06.02

100-Metre Relay

1928	**Canada**	48.4
1932	United States	46.9
1936	United States	46.9
1948	Netherlands	47.5
1952	United States	45.9
1956	Australia	44.5
1960	United States	44.5
1964	Poland	43.6
1968	United States	42.8
1972	West Germany	42.81
1976	East Germany	42.55
1980	East Germany	41.60*
1984	United States	41.65
1988	United States	41.98
1992	United States	42.11

400-Metre Relay

1972	East Germany	3:23.0
1976	East Germany	3:19.23
1980	USSR	3:20.2
1984	United States	3:18.29
1988	USSR	3:15.18*
1992	Unified Team	3:20.20

80-Metre Hurdles

1932	Mildred "Babe" Didriksen, U.S.	11.7
1936	Trebisonda Valla, Italy	11.7
1948	Francina "Fanny" Blankers-Koen, Netherlands	11.2
1952	Shirley Strickland, Australia	10.9
1956	Shirley Strickland, Australia	10.7
1960	Irina Press, USSR	10.8
1964	Karin Balzer, E. Germany	10.5
1968	Maureen Caird, Australia	10.3*

100-Metre Hurdles

1972	Annelie Ehrhardt, E. Germany	12.59
1976	Johanna Schaller, E. Germany	12.77
1980	Vera Komisova, USSR	12.56
1984	Benita Brown-Fitzgerald, U.S.	12.84
1988	Jordanka Donkova, Bulgaria	12.38*
1992	Paraskevi Patoulidou, Greece	12.64

400-Metre Hurdles

1984	Nawal El Moutawakel, Morocco	54.61
1988	Debra Flintoff-King, Australia	53.17*
1992	Sally Gunnell, Great Britain	53.23

High Jump

1928	**Ethel Catherwood, Canada**	1.59 m
1932	Jean Shiley, U.S.	1.657 m
1936	Ibolya Csák, Hungary	1.60 m
1948	Alice Coachman, U.S.	1.68 m
1952	Esther Brand, South Africa	1.67 m
1956	Mildred McDaniel, U.S.	1.76 m
1960	Iolanda Balas, Romania	1.85 m
1964	Iolanda Balas, Romania	1.90 m
1968	Miloslava Rezková, Czechoslovakia	1.82 m
1972	Ulrike Meyfarth, W. Germany	1.92 m
1976	Rosemarie Ackermann, E. Germany	1.93 m
1980	Sara Simeoni, Italy	1.97 m
1984	Ulrike Meyfarth, W. Germany	2.02 m

1988	Louise Ritter, U.S.	2.03 m*
1992	Heike Henkel, Germany	2.02 m

Discus Throw

1928	Halina Konopacka, Poland	39.62 m
1932	Lillian Copeland, U.S.	40.58 m
1936	Gisela Mauermayer, Germany	47.63 m
1948	Micheline Ostermeyer, France	41.92 m
1952	Nina Romaschkova, USSR	51.42 m
1956	Olga Fikotová, Czechoslovakia	53.69 m
1960	Nina Ponomaryeva, USSR	55.10 m
1964	Tamara Press, USSR	57.27 m
1968	Lia Manoliu, Romania	58.28 m
1972	Faina Melnik, USSR	66.62 m
1976	Evelin Schlaak, E. Germany	69.00 m
1980	Evelin Jahl (Schlaak), E. Germany	69.96 m
1984	Ria Stalman, Netherlands	65.36 m
1988	Martina Hellman, E. Germany	72.30 m*
1992	Maritza Marten Garcia, Cuba	70.06 m

Javelin Throw

1932	Mildred "Babe" Didriksen, U.S.	43.68 m
1936	Tilly Fleischer,	45.57 m
1952	Dana Zátopková, Czechoslovakia	50.47 m
1956	Inese Jaunzeme, USSR	53.86 m
1960	Elvira Ozolina, USSR	55.98 m
1964	Mihaela Penes, Romania	60.54 m
1968	Angéla Németh, Hungary	60.36 m
1972	Ruth Fuchs, E. Germany	63.88 m
1976	Ruth Fuchs, E. Germany	65.94 m
1980	Maria Colon Rue{{á}}es, Cuba	68.40 m
1984	Tessa Sanderson, Great Britain	69.54 m
1988	Petra Felke, E. Germany	74.68 m*
1992	Silke Renk, Germany	68.34 m

Shot Put (4 kg)

1948	Micheline Ostermeyer, France	13.75 m
1952	Galina Zybina, USSR	15.28 m
1956	Tamara Tishkevich, US.	16.59 m
1960	Tamara Press, USSR	17.32 m
1964	Tamara Press, USSR	18.14 m
1968	Margitta Gummel, E. Germany	19.61 m
1972	Nadezhda Chizhova, USSR	21.03 m
1976	Ivanka Hristova, Bulgaria	21.16 m
1980	Ilona Slupianek, E. Germany	22.41 m*
1984	Claudia Losch, W. Germany	20.47 m
1988	Natalia Lisovskaya, USSR	22.24 m
1992	Svetlana Kriveleva, Unified Team	21.06m

Long Jump

1948	Olga Gyarmati, Hungary	5.695 m
1952	Yvette Williams, New Zealand	6.24 m
1956	Elzbieta Krzeski;aanska, Poland	6.35 m
1960	Vyera Krepkina, USSR	6.37 m
1964	Mary Rand, Great Britain	6.76 m
1968	Viorica Viscopoleanu, Romania	6.82 m
1972	Heidemarie Rosendahl, W. Germany	6.78 m
1976	Angela Voigt, E. Germany	6.72 m
1980	Tatiana Kolpakova, USSR	7.06 m
1984	Anisoara-cusmir-Stanciu, Romania	6.96 m
1988	Jackie Joyner-Kersee, U.S.	7.40 m*
1992	Heike Drechsler, Germany	7.14 m

Pentathlon

		Points
1964	Irina Press, USSR	5 246
1968	Ingrid Becker, W. Germany	5 098
1972	Mary Peters, England	4 801
1976	Sigrun Siegl, E. Germany	4 745
1980	Nadezhda Tkachenko, USSR	5 083*

Former point system, 1964–68

Heptathlon

		Points
1984	Glynis Nunn, Australia	6 390
1988	Jackie Joyner-Kersee, U.S.	7 291*
1992	Jackie Joyner-Kersee, U.S.	7 044

Marathon

1984	Joan Benoit, U.S.	2:24:52*
1988	Rosa Mota, Portugal	2:25.40
1992	Valentina Yegorova, Unified Team	2:32.41

10-kilometre Walk

1992	Chen Yueling, China	44:32

■ Men's Swimming

50-Metre Freestyle

1904	Zoltán Halmay, Hungary	28.0
1988	Matt Biondi, U.S.	22.14
1992	Alexander Popov, Unified Team	21.91*

100-Metre Freestyle

1896	Alfréd Hajós, Hungary	1:22.2
1904	Zoltán Halmay, Hungary (100 yards)	1:02.8
1906	Charles Daniels, U.S.	1:13.4
1908	Charles Daniels, U.S.	1:05.6
1912	Duke Paoa Kahanamoku, U.S.	1:03.4
1920	Duke Paoa Kahanamoku, U.S.	1:01.4
1924	Johnny Weissmuller, U.S.	59.0
1928	Johnny Weissmuller, U.S.	58.6
1932	Yasuji Miyazaki, Japan	58.2
1936	Ferenc Csik, Hungary	57.6
1948	Wally Ris, U.S.	57.3
1952	Clarke Scholes, U.S.	57.4
1956	Jon Henricks, Australia	55.4
1960	John Devitt, Australia	55.2
1964	Don Schollander, U.S.	53.4
1968	Michael Wenden, Australia	52.2
1972	Mark Spitz, U.S.	51.22
1976	Jim Montgomery, U.S.	49.99
1980	Jörg Woithe, E. Germany	50.40
1984	Rowdy Gaines, U.S.	49.80
1988	Matt Biondi, U.S.	48.63*
1992	Alexander Popov, Unified Team	49.02

200-Metre Freestyle

1900	Frederick Lane, Australia (220 yd.)	2:25.2
1904	Charles Daniels, U.S. (220 yd.)	2:44.2
1906-64		not held
1968	Michael Wenden, Australia	1:55.2
1972	Mark Spitz, U.S.	1:52.78
1976	Bruce Furniss, U.S.	1:50.29

1980	Sergei Kopliakov, USSR	1:49.81
1984	Michael Gross, W. Germany	1:47.44
1988	Duncan Armstrong, Australia	1:47.25
1992	Evgueni Sadovyi, Unified Team	1:46.70*

400-Metre Freestyle

1896	Paul Neumann, Austria (500 m)	8:12.6
1904	Charles Daniels, U.S. (440 yards)	6:16.2
1908	Henry Taylor, Great Britain	5:36.8
1912	**George Hodgson, Canada**	5:24.4
1920	Norman Ross, U.S.	5:26.8
1924	Johnny Weissmuller, U.S.	5:04.2
1928	Albert Zorilla, Argentina	5:01.6
1932	Clarence "Buster" Crabbe, U.S.	4:48.4
1936	Jack Medica, U.S.	4:44.5
1948	William Smith, U.S.	4:41.0
1952	Jean Boiteux, France	4:30.7
1956	Murray Rose, Australia	4:27.3
1960	Murray Rose, Australia	4:18.3
1964	Don Schollander, U.S.	4:12.2
1968	Mike Burton, U.S.	4:09.0
1972	Brad Cooper, Australia	4:00.27
1976	Brian Goodell, U.S.	3:51.93
1980	Vladimir Salnikov, USSR	3:51.31
1984	George DiCarlo, U.S.	3:51.23
1988	Uwe Dassler, E. Germany	3:46.95
1992	Evgeuni Sadovyi, Unified Team	3:45.00**

1 500-Metre Freestyle

1896	Alfred Hajós, Hungary (1 200 m)	18:22.2
1900	John Arthur Jarvis, Great Britain (1 000 m)	13:40.2
1904	Emil Rausch, Germany (1 mile)	27:18.2
1908	Henry Taylor, Great Britain	22:48.4
1912	**George Hodgson, Canada**	22:00.0
1920	Norman Ross, U.S.	22:23.2
1924	Andrew "Boy" Charlton, Australia	20:06.6
1928	Arne Borg, Sweden	19:51.8
1932	Kusuo Kitamura, Japan	19:12.4
1936	Noboru Terada, Japan	19:13.7
1948	James McLane, U.S.	19:18.5
1952	Ford Konno, U.S.	18:30.3
1956	Murray Rose, Australia	17:58.9
1960	Jon Konrads, Australia	17:19.6
1964	Robert Windle, Australia	17:01.7
1968	Mike Burton, U.S.	16:38.9
1972	Mike Burton, U.S.	15:52.58
1976	Brian Goodell, U.S.	15:02.40
1980	Vladimir Salnikov, USSR	14:58.27*
1984	Michael O'Brien, U.S.	15:05.20
1988	Vladimir Salnikov, USSR	15:00.40
1992	Kieren Perkins, Australia	14:43.48**

100-Metre Medley Relay

1960	United States	4:05.4
1964	United States	3:58.4
1968	United States	3:54.9
1972	United States	3:48.16
1976	United States	3:42.22
1980	Australia	3:45.70
1984	United States	3:39.30
1988	United States	3:36.93*
1992	United States	3:36:93*

100-Metre Freestyle Relay

1964	United States	3:33.2
1968	United States	3:31.7
1972	United States	3:26.42
1976-80	not held	
1984	United States	3:19.03
1988	United States	3:16.53*
1992	United States	3:16.74**

200-Metre Freestyle Relay

1908	Great Britain	10:55.6
1912	Australia/New Zealand	10:11.6
1920	United States	10:04.4
1924	United States	9:53.4
1928	United States	9:36.2
1932	Japan	8:58.4
1936	Japan	8:51.5
1948	United States	8:46.0
1952	United States	8:31.1
1956	Australia	8:23.6
1960	United States	8:10.2
1964	United States	7:52.1
1968	United States	7:52.33
1972	United States	7:35.78
1976	United States	7:23.22
1980	USSR	7:23.50
1984	United States	7:15.69
1988	United States	7:12.51
1992	Unified Team	7:11.95**

100-Metre Backstroke

1904	Walter Brack, Germany (100 yds.)	1:16.8
1908	Arno Bieberstein, Germany	1:24.6
1912	Harry Hebner, U.S.	1:21.2
1920	Warren Paoa Kealoha, U.S.	1:15.2
1924	Warren Paoa Kealoha, U.S.	1:13.2
1928	George Kojac, U.S.	1:08.2
1932	Masaji Kiyokawa, Japan	1:08.6
1936	Adolf Kiefer, U.S.	1:05.9
1948	Allen Stack, U.S.	1:06.4
1952	Yoshinobu Oyakawa, U.S.	1:05.4
1956	David Thiele, Australia	1:02.2
1960	David Thiele, Australia	1:01.9
1964	not held	
1968	Roland Matthes, E. Germany	58.7
1972	Roland Matthes, E. Germany	56.58
1976	John Naber, U.S.	55.49
1980	Bengt Baron, Sweden	56.33
1984	Rick Carey, U.S.	55.79
1988	Daichi Suzuki, Japan	55.05
1992	**Mark Tewksbury, Canada**	53.98*

200-Metre Backstroke

1900	Ernst Hoppenberg, Germany	2:47.0
1904-60	not held	
1964	Jed Graef, U.S.	2:10.3
1968	Roland Matthes, E. Germany	2:09.6
1976	John Naber, U.S.	1:59.19
1980	Sándor Wladár, Hungary	2:01.93
1984	Rick Carey, U.S.	2:00.23
1988	Igor Polianski, USSR	1:59.37

1992	Martin Lopez-Zubera, Spain	1:58.47*

100-Metre Breaststroke

1968	Donald McKenzie, U.S.	1:07.7
1972	Nobutaka Taguchi, Japan	1:04.94
1976	John Hencken, U.S.	1:03.11
1980	Duncan Goodhew, Great Britain	1:03.44
1984	Steve Lundquist, U.S.	1:01.65
1988	Adrian Moorhouse, Great Britain	1:02.04
1992	Nelson Diebel, U.S.	1:01.50*

200-Metre Breaststroke

1908	Frederick Holman, Great Britain	3:09.2
1912	Walter Bathe, Germany	3:01.8
1920	Håken Malmroth, Sweden	3:04.4
1924	Robert Skelton, U.S.	2:56.6
1928	Yoshiyuki Tsuruta, Japan	2:48.8
1932	Yoshiyuki Tsuruta, Japan	2:45.4
1936	Tetsuo Hamuro, Japan	2:41.5
1948	Joseph Verdeur, U.S.	2:39.3
1952	John Davies, Australia	2:34.4
1956	Masaru Furukawa, Japan	2:34.7
1960	William Mulliken, U.S.	2:37.4
1964	Ian O'Brien, Australia	2:27.8
1968	Felipe Muñoz, Mexico	2:28.7
1972	John Hencken, U.S.	2:21.55
1976	David Wilkie, Great Britain	2:15.11
1980	Robertas Zhulpa, USSR	2:15.85
1984	**Victor Davis, Canada**	2:13.34
1988	Jozsef Szabo, Hungary	2:13.52
1992	Mike Barrowman, U.S.	2:10.16**

100-Metre Butterfly

1968	Doug Russell, U.S.	55.90
1972	Mark Spitz, U.S.	54.27
1976	Matt Vogel, U.S.	54.35
1980	Pär Arvidsson, Sweden	54.92
1984	Michael Gross, W. Germany	53.08
1988	Anthony Nesty, Suriname	53.00*
1992	Pablo Morales, U.S.	53.32

200-Metre Butterfly

1956	William Yorzyk, U.S.	2:19.3
1960	Michael Troy, U.S.	2:12.8
1964	Kevin Berry, Australia	2:06.6
1968	Carl Robie, U.S.	2:08.7
1972	Mark Spitz, U.S.	2:00.70
1976	Mike Bruner, U.S.	1:59.23
1980	Sergei Fesenko, USSR	1:59.76
1984	Jon Sieben, Australia	1:57.04
1988	Michael Gross, W. Germany	1:56.94
1992	Mel Stewart, U.S.	1:56.26*

200-Metre Individual Medley

1968	Charles Hickcox, U.S.	2:12.0
1972	Gunnar Larsson, Sweden	2:07.17
1976-80	not held	
1984	**Alex Baumann, Canada**	2:01.42
1988	Tamas Darnyi, Hungary	2:00.17*
1992	Tamas Darnyi, Hungary	2:00.76

400-Metre Individual Medley

1964	Dick Roth, U.S.	4:45.4
1968	Charles Hickcox, U.S.	4:48.4
1972	Gunnar Larsson, Sweden	4:31.98
1976	Rod Strachan, U.S.	4:23.68
1980	Aleksandr Sidorenko, USSR	4:22.89
1984	**Alex Baumann, Canada**	4:17.41
1988	Tamas Darnyi, Hungary	4:14.75
1992	Tamas Darnyi, Hungary	4:14.23*

Springboard Diving

		Points
1908	Albert Zürner, Germany	85.5
1912	Paul Günther, Germany	79.23
1920	Louis Kuehn, U.S.	675.40
1924	Albert White, U.S.	696.40
1928	Pete Desjardins, U.S.	185.04
1932	Michael Galitzen (Mickey Riley), U.S.	161.38
1936	Richard Degener, U.S.	163.57
1948	Bruce Harlan, U.S.	163.64
1952	David Browning, U.S.	205.29
1956	Robert Clotworthy, U.S.	159.56
1960	Gary Tobian, U.S.	170.00
1964	Kenneth Sitzberger, U.S.	159.90
1968	Bernie Wrightson, U.S.	170.15
1972	Vladimir Vasin, USSR	594.09
1976	Phillip Boggs, U.S.	619.05
1980	Aleksandr Portnov, USSR	905.025
1984	Greg Louganis, U.S.	754.41
1988	Greg Louganis, U.S.	730.80
1992	Mark Lenzi, U.S.	676.53

Platform Diving

		Points
1904	George Sheldon, U.S.	12.66
1908	Hjalmar Johansson, Sweden	83.75
1912	Erik Adlerz, Sweden	73.94
1920	Clarence Pinkston, U.S.	100.67
1924	Albert White, U.S.	97.46
1928	Pete Desjardins, U.S.	98.74
1932	Harold Smith, U.S.	124.80
1936	Marshall Wayne, U.S.	113.58
1948	Sam Lee, U.S.	130.05
1952	Sam Lee, U.S.	156.28
1956	Joaquin Capilla, Mexico	152.44
1960	Robert Webster, U.S.	165.56
1964	Robert Webster, U.S.	148.58
1968	Klaus Dibiasi, Italy	164.18
1972	Klaus Dibiasi, Italy	504.12
1976	Klaus Dibiasi, Italy	600.51
1980	Falk Hoffmann, E. Germany	835.650
1984	Greg Louganis, U.S.	710.91
1988	Greg Louganis, U.S.	638.61
1992	Sun Shu-wei, China	677.31

■ Women's Swimming

50-Metre Freestyle

1988	Kristin Otto, E. Germany	25.49
1992	Yang Wenyi, China	24.79*

100-Metre Freestyle

1912	Fanny Durack, Australia	1:22.2
1920	Ethelda Bleibtrey, U.S.	1:13.6
1924	Ethel Lackie, U.S.	1:12.4
1928	Albina Osipowich, U.S.	1:11.0
1932	Helene Madison, U.S.	1:06.8
1936	Hendrika "Rie" Mastenbroek, Netherlands	1:05.9
1948	Greta Andersen, Denmark	1:06.3
1952	Katalin Szöke, Hungary	1:06.8
1956	Dawn Fraser, Australia	1:02.0
1960	Dawn Fraser, Australia	1:01.2
1964	Dawn Fraser, Australia	59.5
1968	Jan Henne, U.S.	1:00.0
1972	Sandra Neilson, U.S.	58.59
1976	Kornelia Ender, E. Germany	55.65
1980	Barbara Krause, E. Germany	54.79
1984	(tie) Carie Steinseifer, U.S.	55.92
	Nancy Hogshead, U.S.	55.92
1988	Kristin Otto, E. Germany	54.93
1992	Zhuang Yong, China	54.64*

200-Metre Freestyle

1968	Debbie Meyer, U.S.	2:10.5
1972	Shane Gould, Australia	2:03.56
1976	Kornelia Ender, E. Germany	1:59.26
1980	Barbara Krause, E. Germany	1:58.33
1984	Mary Wayte, U.S.	1:59.23
1988	Heike Friedrich, E. Germany	1:57.65*
1992	Nicole Haslett, U.S.	1:57.90

400-Metre Freestyle

1920	Ethelda Bleibtrey (300 m)	4:34.0
1924	Martha Norelius, U.S.	6:02.2
1928	Martha Norelius, U.S.	5:42.8
1932	Helene Madison, U.S.	5:28.5
1936	Hendrika "Rie" Mastenbroek, Netherlands	5:26.4
1948	Ann Curtis, U.S.	5:17.8
1952	Valéria Gyenge, Hungary	5:12.1
1956	Lorraine Crapp, Australia	4:54.6
1960	S. Christine von Saltza, U.S.	4:50.6
1964	Virginia Duenkel, U.S.	4:43.3
1968	Debbie Meyer, U.S.	4:31.8
1972	Shane Gould, Australia	4:19.44
1976	Petra Thümer, E. Germany	4:09.89
1980	Ines Diers, E. Germany	4:08.76
1984	Tiffany Cohen, U.S.	4:07.10
1988	Janet Evans, U.S.	4:03.85*
1992	Dagmar Hase, Germany	4:07.18

800-Metre Freestyle

1968	Debbie Meyer, U.S.	9:24.0
1972	Keena Rothhammer, U.S.	8:53.68
1976	Petra Thümer, E. Germany	8:37.14
1980	Michelle Ford, Australia	8:28.90
1984	Tiffany Cohen, U.S.	8:24.95
1988	Janet Evans, U.S.	8:20.20*
1992	Janet Evans, U.S.	8:25.52

100-Metre Backstroke

1924	Sybil Bauer, U.S.	1:23.2
1928	Maria Braun, Netherlands	1:22.0

1932	Eleanor Holm, U.S.	1:19.4
1936	Dina Senff, Netherlands	1:18.9
1948	Karen Margrete Harup, Denmark	1:14.4
1952	Joan Harrison, South Africa	1:14.3
1956	Judith Grinham, Great Britain	1:12.9
1960	Lynn Burke, U.S.	1:09.3
1964	Cathy Ferguson, U.S.	1:07.7
1968	Kaye Hall, U.S.	1:06.2
1972	Melissa Belote, U.S.	1:05.78
1976	Ulrike Richter, E. Germany	1:01.83
1980	Rica Reinisch, E. Germany	1:00.86
1984	Theresa Andrews, U.S.	1:02.55
1988	Kristin Otto, E. Germany	1:00.89
1992	Krisztina Egerszegi, Hungary	1:00.68*

200-Metre Backstroke

1968	Lillian "Pokey" Watson, U.S.	2:24.8
1972	Melissa Belote, U.S.	2:19.19
1976	Ulrike Richter, E. Germany	2:13.43
1980	Rica Reinisch, E. Germany	2:11.77
1984	Jolanda de Rover, Netherlands	2:12.38
1988	Krisztina Egerszegi, Hungary	2:09.29
1992	Krisztina Egerszegi, Hungary	2:07.06*

100-Metre Breaststroke

1968	Djurdjica Bjedov, Yugoslavia	1:15.8
1972	Catherine Carr, U.S.	1:13.58
1976	Hannelore Anke, E. Germany	1:11.16
1980	Ute Geweniger, E. Germany	1:10.22
1984	Petra van Staveren, Netherlands	1:09.88
1988	Tania Dangalakova, Bulgaria	1:07.95*
1992	Elena Rudkovskaya, Unified Team	1:08.00

200-Metre Breaststroke

1924	Lucy Morton, Great Britain	3:33.2
1928	Hildegard Schrader, Germany	3:12.6
1932	Clare Dennis, Australia	3:06.3
1936	Hideko Maehata, Japan	3:03.6
1948	Petronella van Vliet, Netherlands	2:57.2
1952	Eva Székely, Hungary	2:51.7
1956	Ursula Happe, Germany	2:53.1
1960	Anita Lonsbrough, Great Britain	2:49.5
1964	Galina Prozumenshikova, USSR	2:46.4
1968	Sharon Wichman, U.S.	2:44.4
1972	Beverly Whitfield, Australia	2:41.71
1976	Marina Koshevaia, USSR	2:33.35
1980	Lina Kačiušyté, USSR	2:29.54
1984	**Anne Ottenbrite, Canada**	2:30.38
1988	Silke Hörner, E. Germany	2:26.71
1992	Kyoko Iwasaki, Japan	2:26.65*

200-Metre Individual Medley

1968	Claudia Kolb, U.S.	2:24.7
1972	Shane Gould, Australia	2:23.07
1984	Tracy Caulkins, U.S.	2:12.64
1988	Daniela Hunger, E. Germany	2:12.59
1992	Lin Li, China	2:11.65**

400-Metre Individual Medley

1964	Donna De Varona, U.S.	5:18.7
1968	Claudia Kolb, U.S.	5:08.5
1972	Gail Neall, Australia	5:02.97

1976	Ulrike Tauber, E. Germany	4:42.77
1980	Petra Schneider, E. Germany	4:36.29*
1984	Tracy Caulkins, U.S.	4:39.24
1988	Janet Evans, U.S.	4:37.76
1992	Krisztina Egerszegi, Hungary	4:36.54

100-Metre Butterfly

1956	Shelley Mann, U.S.	1:11.0
1960	Carolyn Schuler, U.S.	1:09.5
1964	Sharon Stouder, U.S.	1:04.7
1968	Lyn McClements, Australia	1:05.5
1972	Mayumi Aoki, Japan	1:03.34
1976	Kornelia Ender, E. Germany	1:00.13
1980	Caren Metschuck, E. Germany	1:00.42
1984	Mary T. Meagher, U.S.	59.26
1988	Kristin Otto, E. Germany	59.00
1992	Qian Hong, China	59.34

200-Metre Butterfly

1968	Ada Kok, Netherlands	2:24.7
1972	Karen Moe, U.S.	2:15.57
1976	Andrea Pollack, E. Germany	2:11.41
1980	Ines Geissler, E. Germany	2:10.44
1988	Kathleen Nord, E. Germany	2:09.51
1992	Summer Sanders, U.S.	2:08.67

100-Metre Medley Relay

1960	United States	4:41.1
1964	United States	4:33.9
1968	United States	4:28.3
1972	United States	4:20.75
1976	East Germany	4:07.95
1980	East Germany	4:06.67
1984	United States	4:08.34
1988	East Germany	4:03.74
1992	United States	4:02.54**

100-Metre Freestyle Relay

1912	Great Britain	5:52.8
1920	United States	5:11.6
1924	United States	4:58.8
1928	United States	4:47.6
1932	United States	4:38.0
1936	Netherlands	4:36.0
1948	United States	4:29.2
1952	Hungary	4:24.4
1956	Australia	4:17.1
1960	United States	4:08.9
1964	United States	4:03.8
1968	United States	4:02.5
1972	United States	3:55.19
1976	United States	3:44.82
1980	East Germany	3:42.71
1984	United States	3:43.43
1988	East Germany	3:40.63
1992	United States	3:39.46**

Springboard Diving

		Points
1920	Aileen Riggin, U.S.	539.9
1924	Elizabeth Becker, U.S.	474.5
1928	Helen Meany, U.S.	78.62

1932	Georgia Coleman, U.S.	87.52
1936	Marjorie Gestring, U.S.	89.27
1948	Victoria M. Draves, U.S.	108.74
1952	Patricia McCormick, U.S.	147.30
1956	Patricia McCormick, U.S.	142.36
1960	Ingrid Krämer, E. Germany	155.81
1964	Ingrid Engel-Krämer, E. Germany	145.00
1968	Sue Gossick, U.S.	150.77
1972	Micki King, U.S.	450.03
1976	Jennifer Chandler, U.S.	506.19
1980	Irina Kalinina, USSR	725.91
1984	**Sylvie Bernier, Canada**	530.70
1988	Gao Min, China	580.23
1992	Gao Min, China	572.40

Platform Diving

		Points
1912	Greta Johansson, Sweden	39.90
1920	Stefani Fryland-Clausen, Denmark	34.60
1924	Caroline Smith, U.S.	33.20
1928	Elizabeth Becker Pinkston, U.S.	31.60
1932	Dorothy Poynton, U.S.	40.26
1936	Dorothy Poynton Hill, U.S.	33.93
1948	Victoria Draves, U.S.	68.87
1952	Patricia McCormick, U.S.	79.37
1956	Patricia McCormick, U.S.	84.85
1960	Ingrid Krämer, Germany	91.28
1964	Lesley Bush, U.S.	99.80
1968	Milena Duchková, Czechoslovakia	109.59
1972	Ulrika Knape, Sweden	390.00
1976	Elena Vaytsekhovskaya, USSR	406.59
1980	Martina Jäschke, E. Germany	596.25
1984	Zhou Jihong, China	435.51
1988	Yanmei Xu, China	445.20
1992	Fu Mingxia, China	461.43

Men's Basketball

1936	United States	1972	USSR
1948	United States	1976	United States
1952	United States	1980	Yugoslavia
1956	United States	1984	United States
1960	United States	1988	USSR
1964	United States	1992	United States
1968	United States		

■ Women's Basketball

1976	USSR
1980	USSR
1984	United States
1988	United States
1992	Unified Team

■ Boxing

Light Flyweight

1968	Francisco Rodrigues, Venezuela
1972	Georgy Gedo, Hungary
1976	Jorge Hernandez, Cuba
1980	Shamil Sabyrov, USSR

1984	Paul Gonzales, U.S.
1988	Ivalio Hristov, Bulgaria
1992	Rogelio Marcelo Garcia, Cuba

Flyweight

1904	George Finnegan, U.S.
1920	Frank Di Gennara, U.S.
1924	Fidel LaBarba, U.S.
1928	Antal Kocsis, Hungary
1932	Istva Enekes, Hungary
1936	Willi Kaiser, Germany
1948	Pascual Rerez, Argentina
1952	Nathan Brooks, U.S.
1956	Terence Spinks, Great Britain
1960	Gyula Torok, Hungary
1964	Fernando Atzori, Italy
1968	Ricardo Delgado, Mexico
1972	Georgi Kostadinov, Bulgaria
1976	Leo Randolph, U.S.
1980	Peter Lessov, Bulgaria
1984	Steve McCrory, U.S.
1988	Kim Kwang-Sun, South Korea
1992	Su Choi-choi, North Korea

Bantamweight

1904	Kirk Oliver, U.S.
1908	A. Henry Tomas, Great Britain
1920	Clarence Walker, South Africa
1924	William Smith, South Africa
1928	Vittorio Tamagnini, Italy
1936	Ulderico Sergo, Italy
1948	Tibor Csik, Hungary
1952	Pentti Hamalainen, Finland
1956	Wolfgang Behrendt, E. Germany
1960	Oleg Grigoryev, USSR
1964	Takao Sakurai
1968	Valery Sokolov, USSR
1972	Orlando Martinez, Cuba
1976	Yong-jo Gu, China
1980	Juan Hernandez, Cuba
1984	Maurizio Stecca, Italy
1988	Kennedy McKinney, U.S.
1992	Joel Casamayor, Cuba

Featherweight

1904	Oliver Kirk, U.S.
1908	Richard Gunn, Great Britain
1920	Paul Fritsch, France
1924	John Fields, U.S.
1928	Lambertus van Klaveren, Holland
1932	Carmelo Robledo, Argentina
1936	Arthur Casanovas, Argentina
1948	Ernesto Formenti, Italy
1952	John Zachara, Czechoslovakia
1956	Vladimir Safronov, USSR
1960	Francesco Musso, Italy
1964	Stanislav Stepashkin, USSR
1968	Antonio Roldan, Mexico
1972	Boris Kousnetsov, USSR
1976	Angel Herrera, Cuba
1980	Rudi Fink, E. Germany
1984	Meldrick Taylor, U.S.

| 1988 | Giovanni Parisi, Italy |
| 1992 | Andreas Tews, Germany |

Lightweight

1904	Harry Spanger, U.S.
1908	Frederick Grace, Great Britain
1920	Samuel Mosberg, U.S.
1924	Hans Nielsen, Denmark
1928	Carli Orlando, Italy
1932	Lawrence Stevens, South Africa
1936	Imre Harangi, Hungary
1948	Gerald Dreyer, South Africa
1952	Aureliano Bolognesi, Italy
1956	Richard McTaggart, Great Britain
1960	Kazimierz Pazdzior, Poland
1964	Jozef Grudzien, Poland
1968	Ronald Harris, U.S.
1972	Jan Szczepanski, Poland
1976	Howard Davis, U.S.
1980	Angel Herrera, Cuba
1984	Pernell Whitaker, U.S.
1988	Andreas Zvelow, East Germany
1992	Oscar De La Hoya, U.S.

Light-Welterweight

1952	Charles Adkins, U.S.
1956	Vladimir Yengibaryan, USSR
1960	Bohumil Nemecek, Czechoslovakia
1964	Jerzy Kulej, Poland
1968	Jerzy Kulej, Poland
1972	Ray Seales, U.S.
1976	Ray Leonard, U.S.
1980	Patrizio Oliva, Italy
1984	Jerry Page, U.S.
1988	Viatcheslav Janovski, USSR
1992	Hector Vinent, Cuba

Welterweight

1904	Albert Young, U.S.
1920	**Albert Schneider, Canada**
1924	Jean DeLarge, Belgium
1928	Edward Morgan, New Zealand
1932	Edward Flynn, U.S.
1936	Sten Suvio, Finland
1948	Julius Torma, Czechoslovakia
1952	Zygmunt Chychla, Poland
1956	Bucikae Kubcam Rinabua
1960	Giovanni Benvenuti, Italy
1964	Marian Kasprzyk, Poland
1968	Manfred Wolke, Great Britain
1972	Emilio Correa, Cuba
1976	Jochen Bachfeld, Great Britain
1980	Andres Aldama, Cuba
1984	Mark Breland, U.S.
1988	Robert Wangila, Kenya
1992	Michael Carruth, Ireland

Light-Middleweight

1952	Laszlo Papp, Hungary
1956	Laszlo Papp, Hungary
1960	Wilbert McClure, U.S.
1964	Boris Lagutin, USSR

1968	Boris Lagutin, USSR
1972	Dieter Kottysch, Germany
1976	Jerzy Rybicki, Poland
1980	Armando Martines, Cuba
1984	Frank Tate, U.S.
1988	Park Si-Hun, South Korea
1992	Juan Lemus, Cuba

Middleweight

1904	Charles Mayer, U.S.
1908	John Douglas, Great Britain
1920	Harry Mallin, Great Britain
1924	Harry Mallin, Great Britain
1928	Piero Toscani, Italy
1932	Carmen Barth, U.S.
1936	Jean Despeaux, France
1948	Laszlo Papp, Hungary
1952	Floyd Patterson, U.S.
1956	Gennady Schatkov, USSR
1960	Edward Crook, U.S.
1964	Valery Papenchenko, USSR
1968	Christopher Finnegan, Great Britain
1972	Vyacheslav Lemechev, USSR
1976	Michael Spinks, U.S.
1980	Jose Gomez, Cuba
1984	Joun-sup Shin, China
1988	Henry Maske, East Germany
1992	Ariel Hernandez Ascuy, Cuba

Light-Heavyweight

1920	Edward Egan, U.S.
1924	Harry Mitchell, Great Britain
1928	Victor Avendan, Argentina
1932	David Carstens, South Africa
1956	James Boyd, U.S.
1976	Leon Spinks, U.S.
1980	Slobodan Cacar, Yugoslavia
1984	Anton Josipovic, Yugoslavia
1988	Andrew Maynard, U.S.
1992	Torsten May, Germany

Heavyweight

1984	Herny Tillman, U.S.
1988	Ray Mercer, U.S.
1992	Felix Savon, Cuba

Super Heavyweight

1904	Samuel Berger, U.S.
1908	A.L. Oldham, Great Britain
1928	Arturo R. Jurado, Argentina
1956	Peter Rademacher, U.S.
1960	Franco De Piccoli, Italy
1964	Joseph Frazier, U.S.
1968	George Foreman, U.S.
1972	Teofilo Stevenson, Cuba
1976	Teofilo Stevenson, Cuba
1988	**Lennox Lewis, Canada**
1992	Roberto Balado, Cuba

Soccer

| 1900 | Great Britain |
| 1904 | **Canada** |

1908	Great Britain
1912	Great Britain
1920	Belgium
1924	Uruguay
1928	Uruguay
1932	not held
1936	Italy
1948	Sweden
1952	Hungary
1956	USSR
1960	Yugoslavia
1964	Hungary
1968	Hungary
1972	Poland
1976	E. Germany
1980	Czechoslovakia
1984	France
1988	USSR
1992	Spain

■ Mens's Volleyball

1964	USSR
1968	USSR
1972	Japan
1976	Poland
1980	USSR
1988	United States
1992	Brazil

■ Women's Volleyball

1964	Japan
1968	USSR
1972	USSR
1976	Japan
1980	USSR
1984	China
1988	USSR
1992	Cuba

■ Other Summer Olympics Gold Medalists in 1992

Archery

Men: Sebastian Flute, France
Men's Team: Spain
Women: Cho Youn-leong, S. Korea
Women's Team: South Korea

Badminton

Men: Alan Budi Kusuma, Indonesia
Men's Doubles: Kim Soon-Su, Park Joo-Bong, S. Korea
Women: Susi Susanti, Indonesia
Women's Doubles: Hwang Hye-Young, Chung So-Young, S. Korea

Baseball

1. Cuba 2. Taiwan 3. Japan

Men's Canoeing

500m One-Man Canoe: Nikolai Boukhalov, Bulgaria
500m Two-Man Canoe: Alexandre Masseikov, Dmitri Dovgalenok, Unified Team
500m One-Man Kayak: Miko Kolehmainen, Finland
500m Two-Man Kayak: Kay Bluhm, Torsten Gutsche, Germany
1 000m One-Man Kayak: Clint Robinson, Australia
1 000m Two-Man Kayak: Kay Bluhm, Torsten Gutsche, Germany
1 000m Four-Man Kayak: Germany
1 000m One-Man Canoe: Nikolai Boukhalov, Bulgaria
1 000m Two-Man Canoe: Ulrich Papke, Ingo Spelly, Germany
Kayak Slalom: Pierpaolo Ferrazzi, Italy
Two-Man Canoe Slalom: United States
Canoe Slalom: Lukas Pollert, Czechoslovakia

Women's Canoeing

500m One-Woman Kayak: Birgit Schmidt, Germany
500m Two-Woman Kayak: Ramona Portwich, Anke Von Seck, Germany
500m Four-Woman Kayak: Hungary
Kayak Slalom: Elisabeth Micheler, Germany

Cycling

4 000m Individual Pursuit: Christopher Boardman, Great Britain
Individual Road Race: Fabio Casartelli, Italy
1 km Time Trials: Jose Moreno, Spain
4 000m Team Pursuit: Germany
Sprint: Jens Fiedler, Germany
50 km Points Race: Giovanni Lombardi, Italy
100 km Road Team Time Trials: Germany
Women's Sprint: Erika Saloumiae, Estonia
Women's Individual Road Race: Kathryn Watt, Australia
Women's Individual Pursuit: Petra Rossner, Germany

Equestrian

Individual 3-Day Event: Matthew Morgan Ryan, Australia
Team 3-Day Event: Australia
Team Jumping: Netherlands
Team Dressage: Germany
Individual Dressage: Nicole Uphoff, Germany
Individual Jumping: Ludger Beerbaum, Germany

Men's Fencing

Individual Epee: Eric Srecki, France
Individual Foil: Phillipe Omnes, France
Individual Sabre: Bence Szabo, Hungary
Team Foil: Germany
Team Epee: Germany
Team Sabre: Unified Team

Women's Fencing

Individual Foil: Giovanna Trillini, Italy
Team Foil: Italy

Field Hockey

Men: Germany
Women: Spain

Men's Gymnastics

All Around: Vitaly Scherbo, Unified Team
Team: Unified Team
Floor Exercise: Li Xiao-sahuang, China
Horizontal Bar: Trent Dimas, U.S.
Parallel Bars: Vitaly Scherbo, Unified Team
Pommel Horse: Pae Gil-Su, N. Korea; Vitaly Scherbo, Unified Team (tie)
Rings: Vitaly Scherbo, Unified Team
Vault: Vitaly Scherbo, Unified Team

Women's Gymnastics

Floor Exercise: Lavinia Corina Milosovici, Romania
Balance Beam: Tatiana Lisenko, Unified Team
Vault: Henrietta Onodi, Hungary, Lavinia Corina Milosovici, Romania (tie)
Uneven Parallel Bars: Lu Li, China
All-Around: Tatiana Goutsou, Unified Team
Team: Unified Team
Rhythmic: Alexandra Timoshenko, Unified Team

Team Handball

Men: Unified Team
Women: South Korea

Men's Judo

Extra-Lightweight: Nazim Gousseinov, Unified Team
65 kg: Rogerio Sampaio Cardoso, Brazil
71 kg: Toshihiko Koga, Japan
78 kg: Hidehiko Yoshida, Japan
86 kg: Waldemar Legien, Poland
95 kg: Antal Kovacs, Hungary
95 kg plus: David Khakhaleichvili, Unified Team

Women's Judo

Extra Lightweight: Cecile Nowak, France
52 kg: Almudeno Munoz Martinez, Spain
56 kg: Miriam Blasco, Spain
61 kg: Catherine Fleury, France
66 kg: Odalis Reve Jimenez, Cuba
72 kg: Kim Mi-Jung, S. Korea
72 kg plus: Zhuang Xiaoyan, China

Modern Penathlon

Individual: Arkadiusz Skrzypaszek, Poland
Team: Poland

Men's Rowing

Single Sculls: Thomas Lange, Germany
Double Sculls: Stephen Hawkins, Peter Antonie, Australia
Quadruple Sculls: Germany
Pair Oars Without Coxswain: Steven Redgrave, Matthew Pinsent, Great Britain
Pair Oars With Coxswain: Great Britain
Four Oars With Coxswain: Romania
Four Oars Without Coxswain: Australia
Eight Oars With Coxswain: Canada (John Wallace, Bruce Robertson, Michael Forgeron, Darren Barber, Robert Marland, Michael Rascher, Andy Crosby, Derek Porter, Terry Paul)

Women's Rowing

Single Sculls: Elisabeth Lipa, Romania
Double Sculls: Kerstin Koeppen, Kathrin Boron, Germany
Quadruple Sculls: Germany
Pair Oars Without Coxswain: Marnie McBean, Kathleen Heddle, Canada
Four Oars With Coxswain: Canada (Kirsten Barnes, Brenda Taylor, Jessica Monroe, Kay Worthington)
Eight Oars With Coxswain: Canada (Kirsten Barnes, Brenda Taylor, Megan Delehanty, Shannon Crawford, Marnie McBean, Kay Worthington, Jessica Monroe, Kathleen Heddle, Lesley Thompson)

Men's Shooting

Air Pistol: Wong Yifu, China
Air Rifle: Yuri Fedkine, Unified Team
Small Bore Rifle, Prone Position: Lee Eun- chui, S. Korea
Free Pistol: Konstantine Loukachik, Unified Team
Rapid-Fire Pistol: Ralf Schumann, Germany
Running Game Target: Michael Jakosits, Germany
Small Bore Rifle, 3 Positions: Gratchia Petikiane, Unified Team

Women's Shooting

Air Pistol: Marina Logvinenko, Unified Team
Air Rifle: Yeo Kab-Soon, S. Korea
Small Bore Rifle, 3 Positions: Launi Meili, U.S.
Sport Pistol Marina Logvinenko, Unified Team

Shooting—Open

Skeet: Zhang Shan, China
Olympic Trap: Petr Hrdlicka, Czechoslovakia

Synchronized Swimming

Solo: Kristen Babb-Sprague, U.S.
Duet: Karen Josephson, Sarah Josephson, U.S.

Table Tennis

Men's Singles: Jan Ove Waldner, Sweden
Men's Doubles: Lu Lin, Wang Tao, China
Women's Singles: Deng Yaping, China
Women's Doubles: Deng Yaping, Qiao Hong, China

Tennis

Men's Singles: Marc Rosset, Switzerland
Men's Doubles: Boris Becker, Michael Stich, Germany
Women's Singles: Jennifer Capriati, U.S.
Women's Doubles: Gigi Fernandez, Mary Joe Fernandez, U.S.

Water Polo

Championship: Italy

Weight Lifting

Bantamweight: Chun Byung-Kwan, S. Korea
Flyweight: Ivan Ivanov, Bulgaria
Featherweight: Naim Suleymanoglu, Turkey
Lightweight: Israel Militosyan, Unified Team
Middleweight: Fedor Kassapu, Unified Team
Light Heavyweight: Pyrros Dimas, Greece

Middle Heavyweight: Kakhi Kakhiachvili, Unified Team
100 kg: Victor Tregoubov, Unified Team
110 kg: Ronny Weller, Germany
Super Heavyweight: Alexandre Kourlovitch, Unified Team

Freestyle Wrestling

48 kg: Kim II, N. Korea
52 kg: Li Hak-son, N. Korea
57 kg: Alejandro Puerto Diaz, Cuba
62 kg: John Smith, U.S.
68 kg: Arsen Fadzaev, Unified Team
74 kg: Park Jang-Soon, S. Korea
82 kg: Kevin Jackson, U.S.
90 kg: Makharbek Khadartsev, Unified Team

100 kg: Lari Khabelov, Unified Team
130 kg: Bruce Baumgartner, U.S.

Greco-Roman Wrestling

48 kg: Oleg Koutcherenko, Unified Team
52 kg: Jon Ronningen, Norway
57 kg Han-Bong, S. Korea
62 kg Akif Pirim, Turkey
68 kg Attila Repka, Hungary
74 kg Mnatsakan Iskandarian, Unified Team
82 kg Peter Farkas, Hungary
90 kg Maik Bullmann, Germany
100 kg Hector Millan Perez, Cuba
130 kg Alexandre Kareline, Unified Team

Winter Olympics

Year	Location	Date of Competition	Competitors Men	Competitors Women	Nations Represented	Unofficial Winners
1924	Chamonix, France	Jan. 25–Feb. 4	281	13	16	Norway
1928	St. Moritz, Switzerland	Feb. 11–19	468	27	25	Norway
1932	Lake Placid, United States	Feb. 4–15	274	32	17	United States
1936	Garmisch-Partenkirchen, Germany	Feb. 6–16	675	80	28	Norway
1940	Cancelled because of World War II					
1944	Cancelled because of World War II					
1948	St. Moritz, Switzerland	Jan. 30–Feb. 8	636	77	28	Sweden
1952	Oslo, Norway	Feb. 14–25	623	109	30	Norway
1956	Cortina d'Ampezzo, Italy	Jan. 26–Feb. 5	686	132	32	U.S.S.R.
1960	Squaw Valley, United States	Feb. 18–28	521	144	30	U.S.S.R.
1964	Innsbruck, Austria	Jan. 29–Feb. 9	986	200	36	U.S.S.R.
1968	Grenoble, France	Feb. 6–18	1 081	212	37	Norway
1972	Sapporo, Japan	Feb. 3–13	1 015	217	35	U.S.S.R.
1976	Innsbruck, Austria	Feb. 4–15	900	228	37	U.S.S.R.
1980	Lake Placid, United States	Feb. 14–23	833	234	37	East Germany
1984	Sarajevo, Yugoslavia	Feb. 7–19	1 180	409	49	U.S.S.R.
1988	Calgary, Canada[1]	Feb. 13–28	1 128	317	57	U.S.S.R.
1992	Albertville, France	Feb. 8–23	1 545	602	64	Germany
1994[2]	Lillehammer, Norway	Feb. 12–27				
1998	Nagano, Japan					

(1) Including demonstration sports a total of 1 759 athletes competed in Calgary. (2) Beginning in 1994, the summer and winter games will be held 2 years apart, instead of in the same year.

Final Medal Standings of the Winter Olympics, 1992

(Albertville, France, Feb. 8–23, 1992)

Country	Gold	Silver	Bronze	Total	Country	Gold	Silver	Bronze	Total
Germany	10	10	6	26	Japan	1	2	4	7
CIS	9	6	8	23	Netherlands	1	1	2	4
Norway	9	6	5	20	Sweden	1	0	3	4
Austria	6	7	8	21	Switzerland	1	0	2	3
United States	5	4	2	11	China	0	3	0	3
Italy	4	6	4	14	Luxembourg	0	2	0	2
France	3	5	1	9	New Zealand	0	1	0	1
Finland	3	1	3	7	Czechoslovakia	0	0	3	3
Canada	2	3	2	7	Spain	0	0	1	1
South Korea	2	1	1	4	North Korea	0	0	1	1

Canada's 1992 Winter Olympic Medal Winners

■ Gold

Alpine Skiing, Women's Downhill: Kerrin Lee-Gartner
Skating, Women's Short Track Relay: Sylvie Daigle, Nathalie Lambert, Annie Perrault, Angela Cutrone

■ Silver

Skating, Men's Short Track 100 m: Frederic Blackburn
Skating, Men's Short Track Relay: Mark Lackie, Frederic Blackburn, Michel Daignault, Sylvain Gagnon
Ice Hockey: Dave Archibald, Todd Brost, Sean Burke, Kevin Dahl, Curt Giles, Dave Hannan, Gord Hynes, Fabian Joseph, Joe Juneau, Trevor Kidd, Patrick Lebeau, Chris Lindberg, Eric Lindros, Kent Manderville, Adrian Plavsic, Dan Ratushny, Brad Schlegel, Wally Schreiber, Randy Smith, Sam St. Laurent, Dave Tippett, Brian Tutt, Jason Woolley

■ Bronze

Figure Skating, Pairs: Isabelle Brasseur & Lloyd Eisler
Biathlon, Women's 15 km: Myriam Bedard

■ Demonstration Sports Gold

Freestyle Skiing, Men's Aerials: Philippe Laroche

■ Demonstration Sports Silver

Freestyle Skiing, Men's Aerials: Nicolas Fontaine

■ Demonstration Sports Bronze

Curling, Women's: Julie Sutton, Jodie Sutton, Melissa Soligo, Karri Willms, Elaine Dagg-Jackson

Medal Winners, 1992 Winter Olympics

(Albertville, France)

■ Alpine Skiing

Downhill, Men				Downhill, Women		
P. Ortlieb	Austria	1:50.37		K. Lee-Gartner	Canada	1:52.55
F. Piccard	France	1:50.42		H. Lindh	USA	1:52.61
G. Mader	Austria	1:50.47		V. Wallinger	Austria	1:52.64
Combined Competition, Men				**Combined Competition, Women**		
J. Polig	Italy	14.58 pts.		P. Kronberger	Austria	2.55 pts.
G. Martin	Italy	14.90 pts.		A. Wachter	Austria	19.39 pts.
S. Locher	Switz.	18.16 pts.		F. Masnada	France	21.38 pts.
Super-G, Men				**Super-G, Women**		
K.A. Aamodt	Norway	1:13.04		D. Compagnoni	Italy	1:21.22
M. Girardelli	Lux.	1:13.77		C. Merle	France	1:22.63
J.E. Thorsen	Norway	1:13.83		K. Seizinger	Germany	1:23.19
Slalom, Men				**Slalom, Women**		
F.C. Jagge	Norway	1:44.39		P. Kronberger	Austria	1:32.68
A. Tomba	Italy	1:44.67		A. Coberger	N.Z.	1:33.10
M. Tritscher	Austria	1:44.85		B. Fernandez Ochoa	Spain	1:33.35
Giant Slalom, Men				**Giant Slalom, Women**		
A. Tomba	Italy	2:06.98		P. Wiberg	Sweden	2:12.74
M. Girardelli	Lux.	2:07.30		D. Roffe	USA	2:13.71
K.A. Aamodt	Norway	2:07.82		A. Wachter	Austria	2:13.71
Moguls, Men				**Moguls, Women**		
E. Grospiron	France	25.81 pts.		D. Weinbrecht	USA	23.69 pts.
O. Allamand	France	24.87 pts.		E. Kojevnikova	EUN	23.50 pts.
N. Carmichael	USA	24.82 pts.		S. Hattestad	Norway	23.04 pts.

■ Cross Country Skiing

50 km Free Technique, Men				30 km Free Technique, Women		
B. Daehlie	Norway	2:03:41.5		S. Belmondo	Italy	1:22:30.1
M. De Zolt	Italy	2:04:39.1		L. Egorova	EUN	1:22:52.0
G. Vanzetta	Italy	2:06:42.1		E. Valbe	EUN	1:24:13.9
30 km Classical, Men				**15 km Classical, Women**		
V. Ulvang	Norway	1:22:27.8		L. Egorova	EUN	42:20.8
B. Daehlie	Norway	1:23:14.0		M. Lukkarinen	Finland	43:29.9
T. Langli	Norway	1:23:42.5		E. Valbe	EUN	43:42.3

15 km Free—Pursuit, Men				**10 km Free—Pursuit, Women**		
B. Daehlie	Norway	1:05:37.9		L. Egorova	EUN	40:07.7
V. Ulvang	Norway	1:06:31.3		S. Belmondo	Italy	40:31.8
G. Vanzetta	Italy	1:06:32.2		E. Valbe	EUN	40:41.7
10 km Classical—Pursuit, Men				**5 km Classical—Pursuit, Women**		
V. Ulvang	Norway	27:36.0		M. Lukkarinen	Finland	14:13.8
M. Albarello	Italy	27:55.2		L. Egorova	EUN	14:14.7
C. Majback	Sweden	27:56.4		E. Valbe	EUN	14:22.7
Men's Relay, 4x10 km		**Mix**		**Women's Relay, 4x5 km**		**Mix**
Norway		1:39:26.0		EUN		59:34.8
Italy		1:40:52.7		Norway		59:56.4
Finland		1:41:22.9		Italy		1:00:25.9
Nordic Combined, Individual				**Nordic Combined, Team**		
F. Guy	France	0.0 behind			Japan	0.0 behind
S. Guillaume	France	48.4 behind			Norway	1:26.4 behind
K. Sulzenbacher	Austria	1:06.3 behind			Austria	1:40.1 behind

■ Ski Jumping

K90 m				**K120 m**		
E. Vettori	Austria	222.8 pts.		T. Nieminen	Finland	239.5 pts.
M. Hollwarth	Austria	218.1 pts.		M. Hollwarth	Austria	227.3 pts.
T. Nieminen	Finland	217.0 pts.		H. Kuttin	Austria	214.8 pts.
K120 m Team						
Finland		644.4 pts.				
Austria		642.9 pts.				
Czechoslovakia		620.1 pts.				

■ Biathlon

20 km, Men				**15 km, Women**		
E. Redkine	EUN	57:34.4		A. Misersky	Germany	51:47.2
M. Kirchner	Germany	57:40.8		S. Pecherskaia	EUN	51:58.5
M. Lofgren	Sweden	57:59.4		**M. Bedard**	**Canada**	52:15.0
10 km Sprint, Men				**7.5 km Sprint, Women**		
M. Kirchner	Germany	26:02.3		A. Restzova	EUN	24:29.2
R. Gross	Germany	26:18.0		A. Misersky	Germany	24:45.1
H. Eloranta	Finland	26:26.6		E. Belova	EUN	24:50.8
Men's Relay, 4x7.5 km				**Women's Relay, 3x7.5 km**		
	Germany	1:24:43.5			France	1:15:55.6
	EUN	1:25:06.3			Germany	1:16:18.4
	Sweden	1:25:38.2			EUN	1:16:54.6

■ Bobsled

Two Man				**Four Man**		
G. Weder	Switzerland 1	04:03.20			Austria 1	3:53.90
D. Acklin					Germany 1	3:53.92
R. Lochner	Germany 1	04:03.55			Switzerland 1	3:54.13
M. Zimmermann						
C. Langen	Germany 2	04:03.63				
G. Eger						

■ Ice Hockey

Unified Team	(The Unified Team beat Canada 3-1 in the Gold Medal game.)
Canada	
Czechoslovakia	

■ Luge

Singles, Men				Singles, Women		
G. Hackl	Germany	3:02.363		D. Neuner	Austria	3:06.696
M. Prock	Austria	3:02.669		A. Neuner	Austria	3:06.769
M. Schmidt	Austria	3:02.942		S. Erdmann	Germany	3:07.115
Doubles, Men						
S. Krausse	Germany	1:32.053				
J. Behrendt						
Y. Mankel	Germany	1:32.239				
T. Rudolph						
H. Raffl	Italy	1:32.298				
N. Huber						

■ Figure Skating

Men			Women		
V. Petrenko	EUN	1.0 pts.	K. Yamaguchi	USA	1.5 pts.
P. Wylie	USA	2.0 pts.	M. Ito	Japan	4.0 pts.
P. Barna	Czech.	3.0 pts.	N. Kerrigan	USA	4.0 pts.
Pairs			**Ice Dancing**		
N. Michkouteniok	EUN	1.5 pts.	M. Klimova	EUN	2.0 pts.
A. Dmitriev			S. Ponomarenko		
E. Betchke	EUN	3.0 pts.	I. Duchesnay-Dean	France	4.4 pts.
D. Petrov			P. Duchesnay		
I. Brasseur	**Canada**	4.5 pts.	M. Usova	EUN	5.6 pts.
L. Eisler			A. Zhulin		

■ Speed Skating

10000 m, Men			5000 m, Women		
B. Veldkamp	Neth.	14:12.12	G. Niemann	Germany	07:31.57
J. Koss	Norway	14:14.58	H. Warnicke	Germany	07:37.59
G. Karlstad	Norway	14:18.13	C. Pechstein	Germany	07:39.80
5000 m, Men			**3000 m, Women**		
G. Karlstad	Norway	06:59.97	G. Niemann	Germany	04:19.90
F. Zandstra	Neth.	07:02.28	H. Warnicke	Germany	04:22.88
L. Visser	Neth.	07:04.96	E. Hunyady	Austria	04:24.64
1500 m, Men			**1500 m, Women**		
J. Koss	Norway	01:54.81	J. Boerner	Germany	02:05.87
A. Sondral	Norway	01:54.85	G. Niemann	Germany	02:05.92
L. Visser	Neth.	01:54.90	S. Hashimoto	Japan	02:06.88
1000 m, Men			**1000 m, Women**		
O. Zinke	Germany	01:14.85	B. Blair	USA	01:21.90
Y.M. Kim	S. Korea	01:14.86	Q. Ye	China	01:21.92
Y. Miyabe	Japan	01:14.92	M. Garbrecht	Germany	01:22.10
500 m, Men			**500 m, Women**		
U.J. Mey	Germany	00:37.14	B. Blair	USA	00:40.33
T. Kuroiwa	Japan	00:37.18	Q. Ye	China	00:40.51
J. Inque	Japan	00:37.26	C. Luding	Germany	00:40.57

■ Short Track Speed Skating

1000 m, Men			500 m, Women		
K.H. Kim	S. Korea		C. Turner	USA	
F. Blackburn	**Canada**		Y. Li	China	
J.H. Lee	S. Korea		O.S. Hwang	N. Korea	
5000 m Relay, Men			**3000 m Relay, Women**		
	S. Korea		Canada		
	Canada			United States	
	Japan			EUN	

Source: *Canadian Olympic Association*

National Hockey League, 1992–93

Final Standings

Prince of Wales Conference

■ **Adams Division**

	W	L	T	GF	GA	Pts
Boston	51	26	7	332	268	109
Quebec	47	27	10	351	300	104
Montreal	48	30	6	326	280	102
Buffalo	38	36	10	335	297	86
Hartford	26	52	6	284	369	58
Ottawa	10	70	4	202	395	24

■ **Patrick Division**

	W	L	T	GF	GA	Pts
Pittsburgh	56	21	7	367	268	119
Washington	43	34	7	325	286	93
NY Islanders	40	37	7	335	297	87
New Jersey	40	37	7	308	299	87
Philadelphia	36	37	11	319	319	83
NY Rangers	34	39	11	304	308	79

Clarence Campbell Conference

■ **Norris Division**

	W	L	T	GF	GA	Pts
Chicago	47	25	12	279	230	106
Detroit	47	28	9	369	280	103
Toronto	44	29	11	288	241	99
St Louis	37	36	11	282	278	85
Minnesota	36	38	10	272	293	82
Tampa Bay	23	54	7	245	332	53

■ **Smythe Division**

	W	L	T	GF	GA	Pts
Vancouver	46	29	9	346	278	101
Calgary	43	30	11	322	282	97
Los Angeles	39	35	10	338	340	88
Winnipeg	40	37	7	322	320	87
Edmonton	26	50	8	242	337	60
San Jose	11	71	2	218	414	24

NHL Playoff Results, 1993

Prince of Wales Conference

■ **Adams Division Semifinals**

Date	Teams, Result
	Montreal 2 at Quebec 3*
	Montreal 1 at Quebec 4
	Quebec 1 at Montreal 2*
	Quebec 2 at Montreal 3
	Montreal 5 at Quebec 4*
	Quebec 2 at Montreal 6

Montreal defeated Quebec 4-2

	Buffalo 5 at Boston 4*
	Buffalo 4 at Boston 0
	Boston 3 at Buffalo 4*
	Boston 5 at Buffalo 6*

Buffalo defeated Boston 4-0

■ **Adams Division Finals**

	Buffalo 3 at Montreal 4
	Buffalo 3 at Montreal 4*
	Montreal 4 at Buffalo 3*
	Montreal 4 at Buffalo 3*

Montreal defeated Buffalo 4-0

■ **PatrickDivision**

Date	Teams, Result
	New Jersey 3 at Pittsburgh 6
	New Jersey 0 at Pittsburgh 7
	Pittsburgh 4 at New Jersey 3
	Pittsburgh 1 at New Jersey 4
	New Jersey 3 at Pittsburgh 5

Pittsburgh defeated New Jersey 4-1

	NY Islanders 1 at Washington 3
	NY Islanders 3 at Washington 4*
	Washington 3 at NY Islanders 4*
	Washington 3 at NY Islanders 4*
	NY Islanders 4 at Washington 6
	Washington 3 at NY Islanders 5

NY Islanders defeated Washington 4-2

■ **Patrick Division Finals**

	NY Islanders 3 at Pittsburgh 2
	NY islanders 0 at Pittsburgh 3
	Pittsburgh 3 at NY Islanders 1
	Pittsburgh 5 at NY Islanders 6
	NY Islanders 3 at Pittsburgh 6
	Pittsburgh 5 at NY Islanders 7
	NY Islanders 4 at Pittsburgh 3*

NY Islanders defeated Pittsburgh 4-3

▶

Prince of Wales Conference Final

Date	Teams, Result
	NY Islanders 1 at Montreal 4
	NY Islanders 3 at Montreal 4*
	Montreal 2 at NY Islanders 1*
	Montreal 1 at NY Islanders 4
	NY Islanders 2 at Montreal 5

Montreal defeated NY Islanders 4-1

Clarence Campbell Conference

■ Norris Division Semifinals

Date	Teams, Result
	Toronto 3 at Detroit 6
	Toronto 2 at Detroit 6
	Detroit 2 at Toronto 4
	Detroit 2 at Toronto 3
	Toronto 5 at Detroit 4*
	Detroit 7 at Toronto 3
	Toronto 4 at Detroit 3*

Toronto defeated Detroit 4-3

	St. Louis 4 at Chicago 3
	St. Louis 2 at Chicago 0
	Chicago 0 at St. Louis 3
	Chicago 3 at St. Louis 4*

St. Louis defeated Chicago 4-0

■ Norris Division Finals

	St. Louis 1 at Toronto 2*
	St. Louis 2 at Toronto 2*
	Toronto 3 at St. Louis 4
	Toronto 4 at St. Louis 1
	St. Louis 1 at Toronto 5
	Toronto 1 at St. Louis 2
	St. Louis 0 at Toronto 6

Toronto defeated St. Louis 4-3

■ Smythe Division Semifinals

Date	Teams, Result
	Winnipeg 2 at Vancouver 4
	Winnipeg 2 at Vancouver 3
	Vancouver 4 at Winnipeg 5
	Vancouver 3 at Winnipeg 1
	Winnipeg 4 at Vancouver 3*
	Vancouver 4 at Winnipeg 3*

Vancouver defeated Winnipeg 4-2

	Los Angeles 6 at Calgary 3
	Los Angeles 4 at Calgary 9
	Calgary 3 at Los Angeles 2
	Calgary 1 at Los Angeles 3
	Los Angeles 9 at Calgary 4
	Calgary 6 at Los Angeles 9

Los Angeles defeated Calgary 4-2

■ Smythe Division Finals

	Los Angeles 2 at Vancouver 5
	Los Angeles 6 at Vancouver 3
	Vancouver 4 at Los Angeles 7
	Vancouver 7 at Los Angeles 2
	Los Angeles 4 at Vancouver 3*
	Vancouver 3 at Los Angeles 5

Los Angeles defeated Vancouver 4-2

Clarence Campbell Conference Finals

Date	Teams, Result
	Los Angeles 1 at Toronto 4
	Los Angeles 3 at Toronto 2
	Toronto 2 at Los Angeles 4
	Toronto 4 at Los Angeles 2
	Los Angeles 2 at Toronto 3*
	Toronto 4 at Los Angeles 5*
	Los Angeles 5 at Toronto 4

Los Angeles defeated Toronto 4-3

Stanley Cup Championship

Date	Teams, Result
	Los Angeles 4 at Montreal 1
	Los Angeles 2 at Montreal 3*
	Montreal 4 at Los Angeles 3*
	Montreal 3 at Los Angeles 2*
	Los Angeles 1 at Montreal 4

Montreal defeated Los Angeles 4-1

*overtime

Major League Arenas and Stadiums in Canada

■ Hockey

Name, Location	Seating Capacity
Le Collisée, Quebec	15 399
Maple Leaf Gardens, Toronto	15 642
Montreal Forum	16 197
Northlands Coliseum, Edmonton	17 313
Olympic Saddledome, Calgary	20 133
Pacific Coliseum, Vancouver	16 123
Winnipeg Arena	15 393

■ Football/Baseball

Name, Location	Seating Capacity
B.C. Place, Vancouver	59 478
Commonwealth Stadium, Edmonton	60 081
Ivor Wynne Stadium, Hamilton	29 183
Landsdowne Park, Ottawa	30 927
McMahon Stadium, Calgary	38 408
Olympic Stadium, Montreal	43 739
Taylor Field, Regina	27 637
Winnipeg Stadium	32 648
SkyDome, Toronto	53 595[1]

(a) Baseball capacity is approx. 51 000, including restaurant and box seating.

Stanley Cup Champions, 1918–93

The Stanley Cup, the oldest trophy competed for by professional athletes in North America, was donated by Frederick Arthur, Lord Stanley of Preston, in 1893. Originally presented to the ama-teur hockey champions of Canada, it has been awarded to the top professional team since 1910 and, since 1926, has been competed for only by NHL teams.

Year	Champion	Final Opponent	Series Result	Winning Coach	Winning Manager
1918	Toronto Arenas	Vancouver	3-2	Dick Carroll	Charlie Querrie
1919[1]	No decision				
1920	Ottawa Senators	Seattle	3-2	Pete Green	Tommy Gorman
1921	Ottawa Senators	Vancouver	3-2	Pete Green	Tommy Gorman
1922	Toronto St. Pats	Vancouver	3-2	Eddie Powers	Charlie Querrie
1923[2]	Ottawa Senators	Vancouver; Edm.	3-1; 2-0	Pete Green	Tommy Gorman
1924[3]	Montreal Canadiens	Vancouver; Calgary	2-0; 2-0	Leo Dandurand	Leo Danduran
1925	Victoria Cougars	Montreal	3-1	Lester Patrick	Lester Patrick
1926	Montreal Maroons	Victoria	3-1	Eddie Gerard	Eddie Gerard
1927	Ottawa Senators	Boston	2-0	Dave Gill	Dave Gill
1928	New York Rangers	Montreal	3-2	Lester Patrick	Lester Patrick
1929	Boston Bruins	New York	2-0	Cy Denneny	Art Ross
1930	Montreal Canadiens	Boston	2-0	Cecil Hart	Cecil Hart
1931	Montreal Canadiens	Chicago	3-2	Cecil Hart	Cecil Hart
1932	Toronto Maple Leafs	New York	3-0	Dick Irvin	Conn Smythe
1933	New York Rangers	Toronto	3-1	Lester Patrick	Lester Patrick
1934	Chicago Black Hawks	Detroit	3-1	Tommy Gorman	Tommy Gorman
1935	Montreal Maroons	Toronto	3-0	Tommy Gorman	Tommy Gorman
1936	Detroit Red Wings	Toronto	4-0	Jack Adams	Jack Adams
1937	Detroit Red Wings	New York	3-2	Jack Adams	Jack Adams
1938	Chicago Black Hawks	Toronto	4-1	Bill Stewart	Bill Stewart
1939	Boston Bruins	Toronto	4-1	Art Ross	Art Ross
1940	New York Rangers	Toronto	4-2	Frank Boucher	Lester Patrick
1941	Boston Bruins	Detroit	4-0	Cooney Weiland	Art Ross
1942	Toronto Maple Leafs	Detroit	4-3	Hap Day	Conn Smythe
1943	Detroit Red Wings	Boston	4-0	Jack Adams	Jack Adams
1944	Montreal Canadiens	Chicago	4-0	Dick Irvin	Tommy Gorman
1945	Toronto Maple Leafs	Detroit	4-3	Hap Day	Conn Smythe
1946	Montreal Canadiens	Boston	4-1	Dick Irvin	Tommy Gorman
1947	Toronto Maple Leafs	Montreal	4-2	Hap Day	Conn Smythe
1948	Toronto Maple Leafs	Detroit	4-0	Hap Day	Conn Smythe
1949	Toronto Maple Leafs	Detroit	4-0	Hap Day	Conn Smythe
1950	Detroit Red Wings	New York	4-3	Tommy Ivan	Jack Adams
1951	Toronto Maple Leafs	Montreal	4-1	Joe Primeau	Conn Smythe

▶

▶ 1952	Detroit Red Wings	Montreal	4-0	Tommy Ivan	Jack Adams
1953	Montreal Canadiens	Boston	4-1	Dick Irvin	Frank Selke
1954	Detroit Red Wings	Montreal	4-3	Tommy Ivan	Jack Adams
1955	Detroit Red Wings	Montreal	4-3	Jimmy Skinner	Jack Adams
1956	Montreal Canadiens	Detroit	4-1	Toe Blake	Frank Selke
1957	Montreal Canadiens	Boston	4-1	Toe Blake	Frank Selke
1958	Montreal Canadiens	Boston	4-2	Toe Blake	Frank Selke
1959	Montreal Canadiens	Toronto	4-1	Toe Blake	Frank Selke
1960	Montreal Canadiens	Toronto	4-0	Toe Blake	Frank Selke
1961	Chicago Black Hawks	Detroit	4-2	Rudy Pilous	Tommy Ivan
1962	Toronto Maple Leafs	Chicago	4-2	Punch Imlach	Punch Imlach
1963	Toronto Maple Leafs	Detroit	4-1	Punch Imlach	Punch Imlach
1964	Toronto Maple Leafs	Detroit	4-3	Punch Imlach	Punch Imlach
1965	Montreal Canadiens	Chicago	4-3	Toe Blake	Sam Pollock
1966	Montreal Canadiens	Detroit	4-2	Toe Blake	Sam Pollock
1967	Toronto Maple Leafs	Montreal	4-2	Punch Imlach	Punch Imlach
1968	Montreal Canadiens	St. Louis	4-0	Toe Blake	Sam Pollock
1969	Montreal Canadiens	St. Louis	4-0	Claude Ruel	Sam Pollock
1970	Boston Bruins	St. Louis	4-0	Harry Sinden	Milt Schmidt
1971	Montreal Canadiens	Chicago	4-3	Al MacNeil	Sam Pollock
1972	Boston Bruins	New York	4-2	Tom Johnson	Milt Schmidt
1973	Montreal Canadiens	Chicago	4-2	Scotty Bowman	Sam Pollock
1974	Philadelphia Flyers	Boston	4-2	Fred Shero	Keith Allen
1975	Philadelphia Flyers	Buffalo	4-2	Fred Shero	Keith Allen
1976	Montreal Canadiens	Philadelphia	4-0	Scotty Bowman	Sam Pollock
1977	Montreal Canadiens	Boston	4-0	Scotty Bowman	Sam Pollock
1978	Montreal Canadiens	Boston	4-2	Scotty Bowman	Sam Pollock
1979	Montreal Canadiens	New York	4-1	Scotty Bowman	Irving Grundman
1980	N.Y. Islanders	Philadelphia	4-2	Al Arbour	Bill Torrey
1981	N.Y. Islanders	Minnesota	4-1	Al Arbour	Bill Torrey
1982	N.Y. Islanders	Vancouver	4-0	Al Arbour	Bill Torrey
1983	N.Y. Islanders	Edmonton	4-0	Al Arbour	Bill Torrey
1984	Edmonton Oilers	New York	4-1	Glen Sather	Glen Sather
1985	Edmonton Oilers	Philadelphia	4-1	Glen Sather	Glen Sather
1986	Montreal Canadiens	Calgary	4-1	Jean Perron	Serge Savard
1987	Edmonton Oilers	Philadelphia	4-3	Glen Sather	Glen Sather
1988	Edmonton Oilers	Boston	4-0	Glen Sather	Glen Sather
1989	Calgary Flames	Montreal	4-2	Terry Crisp	Cliff Fletcher
1990	Edmonton Oilers	Boston	4-1	John Muckler	Glen Sather
1991	Pittsburgh Penguins	Minnesota	4-2	Bob Johnson	Craig Patrick
1992	Pittsburgh Penguins	Chicago	4-0	Scotty Bowman	Craig Patrick
1993	Montreal Canadiens	Los Angeles	4-1	Jacques Demers	Serge Savard

Source: *National Hockey League*

(1) The series between Montreal Canadiens and Seattle Metropolitans was halted by Spanish influenza epidemic with the series tied at 2 wins each. (2) Ottawa also met and defeated Edmonton Eskimos, champions of the WCHL. (3) Because of an agreement between the NHL and the 2 western leagues (WCHL and PCHA), Canadiens had to play the champions of each league.

Fastest Women on Skates...

*N**athalie Lambert** of Montreal and **Sylvain Gagnon** of Dolbeau, Que. won their respective 1500-metre races at the world short track speed skating championships, March 26 in Beijing. Lambert earlier set a world record of 46.44 seconds in a 500-metre race at Hamar, Norway Jan. 30.*

NHL Scoring Leaders, 1992–93

Player	GP	G	A	Pts	+/-	PIM	PP	SH	S	Pct
Mario Lemieux, Pit	60	69	91	160	55	38	16	6	286	24.1
Pat Lafontaine, Buf	84	53	95	148	11	63	20	2	306	17.3
Adam Oates, Bos	84	45	97	142	15	32	24	1	254	17.7
Steve Yzerman, Det	84	58	79	137	33	44	13	7	307	18.9
Teemu Selanne, Win	84	76	56	132	8	45	24	0	387	19.6
Pierre Turgeon, NYI	83	58	74	132	-1	26	24	0	301	19.3
Alexander Mogilny, Buf	77	76	51	127	7	40	27	0	360	21.1
Doug Gilmour, Tor	83	32	95	127	32	100	15	3	211	15.2
Luc Robitaille, LA	84	63	62	125	18	100	24	2	265	23.8
Mark Recchi, Phi	84	53	70	123	1	95	15	4	274	19.3
Mats Sundin, Que	80	47	67	114	21	96	13	4	215	21.9
Kevin Stevens, Pit	72	55	56	111	17	177	26	0	326	16.9
Pavel Bure, Van	83	60	50	110	35	69	13	7	407	14.7
Rick Tocchet, Pit	80	48	61	109	28	252	20	4	240	20.0
Jeremy Roenick, Chi	84	50	57	107	15	86	22	3	255	19.6
Jeremy Roenick, Chi	80	53	50	103	23	98	22	3	234	22.6
Craig Janney, StL	84	24	82	106	-4	12	8	0	137	17.5
Joe Sakic, Que	78	48	57	105	-3	40	20	2	264	18.2
Joe Juneau, Bos	84	32	70	102	23	33	9	0	229	14.0
Brett Hull, StL	80	54	47	101	-27	41	29	0	390	13.8
Theoren Fleury, Cal	83	34	66	100	14	88	12	2	250	13.6
Ron Francis, Pit	84	24	76	100	6	68	9	2	215	11.2
Dave Andreychuk, Buf/Tor	83	54	45	99	4	56	32	0	310	17.4
Dino Ciccarelli, Det	82	41	56	97	12	81	21	0	200	20.5
Vincent Damphousse, Mon	84	39	58	97	12	81	21	0	287	13.6
Phil Housley, Win	80	18	79	97	-14	52	6	0	249	7.2

GP = Games played; G = Goals; A = Assists; Pts = Points; +/- = Plus/minus statistic, which shows the number of even-strength and shorthanded goals scored by a player's team, minus those scored against it, while he is on the ice; PIM = Penalties in minutes; PP = Power play goals; SH = Shorthanded goals; S = Shots on goal; Pct = Percentage of shots that score goals.

NHL Playoff Scoring Leaders, 1992–93

Player	GP	G	A	Pts	+/-	PIM	PP	SH	S	Pct
Wayne Gretzky, LA	24	15	25	40	6	4	4	1	76	19.7
Doug Gilmour, Tor	21	10	25	35	16	30	4	0	51	19.6
Tomas Sandstrom, LA	24	8	17	25	2-	12	2	0	61	13.1
Vincent Damphousse, Mon	20	11	12	23	8	16	5	0	52	21.2
Luc Robitaille, LA	24	9	13	22	13-	28	4	0	71	12.7
Ray Ferraro, NY Is	18	13	7	20	5	18	4	1	47	27.7
Wendel Clark, Tor	21	10	10	20	15	51	2	0	71	14.1
Dave Andreychuk, Tor	21	12	7	19	6	35	4	0	72	16.7
Mario Lemieux, Pit	11	8	10	18	2	10	3	1	40	20.0
Glenn Anderson, Tor	21	7	11	18	7	31	0	0	46	15.2
Kirk Muller, Mon	20	10	7	17	4	18	3	0	54	18.5
Steve Thomas, NY Is	18	9	8	17	1-	37	1	0	66	13.6
Jari Kurri, LA	24	9	8	17	2	12	2	2	50	18.0
Ron Francis, Pit	12	6	11	17	5	19	1	0	26	23.1
Tony Granato, LA	24	6	11	17	3	50	1	0	77	7.8

NHL Individual Records

(up to the end of the 1992–93 season)

Most seasons . . . . **26, Gordie Howe,** Det, 1946/47 through 1970/71; Htfd, 1979/80
Most games . . . . **1 767, Gordie Howe,** Det, 1946/47 through 1970/71; Htfd, 1979/80
Most goals . . . . **801, Gordie Howe,** Det, Htfd, in 26 seasons and 1 767 games
Most assists . . . . **1 563, Wayne Gretzky,** Edm, LA, in 14 seasons, 1 044 games
Most points . . . . **2 328, Wayne Gretzky,** Edm, LA, in 14 seasons, 1 044 games (765 goals 1 563 assists)
Most penalty minutes . . . . **3 966, Dave Williams,** Tor, Vcr, Det, LA, Htfd, in 14 seasons, 962 games
Most consecutive games . . . . **964, Doug Jarvis,** Mtl, Wash, Htfd from Oct. 8, 1975 through Oct. 10, 1987
Most games appeared in by a goaltender, career . . . . **971, Terry Sawchuk,** Det, Bos, Tor, LA, NYR (1949–70)
Most consecutive complete games by a goaltender . . . . **502, Glenn Hall,** Det, Chi.
    Played 502 games from beginning of 1955/56 season through first 12 games of 1962/63. In his 503rd straight game, Nov. 7, 1962, at
    Chicago, Hall was removed from the game against Boston with a back injury in the first period.
Most shutouts by a goaltender, career . . . . **103, Terry Sawchuk,** Det, Bos, Tor, LA, NYR, in 20 seasons
Most 50-or-more goal seasons . . . . **9, Mike Bossy,** NYI; **Wayne Gretzky,** Edm, LA
Most goals, one season . . . . **92, Wayne Gretzky,** Edm, 1981/82 (80 games)
Most assists, one season . . . . **163, Wayne Gretzky,** Edm, 1985/86 (80 games)
Most goals, one season, by a defenceman . . . . **48, Paul Coffey,** Edm, 1985/86 (79 games)
Most goals, one season, by a centre . . . . **92, Wayne Gretzky,** Edm, 1981/82 (80 games)
Most goals, one season, by a right winger . . . . **86, Brett Hull,** StL, 1990/91 (80 games)
Most goals, one season, by a left winger . . . . **63, Luc Robitaille,** LA, 1992/93 (84 games)
Most goals, one season, by a rookie . . . . **76, Teemu Selanne,** Win, 1992/93 (84 games)
Most points, one season, by a defenceman . . . . **139, Bobby Orr,** Bos, 1970/71 (78 games)
Most points, one season, by a centre . . . . **215, Wayne Gretzky,** Edm, 1985
games)
Most points, one season, by a right winger . . . . **147, Mike Bossy,** NYI, 1981/82 (80 games)
Most points, one season, by a left winger . . . . **125, Luc Robitaille,** LA, 1992/93 (84 games)
Most points, one season, by a rookie . . . . **132,Teemu Selanne,** Win, 1992/93 (84 games)
Most power-play goals, one season . . . . **34, Tim Kerr,** Phi, 1985/86 (76 games)
Most penalty minutes, one season . . . . **472, Dave Schultz ,** Ph, 1974/75 (80 games)
Most shutouts, one season . . . . **22, George Hainsworth,** Mtl, 1928/29 (44 games)

Regular Season NHL Scoring Champions, 1917–93

Season	Player, Team	GP	G	A	Pts	Season	Player, Team	GP	G	A	Pts
1917–18[1]	Joe Malone, Mtl	20	44	—	44	1937–38	Gordie Drillon, Tor	48	26	26	52
1918–19	Newsy Lalonde, Mtl	17	23	9	32	1938–39	Toe Blake, Mtl	48	24	23	47
1919–20	Joe Malone, Que	24	39	6	45	1939–40	Milt Schmidt, Bos	48	22	30	52
1920–21	Newsy Lalonde, Mtl	24	33	8	41	1940–41	Bill Cowley, Bos	46	17	45	62
1921–22	Punch Broadbent, Ott	24	32	14	46	1941–42	Bryan Hextall, NYR	48	24	32	56
1922–23	Babe Dye, Tor	22	26	11	37	1942–43	Doug Bentley, Chi	50	33	40	73
1923–24	Cy Denneny, Ott	21	22	1	23	1943–44	Herbie Cain, Bos	48	36	46	82
1924–25	Babe Dye, Tor	29	38	6	44	1944–45	Elmer Lach, Mtl	50	26	54	80
1925–26	Nels Stewart,					1945–46	Max Bentley, Chi	47	31	30	61
	Mtl Maroons	36	34	8	42	1946–47	Max Bentley, Chi	60	29	43	72
1926–27	Bill Cook, NYR	44	33	4	37	1947–48	Elmer Lach, Mtl	60	30	31	61
1927–28	Howie Morenz, Mtl	43	33	18	51	1948–49	Roy Conacher, Chi	60	26	42	68
1928–29	Ace Bailey, Tor	44	22	10	32	1949–50	Ted Lindsay, Det	69	23	55	78
1929–30	Cooney Weiland, Bos	44	43	30	73	1950–51	Gordie Howe, Det	70	43	43	86
1930–31	Howie Morenz, Mtl	39	28	23	51	1951–52	Gordie Howe, Det	70	47	39	86
1931–32	Harvey Jackson, Tor	48	28	25	53	1952–53	Gordie Howe, Det	70	49	46	95
1932–33	Bill Cook, NYR	48	28	22	50	1953–54	Gordie Howe, Det	70	33	48	81
1933–34	Charlie Conacher, Tor	42	32	20	52	1954–55	Bernie Geoffrion, Mtl	70	38	37	75
1934–35	Charlie Conacher, Tor	48	36	21	57	1955–56	Jean Béliveau, Mtl	70	47	41	88
1935–36	Dave Schriner,					1956–57	Gordie Howe, Det	70	44	45	89
	NY Americans	48	19	26	45	1957–58	Dickie Moore, Mtl	70	36	48	84
1936–37	Dave Schriner,					1958–59	Dickie Moore, Mt l	70	41	55	96
	NY Americans	48	21	25	46	1959–60	Bobby Hull, Chi	70	39	42	81 ▶

Season	Player, Team	GP	G	A	Pts	Season	Player, Team	GP	G	A	Pts
▶ 1960–61	Bernie Geoffrion, Mtl	64	50	45	95	1977–78	Guy Lafleur, Mtl	78	60	72	132
1961–62	Bobby Hull, Chi	70	50	34	84	1978–79	Bryan Trottier, NYI	76	47	87	134
1962–63	Gordie Howe, Det	70	38	48	86	1979–80	Marcel Dionne, LA	80	53	84	137
1963–64	Stan Mikita, Chi	70	39	50	89	1980–81	Wayne Gretzky, Edm	80	55	109	164
1964–65	Stan Mikita, Chi	70	28	59	87	1981–82	Wayne Gretzky, Edm	80	92	120	212
1965–66	Bobby Hull, Chi	65	54	43	97	1982–83	Wayne Gretzky, Edm	80	71	125	196
1966–67	Stan Mikita, Chi	70	35	62	97	1983–84	Wayne Gretzky, Edm	74	87	118	205
1967–68	Stan Mikita, Chi	72	40	47	87	1984–85	Wayne Gretzky, Edm	80	73	135	208
1968–69	Phil Esposito, Bos	74	49	77	126	1985–86	Wayne Gretzky, Edm	80	52	163	215
1969–70	Bobby Orr, Bos	76	33	87	120	1986–87	Wayne Gretzky, Edm	79	62	121	183
1970–71	Phil Esposito, Bos	78	76	76	152	1987–88	Mario Lemieux, Pit	77	70	98	168
1971–72	Phil Esposito, Bos	76	66	67	133	1988–89	Mario Lemieux, Pit	76	85	114	199
1972–73	Phil Esposito, Bos	78	55	75	130	1989–90	Wayne Gretzky, LA	73	40	102	142
1973–74	Phil Esposito, Bos	78	68	77	145	1990–91	Wayne Gretzky, LA	78	41	122	163
1974–75	Bobby Orr, Bos	80	46	89	135	1991–92	Mario Lemieux, Pit	64	44	87	131
1975–76	Guy Lafleur, Mtl	80	56	69	125	1992–93	Mario Lemieux, Pit	60	69	91	160
1976–77	Guy Lafleur, Mtl	80	56	80	136						

Source: *National Hockey League*

(a) Number of assists not recorded.

Top 25 All-Time NHL Point-Scoring Leaders

(to the end of the 1992/93 season; active players in bold type)

Player/Teams	Seasons	Games	Goals	Assists	Points	Points/ Game
Wayne Gretzky, Edm/LA	14	1 044	765	1 563	2 328	2.230
Gordie Howe, Det/Htfd	26	1 767	801	1 049	1 850	1.047
Marcel Dionne, Det/LA/NYR	18	1 348	731	1 040	1 771	1.314
Phil Esposito, Chi/Bos/NYR	18	1 282	717	873	1 590	1.240
Stan Mikita, Chi	22	1 394	541	926	1 467	1.052
Bryan Trottier, NYI/Pit	17	1 238	520	890	1 410	1.139
John Bucyk, Det/Bos	23	1 540	556	813	1 369	.889
Guy Lafleur, Mtl/NYR/Que	17	1 126	560	793	1 353	1.202
Gilbert Perreault, Buf	17	1 191	512	814	1 326	1.113
Alex Delvecchio, Det	24	1 549	456	825	1 281	.827
Jean Ratelle, NYR/Bos	21	1 281	491	776	1 267	.989
Mark Messier, Edm/NYR	14	1 005	452	780	1 232	1.220
Norm Ullman, Det/Tor	20	1 410	490	739	1 229	.872
Peter Stastny, Que/NJ	13	954	444	777	1 221	1.280
Jean Béliveau, Mtl	20	1 125	507	712	1 219	1.084
Dale Hawerchuk, Wpg, Buf	12	951	449	763	1 212	1.274
Bobby Clarke, Phi	15	1 144	358	852	1 210	1.058
Paul Coffey, Edm/Pit	13	953	330	871	1 201	1.260
Denis Savard, Chi/Mtl	13	946	423	769	1 192	1.260
Jari Kurri, Edm, LA	12	909	524	666	1 190	1.307
Mario Lemieux, Pit	9	577	477	697	1 174	2.035
Bobby Hull, Chi, Wpg/Htfd	16	1 063	610	560	1 170	1.101
Bernie Federko, StL/Det	14	1 000	369	761	1 130	1.130
Mike Bossy, NYI	10	752	573	553	1 126	1.497
Michel Goulet, Que, Chi	14	1 033	532	590	1 122	1.086

Source: *National Hockey League*

Top Ten NHL Draft Selections, 1988–93

(Teams selected by in parentheses)

	1988	1989	1990
1.	Mike Modano, Min	Matt Sundin, Que	Owen Nolan, Que
2.	Trevor Linden, Vcr	Dave Chyzowski, NYI	Petr Nedved, Vcr
3.	Curtis Leschyshyn, Que	Scott Thornton, Tor	Keith Primeau, Det
4.	Darrin Shannon, Pit	Stu Barnes, Wpg	Mike Ricci, Phi
5.	Daniel Doré, Que	Bill Guerin, NJ	Jaromir Jag, Pit
6.	Scott Pearson, Tor	Adam Bennett, Chi	Scott Scissons, NYI
7.	Martin Gelinas, LA	Doug Zmolek, Min	Darryl Sydor, LA
8.	Jeremy Roenick, Chi	Jason Herter, Vcr	Derian Hatcher, Min
9.	Rod Brind'Amour, StL	Jason Marshall, StL	John Slaney, Wash
10.	Teemu Selanne, Wpg	Robert Holik, Htfd	Drake Berehowsky, Tor

	1991	1992	1993
1.	Eric Lindros, Que	Roman Hamrlik, TB	Alexander Daigle (Ottawa)
2.	Pat Falloon, SJ	Alexei Yashin, Ott	Chris Pronger (Hartford)
3.	Scott Niedermayer, NJ	Mike Rathje, SJ	Chris Gratton (Tampa Bay)
4.	Scott Lachance, NYI	Todd Warriner, Que	Paul Kariya (Anaheim)
5.	Aaron Ward, Wpg	Darius Kasparaitis, NYI	Rob Neidermayer (Florida)
6.	Peter Forsber, Phi	Cory Stillman, Cal	Viktor Kozlovi (San Jose)
7.	Alex Stojanov, Vcr	Ryan Sittler, Phi	Jason Arnott (Edmonton)
8.	Richard Matvichuk, Min	Brandon Convery, Tor	Niklas Sundstrom (NY Rang.)
9.	Patrick Poulin, Htfd	Robert Petrovicky, Htfd	Todd Harvey (Dallas)
10.	Martin Lapointe, Det	Andrei Mazarov, Min	Jocelyn Thibault (Quebec)

NHL All-Star Teams, 1988–93[1]

First Team	Second Team	First Team	Second Team
1988		**1989**	
Grant Fuhr, Edm, g	Patrick Roy, Mtl, g	Patrick Roy, Mtl, g	Mike Vernon, Cal, g
Raymond Bourque, Bos, d	Gary Suter, Cal, d	Chris Chelios, Mtl, dl	Al MacInnis, Cal, d
Scott Stevens, Wash, d	Brad McCrimmon, Cal, d	Paul Coffey, Pit, d	Raymond Bourque, Bos, d
Mario Lemieux, Pit, c	Wayne Gretzky, LA, c	Mario Lemieux, Pit, c	Wayne Gretzky, LA, c
Hakan Loob, Cal, rw	Cam Neely, Bos, rw	Joe Mullen, Cal, rw	Jari Kurri, Edm, rw
Luc Robitaille, LA, lw	Michel Goulet, Que, lw	Luc Robitaille, LA, lw	Gerald Gallant, Det, lw
1990		**1991**	
Patrick Roy, Mtl, g	Daren Puppa, Buf, g	Ed Belfour, Chi, g	Patrick Roy, Mtl g
Raymond Bourque, Bos, d	Paul Coffey, Pit, d	Raymond Bourque, Bos, d	Chris Chelios, Chi, d
Al MacInnis, Cal, d	Doug Wilson, Chi, d	Al MacInnis, Cal, d	Brian Leetch, NYR, d
Mark Messier, Edm, c	Wayne Gretzky, LA, c	Wayne Gretzky, LA, c	Adam Oates, StL, c
Brett Hull, StL, rw	Cam Neely, Bos, rw	Brett Hull, StL, rw	Cam Neely, Bos, rw
Luc Robitaille, LA, lw	Brian Bellows, Min, lw	Luc Robitaille, LA, lw	Kevin Sevens, Pit, lw
1992		**1993**	
Patrick Roy, Mtl, g	Kirk McLean, Vcr, g	Ed Belfour, Chi, g	Tom Barasso, Pit, g
Brian Leetch, NYR, d	Phil Housley, Wpg, d	Chris Chelios, Chi, d	Larry Murphy, Pit, d
Raymond Bourque, Bos, d	Scott Stevens, NJ, d	Raymond Bourque, Bos, d	Al Iafrate, Wash, d
Mark Messier, NYR, c	Mario Lemieux, Pit, c	Mario Lemieux, Pit, c	Pat LaFontaine, Buf, c
Brett Hull, StL, rw	Mark Recchi, Pit/Phi, rw	Teemu Selanne, Win, rw	Alexander Mogilny, Buf, rw
Kevin Stevens, Pit, lw	Luc Robitaille, LA, lw	Luc Robitaille, LA, lw	Kevin Stevens, Pit, lw

(1) As selected by members of the Professional Hockey Writers' Association at the end of the season.

NHL Individual Award Winners, 1950–93

Hart Trophy (Most Valuable Player)[1]

1950 Charlie Rayner, NYR	1965 Bobby Hull, Chi	1980 Wayne Gretzky, Edm
1951 Milt Schmidt, Bos	1966 Bobby Hull, Chi	1981 Wayne Gretzky, Edm
1952 Gordie Howe, Det	1967 Stan Mikita, Chi	1982 Wayne Gretzky, Edm
1953 Gordie Howe, Det	1968 Stan Mikita, Chi	1983 Wayne Gretzky, Edm
1954 Al Rollins, Chi	1969 Phil Esposito, Bos	1984 Wayne Gretzky, Edm
1955 Ted Kennedy, Tor	1970 Bobby Orr, Bo	1985 Wayne Gretzky, Edm
1956 Jean Béliveau, Mtl	1971 Bobby Orr, Bos	1986 Wayne Gretzky, Edm
1957 Gordie Howe, Det	1972 Bobby Orr, Bos	1987 Wayne Gretzky, Edm
1958 Gordie Howe, Det	1973 Bobby Clarke, Phi	1988 Mario Lemieux, Pit
1959 Andy Bathgate, NYR	1974 Phil Esposito, Bos	1989 Wayne Gretzky, LA
1960 Gordie Howe, Det	1975 Bobby Clarke, Phi	1990 Mark Messier, Edm
1961 Bernie Geoffrion, Mtl	1976 Bobby Clarke, Phi	1991 Brett Hull, StL
1962 Jacques Plante, Mtl	1977 Guy Lafleur, Mtl	1992 Mark Messier, NYR
1963 Gordie Howe, Det	1978 Guy Lafleur, Mtl	1993 Mario Lemieux, Pit
1964 Jean Béliveau, Mtl	1979 Bryan Trottier, NYI	

Calder Trophy (Best Rookie)[1]

1950 Jack Gelineau, Bos	1965 Roger Crozier, Det	1980 Raymond Bourque, Bos
1951 Terry Sawchuk, Det	1966 Brit Selby, Tor	1981 Peter Stastny, Que
1952 Bernie Geoffrion, Mtl	1967 Bobby Orr, Bos	1982 Dale Hawerchuk, Wpg
1953 Lorne Worsley, NYR	1968 Derek Sanderson, Bos	1983 Steve Larmer, Chi
1954 Camille Henry, NYR	1969 Danny Grant, Min	1984 Tom Barrasso, Buf
1955 Ed Litzenberger, Chi	1970 Tony Esposito, Chi	1985 Mario Lemieux, Pit
1956 Glenn Hall, Det	1971 Gilbert Perreault, Buf	1986 Gary Suter, Cal
1957 Larry Regan, Bos	1972 Ken Dryden, Mtl	1987 Luc Robitaille, LA
1958 Frank Mahovlich, Tor	1973 Steve Vickers, NYR	1988 Joe Nieuwendyk, Cal
1959 Ralph Backstrom, Mtl	1974 Denis Potvin, NYI	1989 Brian Leetch, NYR
1960 Bill Hay, Chi	1975 Eric Vail, Atlanta	1990 Sergei Makarov, Cal
1961 Dave Keon, Tor	1976 Bryan Trottier, NYI	1991 Ed Belfour, Chi
1962 Bobby Rousseau, Mtl	1977 Willi Plett, Atl	1992 Pavel Bure, Vcr
1963 Kent Douglas, Tor	1978 Mike Bossy, NYI	1993 Teemu Selanne, Wpg
1964 Jacques Laperrière, Mtl	1979 Bobby Smith, Min	

James Norris Trophy (Best Defenceman)[1]

1954 Red Kelly, Det	1968 Bobby Orr, Bos	1982 Doug Wilson, Chi
1955 Doug Harvey, Mtl	1969 Bobby Orr, Bos	1983 Rod Langway, Wash
1956 Doug Harvey, Mtl	1970 Bobby Orr, Bos	1984 Rod Langway, Wash
1957 Doug Harvey, Mtl	1971 Bobby Orr, Bos	1985 Paul Coffey, Edm
1958 Doug Harvey, Mtl	1972 Bobby Orr, Bos	1986 Paul Coffey, Edm
1959 Tom Johnson, Mtl	1973 Bobby Orr, Bos	1987 Raymond Bourque, Bos
1960 Doug Harvey, Mtl	1974 Bobby Orr, Bos	1988 Raymond Bourque, Bos
1961 Doug Harvey, Mtl	1975 Bobby Orr, Bos	1989 Chris Chelios, Mtl
1962 Doug Harvey, NYR	1976 Denis Potvin, NYI	1990 Raymond Bourque, Bos
1963 Pierre Pilote, Chi	1977 Larry Robinson, Mtl	1991 Raymond Bourque, Bos
1964 Pierre Pilote, Chi	1978 Denis Potvin, NYI	1992 Brian Leetch, NYR
1965 Pierre Pilote, Chi	1979 Denis Potvin, NYI	1993 Chris Chelios, Chi
1966 Jacques Laperrière, Mtl	1980 Larry Robinson, Mtl	
1967 Harry Howell, NYR	1981 Randy Carlyle, Pittsburgh	

Vezina Trophy (Best Goalkeeper)[2]

1950 Bill Durnan, Mtl	1967 Glenn Hall, Chi	1979 Ken Dryden, Mtl
1951 Al Rollins, Tor	Denis Dejordy, Chi	Michel Larocque, Mtl
1952 Terry Sawchuk, Det	1968 Lorne Worsley, Mtl	1980 Bob Suavé, Buf
1953 Terry Sawchuk, Det	Rogie Vachon, Mtl	Don Edwards, Buf
1954 Harry Lumley, Tor	1969 Jacques Plante, StL	1981 Richard Sevigny, Mtl
1955 Terry Sawchuk, Det	Glenn Hall, StL	Denis Herron, Mtl
1956 Jacques Plante, Mtl	1970 Tony Esposito, Chi	Michel Larocque, Mtl
1957 Jacques Plante, Mtl	1971 Ed Giacomin, NYR	1982 Bill Smith, NYI
1958 Jacques Plante, Mtl	Gilles Villemure, NYR	1983 Pete Peeters, Bos
1959 Jacques Plante, Mtl	1972 Tony Esposito, Chi	1984 Tom Barrasso, Buf
1960 Jacques Plante, Mtl	Gary Smith, Chi	1985 Pelle Lindbergh, Phi
1961 Johnny Bower, Tor	1973 Ken Dryden, Mtl	1986 John Vanbiesbrouck, NYR
1962 Jacques Plante, Mtl	1974 Bernie Parent, Phi	1987 Ron Hextall, Phi
1963 Glenn Hall, Chi	Tony Esposito, Chi	1988 Grant Fuhr, Edm
1964 Charlie Hodge, Mtl	1975 Bernie Parent, Phi	1989 Patrick Roy, Mtl
1965 Terry Sawchuk, Tor	1976 Ken Dryden, Mtl	1990 Patrick Roy, Mtl
Johnny Bower, Tor	1977 Ken Dryden, Mtl	1991 Ed Belfour, Chi
1966 Lorne Worsley, Mtl	Michel Larocque, Mtl	1992 Patrick Roy, Mtl
Charlie Hodge, Mtl	1978 Ken Dryden, Mtl	1993 Ed Belfour, Chi
	Michel Larocque, Mtl	

Lady Byng Trophy (Most Sportsmanlike)[1]

1950 Edgar Laprade, NYR	1965 Bobby Hull, Chi	1980 Wayne Gretzky, Edm
1951 Red Kelly, Det	1966 Alex Delvecchio, Det	1981 Rick Kehoe, Pit
1952 Sid Smith, Tor	1967 Stan Mikita, Chi	1982 Rick Middleton, Bos
1953 Red Kelly, Det	1968 Stan Mikita, Chi	1983 Mike Bossy, NYI
1954 Red Kelly, Det	1969 Alex Delvecchio, Det	1984 Mike Bossy, NYI
1955 Sid Smith, Tor	1970 Phil Goyette, StL	1985 Jari Kurri, Edm
1956 Earl Reibel, Det	1971 John Bucyk, Bos	1986 Mike Bossy, NYI
1957 Andy Hebenton, NYR	1972 Jean Ratelle, NYR	1987 Joe Mullen, Cal
1958 Camille Henry, NYR	1973 Gilbert Perreault, Buf	1988 Mats Naslund, Mtl
1959 Alex Delvecchio, Det	1974 John Bucyk, Bos	1989 Joe Mullen, Cal
1960 Don McKenney, Bos	1975 Marcel Dionne, Det	1990 Brett Hull, StL
1961 Red Kelly, Tor	1976 Jean Ratelle, NYR/Bos	1991 Wayne Gretzky, LA
1962 Dave Keon, Tor	1977 Marcel Dionne, LA	1992 Wayne Gretzky, LA
1963 Dave Keon, Tor	1978 Butch Goring, LA	1993 Pierre Turgeon, NYI
1964 Ken Wharram, Chi	1979 Bob MacMillan, Atl	

Conn Smythe Trophy (Most Valuable in Playoffs)[3]

1965 Jean Béliveau, Mtl	1975 Bernie Parent, Phi	1985 Wayne Gretzky, Edm
1966 Roger Crozier, Det	1976 Reggie Leach, Phi	1986 Patrick Roy, Mtl
1967 Dave Keon, Tor	1977 Guy Lafleur, Mtl	1987 Ron Hextall, Phi
1968 Glenn Hall, StL	1978 Larry Robinson, Mtl	1988 Wayne Gretzky, Edm
1969 Serge Savard, Mtl	1979 Bob Gainey, Mtl	1989 Al MacInnis, Cal
1970 Bobby Orr, Bos	1980 Bryan Trottier, NYI	1990 Bill Ranford, Edm
1971 Ken Dryden, Mtl	1981 Butch Goring, NYI	1991 Mario Lemieux, Pit
1972 Bobby Orr, Bos	1982 Mike Bossy, NYI	1992 Mario Lemieux, Pit
1973 Yvan Cournoyer, Mtl	1983 Bill Smith, NYI	1993 Patrick Roy, Mtl
1974 Bernie Parent, Phi	1984 Mark Messier, Edm	▶

Frank J. Selke Trophy (Best Defensive Forward)[1]

▶ 1978 Bob Gainey, Mtl
1979 Bob Gainey, Mtl
1980 Bob Gainey, Mtl
1981 Bob Gainey, Mtl
1982 Steve Kasper, Bos
1983 Bobby Clarke, Phi

1984 Doug Jarvis, Wash
1985 Craig Ramsay, Buf
1986 Troy Murray, Chi
1987 Dave Poulin, Phi
1988 Guy Carbonneau, Mtl
1989 Guy Carbonneau, Mtl

1990 Rick Meagher, StL
1991 Dirk Graham, Chi
1992 Guy Carbonneau, Mtl
1993 Doug Gilmour, Tor

(1) As selected at the end of the regular season by members of the Professional Hockey Writers' Association in the 21 NHL cities. (2) Since the 1981–82 season, Vezina Trophy winners have been selected by general managers of the 21 NHL clubs. In earlier seasons the trophy was awarded to the goalkeeper(s) of the team allowing the fewest goals during the regular season. (3) As selected by members of the Professional Hockey Writers' Association at the end of the last game of the Stanley Cup finals.

Men's World Hockey Championships, 1993

(Munich, Germany)

Team	W	L	T	GF	GA	Team	W	L	T	GF	GA
Canada	5	0	0	31	4	Czech Republic	4	0	1	17	4
Sweden	3	2	0	17	14	Germany	4	1	0	20	12
Russia	2	2	1	15	12	USA	2	1	2	14	10
Italy	1	2	2	8	20	Finland	2	2	1	7	7
Switzerland	2	3	0	11	14	Norway	0	5	0	6	17
Austria	0	4	1	4	22	France	1	4	0	10	24

Semi-finals: Sweden 4, Czech Republic 3 (OT); Russia 7, Canada 4.
Gold Medal: Russia 3, Sweden 1;
Bronze Medal: Czech Republic 5, Canada 1.

World Junior Hockey Tournament

(Sweden)

Team	W	L	T	F	A	Pts	Team	W	L	T	F	A	Pts
Canada	6	1	0	37	17	12	Finland........	3	3	1	31	20	7
Canada	6	1	0	37	17	12	Russia........	2	3	2	26	20	6
Sweden.......	6	1	0	53	15	12	Germany......	1	6	0	16	37	2
Czech-Slovak ..	4	2	1	38	27	9	Japan.........	0	7	0	9	83	0
U.S...........	4	3	0	32	23	8							

Canada wins gold; Sweden silver; Czech–Slovak bronze.

World Junior All–Stars

First Team		Second Team
Manny Legace, Canada*	G	Petter Ronnqvist, Sweden
Brent Tully, Canada	D	Mike Rathje, Canada
Kenny Jonsson, Sweden	D	Janne Gronvall, Finland
Peter Forsberg, Sweden*	C	Saku Koivu, Finland
Markus Naslund, Sweden*	RW	Martin Lapointe, Canada
Paul Kariya, Canada	LW	Ville Peltonen, Finland

▶

* Unanimous choice

Previous winners

▶ 1992	C.I.S. (fomer Soviet Union)	1984	Soviet Union
1991	Canada	1983	Soviet Union
1990	Canada	1982	Canada
1989	Soviet Union	1981	Sweden
1988	Canada	1980	Soviet Union
1987	Finland	1979	Soviet Union
1986	Soviet Union	1978	Soviet Union
1985	Canada	1977	Soviet Union

Memorial Cup Winners, 1919–93

(Canadian Junior Hockey Champions)

1919	University of Toronto Schools	1957	Flin Flon Bombers
1920	Toronto Canoe Club	1958	Ottawa-Hull Canadiens
1921	Winnipeg Falcons	1959	Winnipeg Braves
1922	Fort William War Veterans	1960	St. Catharines Tee Pees
1923	University of Manitoba—Winnipeg	1961	St. Michael's Majors
1924	Owen Sound Greys	1962	Hamilton Red Wings
1925	Regina Pats	1963	Edmonton Oil Kings
1926	Calgary Canadians	1964	Toronto Marlboros
1927	Owen Sound	1965	Niagara Falls Flyers
1928	Regina Monarchs	1966	Edmonton Oil Kings
1929	Toronto Marlboros	1967	Toronto Marlboros
1930	Regina Pats	1968	Niagara Falls Flyers
1931	Winnipeg Elmwoods	1969	Montreal Jr. Canadiens
1932	Sudbury	1970	Montreal Jr. Canadiens
1933	Newmarket	1971	Quebec Ramparts
1934	Toronto St. Michael's	1972	Cornwall Royals
1935	Winnipeg Monarchs	1973	Toronto Marlboros
1936	West Toronto Redmen	1974	Regina Pats
1937	Winnipeg Monarchs	1975	Toronto Marlboros
1938	St. Boniface Seals	1976	Hamilton Fincups
1939	Oshawa Generals	1977	New Westminster Bruins
1940	Oshawa Generals	1978	New Westminster Bruins
1941	Winnipeg Rangers	1979	Peterborough Petes
1942	Portage La Prairie	1980	Cornwall Royals
1943	Winnipeg Rangers	1981	Cornwall Royals
1944	Oshawa Generals	1982	Kitchener Rangers
1945	Toronto St. Michael's	1983	Portland Winter Hawks
1946	Winnipeg Monarchs	1984	Ottawa 67's
1947	Toronto St. Michael's	1985	Prince Albert Raiders
1948	Port Arthur West End Bruins	1986	Guelph Platers
1949	Montreal Royals	1987	Medicine Hat Tigers
1950	Montreal Canadiens	1988	Medicine Hat Tigers
1951	Barrie Flyers	1989	Swift Current Broncos
1952	Guelph Biltmores	1990	Oshawa Generals
1953	Barrie Flyers	1991	Spokane Chiefs
1954	St. Catharines Tee Pees	1992	Kamloops Blazers
1955	Toronto Marlboros	1993	Sault Ste. Marie Greyhounds
1956	Toronto Marlboros		

Source: *Canadian Amateur Hockey Association*

Team Canada in International Hockey Competition

The 1972 Series
(an 8–game series)

Goal: Ken Dryden, Tony Esposito; **Defence:** Don Awrey, Gary Bergman, Guy Lapointe, Brad Park, Serge Savard, Rod Seiling, Pat Stapleton, Bill White; **Forwards:** Red Berenson, Wayne Cashman, Bobby Clarke, Yvan Cournoyer, Ron Ellis, Phil Esposito, Rod Gilbert, Bill Goldsworthy, Vic Hadfield, Paul Henderson, Dennis Hull, Frank Mahovlich, Peter Mahovlich, Stan Mikita, Jean-Paul Parise, Gilbert Perreault, Jean Ratelle

Date	Location	Score	Date	Location	Score
Sept. 2	Montreal	Soviets 7, Team Canada 3	Sept. 22	Moscow	Soviets 5, Team Canada 4
Sept. 4	Toronto	Team Canada 4, Soviets 1	Sept. 24	Moscow	Team Canada 3, Soviets 2
Sept. 6	Winnipeg	Soviets 4, Team Canada 4	Sept. 26	Moscow	Team Canada 4, Soviets 3
Sept. 8	Vancouver	Soviets 5, Team Canada 3	Sept. 28	Moscow	Team Canada 6, Soviets 5

Canada won the series 4 games to 3, with 1 game tied.

The Canada Cup, 1976

Final-Round Results
Canada 6, Czechoslovakia 0
Canada 5, Czechoslovakia 4*
Canada won best 2-out-of-3 final series 2 games to 0.

*overtime

The Canada Cup, 1981

Semi-Final Results
Soviet Union 4, Czechoslovakia 1
Canada 4, United States 1
Final Game Score
Soviet Union 8, Canada 1
The Soviet Union won the series.

The Canada Cup, 1984

Playoff Results
Canada 3, Soviet Union 2Sweden 9, United States, 2
Final Results
Canada 5, Sweden 2
Canada 6, Sweden 5
Canada won best-2-out-of-3 series 2 games to 0.

The Canada Cup, 1987

Semi-Final Results
Canada 5, Czechoslovakia 3
Soviet Union 4, Sweden 2
Final Results
Soviet Union 6, Canada 5*
Canada 6, Soviet Union 5*
Canada 6, Soviet Union 5*
Canada won the best-2-out-of-3 series 2 games to 1.

*overtime

The Canada Cup, 1991

Goal: Ed Belfour, Sean Burke, Bill Ranford; **Defence:** Paul Coffey, Eric Desjardins, Al MacInnis, Jamie Macoun, Larry Murphy, Steve Smith, Scott Stevens; **Forwards:** Shayne Corson, Russ Courtnall, Theoren Fleury, Dirk Graham, Wayne Gretzky, Dale Hawerchuk, Steve Larmer, Eric Lindros, Mark Messier, Luc Robitaille, Brendan Shanahan, Brent Sutter, Rick Tocchet.

Semi-Final Results
United States 7, Finland 3
Canada 4, Sweden 0
Final Results
Canada 4, United States 1
Canada 4, United States 2
Canada won the best-2-out-of-3 series 2 games to 0.

First Lady of Hockey

M anon Rheaume became the first woman to appear in a regular-season professional hockey game Dec. 13, 1992. She played the first 5:49 of the second period for the Atlanta Knights against Salt Lake City. She stopped three shots, allowed one goal, and had another nullified by a penalty in a 4-1 loss. In September, she had played the second period of an NHL exhibition game for the Tampa Bay Lightning, allowing two goals.

The Hockey Hall of Fame and Museum

(Toronto, Ont.)
(year of election to the Hall indicated in brackets)

Abel, Sid (1969)
Adams, Jack (1959)
Apps, Syl (1961)
Armstrong, George (1975)
Bailey, Ace (1975)
Bain, Dan (1945)
Baker, Hobey (1945)
Barber, Bill (1990)
Barry, Marty (1965)
Bathgate, Andy (1978)
Béliveau, Jean (1972)
Benedict, Clinton (1965)
Bentley, Doug (1964)
Bentley, Max (1966)
Blake, Toe (1966)
Boivin, Leo (1986)
Boon, Dickie (1952)
Bossy, Mike (1991)
Bouchard, Butch (1966)
Boucher, Frank (1958
Boucher, Buck (1960)
Bower, Johnny (1976)
Bowie, Russell (1945)
Brimsek, Frank (1966)
Broadbent, Punch (1962)
Broda, Turk (1967)
Bucyk, Johnny (1981)
Burch, Billy (1974)
Cameron, Harry (1962)
Cheevers, Gerry (1985)
Clancy, King (1958)
Clapper, Dit (1945)
Clarke, Bob (1987)
Cleghorn, Sprague (1958)
Colville, Neil (1967)
Conacher, Charlie (1961)
Connell, Alex (1958)
Cook, Bill (1952)
Coulter, Art (1974)
Cournoyer, Yvan (1982)
Cowley, William (1968)
Crawford, Rusty (1962)
Darragh, Jack (1962)
Davidson, Scotty (1950)
Day, Hap (1961)
Delvecchio, Alex (1977)
Denneny, Cy (1959)
Dionne, Marcel (1992)
Drillon, Gordie (1975)
Drinkwater, Charles (1950)
Dryden, Ken (1983)
Dumart, Woody (1992)
Dunderdale, Thomas (1974)
Durnan, Bill (1964)
Dutton, Red (1958)
Dye, Babe (1970)

Esposito, Phil (1984)
Esposito, Tony (1988)
Farrell, Arthur (1965)
Flaman, Fern (1990)
Foyston, Frank (1958)
Frederickson, Frank (1958)
Gadsby, Bill (1970)
Gainey, Bob (1992)
Gardiner, Chuck (1945)
Gardiner, Herb (1958)
Gardner, Jimmy (1962)
Geoffrion, Boom Boom (1972)
Gerard, Eddie (1945)
Giacomin, Ed (1987)
Gilbert, Rod (1982)
Gilmour, Billy (1962)
Goheen, Moose (1952)
Goodfellow, Ebbie (1963)
Grant, Mike (1950)
Green, Shorty (1962)
Griffis, Si (1950)
Hainsworth, George (1961)
Hall, Glenn (1975)
Hall, Joe (1961)
Harvey, Doug (1973)
Hay, George (1958)
Hern, Riley (1962)
Hextall, Bryan (1969)
Holmes, Hap (1972)
Hooper, Tom (1962)
Horner, Red (1965)
Horton, Tim (1977)
Howe, Gordie (1972)
Howell, Syd (1965)
Howell, Harry (1979)
Hull, Bobby (1983)
Hutton, Bouse (1962)
Hyland, Harry (1962)
Irvin, Dick (1958)
Jackson, Busher (1971)
Johnson, Moose (1952)
Johnson, Ching (1958)
Johnson, Tom (1970)
Joliat, Aurel (1947)
Keats, Duke (1958)
Kelly, Red (1969)
Kennedy, Teeder (1966)
Keon, Dave (1986)
Lach, Elmer (1966)
Lafleur, Guy (1988)
Lalonde, Newsy (1950)
Laperrière, Jacques (1987)
Lapointe, Guy (1993)
Laprate, Edgar (1993)
Laviolette, Jack (1962)
Lehman, Hugh (1958)

Lemaire, Jacques (1984)
LeSueur, Percy (1961)
Lewis, Herbie (1989)
Lindsay, Ted (1966)
Lumley, Harry (1980)
Mackay, Mickey (1952)
Mahovlich, Frank (1981
Malone, Joe (1950)
Mantha, Sylvio (1960)
Marshall, Jack (1965)
Maxwell, Steamer (1962)
McDonald, Lanny (1992)
McGee, Frank (1945)
McGimsie, Billy (1962)
McNamara, George (1958)
Mikita, Stan (1983)
Moore, Dickie (1974)
Moran, Paddy (1958)
Morenz, Howie (1945)
Mosienko, Bill (1965)
Nighbor, Frank (1947)
Noble, Reg (1962)
O'Connor, Buddy (1988)
Oliver, Harry (1967)
Olmstead, Bert (1985)
Orr, Bobby (1979)
Parent, Bernie (1984)
Park, Brad (1988)
Patrick, Lynn (1980)
Patrick, Lester (1947)
Perreault, Gilbert (1990)
Phillips, Tommy (1945)
Pilote, Pierre (1975)
Pitre, Didier "Pit" (1962)
Plante, Jacques (1978)
Potvin, Denis (1991)
Pratt, Babe (1966)
Primeau, Joe (1963)
Pronovost, Marcel (1978)
Pulford, Bob (1991)
Pulford, Harvey (1945)
Quackenbush, Bill (1976)
Rankin, Frank (1961)
Ratelle, Jean (1985)
Rayner, Chuck (1973)
Reardon, Ken (1966)
Richard, Henri (1979)
Richard, Maurice "Rocket" (1961)
Richardson, George (1950)
Roberts, Gordon (1971)
Ross, Art (1945)
Russel, Blair (1965)
Russell, Ernest (1965)
Ruttan, Jack (1962)
Savard, Serge (1986)
Sawchuk, Terry (1971)

▶

Scanlan, Fred (1965)
Schmidt, Milt (1961)
Schriner, Sweeney (1962)
Seibert, Earl (1963)
Seibert, Oliver (1961)
Shore, Eddie (1947)
Shutt, Steve (1993)
Siebert, Babe (1964)
Simpson, Bullet Joe (1962)
Sittler, Darryl (1989)
Smith, Alfred (1962)
Smith, Bill (1993)

Smith, Clint (1991)
Smith, Hooley (1972)
Smith, Thomas (1973)
Stanley, Allan (1981)
Stanley, Barney (1962)
Stewart, Black Jack (1964)
Stewart, Nels (1962)
Stuart, Bruce (1961)
Stuart, Hod (1945)
Taylor, Cyclone (1947)
Thompson, Tiny (1959)
Tretiak, Vladislav (1989)

Trihey, Harry (1950)
Ullman, Norm (1982)
Vezina, Georges (1945)
Walker, Jack (1960)
Walsh, Marty (1962)
Watson, Moose (1962)
Weiland, Cooney (1971)
Westwick, Harry (1962)
Whitcroft, Fred (1962)
Wilson, Phat (1962)
Worsley, Lorne "Gump" (1980)
Worters, Roy (1969)

BASEBALL

American League Final Standings, 1993

Eastern Division	W	L	Pct	GB	Home	Away	Western Division	W	L	Pct	GB	Home	Away
Toronto	95	67	.586	—	48-33	47-34	Chicago	94	68	.580	—	45-36	49-32
New York	88	74	.543	7	50-31	38-43	Texas	86	76	.531	8	50-31	36-45
Baltimore	85	77	.525	10	48-33	37-44	Kansas City	84	78	.519	10	43-38	41-40
Detroit	85	77	.525	10	44-37	41-40	Seattle	82	80	.506	12	46-35	36-45
Boston	80	82	.494	15	43-38	37-44	California	71	91	.438	23	45-36	26-55
Cleveland	76	86	.469	19	46-35	30-51	Minnesota	71	91	.438	23	36-45	35-46
Milwaukee	69	93	.426	26	38-43	31-50	Oakland	68	94	.420	26	38-43	30-51

American League Leaders, 1993

Batting

Runs

Rafael Palmeiro, Tex., 124
Paul Molitor, Tor., 121
Ken Lofton, Cle., 116
Devon White, Tor., 116
Ricky Henderson, Tor., 114

Hits

Paul Molitor, Tor., 211
Carlos Baerga, Cle., 200
John Olerud, Tor., 200
Robby Alomar, Tor., 192
Ken Lofton, Cle., 185

Runs Batted In

Albert Belle, Cle., 129
Frank Thomas, Chi., 128
Joe Carter, Tor., 121
Juan Gonzalez, Tex., 118
Cecil Fielder, Det., 117

Doubles

John Olerud, Tor., 54
Devon White, Tor., 42
John Valentin, Bos., 40
Rafael Palmeiro, Tex., 40
Kirby Puckett, Minn. 39

Triples

Lance Johnson, Chi., 14
Joey Cora, Chi., 13
David Hulse, Tex., 10
Tony Fernandez, Tor., 9
Brian McRae, KC, 9

Home Runs

Juan Gonzalez, Tex., 46
Ken Griffey Jr. Sea., 45
Frank Thomas, Chi., 41
Albert Belle, Cle., 38
Rafael Palmeiro, Tex., 37

Slugging Average

Juan Gonzalez, Tex., .632
Ken Griffey Jr., Sea., .617
Frank Thomas, Chi., .607
John Olerud, Tor., .599
Chris Hoiles, Balt., .585

On-Base Pct.

John Olerud, Tor., .473
Tony Phillips, Det., .443
R. Henderson,Oak/Tor,.432
Frank Thomas, Chi., .426
Chris Hoiles, Balt., .416

Stolen Bases

Ken Lofton, Cle., 70
Robby Alomar, Tor., 55
Luis Polonia, Cal., 55
Ricky Henderson, Tor, 53
Chad Curtis, Cal., 48

Pitching

Wins	Earned Run Average	Strikeouts
Jack McDowell, Chi., 22	Kevin Appier, KC, 2.56	Randy Johnson,Sea., 308
Pat Hentgen, Tor., 19	Wilson Alvarez, Chi., 2.95	Mark Langston,Cal., 196
Randy Johnson, Sea., 19	Jimmy Key, NY, 3.00	David Cone, KC, 191
Alex Fernandez, Chi., 18	Alex Fernandez, Chi., 3.13	Chuck Finley, Cal. 187
Kevin Appier, KC, 18	Frank Viola, Bos., 3.14	Kevin Appier, KC, 186
Jimmy Key, NY, 18		

Saves	Shutouts	Innings Pitched
Jeff Montgomery, KC, 45	Jack McDowell,Chi., 4	Cal Eldred, Mil. 258.0
Duane Ward, Tor, 45	Kevin Brown, Tex., 3	J. McDowell, Chi., 256.2
Tom Henke, Tex., 40	Randy Johnson, Sea., 3	M. Langston, Cal., 256.1
Roberto Hernandez, Chi., 38	Mike Moore, Det., 3	R. Johnson, Sea., 255.1
Dennis Eckersley, Oak., 36	5 with 2	David Cone, KC, 254.0

National League Final Standings, 1993

Eastern Division	W	L	Pct	GB	Home	Away	Western Division	W	L	Pct	GB	Home	Away
Philadelphia	97	65	.599	—	52-29	45-36	Atlanta	104	58	.642	—	51-30	53-28
Montreal	**94**	**68**	**.580**	**3**	**55-26**	**39-42**	San Fran	103	59	.636	1	50-31	53-28
St. Louis	87	75	.537	10	48-32	39-43	Houston	85	77	.525	19	44-37	41-40
Chicago	84	78	.519	13	43-38	41-40	Los Angl's	81	81	.500	23	41-40	40-41
Pittsburgh	75	87	.463	22	40-42	35-45	Cincinnati	73	89	.451	31	41-40	32-49
Florida	64	98	.395	33	35-46	29-52	Colorado	67	95	.414	37	39-42	28-53
New York	59	103	.364	38	28-53	31-50	San Diego	61	101	.377	43	34-47	27-54

National League Leaders, 1993

Batting

Runs	Hits	Runs Batted In
Len Dykstra, Phi., 142	Len Dykstra, Phi., 194	Barry Bonds, SF, 123
Barry Bonds, SF, 129	Mark Grace, Chi., 193	Dave Justice, Atl., 120
Ron Gant, Atl., 113	**Marquis Grissom, Mtl., 188**	Ron Gant, Atl., 117
Fred McGriff, Atl.,111	Jay Bell, Pitt., 187	Mike Piazza, LA., 112
Jeff Blauser, Atl.,110	Gregg Jefferies, St.L., 186	Matt Williams, SF, 110

Doubles	Triples	Home Runs
Charlie Hayes, Col., 45	Chuck Finley, Hou., 13	Barry Bonds, SF, 46
Len Dykstra, Phi., 44	Brett Butler, LA, 10	Dave Justice, Atl., 40
Dante Bichette, Col., 43	Jay Bell, Pitt., 9	Matt Williams, SF, 38
Craig Biggio, Hou., 41	Mickey Morandini, Phi., 9	Fred McGriff, SD/Atl., 37
Tony Gwynn, SD, 41	3 with 8	Ron Gant, Atl., 36

Slugging Average	On-Base Pct.	Stolen Bases
Barry Bonds, SF, .677	Barry Bonds, SF, .458	Chuck Carr, Fla., 58
Andres Galarraga,Col., .602	John Kruk, Phi., .430	**Marquis Grissom, Mtl., 53**
Matt Williams, SF, .561	Len Dykstra, Phi., .420	Otis Nixon, Atl., 47
Rick Wilkins, Chi., .561	Orlando Merced, Pitt., 414	Greg Jefferies, StL., 46
Mike Piazza, LA, .561	Greg Jefferies, St.L., 408	Darren Lewis, SF, 46

Pitching

Wins/Losses	Earned Run Average	Strikeouts
John Burkett, SF, 22	Greg Maddux, Atl., 2.36	Jose Rijo, Cin., 227
Tom Glavine, Atl., 22	Jose Rijo, Cin., 2.48	John Smoltz, Atl., 208
Bill Swift, SF, 21	Mark Portugal, Hou., 2.77	Greg Maddux, Atl., 197
Greg Maddux, Atl., 20	Bill Swift, SF. 2.82	Curt Schilling, Phi.186
Steve Avery, Atl., 18	Steve Avery, Atl., 2.94	Pete Harnisch, Hou.,185
Mark Portugal, Hou., 18		

Saves	Shutouts	Innings Pitched
Randy Myers, Chi., 53	Pete Harnisch, Hou., 4	Greg Maddux, Atl., 267.0
Rod Beck, SF, 48	Ramon Martinez, LA, 3	Jose Rijo, Cin., 257.1
Bryan Harvey, Fla., 45	11 with 2	John Smoltz, Atl., 243.2
Lee Smith, St.L., 43		Tom Glavine, Atl., 239.1
John Wetteland, Mtl., 43		Doug Drabek, Hou., 237.2
Mitch Williams, Phi., 43		

Major League Pennant Winners, 1901–92

National League

Year	Winner	Won	Lost	Pct.
1901	Pittsburgh	90	49	.647
1902	Pittsburgh	103	36	.741
1903	Pittsburgh	91	49	.650
1904	New York	106	47	.693
1905	New York	105	48	.686
1906	Chicago	116	36	.763
1907	Chicago	107	45	.704
1908	Chicago	99	55	.643
1909	Pittsburgh	110	42	.724
1910	Chicago	104	50	.675
1911	New York	99	54	.647
1912	New York	103	48	.682
1913	New York	101	51	.664
1914	Boston	94	59	.614
1915	Philadelphia	90	62	.592
1916	Brooklyn	94	60	.610
1917	New York	98	56	.636
1918	Chicago	84	45	.651
1919	Cincinnati	96	44	.686
1920	Brooklyn	93	61	.604
1921	New York	94	59	.614
1922	New York	93	61	.604
1923	New York	95	58	.621
1924	New York	93	60	.608
1925	Pittsburgh	95	58	.621
1926	St. Louis	89	65	.578
1927	Pittsburgh	94	60	.610
1928	St. Louis	95	59	.617
1929	Chicago	98	54	.645
1930	St. Louis	92	62	.597
1931	St. Louis	101	53	.656
1932	Chicago	90	64	.584
1933	New York	91	61	.599
1934	St. Louis	95	58	.621
1935	Chicago	100	54	.649
1936	New York	92	62	.597
1937	New York	95	57	.625
1938	Chicago	89	63	.586

American League

Year	Winner	Won	Lost	Pct.
1901	Chicago	83	53	.610
1902	Philadelphia	83	53	.610
1903	Boston	91	47	.659
1904	Boston	95	59	.617
1905	Philadelphia	92	56	.622
1906	Chicago	93	58	.616
1907	Detroit	92	58	.613
1908	Detroit	90	63	.588
1909	Detroit	98	54	.645
1910	Philadelphia	102	48	.680
1911	Philadelphia	101	50	.669
1912	Boston	105	47	.691
1913	Philadelphia	96	57	.627
1914	Philadelphia	99	53	.651
1915	Boston	101	50	.669
1916	Boston	91	63	.591
1917	Chicago	100	54	.649
1918	Boston	75	51	.595
1919	Chicago	88	52	.629
1920	Cleveland	98	56	.636
1921	New York	98	55	.641
1922	New York	94	60	.610
1923	New York	98	54	.645
1924	Washington	92	62	.597
1925	Washington	96	55	.636
1926	New York	91	63	.591
1927	New York	110	44	.714
1928	New York	101	53	.656
1929	Philadelphia	104	46	.693
1930	Philadelphia	102	52	.662
1931	Philadelphia	107	45	.704
1932	New York	107	47	.695
1933	Washington	99	53	.651
1934	Detroit	101	53	.656
1935	Detroit	93	58	.616
1936	New York	102	51	.667
1937	New York	102	52	.662
1938	New York	99	53	.651

	National League					American League			
Year	Winner	Won	Lost	Pct.	Year	Winner	Won	Lost	Pct.
▶ 1939	Cincinnati	97	57	.630	1939	New York	106	45	.702
1940	Cincinnati	100	53	.654	1940	Detroit	90	64	.584
1941	Brooklyn	100	54	.649	1941	New York	101	53	.656
1942	St. Louis	106	48	.688	1942	New York	103	51	.669
1943	St. Louis	105	49	.682	1943	New York	98	56	.636
1944	St. Louis	105	49	.682	1944	St. Louis	89	65	.578
1945	Chicago	98	56	.636	1945	Detroit	88	65	.575
1946	St. Louis	98	58	.628	1946	Boston	104	50	.675
1947	Brooklyn	94	60	.610	1947	New York	97	57	.630
1948	Boston	91	62	.595	1948	Cleveland	97	58	.626
1949	Brooklyn	97	57	.630	1949	New York	97	57	.630
1950	Philadelphia	91	63	.591	1950	New York	98	56	.636
1951	New York	98	59	.624	1951	New York	98	56	.636
1952	Brooklyn	96	57	.627	1952	New York	95	59	.617
1953	Brooklyn	105	49	.682	1953	New York	99	52	.656
1954	New York	97	57	.630	1954	Cleveland	111	43	.721
1955	Brooklyn	98	55	.641	1955	New York	96	58	.623
1956	Brooklyn	93	61	.604	1956	New York	97	57	.630
1957	Milwaukee	95	59	.617	1957	New York	98	56	.636
1958	Milwaukee	92	62	.597	1958	New York	92	62	.597
1959	Los Angeles	88	68	.564	1959	Chicago	94	60	.610
1960	Pittsburgh	95	59	.617	1960	New York	97	57	.630
1961	Cincinnati	93	61	.604	1961	New York	109	53	.673
1962	San Francisco	103	62	.624	1962	New York	96	66	.593
1963	Los Angeles	99	63	.611	1963	New York	104	57	.646
1964	St. Louis	93	69	.574	1964	New York	99	63	.611
1965	Los Angeles	97	65	.599	1965	Minnesota	102	60	.630
1966	Los Angeles	95	67	.586	1966	Baltimore	97	63	.606
1967	St. Louis	101	60	.627	1967	Boston	92	70	.568
1968	St. Louis	97	65	.599	1968	Detroit	103	59	.636
1969	New York	100	62	.617	1969	Baltimore	109	53	.673
1970	Cincinnati	102	60	.630	1970	Baltimore	108	54	.667
1971	Pittsburgh	97	65	.599	1971	Baltimore	101	57	.639
1972	Cincinnati	95	59	.617	1972	Oakland	93	62	.600
1973	New York	82	79	.509	1973	Oakland	94	68	.580
1974	Los Angeles	102	60	.630	1974	Oakland	90	72	.556
1975	Cincinnati	108	54	.667	1975	Boston	95	65	.594
1976	Cincinnati	102	60	.630	1976	New York	97	62	.610
1977	Los Angeles	98	64	.605	1977	New York	100	62	.617
1978	Los Angeles	95	67	.586	1978	New York	100	63	.613
1979	Pittsburgh	98	64	.605	1979	Baltimore	102	57	.642
1980	Philadelphia	91	71	.562	1980	Kansas City	97	65	.599
1981	Los Angeles	63	47	.573	1981	New York	59	48	.551
1982	St. Louis	92	70	.568	1982	Milwaukee	95	67	.586
1983	Philadelphia	90	72	.556	1983	Baltimore	98	64	.605
1984	San Diego	92	70	.568	1984	Detroit	104	58	.642
1985	St. Louis	101	61	.623	1985	Kansas City	91	71	.562
1986	New York	108	54	.667	1986	Boston	95	66	.590
1987	St. Louis	95	67	.586	1987	Minnesota	85	77	.525
1988	Los Angeles	94	67	.584	1988	Oakland	104	58	.642
1989	San Francisco	92	70	.568	1989	Oakland	99	63	.611
1990	Cincinnati	91	71	.562	1990	Oakland	103	59	.636
1991	Atlanta	94	68	.580	1991	Minnesota	95	67	.586
1992	Atlanta	98	64	.605	1992	**Toronto**	**96**	**66**	**.593**

Canada Wins Down Under

Canada won the under-19 world junior softball championship February 21 in Aukland by defeating the host New Zealand team 4-3.

World Series Results, 1903–92

Year	Champion	Final Opponent	Series Result
1903	Boston Red Sox, AL	Pittsburgh Pirates, NL	5-3
1904	No series		
1905	New York Giants, NL	Philadelphia Athletics, AL	4-1
1906	Chicago White Sox, AL	Chicago Cubs, NL	4-2
1907	Chicago Cubs, NL	Detroit Tigers, AL	4-0; 1 tie
1908	Chicago Cubs, NL	Detroit Tigers, AL	4-1
1909	Pittsburgh Pirates, NL	Detroit Tigers, AL	4-3
1910	Philadelphia Athletics, AL	Chicago Cubs, NL	4-1
1911	Philadelphia Athletics, AL	New York Giants, NL	4-2
1912	Boston Red Sox, AL	New York Giants, NL	4-3; 1 tie
1913	Philadelphia Athletics, AL	New York Giants, NL	4-1
1914	Boston Braves, NL	Philadelphia Athletics, AL	4-0
1915	Boston Red Sox, AL	Philadelphia Phillies, NL	4-1
1916	Boston Red Sox, AL	Brooklyn Dodgers, NL	4-1
1917	Chicago White Sox, AL	New York Giants, NL	4-2
1918	Boston Red Sox, AL	Chicago Cubs, NL	4-2
1919	Cincinnati Reds, NL	Chicago White Sox, AL	5-3
1920	Cleveland Indians, AL	Brooklyn Dodgers, NL	5-2
1921	New York Giants, NL	New York Yankees, AL	5-3
1922	New York Giants, NL	New York Yankees, AL	4-0; 1 tie
1923	New York Yankees, AL	New York Giants, NL	4-2
1924	Washington Senators, AL	New York Giants, NL	4-3
1925	Pittsburgh Pirates, NL	Washington Senators, AL	4-3
1926	St. Louis Cardinals, NL	New York Yankees, AL	4-3
1927	New York Yankees, AL	Pittsburgh Pirates, NL	4-0
1928	New York Yankees, AL	St. Louis Cardinals, NL	4-0
1929	Philadelphia Athletics, AL	Chicago Cubs, NL	4-1
1930	Philadelphia Athletics, AL	St. Louis Cardinals, NL	4-2
1931	St. Louis Cardinals, NL	Philadelphia Athletics, AL	4-3
1932	New York Yankees, AL	Chicago Cubs, NL	4-0
1933	New York Giants, NL	Washington Senators, AL	4-1
1934	St. Louis Cardinals, NL	Detroit Tigers, AL	4-3
1935	Detroit Tigers, AL	Chicago Cubs, NL	4-2
1936	New York Yankees, AL	New York Giants, NL	4-2
1937	New York Yankees, AL	New York Giants, NL	4-1
1938	New York Yankees, AL	Chicago Cubs, NL	4-0
1939	New York Yankees, AL	Cincinnati Reds, NL	4-0
1940	Cincinnati Reds, NL	Detroit Tigers, AL	4-3
1941	New York Yankees, AL	Brooklyn Dodgers, NL	4-1
1942	St. Louis Cardinals, NL	New York Yankees, AL	4-1
1943	New York Yankees, AL	St. Louis Cardinals, NL	4-1
1944	St. Louis Cardinals, NL	St. Louis Browns, AL	4-2
1945	Detroit Tigers, AL	Chicago Cubs, NL	4-3
1946	St. Louis Cardinals, NL	Boston Red Sox, AL	4-3
1947	New York Yankees, AL	Brooklyn Dodgers, NL	4-3
1948	Cleveland Indians, AL	Boston Braves, NL	4-2
1949	New York Yankees, AL	Brooklyn Dodgers, NL	4-1
1950	New York Yankees, AL	Philadelphia Phillies, NL	4-0
1951	New York Yankees, AL	New York Giants, NL	4-2
1952	New York Yankees, AL	Brooklyn Dodgers, NL	4-3
1953	New York Yankees, AL	Brooklyn Dodgers, NL	4-2
1954	New York Giants, NL	Cleveland Indians, AL	4-0
1955	Brooklyn Dodgers, NL	New York Yankees, AL	4-3
1956	New York Yankees, AL	Brooklyn Dodgers, NL	4-3
1957	Milwaukee Braves, NL	New York Yankees, AL	4-3
1958	New York Yankees, AL	Milwaukee Braves, NL	4-3
1959	Los Angeles Dodgers, NL	Chicago White Sox, AL	4-2
1960	Pittsburgh Pirates, NL	New York Yankees, AL	4-3
1961	New York Yankees, AL	Cincinnati Reds, NL	4-1

▶

▶ 1962 . . . . New York Yankees, AL   San Francisco Giants, NL. 4-3
1963 . . . . Los Angeles Dodgers, NL   New York Yankees, AL. 4-0
1964 . . . . St. Louis Cardinals, NL   New York Yankees, AL. 4-3
1965 . . . . Los Angeles Dodgers, NL   Minnesota Twins, AL. 4-3
1966 . . . . Baltimore Orioles, AL   Los Angeles Dodgers, NL. 4-0
1967 . . . . St. Louis Cardinals, NL   Boston Red Sox, AL. 4-3
1968 . . . . Detroit Tigers, AL   St. Louis Cardinals, NL. 4-3
1969 . . . . New York Mets, NL   Baltimore Orioles, AL 4-1
1970 . . . . Baltimore Orioles, AL   Cincinnati Reds, NL 4-1
1971 . . . . Pittsburgh Pirates, NL   Baltimore Orioles, AL 4-3
1972 . . . . Oakland Athletics, AL   Cincinnati Reds, NL 4-3
1973 . . . . Oakland Athletics, AL   New York Mets, NL. 4-3
1974 . . . . Oakland Athletics, AL   Los Angeles Dodgers, NL. 4-1
1975 . . . . Cincinnati Reds, NL   Boston Red Sox, AL 4-3
1976 . . . . Cincinnati Reds, NL   New York Yankees, AL. 4-0
1977 . . . . New York Yankees, AL   Los Angeles Dodgers, NL. 4-2
1978 . . . . New York Yankees, AL   Los Angeles Dodgers, NL. 4-2
1979 . . . . Pittsburgh Pirates, NL   Baltimore Orioles, AL 4-3
1980 . . . . Philadelphia Phillies, NL   Kansas City Royals, AL 4-2
1981 . . . . Los Angeles Dodgers, NL   New York Yankees, AL. 4-2
1982 . . . . St. Louis Cardinals, NL   Milwaukee Brewers, AL. 4-3
1983 . . . . Baltimore Orioles, AL   Philadelphia Phillies, NL 4-1
1984 . . . . Detroit Tigers, AL   San Diego Padres, NL. 4-1
1985 . . . . Kansas City Royals, AL   St. Louis Cardinals, NL 4-3
1986 . . . . New York Mets, NL   Boston Red Sox, AL 4-3
1987 . . . . Minnesota Twins, AL   St. Louis Cardinals, NL 4-3
1988 . . . . Los Angeles Dodgers, NL   Oakland Athletics, AL 4-1
1989 . . . . Oakland Athletics, AL   San Francisco Giants, NL. 4-0
1990 . . . . Cincinnati Reds, NL   Oakland Athletics, AL 4-0
1991 . . . . Minnesota Twins, AL   Atlanta Braves, NL 4-3
1992 . . . . **Toronto Blue Jays,** AL   Atlanta Braves, NL 4-2

World Series MVPs

1955 Johnny Podres, Bklyn	1969 Donn Clendenon, NY (NL)	1981 Steve Yeager, LA
1956 Don Larsen, New York (AL)	1970 Brooks Robinson, Bal	1982 Darrell Porter, StL
1957 Lew Burdette, Mil	1971 Roberto Clemente, Pgh	1983 Rick Dempsey, Bal
1958 Bob Turley, NY (AL)	1972 Gene Tenace, Oak	1984 Alan Trammell, Det
1959 Larry Sherry, LA	1973 Reggie Jackson, Oak	1985 Bret Saberhagen, KC
1960 Bobby Richardson, NY (AL)	1974 Rollie Fingers, Oak	1986 Ray Knight, NY (NL)
1961 Whitey Ford, NY (AL)	1975 Pete Rose, Cin	1987 Frank Viola, Min
1962 Ralph Terry, NY (AL)	1976 Johnny Bench, Cin	1988 Orel Hershiser, LA
1963 Sandy Koufax, LA	1977 Reggie Jackson, NY (AL)	1989 Dave Stewart, Oak
1964 Bob Gibson, StL	1978 Bucky Dent, NY (AL)	1990 Jose Rijo, Cin
1965 Sandy Koufax, LA	1979 Willie Stargell, Pgh	1991 Jack Morris, Min
1966 Frank Robinson, Bal	1980 Mike Schmidt, Pha	1992 **Pat Borders, Tor**
1967 Bob Gibson, StL	1981 Ron Cey, LA	
1968 Mickey Lolich, Det	1981 Pedro Guerrero, LA	

Cy Young Award Winners, 1956–92[1]

Year	Player, club	Year	Player, club
1956[1]	Don Newcombe, Brooklyn Dodgers	1963[1]	Sandy Koufax, Los Angeles Dodgers
1957[1]	Warren Spahn, Milwaukee Braves	1964[1]	Dean Chance, California Angels
1958[1]	Bob Turley, New York Yankees	1965[1]	Sandy Koufax, Los Angeles Dodgers
1959[1]	Early Wynn, Chicago White Sox	1966[1]	Sandy Koufax, Los Angeles Dodgers
1960[1]	Vernon Law, Pittsburgh Pirates	1967 (NL)	Mike McCormick, San Francisco Giants
1961[1]	Whitey Ford, New York Yankees	(AL)	Jim Lonborg, Boston Red Sox
1962[1]	Don Drysdale, Los Angeles Dodgers	1968 (NL)	Bob Gibson, St. Louis Cardinals

▶

► (AL) Dennis McLain, Detroit Tigers
1969 (NL) Tom Seaver, New York Mets
(AL) Dennis McLain, Detroit Tigers
(AL) Mike Cuellar, Baltimore Orioles
1970 (NL) Bob Gibson, St. Louis Cardinals
(AL) Jim Perry, Minnesota Twins
1971 (NL) Ferguson Jenkins, Chicago Cubs
(AL) Vida Blue, Oakland A's
1972 (NL) Steve Carlton, Philadelphia Phillies
(AL) Gaylord Perry, Cleveland Indians
1973 (NL) Tom Seaver, New York Mets
(AL) Jim Palmer, Baltimore Orioles
1974 (NL) Mike Marshall, Los Angeles Dodgers
(AL) Jim (Catfish) Hunter, Oakland A's
1975 (NL) Tom Seaver, New York Mets
(AL) Jim Palmer, Baltimore Orioles
1976 (NL) Randy Jones, San Diego Padres
(AL) Jim Palmer, Baltimore Orioles
1977 (NL) Steve Carlton, Philadelphia Phillies
(AL) Sparky Lyle, New York Yankees
1978 (NL) Gaylord Perry, San Diego Padres
(AL) Ron Guidry, New York Yankees
1979 (NL) Bruce Sutter, Chicago Cubs
(AL) Mike Flanagan, Baltimore Orioles
1980 (NL) Steve Carlton, Philadelphia Phillies
(AL) Steve Stone, Baltimore Orioles

1981 (NL) Fernando Valenzuela, Los Angeles Dodgers
(AL) Rollie Fingers, Milwaukee Brewers
1982 (NL) Steve Carlton, Philadelphia Phillies
(AL) Pete Vuckovich, Milwaukee Brewers
1983 (NL) John Denny, Philadelphia Phillies
(AL) LaMarr Hoyt, Chicago White Sox
1984 (NL) Rick Sutcliffe, Chicago Cubs
(AL) Willie Hernandez, Detroit Tigers
1985 (NL) Dwight Gooden, New York Mets
(AL) Bret Saberhagen, Kansas City Royals
1986 (NL) Mike Scott, Houston Astros
(AL) Roger Clemens, Boston Red Sox
1987 (NL) Steve Bedrosian, Philadelphia Phillies
(AL) Roger Clemens, Boston Red Sox
1988 (NL) Orel Hershiser, Los Angeles Dodgers
(AL) Frank Viola, Minnesota Twins
1989 (NL) Mark Davis, San Diego Padres
(AL) Bret Saberhagen, Kansas City Royals
1990 (NL) Doug Drabek, Pittsburgh Pirates
(AL) Bob Welch, Oakland A's
1991 (NL) Tom Glavine, Atlanta Braves
(AL) Roger Clemens, Boston Red Sox
1992 (NL) Greg Maddux, Chicago Cubs
(AL) Dennis Eckersley, Oakland A's

(1) One award, 1956–66

Most Valuable Player, 1931–92[1]

National League	American League
1931[1] Frank Frisch, St. Louis Cardinals	Lefty Grove, Philadelphia Athletics
1932 Chuck Klein, Philadelphia Phillies	Jimmie Foxx, Philadelphia Athletics
1933 Carl Hubbell, New York Giants	Jimmie Foxx, Philadelphia Athletics
1934 Dizzy Dean, St. Louis Cardinals	Mickey Cochrane, Detroit Tigers
1935 Gabby Hartnett, Chicago Cubs	Hank Greenberg, Detroit Tigers
1936 Carl Hubbell, New York Giants	Lou Gehrig, New York Yankees
1937 Joe Medwick, St. Louis Cardinals	Charley Gehringer, Detroit Tigers
1938 Ernie Lombardi, Cincinnati Reds	Jimmie Foxx, Boston Red Sox
1939 Bucky Walters, Cincinnati Reds	Joe DiMaggio, New York Yankees
1940 Frank McCormick, Cincinnati Reds	Hank Greenberg, Detroit Tigers
1941 Dolph Camilli, Brooklyn Dodgers	Joe DiMaggio, New York Yankees
1942 Mort Cooper, St. Louis Cardinals	Joe Gordon, New York Yankees
1943 Stan Musial, St. Louis Cardinals	Spud Chandler, New York Yankees
1944 Marty Marion, St. Louis Cardinals	Hal Newhouser, Detroit Tigers
1945 Phil Cavarretta, Chicago Cubs	Hal Newhouser, Detroit Tigers
1946 Stan Musial, St. Louis Cardinals	Ted Williams, Boston Red Sox
1947 Bob Elliott, Boston Braves	Joe DiMaggio, New York Yankees
1948 Stan Musial, St. Louis Cardinals	Lou Boudreau, Cleveland Indians
1949 Jackie Robinson, Brooklyn Dodgers	Ted Williams, Boston Red Sox
1950 Jim Konstanty, Philadelphia Phillies	Phil Rizzuto, New York Yankees
1951 Roy Campanella, Brooklyn Dodgers	Yogi Berra, New York Yankees
1952 Hank Sauer, Chicago Cubs	Bobby Shantz, Philadelphia Athletics
1953 Roy Campanella, Brooklyn Dodgers	Al Rosen, Cleveland Indians
1954 Willie Mays, New York Giants	Yogi Berra, New York Yankees
1955 Roy Campanella, Brooklyn Dodgers	Yogi Berra, New York Yankees
1956 Don Newcombe, Brooklyn Dodgers	Mickey Mantle, New York Yankees
1958 Ernie Banks, Chicago Cubs	Jackie Jensen, Boston Red Sox
1959 Ernie Banks, Chicago Cubs	Nelson Fox, Chicago White Sox
1960 Dick Groat, Pittsburgh Pirates	Roger Maris, New York Yankees
1961 Frank Robinson, Cincinnati Reds	Roger Maris, New York Yankees
1962 Maury Wills, Los Angeles Dodgers	Mickey Mantle, New York Yankees
1963 Sandy Koufax, Los Angeles Dodgers	Elston Howard, New York Yankees

►

► **National League**   **American League**

1964	Ken Boyer, St. Louis Cardinals	Brooks Robinson, Baltimore Orioles
1965	Willie Mays, San Francisco Giants	Zoilo Versalles, Minnesota Twins
1966	Roberto Clemente, Pittsburgh Pirates	Frank Robinson, Baltimore Orioles
1967	Orlando Cepeda, St. Louis Cardinals	Carl Yastrzemski, Boston Red Sox
1968	Bob Gibson, St. Louis Cardinals	Denny McLain, Detroit Tigers
1969	Willie McCovey, San Francisco Giants	Harmon Killebrew, Minnesota Twins
1971	Joe Torre, St. Louis Cardinals	Vida Blue, Oakland Athletics
1972	Johnny Bench, Cincinnati Reds	Dick Allen, Chicago White Sox
1975	Joe Morgan, Cincinnati Reds	Fred Lynn, Boston Red Sox
1976	Joe Morgan, Cincinnati Reds	Thurman Munson, New York Yankees
1979	Keith Hernandez, St. Louis Cardinals; Willie Stargell, Pittsburgh Pirates	Don Baylor, California Angels
1980	Mike Schmidt, Philadelphia Phillies	George Brett, Kansas City Royals
1981	Mike Schmidt, Philadelphia Phillies	Rollie Fingers, Milwaukee Brewers
1982	Dale Murphy, Atlanta Braves	Robin Yount, Milwaukee Brewers
1983	Dale Murphy, Atlanta Braves	Cal Ripken, Jr., Baltimore Orioles
1984	Ryne Sandberg, Chicago Cubs	Willie Hernandez, Detroit Tigers
1985	Willie McGee, St. Louis Cardinals	Don Mattingly, New York Yankees
1986	Mike Schmidt, Philadelphia Phillies	Roger Clemens, Boston Red Sox
1987	André Dawson, Chicago Cubs	**George Bell, Toronto Blue Jays**
1988	Kirk Gibson, Los Angeles Dodgers	Jose Canseco, Oakland Athletics
1989	Kevin Mitchell, San Francisco Giants	Robin Yount, Milwaukee Brewers
1990	Barry Bonds, Pittsburgh Pirates	Rickey Henderson, Oakland Athletics
1991	Terry Pendleton, Atlanta Braves	Cal Ripken, Jr., Baltimore Orioles
1992	Barry Bonds, Pittsburgh Pirates	Dennis Eckersley, Oakland A's

(1) 1931: First year award voted by Baseball Writers of America.

Batting Champions, 1924–93

Year	National League Player/Club	Pct	Year	American League Player/Club	Pct
1924	Rogers Hornsby, St. Louis	.424	1924	Babe Ruth, New York	.378
1925	Rogers Hornsby, St. Louis	.403	1925	Harry Heilmann, Detroit	.393
1926	Eugene Hargrave, Cincinnati	.353	1926	Heinie Manush, Detroit	.377
1927	Paul Waner, Pittsburgh	.380	1927	Harry Heilmann, Detroit	.398
1928	Rogers Hornsby, Boston	.387	1928	Goose Goslin, Washington	.379
1929	Lefty O'Doul, Philadelphia	.398	1929	Lew Fonseca, Cleveland	.369
1930	Bill Terry, New York	.401	1930	Al Simmons, Philadelphia	.381
1931	Chick Hafey, St. Louis	.349	1931	Al Simmons, Philadelphia	.390
1932	Lefty O'Doul, Brooklyn	.368	1932	Dale Alexander, Detroit-Boston	.367
1933	Charles Klein, Philadelphia	.368	1933	Jimmie Foxx, Philadelphia	.356
1934	Paul Waner, Pittsburgh	.362	1934	Lou Gehrig, New York	.363
1935	Arky Vaughan, Pittsburgh	.385	1935	Buddy Myer, Washington	.349
1936	Paul Waner, Pittsburgh	.373	1936	Luke Appling, Chicago	.388
1937	Joe Medwick, St. Louis	.374	1937	Charlie Gehringer, Detroit	.371
1938	Ernie Lombardi, Cincinnati	.342	1938	Jimmie Foxx, Boston	.349
1939	John Mize, St. Louis	.349	1939	Joe DiMaggio, New York	.381
1940	Debs Garms, Pittsburgh	.355	1940	Joe DiMaggio, New York	.352
1941	Pete Reiser, Brooklyn	.343	1941	Ted Williams, Boston	.406
1942	Ernie Lombardi, Boston	.330	1942	Ted Williams, Boston	.356
1943	Stan Musial, St. Louis	.357	1943	Luke Appling, Chicago	.328
1944	Dixie Walker, Brooklyn	.357	1944	Lou Boudreau, Cleveland	.327
1945	Phil Cavarretta, Chicago	.355	1945	George Stirnweiss, New York	.309
1946	Stan Musial, St. Louis	.365	1946	Mickey Vernon, Washington	.352
1947	Harry Walker, Philadelphia	.363	1947	Ted Williams, Boston	.343
1948	Stan Musial, St. Louis	.376	1948	Ted Williams, Boston	.369
1949	Jackie Robinson, Brooklyn	.342	1949	George Kell, Detroit	.343
1950	Stan Musial, St. Louis	.346	1950	Billy Goodman, Boston	.354
1951	Stan Musial, St. Louis	.355	1951	Ferris Fain, Philadelphia	.344
1952	Stan Musial, St. Louis	.336	1952	Ferris Fain, Philadelphia	.327
1953	Carl Furillo, Brooklyn	.344	1953	Mickey Vernon, Washington	.337
1954	Willie Mays, New York	.345	1954	Roberto Avila, Cleveland	.341 ►

▶	1955	Richie Ashburn, Philadelphia	.338		1955	Al Kaline, Detroit	.340
	1956	Hank Aaron, Milwaukee	.328		1956	Mickey Mantle, New York	.353
	1957	Stan Musial, St. Louis	.351		1957	Ted Williams, Boston	.388
	1958	Richie Ashburn, Philadelphia	.350		1958	Ted Williams, Boston	.328
	1959	Hank Aaron, Milwaukee	.355		1959	Harvey Kuenn, Detroit	.353
	1960	Dick Groat, Pittsburgh	.325		1960	Pete Runnels, Boston	.320
	1961	Roberto Clemente, Pittsburgh	.351		1961	Norm Cash, Detroit	.361
	1962	Tommy Davis, Los Angeles	.346		1962	Pete Runnels, Boston	.326
	1963	Tommy Davis, Los Angeles	.326		1963	Carl Yastrzemski, Boston	.321
	1964	Roberto Clemente, Pittsburgh	.339		1964	Tony Oliva, Minnesota	.323
	1965	Roberto Clemente, Pittsburgh	.329		1965	Tony Oliva, Minnesota	.321
	1966	Matty Alou, Pittsburgh	.342		1966	Frank Robinson, Baltimore	.316
	1967	Roberto Clemente, Pittsburgh	.357		1967	Carl Yastrzemski, Boston	.326
	1968	Pete Rose, Cincinnati	.335		1968	Carl Yastrzemski, Boston	.301
	1969	Pete Rose, Cincinnati	.348		1969	Rod Carew, Minnesota	.332
	1970	Rico Carty, Atlanta	.366		1970	Alex Johnson, California	.329
	1971	Joe Torre, St. Louis	.363		1971	Tony Oliva, Minnesota	.337
	1972	Billy Williams, Chicago	.333		1972	Rod Carew, Minnesota	.318
	1973	Pete Rose, Cincinnati	.338		1973	Rod Carew, Minnesota	.350
	1974	Ralph Garr, Atlanta	.353		1974	Rod Carew, Minnesota	.364
	1975	Bill Madlock, Chicago	.354		1975	Rod Carew, Minnesota	.359
	1976	Bill Madlock, Chicago	.339		1976	George Brett, Kansas City	.333
	1977	Dave Parker, Pittsburgh	.338		1977	Rod Carew, Minnesota	.388
	1978	Dave Parker, Pittsburgh	.334		1978	Rod Carew, Minnesota	.333
	1979	Keith Hernandez, St. Louis	.344		1979	Fred Lynn, Boston	.333
	1980	Bill Buckner, Chicago	.324		1980	George Brett, Kansas City	.390
	1981	Bill Madlock, Pittsburgh	.341		1981	Carney Lansford, Boston	.336
	1982	**Al Oliver, Montreal**	.331		1982	Willie Wilson, Kansas City	.332
	1983	Bill Madlock, Pittsburgh	.323		1983	Wade Boggs, Boston	.361
	1984	Tony Gwynn, San Diego	.351		1984	Don Mattingly, New York	.343
	1985	Willie McGee, St. Louis	.353		1985	Wade Boggs, Boston	.368
	1986	**Tim Raines, Montreal**	.334		1986	Wade Boggs, Boston	.357
	1987	Tony Gwynn, San Diego	.370		1987	Wade Boggs, Boston	.363
	1988	Tony Gwynn, San Diego	.313		1988	Wade Boggs, Boston	.366
	1989	Tony Gwynn, San Diego	.336		1989	Kirby Puckett, Minnesota	.339
	1990	Willie McGee, St. Louis	.335		1990	George Brett, Kansas City	.329
	1991	Terry Pendleton, Atlanta	.319		1991	Julio Franco, Texas	.341
	1992	Gary Sheffield, San Diego	.330		1992	Edgar Martinez, Seattle	.343
	1993	Andres Galarraga, Colorado	.370		**1993**	**John Olerud, Toronto**	.363

Individual Earned Run Average Leaders, 1901–93

National League

Year	Player/Team	ERA	Year	Player/Team	ERA	Year	Player/Team	ERA
1901	Jesse Tannehill, Pgh	2.18	1922	Rosy Ryan, NY	3.01	1943	Howie Pollet, StL	1.75
1902	Jack Taylor, Chi	1.33	1923	Dolf Luque, Cin	1.93	1944	Ed Heusser, Cin	2.38
1903	Sam Leever, Pgh	2.06	1924	Dazzy Vance, Brooklyn	2.16	1945	Hank Borowy, Chi	2.13
1904	Joe McGinnity, NY	1.61	1925	Dolf Luque, Cin	2.63	1946	Howie Pollet, StL	2.10
1905	Christy Mathewson, NY	1.27	1926	Ray Kremer, Pgh	2.61	1947	Warren Spahn, Bos	2.33
1906	Three Finger Brown, Chi.	1.04	1927	Ray Kremer, Pgh	2.47	1948	Harry Brecheen, StL	2.24
1907	Jack Pfiester, Chi	1.15	1928	Dazzy Vance, Brooklyn	2.09	1949	Dave Koslo, NY	2.50
1908	Christy Mathewson, NY	1.43	1929	Bill Walker, NY	3.09	1950	Jim Hearn, StL/NY	2.49
1909	Christy Mathewson, NY	1.14	1930	Dazzy Vance, Brooklyn	2.61	1951	Chet Nichols, Bos	2.88
1910	George McQuillan, Pha	1.60	1931	Bill Walker, NY	2.26	1952	Hoyt Wilhelm, NY	2.43
1911	Christy Mathewson, NY	1.99	1932	Lon Warneke, Chi	2.37	1953	Warren Spahn, Mil	2.10
1912	Jeff Tesreau, NY	1.96	1933	Carl Hubbell, NY	1.66	1954	Johnny Antonelli, NY	2.30
1913	Christy Mathewson, NY	2.06	1934	Carl Hubbell, NY	2.30	1955	Bob Friend, Pgh	2.83
1914	Bill Doak, StL	1.72	1935	Cy Blanton, Pgh	2.58	1956	Lew Burdette, Mil	2.70
1915	Grover Alexander, Pha	1.22	1936	Carl Hubbell, NY	2.31	1957	Johnny Podres, Brooklyn	2.66
1916	Grover Alexander, Pha	1.55	1937	Jim Turner, Bos	2.38	1958	Stu Miller, SF	2.47
1917	Grover Alexander, Pha	1.86	1938	Bill Lee, Chi	2.66	1959	Sam Jones, SF	2.83
1918	Hippo Vaughn, Chi	1.74	1939	Bucky Walters, Cin	2.29	1960	Mike McCormick, SF	2.70
1919	Grover Alexander, Chi	1.72	1940	Bucky Walters, Cin	2.48	1961	Warren Spahn, Mil	3.02
1920	Grover Alexander, Chi	1.91	1941	Elmer Riddle, Cin	2.24	1962	Sandy Koufax, LA	2.54
1921	Bill Doak, StL	2.59	1942	Mort Cooper, StL	1.78	1963	Sandy Koufax, LA	1.88 ▶

Year	Player/Team	ERA	Year	Player/Team	ERA	Year	Player/Team	ERA
1964	Sandy Koufax, LA	1.74	1974	Buzz Capra, Atl	2.28	1984	Alejandro Pena, LA	2.48
1965	Sandy Koufax, LA	2.04	1975	Randy Jones, SD	2.24	1985	Dwight Gooden, NY	1.53
1966	Sandy Koufax, LA	1.73	1976	John Denny, StL	2.52	1986	Mike Scott, Hou	2.22
1967	Phil Niekro, Atl	1.87	1977	John Candelaria, Pgh	2.34	1987	Nolan Ryan, Hou	2.76
1968	Bob Gibson, StL	1.12	1978	Craig Swan, NY	2.43	1988	Joe Magrane, StL	2.18
1969	Juan Marichal, SF	2.10	1979	J.R. Richard, Hou	2.71	1989	Scott Garrelts, SF	2.28
1970	Tom Seaver, NY	2.81	1980	Don Sutton, LA	2.21	1990	Danny Darwin, Hou	2.21
1971	Tom Seaver, NY	1.76	1981	Nolan Ryan, Hou	1.69	1991	**Dennis Martinez, Mtl**	**2.39**
1972	Steve Carlton, Pha	1.97	1982	**Steve Rogers, Mtl**	**2.40**	1992	Bill Swift, S	2.08
1973	Tom Seaver, NY	2.08	1983	Atlee Hammaker, SF	2.25	1993	Greg Maddux, Atl.	2.36

American League

Year	Player/Team	ERA	Year	Player/Team	ERA	Year	Player/Team	ERA
1901	Cy Young, Bos	1.62	1932	Lefty Grove, Pha	2.84	1963	Gary Peters, Chi	2.33
1902	Ed Siever, Det	1.91	1933	Monte Pearson, Cle	2.33	1964	Dean Chance, LA	1.65
1903	Earl Moor, Cle	1.77	1934	Lefty Gomez, NY	2.33	1965	Sam McDowell, Cle	2.18
1904	Addie Joss, Cle	1.59	1935	Lefty Grove, Bos	2.70	1966	Gary Peters, Chi	1.98
1905	Rube Waddell, Pha	1.48	1936	Lefty Grove, Bos	2.81	1967	Joel Horlen, Chi	2.06
1906	Doc White, Chi	1.52	1937	Lefty Gomez, NY	2.33	1968	Luis Tiant, Cle	1.60
1907	Ed Walsh, Chi	1.60	1938	Lefty Grove, Bos	3.08	1969	Dick Bosman, Wash	2.19
1908	Addie Joss, Cle	1.16	1939	Lefty Grove, Bos	2.54	1970	Diego Segui, Oak	2.56
1909	Harry Krause, Pha	1.39	1940	Bob Feller, Cle	2.61	1971	Vida Blue, Oak	1.82
1910	Ed Walsh, Chi	1.27	1941	Thornton Lee, Chi	2.37	1972	Luis Tiant, Bos	1.91
1911	Vean Gregg, Cle	1.81	1942	Ted Lyons, Chi	2.10	1973	Jim Palmer, Bal	2.40
1912	Walter Johnson, Wash	1.39	1943	Spud Chandler, NY	1.64	1974	Catfish Hunter, Oak	2.49
1913	Walter Johnson, Wash	1.09	1944	Dizzy Trout, Det	2.12	1975	Jim Palmer, Bal	2.09
1914	Dutch Leonard, Bos	1.01	1945	Al Newhouser, Det	1.81	1976	Mark Fidrych, Det	2.34
1915	Smoky Joe Wood, Bos	1.49	1946	Al Newhouser, Det	1.94	1977	Frank Tanana, Cal	2.54
1916	Babe Ruth, Bos	1.75	1947	Spud Chandler, NY	2.46	1978	Ron Guidry, NY	1.74
1917	Eddie Cicotte, Chi	1.53	1948	Gene Bearden, Cle	2.43	1979	Ron Guidry, NY	2.78
1918	Walter Johnson, Wash	1.27	1949	Mel Parnell, Bos	2.77	1980	Rudy May, NY	2.47
1919	Walter Johnson, Wash	1.49	1950	Early Wynn, Cle	3.20	1981	Steve McCatty, Oak	2.32
1920	Bob Shawkey, NY	2.45	1951	Saul Rogovin, Det/Chi	2.78	1982	Rick Sutcliffe, Cle	2.96
1921	Red Faber, Chi	2.48	1952	Allie Reynolds, NY	2.06	1983	Rick Honeycutt, Tex	2.42
1922	Red Faber, Chi	2.80	1953	Ed Lopat, NY	2.42	1984	Mike Boddicker, Bal	2.79
1923	Stan Coveleski, Cle	2.76	1954	Mike Garcia, Cle	2.64	1985	**Dave Stieb, Tor**	**2.48**
1924	Walter Johnson, Wash	2.72	1955	Billy Pierce, Chi	1.97	1986	Roger Clemens, Bos	2.48
1925	Stan Coveleski, Cle	2.84	1956	Whitey Ford, NY	2.47	1987	**Jimmy Key, Tor**	**2.76**
1926	Lefty Grove, Pha	2.51	1957	Bobby Shantz, NY	2.45	1988	Allan Anderson, Min	2.45
1927	Wilcy Moore, NY	2.28	1958	Whitey Ford, NY	2.01	1989	Bret Saberhagen, KC	2.16
1928	Garland Braxton, Wash	2.51	1959	Hoyt Wilhelm, Bal	2.19	1990	Roger Clemens, Bos	1.93
1929	Lefty Grove, Pha	2.81	1960	Frank Baumann, Chi	2.67	1991	Roger Clemens, Bos	2.62
1930	Lefty Grove, Pha	2.54	1961	Dick Donovan, Wash	2.40	1992	Roger Clemens, Bos	2.41
1931	Lefty Grove, Pha	2.06	1962	Hank Aguirre, Det	2.21	1993	Kevin Appier, KC	2.56

Source: *The Baseball Encyclopedia*

Montreal Expos Year-By-Year Record

Year	Won	Lost	Pct.	Pos.	GB	Home Attendance	Manager
1969	52	110	.321	6th	48	1 212 608	Gene Mauch
1970	73	89	.451	6th	16	1 424 683	Gene Mauch
1971	71	90	.441	5th	25¹/2	1 290 963	Gene Mauch
1972	70	86	.449	5th	26¹/2	1 142 145	Gene Mauch
1973	79	83	.488	4th	3¹/2	1 246 863	Gene Mauch
1974	79	82	.491	4th	8¹/2	1 019 134	Gene Mauch
1975	75	87	.463	5th	17¹/2	908 292	Gene Mauch
1976	55	107	.340	6th	46	646 704	K. Kuehl/C. Fox
1977	75	87	.463	5th	26	1 433 757	Dick Williams
1978	76	86	.469	4th	14	1 427 007	Dick Williams
1979	95	65	.594	2nd	8	2 102 173	Dick Williams
1980	90	72	.556	2nd	1	2 208 175	Dick Williams
1981	60	48	.556	—	—	1 534 564	Dick Williams/Jim Fanning
1st half	30	25	.545	3rd	4	—	
2nd half	30	23	.566	1st	+¹/2	—	

►

▶ | | | | | | | | |
|---|---|---|---|---|---|---|---|
| **1982** . . . . 86 | 76 | .531 | 3rd | 6 | 2 318 292 | Jim Fanning |
| **1983** . . . . 82 | 80 | .506 | 3rd | 8 | 2 320 651 | Bill Virdon |
| **1984** . . . . 78 | 83 | .484 | 5th | 18 | 1 606 531 | BillVirdon/Jim Fanning |
| **1985** . . . . 84 | 77 | .522 | 3rd | 16½ | 1 502 494 | Buck Rodgers |
| **1986** . . . . 78 | 83 | .484 | 4th | 29½ | 1 128 981 | Buck Rodgers |
| **1987** . . . . 91 | 71 | .562 | 3rd | 4 | 1 850 324 | Buck Rodgers |
| **1988** . . . . 81 | 81 | .500 | 3rd | 20 | 1 478 659 | Buck Rodgers |
| **1989** . . . . 81 | 81 | .500 | 4th | 12 | 1 783 533 | Buck Rodgers |
| **1990** . . . . 85 | 77 | .525 | 3rd | 10 | 1 421 388 | Buck Rodgers |
| **1991** . . . . 70 | 91 | .441 | 6th | 26½ | 978 045 | Buck Rodgers/Tom Runnells |
| **1992** . . . . 87 | 75 | .537 | 2nd | 9 | 1 731 566 | Tom Runnells/Felipe Alou |
| **1993** . . . . . . 94 | 68 | .580 | 2nd | 3 | 1 641 437 | Felipe Alou |

Montreal Expos Individual Statistics, 1993

Batters

	AVG	OBA	AB	R	H	2B	3B	HR	RBI	BB	SO	SB	CS	E
Pride	.444	.444	9	3	4	1	1	1	5	0	3	1	0	0
Montoyo	.400	.400	5	1	2	1	0	0	3	0	0	0	0	0
Stairs	.375	.375	8	1	3	1	0	0	2	0	1	0	0	0
Grissom	.298	.351	630	104	188	27	2	19	95	52	76	53	10	7
DeShields	.295	.389	481	75	142	17	7	2	29	72	64	43	10	11
Lansing	.287	.352	491	64	141	29	1	3	45	46	56	23	5	24
Alou	.286	.340	482	70	138	29	6	18	85	38	53	17	6	4
Frazier	.286	.340	189	27	54	7	1	1	16	16	24	17	2	2
Walker	.265	.371	490	85	130	24	5	22	86	80	76	29	7	6
Berry	.261	.348	299	50	78	15	2	14	49	41	70	12	2	15
R. White	.260	.321	73	9	19	3	1	2	15	7	16	1	2	0
Fletcher	.255	.320	396	33	101	20	1	9	60	34	40	0	0	8
Colbrunn	.255	.282	153	15	39	9	0	4	23	6	33	4	2	2
Ready	.254	.367	134	22	34	8	1	1	10	23	8	2	1	8
Cordero	.248	.308	475	56	118	32	2	10	58	34	60	12	3	36
Vanderwal	.233	.320	215	34	50	7	4	5	30	27	30	6	3	4
Spehr	.230	.281	87	14	20	6	0	2	10	6	20	2	0	9
Floyd	.226	.226	31	3	7	0	0	1	2	0	9	0	0	0
D. White	.224	.269	49	6	11	3	0	2	4	2	12	2	0	1
Bolick	.211	.298	213	25	45	13	0	4	24	23	37	1	0	8
Marrero	.210	.326	81	10	17	5	1	1	4	14	16	1	3	2
Laker	.198	.222	86	3	17	2	1	0	7	2	16	2	0	2
Wood	.192	.276	26	4	5	1	0	0	3	3	3	0	0	0
Siddall	.100	.143	20	0	2	1	0	0	1	1	5	0	0	0
McIntosh	.095	.095	21	2	2	1	0	0	2	0	7	0	0	0
Team Totals	**.257**	**.326**	**5 493**	**732**	**1 410**	**270**	**36**	**122**	**682**	**542**	**860**	**228**	**56**	**159**

AVG = batting average; OBA = on base average; AB = times at bat; R = runs; H = hits; 2B = doubles; 3B = triples; HR = home runs; RBI = runs batted in; BB = walks; SO = strikeouts; SB = stolen bases; CS = caught stealing; E = errors.

Pitchers

	W	L	ERA	G	GS	SV	IP	H	R	ER	HR	BB	SO
Wetteland	9	3	1.37	70	0	43	85.1	58	17	13	3	28	113
Boucher	3	1	1.91	5	5	0	28.1	24	7	6	1	6	14
Fassero	12	5	2.29	56	15	1	149.2	119	50	38	7	54	140
Rueter	8	0	2.73	14	14	0	85.2	85	33	26	5	18	31
Rojas	5	8	2.95	66	0	10	88.1	80	39	29	6	30	48
Looney	0	0	3.00	3	1	0	6.0	8	2	2	0	2	7
Scott	7	2	3.01	56	0	1	71.2	69	28	24	4	34	65
Hill	9	7	3.23	28	28	0	183.2	163	84	66	7	74	90
Young	1	0	3.38	4	0	0	5.1	4	2	2	1	0	3
Martinez	15	9	3.85	35	34	1	224.2	211	110	96	27	64	138
Heredia	4	2	3.92	20	9	2	57.1	66	28	25	4	14	40
Nabholz	9	8	4.09	26	21	0	116.2	100	57	53	9	63	74
Shaw	2	7	4.14	55	8	0	95.2	91	47	44	12	32	50
Barnes	2	6	4.41	52	8	3	100.0	105	53	49	9	48	60
Gardiner	2	3	5.21	24	2	0	38.0	40	28	22	3	19	21
Risley	0	0	6.00	2	0	0	3.0	2	3	2	1	2	2
Henry	3	9	6.12	30	16	0	103.0	135	76	70	15	28	47 ▶

Jones	4	1	6.35	12	6	0	39.2	47	34	28	6	9	21
Aldred	1	0	9.00	8	0	0	12.0	19	14	12	2	10	9
Valdez	0	0	9.00	4	0	0	3.0	4	4	3	1	1	2
Walton	0	0	9.53	4	0	0	5.2	11	6	6	1	3	0
Team Totals	**94**	**68**	**3.55**	**163**	**163**	**61**	**1 456.2**	**1 369**	**682**	**574**	**119**	**521**	**934**

W = games won; L = games lost; ERA = earned run average; G = games played in; GS = games started; SV = saves; IP = innings pitched; H = hits allowed; R = runs allowed; ER = earned runs; HR = home runs allowed; BB = walks allowed; SO = strikeouts.

Montreal Expos Team Records

Batting

Single Season	Career Leaders
Batting Average: Tim Raines, 1986, .334	**Batting Average:** Al Oliver, .315
At Bats: Warren Cromartie, 1979, 659	**At Bats:** Tim Wallach, 6 529
Games: Rusty Staub, 1971, 162; Ken Singleton, 1973, 162; Warren Cromartie, 1980, 162	**Games:** Tim Wallach, 1 767
Hits: Al Oliver, 1982, 204	**Hits:** Tim Wallach, 1 694
Runs: Tim Raines, 1983, 133	**Runs:** Tim Raines, 934
Singles: Tim Raines, 1986, 140	**Singles:** Tim Raines, 1,148
Doubles: Warren Cromartie, 1979, 46	**Doubles:** Tim Wallach, 360
Triples: Rodney Scott, 1980, 13; Tim Raines, 1985, 13; Mitch Webster, 1986, 13	**Triples:** Tim Raines, 81
Home Runs: Andre Dawson, 1983, 32	**Home Runs:** Andre Dawson, 225
Runs Batted In: Tim Wallach, 1987, 123	**Runs Batted In:** Tim Wallach, 905
Total Bases: Andre Dawson, 1983, 341	**Total Bases:** Tim Wallach, 2 728
Slugging Average: Andre Dawson, 1981, .553	
On-Base Average: Tim Raines, 1987, .431	
Stolen Bases: Ron LeFlore, 1980, 97	**Stolen Bases:** Tim Raines, 634
Strikeouts: Andres Galarraga, 1990, 169	
Walks: Ken Singleton, 1973, 123	**Walks:** Tim Raines, 775
Hit By Pitch: Ron Hunt, 1971, 50	
Hitting Streak: Delino Deshields, 1993, 21	
Pinch Hits: Jose Morales, 1976, 25	

Pitching

Single Season	Career Leaders
Games: Mike Marshall, 1973, 92	**Games:** Tim Burke, 425
Games Started: Steve Rogers, 1977, 40	**Games Started:** Steve Rogers, 393
Complete Games: Bill Stoneman, 1971, 20	**Complete Games:** Steve Rogers, 129
Innings Pitched: Steve Rogers, 1977, 302	**Innings Pitched:** Steve Rogers, 2 839
Wins: Ross Grimsley, 1978, 20	**Wins:** Steve Rogers, 158
Losses: Steve Rogers, 1974, 22	**Losses:** Steve Rogers, 152
Saves: John Wetteland, 1993, 4.3	**Saves:** Jeff Reardon, 152
Earned Run Average: Mark Langston, 1989, 2.39; Dennis Martinez, 1991, 2.39	**Earned Run Average:** Dennis Martinez, 2.93
Earned Run Average (Relief Pitcher): Dale Murray, 1974, 1.03	
Shutouts: Bill Stoneman, 1969, 5; Steve Rogers, 1979, 5; Steve Rogers, 1983, 5; Dennis Martinez, 1991, 5	**Shutouts:** Steve Rogers, 37
Strikeouts: Bill Stoneman, 1971, 251	**Strikeouts:** Steve Rogers, 1 621
Walks: Bill Stoneman, 1971, 146	**Walks:** Steve Rogers, 876
Home Runs Allowed: Carl Morton, 1970, 27; Steve Renko, 1970, 27; Bill Gullickson, 1984, 27	
Hit Batsmen: Bill Stoneman, 1970, 14	

Source: *Montreal Expos*

Montreal Expos Player of the Year

1969	Rusty Staub	1975	Gary Carter	1981	Andre Dawson	1986	Tim Raines
1970	Carl Morton	1976	Woodie Fryman	1982	Al Oliver	1987	Tim Wallach
1971	Ron Hunt	1977	Gary Carter	1983	Andre Dawson;	1988	Andres Galarraga
1972	Mike Marshall	1978	Ross Grimsley		Tim Raines (tie)	1989	Tim Wallach
1973	Mike Marshall	1979	Larry Parrish	1984	Gary Carter	1990	Tim Wallach
1974	Willie Davis	1980	Gary Carter	1985	Tim Raines	1991	Dennis Martinez
						1992	Larry Walker

Toronto Blue Jays Year-By-Year Record

Year	Won	Lost	Pct.	Pos.	GB	Home Attendance	Manager
1977 54	107	.335	7th	45$\frac{1}{2}$	1 701 052	Roy Hartsfield
1978 59	102	.366	7th	50	1 562 585	Roy Hartsfield
1979 53	109	.327	7th	50$\frac{1}{2}$	1 431 651	Roy Hartsfield
1980 67	95	.414	7th	36	1 400 327	Bob Mattick
1981 37	69	.349	—	—	755 083	Bob Mattick
1st half 16	42	.276	7th	19	—	
2nd half . . . 21	27	.438	7th	7$\frac{1}{2}$	—	
1982 78	84	.481	6th[1]	17	1 275 978	Bobby Cox
1983 89	73	.549	4th	9	1 930 415	Bobby Cox
1984 89	73	.549	2nd	15	2 110 009	Bobby Cox
1985 99	62	.615	1st	+2	2 468 925	Bobby Cox
1986 86	76	.531	4th	9$\frac{1}{2}$	2 455 477	Jimy Williams
1987 96	66	.593	2nd	2	2 778 459	Jimy Williams
1988 87	75	.537	3rd	2	2 595 175	Jimy Williams
1989 89	73	.549	1st	+2	3 375 573	Williams/Cito Gaston
1990 86	76	.531	2nd	2	3 885 284	Cito Gaston
1991 91	71	.562	1st	+7	4 001 526	Cito Gaston
1992 96	66	.593	1st	+4	4 028 318	Cito Gaston
1993 95	67	.586	1st	+7	4 057 947	Cito Gaston

(1) Tied.

Toronto Blue Jays Individual Statistics, 1993

Batters

	AVG	OBA	AB	R	H	2B	3B	HR	RBI	BB	SO	SB	CS	E
Olerud	.363	.473	551	109	200	54	2	24	107	114	65	0	2	10
Molitor	.332	.402	636	121	211	37	5	22	111	77	71	22	4	3
Alomar	.326	.408	589	109	192	35	6	17	93	80	67	55	15	14
Fernandez	.306	.361	353	45	108	18	9	4	50	31	26	15	8	7
Henderson	.289	.432	481	114	139	22	2	21	59	120	65	53	8	7
Martinez	.286	.333	14	2	4	0	0	1	3	1	7	0	0	0
White	.273	.341	598	116	163	42	6	15	52	57	127	34	4	3
Butler	.271	.375	48	8	13	4	0	0	2	7	12	2	2	1
Sprague	.260	.310	546	50	142	31	1	12	73	32	85	1	0	17
Borders	.254	.285	488	38	124	30	0	9	55	20	66	2	2	13
Carter	.254	.312	603	92	153	33	5	33	121	47	113	8	3	8
Coles	.253	.319	194	26	49	9	1	4	26	16	29	1	1	7
Knorr	.248	.309	101	11	25	3	2	4	20	9	29	0	0	0
Jackson	.216	.250	176	15	38	8	0	5	19	8	53	0	2	1
Canate	.213	.309	47	12	10	0	0	1	3	6	15	1	1	0
Coles	.253	.319	194	26	49	9	1	4	26	16	29	1	1	7
Griffin	.211	.235	95	15	20	3	0	0	3	3	13	0	0	4
T. Ward	.192	.287	167	20	32	4	2	4	28	23	26	3	3	1
Schofield	.191	.294	110	11	21	1	2	0	5	16	25	3	0	4
Cedeno	.174	.188	46	5	8	0	0	0	7	1	10	1	0	1
Sojo	.170	.231	47	5	8	2	0	0	6	4	2	0	0	2
Delgado	.000	.500	1	0	0	0	0	0	0	1	0	0	0	0
Green	.000	.000	6	0	0	0	0	0	0	0	1	0	0	0
Team Totals	**.279**	**.350**	**5 579**	**847**	**1 556**	**317**	**42**	**159**	**796**	**588**	**861**	**170**	**49**	**107**

AVG = batting average; OBA = on base average; AB = times at bat; R = runs; H = hits; 2B = doubles; 3B = triples; HR = home runs; RBI = runs batted in; BB = walks; SO = strikeouts; SB = stolen bases; CS = caught stealing; E = errors.

Pitchers

	W	L	ERA	G	GS	SV	IP	H	R	ER	HR	BB	SO
Dayley	0	0	0.00	2	0	0	0.2	1	2	0	0	4	2
D. Ward	2	3	2.13	71	0	45	71.2	49	17	17	4	25	97
Eichhorn	3	1	2.72	54	0	0	72.2	76	26	22	3	22	47
Cox	7	6	3.12	44	0	2	83.2	73	31	29	8	29	84
Castillo	3	2	3.38	51	0	0	50.2	44	19	19	4	22	28
Hentgen	19	9	3.87	34	32	0	216.1	215	103	93	27	74	122
Guzman	14	3	3.99	33	33	0	221.0	221	107	98	17	110	194
Flener	0	0	4.05	6	0	0	6.2	7	3	3	0	4	2
Leiter	9	6	4.11	34	12	2	105.0	93	52	48	8	56	66
Williams	3	1	4.38	30	0	0	37.0	40	18	18	2	22	24
Stewart	12	8	4.44	26	26	0	162.0	146	86	80	23	72	96
Timlin	4	2	4.69	54	0	1	55.2	63	32	29	7	27	49
Stottlemyre	11	12	4.84	30	28	0	176.2	204	107	95	11	69	98
Brow	1	1	6.00	6	3	0	18.0	19	15	12	2	10	7
Morris	7	12	6.19	27	27	0	152.2	189	116	105	18	65	103
Team Totals	**95**	**67**	**4.21**	**162**	**162**	**50**	**1 441.1**	**1 441**	**742**	**674**	**134**	**620**	**1 023**

W = games won; L = games lost; ERA = earned run average; G = games played in; GS = games started; SV = saves; IP = innings pitched; H = hits allowed; R = runs allowed; ER = earned runs; HR = home runs allowed; BB = walks allowed; SO = strikeouts.

Toronto Blue Jays Team Records

Batting

Single Season

Batting Average: John Olerud, 1993, .363

At Bats: Tony Fernandez, 1986, 687

Games: Tony Fernandez, 1986, 163

Hits: Tony Fernandez, 1986, 213

Runs: Paul Molitor, 1993, 121

Singles: Tony Fernandez, 1986, 161

Doubles: John Olerud, 1993, 54

Triples: Tony Fernandez, 1990, 17

Home Runs: George Bell, 1987, 47

Runs Batted In: George Bell, 1987, 134

Total Bases: George Bell, 1987, 369

Slugging Average: George Bell, 1987, .605

On-Base Average: John Olerud, 1993, .473

Stolen Bases: Dave Collins, 1984, 60

Strikeouts: Fred McGriff, 1988, 149

Walks: Fred McGriff, 1989, 119

Hit By Pitch: Joe Carter, 1992, 11

Hitting Streak: John Olerud, 1993, 26

Career Leaders

Batting Average: Roberto Alomar, 3.10

At Bats: Lloyd Moseby, 5,124

Games: Lloyd Moseby, 1,392

Hits: Lloyd Moseby, 1,319

Runs: Lloyd Moseby, 768

Singles: Lloyd Moseby, 868

Doubles: Lloyd Moseby, 242

Triples: Tony Fernandez, 70

Home Runs: George Bell, 202

Runs Batted In: George Bell, 740

Total Bases: George Bell, 2,201

Slugging Average: Fred McGriff, .530

On-Base Average: Fred McGriff, .391

Stolen Bases: Lloyd Moseby, 255

Strikeouts: Lloyd Moseby, 1,015

Walks: Lloyd Moseby, 547

Hit By Pitch: Lloyd Moseby, 50

Pitching

Single Season	Career Leaders
Games: Mark Eichhorn, 1987, 89	**Games:** Tom Henke, 446
Games Started: Jim Clancy, 1982, 40	**Games Started:** Dave Stieb, 405
Complete Games: Dave Stieb, 1982, 19	**Complete Games:** Dave Stieb, 103
Innings Pitched: Dave Stieb, 1982, 288.1	**Innings Pitched:** Dave Stieb, 2 822.2
Wins: Jack Morris, 1992, 21	**Wins:** Dave Stieb, 174
Losses: Jerry Garvin, 1977, 18; Phil Huffman, 1979, 18	**Losses:** Jim Clancy, 140
Saves: Duane Ward, 1993, 45	**Saves:** Tom Henke, 217
Earned Run Average: Dave Stieb, 1985, 2.48	**Earned Run Average:** Tom Henke, 2.48
Shutouts: Dave Stieb, 1982, 5	**Shutouts:** Dave Stieb, 30
Strikeouts: Dave Stieb, 1984, 198	**Strikeouts:** Dave Stieb, 1 631
Walks: Jim Clancy, 1980, 128	**Walks:** Dave Stieb, 1 003
Home Runs Allowed: Jerry Garvin, 1977, 33	**Home Runs Allowed:** Jim Clancy, 219
Hit Batsmen: Dave Stieb, 1986, 15	**Hit Batsmen:** Dave Stieb, 124

Source: *Toronto Blue Jays*

Toronto Blue Jays Player of the Year

1977	Bob Bailor	1983	Lloyd Moseby	1989	George Bell
1978	Bob Bailor	1984	Dave Collins	1990	Kelly Gruber
1979	Alfredo Griffin	1985	Jesse Barfield	1991	Roberto Alomar
1980	John Mayberry	1986	Jesse Barfield	1992	Roberto Alomar
1981	Dave Stieb	1987	George Bell		
1982	Damaso Garcia	1988	Fred McGriff		

Canadian Players in Major League Baseball, 1993

Player	G	AB	R	H	2B	3B	HR	RBI	BA	OBA	SA
Larry Walker											
1993 Montreal	138	490	85	130	24	5	22	86	.265	.371	.467
Career	571	1971	292	539	103	14	80	298	.273	.351	.462
Kevin Reimer											
1993 Milwaukee	125	437	53	109	22	1	13	60	.249	.303	.394
Career	478	1455	162	376	85	4	52	204	.258	.321	.430
Rob Ducey											
1993 Texas	27	85	15	24	6	3	2	9	.282	.351	.494
Career	241	464	69	113	26	6	4	41	.244	.318	.351
Joe Siddall[1]											
1993 Montreal	19	20	0	2	0	0	0	1	.100	.143	.100
Rob Butler[1]											
1993 Toronto	17	48	8	13	4	0	0	2	.271	.375	.354

Pitcher	W	L	Pct.	G	ShO	Sv	IP	H	BB	SO	ERA
Real Cormier											
1993 St. Louis	7	6	.538	38	0	0	145.1	163	27	75	4.33
Career	21	21	.500	80	0	0	399.0	431	68	230	3.99
Kirk McCaskill											
1993 Chicago (AL)	4	8	.333	30	0	2	113.2	144	36	65	5.23
Career	94	95	.497	256	11	2	1543.2	1528	579	888	4.01
Mike Gardiner											
1993 Montreal/Detroit	2	3	.400	.37	0	0	49.1	52	26	2.5	4.93
Career	15	25	.375	89	0	0	322.2	340	136	201	5.05 ▶

▶ Paul Quantrill

1993 Boston	6	12	.333	49	0	1	138.0	151	44	66	3.91
Career	8	15	.348	76	0	2	187.1	206	59	90	3.46

Denis Boucher

1993 Montreal	3	1	.750	5	0	0	28.1	24	3	14	1.91
Career	5	10	.332	25	0	0	127.1	146	47	60	5.23

Steve Wilson

1993 Los Angeles	1	0	1.00	25	0	1	25.2	30	14	23	4.56
Career	13.25	18	.419	205	0	6	345.1	348	130	252	4.40

Vince Horsman

1993 Oakland	2	0	1.00	40	0	1	25.0	25	15	17	5.40
Career	4	1	.800	102	0	1	72.1	66	39	37	3.36

(1) First year in 1993.

Career Records of Some Canadian Major League Players of the Past

Player	G	AB	R	H	2B	3B	HR	RBI	BA	OBA	SA
Jeff Heath, 1936–49	1 383	4 937	777	1 447	279	102	194	887	.293	.370	.509
Terry Puhl, 1977–90	1 531	4 855	676	1 361	226	56	62	435	.280	.350	.388
George Gibson, 1905–18	1 213	3 776	295	893	142	49	15	335	.236	.294	.312
Tip O'Neill, 1883–92	1 054	4 255	880	1 386	222	92	52	435	.326	.392	.458
Pete Ward, 1962–70	973	3 060	345	776	136	17	98	427	.254	.342	.405

Pitcher	W	L	Pct.	G	ShO	Sv	IP	H	BB	SO	ERA
Ferguson Jenkins, 1965–83	284	226	.557	664	49	7	4 498	4 142	997	3 192	3.34
Reggie Cleveland, 1969–81	105	106	.498	203	12	25	1 809	1813	543	930	4.01
Russ Ford, 1909–15	99	71	.582	199	15	9	1 487	1 318	376	710	2.59
Phil Marchildon, 1942–50[1]	68	75	.476	185	6	2	1 214	1084	684	4 81	3.93
Oscar Judd, 1941–48	40	51	.440	161	4	7	770	744	397	304	3.90

G: Games played. AB: At bats. R: Runs. H: Hits. 2B: Doubles. 3B: Triples. HR: Home runs. RBI: Runs batted in. BA: Batting average. OBA: On-base percentage. SA: Slugging average.

W: Wins. L: Losses. Pct.: Percentage. G: Games pitched. ShO: Shutouts. Sv: Saves. IP: Innings pitched. H: Hits allowed. BB: Walks. K: Strikeouts. ERA: Earned run average.

(1) Marchildon was in Canadian Armed Forces in 1943–44

FOOTBALL

Canadian Football League

(1992 Standings)

	W	L	T	F	A	Pts		W	L	T	F	A	Pts
Calgary	13	5	0	607	430	26	Winnipeg*	11	7	0	507	499	22
Edmonton	10	8	0	552	513	20	Hamilton	11	7	0	536	514	22
Saskatchewan	9	9	0	505	545	18	Ottawa	9	9	0	484	439	18
B.C.	3	15	0	472	667	6	Toronto	6	12	0	469	523	12

Semi-final: Edmonton 22, Saskatchewan 20
Final: Calgary 23, Edmonton 22

Semi-final: Hamilton 29, Ottawa 28
Final: Winnipeg 59, Hamilton 11

Grey Cup: Calgary 24, Winnipeg 10

*Winnipeg was awarded first place on the basis of more points scored in head-to-head games (115-106).

The Grey Cup

The Grey Cup was donated in 1909 by Governor General Earl Grey for the "Rugby Football Championship of Canada." Since 1954, only teams in the Canadian Foot-ball League have challenged for the trophy, with the winners of the East and West divisions meeting in the championship game.

1909 . . . . . U. of Toronto 26, Parkdale 6
1910 . . . . . U. of Toronto 16, Ham. Tigers 7
1911 . . . . . U. of Toronto 14, Toronto 7
1912 . . . . . Ham. Alerts 11, Toronto 4
1913 . . . . . Ham. Tigers 44, Parkdale 2
1914 . . . . . Toronto 14, U. of Toronto 2
1915 . . . . . Ham. Tigers 13, Tor. R.A.A. 7
1916–19 . . No games held.
1920 . . . . . U. of Toronto 16, Toronto 3
1921 . . . . . Toronto 23, Edmonton 0
1922 . . . . . Queen's U. 13, Edmonton 1
1923 . . . . . Queen's U. 54, Regina 0
1924 . . . . . Queen's U. 11, Balmy Beach 3
1925 . . . . . Ott. Senators 24, Winnipeg 1
1926 . . . . . Ott. Senators 10, U. of Toronto 7
1927 . . . . . Balmy Beach 9, Ham. Tigers 6
1928 . . . . . Ham. Tigers 30, Regina 0
1929 . . . . . Ham. Tigers 14, Regina 3
1930 . . . . . Balmy Beach 11, Regina 6
1931 . . . . . Mtl. A.A.A. 22, Regina 0
1932 . . . . . Ham. Tigers 25, Regina 6
1933 . . . . . Toronto 4, Sarnia 3
1934 . . . . . Sarnia 20, Regina 12
1935 . . . . . Winnipeg 18, Ham. Tigers 12
1936 . . . . . Sarnia 26, Ott. R.R. 20
1937 . . . . . Toronto 4, Winnipeg 3
1938 . . . . . Toronto 30, Winnipeg 7
1939 . . . . . Winnipeg 8, Ottawa 7
1940[1] . . . . Ottawa 12, Balmy Beach 5
. . . . Ottawa 8, Balmy Beach 2
1941 . . . . . Winnipeg 18, Ottawa 16
1942 . . . . . Tor. R.C.A.F. 8, Win. R.C.A.F. 5
1943 . . . . . Ham. F. Wild 23, Win. R.C.A.F. 14
1944 . . . . . Mtl. St. H.D. Navy 7, Ham. F. Wild 6
1945 . . . . . Toronto 35, Winnipeg 0
1946 . . . . . Toronto 28, Winnipeg 6
1947 . . . . . Toronto 10, Winnipeg 9
1948 . . . . . Calgary 12, Ottawa 7
1949 . . . . . Mtl. Als. 28, Calgary 15
1950 . . . . . Toronto 13, Winnipeg 0
1951 . . . . . Ottawa 21, Saskatchewan 14

1952 . . . . . Toronto 21, Edmonton 11
1953 . . . . . Hamilton 12, Winnipeg 6
1954 . . . . . Edmonton 26, Montreal 25
1955 . . . . . Edmonton 34, Montreal 19
1956 . . . . . Edmonton 50, Montreal 27
1957 . . . . . Hamilton 32, Winnipeg 7
1958 . . . . . Winnipeg 35, Hamilton 28
1959 . . . . . Winnipeg 21, Hamilton 7
1960 . . . . . Ottawa 16, Edmonton 6
1961 . . . . . Winnipeg 21, Hamilton 14
1962 . . . . . Winnipeg 28, Hamilton 27
1963 . . . . . Hamilton 21, British Columbia 10
1964 . . . . . British Columbia 34, Hamilton 24
1965 . . . . . Hamilton 22, Winnipeg 16
1966 . . . . . Saskatchewan 29, Ottawa 14
1967 . . . . . Hamilton 24, Saskatchewan 1
1968 . . . . . Ottawa 24, Calgary 21
1969 . . . . . Ottawa 29, Saskatchewan 11
1970 . . . . . Montreal 23, Calgary 10
1971 . . . . . Calgary 14, Toronto 11
1972 . . . . . Hamilton 13, Saskatchewan 10
1973 . . . . . Ottawa 22, Edmonton 18
1974 . . . . . Montreal 20, Edmonton 7
1975 . . . . . Edmonton 9, Montreal 8
1976 . . . . . Ottawa 23, Saskatchewan 20
1977 . . . . . Montreal 41, Edmonton 6
1978 . . . . . Edmonton 20, Montreal 13
1979 . . . . . Edmonton 17, Montreal 9
1980 . . . . . Edmonton 48, Hamilton 10
1981 . . . . . Edmonton 26, Ottawa 23
1982 . . . . . Edmonton 32, Toronto 16
1983 . . . . . Toronto 18, B.C. 17
1984 . . . . . Winnipeg 47, Hamilton 17
1985 . . . . . B.C. 37, Hamilton 24
1986 . . . . . Hamilton 39, Edmonton 15
1987 . . . . . Edmonton 38, Toronto 36
1988 . . . . . Winnipeg 22, B.C. 21
1989 . . . . . Saskatchewan 43, Hamilton 40
1990 . . . . . Winnipeg 50, Edmonton 11
1991 . . . . . Toronto 36, Calgary 21
1992 . . . . . Calgary 24, Winnipeg 10

(1) A 2-game total point series.

CFL Individual Player Records

(up to the end of the 1992 season)

Most games played: . . . . **288, Ron Lancaster,** Ott/Sask (1960–78)

Most career points: . . . . **2 653, Lui Passaglia,** BC (1976–92)

Most points one season: . . . . **236, Lance Chomyc,** Tor, 1991

Most points one game: . . . . **36, Bob McNamara,** Wpg, Wpg at BC, Oct. 13, 1956

Most touchdowns one season: . . . . **20, Pat Abbruzzi,** Mtl, 1956; **Darrell K. Smith,** Tor, 1990;
Blake Marshall, Edm, 1991; **Jon Volpe,** BC, 1991

Most touchdowns one game: . . . . **6, Bob McNamara,** Wpg, Wpg at BC, Oct. 13, 1956

Most touchdown passes one season: . . . . **40, Peter Liske,** Cal, 1967

Most touchdown passes one game: . . . . **8, Joe Zuger,** Ham, Sask at Ham, Oct. 15, 1962

Most touchdowns scored rushing one season: . . . . **18, Gerry James,** Wpg, 1957; **Jim Germany,** Edm, 1981

Most touchdowns scored rushing one game: . . . . **5, Earl Lunsford,** Cal, Edm at Cal, Sept. 3, 1962

Most touchdowns on pass receptions one season: . . . . **20 , Darrell K. Smith,** Tor, 1990

Most touchdowns on pass receptions one game: . . . . **5, Ernie Pitts,** Wpg, Wpg at Sask, Aug. 29, 1959

Most passes thrown one season: . . . . **770, Kent Austin,** Sask, 1992

Most passes thrown one game: . . . . **65, Kent Austin,** Sask, Edm at Sask, Sept. 15, 1991

Most passes completed one season: . . . . **466, Doug Flutie,** BC, 1991

Most passes completed one game: . . . . **41, Dieter Brock,** Wpg, Wpg at Ott, Oct. 3, 1981

Most yards passed one season: . . . . **6 619, Doug Flutie,** BC, 1991

Most yards passed one game: . . . . **586, Sam Etcheverry,** Mtl, Ham at Mtl, Oct. 16, 1954

Most consecutive pass completions: . . . . **18, Joe Paopao,** BC, Tor at BC, Sept. 22, 1979

Longest pass: . . . . **109 yds, Sam Etcheverry to Hal Patterson,** Mtl, Ham at Mtl, Sept. 22, 1956;
Jerry Keeling to Terry Evanshen, Cal, Cal at Wpg, Sept. 27, 1966

Most yards rushing one season: . . . . **1 896, Willie Burden,** Cal, 1975

Most yards rushing one game: . . . . **287, Ron Stewart,** Ott, Ott at Mtl, Oct. 10, 1960

Longest rushing plays: . . . . **109 yds, George Dixon,** Mtl, Ott at Mtl, Sept. 2, 1963;
Willie Fleming, BC, BC at Edm, Oct. 17, 1964

Most carries one season: . . . . **332, Willie Burden,** Cal, 1975

Most carries one game: . . . . **37, Doyle Orange,** Tor, Ham at Tor, Aug. 13, 1975

Most pass reception yardage one season: . . . . **2 003, Terry Greer,** Tor, 1983

Most pass reception yardage one game: . . . . **338, Hal Patterson,** Mtl, Mtl at Ham, Sept. 29, 1956

Most pass receptions one season: . . . . **118, Allen Pitts,** Cal, 1991

Most pass receptions one game: . . . . **16, Terry Greer,** Tor, Tor at Ott, Aug. 19, 1983

Most combined yards one game: . . . . **401, Raghib Ismail,** Tor, Tor at Ott, July 9, 1992

Most field goals one season: . . . . **59, Dave Ridgway,** Sask, 1990

Most field goals one game: . . . . **8, Dave Ridgway,** Sask, 1984 and 1988

Longest field goals: . . . . **60 yds, Dave Ridgway,** Sask, Wpg at Sask, Sept. 6, 1987

Longest punts: . . . . **108 yds, Zenon Andrusyshyn,** Tor, Tor at Edm, Oct. 23, 1977

Best punting average one season: . . . . **50.2, Lui Passaglia,** BC, 1983

Most interceptions one game: . . . . **5, Rod Hill,** Wpg, Ham at Wpg, Sept 9, 1990

Most interceptions one season: . . . . **15, Al Brenner,** Ham, 1972

Most quarterback sacks one season: . . . . **26.5, James Parker,** BC, 1984

Source: *Canadian Football League*

Leading CFL Quarterbacks, by Year

(by number of yards)

Year	Eastern Division	Yards	Western Division	Yards
1954	Sam Etcheverry, Mtl	3 610	Frank Tripucka, Sask	2 003
1955	Sam Etcheverry, Mtl	3 657	Don Klosterman, Cal	2 405
1956	Sam Etcheverry, Mtl	4 723	Frank Tripucka, Sask	3 274
1957	Sam Etcheverry, Mtl	3 341	Frank Tripucka, Sask	2 589
1958	Sam Etcheverry, Mtl	3 548	Frank Tripucka, Sask	2 766
1959	Sam Etcheverry, Mtl	3 133	Joe Kapp, Cal	2 990
1960	Tobin Rote, Tor	4 247	Joe Kapp, Cal	3 060
1961	Tobin Rote, Tor	3 093	Eagle Day, Cal	1 800
1962	Tobin Rote, Tor	2 532	Joe Kapp, BC	3 279
1963	Russ Jackson, Ott.	2 910	Joe Kapp, BC	3 126
1964	Russ Jackson, Ott	2 156	Joe Kapp, BC	2 816
1965	Russ Jackson, Ott	2 303	Joe Kapp, BC	2 961
1966	Russ Jackson, Ott	2 400	Ron Lancaster, Sask	2 976
1967	Russ Jackson, Ott	3 332	Peter Liske, Cal	4 479
1968	Wally Gabler, Tor	3 242	Peter Liske, Cal	4 333
1969	Russ Jackson, Ott	3 641	Jerry Keeling, Cal	3 179
1970	Gary Wood, Ott	2 759	Ron Lancaster, Sask	2 779
1971	Joe Theismann, Tor	2 440	Don Jonas, Wpg	4 036
1972	Chuck Ealey, Ham	2 573	Don Jonas, Wpg	3 583
1973	Joe Theismann, Tor	2 496	Ron Lancaster, Sask	3 767
1974	Mike Rae, Tor	2 501	Peter Liske, Cal/BC	3 259
1975	Tom Clements, Ott	2 013	Ron Lancaster, Sask	3 545
1976	Tom Clements, Ott	2 856	Ron Lancaster, Sask	3 869
1977	Tom Clements, Ott	2 804	Ron Lancaster, Sask	3 072
1978	Jimmy Jones, Ham	2 060	Dieter Brock, Wpg	3 755
1979	Tony Adams, Tor	2 692	Dieter Brock, Wpg	2 383
1980	Mark Jackson, Tor	3 041	Dieter Brock, Wpg	4 252
1981	Tom Clements, Ham	4 536	Dieter Brock, Wpg	4 796
1982	Tom Clements, Ham	4 706	Warren Moon, Edm	5 000
1983	Conredge Holloway, Tor	3 184	Warren Moon, Edm	5 648
1984	Dieter Brock, Ham	3 966	Tom Clements, Wpg	3 845
1984	Joe Barnes, Mtl	3 432	Roy Dewalt, BC	4 237
1986	Brian Ransom, Mtl	3 204	Rick Johnson, Cal	4 379
1987	Tom Clements, Wpg	4 686	Roy Dewalt, BC	3 855
1988	Gilbert Renfroe, Tor	4 113	Matt Dunigan, BC	3 776
1989	Sean Salisbury, Wpg	4 049	Matt Dunigan, BC	4 509
1990	Tom Burgess, Wpg	3 958	Kent Austin, Sask	4 604
1991	Damon Allen, Ott	4 275	Doug Flutie, BC	6 619
1992	Tom Burgess, Ott.	4 026	Kent Austin, Sask.	6 225

Source: *Canadian Football League*

Leading CFL Pass Receivers, by Year

	Eastern Division	Receptions	Western Division	Receptions
1954	Al Pfeifer, Tor	68	Bud Grant, Wpg	49
1955	Red O'Quinn, Mtl	78	Willie Roberts, Cal	59
1956	Hal Patterson, Mtl	88	Bud Grant, Wpg	63
1957	Red O'Quinn, Mtl	61	Jack Gotta, Cal	39
1958	Red O'Quinn, Mtl	65	Jack Hill, Sask	60
1959	Red O'Quinn, Mtl	53	Ernie Pitts, Wpg	68
1960	Dave Mann, Tor	61	Gene Filipski, Cal	47
	Hal Patterson, Mtl	61		
1961	Dave Mann, Tor	53	Farrell Funston, Wpg	47
1962	Dick Shatto, Tor	47	Tommy Joe Coffey, Edm	65
1963	Dick Shatto, Tor	67	Bobby Taylor, Cal	74
1964	Dick Shatto, Tor	53	Tommy Joe Coffey, Edm	81
1965	Terry Evanshen, Mtl	37	Tommy Joe Coffey, Edm	81
1966	Bobby Taylor, Tor	56	Terry Evanshen, Cal	67
1967	Bobby Taylor, Tor	53	Terry Evanshen, Cal	96
1968	Bobby Taylor, Tor	56	Ken Nielsen, Wpg	68
1969	Tommy Joe Coffey, Ham	71	Herman Harrison, Cal	68
1970	Dave Fleming, Ham	56	Herman Harrison, Cal	70
1971	Terry Evanshen, Mtl	50	Herman Harrison, Cal	70
			Jim Thorpe, Wpg	70
1972	Eric Allen, Tor	53	Jim Thorpe, Wpg	70
1973	Johnny Rodgers, Mtl	41	George McGowan, Edm	81
1974	Tony Gabriel, Ham	61	Rudy Linterman, Cal	64
1975	Tony Gabriel, Ott	65	George McGowan, Edm	98
1976	Tony Gabriel, Ott	72	Rhett Dawson, Sask	65
1977	Tony Gabriel, Ott	65	Molly McGee, Sask	68
1978	Tony Gabriel, Ott	67	Joe Poplawski, Wpg	75
1979	Leif Pettersen, Ham	56	Waddell Smith, Edm	74
1980	Bob Gaddis, Tor	68	Mike Holmes, Wpg	79
1981	James Scott, Mtl	81	Eugene Goodlow, Wpg	100
1982	Nick Arakgi, Mtl	89	Joey Walters, Sask	102
1983	Terry Greer, Tor	113	Brian Kelly, Edm	104
1984	Rocky DiPietro, Ham	71	Craig Ellis, Sask	91
	Paul Pearson, Tor	71		
1985	Terry Greer, Tor	78	Craig Ellis, Sask	102
1986	James Hood, Mtl	95	James Murphy, Wpg	116
1987	Marc Lewis, Ott	94	Jim Sandusky, BC	80
1988	James Murphy, Wpg	76	David Williams, BC	83
1989	Tony Champion, Ham	95	Donald Narcisse, Sask	81
1990	Darrell K. Smith, Tor	93	Craig Ellis, Edm	106
1991	Darrell K. Smith, Tor	73	Allen Pitts, Cal	118
1992	Stephen Jones, Ott	75	Allen Pitts, Cal	103

Source: *Canadian Football League*

Leading CFL Rushers, by Year

	Eastern Division	Yards	Western Division	Yards
1954	Alex Webster, Mtl.	984	Howard Waugh, Cal	1 043
1955	Pat Abbruzzi, Mtl.	1 248	Normie Kwong, Edm	1 250
1956	Pat Abbruzzi, Mtl.	1 062	Normie Kwong, Edm	1 437
1957	Gerry McDougall, Ham	1 053	Johnny Bright, Edm	1 679
1958	Gerry McDougall, Ham	1 109	Johnny Bright, Edm	1 722
1959	Dave Thelen, Ott	1 339	Johnny Bright, Edm	1 340
1960	Dave Thelen, Ott	1 407	Earl Lunsford, Cal	1 343
1961	Don Clark, Mtl	1 143	Earl Lunsford, Cal	1 794
1962	George Dixon, Mtl	1 520	Nub Beamer, BC	1 161
1963	George Dixon, Mtl	1 270	Lovell Coleman, Cal	1 343
1964	Ron Stewart, Ott	867	Lovell Coleman, Cal	1 629
1965	Dave Thelen, Ott	801	George Reed, Sask	1 768
1966	Don Lisbon, Mtl	1 007	George Reed, Sask	1 409
1967	Bo Scott, Ott	762	George Reed, Sask	1 471
1968	Bill Symons, Tor	1 107	George Reed, Sask	1 222
1969	Dennis Duncan, Mtl	1 037	George Reed, Sask	1 353
1970	Bill Symons, Tor	908	Hugh McKinnis, Cal	1 135
1971	Leon McQuay, Tor	977	Jim Evenson, BC	1 237
1972	Dave Buchanan, Ham	1 163	Mack Herron, Wpg	1 527
1973	Andy Hopkins, Ham	1 223	Roy Bell, Edm	1 455
1974	Steve Ferrughelli, Mtl	1 134	George Reed, Sask	1 447
1975	Art Green, Ott	1 188	Willie Burden, Cal	1 896
1976	Art Green, Ott	1 257	Jim Washington, Wpg	1 277
1977	Jimmy Edwards, Ham	1 581	Jim Washington, Wpg	1 262
1978	Jimmy Edwards, Ham	840	Mike Strickland, Sask	1 306
1979	David Green, Mtl	1 678	Jim Germany, Edm	1 324
1980	Richard Crump, Ott	1 074	Jimmy Sykes, Cal	1 263
1981	David Overstreet, Mtl	952	Jimmy Sykes, Cal	1 107
1982	Alvin (Skip) Walker, Ott	1 141	William Miller, Wpg	1 076
1983	Alvin (Skip) Walker, Ott	1 431	Willard Reaves, Wpg	898
1984	Dwaine Wilson, Mtl	1 083	Willard Reaves, Wpg	1 733
1985	Ken Hobart, Ham	928	Willard Reaves, Wpg	1 323
1986	Walter Bender, Ham	618	Gary Allen, Cal	1 153
1987	Willard Reaves, Wpg	1 471	Gary Allen, Cal	857
1988	Orville Lee, Ott	1 075	Tony Cherry, BC	889
1989	Gill Fenerty, Tor	1 247	Reggie Taylor, Edm	1 503
1990	Robert Mimbs, Wpg	1 341	Tracy Ham, Edm	1 096
1991	Robert Mimbs, Wpg	1 769	Jon Volpe, BC	1 395
1992	Michael Richardson, Wpg	1 153	Jon Volpe, BC	941

Source: *Canadian Football League*

All-Time Leading CFL Players

(up to the end of the 1992 season)

Touchdowns

	TD	Seasons		TD	Seasons
George Reed, Sask	137	13	(1963–75)	Johnny Bright, Cal/Edm	71	13	(1952–64)
Brian Kelly, Edm	97	9	(1979–87)	Jim Germany, Edm	71	7	(1977–83)
Dick Shatto, Tor	91	12	(1954–65)	Bob Simpson, Ott	70	13	(1950–62)
Tom Scott, Wpg/Edm/Cal	91	11	(1974–84)	Jeff Boyd, Wpg/Tor	70	9	(1983–91)
Jackie Parker, Edm/Tor/BC	88	13	(1954–68)	Jim Young, BC	68	13	(1967–79)
Craig Ellis, Wpg/Cal/Sask/Tor/Edm	88	9	(1982–92)	Ron Stewart, Ott	67	12	(1959–70)
Willie Fleming, BC	86	8	(1959–68)	Tommy Joe Coffey, Edm/Ham/Tor	65	14	(1959–73)
Normie Kwong, Cal/Edm	83	13	(1948–60)	Gerry James, Wpg/Sask	63	11	(1952–64)
Terry Evanshen, Mtl/Cal/Ham/Tor	80	14	(1965–78)	Milson Jones, Wpg/Edm/Sask	63	11	(1982–92)
Virgil Wagner, Mtl.	79	9	(1946–54)	James Murphy, Wpg	62	8	(1983–90)
Leo Lewis, Wpg	75	12	(1955–66)	Lovell Coleman, Cal/Ott/BC	62	10	(1960–70)
Hal Patterson, Mtl/Ham	75	14	(1954–67)	Tom Forzani, Cal	62	11	(1973–83)
Tony Gabriel, Ham/Ott	72	11	(1971–81)				

Points

	Points	TD	Con	FG	Sing		Seasons
Lui Passaglia, BC	2 653	1	682	574	243	17	(1976–92)
Dave Cutler, Edm	2 237	0	627	464	218	16	(1969–84)
Dave Ridgway, Sask	1 882	0	424	453	99	11	(1982–92)
Trevor Kennerd, Wpg	1 840	0	509	394	149	12	(1980–91)
Bernie Ruoff, Wpg/Ham	1 772	0	401	384	219	14	(1975–88)
Gerry Organ, Ott	1 462	2	391	318	105	12	(1971–83)
John T. Hay, Ott/Cal	1 411	0	363	308	124	11	(1978–88)
Lance Chomyc, Tor	1 363	0	377	307	65	8	(1985–92)
Don Sweet, Mtl/Ham	1 342	0	327	314	73	14	(1972–85)
Larry Robinson, Cal	1 030	9	362	171	101	14	(1961–74)
Zenon Andrusyshyn, Tor/Ham/Edm/Mtl	1 010	0	222	21	143	12	(1971–86)
Paul Osbaldiston, BC/Wpg/Ham	978	0	262	264	120	7	(1986–92)
Tommy Joe Coffey, Edm/Ham/Tor	971	65	204	108	53	14	(1959–73)
Dean Dorsey, Tor/Ott	951	0	244	219	50	8	(1982–91)
Mark McLoughlin, Cal	924	0	236	207	67	5	(1988–92)
Jack Abendschan, Sask	863	0	312	59	74	11	(1965–75)
George Reed, Sask	823	137	0	0	1	13	(1963–75)
Jackie Parker, Edm/Tor/BC	750	88	103	40	19	13	(1954–68)
Don Sutherin, Ham/Ott/Tor	714	4	270	114	78	12	(1958–70)
Gerry James, Wpg/Sask	645	63	143	40	21	11	(1952–64)
Ian Sunter, Ham/Tor	626	0	155	135	66	6	(1972–79)
Brian Kelly, Edm	586	97	2	0	0	9	(1979–87)
Cyril McFall, Cal	578	0	131	134	45	5	(1974–78)
Jerry Kauric, Edm	577	0	170	122	65	4	(1987–91)
Bob Macoritti, Wpg/Sask	576	0	145	122	65	6	(1975–80)

Rushing

	Yards	Carries	Avg	Long	TD		Seasons
George Reed, Sask	16 116	3 243	5.0	71	134	13	(1963–75)
Johnny Bright, Cal/Edm	10 909	1 969	5.5	90	69	13	(1952–64)
Normie Kwong, Cal/Edm	9 022	1 745	5.2	60	78	13	(1948–60)
Leo Lewis, Wpg	8 861	1 351	6.5	92	48	11	(1955–66)
Dave Thelen, Ott/Tor	8 463	1 530	5.5	77	47	9	(1958–66)
Jim Evenson, BC/Ott	7 060	1 460	4.8	68	37	7	(1968–74)
Earl Lunsford, Cal	6 994	1 199	5.8	85	55	6	(1956–63) ▶

	Yards	Carries	Avg	Long	TD		Seasons
▶ Dick Shatto, Tor	6 958	1 322	5.3	67	39	12	(1954–65)
Lovell Coleman, Cal/Ott/BC	6 566	1 135	5.8	85	42	10	(1960–70)
Willie Burden, Cal	6 234	1 242	5.0	71	32	8	(1974–81)

Passing
(ranked by total yards)

	Attempts	Comp	Yards	Pct	Avg[1]	Int	TD		Seasons
Ron Lancaster, Ott/Sask	6 233	3 384	50 535	54.3	14.9	396	333	19	(1960–78)
Tom Clements, Ott/Sask/Ham/Wpg	4 657	2 807	39 041	60.3	13.9	214	252	12	(1975–87)
Dieter Brock, Wpg/Ham	4 535	2 602	34 830	57.4	13.4	158	210	11	(1974–84)
Matt Dunigan, Edm/BC/Tor/Wpg	3 591	1 995	28 574	53.6	14.3	157	190	10	(1983–92)
Sam Etcheverry, Mtl	2 829	1 630	25 582	57.6	15.7	163	174	7	(1953–60)
Condredge Holloway, Ott/Tor/BC	3 013	1 710	25 193	56.8	14.7	94	155	13	(1975–87)
Russ Jackson, Ott	2 530	1 356	24 592	53.6	18.1	125	185	12	(1958–69)
Bernie Faloney, Edm/Ham/Mtl/BC	2 876	1 493	24 264	51.9	16.3	201	151	12	(1954–66)
Roy Dewalt, BC/Wpg/Ott	3 130	1 803	24 147	57.6	13.4	96	132	9	(1980–88)
Joe Kapp, Cal/BC	2 709	1 476	22 725	54.5	15.4	130	136	8	(1959–67)
Tom Wilkinson, Tor/BC/Edm	2 662	1 613	22 579	60.6	14.0	126	154	15	(1967–81)
Joe Paopao, BC/Sask/Ott[b]	3 008	1 721	22 474	57.2	13.1	157	117	11	(1978–90)
John Hufnagel, Cal/Sask/Wpg	2 665	1 495	21 594	55.5	14.6	131	127	12	(1976–87)
Peter Liske, Tor/Cal/BC	2 571	1 449	21 266	56.4	14.7	133	130	7	(1 965–75)
Warren Moon, Edm	2 382	1 369	21 228	57.5	15.5	77	144	6	(1978–83)

(1) Yards per pass completed. (2) Did not play in 1988 or 1989.

Pass Receiving

	Rec	Yards	Avg	TD		Seasons
Rocky DiPietro, Ham	706	9 762	13.8	45	14	(1978–91)
Tommy Joe Coffey, Edm/Ham/Tor	650	10 320	15.9	63	14	(1959–73)
Tom Scott, Wpg/Edm/Cal	649	10 837	16.7	88	11	(1974–84)
Tony Gabriel, Ham/Ott	614	9 832	16.0	69	11	(1971–81)
Ray Elgaard, Sask	605	9 860	16.3	61	10	(1983–92)
Terry Evanshen, Mtl/Cal/Ham/Tor	600	9 697	16.2	80	14	(1965–78)
Craig Ellis, Wpg/Cal/Sask/Tor/Edm	578	7 706	13.3	58	9	(1982–92)
Brian Kelly, Edm	575	11 169	19.4	97	11	(1979–87)
James Murphy, Wpg	573	9 036	15.8	61	8	(1983–90)
Tom Forzani, Cal	553	8 285	15.0	62	11	(1973–83)
Joe Poplawski, Wpg	549	8 341	15.2	48	9	(1978–86)
Jim Young, BC	522	9 248	17.7	65	13	(1967–79)
Rick House, Wpg/Edm	522	8 139	15.6	55	13	(1979–91)

Source: *Canadian Football League*

CFL Outstanding Player Awards[1]

Outstanding player

1954	Sam Etcheverry, Mtl	**1962**	George Dixon, Mtl	**1970**	Ron Lancaster, Sask
1955	Pat Abbruzzi, Mtl	**1963**	Russ Jackson, Ott	**1971**	Don Jonas, Wpg
1956	Hal Patterson, Mtl	**1964**	Lovell Coleman, Cal	**1972**	Garney Henley, Ham
1957	Jackie Parker, Edm	**1965**	George Reed, Sask	**1973**	George McGowan, Edm
1958	Jackie Parker, Edm	**1966**	Russ Jackson, Ott	**1974**	Tom Wilkinson, Edm
1959	Johnny Bright, Edm	**1967**	Peter Liske, Cal	**1975**	Willie Burden, Cal
1960	Jackie Parker, Edm	**1968**	Bill Symons, Tor	**1976**	Ron Lancaster, Sask
1961	Bernie Faloney, Ham	**1969**	Russ Jackson, Ott	**1977**	Jimmy Edwards, Ham

▶

1978	Tony Gabriel, Ott	1983	Warren Moon, Edm	1988	David Williams, BC
1979	David Green, Mtl	1984	Willard Reaves, Wpg	1989	Tracy Ham, Edm
1980	Deiter Brock, Wpg	1985	Mervyn Fernandez, BC	1990	Mike Clemons, Tor
1981	Deiter Brock, Wpg	1986	James Murphy, Wpg	1991	Doug Flutie, BC
1982	Condredge Holloway, Tor	1987	Tom Clements, Wpg	1992	Doug Flutie, Cal

Outstanding Canadian

1954	Gerry James, Wpg	1967	Terry Evanshen, Cal	1980	Gerry Dattilio, Mtl
1955	Normie Kwong, Edm	1968	Ken Nielson, Wpg	1981	Joe Poplawski, Wpg
1956	Normie Kwong, Edm	1969	Russ Jackson, Ott	1982	Rocky DiPietro, Ham
1957	Gerry James, Wpg	1970	Jim Young, BC	1983	Paul Bennett, Wpg
1958	Ron Howell, Ham	1971	Terry Evanshen, Mtl	1984	Nick Arakgi, Mtl
1959	Russ Jackson, Ott	1972	Jim Young, BC	1985	Paul Bennett, Ham
1960	Ron Stewart, Ott	1973	Gerry Organ, Ott	1986	Joe Poplawski, Wpg
1961	Tony Pajaczkowski, Cal	1974	Tony Gabriel, Ham	1987	Scott Flagel, Wpg
1962	Harvey Wylie, Cal	1975	Jim Foley, Ott	1988	Ray Elgaard, Sask
1963	Russ Jackson, Ott	1976	Tony Gabriel, Ott	1989	Rocky DiPietro, Ham
1964	Tommy Grant, Ham	1977	Tony Gabriel, Ott	1990	Ray Elgaard, Sask
1965	Zeno Karcz, Ham	1978	Tony Gabriel, Ott	1991	Blake Marshall, Edm
1966	Russ Jackson, Ott	1979	Dave Fennell, Edm	1992	Ray Elgaard, Sask

Outstanding defensive player

1955	Tex Coulter, Mtl	1968	Ken Lehmann, Ott	1981	Dan Kepley, Edm
1956	Kaye Vaughan, Ott	1969	John LaGrone, Edm	1982	James Parker, Edm
1957	Kaye Vaughan, Ott	1970	Wayne Harris, Cal	1983	Greg Marshall, Ott
1958	Don Luzzi, Cal	1971	Wayne Harris, Cal	1984	James Parker, BC
1959	Roger Nelson, Edm	1972	John Helton, Cal	1985	Tyrone Jones, Wpg
1960	Herb Gray, Wpg	1973	Ray Nettles, BC	1986	James Parker, BC
1961	Frank Rigney, Wpg	1974	John Helton, Cal	1987	Gregg Stumon, BC
1962	John Barrow, Ham	1975	Jim Corrigall, Tor	1988	Grover Covington, Ham
1963	Tom Brown, BC	1976	Bill Baker, BC	1989	Danny Bass, Edm
1964	Tom Brown, BC	1977	Dan Kepley, Edm	1990	Greg Battle, Wpg
1965	Wayne Harris, Cal	1978	Dave Fennell, Edm	1991	Greg Battle, Wpg
1966	Wayne Harris, Cal	1979	Ben Zambiasi, Ham	1992	Willie Pless, Edm.
1967	Ed McQuarters, Sask	1980	Dan Kepley, Edm		

Outstanding offensive lineman

1974	Ed George, Mtl	1981	Larry Butler, Wpg	1988	Roger Aldag, Sask
1975	Charlie Turner, Edm	1982	Rudy Phillips, Ott	1989	Rod Connop, Edm
1976	Dan Yochum, Mtl	1983	Rudy Phillips, Ott	1990	Jim Mills, BC
1977	Al Wilson, BC	1984	John Bonk, Wpg	1991	Jim Mills, BC
1978	Jim Coode, Ott	1985	Nick Bastaja, Wpg	1992	Rob Smith, Ott
1979	Mike Wilson, Edm	1986	Roger Aldag, Sask		
1980	Mike Wilson, Edm	1987	Chris Walby, Wpg		

Outstanding rookie

1972	Chuck Ealey, Ham	1979	Brian Kelly, Edm	1986	Harold Hallman, Cal
1973	Johnny Rodgers, Mtl	1980	William Miller, Wpg	1987	Gill Fenerty, Tor
1974	Sam Cvijanovich, Tor	1981	Vince Goldsmith, Sask	1988	Orville Lee, Ott
1975	Tom Clements, Ott	1982	Chris Isaac, Ott	1989	Stephen Jordan, Ham
1976	John Sciarra, BC	1983	Johnny Shepherd, Ham	1990	Reggie Barnes, Ott
1977	Leon Bright, BC	1984	Dwaine Wilson, Mtl	1991	Jon Volpe, BC
1978	Joe Poplawski, Wpg	1985	Michael Gray, BC	1992	Mike Richardson, Win

Source: *Canadian Football League*

(1) Winners are chosen by a vote of the Football Reporters of Canada; prior to 1989 they were known as the Schenley Awards.

Canadian Football League All-Stars, 1992

(voted by Football Reporters of Canada

Offence	Defence
Quarterback: Doug Flutie, Cal*	**Tackle:** Rodney Handing, Tor
Fullback: Blake Marshall, Edm	**Tackle:** Jearld Baylis, Sask
Running Back: Michael Richardson, Wpg	**End:** Will Johnson, Cal*
Slotback: Ray Elgaard, Sask	**End:** Bobby Jurasin, Sask
Slotback: Allen Pitts, Cal*	**Linebacker:** Willie Pless, Edm*
Wide Receiver: Stephen Jones, Ott	**Linebacker:** Angelo Snipes, Ott
Wide Receiver: Jim Sandusky, Edm	**Linebacker:** John Motton, Ham
Centre: Rod Connop, Edm*	**Cornerback:** Less Browne, Ott*
Guard: Pierre Veachevel, Edm	**Cornerback:** Junior Thurman, Cal*
Guard: Rocco Romano, Cal	**Halfback:** Darryl Hall, Cal*
Tackle: Vic Stevenson, Sask	**Halfback:** Anthony Drawhorn, Ott
Tackle: Rob Smith, Ott	**Safety:** Glen Suitor, Sask*
Punter: Hank Ilesic, Tor*	
Kicker: Troy Westwood, Win	
Specialty Teams: Henry Williams, Edm*	

Source: *Canadian Football League. (*) Also All-Stars in 1991*

Canadian Football Hall of Fame[1]

(only payers listed, not builders)

Player / Year Elected / Team(s)	Player / Year Elected / Team(s)
Atchison, Ron, (1978) Sask	**Gall,** Hugh (1963) U of Toronto
Bailey, Byron (1975) BC	**Golab,** Tony (1964) Ott
Barrow, John (1976) Ham	**Gray,** Herb (1983) Wpg
Batstone, Harry (1963) Tor/Queen's	**Griffing,** Dean (1965) Sask/Cal
Beach, Ormond (1963) Sarnia	**Hanson,** Fritz (1963) Wpg
Box, Ab (1965) Balmy Beach/Tor	**Harris,** Wayne (1976) Cal
Breen, Joseph (1963) U of Toronto/Tor	**Harrison,** Herman (1993) Cal
Bright, Johnny (1970) Edm/Cal	**Helton,** John (1985) Cal/Wpg
Brown, Tom (1984) BC	**Henley,** Garney (1979) Ham
Casey, Tom (1964) Wpg	**Hinton,** Tom (1991) BC
Charlton, Ken (1992) Ott/Sask	**Huffman,** Dick (1987) Wpg/Cal
Coffey, Tommy Joe (1977) Edm/Cal	**Isbiste,r** Bob (1965) Ham
Conacher, Lionel (1963) Tor	**Jackson,** Russ (1973) Ott
Copeland, Royal (1988) Tor	**Jacobs,** Jack (1963) Wpg
Corrigal, Jim (1990) Tor	**James,** Eddie (1963) Wpg/Reg
Cox, Ernest (1963) Ham	**James,** Gerry (1981) Wpg
Craig, Ross (1964) Ham	**Kabat,** Greg (1966) Wpg
Cronin, Carl (1967) Wpg	**Kapp,** Joe (1984) Cal/BC
Cutler, Wes (1968) Tor	**Keeling,** Jerry (1989) Cal/Ott/Ham
Dalla Riva, Peter (1993) Mtl	**Kelly,** Brian (1991) Edm
Dixon, George (1974) Mtl	**Kelly,** Ellison (1992) Edm/Ham
Eliowitz, Abe (1969) Ott/Mtl	**Krol,** Joe (1963) Tor/Ham
Emerson, Eddie (1963) Ott	**Kwong,** Normie (1969) Cal/Edm
Etcheverry, Sam (1969) Mtl	**Lawson,** Smirle (1963) U. of Toronto
Evanshen, Terry (1984) Mtl/Cal/Ham/Tor	**Leadlay,** Frank (1963) Queen's/Ham
Faloney, Bernie (1974) Edm/Ham	**Lear,** Les (1974) Wpg/Cal
Fear, Cap (1967) Tor/Mtl/Ham	**Lewis,** Leo (1973) Wpg
Fennell, Dave (1990) Edm	**Lunsford,** Earl (1983) Cal
Ferraro, John (196)6 Ham/Mtl	**Luster,** Marv (1990) Mtl/Tor
Fieldgate, Norm (1979) BC	**Luzzi,** Don (1985) Cal
Fleming, Willie (1982) BC	**McCance,** Chester (1976) Wpg/Mtl
Gabriel, Tony(1984) Ham/Ott	**McGill,** Frank (1965) Mtl

▶

▶ **McQuarters,** Ed (1988) Sask
Miles, Rollie (1980) Edm
Morris, Frank (1983) Tor/Edm
Morris, Ted (1964) Tor
Mosca, Angelo (1987) Ham
Nelson, Roger (1985) Edm
Neumann, Peter (1979) Ham
O'Quinn, Red (1981) Mtl
Pajaczkowski, Tony (1988) Cal/Mtl
Parker Jackie (1971) Edm/Tor/BC
Patterson, Hal (1971) Mtl/Ham
Perry, Gordon (1970) Mtl
Perry, Norman (1963) Sarnia
Ploen, Ken (1975) Wpg
Quilty Silver (1966) U. of Ottawa
Rebholz, Russ (1963) Wpg
Reed, George (1979) Sask
Reeve, Ted (1963) Tor
Rigney, Frank (1984) Wpg
Rodden, Michael (1964) Queen's/Tor
Rowe, Paul (1964) Cal
Ruby, Martin (1974) Sask
Russel, Jeff (1963) Ott
Scott, Vince (1982) Ham

Shatto, Dick (1975) Tor
Simpson, Benjamin (1963) Ham
Simpson, Bob (1976) Ott
Sprague, David (1963) Ham/Ott
Stevenson, Art (1969) Wpg
Stewart, Ron (1977) Ott
Stirling, Bummer (1966) Sarnia
Sutherin, Don (1992) Ham/Ott
Thelen, Dave (1989) Ott/Tor
Timmis, Brian (1963) Ham/Ott
Tinsley, Buddy (1982) Wpg
Tommy, Andrew (1989) Ott/Tor
Trawick, Herb (1975) Mtl
Tubman, Joe (1968) Ott
Tucker, Whit (1993) Ott
Urness, Ted (1989) Sask
Vaughn, Kaye (1978) Ott
Wagner, Virgil (1980) Mtl
Welch, Huck (1964) Ham/Mtl
Wilkinson, Tom (1987) Edm
Wylie, Harvey (1980) Cal
Young, Jim (1991) BC
Zock, William (1984) Tor/Edm

Source: *Canadian Football League*

NFL Final Standings, 1992

National Conference

■ Eastern Division

	W	L	T	Pct	Pts	OP
Dallas *	13	3	0	.813	409	243
Philadelphia#	11	5	0	.688	354	245
Washington#	9	7	0	.563	300	255
NY Giants	6	10	0	.375	306	367
Phoenix	4	12	0	.250	243	332

■ Central Division

	W	L	T	Pct	Pts	OP
Minnesota*	11	5	0	.688	374	249
Green Bay	9	7	0	.563	276	296
Tampa Bay	5	11	0	.313	267	365
Chicago	5	11	0	.313	295	361
Detroit	5	11	0	.313	273	332

■ Western Division

	W	L	T	Pct	Pts	OP
San Francisco*	14	2	0	.875	431	236
New Orleans#	12	4	0	.750	330	202
Atlanta	6	10	0	.375	327	414
LA Rams	6	10	0	.375	313	383

American Conference

■ Eastern Division

	W	L	T	Pct	Pts	OP
Miami*	11	5	0	.688	340	281
Buffalo#	11	5	0	.688	381	283
Indianapolis	9	7	0	.563	216	302
NY Jets	4	12	0	.250	220	315
New England	2	14	0	.125	205	363

■ Central Division

	W	L	T	Pct	Pts	OP
Pittsburgh*	11	5	0	.688	299	225
Houston#	10	6	0	.625	352	258
Cleveland	7	9	0	.438	272	275
Cincinnati	5	11	0	.313	274	364

■ Western Division

	W	L	T	Pct	Pts	OP
San Diego*	11	5	0	.688	335	241
Kansas City#	10	6	0	.625	348	282
Denver	8	8	0	.500	262	329
LA Raiders	7	9	0	.438	249	281
Seattle	2	14	0	.125	140	312

*Division Champion   #Wild Card Team

Miami finished ahead of Buffalo based on better conference record (9-3 to 7-5). Tampa Bay finished ahead of Chicago and Detroit on better conference record (5-7 to Bears' 4-8 and Lions' 3-9). Atlanta finished ahead of LA Rams based on better record versus common opponents (5-7 to 4-8).

▶

Playoffs

▣ First Round
NFC: Washington 24, Minnesota 7
Philadelphia 36, New Orleans 20
AFC: San Diego 17 Kansas City 0
Buffalo 41, Houston 38 (OT)

▣ Divisional Playoffs
NFC: San Francisco 20, Washington 13
Dallas 34, Philadelphia 10
AFC: Buffalo 24, Pittsburgh 3
Miami 31, San Diego 0

▣ Championships
NFC : Dallas 30, San Francisco 20
AFC: Buffalo 29, Miami 10

▣ Super Bowl XXVII
(at Rose Bowl, Pasadena, California)
Dallas 52, Buffalo 17

▣ AFC-NFC Pro Bowl at Aloha Stadium, Honolulu, Hawaii
AFC 23, NFC 20

Source: *National Football League*

All-Time Pro Football Records

(all conferences; up to the start of the 1993 season)

Leading Lifetime Scorers

	Yrs	TD	PAT	FG	Total		Yrs	TD	PAT	FG	Total
George Blanda	26	9	943	335	2 002	Jim Breech	13	0	486	224	1 158
Jan Stenerud	19	0	580	373	1 699	Gino Cappelletti	11	42	350	176	1 130
Pat Leahy	18	0	558	304	1 470	Ray Wersching	15	0	456	222	1 122
Jim Turner	16	1	521	304	1 439	Eddie Murray	12	0	381	244	1 113
Mark Moseley	16	0	482	300	1 382	Don Cockroft	13	0	432	216	1 080
Jim Bakken	17	0	534	282	1 380	Garo Yepremian	14	0	444	210	1 074
Nick Lowery	14	0	449	306	1 369	Matt Bahr	13	0	402	221	1 065
Fred Cox	15	0	519	282	1 365	Bruce Gossett	11	0	374	219	1 031
Lou Groza	17	1	641	234	1 349	Gary Anderson	10	0	323	229	1 010
Chris Bahr	14	0	490	241	1 213	Sam Baker	15	2	428	179	977

Most points, one season . . . . **176, Paul Hornung,** GB, 1960 (15 TD, 41 PAT, 15 FG)
Most points, one game . . . . **40, Ernie Nevers,** Chi Cardinals vs. Chi Bears, Nov. 28, 1929 (6 TD, 4 PAT)
Most touchdowns, career . . . . **126, Jim Brown,** Cleve., 1957–65
Most touchdowns, one season . . . . **24, John Riggins,** Wash, 1984 (24 rushing
Most touchdowns, one game . . . . **6, Ernie Nevers,** Chi Cardinals vs. Chi Bears, Nov. 28, 1929 (6 rushing)
Dub Jones, Clev vs. Chi Bears, Nov. 25, 1951 (4 rushing, 2 pass receptions)
Gale Sayers, Chi Bears vs. SF, Dec. 12, 1965 (4 rushing, 1 pass reception, 1 punt return)
Most points after touchdown, one season . . . . **66, Uwe von Schamann,** Mia, 1984
Most points after touchdown, career . . . . **943, George Blanda,** 4 teams, 1949–75
Most consecutive points after touchdown . . . . **234, Tommy Davis,** SF, 1959–69
Most field goals, one game . . . . **7, Jim Bakken,** StL vs. Pitt, Sept. 24, 1967
Rich Karlis, Minn vs. LA Rams, Nov. 5, 1989
Most field goals, one season . . . . **35, Ali Haji-Sheikh,** NY Giants, 1983
Most field goals, career . . . . **373, Jan Stenerud,** 3 teams, 1967–85
Most consecutive field goals . . . . **24, Kevin Butler,** Chi Bears, 1988–89
Longest field goal . . . . **63 yds, Tom Dempsey,** NO vs. Det, Nov. 8, 1970

Pass Interceptions

Most passes had intercepted, one game . . . . **8, Jim Hardy,** Chi Cardinals vs. Phil, Sept. 24, 1950 (39 attempts)
Most passes had intercepted, one season . . . . **42, George Blanda,** Hou, 1962
Most passes had intercepted, career . . . . **277, George Blanda,** Chi Bears, 1949–58;
Balt, 1950; Hou, 1960–66; Oak, 1967–75
Most consecutive passes attempted without interception . . . . **308, Bernie Kosar,** Clev, 1990–91
Most interceptions by, one season . . . . **14, Dick (Night Train) Lane,** LAs Rams, 1952
Most interceptions by, career . . . . **81, Paul Krause,** Wash, 1964–67; Minn, 1968–79 ▶

Punting

Most punts, one game .... **15, John Teltschick,** Phil vs. N. Giants, Dec. 6, 1987 (OT)
Most punts, career .... **1 154, Dave Jennings,** NY Giants, 1974–84; N.Y. Jets, 1985–87
Most punts, season .... **114, Bob Parsons,** Chi Bears, 1981
Highest punting average, season (20 punts) .... **51.40, Sam Baugh,** Wash., 1940 (35 punts)
Longest punt .... **98 yds, Steve O'Neal,** NY Jets vs. Den, Sept. 21, 1969j2

Miscellaneous Records

Most fumbles, one season .... **18, Dave Krieg,** Sea, 1989; **Warren Moon,** Hou, 1990
Most fumbles, one game .... **7, Len Dawson,** KC vs. SD, Nov. 15, 1964
Most sacks, career .... **121.5, Lawrence Taylor,** NY Giants, 1982–91
Most sacks, season .... **22, Mark Gastineau,** NY Jets, 1984
Most seasons, active player .... **26, George Blanda,** Chi Bears, 1949–58; Balt, 1950; Hou, 1960–66; Oak, 1967–75
Most consecutive games played, career .... **282, Jim Marshall,** Cle, 1960; Minn, 1961–79
Highest punt return average, season .... **23.00 yards, Herb Rich,** Baltimore, 1950
Highest punt return average, career .... **12.78 yards, George McAfee,** Chicago, 1940–41, 1945–50
Highest kickoff return average, season .... **41.06 yards, Travis Williams,** Green Bay, 1967
Highest kickoff return average, career .... **30.56 yards,** Gale Sayers, Chicago, 1965–71

Leading Lifetime Rushers

	Yrs	Att	Yards	Avg		Yrs	Att	Yards	Avg
Walter Payton	13	3 838	16 726	4.4	Marcus Allen	11	2 090	8 545	4.8
Eric Dickersont	10	2 970	13 168	4.4	Joe Perry	14	1 737	8 378	4.8
Tony Dorsett	12	2 936	12 739	4.3	Gerald Riggs	10	1 989	8 188	4.1
Jim Brown	9	2 359	12 312	5.2	Larry Csonka	11	1 891	8 081	4.3
Franco Harris	13	2 949	12 120	4.1	Freeman McNeil	12	1 798	8 074	4.7
John Riggins	14	2 916	11 352	3.9	Roger Craig	10	1 953	8 070	4.5
O.J. Simpson	11	2 404	11 236	4.7	James Brooks	12	1 685	7 962	4.1
O.J. Anderson	14	2 562	10 273	4.0	Mike Pruitt	11	1 844	7 378	4.0
Earl Campbell	8	2 187	9 407	4.3	Leroy Kelly	10	1 727	7 274	4.2
Jim Taylor	10	1 941	8 597	4.4	George Rogers	7	1 692	7 176	4.2

Most yards gained, one season .... **2 105, Eric Dickerson,** LAs Rams, 1984
Most yards gained, one game .... **275, Walter Payton,** Chi Bears vs. Minn, Nov. 20, 1977
Most touchdowns rushing, career .... **110, Walter Payton,** Chi Bears, 1975–87
Most touchdowns rushing, one season .... **24, John Riggins,** Wash, 1983
Most touchdowns rushing, one game .... **6, Ernie Nevers,** Chi Cardinals vs. Chi Bears, Nov. 8, 1929
Most rushing attempts, one season .... **407, James Wilder,** Tam, 1984
Most rushing attempts, one game .... **45, Jamie Morris,** Wash vs. Cin, Dec. 17, 1988
Longest run .... **99 yds, Tony Dorsett,** Dal vs. Minn, Jan. 3, 1983

Leading Lifetime Receivers

	Yrs	No.	Yards	Avg		Yrs	No.	Yards	Avg
Art Monk	13	847	11 620	13.7	Fred Biletnikoff	14	589	8 974	15.2Steve
Largent	14	819	13 089	16.0	Harold Jackson	16	579	10 372	17.9
James Lofton	15	750	13 821	18.4	Lionel Taylor	10	567	7 195	12.7
Charlie Joiner	18	750	12 146	16.2	Wes Chandler	11	559	8 966	16.0
Ozzie Newsome	13	662	7 980	12.1	Roy Green	14	559	8 965	16.0
Charley Taylor	13	649	9 110	14.0	Stanley Morgan	14	557	10 716	19.2
Don Maynard	15	633	11 834	18.7	Mark Clayton	10	550	8 643	15.7
Raymond Berry	13	631	9 275	14.7	Gary Clark	8	549	8 742	15.9
Jerry Rice	8	610	10 273	16.8	Roger Craig	10	547	4 742	8.7
Drew Hill	13	600	9 447	16.3					
Harold Carmichael	14	590	8 985	157					

▶

▶ Most yards gained, one season .... **1 746, Charley Hennigan,** Hou, 1961
Most yards gained, one game .... **336, Willie Anderson,** LA Rams vs. NO, Nov. 26, 1989
Most pass receptions, one season .... **108, Sterling Sharpe,** Green Bay, 1992
Most pass receptions, one game .... **18, Tom Fears,** LA Rams vs. GB, Dec. 3, 1950 (189 yds)
Most consecutive games, pass receptions .... **177, Steve Largent,** Sea, 1976–89
Most touchdown passes, career .... **103, Jerry Rice,** SF, 1985–92
Most touchdown passes, one season .... **22, Jerry Rice, SF,** 1987
Most touchdown passes, one game .... **5, Bob Shaw,** Chi Cardinals vs. Balt, Oct. 2, 1950; **Kellen Winslow,**
SD vs. Oak, Nov. 22, 1981; **Jerry Rice,** SF vs. Atl, Oct. 14, 1990

Leading Lifetime Passers
(Minimum 1 500 attempts)

	Rtg[1]	Yrs	Att	Comp	Yards		Rtg[1]	Yrs	Att	Comp	Yards
Joe Montana	93.5	13	4 600	2 929	35 124	Ken Anderson ..	81.9	16	4 475	2 654	32 838
Steve Young	90.4	8	1 506	908	11 877	Boomer Esiason	81.8	9	3 378	1 897	25 671
Dan Marino	87.8	10	5 284	3 128	39 502	Bernie Kosar ...	81.8	8	3 012	1 774	21 097
Jim Kelly	86.9	7	3 024	1 824	23 031	Danny White ...	81.7	13	2 950	1 761	21 959
Mark Rypien	84.3	5	1 888	1 078	14 414	Ken O'Brien ...	81.0	9	3 465	2 039	24 386
Roger Staubach ..	83.4	11	2 958	1 685	22 700	Warren Moon ...	81.0	9	4 026	2 329	30 200
Neil Lomax	82.7	8	3 153	1 817	22 771	Bart Starr	80.5	16	3 149	1 808	24 718
Sonny Jurgensen .	82.6	18	4 262	2 433	32 224	Fran Tarkenton .	80.4	18	6 467	3 686	47 003
Len Dawson	82.6	19	3 741	2 136	28 711	Dan Fouts	80.2	15	5 604	3 297	43 040
Dave Krieg	82.1	13	3 989	2 326	29 247	R. Cunningham .	79.9	8	2 641	1 464	18 193

Most yards gained, one season .... **5 084, Dan Marino,** Mia, 1984
Most yards gained, one game .... **554, Norm Van Brocklin,** LA Rams vs. NY Giants, Sept. 28, 1951
(27 completions in 41 attempts)
Most touchdowns passing, career ...... **342, Fran Tarkenton,** Minn, 1961–66; NY Giants, 1967–71; Vikings, 1972–78
Most touchdowns passing, one season .... **48, Dan Marino,** Mia, 1984
Most touchdowns passing, one game ...... **7, Sid Luckman,** Chi Bears vs. NY Giants, Nov. 14, 1943; **Adrian Burk,**Phil vs.
Wash, Oct. 17, 1954; **George Blanda,** Hou vs. NY Titans, Nov. 19, 1961;
Y.A. Tittle, NY Giants vs. Wash, Oct. 28, 1962; **Joe Kapp,** Minn vs. Balt, Sept. 28, 1969
Most passing attempts, one season .... **655, Warren Moon,** Hou, 1991
Most passing attempts, one game .... **68, George Blanda,** Hou vs. Buff, Nov. 1, 1964 (37 completions)
Most passes completed, one season .... **404, Warren Moon,** Hou, 1991
Most passes completed, one game .... **42, Richard Todd,** NY Jets vs. SF 49ers, Sept. 21, 1980

Source: *National Football League*

(1) Rating based on performance standards for completion percentage, interception percentage, touchdown percentage and average gains.

Canadian Junior Football Champions, 1908–92

1908	Parkdale Canoe Club 18, Montreal III, 1	**1930**	Toronto Argos 7, Winnipeg Native Sons 1
1909	Toronto St. Michaels College 7, Hamilton Alerts 2	**1931**	Woodstock Grads 14, Moose Jaw Maroons 13
1910	Hamilton Alerts III 4, St. Lambert 3	**1932**	Toronto Varsity 8, Moose Jaw Maroon 6
1911	Petrolia 27, Kingston Royal Military College 20	**1933**	Toronto Argos 14, Montreal Westwards 6
1912	Hamilton Alerts III 13, Ontario Agro College (Guelph) 7		Calgary Altonas 11, Winnipeg Deer Lodge 6 Toronto Argos received trophy.
1913	Ottawa Capitals 17, Montreal Westmounts 2	**1934–35**	No series
1914	Univ. of Western Ontario (London) 23, Ontario Agro College (Guelph) 9	**1936**	No final
		1937	Hamilton Italo Canadians 27, Regina Dales 2
1915–20	No series	**1938**	Regina Dales 4, Montreal Westmounts 3
1921	Toronto St. Aldens 18, Queen's University 8	**1939-45**	No series
1922	Montreal A.A.A.	**1946**	No final
1923	Loyola College (Montreal) 9, Toronto Canoe Club 3	**1947**	Vancouver Blue Bombers 19, Hamilton Tigers 8 (2-game total-point series)
1924	Toronto Canoe Club 7, Ottawa Rideaus 1		
1925	Montreal A.A.A. 6, Regina Pats 4	**1948**	Hamilton Wildcats 23, Saskatoon Hilltops 10
1926	Montreal A.A.A. 16, St. Thomas Tigers 5	**1949**	Hamilton Wildcats 14, Vancouver Blue Bombers 11
1927	Montreal A.A.A. 4, Toronto Varsity 2	**1950**	Hamilton Tigercats 14, Vancouver Blue Bombers, 5
1928	Regina Pats 9, St. Thomas Tigers 6	**1951**	Hamilton Tiger Cats 22, Edmonton Maple Leafs 1
1929	St. Thomas Tigers 14, Moose Jaw Maroons 0	**1952**	Windsor A.K.O. 15, Edmonton Wildcats 12

▶

▶ **1953** Saskatoon Hilltops 34, Windsor A.K.O. 6
1954 Windsor A.K.O. 13, Winnipeg Rods 9
1955 Winnipeg Rods 19, Windsor A.K.O. 13
1956 Winnipeg Rods 21, Toronto Parkdale Lions 10
1957 Toronto Parkdale Lions 20, Winnipeg Rods 13
1958 Saskatoon Hilltops 18, Montreal N.D.G. 14
1959 Saskatoon Hilltops 46, Toronto North York Knights 7
1960 Montreal Rosemount Bombers 22, Saskatoon Hilltops, 20
1961 Winnipeg Rods 16, Montreal Rosemount Bombers 13
1962 Edmonton Huskies 7, Montreal N.D.G. 3
1963 Edmonton Huskies 47, Montreal N.D.G. 27
1964 Edmonton Huskies 48, Montreal N.D.G. 27
1965 Montreal N.D.G. 2, Edmonton Huskies 1
1966 Regina Rams 29, Montreal N.D.G. 14
1967 Edmonton Wildcats 29, Burlington Braves 6
1968 Saskatoon Hilltops 27, Ottawa Sooners 7
1969 Saskatoon Hilltops 28, Ottawa Sooners 7
1970 Regina Rams 39, Burlington Braves 8
1971 Regina Rams 42, Burlington Braves 13

1972 Hamilton Hurricanes 33, Regina Rams 8
1973 Regina Rams 9, Ottawa Sooners 0
1974 Ottawa Sooners 17, Vancouver Meralomas 4
1975 Regina Rams 38, Hamilton Hurricanes 19
1976 Regina Rams 45, Hamilton Hurricanes 23
1977 Edmonton Wildcats 23, Hamilton Hurricanes 0
1978 Saskatoon Hilltops 24, Ottawa Sooners 4
1979 Ottawa Sooners 13, Regina Rams 9
1980 Regina Rams 26, Hamilton Hurricanes 24
1981 Regina Rams 46, Hamilton Hurricanes 24
1982 Renfrew Trojans 46, Montreal Junior Concordes 0
1983 Edmonton Wildcats 30, Ottawa Sooners 11
1984 Ottawa Sooners 46, Richmond Raiders 23
1985 Saskatoon Hilltops 29, Ottawa Sooners 11
1986 Regina Rams 53, Ottawa Sooners 12
1987 Regina Rams 31, St. Vital Mustangs 23
1988 Okanagan Sun 50, Burlington Jr. Tiger-Cats 0
1989 Calgary Colts 23, Burlington Jr. Tiger-Cats 6
1990 Calgary Colts 50, Windsor A.K.O. Fratmen 15
1991 Saskatoon Hilltops 48, Ottawa Sooners 7
1992 Ottawa Sooners 35, Surry Rams 18

Source: *Football Canada*

Note: Canadian Rugby Union, 1908–46; Canadian Amateur Football Association, 1947–74; Leader Post Trophy to winner. Canadian Junior Football League, 1975– ; Armadale Cup 1975–88; Canadian Bowl 1989– .

Major Bowl Games, 1993

Bowl	Site	Result
Cotton	Dallas, TX	Notre Dame 28, Texas A&M 3
Fiesta	Tempe, AZ	Syracuse 26, Colorado 22
Rose	Pasadena, CA	Michigan 38, Washington 31
Orange	Miami, FL	Florida State 27, Nebraska 14
Sugar	New Orleans, LA	Alabama 34, Miami (FL) 13

U.S. College Football Top 20, 1992

	Record	Pts		Record	Pts
1. Alabama	13-0-0	1 550	11. Washington	9-3-0	892
2. Florida St.	11-1-0	1 470	12. Tennessee	9-3-0	819
3. Miami	11-1-0	1 410	13. Colorado	9-2-1	818
4. Notre Dame	10-1-1	1 375	14. Nebraska	9-3-0	771
5. Michigan	9-0-3	1 266	15. Washington St.	9-3-0	618
6. Syracuse	10-2-0	1 209	16. Mississippi	9-3-0	583
7. Texas A&M	12-1-0	1 167	17. N. Carolina St.	9-3-1	582
8. Georgia	10-2-0	1 159	18. Ohio St.	8-3-1	493
9. Stanford	10-3-0	1 058	19. N. Carolina	9-3-0	491
10. Florida	9-4-0	931	20. Hawaii	11-2-0	354

Source: *Associated Press*

BASKETBALL

National Basketball Association, 1992–93

Final Standings

Eastern Conference

■ Atlantic Division

	W	L	Pct	GB
New York	60	22	.732	—
Boston	48	34	.585	12
New Jersey	43	39	.524	17
Orlando	41	41	.500	19
Miami	36	46	.439	24
Philadelphia	26	56	.317	34
Washington	22	60	.268	38

■ Central Division

	W	L	Pct	GB
Chicago	57	25	.695	—
Cleveland	54	28	.659	3
Charlotte	44	38	.532	13
Atlanta	43	39	.524	14
Indiana	41	41	.500	16
Detroit	40	42	.488	17
Milwaukee	28	54	.341	29

Western Conference

■ Midwest Division

	W	L	Pct	GB
Houston	55	27	.671	—
San Antonio	49	33	.598	6
Utah	47	35	.573	8
Denver	36	46	.439	19
Minnesota	19	63	.232	36
Dallas	11	71	.134	44

■ Pacific Division

	W	L	Pct	GB
Phoenix	62	20	.756	—
Seattle	55	27	.671	7
Portland	51	31	.622	11
Los Angeles Clippers	41	41	.500	21
Los Angeles Lakers	39	43	.476	23
Golden State	34	48	.415	28
Sacramento	25	57	.305	37

NBA Playoff Results, 1992–93

Eastern Conference

First Round (best-of-5)
Chicago defeated Atlanta 3-0
Charlotte defeated Boston 3-1
Cleveland defeated New Jersey 3-2
New York defeated Indiana 3-1
Semifinals (best-of-7)
New York defeated Charlotte 4-1
Chicago defeated Cleveland 4-0
Finals (best-of-7)
Chicago defeated New York 4-2

Western Conference

First Round (best-of-5)
Phoenix defeated LA Lakers 3-2
Seattle defeated Utah 3-2
Houston defeated LA Clippers 3-2
San Antonio defeated Portland 3-1
Semifinals (best-of-7)
Portland defeated San Antonio 4-2
Seattle defeated Houston 4-3
Finals (best-of-7)
Phoenix defeated Seattle 4-3

Championship (best-of-7)
Chicago defeated Phoenix 4-2

Source: *NBA News*

NBA Individual Highs, 1991–93

Minutes played, season	**3 323, Johnson,** Char
Minutes played, game	**59, Rice,** Miami vs. Phil., Nov. 20 (3 OT)
Points, game	**64, Jordan,** Chi vs. Orl, Jan 16 (OT)
Field goals, game	**27, Jordan,** Chi vs. Orl, Jan 16
Field goal attempts, game	**49, Jordan,** Chi vs. Orl, Jan 16
3-point field goals, game	**10 Shaw,** Miami vs. Milw, Apr. 8
3-point field goal attempts, game	**19, Scott,** Orl vs. Milw, Apr. 13
Free throws, game	**23, Wilkins,** Atl vs. Chi, Dec. 8 ▶

▶ Free throw attempts, game .... **24, K. Malone,** Utah vs. Miami, Jan 12 (2 OT), **Jordan,** Chi vs. Miami, Dec 30
Rebounds, game .... **34, Seikaly,** Miami vs. Wash, Mar. 3
Offensive rebounds, game .... **12,** by four players
Defensive rebounds, game .... **26, Seikaly,** Miami vs. Wash, Mar. 3
Offensive rebounds, season .... **367, Rodman,** Det
Defensive rebounds, season .... **789, Ewing,** NY
Assists, game .... **23, Blaylock,** Atl vs. Utah, Mar. 6
Blocked shots, game .... **12, Mutombo,** Den vs. LA Clip, Apr. 18
Steals, game .... **9, Jordan,** Chi vs. NJ, Apr. 2
Personal fouls, season .... **332, Roberts,** LA Clip.
Games disqualified, season .... **15, Roberts,** LA Clip.

Source: *National Basketball Association*

NBA Statistical Leaders, 1991–93

■ Scoring

	FG	Pts	Avg
Jordan, Ch	992	2 541	32.6
Wilkins, Atl.	741	2 121	29.9
K. Malone, Utah	797	2 217	27.0
Olajuwon, Hou	848	2 140	26.1
Barkley, Pho	716	1 944	25.6
Ewing, NY	779	1 959	24.2
Dumars, Det	677	1 809	23.5
O'Neal, Orl	733	1 893	23.4
Robinson, SA	676	1 916	23.4
Manning, LA-C	702	1 800	22.8
Petrovic, NJ	587	1 564	22.3
Johnson, Cha	728	1 810	22.1
Hardaway, GS	522	1 419	21.5
Miller, Ind.	571	1 736	21.2
Mourning, Cha.	572	1 639	21.0
Lewis, Bos..	663	1 666	20.8
Coleman, NJ.	564	1 572	20.7
Hawkins, Phi.	551	1 643	20.3
Daugherty, Cle.	520	1 432	20.2
Anderson, Orl	594	1 574	19.9

■ Rebounds

	Def	Total	Avg
Rodman, Det	765	1 132	18.3
O'Neal, Orl.	780	1 122	13.9
Mutombo, Den	726	1 070	13.0
Olajuwon, Hou	785	1 068	13.0
Willis, Atl	693	1 028	12.9
Barkley, Pho	691	928	12.2
Ewing, NY	789	980	12.1
Seikaly, Mia	587	846	11.8
Robinson, SA	727	956	11.7
Coleman, NJ.	605	852	11.2
K. Malone, Utah	692	919	11.2

■ Field Goal Percentage

	FG	FGA	Pct
Ceballos, Pho	381	662	.576
Daugherty, Cle.	520	911	.571
Davis, Ind	304	535	.568
O'Neal, Orl	733	1 304	.562
Thorpe, Hou..	385	690	.558
K. Malone, Utah.	797	1 443	.552
Nance, Cle	533	971	.549
Brickowski, Mil	456	836	.545
Stewart, Was	306	564	.543
Carr, SA	379	705	.538

■ Free Throw Percentage

	FT	FTA	Pct
Price, Cle	289	305	.948
Jackson, Den.	217	232	.935
Johnson, Sea.	234	257	.911
Williams, Min	419	462	.907
Skiles, Orl	289	324	.892
Pierce, Sea	313	352	.889
Miller, Ind	427	485	.880
Smith, Hou	195	222	.878
Petrovic, NJ	315	362	.870
Lewis, Bos	326	376	.867

■ Assists

	G	Ast	Avg
Stockton, Utah	82	987	12.0
Hardaway, GS	66	699	10.6
Skiles, Orl	78	735	9.4
M. Jackson, LA-C	82	724	8.8
Bogues, Cha.	81	711	8.8
Williams, Min	76	661	8.7
Thomas, Det.	79	671	8.5
Blaylock, Atl	80	671	8.4
Anderson, NJ	55	449	8.2
Price, Cle	75	602	8.0

■ 3-Point Field Goal Percentage

	3FG	3FGA	Pct
Armstrong, Chi	63	139	.453
Mullin, GS	60	133	.451
Petrovic, NJ	75	167	.449
Smith, Hou	96	219	.438
Les, Sac	66	154	.429
Price, Cle.	122	293	.416
Porter, Por	143	345	.414
Ainge, Pho	150	372	.403
Scott, Orl	108	268	.403
Smith, Mia.	53	132	.402 ▶

▶ ■ **Steals**

	G	Steals	Avg
Jordan, Chi	78	221	2.83
Blaylock, Atl	80	203	2.54
Stockton, Utah	82	199	2.43
McMillan, Sea	73	173	2.37
Robertson, Mil-Det	69	155	2.25
Harper, LA-C	80	177	2.21
Murdock, Mil	79	174	2.20
Williams, Min	76	165	2.17
Payton, Sea	82	177	2.16
Pippen, Chi	81	173	2.14

■ **Blocked Shots**

	G	Blocks	Avg
Olajuwon, Hou	82	342	4.17
O'Neal, Orl	81	286	3.53
Mutombo, Den	82	287	3.50
Mourning, Cha	78	271	3.47
Robinson, SA	82	264	3.22
Nance, Cle	77	198	2.57
Ellison, Was	49	108	2.20
Bol, Phi	58	119	2.05
Robinson, Por	82	163	1.99
Ewing, NY	81	161	1.99

All-Time NBA Statistical Leaders

(as of the end of the 1991–92 season)

Scoring Average
(400 games or 10 000 points minimum)

	G	FGM	FTM	Points	Avg
Michael Jordan*	667	8 079	5 096	21 541	32.3
Wilt Chamberlain	1 045	12 681	6 057	31 419	30.1
Elgin Baylor	846	8 693	5 763	23 149	27.4
Jerry West	932	9 016	7 160	25 192	27.0
Dominique Wilkins*	833	8 322	5 013	22 096	26.5
Bob Pettit	792	7 349	6 182	20 880	26.4
George Gervin	791	8 045	4 541	20 708	26.2
Karl Malone*	570	5 458	3 725	14 770	25.9
Oscar Robertson	1 040	9 508	7 694	26 710	25.7
Kareem Abdul-Jabbar	1 560	15 837	6 712	38 387	24.6

Source: *National Basketball Association*

*active player

OTHER SPORTS

Canadian Curling Champions

Men

Year	Skip, Province	Year	Skip, Province	Year	Skip, Province
1927	Murray Macneill, N.S.	1941	Howard Palmer, Alta.	1958	Matt Baldwin, Alta.
1928	Gordon Hudson, Man.	1942	Ken Watson, Man.	1959	Ernie Richardson, Sask.
1929	Gordon Hudson, Man.	1946	Billy Rose, Alta.	1960	Ernie Richardson, Sask.
1930	Howard Wood, Man.	1947	Jimmy Welsh, Man.	1961	Hec Gervais, Alta.
1931	Bob Gourley, Man.	1948	Frenchy D'Amour, B.C.	1962	Ernie Richardson, Sask.
1932	Jim Congalton, Man.	1949	Ken Watson, Man.	1963	Ernie Richardson, Sask.
1933	Cliff Manahan, Alta.	1950	Tom Ramsay, N. Ont.	1964	Lyall Dagg, B.C.
1934	Leo Johnson, Man.	1951	Don Oyler, N.S.	1965	Terry Braunstein, Man.
1935	Gordon Campbell, Ont.	1952	Billy Walsh, Man.	1966	Ron Northcott, Alta.
1936	Ken Watson, Man.	1953	Ab Gowanlock, Man.	1967	Alf Phillips, Jr., Ont.
1937	Cliff Manahan, Alta.	1954	Matt Baldwin, Alta.	1968	Ron Northcott, Alta.
1938	Ab Gowanlock, Man.	1955	Garnet Campbell, Sask.	1969	Ron Northcott, Alta.
1939	Bert Hall, Ont.	1956	Billy Walsh, Man.	1970	Don Duguid, Man.
1940	Howard Wood, Man.	1957	Matt Baldwin, Alta.	1971	Don Duguid, Man.

▶

▶

Year	Skip, Province	Year	Skip, Province	Year	Skip, Province
1972	Orest Meleschuk, Man.	1980	Rick Folk, Sask.	1988	Pat Ryan, Alta.
1973	Harvey Mazinke, Sask.	1981	Kerry Burtnyk, Man.	1989	Pat Ryan, Alta.
1974	Hector Gervais, Alta.	1982	Al Hackner, N. Ont.	1990	Ed Werenich, Ont.
1975	Bill Tetley, N. Ont.	1983	Ed Werenich, Ont.	1991	Kevin Martin, Alta.
1976	Jack MacDuff, Nfld.	1984	Mike Riley, Man.	1992	Vic Peters, Man.
1977	Jim Ursel, Que.	1985	Al Hackner, N. Ont.	1993	Russ Howard, Ont.
1978	Ed Lukowich, Alta.	1986	Ed Lukowich, Alta.		
1979	Barry Fry, Man.	1987	Russ Howard, Ont.		

Women

Year	Skip, Province	Year	Skip, Province	Year	Skip, Province
1961	Joyce McKee, Sask.	1972	Vera Pezer, Sask.	1983	Penny LaRocque, N.S.
1962	Ina Hansen, B.C.	1973	Vera Pezer, Sask.	1984	Connie Laliberte, Man.
1963	Mabel DeWare, N.B.	1974	Emily Farnham, Sask.	1985	Linda Moore, B.C.
1964	Ina Hansen, B.C.	1975	Lee Tobin, Que.	1986	Marilyn Darte, Ont.
1965	Peggy Casselman, Man.	1976	Lindsay Davie, B.C.	1987	Pat Sanders, B.C.
1966	Gail Lee, Alta.	1977	Myrna McQuarrie, Alta.	1988	Heather Houston, Ont.
1967	Betty Duguid, Man.	1978	Cathy Pidzarko, Man.	1989	Heather Houston, Ont.
1968	Hazel Jamieson, Alta.	1979	Lindsay Sparkes, B.C.	1990	Alison Goring, Ont.
1969	Joyce McKee, Sask.	1980	Marj Mitchell, Sask.	1991	Julie Sutton, B.C.
1970	Dorenda Schoenhais, Sask.	1981	Susan Seitz, Alta.	1992	Connie Laliberte, Man.
1971	Vera Pezer, Sask.	1982	Colleen Jones, N.S.	1993	Sandra Peterson, Sask.

The World Cup

Soccer's World Cup, a month-long tournament held every four years, is widely regarded as the world's biggest sporting event. More than 100 countries spend two years competing in qualifying rounds to determine which nations earn the distinction of competing in the 24-team final round. Canada has only qualified for the final once, in 1986.

The final 24 teams are divided into six groups of four, with each team playing once against each of the others in its group. The two top teams in each group, plus the four with the next best records, advance to an elimination round leading to the final.

The 1990 final began in Milan June 8 and finished in Rome a month later. On July 8, an estimated one billion world-wide television viewers watched West Germany defeat defending champion Argentina in a 1-0 contest. It was the lowest-scoring final in the 60-year history of the event. Argentina managed only one shot on goal the entire game; West Germany got its only goal on a controversial penalty kick with only six minutes remaining in regulation time.

The 1994 World Cup will be hosted by the United States.

Year	Host nation	Final Game	Third Place	Tournament's Top scorer
1930	Uruguay	**Uruguay** 4, Argentina 2	—	Stabile, Argentina (8)
1934	Italy	**Italy** 2, Czechoslovakia 1	Germany 3, Austria 2	Several (4)
1938	France	**Italy** 4, Hungary 2	Brazil 4, Sweden 2	Leonadis, Brazil (8)
1942–46		Tournament not held because of Second World War		
1950	Brazil	**Uruguay** 2, Brazil 1	Sweden[1]	Ademir, Brazil (8)
1954	Switzerland	**W. Germany** 3, Hungary 2	Austria 3, Uruguay 1	Kocsis, Hungary (11)
1958	Sweden	**Brazil** 5, Sweden 2	France 6, W. Germany 3	Fontaine, France (13)
1962	Chile	**Brazil** 3, Czechoslovakia 1	Chile 1, Yugoslavia 0	Jerkovic, Yugoslavia (5)
1966	England	**England** 4, W. Germany 2	Portugal 2, Russia 1	Eusebio, Portugal (9)
1970	Mexico	**Brazil** 4, Italy 1	W. Germany 1, Uruguay 0	Muller, W. Germany (10)
1974	W. Germany	**W. Germany** 2, Holland 1	Poland 1, Brazil 0	Lato, Poland (7)
1978	Argentina	**Argentina** 3, Holland 1	Brazil 2, Italy 1	Kempes, Argentina (6)
1982	Spain	**Italy** 3, W. Germany 1	Poland 3, France 2	Rossi, Italy (6)
1986	Mexico	**Argentina** 3, W. Germany 2	France 4, Belgium 2	Lineker, England (6)
1990	Italy	**W. Germany** 1, Argentina 0	Italy 2, England 1	Schillaci, Italy (6)

(1) Based on point system.

Canadian Interuniversity Athletic Union Champions

Men

	Basketball	Football	Ice Hockey	Soccer	Swimming & Diving	Volleyball	Track & Field
1975/76	Manitoba	Ottawa	Toronto	Alberta	Toronto	B.C.	—
1976/77	Acadia	Western	Toronto	Concordia	Waterloo	Winnipeg	—
1977/78	St. Mary's	Western	Alberta	York	Waterloo	Manitoba	—
1978/79	St. Mary's	Queen's	Alberta	Manitoba	Waterloo	Saskatchewan	—
1979/80	Victoria	Acadia	Alberta	Alberta	Toronto	Manitoba	—
1980/81	Victoria	Alberta	Moncton	New Brunswick	Toronto	Alberta	Toronto
1981/82	Victoria	Acadia	Moncton	McGill	Calgary	Calgary	Toronto
1982/83	Victoria	B.C.	Saskatchewan	McGill	Calgary	B.C.	York
1983/84	Victoria	Calgary	Toronto	Laurentian	Calgary	Manitoba	York
1984/85	Victoria	Guelph	York	B.C.	Calgary	Manitoba	Toronto
1985/86	Victoria	Calgary	Alberta	B.C.	Toronto	Winnipeg	Toronto
1986/87	Brandon	B.C.	Trois-Rivières	B.C.	Calgary	Winnipeg	Saskatchewan
1987/88	Brandon	McGill	York	Victoria	Calgary	Manitoba	Manitoba
1988/89	Brandon	Calgary	York	Toronto	Calgary	Calgary	Manitoba
1989/90	Concordia	Western	Moncton	B.C.	Calgary	Laval	Manitoba/Toronto
1990/91	Western	Saskatchewan	Trois-Rivières	B.C.	Calgary	Manitoba	Windsor
1991/92	Brock	Wilfrid Laurier	Alberta	B.C.	Toronto	Laval	Manitoba
1992/93	St. Francis Xavier	Queen's	Acadia	B.C.	Toronto	Calgary	Windsor

Women

	Basketball	Field Hockey	Swimming & Diving	Track & Field	Volleyball
1975/76	Laurentian	Toronto	—	—	Western
1976/77	Laurentian	Dalhousie	Acadia	—	B.C.
1977/78	Laurentian	Toronto	Acadia	—	B.C.
1978/79	Laurentian	B.C.	Toronto	—	Saskatchewan
1979/80	Victoria	Toronto	Toronto	—	Saskatchewan
1980/81	Victoria	B.C.	Toronto	Western	Saskatchewan
1981/82	Victoria	Toronto	Toronto	Western	Dalhousie
1982/83	Bishop's	B.C.	Toronto	Western	Winnipeg
1983/84	Bishop's	B.C.	Toronto	York	Winnipeg
1984/85	Victoria	Victoria	B.C.	Alta. & Sask.	Winnipeg
1985/86	Toronto	Toronto	B.C.	Saskatchewan	Winnipeg
1986/87	Victoria	Toronto	Toronto	Calgary	Winnipeg
1987/88	Manitoba	Victoria	Toronto	York	Winnipeg
1988/89	Calgary	Toronto	Toronto	Toronto	Calgary
1989/90	Laurentian	Victoria	Toronto	York	Manitoba
1990/91	Laurentian	B.C.	Toronto	Calgary	Manitoba
1991/92	Victoria	Victoria	Toronto	Windsor	Manitoba
1992/93	Winnipeg	Victoria	Toronto	Windsor	Winnipeg

Source: *Canadian Interuniversity Athletic Union.*

First at U of W

The University of Winnipeg achieved an unprecedented feat when its men's and women's basketball and volleyball teams were all ranked first at the same time during the season by the Canadian Interuniversity Athletic Union.

Canadian Tennis Champions, 1970–93

Men's Singles

1970	Mike Belkin	1978	Harry Fritz	1986	Andrew Sznajder
1971	Peter Burwash	1979	Dale Power	1987	Andrew Sznajder
1972	Mike Belkin	1980	Greg Halder	1988	Andrew Sznajder
1973	Keith Carpenter	1981	Glenn Michibata	1989	Andrew Sznajder
1974	Pierre Lamarche	1982	Glenn Michibata	1990	Brian Gyetko
1975	Tony Bardsley	1983	Derek Segal	1991	Grant Connell
1976	Jim Boyce	1984	Stephane Bonneau	1992	Andrew Sznajder
1977	Harry Fritz	1985	Stephane Bonneau	1993	Andrew Sznajder

Women's Singles

1970	Andree Martin	1978	Marjorie Blackwood	1986	Carling Bassett
1971	Vicki Berner	1979	Marjorie Blackwood	1987	Helen Kelesi
1972	Janice Tindle	1980	Wendy Barlow	1988	Helen Kelesi
1973	Janice Tindle	1981	Nina Bland	1989	Helen Kelesi
1974	Susan Stone	1982	Carling Bassett	1990	Helen Kelesi
1975	Susan Stone	1983	Carling Bassett	1991	Patricia Hy
1976	Susan Stone	1984	Marianne Groat	1992	René Simpson-Alter
1977	Marjorie Blackwood	1985	Jane Young	1993	Patricia Hy

Source: *Tennis Canada*

An Canadian first, almost...

G rant Connell of Vancouver just missed becoming the first Canadian tennis player (other than a junior) to win a Wimbledon title when he and American partner Pat Galbraith lost to the number one pair of Australians Mark Woodforde and Todd Woodbridge, 7-5, 6-3, 7-6 (7-4) in the finals at the All England Club on July 3.

Canadian Swimming Records

(as of August 21, 1993)

Women

Event	Time	Swimmer	Site	Date
Freestyle				
50 m	26.01	Andrea Nugent	Montreal	Mar., 1987
	26.01	Kristin Topham	Havana	Aug. 18, 1991
100 m	56.29	Marianne Limpert	Buffalo	July 14, 1993
200 m	2:00.61	Patricia Noall	Toronto	Aug. 17, 1988
400 m	4:12.83	Julie Daigneault	Montreal	July 29, 1983
800 m	8:36.24	Debbie Wurzburger	Seoul	Sept. 23, 1988
1 500 m	16:40.60	Elissa Purvis	Los Altos, Cal.	July, 1986
Backstroke				
100 m	1:03.28	Nancy Garapick	Montreal	July 21, 1976
200 m	2:14.23	Cheryl Gibson	Berlin	Aug. 24, 1978
Breaststroke				
100 m	1:08.86	Allison Higson	Seoul	Sept. 23, 1988
200 m	2:27.27	Allison Higson	Montreal	May 29, 1988
Butterfly				
100 m	1:01.18	Kristin Topham	Vancouver	Aug. 31, 1991
200 m	2:11.48	Jill Horstead	Montreal	July 31, 1985
Individual Medley				
200 m	2:15.15	Marianne Limpert	Montreal	May 17, 1992
400 m	4:45.58	Nancy Sweetnam	Montreal	May 13, 1992 ▶

Event	Time	Swimmer	Site	Date
▶ **Relays**				
Freestyle				
100 m	3:46.75	1988 Olympic Team . . . . Kathy Bald, Patricia Noall, Andrea Nugent, Jane Kerr	Seoul	Sept. 22, 1988
200 m	8:10.65	1993 Canadian National Team . . . . Kathy Bald, Patricia Noall, Andrea Nugent, Jane Kerr	Kobe	Aug. 13, 1993
Medley				
100 m	4:09.26	1992 Olympic Team . . . . Nikki Dryden, Guylaine Cloutier, Kristin Topham, Andrea Nugent	Barcelona	July 14, 1992

Men

Event	Time	Swimmer	Site	Date
Freestyle				
50 m	22.81	Mark Andrews	Indianapolis	Apr. 10, 1988
100 m	50.45	Sandy Goss	Calgary	Aug. 2, 1989
200 m	1:49.71	Turlough O'Hare	Perth	Jan. 7, 199
400 m	3:50.49	Peter Szmidt	Etobicoke	July 16, 1980
800 m	8:00.22	Chris Bowie	Etobicoke	Aug. 3, 1990
1 500 m	15:12.63	Harry Taylor	Auckland, N.Z.	Jan. 30, 1990
Backstroke				
100 m	53.98[1]	Mark Tewksbury	Barcelona	July 30, 1992
200 m	2:00.54	Kevin Draxinger	Edmonton	Aug. 24, 1991
Breaststroke				
100 m	1:01.99	Victor Davis	Los Angeles	July 29, 1984
200 m	2:13.34	Victor Davis	Los Angeles	Aug. 2, 1984
Butterfly				
100 m	53.73	Marcel Gery	Gothenburg	Feb. 14, 1990
200 m	1:58.14	Tom Ponting	Montreal	May 31, 1988
Individual Medley				
200 m	2:01.42	Alex Baumann	Los Angeles	Aug. 4, 1984
400 m	4:17.41	Alex Baumann	Los Angeles	July 30, 1984
Relays				
Freestyle				
100 m	3:21.74	1987 Canadian National Team . . . . Vlastimil Cerny, Sandy Goss, Blair Hicken, Marcel Gery	Brisbane	Aug., 1987
200 m	7:22.74	1991 World Championships Team . . . . Eddie Parenti, Paul Szekula, Darren Ward, Turlough O'Hare	Perth	Jan. 8, 1991
Medley				
100 m	3:39.28	1988 Olympic Team . . . . Mark Tewksbury, Victor Davis, Tom Ponting, Sandy Goss	Seoul	Sept. 25, 1988

Source: *Swim Magazine*   (1) Olympic record

Canadian kayakers collect...

*C**anadian kayakers collected 12 medals, including seven golds, at the 18-country Paris International regatta, June 20-21, 1993. World champion Renn Crichlow, of Nepean, Ont., swept the singles events, winning the 200-metre, 500-metre, and 1000-metre races. Lizanne Bussieres-Chafe of London, Ont. won the Pittsburgh Marathon May 2 in a time of two hours, 35 minutes and 39 seconds. She collected $20,000 for winning.*

Canadian Boxing Champions, 1950–92

(as of August 1992)

Heavyweight
(79.379 kg and over)

1950–51	Vern Escoe (Edmonton)
1952–56	Earl Walls (Toronto)
1958–59	George Chuvalo (Toronto)
1960–62	Robert Cleroux (Montreal)
1964–77	George Chuvalo (Toronto)
1979–85	Trevor Berbick (Halifax)
1986	Ken Lakusta (Edmonton)
1986–87	Willie de Wit (Grand Prairie, Alta.)
1988–89	Razor Ruddock (Toronto)
1990	Ken Lakusta (Edmonton)
1991–	Conroy Nelson (Calgary)

Light Heavyweight
(79.379 kg max.)

1950–51	Tiger Warrington (Liverpool, N.S.)
1952	Eddie Zastre (Winnipeg)
1953	Yvon Durelle (Baie Ste. Anne)
1954	Doug Harper (Winnipeg)
1955–59	Yvon Durelle (Baie Ste. Anne)
1960–61	Burke Emery (Sherbrooke)
1964–67	Leslie Borden (Montreal)
1968–72	Al Sparks (Winnipeg)
1973–80	Gary Summerhays (Brantford)
1981–82	Roddie McDonald (Toronto)
1983–85	Donnie Lalonde (Winnipeg)
1986	Roddie McDonald (Toronto)
1986–89	Willie Featherstone (Toronto)
1990–91	Danny Stonewalker (Hobbema, Alta.)
1991–	Drake Thadzi (Moncton)

Middleweight
(72.575 kg max.)

1950–51	Roy Wouters (Vancouver)
1953	Yvon Durelle (Baie Ste. Anne)
1954	Charlie Chase (Montreal)
1955	Lou Lawrence (Vancouver)
1958–61	Wilf Greaves (Edmonton)
1962–65	Blair Richardson (Sydney, N.S.)
1966–69	Dave Downey (Halifax)
1970	Gary Broughton (Brantford)
1971–72	Dave Downey (Halifax)
1975	Lawrence Hafey (New Glasgow)
1976–79	Fernand Marcotte (Quebec)
1980–82	Ralph Hollett (Halifax)
1983–84	Alex Hilton (Montreal)
1985–88	Michael Olajide (Vancouver)
1989	Jacques Leblanc
1990–91	Daniel Sherry (Burlington)
1991	Otis Grant (Montreal)

Lightweight
(61.235 kg max.)

1950	Arthur King (Toronto)
1951–52	Armond Savoie (Montreal)
1953	Arthur King (Toronto)
1954–59	Richard Howard (Halifax)
1960–61	Eddie Beatie (Hamilton)
1963–65	Tyrone Gardner (Sydney, N.S.)
1966	Ronnie Sampson (Sydney, N.S.)
1967–73	Al Ford (Edmonton)
1974–75	Johnny Summerhays (Brantford)
1976	Barry Sponagle (New Glasgow, N.S.)
1977	Cleveland Denny (Montreal)
1978	Gaeton Hart (Buckingham, Que.)
1979	Nicky Furlano (Toronto)
1980	Gaeton Hart (Buckingham, Que.)
1981	Michael Lalonde (Hull)
1982	Johnny Summerhays (Brantford)
1983–87	Remo DiCarlo (Toronto)
1987–88	Mark Adams (Parrsboro, N.S.)
1989	John Kalbheen
1990–	Harpal Talhan (Edmonton)
1990–91	Mark Adams (Moncton) [1]
1991–	Howard Grant (Montreal

Welterweight
(66.678 kg max.)

1950–51	Johnny Greco (Montreal)
1952–53	Marcel Brisebois (Montreal)
1954	Claude Fortin (Montreal)
1955	Tony Percy (Montreal)
1956–57	Johnny Salkeld (Calgary)
1958	Gale Kerwin (Ottawa)
1960–61	Gale Kerwin (Ottawa)
1962–63	Peter Schmidt (Toronto)
1964–68	Joey Durelle (Baie Ste. Anne)
1969–70	Donato Paduano (Montreal)
1971–76	Clyde Gray (Toronto)
1977	Guerrero Chavex (Montreal)
1978–79	Clyde Gray (Toronto)
1980	Chris Clarke (Halifax)
1981–83	Mario Cusson (Montreal)
1984	Dave Hilton (Montreal)
1985	Donnie Poole (Toronto)
1986–87	Ricky Anderson (Halifax)
1987–	Donovan Boucher (Toronto) [2]

Featherweight
(57.153 kg max.)

1950–51	Frankie Almond (Vancouver)
1954	Mike Garlash (Kitchener)
1955–57	Gaby Palotti (Montreal)
1958	Gerry Simpson (Montreal)
1959–62	Dave Hilton (Montreal)
1965	Rocky McDougall (Sydney, N.S.)
1966–68	Billy McGrandle (Edmonton)
1969–70	Rocky McDougall (Sydney, N.S.)
1983–84	Tony Salvatore (Montreal)
1985–87	Tony Pep (Vancouver)
1988–90	Barrington Francis (Montreal) [3]
1990–	Vitorio Salvatore (Montreal)

Source: *Canadian Boxing Federation*   (1) Abdicated title due to injury. (2) British Commonwealth champion. (3) WBF World Champion.

Canadian Alpine Skiing Champions

Men

	Downhill	Slalom	Giant Slalom	Super Giant Slalom
1979	Ken Read	Raymond Pratte	Peter Monod	—
1980	Ken Read	Peter Monod	Peter Monod	—
1981	Robin McLeish	Peter Monod	Peter Monod	—
1982	Urs Raeber (SUI)	Peter Monod	Jim Read	—
1983	Steve Podborski	Francois Jodoin	Mike Tommy	—
1984	Steve Podborski	Mike Tommy	Jim Read	Jim Read
1985	Steven Lee (AUS)	Gordon Perry	Jim Read	Mike Brown (USA)
1986	Don Stevens	Jim Read	Jim Read	Derek Trussler
1987	Brian Stemmle	Alain Villiard	Alain Villiard	Jim Read
1988	Steven Lee (AUS)	Jack Miller (USA)	Tiger Shaw (USA)	Leonard Stock (AUT)
1989	Mike Carney	Alain Villiard	Alain Villiard	Felix Belczyk
1990	Felix Belczyk	Rob Crossan	Robbie Parisien	David Duchesne
1991	Edi Podivinsky	Eric Villiard	Eric Villiard	Rob Boyd
1992	Reggie Crist (USA)	Rob Crossan	Thomas Grandi	Reggie Crist (USA)
1993	John Mealey	Rob Crossan	Thomas Grandi	Eric Villiard

Women

	Downhill	Slalom	Giant Slalom	Super Giant Slalom
1979	Lani Kletl	Kathy Kreiner	Judy Richardson	—
1980	Laurie Graham	Lynn Lacasse	Ann Blackburn	—
1981	Gerry Sorensen	Josée Lacasse	Diana Haight	—
1982	Dianne Lehodey	Lynn Lacasse	Lynn Lacasse	—
1983	Gerry Sorensen	Lynn Lacasse	Liisa Savijarvi	—
1984	Diana Haight	Andréa Bedard	Liisa Savijarvi	Laurie Graham
1985	Laurie Graham	Andréa Bedard	Liisa Savijarvi	Karen Percy
1986	Karen Percy	Josée Lacasse	Josée Lacasse	Karen Percy
1987	Liisa Savijarvi	Julie Klotz	Josée Lacasse	Karen Percy
1988	Laurie Graham	Josée Lacasse	Karen Percy	Karen Percy
1989	Lucie LaRoche	Sonja Rusch	Karen Percy	Kendra Kobelka
1990	Lucie LaRoche	Josée Lacasse	Josée Lacasse	Nancy Gee
1991	Kerrin Lee-Gartner	Sonja Rusch	Annie Laurendeau	Michelle McKendry
1992	Kerrin Lee-Gartner	Annie Laurendeau	Michelle McKendry	Michelle McKendry
1993	Kerrin Lee-Gartner	Nanci Gee	Melanie Turgeon	Michelle McKendry-Ruthuen

Source: *Alpine Canada*

Canadian skiing champs

*I**t was a successful year for Canada in international skiing. Kate Pace of North Bay, Ont. captured her first World Cup downhill race. She won March 13 in Lillehammer, Norway, site of
the 1994 Winter Olympics. A week earlier, she captured the women's downhill at the world
championships in Shizukuishi, Japan. Jean-Luc Brassard of Grande-Ile, Que. won the World
Cup in freestyle skiing's Grand Prix Moguls. John Smart of Lions Bay, BC finished second.
Myriam Bedard of Loreteville, Que., who won a surprising bronze medal in the biathlon at the
1992 Winter Olympics, finished second in World Cup standings to Anfisa Revtsova of Russia.
Bedard became the first Canadian to win an international biathlon event with a victory in the 7.5
kilometre sprint in Borovets, Bulgaria Feb. 13, 1993.*

Figure Skating Champions, 1952–93

	Canadian Champions		World Champions	
	Men	**Women**	**Men**	**Women**
1952	Peter Firstbrook	Marlene Smith	Richard Button, U.S.	Jacqueline du Bief, France
1953	Peter Firstbrook	Barbara Gratton	Hayes Jenkins, U.S.	Tenley Albright, U.S.
1954	Charles Snelling	Barbara Gratton	Hayes Jenkins, U.S.	Gundi Busch, W. Germany
1955	Charles Snelling	Carole Jane Pachl	Hayes Jenkins, U.S.	Tenley Albright, U.S.
1956	Charles Snelling	Carole Jane Pachl	Hayes Jenkins, U.S.	Carol Heiss, U.S.
1957	Charles Snelling	Carole Jane Pachl	Dave Jenkins, U.S.	Carol Heiss, U.S.
1958	Charles Snelling	Margaret Crosland	Dave Jenkins, U.S.	Carol Heiss, U.S.
1959	Donald Jackson	Margaret Crosland	Dave Jenkins, U.S.	Carol Heiss, U.S.
1960	Donald Jackson	Wendy Griner	Alain Giletti, France	Carol Heiss, U.S.
1961	Donald Jackson	Wendy Griner	none[1]	none[a]
1962	Donald Jackson	Wendy Griner	Don Jackson, Canada	Sjoukje Dijkstra, Neth.
1963	Donald McPherson	Wendy Griner	Don McPherson, Canada	Sjoukje Dijkstra, Neth.
1964	Charles Snelling	Petra Burka	Manfred Schnelldorfer, W. Germany	Sjoukje Dijkstra, Neth.
1965	Donald Knight	Petra Burka	Alain Calmat, France	Petra Burka, Canada
1966	Donald Knight	Petra Burka	Emmerich Danzer, Austria	Peggy Fleming, U.S.
1967	Donald Knight	Valerie Jones	Emmerich Danzer, Austria	Peggy Fleming, U.S.
1968	Jay Humphry	Karen Magnussen	Emmerich Danzer, Austria	Peggy Fleming, U.S.
1969	Jay Humphry	Linda Carbonetto	Tim Wood, U.S.	Gabriele Seyfert, E. Germany
1970	David McGillivray	Karen Magnussen	Tim Wood, U.S.	Gabriele Seyfert, E. Germany
1971	Toller Cranston	Karen Magnussen	Ondrej Nepela, Czech.	Beatrix Schuba, Austria
1972	Toller Cranston	Karen Magnussen	Ondrej Nepela, Czech.	Beatrix Schuba, Austria
1973	Toller Cranston	Karen Magnussen	Ondrej Nepela, Czech.	Karen Magnussen, Canada
1974	Toller Cranston	Lynn Nightingale	Jan Hoffman, E. Germany	Christine Errath, E. Germany
1975	Toller Cranston	Lynn Nightingale	Sergei Volkov, USSR	Dianne de Leeuw, Neth.-U.S.
1976	Toller Cranston	Lynn Nightingale	John Curry, Gr. Brit.	Dorothy Hamill, U.S.
1977	Ron Shaver	Lynn Nightingale	Vladimir Kovalev, USSR	Linda Fratianne, U.S.
1978	Brian Pockar	Heather Kemkaran	Charles Tickner, U.S.	Anett Poetzsch, E. Germany
1979	Brian Pockar	Janet Morrisey	Vladimir Kovalev, USSR	Linda Fratianne, U.S.
1980	Brian Pockar	Heather Kemkaran	Jan Hoffmann, E. Germany	Anett Poetzsch, E. Germany
1981	Brian Orser	Tracey Wainman	Scott Hamilton, U.S.	Denise Biellmann, Switzerland
1982	Brian Orser	Kay Thomson	Scott Hamilton, U.S.	Elaine Zayak, U.S.
1983	Brian Orser	Kay Thomson	Scott Hamilton, U.S.	Rosalyn Sumners, U.S.
1984	Brian Orser	Kay Thomson	Scott Hamilton, U.S.	Katarina Witt, E. Germany
1985	Brian Orser	Elizabeth Manley	Alexandre Fadeev, USSR	Katarina Witt, E. Germany
1986	Brian Orser	Tracey Wainman	Brian Boitano, U.S.	Debi Thomas, U.S.
1987	Brian Orser	Elizabeth Manley	Brian Orser, Canada	Katarina Witt, E. Germany
1988	Brian Orser	Elizabeth Manley	Brian Boitano, U.S.	Katarina Witt, E. Germany
1989	Kurt Browning	Karen Preston	Kurt Browning, Canada	Midori Ito, Japan
1990	Kurt Browning	Lisa Sargeant	Kurt Browning, Canada	Jill Trenary, U.S.
1991	Kurt Browning	Josée Chouinard	Kurt Browning, Canada	Kristi Yamaguchi, U.S.
1992	Michael Slipchuk	Karen Preston	Victor Petrenko, Russia	Kristi Yameguchi, U.S.
1993	Kurt Browning	Josée Chouinard	Kurt Browning, Canada	Oksana Baiul, Ukraine

Source: *Canadian Figure Skating Association*

(1) The 1961 world championships were cancelled after an air crash killed the entire U.S. team travelling to the competition.

Canadians win gold in Prague

C anadians won two of four gold medals in the world figure skating championships, held in Prague in March, 1993. Kurt Browning of Alberta resurfaced as the men's champion, while Isabelle Brasseur of St-Jean-sur-Richelieu, Que. and Llyod Eisler of Seaforth, Ont. finally captured their elusive first title in pairs competition.

Canadian Open Golf Tournament, 1904–93

	Winner	Score		Winner	Score
1904	J.H. Oke	156	1951	Jim Ferrier	273
1905	George Cumming	146	1952	John Palmer	263
1906	Charles Murray	170	1953	Dave Douglas	273
1907	Percy Barrett	306	1954	Pat Fletcher[1]	280
1908	Albert Murray	300	1955	Arnold Palmer	265
1909	Karl Keffer	309	1956	Doug Sanders	273
1910	Daniel Kenny	303	1957	George Bayer	271
1911	Charles Murray	314	1958	Wesley Ellis Jr.	267
1912	George Sargent	299	1959	Doug Ford	276
1913	Albert Murray	295	1960	Art Wall Jr.	269
1914	Karl Keffer	300	1961	Jacky Cupit	270
1915–1918 No Tournament			1962	Ted Kroll	278
1919	J. Douglas Edgar	278	1963	Doug Ford	280
1920	J. Douglas Edgar	298	1964	Kel Nagle	277
1921	W.H. Trovinger	293	1965	Gene Littler	273
1922	Al Watrous	303	1966	Don Massengale	280
1923	C.W. Hackney	295	1967	Bill Casper	279
1924	Leo Diegel	285	1968	Bob Charles	274
1925	Leo Diegel	295	1969	Tommy Aaron	275
1926	Macdonald Smith	283	1970	Kermit Zarley	279
1927	T.D. Armour	288	1971	Lee Trevino	275
1928	Leo Diegel	282	1972	Gay Brewer	275
1929	Leo Diegel	274	1973	Tom Weiskopf	278
1930	T.D. Armour	277	1974	Bobby Nichols	270
1931	Walter Hagen	292	1975	Tom Weiskopf	274
1932	Harry Cooper	290	1976	Jerry Pate	267
1933	Joe Kirkwood	282	1977	Lee Trevino	280
1934	T.D. Armour	287	1978	Bruce Lietzke	283
1935	Gene Kunes	280	1979	Lee Trevino	281
1936	Lawson Little	271	1980	Bob Gilder	274
1937	Harry Cooper	285	1981	Peter Oosterhuis	280
1938	Sam Snead	277	1982	Bruce Lietzke	277
1939	Harold McSpaden	282	1983	John Cook	277
1940	Sam Snead	281	1984	Greg Norman	278
1941	Sam Snead	274	1985	Curtis Strange	279
1942	Craig Wood	275	1986	Bob Murphy	280
1943–1944 No Tournament			1987	Curtis Strange	276
1945	Byron Nelson	280	1988	Ken Green	275
1946	George Fazio	278	1989	Steve Jones	271
1947	Robert Locke	268	1990	Wayne Levi	278
1948	C.W. Congdon	280	1991	Nick Price	273
1949	E.J. Dutch Harrison	271	1992	Greg Norman	280
1950	Jim Ferrier	271	1993	David Frost	279

Source: *Royal Canadian Golf Association*

(1) Last Canadian winner.

A stroke of luck in paradise...

*W**hen Lisa Walters won the Hawaiian Ladies Open golf title Feb. 20, it was the fourth time in 12 months a Canadian had won an LPGA tournament in Hawaii. Walters, of Prince Rupert, BC defended the title she won the previous year with a one-stroke win over Nancy Lopez. Dawn Coe-Jones, of Lake Cowichan, BC, won two major tournaments in Hawaii—the Women's Kemper Open and the LPGA Match Play championship.*

Du Maurier Ltd. Women's Golf Classic, 1973–93

	Winner	Score		Winner	Score
1973[1]	Jocelyne Bourassa	214	1984	Juli Inkster	274
1974[1]	Carol Jo Skala	208	1985	Pat Bradley	278
1975[1]	JoAnne Carner	214	1986	Pat Bradley	276
1976[1]	Donna Caponi Young	212	1987	Jodi Rosenthal	272
1977[1]	Judy T. Rankin	212	1988	Sally Little	279
1978	JoAnne Carner	278	1989	Tammie Green	279
1979	Amy Alcott	285	1990	Cathy Johnston	276
1980	Pat Bradley	277	1991	Nancy Scranton	279
1981	Jan Stephenson	278	1992	Sherri Steinhauer	277
1982	Sandra Haynie	280	1993	Brandie Burton[2]	277
1983	Hollis Stacy	277			

(1) Three rounds only. (2) Won on first playoff hole vs. Betsy King.

The Queen's Plate, 1920–93

The Queen's Plate, first run in 1860, is North America's oldest annual sports event. The race for 3-year-olds foaled in Canada, is run at Toronto's Woodbine Race Track in late June or July.

	Winner	Jockey	Time[1]		Winner	Jockey	Time[1]
1920	St. Paul	Roxy Romanelli	2:09	1957	Lyford Cay	Avelino Gomez	2:02.3
1921	Herendesy	Jimmy Butwell	2:10	1958	Calendon Beau	Al Coy	2:04.1
1922	South Shore	Kenny Parrington	2:12	1959	New Providence	Robert Ussery	2:04.4
1923	Flowerful	Terry Wilson	2:11	1960	Victoria Park	Avelino Gomez	2:02
1924	Maternal Pride	George Walls	1:57.3	1961	Blue Light	Hugo Dittfach	2:05
1925	Fairbank	Chick Lang	1:56.2	1962	Flaming Page	Jim Fitzsimmons	2:04.3
1926	Haplite	Henry Erickson	1:59.3	1963	Canebora	Manuel Ycaza	2:04
1927	Troutlet	Francis Horn	1:55.4	1964	Northern Dancer	Bill Hartack	2:02.1
1928	Young Kitty	Lester Pichon	1:57	1965	Whistling Sea	Tak Inouye	2:03.4
1929	Shorelint	Jaydee Mooney	1:57.3	1966	Titled Hero	Avelino Gomez	2:03.3
1930	Aymond	Henry Little	1:57.1	1967	Jammed Lovely	Jim Fitzsimmons	2:03
1931	Froth Blower	Frank Mann	1:59.1	1968	Merger	Wayne Harris	2:05.2
1932	Queensway	Frank Mann	1:55.1	1969	Jumpin Joseph	Avelino Gomez	2:04.1
1933	King O'Connor	Eddie Legere	1:56.2	1970	Almoner	Sandy Hawley	2:04.4
1934	Horometer	Frank Mann	1:54.1	1971	Kennedy Road	Sandy Hawley	2:03
1935	Sally Fuller	Herb Lindberg	1:55.1	1972	Victoria Song	Robin Platts	2:03.1
1936	Monsweep	Danny Brammer	1:55	1973	Royal Chocolate	Ted Colangelo	2:08
1937	Goldlure	Sterling Young	1:55.2	1974	Amber Herod	Robin Platts	2:09.1
1938	Bunty Lawless	John Bailey	1:54.2	1975	L'Enjoleur	Sandy Hawley	2:02.3
1939	Archworth	Sydney D. Birley	1:54.2	1976	Norcliffe	Jeffrey Fell	2:05
1940	Willie the Kid	Ronnie Nash	1:55.4	1977	Sound Reason	Robin Platts	2:06.3
1941	Budpath	Bobby Watson	1:56.4	1978	Regal Embrace	Sandy Hawley	2:02
1942	Ten to Ace	Charlie Smith	1:57.4	1979	Steady Growth	Brian Swatuk	2:06.3
1943	Paolita	Pat Remillard	2:02.3	1980	Driving Home	Bill Parsons	2:04.1
1944	Acara	Bobby Watson	1:54.4	1981	Fiddle Dancer Boy	David Clark	2:04.4
1945	Uttermost	Bobby Watson	1:53.4	1982	Son of Briartic	John-Paul Souter	2:04.3
1946	Kingarvie	Johnny Dewhurst	1:55.3	1983	Bompago	Larry Attard	2:04.1
1947	Moldy	Colin McDonald	1:54.1	1984	Key to the Moon	Robin Platts	2:03.4
1948	Last Mark	Howard Bailey	1:52	1985	La Lorgnette	David Clark	2:04.3
1949	Epic	Chris Rogers	1:52.1	1986	Golden Choice	Vince Bracciale	2:07.1
1950	McGill	Chris Rogers	1:52.2	1987	Market Control	Ken Skinner	2:03.2
1951	Major Factor	Alf Bavington	1:53	1988	Regal Intention	Jack Lauzon	2:06.1
1952	Epigram	Gil Robillard	1:58.3	1989	With Approval	Don Seymour	2:03
1953	Canadiana	Eddie Arcaro	1:52.1	1990	Izvestia	Don Seymour	2:01.4
1954	Collisteo	Chris Rogers	1:52	1991	Dance Smartly	Pat Day	2:03.2
1955	Ace Marine	George Walker	1:52.2	1992	Alydeed	Craig Perret	2:04.6
1956	Canadian Champ	Dave Stevenson	1:55	1993	Peteski	Craig Perret	2:04.2

Source: *Ontario Jockey Club*

(1) Fractions of a second are in fifths.

1993 U.S. Triple Crown Winners

Race	Winner	Jockey
Kentucky Derby	Sea Hero	Jerry Bailey
Preakness	Prairie Bayou	Mike Smith
Belmont Stakes	Colonial Affair	Julie Krone

Prince of Wales Stakes, 1960–93

	Winner	Jockey	Time[1]		Winner	Jockey	Time[1]
1960	Bulpamiru	Hugo Dittfach	2:19.4	1977	Dance in Time	Gary Stahlbaum	2:31.4
1961	Song of Even	Jim Fitzsimmons	2:29.0	1978	Overskate	Robin Platts	2:34.2
1962	King Gorm	Hugo Dittfach	2:21.1	1979	Mass Rally	George Ho Sang	2:33.2
1963	Canebora	Hugo Dittfach	2:30.3	1980	Allan Blue	Joe Belowus	2:34.4
1964	Canadillis	Avelino Gomez	2:35.0	1981	Cadet Corps	Robin Platts	2:34.4
1965	Good Old Mort	S. McComb	2:22.4	1982	Runaway Groom	Robin Platts	2:38.2
1966	He's A Smoothie	Hugo Dittfach	2:19.0	1983	Archdeacon	Vince Bracciale	2:32.0
1967	Battling	Hugo Dittfach	2:21.0	1984	Val Dansant	John LeBlanc	2:48.3
1968	Rouletabille	Richard Grubb	2:18.3	1985	Imperial Choice	Irwin Driedger	2:34.3
1969	Sharp-Eyed Quillo	H. Gustines	2:16.3	1986	Golden Choice	Vince Bracciale	2:44.2
1970	Almoner	Sandy Hawley	2:19.4	1987	Coryphee	Brian Swatuk	2:39.3
1971	New Pro	Jim Kelly	2:15.1	1988	Regal Classic	Sandy Hawley	2:00.1
1972	Presidial	John LeBlanc	2:16.3	1989	With Approval	Don Seymour	1:56.4
1973	Tara Road	Sandy Hawley	2:16.4	1990	Izvestia	Don Seymour	1:56.2
1974	Rushton's Corsair	Jim Kelly	2:23.2	1991	Dance Smartly	Pal Day	1:56.3
1975	L'Enjoleur	Sandy Hawley	2:32.2	1992	Benburb	Larry Attard	1:57.2
1976	Norcliffe	Jeff Fell	2:30.1	1993	Peteski	Dave Penna[2]	1:54.4

Source: *Ontario Jockey Club*

(1) Fractions of a second are in fifths. (2) Peteski's regular jockey, Craig Perret, was serving a 15-day suspension.

"Sky" is "Eclipsed"

Sky Classic won a prestigious Eclipse Award as North America's top turf horse for 1992. The awards are given annually by the Thoroughbred Racing Association. Sky Classic is owned by Ernie Samuel's Sam-Son Farm in Oakville, Ont.

Breeders Stakes, 1960–93

Year	Winner	Jockey	Time[1]	Year	Winner	Jockey	Time[1]
1960	Hidden Treasure	Al Coy	2:34.2	1975	Momigi	Gary Melanson	2:38.1
1961	Song of Even	Jim Fitzsimmons	2:31.3	1976	Tiny Tinker	Sandy Hawley	2:31.1
1962	Crafty Lace	Ron Turcotte	2:52	1977	Dance in Time	Gary Stahlbaum	3:01.3
1963	Canebora	Manuel Ycaza	2:32.1	1978	Overskate	Robin Platts	2:29.2
1964	Artic Hills	R. Armstrong	2:33.3	1979	Bridle Path	Sandy Hawley	2:29.3
1965	Good Old Mort	P. Kallai	2:43	1980	Ben Fab	Gary Stahlbaum	2:31.3
1966	Titled Hero	Avelino Gomez	2:31.2	1981	Social Wizard	George Ho Sang	2:48.4
1967	Pine Point	Avelino Gomez	2:32.1	1982	Runaway Groom	Robin Platts	2:32.1
1968	No Parando	John LeBlanc	2:30	1983	Kingsbridge	Robin Platts	2:32.2
1969	Grey Whiz	John LeBlanc	2:29	1984	Bounding Away	David Clark	2:32.3
1970	Mary of Scotland	Richard Grubb	2:38.2	1985	Crowning Honors	Brian Swatuk	2:50
1971	Belle Geste	Noel Turcotte	2:28	1986	Carotene	Richard Dos Ramos	2:32.3
1972	Nice Dancer	Sandy Hawley	2:35.4	1987	Hangin On a Star	Dave Penna	2:30
1973	Come In Dad	Wayne Green	2:33.3	1988	King's Deputy	Sandy Hawley	2:30.3
1974	Haymaker's Jig	Robin Platts	2:30.4	1989	With Approval	Don Seymour	2:29

▶

Year	Winner	Jockey	Time[1]	Year	Winner	Jockey	Time[1]
1990	Izvestia	Don Seymour	2:33.2	1992	Blitzer	Don Seymour	2:35.6
1991	Dance Smartly	Pal Day	2:31.2	1993	Peteski	Craig Perret	2:30.4

Source: *Ontario Jockey Club*

(1) Fractions of a second are in fifths.

Breeder's comes to T.O.

The Breeder's Cup, the World series of throughbred racing, will be held at Toronto's Woodbine race track in 1996. The Cups's board of directors announced Feb. 23 that it had awarded the event to the Ontario Jockey Club. total purses for the seven races is $10 million, with the Breeder's Cup Classic—at $3 million—the world's richest race.

World Track and Field Records

(as of Sept. 17, 1993)

Men

Event	Record	Holder/Country	Date	Where Made
■ Running				
100 m	9.86	Carl Lewis, U.S.	Aug. 25, 1991	Tokyo
200 m	19.72	Pietro Mennea, Italy	Sept. 12, 1979	Mexico City
400 m	43.29	Harry Reynolds, U.S.	Aug. 17, 1988	Zurich
800 m	1:41.7	Sebastian Coe, Gr. Britain	June 10, 1981	Florence
1 000 m	2:12.181	Sebastian Coe, Gr. Britain	July 11, 1981	Oslo
1 500 m	3:28.86	Nourredine Morceli, Algeria	Sept. 6, 1992	Rieti, Italy
1 mile	3:44.39	Nourredine Morceli, Algeria	Sept. 4, 1993	Rieti, Italy
2 000 m	4:50.81	Said Aouita, Morocco	July 16, 1987	Paris
3 000 m	7:29.45	Said Aouita, Morocco	Aug. 20, 1989	Cologne
	*7:28.96	Moses Kiptanui, Kenya	Aug. 16, 1992	Cologne
5 000 m	12:58.39	Said Aouita, Morocco	July 22, 1987	Rome
10 000 m	26:58.38	Yobes Ondieki, Kenya	July 10, 1993	Oslo
20 000 m	56:55.60	Arturo Barrios, Mexico	Mar. 30, 1991	La Fleche
25 000 m	1.13:55.80	Toshihiko Seko, Japan	Mar. 22 1981	Christchurch, N.Z.
30 000 m	1.29:18.80	Toshihiko Seko, Japan	Mar. 22, 1981	Christchurch, N.Z.
3 000 m steeplechase	8:05.35	Peter Koech, Kenya	July 3, 1989	Stockholm
Marathon	2.06:06.50	Belayneh Dinsamo, Ethiopia	Apr. 17, 1988	Rotterdam
■ Hurdles				
110 m	12.91	Colin Jackson, Gr. Britain	Aug. 20 1993	Stuttgart
400 m	46.78	Kevin Young, U.S.	Aug. 6, 1992	Barcelona
■ Relay Races				
100 m	37.40	(Marsh, Burrell, Mitchell, Lewis), U.S.	Aug. 8, 1992	Barcelona
	37.40	(Drummond, Cason, Mitchell, Burrell), U.S.	Aug. 21, 1993	Stuttgart
200 m	1:19.1	Santa Monica, U.S.	Apr. 25, 1992	Philadelphia
400 m	2:54.29	(Valmon, Watts, Reynolds, Johnson), U.S.	Aug. 22, 1993	Stuttgart
800 m	7:03.89	(Elliott, Cook, Cram, Coe), Gr. Britain	Aug. 30, 1982	London
■ Field Events				
High jump	2.44 m	Javier Sotomayor, Cuba	July 27, 1993	Salamanca, Spain
Long jump	8.95 m	Mike Powell, U.S.	Aug. 30, 1991	Tokyo
Triple jump	17.97 m	Willie Banks, U.S.	June 16, 1985	Indianapolis
Pole vault	6.13 m	Sergey Bubka, Ukraine	Aug. 30, 1992	Tokyo
7.26 kg shot put	23.12 m	Randolph Barnes, U.S.	May 20, 1990	Los Angeles
Discus throw	74.08 m	Jurgen Schult, E. Germany	June 6, 1986	E. Germany
Javelin throw	91.46 m	Steve Backley, Gr. Britain	Jan. 25, 1992	Auckland, N.Z.
7.26 kg hammer throw	86.74 m	Yuri Sedykh, USSR	Aug. 30, 1986	Stuttgart

▶ ■ **Walking**

30 km	2.03:56.51	Thierry Toutain, France	Mar. 24, 1991	Hericourt
50 km	3.37:00.41	Andrey Perlov, USSR	Aug. 5, 1989	Leningrad

Women

Event	Record	Holder/Country	Date	Where Made
■ **Running**				
100 m	10.49	Florence Griffith-Joyner, U.S.	July 16, 1988	Indianapolis
200 m	21.34	Florence Griffith-Joyner, U.S.	Sept. 29, 1988	Seoul
400 m	47.60	Marita Koch, E. Germany	Oct. 6, 1985	Canberra
800 m	1:53.28	Jarmila Kratochvilova, Czech.	July 26, 1983	Munich
1 500 m	3:50.46	Qu Yunxia, China	Sept. 11, 1993	Beijing
1 mile	4:15.61	Paula Ivan, Romania	July 10, 1989	Nice
2 000 m	5:28.69	Maricica Puica, Romania	July 11, 1986	London
3 000 m	8:06.11	Wang Junxia, China	Sept. 13, 1993	Beijing
5 000 m	14:37.33	Ingrid Kristiansen, Norway	Aug. 5, 1986	Stockholm
10 000 m	29:31.78	Wang Junxia, China	Sept. 8, 1993	Beijing
30 000 m	1:47:05.6	Karolina Szabo, Hungary	Apr. 22, 1988	Budapest
Marathon	2.21:06.00	Ingrid Kristiansen, Norway	Apr. 21, 1985	London
■ **Hurdles**				
100 m	12.21	Yordanka Donkova, Bulgaria	Aug. 20, 1988	Stara Zagora
400 m	52.74	Sally Gunnell, Gr. Britain	Aug. 19, 1993	Stuttgart
■ **Field Events**				
High jump	2.09 m	Stefka Kostadinova, Bulgaria	Aug. 8, 1987	Rome
Shot put	22.63 m	Natalya Lisovskaya, USSR	June 7, 1987	Moscow
Long jump	7.52 m	Galina Christyakova, USSR	June 11, 1988	Leningrad
Discus throw	76.80	Gabriele Reinsch, E. Germany	July 9, 1988	Neubrandenburg
Javelin	80.00 m	Petra Felke, E. Germany	Sept. 9, 1988	Potsdam
Heptathlon	7 291 pts.	Jackie Joyner-Kersee, U.S.	Sept. 24, 1988	Seoul
Triple jump	15.09 m	Ana Biryukova, Russia	Aug. 21, 1993	Stuttgart
Hammer throw	64.44 m	Alla Fyodorova, USSR	Feb. 26, 1991	Adler, USSR
■ **Relay Races**				
100m	41.37	National team, E. Germany	Oct. 6, 1985	Canberra
200m	1:28.15	National team, E. Germany	Aug. 9, 1980	Jena, E. Germany
400m	3:15.17	National team, USSR	Oct. 1, 1988	Seoul
800m	7:50.17	National team, USSR	Aug. 5, 1984	Moscow
■ **Walking**				
5 000 m	20:17.19	Kerry Saxby, Australia	Jan. 14, 1990	Sydney
10 000 m	41:56.23	Nadezhda Ryashkina, USSR	July 24, 1990	Seattle

Source: *Canadian Track and Field Association*   (1) Record set at high altitude. (*) Pending ratification.

World Track and Field Championships

Stuttgart, Germany, Aug. 14-22, 1993

Men

100 metres—Linford Christie, Britain, 9.87
200 metres—Frank Fredericks, Namibia, 19.85
400 metres—Michael Johnson, US, 43.65
800 metres—Paul Ruto, Kenya, 1:44.71
1500 metres—Noureddine Morceli, Algeria, 3:24.24
5000 metres—Ismael Kirui, Kenya, 13:02.75
10 000 metres—Haile Gebresilasie, Ethiopia, 27:46.02

Marathon—Mark Plaatjes, US, 2:13:57
110-metre hurdles—Colin Jackson, Britain, 12.91*
400-metre hurdles—Kevin Young, US, 47.18
3000-metre steeplechase—Moses Kiptanui, Kenya, 8:06.36
4x100-metre relay—United States, 37.48
4x400-metre relay—United States, 2:54.29*
Decathlon—Dan O'Brien, US, 8817 points.

▶

20-km walk—Valentin Massana, Spain, 1:22:31
50-km walk—Jesus Angel Garcia, Spain, 3:41:41
High jump—Javier Sotomayor, Cuba, 2.40
Long jump—Mike Powell, US, 8.59
Triple jump—Mike Conley, US, 17.86

Pole vault—Sergey Bubka, Ukraine, 6.00
Discus—Lars Riedel, Germany, 67.72
Shotput—Werner Gunthor, Switzerland,, 21.97
Hammer throw—Andrey Abduvaliyev, Tadjikistan, 81.64
Javelin—Jan Zelezny, Czech republic, 85.98

Women

100 metres—Gail Devers, US, 10.81
200 metres—Merelen Ottey, Jamaica, 21.98
400 metres—Jearl Miles, US, 49.82
800 metres—Maria Mutola, Mozambique, 1:55.43
1500 metres—Dong Liu, China, 4:00.50
3000 metres—Yunxia Qu, China, 8:28.71
10,000 metres—Junxia Wang, China, 30:49.30
Marathon—Junko Asari, Japan, 2:30:03
100-metre hurdles—Gail Devers, US, 12.46
400-metre hurdles—Sally Gunnell, Britain, 52.74*

4x100-metre relay—Russia, 41.49
4x400-metre relay—United States, 3:16.71
Heptathlon—Jackie Joyner-Kersee, US, 6837 points
10km walk—Sari Essayeh, Finland, 42:59
High jump—Ioamnet Quintero, Cuba, 1.99
Long jump—Heike Drechsler, Germany, 7.11
Triple jump—Ana Biryukova, Russia, 15.09*
Discus—Olga Burova, Russia, 67.40
Shotput—Zhihong Huang, China, 20.57
Javelin—Trine Hattestad, Norway, 69.18

* world record

Canadian Track and Field Championships

Coquitlam, BC
July 31–Aug. 1, 1993

Men

100 metres—Atlee Mahorn, Que. 10.25
200 metres—Glenroy Gilbert, Ont. 20.63
400 metres—Troy Jackson, Alta 46.69
800 metres—Freddie Williams, Ont. 1:47.13
1500 metres—Kevin Sullivan, Ont. 3:41.58
3000 metres—Graeme Fell, BC 8:28.90
5000 metres—David Reid, Ont. 13:54.64
10,000 metres—David Reid, Ont. 29:00.04
110-metre hurdles—Timothy Kroeker, BC 13.78
400-metre hurdles—Mark Jackson, Ont. 50.82

20-kilometre walk—Tim Berrett, Sask. 1:26:45.3
High Jump—Alex Zaliauskas, Ont. 2.24 metres
Long Jump—Edrick Floreal, Que. 7.89 metres
Triple Jump—Karl Dyer, Ont. 15.46 metres
Pole Vault—Doug Wood, Ont. 5.30 metres
Javelin—Steve Ferady, Ont. 74.66 metres
Hammer—Boris Stoikos, Ont. 67.82 metres
Shotput—Scott Cappos, Ont.17.77 metres
Discus—Ray Lazdina, Ont. 54.52 metres

Women

100 metres—Karen Clarke, Alta 11.66
200 metres—Stacey Bowen, Ont. 23.83
400 metres—Camille Noel, BC 52.98
800 metres—Nicki Knapp, Ont. 2:04.23 1
500 metres—Angela Chalmers, BC 4:15.31
3000 metres—Leah Pell, BC 9:03.13
10,000 metres—Lisa Harvey, Alta 33:40.31
100-metre hurdles—Donalda Duprey, Ont. 13.65
400-metre hurdles—Rosey Edeh, Que. 55.29

10-kilometre walk—Alison Baker, Ont. 46:46.39
High Jump—Wanita Dykstra, Ont. 1.63 metres
Long Jump—Vanessa Monar-Enweani, Sask. 6.42 metres
Triple Jump—Kelly Dinsmore, Ont. 12.99 metres
Javelin—Eileen Volparti, BC 53.24 metres
Hammer—Theresa Brick, Man. 51.80 metres
Shotput—Georgette Reed. Alta 15.07 metres
Discus—Theresa Brick, Man. 51.7 metres

Auto Racing

Molson Indy

Toronto
1986: Bobby Rahal
1987: Emerson Fittipaldi
1988: Al Unser Jr.
1989: Michael Andretti
1990: Al Unser Jr.
1991: Michael Andretti
1992: Michael Andretti
1993: Paul Tracy*

Vancouver
1990: Al Unser Jr.
1991: Michael Andretti
1992: Michael Andretti
1993: Al Unser Jr.

* Canadian

The America's Cup

Competition for the America's Cup grew out of the first contest to establish a world yachting championship, one of the carnival features of the London Exposition of 1851. The race, open to all classes of yachts from all over the world, covered a 60-mile course around the Isle of Wight; the prize was a cup worth about $500, donated by the Royal Yacht Squadron of England, known as the "America's Cup" because it was first won by the United States yacht *America*. Successive efforts of British and Australian yachtsmen had failed to win the famous trophy until 1983 when the Australian yacht *Australia II* defeated the US entry *Liberty*.

Winners of the America's Cup

1851	America
1870	Magic defeated Cambria, England (1-0)
1871	Columbia (first three races) and Sappho (last two races) defeated Livonia, England (4-1)
1876	Madeline defeated **Countess of Dufferin, Canada** (2-0)
1881	Mischief defeated **Atalanta, Canada** (2-0)
1885	Puritan defeated Genesta, England (2-0)
1886	Mayflower defeated Galatea, England (2-0)
1887	Volunteer defeated Thistle, Scotland (2-0)
1893	Vigilant defeated Valkyrie II, England (3-0)
1895	Defender defeated Valkyrie III, England (3-0)
1899	Columbia defeated Shamrock, England (3-0)
1901	Columbia defeated Shamrock II, England (3-0)
1903	Reliance defeated Shamrock III, England (3-0)
1920	Resolute defeated Shamrock IV, England (3-2)
1930	Enterprise defeated Shamrock V, England (4-0)

1934	Rainbow defeated Endeavour, England (4-2)
1937	Ranger defeated Endeavour II, England (4-0)
1958	Columbia defeated Sceptre, England (4-0)
1962	Weatherly defeated Gretel, Australia (4-1)
1964	Constellation defeated Sovereign, England (4-0)
1967	Intrepid defeated Dame Pattie, Australia (4-0)
1970	Intrepid defeated Gretel II, Australia (4-1)
1974	Courageous defeated Southern Cross, Australia (4-0)
1977	Courageous defeated Australia, Australia (4-0)
1980	Freedom defeated Australia, Australia (4-1)
1983	Australia II, Australia defeated Liberty, (4-3)
1987	Stars & Stripes defeated Kookaburra III, Australia (4-0)
1988	Stars & Stripes defeated New Zealand, New Zealand (2-0) (New Zealand awarded forfeit)
1992	America defeated Il Moro de Venezia, Italy (4-1)

Canadian Sports Hall of Fame

(living members as of Sept. 1, 1993)

Anakin, Douglas, bobsled
Apps, Syl, hockey
Arnold, Don, rowing
Athans, George, Jr., water skiing
Balding, Al, golf
Baldwin, Matt, curling
Baumann, Alex, swimming
Béliveau, Jean, hockey
Bell, Florence, track relay
Bell, Marilyn, marathon swimming
Bernier, Sylvie, diving
Bionda, Jack, lacrosse
Blake, Hector (Toe), hockey builder
Boldt, Arnie, field high jump
Boucher, Gaetan, speed skating
Box Ab, footbal
Boys Bev, diving
Brooks Lela, speed skatin
Brouillard, Lou, boxing
Burka, Petra, figure skatin
Burka, Sylvia, speed skating
Callura, Jackie, boxing
Cameron, Michelle, synchro swimming
Chuvalo, George, boxing
Cliff, Leslie, swimming
Clifford, Betsy, skiing
Coleman, Jim, sports journalism

Côté, Gérard, marathon swimming
Cowan, Gary, golf
Cranston, Toller, figure skating
Crothers, Bill, track mid-distance
D'hondt, Walter, rowing
Dafoe, Frances, figure skating
Day, James, equestrian
Dexter, Glen, yachting
Drake, Clare, hockey builder
Drayton, Jerome, marathon running
Dryden, Ken, hockey
Duguid, Don, curling
Dunnell, Milt, all-around builder
Durrelle, Yvon, boxing
Eagleson, Alan, hockey builder
Elder, James, equestrian
Emery, Dr. John, bobsled
Emery, Victor, bobsled
Esaw, Johnny, all-around builder
Esposito, Phil, hockey
Filion, Hervé, harness racing
Fogh, Hans, yachting
Fortier, Sylvie, synchro swimming
Gabriel, Tony, football
Galbraith, Sheldon, figure sk. builder
Gate, George, swimming builder
Gaudaur, Jake, Jr., football builder

►

▶ **Gayford,** Tom, equestrian
Golab, Tony, football
Graham, Laurie, skiing
Greene, Nancy, skiing
Grenier, Jean, speed skating builder
Gwynne, Horace, boxing
Hall, Glenn, hockey
Hanson, Fritz, football
Hartman, Barney, skeet shooting
Heggtveit, Anne, skiing
Hepburn, Doug, weightlifting
Hildebrand, Ike, lacrosse
Howe, Gordie, hockey
Hull, Bobby, hockey
Hungerford, George W., rowing
Huot, Jules, golf
Hutton, Ralph, swimming
Jackson, Donald, figure skating
Jackson, Dr. Roger, rowing
Jackson, Russ, football
Jelinek, Maria, figure skating
Jelinek, Otto, figure skating
Jenkins, Ferguson, baseball
Josenhans, Andreas, yachting
Juckes, Gordon, hockey builder
Kelly, Leonard (Red), hockey
Kidd, Bruce, track mid-distance
Kirby, Kirby, bobsled
Kreiner, Kathy, skiing
Krol, Joe, football
Kwong, Norm, football
Lancaster, Ron, football
Leonard, Stan, golf
Lessard, Lucille, archery
Lévesque, Jean-Louis, equestrian
Lidstone, Dorothy, archery
Loney, Don, football builder
Longden, Johnny, horse racing
Loomer, Lorne, rowing
Lovell, Jocelyn, cycling
Luftspring, Sammy, boxing
MacDonald, Irene, diving
MacDonald, Noel, basketball
McKinnon, Archie, rowing
MacKinnon, Lt. Col. Dan, harness racing builder
McLarnin, Jimmy, boxing
MacMillan, Sandy, yachting
McNaughton, Duncan, field high jump
McPherson, Donald, figure skating
Magnussen, Karen, figure skating
Mahovlich, Frank, hockey
Marchildon, Phil, baseball
Martini, Paul, figure skating
Miles, John C., marathon swimming
Mitchell, Ray, bowling
Nattrass, Susan, trap shooting
Nicholas, Cindy, marathon swimming
Northcott, Ron, curling
O'Donnell, Bill, harness racing
Orr, Robert (Bobby), hockey
Orser, Brian, figure skating

Parker, Jackie, football
Paul, Robert, figure skating
Peden, Doug, multi-sport
Perry, Gordon, football
Podborski, Steve, skiing
Pollock, Sam, hockey builder
Porter, R.A. (Bobby), multi-sport
Post, Sandra, golf
Presley, Gerald, bobsled
Primrose, John, trap shooting
Ramage, Pat, skiing builder
Read, Ken, skiing
Reed, George, football
Richard, Henri, hockey
Richard, Maurice (Rocket), hockey
Richardson, Arnold, curling
Richardson, Ernie, curling
Richardson, Garnet, curling
Richardson, Wes, curling
Robertson, Bruce, swimming
Robinson, Graydon, bowling
Rogers, Doug, judo
Saunders, Claude, rowing builder
Schmidt, Milt, hockey
Schneider, Bert, boxing
Scott, Barbara Ann, figure skating
Seller, Peggy, synchro swimming
Shedd, Marjory, badminton
Smith, Graham, swimming
Sorensen, Gerry, skiing
Steen, Dave, decathlon
Stewart, Marlene, golf
Stewart, Nels, hockey
Stewart, Ron, football
Stirling, Hugh, football
Storey, R.A. (Red), all-around
Stukus, Annis, football builder
Sullivan, Jack, sports journalism
Tanner, Elaine, swimming
Taylor, Ron, baseball
Thom, Linda, shooting
Thompson, James, speedboating builder
Townsend, Cathy, bowling
Trifunov, James, wrestling
Turcotte, Ron, horse racing
Underhill, Barbara, figure skating
Vanderburg, Helen, synchro swimming
Wagner, Barbara, figure skating
Waldo, Carolyn, synchro swimming
Waples, Keith, harness racing
Watson, Ken J., curling
Weslock, Nick, golf
Wheeler, Lucille, skiing
Whitaker, Brig. Gen. Denis, equestrian builder
Wilson, Harold A., speed boating
Worrall, Jim, builder
Wright, Harold, builder
Young, Michael, bobsled

Source: *Canadian Sports Hall of Fame*

Canadian Press Athlete of the Year

	Male (Lionel Conacher Award)	Female
1932	**Somerville,**Sandy, golf	No award
1933	**Komonen,** Dave, track and field	**Mackenzie,** Ada, golf
1934	**Webster,** Harold, track and field	**Dewar,** Phyllis, swimming
1935	**Rankine,**Robert (Scotty), track and field	**Meagher,** Aileen, track and field
1936	**Edwards,** Phil, track and field	**Taylor,** Betty, track and field
1937	**Apps,** Syl, hockey	**Higgins,** Robina, track and field
1938	**Stirling,**Hugh (Bummer), football	**Macdonald,** Noel, basketball
1939	**Hanson,** Fritz, football	**Thacker,** Mary Rose, figure skating
1940	**Cote,** Gerard, track and field	**Walton,** Dorothy, badminton
1941	**Golab,** Tony, football	**Thacker,** Mary Rose, figure skating
	No awards during Second World War	
1946	**Krol,** Joe, football	**Scott,** Barbara Ann, figure skating
1947	**Krol,** Joe, football	**Scott,** Barbara Ann, figure skating
1948	**O'Connor,** Buddy, hockey	**Scott,** Barbara Ann, figure skating
1949	**Filchock,** Frank, football	**Strong,** Irene, swimming
1950	**Conacher,** Lionel named athlete of the half century (no athlete of the year)	**Rosenfeld,** Bobbie, track and field, named athlete of the half century (no athlete of the year)
1951	No award	No award
1952	**Richard,** Maurice, hockey	**Stewart,** Marlene, golf
1953	**Hepburn,** Doug, weightlifting	**Stewart,** Marlene, golf
1954	**Ferguson,** Rich, track and field	**Bell,** Marilyn, swimming
1955	**Kwong,** Normie, football	**Bell,** Marilyn, swimming
1956	**Beliveau,** Jean, hockey	**Stewart,** Marlene, golf
1957	**Richard,** Maurice, hockey	**Stewart,** Marlene, golf
1958	**Richard,** Maurice, hockey	**Wheeler,** Lucile, skiing
1959	**Jackson,** Russ, football	**Heggtveit,** Anne, skiing
1960	**Stewart,** Ron, football	**Heggtveit,** Anne, skiing
1961	**Kidd,** Bruce, track and field	**Stewart,** Mary, swimming
1962	**Kidd,** Bruce, track and field	**Stewart,** Mary, swimming
1963	**Howe,** Gordie, hockey	**Stewart Streit,** Marlene, golf
1964	**Crothers,** Bil,l track and field	**Burka,** Petra, figure skating
1965	**Hull,** Bobby, hockey	**Burka,** Petra, figure skating
1966	**Hull,** Bobby, hockey	**Tanner,** Elaine, swimming
1967	**Jenkins,** Ferguson, baseball	**Greene,** Nancy, skiing
1968	**Jenkins,** Ferguson, baseball	**Greene,** Nancy, skiing
1969	**Jackson,** Russ, football	**Boys,** Beverley, diving
1970	**Orr,** Bobby, hockey	**Boys,** Beverley, diving
1971	**Jenkins,** Ferguson, baseball	**Van Kiekebelt,** Debbie, track and field; **Brill,** Debbie, track and field (tie)
1972	**Esposito,** Phil, hockey	**Bourassa,** Jocelyn, golf
1973	**Esposito,** Phil, hockey	**Magnussen,** Karen, figure skating
1974	**Jenkins,** Ferguson, baseball	**Cook,** Wendy, swimming
1975	**Clarke,**Bobby, hockey	**Garapick,** Nancy, swimming
1976	**Joy,** Greg, track and field	**Kreiner,** Kathy, skiing
1977	**Lafleur,** Guy, hockey	**Nicholas,** Cindy, swimming
1978	**Smith,** Graham, swimming	**Jones-Konihowski,** Diane, track and field
1979	**Villeneuve,** Gilles, auto racing	**Post,** Sandra, golf
1980	**Gretzky,** Wayne, hockey	**Post,** Sandra, golf
1981	**Gretzky,** Wayne, hockey	**Wainman,** Tracey, figure skating
1982	**Gretzky,** Wayn,e hockey	**Sorensen,** Gerry, skiing
1983	**Gretzky,** Wayne, hockey	**Bassett,** Carling, tennis
1984	**Baumann,** Alex, swimming	**Bernier,** Sylvie, diving
1985	**Gretzky,** Wayne, hockey	**Bassett,** Carling, tennis
1986	**Johnson,** Ben, track and field	**Graham,** Laurie, skiing
1987	**Johnson,** Ben, track and field	**Waldo,** Carolyn, synchronized swimming
1988	**Lemieux,** Mario, hockey	**Waldo,** Carolyn, synchronized swimming
1989	**Gretzky,** Wayne, hockey	**Kelesi,** Helen, tennis
1990	**Browning,** Kurt, figure skating	**Kelesi,** Helen, tennis
1991	**Browning,** Kurt, figure skating	**Laumann,** Silken, rowing
1992	**Tewksbury,** Mark, swimming	**Laumann,** Silken, rowing

Source: *Canadian Press*

QUICK REFERENCE

WEIGHTS AND MEASURES

Canadian Imperial Measures

Name	Abbrev.	Equivalent in Related Units	Metric Equivalent
■ Length			
inch	in.	—	2.54 cm
foot	ft.	12 in.	30.48 cm
yard	yd.	3 ft.; 36 in.	0.91 m
mile	mi.	1 760 yd.; 5 280 ft.	1.609 km
■ Mass (Weight)			
grain	gr.	—	0.06 g
dram	dr.	27.343 gr.	1.77 g
ounce	oz.	16 dr.	28.35 g
pound	lb.	16 oz.	0.453 kg
hundredweight			
(short)	cwt.	100 lb.	45.36 kg
(long)	cwt.	112 lb.	50.80 kg
ton (short)	—	2 000 lb.	0.907 t
ton (long)	—	2 240 lb.	1.016 t
■ Volume and Capacity			
fluid dram	fl. dr.	0.22 cu. in.	3.55 cm³
fluid ounce	fl. oz.	8 fl. dr.; 1.7 cu. in.	28.41 cm³
pint	pt.	20 fl. oz.; 34.7 cu. in.	568.3 cm³
quart	qt.	2 pt.; 69.4 cu. in.	1.14 dm³
gallon	gal.	4 qt.; 277 cu. in.	4.55 dm³
peck	pk.	2 gal.; 555 cu. in.	9.09 dm³
bushel	bu.	4 pk.; 2 219 cu. in.	36.37 dm³
barrel (oil)	bbl	35 gal.	0.159 m³
cubic foot	ft.³	1 728 in.³	0.028 m³
cubic yard	yd.³	27 ft.³	0.765 m³
■ Area			
square foot	ft.²	144 sq. in.	0.09 m²
square yard	yd.²	9 sq. ft.	0.836 m²
acre	—	4 840 sq. yd.	4 047 m²
square mile	sq. mi.	640 acres	2.590 km²

Source: *Gage Canadian Dictionary*

Conversion Chart

(approximations)

FROM METRIC:

Symbol	When you know:	Multiply by:	To find:	Symbol
		Length		
mm	millimetres	0.04	inches	in.
cm	centimetres	0.4	inches	in.
m	metres	3.3	feet	ft.
m	metres	1.1	yards	yd.
km	kilometres	0.6	miles	m.

Symbol	When you know:	Multiply by:	To find:	Symbol
		Area		
cm²	square centimetres	0.16	square inches	in.²
m²	square metres	1.2	square yards	yd.²
km²	square kilometres	0.4	square miles	mi.²
ha	hectares (10 000m²)	2.5	acres	
		Mass (Weight)		
g	grams	0.035	ounce	oz.
kg	kilograms	2.2	pounds	lb.
t	tonnes (1 000kg)	1.1	short tons	
		Volume		
mL	millilitres	0.03	fluid ounces	fl.oz.
L	litres	2.1	pints	pt.
L	litres	1.06	quarts	qt.
L	litres	0.26	gallons (US)	gal. (US)
L	litres	0.22	gallons (Imp.)	gal. (Imp.)
m³	cubic metres	35	cubic feet	ft.³
m³	cubic metres	1.3	cubic yards	yd.³
		Temperature (Exact)		
°C	Celsius	9/5 (+32)	Fahrenheit	°F

TO METRIC:

Symbol	When you know:	Multiply by:	To find:	Symbol
		Length		
in.	inches	2.54 (exactly)	centimetres	cm
ft.	feet	30	centimetres	cm
yd.	yards	0.9	metres	m
m.	miles	1.6	kilometres	km
		Area		
in.²	square inches	6.5	square centimetres	cm²
ft.²	square feet	0.09	square metres	m²
yd.²	square yards	0.8	square metres	m²
mi.²	square miles	2.6	square kilometres	km²
	acres	0.4	hectares	ha
		Mass (Weight)		
oz.	ounces	28	grams	g
lb.	pounds	0.45	kilograms	kg
	short tons (2 000 lb.)	0.9	tonnes	t
		Volume		
tsp.	teaspoons	5	millilitres	mL
tbsp.	tablespoons	15	millilitres	mL
f.l oz.	fluid ounces	30	millilitres	mL
c.	cups	0.24	litres	L
pt.	pints	0.47	litres	L
qt.	quarts	0.95	litres	L
gal.	gallons (US)	3.8	litres	L
gal.	gallons (Imp.)	4.5	litres	L
ft.³	cubic feet	0.03	cubic metres	m³
yd.³	cubic yards	0.76	cubic metres	m³
		Temperature (Exact)		
°F	Fahrenheit temp.	(-32) 5/9	Celsius temp.	°C

Temperature Equivalents

(Celsius and Fahrenheit)

°C	°F	°C	°F	°C	°F	°C	°F	°C	°F
-50	-58	-30	-22	-10	14	10	50	30	86
-49	-56.2	-29	-20.2	-9	15.8	11	51.8	31	87.8
-48	-54.4	-28	-18.4	-8	17.6	12	53.6	32	89.6
-47	-52.6	-27	-16.6	-7	19.4	13	55.4	33	91.4
-46	-50.8	-26	-14.8	-6	21.2	14	57.2	34	93.2
-45	-49	-25	-13	-5	23	15	59	35	95
-44	-47.2	-24	-11.2	-4	24.8	16	60.8	36	96.8
-43	-45.4	-23	-9.4	-3	26.6	17	62.6	37	98.6
-42	-43.6	-22	-7.6	-2	28.4	18	64.4	38	100.4
-41	-41.8	-21	-5.8	-1	30.2	19	66.2	39	102.2
-40	-40	-20	-4	0	32	20	68	40	104
-39	-38.2	-19	-2.2	1	33.8	21	69.8	41	105.8
-38	-36.4	-18	-0.4	2	35.6	22	71.6	42	107.6
-37	-34.6	-17	1.4	3	37.4	23	73.4	43	109.4
-36	-32.8	-16	3.2	4	39.2	24	75.2	44	111.2
-35	-31	-15	5	5	41	25	77	45	113
-34	-29.2	-14	6.8	6	42.8	26	78.8	50	122
-33	-27.4	-13	8.6	7	44.6	27	80.6	100	212
-32	-25.6	-12	10.4	8	46.4	28	82.4	150	302
-31	-23.8	-11	12.2	9	48.2	29	84.2	200	392

Large Numbers

1 thousand	= 1 000
1 million	= 1 000 000 or 10^6
1 milliard: used in Europe, USSR, former French possessions	= 1 000 000 000 or 10^9
1 billion:	= 1 000 000 000 000 or 10^{12}
Canada, the United States and France	= 1 000 000 000 or 10^9
1 trillion:	= 1 000 000 000 000 000 000 or 10^{18}
Canada and the United States	= 1 000 000 000 000 or 10^{12}

Source: *World Weights and Measures*

Roman Numerals

I	1	VII	7	XX	20	C	100	V	5 000
II	2	VIII	8	XXX	30	CC	200	X	10 000
III	3	IX	9	XL	40	CD	400	L	50 000
IV	4	X	10	L	50	D	500	C	100 000
V	5	XI	11	LX	60	CM	900	D	500 000
VI	6	XIX	19	XC	90	M	1 000	M	1 000 000

Best foot forward...

*O*ne of the earliest units of length was the foot, first the length of any human foot and later the length of a specific foot (such as the king's). The inch was originally the width of a thumb; the Romans also defined it as 1/12 of a foot.

The International System of Units (SI)

Name	Symbol	Quantity

■ SI Base Units

Name	Symbol	Quantity
metre	m	length
kilogram	kg	mass
second	s	time
ampere	A	electric current
kelvin	K	thermodynamic temperature
mole	mol	amount of substance
candela	cd	luminous intensity

■ SI Supplementary Units

Name	Symbol	Quantity
radian	rad	plane angle
steradian	sr	solid angle

■ Common SI Derived Units With Special Names

Name	Symbol	Quantity
hertz	Hz	frequency
pascal	Pa	pressure, stress
watt	W	power, radiant flux
volt	V	electric potential, electromotive force
newton	N	force
joule	J	energy, work
coulomb	C	electric charge
ohm	Ω	electric resistance
farad	F	electric capacitance

■ Common Units Used With the SI

Name	Symbol	Quantity
litre	L	volume or capacity (= 1 dm^3)
degree Celsius	°C	temperature (= 1 K; 0°C = 273.2 K)
hectare	ha	area (= 10 000 m^2)
tonne	t	mass (= 1000 kg)
electronvolt	eV	energy (= 0.160 aJ)
nautical mile	M	distance (navigation) (= 1852 m)
knot	kn	speed (navigation) (= 1 M/h)
standard atmosphere	atm	atmospheric pressure (= 101.3 kPa)

■ SI Prefixes

Name	Symbol	Quantity
exa-	E	10^{18}
peta-	P	10^{15}
tera-	T	10^{12}
giga-	G	10^9
mega-	M	10^6
kilo-	k	10^3
hecto-	h	10^2
deca-	da	10
deci-	d	10^{-1}
centi-	c	10^{-2}
milli-	m	10^{-3}
micro-	μ	10^{-6}
nano-	n	10^{-9}
pico-	p	10^{-12}
femto-	f	10^{-15}
atto-	a	10^{-18}

* $10^2 = 100$; $10^3 = 1\ 000$
  $10^{-1} = 0.1$; $10^{-2} = 0.01$
  Thus, 2 km = 2 x 1 000 = 2 000 m
  3 cm = 3 x 0.01 = 0.03 m

Source: *Gage Canadian Dictionary*

Birthstones

Month	Stone
January	Garnet
February	Amethyst
March	Aquamarine or bloodstone
April	Diamond
May	Emerald
June	Pearl, moonstone or alexandrite
July	Ruby
August	Sardonyx or peridot
September	Sapphire
October	Opal or tourmaline
November	Topaz
December	Turquoise, zircon or lapis lazuli

Signs of the Zodiac

The movement in the planets causes a variation from year to year in the dates assigned to each sign. The dates listed below are for 1994.

Sign		Dates
Aries	The Ram	Mar. 20 to Apr. 19
Taurus	The Bull	Apr. 20 to May 20
Gemini	The Twins	May 21 to June 20
Cancer	The Crab	June 21 to July 21
Leo	The Lion	July 22 to Aug. 22
Virgo	The Virgin	Aug. 23 to Sept. 22
Libra	The Scales	Sept. 23 to Oct. 23
Scorpio	The Scorpion	Oct. 24 to Nov. 21
Sagittarius	The Archer	Nov. 22 to Dec. 20
Capricorn	The Goat	Dec. 21 to Jan. 19
Aquarius	The Water Bearer	Jan. 20 to Feb. 17
Pisces	The Fishes	Feb. 18 to Mar. 19

Source: *Eugenia Last*

Canada's Food Guide To Healthy Eating[1]

Canada's Food Guide, revised in November of 1992, recognizes that the amount of food each Canadian needs every day from the four food groups and other foods depends on age, body size, activity level, whether the individual is male or female, and if the individual is pregnant or breast-feeding. That's why the Food Guide gives a range of possible servings for each food group—young children can choose the lower number of recommended servings from a particular group, while male teenagers can go to the higher number. Most other people can choose servings somewhere in between.

Canada's Food Guide recommends, every day:

■ 5 to 12 servings from the grain products group. An example of one serving would be one slice of bread; 30 g of cold cereal or 175 mL of hot cereal. Two servings would be a bagel, pita or bun; or 250 mL of rice or pasta.

■ 5 to 10 servings of vegetables and fruit.

One serving would be one medium size vegetable or fruit; 125 mL of fresh, frozen or canned vegetables or fruit; 250 mL of salad; or 125 mL of juice.

■ 2 to 3 servings of meat or alternatives. One serving would be 50-100 g of meat, poultry or fish; 1-2 eggs; 125-250 mL of beans; 100 g of tofu; or 30 mL of peanut butter.

■ Recommended servings of milk products vary according to age: 2-3 servings for children aged 4-9; 3-4 servings for young people aged 10-16; 2-4 servings for adults; and 3-4 servings for pregnant or breast-feeding women. Examples of one serving would be 250 mL of milk, 50 g of cheese or 175 g of yogurt.

Taste and enjoyment can also come from other foods and beverages that are not part of the four food groups. Some of these foods are higher in fat or calories, so it is recommended that these foods be used in moderation. The important things to remember are: enjoy a variety of foods from each group every day and choose lower-fat foods more often.

Source: Health and Welfare Canada *(1) For people four years and over.*

Functions of Nutrients

Calcium aids in the formation and maintenance of strong bones and teeth; promotes healthy nerve function and normal blood clotting.
Carbohydrate supplies energy; assists in the utilization of fats.
Fat supplies energy; aids in the absorption of fat-soluble vitamins.
Fibre provides undigestible bulk, which encourages the normal elimination of body wastes.
Folacin (folic acid) aids red blood cell formation.
Iodine aids in function of the thyroid gland.
Iron combines with protein to form hemoglobin, the red blood cell constituent that transports oxygen and carbon dioxide.
Magnesium aids in formation and maintenance of strong bones and teeth; aids in energy metabolism and tissue formation.
Phosphorus aids in formation and maintenance of strong bones and teeth.

Protein builds and repairs body tissues; builds antibodies, the blood components that fight infection.
Riboflavin (vitamin B_2) maintains healthy skin and eyes; maintains a normal nervous system; releases energy to body cells during metabolism.
Thiamin (vitamin B_1) releases energy from carbohydrate; aids normal growth and appetite.
Vitamin A aids normal bone and tooth development; promotes good night vision; maintains the health of skin and membranes.
Vitamin B_{12} (cobalamin) aids in red blood cell formation; maintains healthy nerve and gastrointestinal tissues.
Vitamin C (ascorbic acid) maintains healthy teeth and gums; maintains strong vessel walls.
Vitamin E (tocopherol)protects the fat in body tissues from oxidation.
Zinc aids in energy and metabolism and tissue formation.

Source: *Canada's Food Guide Handbook*

Cardiovascular Disease Warning Signs

Heart Attack

Any combination of the following symptoms may be a signal of a heart attack about to happen:

- heaviness, pressure, squeezing, fullness, burning, discomfort or pain in the centre of the chest, which may spread to neck, jaw, shoulders, arms and back; these symptoms may not be severe;
- shortness of breath, paleness, sweating or weakness;
- nausea, vomiting and/or indigestion;
- fear, anxiety, denial;
- symptoms may come and go.

Stroke

- a sudden temporary weakness or numbness in the face, leg or arm;
- temporary loss of speech or trouble speaking or understanding speech;
- episodes of double vision;
- unexplained dizziness, headaches, etc. in conjunction with other symptoms.

What to do?

Act immediately.

- Have victim stop activity and sit or lie down.
- Expect denial; take charge; don't rely on the victim's opinion of whether medical help is required.
- If the victim has known heart disease, assist the victim in taking his/her nitroglycerine as prescribed.
- Call your emergency telephone number.
- Take action to get to the nearest hospital with 24-hour emergency cardiac care. Each year more Canadian heart attack victims could have been saved if they had reached a hospital within hours of the signals of a heart attack.

Source: *Heart and Stroke Foundation of Canada*

AIDS

AIDS (Acquired Immunodeficiency Syndrome) is believed to be caused by a virus (HIV) that attacks the body's natural defence mechanism, making a person vulnerable to illnesses that a healthy immune system could prevent. It is not known if infection with the HIV virus always leads to AIDS; the amount of virus, in addition to infection by other viruses, may influence its development.

According to recent estimates, 50 percent of individuals with HIV will have developed AIDS within 10 years of infection, and another 20 to 25 percent will experience AIDS-related illness. Of those diagnosed as having AIDS in Canada and the United States, over 90 percent have died within five years and 80 percent within three years.

AIDS was first identified in the United States in 1981. Canada's first reported case was in 1982. The World Health Organization estimates that more than 650,000 AIDS cases had occurred worldwide by the end of 1990, and that over one million new cases will be identified by 1992 from among persons who have already been infected. It is estimated that 13 million individuals will be infected with HIV by the year 2000. The ultimate health impact of the HIV infection, including effects on future generations, is unknown.

In Canada, 5,308 AIDS cases had been reported by Sept. 1991 and an estimated 25,000 to 50,000 persons had been infected with the HIV virus.

The AIDS virus is transmitted in four known ways: through sexual contact with an infected person; through sharing contaminated needles; through transfusion of infected blood or blood products; from an infected mother to an infant during pregnancy or delivery or during breast-feeding. AIDS cannot be transmitted through casual or social contact, through food or water or by insects.

Cancer Information

Site	Warning Signs	Comments
Lung	Chronic cough; blood may appear in sputum. Fever and chest pains may also occur.	Lung cancer is largely preventable; it is the leading cause of cancer death among men and is predicted to be the leading cause for women by 1993. Don't smoke.
Intestine and Rectum	Bleeding from the rectum; persistent indigestion; a change in bowel habits; vague, dull or annoying abdominal pains.	A balanced, low-fat diet with adequate amounts of green and yellow vegetables, i.e., cabbage, cauliflower, broccoli or brussel sprouts and foods containing Vitamin C and E is recommended. Enjoy a variety of foods; eat more whole grains, vegetables and fruits; choose lower-fat food.
Mouth and Pharynx	Unusual conditions in the mouth; sores that don't heal; trouble swallowing.	Ask your dentist to check unusual conditions. Cytological smears of suspicious areas will detect the presence of many cancers.
Stomach	Indigestion; pain in upper abdomen; persistent loss of appetite; vomiting of blood; unexplained weight loss.	Mortality has declined 50% in the past 20 years. Avoid highly spiced foods.
Skin	A pearly nodule that may grow larger or a red, scaly, sharply outlined patch or a mole-like growth which is dark brown mixed with areas of white, blue, pink or grey. May change shape or color.	Most common of all cancers and is usually caused by over-exposure to the sun. Most cases are simple to treat, but early treatment is important. Protect yourself and your children from too much sunlight.
Breast	Puckered or dimpled skin; bleeding or discharge from the nipples; lump or thickening in the breast.	After age 50 have a mammogram every two years; practice monthly breast self-examination. Reduce fat in diet. 80% of lumps are benign, but early detection and treatment is essential.
Cervix and Uterus	Unusual bleeding or discharge.	The Pap test has made cervical cancer preventable.
Prostate	Pain in the lower back or during urination or ejaculation. Problems during urination; urine may contain blood.	More than half the men over 50 in North America develop a growth in the prostate gland; in most cases the growth is benign. Doctors may do a digital examination during checkup.
Bladder	Blood in urine; frequent urination, strong urges to urinate and discomfort or burning during urination.	Most common in men aged 45–80. Avoid smoking and cancer-causing industrial compounds; limit use of saccharin and coffee.
Leukemia	No distinctive early warning signs. Symptoms resemble those of common less serious diseases (e.g., fatigue, pallor, overall feeling of ill health).	Most common type of cancer in children. Unlike other cancers, there is no tumor. Instead countless immature white blood cells spill into bloodstream from bone marrow and travel throughout body.

The Canadian Cancer Society suggests all Canadians follow the Seven Steps to Health:

- have a medical and dental checkup;
- watch for any change in your normal state of health;
- find out about any lump or sore that doesn't heal
- protect yourself against too much sunlight;
- do not smoke;
- have a Pap test; have a mammogram after age 50; and
- do a monthly breast self-examination.

Source: *Canadian Cancer Society*

How to Poison-Proof Your Home

The average household contains as many as 250 poisons and each year in Canada hundreds of fatalities are caused by poisoning. There are two key steps to poison-proofing your home: identification and storage.

Common Household Poisons:

- Cleaners and bleaches: including detergents, ammonia, naphtha, oven cleaner and bleach.
- Solvents: including paint remover, kerosene and turpentine.
- Polishes and waxes: including paint, car and furniture wax, silver polish.
- Herbicides, insecticides and insect repellents.
- Mercury (from a thermometer).
- Cosmetics and toiletries: including aftershave, bubble bath, nail polish, hair lotions.
- Drugs and medicines: including both prescription and non-prescription drugs such as vitamins, ASA, cough medicines and cold medications.
- House plants, ornamental plants and flower and vegetable garden plants.

How to Store Them:

- Keep products in clearly labelled original containers.
- Store prescription drugs out of the reach of children and in containers with safety lids.
- Store household cleaners on high shelves, not underneath the sink.
- Return medication or cleaning products to a safe place after using them.
- Keep all poisonous liquids and solids out of the reach of children; if possible, install child-proof locking cabinets.
- Never call medicine "candy"; it gives children a distorted idea.
- Warn children at an early age not to eat household plants or wild plants and berries.
- Never keep food and household cleaners next to each other.
- Don't continue to store old products around the house.
- Don't leave a purse or handbag where a child can reach it because there are often prescription drugs inside.
- If poisoning occurs, identify the suspected poison and immediately seek medical help. Many areas have poison information centres. Never attempt to induce vomiting without medical advice.

Safety Information

*E*mergency telephone numbers (e.g. fire, police, ambulance, and poison information centre) are located on the inside cover of your telephone book.

*T*he Canadian Red Cross Society offers a seven-hour program, "ChildSafe," which teaches basic skills for dealing with bleeding and breathing emergencies, choking, poisons, falls, shock and burns. For more information on this program, contact your local branch of the Red Cross, listed in the white pages under "Canadian Red Cross Society."

*S*t. John Ambulance offers programs in both first aid and CPR, including the "Save That Child" program. A new program called "Child Care" offers a 15-hour learning package to teach new parents about infant care, behaviour, safety, first aid, and how to deal with illness. Local branches of St. John Ambulance are listed in the white pages of your telephone directory, and in the Yellow Pages under "First Aid Services."

A Guide to Poisonous Plants

All plants contain small amounts of various toxins. The ingestion of a poisonous plant may cause some of the effects listed below, but it would be rare for a serious poisoning to result.

The following are the most common poisonous plants found in the home, garden or wild.

Plant	Toxic Parts	Possible Effects
House Plants		
Dieffenbachia (Dumbcane) Elephant's ear Philodendron Caladium	All parts	Small sharp crystals may cause intense burning of mouth, tongue and lips. Swollen lips and tongue may interfere with speaking, swallowing or breathing.
Poinsettia	Leaves	Usually produces no ill effects.
Jersualem cherry	Leaves and fruit (especially unripe fruit)	Headache, abdominal pain, vomiting, diarrhea; slowed heart rate.
Garden Plants		
Crocus	All parts, especially bulb	Vomiting, severe diarrhea; bone marrow suppression.
Daffodil Narcissus Hyacinth	All parts, especially bulb. May be mistaken for onion.	Abdominal pain, vomiting, diarrhea, shivering.
Mistletoe	Stem, leaves, berries	Vomiting, diarrhea.
Foxglove	All parts	One of the sources of the cardiac medication digitalis. May cause abdominal pain, vomiting, diarrhea; irregular slow pulse; rarely delirium, convulsions, death. Children have been known to pick the drooping tubular flowers and suck the toxic nectar from the base.
Lily of the valley	All parts, especially the roots	Another source of digitalis-like effects. Stomach upset and irregular heartbeat may occur.
Vegetable Garden Plants		
Tomato	Leaves and vine	Headache, abdominal pain, vomiting and diarrhea. "Tea" made from the leaves may be poisonous.
Potato	Green tubers, vines, leaves, new sprouts, spoiled parts.	Ingestion may cause severe vomiting and diarrhea. Do not eat green or spoiled potatoes.
Rhubarb	Leaves	Small sharp crystals may cause intense burning and irritation of mouth, tongue and lips. Swollen lips and tongue may interfere with speaking, swallowing or breathing.
Ornamental Plants		
English ivy	Berries, leaves	Oral irritation, nausea, vomiting, diarrhea, abdominal pain.
English holly	Berries	Vomiting, diarrhea, drowsiness.
Common privet	Berries, leaves	Nausea, vomiting, severe diarrhea. May cause kidney damage.
Daphne	Fruit	Burning of mouth and throat; abdominal pain, vomiting, diarrhea, kidney damage; rarely convulsions, coma; death.
Rhododendron Azalea	All parts	Poisonings are rare but potentially dangerous. May cause salivation, vomiting, low blood pressure, convulsions.

▶

Plant	Toxic Parts	Possible Effects
▶ **Wisteria**	Pods and seeds	Abdominal pain; vomiting, diarrhea. Symptoms often diminish within 24–48 hours.
Yew	Leaves (needles), bark, seeds, but not pulp of fruit.	Abdominal pain, vomiting. In severe cases, muscular weakness; cardiac and respiratory depression.
Rosary pea	Chewed seeds	Burning pain in mouth; delay in onset of abdominal pain, vomiting, severe diarrhea; kidney failure; death.
Castor bean	Chewed seeds	Delay in onset of burning in mouth and throat; vomiting, diarrhea, blurred vision; convulsions, renal failure; death.

Trees and Shrubs

Plant	Toxic Parts	Possible Effects
Apple	Seeds	Many types of fruit seeds contain a minute amount of cyanide. Very large numbers of seeds, if chewed, may cause death.
Black locust	Bark, leaves, seeds	Burning pain in mouth; abdominal pain, vomiting, severe diarrhea.
Wild black cherry Choke cherry	Leaves, pits, bark	Cyanide is present in large, tender leaves of shoots and sprouts. May cause nausea, vomiting, low blood pressure; coma; death.
Elderberry	Stems, unripe or raw berries	Nausea, vomiting, slow heart beat, low blood pressure; coma, death. The berries are harmless if cooked.
Horse chestnut	All parts	Abdominal pain, vomiting, weakness if large amounts ingested.
Oak	Raw acorns, young sprouts	Abdominal pain, vomiting, diarrhea if large amounts of raw acorns eaten.

Plants in Wooded Areas

Plant	Toxic Parts	Possible Effects
Baneberry (dolls' eyes)	All parts	Headache; abdominal pain, vomiting, diarrhea; delirium, rapid heartbeat.
Jack-in-the-pulpit Skunk cabbage	All parts	Small sharp crystals may cause intense burning of mouth, tongue and lips. Swollen lips and tongue may interfere with speaking, swallowing or breathing.
Water hemlock	Stems, leaves, especially roots	Vomiting, diarrhea, abdominal pain; tremors, dilated pupils, convulsions, death. Root has been mistaken for parsnips.
Mushrooms	All parts	Poisonous and edible mushrooms often grow side by side and are very difficult to distinguish. Any ingestion is potentially toxic.

Plants in Fields

Plant	Toxic Parts	Possible Effects
Jimson weed Thorn apple	All parts	Flushed skin, dry mouth, dilated pupils, nervous excitement with hallucinations, delirium; convulsions.
Death camas	Flowers, especially bulb	Bulbs may be mistaken for onions. May cause headache, abdominal pain, vomiting, diarrhea; weakness, slowed heart beat, low blood pressure.
Nightshade	All parts, especially berries	May cause rapid heartbeat, blurred vision, dilated pupils, flushed skin, delirium, rarely coma, convulsions, respiratory failure.
Poison hemlock	All parts, especially young leaves, unripe fruit, roots, seeds	Root resembles wild carrot. May cause nervousness, trembling, weakness; dilated pupils; diarrhea, vomiting; coma, death.

Source: *Poison Information Centre, The Hospital for Sick Children, Toronto*

First Aid

First aid is the first assistance or treatment given to a casualty before the arrival of expert care. The objective of first aid is to preserve life, to prevent the injury or condition from becoming worse and to promote recovery. In giving first aid, there are three golden rules:

DO NOT approach the casualty if doing so will put your own life in danger;

ALWAYS give your attention to the most seriously injured person first. (This is not necessarily the noisiest casualty.)

NEVER MOVE a casualty unless his or her life is in danger as is.

In a situation where first aid is required, the Red Cross advises:

1. A.B.C. must be established immediately if the casualty is unconscious.

   A. is for airway: the passage between the mouth, nose, throat and windpipe must be kept open and clear.
   B. is for breathing: this must be established and maintained through artificial resuscitation.
   C. is for blood circulation: it must be confirmed that the heart is still beating and the circulation is adequate. Severe bleeding must be stopped, shock treated and the blood circulated by compressing the chest.

2. Broken bones must be immobilized if the casualty is to be moved. A casualty with a suspected back or neck injury should not be moved.

3. Reassure the casualty. Decide which is the most serious injury and treat it first. Then, treat other injuries as required.

4. Call for help or have someone make the call for you. An ambulance should be called in any incident involving difficulty in breathing, heart failure, severe bleeding, unconsciousness, serious burns, suspected broken bones (with the possible exceptions of broken arms, fingers, toes), shock or poisoning.

Here are the recommended first aid procedures for common injuries:

■ Animal bites

Any bite that breaks the skin needs prompt attention to prevent the possibility of either tetanus or rabies infection. Severe bleeding should be controlled with direct pressure and elevation; the wound should be thoroughly cleaned with soap and water and protected with a sterile dressing. Seek medical attention.

■ Back injury

A back injury may occur through strained back muscles, sprained ligaments supporting the spine, damage to the discs between the bones that make up the spine or damage to the bones themselves. In any suspected back injury the casualty should not move; rolled coats and/or pillows should be placed alongside the body to keep the casualty as still as possible until medical help arrives.

■ Blisters (from rubbing)

Never break a blister caused by any form of heat because of the risk of infection. Blisters caused by rubbing, on the foot for example, should be cleaned, punctured in two places with a sterilized needle and covered with clean cotton batting and an adhesive dressing.

■ Bleeding

Apply direct pressure on the wound using a clean bandage or your hand. Raise the site of bleeding above heart level and insist that the casualty lie down. Apply a sterile dressing, making sure that it is large enough to extend well beyond the edges of the wound. If a dressing is not available, use a handkerchief, any available linens or paper tissue. If the blood begins to show through the dressing, apply another on top of the first. Watch for signs of shock and treat accordingly.

■ Broken bones

A broken bone should be suspected if a casualty complains of extreme pain at the site of the injury which is increased by any attempt to move; swelling and later bruising; if the affected body part looks deformed compared with its opposite; if shock sets in. The broken bone should be steadied and supported by the attendant placing one hand above and one below the injured area. If help has been called, make the casualty as comfortable as possible by placing rolled coats/blankets/pillows alongside the injury. If help is not going to arrive quickly, the joints above and below the injury should be immobilized using a sound part of the body as a splint. Also treat for shock.

■ Bug bites and stings/Anaphylactic shock

If the stinger is still in the skin it should be pulled out with tweezers (preferably sterilized), avoiding the poison sac at the top of the stinger. Apply rubbing alcohol or a bicarbonate of soda and water paste or a cold compress. If a casualty shows sign of shock, nausea, has difficulty breathing, is sneezing or has facial swelling, then urgent removal to hospital or medical care is necessary. If this is not possible, apply mouth-to-mouth resuscitation and external chest compression if required.

■ Burns

If a casualty's clothes are on fire, douse the flames with water or smother them with a non- flammable blanket or coat. If the burned area is not large, hold it under cold running water for 10–20 minutes or immerse in a bucket of clean, cold water or other cold, harmless fluid such as milk. At the same time, quickly and carefully remove any rings, watches or tight clothing from the injured area. Remove or cut away any clothing that may interfere with the injury; when chemicals have been involved, remove clothing that has been soaked in the chemical. Do not remove anything that is sticking to the burned area. Protect the burn with a sterile dressing, but never use an adhesive or cotton batting type of bandage. Never put any fats or ointments on a burn. Seek medical attention.

■ Carbon monoxide poisoning

Since the priority is to restore adequate breathing, the casualty should first be removed or dragged away from the fumes. The airway should be opened, the breathing checked and circulation maintained. Call for help.

■ Choking in adults

If caused by a blockage in the windpipe, the casualty will suddenly bring a hand to his or her throat and will be unable to speak. If not relieved, the casualty will turn blue in the face and the veins in the face and neck will begin to stand out. If the blockage is still not removed, the casualty will lose consciousness. When choking begins, allow the person to cough freely if possible; if not, apply four sharp slaps between the shoulder blades with

the heel of your hand. If choking persists, help the casualty to bend forward so the head is lower than the chest and apply four more slaps. If these measures fail, resort to the use of abdominal thrust: stand or kneel behind the casualty and wrap your arms around his or her waist. Put the thumb side of your fist just above the navel and well below the rib cage. Grasp it with your other hand and pull both hands towards you with a quick, hard inward and upward thrust. Repeat up to four times.

■ Choking in babies and small children

Use less force than with adults when slapping the back. Lay a baby along your forearm face down, supporting the head and shoulders with one hand and slapping between the shoulders with the other. A small child should be laid across your thigh with the head lower than the chest and slapped quickly between the shoulders.

■ Drowning

Do not waste time trying to remove water from a drowning victim's lungs. Quickly remove any obstructions such as seaweed from the casualty's mouth and apply mouth-to-mouth resuscitation. When breathing is re-established, remove wet clothes and keep casualty warm until help arrives.

■ Electrical injuries

The casualty must not be touched until the electrical current is broken. If the casualty is unconscious, check breathing and, if necessary, begin mouth-to-mouth and chest compression. Treat burns as described above. Call ambulance.

■ Embedded objects

Do not attempt to pull out objects—of any description—embedded in a wound. The casualty should lie down with the injured part raised and severe bleeding controlled by applying pressure above and below the wound. Cover the wound lightly with a sterile dressing without applying any pressure on the object. Immobilize the injured part and seek medical attention.

■ Eye injuries

If a loose particle is visible on the white of the eye, lift it off with a moistened piece of cotton batting or the corner of a clean tissue. Alternatively, try flushing the eye under clean running water. If both steps fail, or if the object is embedded, lightly cover both eyes to prevent eye movement. Seek medical help.

Fainting

Fainting is a brief period of unconsciousness which may be brought on by pain, emotion or standing still for a long time in a warm atmosphere. A casualty will feel weak, faint and giddy and will have very pale skin and a slow pulse. The casualty should lie down with the feet raised above heart level or, if space does not permit lying down, seated with head bent forward between the knees. Any tight clothing around neck, chest and waist should be loosened and the casualty must have plenty of air; fan, if necessary.

Food poisoning

Food can be contaminated through bacteria or incorrect storage or cooking. Staphylo-cocci bacteria multiply in food and produce a poisonous toxin. Salmonellae bacteria multiply in the bowel and cause a dysentery-type illness. Salmonella is infectious and can be transmitted through poor personal hygiene. Symptoms of staphylococcal poisoning will appear within two to six hours of eating contaminated food: the casualty will feel nauseated and may vomit; there may also be abdominal pain, headache and diarrhea. Shock might also set in. Signs of salmonella poisoning may be seen within a few hours of eating or delayed for a day or two. The casualty will have a fever, abdominal pain, diarrhea, nausea accompanied by vomiting and shock. For both types of poisoning, ensure breathing and circulation is maintained, make sure the casualty rests, give plenty of fluids to drink and when in doubt remove to a hospital.

Frostbite

When frostbite (freezing of the skin and underlying tissues) is accompanied by hypothermia, the latter condition must be treated first. Frostbite can be expected if there is a prickling sensation in the skin followed by a gradual loss of feeling; the affected skin will feel hard or cold and may appear waxy, mottled blue or white. Remove tight clothing or jewellery from the affected area and cover the frostbite with warm, dry clothes or blankets. Frostbitten hands can be placed in the armpits. Do not apply direct heat such as a hot-water bottle to frostbite and do not rub the affected area. If frostbite occurs in the feet, the casualty should not walk. Seek medical help.

Heart attacks

See "Cardiovascular Disease Warning Signs" elsewhere in this book.

Hiccups

It is important to break up the sequence of contractions to counteract hiccups and seek medical help if the attack is prolonged. The casualty should hold his or her breath, take long drinks or place a paper bag over the mouth and nose until hiccups stop.

Hypothermia

This condition develops when the body temperature drops below 35°C (95°F). It can occur quickly in summer as well as winter through being immersed in cold water or by exposure to wind while wearing wet clothes. In its initial stages, a casualty will show signs of shivering and slurred speech. As the hypothermia worsens, the casualty may appear confused, irrational, sleepy or clumsy, and shivering may stop. In babies, there will be signs of drowsiness as well as floppiness, and the face, hands and feet will feel very cold. The casualty should be gradually rewarmed, not through use of a hot-water bottle or electric blanket, but with a warm bath and warm drink. If there are no other means of warmth, use your own body to warm the casualty. The casualty should move to improve circulation, but the skin should not be rubbed.

Nose bleeds

These can cause considerable loss of blood, and further complications can result through the casualty inhaling blood. A sufferer should sit down with head well forward, with any tight clothing around the neck and chest loosened, and the nose should be pinched in the soft area for 10 minutes. The casualty should not talk, swallow, cough, spit or sniff. If the bleeding hasn't stopped, pressure should be applied for further periods of 10 minutes as necessary. The nose should not be plugged during this time. When bleeding has stopped, the casualty should avoid exertion and should not blow the nose for at least four hours. If bleeding persists or resumes after 30 minutes, seek medical aid.

Poisoning

Poisons can enter the body through swallowing, inhalation, injection or absorption through the skin. A person who has been poisoned will show signs of drowsiness, possible burns around the lips, vomiting or diarrhea, convulsions and loss of consciousness. It is important not to leave the casualty alone. If a corrosive poison has been swallowed, do not induce vomiting. When poisoning is suspected, ask the casualty what has been taken and call an ambulance; the person taking the call may tell you what to do while you are waiting for help to arrive. If the casualty is unconscious but breathing, treat for unconsciousness. If mouth-to-mouth is necessary, be careful not to get any of the poison on your mouth. Transfer the casualty to hospital as soon as possible, and bring with you any evidence of the poison consumed (empty bottles, medicines, etc.).

■ Shock
Shock occurs when blood circulation fails, perhaps due to bleeding, heart attacks, loss of body fluids following large burns, severe allergic reaction, serious vomiting or diarrhea. Signs of shock include skin color which is very pale and grey, cold and sweaty skin; a rapid but weak pulse; and shallow and fast breathing. The casualty may also be restless and begin yawning as well as complaining of thirst. In the final stages of shock, a casualty will lose consciousness and die if not treated successfully. Any bleeding should be stopped immediately using direct pressure and elevation. The casualty should be reassured, kept comfortable and warm and laid down with feet raised and head turned to one side. Call an ambulance and treat for unconsciousness if necessary.

■ Smoke inhalation
Remove the casualty from the smoke only if you can be sure there are no toxic fumes present that might endanger you. Extinguish any clothing that is on fire or smouldering and, if the casualty is unconscious, open the airway, check breathing and resuscitate if required. Treat any burns. Call an ambulance.

■ Snake bite
Contrary to popular belief, snake bites are rarely fatal but their bites can produce serious fright that can lead to severe shock. A casualty may experience disturbed vision, nausea, vomiting, puncture wounds with severe pain and local swelling, difficulty in breathing and salivation and sweating. The casualty should lay down and not move, the bitten area should be immobilized and kept below the level of the heart and the wound should be thoroughly washed with soap and water. Be prepared to start artificial respiration if neces-

sary. Obtain immediate medical aid and, if possible, kill or take the snake for identification.

■ Sprains
If doubt exists as to whether the limb is broken or sprained, treat as a broken bone. Signs of a sprain include severe pain, bruising and discoloration, swelling and possible immobility. Keep a casualty comfortable and raise the injured part. If the sprain is recent, cover with a cold compress (either an ice bag or material soaked in cold water) wrap the injury in cotton batting and an elastic bandage or support with an arm sling. Seek medical aid.

■ Suffocation
Immediately remove the cause of the suffocation (plastic bag, earth, etc.) or remove the casualty from the danger (for example, smoke or poisonous gas). If the casualty is buried, clear the earth or sand away from the casualty's chest so that it can expand during breathing. Open and clear the airway, check breathing, begin mouth-to-mouth if necessary, and call for medical aid.

■ Sun stroke/Heat exhaustion
Symptoms of excessive sun or heat are dizziness, nausea or feeling faint. Move a casualty out of the heat into the shade, loosen tight clothing, make him or her lie down and raise feet and legs slightly. If cramps are present give a single glass of slightly salted (1/4 tsp. salt) cool water to drink. A casualty who loses consciousness and has flushed, hot and dry skin is suffering from heat stroke and needs to be cooled with a sponge bath while immediate help is summoned.

■ Unconsciousness
This condition is dangerous because the normal reflexes that allow a person to breathe properly without choking while asleep may not work. The casualty may show signs of confusion and stupor before losing consciousness. When unconscious, the casualty's airway, breathing and circulation must be maintained while waiting for medical help to arrive. If these are established, place the casualty in a position so that the tongue will not fall back and cause choking. Never leave an unconscious person alone and do not give anyone who is, or who has been, unconscious anything to eat or drink.

Sources: *St. John Ambulance; The Red Cross Society*

Code of Ethics for Travellers

1. Travel in a spirit of humility and with a genuine desire to meet and talk with the local people.

2. Be aware of the feelings of other people, thus preventing what might be offensive behaviour. Remember this especially with photography.

3. Cultivate the habit of listening and observing, rather than merely hearing and seeing.

4. Realize that people in the country you visit often have time concepts and thought patterns different from your own. Not inferior, just different.

5. Discover the enrichment that comes from seeing another way of life, rather than looking for the "beach paradise" of the tourist posters.

6. Acquaint yourself with the local customs. Respect local customs; people will be happy to help you.

7. Cultivate the habit of asking questions instead of knowing all the answers.

8. Remember that you are one of thousands of visiting tourists. Do not expect special privileges.

9. If you really want a home away from home, why travel?

10. Spend wisely. Remember when shopping that the bargain you obtain is only possible because of the low wages paid to the maker.

11. Make no promises to local people unless you are certain you can fulfill them.

12. Reflect daily on your experiences; seek to deepen your understanding. "What enriches you may rob or violate others."

Source: *North America Coordinating Center for Responsible Tourism, Box 827, San Anselmo, CA 94979*

Wedding Anniversary Gifts

Year	Traditional	Modern	Year	Traditional	Modern
1st	Paper	Clocks	15th	Crystal or watches	Watches
2nd	Cotton	China	20th	China	Platinum
3rd	Leather	Glass or crystal	25th	Silver	Silver plate or sterling silver
4th	Fruit & flowers	Small electric appliances			
5th	Wood	Silverware	30th	Pearl	Pearl
6th	Sugar & candy	Iron or Wood	35th	Coral	Jade
7th	Wool or pottery	Copper or pen/pencil sets	40th	Ruby	Ruby
8th	Bronze	Linen	45th	Sapphire	Sapphire
9th	Pottery or willow	Pottery	50th	Gold	Gold
10th	Tin	Aluminum	55th	Emerald	Emerald
11th	Steel	Fashion jewellery	60th	Diamond	Diamond (from 60th anniversary on)
12th	Silk or linen	Pearls			
13th	Lace or fur	Textiles	75th	Diamond	
14th	Ivory	Gold jewellery			

Canadian Customs Regulations[1]

Taxes and duties on goods that exceed or do not qualify for the exemptions noted below should be estimated at 30% of the value. This is a guideline only; luxury items such as jewellery may have excise tax applied as well.

Personal Exemptions[2]

Canadian residents returning from another country can bring goods into Canada free of duty and taxes if they qualify for a personal exemption under conditions listed below. Goods brought in under personal exemption must be for personal or household use, and your exemption cannot be pooled with (or transferred to) other people. A parent or guardian may make a customs declaration on behalf of an infant, but the goods declared in the child's name must be for his or her use only.

■ After 24 Hours' Absence or More

Any number of times per year, you may bring in goods to the value of $20 (except tobacco products and alcoholic beverages). A written declaration may be required. If the total value of all goods brought in exceeds $20, this exemption may not be claimed. Rather, you must pay duties on the full value.

■ After 48 Hours' Absence or More

Any number of times per year, you may bring in goods to the value of $100. A written declaration may be required.

■ After 7 Days' Absence or More

Once every calendar year, you may bring in goods to the value of $300. A written declaration will be required. To calculate the number of days exclude the date of departure, but include the date of return. It is dates that matter, not times; for example leave Friday the 7th, return Friday the 14th.

Tobacco Products and Alcoholic Beverages[2]

Subject to certain conditions, you may bring in alcoholic beverages and tobacco products free of duties under the 48-hours ($100) or yearly ($300) exemption, but not under the 24-hour ($20) exemption. The dollar value of these will form part of your exemption. All tobacco products and alcoholic beverages must accompany you in your hand luggage. Any person aged 16 or over may include up to 200 cigarettes and 50 cigars or cigarillos and 400 g of tobacco. More may be brought in, but you must pay the applicable duties on the excess amount. If you meet the age requirements set by the province or territory through which you re-enter Canada, you may bring in 1.14 litres (40 imperial oz.) of wine or liquor, or 24 cans or bottles (355 ml or 12 fl. oz.) of beer or ale or its equivalent (totalling 8.5 litres).

Your Declaration

When you return to Canada, you must declare to Customs all goods you have acquired abroad as purchases, gifts, prizes or awards. You must also include goods purchased at a Canadian or foreign duty-free store. If goods are not declared, or are falsely declared, they may be seized and forfeited and the traveller may face severe penalties.

Goods which you bring in under the $20 or $100 exemption must accompany you in hand or checked luggage in all cases. The goods that you claim under the $300 exemption may follow you by mail or other means.

Source: *Revenue Canada*

(1) For Canadian residents travelling abroad; figures are in Canadian dollars. (2) The Canada-US Free Trade Agreement does not affect personal exemption levels or restrictions on tobacco products and alcoholic beverages.

► **For More Information**

Please contact one of the regional Customs offices listed below or check the telephone book (under "Government of Canada, Customs and Excise") for local offices.

Atlantic: Customs Office, 6169 Quinpool Rd, Halifax, NS B3J 3G6; (902) 426-2911

Quebec: Customs Office, 130 Dalhousie St, Quebec, Que. G1K 7P6; (418) 648-4445

Montreal: Customs Office, 400 d'Youville Sq., Montreal, Que. H2Y 3N4; (514) 283-9900

Ottawa: Customs Office, 360 Coventry Rd, Ottawa, Ont. K1K 2C6; (613) 993-0534 or 991-0526

Toronto: Customs Office, Box 10, Stn A, 1 Front St W, Toronto, Ont. M5W 1A3; (416) 973-8022

Hamilton: Customs Office, 400 Grays Rd N, Stoney Creek, Ont. L8E 3J6; (416) 578-8715

Southwestern Ontario: Customs Office, Box 2280, Walkerville Post Office, Windsor, Ont. N8Y 4R8; (519) 973-8522

Central: Customs Office, Federal Bldg, 269 Main St, Winnipeg, Man. R3C 1B3; (204) 983-6004

Alberta: Customs Office, 220-4th Ave SE, Ste 720, Calgary, Alta. T2P 2M7; (403) 292-4660

Pacific: 1001 W Pender St, Vancouver, BC V6E 2M8; (604) 666-0545

How to Become a Canadian Citizen

Legal Entry: You must have been lawfully admitted to Canada for permanent residence; i.e. as a landed immigrant.

Age: You must be 18 years of age or older to apply on your own behalf.

Residence: You must have resided in Canada for a total of three years within the four years immediately before your application for citizenship.

Freedom from Prohibitions: You cannot receive citizenship or take the oath of citizenship if: you are considered a risk to Canada's security; you are under a deportation order; you are on probation or parole; you are in prison; you have been convicted of an indictable offence within the past three years.

Official Language: You must know either English or French, the official languages of Canada, well enough to make yourself understood in your community.

Knowledge of Canada: You must have some knowledge of your rights and responsibilities as a Canadian citizen and of Canada's political system, geography and history.

Oath of Citizenship: You must take and sign this Oath of Citizenship: "I swear/affirm that I will be faithful and bear true allegiance to Her Majesty Queen Elizabeth the Second, Queen of Canada, Her Heirs and Successors, according to law and that I will faithfully observe the laws of Canada and fulfil my duties as a Canadian citizen."

How to Apply: You apply for citizenship at the offices of a Citizenship Court or to a citizenship officer who may travel to your area. For more information and for locations, dates and times of such visits, contact the nearest Citizenship Court or contact the Registrar of Canadian Citizenship, Department of Multiculturalism and Citizenship, Sydney, NS B1P 646.

Special Birthday and Anniversary Greetings

■ *Greetings from the **Prime Minister** are sent on the occasion of a 25th wedding anniversary or a 70th birthday.*

■ *Greetings from the **Governor General** are sent on the occasion of a 50th wedding anniversary or a 90th or 95th birthday.*

■ *Greetings from **Her Majesty the Queen** are sent on the occasion of a 60th wedding anniversary or a 100th birthday.*

Contact the office of your local Member of Parliament (federal) to arrange for the greetings to be sent. Allow at least 6 weeks notice.

Citizenship Courts

Maritime Region

St John's, Nfld: Box 75, Atlantic Place, 215 Water St, Flr 8 A1C 6C9; (709) 772-5566

Halifax, NS: 5281 Duke St, B3J 3M1; (902) 426-2148; (902) 426-6227 (tollfree in NS)

Moncton, NB: Central Guaranty Trust Bldg, 860 Main St, Ste 503, E1C 1G2; (506) 851-7050

Charlottetown, PEI: Application Centre, Dominion Bldg, 97 Queen St, Ste 316 C1A 4A9; (902) 566-7188

Central Canada

Quebec, Que.: St Amable Complex, 333 St Amable St, Ste 155 G1R 5G2; (418) 648-3831

Montreal, Que.: Guy Favreau Complex, 10th Flr, West Tower, 200 René-Lévesque Blvd. W., H2Z 1X4; (514) 283-6679; Room 100, 5167 Jean Talon St E., H1S 1K8; (514) 283-2817; 6420 St Denis St, H2S 2R7; (514) 283-6835

Ottawa, Ont.: 150 Kent St, Flr 9 K1A 0M5; (613) 992-4485

Kingston, Ont.: 106 Clarence St, Ste 210 K7L 1X3; (613) 545-8015

Oshawa, Ont.: 310 Simcoe St S, Flr 2 L1H 4H7; (416) 723-1216

Toronto, Ont.: 1541 Bloor St W, M6P 1A5; (416) 973-6424; 55 St Clair Ave E, Ste 216 M4T 1M2; (416) 973-6424

Mississauga, Ont.: 77 City Centre Dr, Ste 151 L5B 1M5; (416) 973-6424

North York, Ont.: 4580 Dufferin St, Ste 300 M3H 5Y2; (416) 973-6424

Scarborough, Ont.: 200 Town Centre Court, Ste 217 M1P 4X8; (416) 973-6424

Hamilton, Ont.: 150 Main St W, Ste 412 L8P 1H8; (416) 572-2361

Source: *Multiculturalism and Citizenship Canada*

Waterloo, Ont.: 70 King St N N2J 2X0; (519) 886-3120

London, Ont.: Govt of Canada Bldg, 451 Talbot St, Main Flr N6A 5C9; (519) 645-4334

Windsor, Ont.: 467 University Ave W, Rm 201 N9A 5R2; (519) 252-7852

Sudbury, Ont.: Federal Bldg, 19 Lisgar St S, Rm 326 P3E 3L4; (705) 671-0621

Thunder Bay, Ont.: Federal Building, 33 South Court St, Rm 234 P7B 2W6; (807) 345-2316

Western Canada

Winnipeg, Man.: Canadian Grain Commission Bldg, 303 Main St, Rm 200 R3C 3G7; (204) 983-3792

Regina, Sask.: 2101 Scarth St, Rm 200 S4P 2H9; (306) 780-5535

Saskatoon, Sask.: Financial Bldg, 230-22nd St, Rm 505 S7K 0E9; (306) 975-4115

Calgary, Alta: 220-4th Ave SE, Rm 254 T2P 3C1; (403) 292-5539

Edmonton, Alta: 9700 Jasper Ave, Ste 225 T5J 4C3; (403) 495-3355

Kelowna, BC: 102-1433 St Paul St V1Y 2E4; (604) 861-3317

Surrey, BC: Rm 240, 7093 King George Hwy, V3W 5A2; (604) 585-5730

Vancouver, BC: Sinclair Centre, 757 W Hastings St, Ste 200 V6C 1A1; (604) 666-3971

Victoria, BC: Customs House, 816 Government St, Rm 105 V8W 1W9; (604) 363-3464

Prince George, BC: Royal Bank Bldg, 550 Victoria St, Ste 400A V2L 2K1; (604) 561-5303

Whitehorse, YT: Yukon Centre, 4114-4th Ave, Rm 304 Y1A 4N7; (403) 668-2721

Yellowknife, NWT: Scotia Centre, #4, 5102 50th Ave, Rm 202 X1A 2N5; (403) 920-8270

The Seven Wonders of the World

Ancient	Modern
The Pyramids (Egypt)	The Great Sphinx of Giza and the Pyramid of Khufu (Egypt)
The Hanging Gardens of Babylon (Iraq)	Hagia Sofia (Turkey)
The Statue of Zeus at Olympia (Greece)	The Taj Mahal (India)
The Colossus at Rhodes (Greece)	The Leaning Tower of Pisa (Italy)
The Temple of Artemis (Diana) at Ephesus (Turkey)	The Eiffel Tower (France)
The Mausoleum at Halicarnassus (Turkey)	The Washington Monument (US)
The Pharos (Lighthouse) of Alexandria (Egypt)	The Empire State Building (US)

October 16, 1992–October 1, 1993

ACUFF, ROY, 89; fiddler and singer who starred on *Grand Ole Opry* for more than 50 years. November 23, 1992.

>>>

ANDERSON, Marion, 96; US contralto who drew her nation's attention to the reality of racial discrimination with her 1939 concert at the Lincoln Memorial in Washington. April 8, 1993.

>>>

ANDREWS, Dana, 83; screen actor best known for his role in the 1944 film *Laura*. December 17, 1992.

>>>

ARSENAULT, Bona, 88; former Liberal MP, MNA, and Quebec cabinet minister who recruited René Lévesque for Jean Lesage's liberals. July 4, 1993.

>>>

ASHE, Arthur, 49; US tennis star and 1975 Wimbledon champion. February 6, 1993.

>>>

BAUDOIN, King of Belgium, 62; Europe's longest-serving monarch. July 31, 1993.

>>>

BAXTER, Richard, 87; winner of the 1988 Outstanding Broadcaster Award, he built a broadcasting empire in northern Ontario and helped found Northern Cable TV. February 4, 1993.

>>>

BOMBARDIER, J.A. Germain, 62; eldest son of Bombardier founder Joseph-Armand Bombardier and former president of L'Auto-Neige Bombardier. January 14, 1993.

>>>

BORINSKY, Jacob, 95; founder of Monarch Fine Foods. April 17, 1993.

>>>

BROWN, Kingsley Ewart Sr., 82; reporter and editor who worked for *The Toronto Star*, the *Winnipeg Free Press*, the Paris edition of *The New York Herald-Tribune*, *The Halifax Herald*, *The Halifax Chronicle*, *The Saint John Telegraph-Journal*, *The Hamilton News* and *The Hamilton Spectator* during his career. He was a civil libertarian and acted as executive assistant to Canada's first female cabinet member, Ellen Fairclough. August 30, 1993.

>>>

BURR, Raymond, 76; US actor best known for his television roles in "Perry Mason" and "Ironside." September 12, 1993.

BUTTS, Alfred Mosher, 93; US architect who invented the board game "Scrabble." April 4, 1993.

>>>

CAHN, Sammy, 79; Oscar-winning lyricist whose songs included "Call Me Irresponsible," "Three Coins in a Fountain" and "High Hopes." January 15, 1993.

>>>

CHALMERS, Dr. Everett, 87; New Brunswick doctor who served as cabinet minister in Richard Hatfield's government. April 26, 1993.

>>>

CHALMERS, Floyd, 94; publisher and philanthropist who served as vice-president, president and chairman of the Maclean Hunter publishing empire and donated millions to support the work of Canadian artists and performers. April 26, 1993.

>>>

CHARLAND, Claude, 59; a career diplomat and ambassador, and Canada's ambassador to France. March 4, 1993.

>>>

CHARTERIS, Leslie, 85; mystery writer who created The Saint. April 15, 1993.

>>>

CHAVEZ, Cesar, 66; farm worker and unionist who organized US migrant farm workers and the grape boycott in the 1960s. April 23, 1993.

>>>

CONNORS, Chuck, 71; US actor and former baseball player who starred in TV series *The Rifleman* from 1958 to 1963. November 10, 1992.

>>>

COOK, Charles, 66; Conservative Member of Parliament from North Vancouver. February 23, 1993.

>>>

CROMIE, Donald, 77; former publisher and owner of the *Vancouver Sun*. He became manager of his father's paper, the *Sun*, in 1942 and worked to publish it until he sold it 22 years later. March 17, 1993.

>>>

CURNOE, Greg, 56; one of Canada's most celebrated contemporary artists. November 14, 1992.

>>>

DeRITA, Joe, 83; US comedian who was a member of the Three Stooges – the bald-headed Curly. July 3, 1993.

>>>

DESMEULES, Larry, 53; president of the Métis National of Alberta who was instrumental in the signing of the Métis National Accord (1990) which began the Métis nation's steps towards self-government. February 24, 1993.

DICKENS, Monica, 77; British writer who followed in the footsteps of her great-grandfather Charles Dickens and wrote more than 50 books. December 25, 1992.

>>>

DUBCEK, Alexander, 70; first secretary of the Czechoslovakian Communist Party and reform leader who led the 1968 Prague Spring push for democracy, only to see it crushed by the arrival of Soviet tanks. November 7, 1992.

>>>

ECKSTINE, Billy, 78; US singer and bandleader from the 1940s and 50s. March 8, 1993.

>>>

EMMERSON, Jim, 70; journalist and rewrite specialist for the *Toronto Telegram* and *Toronto Star* for over 40 years. January 11, 1993.

>>>

GALLIVAN, Danny, 75; legendary broadcaster for *Hockey Night in Canada* and the voice of the Montreal Canadiens. February 25, 1993.

>>>

GALLO, Ernest, 82; US winemaker and co-founder of the world's largest wine-making business. May 2, 1993.

>>>

GARDENIA, Vincent, 71; US actor on stage, screen and televi-

sion. December 10, 1992.

>>>

GARRISON, Jim, 71; former US district attorney who insisted that the assassination of John F. Kennedy was the result of a conspiracy. October, 1993.

>>>

GIES, Jan, 87; a member of the Dutch resistance who smuggled food to Anne Frank and her family during their period of hiding in Amsterdam. January 26, 1993.

>>>

GILLESPIE, John Birks (Dizzy), 75; US jazz trumpeter and founding father of style known as bebop. January 6, 1993.

>>>

GISH, Lillian, 99; silent screen star and Hollywood legend who appeared in many of director D.W. Griffith's early films, most notably *Birth of A Nation*, and who continued to perform until 1987. February 27, 1993.

>>>

GOLDING, William, 81; Nobel Prize-winning author of *Lord of the Flies*. June 19, 1993.

>>>

HANI, Chris, 50; secretary-general of the South African Communist Party and former chief of staff of the African National Congress's army. April 10, 1993.

HAYES, Helen, 92; US star of stage, screen and television. March 17, 1993.

>>>

HEARST, William Randolph, 85; Pulitzer Prize-winning journalist and editor-in-chief of the Hearst publishing empire. May 14, 1993.

>>>

HEPBURN, Audrey, 63; US movie star and later ambassador for UNICEF. January 20, 1993.

>>>

HERSEY, John, 78; US World War II correspondent who wrote more than 20 books and won the Pulitzer Prize in 1945 for *A Bell for Adano*. March 24, 1993.

>>>

HOGG, Helen, 87; Canadian astronomer, teacher and scientist who was a leading expert on star clusters. Over her 60-year career she accumulated a number of honours, including an asteroid named after her (Asteroid Sawyer Hogg) and in 1989 the observatory at the National Museum of Science and Technology was dedicated in her name. January 28, 1993.

>>>

HOLLOWAY, Sterling, 87; US actor whose career began in the silent film era but who went on to work for Disney studios as the voice of the Chesire Cat in *Alice in Wonderland* and later created the voice of Winnie the Pooh. November 22, 1992.

HOWSE, Rev. Ernest, 90; controversial liberal preacher and former United Church moderator. February 1, 1993.

>>>

HUNT, James, 45; British racing driver who won the Formula One world championship in 1976. June 15, 1993.

>>>

IRVING, Kenneth Colin, 93; founder of the Irving family empire, estimated to be worth $8.5 billion. Born in Buctouche, NB in 1899, Irving formed the Irving Oil Co. in the 1920s and expanded his business to include transportation, oil refining, mining, pulp and paper and communications. December 13, 1992.

>>>

IVES, George, 111; last living survivor of the Boer War and last living holder of the Queen Victoria Medal. The BC resident was also believed to be the oldest man in Canada at the time of his death. April 12, 1993.

>>>

JEPSON-YOUNG, Dr. Peter, 35; Vancouver doctor and AIDS activist who was considered BC's most effective AIDS educator. November 15, 1992.

>>>

KEELER, Ruby, 83; actress and dancer in a series of Busby Berkeley musicals who starred in such classic films as *42nd Street*, *Gold Diggers of 1933*, *Dames*, and *Shipmates Forever*. February 28, 1993.

➣➣➣

KLEIN, George, 88; scientist who headed the team that designed Canada's first atomic reactor, was chief consultant on the gear design for the Canadarm and was known as the most productive inventor in Canada in the 20th century. November 4, 1992.

➣➣➣

KUTNER, Luis, 84; human rights lawyer and co-founder of Amnesty International. March 1, 1993.

➣➣➣

LACKEY, Archbishop Edwin, 62; Anglican archbishop of the ecclesiastical province of Ontario. January 9, 1993.

➣➣➣

LEE, Brandon, 28; US actor and son of the late martial arts star Bruce Lee. March 31, 1993.

➣➣➣

LEFEBVRE, Tom, 65; Senator who also served as a Quebec Liberal MP for nearly 20 years. November 20, 1992.

➣➣➣

LILLO, Larry, 46; artistic director of the Vancouver Playhouse, Lillo was credited with reviving its fortunes. Prior to that posting, he served as artistic director of The Grand Theatre in London, Ontario. June 2, 1993.

➣➣➣

LLOYD, Gweneth, 91; choreographer and co-founder of the Royal Winnipeg Ballet. January 1, 1993.

➣➣➣

LOMBARDO, Lebert, 86; trumpet player and the last of the three Lombardo brothers who played with the Royal Canadians in the 1920s. June 16, 1993.

➣➣➣

McLEOD, Lionel, 65; doctor who pioneered the development of kidney dialysis in Canada, he established the University of Calgary's school of medicine and later became founding president of the Alberta Heritage Foundation for Medical Research as well as serving as president of the Royal College of Physicians and Surgeons of Canada. April 10, 1993.

➣➣➣

MacMILLAN, Sir Kenneth, 62; principal choreographer of London's Royal Ballet. October 29, 1992.

➣➣➣

MACPHERSON, Duncan, 68; award-winning editorial cartoonist for *The Toronto Star* for nearly 35 years. May 5, 1993.

➣➣➣

MANKIEWICZ, Francis, 49; Canadian film and television director whose work included *Love and Hate, Conspiracy of*

Silence and *Les Bons debarras*.
August 14, 1993.

MARSHALL, Bertha, 93; BC
resident who was one of the last
remaining survivors of the sinking of the *Titanic*. March 4, 1993.

>>>

MARSHALL, Thurgood, 84; the
first black to serve on the US
Supreme Court and leader in that
country's civil rights movement.
January 24, 1993.

>>>

MARSHALL, Tom, 55;
Canadian poet, novelist, teacher
and one of the founders of Quarry
Press. April 27, 1993.

>>>

MILLER, Roger, 56; US singer-
songwriter best remembered for
his 1965 hit "King of the Road."
October 25, 1992.

>>>

MONET-CHARTRAND,
Simonne, 73; longtime Quebec
feminist and peace activist who
helped found two women's organizations in Quebec and cam-
paigned for the No side during the
constitutional   referendum.
January 18, 1993.

>>>

MORI, Taikichiro, 88; Japanese
magnate and number 3 on *Forbes*
magazine's list of the world's bil-
lionaires. January 30, 1993.

NIXON, Patricia, 81; wife of former US President Richard Nixon.
June 22, 1993.

>>>

NUREYEV, Rudolf, 54; Russian-
born international ballet superstar.
January 6, 1993.

>>>

OORT, Jan, 92: Dutch astronomer
who established that the earth's
solar system lies on the outskirts
of a rotating Milky Way.
November 5, 1992.

>>>

PARISH, Mitchell, 92; US lyricist
who put words to Hoagy
Carmichael's "Star Dust" and also
wrote lyrics for "Deep Purple,"
"Moonlight Serenade," and
"Sophisticated Lady." March 31,
1993.

>>>

POLLOCK, Jack Henry, 62;
painter, teacher and art dealer
who helped fuel interest in
Canadian art in the 1960s.
December 10, 1992.

>>>

PUDLAT, Pudlo, 76; one of
Canada's first-known Inuit artists
and the first Inuit to have a one-
person show at the National
Gallery of Canada. December 28,
1992.

>>>

REID, Kate, 62; Canadian classical actress whose 50-year career
included appearances on the

Stratford Festival stage, Broadway, and movie and television roles. March 27, 1993.

>>>

ROACH, Hal, 100; US movie producer who began in the era of Harold Lloyd and was responsible for pairing Laurel and Hardy, who became his greatest stars. November 2, 1992.

>>>

ROSS, Lillian, 113; Canada's oldest person and recognized as one of the oldest women in the world. Ms. Ross could remember her younger sister presenting a bouquet of flowers to Canada's first prime minister, Sir John A. Macdonald. March 20, 1993.

>>>

SABIN, Albert, 86; US scientist who developed an oral vaccine to protect against polio and (with Dr. Salk's injected vaccine) helped to eliminate polio as a health threat. March 3, 1993.

>>>

SABZEVARI, Abdul A'ala, 86; Grand Ayatollah of the world's 200 million Shia Muslims. August 16, 1993.

>>>

SALISBURY, Harrison, 84; longtime reporter and editor for *The New York Times* whose dispatches from the Soviet Union during the Cold War won him the Pulitzer Prize. July 5, 1993.

SAUVÉ, Jeanne, 70; former Liberal MP, cabinet minister and Canada's governor-general from 1984 to 1990. January 26, 1993.

>>>

SINCLAIR, George, 80; Canadian electrical engineer who helped develop the technique that made TV disc antennas and cellular telephones possible. He also organized Canada's first PhD program in electrical engineering and encouraged the growth of radio astronomy as a field of study. August 16, 1993.

>>>

SMALL LEGS, Nelson Sr., 61; former chief of Peigan reserve who challenged Alberta's government over construction of the Oldman River Dam. February, 1993.

>>>

SOLANDT, Dr. Omond, 83; founding chairman of the Science Council of Canada. Dr. Solandt studied in England during the Second World War and he helped establish a blood transfusion service in Britain during that period. May 12, 1993.

>>>

STARK, Dame Freya, 100; one of the world's great travel writers. Her books included *Baghdad Sketches* (1933) and *The Valley of the Assassins* (1934). May 9, 1993.

STEGNER, Wallace, 84; Pulitzer Prize-winning author of *Angle of Repose*, who also wrote *Wolf Willow*, a novella about his childhood on his parents' Saskatchewan farm. April 13, 1993.

≻≻≻

TAIT, Wilma, 103; distinguished journalist in an era when there were few women in journalism. Ms. Tait served as national president of the Women's Press Club in 1945. May 13, 1993.

≻≻≻

TAMBO, Oliver, 75; African National Congress leader-in-exile and ANC president in 1990. April 24, 1993.

≻≻≻

TARNOPOLSKY, Walter, 61; a leading Canadian human-rights scholar who served on the UN Human Rights Committee and various other international bodies. September 15, 1993.

≻≻≻

TEED, Nancy, 43; youngest member of the Canadian Senate, representing New Brunswick. Ms. Teed also served in the New Brunswick legislature. January 29, 1993.

≻≻≻

THOMPSON, Edward Palmer, 69; British historian and anti-nuclear activist best known as author of *The Making of the English Working Class*. August 28, 1993.

≻≻≻

TRACE, Al, 92; American big band songwriter and bandleader who wrote hits of the 40s and 50s, including *If I Knew You Were Coming I'd've Baked a Cake* and *Brush Those Tears from Your Eyes*. August 31, 1993.

≻≻≻

TRITT, William, 40; prominent Montreal-born pianist who formed the Dalart Trio and went on to a busy concert career. October, 1992.

≻≻≻

TURNER, Charlie, 76; MP for the riding of London East from 1968-84, and a member of the Senate from 1984 until 1991. January 10, 1993.

≻≻≻

VEITCH, Elwood, 64; popular BC Socred politician who held the cabinet posts of international business and immigration in the Vander Zalm government. September 18, 1993.

≻≻≻

WILSON, J. Tuzo, 84; eminent geophysicist, professor, founding principal of University of Toronto's Erindale College, chancellor of York University and director of the Ontario Science Centre from 1974 to 1985. April 15, 1993.

≻≻≻

WINCH, Harold, 85; one of the founders of the CCF and the New Democratic Party that followed it, he served in the BC legislature for 20 years and went on to represent the riding of Vancouver East from 1952 to 1972. February 1, 1993.

NEWS EVENTS OF 1992-93

October 1, 1992 to September 30, 1993

October

INTERNATIONAL

Bosnia: Fighting continued throughout the month as the UN High Commission for Refugees (UNHCR) struggled to get supplies to Sarajevo. Relief flights to Sarajevo resumed on Oct. 2, nearly a month after an Italian cargo plane was shot down. **Brazil:** On Oct. 2, Brazilian paramilitary police invaded the overcrowded Casa de Detencao, the largest prison in Brazil, in order to quell a riot; 111 prisoners died during the confrontation. **China**: 88-year premier Deng Xiaoping made his first public appearance since Feb. Beijing continued its war of words with Hong Kong governor Chris Patten who has proposed democratic reforms before the colony is handed back to the Chinese in 1997. Japanese emperor Akihito visited China for the first ever Japanese imperial visit; the emperor acknowledged the suffering that had been caused by Japan's 1931-45 occupation of China, but his remarks fell short of the apology many were hoping for. **Czechoslovakia:** The Czechoslovakian parliament rejected the draft bill on division of the country, throwing the timetable for separation (deadline Jan. 1, 1993) into chaos. **Egypt:** On Oct. 12 an earthquake measuring 5.9 on the Richter scale toppled apartment buildings in Cairo, leaving 557 dead and thousands injured and/or homeless. Over 5,000 buildings were destroyed and the Egyptian government was accused of bungling as survivors lived on the streets for over a week while waiting for assistance and temporary housing. **Germany:** Green party founders Petra Kelly and Gert Bastian were found shot to death in their home; investigators concluded that Kelly was killed by Bastian, who then turned the gun on himself. **Iraq:** Nearly 30 groups (including Shi'ite Muslims, Sunni Muslims and Kurds) opposed to Saddam Hussein and intent on the establishment of a democratic government gathered in Salahuddin, in Kurdish Iraq. **Israel:** Militants among the Shi'ite group Hizballah detonated a roadside bomb that killed five soldiers as part of their ongoing campaign to disrupt Middle East peace talks. Talks continued despite Israeli charges of Syrian complicity in the violence. **Liberia**: The two-year-old ceasefire, monitored by a military contingent made up of soldiers from seven west African neighbours collapsed as rebel commander Charles Taylor fought the peacekeepers and two ethnic Liberian armies. **Lithuania:** In the first parliamentary elections since the country declared independence in 1991, voters elected their former communist leaders. The failure of economic reforms made many citizens turn away from the nationalist Sajudis party that had spearheaded the break with Moscow. **Netherlands**: An El Al cargo plane crashed after takeoff from Amsterdam's Schiphol airport, plowing into two 9-story apartment buildings; the crash and subsequent fire killed many residents and severely injured dozens of others. **Peru:** On Oct. 7 a military tribunal sentenced Abimael Guzman, leader of the Shining Path guerilla movement, to life in prison without parole for his role in Peru's 12-year civil war. **Russia:** The Russian government advised the governments of Latvia, Lithuania and Estonia that the withdrawal of troops from their soil would be temporarily halted because of a shortage of housing for those to be repatriated; Baltic residents voiced suspicion that the troops would remain to protect the interests of Russian minorities. Russian Pres. Boris Yeltsin announced that the National Salvation Front, a party made up of militant nationalists and hardline communists, was banned from any participation in Russian politics. **Somalia**: Leaders of rival factions in Somalia's civil war signalled a willingness to begin serious peace talks after the leader of the provisional government, Ali Mahdi Mohammed, agreed to dissolve his administration. **South Africa:** An internal inquiry into the affairs of the African National Congress's (ANC) security forces confirmed accusations that the organization had been guilty of acts of violence and torture against detainees; ANC president Nelson Mandela vowed immediate action to end the abuses. President F.W. de Klerk pushed a bill through the South African parliament that effectively allowed blacks into the government by permitting unelected people to be appointed to cabinet. **Sweden**: During the week of October 8-16 the following Nobel Prizes were announced: Literature—Derek Walcott; Physiology or Medicine—Edmond H. Fischer and Edwin G. Krebs; Economics—Gary S. Becker; Physics—George Charpak; Chemistry—Rudolph A. Marcus; Peace—Rigoberta Menchu. **Ukraine**: The government of the Ukraine was defeated by a margin of 295 to 6 on a no-confidence motion on October 1, the day after Prime Minister Vitold Fokin resigned. Both the prime minister and the government were blamed for delaying economic reform and creating a serious financial crisis in the fledgling country. **United Kingdom**: The IRA began a random bombing campaign in London on Oct. 7; by Oct. 12, there had been eight explosions and numerous injuries. On Oct. 13, British Coal announced plans to close 31 of 40 mines, touching off a political crisis for Prime Min. John Major. By the 19th, his government was forced to back down after widespread protests and announced that the number of proposed mine closures would be limited to 10. **United States**: Ross Perot, an undeclared candidate for the US presidency earlier in the year, termed his decision to withdraw in July "a mistake" and officially declared himself in the race on Oct. 1. Also on Oct. 1, The *USS Saratoga,* an aircraft carrier taking part in NATO exercises, accidentally fired two missiles that hit a Turkish destroyer, killing five and injuring 14 others. On Oct. 12, the *Pioneer* spacecraft plunged into the scorching atmosphere surrounding the planet Venus and ended a 14-year space mission; on the same day, scientists began scanning the cosmos for signs of intelligent life in space via high-powered radio telescopes.

CANADA

Despite a nearly 2% jump in interest rates the Canadian dollar continued to fall, closing at US$.8006 on Oct. 1, down from US$.8024 the day before. Micmacs in Nova Scotia moved a step closer to having their own justice system when they won the right to have minor criminal cases heard by a native panel on the Indian Brook reserve.

The British Columbia Liberal party split over the constitutional debate when David Mitchell resigned as house leader on Oct. 6, protesting the party's official stand on the "No" side of the referendum on the Charlottetown accord. Former prime minister Pierre Trudeau continued his attacks on the proposed constitutional revision, calling for a "No" vote on Oct. 26.

Business and personal bankruptices in August were at their lowest level in two years, but economists warned that there was no indication that the economy was about to improve significantly.

Early frost at the end of a cold, wet summer was blamed as wheat farmers lost 1.4 millions tonnes of grain and the canola crop was reduced by 18% as well.

On Oct. 8, Manitoba native leaders urged their people to vote against the Charlottetown accord, stating that their existing treaty rights would be eroded by the agreement; national native leader Ovide Mercredi countered their argument, saying that the concern was based on an outdated copy of the legal text. Also, on Oct. 8: former Saskatchewan premier Grant Devine announced that he was leaving politics and the Ottawa Senators made their NHL debut, defeating the Montreal Canadiens in their first regular season game.

On Oct. 9, Canada announced reduced fish quotas for French vessels fishing off southern Newfoundland, setting new catch limits at roughly half of 1992's quota; the French government retaliated by demanding that any Canadian vessel fishing in French waters off St-Pierre-Miquelon carry a French fishing permit. After an eight-month slowdown on construction at the Hibernia offshore oil project, work resumed in anticipation of a new partner entering the deal. Oil industry analysts hailed a find east of Windsor as the best well in a "very, very long time;" the well was producing 500 barrels of high-grade crude a day and the initial survey indicated there was a large pool of oil that could keep up to 10 wells producing for 10 to 15 years.

On Oct. 13, Ottawa laid charges against Tioxide Canada Inc. of Tracy, Que., entering the battle with the long-time polluter of the St. Lawrence River after the company ignored a provincial clean-up order and attempts to shut the plant down by claiming that the river was in federal jurisdiction. Toronto author Michael Ondaatje was named a joint winner of the prestigious Booker Prize for his novel *The English Patient*. On the 14th, the Toronto Blue Jays defeated Oakland to win the American League pennant, the first championship for the Toronto franchise. In New York, Standard and Poor's bond-rating service announced it was downgrading Ottawa's credit rating on a portion of the government's long-term debt from AAA to AA plus.

The C.D. Howe Institute released a study on free trade on Oct. 19 that noted that while traditional, labour-intensive sectors of the economy such as processed food and beverages and household products had suffered under the agreement, producers of telecommunications, office and precision equipment had benefitted from access to the US market.

On Oct. 22, Canadian astronaut Steve MacLean blasted off on a 10-day space voyage. On Oct. 24, the Toronto Blue Jays won the World Series, defeating the Atlanta Braves 4 to 3 in a final game that lasted 11 innings.

On Oct. 26, after an often fractious campaign, Canadian voters went to the polls and rejected the terms of the Charlottetown accord. The "Yes" side of the referendum won by a small margin in Ontario (.2%) and also prevailed in Newfoundland, New Brunswick, PEI and the Northwest Territories. The "No" side won decisively in the remaining provinces with the national figures showing 54.4% voting "No" to 44.6% "Yes." While conceding that the defeat was a major blow, Prime Min. Mulroney announced that he planned to stay on as party leader into the next election.

Following a Federal Court ruling on the rights of homosexuals in the armed services, Chief of Staff John de Chastelain announced on Oct. 27 that all barriers to enlistment and promotion of gays in military service would be dropped. On Oct. 30, PEI Premier Joe Ghiz announced that he would be stepping down as premier and called for a leadership convention in January 1993. On the same day, Inuit, federal and territorial leaders signed an agreement to divide the Northwest Territories and create a new territory, to be called Nunavut, before the year 2000.

November

INTERNATIONAL

Angola: UNITA, the party widely seen as the champion of the country's democratic movement despite being the loser in the Sept. elections, launched attacks on the capital of Luanda and several other Angolan cities. UNITA's leader Jonas Savimbi charged that the election was rigged and raised fears that the country was headed for civil war. **Bosnia:** Attempts by UNICEF to distribute aid to 1 million children in Bosnia during a "week of tranquillity" had to be stopped as Serbian forces intent on consolidating territorial gains ended the effort almost as soon as it began. Serbs and Croats rejected earlier proposals for a partition of the country and demanded a split along ethnic lines as Muslims caught in the middle of the fighting fled in search of sanctuary. Aid to beleaguered Muslims in Srebenica and Gordadze was blocked by Serbian militia and civilians at the border. Western diplomats charged that Serbia repeatedly violated the ban on military flights to ferry troops and supplies. **Brazil**: Criminal charges were filed against Pres. Fernando Collor de Mello and eight associates in connection with the bribery and corruption scandal that led to his suspension by the Chamber of Deputies. **Cambodia**: Khmer Rouge forces continued to violate the ceasefire agreement, threatening the continuing diplomatic talks with China. The UN Security Council proposed economic sanctions on territory held by the Khmer Rouge if the violations did not stop, but neighbouring countries, including Thailand, made it clear they did not support such a move. **Colombia**: Following drug baron Pablo Escobar's escape in July of 1992, police cracked down on business associates and relatives in an effort to find him. Dozens of Escobar's associates were arrested or killed, and the traffickers responded by killing 29 police officers. (Leftist rebels joined in the attacks on government forces and killed over 1,000 police, soldiers and civilians in 1992.) After 30 were killed in bomb attack and 26 police guards were murdered at a remote oil installation, President Gaviria imposed a 90-day state of emergency to deal with the crisis. **El Salvador**: After weeks of UN-sponsored mediation, both government and FMLN rebels agreed to continue to demobilize their forces in accordance with the terms of the peace agreement that ended the 12-year civil war. **Germany:** Over 300,000 demonstrators gathered in Berlin to protest anti-foreigner violence but the show of goodwill was disrupted by a group of 400 anarchists who threw eggs and paint bombs and forced rally organizers to take cover behind anti-riot police. The town of Mölln was the scene of an arson attack on a residence for Turkish migrant workers. The attack, which killed three and injured nine others, signalled a shift in anti-foreigner violence from asylum seekers to workers legally in the country. Germany's federal prosecutor took over the case when it was revealed that the caller claiming responsibility for the blaze had used the phrase "Heil Hitler," and the government banned the far-right Nationalist Front. By month end however, the government had bowed to right wing anti-foreigner protests and begun planning constitutional amendments to tighten Germany's liberal immigration and asylum provisions. **Hong Kong:** Stock market prices in the British colony fell 8% after China's vice-premier hinted that proposed democratic reforms would jeopardize a 1984 agreement to preserve Hong Kong's capitalist culture after the 1997 repatriation. **India:** The Supreme Court upheld former Prime Minister's V.P. Singh's decision to reserve 27% of federal jobs for people of the lower castes. Upper caste students in New Delhi and five other states protested the decision which means that 49.5% of positions are now reserved for those in the lower castes, untouchables and tribal people. **Iran:** Western diplomats raised the alert about a possible arms build up after Iran purchased a Russian-built Kiloclass submarine and was rumoured to be negotiating with the Ukraine, Russia and China for tanks, missiles and jet fighters as well as information on building nuclear weapons. **Ireland:** A general election failed to elect a majority government as the Fianna Fail party won only 67 seats in the 166-member Dail, while Labour took 33. A referendum on abortion held concurrent with the election saw a proposal to legalize abortion defeated, but the ban on travel to other countries for the procedure was lifted. **Italy:** Italian police rounded up 90 suspected members of the mafia in Sicily, using evidence supplied by members of the mob. One of the

prosecution's key witnesses claimed that the organization has control of many politicians. **Japan:** Public confidence in the ruling Liberal-Democrats was further eroded when the latest official forced to resign after a US$4 million bribery scandal received a light sentence. Public protest over the lenient treatment was widespread. **Kenya:** A study sponsored by the Kenyan government and the UN revealed that 9% of the 2.16 million population have been infected with the HIV virus, including 200,000 children under the age of five. **Pakistan:** Former prime minister Benazir Bhutto, now in opposition, launched a march of her party's followers to Islamabad to protest alleged misrule and corruption on the part of her successors. She was arrested by security forces and barred from the capital for a month because of her actions, but vowed to continue. **Panama:** President Guillermo Endara's proposed constitutional reforms were rejected by voters in a national referendum. The country, formerly governed by dictator Manuel Noriega, has suffered from 20% unemployment and widespread crime and corruption. Opponents of President Endara demanded that he step down and allow a constituent assembly to rewrite the constitution. **Peru:** Three bomb explosions in various parts of Lima signalled that the Shining Path guerilas intended to carry on their campaign despite the arrest and conviction of their leader Abimael Guzman. The goal was to disrupt elections for a new national congress to replace the one suspended in April amid charges of corruption. Civilians ignored the terrorist attempts and on Nov. 22 Pres. Fujimori was returned to power with a coalition government that held 44 of the 80 seats in Congress. **Philippines:** The US pulled out of the last military base in the area but pledged to retain a policy of "cooperation without permanent bases" in the area. The former base is to be converted into a free port and industrial zone. **Somalia:** 2,500 Somali refugees crammed aboard a dilapidated cargo ship in an effort to escape the civil war. After travelling for a week the boat was barred from the Yemeni port of Mukalla, but was eventually alllowed to dock at Aden. **Sri Lanka:** Tamil rebels staged a successful suicide attack, killing the Navy chief and 3 of his staff members. **United Kingdom:** The Conservative government was rocked by further revelations that government officials had assisted companies in violating the trade embargo on military equipment to Iraq prior to the Gulf War. The Church of England narrowly approved the ordination of women with clergy and bishops strongly supporting the move while lay delegates barely gave the motion the two-thirds majority it needed. On Nov. 20 a fire at Windsor Castle burned for 30 hours and destroyed the 14th century St. George's Hall. The castle sustained about US$1 million in damages, but the art and other treasures in the castle were saved. On Nov. 26 it was announced that the Queen would pay taxes on her 1993 personal income and the civil list (the list of members of the royal family supported by the state) was trimmed to three— the Queen, Prince Philip and the Queen Mother. **United States**: In the November 3rd presidential election, Bill Clinton and his running mate Al Gore were elected with 43% of the popular vote; incumbent president George Bush received 38% of the support and latecomer Ross Perot trailed with 19%. The Democratic victors received support from across the country and the 54% voter turnout was the best in recent elections. As GATT and other trade talks nearly foundered on the issue of farm subsidies, the US threatened to initiate a trade war by slapping a 200% tariff on white wine from France. EC leaders moved to re-open trade negotiations with the US and avert the move. Vietnamese officials allowed a Senate delegation access to thousands of documents and artifacts during a visit to Viet Nam in an effort to prove there were no POWs still in that country. **Vatican**: Vatican officials acknowledged that the prosecution of the astronomer Galileo in 1633 over his assertion that, contrary to the church's teachings, the earth revolved around the sun, was a mistake. **Yugoslavia**: The UN Security Council voted to impose further sanctions against the Yugoslav government of Slobodan Milosevic in the hope of weakening his country's war efforts, and ignored pleas from Arab countries to lift the sanctions against Bosnia.

CANADA

Citing shrinking tax revenues in both income tax and retail sales tax, the treasurer of the cash-strapped Ontario government announced that C$595 million in spending would have to be cut in order to keep the projected deficit at C$9.9 billion for the fiscal year. In an effort to cut health care costs, the province announced that patients or their employers would begin to pay for medical services that were required by a third party, including examinations required for life insurance or motor vehicle or pilots' licences. Meanwhile in Newfoundland, Premier Clyde Wells unveiled a small program to create short-term jobs for residents hard hit by the cutbacks in the fishery, while the province looked for ways to diversify its economy.

In a referendum on Nov. 3, Inuit of the eastern Arctic approved the land-claim settlement required for the creation of the territory of Nunavut. Title to 350,000 sq. km of land will be given to residents as part of the 2.2 million sq. km territory, along with C$1.15 billion over the next 14 years and the right to hunt, fish and trap in all of the territory.

Environment Canada released figures for the ozone levels in various parts of Canada, noting that levels over Edmonton and Toronto reached record lows early in the year, between 5 and 15% lower than averages measured before 1980.

Manitoba Liberal leader Sharon Carstairs announced she would step down from the post as soon as a new leader could be chosen and would retire from politics when the next provincial election is called.

A poll released on Nov. 7 showed that a majority of Canadians in every region supported a united Canada, despite the rejection of the Charlottetown accord in the constitutional referendum.

The Finance Department announced that the federal deficit could hit C$35 billion for fiscal 1992-3 as the weak economy continued to cut government revenues.

Canadian immigration officials announced a plan to bring 500 Bosnians from detention camps as part of a deal negotiated by the UNHCR to bring people to Canada. In a separate announcement it was promised that thousands of Somali refugees in Canada would be reunited with family members left behind in the war-torn country.

On Nov. 10 RCMP Commissioner Norman Inkster was named president of Interpol, the international criminal police agency. He is the second RCMP commissioner to fill the post.

As fishing vessels from South Korea, Panama, Honduras, Morocco and Venezuela continued to fish just outside Canada's 200-mile limit on the Grand Banks, External Affairs announced plans to withdraw preferential tariffs and take other punitive measures in an effort to stop violations of the ban on cod fishing. Member countries of the Northwest Atlantic Fisheries Organization (NAFO) agreed to honour the ban in an effort to preserve fish stocks; the five countries continuing to fish in the area were not members of NAFO. Meanwhile the Canada-US steel war continued as Revenue Canada announced a dumping investigation into cold-rolled steel imports from Germany, France, Italy, the UK and the US. This brought the number of steel anti-dumping investigations to three in Canada, while the US has four underway involving Canadian steel.

On Nov. 20, Treasury President Gilles Loiselle announced that federal departments had been ordered to cut C$470 million from their operating budgets before the end of the fiscal year in an effort to hold the line on the deficit. On Nov. 24, a revision of the Immigration Act received final approval in parliament. The controversial changes included a limit on the right of appeal for refugee claimants and gave the government the power to decide where immigrants would settle upon arrival.

Federal fisheries minister John Crosbie announced further aid to displaced fishery workers in the form of make-work projects in Quebec and Atlantic Canada to help residents qualify for UIC payments. The package would total about C$5 million. CP Rail applied to the National Transportation Agency for permission to abandon all lines east of Sherbrooke, Que. citing a C$52 million loss in the last three years. The move would mean another 300 jobs lost in an area already devastated by the shutdown of much of the fishery.

On Nov. 27 Elijah Harper announced that he would be leaving provincial politics in Manitoba and would possibly try for a seat in the House of Commons during the next federal election.

On Nov. 29 the Calgary Stampeders won the Grey Cup in a game with the Winnipeg Blue Bombers, beating them 24-10.

December

INTERNATIONAL

Bolivia: On Dec. 1, 150 residents of the mining town of Llipi were killed, along with hundreds of miners, when a mountainside above the town collapsed on the area after heavy rains. **Cambodia:** In response to a UN Security Council limited trade embargo imposed on the area controlled by the Khmer Rouge, guerillas seized a six-member UN peacekeeping team and held them for four days. As the UN prepared to send in a team to supervise free elections, Thailand made it clear it was not happy with the sanctions and would create slowdowns for the UN operation. **Egypt:** Riot police arrested 400 Muslim activists in the face of increased fundamentalist militancy and terrorist attacks directed at both the government and foreign visitors. **El Salvador:** FLMN members used blow torches to destroy weapons as the disarmament program continued in the wake of the peace settlement. **Germany:** Proposals to reform the country's rules for granting asylum were unveiled. The new criteria would bar anyone arriving from a country that observes the Geneva convention on refugees; in those cases, the asylum seekers would be asked to return to the country they arrived from. In the latter half of the month, half a million marchers in various German cities took to the streets to protest against rising violence against refugees and the desecration of a Jewish cemetery. **India:** Hindu devotees destroyed an ancient Muslim mosque in the town of Ayodhya and touched off a week of riots in Calcutta, Bombay and other cities that left an estimated 1,000 dead. Violent protests against the Hindu action spread to Pakistan, Bangladesh and Britain. The mosque, built in 1528, is said to have been on the site of the birthplace of the Hindu god Rama. A crackdown on the violence led to the arrest of 6,000 Hindus and Muslims in a nationwide attempt to restore public order. **Indonesia:** On Dec. 12 a strong earthquake shook the island of Flores in Indonesia. The quake measured 6.8 on the island and 7.5 at the epicentre out in the ocean. The ocean earthquake was followed by a series of tidal waves (tsunamis) that left 2,500 people dead and destroyed over 60,000 buildings. **Israel:** On Dec. 17 Israel deported 415 Palestinians suspected of being activists in Muslim fundamentalist movements. The decision was taken after escalating Arab-Israeli violence but was roundly condemned by the UN. The deportees were taken over the border into the Israeli-controlled territory in Lebanon, but that government's refusal to admit the deportees left them stranded between the two countries. Muslim fundamentalists and the PLO joined forces to protest the deportation, despite the fact that the PLO was engaged in talks with Israel. **Russia**: Deputies to the Congress of People's Deputies held fractious sessions over the degree and direction of economic reform and former communist hardliners attacked Pres. Boris Yeltsin and some of his chief reformers, narrowly failing in an attempt to strip Yeltsin of his power to appoint a government. After eight days of arguing, the Russian president threatened a national referendum on the division of powers in order to force the deputies to choose a prime minister. The congress's choice for prime minister, Victor Chernomyrdin, was eventually agreed upon and the referendum was set for April 11. **Somalia**: On Dec. 9, 1,800 US Marines arrived to begin "Operation Restore Hope" in which American and other UN-sponsored troops would distribute food and other aid throughout the country and attempt a peacemaking role in the country—a sharp departure from the UN's usual peacekeeping duties. By mid-month French and American troops had reached the town of Baidoa; looting in the capital of Mogadishu was sporadic as 30 nations contributed troops in an effort to end the starvation caused by civil war; by the end of the month, UN forces had reached the southern part of the country, closing in on Bardera as clan militia and armed gangs withdrew. **South Africa**: Pres. F.W. de Klerk fired 23 top officers in the military after accusations that the military had been involved in racial violence. **Switzerland**: Voters in Switzerland rejected a proposal to join a 19-nation European free trade zone comprised of the 12-member European Community and the seven Nordic and Alpine members of the European Free Trade Association. **United Kingdom**: On Dec. 9 the prime minister announced that the Prince and Princess of Wales had agreed to a formal separation, but stressed that the agreement did not include plans for divorce. On Dec. 12 Princess Anne

and Commander Tim Laurence married in Scotland. Later in the month a British court ruled that 10 proposed mine closings were unlawful and ordered the government to consult with unions and miners before proceeding. **United States**: Pres. George Bush made a New Year's eve visit to Somalia to inspect troops serving in UN peace mission. **Venezuela**: Voters in the second election to be held in 34 years rejected the ruling party in contests for state governors, mayors and city council members. **Yugoslavia**: Slobodan Milosevic was returned as president of the Serbian republic with 55% of the popular vote in an election that monitors from other European countries charged was marred by smear campaigns, the rigging of electoral lists and other irregularities.

CANADA

On Dec. 2 Finance minister Don Mazankowski announced that the deficit would be C$7 billion higher than expected by the end of the fiscal year (Mar. 31) and proposed spending cuts that included a two-year freeze on civil service salaries and cutbacks in UI payments in an effort to save C$8 billion.

Immigration Minister Bernard Valcourt announced that the number of sponsored refugees for 1993 would be cut by 14,000 while the number of independent and business immigrants allowed into the country would be increased by 7,000. (1991 saw the highest immigration (224,600) since 1957, while emigration fell to the lowest levels in 30 years.)

Provincial trade ministers set 1995 as the target date for dismantling interprovincial trade barriers, hoping for a broad agreement by June of 1994. Meanwhile an international trade panel ruled that the US would have to refund C$15 to C$20 million to Canadian lumber exporters to cover an unfairly imposed export duty equivalent that had been required between October 1991 and March 1992.

A federal constitutional amendment to recognize New Brunswick as the only officially bilingual province was stalled by procedural wrangling in the House of Commons while the government used closure to force a drug patent bill through parliament in an effort to have it become law by Jan. 1. The drug bill will extend drug patent protection for brand-name drugs to 20 years; critics charged that it would threaten Canada's fledgling generic drug industry as well as the overextended health care program. Later in the month the Senate passed the controversial amendments to the Immigration Act and gave unanimous approval to the constitutional resolution guaranteeing French and English language rights in New Brunswick that had stalled in the House of Commons.

On Dec. 11 Statistics Canada revealed that average family income in Canada fell 2.6% during 1991, bringing real income close to 1980 levels and pushing more people below the poverty line.

On Dec. 14, Ralph Klein was sworn is as premier of Alberta; Klein won the Conservative party leadership in a run-off vote after former health minister Nancy Betkowski won the first leadership ballot by one vote.

100 Canadian troops arrived in Somalia on Dec. 15, soon to be joined by 800 more to help distribute food throughout the country. Earlier in the month Ottawa announced that Canada would be withdrawing all troops from Cyprus after 28 years of supplying peacekeepers to patrol the buffer zone separating the Greeks and Turks on the island.

After protracted negotiations to save the airline, PWA announced a deal with American Airlines that would see the US carrier acquire 33% of the stock in Canadian Airlines.

A federal-provincial agreement providing funds for road improvement and compensation for the loss of jobs in the ferry service was signed on Dec. 16, clearing yet another hurdle in the process of approving the construction of the C$800-million bridge linking PEI to the mainland.

Prime Min. Mulroney signed the North American free trade agreement on Dec. 17, although legislation remained to be passed in Canada as well as the US and Mexico to make the deal law.

The European Community accepted a deal to cut back on fishing in the high seas by agreeing to observe quotas that have been in place but ignored since 1986. New quotas were also agreed upon for northern cod, the fishery that was shut down in Canada in July, 1992. Fisheries Minister John Crosbie also announced sweeping cuts on the domestic fishery, up to 70% on other species of cod,

haddock and pollock. On Dec. 29 Crosbie announced that Canada would end the practice of allowing the capture of beluga whales for export.

January

INTERNATIONAL

Bosnia: The deputy prime minister of Bosnia was assassinated by Serbian irregular troops after his UN-escorted convoy was stopped. **Brazil:** Minutes into his impeachment trial, Pres. Fernando Collor de Mello announced his resignation in an effort to protect his political future, however the Brazilian Senate passed a decree barring him from holding public office for eight years; de Mello still faced criminal charges of corruption arising from the scandal. **Colombia:** Medellin drug baron Pablo Escobar indicated he would like to negotiate a conditional surrender in return for American asylum for members of his immediate family; Pres. Trujillo rejected any negotiations and Escobar vowed to escalate his campaign of violence. By the end of the month, two car bombs had exploded in Bogota killing 20 people. **Croatia:** The Peruca hydro dam north of Split was damaged by landmines; as water poured through gaping holes Croatians scrambled to drain the reservoir and make repairs while an estimated 20,000 people prepared to evacuate the area. **Guatemala:** A ceasefire was proposed in that country's 32-year-old civil war that has taken 120,000 lives. Rebels demanded that the military be cut in half; the government proposed a UN-monitored demobilization plan and the repatriation of over 42,000 refugees in neighbouring Mexico during the next two years. **India:** Indian soldiers in the town of Sopore in Kashmir massacred 55 people and set buildings ablaze to avenge the death of a soldier. On Jan. 6 Hindus and Muslims clashed as protests over the destruction of the mosque at Ayodhya escalated; the violence left over 600 dead. **Iraq:** After weeks of Iraqi defiance of the Gulf War ceasefire agreement, UN forces unleashed a missile attack in retaliation; by Jan. 19, the Iraqi president proposed a ceasefire as a gesture of goodwill to the incoming US president. **Israel:** Israeli parliament passed a bill making it legal for citizens to talk to members of the PLO; PLO leader Yasser Arafat immediately called an Israeli TV talk show to suggest peace negotiations. **Japan:** Crown Prince Naruhito announced his engagement to Masako Owada, a career diplomat. **Kenya:** Pres. Daniel Tarap Moi won re-election despite charges of corruption and the fact that all foreign aid had been suspended in protest over his regime; deeply splintered opposition allowed Moi victory with just 38% of the popular vote. **Lebanon:** Deported Palestinians remained stranded as the Red Cross applied for permission to bring in supplies; permission was required from both Israel and Lebanon and was eventually denied. **Malaysia:** Prime Min. Mahathir Mohamad plunged the country into a constitutional crisis when he forced legislation through parliament to eliminate immunity from prosecution and press criticism for the country's various royal families. The move came as some of Malaysia's sultans were accused of appropriating public funds and maintaining their own private armies. **Nicaraugua:** The coalition government of Violetta Chamorro crumbled as her allies deserted her and she added 3 former Sandinistas to her cabinet, devalued the cordoba and froze government spending in an effort to retain power. **Slovakia:** On Jan. 1 Bratislava celebrated Slovakia's new independence with fireworks. **Somalia:** US troops began to pull out late in Jan., hoping to prod the UN Security Council into creating a peacekeeping force to take over the job; a US marine was killed later in the month and helicopter gunships swept the area near Kismayu in an effort to flush out the killers. **United Kingdom:** The oil tanker *Braer* ran aground after its engines failed in rough seas around the Shetland Islands; the tanker broke up as the storm continued and over 600,000 barrels of light crude oil were dumped into the sea. **United States:** Pres. George Bush visited Moscow and joined Russian Pres. Boris Yeltsin in signing the START II treaty which will see both countries retire 66% of their remaining long-range warheads, leaving the US with 3,500 and Russia with 3,000. Bill Clinton was inaugurated as president on Jan. 20; Clinton's nominee for Attorney General, Zoë Baird, was forced to withdraw her name from consideration after revelations of irregularities in her hiring of domestic help. Clinton also came under fire for acting on an election promise to relax the ban on gays in the military. Puerto Rico passed a law declaring the US commonwealth officially bilingual (English and Spanish), and Gov. Pedro Rossello signalled a continuing push for recognition as the 51st state. **Zaïre:** The government of Mobutu Sese Seko issued new banknotes in denominations of 5 million Zaïres (worth about US$2); merchants refused to accept the new currency and troops went on an armed rampage to protest after they were paid with the new banknotes.

CANADA

Quebec premier Robert Bourassa resumed treatments for skin cancer and announced that he would make a decision on his political future some time in February.

On Jan. 6 Gen. John de Chastelain, Canada's chief of defence staff was appointed as Canada's ambassador to Washington, replacing Derek Burney who had earlier announced his plan to return to private business.

50 fishery workers and politicians from St-Pierre-Miquelon were bailed out of jail in St. John's after France paid C$1.4 million to win freedom for them and their fishing trawlers. The residents of the islands had staged a protest over reduced cod quotas and were charged with illegally fishing in Canadian waters after they dropped their nets inside Canada's 200-mile zone.

Canadian peacekeepers moved into Macedonia in mid-January as part of a UN-sponsored effort to contain the war in Bosnia. At the same time Canada joined 125 other nations in Paris to sign a treaty banning chemical weapons. North Korea and most Arab states were absent from the arms control negotiations to eliminate the entire class of weapons.

Canada hit importers of flat-rolled steel from nine countries (Belgium, Brazil, the former Czechoslovakia, Denmark, Germany, Romania, Britain, the US and Macedonia) with dumping penalties in a move that would likely escalate the steel trade battle with the US.

On Jan. 13 the Sahtu Tribe of the Great Bear Lake region in the NWT reached a land claim agreement with Ottawa that would give the group 41,437 sq. km of land and C$75 million over 15 years plus a share of the government's resource royalties from the Norman Wells oilfield and pipeline. The negotiations for self-government of the region continued but were expected to be completed by April. The Cree in Northern Quebec signed a deal with Hydro-Quebec to get a minimum of C$125 million in compensation for the damage caused by the La Grande hydroelectric project in the James Bay region, but vowed to continue the fight against the Great Whale River project in the same area.

The economy continued to lag as car sales were reported to have fallen in 1992, the fourth straight year for such a slide. On Jan. 11 Henry Birks and Sons Ltd. filed for bankruptcy protection while in western Canada Woodward's Ltd. announced a reorganization that would cut 1,200 jobs as part of its effort to avoid bankruptcy.

On Jan. 15 it was announced that Ottawa would be a new partner in the C$5.2 billion Hibernia megaproject, along with Murphy Oil of Arkansas and that Mobil and Chevron Canada would increase their share in the project in an effort to get back on track.

The Quebec government announced a deal to get rid of 10,000 tonnes of PCB waste that have been a source of conflict with environmentalists and residents in the Baie Comeau area since 1988. The waste was to be burned pending environmental hearings and a test burn in the communities where the waste is stored.

In sports, the CFL announced deals with San Antonio, Texas and Sacramento, Calif. that would see the league expand to 10 teams for the 1993 season.

The last Canadian fighter jets in Europe left Baden-Soellingen, Germany on Jan. 19, part of a process that will turn the base over to NATO and the German government by December 31. The Canadian base in Lahr will close in 1994 as Canada implements defence cutbacks and pulls out of NATO.

On Jan. 25 Catherine Callbeck was sworn in as premier of PEI after winning 79% of the vote in a Charlottetown leadership convention.

Statistics Canada announced that in 1992 Canada had the lowest inflation rate in the past 30 years, posting a 1.5% jump; housing starts for the year were up 7.7%, lead by strong growth in BC as the economic recovery continued to limp along. Trade Minister Michael Wilson announced that the NAFTA pact among Canada, the US and Mexico could be expanded to include South American countries within the framework of the existing agreement. Possible new partners were Colombia and Venezuela.

On Jan. 29 Bill Hopper was relieved of his duties as chairman and CEO of Petro-Canada; Hopper, who had lead the company since 1976, was replaced by president James Stanford.

February

INTERNATIONAL

Austria: Voters in a national referendum on regulations to restrict foreigners in that country soundly rejected the idea, with only 7% of ballots cast supporting the plan. **Bosnia:** The Vance-Owen peace plan, which would divide Bosnia into 10 provinces and leave captured territory in the hands of Serbians, was rejected by Washington. By mid-month all sides had increased pressure on civilians by blocking the shipment of relief supplies to Muslims trapped in eastern Bosnia, and to Sarajevo; representatives of various factions boycotted the latest round of peace negotiations. **Brazil:** The convicted killers of environmentalist Chico Mendes escaped from prison amid charges of lax security and government complicity; locals feared that violence between rubber tappers and farmers hoping to harvest the forest would escalate. **Egypt:** A six-month wave of attacks on tourists by Muslim fundamentalists was blamed for a 25% drop in Egypt's tourist revenues; losses were expected to total US$1 billion by June 1993. **France:** Farmers and fishermen protested falling prices by storming a Paris wholesale market and destroying nearly US$3.6 million in produce. **Germany:** The Bundesbank lowered interest rates after months of intense pressure from EC allies; German officials maintained that the threat of inflation at home was more important than economic growth elsewhere, however speculative pressure on the Danish krone finally forced the rates down. Archaeologists announced new evidence confirming that the site of mythic Troy may in fact be the one chosen by Heinrich Schliemann 120 years ago. **India:** An anti-government rally was halted before it reached New Delhi as thousands of Hindu militants were arrested on their way to the city; security forces sealed off New Delhi. **Israel:** Palestinian refugees rejected a proposal that would have repatriated a quarter of those expelled in Dec., vowing to stay until all could return home. Efforts to resume the peace talks were stalled and tensions heightened as the stalemate over the expelled Palestinians continued; a new wave of violence lead to deaths and injuries on both sides of the conflict. **Italy:** The minister of justice was forced to step aside as "Operation Clean Hands" (the government's anti-corruption campaign) entered its 18th month and the scandal continued to spread. **Japan:** Japan's trade surplus reached an all-time high with the rest of the world (US$117.6 billion) and trading partners increased demands for better access to Japanese markets. Meanwhile Nissan announced a plant closing on the outskirts of Tokyo and Fujitsu and NEC announced they would likely end the year with losses. **Netherlands:** The parliament approved the world's most liberal guidelines for doctor-assisted suicide and euthanasia, making it possible for doctors to assist patients without prosecution. **Poland:** Pres. Lech Walesa signed strict anti-abortion provisions into law, second only to the restrictions in Ireland. **Slovakia:** Economic differences in the two former Czech states forced Prague (Czech Republic) and Bratislava to establish their own currencies. **Somalia:** Gunmen launched a successful sneak attack in southern Kismayu that lead to charges of American involvement; General Aidid called for anti-American demonstrations to protest the attack. **South Africa:** The South African government tabled a bill of rights aimed at protecting the minority whites against any possible civil rights abuses by a black government. **United States:** Pres. Clinton's second choice for Attorney General, Kimba Wood, was also forced to withdraw her name from consideration after evidence of illegal babysitting arrangements. Fears of a new strain of non-HIV AIDS were laid to rest when the *New England Journal of Medicine* published a study establishing that the non-HIV patients were suffering from a non-contagious and rare virus not related to AIDS. On. Feb. 26 a car bomb exploded under the World Trade Centre in New York City, killing 5 people and injuring over 1,000 as tens of thousands were evacuated from the area. A standoff began in the town of Waco, Texas after the US Bureau of Alcohol, Tobacco and Firearms launched an assaut on a compound occupied by the Branch Davidians on Feb. 28 that resulted in a gunbattle and the deaths of 4 federal agents and an estimated cult 10 members. **Zaïre:** Pres. Mobutu Sese Seko resisted international pressure to hand power over to a transitional government; nearly 1,000 died in civil unrest protesting Seko's 27-year rule.

CANADA

The Conference Board of Canada announced that while Canada would lead the G-7 industrial nations with a projected growth rate of 3.3% in 1993, it would have one of the worst employment records with 11.3% forecast. The bank rate fell in early Feb. as the dollar improved, but Consumer and Corporate Affairs reported that the number of bankruptcies was another record-breaker in 1992 with 76,139 companies closing their doors.

The federal government announced plans to move the Innu community of Davis Inlet in northern Labrador farther inland to Sango Bay in an effort to improve the living conditions of the residents. The village was relocated to the inlet in 1967 and promised running water and sewage treatment facilities, neither of which materialised. Economic and social problems have plagued the community which has seen a rash of suicides of children and adults in recent years.

On Feb. 12, the federal government gave South Korea until the end of April to stop fishing in the waters off Newfoundland. Failure to leave the area would result in trade and economic sanctions.

The US accused Canada of dumping durum wheat in the US market, but a binational trade panel declined to make a decision on the matter. A group of independent auditors was scheduled to review the Wheat Board's sales contracts and the panel endorsed some of Canada's cost accounting methods, prompting the US National Assoc. of Wheat Growers to threaten to fight ratification of NAFTA.

Employees at the Provincial Papers mill in Thunder Bay voted to buy the mill from Abitibi-Price Inc. While the company and the provincial government will provide funds for the mill's operation and severance packages, the employee-owned company will assume the mill's debts.

Tioxide Canada Inc., a company long accused of being one of the major polluters of the St. Lawrence River, announced on Feb. 1 that it would close its plant in Tracy, Que. and cancelled plans to build a new plant in Becancour after the federal and provincial governments prosecuted the company for polluting the river with its production of titanium dioxide pigment (a whitener for paints, plastics and fine paper). Meanwhile angry workers at the NS plant of Premium Automotive Tanks Inc. received more than C$300,000 in compensation after occupying the plant in protest when the company abruptly shut down the operation and began trucking its equipment to Quebec.

In BC, Liberal Leader Gordon Wilson fired Judy Tyabji, the Liberal House leader, on Feb. 13 after rumours of favouritism and romantic involvement between the two swept party ranks. On Feb. 19 Wilson announced he was stepping down as Opposition leader in the BC legislature, but would remain as leader of the party.

On Feb. 15, Defence Minister Kim Campbell announced a renewal of the agreement to allow US Cruise Missile tests in Canada. The next day she announced that 1,200 Canadian troops would be moved into Sarajevo as part of an armed escort for UN food and medicine convoys.

On Feb. 17, the government announced it would soften some of the more controversial changes in the UI legislation by continuing eligibility for benefits for those who accept a layoff to protect jobs, take early retirement or quit their jobs because of sexual harassment.

In sports, Kurt Browning retained his Canadian men's figure skating championship crown by a narrow margin over Elvis Stojko, while Josée Choinard won the women's championship. Kate Pace of North Bay won the gold medal in the women's downhill at the world alpine ski championships.

On Feb. 24, Prime Min. Brian Mulroney announced that he was stepping down from his post in June, ending months of speculation about his future as Conservative leader.

Treasury Board president Gilles Loiselle indicated that federal spending would rise 1.5% in the coming fiscal year, despite earlier plans for restraint. The total spending for 1993-4 was estimated to be C$160.7 billion. The finance minister announced cuts to transfer payments to Newfoundland, PEI, Nova Scotia, Saskatchewan, Manitoba and Quebec. The cuts were based on revised 1991 census

population figures and the government also demanded repayment of transfer monies given on the earlier figures.

March

INTERNATIONAL

Afghanistan: 10 months after the Russian-backed regime collapsed, fighting continued as the mujahedin leadership tried to work out a power sharing arrangement. **Australia:** Incumbent Prime Min. Paul Keating was re-elected with a larger majority that his pre-election tally. The campaign focussed on the country's economic woes and Keating was widely expected to be defeated, however his promise to transform the country into a republic, and his opponent's proposal for a GST-style consumption tax was credited with giving him the victory. **Bosnia:** UN commander Philippe Morillon finally succeeded in getting aid to the besieged town of Srebrenica after days of negotiations and a final push into the town. Serbian militia continued the drive into Muslim territory as Western diplomats and politicians again shied away from the option of military intervention. Later in the month efforts to relieve the town were abandoned when Serbian militia shelled UN helicopters involved in the mission. **Cambodia:** UN Security Council members (incl. Cambodia's ally, China) voted to hold national elections in May, despite the Khmer Rouge's opposition. The Khmer Rouge stepped up their campaign to disrupt the peace process and drive the ethnic Vietnamese out of Cambodia by killing 33 Vietnamese settlers. **Congo:** 147 illegal aliens returning to Zaïre were drowned as thousands tried to board an aging ferry to make the trip home. **Egypt:** Government forces cracked down on opposition militants in several cities; in the wave of shootouts and arrests 23 were killed and 46 injured. At the same time, the trial for 49 Muslim militants charged with attacking tourists began. **El Salvador:** UN-sponsored Truth Commission issued its final report on atrocities committed during the 12-year civil war, claiming that 85% of the crimes were committed by government-directed forces. Recommendations included the suspension of 40 military officers and the banning of 10 FMLN members from public office for 10 years. **France:** In the first round of parliamentary elections, the ruling Socialists' share of the vote was reduced from 34.7% to 17.6%; the shift was expected to translate into a solid majority for a conservative alliance in the National Assembly. **Georgia:** Violence flared in the breakaway republic of Abkahazi and Georgian leader Eduard Sheverdnadze accused Russian forces of supporting the rebels. **Germany:** Local elections on Mar. 7 showed a shift to the far right as an extremist party headed by a former SS soldier won between 8 and 15% of the vote in various towns and cities, with many of their gains coming at the expense of the left. **India:** Bombay was rocked by explosions from 13 car bombs that killed 300, injured 1,100 and did major damage to downtown buildings during a 2 1/2 hour period. No group claimed responsibility for the attacks. On Mar. 12, a blast in Calcutta killed 86 people; police investigations later traced the Bombay explosions to one of the city's underworld families. **Indonesia:** 71-year-old Pres. Suharto was re-elected to a sixth 5-year-term by the People's Consultative Assembly. His rule over the fourth largest population in the world has been marked by economic development and a steady rise in per capita income. **Kenya:** Pres. Daniel Tarap Moi rejected international demands for economic reform, ensuring that foreign aid would continue to be withheld. Opposition parties boycotted the opening of parliament to protest Moi's presidency. **Netherlands:** News of the recession continued in Europe as Philips NV announced plans to lay off as many as 15,000 workers after the company posted a US$489 million loss. **Russia:** Pres. Boris Yeltsin's battles with the Congress of People's Deputies continued as he threatened to call a referendum on the division of power to settle their disputes; the Congress made it known that such a move would be unconstitutional if done without their consent. Yeltsin retaliated by calling a referendum on a new constitution for April and declared that any legislation adopted by Congress or the Supreme Soviet was subject to his approval. Congress denounced the special rule as unconstitutional but abandoned plans to impeach Yeltsin. **South Africa:** A conference of 26 delegates from across the political spectrum negotiated a return to the formal talks on power sharing, even as violence by extremists was renewed in an effort to derail the process.

Switzerland: The Geneva-based International Labour Organization (ILO) reported that millions of people around the world work as slaves in countries as diverse as Sudan, Haiti, Pakistan, Mauritania, India, Thailand, Peru and Brazil. Many of the workers are sold as children by families desperate for cash or captured during the chaos of war. **Thailand:** One of the last Cambodian refugee camps closed as the last 200 residents began their trip home; the camps were once home to nearly 150,000 people. **United Kingdom:** John Major's government suffered a defeat in a parliamentary vote as a bill amending the ratification of the Maastricht Treaty passed despite government opposition. **United States:** The first arrest was made in the World Trade Centre bombing after the serial number on the van that delivered the bomb lead police to a suspect; by mid-month five more arrests had been made. Researchers announced the discovery of the gene behind Lou Gehrig's disease, raising hopes that a treatment for the crippling and usually fatal illness would eventually be found. An anti-abortion protestor shot and killed Dr. David Gunn, a doctor legally allowed to perform abortions. On Mar. 12 a huge storm system swept eastern North America, affecting territory from Canada to Cuba. The US took most of the punishment as cold, snow and hurricane-force winds stranded travellers; the storm was blamed for 238 deaths, not including 48 people missing at sea.

CANADA

After two years of negative growth the Canadian economy finally showed signs of expansion, but only by a meager 0.9% in 1992. The bulk of the growth came in Dec. and was lead by a very strong showing in exports.

Supplementary estimates tabled in the House of Commons indicated that the constitutional referendum cost taxpayers C$103.9 million; in addition, the chief electoral officer's budget was exceeded by C$19.1 million; however, it was also announced that C$700 million would be saved on interest charges on the public debt because of falling interest rates—those costs were expected to fall from C$40.2 billion to C$39.5.

Western provinces launched cuts and reorganization measures in an effort to curtail rising health care costs: Manitoba served notice it will not pay for abortions at private clinics in spite of a court ruling that it has an obligation to do so; Alberta announced that hospitals as well as municipalities, schools and universities would receive no increases in provincial grants for the coming year, cabinet ministers would have their salaries cut by 5% and civil service salaries would be frozen for two years; Saskatchewan announced plans to establish autonomous boards to run the province's hospitals and clinics to cut duplication and other inefficiencies in the current system.

Statistics Canada released more data from the 1991 census, noting that the marriage rate dropped 9.9% from the previous year to the lowest rate since the 1930s.

On Mar. 9 the Inuit of Labrador presented a proposal to Premier Clyde Wells that would settle a 15-year-old land claim and protect their cultural survival. The claim covers a huge part of northern Labrador and part of the Labrador Sea and would allow the residents to trap, fish and hunt in their traditional area. The Inuit have also asked for a role in ocean management and land conservation and a share of royalties from the economic development. The second stage of the proposal would cover self-government, education, housing and health care issues.

Ontario Hydro chairman Maurice Strong announced that a further 4,500 jobs would be cut as the utility re-organizes to make itself more cost efficient, bringing the reduction in the workforce to 6,000 for 1993.

On Mar. 13 South Korea notified the Fisheries ministry that it would stop fishing off the coast of Newfoundland by April 30.

BC Liberal leader Gordon Wilson announced that he and colleague Judy Tyabji planned to marry once they obtained divorces from their present spouses. The announcement prompted party members to demand that he resign from the Liberal leadership post.

Canadians triumphed at the world figure skating championships as Kurt Browning and Elvis Stojko won the gold and silver medals respectively in the men's competition and Lloyd Eisler and Isabelle Brasseur won the gold medal in the pairs competition.

Catherine Callbeck was elected premier of PEI on Mar. 29 in a strong Liberal victory that saw the opposition reduced to one seat, held by provincial Tory leader Pat Mella.

In the latter half of the month more provinces tackled their financial problems as Newfoundland brought in a budget that shaved spending in nearly all areas while holding the line on tax increases and layoffs; BC hit high-income taxpayers with new income taxes as well as taxes on luxury cars and expensive homes. Gasoline tax hikes and increased levies on medicare premiums, cigarettes and liquor hit the average BC taxpayer as well. Quebec held spending increases to 0.9% and planned to review its public administration in an effort to cut waste, while Alberta announced plans to cut back on pensions for provincial members.

Ontario, PEI and Saskatchewan filed claims for special stabilization payments from the federal government to deal with some of the fiscal damage caused by a sharp decline in revenues due to the economic downturn.

April

INTERNATIONAL

Armenia: Armenians launched an attack on the disputed territory of Nagorno-Karabakh and captured 10% of Azeri land, including thousands of civilians; the UN strongly condemned the move. **Bosnia:** Serbians launched an artillery attack on the town of Srebrenica as NATO warplanes began to patrol a no-fly zone. By mid-month Srebrenica's Muslim defenders had negotiated a ceasefire that would allow the evacuation of the town. Croats and Muslims began fighting over the proposed boundary in the Vance-Owen peace plan; there were reports of both Muslim and Croatian atrocities. **Brazil:** Voters in a referendum rejected a proposal to change to a parliamentary style democracy and supported the existing republican-style structure, however nearly 45% of voters boycotted the referendum or spoiled their ballots. **Cambodia:** Khmer Rouge guerillas stepped up their attacks on Vietnamese settlers, prompting thousands to flee to Vietnam. By mid-month the guerillas had withdrawn from the interim governing body and refused any further co-operation in UN-sponsored peace process. Fears for the safety of UN representatives grew as attacks in the countryside increased. **China:** China and Taiwan announced talks to bring about closer transportation links, marking the beginning of moves to a possible reunification. **El Salvador:** The only military officer to be convicted in a human rights case, the Salvadoran colonel sentenced in the slaying of six Jesuit priests, their housekeeper and her daughter, was freed under a new amnesty law which also precluded any further trials on any war crimes committed during the 12-year civil war. **Ethiopia:** 98% of voters in a referendum on Eritrean sucession supported the move, bringing an end to one of the longest civil wars in Africa. **Germany:** For the first time since the Second World War, Germany sent troops outside its borders to take part in military missions: German airmen flew missions over Bosnia as part of UN surveillance of the region and over 1,600 troops were sent to the UN mission in Somalia. **India:** The World Bank announced that India had failed to supply information necessary for the next loan instalment for the controversial dam on the Narmada River and that it was withdrawing from the project. While environmentalists celebrated the victory, the Indian government vowed to continue the project on its own. Rebel forces in Kashmir clashed with Indian security police on Apr. 10, flattening the commercial centre of Kashmir's capital. 260 buildings were destroyed and 100 died as Hizbul-Mujahedin militants supporting Pakistan's claim over the territory continued a conflict that has raged intermittently since 1948. **Israel:** Escalating violence between Arabs and Jews prompted the Israeli government to close off the Gaza Strip and forbid West Bank Palestinians to enter Israel for an indefinite period. **Italy:** Operation Clean Hands continued as the tally stood at 1,356 arrest warrants issued and investigations into the affairs of 263 MPs, 852 local officials and 1,487 businessmen underway. **Jamaica:** Incumbent Pres. P.J. Patterson won 53 of 60 seats in a national election, hailing the victory as a strong endorsement of his economic program of deregulation. **Pakistan:** Prime Min. Mian Nawaz Sharif was dismissed from his post amid charges of corruption; the business sector staged a one-day strike in protest of Pres. Ghulam Ishaq Khan's move. **Poland:** Ceremonies in Warsaw marked the 50th anniversary of the uprising in the Jewish ghetto in that city; other cities around the world also commemorated the holocaust. **Russia:** Pres. Boris Yeltsin flew to Vancouver for an Apr. 3 summit with US Pres. Bill Clinton, amid speculation over

Yeltsin's political fate on his return. Clinton confirmed US$1.6 billion in technical aid already promised as the Russian Congress failed in another bid to unseat the absent president. A uranium tank at a chemical plant in western Siberia exploded; the subsequent radiation leaks were termed the most serious since Chernobyl, but in no way comparable in scale to the reactor accident. The Apr. 25 referendum gave Pres. Yeltsin support of 58% of the voters and a 53% approval rating for his economic reforms; opposition leaders dismissed the vote, claiming it was not a clear majority of registered voters. **Somalia:** At month end US forces handed command of the peacekeeping duties over to a UN force of personnel from over 20 countries. **South Africa:** The popular leader of the South African communist party, Chris Hani, was assassinated in Johannesburg by a white gunman who surrendered to police. ANC leader Nelson Mandela asked for calm in the wake of the killing, however five mourners were killed and hundreds were injured during the march to commemorate Hani; widespread looting and violence during the demonstrations again threatened to derail negotiations for power sharing. A police investigation into Hani's murder lead back to officials in South Africa's Conservative party and indicated a conspiracy. **Spain:** A post-Olympic recession prompted an election call as the government sought a new mandate to implement new economic measures. **Sri Lanka:** Pres. Ranasinghe Premadasa was killed by a suicide bomber on Apr. 24. **United States:** The jury in the second Rodney King trial returned a split verdict, convicting the supervising officer and the officer who delivered the most blows, but exonerating the other two charged. LA police were on standby, anxious to avoid a repetition of the three days of riots that greeted the first verdict. The stand-off in Waco, Texas ended in tragedy on Apr. 19 when authorities stormed the compound and it erupted in flames; 80 residents died in the fire.

CANADA

Newfoundland premier Clyde Wells announced a provincial election on May 3 and made public sector wages and benefits a target in both the election campaign and the campaign to cut government spending. Newly-elected PEI premier Catherine

Callbeck cut the number of government departments from 13 to eight and dropped one cabinet position.

The federal government announced cost-cutting of its own as External Affairs planned to close Canadian missions in Iraq, Austria and Zaïre; missions in Namibia, the US and Australia were also slated for the axe as the department moved to cut C$31 million from its budget for the coming year.

Time Warner Inc., a New York-based publishing company, circumvented regulations designed to stop American publishers from bringing their product across the border, by writing and editing the new "Canadian" edition of *Sports Illustrated* in New York and sending the pages by modem to a Canadian printer for final production.

On Apr. 6 Revenue Canada revealed that investigators had found 5,000 false tax returns filed from the Toronto area in a massive tax fraud that cheated the government of C$60 million. Investigators stressed that at least 30 tax preparers were involved in unrelated efforts that used minor infractions to try and beat the system. They blamed the unlicensed nature of the field and the new electronic filing system that does not require receipts for a large part of the problem.

BC premier Mike Harcourt announced on Apr. 13 that the government would allow limited logging in the last major old-growth rainforest on Vancouver Island. The proposal to allow any logging in the Clayoquot Sound area outraged environmentalists while the limitations placed on the operations left logging interests dissatisfied as well.

In early April, Canada won both the men's and women's championships at the world curling tournament in Geneva, Switzerland, re-establishing a dominance that has seen the country win 21 out of 35 men's titles and seven of the 15 contests held for women.

The defence department revealed that four Canadian peacekeepers were arrested after a Somali civilian was beaten to death while in their custody in Mar. The accused were released in Ottawa on Apr. 5, but were not allowed to leave the base. On Apr. 26 Defence Minister Kim Campbell announced that the conduct of Canadian soldiers in Somalia would be investigated by a board of inquiry, noting that four civilians had been killed by Canadians since February.

In a pre-election budget that satisfied no

one, Finance Min. Don Mazankowski cut just over C$1 billion from the spending plans for 1993-94, leaving a projected deficit of C$32.6 billion for the fiscal year. In response, the dollar fell the next day on money markets, but stabilized on Apr. 28 when Standard and Poor's Corp. announced that the government's triple-A rating would be maintained. The day before, the Canadian Bond Rating Service cut Ottawa's credit rating a notch. Conservative leadership contenders Kim Campbell and Jean Charest defended the minister's budget, saying that it was inappropriate to introduce a radical plan when a change in leadership was imminent.

New Brunswick and Quebec escalated their long-simmering dispute over provincial protectionism as NB announced that Quebec companies could no longer tender on NB government projects unless specifically asked to do so and that goods, labourers and services originating in Quebec would only be chosen as a last resort for any government work.

Ontario continued efforts to reduce costs by announcing plans to cut up to 11,000 jobs from the public sector and save C$4 billion. In Quebec, the controversial sign law was amended to allow English on commercial signs, as long as the French version of the information was more prominent.

A House of Commons committee on the environment sharply criticized the government's cutbacks in foreign aid, claiming that the changes would reduce Canada's ability to live up to commitments made at the Earth Summit in June of 1992.

On Apr. 29, federal fisheries officials announced that new regulations regarding native fishing rights in federal waters had been drafted. The proposals included provision for communal fishing licences and quotas but did not increase permits to sell fish commercially.

May

INTERNATIONAL

Bosnia: A referendum on the Vance-Owen peace plan was rejected by Bosnian Serb voters. **Cambodia:** Khmer Rouge guerillas stepped up their campaign to disrupt the election process with more attacks in the countryside; UNTAC, the UN body set up to supervise the process, was forced to withdraw personnel from many areas because of the dangers. The elections, held May 23, attracted 90% of registered voters despite the guerilla tactics. The tally from the vote gave the victory to the royalist FUNCINPEC party headed by Prince Norodim Ranariddh; his father, Prince Norodim Sihanouk announced that he would form a government with the defeated Cambodian People's Party sharing power with the victors, however Ranariddh vetoed the idea. Members of the People's Party called for a new vote in five provinces, claiming there were irregularities in the election. **Denmark:** A referendum was held on a revised Maastricht Treaty that exempted Denmark both from using a common EC currency and from supporting a common defence policy; voters supported the new proposal, however victory was marred by rioting by anarchists who opposed the EC. **Germany:** Parliament voted to tighten the liberal immigration laws that allowed up to 1,000 foreigners a day into the country. On the same day, a building housing Turkish workers in Solingen was firebombed and the resulting blaze killed five and injured 14. **Iran:** Iranian military jets bombed two guerilla bases of the Iranian Peoples' Mujahedin in Iraq. **Italy:** The Galleria degli Uffizi, the principal museum in Florence, was the target of a bomb attack that damaged paintings (although the collection's major treasures were untouched) and killed five people; Italian police suspected that the Mafia, battered by the ongoing criminal investigations into political corruption, had resorted to cultural terrorism. **Jordan:** King Hussein announced an end to his support of Iraq's Saddam Hussein, citing the persecution of Iraq's Shi'ite Muslim minority and the Hussein government's disastrous economic policies as prime factors in his decision. **Mexico:** Cardinal Juan Jésus Posadas Ocampo and six others were killed in an attack at the Guadalajara airport; police suspect the killings were a result of mistaken identity in an ongoing feud between drug barons. **Paraguay:** Voters elected Juan Carlos Wasmosy, the first civilian president elected since 1954; observers noted some irregularities in the election, but felt that none were serious enough to have influenced the outcome. **Thailand:** A fire in a toy factory killed at least 200 workers in Bangkok; many of the staff fleeing the fire were trapped

behind doors that were kept locked as a security measure. **United Kingdom:** Britain's House of Commons voted in favour of the Maastricht Treaty, clearing the way for Britain to join the other EC signatories. **United States:** Pres. Clinton's package of reduced spending and tax increases narrowly passed in Congress as the new administration had difficulty getting its programs approved. Clinton attempted to prod the European Community into action in Bosnia, proposing unilateral action in the form of air strikes if other forces would not join. By month end, Clinton had been dissuaded by other governments concerned about the safety of their peacekeepers already in Bosnia.

CANADA

Newfoundland premier Clyde Wells won the provincial election on May 3, as voters supported his proposals to cut benefits and wages in the civil service. Later in the month he sharply criticized federal plans for amendments to fisheries management, demanding that Newfoundland have more control over the resource that is the mainstay of its economy.

Quebec premier Robert Bourassa joined his Liberal caucus for a meeting in early May, confirming that his cancer was in remission and putting off any decision on his political future. Saskatchewan announced plans to cut eight seats from the provincial legislature in a redrawing of riding boundaries to ensure no more than a 5% population variance between constituencies.

Ontario announced legislation to introduce a graduated licensing process for new drivers in an effort to cut the high accident rate among that population. The plan, which would require a new driver to be accompanied by a fully-licensed driver with at least four years' experience for the first year and ban new drivers from major highways and also from driving between midnight and 5 a.m., was hailed as a model for other provinces.

Analysts at Statistics Canada revealed that families had less money after taxes in 1991 than they had in either 1990 or 1980, noting that real after-tax income fell by 2.6%

On May 15 the UN announced its annual ranking of countries in terms of quality of life and Canada lost first place to Japan, although we remained ahead of Norway, Switzerland

and Sweden. Canada was 11th in terms in terms of average income and sexual equality but high levels of education and life expectancy pushed us up to second place overall. Days earlier, Statistics Canada released more studies based on the 1991 census data and noted that in 1991, nearly half of the adult population (15 and older) had attended or graduated from a post-secondary institution. Women registered the greatest increase in educational attainment since 1981 with 86% more holding university degrees, while the number of men with degrees rose 47%.

On May 13, Public Works Minister Elmer MacKay dismissed concerns over the environmental impact of a bridge between PEI and New Brunswick, stating that reports received indicated that all effects would be either insignificant or could be dealt with by existing technology.

Voters in NS sent the Conservative government of Premier Donald Cameron packing and handed John Savage's Liberals 40 of the 52 seats in the legislature. In Ontario, Finance Minister Floyd Laughren brought in his budget on May 19 and raised taxes for every income group, although he hit the high income earners the hardest, in an effort to deal with 1993's ballooning deficit. In Quebec, Finance Minister Gerard-D. Levesque did not introduce any new taxes, but closed enough loopholes to rival the damage done to taxpayers in Ontario.

In Parliament, NAFTA legislation was passed on May 27 after the Conservatives used their majority to force a vote and send the legislation to the Tory-dominated Senate.

The Umbrella Final Agreement, a settlement with the Yukon's 14 First Nations, was signed in Whitehorse on May 29. 41,400 sq. km and C$280 million will be divided among the 8,000 beneficiaries and a joint-management board shared by the aboriginals and the territorial government was established to oversee wildlife and land use. The agreement also paved the way for native self-government and the handing over of jurisdiction over such federal and territorial matters as education, justice and environmental protection.

The Defence department has announced charges against four Canadian soldiers in the beating death of a Somali man who died in their custody on Mar. 16. Two members of the airborne regiment were charged with second-degree murder and torture while two others were charged with torture and negligence in performance of duties.

On May 24, Constitutional Affairs Minister Joe Clark was appointed as special representative for Cyprus, responsible to the UN Secretary-General. Clark was given the task of developing a federal type of government for the island in an effort to solve the long-standing conflict between the Greek and Turkish populations.

US President Bill Clinton appointed former Michigan governor James Blanchard as the new US ambassador to Canada, replacing Peter Teeley, who left the post in February. The new ambassador will take up his post in August.

On May 31, the Canadian International Trade Tribunal found that Canada's steel producers were not being harmed by steel imports from the US or any other countries named in the complaints filed. Temporary duties on the commodity were lifted as a result of the decision although Canadian steel producers vowed to appeal the decision.

The UN committee on Economic, Social and Cultural Rights criticized Canada for the level of poverty and homelessness that persists in the country despite the general high standard of living, noting that little progress has been made on the problem in the past decade.

In the latest move in the federal and Quebec government's dispute with Tioxide Canada Inc., the company was fined C$4 million for polluting the St. Lawrence River.

June

INTERNATIONAL

Bosnia: Bosnian Serbs attacked Goradze, one of the six safe areas established for Bosnian Muslims. A new peace plan that suggested dividing Bosnia into three ethnic regions was widely criticized for appearing to reward Serbian agresssion and was rejected by Bosnian Muslim leaders. **Cambodia:** The leader of the Cambodian People's Party, Prince Norodim Chakrapong, a son of Sihanouk and loser in the May elections agreed to share power with his brother Prince Norodim Ranariddh; Chakrapong had threatened to secede with seven provinces under his control, sparking fears of a possible civil war. **France:** An Algerian national took three- and four-year-old children hostage in a nursery school and threatened to blow up himself and the children if his demands were not met. The standoff ended some 42 hours later when the lone gunman fell asleep and police stormed the room, rescuing the children and killing the intruder. **Guatemala:** Rocked by coup and countercoup in a bewildering series of events, Guatemala's president declared himself dictator, and then was deserted by the army after the withdrawal of foreign aid and the threat of international economic sanctions if the government was not restored. After days of confusion, during which a number of people claimed power and the former president fled the country, Ramiro de León Carpio, the country's former human rights ombudsman was inaugurated as president by Congress. **Haiti:** Prime Min. Marc Bazin resigned after an attempt to shuffle his cabinet failed. Members of the military junta finally agreed to meet with deposed Pres. Jean Bertrand Aristide after the international community threatened economic sanctions if Aristide was not returned to power. **Japan:** Crown Prince Naruhito wed commoner Masako Owada on June 9th. The town of Ito reported a series of 140 earth tremors strong enough to be felt, while a total of 9,000 were recorded by more delicate sensing devices. Prime Min. Kiichi Miyazawa lost a no confidence motion amid charges that he had failed to deliver on promises to clean up corruption; the loss forced him to dissolve the Diet and schedule elections. **Nigeria:** Military dictator Ibrahim Babangida annulled the results of an election held on June 12. **Russia:** An agreement was reached with the Ukraine to split the Black Sea fleet, ending months of tense dispute over the fleet's fate. **Somalia:** There were a series of clashes between supporters of Gen. Aidid and UN troops in Mogadishu; 23 peacekeepers were killed in a raid on June 5 and US and UN forces struck back in attacks of their own. UN forces stormed Aidid's headquarters, forcing him to flee and operate his organization on the run. Food distribution resumed after two weeks of fighting. **Turkey:** Tansu Ciller won the leadership of Turkey's ruling party on June 13, to take office as the country's prime minister in July. Ciller, an economist educated in the US, will be the country's first female prime minister. **United States:** President Clinton launched a cruise missile attack on Baghdad on June 26 in an effort to destroy the headquarters of Saddam Hussein's intelligence network; the attack was in retaliation for Hussein's planned attempt to kill former US president George Bush in April. FBI agents arrested eight men suspected to be plotting a bombing campaign in New York City that included such varied sites as the UN headquarters, the Holland and Lincoln tunnels and the headquarters of the FBI. The conspirators were linked to Egyptian cleric Sheik Omar Abdel Rahman and two of the accused were thought to be involved in the bombing of the World Trade Centre.

CANADA

More census statistics were released on June 1, showing that only 48% of the country's 7.4 million families were characterised by a married mom and dad living together with their children. New trends of common-law unions, single parent families, an aging population and an increase in childless couples all contributed to the change. A second study on religious affiliation was also released, showing 13% of Canadians now reported no religious affiliation, a 90% increase in that category since 1971.

The Montreal Canadiens won their 24th Stanley Cup on June 9 with a fifth game victory over the Los Angeles Kings. Celebrations in the streets of Montreal quickly turned into a riot as fans smashed windows, overturned cars and looted stores. Damage was estimated at C$10 million.

On June 13 Defence Minister Kim Campbell won the Conservative party leadership on the second ballot, defeating a strong but late challenge by Environment Minister Jean Charest. She was sworn in as Canada's prime minister on June 25, along with a 24-member cabinet that cut 10 positions and dropped 17 veteran members who had already announced plans to retire.

On June 15 Alberta's Conservatives, under new leader Ralph Klein, won 51 seats in the legislature to the Liberals' 32, shutting out the NDP completely. In Ontario, the NDP government served notice that those public sector employees refusing to negotiate contract concessions by Aug. 1 would automatically have their wages and benefits frozen for three years and be given up to 12 days off a year without pay.

Meanwhile Quebec and New Brunswick agreed to work on a bilateral agreement to eliminate trade barriers and end their long-standing trade war over goods and services.

On June 15 Canada officially ended its role in Cyprus after 29 years of peacekeeping on the island, the remaining soldiers were to head home by the end of the month.

The latest figures on Newfoundland's devastated cod fishery indicated that, one year after a two-year moratorium was imposed on the fishery, stock had continued to decline. Officials predicted that there would be no significant recovery of fish stocks until the late 1990s.

The US International Trade Tribunal investigating dumping charges against Canadian, Japanese and Brazilian steelmakers came down on the side of American steelmakers, ruling that they had been injured by the dumping of steel wire rods in the US. The US Commerce Department was given the go-ahead to investigate the charges further and the option of imposing anti-dumping tariffs was not ruled out.

On June 23 the Senate approved a controversial measure that gave Senators a C$6,000 increase in their expense allowance. The provision was approved in a 26-24 vote (the Senate has 104 members) and prompted such a degree of public and parliamentary protest that Senate leaders announced the chamber would reconvene on July 12 to rescind the decision. Retiring Prime Min. Mulroney brought the Senate up to full complement, appointing 15 new senators since February to fill all vacancies and establish a solid Conservative majority in the upper house.

The BC Court of Appeal ruled that Gitksan and Wet'suwet'en Indians have a legitimate claim to a massive piece of land in northwestern BC. Although the rights did not include ownership, native leaders hailed the ruling as a breakthrough that would strengthen their position in upcoming talks with both Ottawa and the BC government.

US-Canada trade disputes widened to include wheat as the US Department of Agriculture announced plans to increase its Export Enhancement Program to subsidize the export of 1.4 million of tonnes of wheat to Mexico in order to combat Canada's growing market share in that country. Previously the program was aimed at European wheat; members of the Canadian Wheat Board estimated that prices could fall by as much as C$21/tonne, partly because of the US subsidy program.

July

INTERNATIONAL

Bosnia: US President Clinton again suggested that air strikes be used to protect UN forces and civilians in Sarajevo, however European allies did not support the move. **Brazil:** Three military policemen were arrested in Rio de Janeiro and charged in a gun attack on 50 sleeping street children that left eight dead. **Georgia:** Georgia's leader Eduard Shevardnadze declared martial law in the Black Sea region of Abkhazi in an attempt to end the fighting in the region. **Haiti:** A UN-brokered plan to restore deposed President Jean-Bertrand Aristide was accepted by all parties, paving the way for the president's return. **Israel:** Israeli warplanes and artillery fired into southern Lebanon for a week to retaliate for rocket attacks by Hizballah guerillas. More than half a million villagers fled to safety during the barrage which stopped only after the guerillas agreed to stop the attacks. **Italy:** As Italy's anti-corruption investigation continued to sweep up politicians and prominent business people, a new wave of cultural bombings killed five people near the museum of contemporary art in Milan and two more bombs targeted historic churches in Rome. **Japan:** An earthquake measuring 7.8 on the Richter scale hit a small island SW of Hokkaida; most of the 166 casualties were killed by the tidal waves that followed. A coalition of seven political parties agreed to form a government that would shut out the Liberal Democratic Party, which had governed since 1955. Morihito Hosakawa was slated to become the new prime minister. **Nepal:** Flash floods and landslides swept through mountain villages, killing at least 1,800 people. **Nigeria:** Three days of rioting that left nearly 75 people dead came to an end when the two political parties agreed to form an interim civilian coalition government. Elections held in June were nullified by the country's military leader and Nigerians rallied to demand that the democratically-elected government be allowed to take office. **Norway:** In defiance of a ban by the International Whaling Commission, the Norwegian government sanctioned the resumption of commercial hunting of minke whales. **Somalia**: Somali warlord General Mohammed Farrah Aidid's forces ambushed a UN search party on July 2, killing 3 soldiers and wounding 21. Aidid is considered responsible for 26 peacekeeping deaths since June. **South Africa**: Negotiators for South Africa's first non-racial elections chose April 27, 1994 as the date for the vote. The announcement prompted both black and white extremists to denounce the process and vow to intensify the struggle to eliminate the opposition. **United States**: The US International Trade Commission finally cleared foreign steel firms of most of the charges of unfair trade practices and ordered the stiff tariffs aimed at foreign steel (including Canadian products) be rescinded. US President Clinton dropped his country's opposition to a Vietnamese request for loans from the International Monetary Fund, a move that analysts interpreted as a gesture to improve relations. New York police announced the arrest of eight Muslims accused of planning a series of bombings in New York City, including one in a tunnel linking Manhattan to New Jersey. Sheik Omar Abdel Rahman was later detained as the suspects in the most recent arrests and one of the suspects in the World Trade Centre bombing were linked with the religious leader. Record-breaking floods swamped areas in nine states along the Mississippi River as an unseasonally rainy summer continued to pour water over the region.

CANADA

On July 1, Greenpeace activists staged protests against the BC government's decision to allow logging along the Clayoquot Sound in several Canadian cities and outside 11 Canadian embassies abroad. Meanwhile, Prime Min. Kim Campbell marked Canada Day by crossing the country to visit celebrations, beginning with a sunrise ceremony in St. John's and finishing the day at an evening concert in her Vancouver riding.

On July 6, Karla Homolka, estranged wife of accused murderer Paul Teale, was found guilty of two charges of manslaughter in connection with the deaths of two southern Ontario teenage girls. The Ontario courtroom was closed to the public and the judge imposed a publication ban on detail, pending Teale's trial.

Quebec Prem. Robert Bourassa was given a clean bill of health by his doctors, confirming that his melanoma, the deadliest form of skin cancer, was in remission.

The Senate reconvened on July 12 and voted 80 to 1 in favour of rescinding the unpopular C$6,000 increase in their tax-free expense allowance.

The National Capital Commission confirmed that it had agreed to pay the departing Mulroneys C$150,000 for used furniture, drapes and carpets, but after a public outcry Mila Mulroney returned the cheque and cancelled the deal.

Ontario's NDP government used closure to pass its controversial Social Contract Act. The legislation was designed to cut C$2 billion from Ontario's payroll for the next three years by freezing wages and giving many provincial and municipal employees up to 12 days of unpaid leave. Meanwhile, Alberta's newly-elected Conservative government announced spending cuts of its own including a reduction in hospital funding that could eliminate up to 2,000 jobs.

Nineteen senior citizens from a small Quebec town were killed when the van they were riding in collided with a pickup truck towing tanks filled with diesel fuel. The road accident was the worst in Canada since 1980.

August

INTERNATIONAL

Belgium: After heavy pressure from currency speculators, on Aug. 2 EC officials scrapped the exchange rate mechanism designed to bring the currencies of EC member countries into a fiscal equilibrium and a single currency by 1999. **Bosnia**: NATO forces threatened air strikes against Serbian positions if they did not withdraw from two mountains overlooking Sarajevo. Nations with troops on the ground in Bosnia, including Canada, expressed cautious support for the plan, fearing their troops would become hostages (or targets) in the battle. Bosnia's Muslim negotiator refused to attend peace talks aimed at partitioning his country until the siege of Sarajevo was lifted. By Aug. 14, Serbian troops appeared to have withdrawn and peacekeepers had moved in to patrol the area. On Aug. 26 a UN convoy with food and medical supplies reached the Muslim city of Mostar after making its way through Croats attempting to block entry to the city; once the materials were unloaded residents of the city tried to prevent the convoy from leaving, fearing a massacre once the UN workers left the region. **China:** Officials acknowledged that a series of chemical and gas explosions had ignited a blaze that burned for 15 hours in the southern town of Shenzhen which adjoins Hong Kong. The accident, which claimed up to 70 lives and injured hundreds more, was blamed on leaking nitric acid which exploded and ignited a nearby natural-gas reservoir. A dam in a remote western province collapsed and killed 1,257 people, with more than 300 others injured. **Germany:** For the first time in its modern history the safety net of social benefits was to be reduced as the government announced plans to redirect money to rebuilding the economy in former East Germany. **Israel:** Three negotiators in the Middle East peace talks, representing Palestinians in the Israeli-occupied territories, threatened to resign from the PLO after leader Yasser Arafat indicated that some concessions might be in order in the quest for peace. The negotiators eventually returned to the talks and the Israeli government made it clear that Cabinet members could deal directly with PLO leaders in an effort to gain a settlement. Meanwhile, the 396 remaining Palestinians deportees trapped just inside the border of southern Lebanon appeared likely to accept a proposal for a two-stage return home. On Aug. 19 Israel sent fighter-bombers to attack targets in southern Lebanon in an attempt to destroy the fundamentalist Shi'ite group that was held responsible for recent attacks on Israeli soldiers. **Italy:** On Aug. 4, the Italian parliament approved sweeping electoral reforms that scrapped proportional representation in time for an early 1994 general election. The changes in the system mean that 75% of the deputies in the 945-seat lower chamber would now be directly elected. **Japan:** A series of political scandals forced the ruling Liberal Democrats to relinquish office and Morihiro Hosokawa became prime minister on Aug. 6, leading a reform coalition made up of seven parties, including socialists, conservatives, reformers and centrists. After much prodding the Japanese government acknowledged that during the Second World War the Imperial Army forced thousands of Asian women to serve as "comfort women"

for Japanese soldiers. There was no mention of compensation for those who had been forced into prostitution, but the admission that force was used was a breakthrough for the Korean victims, who were offered an apology. **Nigeria:** Long-time dictator General Ibrahim Babangida announced that he would not honour his promise to restore civilian government by Aug. 27, but instead pledged to install an interim government of soldiers and civilians. The Nigerian people continued to demand that the results of the June election be honoured and demonstrated their displeasure at the latest move with a three-day general strike that shut down the capital of Lagos. **Russia:** The administrator for southwest Russia was assassinated during an Aug. 2nd ambush, raising fears that the area will dissolve into yet another violent ethnic feud. **Somalia:** US troops intent on capturing Somali General Aidid attacked UN Development Program buildings in a mistaken attempt to capture him. **Thailand:** 136 people were killed and hundreds injured when a hotel under renovation collapsed. The hotel, which was originally three storeys but had recently added three more floors, was completely destroyed. **United Kingdom:** Buckingham Palace opened 18 rooms for tourist viewing for eight weeks in a bid to raise money to pay for the repairs at Windsor Castle. Early crowds were not as heavy as expected, but the gift shop was reported to be doing strong business. **United States:** Pres. Bill Clinton's budget package was passed by one vote in the Senate with the Vice-President casting the tie-breaking vote. Hollywood was fascinated by a call-girl scandal expected to touch the top ranks of the entertainment industry. A Titan IV rocket carrying a US$1 billion intelligence and satellite system exploded two minutes after lift-off and raised further doubts about the reliability of the newly-designed Titan IV booster rocket. Pope John Paul II visited Denver, Colorado for a four-day mid-August Catholic youth festival that drew participants from 70 countries.

CANADA

Prime Min. Campbell announced she would not endorse the nominations of three Quebec candidates currently facing charges of fraud, influence peddling and breach of trust.

On Aug. 3 an earthquake measuring 5.7 on

the Richter scale and centred under the Pacific Ocean 310 km south of Prince Rupert was felt in the Queen Charlotte Islands and as far as Bella Bella on the mainland. No damage or injury was reported and the quake was not strong enough to generate a tidal wave.

Trade Minister Tom Hockin and his US counterpart announced an end to the "beer wars" on Aug. 5. The draft agreement removed US duties on Ontario beer and took Canadian tariffs off some US beer but the C$.10/can environmental levy was to remain.

An Ontario government report estimated that health card fraud was costing the province as much as C$284 million a year with thousands of residents having two health cards, and cards in the hands of deportees, non-residents and in some cases, issued in the name of deceased residents.

BC MLA Judy Tyabji was dropped by the executive in her riding of Okanagan East on Aug. 6 amid criticism of her work as a representative and her romance with party leader Gordon Wilson.

On Aug. 11, Valery Fabrikant was pronounced guilty of first-degree murder in the shooting deaths of four Concordia University professors and given an automatic life sentence.

On Aug. 12, Federal Court judges rejected demands for a full environmental assessment of the effects of the proposed bridge across the Northumberland Strait, clearing the way for contract talks for the C$840 million project. On Aug. 18, Prime Min. Campbell and PEI Premier Catherine Callbeck pledged to go ahead with the bridge despite last-ditch bids to block the project.

On Aug. 20, 18 protesters were arrested at the Clayoquot Sound anti-logging blockade as activists vowed to continue their protests despite the 470 charges already laid in connection with violation of the BC Supreme Court injunction banning interference with logging in the area.

As part of its program of cutbacks, the Ontario government announced that government offices would be shut down for three successive Fridays, starting Aug. 27, and would likely be shut down for three more during the December holiday period.

On Aug. 27 the defence department revealed that the family of a slain Somali man had received the settlement it requested in March when compensation of C$15,000

was paid in early June. The department's investigation into the death of four Somalis was not complete at the time of the settlement.

On Aug. 31, Fisheries minister Ross Reid announced that the east coast fishery would be shut down in five more areas until the end of the 1993 fishing season and that quotas would be slashed in three others.

September

INTERNATIONAL

Argentina: A federal judge filed preliminary charges of child abuse against 17 members of a religious cult that claimed status as fundamentalist Christians living on a commune. **Azerbaijan:** Parliament voted to rejoin the Commonwealth of Independent States (CIS) in the hope of enlisting Russian aid in the eight-year-old war with Armenia over the disputed Nagorno-Karabakh region. **Bosnia:** Peace talks that appeared to be headed for success collapsed on Sept. 1 as the three factions failed to agree on how the country would be divided. On Sept. 16 yet another ceasefire failed to hold as renewed fighting broke out. **Croatia:** Charges of a Muslim massacre of 27 Croat civilians surfaced as a shaky ceasefire continued to hold. **France:** Carmaker Renault announced plans to merge with Sweden's Volvo AB by Jan. 1, 1994 in an effort to save both companies from the effects of the depression in the European car market; Renault's largest trade union announced it would do everything possible to scuttle the deal. The French government continued to fight a deal on farm trade between EC members and the US, threatening to veto the deal unless terms were improved; French farmers joined the fray by setting up blockades. **Georgia:** Leader Eduard Scheverdnadze threatened to resign if the government would not allow him to declare a state of emergency necessary to deal with the fighting in the Abkhazi region. By month end a civil war raged around the embattled town of Sukhumi and Scheverdnadze went to the city to bolster the defence and call for volunteers to help resist the Abkhazi rebel attack. Sukhumi fell to the rebels on Sept. 27 and Schevernadze returned to Tiblisi as thousands of refugees attempted to flee to safety. **Greece:** The government of Prime Min. Constantine Mitsotakis lost its one-seat majority as another deputy deserted the governing party and forced an election call for Oct. 10. **Israel:** Rumours of a deal on mutual recognition between Israel and the PLO swirled as thousands of people demonstrated outside the offices of Israeli Prime Min. Yitzhak Rabin to protest possible Palestinian autonomy. Nearly 200 of the Palestinians exiled in Dec. headed for home on Sept. 9. Also on Sept. 9, the PLO issued a statement recognizing the right of Israel to exist and renouncing violence as a means of dealing with the state; Israel issued a similar statement recognizing the PLO a day later. On Sept. 13, PLO leader Yasser Arafat and Israeli Prime Min. Yitzak Rabin met in Washington to sign a peace agreement that had been negotiated in secret over several months in Norway. Many Palestinians took to the streets in Jericho to celebrate the pact while protests were mounted in the Gaza Strip and Beirut. On Sept. 14, Jordan signed a pact with Israel that set up an agenda for negotiations for a peace treaty. On Sept. 20 a senior PLO leader in Gaza was assassinated by factions opposed to the peace plan. **India:** On Sept. 29 an earthquake measuring 6.4 on the Ricther scale hit a densely populated area SW of Bombay, causing widespread damage and killing hundreds of people. **Iraq:** Pres. Saddam Hussein reportedly foiled a coup attempt; dozens of people from a clan in his home region were arrested or executed. **Japan:** Typhoon Yancy slammed into southern Japan, killing at least 11 people and burying 20 in a mudslide. **Philippines:** The body of former president Ferdinand Marcos was brought from Hawaii to his home village for burial; an estimated 30,000 people were on hand to witness the Sept. 9 ceremony. On Sept. 25, former first lady Imelda Marcos was sentenced to 18 years in jail for corruption. **Poland:** A national election saw the return of former communist bosses to power as the electorate rejected the hard times that economic reform created. **Russia:** Pres. Boris Yeltsin suspended Vice-Pres. Alexander Rutskoi after charges of corruption surfaced; the Russian parliament refused to accept the suspension, asking the constitutional court to overturn the decree. In an attempt to break the deadlock Yeltsin dissolved parliament and called for elections in mid-December. Parliamentary members responded by stripping Yeltsin of his powers and appointing

Rutskoi as acting president. By Sept. 24 parliamentarians were barricaded in their building as forces loyal to Yeltsin surrounded the parliament; by Sept. 30 only 150 hardline deputies remained holed up in the parliamentary buildings. **Somalia:** Battles between Somalis and UN peacekeeping forces escalated as youths fired grenades at UN units and militia forces shot and killed seven Nigerian members of the UN forces. Gunbattles later in the month claimed the lives of more than 100 Somalis and one Pakistani soldier. Somali forces retaliated by shooting down a US military helicopter, killing the crew. **South Africa:** Negotiators announced an agreement to establish a multi-party transitional council to oversee the transition to democracy, paving the way for blacks to be appointed to the ruling body. ANC leader Nelson Mandela called for an end to economic sanctions against his country during an address to the UN. **Ukraine:** On Sept. 3 the Ukranian president renegotiated an earlier deal on the Black Sea fleet, agreeing to turn over the entire fleet in exchange for Russia writing off a major portion of Ukraine's debt. Thousands of protestors gathered in Kiev to demand that the government resign over their poor economic performance, and Sept. 21 parliament accepted the resignations of Prime Min. Leonid Kuchma and his entire cabinet; Kuchma had offered to resign twice before saying that the conservative forces in the government were preventing him from bringing about any economic reform. Pres. Leonid Kravchuk took over as government leader late in the month, hoping to break the deadlock over economic reforms. **United States:** US defence chief, Gen. Colin Powell, announced major changes to slash military spending and reduce the size of the American military; the Pentagon stated that the changes would prepare the US for the likelihood of regional conflicts throughout the world rather than the previously anticipated massive war with a single enemy. Pres. Clinton appointed a new chief for the FBI, with Louis Freeh replacing the ousted William Sessions. A German tourist became the 8th foreigner to be killed in Miami in the past 10 months as state official scrambled to increase protection for visitors and minimize the damage to their tourist industry. Later in the month two British tourists were shot, one fatally. On Sept. 20 and series of earthquakes in Oregon killed two and left many buildings badly damaged; the governor declared a state of emergency. On Sept. 22 Pres. Clinton unveiled his program for health-care reform, making good on his promise to come up with proposals to provide health care for all Americans.

CANADA

On Sept. 2nd, Prime Min. Campbell announced that the much-maligned purchase of 50 helicopters for the armed forces would be trimmed to 43, in the hope of saving C$1 billion.

Federal Fisheries minister Ross Reid pressured other members of (Northwest Atlantic Fishing Organization) NAFO to end overfishing off the east coast, and although members agreed to quotas, a suspension of fishing activity was rejected.

On Sept. 8, Prime Min. Kim Campbell announced a federal election for Oct. 25; politicians of all stripes began campaigning in the much-anticipated election immediately, citing the economy as the most important issue.

The Canadian Grain Commission released figures showing that Russia's cash shortage had cut that country's Canadian grain purchases from an annual average of 4.5 million tonnes over the past few years to 1.8 million, moving the former number one customer to third place behind China (3.5) and South Korea (2).

On Sept. 9 John Savage's new Liberal government in Nova Scotia trimmed the ranks of its civil service by nine when that number of deputy ministers were asked for resignations or were fired. On the same day, Canada's military also cut costs by closing a luxury fishing camp in Labrador in a move that was estimated to save C$1 million annually. Two more soldiers were charged in connection with the beating death of a Somali prisoner, bringing the number charged in the torture and beating death to six.

On Sept. 11 a meeting of the Royal College of Physicians and Surgeons of Canada was told that tuberculosis was re-emerging in Canada's three largest cities, with 2,000 new cases diagnosed in 1991, and that the new strain appeared to be resistant to the drugs commonly used to treat the disease.

On Sept. 14 Quebec Premier Robert Bourassa announced he was stepping down as leader of the Quebec Liberals after leading them from 1970 to 1976 and again from 1983 to 1993.

On Sept. 15 the remaining nine provinces and both territories announced compensation packages for residents who contracted AIDS from contaminated blood supplies during transfusions; Nova Scotia lead the way in compensation with a package in April. On the same day, Canada and Australia announced plans to run joint embassies in jurisdictions where feasible; Canadian embassies in the Caribbean, where Australia has minimal presence, were the first slated to be shared.

Five by-elections in Manitoba, held Sept. 21, reduced Premier Gary Filmon's majority to one seat as voters rejected Liberal candidates in all ridings.

Two Canadian authors were nominated for Britain's prestigious Booker Prize—Carol Shields's *The Stone Diaries* and Michael Ignatieff's *Scar Tissue* joined a field of six contenders.

On Sept. 26 the first hearings in Ontario's Royal Commission on Learning were held in Thunder Bay as that province prepares to evaluate the quality of education in the face of widespread complaints. On Sept. 28 Bell Canada announced a major restructuring that is expected to cut 10% of its 46,000-member workforce.

On Sept. 30, the Supreme Court of Canada handed down its decision in the Sue Rodriguez case. The members of the court voted 5-4 that the federal law against assisted suicides did not violate her constitutional rights, and upheld the criminalization of such an act. Ms. Rodriguez, who suffers from ALS, an incurable motor neuron disease, is expected to live only weeks after the decision, but had hoped that the courts would allow her to choose to end her life on her own terms.

In another decision on Sept. 30, the Supreme Court ruled that the Nova Scotia ban on free-standing abortion clinics was unconstitutional, largely because the ban dealt with an area of criminal law which falls under federal authority, and the province had enacted a ruling outside its jurisdiction.

Index

A

Abbott, Sir John 106-7, 129
Abortions 61
Academy Awards 565-69
Acadians 93
Accidents,
  cause of death 59, 60
  first aid 703-6
  motor vehicles 60
  poison-proofing 700
  (see also Disasters)
Acquired Immune Deficiency Syndrome
  (see AIDS)
Addresses (see Directories)
Adventist church 73
Afghanistan 297, 307-8
  (see also History, world)
Africa,
  area 236
  highest, lowest points 236
  map 303
  mountains 238
  population 236, 242
Agriculture 204-7
  by province 29-34
  by region 10-11
  cash receipts by province 204-5
  food aid 249
  fruit production 210
  labour force 198, 202
  livestock 246-47
  top Can. corporations 193
  value of production 204
  vegetable production 207
  wheat production 206
  world dairy producers 248
  world grain producers 246
AIDS 61-62, 697
  recognized 293
Air Force (see Canadian Armed Forces)
Aircraft (see Aviation)
Airports,
  busiest world 235
  weather at 27
Albania 308-9
Alberta 33
  agriculture 204, 205, 207
  cabinet 148-49
  education 72, 73, 79-80
  election results 152-54, 155
  energy production 212, 213, 214
  formed (1905) 95
  geography 28, 33

joins Confederation 33
labour force 199, 200, 202
languages 33, 70
lieutenant-governor 141
MPs 137-38
party leaders 160
population 33, 42
  native 68-69
  towns and cities 50
  urban/rural 46
premier 144
religions 33
resource industries 208-10
revenues/expenditures 184
surplus/deficit 185
  (see also Provinces and territories)
Alexander the Great 280
Algeria 309-10
  (see also History, world)
Altitudes,
  highest, lowest (Canada) 7
  highest, lowest (world) 235, 236
  mountains 238-39
Ambassadors, Canadian, to UN 251
American League (baseball) 643-44,
                649-51, 652, 655-57
American Revolution 270
American Samoa 310-11, 508
America's Cup (yachting) 689
Andaman Sea 237
Andorra 312-13
Anglican Church 71
Angola 312-13
  (see also History, world)
Anguilla 313, 506
Animals,
  collective names 561
  endangered species 558
  names of young 560
  vital statistics 560
Anniversary gifts and greetings 707, 709
Antarctica,
  area 236
  highest, lowest points 236
  mountains 238
Anthem of Canada 88
Antigua and Barbuda 313-14
Appalachian Region (Canada) 3
Appliances, households owning 85, 86
Aquariums 562
Arab League 255
Aral Sea 237
Archery 622
Archimedes 260

Arctic Ocean 236
Arenas 631
Argentina 314-15
  (see also History, world)
Aristotle 260
Armed forces (see Canadian Armed Forces)
Armenia 315-16
  (see also History, world)
Arms, first nuclear bombs 286
Army (see Canadian Armed Forces)
Arrow Airlines crash (1985) 105
Artists 590
Arts and Entertainment 563-600
  govt culture spending 589-90
  (see also History, world)
Aruba 316-17, 442
ASEAN 255
Ashmore and Cartier Islands 317
Asia,
  area 236
  highest, lowest points 236
  map 301
  mountains 238
  population 236, 242-43
Association of Southeast Asian Nations
  (ASEAN) 255
Astrological signs 696
Astronauts 533
Astronomy 523-35
  constellations 534
  eclipses 530
  events of 1994 528-29
  glossary of terms 527
  organizations 530
  solar system 523-26
Atlantic Ocean 236
Atomic energy (see Nuclear energy)
Australia 236, 317-18
  map 305
  population 243
Australian Antarctic Territory 317
Austria 318-19
  (see also History, world)
Auto racing 688
Automobiles,
  Can. production 189
  households owning 86
  sales 189, 190
  top Can. corporations 194
  traffic deaths 60
Aviation,
  airports, busiest overseas 235
  disasters 104-5
  Lindbergh 282

Wright brothers 277
Avro Arrow 96
Awards and prizes,
  Booker Prize 598
  Can. Country Music 577
  Cannes Film Festival 564-65
  CASBY Awards 577
  Emmy Awards 571-72
  Gairdner Awards 547
  Gemini Awards 570-71
  Genie Awards 563-64
  Gov. Genl's Literary Awards 592-97
  Grammy Awards 578
  honors and decorations 126-28
  Juno Awards 574-76
  Manning Awards 555
  Montreal Film Festival 564
  Music Video Awards 581
  National Magazine 600
  National Newspaper 599
  Nobel 553
  Oscars 565-69
  Pulitzer Prizes 598
  sports *(see individual sports)*
  Toronto Film Festival 564
  Video Music Awards 582
Azerbaijan 319-20
Aztecs 266, 267

B

Baby names 55
Babylon 259-60
Bach, J. S. 270
Badminton 622
Baha'i religion 71
Bahamas 320-21
Bahrain 321-22
Baker Island 508
Balance of payments, Canada 216
Balance of trade, Canada 217
Ballet, Can. companies 586
Bangladesh 322-23
Bankruptcies 190
Banks,
  Canadian 188
  interest rates 182, 227, 228
  world's largest 245
Baptist churches 71
Barbados 323-24
Barbuda 313-14
Barrie (Ont.) tornado 105
Baseball 643-58
  American League 643-44, 645-46,
                            649-51, 652
  awards 648-49
  batting champions 650-51

Canadian players 657-58
earned-run avg. leaders 651-52
league standings (1993) 643
Montreal Expos 652-54
most valuable players 648, 649-50
National League 644-45, 649-54
Olympics 622
pennant winners 645-46
stadiums 631
Toronto Blue Jays 655-57
World Series 647-48
Basketball 673-75
  all-time leaders 675
  individual highs 1992-93 673-74
  NBA 1992-93 standings 673
  Olympics 620
  playoff results 673
  statistical leaders 674-75
Beethoven, Ludwig van 271
Belarus 324-25
Belau (Palau) 325, 508
Belgium 325-26
  (see also History, world)
Belize 326-27
Benin 327-29
Bennett, R.B. 94, 109-10, 129
Bering Sea 237
Berlin Wall 289, 296
Bermuda 329, 506
Beverages, world producers 249
Bhutan 329-30
Biathlon 627
Bilingualism, official 96
Biodiversity Convention 557
Birds, endangered species 558
Birthday greetings 709
Births,
  baby names 55
  by age of mother 54, 55
  first test-tube baby 292
  rates, Canada 29-34, 53
Birthstones 696
Black Death 266
Black Sea 237
Bloc Québécois 99, 150
Bobsledding 627
Boer War 92, 276, 277
Bolívar, Simón 271
Bolivia 330-31
Bonds, government 233
Booker Prize 598
Books *(see Literature)*
Bophuthatswana 331
Borden, Sir Robert 108, 129
Bosnia 298
  (see also Yugoslavia)
Botswana 331-33
Bowell, Sir Mackenzie 107, 129

Boxing,
  Can. champions 680
  Olympic champions 621-22
Bravery awards 128
Brazil 333-34
Breeders Stakes (racing) 685-86
Britain *(see United Kingdom)*
British Antarctic Territory 506
British Columbia 33-34
  agriculture 204, 205, 207
  cabinet 149
  education 72, 73, 80
  election results 151-54, 158
  energy production 212, 213, 214
  geography 28, 33
  joins Confederation 33, 92
  labour force 199, 200, 202
  languages 33, 70
  lieutenant-governor 141
  MPs 138
  party leaders 160
  population 33, 42
    native 68-69
    towns and cities 50
    urban/rural 46
  premier 145
  religions 33
  resource industries 208-10
  revenues/expenditures 184
  surplus/deficit 185
  (see also Provinces and territories)
British Honduras *(see Belize)*
British Indian Ocean Territory 334, 506
British North America Act 91, 120-21
British Virgin Islands 334, 506
Bronze Age 259
Brunei Darussalam 334-35
Buddhism 71, 260
Bulgaria 335-36
Burkina Faso 337-38
Burma 437-38
Burundi 338-39
Business, Canada 193-97
  bankruptcies 190
  foreign investment in 186
  investment abroad 185
  leading firms, by industry 193-95
  small business 203
  (see also Corporations; Industries)
Business and labour 193-202
Byelorussia 324-25
Byzantium 262-64

C

Cabinet members (Canada) 117-18, 130
Cabot, John 89

Caesar, Julius 261
Calendar (1994) 760
  (1993), (1995) 759
Calgary (Alta.) 35
  population 50, 51, 52
Calvin, John 268
Cambodia 339-40
Cameroon 340-41
Campbell, Kim 113, 129
Canada 1, 341-42
  agriculture 204-7
  area 28
  bilingualism 96
  centennial 96
  cities 35-39
  citizenship 65, 709-10
  Constitution 98, 99, 120-26
  courts 118-19
  currency 220
  economy 178-92
  federal elections (see Elections)
  flag 88
  foreign trade 216-19
  geography 1, 2-9, 28
  geology 3-4
  government (see Federal government)
  Governors General 114-15, 129
  gross domestic product 179
  health insurance 96
  history 89-99
  immigration 63-68
  landforms 3-4
  military (see Canadian Armed Forces)
  minerals 208-9
  monarchy 114
  national anthem 88
  national parks 40-41
  native people (see Native people of
    Canada)
  official languages 70, 96
  Parliament 115-16, 120, 131-40
  pension policy 96, 166
  petroleum production 213
  population (see Population, Canada)
  poverty 87
  prime ministers 106-13, 116, 129
  railways 91, 92
  social security 164-70
  superlative facts 2
  system of government 114-26
  time zones 1, 2
  unemployment 199, 202
  unemployment insurance 94, 165
  universities and colleges 75-80
  vegetation 8
  vital statistics 53-60
  weather 11-27
  (see also Provinces and territories)
Canada Assistance Plan 164

Canada Cup 641
Canada Pension Plan 166
Canadian Armed Forces 163
  bases 163
  Boer War 93
  defence spending 162
  Korean War 95
  medals 126-28
  navy 93
  ranks 162
  senior personnel 161
  stations 162
  strength 161
  unified 96
  veterans benefits 168
  World War I 93
  World War II 94-95, 168
Canadian Broadcasting Corporation (CBC),
  early history 569
Canadian Country Music Assn Awards . 577
Canadian Football League (CFL) 658-68
Canadian Interuniversity Athletic Union
  (CIAU) 677
Canadian National Railways 94
Canadian Pacific Railway 92
Canadian Shield 3
Cancer,
  cause of death 59, 62
  new Can. cases 62
  warning signs 699
Cannes Film Festival 564-65
Canoeing 623
Cape Verde 342-43
Carbohydrates in foods 697
Cardiovascular diseases 59, 62, 698
Caribbean Community 255
Caribbean islands, map 306
Caribbean Sea 237
CARICOM 255
Cars (see Automobiles)
Cartier, Jacques 89, 268
CASBY Awards 577
Caspian Sea 237
Castro, Fidel 288
Cayman Islands 343, 506
CCF 94
Celsius scale 694
Central African Republic 343-45
Ceylon (see Sri Lanka)
Chad 345-46
Challenger explosion 295
Champlain, Samuel de 89
Channel Islands 346, 506
Charge cards 226-27
Charlemagne 264
Charlottetown (PEI) 47
Charlottetown Conference (1864) 91
Charter of Rights and Freedoms . 98, 121-26
Chaucer 266

Chemistry 546-48, 550-51
Chernobyl accident 295
Chiang Kai-Shek 282
Chicoutimi-Jonquière (Que.) 35
  population 47, 51, 52
Chile 346-47
China (People's Republic) 347-48
  (see also History, world)
China Sea 237
Chokings, deaths (Canada) 60
Christian Heritage Party 150
Christian and Missionary Alliance 71
Christianity,
  birth of Jesus 261
  population, Canada 71
Christmas Island 317, 348-49
Church of Christ (Disciples) 71
Churchill, Winston 281-86
Ciskei 349
Cities, Canada 35-39
  average income 220
  Consumer Price Index 181
  fuel costs 215
  incorporation dates 51-52
  labour force 198
  latitude, longitude, elevation 28
  population 51-52
  population, area 47-50
  resale value of homes 230
  weather 18, 24-26
Cities, world 236, 240, 243
  elevations 236
  population, largest 240
  superlative statistics 235
  weather 18
Citizenship, Canadian,
  persons granted 65
  requirements 709
Clark, Joe 97, 112, 129
Climate 11
  global warming 557
  (see also Weather)
CN Tower 97
Coal,
  exports/imports 214
  production 214
Cocos (Keeling) Islands 317, 349
Cold War ends 296
Colleges (see Universities and colleges)
Colombia 349-50
Columbia River 6
Columbus, Christopher 267
Commerce (see Trade)
Commodities (see Agriculture)
Commonwealth (British) 258
Communications,
  top Can. corporations 192
  (see also Utilities)
Communist Manifesto 273

Communist Party .....,................ 150
Community colleges 72, 77-80
Comoros 350-51
Computers, households owning 86
Confederation (1867) 92, 105
  fathers of 102
Confederation of Regions Western Party 150
Confucianism 71, 260
Conglomerates, top Canadian 195
Congo 351-52
Congo, Dem. Republic of *(see Zaire)*
Conscription Crisis (1917) 93
Conscription Crisis (1942) 95
Conservatives
  (see Progressive Conservative Party)
Constantine the Great 263
Constellations 534
Constitution of Canada 99, 120-26
  patriation 98
Construction,
  disasters 103-4
  labour force 198, 202
  small businesses 203
  tallest structures 235
  value 191
Consumer goods and services,
  credit 226-27
  personal expenditures 85, 86
  prices 180-81
  purchasing power 220
Consumer Price Index 180-81
Continents,
  area 235, 236
  highest, lowest points 236
  mountains 238-39
  population 236
Cook Islands 353, 443
Cooperative Commonwealth Federation
  (CCF) 94
Coral Sea Islands Territory 317
Corporations,
  income tax 225
  world's largest 244
Corporations, Canada,
  addresses 196-97
  bankruptcies 190
  foreign-owned 195
  largest overall 193
  largest profits/losses 195
  leaders, by industry 193-95
  stock performance 233
  subsidiaries 196
Costa Rica 353-54
Côte d'Ivoire 354-55
Countries of the world 299-522
  events of 1993 719-43
  history 258-98
  maps 299-306
  most populous 240

superlative statistics 235
County courts 118
Courts, Canada 118-19
  citizenship 710
Credit cards 226-27
Crete, ancient 259
Crime,
  adults charged 173-74
  drug crimes 173-74
  homicides 172, 173
  prison inmates 172
  property crimes 173-74
  rates 173-74
  sexual assault 173
  young offenders 171, 173-74
Crime and Justice 171-74
Crimean War 273
Croatia 355-56
  (see also Yugoslavia)
Cromwell, Oliver 270
Crops, *(see Agriculture)*
Crusades 265
Cuba 356-57
Cuban Missile Crisis 289
Cultural Revolution 289
Culture, *(see Arts and Entertainment)*
Curling 675-76
Currency,
  foreign exchange rates 187
  official reserves 187
Customs regulations (Can.) 708-9
Cy Young Awards 648-49
Cycling, Olympics 623
Cyprus 357-58
Czechoslovakia 297, 358-59

national, per capita 183
Defence 161-63
  (see also Canadian Armed Forces)
Denmark 359-60
Deserts, world 235
Diefenbaker, John 95-96, 110-11, 129
Dieppe raid (1942) 94
Diet and Health 697-706
Dietary allowances, recommended 697
Dinosaurs 542-43
Dionne quintuplets 94
Diplomacy, UN ambassadors 251
Directories,
  aquariums 562
  art galleries 591
  astronomy organizations 530
  corporations 196-97
  dance companies 586
  dance service orgs 587
  earth science museums 545
  federal political parties 150-51
  inventors' orgs 556
  jazz festivals 583
  labour unions 201-2
  museums 591
  observatories 535
  opera cos. 586
  orchestras 584-85
  planetariums 535
  science museums 545, 552
  theatre companies 587-88
  TV networks 573
  universities and colleges 75-80
  zoos 562
Disability benefits 168
Disasters,
  aviation 104-5
  Bhopal gas leak 294
  Canadian 103-4
  Challenger explosion 295
  Chernobyl accident 295
  earthquakes 537-41
  Empress of Ireland 93, 103
  fires 103-5
  Hurricane Andrew (1992) 18, 298
  Hurricane Hazel (1954) 104
  Korean airliner 294
  marine 103-5
  mining 103-5
  Ocean Ranger 105
  oil spills 296
  railways 103-5
  Titanic 278
  (see also Accidents; News events of 1993)
Diseases,
  AIDS 61-62, 698
  cancer 699
  cause of death 59
  first aid 703-6

D

da Vinci, Leonardo 267
Dahomey *(see Benin)*
Dairy producers 248
Dance,
  Can. service orgs 587
  Canadian companies 586
Dark Ages 262-66
Darwin, Charles 272, 273, 274
Deaths,
  accidental, Canada 60
  causes among females 59
  causes among males 59
  motor vehicles 60
  rates, Canada 29-34, 58
  suicides, Canada 60
  (see also Crime; Disasters; Obituaries)
Debt,
  bankruptcies 190
  national 183

heart 698
District courts 118
Diving, Olympic champions 618-19, 620
Divorces,
  by length of marriage 81
  by province 81
  number (Canada) 81
  rates, by province 29-34
Djibouti 360-61
Dollar, Canadian,
  exchange rates 187
  purchasing power 220
Dominica 361-62
Dominican Republic 362-63
Doukhobors 71
Dreyfus affair 276
Drownings (number) 60
Drug abuse, drug trade 173-74
Durham, Lord, Report (1839) 91

E

Earth (planet), composition 536
Earth Sciences 536-45
  museums 545
Earth Summit (1992) 297, 557
Earthquakes 537-41
East China Sea 237
Eclipses (1994) 530
Economics 178-92
  by province 29-34
  Consumer Price Index 180-81
  exchange rates 187
  federal surplus/deficit 183
  foreign investment 186, 216
  foreign ownership 195, 196
  glossary of terms 178-79
  gross domestic product 179
  interest rates 182, 227, 228
  investment abroad 185, 216
  monetary reserves 187
  national debt 183
  rates at a glance 1
  trade balance 217
  unemployment .. 191, 198, 199, 202, 221
  wage/price controls 97
Ecuador 363-65
Edison, Thomas 275
Edmonton (Alta.) 35
  population 50, 51, 52
Education 72-80
  attainment 72
  continuing 80
  and employment 73, 74, 75
  enrolment,
    community colleges 72
    elem. and sec. schools 72, 73

  univ. and colleges 72
French immersion 73
  literacy and numeracy 74
  provincial statistics 29-34
  spending 73
  universities and colleges 75-80
Edward VIII 283
Egypt 365-66
  ancient 259-61
  (see also History, world)
Einstein, Albert 277
El Salvador 366-67
Elections,
  federal 151-54
  provincial 157-58
  voter turnout 154
Electricity,
  costs 215
  exports/imports 214
  nuclear production 212, 213
  production, by source 212
  (see also Utilities)
Elements 550-51
Elizabeth II 114, 287
Emigration, by province 68
Emmy Awards 571-72
Employment,
  by industry 198, 202
  by small business 203
  and education 73, 74, 75
  unemployment insurance 165
  (see also Labour force)
Empress of Ireland (1914) 93, 103
Endangered species 558-59
Energy 212-15
  Can. production 213-14
  fuel costs 215
  household heating 215
  nuclear power 212-13
  top Can. corporations 194
Engineering 556
England *(see United Kingdom)*
Environment 557-62
Equality Party (Que.) 159
Equatorial Guinea 367-68
Equestrian sport, Olympics 623
Ericsson, Leif 89, 264
Erie, Lake 5
Estonia 368-69
Ethiopia 369-70
  (see also History, world)
Europe,
  area 236
  highest, lowest points 236
  map 301
  mountains 238
  population 236, 243
European Community (EC) 256-57
Everest, Mount 235, 236

Expenditures, consumer 85, 86
Expenditures, government 182
  by provinces 29-34
  on culture 589-90
  education 73
  health care 169-70
  public works 174-75
  social programs 164-70
Explorations, North America . 89-90, 267-68
Expo 67 96
Expo 86 98
Exports/imports 216-19
  Can. exports by country 219
  Can. imports by country 218
  energy 214
  petroleum 214
  wheat 206
Exxon Valdez 296

F

Faeroe Islands 360, 370
Fahrenheit scale 694
Falkland Islands 370, 506
Falklands War 293
Families and Income 81-87
Family composition 71
Family size 83
FAO 252
Farms *(see Agriculture)*
Fats in foods 697
Federal Court of Canada 118
Federal government,
  cabinet and departments 117, 130
  labour force 202
  legislative authority 119
  legislative costs 140
  mechanics 120
  Parliament 115-16, 120, 131-40
  prime ministers 106-13, 129
  public works 174-75
  social security programs 164-70
  spending 182
  surplus/deficit 183
  system 114-26
Federated States of Micronesia 508
Fencing 623
Festival of Festivals (Toronto) 564
Fibre in foods 697
Field hockey 623
Fiji 370-71
Films *(see Movies)*
Finance industry,
  labour force 198, 202
  largest institutions 188
  small businesses 203
Finance, Personal 220-34

Finland 371-72
FIRA 97
Fires,
   deaths, Canada 60
   disasters 103-5
First aid 703-6
Fish, endangered species 558
Fishing,
   by region, species 211
   cutbacks 210
   industry statistics 210-11
   labour force 198, 202
   small businesses 203
   world producers 248
Flag, Canada 88
FLQ 95, 96
Food 697
   aid requirements 249
   Canada's Food Guide 697
   top Can. corporations 194
   world producers 246-49
Food and Agriculture Org. (FAO) 252
Football, American,
   all-time records 669-71
   bowl games 672
   National Football League 668-71
   season standings (1992) 668-69
   Super Bowl 669
   top college teams 672
Football, Canadian 658-68
   all-time records 664-65
   CFL all-stars 667
   Grey Cup 659
   Hall of Fame 667-68
   individual records 660
   junior champions 671-72
   leaders by year 661-63
   1992 standings 658
   Outstanding Player Awards 665-66
   stadiums 631
Ford, Henry 278
Foreign aid,
   Canadian 175-77
   food needs 249
   world 177
Foreign Investment Review Agency (FIRA)
   97
Foreign Trade 216-19
Forestry 8
   industry statistics 209-10
   labour force 198, 202
   small businesses 203
   top Can. corporations 194
Fox, Terry 98
France 373-74
   (see also History, world)
Francophonie 255
Free Methodists 71
Free trade agreement 98

French Guiana 373, 374
French immersion schools 73
French and Indian War 90
French Polynesia 373, 374
French Revolution 270
Freud, Sigmund 276
Front de Libération du Québec (FLQ) 96
Frost dates 8-9
Fruit production 207
Fuels,
   coal production 214
   consumer costs 215
   electricity production 212-13
   exports/imports 214
   household heating, by province 215
   natural gas production 213
   petroleum production 213
   (see also Nuclear energy)

G

Gabon 375-76
Gairdner Awards 547
Galileo 269
Galleries 590-91
Gambia 376-77
Gandhi, Mohandas 280, 281, 285, 287
Gas *(see Natural gas)*
Gasoline prices 215
GATT 252
Gemini Awards 570-71
General Agreement on Tariffs and Trade
   (GATT) 252
Genghis Khan 265
Genie Awards 563-64
Geography 1, 2-9, 235-39
   by province 29-34
   world maps 299-306
Geological Survey of Canada 536
Geology 536-45
   glossary of terms 537
   time periods 541-42
Georgia (CIS) 377
Germany 378-79
   reunification 296
   (see also History, world)
Gesner, Abraham 546
Ghana 379-80
Gibraltar 380, 506
Glaciers 4
Gold, official reserves 187
Golf 683-84
Goods and services tax (GST) 99
Gorbachev, Mikhail 294-97
Gouzenko affair 95
Government of Canada 114-49
   (see also Federal government)

Governor General's Literary Awards . 592-97
Governors General,
   salary 139
   terms 129
Grains 208
   Can. exports 205
   world producers 246
Grammy Awards 578
Grand Trunk Railway 91
Great Bear Lake 4
Great Britain *(see United Kingdom)*
Great Depression 94, 282
Great Lakes 5
Great Slave Lake 5
Greece 380-81
   ancient 259-62
Greek Orthodox Church 71
Green Party 151
Greenland 360, 381-82
Grenada 382-83
Grenadines 468-69
Grey Cup 659
Gross domestic product, Canada 179
Group of Seven 590
GST *(see Goods and services tax)*
Guadeloupe 373, 383
Guam 383, 508
Guaranteed Income Supplement 167
Guatemala 384-85
Guernsey 346, 506
Guiana (French) 373, 374
Guinea 385-86
Guinea-Bissau 386-87
Gulf of Mexico 237
Gulf War 99, 297
Guns, cause of death 60
Guyana 387-88
Gymnastics 623

H

Hagersville fire (1990) 105
Haiti 388-89
Halifax (NS) 35
   Explosion (1917) 104
   founding (1749) 90
   population 47, 51, 52
Halls of Fame,
   Canadian Football 667-68
   Canadian Sports 689-90
   Hockey 642-43
   Rock and Roll 582-83
   Science and Engineering 556
Hamilton (Ont.) 35-36
   population 49, 51, 52
Hammurabi 259
Handball 623

Heads of state, govt *(see individual nations)*
Health care 169-70, 698-99
Heard and McDonald Islands 317
Heart disease,
   cause of death 59, 62
   warning signs 698
Heating oil prices 215
Henry VIII 267-68
Hinduism 71
Hinton train crash (1986) 105
Hiroshima bombing 286
History,
   ancient 259-62
   events of 1993 719-43
   world 259-98
History, Canadian 89-99
   events of 1993 719-43
   quotations 100-102
Hitler, Adolph 280-86
Hnatyshyn, Ray 129
Hockey 629-42
   all-star teams 636
   arenas 631
   Canada Cup 641
   Canada-USSR series 641
   Hall of Fame 642-43
   individual records 634
   junior championships 639-40
   National Hockey League 629-39
   Olympics 627
   playoffs (1993) 629-30
   scoring leaders,
     all-time 635
     1992-93 633
     regular season 634-35
   season standings (1992-93) 629
   Stanley Cup 630, 631-32
   top draft choices 636
   trophy winners 637-39
   world championships 639-40
Hockey, field 623
Holidays (1994) 760
Holland *(see Netherlands)*
Home electronics 86
Homer 259
Homicides *(see Crime)*
Honduras 389-90
Honduras, British *(see Belize)*
Hong Kong 390-91, 506
Honors and decorations 126-28
Horse racing 684-86
House of Commons 116, 120
   expenses 139-40
   members 133-38
   pensions 140
   salaries 139
Housing,
   affordability 229
   mortgages 227, 228-29

resale value of homes 230
   (see also Construction)
Howland Island 508
Hudson Bay 237
Hudson's Bay Company 89
Hull (Que.) 36-37, 47, 51, 52
Hundred Years' War 266
Hungary 391-92
   (see also History, world)
Huron, Lake 5, 237
Hurricane Andrew (1992) 18, 298
Hurricane Hazel (1954) 95, 104
Hutterites 71
Hydroelectric power 212

I

IAEA 252
IBRD 252
ICAO 252
Iceland 392-93
IFAD 252
ILO 252
IMF 252
Immigration 63-68
   by destination 64
   by origin 44-45, 67
   by province 65
   interprovincial migration 67
   refugees 66-67
IMO 252
Incas 267
Incomes 221, 225
   by family, province 84
   by gender 84
   by occupation 225
   cities, selected 220
   family and individual 221
   poverty 87
   (see also Social security)
India 393-94
   (see also History, world)
Indian Ocean 236
Indians, Canadian
   (see Native people of Canada)
Indochina *(see Cambodia; Laos; Vietnam)*
Indonesia, 394-95
Industrial Revolution 270-73
Industries,
   labour force 198, 202
   manufacturing 188
   resource 208-10
   small businesses 203
   top Can. corporations 193-95
   world's largest cos. 244
   (see also Trade)

Inflation,
   Can. annual 180, 180-81
   and wages 86
Innuitian Region 4
Inquisition 265, 267
Insulin discovered 94
Intercolonial Railway 92
Interest rates 180, 227, 228-29
   credit cards 226-27
   and mortgages 182, 227, 228-29
Interior Plains (Canada) 3
International Atomic Energy Agency (IAEA)
   252
International Bank for Reconstruction and
   Development (IBRD) 252
International Civil Aviation Org. (ICAO) . 252
International Court of Justice 250-51
International Fund for Agricultural
   Development (IFAD) 252
International Labour Org. (ILO) 252
International Maritime Org. (IMO) 252
International Monetary Fund (IMF) 252
International organizations 250-58
   Canadian representatives 251
International System of Units 695
International Telecommunication Union (ITU)
   252
Inuit *(see Native people of Canada)*
Inventions 547, 548, 549, 553-56
   (see also History, world)
Investment,
   abroad, by Canada 185, 216
   bond yields 233
   foreign, in Canada 186, 216
   glossary of terms 230-32
Iran 395-96
   (see also History, world)
Iran-Iraq War 293
Iraq 396-97
   (see also History, world)
Ireland 397-98
Iron Age 259
Iroquois Confederacy 268
Islam 71
   founded 263
Islands 5, 235, 237
Isle of Man 398-99, 506
Israel 399-400
   ancient 259-61
   (see also History, world)
Italy 400-401
   (see also History, world)
ITU 252
Ivan the Terrible 268
Ivory Coast 354-55

J

Jamaica 401-2
Japan 402-3
  (see also History, world)
Japan, Sea of 237
Jarvis Island 508
Jay's Treaty 90
Jazz festivals 583
Jehovah's Witnesses 71
Jersey 346, 506
Joan of Arc 266
Jobs (see Employment; Labour force)
Johnston Atoll 508
Jordan 403-4
  (see also History, world)
Judaism 71
  founded 259-61
Judges and justices 118-19, 130
Judo 623
Juno Awards 574-76
Justice system 118-19

K

Kampuchea (see Cambodia)
Kayaking 679
Kazakhstan 404-5
Keeling Islands 317, 349
Kenya 405-6
Kermadec Islands 443
Khrushchev, Nikita 288
King, W.L. Mackenzie 94, 109, 129
Kingman Reef 508
Kiribati 406-7
Kitchener (Ont.) 36, 49, 51, 52
Korea, North 407-8
Korea, South 408-10
Korean War 95, 287-88
Kuwait 410-11
Kyrgyzstan 411-12

L

Labour force,
  by age 199
  by industry 198, 202
  by province 199
  incomes by occupation 225
  metropolitan areas 198
  minimum wages 200
Labour unions,
  directory 201-2
  membership 200-201

Lakes,
  Canada 5, 237
  world 235, 237
Languages, Canada,
  mother tongues 70
  official 70, 96
Laos 412-13
Latin America (see South America)
Latter-Day Saints 71
Latvia 413
Laurier, Wilfrid 92, 107, 129
Law enforcement 171-72
League of Arab States 255
League of Nations 280
Lebanon 413-14
Lenin, Vladimir 277, 278, 279
Lesotho 415-16
Lévesque, René 97
Liberal Party 150
  leaders 155
  leadership conventions 156
  provincial leaders 159-60
Liberia 416-17
Libertarian Party 150
Libya 417-18
Liechtenstein 418-19
Lieutenant-governors, by province .. 141
Life expectancy, Canada 56-57
Lincoln, Abraham 273
Lindbergh, Charles 282
Literacy and numeracy 74
Literature,
  bestsellers in Canada 1992 598
  Booker Prize 598
  Governor General's Awards 592-97
  Pulitzer Prizes 598
Lithuania 419-20
Livestock 204-5, 246-47
Logging 209
  (see also Forestry)
London (Ont.) 36
  population 49, 51, 52
London Conference (1866) 106
Loudness of sounds 552
Luge 628
Luther, Martin 267-68
Lutheran churches 71
Luxembourg 420-21

M

Maastricht Treaty 256-57, 297
Macdonald, John A. 92, 106-8, 129
Mackenzie, Alexander (explorer) 90
Mackenzie, Alexander (prime minister)
  .... 106, 129
Mackenzie, William Lyon 91

Mackenzie River 6
Madagascar 421-22
Magazines 600
Magna Carta 265
Malagasy Republic (see Madagascar)
Malawi 422-23
Malaysia 423-24
Maldives 424-25
Mali 425-27
Malta 427-28
Mandela, Nelson 296
Manitoba 32
  agriculture 204, 205, 207
  cabinet 148
  created 92
  education 72, 73, 79
  election results 151-54, 158
  electricity production 212
  geography 28, 32
  joins Confederation 32
  labour force 199, 200, 202
  languages 32, 70
  lieutenant-governor 141
  MPs 137
  party leaders 160
  population 32, 42
    native 68-69
    towns and cities 50
    urban/rural 46
  premier 143
  religions 32
  resource industries 208-10
  revenues/expenditures 184
  Schools Question 107
  surplus/deficit 185
  (see also Provinces and territories)
Manning Awards 555
Manufacturing,
  employees, value 188
  labour force 198, 202
  small businesses 203
  top Can. corporations 194-95
Mao Tse-Tung (Zedong) 283, 287, 291
Maple Leaf flag 88
Maps of the world 299-306
Marco Polo 265
Marriages,
  ages of bride and groom 81
  by province 81
  number (Canada) 81
  rates, by province 29-34
Mars (planet) 525-26
Marshall Islands 508
Martinique 373, 428
Marx, Karl 273, 274
Marxist-Leninist Party 150
Mauritania 428-29
Mauritius 429-30
Mayans 260-62

Mayflower voyage 270
Mayotte 373, 430
Measures *(see Weights and measures)*
Meats, world producers 246-47
Medals (military, etc.) 126-28
Media, top Can. corporations 194
Medical science 547
Mediterranean Sea 237
Meech Lake Accord 98, 122
Meighen, Arthur 108-9, 129
Memorial Cup 640
Mennonites 71
Mesopotamia 279
Métis *(see Native people of Canada)*
Metric system 692-94
Mexico 431-32
   Aztecs 266, 267
   Mayans 260-62
   (see also History, world)
Michelangelo 267
Michigan, Lake 5, 237
Micronesia 508
Middle Ages 262-66
Midway Islands 508
Military *(see Canadian Armed Forces)*
Minerals 543-44
   in foods 697
Mining 208-9, 543-44
   coal production 214
   disasters 103-5
   labour force 198, 202
   small businesses 203
   top Can. corporations 193
Mohammed 263
Moldova 432
Monaco 433
Mongolia 433-34
Montcalm, Marquis de 90
Montezuma 266
Montreal (Que.) 36
   Expo 67 96
   Film Festival 564
   founding (1642) 89
   population 48, 51, 52
Montreal Expos,
   individual stats 653
   player of the year 654
   team records 654
   year-by-year record 652-53
Montreal massacre (1989) 105
Montserrat 334-35, 506
Moon, the, phases 529
Mormons 71
Morocco 435-36
Mortgages,
   interest rates 182, 227, 228-29
   qualifying for 229
Moses 259
Moslems, Can. population 71

Mountains 238-39
   Canada 7
Movies,
   Academy Awards (Oscars) 565-69
   Canadian 563-64
   Cannes Film Festival 564-65
   Genie Awards 563-64
   Montreal Festival 564
   Toronto Festival 564
Mozambique 436-37
Mulroney, Brian 98, 98-99, 112-13, 129
Murders *(see Crime)*
Muscat *(see Oman)*
Museums,
   art 590-91
   science 545, 552
Music 574-86
   Can. Country 577
   Can. sales 579
   CASBY Awards 577
   dance companies 586
   Grammy Awards 578
   jazz festivals 583
   Juno Awards 574-76
   Music Video Awards 581
   new recordings in Can. 579-80
   opera companies 586
   orchestras 584-85
   recording formats 581
   records, best-selling 579, 580-81
   rock hall of fame 582-83
   Video Music Awards 582
Music Video Awards 581
Myanmar 437-38

N

Names, baby 55
Namibia 438-39
Napoleon 271
National anthem 88
National Basketball Association (NBA)
   673-75
National defence
   (see Canadian Armed Forces)
National Energy Program 97
National Football League (NFL) 668-71
National Hockey League (NHL) 629-39
National League (baseball) . 644-46, 649-54
National parks 40-41
Nations of the world 307-522
   events of 1993 719-43
   maps 299-306
   most populous 240
   superlative statistics 235
   world history 259-98
Native people of Canada 68-69

Iroquois Confederacy 268
   largest bands 69
   Métis 92
   suffrage 96
NATO 255
Natural gas,
   exports/imports 214
   prices 215
   production 213
Natural resources 208-11
Nauru 439-40
Navy *(see Canadian Armed Forces)*
Nelson River 6
Nepal 440-41
Netherland Antilles 442-43
Netherlands 441-42
   (see also History, world)
Nevis 466-67
New Brunswick 30
   agriculture 204, 207
   cabinet 146
   education 72, 73, 77
   election results 151-54, 157
   geography 28, 30
   joins Confederation 30
   labour force 199, 200, 202
   languages 30, 70
   lieutenant-governor 141
   MPs 133
   party leaders 159
   population 30, 42
      native 68-69
      towns and cities 47
      urban/rural 46
   premier 142-43
   religions 30
   resource industries 208-10
   revenues/expenditures 184
   surplus/deficit 185
   (see also Provinces and territories)
New Caledonia 373, 443
New Democratic Party 96, 150
   leaders 155
   leadership conventions 156
   provincial leaders 159-60
New Zealand 443-44
   map 305
Newfoundland 29
   agriculture 204, 207
   cabinet 145-46
   education 72, 73, 77
   election results 152-54, 157
   electricity production 212
   geography 28, 29
   joins Confederation 29, 95
   labour force 199, 200, 202
   languages 29, 70
   lieutenant-governor 141
   MPs 133

party leaders 159
population 29, 42
native 68-69
towns and cities 47
urban/rural 46
premier 141
provincial police 171
religions 29
resource industries 208-10
revenues/expenditures 184
surplus/deficit 185
(see also Provinces and territories)
News events of 1993 719-43
obituaries 711-18
Newspapers 599
Newton, Isaac 270
Niagara Falls 6
Nicaragua 444-45
Niger 445-46
Nigeria 446-47
Niue 443, 448
Nobel Prizes 276, 553
Noise levels 552
Norfolk Island 317, 448
North America,
  area 236
  explorations 89-90, 267-68
  highest, lowest points 236
  lakes 5
  map 299
  mountains 239
  population 236, 242
North Atlantic Treaty Organization (NATO)
  255
North Korea 407-8
North West Company 90
Northern Ireland *(see United Kingdom)*
Northern Marianas 448, 508
Northwest Territories 34
  area 28
  cabinet 149
  education 72, 73
  election results 151-54
  energy production 213
  government 119-20
  govt leader 145
  joins Confederation 34
  labour force 200
  languages 34, 70
  mining production 208-9
  MPs 138
  population 34, 42
    native 68-69
    towns and cities 50
    urban/rural 46
  religions 34
  revenues/expenditures 184
  surplus/deficit 185
Norway 448-50

Nova Scotia 30
  agriculture 204, 207
  cabinet 146
  education 72, 73, 77
  election results 151-54, 157
  energy production 214
  geography 28, 30
  joins Confederation 30
  labour force 199, 200, 202
  languages 30, 70
  lieutenant-governor 141
  MPs 133
  party leaders 159
  population 30, 42
    native 68-69
    towns and cities 47
    urban/rural 46
  premier 142
  religions 31-32
  resource industries 208-10
  revenues/expenditures 184
  surplus/deficit 185
  (see also Provinces and territories)
Nuclear energy,
  accidents 292, 295
  Can. generating stations 213
  electricity production 212-13
Nuclear weapons 286
Numbers,
  large numbers 694
  Roman numerals 694
  (see also Weights and measures)
Numeracy in Canada 74
Nutrition,
  Canada's Food Guide 697
  recommended daily intakes 697

O

O Canada 88
OAS 255
Obituaries (1993) 711-18
Observatories 535
Ocean Ranger sinking (1982) ... 98, 105
Oceania,
  mountains 239
  population 243
Oceans and seas,
  areas, depths 236
  pollution 559
  superlative statistics 235
October Crisis (1970) 96, 290
OECD 255-56
Official Languages Act 96
Oil *(see Petroleum)*
Oil spills 296
Oka crisis (1990) 99

Okhotsk, Sea of 237
Old Age Security 167
Olympic Games,
  Albertville (1992) 625-28
  Barcelona (1992) 608-9, 610
  Canadian medalists 609-10, 626
  first ancient 259
  summer 608-24
  winter 609, 625-28
Oman 450-51
Ontario 31
  agriculture 204, 205, 207
  cabinet 147-48
  education 72, 73, 78-79
  election results 158
  energy production 212, 213
  geography 28, 31
  joins Confederation 31
  labour force 199, 200, 202
  languages 31, 70
  lieutenant-governor 141
  MPs 135-36
  party leaders 159
  population 31, 42
    native 68-69
    towns and cities 48-50
    urban/rural 46
  premier 143
  provincial police 171
  religions 31
  resource industries 208-10
  revenues/expenditures 184
  surplus/deficit 185
  (see also Provinces and territories)
Ontario, Lake 5
OPEC 255
Opera, Can. companies 586
Option Canada Party 151
Orchestras 584-85
Order of Canada 126
Organization of American States (OAS) . 255
Organization for Economic Cooperation and
  Development (OECD) 255-56
Organization of Petroleum Exporting
  Countries (OPEC) 255
Orthodox churches, population, Canada . 71
Oscars 565-69
Oshawa (Ont.) 36, 49, 51
Ottawa (Ont.) 36-37
  population 49, 51, 52
Ottoman Empire 266, 268
Outstanding Player Awards (CFL) ... 665-66

P

Pacific Ocean 236
  map 305

Pacific Scandal 106
Pakistan 451-52
Palau 325, 508
Palymyra Atoll 508
Panama 452-53
Panama Canal 279
Papineau, Louis-Joseph 91
Papua New Guinea 453-54
Paraguay 454-55
Parks, national 40-41
Parliament of Canada . 115-16, 120, 131-40
  (see also House of Commons; Senate)
Parti Libéral (Quebec) 159
Parti Nationaliste du Québec 151
Parti Québécois 97, 159
Parti Rhinocéros 151
Party for the Commonwealth of Canada . 151
Pasteur, Louis 273
Patents 554-55
Peace Prizes, Nobel 95
Peace River 6
Pearson, Lester 95, 111, 129
Pensions *(see Social security)*
Pentathlon, Olympic champions 623
Pentecostal churches 71
Performing Arts 584-88
Persian empire *(see History, world)*
Personal Finance 220-34
Persons case (1928) 282
Peru 455-56
Petroleum,
  Can. production 213
  exports/imports 214
  gasoline prices 215
  heating oil 215
  in Ontario 213
  top Can. corporations 194
Philippines 456-57
Phoenicia 259
Physical Sciences 546-52
Physics 546, 548-49
Pipeline Debate (1956) 96
Pitcairn Islands 506, 548
Plains of Abraham (1759) 90
Planetariums 535
Planets 523-26, 528
Plants,
  endangered species 558-59
  poisonous 701-2
Plato 260
Poetry, Governor General's Awards . 592-97
Poisons,
  deaths (Canada) 60
  poison-proofing 700
  poisonous plants 701-2
Poland 458-59
  (see also History, world)
Police,
  by province 172

provincial (Ont., Que.) 171
RCMP 171
Political parties,
  federal 150-51
  leaders 155
  leadership conventions 156
  provincial leaders 159-60
  (see also Elections)
Politics and Elections 1, 150-60
Pollution 559
Population, Canada 42-53
  age structure 56, 58
  below poverty line 87
  births and deaths 45, 53-60, 59, 60
  by age group 42-43, 56
  by country of birth 44-45
  by mother tongue 70
  by official language 70
  by province 29-34
  by religion 71
  cities, in detail 34-38
  family size 83
  growth 45
  immigration 63-68
  interprovincial migration 67
  languages 70
  life expectancy 56-57
  lone parents 82
  marital status 82
  metropolitan areas 52
  native people 68-69
  persons granted citizenship 65
  projections 43
  towns and cities 47-52
  urban and rural 46
Population, world,
  continents 236
  endangered groups 241
  largest cities 240
  most pop. nations 240
  projections 242-43
Populist Party 151
Portugal 459-60
  (see also History, world)
Poverty 87
Precambrian Shield 3
Precipitation,
  Canada 18
  in cities 24-26
  provincial averages 19, 21
  records 17, 21, 26, 235
  snowfall 17, 18, 19, 21, 24, 26
  storms 17, 19
  superlative statistics 235
  world cities 18
Premiers, provincial 141-45
Presbyterian churches 71
Prime Ministers of Canada 116, 129
  biographies 106-13

birth, death dates 129
  salary 139
  terms 129
Prince Edward Island 29-29
  agriculture 204, 207
  cabinet 146-47
  education 72, 73, 77
  election results 151-54, 157
  geography 28, 29
  joins Confederation 29, 92
  labour force 199, 200, 202
  languages 29, 70
  lieutenant-governor 141
  MPs 133
  party leaders 159
  population 29, 42
    native 68-69
    towns and cities 47
    urban/rural 46
  premier 141-42
  religions 29
  revenues/expenditures 184
  surplus/deficit 185
  (see also Provinces and territories)
Prince of Wales Stakes (racing) 685
Principe 470-71
Prisons 172
Privy Council Office 117
Prizes *(see Awards and prizes)*
Progressive Conservative Party 151
  leaders 155
  leadership conventions 156
  provincial leaders 159-60
Protein in foods 697
Provinces and territories 28-34
  agricultural statistics 204-5, 207
  births and deaths 53, 58
  coal production 214
  courts 118-19
  economy 29-34
  education 72, 73
  election results 157-58
  electricity production 212-13
  emigrants 68
  family income 84
  fishing statistics 210-11
  forestry statistics 209-10
  gas production 213
  geography 28, 29-34
  health care 169-70
  highest points 7
  household heating 215
  immigration 65
  income 29-34
  join Confederation 29-34
  labour force 199, 202
  languages 29-34, 70
  legislative authority 119-20
  legislative costs 140

lieutenant-governors 141
marriages/divorces 81
mineral reserves 209
minimum wages 200
mining production 208-9
party leaders 156-57
petroleum production 213
police, number of 171-72
population 29-34
   native 68-69
   towns/cities 47-50
   urban/rural 46
premiers 141-45
revenues/expenditures 29-34, 184
surplus/deficit 185
system of government 120
taxes 221, 223
vital statistics 29-34, 53, 58
weather records 20-22, 26
Ptolemy 261
Public works projects 174-75
Puerto Rico 460-61, 508
Pulitzer Prizes 598
Purchasing power of dollar 220

Q

Qatar 461-62
Quebec 31
   agriculture 204, 207
   cabinet 147
   constitutional negotiations 121-22
   education 72, 73, 77-78
   election results 151-54, 157
   electricity production 212, 213
   geography 28, 31
   income tax 223
   joins Confederation 31
   labour force 199, 200, 202
   languages 31, 70
   lieutenant-governor 141
   MPs 133-35
   party leaders 159
   population 31, 42
      native 68-69
      towns and cities 47-48
      urban/rural 46
   premier 143
   provincial police 171
   Quebec Pension Plan 166
   Quiet Revolution 96
   referendum (1980) 97, 121
   religions 31
   resource industries 208-10
   revenues/expenditures 184
   surplus/deficit 185
   (see also Provinces and territories)

Quebec Act (1774) 90
Quebec City (Que.) 37
   founding (1608) 89
   population 48, 51, 52
Queen Elizabeth II 114
Queen's Plate 684
Quiet Revolution 96
Quotations, Canadian 100-102

R

Racing (horses) 684-86
Radio 574
Railways, Canada,
   Canadian National 94
   Canadian Pacific 92
   disasters 103-5
   Grand Trunk 91
   Hinton crash (1986) 105
   Intercolonial 92
RCMP 171
Rebellions of 1837 91
Reciprocity Treaty (1854) 91
Red Sea 237
Reform of the Monetary Law Party 151
Reform Party 151
Refugees,
   in Canada 66-67
   special movements 67
Regina (Sask.) 37
   population 50, 51, 52
Registered Retirement Savings Plans (RRSPs)
   234
Religions,
   population, Canada 71
   (see also History, world)
Renaissance 266-70
Resale value of homes 230
Respiratory disease, cause of death 59
Retail trade,
   labour force 202
   small businesses 203
   top Can. corporations 194
Reunion 373, 462
Rheaume, Manon 641
Rhodesia (see Zimbabwe)
Riel, Louis 92
Rivers,
   Canada 6
   world 235, 237
Rock and Roll Hall of Fame 582-83
Roman Catholicism, population, Canada . 71
Roman numerals 694
Romania 462-63
Rome, ancient 259-62
Roosevelt, Franklin 282-86
Ross Dependency 443

Rowing 623-24
Royal Canadian Mounted Police (RCMP)
   171
Royal Newfoundland Constabulary 171
RRSPs 234
Rush-Bagot agreement (1817) 89
Russia 463-64
   (see also History, world)
Russian Revolution 279-80
Rwanda 464-65

S

Safety information 700
St. Catharines (Ont.) 37, 49, 52
Saint Helena 465, 506
Saint John (NB) 37
   population 47, 52
St. John's (Nfld.) 37-38
   population 47, 52
Saint Kitts and Nevis 466-67
St. Laurent, Louis 95, 110, 129
St. Lawrence River 6
St. Lawrence Seaway 96
Saint Lucia 467-68
St. Pierre and Miquelon 373, 468
Saint Vincent and the Grenadines ... 468-69
Salaries (see Incomes)
Salvation Army 71
San Marino 469-70
Sao Tome and Principe 470-71
Saskatchewan 32-33
   agriculture 204, 205
   cabinet 148
   education 72, 73, 79-80
   election results 152-54, 158
   formed (1905) 93
   geography 28, 32
   joins Confederation 32
   labour force 199, 200, 202
   languages 32, 70
   lieutenant-governor 141
   MPs 137
   party leaders 160
   petroleum production 213
   population 32, 42
      native 68-69
      towns and cities 50
      urban/rural 46
   premier 144
   religions 32
   resource industries 208-10
   revenues/expenditures 184
   surplus/deficit 185
   (see also Provinces and territories)
Saskatchewan River 6
Saskatoon (Sask.) 38

population 50, 52
Satellites 531-32
   Sputnik 288
Saudi Arabia 471-72
Schools *(see Education)*
Science and Nature 523-62
Scotland *(see United Kingdom)*
Seas *(area, depth)* 237
Secord, Laura 91
Senate of Canada 115-16
   members 131-32
   salaries 139
Senegal 472-73
Serbia *(see Yugoslavia)*
Service industries,
   labour force 202
   small businesses 203
Seven Wonders of the World 710
Seven Years' War 90, 270
Seychelles 473-74
Shakespeare, William 268-69
Sherbrooke (Que.) 38
Ships, disasters 103-5
Shooting, Olympics 624
Sierra Leone 474-75
Sikhism 71, 268
Singapore 475-76
Six Day War 290
Skating, figure 682
   Olympics 628
Skating, speed, Olympics 628
Skiing,
   Can. champions 681
   Olympics 626-27
Slovenia 477
Small business 203
Snowfall *(see Precipitation)*
Soccer,
   Olympics 622
   World Cup 676
Social Credit Party 151
   British Columbia 160
   provincial leaders 160
Social security 164-70
   Canada Assistance Plan 164
   Canada Pension Plan 166
   disability benefits 168
   family allowances 95
   Guaranteed Income Supplement 167
   health care 169-70
   Old Age Security 167
   Quebec Pension Plan 166
   Spouse's Allowance 167
   unemployment insurance 165
   veterans benefits 168
Socrates 260
Solar system 523-26
Solomon Islands 477-78

Somalia 298, 479-80
   (see also News events of 1993)
South Africa 480-81
   (see also News events of 1993)
South America,
   area 236
   highest, lowest points 236
   map 304
   mountains 239
   population 236, 242
South China Sea 237
South Georgia 506
South Korea 408-10
South Sandwich Islands 506
South-West Africa *(see Namibia)*
Southern and Antarctic Territories 373
Sovereignty-association 121
Soviet Union,
   becomes CIS 297
   democratization 294-97
   population 243
   (see also History, world; Russia)
Space exploration,
   Can. achievements 533
   Challenger explosion 295
   crewed flights 532
   glossary of terms 526
   men on moon 289-91
   satellites and probes 288, 531-32
   space junk 530
Spain 481-82
   Civil War 283-84
   (see also History, world)
Species, endangered 558-59
Speed skating 628
Sports 601-91
   1993 events 601-7
   arenas and stadiums 631
   Can. Hall of Fame 689-90
   CIAU champions 677
   CP Athlete of Year 691
   Olympics 608-28
   (see also individual sports)
Spouse's Allowance 167
Springhill mine disasters 103, 104
Sri Lanka 482-83
Stadiums 631
Stalin, Joseph 282-88
Stanley Cup 630
Status Indians 69
Statute of Westminster (1931) 94, 121
Stock exchanges,
   Can., trading 232-33
   glossary of terms 230-32
   most traded stocks 233
   top gainers/losers 233
   Toronto, price index 234
   world trading 245
Storms 17, 19

Stroke,
   cause of death 59, 63
   warning signs 698
Sudan 483-84
Sudbury (Ont.) 49, 52
Suez Crisis 288
Suffrage,
   native people 96
   women 93
Suicide rates 60
Sumeria 259
Super Bowl 669
Superior, Lake 5, 237
Superior Courts 118
Supreme Court of Canada 118, 130
Suriname 484-86
Svalbard 449, 486
Swaziland 486-87
Sweden 487-88
Swimming,
   Can. records 678-79
   Olympic champions 616-20
   synchronized 624
Switzerland 488-89
Synchronized swimming 624
Syria 489-90

T

Table tennis 624
Taiwan 490-91
Tajikistan 491-92
Tampa Bay Lightning 641
Tanzania 492-93
Taxes 221-25
   average paid 221
   by occupation 225
   by province 222, 223
   federal rates 223
   goods and services tax 99
   individual and corporate 225
   1993 tables 224
   personal credits 224
   provincial rates 223
   tax freedom day 223
Team Canada (hockey) 641
Technology, top Can. corporations 194
Television 569-73
   Canadian shows 569-70
   Emmy Awards 571-72
   Gemini Awards 570-71
   households owning 87
   most-watched programs 571
   network addresses 573
   time spent viewing 572
Temperature,
   Canada 18

Celsius/Fahrenheit 694
in cities 18, 24-26
heat waves 26
provincial averages 20
records 17, 20
Tennis,
Can. champions 678
Olympics 624
Thailand 493-95
Theatre,
Can. companies 587-88
Governor General's Awards 592-97
Thomas Aquinas 265
Thompson, Sir John 107, 129
Three Mile Island 292
Thunder Bay (Ont.) 38, 49, 52
Thunderstorms 19, 26
Tiananmen massacre 296
Tide, greatest 235
Time,
geological periods 541-42
time zones 1, 2
Titanic sinks 278
Tobago 497-98
Togo 495-96
Tokelau 443, 496
Tonga 496-97
Tornados,
Barrie, Ont. (1985) 105
Edmonton (1987) 105
Toronto (Ont.) 38
Film Festival 564
population 49, 52, 53
Toronto Blue Jays,
individual stats 655-56
player of the year 657
team records 656-57
year-by-year record 655
Toronto Stock Exchange,
price index 234
top gainers/losers 233
Tourism 192
national parks 40-41
(see also Travel)
Towns, Canada 47-50
(see also Cities, Canada)
Track and field,
Can. champions 688
Olympic champions 611-16
world champions 687-88
world records 686-87
Trade 216-19
balance of payments 216
exports/imports 186, 216-19
free trade agreement 98
trade balance 217
Transkei 497
Transportation, top Can. corporations ... 192

Travel,
Can. customs regulations 708-9
code of ethics 707
(see also Tourism)
Treasury Board 117
Treaties, Canada,
Ghent (1814) 91
Jay's (1794) 90
Reciprocity (1854) 91
Utrecht (1713) 90
Webster-Ashburton 272
Tree, oldest 235
Trinidad and Tobago 487-98
Triple Crown (racing) 685
Trois-Rivières (Que.) 39, 48, 52, 53
Trucks and vans, Can. production 189
Trudeau, Pierre 96, 111-12, 129
Tunisia 498-500
Tupper, Sir Charles 107, 129
Turkey 500-501
(see also History, world)
Turkmenistan 501-2
Turks and Caicos Islands 502, 508
Turner, John 112, 129
Tuvalu 502-3

U

Uganda 503-4
Ukraine 504-5
Ukrainian Orthodox church 71
Unemployment 191
by industry 198
by province 202
UNESCO 252
UNICEF 252
UNIDO 252
Union of Soviet Socialist Republics
(see Soviet Union)
Unions *(see Labour unions)*
Unitarianism 71
United Arab Emirates 505-6
United Church 71
United Kingdom 506-7
(see also History, world)
United Nations 250-55
agencies 252-53
Can. ambassadors to 251
founded 286
roster (members) 254-55
Secretaries General 252
United Nations Children's Fund (UNICEF)
.... 252
United Nations Industrial Development
Organization 252
United States of America 507-9
American Revolution 270

Civil War 273-74
map 300
(see also History, world)
United States Virgin Islands 508, 515-16
Units of measure *(see Weights and measures)*
Universal Postal Union (UPU) 252
Universities and colleges,
addresses 75-80
community colleges 77-80
degrees awarded 75
enrolment 72
Upper Volta *(see Burkina Faso)*
UPU 252
Uruguay 509-10
Utilities, labour force 198, 202
Uzbekistan 510

V

Vancouver (BC) 39
population 50, 52, 53
Vanuatu 510-11
Vatican City 512
Vegetable production 207
Vegetation 8
Venda 512-13
Venezuela 513-14
Veterans benefits 168
Victoria (BC) 39
population 50, 52, 53
Victoria Cross 127
Video Music Awards 582
Vietnam 514-15
Vietnam War 289-91
Viking explorers 89, 264
Vimy Ridge (1917) 93
Virgin Islands (U.S.) 508, 515-16
Vital statistics, Canada 1, 53-62
by province 29-34
Vitamins in foods 697
Volcanoes 235
Volleyball 622
Voltaire 270
Voyager space probes 531

W

Wages,
controls 97
growth in 86
minimum, federal and provincial 200
(see also Incomes)
Wake Island 508
Wales *(see United Kingdom)*
Wallis and Futuna Islands 373, 516

War Measures Act 96
Wars,
　Austrian Succession 90
　Boer 93, 276, 277
　Crimean 273
　current 241
　Gulf 99, 297
　Hundred Years' 266
　Iran-Iraq 293
　Korean 95, 287-88
　Seven Years' 90, 270
　Six Day 290
　Spanish Succession 89
　Vietnam 289-91
　War of 1812 .... 91, 271
　World War I 93, 278-80
　World War II 94-95, 284-86
　Yom Kippur 291
　(see also History, world)
Water polo 624
Water use 6
Waterfalls 6, 235, 237
Watergate scandal 291
Weapons, nuclear 286
Weather,
　measuring 10
　(see also Climate)
　terms 12-13, 21
　world 17, 18, 235
Weather, Canadian 11-27
　at airports 27
　by city 18, 24-26
　frost dates 8-9
　frost, fog, hail 19
　1992-93 highlights 14-16
　records 17, 20-22, 26
　watchers 25
Webster-Ashburton Treaty 272
Wedding anniversary gifts and greetings
　.................................... 707, 709
Weight lifting, Olympics 624
Weights and measures,
　imperial 692
　International System 695
　metric conversion 692-94
　temperature 694
Welfare *(see Social security)*
Western Cordillera (Canada) 4
Western Samoa 516-17
Westray mine disaster (1992) 105
WFP 252
Wheat 206
　exports/imports 206
　world producers 246
WHO 252
Wildlife *(see Animals; Plants)*
William the Conqueror 264
Wind,
　provincial averages 22

records 17, 22
wind chill 22-23
Windsor (Ont.) 39, 50, 52, 53
Winnipeg (Man.) 39
　General Strike 93
　population 50, 52, 53
Winnipeg, Lake 5
WIPO 252
WMO 252
Wolfe, General (1759) 90
Women,
　first NHL player 641
　suffrage 93
Wonders of the World 710
Wood industries 210
　(see also Forestry)
World,
　countries 307-522
　events of 1993 719-43
　global information 235-58
　history 259-98
　maps 299-306
　populations in danger 241
　Seven Wonders of 710
World Court (ICJ) 250-51
World Cup (soccer) 676
World Food Programme (WFP) 252
World Health Org. (WHO) 252
World Intellectual Property Org. (WIPO) 252
World Meteorological Org. (WMO) 252
World Series (baseball) 647-48
World War I 93, 278-80
World War II 94-95, 168, 284-86
World's fairs,
　Expo 67 96
　Expo 86 98
Wrestling, Olympics 624

minimum wage 200
mining production 208-10
MP 138
population 34, 42
　native 68-69
　towns and cities 50
　urban/rural 46
religions 34
revenues/expenditures 184
surplus/deficit 185
(see also Provinces and territories)
Yukon River 6

Z

Zaire 519-20
Zambia 520-21
Zimbabwe 521-22
Zodiac signs 696
Zoos 562

Y

Yacht racing,
　America's Cup 689
　Olympics 624
Yemen 517-18
Yom Kippur War 291
Young offenders 171, 173-74
Yugoslavia 298, 518-19
　(see also News events of 1993)
Yukon 34
　cabinet 149
　education 72, 73, 80
　election results 151-54
　geography 28, 34
　government 119-20
　govt leader 145
　joins Confederation 34
　languages 34, 70

1993

JANUARY	FEBRUARY	MARCH	APRIL
S M T W T F S	S M T W T F S	S M T W T F S	S M T W T F S
[1] 2	1 2 3 4 5 6	1 2 3 4 5 6	1 2 3
3 4 5 6 7 8 9	7 8 9 10 11 12 13	7 8 9 10 11 12 13	4 5 6 7 8 [9] 10
10 11 12 13 14 15 16	14 15 16 17 18 10 20	14 15 16 17 18 19 20	11 12 13 14 15 16 17
17 18 19 20 21 22 23	21 22 23 24 25 26 27	21 22 23 24 25 26 27	18 19 20 21 22 23 24
24 25 26 27 28 29 30	28	28 29 30 31	25 26 27 28 29 30
31			

MAY	JUNE	JULY	AUGUST
S M T W T F S	S M T W T F S	S M T W T F S	S M T W T F S
1	1 2 3 4 5	[1] 2 3	1 2 3 4 5 6 7
2 3 4 5 6 7 8	6 7 8 9 10 11 12	4 5 6 7 8 9 10	8 9 10 11 12 13 14
9 10 11 12 13 14 15	13 14 15 16 17 18 19	11 12 13 14 15 16 17	15 16 17 18 19 20 21
16 17 18 19 20 21 22	20 21 22 23 24 25 26	18 19 20 21 22 23 24	22 23 24 25 26 27 28
23 [24] 25 26 27 28 29	27 28 29 30	25 26 27 28 29 30 31	29 30 31
30 31			

SEPTEMBER	OCTOBER	NOVEMBER	DECEMBER
S M T W T F S	S M T W T F S	S M T W T F S	S M T W T F S
1 2 3 4	1 2	1 2 3 4 5 6	1 2 3 4
5 [6] 7 8 9 10 11	3 4 5 6 7 8 9	7 8 9 10 11 12 13	5 6 7 8 9 10 11
12 13 14 15 16 17 18	10 [11] 12 13 14 15 16	14 15 16 17 18 19 20	12 13 14 15 16 17 18
19 20 21 22 23 24 25	17 18 19 20 21 22 23	21 22 23 24 25 26 27	19 20 21 22 23 24 [25]
26 27 28 29 30	24 25 26 27 28 29 30	28 29 30	[26] 27 28 29 30 31
	31		

1995

JANUARY	FEBRUARY	MARCH	APRIL
S M T W T F S	S M T W T F S	S M T W T F S	S M T W T F S
[1] 2 3 4 5 6 7	1 2 3 4	1 2 3 4	1
8 9 10 11 12 13 14	5 6 7 8 9 10 11	5 6 7 8 9 10 11	2 3 4 5 6 7 8
15 16 17 18 19 20 21	12 13 14 15 16 17 18	12 [13] 14 15 16 17 18	9 10 11 12 13 [14] 15
22 23 24 25 26 27 28	19 20 21 22 23 24 25	19 20 21 22 23 24 25	16 17 18 19 20 21 22
29 30 31	26 27 28	26 27 28 29 30 31	23 24 25 26 27 28 29
			30

MAY	JUNE	JULY	AUGUST
S M T W T F S	S M T W T F S	S M T W T F S	S M T W T F S
1 2 3 4 5 6	1 2 3	[1]	1 2 3 4 5
7 8 9 10 11 12 13	4 5 6 7 8 9 10	2 3 4 5 6 7 8	6 7 8 9 10 11 12
14 15 16 17 18 19 20	11 12 13 14 15 16 17	9 10 11 12 13 14 15	13 14 15 16 17 18 19
21 [22] 23 24 25 26 27	18 19 20 21 22 23 24	16 17 18 19 20 21 22	20 21 22 23 24 25 26
28 29 30 31	25 26 27 28 29 30	23 24 25 26 27 28 29	27 28 29 30 31
		30 31	

SEPTEMBER	OCTOBER	NOVEMBER	DECEMBER
S M T W T F S	S M T W T F S	S M T W T F S	S M T W T F S
1 2	1 2 3 4 5 6 7	1 2 3 4	1 2
3 [4] 5 6 7 8 9	8 [9] 10 11 12 13 14	5 6 7 8 9 10 11	3 4 5 6 7 8 9
10 11 12 13 14 15 16	15 16 17 18 19 20 21	12 13 14 15 16 17 18	10 11 12 13 14 15 16
17 18 19 20 21 22 23	22 23 24 25 26 27 28	19 20 21 22 23 24 25	17 18 19 20 21 22 23
24 25 26 27 28 29 30	29 30 31	26 27 28 29 30	24 [25] [26] 27 28 29 30
			31

1994 CALENDAR AND HOLIDAYS

JANUARY

S	M	T	W	T	F	S
					1	
2	3	4	5	6	7	8
9	10	11	12	13	14	15
16	17	18	19	20	21	22
23	24	25	26	27	28	29
30	31					

FEBRUARY

S	M	T	W	T	F	S
		1	2	3	4	5
6	7	8	9	10	11	12
13	14	15	16	17	18	19
20	21	22	23	24	25	26
27	28					

MARCH

S	M	T	W	T	F	S
		1	2	3	4	5
6	7	8	9	10	11	12
13	14	15	16	17	18	19
20	21	22	23	24	25	26
27	28	29	30	31		

APRIL

S	M	T	W	T	F	S
					1	2
3	4	5	6	7	8	9
10	11	12	13	14	15	16
17	18	19	20	21	22	23
24	25	26	27	28	29	30

MAY

S	M	T	W	T	F	S
1	2	3	4	5	6	7
8	9	10	11	12	13	14
15	16	17	18	19	20	21
22	**23**	24	25	26	27	28
29	30	31				

JUNE

S	M	T	W	T	F	S
			1	2	3	4
5	6	7	8	9	10	11
12	13	14	15	16	17	18
19	20	21	22	23	24	25
26	27	28	29	30		

JULY

S	M	T	W	T	F	S
					1	2
3	4	5	6	7	8	9
10	11	12	13	14	15	16
17	18	19	20	21	22	23
24	25	26	27	28	29	30
31						

AUGUST

S	M	T	W	T	F	S
	1	2	3	4	5	6
7	8	9	10	11	12	13
14	15	16	17	18	19	20
21	22	23	24	25	26	27
28	29	30	31			

SEPTEMBER

S	M	T	W	T	F	S
				1	2	3
4	**5**	6	7	8	9	10
11	12	13	14	15	16	17
18	19	20	21	22	23	24
25	26	27	28	29	30	

OCTOBER

S	M	T	W	T	F	S
						1
2	3	4	5	6	7	8
9	**10**	11	12	13	14	15
16	17	18	19	20	21	22
23	24	25	26	27	28	29
30	31					

NOVEMBER

S	M	T	W	T	F	S
		1	2	3	4	5
6	7	8	9	10	11	12
13	14	15	16	17	18	19
20	21	22	23	24	25	26
27	28	29	30			

DECEMBER

S	M	T	W	T	F	S
				1	2	3
4	5	6	7	8	9	10
11	12	13	14	15	16	17
18	19	20	21	22	23	24
25	**26**	27	28	29	30	31

New Year's Day (January 1), Good Friday (April 1), Victoria Day (May 23), Canada Day (July 1), Labour Day (September 5), Thanksgiving (October 10), Christmas Day (December 25) and Boxing Day (December 26).

Other Holidays and Holy Days

Jewish Holy Days: Purim—February 25; Passover—March 27; Shavouth—May 16; Rosh Hashanah—September 6; Yom Kippur—September 15; Sukkoth—September 20; Hanukkah—November 28.
Muslim Holy Days: Ramadam—February 12; Id al-Fitr—March 14; Id al-Adha—May 21; New Year's Day—June 9.
St. Jean Baptiste Day (Quebec)—June 24.

Newfoundland Holidays: St. Patrick's Day—March 14; St. George's Day—April 25; Discovery Day—June 20; Orangeman's Day—July 11.
Government and bank holidays: April 4 (Easter Monday), November 11 (Remembrance Day).